NOTABLE
TWENTIETH-CENTURY
SCIENTISTS

SUPPLEMENT

Kristine M. Krapp, Editor

GALE

DETROIT · NEW YORK · TORONTO · LONDON

Editor
Kristine M. Krapp

Contributing Senior Editors
Donna Olendorf
Bridget Travers

Contributing Editors
Jacqueline L. Longe
Pamela Proffitt
Robyn V. Young

Associate Editors
Nicole Beatty
Zoran Minderovic

Managing Editor
Christine B. Jeryan

Picture Permissions Supervisor
Susan Trosky

Picture Permissions Assistant
Jessica Ulrich

Art Director
Cynthia Baldwin

Cover Design
Gary Leach

Contents

Introduction

Every year, Gale Research receives numerous requests from librarians for sources providing biographical information. *Notable Twentieth-Century Scientists* and its accompanying volume, *Notable Twentieth-Century Scientists Supplement*, have been designed specifically to fill a niche for scientific biographies. The set provides students, educators, librarians, researchers, and general readers with an affordable and comprehensive source of biographical information on approximately 1,600 scientists active in this century in all of the natural, physical, and applied sciences, including the traditionally studied subjects of astronomy, biology, botany, chemistry, earth science, mathematics, medicine, physics, technology, and zoology, as well as the more recently established and as yet sparsely covered fields of computer science, ecology, engineering, and environmental science. International in scope, *Notable Twentieth-Century Scientists* coverage ranges from the well-known scientific giants of the early century to contemporary scientists working on the latest advances in their fields. *Notable Twentieth-Century Scientists Supplement* provides updated biographical information on 65 scientists included in the first four-volume set. In addition, it lists almost 250 new biographies of modern scientists.

Superior Coverage of Women, Minority, and Non-Western Scientists

Addressing the growing interest in and demand for biographical information on women, minority, and non-Western scientists, *Notable Twentieth-Century Scientists Supplement* also seeks to bring to light the achievements of women scientists, Asian American, African American, Hispanic American, and Native American scientists, and scientists from countries outside North America and Western Europe. Due to the scarcity of published information on these scientists, information for many of the sketches on these listees has been obtained through telephone interviews and correspondence with the scientists themselves or with their universities, companies, laboratories, or families. Our hope is that in presenting these entries, we are providing a basis for future research on the lives and contributions of these important and historically marginalized segments of the scientific community.

Inclusion Criteria

A preliminary list of scientists was compiled from a wide variety of sources, including established reference works, history of science indexes, science periodicals, awards lists, and suggestions from organizations and associations. The advisory board evaluated the names and made suggestions for inclusion. Final selection of names to include was made by the editors on the basis of the following criteria:

- Discoveries, inventions, overall contributions, influence, and/or impact on scientific progress in the twentieth century
- Receipt of a major science award, including Nobel Prizes in Physics, Chemistry, and Physiology or Medicine, the Fields Medal (mathematics), Albert Lasker awards (medicine), the Tyler Prize (environmental science), the National Medal of Science, and the National Medal of Technology
- Involvement or influence in education, organizational leadership, or public policy
- Familiarity to the general public

- Notable "first" achievements, including degrees earned, positions held, or organizations founded; several listees involved in the first space flights are also included

Entries Provide Easy Access to Information

Entries are arranged alphabetically by surname. The typical *Notable Twentieth-Century Scientists Supplement* entry provides the following information:

- **Entry head**—offers at-a-glance information: name, birth/death dates, nationality and primary field(s) of specialization.

- **Biographical essay**—ranges from 400 to 2500 words and provides basic biographical information [including date and place of birth, name(s) of spouse(s) and children, educational background and degrees earned, etc.] along with scientific endeavors and achievements, all explained in prose accessible to high school students and readers without a scientific background. Intratextual headings within the essays highlight the significant events in the listee's life and career, allowing readers to easily find information they seek. **Bold-faced** names in *Notable Twentieth-Century Scientists Supplement* entries direct readers to other entries found in *Notable Twentieth-Century Scientists* or the *Supplement*.

- **Selected Writings** by the Scientist section—lists representative publications, including important papers, textbooks, research works, autobiographies, lectures, etc.

- **Further Reading** section—provides citations of biographies, interviews, periodicals, obituaries, and other sources about the listee for readers seeking additional information.

Indexes Provide Numerous Points of Access

In addition to the complete list of scientists found at the beginning of the book, readers seeking more information can consult the four indexes at the end of the book for additional listings. These indexes are cumulative with the first *Notable Twentieth-Century Scientists* set. They contain all the references from the original set of indexes, as well as including indexed information from those scientists listed only in *Notable Twentieth-Century Scientists Supplement*.

- **Field of Specialization Index**—groups listees according to the scientific fields to which they have contributed
- **Gender Index**—provides lists of the women and men covered
- **Nationality/Ethnicity Index**—arranges listees by country of birth and/or citizenship and/or ethnic heritage
- Comprehensive **Subject Index**—provides volume and page references for scientists and scientific terms used in the text. Includes cross references.

Photographs

Individuals in *Notable Twentieth-Century Scientists Supplement* come to life in the 153 photos of the scientists.

Advisory Board

Contributors

Ethan E. Allen, Julie Anderson, Jeffrey Bass, Karl Leif Bates, Maurice Bleifeld, Barbara Boughton, Barbara A. Branch, Tammy J. Bronson, Leonard C. Bruno, Bryan H. Bunch, Jill Carpenter, Chris Cavette, Kenneth Chiacchia, Mujoko Chu, Jane Stewart Cook, Tom Crawford, John Henry Dreyfuss, Thomas Drucker, Martin R. Feldman, Jerome P. Ferrance, C. J. Giroux, Chris Hables Gray, Bridget K. Hall, Elizabeth Henry, Fran Nicholson Hodgkins, Kelley Reynolds Jacquez, J. Sydney Jones, D. George Joseph, Janet Kieffer Kelley, Jennifer Kramer, Marc Kusinitz, Penelope Lawbaugh, Benedict A. Leerburger, Laura Mangan-Grenier, Gail B.C. Marsella, Liz Marshall, Avril McDonald, Carla Mecoli-Kamp, Sally M. Moite, Patrick Moore, Paula M. Morin, Angie Mullig, David Newton, Joan Oleck, Donna Olshansky, Kristin Palm, Daniel Pendick, David A. Petechuk, Annette Petrusso, Karl Preuss, Rayma Prince, Lewis Pyenson, Leslie Reinherz, Vita Richman, Larry Riddle, Shari Rudavsky, Karen Sands, Neeraja Sankaran, Michael Sims, Linda Wasmer Smith, Monica Stevens, R.F. Trimble, Katherine Williams

Photo Credits

Photographs appearing in *Notable Twentieth-Century Scientists Supplement* were received from the following sources. Every effort has been made to trace copyright, but if omissions have been made, please let us know.

Page 1: University of Oxford, reproduced by permission; **Page 3:** Mathematisches Forschungsinstitut, Oberwolfach, Germany, 1988, reproduced by permission; **Page 4:** Nordisk Pressefoto/Archive Photos, Inc., reproduced by permission; **Page 6:** Reproduced by permission of Ralph A. Alpher; **Page 10:** AP/Wide World Photos, Inc., reproduced by permission; **Page 12:** The Mount Holyoke Archives and Special Collections, reproduced by permission; **Page 15** (left) Mathematisches Forschungsinstitut, Oberwolfach, Germany, 1977, reproduced by permission; **Page 15** (right): AP/Wide World Photos, Inc., reproduced by permission; **Page 18:** UPI/Corbis-Bettmann, reproduced by permission; **Page 20:** Reproduced by permission of Mary Ellen Avery; **Page 23:** Archive Photos, Inc., reproduced by permission; **Page 25:** Photo by Francois Gohier, Photo Researchers, Inc., reproduced by permission; **Page 27:** UPI/Corbis-Bettmann, reproduced by permission; **Page 33:** Mathematisches Forschungsinstitut, Oberwolfach, Germany, reproduced by permission; **Page 36:** Photo by Stephan Savoia, AP/Wide World Photos, Inc., reproduced by permission; **Page 43:** University of Maryland, reproduced by permission; **Page 45:** Mathematisches Forschungsinstitut, Oberwolfach, Germany, reproduced by permission; **Page 48:** Berkely, California, Mathematisches Forschungsinstitut Oberwolfach, reproduced by permission; **Page 51:** U.S. National Aeronautics and Space Administration; **Page 53:** Reproduced by permission of Paul Boyer; **Page 55:** Reproduced by permission of Carl Brans; **Page 58:** Berkely, California, 1984, Mathematisches Forschungsinstitut Oberwolfach, reproduced by permission; **Page 61:** National Academy of Sciences, reproduced by permission; **Page 66:** Reproduced by permission of D. Allan Bromley; **Page 71:** London Daily Express/Archive Photos, Inc., reproduced by permission; **Page 74:** Deutche Presse/Archive Photos, Inc., reproduced by permission; **Page 77:** The Library of Congress; **Page 81:** Mathematisches Forschungsinstitut, Oberwolfach, 1920, reproduced by permission; **Page 86:** UPI/Corbis-Bettmann, reproduced by permission; **Page 94:** Photo by L. A. Cicero, Stanford University News Service, reproduced by permission; **Page 98:** AP/Wide World Photos, Inc., reproduced by permission; **Page 101:** Agence France Presse/Corbis-Bettmann, reproduced by permission; **Page 103:** Reproduced by permission of Theo Colburn; **Page 105:** National Academy of Sciences, reproduced by permission; **Page 111:** AP/Wide World Photos, Inc., reproduced by permission; **Page 114:** Agence France Presse/Corbis-Bettmann, reproduced by permission; **Page 116:** Reuters/Andrees A. Latif/Archive Photos, Inc., reproduced by permission; **Page 125:** UPI/Corbis-Bettmann, reproduced by permission; **Page 128:** Reuters/News Limited/Archive Photos, Inc., reproduced by permission; **Page 130:** Reproduced by permission of Harry Drickamer; **Page 132:** AP/Wide World Photos, Inc., reproduced by permission; **Page 137:** The Library of Congress; **Page 139:** AP/Wide World Photos, Inc., reproduced by permission; **Page 146:** Mathematisches Forschungsinstitut Oberwolfach, reproduced by permission: **Page 150:** AP/Wide World Photos, Inc., reproduced by permission; **Page 153:** UPI/Corbis-Bettmann, reproduced by permission; **Page 155:** UPI/Corbis-Bettmann, reproduced by permission; **Page 157:** Reproduced by permission of Etta Falconer; **Page 160:** A.K. Peters Ltd., reproduced by permission; **Page 164:** UPI/Corbis-Bettmann, reproduced by permission; **Page 166:** Photo by Randy Baum, courtesy of C&EN News, reproduced by permission; **Page 168:** The Library of Congress; **Page 170:** Mathematisches Forschungsinstitut Oberwolfach, reproduced by permission; **Page 173:** Mathematisches Forschungsinstitut Oberwolfach, reproduced by permission; **Page 175:** The Library of Congress; **Page 178:** AP/Wide World Photos, Inc., reproduced by permission; **Page 183:** EG&G, Inc., reproduced by permission; **Page 198:** Corbis-Bettmann, reproduced by permission; **Page 199:** The Library of Congress; **Page 206:** The Library of Congress; **Page 209:** Reproduced by permission of David Ho; **Page 212:** Archive Photos, Inc./Express Newspapers, reproduced by permission; **Page 214:** The Library of Congress; **Page 217:** Reproduced by permission of Ariel Hollinshead; **Page 219:** The Library of Congress; **Page 221:** Reproduced by permission of John Hughes; **Page 223:** Brandeis University Photography Department, reproduced by permission; **Page 227:** AP/Wide World Photos, Inc.,

Entry List

Abraham, Edward P.
Ahlfors, Lars V.
Alfvén, Hannes Olof Gösta
Alpher, Ralph Asher
Anastasi, Anne
Anfinsen, Christian Boehmer
Antonelli, Kay McNulty Mauchly
Apgar, Virginia
Askey, Richard
Atanasoff, John
Auerbach, Charlotte
Auger, Pierre V.
Avery, Mary Ellen

Babcocke, Horace W.
Bakker, Robert T.
Barghoorn, Elso Sterrenberg, Jr.
Bari, Nina
Bari, Ruth Aaronson
Baxter, Agnes
Bell, John Stewart
Bellow, Alexandra
Beltrán, Enrique
Berners-Lee, Tim
Bernstein, Richard B.
Berry, Leonidas Harris
Bers, Lipman
Bird, R. Byron
Birkhoff, Garrett
Blout, Elkan R.
Blum, Lenore
Bodmer, Walter F.
Bondar, Roberta L.
Boyer, Paul D.
Brans, Carl Henry
Branson, Herman
Bremermann, Hans-Joachim
Breslow, Ronald C.
Bridges, Calvin B.
Brockhouse, Bertram Neville
Broecker, Wallace S.
Bromley, D. Allen
Brown, Robert Hanbury

Burger, Alfred
Burkitt, Denis Parsons
Butement, William
Butenandt, Aldolf

Calvin, Melvin
Carothers, E. Eleanor
Cartan, Élie Joseph
Cartan, Henri Paul
Cartwright, Mary Lucy
Chandrasekhar, Subrahmanyan
Chang, Sun-Yang Alice
Charnley, John
Chase, Mary Agnes Meara
Chu, Steven
Chung, Fan R.K.
Church, Alonzo
Clemence, Gerald M.
Cocke, John
Cohen-Tannoudji, Claude
Colburn, Theodora E.
Condon, Edward U.
Coster, Dirk
Cousteau, Jacques
Cray, Seymour
Crutzen, Paul J.
Curl, Robert Floyd, Jr.

Daubechies, Ingrid
Davidson, Norman R.
Diacumakos, Elaine
Dick, Gladys Henry
Dicke, Robert Henry
Diggs, Irene
Doherty, Peter C.
Drickamer, Harry G.
Durrell, Gerald

Eagle, Harry
Eastwood, Alice

Eccles, John C.
Eckert, J. Presper
Einstein-Marić, Mileva
Elsasser, Walter M.
Elton, Charles Sutherland
Emerson, Gladys Anderson
Erdös, Paul
Erlang, Agner Krarup
Evans, James C.
Ewing, William Maurice

Fabry, Charles
Fairbank, William
Falconer, Etta Zuber
Farman, Joseph C.
Fasenmyer, Mary Celine
Fenchel, Käte
Ferguson, Margaret Clay
Fieser, Mary Peters
Flanagan, James L.
Folkers, Karl A.
Fowler, William A.
Fredholm, Erik Ivar

Gelfond, Aleksandr Osipovich
Gentry, Ruth
Gibbs, Josiah Willard
Gilman, Alfred Goodman
Goldreich, Peter
Gorer, Peter
Grier, Herbert E., Jr.
Guthrie, Mary Jane

Hackerman, Norman
Hammond, George S.
Harvey, Ethel Browne
Haus, Hermann A.
Hay, Louise Schmir
Hayes, Ellen Amanda

Hazlett, Olive Clio
Heezen, Bruce C.
Hermite, Charles
Hershey, Alfred Day
Hewitt, Jacqueline N.
Hibbard, Hope
Higgs, Peter Ware
Hill, George William
Hill, Robert (Robin)
Ho, David Da-I
Hodgkin, Dorothy Crowfoot
Holley, Robert William
Hollinshead, Ariel Cahill
Huggins, Charles B.
Hughes, John
Huxley, Hugh Esmor

Janovskaja, Sof'ja Aleksandrovna
Jeffreys, Alec John
Jencks, William P.
Jerne, Niels K.
Johnson, William Summer
Jones, Mary Ellen
Jordan, Ernst Pascual

Kandel, Eric R.
Karp, Richard M.
Keen, Linda
Keller, Evelyn Fox
Kimura, Motoo
King, Helen Dean
King, Louisa Boyd Yeomans
King, Reatha Clark
Klein, Christian Felix
Koehl, Mimi A. R.
Köhler, Georges
Koshland, Daniel E., Jr.
Kouwenhoven, William B.
Kramer, Fred Russell
Krieger, Cecilia
Kroto, Harold Walter
Kuperberg, Krystyna
Kusch, Polycarp

L'Esperance, Elise Depew Strang
Landau, Edmund
Langlands, Robert P.
Leakey, Mary
Lee, David M.
Levi-Montalcini, Rita
Lévi-Strauss, Claude

Lewis, Edward B.
Lindemann, Carl Louis Ferdinand von
Litvinova, Elizaveta Fedorovna
Lovejoy, Thomas Eugene
Lubchenco, Jane
Lwoff, André

Macintyre, Sheila Scott
Macklin, Madge Thurlow
MacPherson, Robert
Maddison, Ada Isabel
Malone-Mayes, Vivienne
McAfee, Walter S.
McDuff, Margaret Dusa
Méray, Hugues Charles Robert
Merrill, Helen Abbot
Merrill, Winifred Edgerton
Mexia, Ynes
Mitchell, Peter D.
Mordell, Louis Joel
Morgan, Ann Haven
Mott, Nevil Francis
Moulton Browne, Barbara

Nakanishi, Koji
Nash, John Forbes
Ne'eman, Yuval
Needham, Joseph
Nelson, Evelyn
Neumann, Hanna
Nicholson, Seth Barnes
Nier, Alfred O. C.
Noether, Max
Nozoe, Tetsuo
Nüesslein-Volhard, Christiane

O'Neill, Gerard K.
Ochoa, Severo
Olah, George A.
Oleinik, Olga
Osheroff, Douglas D.

Packard, David
Parker, Arthur C.

Parker, Eugene Newman
Patel, C. Kumar N.
Paul, Wolfgang
Peebles, Phillip James Edwin
Peierls, Rudolf
Peirce, Charles Sanders
Penry, Deborah L.
Perl, Martin L.
Pettersson, Hans
Phillips, William D.
Pierce, George Edward
Pierce, Naomi E.
Pilbeam, David R.
Pless, Vera
Plotkin, Mark
Ponnamperuma, Cyril
Press, Frank
Profet, Margie
Prusiner, Stanley B.
Puck, Theodore T.
Purcell, Edward Mills

Quate, Calvin F.

Rees, Mina S.
Rich, Alexander
Richardson, Robert C.
Rodbell, Martin
Roddy, Leon Raymand
Rudin, Mary Ellen
Runcorn, S. K.

Sagan, Carl
Sager, Ruth
Salam, Abdus
Sanford, Katherine Koontz
Schafer, Alice T.
Scharrer, Berta
Schick, Bela
Schwarz, John Henry
Scott, Charlotte Angas
Selberg, Atle
Shepard, Roger N.
Shull, Clifford Glenwood
Sierpiński, Waclaw
Silbergeld, Ellen Kovner
Simmons, Howard Ensign, Jr.
Sinclair, Clive Marles
Skou, Jens C.
Smalley, Richard Errett
Snyder, Solomon H.

Sperry, Roger W.
Spitzer, Lyman, Jr.
Stanley, Richard
Steitz, Joan Argetsinger
Stibitz, George R.
Stokes, George Gabriel
Stott, Alicia Boole
Suomi, Verner E.
Synge, Richard
Szegö, Gabor

Taussky-Todd, Olga
Telkes, Maria
Tishler, Max
Todd, Alexander
Tombaugh, Clyde W.
Topchiev, Alexsandr Vasil'evich
Tsui, Lap-Chee
Twort, Frederick

Uvarov, Boris Petrovitch

Vallée-Poussin, Charles Jean
   Gustave de la
Van de Kamp, Peter
Vedder, Edward Bright
Velez-Rodriguez, Argelia
Vine, Frederick John

Wahl, Arnold C.
Wald, George
Walker, John E.
Walton, Ernest
Weber, Ernst
Weiss, Mary Catherine Bishop
Wheeler, Anna Johnson Pell
Whinfield, John R.
White, Raymond L.
Whittle, Frank
Wieschaus, Eric F.
Wigner, Eugene Paul
Williams, Cicely Delphin
Williams, Evan James
Williams, Heather
Wilmut, Ian
Wu, Chien-Shiung

Young, J. Z.
Young, Lai-Sung
Young, William Henry

Zamecnik, Paul Charles
Zinkernagel, Rolf M.
Zinn, Walter Henry

Chronology of Scientific Advancement

1895 Scottish physicist *C.T.R. Wilson* invents the cloud chamber

French physicist *Jean Baptiste Perrin* confirms the nature of cathode rays

1896 American agricultural chemist *George Washington Carver* begins work at the Tuskegee Institute

1897 English physicist *J.J. Thomson* discovers the electron

1898 Polish-born French radiation chemist *Marie Curie* and French physicist *Pierre Curie* discover polonium and radium

1900 German physicist *Max Planck* develops Planck's Constant

1901 Austrian American immunologist *Karl Landsteiner* discovers A, B, and O blood types

German geneticist *Wilhelm Weinberg* outlines the "difference method" in his first important paper on heredity

1902 English geneticist *William Bateson* translates Austrian botanist Gregor Mendel's work

1903 Polish-born French radiation chemist *Marie Curie* becomes the first woman to be awarded the Nobel Prize

German chemist *Otto Diels* isolates molecular structure of cholesterol

1904 English electrical engineer *John Ambrose Fleming* develops the Fleming Valve

Russian physiologist *Ivan Petrovich Pavlov* receives the Nobel Prize for digestion research

1905 German-born American physicist *Albert Einstein* publishes the theory of relativity

German chemist *Fritz Haber* publishes *Thermodynamics of Technical Gas Reactions*

German chemist *Walther Nernst's* research leads to the Third Law of Thernodynamics

1906 Danish physicist and chemist *Johannes Nicolaus Brønsted* publishes his first paper on affinity

English neurophysiologist *Charles Scott Sherrington* publishes *The Integrative Action of the Nervous System*

1907 Prussian-born American physicist *Albert Michelson* becomes the first American to receive the Nobel Prize for Physics

1908 American astrophysicist *George Ellery Hale* discovers magnetic fields in sunspots

1909 German bacteriologist and immunologist *Paul Ehrlich* discovers a cure for syphilis

American engineer and inventor *Charles Franklin Kettering* successfully tests the first prototypes of the electric automobile starter

1910 English American mathematician *Alfred North Whitehead* and English mathematician and philosopher *Bertrand Russell* publish the first volume of *Principia Mathematica*

American engineer and inventor *Lee De Forest* attempts the first live broadcast of radio

New Zealand-born English physicist *Ernest Rutherford* postulates the modern concept of the atom

1911 English mathematician *Godfrey Harold Hardy* begins his collaboration with J. E. Littlewood

Polish-born French radiation chemist *Marie Curie* becomes the first scientist to win a second Nobel Prize

1912 Danish physicist *Niels Bohr* develops a new theory of atomic structure

Austrian physicist *Victor Hess* discovers cosmic rays

English biochemist *Frederick Gowland Hopkins* publishes a groundbreaking work illustrating the nutritional importance of nutrients

German physicist *Max von Laue* discovers x-ray diffraction

Austrian physicist *Lise Meitner* becomes the first woman professor in Germany

German meteorologist and geophysicist *Alfred Wegener* proposes the theory of continental drift

1913 German bacteriologist and immunologist *Paul Ehrlich* gives an address explaining the future of chemotherapy

English physicist *Henry Gwyn Jeffreys Moseley* discovers atomic number of the elements

French physicist *Jean Baptiste Perrin* verifies German-born American physicist *Albert Einstein's* calculations of Brownian Motion

American astronomer and astrophysicist *Henry Norris Russell* publishes the Hertzsprung-Russell diagram

Russian-born American aeronautical engineer *Igor I. Sikorsky* designs the *Ilya Mourometz* bomber

German chemist *Richard Willstätter* and Arthur Stoll publish their first studies of chlorophyll

American geneticist *A.H. Sturtevant* develops gene mapping

1916 American chemist and physicist *Irving Langmuir* receives a patent for an energy-efficient, longer-lasting tungsten filament light bulb

American geneticist and embryologist *Thomas Hunt Morgan* publishes *A Critique of the Theory of Evolution*

German theoretical physicist *Arnolde Sommerfeld* reworks Danish physicist *Niels Bohr's* atomic theory

American anatomist *Florence Rena Sabin* publishes *The Origin and Development of the Lymphatic System*

1918 Daniel physical chemist *Johannes Nicolaus Brønsted* publishes his thirteenth paper on affinity

1919 New Zealand-born English physicist *Ernest Rutherford* determines that alpha particles can split atoms

1920 American astronomer *Harlow Shapley* convinces the scientific community that the Milky Way is much larger than originally thought and the Earth's solar system is not its center

1921 Canadian physiologist *Frederick G. Banting* and Canadian physiologist *Charles Herbert Best* discover insulin

1923 Danish physical chemist *Johannes Nicolaus Brønsted* redefines acids and bases

English astronomer *Arthur Stanley Eddington* publishes *Mathematical Theory of Relativity*

American astronomer *Edwin Hubble* confirms the existence of galaxies outside the Milky Way

American physicist *Robert A. Millikan* begins his study of cosmic rays

1924 French theoretical physicist *Louis Victor de Broglie* publishes findings on wave mechanics

English astronomer *Arthur Stanley Eddington* determines the mass-luminosity law

1925 German-born American physicist *James Franck* and German physicist *Gustav Hertz* prove Danish physicist *Niels Bohr's* theory of the quantum atom

Italian-born American physicist *Enrico Fermi* publishes a paper explaining Austro-Hungarian-born Swiss physicist *Wolfgang Pauli's* exclusion principle

English statistician and geneticist *Ronald A. Fisher* publishes *Statistical Methods for Research Workers*

1926 German-born English physicist *Max Born* explains the wave function

American physicist and rocker pioneer *Robert H. Goddard* launches the first liquid-propellant rocket

American geneticist *Hermann Joseph Muller* confirms that x rays greatly increase the mutation rate in *Drosophila*

Austrian physicist *Erwin Schrödinger* publishes his wave equation

1927 American physicist *Arthur Holly Compton* receives the Nobel Prize for x-ray research

English physiologist *Henry Hallett Dale* identifies the chemical mediator involved in the transmission of nerve impulses

German chemist *Otto Diels* develops a successful dehydrogenating process

German physicist *Werner Karl Heisenberg* develops the Uncertainty Principle

Belgian astronomer *Georges Lemaître* formulates the big bang theory

Hungarian American mathematical physicist *Eugene Paul Wigner* develops the law of the conservation of parity

American astronomer *Edwin Hubble* puts together the theory of the expanding universe, or Hubble's Law

1928 German chemist *Otto Diels* and German chemist *Kurt Alder* develop the Diels-Alder Reaction

Scottish bacteriologist *Alexander Fleming* discovers penicillin

Austro-Hungarian-born German physicist *Hermann Oberth* publishes a book explaining the basic principles of space flight

Indian physicist *C. V. Raman* discovers the Raman Effect

1929 American physicist *Robert Van de Graaff* constructs the first working model of his particle accelerator

Danish astronomer *Ejnar Hertzsprung* receives the Gold Medal Award for calculating the first intergalactic distance

Norwegian American chemist *Lars Onsager* develops the Law of Reciprocal Relations

German-born American mathematician *Hermann Weyl* develops a mathematical theory for the neutrino

Russian-born American physicist and engineer *Vladimir Zworkin* files his first patent for color television

1930 English statistician and geneticist *Ronald A. Fisher* publishes *The Genetical Theory of Natural Selection*

Austrian-born American mathematician *Kurt*

Friedrich Gödel proves the incompleteness theorem

Austro-Hungarian-born Swiss physicist *Wolfgang Pauli* proposes the existence of the neutrino

1931 American engineer *Vannevar Bush* develops the differential analyzer with colleagues

American chemist *Wallace Hume Carothers* founds the synthetic rubber manufacturing industry with his research

South African-born American virologist *Max Theiler's* research leads to the production of the first yellow-fever vaccine

German biochemist *Otto Warburg* establishes the Kaiser Wilhelm Institute for Cell Physiology

1932 English atomic physicist *John Cockcroft* and Irish experimental physicist *Ernest Walton* split the atom

American physicist *Carl David Anderson* discovers the positron

English-born Indian physiologist and geneticist *John Burdon Sanderson Haldane* publishes *The Causes of Evolution*

American physicist *Ernest Orlando Lawrence* develops the cyclotron and disintegrates a lithium nucleus

1933 Canadian-born American biologist and bacteriologist *Oswald Theodore Avery* identifies DNA as the basis of heredity

English physicist *Paul Adrien Maurice Dirac* wins the Nobel Prize for his work on the wave equation

Italian-born American physicist *Enrico Fermi* proposes his beta decay theory

German inventor *Felix Wankel* successfully operates the first internal combustion, rotary engine

1934 French nuclear physicist *Frédéric Joliot-Curie* and French chemist and physicist *Irène Joliot-Curie* discover artificial radioactivity

American inventor *Edwin H. Land* develops a commerical method to polarize light

New Zealand-born English physicist *Ernest Rutherford* achieves the first fusion reaction

American chemist and physicist *Harold Urey* receives the Nobel Prize in Chemistry for his discovery of deuterium, or heavy hydrogen

1935 American seismologist *Charles F. Richter* and German American seismologist *Beno Gutenberg* develop the Richter(-Gutenberg) Scale

English physicist *James Chadwick* receives the Nobel Prize for the discovery of the neutron

1936 German experimental physicist *Hans Geiger* perfects the Geiger-Mueller Counter

Russian biochemist *Aleksandr Ivanovich Oparin* publishes his origin of life theory

English mathematician *Alan Turing* publishes a paper detailing a machine that would serve as a model for the first working computer

1937 Russian-born American biologist *Theodosius Dobzhansky* writes *Genetics and the Origin of Species*

Australian English pathologist *Howard Walter Florey* discovers the growth potential of polymeric chains

German-born English biochemist *Hans Adolf Krebs* identifies the workings of the Krebs Cycle

Hungarian American biochemist and molecular biologist *Albert Szent-Gyorgyi* receives the nobel Prize for isolating vitamin C

1938
German chemist *Otto Hahn*, Austrian physicist *Lise Meitner*, and German chemist *Fritz Strassmann* discover nuclear fission

American physicist *Carl David Anderson* discovers the meson

1939
Swiss-born American physicist *Felix Bloch* measures the neutron's magnetic movement

American chemist *Wallace Hume Carothers* founds the synthetic fiber industry with his research

French-born American microbiologist and ecologist *René Dubos* discovers tyrothricin

American chemist *Linus Pauling* develops the theory of complimentarity

Russian-born American aeronautical engineer *Igor I. Sikorsky* flies the first single-rotor helicopter

1940
American physicist and inventor *Chester Carlson* receives a patent for his photocopying method

English experimental physicist *George Paget Thomson* forms the Maud Committee

1941
German-born English biochemist *Ernst Boris Chain* and Australian English pathologist *Howard Walter Florey* isolate penicillin

German-born American physicist *Hans Bethe* develops the Bethe Coupler

American biochemist *Fritz Lipmann* publishes "Metabolic Generation and Utilization of Phosphate Bond Energy"

1942
Hungarian American physicist and biophysicist *Leo Szilard* and Italian-born American physicist *Enrico Fermi* set up the first nuclear chain reaction

German-born American biologist *Ernst Mayr* proposes the theory of geographic speciation

American physicist *J. Robert Oppenheimer*

becomes the director of the Manhattan Project

1943
German-born American molecular biologist *Max Delbrück* and Italian-born American molecular biologist *Salvador Edward Luria* publish a milestone paper regarded as the beginning of bacterial genetics

English physicist *James Chadwick* leads the British contingent of the Manhattan Project

French oceanographer *Jacques-Yves Cousteau* patents the Aqualung

Italian-born American molecular biologist *Salvador Edward Luria* devises the fluctuation test

1944
German American rocket engineer *Wernher Von Braun* fires the first fully operational V-2 rocket

Austrian-born American biochemist *Erwin Chargaff* discovers the genetic role of DNA

American nuclear chemist *Glenn T. Seaborg* successfully isolates large amounts of plutonium and develops the actinide concept

American paleontologist *George Gaylord Simpson* publishes *Tempo and Mode in Evolution*

Russian-born American microbiologist *Selman Waksman* develops streptomycin

1945
English physicist *James Chadwick* witnesses the first atomic bomb test

American biochemist *Fritz Lipmann* discovers coenzyme A

Hungarian American mathematician *Johann Von Neumann* publishes a report containing the first written description of the stored-program concept

American chemist *Linus Pauling* determines the cause of sickle-cell anemia

Austrian physicist *Erwin Schrödinger* publishes *What is Life?*

1946   American geneticist *Joshua Lederberg* and American biochemist *Edward Lawrie Tatum* show that bacteria may reproduce sexually

English zoologist *Julian Huxley* becomes the first director-general of UNESCO

1947   French oceanographer *Jacques-Yves Cousteau* breaks the free diving record using his Aqualung

Hungarian-born English physicist *Dennis Gabor* discovers holography

American inventor *Edwin H. Land* demonstrates the first instant camera

American mathematician *Norbert Wiener* creates the study of cybernetics

1948   American physicist *John Bardeen* develops the transistor

American chemist *Melvin Calvin* begins research on photosynthesis

Russian-born American physicist *George Gamow* publishes "Alpha-Beta-Gamma" paper

American zoologist and sex researcher *Alfred Kinsey* publishes *Sexual Behavior in the Human Male*

American biochemist *Wendell Meredith Stanley* receives Presidential Certificate of Merit for developing an influenza vaccine

Swedish chemist *Arne Tiselius* receives the Nobel Prize for research in electrophoresis

1949   Hungarian-born American physicist *Edward Teller* begins developing the hydrogen bomb

American astronomer *Fred Lawrence Whipple* suggests the "dirty snowball" comet model

1950   American geneticist *Barbara McClintock* publishes the discovery of genetic transposition

1951   American chemist *Katherine Burr Blodgett* receives the Garvan Medal for women chemists

American biologist *Gregory Goodwin Pincus* begins work on the antifertility steroid the "pill"

Dutch-born English zoologist and ethologist *Nikolaas Tinbergen* publishes *The Study of Instinct*

1952   German-born American astronomer *Walter Baade* presents new measurements of the universe

French-born American microbiologist and ecologist *René Dubos* publishes a book linking tuberculosis with certain environmental conditions

American microbiologist *Alfred Day Hershey* conducts the "Blender Experiment" to demonstrate that DNA is the genetic material of life

Italian-born American molecular biologist *Salvador Edward Luria* discovers the phenomenon known as restriction and modification

American microbiologist *Jonas Salk* develops the first polio vaccine

English chemist *Alexander Todd* establishes the structure of flavin adenine dinucleotide (FAD)

1953   Russian theoretical physicist *Andrei Sakharov* and Russian physicist *Igor Tamm* develop the first Soviet hydrogen bomb

English molecular biologist *Francis Crick* and American molecular biologist *James D. Watson* develop the Watson-Crick model of DNA

English molecular biologist *Rosalind Elsie Franklin* provides evidence of DNA's double-helical structure

American physicist *Murray Gell-Mann* publishes a paper explaining the strangeness principle

American zoologist and sex researcher *Alfred Kinsey* publishes *Sexual Behavior in the Human Female*

French microbiologist *André Lwoff* proposes that "inducible lysogenic bacteria" can test cancerous and noncancerous cell activity

English biologist *Peter Brian Medawar* proves acquired immunological tolerance

American chemist *Stanley Lloyd Miller* publishes "A Production of Amino Acids under Possible Primitive Earth Conditions"

Austrian-born English crystallographer and biochemist *Max Perutz* develops method of isomorphous replacement

1955 English chemist *Alexander Todd* and English chemist and crystallographer *Dorothy Crowfoot Hodgkin* determine the structure of vitamin B_{12}

American biochemist *Sidney W. Fox* begins identifying properties of microspheres

American microbiologist *Jonas Salk's* polio vaccine pronounced safe and ninety-nine percent effective

English biochemist *Frederick Sanger* determines the total structure of the insulin molecule

1956 American biochemist *Stanley Cohen* extracts NGF from a mouse tumor

American experimental physicist *Leon Max Lederman* helps discover the "long-lived neutral kaon"

1957 American biochemist *Arthur Kornberg* and Spanish biochemist *Severo Ochoa* use DNA polymerase to synthesize DNA molecules

1958 American physicist *James Van Allen* discovers

Van Allen radiation belts

American geneticist *George Wells Beadle* receives the Nobel Prize for the One Gene, One Enzyme Theory

American population biologist *Paul R. Ehrlich* makes his first statement regarding the problem of overpopulation

German physicist *Rudolf Mössbauer* discovers recoilless gamma ray release

1959 American computer scientist *Grace Hopper* develops the COBOL computer language

German physicist *Rudolf Mössbauer* uses the Mössbauer Effect to test the theory of relativity

1960 English physicist and biochemist *John Kendrew* and Austrian-born English crystallographyer and biochemist *Max Perutz* formulate the first three-dimensional structure of the protein myoglobin

American chemist *Willard F. Libby* receives the Nobel Prize for his development of radiocarbon dating

Russian-born American virologist *Albert Sabin's* oral polio vaccine is approved for manufacture in the United States

1961 French biologists *François Jacob* and *Jacques Monod* discover messenger ribonucleic acid (mRNA)

American chemist *Melvin Calvin* receives the Nobel Prize in Chemistry for his research on photosynthesis

American biochemist *Marshall Warren Nirenberg* cracks the genetic code

1962 American marine biologist *Rachel Carson* publishes *Silent Spring*

Russian theoretical physicist *Lev Davidovich Landau* receives the Nobel Prize for his research into theories of condensed matter

Hungarian-born American physicist *Edward Teller* becomes the first advocate of an "active defense system" to shoot down enemy missiles

New Zealand-born English biophysicist *Maurice Hugh Frederick Wilkins* shows the helical structure of RNA

1963
German American physicist *Maria Goeppert-Mayer* becomes the first woman to receive the Nobel Prize for theoretical physics

American chemist *Linus Pauling* becomes the only person to receive two unshared Nobel Prizes

1964
American psychobiologist *Roger W. Sperry* publishes the findings of his split-brain studies

1965
American geneticist *A.H. Sturtevant* publishes *The History of Genetics*

1967
English astrophysicist *Antony Hewish* and Irish astronomer *Jocelyn Susan Bell Burnell* discover pulsars

South African heart surgeon *Christiaan Neethling Barnard* performs the first human heart transplant

American primatologist *Dian Fossey* establishes a permanent research camp in Rwanda

1968
American physicist *Luis Alvarez* wins the Nobel Prize for his bubble chamber work

1969
American astronaut *Neil Armstrong* becomes the first man to walk on the moon

1970
Indian-born American biochemist *Har Gobind Khorana* synthesizes the first artificial DNA

American biologist *Lynn Margulis* publishes *Origins of Life*

1971
English ethologist *Jane Goodall* publishes *In the Shadow of Man*

1972
American evolutionary biologist *Stephen Jay Gould* and American paleontologist *Niles Eldredge* introduce the concept of punctuated equilibrium

American physicist *John Bardeen* develops the BCS theory of superconductivity

American inventor *Edwin H. Land* reveals the first instant color camera

1973
American radio engineer *Karl Jansky* receives the honor of having the Jansky unit adopted as the unit of measure of radiowave intensity

Austrian zoologist and ethologist *Konrad Lorenz* receives the Nobel Prize for his behavioral research

American biochemist and geneticist *Maxine Singer* warns the public of gene-splicing risks

1974
English astrophysicist *Antony Hewish* receives the first Nobel Prize awarded to an astrophysicist

1975
French oceanographer *Jacques-Yves Cousteau* sees his Cousteau Society membership reach 120,000

American zoologist *Edward O. Wilson* publishes *Sociobiology: The New Synthesis*

1976
American computer engineer *Seymour Cray* introduces the CRAY-1 supercomputer

1977
Russian-born Belgian chemist *Ilya Prigogine* receives the Nobel Prize in Chemistry for his work on nonequilibrium thermodynamics

1980
American biochemist *Paul Berg* receives the Nobel Prize for the biochemistry of nucleic acids

1981   American virologist *Robert C. Gallo* develops a blood test for the AIDS virus and discovers human T-cell leukemia virus

1982   American astronaut and physicist *Sally Ride* becomes the first American woman in space

1983   Italian-born American astrophysicist and applied mathematician *Subrahmanyan Chandrasekhar* receives the Nobel Prize for research on aged stars

American primatologist *Dian Fossey* publishes *Gorillas in the Mist*

French virologist *Luc Montagnier* discovers the human immunodeficiency virus (HIV)

American astronomer and exobiologist *Carl Sagan* publishes an article with others suggesting the possibility of a "nuclear winter"

1986   American physicist *Richard P. Feynman* explains why the space shuttle *Challenger* exploded

1987   Chinese American physicist *Paul Ching-Wu Chu* leads a team that discovers a method for higher temperature superconductivity

1988   English theoretical physicist *Stephen Hawking* publishes *A Brief History of Time: From the Big Bang to Black Holes*

English pharmacologist *James Black* receives the Nobel Prize for his heart and ulcer medication work

1989   German-born American physicist *Hans Dehmelt* and German physicist *Wolfgang Paul* share the Nobel Prize for devising ion traps

1990   American physicists *Jerome Friedman, Henry W. Kendall,* and *Richard E. Taylor* are awarded the Nobel Prize for confirming the existence of quarks

American surgeon *Joseph E. Murray* receives

the Nobel Prize for performing the first human kidney transplant

1991   German physician and cell physiologist *Bert Sakmann* and German biophysicist *Erwin Neher* are awarded the Nobel Prize for inventing the patch clamp technique

1993   English biochemist *Richard J. Roberts* and American biologist *Phillip A. Sharp* share the Nobel Prize for their research on DNA structure

American astrophysicists *Russell A. Hulse* and *Joseph H. Taylor, Jr.* receive the Nobel Prize for their work on binary pulsars

1994   American researchers *Alfred G. Gilman* and *Martin Rodbell* win the Nobel Prize for their discovery of the role of G-proteins in cellular communication

1995   American biologists *Edward B. Lewis* and *Eric F. Wieschaus* and German biologist *Christiane Nusslein-Volhard* are awarded the Nobel Prize for discoveries concerning the embryonic development of fruit flies

1996   American paleobiologist *J. William Schopf* determines that a Martian meteorite which struck Antarctica 16 million years ago did not contain evidence of life on Mars.

American medical researcher *David Ho* heads a research group that announces the results of a study in which nine HIV-infected men were treated with a combination of drugs that halted the progression of AIDS so that HIV was not detected in blood tests a year after treatment ended

1997   English embryologist *Ian Wilmut* at the Roslin Institute reports that a sheep named Dolly is the first mammal successfully cloned from adult tissue

American biologist *Stanley Prusiner* wins the Nobel Prize for his discovery of prions, cellular proteins capable of causing disease

NOTABLE
TWENTIETH-CENTURY
SCIENTISTS

A

Edward P. Abraham

Edward P. Abraham
1913–

English biochemist

Sir Edward P. Abraham is best known for his research on antibiotics, particularly penicillin and cephalosporin. He was part of a team that included **Howard W. Florey** and **Ernest B. Chain** that followed up on **Alexander Fleming**'s initial discovery of the antibiotic properties of penicillin. This team determined the biological properties and chemical structure of penicillin, an accomplishment that won Fleming, Florey, and Chain shares of the 1945 Nobel Prize in Medicine or Physiology. Abraham first accepted an appointment at Oxford University in 1948 and has continued his affiliation with Oxford ever since. He was knighted by Queen Elizabeth II in 1980.

Edward Penley Abraham was born in Southampton, England, on June 10, 1913, the son of Albert Penley Abraham and the former Mary Hearn. He attended King Edward VI School in Southampton and then matriculated at The Queen's College, Oxford, from which he received First Class Honors in the School of Natural Science in 1935. Upon graduation, Abraham took a position in the laboratory of 1947 Nobel Prize winner **Robert Robinson**. There, he studied a substance called lysozyme, an antibiotic that occurs naturally in tears and that had been discovered by Alexander Fleming in 1921.

In 1938, Abraham was awarded a Rockefeller Travelling Scholarship which he used to spend a year at the University of Stockholm. At the end of that scholarship year, he returned to Oxford, where he joined the laboratory at which Florey and Chain were studying penicillin.

The Penicillin Problem

Penicillin had been discovered in 1928 by Fleming in one of the most dramatic and famous examples of serendipity in scientific history. Fleming found that the presence of a particular genus of the mold *Penicillium* prevented the growth of bacteria in a petri dish. He worked for nearly a year to find out how the mold exerted its antibacterial action. Unfortunately, he had relatively modest success and had neither the scientific background nor the interest to pursue his studies on the material. Fleming did publish and speak about his discovery, but with so little effectiveness that it nearly became lost in the archives of science.

Fortunately, Fleming's work was resurrected in 1935 by Florey and Chain, who were then working on the broader problem of the development of antibacterial agents. Between them Florey and Chain decided to test the biological properties and chemical structure of the antibacterial agent produced by *Penicillium*. In order to carry out either of these tasks, the first step was to prepare the agent in a pure form, a responsibility that fell largely to Abraham. He was eventually able to crystallize the sodium salt of penicillin, making it possible for him to eventually determine the chemical structure of the penicillin molecule. It was this step that made it possible to obtain, study, and ultimately to synthesize the antibiotic.

Abraham's work on penicillin came at a critical time in history. World War II was just about to begin, and the scientists immediately recognized the enormous potential of the antibiotic as an anti-infective agent. Commercial production was not possible in Great Britain during the year, but the compound was put into commercial production almost immediately in the United States so that it would be available for the treatment of battle injuries.

Research on Cephalosporin

After completing his work with penicillin, Abraham continued his studies of antibacterial agents. In the 1950s, he collaborated with Guy Newton to discover the antibiotic known as cephalosporin C, obtained from the mold *Cephalosporium acremonium*. This compound turned out to be only one member of a large collection of antibiotics with similar chemical structures. Abraham and Newton obtained a patent for cephalosporin C and for the basic chemical structure of its molecule. The two discoverers eventually made fortunes from their patent, but both created charitable foundations for the distribution of their profits. Both the E. P. Abraham Research Fund and the Guy Newton Trust are dedicated to the support of medical, biological, and chemical research at the Sir William Dunn School of Pathology and Lincoln College of Oxford University and at the university itself.

Abraham was made a Fellow of Lincoln College in 1948, a post he held until 1980, when he was made an Honorary Fellow of the College. He also served as Reader in Chemical Pathology at Oxford from 1960 to 1964 before being promoted to Professor of Chemical Pathology. He held that post from 1964 to 1980 and is now Emeritus Professor at the university. He is also an Honorary Fellow at Linacre, Lady Margaret Hall, Wolfson, and St. Peter's Colleges at Oxford, and an Honorary Foreign member of the American Academy of Arts and Sciences. He was awarded the Royal Medal of the Royal Society in 1973, the Mullard Prize and Medal of the Royal Society in 1980, the Scheele Medal of the Swedish Academy of Pharmaceutical Sciences in 1975, the Chemical Society Award in Medicinal Chemistry in 1975, the International Society of Chemotherapy Award in 1983, and the Sarton Medal in 1989.

Abraham was Rennebohm Lecturer at the University of Wisconsin in 1966-67, the Squibb Lecturer at Rutgers University in 1972, the Perlman Lecturer at Wisconsin in 1985, and the Sarton Lecturer at the University of Gent in 1989. He was elected a Fellow of the Royal Society in 1958, was made a companion of the Order of the British Empire in 1973, and was knighted in Queen Elizabeth II in 1980.

Abraham is the author or coauthor of five books on antibiotics and of biographies of important figures in the field of medicinal chemistry, including contributions to the *Biographical Memoirs of Fellows of the Royal Society* for Florey and Chain. He was married in 1939 to the former Asbjörg Harung in Bergen, Norway. The couple has one son.

SELECTED WRITINGS BY ABRAHAM:

Books

(with others) *Antibiotics*, 1949.
Biochemistry of Some Peptide and Steroid Antibiotics, 1957.
Biosynthesis and Enzymic Hydrolysis of Penicillins and Cephalosporins, 1974.
Cephalosporins and Penicillins, 1972.
General Pathology, 1957, 4th ed., 1970.

FURTHER READING:

Books

Abbott, David, general editor. *Biographical Dictionary of Scientists*. New York: Bedrick Books, 1994, p. 2.
Muir, Hazel, editor. *Larousse Dictionary of Scientists*, Edinburgh: Larousse, 1994, pp. 2-3.

Other

"Penicillin." http://cygnus.uwa.edu.au/.wmbest/mo-month/mom-5-97.htm.
"The Sir William Dunn School of Pathology." http://www.path.ox.ac.uk/wsj/history.html.

—Sketch by David E. Newton

Lars V. Ahlfors
1907–1996
Finnish-born American mathematician

Lars V. Ahlfors was a mathematician whose major area of research was complex analysis. In 1936, he was one of the first to receive a Fields Medal. Often considered the equivalent of the Nobel Prize, the Fields Medal is given every four years to a mathematician under the age of forty who has achieved important results in his or her work. Ahlfors received this award for his work on Riemann surfaces, which are schematic devices for mapping the relation between complex numbers according to an analytic function. Ahlfors's results led to new developments in the field of meromorphic functions (functions that are analytic everywhere in a region except for a finite number of poles); the methods he developed to obtain these results created an entirely new field of analysis.

Lars Valerian Ahlfors was born on April 18, 1907 in Helsingfors (now Helsinki), Finland. His mother, Sievä Helander Ahlfors, died giving birth to him. His father, Axel Ahlfors, was a mechanical engineering

Lars V. Ahlfors

professor at the Polytechnical Institute. Even as a child, Ahlfors was interested in mathematics; his high school did not offer calculus courses, but Ahlfors taught himself by reading his father's engineering books.

He did not have access to mathematical books until he began his studies in 1924 at the University of Helsingfors, where he was taught by Ernst Lindelöf and Rolf Nevanlinna. Lindelöf worked in complex analysis and was known as the father of mathematics in Finland—mostly because, in the 1920s, all Finnish mathematicians were his students. Ahlfors received his degree in the spring of 1928, and he also began his graduate work that year. Although there were no official graduate courses in mathematics at the university, Lindelöf supervised students' advanced readings.

Proposes Geometric Interpretation of Nevalinna Theory

Ahlfors took his first official graduate course in mathematics in the fall of 1928, when he accompanied Nevanlinna to Zürich. The class Nevanlinna taught was on contemporary function theory. Topics included the major parts of Nevanlinna's theory of meromorphic functions and Denjoy's conjecture on the number of asymptotic values of an entire function, as well as Carleman's partial proof of it. During his study of this subject, Ahlfors proved the full Denjoy conjecture after he discovered a new approach

based on conformal mapping. A conformal map is a function in which, if two curves intersect at an angle, then the images of the curves in the map will also intersect at the same angle.

When the course ended, Ahlfors travelled to Paris, where he continued his work for three months before returning to Finland. His research there led to a geometric interpretation of the Nevanlinna theory, which he would publish in 1935. Although this interpretation was also discovered independently in Japan, it was the beginning of Ahlfors's concentration on meromorphic functions.

When he returned to Finland, Ahlfors was given the position of lecturer at Åbo Akademi, Finland's Swedish-language university. He also began work on his thesis, the subject of which was conformal mapping and entire functions. He had finished his thesis by the spring of 1930, and received his Ph.D. in 1932. Ahlfors was named a fellow of the Rockefeller Institute in 1932, which allowed him to live and do research in Paris for a year. In July of 1933, he married Erna Lehnert; they would have three daughters. He returned to the University of Helsingfors that same year as an adjunct professor and taught there until the fall of 1935, when he began a three-year assignment as assistant professor at Harvard University.

Receives Fields Medal

For his research in Riemann surfaces of inverse functions in terms of covering surfaces, Ahlfors was awarded the Fields Medal by the International Congress of Mathematicians in 1936. Ahlfors was attending the ceremony in Oslo, but he learned only hours before it began that he had been chosen as the recipient. In the talk about Ahlfors's work he gave to the congress, German mathematician Constantin Carathéodory specifically noted the contribution of Ahlfors's paper, "On the Theory of Covering Surfaces," which explained the methods Ahlfors had developed in his work on Riemann surfaces. Carathéodory pointed out that these methods were also the start of a new branch of analysis, which he termed "metrical topology."

In the spring of 1938, Ahlfors left the United States and returned to Finland to take a position as a professor at the University of Helsinki. World War II soon spread to Finland, however, and the university closed because there were not enough students. Although his family was evacuated to Sweden, Ahlfors stayed in Helsinki. He was not called for military duty because of a physical condition, but he participated in the military's communications setup.

In the summer of 1944, the University of Zürich offered Ahlfors a professorship, and he accepted the position. After an arduous journey from Sweden to

Switzerland because of the war, he began teaching in the summer of 1945. He was not happy there, however, so when Harvard University asked him to return he gladly accepted. He began teaching there in the fall of 1946 and became a naturalized United States citizen in 1952. In 1953, Ahlfors's book *Complex Analysis* was published. It is still widely used as a basic text in graduate courses. In 1964, he was named William Caspar Graustein Professor of Mathematics. Ahlfors remained at Harvard until his retirement as Professor Emeritus in 1977, subsequently moving to Boston. He died in Pittsfield, Massachusetts.

SELECTED WRITINGS BY AHLFORS:

Books

Complex Analysis. New York: McGraw-Hill, 1953.
Riemann Surfaces. Princeton: Princeton University Press, 1960.
Lectures on Quasiconformal Mappings. New York: Van Nostrand, 1966.
Conformal Invariants. New York: McGraw-Hill, 1973.
Lars Valerian Ahlfors: Collected Papers. Vol. 1, 1929–1955. Vol. 2, 1956–1979. Klosterberg, Switzerland: Birkhäuser, 1982.

FURTHER READING:

Saxon, Wolfgang."Lars V. Ahlfors, 89, Pioneer in the Outer Reaches of Higher Math" (obituary). *New York Times* (20 October 1996): A40.

—*Sketch by Laura Mangan-Grenier*

Hannes Olof Gösta Alfvén

fields. The first space scientist to receive the Nobel, Alfvén's discoveries grew out of his research in sunspots.

Hannes Olof Gösta Alfvén was born in Norrköping, Sweden, May 30, 1908. His parents, Johannes Alfvén and Anna-Clara (Romanus) Alfvén, were both physicians. After completing elementary and secondary school in Norrköping, Alfvén enrolled at the University of Uppsala and received his Ph.D. in physics in 1934. He became a lecturer in physics at Uppsala, and three years later was appointed research physicist at the Nobel Institute of Physics. In 1940, he became a member of the faculty at the Royal Institute of Technology in Stockholm, where he held successively the titles of professor of the theory of electricity from 1940 to 1945, professor of electronics from 1945 to 1963, and professor of plasma physics from 1963 to 1967. In 1935, Alfvén was married to Kerstin Maria Erikson, a social science teacher. They had five children.

Sunspot Research Leads to Magnetohydrodynamics

Alfvén's primary research interest was the application of physical principles to astronomical phenomena. In the early 1940s, he began a long-term study of sunspots. One of the consequences of his research was his discovery of hydromagnetic waves (named Alfvén waves in his honor), which challenged some long-held and widely-accepted physical concepts, including James Clerk Maxwell's electromagnetic theory. Tradi-

Hannes Olof Gösta Alfvén
1908–1995
Swedish physicist

Hannes Olof Gösta Alfvén made a number of important discoveries in the fields of plasma physics, space physics, and astrophysics, and is considered the founder of magnetohydrodynamics (MHD), a field of study whose applications are as diverse as the properties of stars and the production of fusion power by artificial means. In 1970, he was awarded the Nobel Prize with **Louis Néel** in physics for his achievements in MHD and their practical uses in plasma physics. MHD deals with the behavior of electrically conducting gases and liquids as they interact with magnetic

tionally, electromagnetic waves were believed to be incapable of penetrating a conductor to any significant degree. For example, light (a form of electromagnetic radiation) is almost perfectly reflected by a conductor such as copper or silver metal.

During his study of sunspots, however, Alfvén came to a very different conclusion. He hypothesized that electromagnetic waves were very good conductors, able to extend through the highly ionized solar gas. In 1942, he published a detailed and elegant demonstration of his theory; however, his observations were either ignored or rejected by most of his colleagues. His biographer, A. J. Dessler, explains that Alfvén's theory of hydromagnetic waves was not taken seriously until six years later, when he presented his ideas in a lecture at the University of Chicago. **Enrico Fermi** is said to have nodded in approval after Alfvén had delivered his paper, remarking, "Of course." Dessler claims that on the next day, "the entire world of physics said, 'Oh, of course' also."

That bit of recognition did not push Alfvén to the forefront of the physics community, however. He continued to work for the most part in private, publishing a relatively small number of papers on his discoveries. Out of that work, however, grew an important new field of physics now known as magnetohydrodynamics (MHD).

Discoveries in Plasma Physics Applied to Fusion Research

An important aspect of Alfvén's work in MHD has been his study of plasma, sometimes referred to as the fourth state of matter. A gas-like mixture of electrons and positively-charged ions, plasma exists only at very high temperatures, such as those found in stars. At such extreme temperatures, atoms and molecules are completely ionized. Most of Alfvén's early research on plasma was based on studies of sunspots, magnetic storms, and other stellar phenomena. One of his most important discoveries in this area came in the 1930s, when he proposed the concept of magnetic field lines that become "frozen" within a plasma. He showed that under certain circumstances in which a plasma moves, the magnetic field associated with it moves as well. The primary goal of Alfvén's work with plasma and MHD has been to better understand the origin of the universe, which he believes was formed from plasma. By studying properties of primordial plasma through exploration of asteroids, for example, Alfvén felt more could be learned about how stars, planets, and other astronomical bodies were formed. Consequently, he was a strong supporter of space research programs, such as those carried out by the U.S. National Aeronautics and Space Administration. Such programs, he believed, provide an invaluable way of testing theoretical concepts like those he developed.

Although Alfvén's own research centered on outer space, many of his discoveries have had important practical applications. For example, developing fusion power plants that can supply energy on a commercial basis depends on the ability to produce and contain very hot masses of material within which fusion reactions can occur. At the high temperatures inside a fusion reactor, these materials exist in the form of plasma, inviting the many important applications of Alfvén's discoveries.

Alfvén left Sweden in 1967 to accept an appointment as professor of physics at the University of California at San Diego. His decision to leave his native country was supposedly based on disagreements with the Swedish government over certain policies, particularly those involving education and nuclear power. For instance, although he had originally been a strong supporter of the construction of nuclear power plants, he later developed concerns about the environmental risks posed by such plants. He argued against the increasing dependence on nuclear power in Sweden, and eventually decided that all applications of nuclear power—both peaceful and military—were dangerous. He became active in the anti-nuclear movement of the 1970s and 1980s. At the time of his death, Alfvén was teaching part-time at the University of California in San Diego. He died at his home in Djursholm, Sweden. In addition to his Nobel Prize, Alfvén received the Gold Medal of the Royal Astronomical Society in 1967, the Lomonosov Gold Medal of the Soviet Academy of Sciences in 1971, the Franklin Medal of the Franklin Institute in 1971, and the Bowie Gold Medal in 1987. Alfvén's memberships included the National Academy of Sciences and the Royal Society.

SELECTED WRITINGS BY ALFVÉN:

Books

Cosmical Electrodynamics. 2nd ed. (with Carl-Gunne Fälthammer). Oxford: Clarendon Press, 1963.

On the Origin of the Solar System. Oxford: Clarendon Press, 1954.

Worlds-Antiworlds: Antimatter in Cosmology. New York: W. H. Freeman, 1966.

Sagan om de stora datamaskinen. (Novel written under pseudonym Olaf Johanneson). Stockholm: Bonniers, 1968. Translated by Naomi Wallford as *The Tale of the Big Computer.* New York: Coward-McCann, 1969.

Living on the Third Planet. New York: W. H. Freeman, 1972.

Structure and Evolutionary History of the Solar System. (Written with Gustaf Arrhenius). Dordrecht, The Netherlands: Reidel, 1975.

FURTHER READING:

Books

Contemporary Authors. Vols. 29–32 Detroit: Gale, 1972.
McGraw-Hill Modern Scientists and Engineers. Vol. 1. New York: McGraw-Hill, 1980, pp. 10–12.

Periodicals

Dessler, A. J. "Nobel Prizes: 1970 Awards Honor Three in Physics and Chemistry." *Science* (6 November 1970): 604–06.
Sullivan, Walter. "Hannes Alfven, 86, Founder of Field in Physics, Is Dead" (obituary). *New York Times* (2 April 1995): B22.

—*Sketch by David E. Newton*

Ralph Asher Alpher

Ralph Asher Alpher
1921–
American physicist

Very early in his career, Ralph Alpher conducted important theoretical studies on the origin and evolution of the universe with his Ph.D. advisor, Russian-American physicist **George Gamow**. Together with Gamow, he proposed the theory that explains the abundance of chemical elements resulting from thermonuclear processes that occurred in the early stages of a hot, evolving universe. This theory was to become an integral part of the "Big Bang" model of the universe. Alpher and another colleague also predicted in 1948 that if the universe began with a hot "Big Bang," it would have produced intense electromagnetic radiation which would have cooled by now. This predicted background radiation was observed by others in 1965, and is considered one of the most important scientific discoveries of this century.

As the youngest of four children born to Samuel Alpher, a building contractor, and Rose Maleson Alpher, Ralph Alpher was born in Washington, D.C. on February 3, 1921. He attended Theodore Roosevelt High School, where his interest in science was stimulated by his English teacher, Matilde Eiker, who was an amateur astronomer, as well as by his chemistry teacher, Sarah Branch, and physics teacher, Richard Feldman. After entering George Washington University in Washington, D.C. in 1938, Alpher was compelled by economic circumstances as well as by the start of World War II to continue his education at night. From that year until he received his Ph.D.,

Alpher worked during the day and attended school at night. One of the earliest of his many jobs was as a secretary at National Cash Register where, being underage, he worked with a special permit. He also was a secretary at the Carnegie Institute of Washington's Department of Terrestrial Magnetism, a statistical clerk at the Bureau of Immigration and Naturalization, and an abstract writer for the War Department. In 1942, Alpher married Louise Ellen Simons, with whom he had two children, Harriet and Victor.

Meets George Gamow and Begins Work on Primordial Nucleosynthesis

After receiving his B. S. in 1943, Alpher began work on his Ph.D. at George Washington University with Gamow as his advisor. He was, however, a part-time student and took evening courses at the university. At the same time, he was also working since 1940 as a civilian contract physicist with the U. S. Navy Department, and then later, in 1944, he joined the Applied Physics Laboratory of The Johns Hopkins University. His wartime projects at the Naval Ordnance Laboratory and later at the Navy Bureau of Ordnance involved degaussing ships (protecting them against magnetic mines) and the detection of submarines by airborne magnetometers. After the war, he continued at Johns Hopkins where he conducted research on supersonic and hypersonic guided missile aerodynamics, nuclear weapons effects, and operations analysis applied to ship-to-ship guided missile systems.

By 1946, he had completed his research and was about to begin writing his dissertation when Gamow suddenly showed him a recently completed dissertation on the same subject whose results had already been published in the *Soviet Journal of Physics*. Since Alpher had to start over with another topic, Gamow suggested that he pursue one of his unformulated ideas concerning the synthesis of elements in the early stages of an expanding universe ("primordial nucleosynthesis"). Alpher agreed to pursue this topic and undertook his research immediately. As his dissertation progressed, the opinions of physicists concerning the creation of the known elements found in the universe varied between those who argued for an evolving, expanding universe and those who preferred a static or steady-state model. One who shared the expanding universe notion of Gamow and Alpher was Robert Herman, a Princeton Ph.D. who also worked with Alpher at the Applied Physics Lab. As a colleague of Alpher's and an eventual collaborator, Herman provided a valuable sounding board for Alpher. They began a friendship and working relationship that lasted for over forty years. Their first joint paper published in 1948 included the now-famous prediction of the remnant cosmic background radiation. Alpher's dissertation also was completed that year.

It was also in 1948 that what was to become known as the "alpha-beta-gamma" theory was published. As a result of Alpher's dissertation findings, he and Gamow collaborated on a paper in which they suggested for the first time the possibility that the abundances of chemical elements could be explained as being the byproduct of thermonuclear processes that occurred during the beginning of a universe that is still evolving. Gamow was an intuitive physicist with a fun-loving and almost irreverent approach to his work, and it was his idea to add the name of **Hans Albrecht Bethe**, the German-American physicist, as coauthor "in absentia." The sound of Alpher-Bethe-Gamow (or alpha-beta-gamma as it came to be called) was simply too tempting for the playful Gamow not to use as the popular name for a theory that dealt with the beginning of the universe. Although Bethe's research focused on the nuclear mechanisms that power stars, he did not actually contribute to this important paper. Alpher later recounted in a 1988 *Physics Today* article that when the editor of the *Physical review* chose to remove "in absentia" from Bethe's name, Bethe did not object, and even listed the paper in his curriculum vitae. Alpher also quotes Bethe as saying that, "I felt at the time that it was rather a nice joke, and that the paper had a chance to be correct, so that I did not mind my name being added to it." The paper—based on Alpher's dissertation results—was published in *Physical Review* just before Alpher's dissertation defense, and his association with Gamow combined with several major newspapers having picked up a short news summary

of the paper, made an unusually large audience appear for Alpher's successful dissertation defense. It also prompted *The Washington Post* to publish a Herblock cartoon that focused on Alpher's statement that all the elements in the universe were produced in a period that lasted about five minutes.

Collaborates with Herman and Predicts Cosmic Background Radiation

In the first of their many papers together, Alpher and Robert Herman suggested that if the "Big Bang" model were indeed correct in describing the beginnings of the universe, then the early stages of the universe must have been dominated by especially intense electromagnetic radiation. They further theorized that with the continuous expansion of the universe, this radiation would have cooled, and they offered a predicted temperature (5 degrees kelvin) that it would register were it to be discovered. This primordial or relic background radiation was eventually found in 1965 by **Arno A. Penzias** and **Robert W. Wilson**. It was actually "heard" by them rather than seen, since they were using a radio telescope. However, for nearly a year they could not account for this steady noise that appeared uniform from all directions. Baffled, they finally obtained help from Princeton scientists **Robert Dicke** and **P. J. Peebles** and eventually measured the noise, finding it was typical of an object radiating at about 3 degrees kelvin—close to what Alpher and Herman predicted in 1948. The measurement of background radiation has been called one of the most significant discoveries of this century, and for it, Penzias and Wilson were awarded the Nobel Prize for physics in 1978. It is ironic that this celebrated award was given to two scientists (Penzias and Wilson) who accidentally discovered something that two others (Alpher and Herman) had openly predicted decades before. In their 1988 article, Alpher and Herman reflected on this apparent injustice and said good-naturedly, "Thinking back, we could not help but be struck by the observation that contrary to what is so often presented, science does not necessarily proceed in an orderly and logical fashion."

The existence of this background radiation is now widely regarded as offering very strong evidence for the validity of the "Big Bang" model, of which Alpher must certainly be considered a pioneer. Its discovery also stimulated an enormous amount of interest and research in the scientific community, lending even further significance to Alpher's early work. Recognition of this fact came somewhat late for Alpher, but in 1980 the Franklin Institute awarded Alpher and Herman the John Price Wetherill Medal for their prediction of the existence of residual cosmic radiation as well as for their work on nucleosynthesis. Later, in the highly regarded book, *The First Three Minutes*, Nobel Prize-winning physicist **Steven Weinberg** described a paper by Alpher and his colleagues

Herman and Follin as, "the first thoroughly modern analysis of the early history of the universe." Finally in 1993, Alpher and Herman were awarded the highly prestigious Henry Draper Medal of the National Academy of Sciences.

In 1986, Alpher left the General Electric Company, where he had worked since 1955, and returned to academia as Distinguished Research Professor of Physics at Union College in Schenectady, New York as well as Administrator and Distinguished Scientist at the Dudley Observatory there.

SELECTED WRITINGS BY ALPHER:

Books

(With Robert C. Herman) "Reflections on 'Big Bang' Cosmology," *Cosmology, Fusion and Other Matters.* ed. by Frederick Reines. Boulder: Colorado Associated University Press, 1972.

Periodicals

"Reflections on Early Work on 'Big Bang' Cosmology." *Physics Today* (August 1988): 24-34.

FURTHER READING:

Books

Millar, David. *The Cambridge Dictionary of Scientists.* Cambridge, England: Cambridge University Press, 1996, pp 4-5.
Porter, Roy. *The Biographical Dictionary of Scientists.* New York: Oxford University Press, 1994, pp. 9-10.

Periodicals

"Franklin Institute Awards Eleven Medals." *Physics Today* (December 1980), pp.73-74.

—*Sketch by Leonard C. Bruno*

Anne Anastasi
1908–

American psychologist

In her long and productive career, Anne Anastasi has produced not only several classic texts in psychology but has been a major factor in the development of psychology as a quantitative behavioral science. To psychology professionals, the name Anastasi is synonymous with psychometrics, since it was she who pioneered understanding how psychological traits are influenced, developed, and measured. In 1987 she was rated by her peers as the most prominent living woman in psychology in the English-speaking world.

Anne Anastasi was born December 19, 1908, in New York City, the only child of Anthony and Theresa Gaudiosi. Her father, who died when she was only one year old, worked for the New York City Board of Education. Soon after his death, her mother experienced such a deep split with her father's relatives that they would never be a part of her life. From then on, she was raised by her mother, grandmother, and great uncle. Her mother was compelled to find a job, and eventually she became office manager of one of the largest foreign newspapers in New York, *Il Progresso Italo-Americano.* Meanwhile, the precocious and intelligent young Anastasi was educated at home by her grandmother, and it was not until the sixth grade that she entered the public school system. After graduating from P.S. 33 in the Bronx at the top of her class, she attended Evander Childs High School, but found the entire experience dispiriting and dropped out after two months.

Skips High School and Discovers Psychology at Barnard College

The dilemma of a 13-year old girl leaving high school after only two months was solved by an insightful family friend, Ida Stadie, who suggested that she prepare to skip high school and go directly to college. Since Barnard College in New York City did not specify a high school degree as an admissions requirement, Anastasi decided she need only submit the results of her College Entrance Examination Board tests. After taking two years to prepare at the Rhodes Preparatory School in Manhattan, she took the tests and was admitted to Barnard College in 1924 at the age of 15.

Mathematics had been her first love since elementary school, and at Barnard she was placed in all the advanced math classes. During her sophomore year however, she took a course in developmental psychology with the department chairman, Harry L. Hollingworth, whose stimulating lectures made her intellectually curious about the discipline. In that course, she encountered a psychology article by Charles Spearman, whose intriguing work on correlation coefficients showed her that it was possible to combine mathematics and psychology. Convinced she had found the best of both worlds, she enrolled in the Barnard's Honors Program in psychology for her last two years, and received her B.A. in 1928 at the age of 19, having been elected to Phi Beta Kappa and having won the Caroline Duror Graduate Fellowship, "awarded to the member of the graduating class showing the greatest promise of distinction in her chosen line of work."

Receives Ph.D., Teaches at 21, and Writes Classic Text at 29

Having taken graduate courses at Columbia University while still at Barnard, she applied there after graduation and was allowed to skip the Master's degree and to go directly for her Ph.D. in general experimental psychology. At this time, Columbia's psychology department provided a stimulating and lively environment, made more enlightening by its summer sessions that were visited by eminent psychologists. During her second year at Columbia, Anastasi began to specialize, and it was then that she decided on the complex field of differential psychology. As the branch of psychology that deals with individual and group differences in behavior, it is a highly quantitative field of study, and therefore much to her liking.

As she had planned, Anastasi received her Ph.D. from Columbia in only two years, and in 1930 returned to Barnard to begin teaching. Three years later, she married psychologist John Porter Foley Jr., a fellow Columbia Ph.D. student. In 1939 she left Barnard to become assistant professor and sole member of the newly created Psychology Department at Queens College of the City of New York. After the war, she left Queens College in 1947 to become associate professor of psychology in the Graduate School of Arts and Sciences at Fordham University, and full professor in 1951. She remained there until her retirement in 1979, when she became a professor emeritus.

The focus of her research, writing, and teaching has been on the nature and measurement of psychological traits. In her landmark work *Psychological Testing*, Anastasi emphasizes the ways education and heredity influence trait development, and then goes on to demonstrate how the measurement of those traits is affected by such variables as training, culture, and language differences. Throughout her work, the "nature-nurture" controversy is dominant, and typically, she argues that psychologists have been incorrect seeking to explain behavior by using one or the other. She states rather, that neither exists apart from the other, and that psychologists should be questioning how the two interact.

At least two of Anastasi's other books are considered classics in the field and are found in many translations around the world. The recipient of several honorary degrees, she became in 1972 the first woman to be elected president of the American Psychological Association in 50 years. In 1987 her career achievements were recognized when she was presented the National Medal of Science by President Ronald Reagan.

Anastasi's life has not been entirely trouble-free, as she had to survive a diagnosis of cervical cancer in 1934. When the successful radiation therapy left her unable to have children, she looked only at the positive aspects of her condition and stated that she was able to focus solely on her career without guilt. A well-rounded individual with an avocational interest in art, she continued her professional writing, speaking, and organizational activities long past the time when most people have fully retired.

SELECTED WRITINGS BY ANASTASI:

Books

Differential Psychology. New York: The Macmillan Company, 1937.
Fields of Applied Psychology. New York: McGraw-Hill Book Company, 1979.
Psychological Testing. New York: Macmillan Publishing Co., Inc., 1982.

FURTHER READING:

Books

Metzger, Linda and Deborah A. Straub, editors. *Contemporary Authors.* New Revision Series, Volume 17. Detroit, MI: Gale Research Co., p 21.
O'Connell, Agnes N. and Nancy Felipe Russo, editors. *Women in Psychology.* New York: Greenwood Press, 1990, pp. 13-22.
Sheehy, Noel, Antony J. Chapman, and Wendy A. Conroy, editors. *Biographical Dictionary of Psychology.* New York: Routledge Reference, 1997, pp. 13-14.

Periodicals

"American Psychological Foundation Awards for 1984." *American Psychologist* (March 1985): 340-341.
"Distinguished Scientific Award for the Applications of Psychology: 1981." *American Psychologist* (January 1982): 52-59.

—*Sketch by Leonard C. Bruno*

Christian Boehmer Anfinsen
1916–1995
American biochemist

Biochemist Christian Boehmer Anfinsen is known for establishing that the structure of an

Christian Boehmer Anfinsen

enzyme is intimately related to its function. This discovery was a major contribution to the scientific understanding of the nature of enzymes. For this achievement, Anfinsen shared the 1972 Nobel Prize for Chemistry with the research team of **Stanford Moore** and **William Howard Stein.**

Anfinsen was born on March 26, 1916, in Monessen, Pennsylvania, a town located just outside of Pittsburgh. He was the child of Christian Anfinsen, an engineer and emigrant from Norway, and Sophie Rasmussen, who was also of Norwegian heritage. Anfinsen earned his B.A. from Swarthmore College in 1937. Subsequently, he attended the University of Pennsylvania, earning an M.S. in organic chemistry in 1939. After earning his master's degree, Anfinsen received a fellowship from the American Scandinavian Foundation to spend a year at the Carlsberg Laboratory in Copenhagen, Denmark. Upon his return in 1940, he entered Harvard University's Ph.D. program in biochemistry. His doctoral dissertation involved work with enzymes; he described various methodologies for discerning the enzymes present in the retina of the eye, and he earned his Ph.D in 1943.

After receiving his Ph.D., Anfinsen began teaching at Harvard Medical School, in the department of biological chemistry. From 1944 to 1946 he worked in the United States Office of Scientific Research and Development. He then worked in the biochemical division of the Medical Nobel Institute in Sweden under Hugo Theorell, as an American Cancer Society

senior fellow, from 1947 to 1948. Harvard University promoted him to associate professor upon his return, but in 1950 he accepted a position as head of the National Institutes of Health's (NIH) National Heart Institute Laboratory of Cellular Physiology. He served in this position until 1962. Anfinsen returned to teaching at Harvard Medical School in 1962, but he returned to NIH a year later. This time he was named director of the Laboratory of Chemical Biology at the National Institute of Arthritis, Metabolism, and Digestive Diseases. He held this position until 1981; he spent a year at the Weizmann Institute of science and then in 1982 accepted an appointment as professor of biology at Johns Hopkins University, where he remained until his death. A former editor of *Advances in Protein Chemistry*, he was also on the editorial boards of the *Journal of Biological Chemistry, Biopolymers*, and the *Proceedings of the National Academy of Sciences.*

Anfinsen began his research concerning the structure and function of enzymes in the mid–1940s. Enzymes are a type of protein; specifically, they are what drives the many chemical reactions in the human body. All proteins are made up of smaller components called peptide chains, which are amino acids linked together. Amino acids are, in turn, a certain class of organic compounds. The enzymes take on a globular, three-dimensional form as the amino acid chain folds over. The unfolded chain form of an enzyme is called the primary structure. Once the chain folds over, it is said to be in the tertiary structure. From one set of amino acids for one particular enzyme there are 100 different possible ways in which these amino acids can link together. (Only certain amino acids can "fit" next to other amino acids.) However, only one configuration will result in an active enzyme. In general, Anfinsen's research concerned finding out how a particular set of amino acids knows to configure in a way that results in the active form of the enzyme.

Anfinsen chose to study the enzyme ribonuclease (RNase), which contains 124 amino acids and is responsible for breaking down the ribonucleic acid (RNA) found in food. This reaction enables the body to recycle the resultant smaller pieces. He felt that by determining how a particular enzyme assumes its particular active configuration, the structure and function of enzymes could be better understood. He reasoned that he could determine how an enzyme protein is built and when the enzyme becomes functional by observing it adding one amino acid at a time. He utilized techniques developed by Cambridge University's **Frederick Sanger** to conduct this research. Another research team headed by Stanford Moore and William Howard Stein was working simultaneously on the same enzyme as Anfinsen, ribonuclease; in 1960, using ribonuclease, Moore and Stein were the first to determine the exact amino acid sequence of an enzyme. However, Anfinsen remained more concerned with how the enzyme forms into its active configuration.

Anfinsen eventually changed his methodology of research during an opportunity to study abroad. While at the NIH, Anfinsen took yet another leave of absence when a Rockefeller Public Service Award allowed him to spend 1954 to 1955 at the Carlsberg Laboratory studying under the physical chemist Kai Linderstrøm-Lang. Anfinsen had been studying ribonuclease by building it up; Linderstrøm-Lang convinced him to start with the whole molecule and study it by stripping it down piece by piece. Anfinsen began with the whole ribonuclease molecule and then successively broke the various bonds of the molecule. The process is called denaturing the protein or, in other words, causing it to lose its functional capacity. By breaking certain key bonds, other bonds formed between the amino acids resulting in a random, inactive form of ribonuclease. By 1962, Anfinsen had confirmed that when this inactive form is placed into an environment that mimics the environment in which ribonuclease normally appears in the body, that inactive form would slowly revert to the active configuration on its own and thus regain its enzymatic activity. This discovery revealed the important fact that all the information for the assembly of the three-dimensional, active enzyme form was within the protein's own sequence of amino acids.

Receives Nobel Prize for Enzyme Research

For uncovering the connection between the primary and tertiary structure of enzymes, Anfinsen received half of the 1972 Nobel Prize for Chemistry. Moore and Stein were awarded the other half. In addition to his numerous journal articles on protein structure, enzyme function, and related matters, in 1959, Anfinsen published a book entitled *The Molecular Basis of Evolution*. After receiving the Nobel Prize, Anfinsen began focusing his research on the protein interferon, known for its key role as part of the body's immunity against both viruses and cancer. He succeeded in isolating and characterizing this important human protein.

Anfinsen's honors in addition to the Nobel Prize include The Rockefeller Foundation Public Service Award, a Guggenheim Fellowship, as well as honorary degrees from Georgetown University and New York Medical College and five other universities. Anfinsen was a member of the National Academy of Sciences, the American Society of Biological Chemists, and the Royal Danish Academy. As an opponent of biological weapons, he belonged to the Committee for Responsible Genetics. He married Florence Bernice Kenenger in 1941, and they had three children. Anfinsen and Kenenger divorced in 1978. In 1979, Anfinsen married Libby Esther Schulman Ely. He died on May 14, 1995, at Northwest Hospital Center in Randallstown, Maryland.

SELECTED WRITINGS BY ANFINSEN:

Books

The Molecular Basis of Evolution. New York: Wiley, 1959.

FURTHER READING:

Books

Wasson, Tyler, ed. *Nobel Prize Winners* New York: H. W. Wilson, 1987, pp. 24–26.

Periodicals

Richards, Frederic M. "The 1972 Nobel Prize for Chemistry." *Science* (3 November 1972): 492–92.
Saxon, Wolfgang. "Christian B. Anfinsen, Nobel Winner in Chemistry, Dies at 79" (obituary). *New York Times* (14 May 1995).
Wasson, Tyler. "Nobel Prize Winners in Physics, Chemistry." *New York Times* (21 October 1972): 14.

—Sketch by Carla Mecoli-Kamp

Kay McNulty Mauchly Antonelli
19??–
American applied mathematician

Kay McNulty Mauchly Antonelli was one of about 75 young women mathematicians hired to serve as "computers" for United States government military projects during World War II. As such, these women calculated weapons firing and bombing trajectories for the U. S. Army at the University of Pennsylvania. With the development of the first electronic digital computer (ENIAC), those calculations became automated, and the women switched from tedious hand computing (each trajectory calculation took five days) to configuring the monster machine for every trajectory calculation.

Kay McNulty graduated from Chestnut Hill College in Philadelphia. The young math major heard that the Moore School of Engineering at the University of Pennsylvania in Aberdeen, a pioneer in computer development, was hiring mathematicians. It was there that she began her "computing" work. When the brilliant physicist team of **John Mauchly** and **Presper Eckert** created the ENIAC, McNulty became one of its programmers.

Thomas Petzinger, Jr., in a *Wall Street Journal* article, talks about the enormous complexity of the women's work: "The first task was breaking down complex differential equations into the smallest possible steps. Each of these had to be routed to the proper bank of electronics and performed in sequence — not simply a linear progression but a parallel one, for the ENIAC, amazingly, could conduct many operations simultaneously. Every datum and instruction had to reach the correct location in time for the operation that depended on it, to within 1/5,000th of a second."

That the Army considered this complex task "women's work" is evident in the job rating — SP, meaning subprofessional. In the beginning, the women were not allowed into the room which housed the ENIAC. Regarded as security risks, they had to work from wiring diagrams. Possessing no operating system or computer language, they were guided by only by human logic.

It is ironic that history has largely ignored the contributions of the "ENIAC girls." The huge machine (100 feet long, 10 feet high, built of 17,480 vacuum tubes)—the hardware—became the dramatic focus of all who witnessed its flawless premier performance in February 1946.

Today, it is the programmers and software that are recognized as the "brains" behind computers. Quoted in the *Wall Street Journal* article, Kathryn Kleiman, who has produced a documentary film about the ENIAC programmers, says, "I absolutely think that computing and programming would be different today [without their contributions]."

McNulty married John Mauchly in 1948. They lived on a farm in Ambler, Pennsylvania. Several years after Mauchly's death in 1980, she married Severo Antonelli.

FURTHER READING:

Books

Ritchie, David. *The Computer Pioneers: The Making of the Modern Computer.* New York: Simon and Schuster, 1986.

Shurkin, Joel. *Engines of the Mind: A History of the Computer.* New York: W. W. Norton & Company, 1984.

Periodicals

Petzinger, Thomas Jr. "History of Software Begins with the Work of Some Brainy Women."

Virginia Apgar

Wall Street Journal (November 1996).

Other

"Kay McNulty Mauchly Antonelli." *Past Notable Women of Computing.* http://www.cs.yale.edu/homes/tap/past–women–cs.html (July 22, 1997).

—*Sketch by Jane Stewart Cook*

Virginia Apgar
1909–1974
American physician

Within minutes of birth, virtually every child today receives an Apgar Score from a delivery nurse or midwife. This simple but crucial test devised in 1952 by Virginia Apgar evaluates infants immediately after birth and is able to identify babies that may be at risk during their first few minutes and hours of life. As an anesthesiologist who attended over 17,000 births, Apgar felt the need to act on her conviction that birth is the most hazardous time of life. Apgar's own life and achievements ranged far beyond her internationally recognized test of newborn health, resulting in the 1997 release of a twenty-cent U. S.

postage stamp commemorating her many accomplishments.

Virginia Apgar was born in Westfield, New Jersey, to a very musical family. Her father, Charles Emory Apgar, a businessman and automobile salesman, was an amateur musician. Her mother, Helen May, shared the family's interest in music as did Virginia's brother. Apgar began studying the violin at six and soon was able to join in the family's living room concerts. Apgar eventually became a member of the local Amateur Chamber Music Players, performing with the Teaneck (N.J.) Symphony, and even learned how to build her own stringed instruments. Despite her love of music, Apgar set her sights on a career in medicine as early as high school. After graduating from Westfield High School in 1925, she entered Mount Holyoke College, majoring in zoology and undertaking a rigorous premedical curriculum. During her college years, she demonstrated her abilities and versatility by working as both a librarian and waitress, while still having time to earn a letter in athletics, work as a reporter for the school paper, and play the violin in the school orchestra. After graduating in 1929, she entered Columbia University College of Physicians and Surgeons in New York and was awarded a degree in medicine in 1933.

Apgar First Encounters Gender Bias

As one of very few female medical students at Columbia during the early 1930s and one of the first women to graduate from its medical school, Apgar knew that her goal of becoming a surgeon would not be achieved easily in a male-dominated profession. Nonetheless, her record of excellence enabled her to become a surgical intern at Columbia Presbyterian Medical Center—only the fifth woman to be awarded that coveted internship. Yet after laboring for two years as an intern and performing many successful operations, she realized that the advice given to her by a professor of surgery, that a female surgeon would never have enough patients to make a living, was unfortunately true. Apgar herself summed up the situation realistically, saying that "even women won't go to a woman surgeon. Only the Lord can answer that one."

Switches to Anesthesiology

Although she reluctantly switched her medical specialty to anesthesiology, she embraced her new field with typical intelligence and energy. At this time, anesthesiology was a relatively new field, having been left by the doctors mostly to the attention of nurses. Apgar realized immediately how much in need of scientifically trained personnel was this significant part of surgery, and she set out to make anesthesiology a separate medical discipline. By 1937, she had become the fiftieth physician to be certified as an

anesthesiologist in the United States. The following year she was appointed director of anesthesiology at the Columbia-Presbyterian Medical Center, becoming the first woman to head a department at that institution. It was mostly due to Apgar's hard work, excellent credentials, and growing national reputation that anesthesiology was established at Columbia-Presbyterian as an entirely new academic department. In 1949, when Columbia made her a full professor, she became the first full professor of anesthesiology ever.

Develops the Apgar Score System

As the attending anesthesiologist who assisted in the delivery of thousands of babies during these years, Apgar noted two post-delivery habits that she came to realize were sometimes detrimental to the health and survival of newborns. The first of these was the inclination of most medical staff to focus their immediate attention on the mother's condition and needs, leaving examination of the infant to be done later in the nursery. Second, she noticed that unless the newborn had suffered some obvious trauma during birth, its condition was assumed to be good. Many a time she realized that an infant had died from respiratory or circulatory complications that early treatment could have prevented. These endangered but seemingly normal babies were failing to receive the immediate medical care that could save their lives simply because no one knew enough to give their vital functions a quick, routine check.

Apgar then decided to bring her considerable research skills to this childbirth dilemma, and her careful study resulted in her publication of the Apgar Score System in 1952. Designed to assure that correctable problems are discovered immediately and addressed on the spot, her system enables the attending nurse or doctor to take a quick reading of a newborn's pulse, respiration, muscle tone, color, and reflexes. The Apgar System rates an infant from 0 to 2 in each of these five areas, with the test being performed from one minute to five minutes after birth. For each vital sign, 0 means no response, 1 is marginal, and 2 is normal or the best response. A newborn that is doing well would receive between 8 and 10, with lower scores suggesting that the baby might need some attention. A score of 4 or below would alert a physician to possible risk factors.

Apgar's quick and easy assessment soon was adopted worldwide, and medical schools adopted Apgar's own name as an acronym for teaching her test: Appearance (skin color), Pulse (heart rate), Grimace (reflex irritability), Activity (muscle tone), and Respiration (breathing). For her work in obstetrical anesthesia and for her development of the Apgar score, she is credited with laying the foundation for the new science called perinatology.

Becomes Director of Birth Defects Research

Although Apgar later published a book titled *Is My Baby All Right?*, she made no money from her test. She did, however, become well-known internationally, and in 1959, after 30 years at Columbia, teaching, administering, and assisting in the birth of some 20,000 babies, she became director of birth defects research for the March of Dimes Foundation. As the head of its division of clinical malformations, her work focused on birth defects and prenatal care.

Part of her responsibilities as director included the distribution of more than $5 million annually in research grants. She also realized that to be really effective, she herself would have to preach the gospel of good prenatal care. So Apgar, a woman of science who nonetheless was afraid of elevators, took to traveling a hundred thousand miles a year lecturing mothers-to-be about the benefits of seeking early prenatal care. She also warned of the dangers of drugs and radiation to the developing fetus. Today's awareness and emphasis on avoiding preventable birth defects owes much to the programs initiated by Apgar. She also proved to be more than a popular and visible proselytizer, as she doubled the annual March of Dimes income. Remaining with the Foundation until her death in 1974, she became vice-president and director of basic research in 1967. In 1973, she was elevated to senior vice-president in charge of medical affairs.

Although she had become internationally known and respected, Apgar remained a modest and unassuming individual. Despite never marrying—"I haven't found a man who can cook," —and living in an apartment in Tenafly, New Jersey, where she cared for her mother, she was by no means a one-dimensional person. She took up flying lessons when she was well over 50 and had as her goal being able to fly under New York City's George Washington Bridge. Described by many as a warm and compassionate person, she died in New York City of cirrhosis of the liver. The recipient of numerous awards and honors, Apgar is today silently acknowledged by the countless (and still-growing) numbers of individuals around the world who owe their lives and well-being to the physician who regarded birth as "the most hazardous time of life."

SELECTED WRITINGS BY APGAR:

Books

(With Joan Beck) *Is My Baby All Right? A Guide to Birth Defects.* New York: Trident Press, 1972.

FURTHER READING:

Books

Bailey, Brooke. *The Remarkable Lives of 100 Woman Healers and Scientists.* Holbrook, MA: Bob Adams, Inc., 1994, pp. 10-11.
Forbes, Malcolm. *Women Who Made A Difference.* New York: Simon and Schuster, 1990, pp. 17-19.

Periodicals

"Newborn Care: Starting with the Apgar Score, Modern Medicine Offers Babies the Best Start in Life." *American Baby* (May 1988): 55-58.

—Sketch by Leonard C. Bruno

Richard Askey
1933–
American mathematician

Richard Askey has kept up the momentum of classical mathematics in an age where much attention has been placed to abstract mathematics. He is best known for providing a crucial element in the proof of a longstanding conjecture in the field of complex analysis.

Richard Allen Askey was born on June 4, 1933 in St. Louis, Missouri, to Philip Edwin and Bessie May Yates Askey. He received his undergraduate education there at Washington University, where the mathematics department held a strong tradition in analysis. Askey carried that strength and interest with him to Harvard University, where he earned a master's degree in 1956 and a doctorate from Princeton University in 1961.

Askey taught at the University of Chicago for two years before joining the faculty at the University of Wisconsin in 1963, where he has remained. His work has been largely in the area of special functions (generalizations of the ordinary trigonometric and exponential functions to solve differential equations) and orthogonal polynomials (simple functions which can be added up to represent any function). This has provided for plenty of exposure to results from classical mathematics, the importance of which Askey never tires of stressing to his students. As a faculty member he has been known to roam the halls of the mathematics department at Wisconsin, looking for students unsure of their area of specialization.

Richard Askey

John Atanasoff

Provides Link to Bieberbach Conjecture

Askey attracted attention in 1984, when a paper of his provided a necessary link in the proof by Louis de Branges of the Bieberbach conjecture, a problem having to do with functions of a complex variable. The German mathematician Ludwig Bieberbach had claimed that if a function of a complex variable were well–behaved in the circle of radius one in the complex plane, then there was a limit as to how large the coefficients of the terms in the polynomial representation of the function could be. Askey's results proved to be what de Branges needed to complete his proof.

Askey was a Guggenheim Fellow during 1969–70 and has served as vice president of the American Mathematical Society in 1986–87.

SELECTED WRITINGS BY ASKEY:

Orthogonal Polynomials and Special Functions, 1975.
The Bieberbach Conjecture: Proceedings of the Symposium on the Occasion of the Proof. Edited by Albert Baernstein II, et al, editors. New York: American Mathematical Society, 1986, pp. 7–32, 213–215.

FURTHER READING:

Aspray, William, and Philip Kitcher, editors. *History and Philosophy of Modern Mathematics.* Minneapolis: University of Minnesota Press, 1988, pp. 201–217.

—Sketch by Thomas Drucker

John Atanasoff
1903–1995
American physicist

John Atanasoff was a pioneer in the field of computer science. In the late 1930s, while teaching at Iowa State University, he designed and built an electronic computing machine with one of his graduate students, Clifford Berry. The Atanasoff-Berry Computer (ABC) was probably the first machine to use vacuum tubes to perform its calculations. Although he abandoned his work on the ABC to do war work during World War II, Atanasoff became involved with computers again in 1971 when a suit was filed by Sperry Rand, which held the patent of the Electronic Numerical Integrator and Computer (ENIAC) built during the War, against Honeywell.

John Vincent Atanasoff was born on October 4, 1903, in Hamilton, New York, the son of Ivan (John) Atanasoff, a Bulgarian immigrant who worked as a mining engineer, and an American mother, a teacher. Atanasoff became interested in calculating devices at an early age—he began studying his father's slide rule when he was only nine, and read technical books on mathematics, physics, and chemistry. He decided to be a theoretical physicist while in high school, and went on to the University of Florida, obtaining a degree in electrical engineering. He then received a graduate assistantship at Iowa State College (now Iowa State University), earning a master's degree in mathematics, with a minor in physics, in 1929. He transferred to the University of Wisconsin to complete his doctoral work, receiving his Ph.D. in 1930, and then returned to Iowa State to teach both physics and mathematics.

Constructs a Calculating Machine

Atanasoff's interest in building a calculating machine arose from his need to solve partial differential equations without doing the number crunching by hand, a very slow method. He decided that his machine would have to use base two, in which the only two digits are zero and one, a convention that may be represented electronically in a number of different ways. In particular, the machine that Atanasoff and Berry built did arithmetic electronically, using vacuum tubes to perform the arithmetic operations and capacitors to store the numbers. Numbers were input with punched cards. The primary innovation was that numbers in the computer were digital, and not analog, in nature. The difference between an analog computer—several working versions of which existed at the time—and a digital one is that an analog machine stores its data in terms of position, such as the exact degree of rotation of a numbered wheel, but a digital computer stores its data as a series of binary digits, the zeros and ones of base two. Atanasoff claims to have originated the term "analog" in this application.

The ABC was never expanded or used other than as a calculator. Although Atanasoff and Berry had plans to create a larger machine using the ABC as a building block, those plans were set aside because of World War II, and were never resumed. During the war, Atanasoff worked at the Naval Ordnance Laboratory in Maryland. His only connection with computers at this time occurred when the Navy needed a computer and asked Atanasoff to construct it. Eventually, however, the Navy gave up on the project. Atanasoff then left the computer field. In 1952, he started a firm of his own, Ordnance Engineering Corp., in Frederick, Maryland, and, four years later, sold it to Aerojet General Corp., becoming the firm's vice president and manager of its Atlantic division. Atanasoff retired from Aerojet in 1961 to become a consultant in package handling automation. He founded another company, Cybernetics, Inc., which his son oversaw.

Wins Sperry Rand-Honeywell Suit

Sperry Rand's 1971 suit alleged that Honeywell had violated the ENIAC patent by not paying Sperry Rand royalties. Honeywell filed a counter-suit charging, among other things, that the inventors of the ENIAC machine were not the inventors of the electronic computer but that Atanasoff was, a fact that would render the ENIAC patent invalid. The judge handed down his decision on October 19, 1973, finding for Honeywell and also specifically ruling that Atanasoff was the inventor of the electronic computer.

This decision touched off a great deal of controversy. Many people believe that Atanasoff did not really invent the computer but that he was responsible for designing and building a number of early computer components (such as a memory drum). It is recognized that Atanasoff did make significant contributions to the development of the electronic computer despite the fact he never built a general-purpose computing machine. After his retirement, Atanasoff worked on a variety of inventions; among his completed invention is a phonetic alphabet for computers. He died on June 15, 1995, in Frederick, Maryland. Atanasoff's honors include, five honorary doctoral degrees, the Navy's Distinguished Civilian Service Award, the Computer Pioneer Medal of the Institute of Electrical and Electronic Engineers, the Holley Medal of the American Society of Mechanical Engineers, the Distinguished Citation of Iowa State University, membership in the Iowa Inventors' Hall of Fame, membership in the Bulgarian Academy of Science, and Bulgaria's highest science award. In 1990, he received the National Medal of Technology from President George Bush.

FURTHER READING:

Books

Shurkin, James. *Engines of the Mind: A History of the Computer.* New York: W. W. Norton, 1984.

Slater, Robert. *Portraits in Silicon.* Cambridge: MIT Press, 1987.

Periodicals

Baranger, Walter R. "John V. Atanasoff, 91, Dies; Early Computer Researcher" (obituary). *New York Times* (17 June 1995): A11.

Levy, Claudia. "John Atanasoff Dies at Age 91; Invented First Electronic Computer" (obituary). *Washington Post* (19 June 1995): B4.

—*Sketch by Alan R. Shepherd*

Charlotte Auerbach
1899-1994
German geneticist

Charlotte Auerbach was a German-born geneticist best known for her work on chemical mutagenesis, that is, the use of chemicals to induce genetic mutations in living things. Notable among her research efforts are her study of mutagens and other genes on the fruit-fly, or *Drosophila*. While her work was part of an ongoing research effort to discover the nature of genetic mutation, Auerbach made important contributions to the study of mutagenesis, receiving high, albeit belated, recognition for her efforts.

Auerbach was born in Krefeld, Germany, on May 14, 1899, to a scientifically inclined German-Jewish family. Her own father was a chemist and one of her uncles a physicist. Her grandfather, an anatomist, identified the Auerbach's plexus in the human intestine. After being educated in Germany, Auerbach had to flee Germany in 1933 with the rise of Nazism. She went to Scotland and joined the Institute of Animal Genetics in Edinburgh, where she obtained her Ph.D. in 1935. Although her position at the Institute was for a long time rather vague, poorly paid, and not particularly secure, she remained there throughout her career except for several sabbaticals taken in the United States and Japan. Recognition came very slowly: named lecturer in 1947, she became a Reader on 1958, attaining a professorship in 1967.

Begins Studies on Mutagenesis

In 1938 Auerbach became familiar with the research of **Hermann Joseph Muller**, an American geneticist who spent a year at the Institute of Animal Genetics. In 1927 Muller had shown how x rays could be used to induce mutations in the fruit fly *Drosophila melanogaster*. Mutations are changes or breakage in parts of the chromosomes, the cell organelles that contain deoxyribonucleic acid (DNA), the source of genetic information and inheritance. Mutations spontaneously occur in nature, giving rise to different characteristics. However, when an organism is exposed to a mutagenic agent, the mutation rate increases dramatically. Many mutations can be lethal for the organism.

At the University of Edinburgh, Auerbach was asked to research the effects of mustard gas on *Drosophila*. Mustard gas, a compound used in chemical warfare during World War I and then outlawed, appeared to have pharmacological effects similar to x rays, so it was thought that its mutagenic effects might be similar. To this end, Auerbach designed and executed many experiments, the results of which were more dramatic than expected. Although other mutagens were being discovered in Germany, Switzerland, and the Soviet Union at about the same time, Auerbach's research on chemical mutagenesis was conducted with greater depth. Rarely hypothesizing, and carefully progressing from one conclusion to another, Auerbach discovered the relationship between chromosome breakage and gene mutation by experimenting on fruit flies. She noted how chemical mutagens have a slower action than the immediate effect of x rays. Auerbach also conducted experiments using yeast—one-celled fungi—to try to explain replication of unstable genes. She also used yeast in experiments to study how one-strand lesions in DNA are changed into two-strand mutations.

While visiting the United States at one time, Auerbach visited the national laboratory in Oak Ridge, Tennessee. There, she began experimenting on the bread mold *Neurospora;* she wished to show that spontaneous mutations can happen without DNA replication. Her work on fungi also focused on the analysis of mutagen specificity—that is, the selective action of certain mutagens on certain genes. This line of research on the metabolic and physiological influence on the action of mutagens was carried out by her successor, B. J. Kilbey.

During the early 1950s, when DNA was discovered as the compound that carries the genetic code, Auerbach was able to explain how chemical mutagenesis is a process that occurs in many steps, the first of which is a chemical change in DNA. Because of her expertise on the effects of chemical mutagens, Auerbach has been involved in the detection and analysis of environmental mutagens. She served as a member of a government committee, honorary president of the second International Congress on Environmental Mutagen Research, and acted as sponsor and advisor to the European Economic Community Program. Auerbach, who retired in 1969, strove to make her field understandable to non-specialists. She died on March 17, 1994.

For her outstanding work, Auerbach won several honorary degrees from such institutions as the universities of Leiden, Cambridge, and Dublin. She received the Keith Medal from the Royal Society of Edinburgh in 1947 and the Darwin Medal from the Royal Society of London in 1977. The University of Edinburgh awarded her a D.Sc. in 1947, and in 1967 gave her a personal chair. Other honors include election to the Genetical Society of Japan in 1966, the Danish

Academy of Science in 1968, and an appointment as foreign associate of the U.S. National Academy of Sciences in 1970. She also won awards of the Environmental Mutagen Society of the United States (1972) and Europe (1974).

SELECTED WRITINGS BY AUERBACH:

Books

Genetics in the Atomic Age. Illustrated by I. G. Auerbach. Harlow, England: Oliver and Boyd, 1956.
The Science of Genetics Illustrated by I. G. Auerbach. New York: Harper, 1962.

FURTHER READING:

Periodicals

Genetics 141 (September 1995): 1–5.
"Professor Charlotte Auerbach" (obituary). *Times* (9 April 1994).

—*Sketch by Barbara A. Branca*

Pierre V. Auger

Pierre V. Auger
1899–1993
French physicist

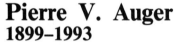

Pierre Auger was an active participant in the development of modern physics. He took a leadership role in many fields, from nuclear energy to space exploration, but he is best known for his research into the nature of cosmic rays. In one of his most famous experiments with cosmic rays, he discovered the existence of particles with a billion times more energy than anything that could be produced on Earth at the time.

Pierre Victor Auger was born on May 14, 1899, in Paris, France. His father, Victor Auger, was a university professor. His mother's maiden name was Eugenie Blanchet. Auger attended school in Paris, first at the Ecole Normale Supérieure and later at the University of Paris, where he studied for his doctorate. He married Suzanne Motteau on July 7, 1921, and they had two children, Mariette and Catherine.

While working on his doctorate, Auger began conducting experiments on the effects of bombarding various gases with x rays. Using a cloud chamber, which allowed him to track the path of electrically charged particles, Auger filled the chamber with

hydrogen gas and photographed the results. Based on previous experiments with a mixture of air and water vapor, he expected the x ray would cause one of the gas molecule's electrons to be ejected, and the ionized molecule would then emit a short burst of radiation, called a photon, to restabilize itself. Instead he found that the impacted hydrogen molecule ejected a second electron from one of its outer orbits rather than emitting a photon. Further experiments with other gases showed that this process was most pronounced in molecules whose atoms had only a few orbiting electrons, like hydrogen. Molecules with a greater number of electrons in their structure, like carbon dioxide, emitted a photon instead of ejecting the second electron. Auger published his findings in 1925. The newly discovered process was named the Auger effect and gave scientists further insights into the internal structure and functions of atoms.

Investigates Cosmic Rays

After graduating from the University of Paris, Auger joined the faculty there. He held several positions, finally becoming a professor of physics in 1937. During his stay at the university, he became interested in the phenomenon of cosmic rays. Initial observations of this phenomenon by researchers starting in 1912 had led them to believe they were detecting radiation from space, hence the name cosmic rays. Later observations in the 1930s revealed that the so-called cosmic rays were not a form of radiation at all, but were actually subatomic particles of great energy. In 1938 Auger was studying these particles in a laboratory located high on a ridge of the Jungfrau in the Swiss Alps. He noticed that two particle detectors, located many meters apart, both detected particles at the same instant. After further study he discovered that the particles were part a much larger shower of particles caused by the impact of high-energy particles from space with air molecules in Earth's atmosphere. These extensive air showers, as they were called, could contain tens of millions of particles and be spread over thousand of square meters. Based on his measurements, Auger came to the staggering conclusion that the particles from space that initially caused these showers must have had energies equivalent to 10^{15} electronvolts—more than a million times more energy than any particle accelerator in a laboratory could produce at the time. Later observations increased those figures to 10^{20} electronvolts. His discovery rocked the scientific world, set off decades of research, and generated numerous theories regarding the source of these cosmic ray particles.

Participates in the Development of Atomic Energy

From 1939 to 1941, Auger was a founder and director of the documentation service of the French National Center of Scientific Research. In 1941 he came to the United States to work on the development of atomic energy with the research team at the University of Chicago. Later he joined the Anglo-Canadian Atomic Energy Research group in Montreal. In 1945 Auger returned to France to help form the Commission de l'Energie Atomique (Atomic Energy Commission).

Realizing the need to coordinate research activities among the growing international family of countries involved in the development of atomic energy, Auger became the Director of the Department of Sciences of the United Nations Educational, Scientific, and Cultural Organization (UNESCO) in 1948. He held that position until 1959, and in 1952, he was instrumental in setting up the European Nuclear Research Organization.

Turns His Attention to Space Exploration

After leaving UNESCO in 1959, Auger joined the growing scientific interest in space exploration. He helped organize the French National Space Study Center in 1959 and was its president from 1961 to 1962. He also had an important role in organizing the European Space Research Organization, and served its Director-General starting in 1962.

Throughout his career, Auger was an enthusiastic promoter of science to the French general public. He founded a science museum in Paris, the Palace of Discovery, and hosted a weekly science radio show for

many years. In 1966 Auger became concerned about the increasing number of scientific articles being written in English, and he joined a committee to encourage the continued use of the French language for scientific work.

For his contributions to modern physics, Auger was awarded the French Commander of the Legion of Honor medal. In 1977 he was elected to the French Academy of Sciences.

Pierre Auger died on December 24, 1993, at the age of 94. In 1995 an international group of physicists began studies for a new cosmic ray observatory, named the Pierre Auger Project. The observatory was designed to detect and measure high-energy cosmic rays and attempt to determine their source—a quest first started by Auger in 1938.

SELECTED WRITINGS BY AUGER:

Books

L'homme Microscopique, 1951.
Dynamics and Thermodynamics in Hierarchically Organized Systems: Applications in Physics, Biology, and Economics. Pergamon Press, 1989.
Main Trends in Scientific Research. UNESCO, 1961.
Rayons Cosmiques.

FURTHER READING:

Other

"The Story of High Energy Cosmic Rays." http://cosmicray.dtc.millard.k12.ut.us/Backgrnd/PA-story.html (January 8, 1998).
English translation of an excerpt from an article on cosmic rays written by Pierre Auger in the French *Journal de Physique*. http://www.lafex.cbpf.br/~auger/etc/pierre_auger.html (January 8, 1998).

—*Sketch by Chris Cavette*

Mary Ellen Avery
1927–
American pediatrician

Mary Ellen Avery is most known for discovering the main cause of respiratory distress syndrome (RDS) in premature infants. Avery found that prema-

Mary Ellen Avery

ture babies with immature lungs lack a substance called pulmonary surfactant, which normally lines the tiny air sacs in the lungs and keeps them from closing. Without this substance, the lungs cannot properly expand and take in oxygen. The result is the severe breathing impairment called RDS. Once the problem was identified, Avery also led the search for life-saving therapies. In 1970, there were about 10,000 infant deaths a year in the United States from RDS. By 1995, that number had been slashed to only 1,460 deaths a year. Much of the credit for this dramatic drop goes to Avery.

Avery was born on May 6, 1927, in Camden, New Jersey. Her parents were William Clarence Avery, the owner of a manufacturing company in Philadelphia, and Mary Catherine Miller Avery, the vice principal of a high school in Newark, New Jersey. Avery was the younger of two sisters. While growing up, she was lucky enough to have a role model living right next door, a pediatrician named Emily Bacon. As Avery later recalled in a November 7, 1997, telephone interview with writer Linda Wasmer Smith. "She used to talk to me about medicine and take me into the hospital occasionally. Actually, she showed me the first premature baby I ever saw. There weren't many women in pediatrics in those days, and I greatly admired her."

After high school, Avery attended Wheaton College in Norton, Massachusetts, where she graduated summa cum laude with a bachelor's degree in chemis-

try in 1948. From there, Avery went to the Johns Hopkins University School of Medicine in Baltimore, where she received her M.D. degree in 1952. Up until this point, Avery had not been especially interested in respiratory problems. Soon after graduation from medical school, however, she was diagnosed with tuberculosis, which kept her at home in bed for six months. When Avery finally recovered her health, she had a newfound fascination with the workings of the lungs.

Landmark Research on Respiratory Distress Syndrome

Avery stayed at Johns Hopkins for her internship and residency in pediatrics, during which she grew interested in newborns. Next came a research fellow-ship at Harvard Medical School, where Avery made a crucial observation. Upon comparing the lungs of infants who had died of RDS to those of healthy experimental animals, she noticed that the latter contained a foamy substance that looked like egg white. Since the lungs of the dead infants lacked this foam, Avery deduced that it must play a critical role. As it turned out, the foam was the result of what came to be called pulmonary surfactant. Avery's observa-tion formed the basis of a breakthrough paper pub-lished in the *American Journal of Diseases of Children* in 1959.

Avery also spearheaded the effort to find better therapies for RDS. She and her coworkers showed that giving glucocorticoid hormones to fetal lambs sped up the development of their lungs. This led to the use of glucocorticoids in pregnant women who are at risk for premature birth. In addition, Avery and her colleagues laid much of the groundwork for the introduction of replacement surfactant in 1991. A pamphlet published the next year by the American Lung Association noted, "The availability of surfac-tant, a key to the survival of thousands of babies gasping for their first breath, is an achievement that owes a great deal to Mary Ellen Avery."

In 1960, Avery joined the faculty at Johns Hopkins University as an assistant professor of pediatrics. At Johns Hopkins Hospital, she also assumed the role of pediatrician in charge of newborn nurseries. In 1969, she moved to McGill University in Montreal, where she served as professor and chair-man of the department of pediatrics. Then in 1974, Avery began a long stint as a pediatrics professor at Harvard Medical School. While at Harvard, she simultaneously served as physician-in-chief at Chil-dren's Hospital in Boston. Over the years, Avery has also traveled widely as a guest speaker and visiting professor in countries including Canada, Mexico, Japan, Korea, Singapore, Pakistan, New Zealand, Australia, Argentina, Chile, Brazil, Cuba, Portugal,

Finland, France, Italy, Switzerland, and the United Kingdom.

Pioneering Work in Newborn Medicine

Avery made her mark not only as a researcher but also as an educator. She established a joint program in neonatology, the branch of pediatrics that deals with the diseases and care of newborns, at Harvard Medical School, Children's Hospital, and two other hospitals. At least 10 of her trainees in this program and elsewhere went on to head neonatology divisions at various hospitals around the United States and Canada. Avery's textbook *The Lung and Its Disorders in the Newborn Infant*, first published in 1964, is considered a classic in the field.

Avery has received numerous honors in a long and distinguished career. In 1991, she was presented the National Medal of Science by President George Bush. The citation recognized her contributions to the understanding, treatment, and prevention of RDS. In addition, it stated that "Avery is one of the founders of neonatal intensive care, and a major advocate of improving access to care for all premature and sick infants." Avery's other awards include the 1984 Edward Livingston Trudeau Medal from the American Lung Association, the 1991 **Virginia Apgar** Award from the American Academy of Pediatrics, and the 1997 Medical Alumnus Award from Johns Hopkins Medical School. Avery is a member of the National Academy of Sciences. She has received honorary degrees from a dozen colleges and served on a number of national and international committees.

Avery, who never married, lives in Wellesley, Massachusetts. She enjoys regular visits to her vacation home on a lake in Maine, where she fishes, swims, boats, and eats lobster. However, in an interview at age 70, the still very busy pediatrician told Smith that "work is really my relaxation."

SELECTED WRITINGS BY AVERY:

Books

(With B.D. Fletcher and R. Williams) *The Lung and Its Disorders in the Newborn Infant*. Philadelphia: W.B. Saunders, 1964, 4th edition, 1981.

(Editor with A.J. Schaffer) *Diseases of the Newborn*. Philadelphia: W.B. Saunders, 1971, 4th edition, 1977.

(Editor with H.W. Taeusch Jr.) 5th edition,, *Schaffer's Diseases of the Newborn*, 5th ed. Philadelphia: W.B. Saunders, 1984.

(Editor with H.W. Taeusch Jr. and R.A. Ballard) *Schaffer and Avery's Diseases of the Newborn*, 6th ed. Philadelphia: W.B. Saunders, 1991.

(Editor with H.W. Taeusch Jr. and R.A. Ballard) *Avery's Diseases of the Newborn*, 7th ed. Philadelphia: W.B. Saunders, to be published 1998.

(With Georgia Litwack) *Born Early: The Story of a Premature Baby*. Boston: Little, Brown, 1982.

(Editor with Lewis R. First) *Pediatric Medicine*. Baltimore: Williams and Wilkins, 1989, 2nd edition, 1994.

Periodicals

(With J. Mead) "Surface Properties in Relation to Atelectasis and Hyaline Membrane Disease." *American Journal of Diseases of Children* (1959): 517-523.

FURTHER READING:

Books

Harvey, A. McGehee. *Adventures in Medical Research: A Century of Discovery at Johns Hopkins*. Baltimore: Johns Hopkins University Press, 1976, pp. 244-247.

May, Hal, ed. *Contemporary Authors*, Vol. 188. Detroit: Gale Research, 1986, pp. 29-30.

Other

National Medal of Science, citation dated August 21, 1991.

"Profile of a Researcher: Mary Ellen Avery, M.D." American Lung Association, 1992.

—Sketch by Linda Wasmer Smith

Horace W. Babcock

Horace W. Babcock
1912–

American astronomer

As an astronomer, Horace W. Babcock was most noted for his many inventions and innovations that furthered astronomical discovery and explanation. With his father, Babcock invented the solar magnetograph, an instrument used to study and measure the Sun's magnetism as well as the magnetism of other stars. Based on his observations, he established a paradigm for solar activity and was the first to indicate the possibility of adaptive optics (correction of the blurring effect Earth's atmosphere has on telescopic images). His scientific inquiry was crucial to astronomy as well as his leadership role at several important observatories, most notably Mount Wilson in Pasadena, California.

Horace Welcome Babcock was born on September 13, 1912, in Pasadena, California. His father was Harold Delos Babcock, a notable astronomer in his own right. Babcock began his college education at the California Institute of Technology, where he gradu-

ated in 1934 with a B.S. degree in physics and engineering. Even at this early date, Babcock was interested in the study of radiation polarization and its potential relationship to stellar magnetism. He did his graduate work at the University of California at Berkeley, and was awarded his Ph.D in astronomy in 1938. His thesis used observations culled from previous experiences at Lick Observatory, where he spent a year working after graduation. For the next two years, Babcock was a staff member at the Yerkes and McDonald Observatories. He also taught at the University of Chicago and the University of Texas in the same years.

World War II Temporarily Squelches Astronomy Career

During World War II, Babcock's astronomy career was temporarily interrupted. Instead of astronomy research, he conducted war-related experiments for the military in the radiation laboratory at two prestigious institutions, the Massachusetts Institute of Technology from 1941-42 and the California Institute of Technology from 1942-45. Babcock's work focused on aircraft-related technology. He developed systems that controlled the launching and aiming of rockets. He also did some experimentation related to airborne radar.

Creates Magnetograph to Measure Sun's Magnetic Fields

At the end of World War II Babcock returned to astronomy, and he was hired as a staff member at Mount Wilson and Palomar Mountain Observatories in 1946. During the same year, Babcock also designed and built a differential analyzer for the Mount Wilson 8.2-foot (2.5-meter) telescope and its high-dispersion spectrograph. He used it to study sharp-line stars and their magnetic fields more closely. Babcock wanted to find stellar magnetic fields via an anomaly in the stars' spectra, specifically the magnetic splitting of spectrum lines into polarized components. He was given an award for his groundbreaking work by the United States Navy.

When he joined the staff at Mount Wilson, Babcock's father was already an astronomer at the observatory. It was at Mount Wilson that the father/son astronomers began their collaboration that resulted in the invention, construction, and use of the ultrasensitive solar (or stellar) magnetograph, with their most important results announced in the mid-

1950s. The solar magnetograph measured data about magnetic fields and velocity fields of the Sun. Specifically, the magnetograph observed the fields' strength, polarity, and distribution on the surface of the Sun. They also used their invention to measure the magnetic fields of sunspots. Another area of research for both men was the polarity of the Sun. They proved that the magnetic poles of the Sun reverse every 22 years, and is related to the 11-year cycle of sunspots.

Together with his father, Babcock devised his own polarizing analyzer that, when used in combination with a spectrograph, allowed them to study the magnetic fields of other stars. These magnetic fields varied in strength and size among stars. Also like the Sun, most stars periodically reversed their polarity. The Babcocks discovered that a small number of stars do not reverse their polarity at all. By 1966, they had collected data on the magnetic fields of nearly 130 stars, using Palomar Mountain's 16.4-foot (5-meter) Hale Telescope. This research supported the theory that stars other than the Sun could have planetary systems. The Babcocks' work in this area expanded astrophysical research on magnetohydrodynamics and its related theory.

Singularly, Babcock went on to derive important models related to the magnetism of sunspots and other solar activity. He published theories related to the magnetic cycle of the Sun in 1960s. The Babcock model is based on his discovery of the Sun-encircling magnetic field lines, as well as his work on solar magnetism. There are two key characteristics of the Sun's atmosphere, differential rotation and convection. These two characteristics interact with the magnetic field of the Sun to produce small-scale flashing and sizzling activity on the surface of the Sun. Also in this model, Babcock describes the north-south pole orientation of the magnetic field of the Sun and its related 22-year polarity reversals. Still utilized, the Babcock Model has been expanded, and recently even questioned, by other astronomers over the years.

During his career, Babcock also invented many astronomical instruments. Among them are a ruling engine that produced exceptional diffraction gratings; several guides and meters for 100-inch (254-cm) and 200-inch (508-cm) telescopes, such as exposure meters, microphoto meters, and automatic guiders; and the cylindrical monorail. Babcock also developed an automatic star tracker, a binary number system translator for Morse code, and astronomical observing equipment that continuously measures and records data in the field. Many of these innovations were produced between 1948 and 1963 and helped advance the capabilities of astrophysical research.

Pioneers Techniques in Adaptive Optics

Related to his important developments in astronomical instrumentation was Babcock's 1953 paper that introduced a system to correct the view through telescopes. Specifically, he described an early method of adaptive optics. Adaptive optics corrects the blurring effect Earth's atmosphere has on light rays from a distant star or galaxy. Babcock's method measured the wavefront's distortions and quickly corrected them based on the ever-changing turbulence of the atmosphere.

Because of his numerous discoveries and innovations, Babcock became a member of the National Academy of Sciences in 1954. Three years later, in 1957, he won the organization's Henry Draper medal.

In the 1960s, Babcock became involved in the administration of observatories. In 1963, he helped establish a Southern hemisphere telescope in Chile, the Las Campanas Observatory for Washington's Carnegie Institution. Babcock was involved in its construction, and he also served as director of this facility from 1963 until 1978. In 1964, Babcock was named head of Mount Wilson and Palomar Mountain Observatories (now known as the Hale Observatories), a position he held until he retired in 1978.

As befitting such a varied astronomical career, including numerous publications in such prestigious journals as the *Astrophysical Journal*, Babcock won numerous prizes and awards. He received an honorary Doctorate from the University of Newcastle-upon-Tyne in 1965. He was awarded the Astronomical Society of the Pacific's Bruce Medal in 1969. His father had won the same award in 1953. In 1970, Babcock won the Royal Astronomical Society's Gold Medal. In 1992, Babcock received the George Hale Prize from the American Astronomical Society for his many years and contributions to solar research.

Babcock was married twice, once in 1940, and again in 1958. He has three children: a daughter, Ann, and two sons, Bruce and Kenneth.

SELECTED WRITINGS BY BABCOCK:

Books

Ira Sprague Bowen, 1898-1973: A Biographical Memoir. Washington, D.C.: National Academy Press, 1982.

Periodicals

"Adaptive Optics Revisited." *Science* (July 20, 1990): 253-58.

FURTHER READING:

Books

"Babcock, Horace W." *American Men & Women of Science*, 19th ed. New Providence, NJ: R.R. Bowker, 1995-96, p. 285.

Robert T. Bakker

"Babcock, Horace Welcome." *A Biographical Encyclopedia of Scientists.* New York: Facts on File, Inc., 1981, p. 38.

"Babcock, Horace Welcome." *Biographical Dictionary of Scientists.* 2nd ed. New York: Oxford University Press, 1994, p. 24.

Periodicals

Addison, Doug. "The Sun also Surprises; Solar Astronomer Patrick McIntosh." *Weatherwise* (December 1993): 32.

"Astronomical Society Honors Paczynski, Babcock." *Physics Today* (July 1992): 80.

Jastrow, Robert and Sallie Baliumas. "Mount Wilson: America's Observatory." *Sky & Telescope* (March 1993): 18.

—*Sketch by Annette Petrusso*

Robert T. Bakker
1945–

American paleontologist

Robert T. Bakker is a renowned paleontologist who has spent most of his life studying the fossil record of the Mesozoic Era in an effort to discover what dinosaurs looked like, how they functioned, and how they interacted with their environment. As a result of his studies, he maintains that many of the conclusions drawn by traditional paleontologists are in error. Bakker has many critics who maintain that his theories lack the evidence of the fossil record, but he has not spent his time and energy trying to convince the academics. Instead, he works to bring his ideas directly to the public.

Among dinosaur enthusiasts Bakker has widespread appeal. He is distinctive in both appearance and personality. His brown ponytail extends to his waist, and he wears an unkempt beard. His usual attire includes jeans and cowboy boots; he is seldom seen without his cowboy hat. Bakker captivates his audiences with his almost religious fervor, and his frequent television appearances have earned him the support of many amateur dinosaur lovers.

Early Life

Bakker was born in Ridgewood, New Jersey, the younger of two sons. His father, an electrical engineer, and his mother, a homemaker, were conservative Christians, never allowing alcohol or tobacco in their home. Bakker's mother prayed with her sons every morning before they went to school, and the family spent Sundays in church, attending services, Bible classes, and church meetings. His elder brother, Donald, now teaches high school history classes in Massachusetts. Bakker's fascination with dinosaurs started at the age of ten, when he found a *Life* magazine at his grandfather's house. In it was an article entitled "The World We Live In" that featured an illustration of a great dinosaur in a swampy Jurassic landscape. Young Robert was so intrigued by the image that he resolved to spend the rest of his life studying these creatures. Though his family assumed he would eventually "grow out of it," Bakker's resolve never faded. Twice a year, his mother took the youngster to the American Museum of Natural History in New York, which had an extensive collection of dinosaur fossils, to feed his fascination. Bakker has always tread his own path. When he was in high school, he researched his Dutch heritage and discovered that his family name, which is pronounced "baker," was pronounced "bocker" in Dutch. He has used that pronunciation since.

In his college years at Yale University, Bakker became a self-described "sixties radical." He spent time as an evangelical street preacher during those years and maintains that the Bible's book of Genesis can be interpreted in a way that does not disagree with evolutionary theory. Bakker has never even clashed with his mother, a strict creationist, on his views. Though often labeled a hippie, he has never smoked or drunk alcohol. His long hair and full beard were inspired by Old Testament writings. Bakker, a pacifist, was drafted during the Vietnam conflict, but he was conscientious objector and never served.

Bakker Challenges Dinosaur Theory

Bakker's revolutionary theories about dinosaurs began to evolve during his years at Yale. At the time, dinosaurs were believed to be cold-blooded animals related to modern lizards. They were thought to be slow-moving and unintelligent. One of Bakker's professors, John Ostrom, was among the first to challenge these notions. Bakker's own analysis of dinosaur fossils also led him away from traditional theory. He found that dinosaur skeletons were more similar to those of the elephant and other large mammals than they were to any lizard. He concluded that the animals were endothermic, or capable of maintaining their own body temperatures. He also concluded that some dinosaurs were energetic, swift-moving predators. Bakker published these findings in 1968, when he finished his B.A. course work at Yale. While many of his peers were intrigued by his findings, the majority remained unconvinced that they were accurate.

After graduation, Bakker continued his work at Yale's Peabody Museum of Natural History for three years, looking for more evidence to back his proposed theories. He then went on to Harvard University for doctoral studies. Following his work at Harvard, Bakker taught at Johns Hopkins University, serving as professor from 1976 to 1984. He then moved to Colorado.

Bakker developed many theories that directly disagree with conventional dinosaur lore. Along with his original hypothesis that dinosaurs were intelligent, warm-blooded animals and not dim-witted lizards, he suggested that some of the dinosaurs evolved into modern birds, a view that is now generally accepted. Bakker claims that dinosaurs were brightly colored, not dull brown and green. He also disagrees that the demise of dinosaurs was caused by a meteorite that hit Earth 65 million years ago, causing thick dust to fill the air, blocking sunlight, and lowering air temperatures. He proposed instead that land bridges appearing at the end of the Cretaceous period allowed new migration routes. As dinosaur populations from different areas intermingled, each population brought with it diseases to which other populations had no resistance. Widespread disease would cause a series of species extinctions, which Bakker says is evidenced in the fossil record.

Achievements and Writings

Bakker's life's work has been difficult to ignore. His digs have uncovered two new species of dinosaurs and 11 species of ancient mammals. In searching the bones collected by museums, he discovered new species that had previously gone unrecognized. He has also written two books. *The Dinosaur Heresies: New Theories Unlocking the Mystery of the Dinosaurs and Their Extinction*, demonstrates his theories in graphic detail. It is well-illustrated and depicts the behavior of dinosaurs, including how they fought and courted. Packaged with extras like an inflatable Stegosaurus and dinosaur egg soap, it became a bestseller despite critics' protests. His second book, *Raptor Red*, was perhaps even more controversial. Written from the dinosaur's point of view, the book relates the life a young female dinosaur whose mate is killed by a beast he is trying to bring home for dinner. The lonely dinosaur then roams North America looking for love and happiness. Paleontologists argue that such details about dinosaurs' behavior and motivation are entirely speculation; however, Bakker expounds his theories unreservedly.

Bakker is now a highly sought lecturer who commands thousands of dollars per appearance. He also leads amateurs on fossil expeditions. He has been a consultant for Dinamation, a company that designs and builds robotic dinosaurs in California, as well as for Sega, a video game company. He also served as an unofficial technical advisor for special effects for the movie *Jurassic Park*. In April 1996, Bakker was the first Scientist-in-Residence at the Disney Institute, a program that examines the processes behind scientific discoveries. Thrice divorced, Bakker now lives with his fourth wife, Constance Clark, and his dog in Boulder, Colorado.

SELECTED WRITINGS BY BAKKER:

Books

The Dinosaur Heresies: New Theories Unlocking the Mystery of the Dinosaurs and Their Extinction. New York: Morrow, 1986.
Raptor Red. New York: Bantam, 1995.

Periodicals

"The Superiority of Dinosaurs." *Discovery* (1968).

FURTHER READING:

Books

Current Biography Yearbook 1995. New York: H.W. Wilson, 1995.
Newsmakers: The People Behind Today's Headlines. 1991, Issue 3. Detroit: Gale Research, 1991.

Elso Sterrenberg Barghoorn, Jr.

Periodicals

"The Dinosaur Heretic." *The New Yorker* (May 31, 1993): 42-5.

"Extinctions: The Early Argument." *Science News* (August 23, 1986): 121.

"Robert Bakker." *Omni.* (March 1992): 65-6, 90.

"Were Dinosaurs Cold-Blooded?" *U.S. News & World Report* (August 18, 1997): 40.

—*Sketch by Monica Stevens and Kris Krapp*

Elso Sterrenberg Barghoorn, Jr.
1915–1984
American paleobiologist

Elso Sterrenberg Barghoorn Jr. is most renown for finding, with J. William Schopf, the earliest evidence of life on Earth. As a specialist in very early plants, plant-like organisms, and fungi, Barghoorn found fossils in an African rock formation that dated back to 3.5 billion years ago. He also studied the process of plant decay in marine environments during his career.

Barghoorn was born in New York City on June 30, 1915, the son of Elso Sterrenberg Barghoorn Sr. and his wife, the former Elizabeth Brust. After taking his B.A. from Miami University in Oxford, Ohio (1937), Barghoorn obtained a Ph.D. in botany from Harvard University in Cambridge, Massachusetts in 1941, just as the disruption of World War II was about to pervade life in the United States. Barghoorn also married for the first time during this period, marrying Margaret Alden MacLeod on August 16, 1941. They produced one son who survived, after an earlier son died in infancy. Although Barghoorn was not in the armed service, he was later awarded a Civilian Service Medal from the U.S. Navy for his contribution to the war effort as a field consultant during the period 1944 through 1946. During the war, however, Barghoorn's main occupation was teaching botany at Amherst College in Massachusetts, where he was an instructor during 1941 through 1943 and an assistant professor from 1944 though 1946.

After the World War II, Barghoorn left Amherst in 1946 and returned to his alma mater, Harvard, where he continued teaching and using the university as a research base for the remainder of his life, eventually holding the chair of the Fisher Professor of Natural History. He also was the curator of Harvard's large collection of botanical fossils from 1949 on and regularly consulted with the U.S. Geological Survey on identification of rock strata from botanical fossils. Barghoorn was divorced from his first wife in 1951 and married Teresa Joan La Croix two years later. That marriage, like his first, lasted 10 years and ended in divorce. In 1964 he married Dorothy Delimer Osgood, who died in 1982. Barghoorn himself died two years later on January 27, 1984.

Barghoorn studied several kinds of changes that occur when plants or plant-like organisms, such as algae and fungi, decay in aquatic or marine environments. One of the most familiar examples of this occurs when swamps or pond bottoms gradually turn to peat and later to coal. These studies led naturally to looking for the final result of such processes in various rock formations, where the plants and plant-like organisms have become fossils.

Discovers Oldest Fossilized Life Forms on Earth

Although Barghoorn's research specialty of very early plants, fungi, and other plantlike organisms seems somewhat obscure, it has had interesting repercussions. When scientists in 1996 discovered evidence in a meteorite that originated in Mars that suggested that there had been life on Mars, the analysis was largely based on the research that Barghoorn had conducted throughout his career, and especially on his discoveries in the 1950s and 1960s.

In 1954 Barghoorn and Stanley A. Tyler found evidence of early colonial cyanobacteria, also known as blue-green algae, from the period of about 2.7 billion years ago in a rock formation near the Canadian shore of Lake Superior named the Gunflint chert. There were also some fossils identified as primitive fungi. The Gunflint chert formation is part of the Canadian shield, one of the oldest regions of continental rock that has not been reformed by plate tectonics. The fossils were about one and a half billion years earlier than any evidences of life found before the 1950s, and many scientists thought that it was impossible for any evidence of life to have survived from that early in Earth's history.

Barghoorn, working with J. William Schopf of the University of California at Los Angeles, found evidence of even earlier life forms in the 1960s. These fossils were small bodies that were about a hundredth of a millimeter in diameter that appeared in an ancient rock formation from South Africa called the Fig Tree chert. Eventually, in 1977, the age of some Fig Tree fossils was determined to be about 3.5 billion years ago, nearly a billion years earlier even than the fossils from the Gunflint chert.

Although these discoveries were controversial at first, continued analysis demonstrated that the fossils had chemical characteristics that were highly indicative of organic life. In 1968 Barghoorn and collaborators showed that very early cherts contained amino acids, a significant chemical signal of life, in this case life from about 3 billion years ago. Another telling analysis examined the ratio of carbon-12 to the rarer carbon-13. In the chert inclusions, this number was like the ratio found in living things, not like that of carbon from inorganic processes. Thus, the small inclusions are now recognized as the earliest forms of life on Earth that scientists have ever found. The only evidence of life any earlier than this consists of ambiguous chemicals that might have been produced by living organisms.

When small bodies were found in the Murchison meteorite that fell on Australia in 1969, some scientists thought it might be evidence of life from an asteroid or comet. Barghoorn was called upon as an expert. He showed that the small bodies were not pollen contaminations, as skeptics had claimed, but that they were definitely part of the meteorites. Some of these bodies resemble the cyanobacteria from the old cherts on Earth, while others resemble other simple life forms, such as slime molds. With the 1996 discovery of possible fossils in a meteorite from Mars, the Murchison inclusions have be re-examined, and some scientists agree that they appear to be organic in nature.

In addition to the Navy's Civilian Service Medal, Barghoorn received a number of prizes and awards reflecting his discoveries in paleobotany. This included the Hayden Memorial Award Medal of the Philadelphia Academy of Natural Sciences and in 1972 the

C.D. Walcott Medal of the U.S. National Academy of Sciences, of which Barghoorn was a member.

FURTHER READING:

Periodicals

"Elso Barghoorn, 68; Found Oldest Signs of Life on the Earth." *The New York Times* (January 31, 1984).

Other

Dooling, Dave. "The Extremophiles from Space." July 25, 1997.

—Sketch by Bryan Bunch

Nina Bari
1901–1961
Russian mathematician

Nina Bari's work focused on trigonometric series. She refined the constructive method of proof to prove results in function theory, and her work is regarded as the foundation of function and trigonometric series theory.

Nina Karlovna Bari was born in Moscow on November 19, 1901, the daughter of Olga and Karl Adolfovich Bari, a physician. In the Russia of her youth, education was segregated by gender and the best academic opportunities reserved for males only. Bari attended a private high school for girls, but in 1918 she defied convention and sat for—and passed—the examination for a boy's high school graduation certificate.

In 1917, Russia's political and social structure was shattered by the Russian Revolution. The power vacuum left the country at the mercy of the czarists, socialist revolutionaries, and Bolsheviks. While many of Russia's universities closed at the beginning of the Revolution, the Faculty of Physics and Mathematics of Moscow State University reopened in 1918, and began accepting applications from women. Records show that Bari was the first woman to attend the university and was probably the first woman to graduate from it. Russia's educational institutions were in the same turmoil as the society around them. Graduation exams were scheduled on a catch–as–can basis, and Bari took advantage of the disorder to sit for her examinations early. She graduated from Moscow State in 1921—just three years after entering the university.

Finds a Mentor and a Movement

After graduation, Bari began her teaching career. She lectured at the Moscow Forestry Institute, the Moscow Polytechnic Institute, and the Sverdlov Communist Institute. Bari applied for and received the only paid research fellowship awarded by the newly created Research Institute of Mathematics and Mechanics. (Ten postgraduate students were accepted at the Research Institute; Bari won the stipend because her name appeared first on the alphabetically arranged list. According to a colleague, she shared the stipend with her fellow students.)

As a student, Bari was drawn to an elite group nicknamed the Luzitania—an informal academic and social organization. These scholars clustered around Nikolai Nikolaevich Luzin, a noted mathematician who rejected any area of mathematical study but function theory. With Luzin as her inspiration, Bari plunged into the study of trigonometric series and functions. She developed her thesis around the topic and presented the main results of her research to the Moscow Mathematical Society in 1922—the first woman to address the society. In 1926, she defended her thesis, and her work earned her the Glavnauk Prize.

In 1927, Bari took advantage of an opportunity to study in Paris at the Sorbonne and the College de France. She then attended the Polish Mathematical Congress in Lvov, Poland; a Rockefeller grant enabled her to return to Paris to continue her studies. Bari's decision to travel may have been influenced by the disintegration of the Luzitanians. Luzin's irascible, demanding personality had alienated many of the mathematicians who had gathered around him. By 1930, all traces of the Luzitania movement had vanished, and Luzin left Moscow State for the Academy of Science's Steklov Institute.

Gains Recognition at Home and Abroad

Bari returned to Moscow State in 1929 and in 1932 was made a full professor. In 1935, she was awarded the degree of Doctor of the Physical–Mathematical Sciences, a more prestigious research degree than the traditional Ph.D.

In 1936, during the dictatorship of Josef Stalin, Bari's mentor, Luzin, was charged with ideological sabotage. For some reason—possibly Stalin's preoccupation with more important enemies of the state—Luzin's trial was canceled. Luzin was officially reprimanded and withdrew from academia.

Bari managed to avoid the taint of association. She and D.E. Men'shov took charge of function theory work at Moscow State during the 1940s. In 1952, she published an important piece on primitive functions, and trigonometric series and their almost everywhere convergence. Bari also presented works at the 1956 Third All–Union Congress in Moscow and the 1958 International Congress of Mathematicians in Edinburg.

Mathematics was the center of Bari's intellectual life, but she enjoyed literature and the arts. She was also a mountain hiking enthusiast and tackled the Caucasus, Altai, Lamir, and Tyan'shan' mountain ranges in Russia. Bari's interest in mountain hiking was inspired by her husband, Viktor Vladmirovich Nemytski, a Soviet mathematician, Moscow State professor, and an avid mountain explorer. There is no documentation of their marriage available, but contemporaries believe the two married later in life.

Bari's last work—her 55th publication—was a 900–page monograph on the state of the art of trigonometric series theory, which is recognized as a standard reference work for those specializing in function and trigonometric series theory.

Bari died July 15, 1961, when she fell in front of a train at the Moscow Metro. Colleagues, however, suspect her death was suicide; they speculate she was despondent over the death of Luzin in 1950, who some believe had been not only her mentor but her lover.

SELECTED WRITINGS BY BARI:

Books

A Treatise on Trigonometric Series. Translated by Margaret F. Mullins, 1964.

Periodicals

"Sur l'uncite du developpement trigonometrique." *Comptes rendus hebdomadaires des seances de l'Academie des Sciences* 177 (1923): 1195–1197.

"Sur la nature diophantique du probleme d'uncite du developpement trigonometrique." *Comptes rendus hebdomadaires des seances de l'Academie des Sciences* 202 (1936): 1901–1903.

"The Uniqueness Problem of the Representation of Functions by Trigonometric Series." *Uspekhi Matematicheskikh Nauk* 3, no. 31, (1949): 3–68. Supplement, 7 (1952): 193–196. (Translation: American Mathematical Society Translation no. 52, (1951.)

"On primitive functions and trigonometric series converging almost everywhere" (in Russian). *Matematicheskii Sbornik* 31, no. 73, (1952): 687–702.

"Trigonometric Series" (in Russian). *Trudy III Vzesoyuznogo Matematicheskoga S'ezda* 2 (1956): 25–26.

"Trigonometric Series" (in Russian). *Trudy III Vzesoyuznogo Matematicheskoga S'ezda* 3 (1957): 164–177.

(With D. E. Men'shov) "On the International Mathematical Congress in Edinburgh" (in Russian). *Upsekhi Matematicheskikh Nauk*, 14, no. 2, (1959): 235–238.

"Subsequences converging to Zero Everywhere of Partial Sums of Trigonometric Series" (in Russian). *Izvestiya Akademii Nauk SSSR. Seriya Matematika* 24 (1960): 531–548.

FURTHER READING:

Books

Fang, J. *Mathematicians From Antiquity to Today.* Memphis State University: Paideia, 1972, p. 185.

Spetich, Joan and Douglas E. Cameron. "Nina Karlovna Bari," in *Women of Mathematics: A Bibliographic Sourcebook.* Edited by Louise S. Grinstein and Paul J. Campbell. Westport, CT.: Greenwood Press, 1987, pp. 6–12.

Zdravkovska, Smilka and Peter L. Duren, editors. *Golden Years of Moscow Mathematics, History of Mathematics*, Volume 6, Providence, RI: American Mathematical Society, 1993, pp. 35–53.

Other

Soublis, Giota. "Nina Karlvona Bari." *Biographies of Women Mathematicians.* June 1997. http:// www.scottlan.edu/lriddle/women/chronol.htm (July 22, 1997).

—*Sketch by A. Mullig*

Ruth Aaronson Bari
1917–

Polish–American algebraist

Ruth Bari is considered the world expert on chromatic polynomials. She was born November 17, 1917 in Brooklyn, New York, the daughter of Polish immigrants Israel Aaronson and Becky Gursky. She has one younger sister, Ethel. Bari attended the all–girls Bay Ridge High School in Brooklyn, where it was thought that mathematics was not important for the girls' education. When Bari requested a more in-depth class on algebra, her teacher offered her only a book with higher algebra problems that she had to study on her own. Bari persisted and went on to earn a medal for her mathematics work at graduation.

Bari enrolled at Brooklyn College and graduated in 1939 with a B.A. in mathematics. That summer she met Arthur Bari, a diamond setter, while working on Staten Island, and they were married on November 22, 1940. Bari switched gears at this point in her life, taking and passing a civil service exam. She went to Washington, D.C. and worked as a statistical clerk for the Bureau of Census. At night, Bari continued to take classes and obtained a master's degree from Johns Hopkins University in 1943. During World War II, Bari worked for her department chairman grading papers for $25 a month, but money was tight with her husband away in the Marines, so she left the university and went to work for Bell Telephone Laboratories in New York City. Bari was employed as a technical assistant for a short time and was then hired as an instructor at the University of Maryland. Bari resigned when she became pregnant with her first daughter, Gina, in 1948. The Baris had two more daughters, in 1949 and 1951, respectively, before she returned to the University of Maryland to pursue her doctorate, which she received in 1966.

Bari's work with Ph.D. candidates at George Washington University has earned her the title of "doctoral mother" due to her patience and encouragement. She has also given numerous lectures on graphs and polynomials. Her work chairing the American Mathematical Society in 1975 and 1981 gained her additional recognition and invitations to lecture abroad at such prestigious universities as the Mathematical Institute at Oxford.

SELECTED WRITINGS BY BARI:

(Editor, with Frank Harary) *Graphs and Combinatorics: Proceedings*, 1974.

FURTHER READING:

Fasanelli, Florence D. "Ruth Aaronson Bari," in *Women of Mathematics: A Biobibliographic Sourcebook.* Edited by Louise S. Grinstein and Paul J. Campbell. Westport, CT: Greenwood Press, 1987, pp. 13–16.

Harrary, Frank. "Academic Roots." *The Mathematical Intelligencer* 7, no. 1, (1985): 7.

Other

"Ruth Aaronson Bari." *Biographies of Women Mathematicians.* June 1997. http:// www.scottlan.edu/lriddle/women/chrono.htm (July 22, 1997).

—*Sketch by Nicole Beatty*

Agnes Baxter
1870–1917
Canadian algebraist

Agnes Sime Baxter was the second Canadian woman to earn a doctoral degree in mathematics and the fourth to receive such a honor in North America. Her award–winning undergraduate career was capped with historic higher degrees. Even though Baxter abandoned mathematics to support her husband's academic career, her name now adorns a reading room in the Department of Mathematics, Statistics and Computing Science at her alma mater, Dalhousie University.

Baxter was born on March 18, 1870, in Halifax, Nova Scotia to Mr. and Mrs. Robert Baxter. Little is known of her early life. She enrolled at Dalhousie at the age of 17, majoring in mathematics. In 1891, Baxter was granted a B.A. degree with a first class distinction, making her the first female honors student at the university. She also won the Sir William Young prize, a gold medal, that year. In 1882, Baxter earned an M.A. in the same field, specializing in mathematical physics, from the same institution. She then studied at Cornell University, funded by a fellowship, and received her Ph.D. in 1895. Baxter's doctoral thesis was on Abelian integrals.

An Early "Retirement"

As Mrs. A. Ross Hill, whom she became just a year later, Baxter assisted her husband's presidency at the University of Missouri. She apparently raised a family, hosted university functions, and quietly nursed a wasting illness never specified in the press. After a long medical struggle she seemed to be cured, but was then succumbed to an infection on March 9, 1917.

Her widower, also a Dalhousie graduate, thought Baxter's memory would best be served by his endowment of the sum of $1000, intended to fund a collection of books. Obituaries at the time noted her aptitude for a subject not widely considered as within a female's natural intellectual realm. Hill was quoted as intending his gift to bring recognition to Baxter for supporting his career, "instead of making an independent record for herself."

Medal in Safe Keeping

The Agnes Baxter Reading Room was dedicated with an afternoon ceremony on March 15, 1988. Dr. John Roberts of the University of California, Berkeley, a grandson of the Hills, was present for the event. The gold medal Baxter had won as an undergraduate was given to the Department of Mathematics, Statistics and Computing Science soon after.

SELECTED WRITINGS BY BAXTER:

"On Abelian Integrals, a Resume of Neumann's Abelsche Integral with Comments and Applications." Unpublished thesis, circa 1895.

FURTHER READING:

Periodicals

A.M.M. "Agnes Sime Baxter." *The Dalhousie Gazette* (June 15, 1917): 1, 3.
Anonymous. "The Agnes Baxter Library." *The Dalhousie Gazette* (June 15, 1917): 1.

Other

"Agnes Baxter." *Biographies of Women Mathematicians*. June 1997. http://www.scottlan.edu/lriddle/women/chronol.htm (July 22, 1997).
The Dalhousie President's Report. Halifax, N. S.: Dalhousie University, 1917, p. 12.
Wilkins, Gina. "Dalhousie University Honours Alumna with Room Dedication." *Dalhousie University Public Relations Office Press Release*, March 11, 1988.

—Sketch by Jennifer Kramer

John Stewart Bell
1928–1990
Irish theoretical physicist

John Stewart Bell is considered to be among the first rank of theoretical physicists, although his fame with the general public rests on one mathematical proof, called Bell's theorem, which has been highly praised. In 1975 physicist Henry Pierce Stapp of Lawrence Berkeley Laboratory described Bell's theorem as "the most profound discovery of science."

Bell would have made no such sweeping claim. He was a modest theoretician with red hair, a red beard, and a lilting Irish accent. He had a teasing, dry wit that led him to title a paper on his theorem addressed to laypersons as "Bertlmann's Socks and the Nature of Reality." In his time he discussed the nature of reality with both the Dalai Lama and the Maharishi Mahesh Yogi, the founder of transcendental meditation.

Bell was born in Belfast, Northern Ireland, on July 28, 1928, to working-class parents John and Mary Ann (Brownlee) Bell. Bell's parents could not afford to send him to college, so he worked his way through his education. Encouraged by his mother, Bell enrolled in Queen's University in Belfast where he had been employed as a laboratory assistant in the physics department. He graduated with a degree in physics in 1949. After graduating, he went right back to work at the United Kingdom Atomic Research Establishment at Harwell, England, where he consulted on the design of the Proton Synchrotron, CERN'S (the European nuclear research organization) first accelerator. During this time he was given a leave of absence to work on his Ph.D. at Birmingham University. When he returned to Harwell, his work took a more theoretical turn.

The United Kingdom Atomic Energy Research Establishment sent Bell to work at one of their substations, in Malvern, Worcestershire. There, Bell met and married his wife and physics partner, a Scottish physicist from Glasgow named Mary. Bell and his wife continued to work together, generally in the same office, until she retired from physics. They had no children.

When Bell was 32, he and Mary left the UK Atomic Energy Organization to join the staff at CERN. They became designers for the CERN particle accelerator operation in Geneva, Switzerland, where Bell continued to work until his sudden death from a stroke in October of 1990. Since CERN is devoted primarily to experimental physics, Bell computed the various quantities needed to design particle accelerators and accelerator experiments as well as doing his more fundamental work. He once listed his occupation as "particle accelerator designer." While in Harwell, for example, he had worked out the stability of various particle paths in the synchrotron.

Resolves Long Time Physics Problem

The work that made Bell famous among quantum physicists and a certain segment of the general public was inspired by the attempts of **Albert Einstein** to show that quantum theory is incomplete. Along with two co-authors, Boris Podolsky and Nathan Rosen, Einstein envisioned a thought experiment, known to physicists as EPR after the authors' initials, that suggested there must be unknown parts of reality that quantum theory has not plumbed.

The EPR problem can be understood by imagining an object breaking down into two particles that fly rapidly apart in opposite directions. Quantum mechanics states that the two particles will be at equal, but opposite distances from the point at which they broke down. What Einstein felt was missing from quantum theory was whether or not the particles communicated in some way. Bell proposed that there must be unknown and unobservable factors affecting the particles and in fact, that the particles do communicate at a distance. This kind of communication is described as "non-local." Pushing a pencil across the

table with your finger would be an example of "local" (direct) communication. Non-local communication is instant and between two distant objects. It is often explained using the example of voodoo—someone sticks a pin in a doll that resembles you and you feel pain. Bell showed in 1964 that EPR could be understood better with the assumption that some kind of instantaneous communication at a distance is allowed in nature.

Bell later described his original intent in a letter to Nick Herbert, quoted in Herbert's book *Quantum Reality:* "I had for long been fascinated by EPR. Was there a paradox or not? I was deeply impressed by Einstein's reservations about quantum mechanics and his views of it as an incomplete theory. For several reasons the time was ripe for me to tackle the problem head on. The result was the reverse of what I had hoped. But I was delighted in a region of woolliness and obscurity to have come upon something hard and clear."

Bell explained his theory in a paper entitled, "On the Einstein-Podolsky-Rosen Paradox." It did not cause much comment at the time, partly because it was published in the first issue of *Physics,* a little-read journal that ceased publication after one year. When various experiments later demonstrated that Bell's theorem correctly predicts results, the importance of his work came to be understood.

Bell's original theorem, also known as Bell's inequalities, predicted how measurements on one electron affect the state of a distant electron with which its quantum fate has become entangled. John Clauser of the University of California at Berkeley tested Bell's theorem using entangled photons instead of electrons. By 1972, Clauser and associates had performed experiments and demonstrated that at heart quantum theory is not local and that certain information is transmitted instantly from one particle to another. This conclusion was later verified by other physicists in a series of increasingly exact experiments that are still ongoing.

One of the reasons for the great interest in Bell's theorem comes from the common assumption that it would enable signals to be transmitted faster than the speed of light. The U.S. Navy became interested because it thought such signals would also be incapable of interception. Bell himself, however, did not believe that his theory could be used to send signals in this way. Other interpretations of his theorem have also aroused great interest. One interpretation is that everything in the universe has been determined since the beginning of time. A second is that each time an act occurs in one particular way, a parallel universe is created in which the act occurs in a different way. The third implication, which is closest to what most quantum physicists would accept, is that Bell's theorem shows that the true nature of reality can never be found by quantum physics nor, by extension, by any form of science.

SELECTED WRITINGS BY BELL:

Speakable and Unspeakable in Quantum Mechanics: Collected Papers on Quantum Mechanics. Cambridge, UK: Cambridge University Press, 1989.

FURTHER READING:

Books

Adair, Robert K. *The Great Design: Particles, Fields, and Creation.* New York: Oxford University Press, 1987.
Bernstein, Jeremy. *Quantum Profiles.* Princeton: Princeton University Press, 1991.
Herbert, Nick. *Quantum Reality: Beyond the New Physics.* New York: Doubleday Anchor, 1985.
Zukav, Gary. *The Dancing Wu Li Masters: An Overview of the New Physics.* New York: William Morrow, 1979.

—*Sketch by Bryan Bunch*

Alexandra Bellow

Alexandra Bellow
1935–
Romanian–American mathematician

Ergodic theory, Alexandra Bellow's field of specialization, deals with the long term averages of the successive values of a function on a set when the set is mapped into itself, and whether these averages equal (converge to) a reasonable function on the set. The theory applies to probability and time series, and to the concept of entropy in physics and information theory. Bellow has proved significant results in this field.

Alexandra Bellow was born in Bucharest, Romania, on August 30, 1935. Her father, Dumitru Bagdasar, had studied medicine in the United States. He was a famous neurosurgeon who founded a school of neurosurgery in Romania in that year. Her mother, Florica Bagdasar, was a psychiatrist specializing in the treatment of mentally retarded children. The Romanian philosopher Nicolae Bagdasar was Bellow's uncle. After World War II, the politics of Romania were extremely unstable as the communists took control of the country. Bellow's parents supported the communists, and in 1946, her father was appointed minister of health in the Groza government. Bellow's father was soon accused of "defection," removed from the ministry, and imprisoned. He died in 1946, reportedly of cancer. Bellow's mother succeeded him as minister of health. According to the *New York Times*, she was the first woman to hold a ministerial position in Romania. However, by 1948 she was removed from that post. Bellow told Ruth Miller (a biographer of her second husband, Saul Bellow) that her mother was accused of "cosmopolitanism" and was prohibited from doing any work or practicing medicine.

In spite of these problems, Bellow studied mathematics at the University of Bucharest. In 1956, she married Cassius Ionescu Tulcea, a professor of mathematics at the university. She received a M.S. in mathematics in 1957. In that year, Bellow and her husband came to the United States to study at Yale University. He was a research associate at Yale while they were students. They both received Ph.D.s in mathematics from Yale in 1959. Bellow's thesis was titled "Ergodic Theory of a Random Sequence." After graduation, Bellow became a research associate at Yale from 1959 to 1961 and at the University of Pennsylvania from 1961 to 1962. She taught at the University of Illinois at Urbana as an assistant professor from 1962 to 1964, then as associate professor from 1964 to 1967. In 1967, Bellow went to Northwestern University as a professor. Her husband held positions at the same schools, although not exactly in the same years. Both remained at the mathematics department at Northwestern for the rest of their careers. Their book, *Topics in the Theory of Liftings*, appeared in 1969. They were divorced in that year.

Starting in 1971, Bellow published papers on ergodic theory. In 1974 she married the writer Saul Bellow, and in the following year they traveled to Israel, where she taught and worked with colleagues in mathematics at the University of Jerusalem. Saul Bellow won the Nobel Prize for literature in 1976. In the late 1970s Bellow published several papers on asymptotic martingales. Bellow edited, with D. Kolzow, the proceedings of a conference on Measure Theory held in Oberwolfach in 1975. She was an editor for the *Transactions of the American Mathematical Society* from 1974 to 1977, associate editor of the *Annals of Probability* from 1979 to 1981, and associate editor for *Advances in Mathematics* since 1979. Bellow's 1979 paper with Harry Furstenberg on applying number theory to ergodic theory contains the Bellow–Furstenberg Theorem.

Bellow was a Fairchild scholar at CalTech in 1980, and also visited the University of California at Los Angeles. She was divorced from Saul Bellow in 1986. Bellow received an award from the Alexander von Humboldt Foundation, which sponsors visits to Germany by scholars, in 1987. In 1989, she and Roger L. Jones of De Paul University organized a conference on "Almost Everywhere Convergence in Probability and Ergodic Theory" at Northwestern University and edited the conference proceedings. In that same year, Bellow married **Alberto P. Calderón**, a distinguished mathematician and civil engineer retired from the University of Chicago, whose fields of research are partial differential equations, functional analysis and harmonic analysis.

In 1991, Bellow gave the **Emmy Noether** Lecture for the Association for Women in Mathematics. Bellow, Jones, and others have collaborated on eight recent papers that deal primarily with partial sequences of observations. This work consists of their attempts to identify when averages based on partial observations are probably valid for the whole population, when they are not valid, and by how much. A 1996 paper in this series had six authors, unusual for a paper in mathematics, which was featured in the *Mathematical Reviews*. It describes averages that behave very badly. Jones describes Bellow as an excellent collaborator who is extremely knowledgeable, "very clever and very careful," and, according to another colleague, "never seems to make a mistake." Jones also reports that Bellow enjoyed her teaching and was a very good instructor who supervised at least four Ph.D. students. A conference was scheduled at Northwestern in October 1997 on the occasion of Bellow's retirement. Bellow plans to continue her research in mathematics.

SELECTED WRITINGS BY BELLOW:

Books

(With Cassius Ionescu Tulcea) *Topics in the Theory of Lifting*, 1969.

Periodicals

(With H. Furstenberg) "An Application of Number Theory to Ergodic Theory and the Construction of Uniquely Ergodic Models." *Israel Journal of Mathematics* 33 (1979): 231–40.
(With Roger L. Jones) "A Banach Principle for L^∞." *Advances in Mathematics* 120 (1996): 155–72.
(With Mustafa Akcoglu et al.) "The Strong Sweeping Out Property for Lacunary Sequences, Riemann Sums, Convolution Powers and Related Matters." *Ergodic Theory and Dynamical Systems* 16 (1996): 207–53.

FURTHER READING:

Books

Green, Judy and Jeanne Laduke. "Women in American Mathematics: A Century of Contributions." *A Century of Mathematics in America, Part II.* Edited by Peter Duncan. Providence, RI: American Mathematical Society, 1989: pp. 379–398.
James, Robert C. *Mathematics Dictionary.* Fifth Edition. New York: Van Nostrand Reinhold, 1992.
Mathematical Society of Japan. *Encyclopedic Dictionary of Mathematics.* Second Edition. Edited by Kiyosi Ito. Cambridge, MA: MIT Press, 1987.
Petersen, Karl. *Ergodic Theory.* Cambridge, England: Cambridge University Press, 1983.

Periodicals

Blum, Lenore. "A Brief History of the Association for Women in Mathematics: The Presidents' Perspectives." *Notices of the American Mathematical Society* (September 1991): 738–54.

Other

"Alexandra Bellow." *Biographies of Women Mathematicians.* June 1997. http://www.scottlan.edu/ riddle/women/bellow.htm. (July 22, 1997).
American Mathematical Society. *Mathematical Reviews: MathSci Disc.* (CD-ROM). Boston: SilverPlatter Information Systems.

Jones, Roger L., interview with Sally Moite, conducted May 1–May 2, 1997.

—Sketch by Sally M. Moite

Enrique Beltrán
1903–1994
Mexican biologist

Enrique Beltrán was Mexico's first professionally trained biologist. He was an authority on single-celled organisms and united the different disciplines of zoology, agriculture, and public health in his work. His importance derives not only from his work as a research scientist, however, but also from his administrative efforts in a wide variety of fields. He was largely responsible for the establishment of biology as a science in its own right in Mexico. Later in his career, Beltrán became interested in conservation and served as Mexico's first secretary of forests and game for several years. His work in the history of science led to the creation of the Mexican Society for the History of Science and Technology.

Beltrán was the grandson of a French colonel who had been sent to Mexico with the expeditionary force of Napoleon III. His father, an official in the Mexican navy who had diplomas in both civil engineering and law, was part of the group that constructed the corvette "Zaragoza," a Mexican training ship, in France. From the time of his youth, Beltrán was familiar with the literature of both France and Mexico. He formed the notion of a biological vocation from Luis Murillo's *Animales de Mexico,* featuring chromolithographic illustrations, as well as from books by Paul Bert, Henri Milne Edwards, and Georges Cuvier.

Becomes Mexico's First Professional Biologist

In the second decade of the twentieth century, professional biology as such did not exist in Mexico. Biologists and naturalists all held positions unrelated to their discipline. Upon graduating from secondary school, Beltrán went to the National University of Mexico, which had just been reorganized following the Mexican revolution. There, he matriculated in the Facultad de Altos Estudios, the university faculty where students could prepare for a career in science. He took basic courses with botanist Guillermo Gándara and zoologist Agustín Reza (by training as a surgeon), and he was assistant to the botanist Ezequiel Chávez. In 1921, as Chávez's assistant, eighteen-year-old Beltrán gave the first biology lectures in the faculty. (In 1902, Alfonso L. Herrera, a parasitologist, had given the first biology lectures in Mexico at the teacher's college in the capital.) Beltrán's wages were four pesos per day. Then he studied advanced biology with parasitologist Herrera and also with Carlos Reiche.

In 1923, under Herrera, Beltrán began to work on a thesis dealing with protozoans in Lake Xochimilco. Single-celled animals thereafter became the focus of Beltrán's scientific research, allowing him to move freely among specialists in zoology, agriculture, and public health. Beltrán's thesis was completed in 1925 under extreme conditions, for at the end of 1924 the government had suspended the faculty's budget and then changed its name to the more conventional Facultad de Filosofia y Letras en la Especialidad de Ciencias Naturales. Near the close of 1926, Beltrán graduated from the faculty with the diploma Profesor Académico en Ciencias Naturales. The diploma was the Mexican equivalent of a doctorate.

Having received certification as Mexico's first trained biologist, Beltrán began teaching in a succession of posts in the capital. (Mexico's system of higher education resembled that of France in its multiplicity of independent schools for advanced study and in the academic practice of teachers simultaneously holding positions at several schools.) Beltrán directed the Marine Biological Station at Veracruz until it was suppressed in 1927, but by then he had attracted the attention of administrators in both the educational and agricultural ministries, each of which funded schools of science. In 1931, he received a part-time professorship for biology at the Escuela Nacional Preparatoria. However, the Mexican political climate induced him to spend 1932 at Columbia University, where he worked as a Guggenheim fellow with the senior protozoologist Gary Nathan Calkins. His research netted him a Ph.D. there. Beltrán returned to Mexico in 1933, where for the next twenty years he trained students and carried out research in a succession of posts, notably a chair in the faculty of sciences at the national capital. In 1936 he entered the Mexican National Academy of Medicine—an unusual honor for someone who was not a physician, and from 1937 to 1939 he served as the head of secondary instruction in Mexico.

Promotes Study of Life Sciences

Between 1939 and 1952 Beltrán served as head of the Department of Protozoology of the Institute for Tropical Health and Disease. His output in the 1940s alone was remarkable—127 papers and 10 books. In the following year, he founded the independent Mexican Institute of Renewable Resources, and over the next decades he focused his efforts on guiding its fortunes. His organizing ability led to his appointment in 1958 as head of the new ministry of state (*subsecretaría*) of forests and game. In the 1960s, he revived a long-standing interest in the history of science to organize a series of colloquia and publications leading to the creation in 1964 of the Mexican Society for the History of Science and Technology; he was the society's first president.

Enrique Beltrán occupies a unique position in the history of modern Mexico. For the life sciences, he was the *bucinator* —the trumpeting herald—the value of whose patronage may be measured in the work of scores of talented colleagues. He died in 1994.

SELECTED WRITINGS BY BELTRÁN:

Books

Medio siglo de ciencia mexicana, 1900–1950. Secretaria de Educación Pública, Mexico City, 1952.
Medio siglo de recuerdos de un biólogo mexicano. Sociedad Mexicana de Historia Natural, 1977.
Contribución de Mexico a la biologia. Mexico City, 1982.

Periodicals

"Curriculum vitae de Enrique Beltrán." "Bibliografía de Enrique Beltrán: 1924-1949." "Veinticinco años de ciencias biológicas en Mexico." *Revista de la Sociedad Mexicana de Historia Natural.* 10 (1949): 5-26.
"Cómo y cuándo me interesé en la historia de la ciencia" *Quipu* 2, no. 2 (1985): 319-28.

FURTHER READING:

Books

Villa Salas, Avelino B., ed. *Homenaje al Dr. Enrique Beltrán.* Academia Nacional de Ciencias Forestales. Mexico City, 1980.

Periodicals

"Enrique Beltrán" (obituary). *Journal of Eukaryotic Microbiology* 42 (September-October 1995): 655-56.

—*Sketch by Lewis Pyenson*

Tim Berners-Lee
1955–

English computer scientist

Tim Berners-Lee, who in 1989 invented the software program known as the World Wide Web, is a

Tim Berners-Lee

scientist in the true sense of the word—idealistic, interested in the pure pursuit of knowledge, and uncomfortable in the media spotlight. Yet his invention, which provides an easy way to access the Internet, has made a huge impact on twentieth-century business and communications. Some experts would even go so far as to say the World Wide Web has revolutionized the ability of computer users around the world to connect to each other. It makes sharing information worldwide possible in a split second—at the click of a mouse. Indeed, in a 1997 article, one *Time* writer compared the importance of the Web to the Gutenberg printing press, which heralded the Scientific Revolution.

The Web has made money for some computer scientists, but Berners-Lee refuses to cash in on his invention. The Web has also become a way for many businesses—from Pepsi to publishers—to sell themselves or their products. Inventor Berners-Lee, however, is a man who shuns the spotlight, only rarely giving press interviews. He remains a conscientious scientist, and an advocate for using the Web as a way to link the world for the benefit of all.

"The World Wide Web is not about connections and cables and PCs," Berners-Lee told a reporter from *Forbes* in 1996. "The Web is where people who can't physically sit next to each other can meet to share their hopes and dreams. It's our global village." Berners-Lee, though all too aware of the commercial exploitation of the Web, is also working actively to promote the best aspects of the Web—its instant communication capabilities and its capacity to unite people all over the world. To that end he heads the World Wide Web Consortium, a group of 120 companies that set standards and guide the growth of the Web. "The Web is like an adolescent," Berners-Lee told *Forbes*. "You can't control it, yet you can't trust it entirely to fend for itself."

Simply put, the Web provides a way to retrieve and access documents on the Internet, the bare-bones network devised by the Pentagon that that links computers—all in networks of their own—around the world. On the original Internet, there were no easy ways to retrieve data. But Berners-Lee developed software which contained processes for encoding documents (HTML, hypertext markup language), linking them (HTTP, hypertext transfer protocol), and addressing them (URL, universal resource locator). Documents could then be linked worldwide. He then posted this software, free to anyone who wanted it, on the Internet.

Develops an Affinity For Computers

Berners-Lee developed a hunger for knowledge and a fascination with computers early in his life. His English parents helped design the first computer that was commercially available worldwide, the Ferranti Mark I. As a boy, he spent his time making toy computers out of boxes. He remembers conversation at dinner time as centering around mathematics; it was more likely to be about the square root of four than the neighbors down the block.

As a teenager, Berners-Lee read science fiction voraciously and was fascinated with Arthur C. Clarke's short story "Dial F for Frankenstein" in which computers are networked together to form a living, breathing human brain. It was only a short step from this type of fiction to his study of physics and computers at Queen's College at Oxford University England. There he built his first computer with a soldering iron, an M6800 processor (the "brain" that runs the computer), and an old television.

Creating the Building Blocks of the Web

After graduating from Queens College with a degree in physics in 1976, Berners-Lee got his first job with Plessey Telecommunications, Ltd. in Dorset. In 1980, after working at D.G. Nast Ltd. in Dorset, he served a six-month stint as an independent consultant at the European particle physics laboratory, CERN, which sits on the French-Swiss border. When he realized he had to master the lab's huge and confusing information system in six months, he created a software program called Enquire. It allowed him to put words in a document that, when clicked, would send the user on to other documents with a fuller explanation. This device, which Berners-Lee used to assist his memory, is now known as "hypertext." It was not a new invention, but like most hypertext software of the 1980s, it needed a centralized database to eliminate links that went nowhere. In such a system, if one document was deleted all the links to it would be deleted. Because of this need for a centralized clearinghouse, hypertext documents couldn't be linked worldwide, Berners-Lee learned during his work on Enquire.

It was not until the birth of the Internet in 1989, that Berners-Lee proposed that CERN's computer resources—whether graphics, text, or video—could be linked with software based on Enquire. Eventually the system could go worldwide, he proposed.

It wasn't long before it did. After developing a language to encode documents, a way to link documents and a way to address documents (the www.whatever address seen on Web pages), Berners-Lee posted his property on the Internet. The software, accompanied by a simple browser (a device that helps the user cruise the Web, looking for subject matter) was also put on the Internet.

Appointed Director of Web Consortium

Over the next several years, Berners-Lee continued working on his design for the Web, accepting feedback from people who used the system. Then in 1994, as the popularity of the Web really began growing, he joined the Laboratory for Computer Science at the Massachusetts Institute of Technology. There he became director of the W3 Consortium. His dream is to ensure the stability of the Web by making sure it remains a tool that can evolve with the times.

He is most proud of his W3 Consortium achievements over the last few years—making the encoding language HTML 3.2 a widely used standard, for instance, which helps make traveling the Web easy for the average computer user. He has also proposed a chip that would let parents keep offending Websites from their computers—and their children's eyes. The idea is that individual parents would use the chip and get ratings of Web sites by subscribing to a rating service of their choice.

Campaigns for a Better World Wide Web

The growing lack of intimacy and the increasing number of companies who charge for access to their sites, are two new developments on the Web that disappoint him. "The Web was supposed to be a creative tool, an expressive tool," he says.

Berners-Lee remains an avid campaigner for keeping the Web open, for making sure no one company dominates it. "He has a real commitment to keep the Web open as a public good, in economic terms," the director of the MIT computer science lab, Michael Dertouzos told the *New York Times* in 1995. Berners-Lee has said he thought about trying to commercialize the Web as he was designing it and was approached by several software companies who wanted to buy it. But in the end, he remained an idealist and refused all offers, instead making the Web available to all.

One of his biggest fears about the Internet is that various competing browsers or competing programming languages could eventually all set up their own turfs, so that users would need several types of browsers or languages to access the entire Web. "The navigation of the Web has to be open," he insists. "If the day comes when you need six browsers on your machine, the World Wide Web will no longer be the World Wide Web."

Receives Awards for Web Work

Berners-Lee has his own Web site (www.W3.org/People/Berners-Lee), and he's continually bombarded by requests from the press for interviews as well as questions from inveterate Web users. He has received numerous awards for his work on the Web, including the Kilby Foundation's "Young Innovator of the Year Award" in 1995. He has honorary degrees from the Parsons School of Design and Southhampton University and is a Distinguished Fellow of the British Computer Society. Yet in public he remains a diffident man, who reveals very little personal information in interviews. He is married to Nancy Carlson, an American. They met in Europe while both were taking an acting class; she was then working for the World Health Organization. They have two children, one born in 1991, the other in 1994. Despite his diffidence with the press, he is a warm, artistic man who can be the life of a party, his friends say.

SELECTED WRITINGS BY BERNERS-LEE:

Periodicals

"What Will the Internet Look Like in the Year 2000?" *OEM Magazine* (June 1996): 36.
"The World Wide Web." *Communications of the ACM* (August 1994): 76.

FURTHER READING:

Periodicals

Daly, James. "Tim Berners-Lee." *Forbes ASAP* (April 8, 1996): 64.
Lohr, Steve. "His Goal: Keeping the Web Worldwide." *New York Times* (Feb. 18, 1995): D1.

Wright, Robert. "The Man Who Invented the Web." *Time* (May 19, 1997):64

Other

"Tim Berners-Lee." http://www.w3.org/People/Berners-Lee (7 October 1997).

—Sketch by Barbara Boughton

Richard B. Bernstein
1923–1990
American physical chemist

Richard B. Bernstein is best known for his invention of methods for studying the interaction of molecular interactions with each other. His techniques made it possible to study the changes that take place in molecules over very brief periods of time, generally no more than a few femtoseconds. (A femtosecond is one quadrillionth of a second). Later in his life, Bernstein focused more specifically on the changes that take place during chemical reactions, particularly with regard to the effects arising as a result of the orientation of atoms and molecules with respect to each other.

Bernstein was born in New York City on October 31, 1923. He attended Columbia University, from which he received his bachelor of arts degree with honors in chemistry and mathematics in 1943, his master of arts degree in 1944, and his Ph.D. in chemistry in 1948. At the conclusion of his undergraduate work, Bernstein joined the Manhattan Project, working on the development of the first fission (atomic) bomb. His work was located at Columbia, where he studied methods for separating uranium-235 from uranium-238.

Academic Appointments at Various Institutions

Bernstein's first academic appointment was as Assistant Professor of Chemistry at the Illinois Institute of Technology in Chicago in 1948. After five years in Chicago, he accepted a position as Assistant Professor of Chemistry at the University of Michigan. He remained at Michigan until 1963, eventually reaching the position of Professor of Chemistry. After leaving Michigan, Bernstein held posts as W. W. Daniells Professor of Chemistry at the University of Wisconsin at Madison (1963-1973), W. T. Doherty Professor of Chemistry at the University of Texas at Austin (1973-1977), Higgins Professor of Natural Sciences at Columbia (1977-1981), and as Professor of Chemistry at the University of California at Los

Angeles (1983-1990). Between 1981 and 1983, Bernstein was Senior Vice President at the Occidental Research Corporation.

Molecular Beam Studies

Bernstein's molecular beam studies were designed to discover how the speed, direction, and orientation of individual molecules affected the way in which those molecules reacted with each other. He once explained that his interest in this kind of research was a result of his contact with two Columbia professors, **Willis E. Lamb, Jr.** and **Norman Ramsey.** Lamb and Ramsey had done pioneer work in the analysis of molecular beams and were both awarded Nobel Prizes for their discovery.

Bernstein's success in molecular beam studies resulted from his ability to design sophisticated equipment with which the movement of individual molecules could be controlled. He forced molecular beams to pass through electrical and magnetic fields that controlled the speed and direction in which they moved, as well as the way they aligned themselves with other molecules in a sample. He then observed the changes that took place when molecules within beams collided with each other by taking femtosecond "snapshots" using very brief pulses of laser light.

By using these techniques, Bernstein was able to follow the discrete steps involved in any chemical reaction, including the way two molecules collided with each other, energy was exchanged, chemical bonds broke, new bonds formed, and new molecules produced in the reaction separated from each other. In other experiments, Bernstein studied the way in which molecules bounced off each other (scattered) both elastically and inelastically.

One of the interesting discoveries made by Bernstein during his study of elastic scattering of molecules was a phenomenon now known as "glory undulations." This effect occurs as the result of interference between two beams at the quantum level and was originally known as "Bernstein's wiggles."

Bernstein also studied the effects of steric hindrance in chemical reactions. Steric hindrance occurs when two molecules are oriented toward each other in such a way that they are unable to react. Their formulas may appear that a reaction *should* occur, but the physical structures or alignments of the molecules prevent a reaction from actually occurring. Again, Bernstein devised equipment and techniques that allowed him to arrange molecules in various orientations with each other in order to study how steric hindrance affects chemical reactions.

Bernstein was the author or co-author of three books and 326 papers dealing with molecular beam reaction dynamics and related topics.

National Medal of Science and Other Awards

In recognition of his scientific accomplishments, Bernstein was awarded the National Medal of Science by President George Bush in October 1989. Less than a year later, Bernstein died while attending a Soviet-American conference on laser chemistry. He collapsed of a heart attack at the conference and was flown to Helsinki for medical treatment. While in Helsinki, he suffered a second heart attack and died on July 8, 1990. He left his wife of 42 years, Norma, a son, Neil, and three daughters, Minda, Beth, and Julie.

In addition to the National Medal of Science, Bernstein was awarded a number of high honors in chemistry, including the American Chemical Society's Debye Award in 1981, the Robert A. Welch Award in 1988, the **Irving Langmuir** Award in Chemical Physics, and the Willard Gibbs Medal in 1989. He had been elected a member of the National Academy of Sciences in 1968 and was given the Academy's Award in Chemistry in 1988. Bernstein was chosen as the Hinshelwood Lecturer at Oxford in 1980, and was named Sherman Fairchild Distinguished Scholar at California Institute of Technology in 1986.

Bernstein was highly respected not only because of his scientific achievements, but also because of what one his colleagues called his "intense devotion to science and awesome vitality." He was, the colleague reported, "perpetually in an excited state and got everyone associated with him excited also about new ideas, approaches, and perspectives."

SELECTED WRITINGS BY BERNSTEIN:

Books

(With R. D. Levine) *Molecular Reaction Dynamics*, 1974.
Atom-Molecule Collision Theory, 1979.
Chemical Dynamics via Molecular Beam and Laser Techniques, 1982.

Periodicals

"Oriented Molecule Beams Via the Electrostatic Hexapole: Preparation, Characterization and Reactive Scattering." *Annual Review of Physical Chemistry* 40 (1989): 561-595.
"The Elementary Act of Chemical Creation, a Citation Classic Commentary." *Current Contents* 29 (1989): 14.

FURTHER READING:

Books

Muir, Hazel, ed. *Larousse Dictionary of Scientists*, Edinburgh: Larousse, 1994, p. 50.

Periodicals

Brown, Malcolm W. "Richard B. Bernstein, 66, Is Dead; A Pioneer in Modern Chemistry." *The New York Times* (July 9, 1990): D20.

Herschbach, Dudley. "Richard Bernstein: Zestful Explorer of Collision Dynamics." *Journal of Physical Chemistry* 5 (1991): 7961.

—*Sketch by David E. Newton*

Leonidas Harris Berry
1902–1995
American physician

As a leading physician and educator, Leonidas Harris Berry was an active force in the Chicago-area medical community for more than forty years. The first African American internist at Cook County Hospital and the first black doctor at Michael Reese Hospital and Medical Center, Berry was an inspiration to minority medical students throughout his long career. In 1955 Berry invented the gastrobiopsyscope, a first-of-its-kind instrument for exploring the digestive tract, now part of the medical collection at the Smithsonian Institution. In 1993 a scholarship fund was established at Rush Medical College in Berry's name.

Berry was born on July 20, 1902, in Woodsdale, North Carolina, to Lewellyn and Beulah Anne Harris Berry. He received a B.S. degree from Wilberforce University in Ohio in 1924. At the University of Chicago, he earned a second B.S. in 1925 and an M.D. in 1930. The University of Illinois awarded him an M.S. in pathology in 1933. After an internship at Freedmen's Hospital in Washington, he served a residency in internal medicine and gastroenterology, then joined the medical staff at Cook County Hospital in Chicago. Following his residency, he joined the medical staff of Provident Hospital in 1935, founded the division of gastroenterology, and served thirty-four years as its chairperson. For eight of those years, 1966 to 1974, Berry also was chief of Cook County Hospital's gastrointestinal endoscopy service. He taught at the University of Illinois Medical School from 1950 to 1957, then at the Cook County Graduate School of Medicine until 1967. In 1955, he invented the direct-vision gastrobiopsyscope, the first instrument for viewing the inside of the digestive tract.

Known for his long involvement in medical and civic affairs from the local to the international level, Berry organized and coordinated clinics for medical counseling on narcotics for the Illinois Department of Health, helped found the Council on Medical Careers, served as chairperson of the health committee for the Chicago Commission on Human Relations, and organized Flying Black Medics in Chicago and Cairo, Illinois. At the national level he served from 1966 to 1968 on the U.S. Department of Health, Education, and Welfare's first national advisory council on regional medical programs in heart disease, cancer, and stroke. Sponsored by the U.S. Department of State, he traveled to East Africa, West Africa, Japan, Korea, the Philippines, and France as a foreign cultural exchange lecturer in 1965, 1966, and 1970.

Berry also served as senior author and editor of the textbook *Gastrointestinal Panendoscopy*, published in 1974, and contributed various articles to medical publications and books. He conducted research on racial, sociological, and pathological aspects of tuberculosis, on gastroscopy techniques, gastro-biopsy instrumentation, therapy for chronic gastritis and peptic ulcer, gastric cancer, and narcotic rehabilitation. In 1977 he was the recipient of the Rudolph Schindler Award. Berry wrote a personal chronicle entitled *I Wouldn't Take Nothin' for My Journey: Two Centuries of an Afro-American Minister,* published in 1981.

In 1937 Berry married Ophelia Flannagan Harrison, with whom he had a daughter, Judith Berry Griffin. After the marriage ended, he wed Emma Ford Willis in 1959. For his energy, dedication, and achievement in the medical profession, Berry received two honorary doctorate degrees and many other awards and honors. Chief among these are the first Clinical Achievement Award from the American College of Gastroenterology; professional achievement and distinguished service awards from the Cook County Physicians Association; and the Marshall Bynum Service Award from the Chicago branch of the NAACP. The Leonidas Berry Society for Digestive Diseases was organized in his honor in 1983. In 1993 graduates and members of the staff of Rush Medical College established a fund in Berry's name to provide scholarships to promising minority students, and kicked off a fund-raising campaign on the occasion of his ninety-first birthday. Berry died on December 4, 1995, at his home in Chicago.

SELECTED WRITINGS BY BERRY:

Books

Gastrointestinal Panendoscopy. Springfield, IL: Charles C. Thomas, 1974.

I Wouldn't Take Nothin' for My Journey: Two Centuries of an Afro-American Minister. Johnson, 1981.

Periodicals

"The Continuing Task of Medicine in a Great Democratic Society." *Journal of the National Medical Association* 57 (1965): 412-15.
"How Important Is Endoscopic Premedication?" *Gastrointestinal Endoscopy* 51 (1969): 170-71.

FURTHER READING:

Periodicals

Carwell, Hattie. "Blacks in Science." *Exposition* (1977): 30.
_____. "Rush Medical College Sets up Scholarship Fund for Minorities in Honor of Dr. Leonidas Berry." *Jet* (13 December 1993).
Saxon, Wolfgang. "Leonidas H. Berry is Dead at 93; Medical Expert Helped Blacks" (obituary). *New York Times* (12 December 1995).

—Sketch by Penelope Lawbaugh

Lipman Bers
1914–1993
Latvian American mathematician

Lipman Bers had a long and prolific career as a mathematician which covered nearly all aspects of the field of analysis, or theoretical calculus. His work in the mathematical aspects of gas dynamics, partial differential equations, and complex function theory redefined several applied mathematical fields. The American Mathematical Society recognized his achievements in 1974 when they awarded him the Steele Prize. A leader in the mathematical community, Bers also used his position to speak out for human rights and equality.

Born in Riga, Russian Latvia (now Latvia), on May 22, 1914, his youth was less than ideal. His parents, Isaac A. Bers and Bertha Weinberg Bers, separated when Bers was still very young, and he spent much time being shuttled back and forth between his father, who was an engineer, and his mother, who was studying to be a psychoanalyst in Berlin. While in Berlin, the eleven-year-old Bers was told by a teacher that he was destined to be a mathematician. Bers did not believe him, and it was only in high school, after discovering that he had unknowingly duplicated the results of the mathematician Kamke, that he withdrew his application to engineering school.

Bers entered the University of Zurich in 1932 to study mathematics, but for economic reasons he was only able to stay in Switzerland for one term. He returned home and entered the University of Latvia. The mathematics department there was poor, however, and Bers devoted much of his time to underground political activities. He became involved in the socialist youth and anti-fascist movements, which made it dangerous for him to stay in Latvia after the coup by the fascists in 1934. Bers escaped to Czechoslovakia, where he completed his schooling at the University of Prague. His dissertation adviser, Karl Löwner (later known as Charles Loewner) was an important mentor, and Bers later had the opportunity to help him.

Escapes from Nazis and Finds Refuge in America

By 1938, the shadow of Hitler and the Nazis had fallen across Czechoslovakia. It was clear that the country would not be a haven for Bers, who was Jewish, for long; his mother had already left Latvia for America. Bers married Mary Kagan in 1938, and they tried to emigrate to the United States. However, conditions all over Europe had worsened, and the pair could only get as far as France, where they spent a tense time waiting and wondering, as war broke out and France seemed about to fall. Their first child, a daughter, was born during this period; their son, however, was born in America. After the fall of Paris, Eleanor Roosevelt convinced her husband to issue special visas for European intellectuals who wished to escape the Nazi regime. In an interview with the *College Mathematics Journal,* Bers said, "I literally owe my life to Mrs. Roosevelt." He and his wife reached the United States in December of 1940.

However, the country was still in an economic depression at that time and jobs were scarce. Bers could only manage to find a poorly paid summer research appointment at Brown University. The couple had to live with Bers's mother, who was in New York City, practicing psychoanalysis. But the need for applied mathematicians increased when America entered World War II, and in 1942 Bers was appointed research director at Brown.

Career Unites Theoretical and Applied Mathematics

The war work Bers did at Brown was largely concerned with gas laws and fluid dynamics, as well as applications of partial differential equations to these fields. His research during this time not only furthered the American war effort, it laid the foundation for his later insistence on the importance of applied as well as theoretical mathematics. Bers also had the pleasure of welcoming his former mentor, Charles Loewner, to Brown. R. G. D. Richardson, Brown's graduate dean, had rescued Loewner from a position at the University of Louisville where he had a heavy teaching load, including remedial classes. Bers and Loewner worked together for many years at various institutions.

After the war, Bers accepted an assistant professorship at Syracuse University, where he remained from 1945 to 1951. Many excellent mathematicians were there, including Loewner and **Paul Erdös,** and Bers found the atmosphere stimulating. He also did research at the prestigious Institute for Advanced Study at Princeton University between 1949 and 1951. During this time, Bers began publishing his first major research papers, which dealt with partial differential equations, analytic functions, and the mapping of "minimal" surfaces (so called because a minimal surface generally defines the smallest area spanned by a curve).

In 1951 Bers moved to New York University, where he gained a full professorship in 1953. During 1953 he also published the first of a series of important papers on his theory of pseudoanalytic functions and their applications, which he termed quasi-conformal mappings. This theory involved a series of exceptions to classical analytic functions, whose applications are called conformal mappings. Conformal mappings display a smooth curvature when graphed, but the pseudoanalytic functions described by Bers had irregularities—breaks or changes of direction—that necessitated new rules and a new terminology.

Before Bers did his research on pseudoanalytic functions, engineers and other applied mathematicians had been forced to utilize the classical framework when confronted by these exceptions in practical situations, and often their results were imperfect. Bers's quasi-conformal mappings were more readily suited to practical problems. But his theories were not simply practical; they also dealt with the more abstract topological concept of Riemann surfaces, providing connections between the fields of topology and differential equations.

In the late 1960s, Bers published a textbook, *Calculus,* which was a standard for many years. His continuing interest in topology, however, led his research in new directions, and he began the study of Kleinian groups. Kleinian groups are an algebraic method for describing rotations and motions of objects. Bers lectured on this subject at a 1974 meeting of the American Mathematical Society, where he was presented with the Steele Prize.

Also during 1974, *Contributions to Analysis* was published in honor of Bers's sixtieth birthday, written by his colleagues and former students. In the dedication, the editors commented not only on Bers's mathematical achievements, but also on his activism in support of human rights and his love of literature and the theatre. The members of the American Mathematical Society showed their appreciation by electing him president from 1975 to 1977. One of Bers's most important contributions to the field of mathematics has been his encouragement of women students, and the Association of Women in Mathematics has honored him by holding a symposium on his teaching. In 1984 Bers was awarded an honorary doctorate at the State University at Stony Brook. The following year, he Bers received the Mayor's Award of Honor for Science and Technology from the City of New York, in recognition for his dedication in helping persecuted Soviet scientists and supporting women mathematicians

In 1988, Bers retired from teaching at the City University of New York, where he had been visiting professor since 1984. However, he continued to giving lectures and seminars on various subjects, from Kleinian groups to his experience with the Nazi regime. Bers died on October 29, 1993, at New Rochelle Hospital in New York.

SELECTED WRITINGS BY BERS:

Books

Theory of Pseudoanalytic Functions. New York: New York University Press, 1952.
Introduction to Several Complex Variables. Courant Institute of Mathematical Sciences, 1964.
Calculus. New York: Holt, Rinehart and Winston, 1969.
A Crash Course on Kleinian Groups. New York: Springer-Verlag, 1974.

FURTHER READING:

Books

Ahlfors, L., I. Kra, B. Maskit, and L. Nirenberg, eds. *Contributions to Analysis: A Collection of Papers Dedicated to Lipman Bers.* Academic Press, 1974.
Furtmuller, L., and M. Pinl, *Mathematicians Under Hitler.* Secker and Warburg, 1973.

Periodicals

Albers, D. J., and C. Reid. "An Interview with Lipman Bers." *College Mathematics Journal.* (September 1987): 266-90.

—Sketch by Karen Sands

R. Byron Bird

R. Byron Bird
1924–

American chemical engineer

Robert Byron Bird, known professionally as R. Byron Bird, is widely recognized for his research into the properties and processes that affect the behavior of fluids. He is especially noted for his studies of complex fluids, such as the molten polymers used to form plastics. Not only has his work significantly expanded the knowledge of these areas, but the textbooks he coauthored have been used by generations of science and engineering students around the world.

Bird, known to his friends and colleagues as Bob, was born on February 5, 1924, in Bryan, Texas. His father, Byron, a professor of civil engineering, and mother, the former Ethel Antrim, moved their family to Iowa in 1925. In 1929, Bird's brother John was born. In 1936, the family moved to Washington, D.C., where his father began a long career with the U.S. Army Corps of Engineers.

Bird enrolled in the University of Maryland in 1941 to major in chemical engineering, but his studies were interrupted when he enlisted in the Army in 1943. He achieved the rank of First Lieutenant with the 90th Chemical Mortar Battalion in Europe, where his distinguished service earned him a Bronze Star medal.

After his discharge from the military in 1946, Bird resumed his studies at the University of Illinois, where he received a B.S. degree in chemical engineering in 1947. He received a Ph.D. in chemistry from the University of Wisconsin in 1950.

Begins Dual Role as Researcher and Educator

While working on his Ph.D., Bird began investigating the field of transport phenomena—the methods by which mass, energy, and momentum move, or are transported, through a fluid as the result of differences in chemical composition, temperature, and velocity. Bird continued looking at transport phenomena in his post-doctoral research from 1950-53. In 1953 he joined the faculty of the University of Wisconsin, where he collaborated with J. O. Hirschfelder and C. F. Curtiss to make further contributions to the field. The results of their work were presented in the 1954 book *Molecular Theory of Gases and Liquids.*

Bird soon realized that transport phenomena was such a complex field that very few practicing scientists and engineers understood much about it. This education gap was confirmed for Bird when he worked at the Du Pont Experimental Station for a summer. It was clear that a course covering some of the basic fundamentals of transport phenomena needed to be included in the chemical engineering curriculum. After several years of work, Bird joined W. E. Stewart and E. N. Lightfoot in coauthoring *Transport Phenomena*, which was published in 1960. This book was designed to present a basic but comprehensive introduction to the subject, and it quickly became a standard text for undergraduate students. In the years that followed, it went through 52 printings and achieved the status of a best seller in the academic world. The English language edition sold over 200,000 copies, and was translated into Spanish, Italian, Czech, Russian, and Chinese.

Bird became a full professor at the University of Wisconsin in 1957. Shortly thereafter he focused his attention on research into the transport phenomena of liquid polymers used in the plastics industry. These liquids are unique because their molecules consist of hundreds or thousands of atoms linked together in long chains. As a result, they do not behave the same ways as other liquids do. Instead they exhibit widely different characteristics depending on temperature, pressure, chemical composition, and time. Bird's initial efforts were to understand the fluid dynamics of polymer flow based on the physical properties of the materials.

In 1968, after being chairman of the chemical engineering department at the University of Wisconsin for four years, he returned to teaching and research. This time he approached the problem of polymer flow from a molecular point of view in an effort to calculate the relationship between the structure of the long chain-like molecules and their fluid flow properties.

After nearly 15 years of research on polymers, Bird coauthored another landmark book, *Dynamics of Polymeric Liquids,* which was published in two volumes in 1977. Its detailed treatment of the subject made it a standard reference for those working with polymers. A second edition of this book was published in 1987.

Travels Spark Interest in Languages

At the same time Bird was involved with his research and education activities, he was also pursuing an interest in languages. In 1958, while he was a Fulbright visiting professor and Guggenheim scholar at the Technical University of Delft in the Netherlands, he became interested in Dutch literature. He coedited *Een Goed Begin—A Contemporary Dutch Reader*, a book of short stories, poems, and other writings by several Dutch authors, in 1963. In 1985, he coedited a second collection of Dutch stories.

A second Fulbright appointment in 1962, this time as a lecturer, took him to Kyoto and Nagoya Universities in Japan. Seeing the tremendous amount of scientific work being published in Japanese, he coauthored *Comprehending Technical Japanese* in 1975 to assist English-speaking researchers. In 1990, he coauthored another book on this topic, *Basic Technical Japanese.*

Continues His Research Into Polymer Flows

Bird's long career has been punctuated with numerous awards and honorary degrees. In 1987, he was awarded the prestigious National Medal of Science for his work. Today he is a Professor Emeritus in the department of chemical engineering at the University of Wisconsin, where he continues to investigate the behavior of large (macro)-molecule, liquid polymers. Education has always been an significant part of Bird's work. He has endeavored to make unknown or difficult scientific concepts accessible to students. In a lecture at the Massachusetts Institute of Technology, subtitled Funny Fluid Flow Fenomena, Bird explained his research on polymer fluid dynamics in a poem that first appeared in the 2nd edition of *Dynamics of Polymeric Liquids*: "A fluid that's macromolecular / Is really quite weird — in particular / The big normal stresses / The fluid possesses / Give rise to effects quite spectacular."

SELECTED WRITINGS BY BIRD:

Books

(With R.C. Armstrong, O. Hassager, and C.F. Curtiss) *Dynamics of Polymeric Liquids.* Wiley, 1977. 2nd edition 1987.

(With E.E. Daub and N. Inoue) *Basic Technical Japanese.* University of Wisconsin Press and University of Tokyo Press, 1990.
(With E.E. Daub and N. Inoue) *Comprehending Technical Japanese.* University of Wisconsin Press and University of Tokyo Press, 1975.
(With J.O. Hirschfelder and C.F. Curtiss) *Molecular Theory of Gases and Liquids.* Wiley, 1954.
(With W.E. Stewart and E.N. Lightfoot) *Transport Phenomena.* Wiley, 1960.

FURTHER READING:

Books

American Men and Women of Science, 19th edition, 1995-96, New York: R.R. Bowker, 1994.

Other

http://www.engr.wisc.edu/centers/rrc/faculty/bird_byron (updated May 4, 1997). This web site includes a list of many of Bird's most recent publications.

—Sketch by Chris Cavette

Garrett Birkhoff
1911–1996
American algebraist and applied mathematician

Garrett Birkhoff's most important contribution to modern mathematics is his theory of lattices, which helped simplify abstract algebraic concepts. His work in this field influenced the development of quantum theory.

Born January 19, 1911, in Princeton, New Jersey, Garrett Birkhoff was the son of noted mathematician **George David Birkhoff**, considered by many the leading mathematician of his day for his work in mathematical analysis and metric transitivity. Birkhoff was home–schooled until age eight. He then attended a public grammar school and Brown and Nichols, a private high school. His mother, a librarian, seemed to be less of an influence than his famous father; in a 1982 interview with G. L. Alexanderson and Carroll Wilde, Birkhoff said, "I think (my mother) was more social than intellectual, really . . . my father was a stimulating person at all ages. He took my sister and me on excursions, particularly when we were very young, and made life interesting for us somewhat later by telling us exciting stories,

Garrett Birkhoff

having opinions on controversial questions. . . . I sometimes think I was trained to be precocious."

Birkhoff's youth was comfortable, if not privileged. In reminiscing about his teens, he mentions that his Euclidean geometry was "a little sloppy" because he joined his parents in Europe in February of his third year of high school. In order to meet language requirements for graduation, Birkhoff remained in high school for a fifth year. "My parents suggested I take my college board exams early. After passing them, I had a wonderful fifth year at Lake Placid where I did much skiing . . . while my family went around the world."

At age 17, Birkhoff enrolled at Harvard University. His father's influence was pervasive; the summer before entering college, Birkhoff's father tutored him in calculus. During his college career, several of his instructors completed their doctoral work under his father's supervision. "My Harvard undergraduate training was almost an inside job," Birkhoff said. It was not until after he graduated from Harvard in 1932 and won a Henry Fellowship to Cambridge University that Birkhoff switched his focus from mathematical physics and quantum mechanics—an interest encouraged by his father—to abstract algebra.

Foreign Studies Spark New Perspectives

At Cambridge, Birkhoff discovered the work of B. L. van der Waerden and Constantin Caratheordo-

ry. His research supervisor, Phillip Hall, had already achieved some recognition for his work in group theory. Birkhoff gradually developed his theory of lattices, which explored the relationship of subdomains within algebraic domains and how operations of union and intersection are defined for such subgroups.

Birkhoff published his first major work on the theory of abstract integrals in 1935. He completed much of his work before discovering Julius Dedekind, who in 1897 developed a system to define a special type of lattice. Dedekind's work was largely ignored until Birkhoff and mathematicians of his generation pushed the boundaries of algebraic theory. "I was lucky to have gone beyond Dedekind before I discovered his work," Birkhoff said. "It would have been quite discouraging if I had discovered all my results anticipated by Dedekind."

Birkhoff completed his Cambridge fellowship in 1933; he carried the enthusiasm and new ideas absorbed during his time abroad with him to Munich in July 1933, where he continued to pursue his research in group theory and met Caratheoedory (who invited him to family tea), who encouraged him. Birkhoff continued his work in the United States. In 1936, he became a mathematics instructor at Harvard University, and father and son teaching appointments overlapped until 1944, when George Birkhoff died. Before his father's death, however, Birkhoff firmly established his international reputation with the publication of *Lattice Theory* in 1940.

Collaborations Prove to be Productive

Birkhoff attracted more attention when he teamed up with Saunders MacLane in 1941. A Benjamin Pierce instructor at Harvard from 1934 to 1936, MacLane returned to Harvard in 1938, which coincided with Birkhoff's first experience teaching "modern" algebra at Harvard. MacLane added a different perspective on teaching to Birkhoff's understanding of theory and research; their textbook, *Survey of Modern Algebra*, first published in 1941, quickly became the standard college text. It was reprinted in 1953 and 1965. Birkhoff and MacLane developed a new text, *Algebra*, which they published in 1967.

In the late 1960s, Birkhoff entered another collaborative agreement, this time with Thomas Bartee; the result was *Modern Applied Algebra*, published in 1970. One of the earliest works to connect algebraic concepts to practical problems, the book included finite groups, Boolean algebra, lattices, combinatorial analysis, and correlated algebraic coding theory with basic abstract principles.

Pursuit of Practical Applications

Throughout his career, Birkhoff sought to link theory with applications. "I feel strongly that it is very dangerous for mathematics to detach itself from the rest of the world; to be part of the world around one is much healthier," Birkhoff stated. As a Harvard freshman, he wrote an essay on the bounce of a spinning tennis ball; during World War II, he contributed his talents to weapons systems such as the "proximity faze" (a device to determine target distance by timing the reflection of radio waves), and antitank charges. Of his work during that era, Birkhoff said simply, "I am proud of having contributed to the defeat of Hitler."

In the 1950s, Birkhoff served as a consultant to the Westinghouse Corporation, working with scientific computing and problems of vector lattices related to nuclear reactors. Birkhoff became an ardent proponent of the development and use of computers as tools to solve mathematical puzzles. "If you have a thousand equations in a thousand unknowns, you know there exists a solution, but how do you compute it? With it [computer programming] you can do for $5 what would have cost $10,000."

Birkhoff authored numerous works on applied mathematics, including *Hydrodynamics* (1950) and *Jets, Wakes and Cavities* (1957). Throughout his career, Birkhoff continued as a consultant to military and industrial institutions, including the Los Alamos Science Laboratory, the General Motors Corporation, and the Rand Corporation.

In the 1980s, Birkhoff remained active, working with the Naval Postgraduate School in Monterey, California, conducting research, studying fluid dynamics and teaching. A member of the National Academy of Sciences, the American Academy of Arts and Sciences, and numerous other academic organizations, Birkhoff was named George Putnam Professor of pure and applied mathematics at Harvard in 1969, a post he held until he retired from teaching in 1981. Birkhoff died November 22, 1996, at his home in Water Mill, New York.

SELECTED WRITINGS BY BIRKHOFF

Books

Lattice Theory, 1940.
(With Saunders MacLane) *Survey of Modern Algebra*, 1941.
(With E. Zarantello) *Jets, Wakes & Cavities*, 1957.
(With G. C. Rota) *Ordinary Differential Equations*, 1962.
(With S. MacLane) *Algebra*, 1967.
(With Thomas Bartee) *Modern Applied Algebra*, 1970.
Source Book in Classical Analysis, 1973.

FURTHER READING:

Books

Albers, Donald J and G. L. Alexanderson, editors. *Mathematical People: Profiles and Interviews.* Cambridge, MA: Birkhauser Boston, Inc., 1985, pp. 3–15.
Bell, E. T. *The Development of Mathematics.* New York: McGraw–Hill Book Co., Inc., 1945, pp. 258–265.
Fang, J. *Mathematicians from Antiquity to Today.* Hauppauge, NY: Paideia Press, 1972, pp. 211–212.

Periodicals

The New York Times (obituary). Nov. 28, 1996.
Harvard Magazine (obituary). New England Regional Edition, January/February 1997, p.76P.

—Sketch by A. Mullig

Elkan R. Blout
1919–

American biochemist

Elkan R. Blout has been one of the pioneers in developing methods for studying the three-dimensional conformation of proteins. This subject holds the key to understanding the structure and function of some of the most important molecules that occur in living organisms. It remains one of the most active fields of research in biochemistry today, a field that owes much to the creative ideas and research of Blout. In addition to his work in the laboratory, Blout has served on a wide range of academic and governmental policy-making and administrative bodies.

Blout was born in New York City on July 2, 1919. He graduated from high school at the age of 14 and then attended the famous preparatory school, Phillips Exeter Academy, for one year before enrolling at Princeton University. He received his B.A. degree from Princeton and then continued his education at Columbia University, from which he earned a Ph.D. in chemistry in 1942 at the age of 24. He then spent a year at Harvard University as a National Research Council Fellow in Chemistry. He was later to receive an honorary A.M. degree from Harvard in 1962, as well as an honorary D.Sc. degree from Loyola University in 1976.

Begins Career at Polaroid

Upon completion of his postgraduate work at Harvard, Blout accepted a position at the Polaroid

Corporation, where he became involved in work on the new instant photographic processes. Over a period of 19 years, he served as a research scientist, Associate Director of Research, and finally Vice President and General Manager of Research. Blout can take much of the credit for the development of the processes used in color photography that became part of the Polaroid film product line. Much of Blout's work during this period involved the painstaking analysis of more than 5,000 compounds in the search for acceptable dye developers. These compounds are the agents needed in an instant color photographic process that makes it possible for colors to develop once a picture has been taken. Blout currently holds more than 50 patents on processes and materials developed during his time at Polaroid.

Work on Protein Structure

Beginning in 1950, Blout held an appointment as Research Associate at the Harvard Medical School and the Children's Cancer Research Foundation of The Children's Hospital Medical Center in Boston along with his position at Polaroid. It was at these two institutions that he continued his longtime interest in the structure of proteins. The basis of this work was the belief that one way to develop a better understanding of proteins was to construct somewhat simpler polypeptides that could be manipulated more easily than could protein molecules themselves.

Following up on this theoretical basis, Blout constructed a variety of polypeptides and then studied the effect of changing pH and solvents on their structure. He used, developed, and modified a variety of techniques to obtain images of these polypeptide structures under a wide range of conditions. One of the most striking results of his early research was x-ray evidence for the existence of alpha helices in polypeptides, confirming a theoretical speculation of **Linus Pauling**'s. Eventually, Blout was able to obtain crystallographic evidence for the three primary protein conformations known, the α-helix, β-sheet, and random coil. One review of Blout's work claims that as many as 20,000 papers on polypeptides have been written, representing a field whose development Blout can lay considerable claim to.

In the 1970s and 1980s, Blout turned his attention to a related problem, the structure of cyclic peptides. Cyclic peptides differ from polypeptides and proteins in that they have less structural flexibility. Blout discovered that cyclic peptides have a limited number of conformations that differ significantly from each other in the way they bind to ions. This finding may prove to have important applications in the development of drugs and in other industrial situations.

Academic, Professional, and Governmental Pursuits

When Blout left Polaroid in 1962, he accepted an appointment as Professor of Biological Chemistry at the Harvard Medical School. Over the next two decades, he served as Edward S. Harkness Professor of Biological Chemistry (1964-90) and Chair of the Department of Biological Chemistry (1965-69), both at the Harvard Medical School, and Dean for Academic Affairs (1978-89), Chair of the Department of Environmental Science and Physiology (1986-88), and Director of the Division of Biological Sciences (1987-), all at the Harvard School of Public Health.

In 1980, Blout was appointed Treasurer of the National Academy of Sciences (NAS). In that position, he held overall responsibility for managing the Academy's endowment and ongoing finances. When he left that position in 1992, Blout accepted a similar appointment with the American Academy of Arts & Sciences, a post he still holds.

In addition to his research interests and work with professional organizations, Blout has long been involved with a variety of national and international governmental agencies. For example, he was a longtime member of the Advisory Committee on the USSR and Eastern Europe of the NAS, the International Organization for Chemical Sciences in Development of UNESCO, and the Board of Governors of the Weizmann Institute of Science, in Rehovot, Israel. In 1992, Blout was appointed the first senior science adviser to the U.S. Food & Drug Administration (FDA). His role at the FDA was to ensure the accuracy of the science underlying the FDA's decision-making processes.

In 1990, Blout was awarded the National Medal of Science by President George Bush. A year later, he also received the American Chemical Society's Ralph F. Hirschmann Award for Peptide Chemistry.

SELECTED WRITINGS BY BLOUT:

Books

(With G.-C. Zanotti, B. Campbell, M. Staples, and E. Fossel) "Bicyclic Nonapeptides: Synthesis, Conformation and Ion-Binding," in *Proceedings of the Ninth American Peptide Symposium*. Edited by V. J. Hurby, C. M. Deber, and K. D. Kopple. Pierce Chemical Company, 1985.

Periodicals

(With S. Weinstein, J. T. Durkin, and W. R. Veatch) "Confirmation of the Gramicidin A Channel in Phospholipid Vesicles: A Fluorine-19 Nuclear Magnetic Resonance Study." *Biochemistry* 24, (1985): 4374-4382.

Lenore Blum

FURTHER READING:

Periodicals

"Elkan Blout's Latest Reincarnation: FDA Science Adviser." *Chemical & Engineering News* (June 17, 1996). Also available online at http://pubs.acs.org/hotartcl/cenear/960617/blout.html.

Other

"Elkan R. Blout." http://twod.med.harvard.edu/biophysics/faculty/Blout96.html.

—*Sketch by David Newton*

Lenore Blum
1943–
American mathematician

Lenore Blum has played an integral role in increasing the participation of girls and women in mathematics. She was one of the founders of the Association for Women in Mathematics (AWM), acting as its president from 1975 to 1978. The AWM has membership totaling over 1,500 women and men. In addition to local, national and international meetings, the AWM sponsors the **Emmy Noether** Lecture series and has organized symposiums. It provides a list of women who are available to speak at high schools and colleges and also contributes to the *Dictionary of Women in the Mathematical Sciences.*

Educational Pursuits

Blum was born in 1943, and as a child, she enjoyed math, art, and music. Finishing high school at 16, Blum applied to Massachusetts Institute of Technology (MIT), but was turned down, several times, in fact. After being turned down by MIT, Blum attended Carnegie Tech in Pittsburgh, Pennsylvania. She began studying architecture, then changed her major to mathematics. For her third year, Blum enrolled at Simmons, a Boston area college for women. However, Blum found that she did not have to put forth much effort in the math classes. She then cross–registered at MIT, graduated from Simmons, and received her Ph.D. in mathematics from MIT in 1968. Blum continued her education as a postdoctorate student and lecturer at the University of California at Berkeley.

According to a biography written by Lisa Hayes, a student at Agnes Scott College, "Blum's research, from her early work in model theory, led to the formulation of her own theorems dealing with the patterns she found in trying to use new methods of logic to solve old problems in algebra." The work she did on this project became her doctoral thesis, which earned her a fellowship. Blum has also had the honor of reporting on work she did with **Stephen Smale** and Mike Shub in developing a theory of computation and complexity over real numbers.

Blum has written mathematical books with her husband, Manuel, a mathematician as well. They collaborated on a paper that proposed designing computers that had the ability to learn from example, much in the way young children learn. Blum has studied this project to discover why some computers learn the methods they do. Blum has been involved in other fields of research, in addition to working with her husband, which includes work in developing a new (homotopy) algorithm for linear programming.

When Blum was hired to teach algebra at Mills College, she was not happy with the program and sought a way to make the classes more interesting to the students and to the instructors. In 1973, she founded the Mills College Mathematics and Computer Science Department. Blum served as Head or Co–Head of the department for 13 years. While at Mills, Blum received the Letts–Villard Research professorship. Since 1988, she has been a research scientist in the Theory Group of the International Computer Science Institute (ICSI). In 1989, Blum was employed as an adjunct professor of Computer Science at Berkeley. During the 1980s, Blum became a research mathematician full–time, giving numerous talks at international conferences.

To further girls and women's participation in mathematics, Blum founded the Math/Science Network and its "Expanding Your Horizons" conferences. The Network began as an after–school problem–solving program. The aim of the program is to get high school girls interested in math and logic. The conference now travels nationwide. Blum served as its Co–Director from 1975–1981. Blum has written books and produced films, including *Count Me In, The Math/Science Connection*, and *Four Women in Science*, for the Network.

In addition to her work with the Math/Science Network, Blum is involved in the Mills College Summer Mathematics Institute for Undergraduate Women (SMI). The SMI is a six–week intensive mathematics program. Twenty–four undergraduate women are selected from across the nation to participate. According to the Mills College SMI page on the World Wide Web, the program aims "to increase the number of bright undergraduate women mathematics majors that continue on into graduate programs in the mathematical sciences and obtain advanced degrees."

Energetic Society Member

Blum is an active member of several mathematical societies. She is a fellow of the American Association for the Advancement of Science and the American Mathematical Society (AMS), where she served as Vice President from 1990 to 1992. Blum represented the AMS at the Pan African Congress of Mathematics held in Nairobi, Kenya, in the summer of 1991. At that time she became dedicated to creating an electronic communication link between American and African mathematics communities. Blum also served as a member of the Mathematics Panel of Project 2061. The project was to determine how much a typical adult must know about science and technology to be prepared for the return of Halley's Comet. Blum also served as the first woman editor of the *International Journal of Algebra and Computation* from 1989 to 1991.

Blum is currently the deputy director at the Mathematical Sciences Research Institute (MSRI) at U.C. Berkeley. She has participated in MSRI's Fermat Fest and has been an organizer of MSRI's "Conversations" between mathematics researchers and mathematics teachers.

SELECTED WRITINGS BY BLUM:

(With Manuel Blum) "Toward a Mathematical Theory of Inductive Inference." *Information and Control* 28, no. 2, (1975): 125–155.

(With Mike Shub) "Evaluating Rational Functions: Infinite Precision is Finite Cost and Tractable on Average" (Extended Abstracts). *FOCS* (1984): 261–267.
(With Manual Blum and Mike Shub) "A Simple Unpredictable Pseudo–Random Number Generator." *SIAM J. Comput.* 15 no. 2, (1986): 364–383.
(With Mike Shub) "Evaluating Rational Functions: Infinite Precision is Finite Cost and Tractable on Average." *SIAM J. Comput.* 15 no. 2, (1986): 384–398.
(With Mike Shub and Stephen Smale) "On a Theory of Computation over the Real Numbers; NP Completeness, Recursive Functions and Universal Machines" (Extended Abstracts). *FOCS* (1988): 387–397.

FURTHER READING:

Books

Perl, Teri. *Women and Numbers: Lives of Women Mathematicians*. Wide World Publishing, 1993.

Periodicals

Blum, Lenore. "Women in Mathematics: An International Perspective, Eight Years Later: Association for Women Mathematics Panel." *The Mathematical Intelligencer* 9, no.2, (1987): 28–32.

Other

"DB&LP: Lenore Blum." *Database Systems & Logic Programming.* http://sunsite.ust.hk/dblp/db/indices/a–tree/b/ Blum:Lenore.html. (April 29, 1997).
Hayes, Lisa. "Lenore Blum." *Biographies of Women Mathematicians.* http://www.scotlan.edu/lriddle/women/blum.html. (April 29, 1997).
Lenore Blum's Home Page. http://www.msri.org/ staff/bio/lblum.html. (April 29, 1997).
Mills College Summer Mathematics Institute for Undergraduate Women. http:// aug3.augsburg.edu/pkal/resources/ptw/mills.html. (April 29, 1997).

—Sketch by Monica L. Stevens

Walter F. Bodmer
1936–
German-born English geneticist

Walter Fred Bodmer is a geneticist whose greatest contribution lies in spearheading the worldwide scientific effort to catalogue human genes, called the Human Genome Project, and in writing both popular and technical books that communicate his fascination with genetics. He also broke new ground in the 1960s, when he defined new ways of mapping human chromosomes and genes.

Bodmer was born on January 10, 1936, in Frankfurt, Germany, the son of a Jewish physician, Ernest Julius, and a modern dancer, Sylvia Emily. Bodmer's father wanted at least one of his three sons to follow in his footsteps and study medicine. However, Bodmer was interested in other things, as were his brothers. He eventually studied mathematics at Cambridge University, where he received a B.A. in 1956 and a Ph.D. in 1959.

While at Cambridge, Bodmer met Sir **Ronald Fisher**, then a professor of genetics. Fisher was famous for proposing a quantititative theory of evolution based on the work of Gregor Mendel, but also was the founder of the science of statistics. Bodmer decided to study under Fisher for his Ph.D., specializing in the mathematical study of the behavior of genes. The field of genetics was just beginning at this time; scientists **James Watson** and **Francis Crick** had recently established the function and molecular structure of deoxyribonucleic acid (DNA). For Bodmer, it was an exciting time of experimentation and intensive learning. Under Fisher, he learned the best qualities of a researcher, the ability to immerse himself in his work and the judgement to analyze his own data. In his 1995 work, *The Book of Man: The Human Genome Project and the Quest to Discover our Genetic Heritage*, Bodmer recounts Fisher's influence: "He was one of the great intellects of the twentieth century and a profound influence on my career."

Although Bodmer had no background in biology, he wanted to continue working as a geneticist after earning his Ph.D; that meant learning about the structure of DNA as well as molecular biology. Bodmer visited Francis Crick to ask him how to combine the two fields he loved. Crick advised Bodmer to try to find out how DNA codes and organizes proteins, the substances which form the building blocks of cells and vital organs.

Bodmer regarded this problem as unsolvable, however, so he decided instead to study and work under **Joshua Lederberg** at the Stanford University Medical School in California. Lederberg, along with his partner, **George Beadle**, had won the 1958 Nobel Prize in physiology or medicine for revealing the ways in which bacteria reproduce sexually—laying the foundation for the study of bacterial genetics.

When Bodmer reached Stanford, he was inspired by Lederberg and **Arthur Kornberg** to pursue work in genetic experimentation. The two scientists were worthwhile role models, Bodmer would say later, for together they had all the qualities of great scientists,

Lederberg's flair and imagination and Kornberg's dogged persistence. At Stanford, Bodmer first performed his ground-breaking work using human-mouse hybrid cells to distinguish and find the specific genes on human chromosomes.

In 1970 Bodmer returned to England to work on cell genetics at Oxford University, where his studies intensified. In 1979, he moved to the Imperial Cancer Research Fund in London, where he began applying DNA technology to the study of human diseases, especially cancers. By 1979, the field of genetics had progressed so much—at Bodmer's lab and others around the world—that researchers began to talk of spearheading an effort to locate and identify the entire genetic map of humans. The idea was that scientists could better understand human diseases—and devise new ways to treat them—once they understood which abnormal genes were responsible for certain types of illness.

In 1986, Bodmer chaired a meeting in Washington, D.C., which brought together scientists interested in creating a human genetic map. The meeting eventually resulted in the creation of the Human Genome Project in the United States. Bodmer himself, however, was having a difficult time persuading scientific organizations to fund a similar project in England. While attending an Imperial Cancer Research fund reception, however, he suggested the human genome project to a cabinet member, who agreed to sponsor the project and suggest it for funding.

By now, genome projects all over the world were being considered. In April 1988, a group of scientists interested in the effort suggested that the work be supervised by an international group of scientists, subsequently called the Human Genome Organization. In 1990, Bodmer became its second president. The Genome Project is now active in many countries and has already contributed much knowledge to the treatment of genetic disease, such as cancer and diabetes.

Over the years, Bodmer has written a variety of books about genetics for his fellow scientists and the general public. One reviewer in the *New England Journal of Medicine* praised *The Book of Man* for its levelheaded treatment of the search for the human genome, stating "Bodmer makes a strong case for a calm and rational appraisal of genetic engineering and for the public to become sufficiently DNA-literate."

In 1997 Bodmer retired as director-general of the Imperial Cancer Research Fund to take on a new position as Principal of Hertford College in Oxford. His wife, Julia Bodmer, a research scientist who was head of the Fund's tissue antigen laboratory, retired in 1998. The couple married on August 11, 1956, and have three children, Mark, Helen, and Charles.

Bodmer is a member of the Royal Society and a past chairman of the British Association Working Party on Social Concern and Biological Advances. In 1980, he received the William Allen Memorial award from the American Society of Human Genetics. He was also awarded the Conway Evans Prize from the Royal College of Physicians in 1982. In 1986, he was knighted by Queen Elizabeth II for his contributions to genetics.

SELECTED WRITINGS BY BODMER:

Books

(With Alan Jones) *Our Future Inheritance: Choice or Chance?* Oxford: Oxford University Press, 1976.

(With L.L. Cavalli-Sforza) *Genetics, Evolution, and Man.* W.H. Freeman, 1976.

(With Robin McKie) *The Book of Man: The Human Genome Project and the Quest to Discover our Genetic Heritage.* New York: Charles Scribner's Sons, 1995.

—*Sketch by Barbara Boughton*

Roberta L. Bondar

Roberta L. Bondar
1945–
Canadian neurologist and astronaut

Only the second Canadian astronaut and the first Canadian woman to travel in space, Roberta Bondar is also the first foreign woman to fly on a United States space flight. As one of the original six astronauts selected by the Canadian Space Agency in 1983, Bondar was chosen in 1989 to begin training as a payload specialist for the International Microgravity Laboratory mission (IML-1). In January 1992, she was part of a seven-person crew that spent eight days conducting zero-gravity experiments aboard the Space Shuttle *Discovery* in what resulted in an extremely smooth and highly successful mission.

Roberta Lynn Bondar was born in Sault Ste. Marie, Ontario, Canada on December 4, 1945. She attended elementary and secondary school in her home town, and it was there, in the eighth grade, that she was first driven to prove that she was as capable as any male. Bondar recalled that although she had received the highest score on a test for candidate crossing-guards, her teacher appointed a boy to be safety patrol captain instead of her, simply because he was male. Remembering this and other slights in a 1992 interview with *Macleans*, Bondar said that each

made her more determined, "to be as qualified as possible, so if people didn't want me, they'd have to say, look, you're a woman and I don't think you can do it."

Obtains Ph.D., M.D., and Specializes in Neuro-ophthalmology

In her 1994 book *Touching the Earth*, Bondar recounts how she was always interested in science and spaceflight, saying, "Every birthday, I asked for a plastic model-rocket kit, a chemistry set, or a doctor's bag." After attending the University of Guelph in Ontario and majoring in zoology and agriculture, she received her B.S. with honors in 1968. As an undergraduate at Guelph, she worked as a research assistant with the Canadian Department of Fisheries and Forestry. She also coached the archery team and was a physical education lecturer and a part-time histology technician. By 1971, she had received her master's degree in experimental pathology from the University of Western Ontario. Three years later, she obtained a Ph.D. in neurobiology from the University of Toronto.

From there, she went directly to medical school and graduated from McMaster University as a medical doctor in 1977. Her medical internship was spent at Toronto General Hospital (1977-78), and she then completed her postgraduate medical training in neurology at the University of Western Ontario in 1980. In 1981 she became a neuro-ophthalmology fellow at

Tuft's New England Medical Center in Boston, Massachusetts, and also trained at the Playfair Neuroscience Unit of Toronto Western Hospital from 1981 to 1982. For the next two years she served as assistant professor of medicine (neurology) and Director of the Multiple Sclerosis Clinic for the Hamilton-Wentworth Region at McMaster University. It was during this time at McMaster that she applied for and was chosen as one of the six original Canadian astronauts.

Competes, Trains, and Receives a Flight Mission

Bondar was selected in December 1983 to represent her country as an astronaut, and in February 1984 she began training. Already a licensed pilot, Bondar was trained from 1984 to 1985 as a back-up payload specialist for a shuttle mission then scheduled for launch in 1987. Being only a back-up meant that she would only fly if the person who was part of the first team was unable to perform. In 1989 she was named a candidate payload specialist for the International Microgravity Laboratory (IML) mission, and in March 1990 she was selected as one of two prime payload specialists for that planned flight. Her goal of flying in space was closer than ever.

During these years of astronaut training, she was also involved in teaching, research, and administration. As the time neared for her actual mission, her training hours necessarily increased, as did the hard work. Recalling these years in a December 1992 interview with the Canadian journal, *Macleans*, she stated that she encountered sexism at NASA as well as with her own group of Canadian astronauts. Remembering her Canadian colleagues, she stated that, "Sometimes they would ask someone who was not an M.D. a medical question and I'd say, excuse me, but it really works this way." In another interview in the same magazine, she recounted that once in space, "Our lives depended on one another—there was a bond there. We may have had disagreements, but the wagons circle when someone fails. It is a tightly knit group and there is a tight bond. We respect one another's strengths and weaknesses. I enjoyed the orbiter crew. They are really good friends and pals."

Becomes the First Canadian Woman to Fly in Space

Only six years after the space shuttle *Challenger* exploded in January 1986, killing all seven astronauts only minutes after lift-off, Bondar found herself on January 22, 1992, strapped into her launch couch listening to the countdown and thinking about that other fateful January. During the difficult and trying times of preparation and training, she often asked herself if this was the way she wanted to live her life. Each time she witnessed another successful shuttle flight however, she found the answer to that question by realizing, "I'm one more [flight] closer to the pad."

After the crucial 8.5 minute launch and separation phase when the shuttle entered orbit, Bondar and her colleagues set about to do what they had trained to do. For seven days, Bondar worked 16- and 18-hour days conducting scientific experiments aimed at understanding the physical changes that take place in the human body in the weightless conditions of zero gravity. Working in an often cramped shuttle laboratory, she was spun in a rotating chair in an experiment designed to measure the effects of weightlessness on her body. She also evaluated the spread of the vertebra in her crew members' backs that would cause them painful muscle spasms and backaches. Among her other scientific responsibilities was the measurement of the effect of gravity on the growth of fertilized frog eggs.

The entire crew worked so hard and the mission went so smoothly, that NASA permitted them to stay one day beyond the planned seven so that they might be able to simply enjoy the phenomenon of flying in space without having to perform an experiment or execute some duty. It was then that Bondar was able to reflect on this unique experience, to view Earth from afar, and to realize how strongly she felt about her native land. Putting her experience in perspective for *Macleans*, she said that, "The science was great and you come back with a successful feeling, but the special part is seeing Earth."

Bondar returned to Earth and found herself ecstatically received by her fellow Canadians. Among the scores of honors she received were the Officer of the Order of Canada and the Order of Ontario, as well as honorary degrees from over 20 universities. She has also had elementary schools in Canada named after her and received awards from France and the United States. As a highly successful role model for all young women interested in careers in science and engineering, she does admit however, that being an unmarried woman made her job both easier and doable. She told *Macleans* that, "If I had had kids and a family, I don't know how I would have coped." After leaving the space program in August 1992, she eventually became CIBC Distinguished Professor, Faculty of Kinesiology at the University of Western Ontario. She also has more time to pursue such recreational interests as flying, photography, biking, hot-air ballooning, and roller blading. She still lives by the words she told *Macleans* in 1992, "It would be pretty dull if one hadn't taken risks in one's life."

SELECTED WRITINGS BY BONDAR:

Books

Touching the Earth. Toronto: Key Porter, 1994.

FURTHER READING:

Books

Cassutt, Michael. *Who's Who In Space.* New York: MacMillan Publishing Company, 1993, p. 343.
Hawthorne, Douglas B. *Men and Women of Space.* San Diego, CA: Univelt, Inc., 1992, pp. 85-87.
Shearer, Benjamin F. and Barbara S. Shearer, eds. *Notable Women in the Life Sciences.* Westport, CT: Greenwood Press, 1996, pp. 51.

Periodicals

"A Report From Space." *Macleans* (February 24, 1992): 52-53.
"An Odyssey In Learning." *Macleans* (December 28, 1992): 16-17.

Other

Press Release. "Biographical Data: Roberta Lynn Bondar." National Aeronautics and Space Administration, Lyndon B. Johnson Space Center. Houston, TX: July 1997.

—*Sketch by Leonard C. Bruno*

Paul D. Boyer

Paul D. Boyer
1918–
American biochemist

Paul Boyer, professor emeritus of chemistry at the University of California at Los Angeles (UCLA), shared 1997's Nobel Prize in chemistry with **John E. Walker** of England, for their discovery of how enzymes synthesize the compound adenosine triphosphate (ATP), an essential part of how cells store and release energy.

Paul D. Boyer was born July 31, 1918, in Provo, Utah, son of a physician, Daryl D. Boyer, and Grace (Guymon) Boyer. Paul graduated from Provo High School's college preparatory course in 1935, and went on to study chemistry at Brigham Young University (BYU); he did not follow in his father's footsteps, he says, "because I didn't want to have to worry about people." While a student at BYU, he met Lyda Whicker; they were married in 1939, the same year Paul earned his bachelor of science degree. They have three children.

While at BYU, Boyer noticed a flyer for a scholarship to the University of Wisconsin. He ap-

plied, and won the scholarship. "Sometimes one has to make a choice, and just hope that it's the right one," he said in a 1997 interview with contributor Fran Hodgkins. "I've been lucky, that all my choices seem to have been right choices."

The atmosphere at the University of Wisconsin was "superb," stimulating Boyer's interest in enzymes. After college graduation, Boyer decided to study biochemistry at the University of Wisconsin at Madison. He received his master's in 1941, and his Ph.D. in 1943.

He then became a research associate at Stanford University, working there from 1943 to 1945. From there, he went to the University of Minnesota. He remained with the University of Minnesota from 1945 to 1963, rising from assistant professor in the department of biochemistry to full professor (in 1953); from 1956-1963, he was the Hill Professor of biochemistry.

From 1963 to 1990, he was a professor in the department of chemistry and biochemistry at the University of California at Los Angeles. During his time at UCLA, he was a member of the UCLA Molecular Biology Institute, of which he served as director from 1965 to 1983. He was also director of the University of California Program for Research and Training in Biotechnology from 1985 to 1989. He is now professor emeritus at UCLA.

Interest in Enzymes

Since the 1950s, Boyer has been studying enzymes, proteins that cause most of the chemical reactions that take place in a cell. He was especially interested in the enzymes at work in the process of converting food nutrients to ATP. ATP serves as the energy source for everything that cells do—from building bones to transmitting nerve impulses.

"My interest in how ATP is made likely arose from my graduate student studies that included the first demonstration of a requirement of K^+ by an enzyme, in this instance the transphosphorylation from phosphoenolpyruvate to ADP to form ATP," Boyer wrote in "From Human Serum Albumin to Rotational Catalysis by ATP Synthase." "The intellectual milieu at the University of Wisconsin, where I was enrolled over 50 years ago, was superb. My studies were stimulated by a symposium on Respiratory Enzymes at which Cori and others mentioned the exciting reports of Ochoa and of Beitzer and Tsibakova showing that more than one ATP was made for each oxygen atom consumed. Although much of my subsequent career has concerned studies with other enzymes, that later portion increasingly focused on the mechanism of the ATP synthase."

ATP was discovered in 1929 by Karl Lohmann, a German chemist. **Fritz Lippman**, who studied ATP extensively during 1939 to 1941, discovered that the compound carries chemical energy in the cell (he received the Nobel Prize in medicine in 1953). It has been called the cell's "energy currency." In 1948 **Alexander Todd** synthesized ATP chemically (he received the Nobel Prize in chemistry in 1957). Researchers during these decades learned that the mitochondria of animal cells and the chloroplasts of plant cells form most ATP, through cell respiration and photosynthesis, respectively. In 1960 researcher Efraim Racker discovered ATP synthase, the enzyme that creates ATP, and described its structure.

Further research showed that the concentration of hydrogen ions (also known as pH) inside and outside the mitchondria's membrane changes during cell respiration. A stream of hydrogen ions drives the formation of ATP, suggested **Peter Mitchell** in 1961—a suggestion that Boyer was, at first, "reluctant to accept." Yet despite all this vital information about the compound's structure and function, no one knew how it was created from phosphate and adenosine diphosphate (ADP).

Structure of ATP Synthase

Racker and his co-workers discovered that ATP synthase consists of two major parts: one that anchors the enzyme to the cell membrane (which he called the F_0 part) and the part containing the "engine" or catalytic center (the F_1 part). Racker called ATP synthase "F_0 F_1 ATPase."

The F_0 part is disc-shaped and consists of smaller units (called "c" subunits). Jutting from the center of this disk is the asymmetrical main shaft of the F_1 part, called the "gamma" subunit. Surrounding the gamma subunit are three alpha and beta subunits, forming a cylinder around the gamma subunit. Over decades, Boyer created a model of how the parts of ATP synthase work together to generate energy.

ATP synthase's structure is like a mixer's. The F_0 part is like the part of the mixer that holds the beaters firmly attached to the mixer's body. The shaftlike, asymmetrical "gamma" subunit is attached to the F_0 like a beater, and projects into the main part of the F_1 as a beater sticks into a bowl. Just like a beater moves with the movement of its base, so does the gamma section move with the F_0 part when a stream of H ions hits it.

However, the alpha and beta parts of F_1 do not move. The gamma section "beater" strikes them as it moves and makes them change shape—like a beater changes the shape of a hard stick of butter in the bowl (unlike the butter, the alpha and beta sections bounce back to their original shapes once the gamma subunit has spun by). This shape changing creates energy, which binds ADP and phosphate into the ATP molecule. The ATP molecule stores extra energy from the reaction. (Walker, who shared the 1997 Nobel with Boyer, verified the model.)

In addition to the Nobel Prize, Paul Boyer and his work have been recognized many times over the years. He received the American Chemical Society Award in Enzyme Chemistry in 1955, the same year he was named a Guggenheim Fellow. He received UCLA's McCoy Award in 1976, the Tolman Medal from the Southern California chapter of the American Chemical Society in 1981, and the Rose Award from the American Society of Biochemistry and Molecular Biology in 1989. He has received honorary doctorates from the University of Stockholm (1974) and the University of Minnesota (1996). He had also been a member of the National Academy of Sciences and a fellow of the American Academy of Arts and Sciences.

Boyer has also served on the editorial board of the journals *Archives of Biochemistry and Biophysics, Biochemistry,* and the *Journal of Biological Chemistry.* He also served as coeditor of *The Enzymes* (as well as editor of its third edition), coeditor of *Biochemical and Biophysical Research Communications*, and associate editor and editor of the *Annual Review of Biochemistry.*

From 1957 to 1961, Boyer was a member of the biochemistry study section of the National Institutes of Health and chairman of that group from 1962-1967. He was chairman of the American Chemistry Society's biological chemistry division (1959-60), and a member of the U.S. National Committee for Biochemistry (1965-1971). With the American Society of Biological Chemists, he was a council member from 1965-1971, president 1969-1970, and chairman of the public affairs advisory committee, 1982-1987. He also was a councilor of the American Academy of Arts and Sciences (1981-1985), and vice president, biological sciences, 1985-1987.

SELECTED WRITINGS BY BOYER:

Books

"The binding change mechanism of ATP synthesis." *Membrane Bioenergetics.* Reading, MA: Addison-Wesley, 1979, p. 461-479.

Periodicals

"From human serum albumin to rotational catalysis by ATP synthase." *The FASEB Journal* 9 (April 1995): 559-561.
"The ATP synthase - a splendid molecular machine." *Annual Review in Biochemistry* (1997): 66, 717-749.
"The binding change mechanism for ATP synthase: Some probabilities and possibilities." *Biochimica et Biophysica Acta* (1993): 1140, 215-250.
"The combination of fatty acids and related compounds with serum albumin. II. Stabilization against urea and guanidine denaturation." *Journal of Biological Chemistry* 162 (1946): 199-208.
(With D.D. Hackney and K.E. Stempel) "Oxygen-18 probes of enzymic reactions of phosphate compounds." *Methods in Enzymology* 64 (1980): 60-83.

FURTHER READING:

Periodicals

Broad, William. "Six Researchers Awarded Nobel Prizes in Chemistry and Physics." *The New York Times.* October 16, 1997.

Other

The Nobel Prize Internet Archive. "Paul D. Boyer." http://www.almaz.com/nobel (January 5, 1998).
1997 Nobel Prize in Chemistry announcement. http://www.nobel.se/announcment-97/chemistry97.html (January 5, 1998).
Press Release from UCLA; "UCLA Biochemist Paul Boyer Wins 1997 Nobel Prize in Chem-

Carl Henry Brans

istry." http://www.bruin.ucla.edu/News/Docs/HLSW480.html (January 5, 1998).

—*Sketch by Fran Hodgkins*

Carl Henry Brans
1935–
American physicist

Carl Henry Brans is one of the world's leading theoretical physicists and is well known among those interested in the study of gravity. As codeveloper of the Brans-Dicke theory, he produced one of the first variants of Einstein's theory of gravitation. A quiet man with a sense of humor, he has spent over three decades conducting research and teaching physics at his undergraduate alma mater, Loyola University in Louisiana.

While Brans is best known for the Brans-Dicke theory, his research career has covered a broad spectrum of interests, from the philosophy of science concerned with the foundations of quantum theory and topology to the overall field of physics, as well as cosmology. He was also one of the early developers of computer algebra for executing complicated formulas which would be, for the most part, otherwise unmanageable.

Brans was born in Dallas, Texas, on December 13, 1935, the only child of Carl and Delia Murrah Brans. He became interested in physics in 1945 when the United States used an atomic bomb to end the war with Japan in World War II. "I remember hearing adults talking about the bomb and how it really impressed them because it ended the war," Brans told contributor David Petechuk in a December 10, 1997 phone interview. "They said it had something to do with **[Albert] Einstein**. That was the first time I had heard of him."

His interest piqued, Brans became a regular at the local public library, reading about Einstein and the field of physics. By the time he began attending a Jesuit high school, Brans was far ahead of the rudimentary calculus and physics taught there. Recognizing Brans's potential, his teachers let him branch out on his own course of study. In algebra and physics classes, he would sit quietly reading about calculus and relativity. Upon graduation, Loyola University in Louisiana granted him a scholarship. Again, Brans was allowed, as he describes, "to do his own thing" in math and physics. As he neared graduation, he applied for postgraduate work at Princeton University when he learned the school was a leading academic institution in the study of theoretical physics. In 1957 he received a National Science Foundation Predoctoral Fellowship to study theoretical physics and relativity at Princeton, where he would gain international recognition in a few short years.

Attains Recognition with the Brans-Dicke Theory

As Brans neared the time when he had to decide on a focus for his Ph.D., a faculty member at Princeton introduced him to **Robert H. Dicke**, one of the world's foremost experimentalists in physics. At the time, Brans was not particularly interested in Dicke's focus on testing Einstein's general theory of relativity. According to Brans, most physicists had become "complacent" about the theory, considered it the definitive work in the field, and had little interest in testing it. Still, the area seemed suitable for writing his thesis, and the two began working together. As a result of his collaboration with Dicke, Brans wrote his thesis on an alternative theory of gravitation in 1961. The thesis became the foundation for the Brans-Dicke theory, which led to a scalar-tensor modification of the standard Einstein theory. The work also spurred on a new generation of experimentalists in relativity.

Despite the wide-spread interest in the theory, Dicke was somewhat ambivalent about the work. After all, this first viable, public alternative to Einstein's theory set out, in a sense, to prove his boyhood idol wrong. "At the time, I didn't think this was terribly profound work, and it was relatively trivial mathematically," Brans told Petechuk. "Also, it

didn't really address some of the basic fundamental issues in physics that I was interested in."

Begins Lifelong Career at Loyola

After writing a few papers on the Brans-Dicke theory, Brans left its further development to his mentor and accepted a faculty position at his undergraduate alma mater, Loyola. Since that time, he has conducted a wide range of research in general relativity and related mathematical problems. In the 1970s and 1980s, he turned his attention to quantum theory and its interaction with the physics of space-time. He went on to write groundbreaking papers on the subject of finding and classifying exact solutions of Einstein's field equations. Brans was also one of the first "relativists" to develop computer algebra systems and has maintained a continuing interest in the field of computer algebra in relativity. He has also investigated the foundations of quantum theory, especially in relation to the true operational significance of Bell's theorem. His most recent work has focused on the possible applications of the discovery of exotic (non-standard) differential structures on R^4 and other topologically simple manifolds to physics. He has also gone full circle and is currently writing a review book about scalar-tensor theories, which are synonymous with the Brans-Dicke theory.

Brans married Anna Monteiro on February 9, 1957, and the couple have four surviving children. Outside of his family and his work in physics, his only other "serious" interest is tennis. Brans, who has his own tennis court, played briefly on the amateur circuit at the state level when he was younger. In his early 60s, he renewed his interest in the game, going as far as to get a personal trainer.

From the time of his youth, when he first learned of Einstein and relativity, Brans has maintained his lifelong interest in Einstein's work. A true scholar, Brans spends many hours in the library keeping up on the latest advances in the field of physics. "He's also a great teacher because, like all good theorists, he goes back to basics to explain things," Creston King, chairman of the physics department at Loyola, told Petechuk. "For example, he recently gave a talk to high school students on worm holes and the physics of traveling in time, and he was able to present the concept on a level the students could understand."

"Einstein first opened my eyes to a lot of possibilities, and since then I've been driven by the profound beauty and simplicity of mathematics," Brans told Petechuk during his interview. "Its congruence with reality is absolutely shocking."

SELECTED WRITINGS BY BRANS:

Periodicals

"Bell's Theorem Does Not Eliminate Fully Causal Hidden Variable Theories." *International Journal of Modern Physics* 27 (1988): 219.

"Exotic Smoothness in Physics." *Journal of Mathematics and Physics* 35 (1994): 5494.

"Localized Exotic Smoothness." *Classical and Quantum Gravity* 11 (1994): 1785.

(With R. H. Dicke) "Mach's Principle and a Relativistic Theory of Gravitation." *Physical Review* 124 (1961): 925.

FURTHER READING:

Periodicals

Zirker, J. "A Radical in Tweeds: Robert H. Dicke and the General Theory of Relativity." *Mercury* (July-August 1994).

—*Sketch by David Petechuk*

Herman Branson
1914–1995
American physicist

Herman Branson was one of few African Americans to direct graduate research in physics. He collaborated with chemist **Linus Pauling** on defining the structure of proteins, which was a significant contribution to the fields of biochemistry and biology. As head of the physics department at Howard University and president of Central State University and Lincoln University, Branson has been devoted to the development of black scientists and other scholars.

Herman Russell Branson was born on August 14, 1914, in the small town of Pocahontas, Virginia, and he received his early education there. His family moved to Washington, D.C., and Branson graduated as valedictorian in 1932 from segregated Dunbar High School, which was famous for its outstanding faculty and curriculum. He attended the University of Pittsburgh for two years, then transferred to Virginia State College in Petersburg. He graduated *summa cum laude* in 1936, and received a fellowship to study physics in the graduate program at the University of Cincinnati. His dissertation included a practical section, on measuring x-ray intensity, and a theoretical section, on the quantization of mass. Branson was the first African American to obtain a Ph. D. in a physical science at the University of Cincinnati when he graduated in 1939. He left for New Orleans, Louisiana, to teach mathematics and physics at Dillard University for two years, then accepted an appointment as assistant professor of physics and chemistry at Howard University in Washington, D.C., in 1941.

He was named professor in 1944, and served as head of the Physics Department from 1941 to 1968.

At Howard University, Branson was able to obtain research grants and develop an undergraduate major in physics as well as a graduate program, both of which were rare in black colleges. In the 1940s, physics courses at those colleges were for the most part service courses for premedical students and other science majors, but Branson was able to expand the department at Howard, and to offer an accredited physics major. Later, he added graduate courses and provided research opportunities at the University and at nearby government laboratories in Washington. Branson's own research at Howard was varied. He investigated biological reaction kinetics using isotopic labeling (isotopes are species of an element having identical atomic numbers, but varying masses), and he studied mass spectral fragmentation on an instrument he acquired for Howard. In the 1948-49 academic year, he received a National Research Council Senior Fellowship to travel to the California Institute of Technology, where he worked with Linus Pauling. His research led to one of Pauling and Robert B. Corey's first papers on the helical structure of proteins, which had a profound effect on the development of molecular biology and biochemistry, and to the understanding of diseases like sickle cell anemia, which are the result of aberrant protein structure.

Branson was always involved in the educational and economic improvement of African Americans, and he believed that the nation's demand for scientists would provide great opportunities for them. In World War II, he directed a program in physics in the Engineering, Science and Management War Training Program at Howard, to provide science education for civilians in the war effort. It was one of the few programs of its kind in physics at a black college. He was also involved in programs for increasing the number of African Americans enrolled in science courses in high school, and in the health professions. He served on many boards which gave scholarship aid and research grants, as well as in other civic and professional organizations.

In 1968, Branson accepted an offer from Central State University, in Wilberforce, Ohio, to serve as its president, and after two years, left to become president of Lincoln University, near Philadelphia, Pennsylvania. Lincoln University was the first college for black students in the United States, founded for the training of ministers. The appointment of Branson as president indicated that the University hoped to improve its science curriculum, and increase its prestige. Branson served as president until his retirement in 1985, at the age of 71. He returned to Howard at that time, and supervised a program which recruited bright high school students into science careers. Branson has received many awards and honors, including honorary degrees from institutions such as Brandeis University, Western Michigan University, Shaw College at Detroit, Virginia State University, Drexel University, University of Cincinnati, and Lincoln University. In 1939, Branson married Corolynne Gray of Cincinnati, Ohio, at the end of his graduate studies. They had one son, Herman Edward, and one daughter, Corolynne Gertrude, both physicians.

After his retirement, Branson lived in Silver Springs, Maryland. He died on June 7, 1995, at Washington Hospital Center.

SELECTED WRITINGS BY BRANSON:

Periodicals

"Structure of Proteins: Two Hydrogen-Bonded Helical Configurations of the Polypeptide Chain." *Proceedings of the National Academy of Sciences of the U. S.* 37 (1951): 205-11.

FURTHER READING:

Periodicals

Elliott, Michael J. "Herman Branson, 80, a Scientist who Headed Lincoln University" (obituary). *New York Times* (10 June 1995): H10.

—*Sketch by Martin R. Feldman*

Hans–Joachim Bremermann

Hans–Joachim Bremermann
1926–1996

German–born American mathematical physicist and biologist

Hans–Joachim Bremermann made his home in many American universities throughout his career. To them all he brought the benefits of his training in the famed Müenster school of thought in complex analysis, as well as his enthusiasm for new fields ripe for mathematical modeling. Although he began his work in pure mathematics, Bremermann published papers on such varied and controversial subjects as artificial intelligence, human evolution, and the AIDS crisis. He was a leader among those inventing new buzzwords for the dawn of the 21st century: complexity theory; fuzzy logic; neural nets. He even speculated on an eponymous "Bremermann limit" to the ultimate computational capacity of all matter in the universe—a sort of intellectual thermodynamics.

Bremermann was born to Bernard and Berta (nee Wicke) Bremermann in Bremen, Germany, on September 14, 1926. His education was apparently unremarkable, perhaps even interrupted during World War II, but that changed in the late 1940s. Once Bremermann turned 20 and began his doctoral work at the University of Müenster, he joined the circle of analysts led by Heinrich Behnke. The year 1949 was an especially active one, in which many German mathematicians and physicists returned to Germany or emigrated to other European countries. They brought with them a mix of new ideas and inventions.

By the early 1950s, Bremermann had devised a general solution to what was known as the Levi problem, previously only solvable in two dimensional forms. He had also emigrated to the United States and married Maria Isabel Lopez Perez–Ojeda. Their marriage would last 42 years, until his death.

A new set of functions introduced by Pierre Lelong and Kiyoshi Oka in the early 1940s set the foundation for Bremermann's continued investigations. He disproved a generalization of the Bochner and Martin conjecture of 1948, offering a simpler proof instead. It was later incorporated into a 1966 textbook on complex analysis that remained in use for many years. By 1959, Bremermann had attacked an even older problem of Peter Dirichlet's, involving continuous functions, proving it could be solved in two classes of domains.

MANIAC

Bremermann and a few other ambitious colleagues were already experimenting with aspects of quantum field theory. By the 1960s, he was involved in biology and computer science as well. Graduate classes in programming and Turing machines had sparked Bremermann's interest in the new technology, but a more practical motivation came in the form of **John von Neumann**'s computer, nicknamed MANIAC. While attempting to program the machine, Bremermann quickly saw the need for the introduction of more subtle algorithms into MANIAC's brute computational processes. He was inspired to set out an agenda for the development of artificial intelligence, in a publication funded by the Office of Naval Research and distributed throughout Europe and the United States. One tactic Bremermann used was to devise and employ evolutionary or "genetic" search procedures. He saw their future in training what he called "perceptrons," and finally witnessed their implementation in automated reasoning or "neural nets" in 1989.

The Red Queen Hypothesis

During the 1980s Bremermann had moved from genetic algorithms in computing to computer models of evolution. Arguing against group–selection models, he supported the Red Queen hypothesis. This still–controversial vision of the human body posits a complex system as host to a churning population of rapidly mutating parasites. Biology and computer analysis continued to overlap as his "Bremermann optimizer" method came to be used in the fields of genetics, bioscience, and cybernetics.

Bremermann took memberships in a variety of scientific clubs and organizations devoted to mathematics both pure and applied. He published in just as wide a variety of publications including one he co–founded, the *Journal of Mathematical Biology.*

Aside from teaching and conducting research at Stanford and Harvard universities, the University of Washington, and the Institute for Advanced Study at Princeton, New Jersey, Bremermann returned to the University of Müenster to teach, before settling permanently in California. He held joint professorships in mathematics and biophysics at the Berkeley campus of the University of California until his retirement in 1991. Bremermann's wife served at San Francisco State as professor emeritus of romance language literature. She survived him upon his death from cancer on February 21, 1996 in Berkeley. The year before Bremermann's death he was feted with such honors as the Evolutionary Programming Society's lifetime achievement award, and an invitation to speak at the Dalai Lama's 60th birthday celebration.

SELECTED WRITINGS BY BREMERMANN:

Books

Distributions, complex variables, and Fourier transforms, 1965.

Periodicals

"On the Conjecture of the Equivalence of the Plurisubharmonic Functions and the Hartogs Functions." *Mathematics Annual* 131 (1956): 76–86.
"Parasites at the Origin of Life." *Journal of Mathematical Biology* 16, no. 2 (1983): 165–180.
"The Adaptive Significance of Sexuality." *Experientia* (1985): 1245–1253.

Other

"Cybernetic Functionals and Fuzzy Sets." *Proceedings of the IEEE Conference on Man, Systems and Cybernetics.* Anaheim, CA: IEEE, 1971.

FURTHER READING:

Anderson, R.W. and Conrad, M. "Hans J. Bremermann: A Pioneer in Mathematical Biology." *Biosystems* 34 (1995):1–10.
Conrad, Michael. "Interview with Bremermann." *Society for Mathematical Biology Newsletter* (April 1992).

Other

Anderson, Russell W. and Range, R. Michael. "Hans–Joachim Bremermann, 1926–1996." *Notices of the AMS* (September 1996).
http://e–math.ams.org/notices/199609/comm–bremer.html
BHN. "99.31 Deaths." *IMU Canberra Circular no. 99.* http://wwwmaths.anu.edu.au/imu/99/personal.html
Jackson, Allyn. "Biographical Sketch." *Notices of the AMS* (September 1996).
http://e–math.ams.org/notices/199609/comm–bremer.html

—Sketch by Jennifer Kramer

Ronald C. Breslow
1931–

American organic chemist

Ronald C. Breslow's accomplishments are multifaceted, ranging from work on the biochemical function of thiamine (vitamin B1) to studying the synthesis of unusual organic compounds and the study of the properties of those compounds. His research on antiaromatic compounds and synthetic enzymes are examples of this line of inquiry. Breslow has also long been active in a wide range of professional activities. Most prominent among these was his election as president of the American Chemical Society in 1996.

Ronald Charles Breslow was born on March 14, 1931, in Rahway, New Jersey. His parents were Alexander E. Breslow and the former Gladys Fellows. He attended Harvard University, from which he received his A.B. degree in 1952. Breslow remained at Harvard to complete a master's degree in 1954 and a Ph.D. in Chemistry in 1956. His doctoral research was conducted under the direction of the famous organic chemist **Robert B. Woodward**.

After completing his doctoral studies, Breslow spent a year of postdoctoral research in the laboratories of Scottish chemist Sir **Alexander Todd**. He then returned to the United States to accept a position as Instructor of Chemistry at Columbia University in 1956. He has remained at Columbia ever since, becoming a full professor in 1962. Breslow is now Samuel Latham Mitchill Professor of Chemistry, a post to which he was appointed at the age of 36. (At the time, Breslow was the youngest holder of a named professorship at Columbia.) He also served as chair of the chemistry department from 1976 to 1979.

Fields of Research

Much of Breslow's research falls into one of three large areas. The first area involves the somewhat traditional investigation of research mechanisms, most notably the discovery the chemical role played by thiamine (vitamin B1) in metabolic processes. Breslow confirmed that thiamine acts as a coenzyme in the formation of a variety of decarboxylases which are involved in the oxidation of pyruvic acid and the release of energy in the metabolism of glucose. In the absence of thiamine, these reactions do not occur normally and a deficiency disorder known as beriberi develops.

Breslow has also long been interested in the properties of aromatic and anti-aromatic systems. Benzene is perhaps the best known example of an aromatic compound. Breslow prepared a number of aromatic systems, including the simplest that can possibly exist, the cyclopropenyl cation. This system consists of three carbon atoms arranged in a ring. Breslow also discovered a number of compounds that do not meet the definition for aromaticity and that he called, therefore, anti-aromatic compounds. A common example of an anti-aromatic compound is cyclobutadiene. The chemical structure of anti-aromatics is similar to that of the aromatic compounds, although the atomic arrangement is slightly different.

A third area of Breslow's research involves a category of compounds now known as biomimetics. The term biomimetic refers to any synthetic compound that has properties similar to ("mimics" the properties of) a naturally occurring compound. This research has provided an enormous and illuminating breakthrough in the study of natural biochemical reactions. For many years, enzymes were regarded as complex molecules whose precise biochemical structure was not entirely clear. By constructing synthetic analogs of naturally occurring enzymes, Breslow has made it possible to develop a far more detailed understanding of the changes that enzymes bring about. Indeed, some of his synthetic enzymes actually perform more efficiently than natural enzymes and, thus, have important practical applications in medicine and industry.

Professional Organizations and Responsibilities

Breslow has assumed positions of responsibility in a number of scientific organizations. He served as Chair of the Chemistry Division of the National Academy of Sciences from 1974 to 1977, as Chair of the Board of Science Advisors of the Alfred P. Sloane Foundation from 1981 to 1985, and as a Member of the Science Advisory Committee for General Motors Corporation from 1982 to 1989. He continues to serve on the Board of Trustees of Rockefeller University (since 1981) and as a Councilor for the American Philosophical Society (since 1987). In 1996, he was elected to serve a one-year term as President of the American Chemical Society, the largest single-science professional organization in the world.

Among the many honors bestowed to Breslow include the American Chemical Society Award in Pure Chemistry (1966), the Fresenius Award of Phi Lambda Upsilon (1966), the Baekeland Medal (1969), the Centenary Medal (1972), the Harrison Howe Award (1974), the Remsen Prize (1977), the Roussel Prize in Steroids (1978), the James Flack Norris Prize in Physical Organic Chemistry of the American Chemical Society (1980), the Richards Medal (1984), the Arthur C. Cope Award (1987), the Kenner Award (1988), the Nichols Medal (1989), the National Academy of Sciences Award in Chemistry (1989), the Allan Day Award (1990), the Paracelsus Award and Medal of the Swiss Chemical Society (1990), and the U.S. National Medal of Science (1991). He has written or co-written more than 300 publications.

Breslow was married to Esther Greenberg on September 7, 1955. The couple has two daughters, Stephanie and Karen.

SELECTED WRITINGS BY BRESLOW:

Books

"Hydrophobic and Antihydrophobic Effects on Organic Reactions in Aqueous Solution," in

Structure and Reactivity in Aqueous Solution. Edited by C. J. Cramer and D. G. Truhlar. Washington, D.C.: American Chemical Society, 1994, pp. 291-302.

Periodicals

"Bifunctional Acid-Base Catalysis by Imidazole Groups in Enzyme Mimics." *Journal of Molecular Catalysis* 91, (1994): 161-174.
"Biomimetic Chemistry." *Pure and Applied Chemistry* 66, (1994): 1573-1582.

FURTHER READING:

Books

Muir, Hazel, ed. *Larousse Dictionary of Scientists.* Edinburgh: Larousse, 1994, p. 76.

Periodicals

"Breslow to Lead Chemical Society." *Columbia University Record* (December 9, 1994). Also online at http://www.columbia.edu/cu/record/record2012.14.html.

Other

"Ronald Breslow." http://www.columbia.edu/cu/chemistry/breslow/boss.html and http://www.columbia.edu/cu/chemistry/breslow/research.html
"Ronald C. Breslow." http://www.columbia.edu/cu/chemistry/faculty/rcb.html.

—*Sketch by David E. Newton*

Calvin B. Bridges
1889–1938
American geneticist

Orphaned at three years old and unable to graduate from high school until he was 20, Calvin Blackman Bridges nonetheless became an original researcher whose work led to the formulation of many of the concepts of modern genetics, including proof of the part played by chromosomes in conveying hereditary characteristics. Described by his friends as a gentle, absent-minded, and even naive individual, Bridges combined tireless laboratory research, breeding some 800 generations of the small tropical fruit fly *Drosphila*, with brilliant theoretical insights.

Calvin B. Bridges

Bridges was born in Schuyler Falls, New York, a small town in the wilds of Lake Champlain. He was the only child of Leonard Victor Bridges, a man of modest means, and his wife, Amelia Charlotte Blackman. Although his great-great-grandfather Hosea Bridges had emigrated to pre-Revolutionary America from Leeds, England, Bridges also had some strains of Native American in his background. When young Calvin was two, his mother died, followed by his father a year later. The boy was taken in by his paternal grandmother who placed him in a small district school but sent him only when it was convenient. Finally sent to school regularly in nearby Plattsburg when he was 14, Bridges still was not ready for high school and had to spend two additional years catching up. Because of this and the fact that he had to help support himself during school, he did not graduate from high school until he was 20.

Enters Columbia and Studies with Future Nobel Prize Winner

Besides compiling an excellent record in high school, Bridges read widely on his own, and when he took regional scholarship examinations for Cornell and Columbia Universities, both schools offered him a scholarship. He chose Columbia in order to live near an aunt in New Jersey, and became a freshman in 1909. Making up for lost time, Bridges graduated in three years despite supporting himself with outside jobs like tutoring. It was in his first year at Columbia that he met **Thomas Hunt Morgan**, who would win the Nobel Prize for Medicine and Physiology in 1933 for his discoveries concerning the function of the chromosome in the transmission of heredity.

In Morgan's 24 years at Columbia, he taught the beginning course in zoology only once, and Bridges was fortunate to be in that class. By 1910, Bridges had so impressed Morgan that he was made his personal assistant, despite being only a sophomore. Morgan was just beginning his great work on the fruit fly *Drosophila*, which eventually would lead to the creation of the modern science of genetics, and to Bridges he gave the task of searching for and testing mutations. Bridges quickly became the leader in this specialty and came to so dominate it that he turned it into an entire career. For five years he worked as research assistant to Morgan and obtained his Ph.D. in zoology in 1916. He continued his studies as a fellow, under grants from the Carnegie Institution, and worked with Morgan until 1919. From then until his death, he was the geneticist on staff at the Carnegie Institution, remaining at Columbia until 1928 and then working with Morgan again at the California Institute of Technology in Pasadena, California.

Influences and Contributes to Morgan's Work

Bridges soon became a close associate of Morgan's. As Bridges became the authority specializing in *Drosophila* to demonstrate and prove the chromosome theory, he became increasingly valuable to Morgan's work and often would co-publish with that eminent biologist. In one of the several obituaries Morgan wrote for his friend and colleague who died before he turned 50, Morgan expressed his admiration for Bridges' scientific abilities, saying, "It would be hard to find in the history of genetic research a more convincing demonstration of the combination of factual evidence and masterly interpretation of it." Morgan also praised Bridges' total lack of concern with priority claims, describing how he would openly distribute results of his long efforts, "without even claiming credit from others for its use."

Although single-minded in his scientific research, Bridges had an altogether different hobby which he pursued with the same detail and thoroughness he gave his profession. He designed and built an early streamlined automobile with an aerodynamic "teardrop" shape. This futuristic vehicle had at first a two-cylinder engine, but when he changed it to a four-cylinder motor, he achieved speeds of 60 miles per hour (97 km per hour) while using gas at a rate of over 40 miles (64 km) per gallon.

When Bridges died in Los Angeles, California after being ill for four months, he left behind many grieving colleagues, some of whom chose to write of his life and accomplishments. Besides Morgan, who wrote four separate biographical accounts of Bridges, others who worked closely and wrote about Bridges were the American zoologist, **Alfred H. Sturtevant** (1891-1970) and the American geneticist and Nobel Prize winner, **Hermann Joseph Muller** (1890-1967). Sturtevant called Bridges a scientist of great patience and ingenuity who was also "a friendly and generous person." He also said Bridges was a nonconformist both personally and socially who moved politically far to the left after visiting the Soviet Union in 1931-32. Muller described his colleague as an uncompromising individual, "where his theoretical convictions were concerned," and one who substituted an ardent faith in human nature rather than in institutions and ideologies. Muller also emphasized the lack of any scientific rivalry in a man who managed to preserve "his early freshness of attitude, boyish enthusiasm, sunniness of character and friendliness." From the tone of everything written about Bridges after his death on December 27, 1938, his passing was not only a shock to his colleagues and friends but a great loss to science. Still, Bridges left behind a body of work not only to be proud of, but one which was able to contribute significantly to the founding concepts of modern genetics.

Bridges was a member of the National Academy of Sciences and a fellow of the American Association for the Advancement of Science, and also belonged to the Birth Control League, the Genetics Society of America, and the Cooperative League of America.

SELECTED WRITINGS BY BRIDGES:

Periodicals

"Non-disjunction as Proof of the Chromosome Theory of Heredity." *Genetics* (1916): 1-52.

FURTHER READING:

Books

Sturtevant, Alfred H. *A History of Genetics*. New York: Harper & Row, 1965, pp. 46-56, 80-82, 137-141.

Periodicals

Morgan, T. H. "Calvin Blackman Bridges: 1889-1938." *Biographical Memoirs. National Academy of Sciences* (1941): 31-48.
Muller, H. J. "Dr. Calvin B. Bridges." *Nature* (February 4, 1939): 191-192.
"Dr. Calvin Bridges, Scientist, Is Dead." *The New York Times* (December 28, 1938): 26.

                                                           —Sketch by Leonard C. Bruno

Bertram Neville Brockhouse
1918–
Canadian physicist

Bertram Neville Brockhouse, along with fellow researcher **Clifford Shull**, received the 1994 Nobel Award in recognition for work he had done more than 40 years earlier. Brockhouse developed the triple axis spectrometer, which enables the user to focus a beam of neutrons on materials such as crystals and understand their exact nature. The apparatus had been compared to a very powerful flashlight which allows one to "see" into a structure. Brockhouse's apparatus and research led to fundamental developments in the knowledge of solid state physics.

Brockhouse was born in Lethbridge, Alberta, Canada, on July 15, 1918, to homestead farmers Israel Bertram Brockhouse and Mable Emily Neville. Brockhouse had one sister, Alice Evelyn, and two brothers, one of whom died in infancy, and another who later became a railroad civil engineer. In 1926 the Brockhouse family moved to Vancouver, British Columbia, where Bertram and his siblings grew up.

Financial difficulties during the Great Depression caused Brockhouse's family to move to Chicago, Illinois in 1935 in search of better opportunities. Brockhouse began attending Central YMCA College (later renamed Roosevelt University), taking technical courses. He learned to repair and design radios and worked for a short time in the laboratory of a small electronics firm. In 1938 the family decided to return to Vancouver, where Brockhouse continued to repair radios for a living.

Anti-totalitarian and anti-Communist feelings inspired Brockhouse to enlist in the Royal Canadian Navy in 1939. He was in the navy for six years, during which he spent most of his time repairing equipment at a shore base. In 1944 the navy enrolled him in electrical engineering courses at Nova Scotia Technical College and assigned him to the test facilities at the National Research Council in Ottawa. It was during this time that Brockhouse met his future wife, Doris Miller. They would lose contact for a while after the war was over and Brockhouse was released from the navy in 1945.

In September 1945 Brockhouse began studying at the University of British Columbia. He felt that engineering or physics were obvious choices for study considering his background, but decided the combination of physics and mathematics was the best choice. In the summer of 1946 Brockhouse took a motorcycle trip to Ottawa. In an autobiography published on the Nobel Foundation's web site, Brockhouse describes the trip as an important turn in his life because he was reunited with Doris Miller, who worked as a film cutter for the National Film Board there. He gradu-

ated with a B.S. from the University of British Columbia in April of 1947 and took a summer job at the National Research Council Laboratory in Ottawa. Brockhouse renewed his acquaintance with Miller, and they finally became engaged, marrying in May of that year.

Brockhouse entered the University of Toronto at the age of 29 and began studying the effects of stress and temperature on ferromagnetism. He ran into some difficulties, though, when three faculty members left to take other positions, and he was left unsupervised. In his autobiography, Brockhouse recalls that he and his wife should have left Toronto, but they were expecting their first child, Ann.

Begins Nobel Prize-Winning Work

Brockhouse earned his Ph.D. in 1950 and then joined the Atomic Energy Project of the National Research Council of Canada (later renamed the Atomic Energy of Canada Limited), in Chalk River, Ontario. His second child, Gordon, was born that October. It was during this period that Brockhouse conducted his ground-breaking research in neutron physics. He had been reading a paper about neutrons, whose existence had only been verified 20 years before. He was supposed to be working on another project, but could not stop thinking about testing the theories he had read about in the laboratory. He began working on an apparatus that would focus a neutron beam on solids like minerals, metals, and gems and would therefore reveal their structure. Brockhouse would go on to improve this neutron beam, and his apparatus, the triple-axis neutron spectrometer, is now used all over the world to examine the structure of crystals.

Brockhouse had only planned to stay a few years in Chalk River, but ultimately, he and his wife lived there for twelve years and had four more children, Ian, James, Beth, and Charles. After the success of the triple-axis spectrometer, Brockhouse began to get invitations to give lectures and attend conferences. In 1957 he made his first trip to Europe, attending seminars and giving a paper at a physics conference in Italy.

In 1962, he accepted a position as professor of physics at McMaster University in Hamilton, Ontario, which had a "swimming pool" reactor that would allow him to continue his research. Brockhouse also chose this smaller school and community because he thought it would be good place to raise his six children. He continued to conduct preliminary research for experiments that would be conducted at the atomic research lab in Chalk River, but now his work included teaching and training students to work with the reactor. In 1962 he won the Buckley Prize of the American Physical Society and in 1963 the British Institute of Physics and Physical Society's prize. In

1971 he supervised a group of talented students in the building of the university's own triple-axis spectrometer.

Wins Nobel Prize

Brockhouse retired from McMaster University as a professor emeritus in 1984. In retirement he pursued interests in the philosophy of physics. Exactly ten years after his retirement, Brockhouse awoke on a Wednesday morning to find a message on his answering machine. The message said that B.N. Brockhouse and C.G. Shull had been chosen for the 1994 Nobel Prize for physics. Brockhouse was stunned and called his wife in to listen to the message. Because of the award, he was promptly called out of retirement for a year of lectures, awards, and travel, all for work he had completed over 40 years ago.

In addition to the Nobel, Brockhouse won the Tory Medal of the Royal Society of Canada in 1973. He won the Duddell Medal and Prize of the British Institute of Physics and Physical Society "for excellence in experimental physics." He is also a Fellow of the Royal Societies of Canada and London, and a foreign member of the Royal Swedish Academy of Sciences. A religious man, Brockhouse is quoted in the GCS Research Society's web page as saying that "Science is an act of faith. Without faith, how can understanding the existence of a neutron help with the larger moral issues in life?"

FURTHER READING:

Periodicals

Corelli, Rae. "The neutron man: a Canadian scientist wins a Nobel Prize." *Maclean's* (October 24, 1994).

Service, Robert F. "Physics: Neutron Cartographers Lauded for Mapping Materials." *Science* (October 21, 1994).

Silverman, Edward R. "Colleagues Laud 1994 Nobelists As Overdue for Coveted Prize." *The Scientist,* (November 28,1994).

Suplee, Curt F. "Molecular Research Wins Prize, American, Canadian Share Physics Nobel." *Boston Globe*, October 13, 1994.

—Sketch by Pamela Proffitt

Wallace S. Broecker
1931–

American geochemist

A sought-after public speaker and author of several articles and books, Wallace S. Broecker is considered one of the world's foremost geologists. He has made great contributions to the understanding of climate change through his research of oceanic cycles and the relationship between the oceans and the atmosphere. Broecker also conducts research in paleoclimatology, ocean chemistry, isotope dating, and environmental science. He is currently a geochemist at Columbia University's Lamont-Doherty Earth Observatory.

Broecker, who is called Wally by friends, was born in Chicago, Illinois, on November 29, 1931, to Wallace Charles and Edith M. (Smith) Broecker. He studied at Wheaton College from 1949 to 1952 before transferring to Columbia College of Columbia University, in Palisades, New York, where he obtained his B.A. degree. Broecker earned his doctorate from Columbia's Lamont-Doherty Earth Observatory in 1958. He began his teaching career at Columbia as an assistant professor in 1959, becoming a full professor in 1964. In 1977, Broecker was named the Newberry Professor of Geological Sciences at Columbia's Lamont-Doherty Earth Observatory.

"No Time for Complacency"

Broecker has spent more than 40 years studying present-day climate systems and those of the past. He likens his theories on global warming to playing Russian roulette, being one of the first to warn of impending global crisis: "If humankind, for some reason or other, had decided that it was necessary to warm the planet, no other plan of action would have come anywhere near matching the potential offered by adding CO_2, methane, and Freons to the atmosphere."

In his book, *How to Build a Habitable Planet*, Broecker does not indicate his optimism that increased knowledge will alter the course of nature. He writes, "Man fiddles and hopes that somehow the future will take care of itself. It surely will, but mankind may not like the course it takes." In spite of his pessimism, however, he works diligently warning of the greenhouse gasses in the Earth's atmosphere.

Research and Theories

Since his student years at Columbia, Broecker's research has focused on the role of oceans in climate changes. He began experimenting with techniques of measuring the radiocarbon content of ocean water along with the ages and accrual rates of deep sea and lake sediments, using the data collected to trace ocean circulation patterns over a period of time. By researching climate change with radiocarbon dating of marine shells found in sediment deposits on the ocean floor, Broecker estimated that the end of the most recent ice age occurred approximately 11,000 years ago. By the 1970s, Broecker was a leader of the

Geochemical Ocean Sections, or the GEOSECS, program. The GEOSECS program has since used radiocarbon dating to accumulate information from the world's oceans.

In addition, Broecker has studied the thermohaline circulation, which he has compared to a conveyor belt. Thermohaline circulation conveys heat to the North Atlantic Ocean and carries salt out of it, much in the same way a conveyor belt does. It is now known as Broecker's Conveyor Belt.

In May 1996, Broecker unveiled his theory that water vapor was a force that may be contributing to the hasty climate changes on Earth, citing evidence that moisture levels in the atmosphere in the tropics dropped significantly during the last ice age. "In the past," Broecker commented in the *Columbia University Record*, "most thinking has focused on water vapor changes as secondary; that is, as the Earth warms or cools, evaporation rates change, and the amount of moisture in the air rises and falls. We opt to turn this thing around and make water vapor the driver that changes global temperatures." He further noted that as a greenhouse gas, water vapor is potentially more heat-trapping than carbon dioxide and that change in water vapor could be "the missing link" that encourages the changes in climates.

Broecker shifts the question of whether or not the Earth is warming to what will life be like if the Earth warms at a pace suggested by computer simulations. Predicting that with the doubling of the Earth's population during the 21st century, the carbon dioxide (CO_2) content of the Earth's atmosphere will double. Broecker suggests that the world prepare for the consequences.

Awards and Honors

The year 1996 brought Broecker two prestigious awards, the Blue Planet Prize and the National Medal of Science. The Blue Planet Prize is an international award that recognizes individuals, groups, and organizations whose achievements have contributed to the resolution of global environmental problems. Broecker received this honor based on his "major contributions to our understanding of climate change and global warming through his research into global ocean currents and ocean chemical cycles, particularly the carbon cycle." In June of 1996, Broecker was one of eight scientists to be awarded the National Medal of Science, again for his contributions to the understanding of chemical changes in the ocean and atmosphere. Broecker is the 13th Columbia University scientist to receive this award.

In addition to the Blue Planet Prize and National Medal of Science, Broecker has been awarded The Roger Revelle Medal of the American Geophysical Union, 1995; the Wollaston Medal of the Geological Society of London, 1990; and the Vetlesen Prize from the G. Unger Vetlesen Foundation in 1987, among others. In 1979 Broecker was elected to the National Academy of Sciences in the United States and was elected chairman of the Geochemical Society.

Broecker married Grace Ellen Cardner on April 7, 1952. The couple have six children: Suzanne, Sandra, Cynthia, Kathleen, Scott, and Cheryl.

SELECTED WRITINGS BY BROECKER:

Books

The Glacial World According to Wally. (Self-published).
How to Build a Habitable Planet. Columbia University, 1985.

Periodicals

(With G.H. Denton) "What Drives Glacial Cycles?" *Scientific American* 262, (1990): 49-56.
"The Great Ocean Conveyor." *Oceanography* 4, (1991): 79-89.

Other

"Wallace S. Broecker." http://imager.ldeo.columbia.edu/geol_sci/html/wallace_broecker.html (November 23, 1997).
"The Coming Warmup: No Time for Complacency." http://columbia.edu/cu/21stC/issue-1.3/warmimg.html (November 23, 1997).

FURTHER READING:

Periodicals

Kunzig, Robert. "In Deep Water." *Discover* (December 1996): 86.
"Broecker Awarded National Medal of Science." *GEOTIMES* (August 1996): 10-11.

Other

"Lamont Scientist Cites Water Vapor in Climate Shifts." http://www.columbia.edu/cu/record21/record2128.14.html (November 23, 1997).
"1996 Blue Planet Prize: Announcement of Award Winners." http://www.af-info.or.jp/eng/whatnew/hot/enr961.html (October 7, 1997).
"Dr. Wallace S. Broecker." http://www.af-info.or.jp/eng/whatnew/hot/enrbro.html (October 3, 1997).
"Press Release: Columbia Geochemist Wins National Medal of Science." Office of Public In-

D. Allan Bromley

formation and Communications, Columbia University. June 10, 1996.

—Sketch by Monica Stevens

D. Allan Bromley
1926–
Canadian-born American physicist

For his pioneering work on the structure of nuclei and heavy ions, D. Allan Bromley is considered the father of modern heavy ion science. He also played a major role in developing particle accelerators, detection systems, and computer-based data acquisition and analysis systems. After a long and highly successful career in academia and service on numerous national and international science policy boards, he was appointed science advisor to President George Bush in 1989. In that crucial position, he played a central role in expanding cooperation between the federal government and the private sector toward the more effective utilization of technology throughout the United States.

David Allan Bromley was born in Westmeath, Ontario, Canada on May 4, 1926. His parents were Milton Escourt Bromley and Susan Anne Anderson.

In 1948 he graduated from Queen's University in Kingston, Ontario with a B.S. in engineering with highest honors. Turning from electrical engineering to experimental nuclear physics, he was awarded his M.S. in nuclear physics two years later from the same university. While an undergraduate, he worked as an operating engineer at the Hydro Electric Power Commission in Niagara Falls, Ontario. In 1949, he married Patricia Jane Brassor, with whom he had two children, David John and Karen Lynn. In 1952, he was awarded his Ph.D. in nuclear physics from the University of Rochester, in Rochester, New York. After graduation, he accepted a position there as assistant professor of physics and remained on the faculty until 1955.

Makes Accelerator Breakthroughs

In 1955, Bromley joined Atomic Energy of Canada Ltd. as a senior research officer and section head at the Chalk River facility, where he remained until 1960. While there, he installed the first tandem Van de Graaff accelerator. This particle accelerator was a forerunner of today's cyclotrons and synchrotrons. These accomplishments led him to Yale University in 1960, where he became associate professor of physics and associate director of the Heavy Ion Accelerator Lab. At that time, Yale required its faculty to have a Yale degree; Bromley was therefore awarded an honorary master's degree in 1961 and thus was "licensed" to teach there.

At Yale, Bromley quickly became recognized as a gifted teacher and outstanding researcher. After only one year at that university, he was appointed professor of physics, and in 1963 became the founder and director of the A. W. Wright Nuclear Structure Laboratory at Yale. It was there that Bromley was able to investigate the structure and dynamics of nuclei and earned the title of "father" of modern heavy-ion work. Under Bromley's leadership, the Wright Lab produced more Ph.D.s in experimental nuclear physics than any other facility in the world. In 1970, Bromley was made chairman of the department of physics. One of Yale's most popular teachers, he taught a science policy course for a dozen years that regularly filled a large lecture hall. A *Physics Today* article quotes a fellow professor as describing him as, "an imposing figure . . . a showman as well as a serious world-class scientist."

Gains National and International Experience and Recognition

Bromley remained director of the Wright Lab from 1961 to 1989, and it was during those years that he became especially active on numerous national and international science policy boards and committees, gaining experience and insight into the industrial and scientific communities. From 1966 to 1974, he chaired the National Academy of Sciences Committee on Nuclear Science, and did the same for its Physics Survey from 1969 to 1974. These influential posts allowed him to contribute in a central way to charting the future of nuclear science and physics. In 1981, he was chosen to be president of the American Association for the Advancement of Science (AAAS), the world's largest scientific society, and in 1984 he became president of the the International Union of Pure and Applied Physics, the world coordinating body for physics.

In 1980, Dr. Bromley became a member of the White House Science Council, a group which gave advice to the President's science advisor. He remained a member until 1989. As vice-chairman of this group, he played a leading role in an influential report on universities that soon became regarded as the "bible" on what the federal government should do to keep universities strong. He was also the principal author of another major report that urged signficant changes be made in the missions and practices of government laboratories. In the last years of the Reagan admistration, Bromley served as a sort of minister without portfolio for the White House and the State Department. He counts as his successes during that time negotiating science and technology exchanges with Brazil, India, and the former U.S.S.R. In 1988, Bromley was awarded the National Medal of Science, this nation's highest scientific honor.

Appointed Science Advisor to President Bush

During the 1988 George Bush presidential campaign, it was Bromley who drafted Bush's only major speech on science. In this speech, Bush voiced his commitment to government investment in basic research and in science and mathematics education. Significantly, this same speech contained a pledge to upgrade the President's science advisor position to assistant to the President. Four months after taking office, President Bush selected Bromley in 1989 to fill the dual roles of director of the White House Office of Science and Technology Policy (OSTP) and as assistant to the President for science and technology. This upgrading of the nation's top science position makes it a Cabinet-level position and gives its holder direct access to the President.

As the first person to hold such a position, Bromley increased the staff and budget of the White House Office of Science and Technology Policy and revitalized and chaired the Federal Coordinating Council for Science, Engineering and Technology (FCCSET). Bromley considers this revitalization one of his proudest achievements. He is also credited with achieving an unprecedented level of communicaton and cooperation among the more than 20 federal agencies that support science and technology in the United States.

In one of his final acts as President Bush's science advisor, Bromley released two reports that were seen as the first step of an examination of the nation's research and development system in a post Cold War environment. Both reports called for university reform, warning that the expansion of academic growth that had occurred since World War II was over, and that universities as well as federal research agencies would be required to make some painful cuts and changes in this coming new era. Having left this legacy of realism for successor administrations, Bromley departed from the federal scene in early 1993 and was appointed The Sterling Professor of Sciences and Dean of Engineering at Yale University. There he oversees all teaching and research within the chemical, electrical, and mechanical engineering departments as well as the department of applied physics.

In his long and varied career, Bromley has published more than 475 papers on science and technology and edited or authored 19 books. He has received 28 honorary degrees from universities around the world, and is a member of all of the most prestigious scientific societies. In 1997 he became president of the American Physical Society and also joined the Washington Advisory Group as consultant.

SELECTED WRITINGS BY BROMLEY:

Books

Treatise on Heavy Ion Science. 8 vols. New York: Plenum Press: 1981-84.
The President's Scientists: Reminiscences of a Presidential Science Advisor. New Haven, CT: Yale University Press, 1994.

FURTHER READING:

Periodicals

Agres, Ted. "D. Allan Bromley – Point Man For U.S. Technology." *R&D Magazine* (July 1992): 40-44.
Cordes, Colleen. "Nuclear Physicist at Yale U. Is Named Science Advisor to President Bush." *The Chronicle of Higher Education* (April 26, 1989): A17, A21.
Culliton, Barbara. "A Conversation with D. Allan Bromley." *Science* (October 13, 1989): 203-204.
Goodwin, Irwin. "President Bush Picks Yale's Bromley For Cabinet-Level Science Adviser." *Physics Today* (June 1989): 39-41.

—*Sketch by Leonard C. Bruno*

Robert Hanbury Brown
1916–
English radio astronomer

Robert Hanbury Brown, trained in engineering, was a key participant in the development of radar technology before and during World War II. After the war, he turned his efforts to radioastronomy at the University of Manchester. By adapting a 218-foot (66-m) diameter fixed parabolic antenna at Jodrell Bank, he became the first to construct a radio map of the sky, from galactic and extragalactic sources. Having mapped the sky accessible to the Jodrell Bank antenna, he turned his attention to development of an intensity interferometer to measure the angular size of distant radio sources. With mathematician Richard Q. Twiss, he wrote about the correlation of photons in two coherent beams of light, a phenomenon essential to the operation of the intensity interferometer and now known as the "Hanbury Brown-Twiss effect." In 1962 he moved to Australia, beginning a long career at the astronomical observatory at Narrabri in New South Wales.

Hanbury Brown was born August 31, 1916, in Aruvankadu, India, to Basil Hanbury and Joyce Blaker Brown. His father was an army officer who had been born in Bengal; his paternal grandfather, Sir Robert Hanbury Brown, had helped to irrigate India and supervised construction of the first Aswan Dam. His maternal grandfather, Rev. Cecil Blaker, helped build the church at Turner's Hill in Sussex. In England, Hanbury Brown attended Tonbridge preparatory school as a boarder with a scholarship in classics, then left at age 16 to study electrical engineering at Brighton Technical College in Sussex. He received degrees from Brighton Technical College in 1935 and the University of London in 1936, and did post-graduate work at City and Guilds. At the University of London, he was a member of the Air Squadron.

Work on the Development of Radar

Hanbury Brown had received a scholarship for his doctoral studies at Imperial College, but Sir Henry Tizard, the Rector, persuaded him to join a research group of the Air Ministry, which needed people with his expertise. From 1936 through 1942, Hanbury Brown was a scientific officer at the Air Ministry's Bawdsey Research Station and at Orfordness, working on the development of radio location and detection methods (radar). The approach being developed consisted of transmitting radio waves toward aircraft, then via antennae detecting "echoes" of the original beam, reflected by the aircraft. The radar was a success, and since war had been declared in September 1939, Hanbury Brown worked on short-range and long range uses of the device, including the develop-ment and installation of experimental radar in aircraft and ships. He also worked on the use of radar for detecting towns and for contour navigation, an idea that was later developed into missile guidance systems. Writing in his 1991 autobiography, Hanbury Brown noted, "Nothing which I have done since then has been so exciting, so absorbing or so worthwhile."

In 1942 Hanbury Brown came to Washington, D.C., as assistant head of the combined research group of the British Air Commission, advising on manufacture of radar equipment and making sure that the American and British equipment would work together. The equipment enabled night-fighting, and pinpointed the dropping of airborne troops.

Radioastronomy and the Intensity Interferometer

At the end of the war, Hanbury Brown returned to England and worked for the Telecommunications Research Establishment in Malvern, helping the Air Historical Branch of the Air Ministry write the history of airborne radar. In 1947 he joined a firm of consultants who advised on how to design and conduct research. When the consulting firm moved to Canada in 1949, Hanbury Brown went to Victoria University of Manchester and, funded by an ICI scholarship, joined Bernard Lovell's research group at the Jodrell Bank Observatory in Cheshire, where they were applying radio techniques to astronomy. At Jodrell Bank, Hanbury Brown converted a 218-foot (66-m) paraboloid into a radiotelescope, which he used to study "cosmic noise" from space. Hanbury Brown's work was pioneering. Over two years, he made a radio map of the sky within the view of the telescope, then used the big dish to scan familiar objects, relating the radio sky to the sky seen by optical astronomers. He created the first radio map of several extragalactic sources, including the spiral nebula in Andromeda. To measure the angular size of radio sources, he invented an intensity interferometer that compared fluctuations in the intensity of two signals. In 1960 Hanbury Brown received his doctorate in science from the University of Manchester. The same year he was appointed professor of radioastronomy, and was named a Fellow of the Royal Society.

On January 5, 1952, Hanbury Brown married Hilda Heather Chesterman, whose father was a medical missionary in Africa. They had three children: a daughter, Marion, and twin boys, Jordan and Robert.

Directs Narrabri Observatory in the Australian Bush

In 1962 Hanbury Brown left for Australia to supervise the completion of an observatory and stellar interferometer at the remote site of Narrabri in New South Wales, 360 miles (576 km) from the University of Sydney. His two-year leave of absence from the University of Manchester extended to 27 years, and in 1964 he joined the University of Sydney as a professor of physics. At Narrabri, Hanbury Brown made fundamental contributions to stellar astronomy, including the first measurements of main sequence stars and the establishment of an empirical temperature scale for hot stars. It was here that he and his team explored the application of intensity interferometry to optical astronomy. After the successful development of a large optical intensity interferometer, he sought higher resolution and went on to develop a pilot model that was a modernization of Michelson's stellar interferometer. In 1974, he published *The Intensity Interferometer*, a scientific work, and in 1977, *Man and the Stars*, a popular book about astronomy, stimulated by questions asked by visitors to Narrabri.

Hanbury Brown retired from his position at the University of Sydney in 1981. In 1982 he received the Albert Michelson Medal from the Franklin Institute for his work in quantum optics. From 1982 through 1985, he served as president of the International Astronomical Union, and in 1986 published *The Wisdom of Science*, a book about the relationship of science to culture and religion. In retirement he spent more and more time in England, and in the late 1980s moved back permanently, to Hampshire. His autobiography, *Boffin: A Personal Story of the Early Days of Radar, Radio Astronomy and Quantum Optics*, was published in 1991. A "boffin," he notes, "is someone who does not stay in the back room, but emerges to poke his nose into other people's business; a boffin is a bridge between two worlds."

Hanbury Brown has lectured as Raman Professor at the Raman Institute in Bangalore. He is a fellow of the Australian Academy of Sciences, the Royal Astronomical Society, the Indian National Science Academy, and the Institute of Electrical Engineers. His awards include the Holweck Prize from the French Physical Society (1959), the Eddington Medal from the Royal Astronomical Society (1968), the Lyle Medal from the Australian Academy of Sciences (1971), the Britannica Medal (1971), the Hughes Medal from the Royal Society (1971), the Flinders Medal (1982), and the Aanzas Medal (1984). In 1997 a symposium of the International Astronomical Union was held at the University of Sydney to mark his eightieth birthday.

SELECTED WRITINGS BY HANBURY BROWN:

Books

Boffin: A Personal Story of the Early Days of Radar, Radio Astronomy and Quantum Optics. Bristol: Adam Hilger, 1991.

The Intensity Interferometer. Chapman and Hall, 1974.
Man and the Stars. Oxford: Oxford University Press, 1978.
The Wisdom of Science: Its Relevance to Culture and Religion. Cambridge: Cambridge University Press, 1986.

Periodicals

"The Nature of Science." *Zygon* (September 1979): 201-215.

FURTHER READING:

Books

Contemporary Authors. Vol. 112. Detroit: Gale Research, 1985, pp. 80-81.
Who's Who in Theology and Science. Framingham, MA: Winthrop Publishing, 1992, pp. 284-285.

—Sketch by Jill Carpenter

Alfred Burger
1905–
Austrian-born American chemist

Alfred Burger spent close to 70 years researching drugs, their effects on the human body, their chemical design, and their abuse. By methodically analyzing their chemical makeup, Burger did much to expand the knowledge of medicinal chemistry and its far reaching effects on the human population. Humans live longer today than 50 years ago because of a greater understanding of the medicinal qualities of some drugs. Effective treatments for addiction have been developed because of a greater knowledge of some chemicals' addictive qualities. Drugs can either help or hinder human beings through their reactions with other chemicals. As Burger explained in an article for the *Charlottesville Daily Progress*, "Drugs are just chemicals. They can't do anything else but react with other chemicals. They can't subdue your pain or raise your expectations by themselves. They can only react with other substances." Through his studies, Burger helped to broaden our understanding of medicinal chemicals, an understanding that has led to new cures, treatments, and therapies.

Alfred Burger was born on September 6, 1905, in Vienna, Austria, the son of S. L. Burger (a civil servant) and Clarisse Burger. After receiving his

Ph.D. in chemistry from the University of Vienna and conducting postdoctoral research in Switzerland in 1928, Burger immigrated to the United States the following year. On August 1, 1936, he married Frances Page Morrison, who eventually bore him one daughter, Frances. In 1937 Burger became a naturalized citizen of the United States.

Upon arrival in the United States in 1929, Burger went to work as a research associate at the newly created Drug Addiction Laboratory at the University of Virginia. Burger's research career spanned over 60 sixty years and would forever link him to the University. Burger conducted research at the laboratory from 1929 through 1938, when he broadened his focus to include teaching. From 1938 to 1939, he was an assistant professor, associate professor from 1939 to 1952, and from 1952 to 1970, he was a full professor, acting as department chair from 1962-1963. In 1970 he was bestowed with the honor of professor emeritus from the University.

Career Focused on the Advancement of Medicinal Chemistry

Burger spent the whole of his career studying chemicals and their medicinal properties. He was an expert in organic chemistry: pinpointing the chemistry of opium alkaloids; analyzing the syntheses of morphine substitutes; and researching and designing antimalarials, antituberculous drugs, organic phosphorus compounds, antimetabolites, and psychopharmacological drugs. He also did much to further the advancement of chemotherapy, acting as a member of the chemistry panel and then as a medical chairman of the Cancer Chemotherapy National Service Center from 1956 through 1964. His most recent work focused on monoamine oxidase inhibitors and antidepressant drugs.

In 1958 Burger founded the *Journal of Medicinal Chemistry*, providing a formal communication venue for his discipline. He acted as editor of the journal from its inception through 1971. Today, the journal still remains a voice for medicinal chemists from around the globe.

Distinguished Career Highlighted by Prestigious Honors

Burger's volume of work did not go unnoticed by his peers. In 1953 he was awarded the Pasteur Medal from the Pasteur Institute in Paris, France. In 1971 he received an honorary degree from the Philadelphia College of Pharmacy and Science as well as an award from the American Pharmacological Society Foundation. In 1977 his contribution to medicinal chemistry was recognized with a Smissman Award from the American Chemical Society. By far, the greatest accolade Burger received was when the American

Chemical Society Alfred Burger Award in Medicinal Chemistry was created in his honor.

Burger was a member of the American Chemical Society and the American Pharmacological Society. A prolific writer, he published close to 200 articles in various scientific journals as well as authored nine books.

SELECTED WRITINGS BY BURGER:

Books

A Chemical Guide to Drug Design. Wiley, 1984.
Drugs Affecting the Peripheral Nervous System. Dekker, 1967.
Drugs and People. University Press of Virginia, 1986.
German for Chemists. Prentice-Hall, 1938.
Medicinal Chemistry. Wiley, 1980.

FURTHER READING:

Books

American Men and Women of Science. New Providence, NJ: R. R. Bowker, 1994.
Contemporary Authors. Detroit: Gale Research, 1988.

Periodicals

Becker, Robert. "From Marijauna to Aspirin, Book Tells How Drugs Work." *Charlottesville Daily Progress* (August 18, 1986).

Other

University of Virginia. "Emeritus Faculty." http://www.virginia.edu/.chem/EMERITUS.HTML (December 3, 1997).

—*Sketch by Jacqueline L. Longe*

Denis Parsons Burkitt
1911–1993
Irish-born English surgeon

Although he has been called "just a surgeon," Denis Parsons Burkitt made an observation that led to the discovery of a new kind of cancer, and to the realization that viruses could cause cancers in human beings. His name is forever attached to the illness that he recognized, Burkitt's lymphoma. He also deserves

Denis Parsons Burkitt

much of the credit for the recent recognition of dietary fiber's role in preventing colon cancer and other illnesses.

Denis Parsons Burkitt was born February 28, 1911, in the small town of Enniskillen, in what is now Northern Ireland. The son of a railroad engineer named James Burkitt, Denis attended local schools, and later schools in Angelsey and Cheltenham. Despite poor grades and the loss of an eye in an accident when he was 11, he persisted at his schoolwork, and at 18 entered Dublin University to study engineering. However, he became interested in medicine, changed his course of study, graduated with his B.A. in 1933, and earned his M.D. in 1935. After a two-year internship he became a fellow in the Royal College of Surgeons in 1938. He served briefly as a ship's surgeon, and then returned to Plymouth, England, for further training. During this time, he met Olive Rogers. They were married in July 1943 while Denis was on a 48-hour leave. A few weeks later, he was sent overseas, and did not see Olive for another two and a half years.

Following his postgraduate training in surgery, he attempted to join the Colonial Service, but was turned down because of his missing eye. Instead, he joined the Royal Army Medical Corps and served as an army surgeon from 1941 to 1946. During much of this time, he was stationed in East Africa.

After the war, he once again applied to join the Colonial Service. This time—with his war experience

on his side—he was accepted. He arrived in Uganda in 1946 to work as a surgeon at a small rural hospital, and then moved to Mulago Hospital in Kampala. He would remain in Uganda until 1964.

Insight into Virus-Caused Cancers

One day in 1957, a colleague asked Burkitt his opinion of a child who had come to the hospital. The boy's face was terribly swollen and marked with lesions. The illness, whatever it was, had distorted his features and loosened his teeth. Burkitt ruled out infection as the cause of the child's distress. Neither his surgical efforts or the other doctors' attempts saved the boy. Burkitt later met another child with similar symptoms (besides her swollen face she suffered from an abdominal mass) and a similar fate.

At the time, it was believed that cancers were unique to organs—that is, that a tumor found in the colon was not the same as a tumor found in the face. As he searched hospital records, he became convinced that many of the tumors reported in children in such diverse sites as the face, the long bones of the arms and legs, the kidneys, the ovaries, and the testicles were related. Studies by other physicians confirmed his suspicion; the tumors were all the same type, composed of lymphoid cells. First referred to as Burkitt's tumor, the disease eventually came to be called Burkitt's lymphoma.

Burkitt did not end his investigation there, however. A colleague from South Africa told him that the tumors were unknown there. Burkitt was curious as to how widespread the lymphoma was. With 25 pounds in grant money, Burkitt prepared and sent out a survey, asking medical personnel whether they knew of these tumors. Over the next three years, he got back several hundred surveys. He plotted each response on a map and found that the tumors occurred in a band across the continent, from 15 degrees north of the equator to 15 degrees south, from Senegal to Somalia and southward to Zambia and Mozambique. They affected children of all races and tribes. Burkitt began to suspect that the environment or climate might have something to do with the tumors—an uncommon idea at the time.

The answer lay at the end of a remarkable road trip Burkitt called the "Long Safari." In 1961 he and his colleagues Clifford Nelson and Edward Wilson packed themselves into an old Ford and set out to drive across Africa. They stopped at almost 60 hospitals, where they examined patients and medical records.

"We suddenly realized that we weren't finding an *edge* to the belt," Burkitt recalled. "We were finding an *altitude* barrier." Even more intriguing was that the map Burkitt had made of the tumors' occurrence matched the incidence of malaria. Although researchers had known that some animal tumors had been caused by viruses transmitted by insects, it was thought not to happen in humans. Burkitt's work disclosed that an insect-borne virus did indeed cause the tumors. This virus is now known as the Epstein-Barr virus. This groundbreaking work was recognized in 1972, when Burkitt was named a fellow of the Royal Society.

Burkitt also discovered that the tumors of Burkitt's lymphoma could be treated with drugs, and that many patients could be cured. No other cancer is as sensitive to chemotherapy as Burkitt's lymphoma. His research here sparked further investigation into the use of chemotherapy to treat cancer.

Dietary Fiber's Link to Good Health Discovered

Burkitt and his family returned to England in 1966, where he became interested in the work of T. L. Cleave. Cleave noted that diseasees common in Western nations were rare in less-developed countries. Among illnesses rarely seen in African countries, for example, were appendicitis, colon cancer, and diverticulitis, an inflammation of the digestive tract.

By studying the volume of stools produced by Africans, Burkitt deduced that their high-fiber diet allowed the food they ate to pass much more quickly through the digestive system than did the typical Westerner's low-fiber, high-cholesterol diet. This work earned him the Bower Award from the Franklin Institute in Philadelphia in 1992.

After spending 12 years as a member of England's Medical Research Council, more than 20 years lecturing around the world, and writing over 300 articles and seven books, Burkitt suffered a stroke and died at home in Gloucester, England, on March 23, 1993, at age 82. Always modest about his accomplishments, Burkitt kept a quote from the Bible hung on his study wall that read "What do you possess that was not given to you? If then you really received it all as a gift, why take the credit to yourself?" (I Corinthians 4:7).

SELECTED WRITINGS BY BURKITT:

Books

Burkitt's Lymphoma. Livingstone, 1970.
Don't Forget Fiber in Your Diet. Arco Publishing, 1985.
(With Norman J. Temple) *Western Diseases: Their Dietary Prevention and Reversibility.* Humana Press, 1994.
Refined Carbohydrate Foods and Disease: Some Implications of Dietary Fibre. Academic Press, 1975.

Periodicals

"The Discovery of Burkitt's Lymphoma," *Cancer* 51 (1983): 1777-1786.

FURTHER READING:

Books

Glemsir, B. *Mr. Burkitt and Africa.* New York: World Publishing Company, 1970.
Spagenburg, Ray and Diane K. Moser. *Disease Fighters Since 1950.* New York: Facts on File, 1996.

Periodicals

Nelson, Ethel R. "Out of Africa . . . Major Medical Discoveries." *Saturday Evening Post.* (March-April 1995): 86.

—Sketch by Fran Hodgkins

William Butement
1904–1990
New Zealand-born Australian physicist

William Butement was a pioneer in radar communication during the 1930s through World War II. While developing radar, he also invented the radar proximity fuse, another important war-time innovation. After the end of World War II, Butement moved to Australia and developed weapons, specifically guided missiles, including anti-tank and anti-submarine weapons.

William Alan Stewart Butement was born on August 18, 1904, in Masterson, New Zealand, to William (a doctor and surgeon) and Amy (nee Stewart) Butement. He began his education in Sydney, Australia, at Scots College which he attended from 1913-15. It continued in London, England, at the University College School from 1916-22. He earned his Bachelor of Science degree from the University College in London in 1928.

After earning his undergraduate degree, Butement went to work in the War Office (specifically, the Signals Experimental Establishment) at Woolwich London, from 1928 until 1938. He began as a Science Officer, then was promoted to Senior Science Officer. While working there, Butement married Ursula Parish on March 17, 1933. Eventually, they had two daughters together, Ann and Jane.

In 1930 Butement began his groundbreaking work on radar, which he developed with P.E. Pollard while in the employ of the Signals Experimental Establishment. Butement's idea was to use radio waves in long-range detection. Butement and Pollard, working in their spare time, devised a crude radio transmitter that used pulses to detect a corrugated iron sheet. Their distance was short, only about 100 yards (91 m), but it opened up new possibilities. However, they were forced to give up because the War Office did not support their experiments. Butement's primary work done for the Office concerned radio and television communication development.

For a short time, 1938-39, Butement worked at the War Office's Bawdsey Research Station. Butement was allowed and encouraged to continue his research on radar. Here, he was involved in the development of CHL Radar, which was used to protect coastal areas from low-flying aircraft. He also experimented with searchlight radar while at Bawdsey, something he continued to plan through 1940.

Invents Proximity Fuse

In 1939 Butement was transferred to the Ministry of Supply (specifically, the Air Defence Experimental Establishment) in Christchurch, Hampshire, where he was given the position of Principal Science Officer, and promoted to Chief Science Officer, then to Assistant Director of Scientific Research, before the war ended in 1947. That same year, he devised what might be considered his greatest invention, a proximity radar fuse used on a guided anti-aircraft weapon. The fuse was used to automatically detonate shells when the weapon had the target in range.

Though Butement directed the research for the development of this fuse in England, the details of his discovery were given to the United States, where the project was completed without him. Traded to the United States for Lend-Lease destroyers, the fuse was used by the American Navy as early as 1941, and by Britain in 1944.

During the war, in 1942, Butement also worked with wavelength radio beams and their use in communication. Butement served his country by being a member of the Home Guard from 1940-43.

After the war, Butement's focus shifted to guided missiles. For two years, 1947-49, he worked with the Long Range Weapons Establishment as the first chief superintendent, until he moved to Australia.

Moves to Australia; Develops Weapons

In 1949 Butement went to Australia, where he was the Chief Scientist in the Department of Supply, and was in executive charge of the Australian Defense Scientific Service (later known as the Defence Science

and Technology Organization). He was very involved with Woomera's Rocket Range. (In fact, in 1946, he was one of the scientists who came to Australia to examine and develop the site that became the Rocket Range.) He held his Supply post until 1967.

After coming to Australia, Butement developed several weapons. He devised the anti-tank weapon, the Malkara, in 1950. Nine years later, he developed the anti-submarine weapon called the Ikara. He also worked on the Barran sonobuoy. In that same year, in recognition of his work, Butement was awarded the Commander of the Order of the British Empire (CBE). In 1960 he finally earned his doctorate from Adelaide University in Australia. He also was instrumental in the founding of the Australian Academy of Technological Sciences, of which he was a member.

In 1967 Butement became the executive director of research for the Plessey Pacific Pty, Ltd. of Sydney and Melbourne, Australia. He later became Director of the Company. He worked at Plessey until retirement in 1981. Butement died in Victoria, Australia, on January 25, 1990.

SELECTED WRITINGS BY BUTEMENT:

Books

Precision Radar.

FURTHER READING:

Books

"Butement, William Alan Stewart." *Biographical Dictionary of Scientists.* New York: Oxford University Press, 1994, pp. 84-85.
"Butement, William Alan Stewart." *The Modern Encyclopedia of Australia and New Zealand.* Sydney, Australia: Horwitz-Grahame, Ltd., 1964, pp. 204-05.

Periodicals

"Australian Pioneer: Dr. William Alan Butement." *Defense & Foreign Affairs–Strategic Policy Australia* (October 1990): 51.
Buderi, Robert. "The V-1 Menace Secret Weapons that saved Britain." *New Scientist* (June 4, 1994): 28.

—*Sketch by Annette Petrusso*

Adolf Butenandt

Adolf Butenandt
1903–1995
German biochemist

Adolf Butenandt's groundbreaking research into sex hormones led to the formulation of the compounds estrone and androsterone, hormones involved in the regulation of sexual processes in the body. He has worked on both male and female sex hormones using microanalytical methods developed by the Austrian chemist **Fritz Pregl.** By uncovering the underlying structure of sex hormones, Butenandt opened biochemical study to the relationship of the chemical structure of sex hormones and carcinogenic substances. For his work, Butenandt was awarded the Nobel Prize in chemistry in 1939, an award that he shared with **Leopold Ružička** but was unable to receive until 1949 because the Nazi government did not allow him to accept it.

Adolf Friedrich Johann Butenandt was born in Bremerhaven-Lehe (now Wesermünde), Germany, on March 24, 1903, to Otto Louis Max Butenandt, a businessman, and Wilhelmina Thomfohrde Butenandt. He received his basic education in Bremerhaven at the Oberrealschule, after which he went to the University of Marburg in 1921 to study chemistry and biology. When he continued his studies at the University of Göttingen in 1924, he was inspired to study biochemistry by his professor, **Adolf Windaus.**

Upon completion of his dissertation on a compound used in insecticides, Butenandt was granted a doctorate by the University of Göttingen in 1927. He was also made an assistant at the Institute of Chemistry in Göttingen in 1931. He remained in Göttingen until 1933, when he was appointed professor of organic chemistry at the Danzig Institute of Technology. He remained in Danzig until 1936, having been coerced by the Nazi government to reject an appointment to Harvard University in 1935. By 1929 Butenandt had isolated a female sex hormone in pure crystalline form. This research was made possible by his association with Walter Schoeller, the director of research for a pharmaceutical firm, Schering Corporation. Schoeller had asked Windaus for help to investigate the female sex hormones and their chemical structures. Windaus recommended his student, Butenandt, for this research. Schoeller provided Butenandt with the necessary hormonal substances needed to carry out the study. Butenandt first called the hormone he isolated folliculin, because it is secreted in the lining of the follicles of the ovary. It was later renamed estrone, however, because it is an estrogen hormone that controls a number of female processes.

In 1931 Butenandt married Erika von Ziegner, his assistant in his early research. They had two sons, Otfrid and Eckart, and five daughters, Ina, Heide, Anke, Imme, and Maike. Also in 1931, Butenandt was able to confirm the existence of another female sex hormone, estriol, which had been discovered in London by G. F. Merrian. (Another biochemist, the American **Edward A. Doisy**, had also isolated estrone at about this time.) He also isolated and purified in crystalline form the male sex hormone androsterone, which is secreted from the testes. This hormone is related to testosterone, the main male sex hormone. He continued his research with sex hormones, and by 1934 he and his associates had isolated the hormone progesterone. In five years he was able to synthesize progesterone from its cholesterol precursor.

An important aspect of Butenandt's research with sex hormones was the discovery that the exact location of male sex hormone activity is in the nucleus of the carbon atoms. This was a major contribution to the study of human biochemistry; it enabled scientists to produce various medical products that alleviate the symptoms of major diseases. Cortisone, a synthetic product closely related to some of the hormones Butenandt researched, has been used in the treatment of arthritis and is one example of the medical applications of hormone research. By 1935 Butenandt completed some significant research on testosterone (the main male sex hormone) that led to his discovery of the chemical sites of biological activities. He found that male and female sex hormones were chemically related by a common sterol nucleus.

Wins Nobel Prize for Chemistry

Butenandt was asked to become director of the Kaiser Wilhelm Society, which oversaw all scientific research in Germany, in 1936. He accepted this position from the physicist **Max Planck,** and the institution now bears Planck's name. The award of the Nobel Prize in chemistry in 1939 was made to Butenandt and Leopold Ružička for their contributions to the study of sex hormones. Because of the outbreak of World War II and the intervention of the Nazi government, Butenandt was not able to receive his award until 1949.

During the war Butenandt worked on genetic problems relating to eye pigmentation in insects. This research led Butenandt to the one-gene-one-enzyme theory that was shared by other researchers. After the war the Kaiser Wilhelm Institute moved to Tübingen; Butenandt became professor of physiological chemistry there and continued his research with insects. By 1953 he had isolated the first insect hormone, ecdysone, which stimulates the transformation of a caterpillar into a butterfly. His associate, Peter Karlson, later showed that ecdysone is derived from cholesterol and is also related to sex hormones in mammals.

In 1956 the Kaiser Wilhelm Institute moved again, this time to Munich, and Butenandt became professor of physiological chemistry at the University of Munich. There, he studied a substance that is synthesized by female silkworms to attract males. Butenandt continued his association with the Max Planck Society for the Advancement of Science, serving as its president from 1960 until 1972. He retired from his position at the University of Munich in 1971. Butenandt died in Munich on January 18, 1995.

Butenandt received many awards, including the Grand Cross for Federal Services of West Germany and the Adolf von Harnack Medal of the Max Planck Society. He was made a commander of the Legion of Honor of France in 1969. He received honorary degrees from many universities throughout Europe and held honorary memberships in scientific societies all over the world. He published numerous articles in scientific journals and wrote a number of books.

SELECTED WRITINGS BY BUTENANDT:

Books

Untersuchungen über das Weibliche Sexualhormon (Follikel-oder Brunsthomon). Berlin: Weidmannsche Buchhandlung, 1931.
Die Biologische Chemie im Dienste der Volksgesundheit. Berlin: W. de Gruyter, 1941.
Zur Feinstruktur des Tabakmosaik-Virus. Berlin: W. de Gruyter, 1944.

FURTHER READING:

Books

Farber, Eduard. *Nobel Prize Winners in Chemistry: 1901–1961.* Abelard-Schuman, 1963, pp. 168-70.
Wasson, Tyler, ed. *Nobel Prize Winners* New York: H. W. Wilson, 1987, pp. 172-74.

Periodicals

Binder, David. "Adolf Butenandt is Dead at 91; Won Nobel for Hormone Work" (obituary). *New York Times* (19 January 1995): B11.

—*Sketch by Vita Richman*

Melvin Calvin

Melvin Calvin
1911–1997
American chemist

Melvin Calvin began his academic career with an interest in the practical and physical aspects of chemistry. His greatest accomplishments, however, have been in the interactions between chemistry and the life sciences. In 1961, Calvin was honored with the Nobel Prize in chemistry for his elucidation of the mechanism by which carbon dioxide is incorporated into green plants. In the years that followed, he pursued his interest in some unusual applications of chemistry, such as researching oil-bearing plants for their possible development as alternative energy sources and in the search for other forms of life that may exist in the universe.

Calvin was born in St. Paul, Minnesota, on April 8, 1911, to Elias and Rose Irene (Hervitz) Calvin. Both Calvin's parents had emigrated from Russia in the 1880s—his father from an urban area in northern Russia and his mother from a rural region in southern Russia. Calvin's father had apparently been well-educated before coming to the United States and, in spite of the fact that he ended up as a factory worker, always put a high value on developing intellectual skills.

The Calvins moved to Detroit, Michigan, when Melvin was a young boy so that his father could take a job at the Cadillac factory there. Calvin received both his grade school and high school education in the Detroit Public Schools, but his studies made little lasting impact on him. Calvin's only recollection from his high school science classes was a physics teacher telling him that he would never become a scientist because he was too impulsive, because he didn't wait to collect *all* the data needed to solve a problem. Calvin observed that the physics teacher didn't really understand the process of scientific advancement: if one were really to know *all* the data, a computer alone would be all that would be necessary to derive a conclusion.

Calvin's interests in science developed as a result of internal forces. He describes walking home from school with a friend and, in a sudden flash of insight, suddenly understanding the role of atoms as the building blocks of all matter in the universe. For Calvin, that moment was a great thrill because it was his own "personal discovery." By the time he reached high school, Calvin knew that he wanted to become a chemist or, more precisely, a chemical engineer.

The Great Depression Pushes Calvin into Chemical Engineering

Calvin pursued his dream of becoming a chemist after he graduated from high school in 1927. He enrolled at the Michigan College of Mining and Technology (now Michigan Technological University) in Houghton, but had to leave at the end of two years. The first rumblings of the Great Depression were being felt, and Calvin could not afford to stay in school. Instead, he got a job at a brass factory in Detroit where he rapidly became familiar with a number of chemical procedures. The experience convinced him to continue with his plans to major in chemical engineering because "I figured I would always be in demand." He looked closely at the world in which he lived and saw chemical applications everywhere. In a time of economic depression, with his father out of work, it was the possibility of making a living rather than "grand questions about the universe," that, he told Swift, determined his career choice.

In any case, Calvin soon returned to the Michigan College of Mining and completed his bachelor of science degree in 1931. He then entered the doctoral program in chemistry at the University of Minnesota. At Minnesota, he gave evidence of the wide-ranging chemical interests that later characterized his professional career. After pursuing problems in both physical and organic chemistry, he finally settled on a problem involving the electron affinity of iodine and bromine for his doctoral thesis. Successful completion of that research earned him a Ph.D. degree in 1935.

In the same year, Calvin was awarded a Rockefeller Foundation fellowship allowing him to spend two years of postgraduate study at the University of Manchester, England. At Manchester, Calvin worked under **Michael Polanyi**, professor of physical chemistry. One of Calvin's research assignments involved studying the role of metalloporphyrins—organic molecules from which are derived chlorophyll and hemoglobin—in various catalytic reactions. Such assignments were a modest preview of the research he would undertake three decades later when studying chlorophyll and that compound's role in photosynthesis. According to *Nobel Prize Winners,* Calvin's interest in coordination catalysis remained "paramount" for many years after his work at Manchester, eventually resulting "both in theoretical (the chemistry of metal chelate compounds) and practical (oxygen-carrying synthetic chelate compounds) applications."

Appointment to the University of California at Berkeley

At the conclusion of his two years in Manchester, Calvin accepted an appointment as instructor of chemistry at the University of California at Berkeley. Two important influences at Berkeley were **Gilbert N. Lewis** and G. E. K. Branch, fellow chemists who spurred Calvin's interests in the structure and behavior of organic molecules.

Calvin's first promotion at Berkeley—to assistant professor—came in 1941, only months before the United States' entry into World War II. Although he continued to teach during the war, Calvin became actively involved in the national war effort, first as an investigator for the National Defense Research Council, and later as a researcher in the Manhattan Project. His most important wartime contribution was the development of a process for obtaining pure oxygen directly from the atmosphere. Variations of that process now have a number of applications, as in machines that provide a continuous supply of oxygen for patients with breathing problems.

After the war, Calvin remained active in national and military organizations. He served as a member of the chemistry advisory committee of the Air Force Office of Scientific Research from 1951 to 1955 and as a delegate to the International Conference on Peaceful Uses of Atomic Energy in Geneva in 1955. In 1942, Calvin was married to Marie Genevieve Jemtegaard, a social worker whose parents were Norwegian immigrants. The Calvins had two daughters, Elin Bjorna and Karole Rowena, and one son, Noel Morgen.

Calvin was promoted to the position of associate professor in 1945 and to full professor in 1947. In the intervening years, he was also appointed director of the Bio-organic Chemistry Group at the University of California's Lawrence Radiation Laboratory. Calvin pointed out to Swift that this appointment was one of the very few administrative positions he had ever held because "You can't do both jobs [research and administration]." He only agreed to the Lawrence post, he said, in order to insure that he would have "an infrastructure on which I could do my job."

Research on Photosynthesis Brings the Nobel Prize in Chemistry

By 1948, Calvin had begun the research for which he is most famous, the elucidation of the process of photosynthesis. Scientists had known the general outlines of that process since the late eighteenth century, a process with which all beginning science students are familiar. In that process, carbon dioxide and water combine with each other in the presence of sunlight to form complex organic compounds known as carbohydrates. Scientists had also long known that photosynthesis is a far more complex process than is suggested by this simple summarizing statement. They knew that the conversion of carbon dioxide to carbohydrates involves many discrete chemical reactions, some of which were then vaguely known, but most of which were not.

Calvin's foray into the photosynthesis question was not without its problems. The only instruction in biology he had ever received came by way of a course in paleontology at Michigan Tech. Thus, when colleagues in the biology department at Berkeley learned that Calvin was about to take on one of the fundamental problems in biology, they could have been forgiven for some doubts about the successful conclusion of that work. Still, Calvin applied himself to mastering the study of biology for more than a decade, from about 1945 to the late 1950s. Eventually, he was able to convince biologists that he knew what he was talking about when he spoke to them about photosynthesis.

As with most scientific discoveries, unraveling the process of photosynthesis was possible only after the development of certain essential research tools and techniques. In this case, the most important of those tools and techniques were radioactive tracer isotopes and chromatography, the ability to separate the compounds within a solution. The radioactive tracer isotope that Calvin needed—carbon-14—had been available only since 1945. Carbon-14 is an extremely valuable research tool in biological research since, while it behaves in plants and animals in exactly the same way as non-radioactive carbon does, its emission of beta and gamma radiation make it continuously detectable to a researcher.

The design of Calvin's research on photosynthesis was elegantly simple. He maintained a water suspension of the green alga called chlorella in a thin glass flask that could be exposed to light. He then introduced to the flask, under controlled conditions, a certain amount of carbon dioxide consisting of carbon-14. As it carried out its normal life processes, the chlorella incorporated the radioactive carbon-14, converting it to carbohydrate. All Calvin had to in order to study the photosynthesis taking place was to stop the reaction at various points and analyze the compounds present in the chlorella.

The analysis required the use of the second new research tool, chromatography. In paper chromatography—one of many methods available—a mixture of compounds such as that obtained from the chlorella is allowed to diffuse along a strip of paper. Each compound diffuses at its own characteristic rate and can be identified by its position on the strip after a given period of time. The presence of a tracer isotope such as carbon-14 makes the process even simpler. By placing a photographic film in contact with the paper strip, the radioactive isotope "takes its own picture" as a result of the radiation it releases. The film offers a distinct record of the isotope's position on the paper strip.

Probably the greatest technical problem Calvin faced was deciding what compound was represented by each spot on the chromatogram. A decade after beginning his research, however, he had the answer he was seeking. The first set of reactions and compounds he proposed were not entirely accurate, but he reworked the series of reactions until correct. That set of reactions is now known to all biochemists as the Calvin cycle. It was in recognition of his determination of the cycle of carbon in photosynthesis that Calvin was awarded the 1961 Nobel Prize in chemistry, as well as a number of other honors, including his 1959 election to the Royal Society and receipt of its prestigious Davy Medal five years later.

But receiving the Nobel Prize did not end Calvin's career in chemistry. Shortly after he traced the path of carbon through the photosynthetic process, Calvin did the same for oxygen, this time using a radioactive isotope of that element.

In 1960, Calvin assumed the directorship of the Laboratory of Chemical Biodynamics at Berkeley, a place where many new and exciting types of research were taking place, including studies on brain chemistry, radiation chemistry, solar energy conversion, and the origins of life on Earth. The last of these topics was one in which Calvin had been particularly interested for some time. During the 1950s, a vigorous debate had been going on among scientists as to whether the earth's primitive atmosphere had consisted exclusively of reducing gases, such as hydrogen, methane, and ammonia, or whether it was an oxidizing atmosphere that also included gases such as carbon dioxide. During this time, Calvin carried out a series of experiments in which a hypothetical primitive atmosphere consisting of hydrogen, carbon dioxide, and water was exposed to intense radiation provided by Berkeley's 60-inch cyclotron. The experiment resulted in the formation of a number of simple organic molecules, such as formaldehyde, formic acid, and glycolic acid. When a similar experiment was later repeated by Calvin's student **Cyril Ponnamperuma,** with nitrogen included this time, simple amino acids—the building blocks of life—were also found among the products.

Calvin's interest in the origins of life on Earth led him in another direction also: the possibility of life elsewhere in the universe. His own feeling has been that the conditions that led to the formation of life on Earth could hardly have been unique in the universe. Instead, he has argued, "we can assert with some degree of scientific confidence that cellular life as we know it on the surface of the Earth does exist in some millions of other sites in the universe."

During the 1970s, Calvin began research on yet another somewhat unusual application of chemistry, the development of alternative fuels. He discovered that certain members of the rubber tree family produce a sap-like material that can be burned in much the same way as petroleum. He suggested the possibility that such trees could be grown on huge plantations in order to provide an alternative source of energy as our supply of crude oil continues to diminish. With his wife, Calvin eventually established an experimental farm in Northern California to test out this idea.

As Calvin's academic career came to a close, he continued to receive the recognition of his peers in the field of science. In 1978, he was awarded the Priestley Medal of the American Chemical Society (ACS) and the Gold Medal of the American Institute of Chemists. In 1981, Calvin was awarded the Oesper Prize by the ACS. To balance a public life dedicated to science, Calvin maintained a number of personal interests, including photography, gardening, politics, and sports. Although he retired as University Professor of Chemistry in 1980, he continued his scientific work. Calvin died on January 8, 1997 at Alta Bates Hospital in Berkeley, California.

SELECTED WRITINGS BY CALVIN:

Books

The Theory of Organic Chemistry. Prentice-Hall, 1941.
Chemistry of the Chelate Compounds. Prentice-Hall, 1949.
Isotopic Carbon New York: Wiley, 1949.
The Path of Carbon in Photosynthesis. Prentice-Hall, 1957.
Chemical Evolution, Oxford University Press, 1961.

FURTHER READING:

Books

Current Biography 1962. New York: H. W. Wilson, 1962, pp. 68-70.
McGraw-Hill Modern Men of Science. Vol. 1.New York: McGraw-Hill, 1984, p. 85.
Nobel Lectures in Chemistry, 1942–1962. Amsterdam, 1964, pp. 645-46.
Swift, David. *SETI Pioneers.* Tucson: University of Arizona Press, 1990, pp. 116-35.
————, ed. *Nobel Prize Winners.* New York: H. W. Wilson, 1987, pp. 176-77.

Periodicals

Oliver, Myrna. "Melvin Calvin; Nobel-Winning Chemist" (obituary). *Los Angeles Times* (11 January 1997): A20.
Saxon, Wolfgang. "Melvin Calvin Dies at 85; Biochemist Won Nobel Prize" (obituary). *New York Times* (10 January 1997): B6.

—*Sketch by David E. Newton*

E. Eleanor Carothers
1882–1957
American zoologist

Eleanor Carothers focused her scientific endeavors in cytology, the study of cells and their inner workings. Particularly concerned with the relationship between cytology and genetics, and the effect x rays have on cells, she was most noted for her precise research methodologies. Carothers contributed much data on the subject and published prolifically in many prestigious journals. Carother's career was also remarkable because she was female in a predominantly male arena.

At birth, she was named Estella Eleanor Carothers on December 4, 1882, in Newton, Kansas. Her parents were Z. W. Carothers and Mary E. Bates Carothers. Carothers attended the Kansas-based Nickerson Normal College, a teacher's school, then after several years after graduating, entered the University of Kansas. Carothers earned her undergraduate degree at age 28 in 1911, and her Masters at the same institution a year later. Carothers attended University of Pennsylvania for the remainder of her graduate work, and was awarded her Ph.D. in 1916.

While still a graduate student, Carothers worked as an assistant in the zoology department at the University of Pennsylvania, from 1913. In 1926, she was promoted to a lecturer position. While at the University of Pennsylvania, Carothers was part of two scientific expeditions conducted in the south and southwestern United States, in 1915 and 1919. This was a prestigious accomplishment for a female student and scientist in this era.

Carothers was afforded many such honors from the time she was a graduate student and onward. In **Thomas Morgan**'s 1915 book, *The Mechanism of Mendelian Heredity*, she was named as a primary investigator, one of only seven women to be so cited. She won the 1921 Ellen Richards Research Prize (sponsored by the Naples Table Association) for her work. Her name was starred in the 1926 edition of the *American Men of Science*, meaning that she was considered one of the United States' 1,000 most distinguished scientists.

The reason for the many honors bestowed upon Carothers was the thoroughness of her research in cytology. In focusing on the genetics of the order Orthoptera (which includes crickets and grasshoppers), Carothers answered many questions concerning cytological heredity. Carothers published her findings in many leading journals such as the *Journal of Morphology, The Biological Bulletin, Quarterly Review of Biology,* and *Proceedings of the Entomolgocial Society.* As befitting such a honored scientist, Carothers was a member of the National Academy of Sciences and the Academy of Natural Sciences of Philadelphia, as well as many related organizations.

Carothers left the University of Pennsylvania in 1933 to become a research associate in zoology at the University of Iowa. She retired in 1941. A lover of the outdoors who favored activities like horseback riding, hiking, and canoeing, Carothers died in 1957 at the age of 75.

SELECTED WRITINGS BY CAROTHERS:

Books

The Segregation and Recombination of Homologous Chromosomes as Found in Two Genera of Acrididae (Orthoptera). Baltimore: Waverly Press, 1917.

Élie Joseph Cartan

FURTHER READING:

Books

Bailey, Martha J. *American Women in Science.* Denver: ABC-CLIO, 1994, p. 55.

Ogilvie, Marilyn Bailey. *Women in Science: Antiquity through the Nineteenth Century.* Cambridge, Massachusetts: MIT Press, 1986, pp. 52-53.

Siegel, Patricia Joan, and Kay Thomas Finley. *Women in the Scientific Search: An American Bio-Bibliography, 1724-1979.* Metuchen, New Jersey: The Scarecrow Press, Inc., 1985, pp. 363-64.

—*Sketch by Annette Petrusso*

Élie Joseph Cartan
1869–1951
French mathematician

Élie Joseph Cartan is one of the most important mathematical figures in the first half of the 20th century. Although recognition for his many accomplishments did not come until late in his career, his intellectual influence is still felt as modern mathemat-

ics develops. From the earliest point in his career, Cartan further developed Norwegian mathematician Marius Sophus Lie's group theory which concerned continuous groups and symmetries within them. He interworked Lie's theory and the original means in which he studied its global properties with differential geometry, classical geometry, and topology. These combined areas are still a vital part of contemporary mathematics. Cartan also formulated many original theories based on his studies. Despite making such vital contributions to mathematics, Cartan was quite modest, good humored, and easy going. He was also a gifted and well-liked teacher who could break down his intricate theories for the consumption of an average student.

Cartan was born April 9, 1869, in Dolomieu Isère, France, a village in the Alps. Of peasant descent, he was the son of the village blacksmith, Joseph, and his wife, Anne (Cottaz) Cartan. Cartan was the second oldest of four children. An inspector of primary schools, Antonin Dubost, noticed Cartan's impressive scholastic aptitude while on a visit to Cartan's school. Though most children from poor families were not put on the track to attend university, Dubost helped Cartan to win a scholarship to attend lycée (secondary school). Cartan's success as a student inspired his youngest sister, Anna, to follow in his intellectual footsteps, and become a mathematics teacher. She also published several texts on geometry.

After attending three lycées, Cartan went on to the l'Ecole Normale Supérieure in Paris in 1888, obtaining his doctorate in 1894. In his graduate thesis, Cartan began the first phase of his life's research, that of Lie's theory of continuous groups, a topic neglected by most of his contemporaries. In his thesis Cartan completed the classification of semisimple algebras begun by Wilhelm Killing during the last two decades of the 19th century, and gave a rigorous foundation for the types of Lie algebras that Killing had shown to be possible.

Before pursuing a career as a mathematician, Cartan was drafted into the French Army for one year after his graduation, rising to the rank of sergeant before his discharge. Cartan then served as a lecturer at two successive institutions, the University of Montpellier (1894 to 1896), and the University of Lyons (1896 to 1903). While a lecturer, he continued his mathematical studies based on Lie's theory, and began bringing together the four disparate disciplines that became the hallmark of Cartan's work: differential geometry, classical geometry, topology, and Lie theory. Cartan began by exploring the structure for associative algebras, then moved onto semisimple Lie groups and their representations. In this period (roughly from 1894 to 1904), Cartan also helped create and develop the calculus of exterior differential forms. This calculus became an important tool Cartan used in his research and he applied it to various differential geometric problems.

In 1903, Cartan's life changed in two fundamental ways. He married Marie–Louise Bianconi in that year. With her he had four children (three sons and one daughter), and enjoyed a happy home life. His eldest son, **Henri Paul Cartan**, born in 1904, became a prominent mathematician in his own right. His daughter Hélène also became a mathematician who taught at lycées and published some mathematical papers. Cartan's two other sons died tragic deaths. Jean, a composer, died at 25 of tuberculosis; Louis, a physicist, was arrested and imprisoned by the Nazis for his activities in the French Resistance. Louis Cartan was executed by the Nazis in 1943, but his family did not learn of his death until 1945.

In 1903, Cartan also became a professor at the University of Nancy, where he worked until 1909. Cartan moved on to the University of Paris (the Sorbonne) in 1909, where he was a lecturer from 1909 to 1912 before becoming a full professor in 1912. He remained a professor there until he retired in 1940. In his first years at the Sorbonne, in 1913, Cartan made one of his most significant contributions to math when he discovered spinors. The spinors are complex vectors used to make two–dimensional representations out of three–dimensional rotations. The spinors were important in the development of quantum mechanics.

Though Cartan continued to intertwine the four subjects mentioned earlier, at the height of his career, he continued to look at them from different perspectives. For example, after 1916, Cartan's publications focused mainly on differential geometry. Cartan developed a moving frames theory and a generalization of Daboux's kinematical theory. In 1925, Cartan refocused his attention to the study of topology. In his paper "La géométrie des espaces de Riemann" ("The Geometry of Riemann Spaces"), Cartan came up with innovative ways to study Lie groups' global properties. He demonstrated, in topological terms, that a Euclidean space and a compact group can produce a connected Lie group. And, from 1926 to 1932, Cartan published treatises concerning his geometric theory of symmetric spaces.

Cartan's continual output of important work led to his appointment as a member of the Académie Royale des Sciences in 1931, one of many honors he received late in his career. About the same time, Cartan began collaborating with his son Henri on mathematical problems, building on his son's theorems. On Cartan's 70th birthday, in 1939, the Sorbonne honored him with a celebratory symposium which praised his many mathematical accomplishments. Although Cartan retired from the Sorbonne in 1940, he remained an honorary professor there until his death. He also continued to publish mathematical

treatises, and his love of classroom instruction led him to teach math at the l'Ecole Normale Supérieure for Girls. Cartan died in Paris on May 6, 1951, after a long illness.

SELECTED WRITINGS BY CARTAN:

"La géométrie des espaces de Riemann," in *Mémorial des Sciences Mathématiques*. Volume 9, 1925.

FURTHER READING:

Books

Akivis, M.A., and B.A. Rosenfeld. *Translations of Mathematical Monographs: Élie Cartan*. Volume 123. Providence, RI: American Mathematical Society, 1991.

Daintith, John, Sarah Mitchell, and Elizabeth Tootill, editors. *A Biographical Encyclopedia of Scientists*. Volume 1. New York: Facts on File, Inc., 1981, pp. 144–45.

Dieudonné, Jean. "Élie Cartan." *Dictionary of Scientific Biography*. Volume 3. Edited by Charles Coulston Gillispie. New York: Charles Scribner's Sons, 1970, pp. 95–96.

Periodicals

Shiing–Shen and Claude Chevalley. "Élie Cartan and his Mathematical Work." *Bulletin of the American Mathematical Society* (March 1952): 217–250.

—*Sketch by Annette Petruso*

Henri Paul Cartan
1904–
French algebraist

Henri Cartan has made monumental contributions in essentially every field of algebraic topology, including analytical functions, the theory of sheaves, homological theory, and potential theory. His most important works include *Homological Algebra* (1956) and *Elementary Theory of Analytic Functions of One or Several Complex Variables* (1963). He also worked on a definitive convergence theorem on decreasing potentials of positive masses, which became a fundamental instrument for improving potential theory. Cartan is the recipient of the 1980 Wolf Prize in Mathematics.

Cartan was born in Nancy, France, in 1904. His father was **Elie Joseph Cartan**, a French mathematician who made significant contributions to the theory of subalgebras. Cartan was educated at the École Normal Superieure in Paris, one of the finest schools for mathematics. Cartan attended the École from 1923–1926. He was a protégée of **Jules Henri Poincare**, who is considered the founder of algebraic topology and the theory of analytic functions of several complex variables. Along with **Albert Einstein** and Hendrik Lorentz, Poincare is considered a co–discoverer of the special theory of relativity. Cartan's studies with Poincare may explain his own interest in algebraic topology.

The "Birth" of Nicholas Bourbaki

In 1935, Cartan was one of the founders of a group of young French mathematicians who had all graduated from the École Normal Superieure. Other members included Claude Chevalley (or Chevallier), Jean Dieudonné, Jean Deslarte, and **Andre Weil.** All members were brilliant in their own right, however, Weil was the only "universalist" among them, accomplished in every area of mathematics. At the beginning, Cartan was not a universalist, although he did become more accomplished later in his career.

The group wrote under the pseudonym of Nicolas Bourbaki. In "Nicholas Bourbaki, Collective Mathematician," Claude Chevalley, as told to Denis Guedj, explains how Bourbaki got his name: "Weil had spent two years in India and for the thesis of one of his pupils he needed a result he couldn't find anywhere in the literature. He was convinced of its validity, but he was too lazy to write out the proof. His pupil, however, was content to put a note at the bottom of the page which referred to 'Nicolas Bourbaki, of the Royal Academy of Poldavia'." The "real" Bourbaki liked to pretend he was in a secret society when he was young. From this, Weil tried to get the members of the group to stay anonymous. Members refused to answer questions about other members and of projects they were working, and even how the name of Bourbaki originated. The group did not remain anonymous for very long.

The Bourbaki group produced *Elements de mathematique*, a 30–volume textbook on analysis geared toward French university students, in 1939. It was intended to replace the class analysis textbook used in France written by Edouard Goursat. Bourbaki's book aimed to achieve the same high standards that Goursat set forth in his text, yet it also included mathematical advances. By 1968, there were 33 volumes in print. Early editions of *Elements* did not include credit to other contributors, so in 1960, *Elements d'historique des mathematiques* was published to rectify the situation.

The group sought the best way to produce the work together. They did not just want to assign topics to the person most qualified to write it, believing if they did, the book would turn out like an encyclopedia, which they did not want. Each member studied the same areas of mathematics, from the beginning. During the Bourbaki–congres, as their thrice yearly meetings were called, the group would discuss sections of the book, making numerous revisions. Bourbaki members had to retire from the group by the age of 50. This assurance was made to keep Bourbaki from "growing old," keeping him young in spirit. Women were not allowed to join the Bourbaki group. Through the Bourbaki members, a new kind of algebraic topology was born. Bourbaki played a key role in the rethinking of structural mathematics.

IMU and Academia

Cartan became president of the International Mathematical Union (IMU) in 1967, serving in that capacity until 1970. He then became the past–president, holding a seat on the executive committee for the following four years. The IMU is a scientific organization with the purpose of promoting international cooperation in mathematics and is part of the International Council of Scientific Unions. Founded in 1919, the IMU was disbanded in 1936, then reconstituted in 1951. Cartan was an invited speaker for a May 1995 IMU conference taking place at the Institut Henri Poincaré.

Cartan's academic career began at the Lyceé Caen in 1928, where he was a professor of mathematics. He left the Lycee in 1929, and was appointed a deputy professor at the University of Lille. From there, he went to the University of Strasbourg, which named him a professor of mathematics in 1931. From 1940 until 1969, Cartan was on the faculty at the University of Paris. After the University of Paris, Cartan taught at Orsay for about five years, until 1975.

A Warning to Humanity

In 1992, Cartan was part of a group of international scientists issuing a warning to humanity. The warning urged changes to protect the living world. According to the Worlds' Scientists Warning to Humanity, found on the World Wide Web, "Human beings and the natural world are on a collision course. . . . If not checked, many of our current practices put at serious risk the future that we wish for human society and the plant and animal kingdoms, and may so alter the living world that it will be unable to sustain life in the manner that we know. . . . Fundamental changes are urgent if we are to avoid the collision our present course will bring about." The warning lists several environments in need of help. Cartan's name is among the 1,500 signatories, all of which are members of regional, national, and international science academies.

SELECTED WRITINGS BY CARTAN:

Books

Homological Algebra, 1956.
Elementary Theory of Analytic Functions of One or Several Complex Variables, 1963.
Differential Forms, 1971.

Periodicals

"Colloque 'Analyse et Topologie' en l'Honneur de Henri Cartan." *Asterisque 32-33, Soc. Math. France* (1976): 3-4.
"Sixteen French Intellectuals On: The Joys of Being Jewish in the USSR." *The New Leader* (November 28, 1983): 5-6.

As Nicolas Bourbaki

Elements de Mathematique, 1939.
Elaements d'histoire des mathaematiques, 1960, 1969.
General Topology, 1966.
Cummutative Algebra, 1972.

FURTHER READING:

Books

Fang. J. *Mathematicians From Antiquity to Today.* Hauppauge, NY: Paideia Press, 1972, pp. 269-270.

Periodicals

"Breve analyse des travaux de Henri Cartan, Colloque 'Analyse et Topologie' en l'Honneur de Henri Cartan." *Asterisque 32-33, Soc. Math. France* (1976): 5-21.
Dimiev, S. and R. Lazov. "Henri Cartan: On the Occasion of His 80th Birthday." *Fiz.–Mat. Spis. Bulgar. Akdad. Nauk.* 26 (59) (2) (1984): 222-225.
Guedj, Denis. "Nicholas Bourbaki, Collective Mathematician, An Interview with Claude Chevalley." Translated by Jeremy Gray. *The Mathematical Intelligencer* 7, no. 2, (1985): 18-22.
"Liste des travaux de Henri Cartan." *Asterisque 32-33, Soc. Math. France* (1976): 22-27.

Other

Conlay, Mike. "Nicolas Bourbaki." http://www.mcs.csuhayward.edu/~malek/Mathlinks/Bourbaki.html (May 9, 1997).

"The Bourbaki View." http://www.rbjones.com/rbjpub/logic/jrh0105.html (May 9, 1997).
"Henri Paul Cartan." *MacTutor History of Mathematician.* http://www–groups.dcs.st–and.ac.uk/~history/Mathematicians/Cartan_Henri.html. (April 25, 1997).
"The International Mathematical Union (IMU)." Online. Available at http://130.225.112.194:8000/0x82e170c2_0x00000b59;sk=311225BD (May 16, 1997).
"IMU Executive Committees 1952–1998." http://130.225.112.194:8000/0x82e170c2_0x00000b59a;sk=311225BD (May 16, 1997).
"World Scientists' Warning to Humanity." http://www.livelinks.com/sumeria/warning.html (April 29, 1997).

—*Sketch by Monica L. Stevens*

Mary Lucy Cartwright
1900–
English mathematician

Dame Mary Lucy Cartwright's research and contributions to the field of mathematics have spanned more than seven decades. England claims her as one of its most brilliant citizens and has honored her for the past 50 years. As late as 1996, she was featured, along with two other women scientists, on British television, modestly answering questions about her impressive achievements.

Cartwright was born in Aynho, Northamptonshire, England, on December 17, 1900. Her father, William Digby Cartwright, served as a curate to his uncle, who was a rector at a church. Her mother was Lucy Harriette Maud Bury. The youngest of three children, Cartwright's two other brothers, John and Nigel, were both killed in World War I. When Cartwright was 11 years old, she was sent to live with her maternal uncle, Fred Bury, and his wife Annie, so she could attend Leamington High School, now known as the Kingsley School. There, she learned mathematics from a teacher she remembers as Miss Hancock, to whom she still pays tribute as "an excellent teacher of mathematics." In 1919, Cartwright entered St. Hughes College at Oxford and remained there until 1923. At the age of 23 she graduated from the University of Oxford, then taught first at the Alice Ottley School in Worcester, then at the Wycombie Abbey School for four years before returning to Oxford to complete her doctorate in mathematics. In 1925 Cartwright received the Hurry Prize for mathematics.

One of only five students, Cartwright began study and research with **Godfrey Hardy** in 1928 and it was under his supervision (as well as of E.C. Titchmarsh) that she pursued her degree. Initially, Hardy was Cartwright's advisor on her thesis, then Titchmarsh took over when Hardy left to spend some time at Princeton University. Hardy is best known for the Hardy–Weinberg law, which resolved the controversy over what proportions of dominant and recessive genetic traits would be reproduced in a large mixed population. Cartwright had great admiration for Hardy, both for his work and for the pains he took in instructing his students. Hardy also collaborated with John E. Littlewood on a series of papers that contributed fundamentally to the theory of Diophantine analysis, divergent series summation, and Fourier series.

Collaboration and Accomplishment

Littlewood was Cartwright's examiner for her Ph.D. in 1930. She was the first woman to read for finals in mathematics at Oxford. The meeting was the first in a long series of conferences that would eventually lead to more than ten years of collaboration on a number of projects. Together, Cartwright and Littlewood published four papers on large parameters, differential equations combining topological and analytical methods, solutions for the Van der Pol equation, and chaos theory. They published several other papers, but the content was based on their collaborative work. Based on her own research, Cartwright also published a number of papers concerning classical analysis. Cartwright was a prolific writer; besides mathematical papers, she produced biographical essays on other women mathematicians such as **Shelia Scott Macintyre** and **Grace Chisholm Young** for the London Mathematical Society's *Journal*.

Also in 1930 Cartwright became a Yarrow Research Fellow of Girton. During her fellowship she attended lectures given by Edward Collingwood concerning integral and metamorphic functions. She worked closely with Collingwood on cluster sets in the theory of functions of one complex variable and these papers were also published. Other publications by Cartwright include *Religion and the Scientist, Specialization in Education, The Mathematical Mind,* and *Integral Functions*.

In 1935, Cartwright was given a Faculty Assistant Lectureship at Cambridge University and her Yarrow Research Fellowship was extended. Cartwright contributes the appointments to a paper she published entitled "Mathematische Zeitschrift" in early 1935. An earlier version of the paper had been shown to Hardy and Littlewood, and Cartwright believes it was upon their joint recommendations that she was given her position at Cambridge.

During World War II, Cartwright volunteered and served with the British Red Cross Detachment from 1940 to 1944. Cartwright was elected to the Council of the London Mathematical Society for the first time in 1933 and served as a member until 1938. She was again elected in 1961 and served as president until 1963.

In 1949, she was appointed Mistress of Girton College and held that position until her retirement in 1968. During that time she received many honors, including an honorary Doctor of Laws degree from Edinburgh in 1953 and Doctor of Science degrees from Leeds in 1958 and from the University of Wales in 1967. Cartwright was elected to the Royal Society of London in 1955 and received the Sylvester Medal of the Royal Society in 1964. Succeeding her Yarrow Fellowships and Lectureship appointments, she became a Reader in Theory of Functions in 1959. At the same time, she additionally served as director of studies in mathematics. In 1968, she was awarded the De Morgan Medal of the London Mathematical Society.

Earns Worldwide Recognition

Cartwright has visited numerous countries around the world, sharing and acquiring knowledge. She was a consultant on the United States Navy Mathematical Research Project at Stanford and Princeton Universities in 1949. Cartwright returned to the United States in 1968 after her retirement and spent two years at Brown University in Providence, Rhode Island, as a Resident Fellow. While at Brown, she also lectured at Clairmont Graduate School and Case Western Reserve University. Cartwright's years in America made a lasting impression on her. She wrote extensively in her memoirs of the killing of three students at Kent State University and of the many college protests she witnessed, including those at the University of California at Berkeley and the Madison Army Research Centre.

In 1973, she received recognition for her lifetime achievements from the University of Jyvaskyla, Finland. The culmination of Cartwright's recognition came in 1969, when she was ordained Dame Commander of the British Empire by Queen Elizabeth II. Cartwright has henceforth been known as Dame Cartwright. She currently leads a sequestered life in Cambridge.

SELECTED WRITINGS BY CARTWRIGHT:

"Moments in a Girl's Life," in *Bulletin of the Institute of Mathematics and Its Applications* 25 (March–April 1989): 63–67.

FURTHER READING:

Kay, Ernest. *The World's Who's Who of Women.* Volume 1. Cambridge and London: Melrose Press Limited, 1973, p. 140.

McMurran, Shawnee L. and James Tattersall. "Mr. Littlewood and I": The Mathematical Collaboration of M.L. Cartwright and J.E. Littlewood. *The American Mathematical Monthly* 103, no. 10 (December 1996): 833–43.

Other

"Dame Mary Lucy Cartwright." *Biographies of Women Mathematicians.* http://www.scottlan.edu/lriddle/women/chronol.htm

—*Sketch by Kelley Reynolds Jacquez*

Subrahmanyan Chandrasekhar

Subrahmanyan Chandrasekhar
1910–1995

Indian-born American astrophysicist and applied mathematician

Subrahmanyan Chandrasekhar was an Indian-born American astrophysicist and applied mathematician whose work on the origins, structure, and dynamics of stars has secured him a prominent place in the annals of science. His most celebrated work concerns the radiation of energy from stars, particularly white dwarf stars, which are the dying fragments of stars. Chandrasekhar demonstrated that the radius of a white dwarf star is related to its mass: the greater its mass, the smaller its radius. Chandrasekhar made numerous other contributions to astrophysics. His expansive research and published papers and books include topics such as the system of energy transfer within stars, stellar evolution, stellar structure, and theories of planetary and stellar atmospheres. For nearly twenty years, he served as the editor-in-chief of the *Astrophysical Journal,* the leading publication of its kind in the world. For his immense contribution to science, Chandrasekhar received numerous awards and distinctions, most notably, the 1983 Nobel Prize for Physics for his research into the depths of aged stars.

Chandrasekhar, better known as Chandra, was born on October 19, 1910, in Lahore, British India (now Pakistan), the first son of C. Subrahmanyan Ayyar and Sitalakshmi née (Divan Bahadur) Balakrishnan. Chandra came from a large family; he had two older sisters, four younger sisters, and three younger brothers. As the firstborn son, Chandra inherited his paternal grandfather's name, Chandrasekhar. His uncle was the Nobel Prize-winning Indian physicist, Sir C. V. Raman.

Chandra received his early education at home, beginning when he was five. From his mother he learned Tamil, from his father, English and arithmetic. He set his sights upon becoming a scientist at an early age, and to this end, undertook at his own initiative some independent study of calculus and physics. The family moved north to Lucknow, in Uttar Pradesh, when Chandra was six. In 1918, the family moved again, this time south to Madras. Chandrasekhar was taught by private tutors until 1921, when he enrolled in the Hindu High School in Triplicane. With typical drive and motivation, he studied on his own and steamed ahead of the class, completing school by the age of fifteen.

After high school, Chandra attended Presidency College in Madras. For the first two years, he studied physics, chemistry, English, and Sanskrit. For his B.A. honors degree he wished to take pure mathematics but his father insisted that he take physics. Chandra resolved this conflict by registering as an honors physics student but attending mathematics lectures. Recognizing his brilliance, his lecturers went out of their way to accommodate Chandra. Chandra also took part in sporting activities and joined the debating team. A highlight of his college years was the publication of his paper, "The Compton Scattering and the New Statistics." These and other early successes while he was still an eighteen-year-old undergraduate only strengthened Chandra's resolve to pursue a career in scientific research, despite his father's wish that he join the Indian civil service. A meeting the following year with the German physicist **Werner Heisenberg**, whom Chandra, as the secretary of the student science association, had the honor of showing around Madras, and Chandra's attendance at the Indian Science Congress Association Meeting in early 1930, where his work was hailed, doubled his determination.

Leaves India for Cambridge, England

Upon graduating with a M.A. in 1930, Chandra set off for Trinity College, Cambridge, as a research student, courtesy of an Indian government scholarship created especially for him (with the stipulation that upon his return to India, he would serve for five years in the Madras government service). At Cambridge, Chandra turned to astrophysics, inspired by a theory of stellar evolution that had occurred to him as he made the long boat journey from India to Cambridge. It preoccupied him for the next ten years. He also worked on other aspects of astrophysics and published many papers.

In the summer of 1931, he worked with physicist **Max Born** at the Institut für Theoretische Physik at Göttingen in Germany. There, he studied group theory and quantum mechanics (the mathematical theory that relates matter and radiation) and produced work on the theory of stellar atmospheres. During this period, Chandra was often tempted to leave astrophysics for pure mathematics, his first love, or at least for physics. He was worried, though, that with less than a year to go before his thesis exam, a change might cost him his degree. Other factors influenced his decision to stay with astrophysics, most importantly, the encouragement shown him by astrophysicist **Edward Arthur Milne**. In August 1932, Chandra left Cambridge to continue his studies in Denmark under physicist **Niels Bohr.** In Copenhagen, he was able to devote more of his energies to pure physics. A series of Chandra's lectures on astrophysics given at the University of Liège, Belgium, in February 1933 received a warm reception. Before returning to Cambridge in May 1933 to sit for his doctoral exams, he went back to Copenhagen to work on his thesis.

Chandrasekhar's uncertainty about his future was assuaged when he was awarded a fellowship at Trinity College, Cambridge. During a four-week trip to Russia in 1934, where he met physicists **Lev Davidovich Landau**, B. P. Gerasimovic, and Viktor Ambartsumian, he returned to the work that had led him into astrophysics to begin with, white dwarfs. Upon returning to Cambridge, he took up research of white dwarfs again in earnest.

As a member of the Royal Astronomical Society since 1932, Chandra was entitled to present papers at its twice monthly meetings. It was at one of these that Chandra, in 1935, announced the results of the work that would later make his name. As stars evolve, he told the assembled audience, they emit energy generated by their conversion of hydrogen into helium and even heavier elements. As they reach the end of their life, stars have progressively less hydrogen left to convert and emit less energy in the form of radiation. They eventually reach a stage when they are no longer able to generate the pressure needed to sustain their size against their own gravitational pull and they begin to contract. As their density increases during the contraction process, stars build up sufficient internal energy to collapse their atomic structure into a degenerate state. They begin to collapse into themselves. Their electrons become so tightly packed that their normal activity is suppressed and they become white dwarfs, tiny objects of enormous density. The greater the mass of a white dwarf, the smaller its radius, according to Chandrasekhar. However, not all stars end their lives as stable white dwarfs. If the mass of evolving stars increases beyond a certain limit, eventually named the *Chandrasekhar limit* and calculated as 1.4 times the mass of the sun, evolving stars cannot become stable white dwarfs. A star with a mass above the limit has to either lose mass to become a white dwarf or take an alternative evolutionary path and become a supernova, which releases its excess energy in the form of an explosion. What mass remains after this spectacular event may become a white dwarf but more likely will form a neutron star. The neutron star has even greater density than a white dwarf and an average radius of about 0.18 m (0.15 km). It has since been independently proven that all white dwarf stars fall within Chandrasekhar's predicted limit, which has been revised to equal 1.2 solar masses.

Theory of Stellar Evolution Unexpectedly Ridiculed

Unfortunately, although his theory would later be vindicated, Chandra's ideas were unexpectedly undermined and ridiculed by no less a scientific figure than astronomer and physicist **Sir Arthur Stanley Eddington,** who dismissed as absurd Chandra's notion that stars can evolve into anything other than white dwarfs. Eddington's status and authority in the community of astronomers carried the day, and Chandra, as the junior, was not given the benefit of the doubt. Twenty years passed before his theory gained general acceptance among astrophysicists, although it was quickly recognized as valid by physicists as noteworthy as **Wolfgang Pauli, Niels Bohr,** Ralph H. Fowler, and **Paul Dirac.** Rather than continue sparring with Eddington at scientific meeting after meeting, Chandra collected his thoughts on the matter into his first book, *An Introduction to the Study of Stellar Structure,* and departed the fray to take up new research around stellar dynamics. An unfortunate result of the scientific quarrel, however, was to postpone the discovery of black holes and neutron stars by at least twenty years, and Chandra's receipt of a Nobel Prize for his white dwarf work by fifty years. Surprisingly, despite their scientific differences, he retained a close personal relationship with Eddington.

Chandra spent from December 1935 until March 1936 at Harvard University as a visiting lecturer in cosmic physics. While in the United States, he was offered a research associate position at Yerkes Observatory at Williams Bay, Wisconsin, starting in January 1937. Before taking up this post, Chandra returned home to India to marry the woman who had waited for him patiently for six years. He had known Lalitha Doraiswamy, daughter of Captain and Mrs. Savitri Doraiswamy, since they had been students together at Madras University. After graduation, she had undertaken a masters degree. At the time of their marriage, she was a headmistress. Although their marriage of love was unusual, neither of their families had any real objections. After a whirlwind courtship and wedding, the young bride and groom set out for the United States. They intended to stay no more than a few years, but, as luck would have it, it became their permanent home.

Joins Staff of Yerkes Observatory in the United States

At the Yerkes Observatory, Chandra was charged with developing a graduate program in astronomy and astrophysics and with teaching some of the courses. His reputation as a teacher soon attracted top students to the observatory's graduate school. He also continued researching stellar evolution, stellar structure, and the transfer of energy within stars. In 1938, he was promoted to assistant professor of astrophysics. During this time Chandra revealed his conclusions regarding the life paths of stars.

During the World War II, Chandra was employed at the Aberdeen Proving Grounds in Maryland, working on ballistic tests, the theory of shock waves, the Mach effect, and transport problems related to neutron diffusion. In 1942, he was promoted to associate professor of astrophysics at the University of Chicago and in 1943, to professor. Around 1944, he switched his research from stellar dynamics to radiative transfer. Of all his research, the latter gave him, he recalled later, more fulfillment. That year, he also achieved a lifelong ambition when he was elected to the Royal Society of London. In 1946, he was elevated to Distinguished Service Professor. In 1952, he became Morton D. Hull Distinguished Service Professor of Astrophysics in the departments of astronomy and physics, as well as at the Institute for Nuclear Physics at the University of

Chicago's Yerkes Observatory. Later the same year, he was appointed managing editor of the *Astrophysical Journal,* a position he held until 1971. He transformed the journal from a private publication of the University of Chicago to the national journal of the American Astronomical Society. The price he paid for his editorial impartiality, however, was isolation from the astrophysical community.

Chandra became a United States citizen in 1953. Despite receiving numerous offers from other universities, in the United States and overseas, Chandra never left the University of Chicago, although, owing to a disagreement with Bengt Strömgren, the head of Yerkes, he stopped teaching astrophysics and astronomy and began lecturing in mathematical physics at the University of Chicago campus. Chandra voluntarily retired from the University of Chicago in 1980, although he remained on as a post-retirement researcher. In 1983, he published a classic work on the mathematical theory of black holes. Following work on this book, he studied colliding waves and the Newtonian two-center problem in the framework of the general theory of relativity. His semi-retirement also left him with more time to pursue his hobbies and interests: literature and music, particularly orchestral, chamber, and South Indian. Chandrasekhar died on August 21, 1995, at the University of Chicago Hospitals.

Received Numerous Honors and Awards

During his long career, Chandrasekhar received many awards. In 1947, Cambridge University awarded him its Adams Prize. In 1952, he received the Bruce Medal of the Astronomical Society of the Pacific, and the following year, the Gold Medal of the Royal Astronomical Society. In 1955, Chandrasekhar became a Member of the National Academy of Sciences. The Royal Society of London bestowed upon him its Royal Medal seven years later. In 1962, he was also presented with the Srinivasa Ramanujan Medal of the Indian National Science Academy. The National Medal of Science of the United States was conferred upon Chandra in 1966; and the Padma Vibhushan Medal of India in 1968. Chandra received the Henry Draper Medal of the National Academy of Sciences in 1971 and the Smoluchowski Medal of the Polish Physical Society in 1973. The American Physical Society gave him its Dannie Heineman Prize in 1974. The crowning glory of his career came nine years later when the Royal Swedish Academy awarded Chandrasekhar the Nobel Prize for Physics. ETH of Zurich gave the Indian astrophysicist its Dr. Tomalla Prize in 1984, while the Royal Society of London presented him with its Copley Prize later that year. Chandra also received the R. D. Birla Memorial Award of the Indian Physics Association in 1984. In 1985, the Vainu Bappu Memorial Award of the Indian National Science Academy was conferred upon Chandrasekhar. In May 1993, Chandra received the state of Illinois's highest honor, Lincoln Academy Award, for his outstanding contributions to science.

While his contribution to astrophysics was immense, Chandra always preferred to remain outside the mainstream of research. He described himself to his biographer, Kameshar C. Wali, as "a lonely wanderer in the byways of science." Throughout his life, Chandra strove to acquire knowledge and understanding, according to an autobiographical essay published with his Nobel lecture, motivated "principally by a quest after perspectives."

SELECTED WRITINGS BY CHANDRASEKHAR:

Books

An Introduction to the Study of Stellar Evolution. Chicago: University of Chicago Press, 1939. Reprint, New York: Dover 1967.
Principles of Stellar Dynamics. Chicago: University of Chicago Press, 1943. Reprint, New York: Dover, 1960.
Radiative Transfer. Oxford: Clarendon Press, 1950. Reprint, New York: Dover, 1960.
Plasma Physics. Chicago: Chicago University Press, 1960.
Hydrodynamic and Hydromagnetic Stability. Oxford: Clarendon Press, 1961. Reprint, New York: Dover, 1987.
Ellipsoidal Figures of Equilibrium. New Haven, CT: Yale University Press, 1968. Reprint, New York: Dover, 1987.
The Mathematical Theory of Black Holes. Oxford: Clarendon Press, 1983.
Eddington: The Most Distinguished Astrophysicist of His Time. Cambridge: Cambridge University Press, 1983.
Truth and Beauty: Aesthetics and Motivations in Science. Chicago: University of Chicago Press, 1987.
Selected Papers. 2 vols. Chicago: University of Chicago Press, 1989-90.
Truth and Beauty: Aesthetics and Motivations in Science. Chicago: University of Chicago Press, 1987.

Periodicals

"The Compton Scattering and the New Statistics." *Proceedings of the Royal Society* 125 (1929).
"Stochastic Problems in Physics and Astronomy." *Review of Modern Physics* 15 (1943): 1-89. Reprinted in *Selected Paper on Noise and Stochastic Processes*, edited by Nelson Wax. New York: Dover Publications, 1954.

FURTHER READING:

Books

The Biographical Dictionary of Scientists, Astronomers. London: Blond Educational Company, 1984, p. 36.
Chambers Biographical Encyclopedia of Scientists. New York: Facts-on-File, 1981.
Goldsmith, Donald, *The Astronomers.* New York: St. Martin's Press, 1991.
_____. *Great American Scientists.* Prentice-Hall, 1960.
Land, Kenneth R., and Owen Gingerich, eds. *A Sourcebook in Astronomy and Astrophysics,* Cambridge: Harvard University Press, 1979.
_____, eds. *Modern Men of Science.* New York: McGraw-Hill, 1966, p. 97.
Wali, Kameshwar C. *Chandra: A Biography of S. Chandrasekhar* Chicago: Chicago University Press, 1991.

Periodicals

Sullivan, Walter. "Subrahmanyan Chandrasekhar, 84, Is Dead; Nobel Laureate Discovered 'White Dwarfs'" (obituary). *New York Times* (22 August 1995): D20.

—*Sketch by Avril McDonald*

Sun–Yung Alice Chang
1948–
Chinese–born American mathematician

Sun–Yung Alice Chang, working with Paul Yang, Tom Branson, and Matt Gursky, has produced what the American Mathematical Society has termed "deep contributions" to the study of partial differential equations in relation to geometry and topology.

Sun–Yung Alice Chang was born in Ci–an, China, on March 24, 1948, and studied for her bachelor's degree at the National University of Taiwan, which she received in 1970. Chang emigrated to the United States for graduate work and a series of teaching jobs. In 1974, Chang earned her Ph.D. from the University of California at Berkeley. She has served as assistant professor at SUNY–Buffalo, the University of California at Los Angeles, and the University of Maryland. Chang returned to UCLA as an associate professor, and she became a full professor in 1980. Her most visible performance was as a speaker at the International Congress of Mathematicians, held in Berkeley in 1986.

Wins Satter Prize

In 1995, Chang was awarded the third the Ruth Lyttle Satter Prize at the American Mathematical Society's 101st annual meeting in San Francisco (the previous two recipients were **Lai-Sung Young** and **Margaret McDuff**). Young was on the selection committee that recommended Chang for that year's prize. In her acceptance speech, Chang acknowledged her debt to her collaborators and promised to "derive further geometric consequences" in various problems currently under study.

Reflecting momentarily on her own school years, Chang admitted that it had been important for her to have role models and female companionship. However, she stated, the deciding factor in the future will be to have more women proving theorems and contributing to mathematics as a whole. To that end, she has joined with a number of steering committees and advisory panels at the national level. After being a Sloan Fellow for the National Academy of Sciences in 1980, she returned ten years later as a member of their Board of Mathematical Sciences. Chang also advised the National Science Foundation and the Association for Women in Mathematics throughout the early 1990s.

Chang always finds time to involve her students in the sometimes arcane world of her specialty. At the University of Texas, she took part in their Distinguished Lecturer Series of 1996–97, a program that successfully targets an audience of young graduate students. She has been most active with the American Mathematical Society, working on a range of committees and speaking at a number of their meetings. Chang's most current professional positions include a three-year term on the Editorial Boards Committee of the AMS, expiring in 1998.

Chang was married in 1973 and has two children.

FURTHER READING:

"1995 Ruth Lyttle Satter Prize in Mathematics." *Notices of the AMS* (April 1995) http://e-math.ams.org/notices/199504/prize-e-satter.html

"Sun-Yung Alice Chang." *Biographies of Women Mathematicians.* http://www.scottlan.edu/lriddle/women/chronol.htm (July 1997).

—*Sketch by Jennifer Kramer*

John Charnley
1911–1982
English orthopedic surgeon

John Charnley was a pioneer in the treatment of bone and joint disease—one of the most important orthopedic surgeons of the twentieth century. His most significant contribution was the development of successful total hip joint replacement surgery. This ground-breaking operation enabled thousands of older people to remain active even after irreversible hip damage. For the knee and hip, he also pioneered arthrodeses (surgically attaching a joint to encourage bones to fuse).

Considered a scientific genius and an artist as a surgeon, Charnley was single-minded in his attempts to study and perfect the treatment of degenerative hip disease. Yet he was also not an easy man to get along with, and, for an educated man, could be narrow in his views. Still, he was devoted to his patients and family, and his unbounded energy and enthusiasm for science earned him the respect of his colleagues.

Charnley was born in Bury, England, the son of a pharmacist, Arthur Walker Charnley, and a nurse, Lily Hodgson Charnley. The young boy initially dreamed of being a dentist, but his schoolteacher, Leonard R. Strangeways, encouraged him to apply himself and become a physician. Though Charnley did not excel academically at the time, Strangeways realized he had both tenacity and promise.

Charnley fulfilled his intellectual potential as an undergraduate at the University of Manchester, winning most of the college's academic honors. He later went on to study medicine at Manchester, passing the first part of the exam for the Fellowship of Royal College of Surgeons of England while still a medical student. A year later he obtained his fellowship to practice surgery, an exceptional accomplishment.

Like many noted surgeons, Charnley spent time in military service. He was a major working in the Royal Army Medical Corps from 1939 to 1945. With Brian Thomas, he ran a renowned orthopedic clinic in Helopolis in the Middle East from 1942 to 1943. There he came up with his first invention, called the Charnley caliper (a splint for the leg). It could be fitted to a soldier within minutes.

During the early years of his career, Charnley published many important papers about trauma and arthritis. The most significant were texts written about closed treatment of fractures in 1950 and compression arthrodesis in 1953.

After the war he returned to Manchester to work as a lecturer, and in 1947 became a surgeon at the Manchester Royal Infirmary. In the 1950s, surgeons first began experimenting with surgical hip replacements. Among the replacements used was the French Judet, a prosthesis which had an acrylic head. But the prosthesis often became loose after it was implanted. Charnley, after hearing the prosthesis squeak on one of his patients, deduced that internal friction at the connecting surfaces was the cause.

Charnley was puzzled as to how to correct the problem, but for years he continued to look for better alternatives. Finally he developed what he thought would be a solution—a new kind of prosthesis and surgery, called low friction arthroplasty, to put it in place. The prosthesis was made of a small metal ball placed in a plastic cup, both secured with methyl methacrylate cement. He first used Teflon as the material for the cup, but then abandoned the material after disastrous results. The cup produced quite a lot of wear on the bone, and fine debris from it caused tissue reaction in the patient's hip. Finally a new material, high density polythene, became available and proved to be the right ingredient. Charnley's surgery, first performed in 1959, then became increasingly successful.

Charnley never intended to marry, but in 1957 he made the acquaintance of Jill Heaver during a ski vacation in Austria. Three months later they were married. According to his colleagues, his best work occurred after his marriage. He was a family man and had a daughter, Henrietta, and a son, Tristan. But the Charnley family made a number of sacrifices to accommodate the surgeon. He was a workaholic, who was single-minded in his search for better treatments for arthritic and hip disease. He had a lab at home, where he spent a great deal of his time trying out his inventions. An extremely ethical man, he was devoted to science.

With the approval of his wife, he concentrated entirely on research about degenerative hip disease during the 1960s and 1970s, continuing to refine the joint surgery he invented. He established a practice at Wrightington Hospital, where he directed a hip surgery center.

During his career, Charnley also pioneered a way to surgically fuse joint surfaces (arthrodesis) to immobilize the knee joint. In this operation, the surgeon passes a metal pin through the lower femur bone and another through the upper tibia bone. These bones are then clamped together to hold the joint surfaces against each other until they fuse. The result is that people with rheumatoid arthritis, a very debilititating, painful type of arthritis, would end up with an immobile but pain-free joint.

Charnley developed a number of effective surgical instruments that advanced the art of orthopedic surgery. When he noticed that some of his surgeries produced poor results because of infection, he became a strong advocate for a more sterile environment in operating rooms. He employed air "tents"—glass enclosures into which filtered air was piped–to keep the surgeon and wound sterile during the operation. The rate of infection among his patients began to drop because of this tactic, but still Charnley was not satisfied. Organisms on skin scales could still pass through conventional surgical clothing. In 1970 he began to wear a ventilated sterile body suit. These measures, as well as the use of antibiotics, reduced the infection rate for hip replacement surgery to about 0.5%.

In his later years, Charnley revealed narrow-minded political views when he wrote a letter to the *Manchester Guardian* about the weakness of the national health system—putting the blame on immigrant employees. But most of the time, Charnley was a kind, caring man, witty and humorous. After his death, one researcher writing in a scientific journal recalled that he was a man who loved a party.

In 1977, Charnley was knighted by Queen Elizabeth II and in 1978 received the Gold Medal of the British Medical Association for his outstanding achievements. He was the first orthopedic surgeon to become a member of the Fellowship of the Royal Society. But the honor that meant the most to him came from the small town of Bury, where he was born. In 1974, he became a "Freeman of Bury."

Charnley died on August 5, 1982. Though in some ways he was a driven and eccentric man, he was also a genius as a surgeon, researcher, and teacher. He never hesitated to give his utmost contribution to medicine. Because of Charnley, orthopedics took a giant step forward, enabling untold numbers of patients to move with freedom in their later years.

SELECTED WRITINGS BY CHARNLEY:

Books

The Closed Treatment of Common Fractures, 2nd ed. Edinburgh: E. & S. Livingstone, 1950.
Compression Arthrodesis, Including Central Dislocation as a Principle in Hip Surgery. Edinburgh: E. & S. Livingstone, 1953.

Periodicals

"Arthroplasty of the hip. A new operation." *Lancet* 1 (1961): 1129.
"A Sterile Operating Theatre Enclosure." *British Journal of Surgery* 51 (1964): 195.

FURTHER READING:

Books

William, Trevor, I., ed. *A Biographical Dictionary of* Scientists. New York: Wiley, 1982, pp 131-132.

Periodicals

Eftekhar, Nas S., M.D. "The Life and Work of John Charnley." *Clinical Orthopedics and Related Research* (October 1986): 10-14.

Older, John. "A Tribute to Sir John Charnley." *Clinical Orthopedics and Related Research* (October 1986): 23-29.

—*Sketch by Barbara Boughton*

Mary Agnes (Meara) Chase
1869–1963
American botanist

Although she had only a grammar-school education, botanist Agnes Chase became one of the most important researchers to ever work in agrostology, the study of grasses. She cataloged more than 10,000 members of the grass family, discovered many previously unknown species, and added immeasurably to the world's knowledge of this important plant family.

Born Mary Agnes Meara on April 20, 1869, in Iroquois County, Illinois, she was the second-youngest child of Martin Meara, from Tipperary, Ireland, and Mary (Cassidy) Brannick Meara, from Louisville, Kentucky. Martin Meara, a railroad blacksmith, died in 1871. Mrs. Meara moved her five surviving children to Chicago (the youngest child had died in infancy). There they lived with Mary Agnes's maternal grandmother.

Mary Agnes completed grammar school and then went to work to help support the family. Among her jobs was proofreading and setting type at the *School Herald*, a periodical for rural school teachers edited by William I. Chase. They married on January 21, 1888. Mary Agnes was not quite 19; her new husband was 34. Chase, ill with tuberculosis, died several weeks short of their first anniversary. His death left his young widow with considerable debt.

The tiny woman—she stood less than five feet tall and weighed about 98 pounds—threw herself into work to pay off the bills. She worked as a proofreader at Chicago's *Inter-Ocean* newspaper while living on a diet of beans and oatmeal. Briefly, she worked at her brother-in-law's general store—a job that was to be a turning point in her life.

Discovers Her Interest in Botany

While working at the store, Chase became very fond of her nephew Virginius Chase. The boy enlisted his aunt's help in using a manual to identify some local plants. Chase was fascinated and continued her botany studies whenever she could. She began to collect in the field and record her observations. On one collecting trip, she met the Rev. Ellsworth Hill, who studied mosses. They became fast friends. Hill recognized Chase's talent as a botanical illustrator, and enlisted her help in illustrating some of his scientific papers. He introduced her to Charles Millspaugh of the Field Museum of Natural History in Chicago, who then hired her to illustrate two museum publications.

Hill also taught Chase how to use a microscope. He encouraged her to take a position as a meat inspector in the Chicago stockyards, where she used her newly acquired skill. She worked there from 1901 to 1903, when she applied—reluctantly, but at Hill's urging—for the position of botanical illustrator at the United States Department of Agriculture (USDA) Bureau of Plant Sciences in Washington D.C. To her surprise, she got the job.

At the USDA, she illustrated publications, and after hours studied grasses in the herbarium. These after-hours studies culminated in the publication of her first scientific paper in 1906.

A Lifelong Partnership

In 1905 Chase began what was to be a lifelong collaboration with Albert Spear Hitchcock, the principal scientist in systematic agrostology. In 1907, she became his assistant. Hitchcock and Chase worked well together, and their professional friendship lasted 30 years until Hitchcock's death. Without her, "it is doubtful if Hitchcock could have accomplished as much as he did," wrote Dr. Jason R. Swallen in *Taxon*. Indeed, the thousands of specimens she gathered on her many collecting trips added immeasurably to the value of Hitchcock's book, *A Manual of Grasses of the United States*, published in 1935, shortly before his death.

A Traveling Woman

Chase financed her collecting trips out of her own pocket (even when she was earning $720 a year) and donated her specimens to the herbarium. Her horizons spread beyond America's borders. In 1913, she made her first overseas collecting trip to Puerto Rico, where she discovered a new species of fern. While she was in Europe visiting herbaria in 1922, Chase's book, *A First Book of Grasses*, was published; a year later, she was promoted to assistant botanist.

In 1924, at age 56, she made the first of her two trips to Brazil. She explored areas botanists had never researched, searching jungles and climbing mountains in pursuit of specimens. After six months in Brazil, she returned home with 20,000 specimens, including 500 grasses. She was named associate botanist when she returned. Four years later she went back to Brazil, doing much of her exploring alone, and returning with 10 new species. All together, Chase brought 4,500 grass specimens back from Brazil, many of which had been previously unknown to exist in that country. The trips earned her the title "Uncle Sam's chief woman explorer." In 1936, she became senior botanist, succeeding her friend and mentor Hitchcock.

Although grasses were her consuming passion, they were not the only thing she cared about. She was active in the suffragist movement in 1918 and 1919, and was even arrested and force-fed. She supported prohibition and socialism and contributed to such organizations as the National Association for the Advancement of Colored People (NAACP) and the Woman's International League for Peace and Freedom.

Agnes Chase retired officially from the USDA in 1939, but "retired" was just a word to her. She continued working as a herbarium research associate. At 71, she traveled to Venezuela at the government's invitation to help develop its range management program. In 1950, she updated Hitchcock's *Manual*. She fostered the careers of many young botanists, urging them to come to the United States to study and even allowing some to board at her home.

She was recognized for her contributions to science by the Botanical Society of America, which awarded her a certificate of merit in 1956; the University of Illinois, which gave her an honorary Doctor of Science degree in 1958; the Smithsonian Institution, which named her an honorary fellow in 1958; and the Linnean Society, by which she was made a fellow in 1961.

Time finally caught up with this tireless investigator. On September 24, 1963, her first day in Bethesda, Maryland, nursing home, Mary Agnes Chase died. She was 94.

SELECTED WRITINGS BY CHASE:

Books

A First Book of Grasses: The Structure of Grasses Explained for Beginnners. New York: Macmillian, 1922. (Revised in 1937 and 1968, and reissued in 1977.)
(With Cornelia D. Niles) *Index to Grass Species.* 1962.

Periodicals

"Eastern Brazil Through an Agrostologist's Spectacles," *in Annual Report of the Smithsonian Institution*, 1926.

Other

In addition, Chase's papers are collected in the Albert S. Hitchcock and Mary Agnes Chase Papes, Hunt Institute for Biological Documentation, Carnegie Mellon University. Other materials, including her field notebooks, are part of the Hitchcock-Chase Library at the Smithsonian.

FURTHER READING:

Books

Bonta, Marcia Myers. *Women in the Field: America's Pioneering Women Naturalists.* 1991.

Periodicals

Fosberg, F.R., and J.R. Swallen. "Agnes Chase." *Taxon*, 8, (June 1959): 145-51.
Furman, Bess. "Grass Is Her Liferoot." *The New York Times* (June 12, 1956): 37.
Hillenbrand, Liz. "87-Year-Old Grass Expert Still Happy with Subject." *The Washington Post and Times Herald* (April 30, 1956): 7.

—Sketch by Fran Hodgkins

Steven Chu
1948–
American atomic physicist

Steven Chu's research has been at the forefront of contemporary efforts to study the structure and behavior of individual particles, such as atoms and molecules. Until very recently, scientists were able to investigate the nature of matter only in bulk form, that is, as collections of millions or billions of individual particles. The properties for an element or compound listed in a standard reference book, for example, are really averages obtained by the analysis of gram or milligram quantities of the material, and little or nothing is known about the properties of individual atoms or molecules of the element or compound. For more than a decade, Chu has been developing techniques for the manipulation of individual particles in order to understand their properties and to compare those properties with their properties in bulk. For his work in this area, Chu was awarded a share of the 1997 Nobel Prize in Physics.

Steven Chu was born in St. Louis, Missouri, on February 28, 1948. His parents were Ju Chin Chu and the former Ching Chen Li. He attended the Universi-

Steven Chu

ty of Rochester, from which he received a B.S. in physics and A.B. degree in mathematics. He then continued his education at the University of California at Berkeley, which awarded him a Ph.D. in Physics in 1976.

Research at AT&T Bell Laboratories

Chu remained at Berkeley as a postdoctoral fellow for two years, and then accepted an appointment as a member of the technical staff at the Bell Laboratories in Murray Hill, New Jersey. In 1983, he was appointed head of the quantum electronics research department at the AT&T Bell Laboratories in Holmdel, New Jersey. It was during this time that Chu conducted the experiments for which he was awarded the 1997 Nobel Prize for Physics.

This research was motivated by a growing interest on the part of scientists to study the properties of individual particles, such as atoms, molecules, and ions. Such an objective would have seemed absurd only a few decades ago. In the first place, there are almost no mechanisms for viewing or otherwise measuring individual particles as small as atoms and molecules. In the second place, even if such instruments were available, they would be difficult to use with individual particles since such particles normally move at very great speeds. For example, the molecules of which air is composed move at speeds of about 2,480 miles (4,000 km) per hour at room temperature.

Chu developed a method for slowing down the motion of atoms and molecules so that their properties could be studied more carefully. The technique that he developed has been termed "atom traps" or "optical molasses" because it restrains atoms and molecules to a relatively small space and prevents them from moving out of that space for a period of time. The principle behind this technique is that a moving particle can be slowed down if it can be bombarded by a pulse of radiation. For example, suppose that an atom is moving from left to right across this page with a speed of 2,480 miles (4,000 km) per hour. Then suppose that one was to fire a pulse of laser radiation from the right to the left, aimed directly at the oncoming atom. When the laser pulse strikes the atom, the atom will absorb energy from the laser pulse and slow down (that is, have an increased energy in the backward direction). In theory, one might hope to stop the atom simply by hitting it with repeated bursts of radiation.

In fact, the process is not quite that simple. Very shortly after the atom absorbs energy from the laser beam, it emits a photon that contains as much energy as was absorbed. That energy may be given off in any direction. As it does so, the atom recoils in some random direction. Its left-to-right speed has been reduced, but a second laser pulse cannot be used to reduce its speed further in the same way.

Chu solved this problem by designing a "box" whose "walls" consisted of six laser beams arranged in three pairs. The beams were arranged along three parallel axes in such a way that an atom placed in the middle of the system was trapped. No matter which direction the atom tried to move, it was struck with one of the laser beams and was suspended in space. Even with this arrangement, atoms are not brought to a complete standstill. The system is able, however, to reduce the speed of particles to about 30 centimeters per second, a speed that corresponds to a temperature of about 240 micro kelvin, or 240 millionths of a degree kelvin. Calculations suggest that this temperature may be the lowest that can be obtained by the process described here.

If the above experiment is continued over a period of time, a second effect is observed. Instead of trapping a single particle, groups of particles are collected, all with similar energies and properties. This collection of particles acts like a very thin gas consisting of slowly moving particles. It corresponds to a new state of matter predicted in 1927 by **Albert Einstein** and now known as a Bose-Einstein condensate (BSC). The BSC has properties distinct from those of the other four states of matter (solid, liquid, gas, and plasma) and appears to behave in some respects like a single "super-atom."

Chu Joins Stanford Faculty

In 1987, Chu was offered an appointment as Professor of Physics and Applied Physics at Stanford

University, a position that he accepted. In 1990, he was appointed the first Theodore and Frances Geballe Professor of Physics and Applied Physics at the university. At Stanford, Chu has continued his work on atom traps and optical molasses, but has also found new applications of these techniques. In these applications, laser beams are used to trap the ends of molecules and hold them in suspension long enough for their properties to be studied. The laser beams used in this way are sometimes referred to as "optical tweezers."

One of the interesting aspects of Chu's work with optical tweezers has been the study of deoxyribonucleic acid (DNA) molecules. As with protein molecules, DNA molecules consist of very long polymeric chains that have complex levels of organization. For example, they form spiral staircase-like coils whose structures, in that configuration, are sometimes difficult to study. Chu has found ways to use his "optical tweezers" laser beams to stretch DNA molecules out to a straight, spaghetti-like string, and then to study their properties in that form. One of the interesting discoveries he has made is that unraveled DNA molecules tend to vibrate, when agitated, in much the same way as a guitar string. His team had expected, Chu explains, that the vibration of a single DNA molecule might be more complex or, at least, different from that of a plucked string. Instead, the team has discovered that the behavior of a plucked strand of DNA can be described completely, simply by applying well known and traditional laws of simple harmonics.

In another series of experiments, Chu and his co-workers have found that identical DNA strands unravel when exposed to mild perturbations in completely different ways. This discovery is remarkable since one would assume that two molecules with identical chemical structures would behave in the same way. These results indicate that some factors are responsible for differences in the unraveling process that DNA molecules experience.

In his relatively short professional career, Chu has already received a number of important awards. Besides the Nobel Prize, these include the American Physical Society's Broida Prize for Laser Spectroscopy in 1987, the APS/AAPT Richtmyer Memorial Prize in 1990, the King Faisal International Prize for Science (co-winner) in 1993, the American Physical Society's **Arthur Schawlow** Prize for Laser Science in 1994, the Optical Society of America's William F. Meggers Award for Spectroscopy in 1994, and the Guggenheim Award in 1996. Chu has been elected to the American Academy of Arts and Sciences (1992), the National Academy of Sciences (1993), and the Academia Sinica (1994).

SELECTED WRITINGS BY CHU:

"Laser Trapping of Neutral Particles." *Scientific American* 71 (February 1992).

FURTHER READING:

Periodicals

Lubkin, G. B. "Experimenters Cool Helium Below Single-Photon Recoil Limit in Three Dimensions." *Physics Today* (January 1996): 22-24.

Other

"Press Release: the Nobel Prize in Physics 1997." http://www.nobel.se/announcement-97/ physics97.html.
Salisbury, David F. "Steven Chu: Uncovering the Secret Life of Molecules." http://www-leland.stanford.edu/dept/news/report/news/july16/ polymers.html.
Salisbury, David F. "Steven Chu Wins Nobel Prize for Research on Interplay of Light and Atoms." http://www-leland.stanford.edu/dept/ news/release/971015chu.html.
"Steven Chu." http://www-leland-stanford.edu/dept/ physics/Faculty/chu.steven.shtml.

—*Sketch by David E. Newton*

Fan R. K. Chung
1949(?)–
Taiwan–born American number theorist

For Fan Chung, mathematics is more than a career. It is sometimes an obsession, and it is always fun. During her 20 years in a corporate research environment at Bell Laboratories or in her academic position as an endowed professor at the University of Pennsylvania, Chung seeks interesting problems in mathematics that make new connections between fields. She has made another kind of connection as well, doing work that helped lay the foundation for modern computer networks and wireless communication.

A Math–Friendly Upbringing

Chung's father was an engineer who encouraged her to pursue mathematics while she was growing up in Kaoshiung, Taiwan. As an undergraduate at the National Taiwan University, many of her classmates were women, and their successes at mathematics further encouraged her. She was drawn to combinatorics, a field that focuses on manipulating sets of numbers, which is useful in figuring permutations and some statistical analyses. Chung earned her bachelor's degree in Taiwan in 1970 and then came to the United States for her graduate education, earning a master's in 1972 and a Ph.D. in 1974 from the University of Pennsylvania.

Chung began working at Bell Laboratories in Murray Hill, New Jersey, which at the time had a staff that included several Nobel prize winners. In an 1995 interview for the journal *Math Horizons*, she told Don Albers that she was initially intimidated by the caliber of her co–workers. "But I got over it. And very soon I discovered that if you just put your hands out in the hallway, you'd catch a problem." Listening to what others were working on and making those connections between fields that she always seeks furthered her research as a member of the technical staff at Bell Labs.

Following the breakup of the Bell Telephone Company in 1984, Chung was promoted to research manager at Bell Communications Research in Morristown, New Jersey, and aided in the formation of a new Discrete Mathematics Research Group there directed by her mentor from Bell Labs. Within two years, she had been promoted again, to division manager for Mathematics, Information Sciences and Operations Research. In addition to her own research, Chung has to supervise the work of other mathematicians, and help recruit new talent to the lab. "Usually with positions in management you obtain more influence and you certainly have more power to make decisions," she told Albers. "But I do not want people to respect me because of that power. I'd rather win their admiration because of the mathematics I'm doing."

Chung's work at Bell Labs focused on practical problems and applications, though the fun of mathematics was never lost for her. Chung devised a method of encoding and decoding signals that is crucial to digital cellular phones which use "code division multiple access," or CDMA. This scheme, which was patented in 1988, allows several conversations to share the same radio frequency with complete security, because each call is encoded for sending to the cellular antenna. The encoding and decoding has to be done very rapidly and accurately to ensure that the caller's voice sounds natural. Chung also holds a patent on a method for routing network traffic, issued in 1993.

A Second Career in Academics

In 1989, Chung began teaching as a visiting professor in the computer science department at nearby Princeton University. In 1990, she became a Bellcore Fellow, studying at Harvard University. She also served as a visiting professor at Harvard from 1991 to 1993.

In 1995, Chung accepted an endowed chair in the mathematics department at the University of Pennsylvania. She began teaching as a full professor in both the math and computer science departments. Chung encourages her students to explore and to make connections between fields, as she has done. Too much exposure to academic mathematics, she contends, makes one feel isolated. "Professors train students to work in their areas and thus, there is a danger of narrowing down instead of broadening and making connections," she told Albers. The curriculum has not always kept pace with the fast–changing world, either, Chung noted. "It is essential for the students to be able to connect the mathematics you learn in the classroom to problems we face in this information age."

Chung has authored or coauthored more than 180 papers, including several with her second husband, mathematician Ron Graham, whom she met at Bell Labs. Her sense of fun is reflected in a 1993 paper in *American Scientist*, in which she and Shlomo Sternberg included a paper cutout for readers to make their own model of the molecule Carbon–60, or the Buckyball, after they read about its mathematical properties.

Chung has two children by her first marriage, which ended in divorce in 1982. They were born in 1974 and 1977.

Chung is an editor for nine academic journals and has served as editor–in–chief of the *Journal of Graph Theory* and chair of the editorial board committee for the American Mathematical Society. In 1990, she was awarded the Allendoerfer Award from the Mathematical Association of America.

SELECTED WRITINGS BY CHUNG:

"Should You Prepare Differently for a Non–Academic Career?" *The Notices of the American Mathematics Society* 38, no. 6, (August 1991): 560–61.
(With Shlomo Sternberg) "Mathematics and the Buckyball." *American Scientist* 81, no. 1, (1993): 56–71.

FURTHER READING:

Albers, Don. "Making Connections: A Profile of Fan Chung." *Math Horizons* (September 1995): 14–18.
"Fan Chung." *Biographies of Women Mathematicians.* June 1997. http://www.scottlan.edu/lriddle/women/chronol.htm (July 22, 1977).

—Sketch by Karl Leif Bates

Alonzo Church
1903–1995
American mathematician and logician

Alonzo Church was an American mathematician and logician who provided significant innovations in number theory and decision theory, the foundation of computer programming. His most important contributions focus on the degrees of decidability and solvability in logic and mathematics.

Church was born in Washington, D.C., on June 14, 1903, to Samuel Robbins Church and Mildred Hannah Letterman Church. He took his undergraduate degree from Princeton University in 1924. On August 25, 1925, he married Mary Julia Kuczinski. They had three children: Alonzo, Mary Ann, and Mildred Warner. Church completed his Ph.D. in mathematics at Princeton in 1927. After receiving his doctorate, he was a fellow at Harvard from 1927 to 1928. He studied in Europe from 1928 to 1929 at the University of Göttingen, a prestigious center for the study of mathematics and physics. He taught mathematics and philosophy at Princeton from 1929 to 1968. Among his Ph.D. students at Princeton was the British mathematician **Alan Turing**, who was to crack the German's World War II secret code, called Enigma, which significantly contributed to the Allied victory over Nazi Germany. In 1944, Church published his influential *Introduction to Mathematical Logic*. Upon his retirement, however, he became professor of philosophy and mathematics at the University of California, where he remained until his second retirement 1990. Church later moved to Hudson, Ohio, to be near his son. He died in Hudson on August 11, 1995. In addition to his work as a teacher, Church edited the *Journal of Symbolic Logic* from 1936 to 1979. His wife died in February 1976.

A very private person, Church led a quiet life. As Andrew Hodges said in his biography of Alan Turing (Church's famed student who killed himself in 1954 after being arrested on homosexual charges), Church "[is] a retiring man himself, not given to a great deal of discussion."

Addressing the Problem of Decidability

One of the key problems concerning foundations of mathematics was stated by the German mathematician **David Hilbert** (1862–1943) when he asked whether the arithmetic is consistent. The belief that formal systems, such as arithmetic, are consistent had been the cornerstone of mathematics for more than 2,000 years, and Hilbert devoted much energy to the task of showing the power of formal systems. The foundational idea of consistent formal systems, crucial to both mathematics and logic, was shattered in 1931, when **Kurt Gödel** published his epoch-making

article "On the Formal Undecidability Thesis of *Principia Mathematica* and Related Systems." In essence, Gödel demonstrated that proof of consistency cannot be found within a formal system. Indeed, one can look for proof outside the system, perhaps within a larger system, but this still would not solve the problem of inconsistency, because there would be no way of proving that the larger system is consistent. Influenced by Gödel's work, Church provided the proof, in 1936, that elementary quantification theory, the basic method that logicians use to express general statements, is not decidable. This means that in elementary quantification theory, there is no method, containing a finite number of steps, of proving a given statement.

Laying the Foundations of Computer Programming

For computer programs to run, programmers have to be able to reduce all problems to the kinds of simple binary logical (or on/off) statements that can be processed by the electronic circuits inside the computer. For a problem to be solvable by a computer, it must be possible to break it down into an operational set of rules and terms. Next it must be possible to apply these rules recursively—that is repeatedly—to the problem until it is solved in terms of the existing set of rules. In short, a computer's binary circuits can only solve a problem under three conditions: (1) if the problem can be expressed as a meaningful set of rules (i.e., meaningful to the computer); (2) if the result of each step is also meaningful in terms of the computer's predefined set of rules; (3) if the computer's set of rules can be applied repeatedly to the problem. For example, in a simple addition or subtraction computer program, it must be possible for a small number (e.g., 1) to be repeatedly added to or subtracted from a larger number (e.g., 100) to get some result, say 10 or 10,000. If any of these three conditions mentioned above is absent, then a computer program cannot solve the problem.

Church's contribution to the foundation of computer programming is that he discovered—as did Alan Turing and Emil Post simultaneously and independently—the importance of recursiveness in solving logical problems. That is, for calculations to take place, some actions (e.g., adding or subtracting) have to be repeated a certain number of times. In 1936, the same year he shook the foundations of logic, Church formulated the thesis that every intuitively calculable function is recursive. (which is often called the Church-Turing thesis) is that a function is computable or calculable if it is recursive. That is, the idea of recursiveness (repeatability) is tightly bound up with computability. Church's thesis is important because the repetition of a simple action can result in significant changes. It also means that one simple action can be useful over a broad range of problems, and at different levels of a problem.

Church's contributions to decidability theory earned him many honors, including induction into the National Academy of Science and the American Academy of Arts and Sciences. He received honorary doctorates from Case Western Reserve University in 1969, Princeton University in 1985, and the State University of New York at Buffalo in 1990.

SELECTED WRITINGS BY CHURCH:

Books

Introduction to Mathematical Logic, Princeton: Princeton University Press, 1944.

Periodicals

American Journal of Mathematics, An Unsolvable Problem of Elementary Number Theory, 58 (1936): 345–63.
Annals of Mathematics, Set of Postulates for the Foundation of Logic, 33 (1932): 346–66.

FURTHER READING:

Books

Eves, Howard. *Foundations and Fundamental Concepts of Mathematics.* Third edition. Mineola, NY: Dover, 1997.
Hodges, Andrew. *Alan Turing: The Enigma.* New York: Simon & Schuster, 1983.
Gödel, Escher, and Bach: An Eternal Golden Braid. New York: Basic Books, 1979.
Tipler, Frank J. *The Physics of Immortality.* New York: Doubleday, 1994.

Periodicals

Wade, Nicholas. "Alonzo Church, 92, Theorist of the Limits of Mathematics" (obituary). *New York Times.* (5 September 1995): B6.

—*Sketch by Patrick Moore*

Gerald M. Clemence

Gerald M. Clemence
1908–1974
American astronomer

Gerald M. Clemence's major achievement during his 30 years at the United States Naval Observatory was the redefinition of time by using the orbital positions of the Moon and Earth rather than with Earth's rotation. Ephemeris time—as it was called—

allowed Clemence to improve the definition of a second. Clemence's work in planetary motion extended beyond Earth, and through all our known planets; Mars was the planet Clemence spent the most time studying.

He was born Gerald Maurice Clemence, in Smithfield, Rhode Island, on August 16, 1908, the son of Richard R. Clemence (a farmer) and his wife Lora Oatley Clemence. Because his mother was a certified teacher, Clemence received his elementary education at home. He earned his Ph.D. degree in mathematics from Rhode Island's Brown University in 1930. The year before he graduated, Clemence married Edith Melvina Vail, on August 17, 1929. They eventually had two sons, Gerald Vail Clemence and Theodore Grinnell Clemence.

After earning his doctorate, Clemence went to work as an astronomer at the United States Naval Observatory in Washington. He held this position from 1930-63. While he worked at the Naval Observatory, he was the Nautical Almanac Director and Head Astronomer from 1945 until 1958, when he was named Science Director of the Observatory. The first to serve in that capacity, Clemence remained in that position until he retired from the Observatory in 1963.

When he initially joined the Observatory, Clemence had to learn the basics of observational work and star cataloging. Indeed, he was basically a self-taught astronomer, who learned much about the field of celestial mechanics on his own. Beginning in the mid 1930s, Clemence began his investigation of the motion of Mars. This research, conducted intermittently over the next 20 years, resulted in the most accurate study and general theory of any of the principal planets.

During World War II, Clemence, working with his life-long collaborator W. J. Eckert, devised an early computerized system involving Long Range Navigation (LORAN) for the Coast Guard. Beginning in 1948, Clemence, in collaboration with Dirk Brouwer and Eckert, calculated the exact locations of the outer planets of our solar system, in four-day intervals, for a 400-year period. Clemence and his colleagues improved on work done a half century earlier by Simon Newcomb and George W. Hill. Their work was accomplished with the help of an early high-speed IBM computer. What made Clemence's work unique was that every interval of the planets' influences on each other was calculated. Previously, astronomers assumed advance knowledge of all the paths to be taken but one. The trio's work was first published in the 1951 publication of *Coordinates of the Five Outer Planets 1653-2060*. This research remained a standard touchstone for astronomers for many years after it was first published.

Time Redefined as Ephemeris Time

Clemence's major contribution to science was the development of the idea of called Ephemeris Time, coined by his colleague Brouwer. After it was substantiated in 1939 that Earth did not rotate at a constant or predictably irregular rate, Clemence ascertained that the Moon and Earth's orbital positions, in relation to Earth's rotation around the Sun, could be the basis for a more accurate determination of time.

In 1948, Clemence defined the equations necessary to determine these values. Ephemeris Time began to be used in 1956. Later, the development of the atomic time scale proved even more accurate than Ephemeris Time, and was adopted in its place. With the development of ephemeris time, Clemence also redefined a second. Before Clemence, a second was equivalent to the 1/86,400 of a day. He defined a second as 1/31,556,925.9747 of a year.

It was also during this time that Clemence began his association with the *Astronomical Journal*. He assumed an editorial role in 1949, and continued to be associated with the publication until 1973.

Second Career at Yale University

In his later years at the Naval Observatory, Clemence won several awards from the United States Navy for his important work, including the Conrad Medal, 1962, and the Distinguished Service Award and Medal, 1963. In 1963, Clemence also began an

academic career at Yale University. He worked for three years as a senior research associate and lecturer in the astronomy department, before being made a full professor in 1966. While at Yale, Clemence wanted to developed a theory of motion for Earth, as he had done for Mars. This research was never fully completed. He also published a book, co-written with E. W. Woolard, entitled *Spherical Astronomy* in 1966.

Clemence was associated with a number of academic societies for his work on ephemeris time and other research, including the American Academy of Arts and Sciences and the International Astronomical Union. Among these societies, the National Academy of Science (of which he was a member, elected in 1952) awarded him the James Craig Watson Medal, and the Royal Academy of Science (of which he was an associate) awarded him a Gold Medal in 1965.

Clemence held his professorship at Yale University until an illness led to his death on November 22, 1974, in Providence, Rhode Island. In a tribute to him published in *Sky & Telescope*, colleague Paul Herget praised Clemence. "His commanding presence, his quick and lucid mind, and dry sense of humor made him a prominent figure at scientific meetings, national and international."

SELECTED WRITINGS BY CLEMENCE:

Books

(With Dirk Brouwer) *Methods of Celestial Mechanics*. New York: Academic Press, 1961.
(With E. W. Woolard) *Spherical Astronomy*. New York: Academic Press, 1966.

FURTHER READING:

Books

"Clemence, Gerald Maurice." *A Biographical Encyclopedia of Scientists*, 2nd edition. Bristol: Institute of Physics Publishing, 1994, p. 169.
"Clemence, Gerald Maurice." *McGraw-Hill Modern Scientists and Engineers*. New York: McGraw-Hill, Inc., p. 209.

Periodicals

Herget, Paul. "The Keeper of Mars." *Sky and Telescope* (April 1975): 215-16.
"Obituaries: Gerald M. Clemence." *Physics Today* (March 1975): 59.

—Sketch by Annette Petrusso

John Cocke
1925–

American computer scientist

John Cocke laid the groundwork for today's generation of super-computers with his work in reduced instruction set computer technology, or RISC. As a researcher for International Business Machines (IBM), Cocke pioneered the theory and applications for software that translate user programs into machine-readable systems, or compilers, and simplify instructions in order to reduce operating cycles.

The youngest of three sons, Cocke was born May 25, 1925, in Charlotte, North Carolina. As a youngster, he was a poor student, and his parents hired a private tutor to instruct him while he was in elementary school. Cocke's lack of enthusiasm and curiosity, however, was confined to the classroom, and he tinkered with mechanical solutions to problems. Although he failed in his attempt to develop a gadget to catch birds by spraying salt on their tails, he jerry-rigged an electromagnetic window-washer and a hydraulic pipe wrench. In high school, he discovered science and mathematics and, perceiving their potential as tools for problem-solving, he developed abilities in these fields to match his interest in finding better, faster ways to tackle tasks.

Cocke entered Duke University in Durham, North Carolina, under the auspices of the U.S. Navy's V-12 program. The V-12 program was instituted during World War II in an effort to meet the military's need for college-educated officers. Cocke graduated with a bachelor's degree in mechanical engineering in 1946; he worked for several companies—including General Electric Company—until 1952, when the Navy called him to service. Cocke served two years with the Navy and returned to Duke in 1954, where he completed a doctorate in mathematics in 1956.

Ushering in the Computer Era

Cocke joined IBM in 1956, when computer science was in its infancy. The field was so new there were few, if any, rules governing research, theory, applications, and procedures. The freedom Cocke and colleagues such as Frederick P. Brooks, Jr., and Harwood Kolsky enjoyed spawned a productive period of scientific discovery. Cocke and Kolsky developed one of the first simulation programs used in computer design, and Cocke helped craft a "look-ahead" feature for programming.

Assigned to IBM's STRETCH project team, Cocke combined academic training with natural intuition to tease out solutions to computing problems. Many innovations envisioned and developed by Cocke and his colleagues are standard on today's high-performance computers and have played a key role in the development of super-computers.

By the mid-1960s, Cocke was working on advanced computer system design. He demonstrated how multiple instructions could be executed in a single cycle and developed a new branching structure that eliminated bottlenecks which previously hampered the performance of look-ahead systems. He also developed compiler techniques for look-ahead machines that dramatically improved the code produced-techniques that served as the foundation of optimization strategies essential for today's systems. Cocke contributed to advances in logic simulation, parallel processing or "pipelining," and large-system architecture. As an academic field supported by a legitimate research base, computer science grew rapidly, and as the field grew, researchers turned their attention to creating systems that were faster and physically smaller.

Growing into Smallness

In the 1970s, Cocke led a team charged with developing a small computer based on RISC architecture. This search was fueled by practicality; in the 1960s, computer systems with the memory and power of modern personal computers were physical behemoths that took up entire rooms (sometimes whole floors) in office buildings. Size was a sticking point for sales; developing a computer that could do more tasks in less space was an industry imperative.

Cocke and his team at IBM's T. J. Watson Research Center in Yorktown Heights, New York, tackled the challenge. In the late 1970s, the team introduced the 801, a computer system that integrated RISC and optimizing compiler technology in a (for the time) modestly-sized package that came close to executing an instruction per cycle. The 801 was a prototype that established IBM as a market leader and served as the basis for applications that made modern high-performance systems and workstations possible.

Cooke managed to find time for other achievements. He and Richard Malm developed a special-purpose, high-speed logic simulator; descendants of that simulator are used today to verify and fix logical design before it is imbedded in silicon. Cocke also probed signal processing, cryptography, magnetic storage devices and coding processes, switching systems, and the mathematics of speech recognition.

The 1970s were also Cocke's most productive for publishing. In addition to numerous articles and papers, Cocke and his colleague Jack Schwartz published *Computers*, a series of IBM programming books that were widely distributed and proved to be highly influential beyond the academic community.

Cocke's work earned him numerous honors. IBM recognized his contributions in 1972 by naming him an IBM fellow, the company's highest honor for scientific and technical achievement. In 1976, he received the ACM Programming Systems and Language Awards; he was elected to the National Academy of Engineering in 1979 and named a fellow of the American Academy of Arts and Sciences in 1988. The recipient of the ACM/IEEE Computer Society Eckert-Mauchly Award in 1985, the National Medal of Technology in 1991, the National Medal of Science in 1994, and the IEEE **John von Neumann** Medal in 1994, Cocke was named inventor of the year by the Intellectual Property Owners Association in 1992.

When Cocke retired in 1993 after a 37-year career at IBM, he owned 22 patents.

SELECTED WRITINGS BY COCKE:

Books

(With Jack Schwartz) *Computers*. New York: IBM Research Center, 1972.

Periodicals

"A Global Common Subexpression Elimination." *Proceedings of the Symposium of Compiler Optimization* SIGPLAN Notices (July 1970).
"An Algorithm for Reduction of Operator Strength." *Comm. Association for Computing Machinery* 20, no. 11, (1977): 850-856.
"The Search for Performance in Scientific Processors (Turing Award Lecture)." *Comm. Association for Computing Machinery* 31, no. 3, (1988): 250-253.

FURTHER READING:

Books

American Men & Women of Science 18th Edition. New Providence, New Jersey: R. R. Bowker, 1992-93, Volume 2, p. 302.
Eckes, Kristin A., ed. *Who's Who in Science and Engineering*. New Providence, New Jersey: Reed Publishing, 1996, pp. 182-183.
Lee, J.A.N., ed. *International Biographical Dictionary of Computer Pioneers*. Chicago: Fitzroy Dearborn, 1995, pp. 179-183.

Other

"John Cocke." http://sunsite.informatik.rwth-aachen.dc/dblp/db/indiccs/a-tree/c/Cock:john.html (November 21, 1997).

—*Sketch by A. Mullig*

Claude Cohen-Tannoudji

Claude Cohen-Tannoudji
1933–
French physicist

It took a Nobel Prize for Claude Cohen-Tannoudji to receive popular attention, though he had been long recognized for his accomplished research by his peers. The French physicist was one of the winners of the Nobel Prize in 1997 (with Americans **Steven Chu** and **William Phillips**), but even before then had a distinguished career. While Cohen-Tannoudji's research focused on the general areas of atomic and molecular physics as well as quantum optics, his award-winning work narrowly concerned cooling atoms to near absolute zero (or ultracold) temperatures (such a measurement describes the rate of movement of atoms within matter) and trapping them, via the light of a laser. By slowing (i.e., cooling) the atoms, scientists can study them in more detail.

Cohen-Tannoudji was born April 1, 1933, in Constantine, Algeria, to Abraham Cohen-Tannoudji and Sarah (nee Sebba) Cohen-Tannoudji. He studied at Ecole Normale Superieure from 1953 until 1957, when he received his *agrégation*. He married Jacqueline Veyrat on November 24, 1958, and with her had three children, Alain, Joelle, and Michel. He earned his D.Sc. (Ph.D.) from the University of Paris in physics in 1962. While a graduate student, he studied under 1966 Nobel Prize winner **Alfred Kastler**. His thesis advisor was Jean Brossel. Following in both of his mentors' theoretical footsteps, Cohen-Tannoudji has arguably become their most distinguished student. Also, while still a student as well as shortly after graduation, from 1960-64, Cohen-Tannoudji worked as a researcher at the Centre National La Recherche Scientifique in Paris. He then served as a professor at the University of Paris from 1964-73.

Discovers Light Shift

In his early research, Cohen-Tannoudji studied the phenomenon that formed the foundation of his later work. Even at this stage of his career, Cohen-Tannoudji worked methodically, predicting theoretically, then demonstrating his theories through experiments. His investigations concerned atoms and their energy levels. He found that energy levels shifted a small amount when, in a field intensely radiated with light, they absorbed and emitted photons of light. (Photons are the smallest pieces of electromagnetic energy.) This is Cohen-Tannoudji's so-called light shift discovery.

In 1973, in addition to publishing his seminal book on quantum mechanics, Cohen-Tannoudji began working at the atomic and molecular physics laboratory, and as chair of the atomic and molecular physics department at the College of France. The laboratory has become recognized worldwide as a leader in research; many of the best physicists have done research there.

Researches Atomic Fields

It was in the 1970s that Cohen-Tannoudji came up with another theory that eventually was applied specifically to lasers. His theory explained the interactions between high-intensity electromagnetic fields and the atoms within them. When an atom is surrounded by photons, it is constantly absorbing and re-emitting them. He described the atom as being "dressed" by the photons, so to speak. This observation became important when it was applied to lasers in the late 1970s and beyond.

In recognition of the continuing importance of his work, Cohen-Tannoudji became member of the Academy of Sciences in 1981. He also held memberships in other scholarly societies, among them the American Academy of Arts and Sciences, and the National Academy of Sciences.

Describes "Sisyphus Cooling" Effect

By the 1980s, Cohen-Tannoudji theorized specifically about the light (of a laser) and its effect on the motion of an atom. His experiments in laser cooling were a response to other scientists' work with laser beams, cooling atoms, and trapping atoms. Cohen-Tannoudji, leading his own team of experts, focused on the modification of atomic motion when it interacted with photons. He had his first breakthrough in 1985, when he saw that an atom in motion slows in a standing light wave. As the laser beam intensifies, the atom slows increasingly. Because a material's temperature measures how fast its atoms are moving, this effect came to be known as "Sisyphus cooling," named for the Greek mythological personage who had to roll a stone up a hill for eternity. However, this method was limited in its cooling effects.

By 1988 Cohen-Tannoudji brought together his "dressed" atom ideas with the problems raised by the cooling and trapping atoms theories in order to try to bring the temperature of atoms closer to absolute zero. A few years later, Cohen-Tannoudji had an unexpected breakthrough when studying an atom trapped in a standing light wave. He found that it was dependent on optical pumping, an advanced laser technology in which emits light energy in pulses. This approach keeps the atoms from rebounding, in effect "trapping" them. This type of Sisyphus cooling brought the temperature to 0.18 millionths of degree above absolute zero. The phenomenon had been anticipated by **Albert Einstein** and others.

Lauded for his Research

In the 1990s, Cohen received important recognition for his work. In 1992 he won the Julius Edgar Lilienfeld Prize from the American Physics Society. In 1993 he won the Charles Hard Townes medal from the Optical Society of America. In 1996 he won the Harvey prize in science and technology from Technion, Israel. In that same year, Cohen-Tannoudji also won the Médaille d'Or of the National Center for Scientific Research, the highest honor a scientist can receive in France. (He was President of the organization for four years at one point.) He won the Médaille specifically for his research in atoms and related cooling methods. In 1997 Cohen-Tannoudji shared the Nobel Prize in physics for his explanation of the phenomenon and his "trapping" discovery.

Cohen-Tannoudji's work has opened up long range research possibilities, but affects basic physics as well. It can be used to study atomic structure, as well as help bridge the frontier between classical and quantum physics. Cohen-Tannoudji's theories also have proven useful for practical technology now and in the future. Ultracold atoms can be used to create more precise atomic clocks. (Atomic clocks are devices which use the constant frequency associated with some atomic and subatomic phenomena to define an accurate and reproducible time scale.) His theories are also influential in the development of measuring instruments of extreme precision. Indeed, an atomic laser might be possible. (An atomic laser would be like an ordinary one, save atoms would take the place of photons used in ordinary lasers.)

In 1994 Cohen-Tannoudji's 30 plus years of papers were published in one book, *Atoms in Electromagnetic Fields*. By putting them in one book, with some comments from Cohen-Tannoudji, the spectrum and development of his ideas over the period is clearly shown. Certainly, this does not mean he is finished with this area of research. Cohen-Tannoudji continued to try to cool atoms even further. As Cohen-Tannoudji told *Science* magazine, "It's exciting to see how far one can go."

SELECTED WRITINGS BY COHEN-TANNOUDJI:

Books

Atoms in Electromagnetic Fields. River Edge, NJ: World Scientific, 1994.

Periodicals

"New Mechanism for Laser Cooling." *Physics Today* (October 1990): 33.

FURTHER READING:

Periodicals

"Energy and its Absence." *Economist* (October 18, 1997): 83.
Forman, Paul. "The dressed-atom approach – Atoms in Electromagentic Fields by C. Cohen-Tannoudji." *Science* (May 26, 1995): 1212-14.
Glanz, James. "Masters of atom manipulation win physics prize." *Science* (October 24, 1997): 578.

Other

Nobel Prize web site. http:// www.nobel.se/announcement-97/ (December 19, 1997). This web site provides information, background, and hyperlinks related to the Nobel Prize and Claude Cohen-Tannoudji.

—*Sketch by Annette Petrusso*

Theodora E. Colborn
1927–

American environmentalist

Theodora Emily Decker Colborn, better known as Theo Colborn, is a leading proponent of the theory

Theodora E. Colborn

of endocrine disruption. This theory states that some synthetic chemicals interfere with the ways that hormones work in humans and animals. Colborn argues that such disruption can have profound adverse effects, especially when a mother passes a contaminating agent to a growing fetus, and the contamination interferes with the hormonal signals used by the fetus to direct its growth. Colborn says the possible adverse effects, which in some cases are not apparent until adulthood, include impaired ability to reproduce, diminished intelligence, altered behavior, and reduced ability to resist disease. Colborn, along with journalist Dianne Dumanoski and zoologist John Peterson Myers, presented her argument in a controversial 1996 book titled *Our Stolen Future: Are We Threatening Our Fertility, Intelligence, and Survival?—A Scientific Detective Story.*

Colborn was born on March 28, 1927, in Plainfield, New Jersey. Her parents were Theodore Decker and Margaret L. DeForge Decker. As a girl, Colborn was fascinated by water, spending many hours playing in the river by the farm where her family lived. This early love for the outdoors laid the groundwork for an enduring commitment to the environment. However, it was many years before Colborn found her calling as a professional environmental activist. Her bachelor's degree, earned from Rutgers University in 1947, was in pharmacy.

While studying at Rutgers, Colborn met Harry R. Colborn, and the couple married on January 20, 1949.

Colborn and her new husband took over his father's drugstore in Newton, New Jersey. Over the years, they added two more stores to their business. At the same time, their family expanded with the births of their children, Harry, Christine, Susan, and Mark. By 1962, the demands of running three drugstores and raising four children had become so overwhelming that the couple felt they needed a change. They sold their New Jersey business and moved to Colorado, where they sought a simpler lifestyle in a sunnier climate.

Colborn and her husband owned pharmacies and raised sheep in western Colorado. It was during this period that Colborn first began to champion environmental causes. Her farm was located in a valley that was rich in coal. During the oil shortage of the 1970s, the coal began to be mined on a massive scale. Combined with the mining of other minerals, this led to significant damage of the local river, the Gunnison's North Fork. Colborn became active as a volunteer on western water issues. However, she felt hampered by the lack of official credentials. As she and her coauthors later wrote in *Our Stolen Future*, "Without a degree behind you, it was easy for opponents to dismiss you as a do-gooder, a 'little old lady in tennis shoes,' even though she was tall, middle-aged, and shod in cowboy boots."

In 1978, at age 51, Colborn entered the graduate program at Western State College of Colorado. For her master's degree in freshwater ecology, completed in 1981, she studied whether aquatic insects such as stone flies and mayflies could serve as indicators of river and stream health. For her doctoral work, Colborn moved to the University of Wisconsin at Madison, where she earned a Ph.D. degree in zoology in 1985. Her children were now grown, and her husband had died in 1983. Colborn was ready to embark upon a new stage of her life.

Promotes the Theory of Endocrine Disruption

In 1985, Colborn began a two-year stint with the Office of Technology Assessment of the U.S. Congress. As a congressional fellow and science analyst there, Colborn worked on studies of air pollution and water purification. Then in 1987, she joined the research team at the Conservation Foundation, a think tank in Washington, D.C. There, in the breakthrough assignment of her career, Colborn studied the environmental health of the Great Lakes. Her job involved sifting through hundreds of papers, trying to determine how well the Great Lakes were recovering from decades of acute pollution. At first, Colborn looked for a link between toxic chemicals in the lakes and cancer among people living in the region, but this proved to be a dead end. Yet she was still convinced that something was wrong. Colborn gradually came to believe that a disruption in hormones was the key to understanding the ill health effects seen in a long list of animals across the Great Lakes basin.

In 1988, Colborn accepted a position at the World Wildlife Fund in Washington, D.C., where she now serves as a senior scientist and director of the Wildlife and Contaminants Program. On sabbatical from 1990-1993, she served as a senior fellow of the W. Alton Jones Foundation, a private philanthropic trust. By this point, dozens of scientists around the world had begun collecting isolated pieces to the puzzle of hormonal disruption, but their work still had not been assembled into a single, coherent picture. In July 1991, Colborn helped bring together 21 key researchers from various disciplines for the Wingspread Conference in Racine, Wisconsin. Participants issued the Wingspread Statement, which warned that hormone-disrupting chemicals could jeopardize the future of humanity.

Not everyone agrees with Colborn's theory or her method of communicating it. For example, in a review of *Our Stolen Future* for *Scientific American*, Michael A. Kamrin wrote: "The authors present a very selective segment of the data that have been gathered about chemicals that might affect hormonal functions. They carefully avoid evidence and interpretations that are not in accord with their thinking." Even the critics admit, however, that Colborn has been remarkably successful at raising public awareness of her theory. *Our Stolen Future* has been debated in publications ranging from *Environmental Science and Technology News* and *Science* to the *New York Times Book Review* and *Business Week*.

Colborn is in heavy demand as a speaker on environmental health issues. Her honors include the Women Leadership in the Environment Award from the United Nations Environment Programme in 1997 and the National Conservation Achievement Award in Science from the National Wildlife Federation in 1994. In her leisure time, Colborn enjoys bird-watching, a lifelong passion that has undoubtedly contributed to her choice of career path.

SELECTED WRITINGS BY COLBORN:

Books

(With Dianne Dumanoski and John Peterson Myers) *Our Stolen Future: Are We Threatening Our Fertility, Intelligence, and Survival?—A Scientific Detective Story.* New York: Dutton, 1996.

Periodicals

(With Dianne Dumanoski and John Peterson Myers) "Hormone Impostors." *Sierra* (January/February 1997): 28-35.

FURTHER READING:

Periodicals

Carey, John. "A Scary Warning—Or Scare Story?" *Business Week* (April 8, 1996): 18.

Cortese, Anthony D. "Endocrine Disruption." *Environmental Science and Technology News* 30, no. 5 (1996): 213A-215A.

Frazier, Deborah. "Drugstore Curiosity Pays Off: Colorado Pharmacist Learns about Chemicals' Effect on Reproduction." *Rocky Mountain News* (May 30, 1996): 50A.

Hertsgaard, Mark. "A World Awash in Chemicals." *New York Times Book Review* (April 7, 1997): 25.

Hirshfield, Anne N., Michael F. Hirshfield, and Jodi A. Flaws. "Problems Beyond Pesticides." *Science* (June 7, 1996): 1444-1445.

Kamrin, Michael A. "The Mismeasure of Risk." *Scientific American* (September 1996): 178, 180.

Wapner, Kenneth. "Chemical Sleuth." *The Amicus Journal* (Spring 1995): 18-21.

Other

"Follow the Facts . . . About Endocrine Disruption and *Our Stolen Future*." http://www.osf-facts.org/ (November 14, 1997). This site contains extensive information about Colborn's book and endocrine disruption.

—*Sketch by Linda Wasmer Smith*

Edward U. Condon
1902–1974
American physicist

Despite his scientific contributions in the fields of molecular and nuclear physics, Edward Condon is perhaps best remembered as being one of the first scientists after World War II to come under scrutiny as a security risk. Although frequent clashes with politicians and government officials often overshadowed his accomplishments and led to his being treated unfairly, Condon remained true to himself and his science throughout his career. He was a brilliant and highly moral scientist who was brave enough to speak out on the difficult questions of public policy and also was willing to face the consequences.

Edward Uhler Condon was born in Alamogordo, New Mexico on March 2, 1902. His father, William

Edward U. Condon

Edward Condon, was a civil engineer who worked for the railroad and moved his family from one construction job to another with such frequency that the young Condon attended fourteen grammar schools. His parents eventually separated, and Condon settled with his mother, Caroline Barr Uhler, in the San Francisco Bay Area where he attended junior high and high school. After graduating from Fremont High School in Oakland in 1918, Condon spent three years as a newspaper reporter before deciding to go to college.

Condon Turns to Science and Excels at Physics

Disillusioned with the sensational and often lurid stories he wrote as a newspaperman, Condon entered the University of California at Berkeley in 1921 and continued as a part-time reporter. Initially an astronomy major, Condon soon switched to chemistry and then again to physics. During his second year, Condon married Emilie Honzik with whom he would have three children. He so excelled in school that he was able to complete his bachelor's degree in three years with highest honors in physics. Only two years later, in 1926, he received a Ph.D. from Berkeley for a thesis based on an extension of the work of German physicist **James Franck**, which contained what soon became widely known as the Franck-Condon principle. That same year, Condon obtained a National Research Council fellowship that allowed him to study in Germany for six months at a time in

Gottingen and Munich, the homes of quantum mechanics. While there, Condon learned the power and significance of the new quantum theory, and when he returned to the United States in 1927 with his wife and infant daughter Marie, it was with a greater appreciation and understanding of the future of theoretical physics.

Although Condon took a public relations job with Bell Telephone Laboratories upon his return, his lecturing and scholarly connections soon brought him back to academic life. Since most Americans were having trouble understanding the new physics, Condon found he was in great demand, and soon took a teaching position at Princeton University in the spring of 1928. While there he continued his productive work in physics and co-authored with P. M. Morse the first English language book on quantum mechanics. By the time he was 27 years old, he had become a full professor of theoretical physics at the University of Minnesota. A year later, he returned to Princeton and remained there until 1937. During these years his major contributions were in the field of atomic spectroscopy. As a lecturer, he was considered an inspiring and even nurturing teacher whose clarity, enthusiasm, and wit made difficult concepts seem easy.

Enters the World of Wartime Physics

In the summer of 1937, Condon was offered the position of associate director of research at Westinghouse Electric Corporation, and he moved his family, which now included sons Paul and Joseph, to Pittsburgh. While strengthening that company's work in fundamental physics, Condon became a member of a group that founded the Radiation Laboratory at Massachusetts Institute of Technology. This lab was devoted to developing airborne microwave radar under the auspices of President Franklin D. Roosevelt's National Defense Research Committee, which had been formed soon after Germany invaded France. With the Japanese attack on Pearl Harbor, President Roosevelt approved the large-scale project on uranium fission called the Manhattan Project. In 1943, Condon spent only six weeks as associate director of the Los Alamos Laboratory under American physicist J. Robert Oppenheimer. Condon chafed under the tight security imposed by General Leslie Groves and returned to his radar project, working only as an atomic consultant away from Los Alamos.

After the war, President Harry S. Truman appointed him as director of the National Bureau of Standards. This agency was engaged in fundamental and applied research in chemistry, physics, and engineering, and it was Condon's charge to modernize the bureau. After taking over in November 1945, Condon also served as advisor to the Senate Committee on Atomic Energy. It was this connection with the

political process that would determine virtually the rest of his career, for Condon believed firmly in the idea that nuclear energy should be under civilian and not military control. In August 1946 when Congress placed control of nuclear energy in the hands of the civilian Atomic Energy Commission, it was partly because of Condon's advice and help in drafting the bill.

In a postwar America that was soon to witness a communist China and the successful detonation of a Soviet atomic bomb, it is no surprise that suspicion, paranoia, and the search for scapegoats abounded. To a nation turning inward against external threats and enemies, the liberal politics of Edward Condon became highly suspect. Condon's internationalist notions of science and his opposition to secrecy were well documented, and he became a highly visible target for the right-wing members of the House Un-American Activities Committee (HUAC). Beginning in March 1947, that committee began its public attacks on Condon, calling him a security risk. Despite public support by President Truman and no proof of any kind that Condon was anything but a loyal and honest individual, Condon eventually left the National Bureau of Standards in 1951 after years of harassment. He became director of research at Corning Glass Works, but his persecution by HUAC continued since Corning held government contracts for defense research. Condon eventually resigned to return to teaching.

During his career, Condon served as president of the American Association for the Advancement of Science, the American Institute of Physics, the Society for Social Responsibility in Science, and the American Association of Physics Teachers. He was also editor of the *Reviews of Modern Physics* and co-editor of the *Handbook of Physics*. In 1966, Condon let the University of Colorado persuade him into heading a project for the U. S. Air Force to investigate unidentified flying objects. This report, issued in January 1969, concluded that there was no evidence to justify further efforts to investigate reports of such phenomena. This report has been criticized by some as a government whitewash or cover-up, and it is ironic that the final public act of a man who all his life fought for openness in government should be so tarnished. Condon died in Boulder, Colorado on March 26, 1974. He is remembered by those who knew him as a straight-forward, squarely-built man with a perpetual crew-cut who, as described by American physicist Hugh Odishaw, was "outgoing, warm, a wit, a raconteur with a gift of gab. He could lecture to any audience, from children to his peers, without condescension."

SELECTED WRITINGS BY CONDON:

Books

(With Philip M. Morse) *Quantum Mechanics.* McGraw-Hill, 1929.

Scientific Study of Unidentified Flying Objects.
Dutton, 1969.

FURTHER READING:

Books

Brittin, Wesley E. and Halis Odabasi. *Topics in Modern Physics: A Tribute to Edward U. Condon.* London: Adam Hilger Ltd., 1971.
McGraw-Hill Modern Scientists and Engineers. New York: McGraw-Hill, 1980, pp.221-22.

Periodicals

"Edward Condon, Leader in A-bomb Creation, Dies." *The New York Times* (March 27, 1974): 46.
Morse, Philip M. "Edward Uhler Condon." *Biographical Memoirs. National Academy of Sciences* (1976): 125-151.
Wang, Jessica. "Science, Security, and the Cold War." *ISIS* (June 1992): 238-269.

—Sketch by Leonard C. Bruno

Dirk Coster
1889–1950
Dutch physicist

Dirk Coster was born in Amsterdam, and lived and worked almost all his life in various parts of the Netherlands. He is known today primarily for a discovery he and a coworker made during a year he conducted research outside of his native Netherlands.

Dirk Coster was born on October 5, 1889, in Amsterdam, Holland, the son of Barend and Aafje (van der Mik) Coster. Coster first began work a primary school teacher, then, with some outside financial support, began his studies in physics at the University of Leiden in the Netherlands from 1913 to 1916. He was already in his twenties.

Coster's student years were an exciting time in the field of physics. **Ernst Rutherford** and his coworkers had gained a general picture of the atom in 1911 by bombarding atoms with alpha particles. Two years later **Niels Bohr** worked out his now-familiar model of the hydrogen atom and the concept of an atomic nucleus circled by electrons. Another group of scientists were using a different tool, still-new x rays, to explore atomic structure. In 1914, the English physicist **Henry Gwyn-Jeffreys Moseley** developed the concept of atomic number based on such x ray

studies. Moseley showed that each element was determined by the number of positive charges in the nucleus. This greatly clarified the periodic table of the elements, which had previously been based on the atomic weights of elements. Atomic numbers are all whole numbers, which means that they identify all the possible elements from hydrogen at number one to uranium at number 92. For example, helium is atomic number two and lithium is atomic number three, so there can be no element in the periodic table between helium and lithium.

Coster recognized that he might be a better physics experimentalist with some knowledge of electrical engineering, so he pursued a degree in that subject from Delft Technological University between his undergraduate work at Leiden University and the start of his graduate studies there. At the time, he was also employed as an assistant in physics at the Technical High School in Delft. It was also during this time that he married Lina Maria Wijsman in 1919. The Costers later had four children.

In 1922 Coster obtained his Ph.D. degree from the University of Leiden. He then left the Netherlands for nearby Denmark to do some post-doctoral work at the Copenhagen Institute headed by Niels Bohr, where much of the important theoretical work in quantum mechanics was soon to take place. Fellowships then supported his work in x ray studies at Lund University in Sweden, while he was still obtaining his doctorate from Leiden, and then for his year of post-doctoral study at Copenhagen. At Copenhagen he succeeded in applying Moseley's idea of atomic number to Bohr's theory of atomic structure. Whereas Moseley had used x rays to study known elements to work out their structure, Coster was able with Bohr's theory to use a similar technique on an unknown element to identify its atomic number.

Bohr set Coster to work on the problem of finding one of the half-dozen elements that should, according to the new and improved periodic table, exist, although they had not been observed. The gaps in 1922 were at atomic numbers 43, 61, 70, 72, 75, and 87. Bohr suggested that his newly developed theory of atomic structure predicted that element 72 should be chemically similar to zirconium, which is in the same column in the periodic table. If so, the missing element 72 would be found in zirconium ores, where there already was suspicion of a new element.

Zirconium had been known since 1799, but the metal had not been purified until 1914. Chemists thought that there was another, heavier element in the zirconium compounds, but they were unable to separate it. Bohr assigned **György Hevesy** (1885-1966) the task of chemically separating the heavier element from some imported Norwegian zirconium ore. Hevesy and an assistant repeatedly crystallized a compound of zirconium until they had a sample rich in the heavier metal. Coster then analyzed the sample by passing x rays through the crystals. The angle of refraction identified the material as element 72.

It is customary to identify Coster and Hevesy as the co-discoverers of the element, which they named hafnium after *Hafnia*, a Latin version of the name for the city of Copenhagen, where the metal was discovered. Hafnium was the first element to be identified as new on the basis of its atomic number and its characteristic x-ray pattern. Today hafnium is still very difficult to separate from zirconium, but because it is hard, corrosion resistant, and has other useful properties, it is commercially important, with hundreds of tons of the metal in use around the world.

After leaving Copenhagen at the end of his fellowship in 1922, Coster returned to the Netherlands, where he worked for the rest of his life. At first he was an assistant to Konrad Lorentz at the Teyler Laboratory in Haarlem, but in 1924 he took the chair of experimental physics at Groningen University, where he remained until shortly before his death. While at Groningen, he directed important x ray studies that led to methods for determining the handedness of molecules in crystals and that elucidated and confirmed quantum mechanics theory, which was being developed during the 1920s and 1930s.

Coster developed a progressive spinal disease, which hampered his activities increasingly in the 1940s. He retired from Groningen in 1949 and died from the effects of the disease on February 12, 1950.

FURTHER READING:

Books

Levi, H. *George De Hevesy: Life and Work.* Adam Hilger, 1986.

—Sketch by Bryan Bunch

Jacques Cousteau
1910–1997
French oceanographer

Jacques Cousteau was known worldwide through his television programs, feature-length films, and books, all of which have focused on the wonders and tragedies of the marine world. Through these films and publications, Cousteau helped demystify undersea life, documenting its remarkable variety, its interdependence, and its fragility. Through the Cousteau Society, which he founded in the 1970s, he led efforts to call attention to environmental problems, to reduce marine pollution, and perhaps most importantly, to bring lasting peace to the world.

Jacques-Yves Cousteau was born in St. André-de-Cubzac, France, on June 11, 1910, to Elizabeth Duranthon and Daniel Cousteau. At the time, the elder Cousteau worked as a legal adviser to American entrepreneur James Hyde, founder of the Equitable Life Assurance Society. In 1917, after a heated argument, Hyde fired Daniel and the family briefly fell on hard times, their problems compounded by the poor health of Jacques, who for the first seven years of his life suffered from chronic enteritis, a painful intestinal condition. In 1918, after the Treaty of Versailles, Daniel found work as legal adviser to Eugene Higgins, a wealthy New York expatriate. Higgins traveled extensively throughout Europe, with the Cousteau family in tow. Cousteau recorded few memories from his childhood; his earliest impressions, however, involve water and ships. His health greatly improved around this time, thanks in part to Higgins, who encouraged young Cousteau to learn how to swim.

In 1920 the Cousteaus accompanied Higgins to New York City. Here, Jacques attended Holy Name School in Manhattan, learning the intricacies of stickball and roller skating. He spent his summers at a camp on Vermont's Lake Harvey, where he first learned to dive underwater. At age thirteen, after a trip south of the American border, he authored a hand-bound book he called "An Adventure in Mexico." That same year, he purchased a Pathé movie camera, filmed his cousin's marriage, and began making short melodramatic films.

During his teens, Cousteau was expelled from a French high school for "experimenting" on the school's windows with different-sized stones. As punishment, he was sent to a military-style academy near the French-German border, where he became a dedicated student. He graduated in 1929, unsure of which career path to follow. The military won out over filmmaking simply because it offered the opportunity for extended travel. After passing a rigorous entrance examination, he was accepted by the Ecole Navale, the French naval academy. His class embarked on a one-year world cruise, which he documented, filming everything and everyone—from Douglas Fairbanks, the famous actor, to the Sultan of Oman. After graduating second in his class in 1933, he was promoted to second lieutenant and sent to a naval base in Shanghai, China. His assigned duty was to survey and map the countryside, but in his free time he filmed the locals in China and Siberia.

In the mid–1930s, Cousteau returned to France and entered the aviation academy. Shortly before graduation, in 1936, he was involved in a near-fatal automobile accident that mangled his left forearm.

His doctors recommended amputation but he steadfastly refused. Instead, he chose rehabilitation, using a regimen of his own design. He began taking daily swims around Le Mourillon Bay to rehabilitate his injured arm. He fell in love with goggle diving, marveling at the variety and beauty of undersea life. He later wrote in his book *The Silent World:* "One Sunday morning . . . I waded into the Mediterranean and looked into it through Fernez goggles. . . . I was astonished by what I saw in the shallow shingle at Le Mourillon, rocks covered with green, brown and silver forests of algae and fishes unknown to me, swimming in crystalline water. . . . Sometimes we are lucky enough to know that our lives have been changed, to discard the old, embrace the new, and run headlong down an immutable course. It happened to me at Le Mourillon on that summer's day, when my eyes were opened on the sea."

During his convalescence he met seventeen-year-old Simone Melchior, a wealthy high-school student who was living in Paris. After a one-year courtship, the couple married on July 12, 1937, and moved into a house near Le Mourillon Bay. The Cousteaus' first son, Jean-Michel, was born in March of 1938. A second son, Philippe, was born in December of 1939. Around this time, the new family's tranquil life on the edge of the sea was threatened by world events. In 1939 France began preparing for war, and Cousteau was promoted to gunnery officer aboard the *Dupleix.* The war was largely limited to ground action, however, and Germany quickly overran the ill-prepared French Army. Living in the unoccupied section of France enabled Cousteau to continue his experiments and allowed him to spend many hours with his family. In his free time, he experimented with underwater photography devices and tried to develop improved diving apparatuses. German patrols often questioned Cousteau about his use of diving and photographic equipment. Although he was able to convince authorities that the equipment was harmless, Cousteau was, in fact, using these devices on behalf of the French resistance movement. For his efforts, he was later awarded the Croix de Guerre with palm.

Undersea Work Leads to Development of the Aqualung

Although he loved diving, Cousteau regretted the limitations of goggle diving; he simply could not spend enough time under water. The standard helmet and heavy suit apparatus had similar limitations; the diver was helplessly tethered to the ship, and the heavy suit and helmet made Cousteau feel like "a cripple in an alien land," as cited in *Contemporary Authors New Revision Series.* A number of experiments with other diving equipment followed, but all the existing systems proved unsatisfactory. He designed his own "oxygen re-breathing outfit," which was less physically constrictive but which ultimately proved ineffective and dangerous. Also during this period he began his initial experiments with underwater filmmaking. Working with two colleagues, Philippe Taillez, a naval officer, and Frédéric Dumas, a renowned spearfisherman, Cousteau filmed his first underwater movie, *Sixty Feet Down,* in 1942. The eighteen-minute film reflects the technical limitations of underwater photography but was quite advanced for its time. Cousteau entered the film in the Cannes Film Festival, where it received critical praise and was purchased by a film distributor.

As pleased as he was with his initial efforts at underwater photography, Cousteau realized that he needed to spend more time underwater to accurately portray the ocean's mysteries. In 1937 he had begun a collaboration with Emile Gagnan, an engineer with a talent for solving technical problems. In 1942 Cousteau again turned to Gagnan for answers. The two spent approximately three weeks developing an automatic regulator that supplied compressed air on demand. This regulator, along with two tanks of compressed air, a mouthpiece, and hoses, was the prototype Aqualung, which Gagnan and Cousteau patented in 1943.

That summer, Cousteau, Talliez, and Dumas tested the Aqualung off the French Riveria, making as many as five hundred separate dives. This device was put to use on the group's next project, an exploration of the *Dalton,* a sunken British steamer. This expedition provided material for Cousteau's second movie, *Wreck.* The film deeply impressed French naval authorities, who recruited Cousteau to assist with the dangerous task of clearing mines from French harbors. When the war ended, Cousteau received a commission to continue his research as part of the Underwater Research Group, which included both Talliez and Dumas. With increased funding and ready access to scientists and engineers, the group expanded its research and developed a number of innovations, including an underwater sled.

In 1947 Cousteau, using the Aqualung, set a world's record for free diving, reaching a depth of 300 feet. The following year, Dumas broke the record with a 306-foot dive. The team developed and perfected many of the techniques of deep-sea diving, working out rigorous decompression schedules that enabled the body to adjust to pressure changes. This physically demanding, dangerous work took its toll; one member of the research team was killed during underwater testing.

Begins World Adventures Aboard *Calypso*

On July 19, 1950, Cousteau bought *Calypso,* a converted U.S. minesweeper. On November 24, 1951, after undergoing significant renovations, *Calypso* sailed for the Red Sea. The *Calypso* Red Sea Expedition (1951–52) yielded numerous discoveries, including the identification of previously unknown plant and animal species and the discovery of volcanic basins beneath the Red Sea. In February of 1952, *Calypso* sailed toward Toulon. On the way home, the crew investigated an uncharted wreck near the southern coast of Grand Congloué and discovered a large Roman ship filled with treasures. The discovery helped spread Cousteau's fame in France. In 1953, with the publication of *The Silent World,* Cousteau achieved international notice. The book, drawn from Cousteau's daily logs, was written originally in English with the help of U.S. journalist James Dugan and later translated into French. Released in more than twenty languages, *The Silent World* eventually sold more than five million copies worldwide.

In 1953 Cousteau began collaborating with **Harold Edgerton**, a pioneer in high-speed photography who had invented the strobe light and other photographic devices. Edgerton and his son, William, spent several summers aboard *Calypso,* outfitting the ship with an innovative camera that skimmed along the ocean floor, sending back blurry but intriguing photos of deep-sea creatures. The death of William Edgerton in an unrelated diving accident effectively ended the experiments, but Cousteau had already realized the limitations of such a method of exploring the ocean depths. Instead, he and his team began work on a small, easily maneuverable submarine, which he called the diving saucer, or DS–2. The sub has made more than one thousand dives and has been part of countless undersea discoveries.

In 1955 *Calypso* embarked on a 13,800-mile journey that was recorded by Cousteau for a film version of *The Silent World.* The ninety-minute film premiered at the 1956 Cannes International Film Festival, where it received the coveted Palme d'Or. The following year, the film won an Oscar from the American Academy of Motion Picture Arts and Sciences. In 1957, in part due to his film's success, Cousteau was named director of the Oceanographic Institute and Museum of Monaco. He filled the museum's aquariums with rare and unusual species garnered from his ocean expeditions.

Cousteau addressed the first World Oceanic Congress in 1959, an event that received widespread coverage and led to his appearance on the cover of *Time* magazine on March 28, 1960. The highly favorable story painted Cousteau as a poet of the deep. In April of 1961 he received the National Geographic Society's Gold Medal at a White house ceremony hosted by President John F. Kennedy. The medal's inscription reads: "To earthbound man he gave the key to the silent world."

Television Programs Bring Worldwide Recognition

After the White House ceremony, Cousteau appeared to be at the pinnacle of his career, but bigger

things were still to come. During the early 1960s he and his crew participated in the Conshelf Saturation Dive program, which was intended to prove the feasibility of extended underwater living. The success of the first mission led to Conshelf II, a month-long project involving five divers. The Conshelf program and the DS–2 project provided material for the fifty-three-minute film *World without Sun,* which debuted in the United States in December of 1964.

Cousteau's first hour-long television special, "The World of Jacques-Yves Cousteau," was broadcast in April of 1966, with Orson Welles providing the narration. The program's high ratings and critical acclaim helped Cousteau land a lucrative contract with the American Broadcasting Company (ABC). The *Undersea World of Jacques Cousteau* premiered in 1968 and has since been rebroadcast in hundreds of countries. The program starred Cousteau and his sons, Philippe and Jean-Michel, and sea creatures from around the globe. The show ran for eight seasons, with the last episode airing in May of 1976. In 1977 the *Cousteau Odyssey* series premiered on the Public Broadcasting System. The new show reflected Cousteau's growing concern about environmental destruction and tended not to focus on specific animal species.

In the 1970s the Cousteau Society, a nonprofit environmental group that also focuses on peace issues, opened its doors in Bridgeport, Connecticut. By 1975 the society had more than 120,000 members and had opened branch offices in Los Angeles, New York, and Norfolk, Virginia. Eventually, Cousteau decided to make Norfolk the homebase for *Calypso.*

On June 28, 1979, Philippe Cousteau was killed when the seaplane he was piloting crashed on the Tagus River near Lisbon, Portugal. Philippe's death deeply affected Cousteau, who was to his death unable to talk about the accident or the loss of his son. Philippe was expected to eventually take command of his father's empire; instead, Jean-Michel was given increased responsibility for overseeing the Cousteau Society and his father's other ventures.

Finds New Outlet on Cable TV

In 1980 Cousteau signed a one-million-dollar contract with the National Office of Canadian Film to produce two programs on the greater St. Lawrence waterway. In 1984 the *Cousteau Amazon* series premiered on the Turner Broadcasting System. The four shows were enthusiastically reviewed, and called attention to the threatened native South American cultures, Amazon rain forest, and creatures who lived in one of the world's great rivers. The final show of the series, "Snowstorm in the Jungle," explored the frightening world of cocaine trafficking. In the mid–1980s "Cousteau/Mississippi: The Reluctant Ally" received an Emmy for outstanding informational special. In all, Cousteau's television programs have earned more than forty Emmy nominations.

In addition to his television programs, Cousteau continued to produce new inventions. The Sea Spider, a many-armed diagnostic device, was developed to analyze the biochemistry of the ocean's surface. In 1980 Cousteau and his team began work on the Turbosail, which uses high-tech wind sails to cut fuel consumption in large, ocean-going vessels. In spring of 1985 he launched a new wind ship, the *Alcyone,* which was outfitted with two 33-foot-high Turbosails.

In honor of his achievements, Cousteau received the Grand Croix dans l'Ordre National du Mérite from the French government in 1985. That same year, he also received the U.S. Presidential Medal of Freedom. In November of 1987 he was inducted into the Television Academy's Hall of Fame and later received the founder's award from the International Council of the National Academy of Television Arts and Sciences. In 1988 the National Geographic Society honored him with its Centennial Award for "special contributions to mankind throughout the years."

While some critics challenged his scientific credentials, Cousteau never claimed "expert" status in any discipline. His talents seemed to be more poetic than scientific; his films and books—which include the eight-volume "Undersea Discovery" series and the twenty-one-volume "Ocean World" encyclopedia series—have a lyrical quality that conveys the captain's great love of nature. This optimism was tempered by his concerns about the environment. He emphatically demonstrated, perhaps to a greater degree than any of his contemporaries, how the quality of both the land and sea is deteriorating and how such environmental destruction is irreversible.

Cousteau continued to speak publicly about environmental issues until he was well into his eighties, although he had given up diving in cold water. In the years before his death, he had been planning for the construction of the *Calypso 2* to replace the original *Calypso,* which had sunk in a Singapore shipyard in 1994. The $20 million vessel was to be powered by solar energy and include equipment for a television studio, marine laboratory, and satellite transmission facility. The oceanographer died of a heart attack on June 25, 1997, at his home in Paris. He had been suffering from a respiratory ailment for which he had been hospitalized for several months. He was 87.

SELECTED WRITINGS BY COUSTEAU:

Books

The Silent World, Harper, 1953.
The Living Sea, Harper, 1963.

Seymour Cray

Le Monde sans soleil, Hachette, 1964, English-language version edited by James Dugan, published as *World without Sun,* Harper, 1965.

FURTHER READING:

Books

Contemporary Authors New Revision Series, Volume 15, Gale, 1985, pp. 90–93.
Cousteau, Jean-Michel, *Cousteau's Papua New Guinea Journey,* Abrams, 1989.
Munson, Richard, *Cousteau: The Captain and His World,* Morrow, 1989.

—Sketch by Tom Crawford

Seymour Cray
1925–1996
American computer engineer

Seymour Cray was an electronics engineer and one of the founding fathers of the computer industry. His seminal work in computer design features the semiconductor as a component to store and process information. Cray's dense packing of hundreds of thousands of semiconductor chips, which reduced the distance between signals, enabled him to pioneer very large and powerful "supercomputers." Among his accomplishments was the first computer to employ a freon cooling system to prevent chips from overheating. However, Cray's most significant contribution was the supercomputer itself. Seeking to process vast amounts of mathematical data needed to simulate physical phenomena, Cray built what many consider the first supercomputer, the CDC 6600 (with 350,000 transistors). To such fields as engineering, meteorology, and eventually biology and medicine, the supercomputer represented a technological revolution, akin to replacing a wagon with a sports car in terms of accelerating research.

A maverick in both his scientific and business pursuits, Cray eventually started his own company devoted entirely to the development of supercomputers. For many years Cray computers dominated the supercomputer industry. A devoted fan of "Star Trek," a 1960s television show about space travel, Cray included aesthetically pleasing touches in his computers, such as transparent blue glass that revealed their inner workings.

Early Computer Innovations

Cray was born on September 28, 1925, in Chippewa Falls, Wisconsin, a small town situated in the heart of Wisconsin's dairy farm country. The eldest of two children, Cray revealed his talent for engineering while still a young boy, tinkering with radios in the basement and building an automatic telegraph machine by the time he was ten years old. Cray's father, a city engineer, and his mother fully supported his scientific interests, providing him with a basement laboratory equipped with chemistry sets and radio gear. Cray's early aptitude for electronics was evident when he wired his laboratory to his bedroom, and included an electric alarm that sounded whenever anyone tried to enter his inner sanctum. While attending Chippewa Falls High School, Cray sometimes taught the physics class in his teacher's absence. During his senior year, he received the Bausch & Lomb Science Award for meritorious achievement in science.

While serving in the U.S. Army during the final years of World War II, Cray utilized his natural gifts in electronics as a radio operator and decipherer of enemy codes. After the war, he enrolled in the University of Wisconsin, but later transferred to the University of Minnesota in Minneapolis, where he received his bachelor's degree in electrical engineering in 1950 and a master's degree in applied mathematics the next year. Cray began his corporate electronics career when he was hired to work for Engineering Research Associates (ERA). When Cray joined the company, it was among a small group of firms on the cutting edge of the commercial computer industry. One of his first assignments with ERA was to build computer pulse transformers for Navy use. Cray credited his success on the project to a top-of-the-line circular slide rule that enabled him to make a multitude of calculations needed to build the transformers. In a speech before his colleagues at a 1988 supercomputer conference, Cray recalled feeling "quite smug" about his accomplishment until he encountered a more experienced engineer working at the firm who told Cray that he did not use complicated slide rules or many of the other standard engineering approaches in his work, preferring to rely on intuition. Intrigued, Cray put away his slide rule and decided that he would do likewise.

For his next computer project, Cray and his colleagues developed a binary programming system. With the addition of magnetic core memory, which allowed Cray and his coworkers to program 4,096 words, the age of the supercomputer dawned. Although devoted to his laboratory work, Cray was also interested in the business side of the industry; his efforts to market ERA's new technology resulted in the Remington Rand typewriter company buying out ERA. With a formidable knowledge of circuits, logic, and computer software design, Cray designed the UNIVAC 1103, the first electronically digital computer to become commercially available.

Despite his growing success, Cray became dissatisfied with the large corporate atmosphere of ERA, which had been renamed the Sperry Rand Corporation. A friend and colleague, William Norris, who also worked at Sperry Rand, decided to start his own company, Control Data Corporation (CDC), and recruited Cray to work for him. Lacking the financial resources of larger companies, Cray and Control Data set out to make affordable computers. Towards this end, Cray built computers out of transistors, which he purchased at an electronics outlet store for 37 cents each. Although the chips were of diverse circuitry, Cray successfully replaced the cumbersome and expensive tubes and radio "valves" which were then standard in the industry.

Control Data began developing a line of computers like the CDC 1604, which was immensely successful as a tool for scientific research. Cray went on to develop the CDC 6600, the most powerful computer of its day and the first to employ freon to cool its 350,000 transistors. In 1969, the corporation introduced the CDC 7600, which many considered to be the world's first supercomputer. Capable of 15 million computations per second, the 7600 placed CDC as the leader in the supercomputer industry to the chagrin of the IBM corporation, CDC's primary competitor. Even with a legion of researchers, IBM was unable to match CDC's productivity, and eventually resorted to questionable tactics to overtake CDC, which eventually filed and won an antitrust suit against IBM. But as Control Data grew, so did its bureaucracy. As Russell Mitchell recounted in *Business Week,* Norris once asked Cray to develop a five-year plan. What Norris received in return was a short note that said Cray's five-year plan was "to build the biggest computer in the world," and his one-year plan was "to achieve one-fifth of the above." After developing the CDC 8600, which the company refused to market, Cray, in 1972, decided to leave CDC and set up his own company, Cray Research Corporation. Norris and CDC graciously invested $500,000 to assist Cray in his fledgling business effort.

The Supercomputer Emerges

Cray Research immediately set out to build the fastest supercomputer. In 1976, the CRAY-1 was introduced. Incorporating a revolutionary vector processing approach, which allowed the computer to solve various parts of a problem at once, the CRAY-1 was capable of performing 32 calculations simultaneously, outpacing even the best CDC computer. When the National Center for Atmospheric Research met the computer's $8.8 million price tag, Cray Research finally had solid financial footing to continue building faster and more affordable computers. For Cray, this meant manufacturing one product at a time, a radical approach in the computer industry. The first CRAY-2 was marketed in 1985 and featured a phenomenal 2-billion byte memory that could perform 1.2 billion computer operations per second, a tenfold performance increase over the Cray-1. Capable of providing computerized models of physical phenomena described mathematically, the CRAY computers were essential catalysts in accelerating research. For example, in such areas as pharmaceutical development, supercomputer modeling of a drug's molecules and its biological components eliminated much trial and error, reducing the time necessary to solve complicated mathematical equations.

In 1983, Cray turned his attention to developing gallium arsenide (GaA) circuits. Although the CRAY-2 was based on silicon chips, Cray continued to develop GaA chips in the spin-off Cray Computer Corporation. Although extremely difficult to work with because of their fragility, gallium arsenide computer chips marked a major advance in computer circuitry with their ability to conduct electrical impulses with less resistance than silicon. Adding even more speed to the computer, the GaA chip also effectively reduced both heat and energy loss. However, his company was a financial failure, because the GaA chip was expensive to develop. Undaunted, he started a new company, SRC Computers. He died on October 5, 1996, at Penrose Hospital in Colorado Springs, Colorado.

While Cray's advances in computer technology enabled him to corner the market on the supercomputer industry for many years, the advent of parallel processing allowed others in the industry to make inroads into the same market. Utilizing hundreds of mini-computers to work on individual aspects of a problem, parallel processing is a less expensive approach to solving huge mathematical problems. Although Cray for many years denounced parallel processing as impractical, he eventually accepted this approach.

Cray's first wife, Verene, was a minister's daughter. Married shortly after World War II, they had two daughters and two sons, who characterized their father as a man intensely dedicated to his work; in fact, Cray demanded their absolute silence while traveling in the car so that he could think about the next advance in supercomputers. In 1975, Cray and Verene divorced, and he wed Geri M. Harrand five years later. Although he engaged in outdoor pursuits with his new wife, such as windsurfing and skiing, Cray remained devoted to his research. In 1972, he was awarded the Harry Goode Memorial Award for "outstanding achievement in the field of information processing." As Cray looked forward to the future of supercomputers, especially to the use of GaA computer chips, many experts in the field characterized his vision as impractical. Nonetheless, Cray's numerous conceptual breakthroughs in computer and information science have firmly established him as an innovator in computer technology.

FURTHER READING:

Books

Slater, R. *Portraits in Silicon.* Cambridge: MIT Press, 1989, pp. 195–204

Spenser, Donald. *Macmillan Encyclopedia of Computers.* Macmillan, 1992.

Periodicals

Anthes, Gary H. "Seymour Cray: Reclusive Genius." *Computerworld* (22 June 1992): 38.

Babcock, Charles. "Cray Left behind Powerful Example" (obituary). *Computerworld* 30, no. 45 (4 November 1996): 157.

Cohen, Sarah. "Supercomputer Legend Seymour Cray Dies at 71" (obituary). *Electronic News* 42, no. 2138 (14 October 1996): 1.

Corcoran, Elizabeth. "Seymour Cray: The Man with Gigabytes of Genius" (obituary). *Washington Post* (7 October 1996): C1.

Elmer-Dewitt, Philip. "Computer Chip Off the Old Block: Genius Seymour Cray and the Company He Founded Split Up." *Time* (29 May 1989): 70.

Kanell, Michael E. "The World Has Lost a Visionary" (obituary). *Atlanta Constitution* (23 October 1996): F2.

Krepchin, Ira. "Datamation 100 North American Profiles." *Datamation* (15 June 1993): 81.

Markoff, John. "Seymour Cray, Computer Industry Pioneer and Father of the Supercomputer, Dies at 71" (obituary). *New York Times* (6 October 1996).

Miller, A. Ray. "Seymour Cray, the Father of Supercomputing and a True National Treasure, Has Died" (obituary). *Computer* 29 (November 1996): 89.

Mitchell, Russell. "The Genius." *Business Week* (30 April 1990): 80-88.

Pearson, Richard. "Computer Pioneer Seymour Cray Dies" (obituary). *Washington Post* (6 October 1996): B6.

Pitta, Julie. "Seymour Cray, Supercomputer Inventor, Dies" (obituary). *Washington Post* (6 October 1996): A1.

—*Sketch by David Petechuk*

Paul J. Crutzen

Paul J. Crutzen
1933–

Dutch meteorologist

Paul Crutzen is one of the world's leading researchers in mapping the chemical mechanisms that affect the ozone layer. He has pioneered research on the formation and depletion of the ozone layer and threats placed upon it by industrial society. Crutzen has discovered, for example, that nitrogen oxides accelerate the rate of ozone depletion. He has also found that chemicals released by bacteria in the soil affect the thickness of the ozone layer. For these discoveries he has received the 1995 Nobel Prize in Chemistry, along with **Mario Molina** and **Sherwood Rowland** for their separate discoveries related to the ozone and how chlorofluorocarbons (CFCs) deplete the ozone layer. According to Royal Swedish Academy of Science, "by explaining the chemical mechanisms that affect the thickness of the ozone layer, the three researchers have contributed to our salvation from a global environmental problem that could have catastrophic consequences."

Paul Josef Crutzen was born December 3, 1933, to Josef C. Crutzen and Anna Gurek in Amsterdam. Despite growing up in a poor family in Nazi-occupied Holland during 1940-1945, he was nominated to attend high school at a time when not all children were accepted into high school. He liked to play soccer in the warm months and ice skate 50-60 miles (80-97 km) a day in the winter. Because he was unable to afford an education at a university, he attended a two-year college in Amsterdam. After graduating with a civil engineering degree in 1954, he designed bridges and homes.

Crutzen met his wife, Tertu Soininen, while on vacation in Switzerland in 1954. They later moved to Sweden where he got a job as a computer programmer for the Institute of Meteorology and the University of Stockholm. He started to focus on atmospheric chemistry rather than mathematics because he had lost interest in math and did not want to spend long hours in a lab, especially after the birth of his two daughters, Illona and Sylvia. Despite his busy schedule, Crutzen obtained his doctoral degree in Meteorology at Stockholm University at the age of 35.

Crutzen's main research focused on the ozone, a bluish, irritating gas with a strong odor. The ozone is a molecule made up of three oxygen atoms (O_3) and is formed naturally in the atmosphere by a photochemical reaction. The ozone begins approximately 10 miles (16 km) above Earth's surface, reaching between 20-30 miles (32-48 km) in height, and acts as a protective layer that absorbs high-energy ultraviolet radiation given off by the sun.

In 1970 Crutzen found that soil microbes were excreting nitrous oxide gas, which rises to the stratosphere and is converted by sunlight to nitric oxide and nitrogen dioxide. He determined that these two gases were part of what caused the depletion of the ozone.

This discovery revolutionized the study of the ozone and encouraged a surge of research on global biogeochemical cycles.

In 1977, while he was the director of the National Center for Atmospheric Research (NCAR) in Boulder, Colorado, Crutzen studied the effects of burning trees and brush in the fields of Brazil. Every year farmers cleared the forests by burning everything in sight. The theory at the time was that this burning caused more carbon compounds or trace gases and carbon monoxide to enter the atmosphere. These gases were believed to cause the greenhouse effect, or a warming of the atmosphere. Crutzen collected and examined this smoke in Brazil and discovered that the complete opposite was occurring. He stated in *Discover* magazine: "Before the industry got started the tropical burning was actually decreasing the amount of carbon dioxide in the atmosphere." The study of smoke in Brazil led Crutzen to further examine what effects larger amounts of different kinds of smoke might have on the environment, such as smoke from a nuclear war.

The journal *Ambio* commissioned Crutzen and John Birks, his colleague from the University of Colorado, to investigate what effects nuclear war might have on the planet. Crutzen and Birks studied a simulated worldwide nuclear war. They theorized that the black carbon soot from the raging fires would absorb as much as 99% of the sunlight. This lack of sunlight, coined "nuclear winter," would be devastating to all forms of life. For this theory Crutzen was named "Scientist of the Year" by *Discover* magazine in 1984 and awarded the prestigious Tyler Award four years later.

As a result of the discoveries by Crutzen and other environmental scientists, a very crucial international treaty was established in 1987. The Montreal Protocol was negotiated under the auspices of the United Nations and signed by 70 countries to slowly phase out the production of chlorofluorocarbons and other ozone-damaging chemicals by the year 2000. However, the United States had ended the production of CFCs five years earlier, in 1995. According to the *New York Times,* "the National Oceanic and Atmospheric Administration reported in 1994, while ozone over the South Pole is still decreasing, the depletion appears to be leveling off." Even though the ban has been established, existing CFCs will continue to reach the ozone, so the depletion will continue for some years. The full recovery of the ozone is not expected for at least 100 years.

From 1977-80, Crutzen was director of the Air Quality Division, National Center for Atmospheric Research (NCAR), located in Boulder, Colorado. While at NCAR, he located he taught classes at Colorado State University in the department of Atmospheric Sciences. Since 1980 he has been a member of the Max Planck Society for the Advancement of Science, and he is the director of the Atmospheric Chemistry division at Max Planck Institute for Chemistry. In addition to Crutzen's position at the institute, he is a part-time professor at Scripps Institution of Oceanography at the University of California. In 1995 he was the recipient of the United Nations Environmental Ozone Award for outstanding contribution to the protection of the ozone layer. Crutzen has co-authored and edited several books, as well as having published several hundred articles in specialized publications.

SELECTED WRITINGS BY CRUTZEN:

Books

Atmosphere, Climate, and Change. Scientific American Library, 1995
Atmosphere Change: An Earth System Perspective. W.H. Freeman, 1993
Environmental Consequences of Nuclear War 1985. Schwarzer Himmel, 1986

—*Sketch by Sheila M. Dow*

Robert Floyd Curl, Jr.
1933–
American physical chemist

American scientist Robert F. Curl, Jr., a professor of physical chemistry at Rice University, won the 1996 Nobel Prize for Chemistry, along with fellow Rice professor **Richard E. Smalley** and Briton **Harold W. Kroto** from the University of Sussex, for the discovery of a new form of the element carbon, called Carbon 60. The third molecular form of carbon (the other two forms are diamonds and graphite), C60 consists of 60 atoms of carbon arranged in hexagons and pentagons and is called a "buckminsterfullerene," "fullerene," or by its nickname "Buckyball" in honor of Buckminster Fuller, whose geodesic domes it resembles.

Fullerenes, which consist of 60 atoms of carbon arranged in hexagons and pentagons in a structure resembling a soccer ball, have practical applications. Extraordinarily stable and resistant to radiation and chemical destruction, fullerenes promise to be the basis for remarkably strong but lightweight materials, new drug delivery systems, computer semiconductors, solar cells, and superconductors.

Curl was born in Alice, Texas, on August 23, 1933, to Robert and Lessie (Merritt) Floyd. His father

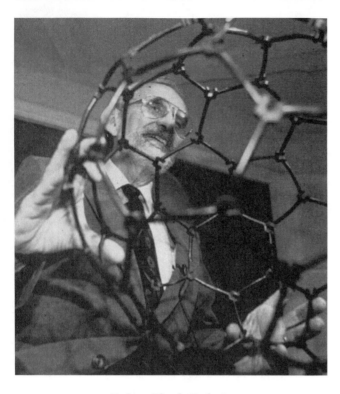

Robert Floyd Curl, Jr.

was a Methodist minister and moved the family all around southern and southwest Texas while Curl was young. Curl credits receiving a chemistry set for Christmas when he was nine years old for sparking his interest in chemistry. According to a biography of Curl on Rice University's web site, Curl decided to get his B.A. from Rice University because of their famous football team. He graduated in 1954 and a year later, on December 21, he married Jonel Whipple. They would have two sons, Michael and David.

Begins Fruitful Collaboration

Scientific interest, rather than football, led him to work with Kenneth Pitzer at the University of California at Berkeley, whom he had read about in an undergraduate course. Pitzer became Curl's research advisor and remembered him as a quiet student with exceptional skills. Curl and Pitzer shared the Clayton Prize of the Institution of Mechanical Engineers, and this began a fruitful collaboration that would continue throughout Curl's career. Curl excelled in graduate school, publishing five research papers and obtaining a National Science Foundation fellowship. After completing his Ph.D. in 1957, he decided to go to Harvard to study with E.B. Wilson, who was working on microwave spectroscopy. His talents then landed him an assistant professorship at his alma mater. In 1967 Curl became a full professor at Rice and again joined Pitzer, who was president of the university. They would collaborate on papers again, although not on the research that led to the Nobel Prize.

At the same time Curl was researching and publishing papers on microwave and infrared spectroscopy at Rice, his acquaintance Harold Kroto, a professor in Sussex, England, was researching chains of carbons in space. Kroto thought these chains might be the products of red-giant stars, but wasn't sure how the chains actually formed. In 1984, Kroto contacted Curl, who told him about fellow Rice professor Richard Smalley. Smalley had designed and built a special laser beam apparatus that could break materials down into a plasma of atoms that could then be controlled and studied. Curl often worked with Smalley on experiments using Smalley's microwave and infrared spectroscopy expertise. Kroto thought that he could use Smalley's apparatus to simulate the temperatures in space needed to form the carbon chains he was interested in, so Curl introduced the two and began what would later make science history.

Unusual Collaboration Leads to Discovery of "Buckyballs"

Smalley and Curl had been looking at semiconductors like silicon and germanium in Smalley's laser apparatus, and had no reason to look at simple carbon. It was something of a favor as well as a break in their research when Kroto asked them to look at carbon in order to verify his research. So that September, the scientists turned the laser beam on a piece of graphite and found something they were not looking for, a molecule that had 60 carbon atoms. Carbon had previously been known to have only two molecular forms, diamond and graphite. They surmised correctly that the molecule had a cage-like structure that looked like a soccer ball. They named the structure buckminsterfullerene, which later became fullerenes, and then by the nickname "buckyballs." It was Curl who attained the right degree of equilibrium in the carbon vapor that permitted the scientists to look at how the carbon molecule differed from all the rest. Curl examined the spectroscopic graph and saw the Carbon 60 had the largest peak on the graph. Evidence for the existence of large carbon clusters had existed before, but Curl, Smalley, and Kroto were the first scientists to fully identify and stabilize Carbon 60. In October of 1996, all three were recognized for this remarkable discovery with the Nobel Prize in Chemistry.

Fullerene research took off quickly and today scientists are manufacturing pounds of buckyballs every day. Extraordinarily stable because of their molecular structure and resistant to radiation and chemical destruction, fullerenes promise to be the basis for remarkably strong but lightweight materials, new drug delivery systems, computer semiconductors, solar cells, and superconductors.

In addition to the Nobel Prize, Curl has also received the Alexander von Humboldt Senior Scientist Award and the APS International Prize for New Materials in 1992. He has also been a NATO fellow, an Alfred P. Sloan fellow, and an Optical Society of America fellow. Curl was the chairman of the chemistry department at Rice from 1992 to 1996. He continues to study how molecules react with each other in combustion processes. This research promises to offer solutions to monitoring emissions monitoring from cars, forest fires, and chemical plants.

SELECTED WRITINGS BY CURL:

Periodicals

(With J. D. Adamson, S. K. Farhat, C. L. Morter, G. P. Glass, and L. F. Phillips) "The Reaction of NH_2 with O." *Journal of Physical Chemistry*, 1994.

(With M. D. Barnes, P. R. Brooks, and B. R. Johnson) "Probing Chemical Reaction: Evidence for Exploration of an Excited Potential Energy Surface at Thermal Energies." *Science*, 1993.

(With C. E. Miller and W. C. Eckhoff) "Quasi-Linearity in HCCN: Effects of the nu2 Fundamental." *Journal of Molecular Structure*, 1995.

(With C. L. Morter, S. K. Farhat, J. D. Adamson, and G. P. Glass) "Rate Constant Measurement of the Recombination Reaction $C_3H_3 +$ C_3H_3." *Journal of Physical Chemistry*, 1994.

FURTHER READING:

Periodicals

Nash, Madeleine. "SCIENCE: Great Balls of Carbon." *Time* (May 6, 1991).

Wu, Corinna. "Buckyballs Bounce into Nobel History." *Science News*, Vol. 150 (October 19, 1996): 247.

Zimmer, Carl. "Buckyballs From Space" *Discover Magazine*, (August 1, 1996).

Other

"Robert F. Curl." *Rice Chemistry.* 1996. http://pchem1.rice.edu/FacultyStaff/Curl.html (09 Oct. 1996).

"Chemistry, physics Nobel winners announced." *CNN Interactive.* 1996. http://cnn.com/WORLD/9610/09/nobel.physics/index.html (09 Oct. 1996)..

—*Sketch by Pamela Proffitt*

Ingrid Daubechies
1954–
Belgian–born American applied mathematician

Ingrid Daubechies was born August 17, 1954, in Houthalen, Belgium. Her father, Marcel Daubechies, is a retired civil engineer and her mother, Simone, is a retired criminologist. Daubechies credits her parents with giving her a love of learning and her mother with teaching her by example to be her own person. Her father always encouraged her to pursue her interest in science. She has one brother.

As a small child, Daubechies displayed an insatiable interest in how things worked and in making things with her hands. She took up the hobbies of weaving and pottery at a young age and continues to produce *objets d'art* in both crafts. At the age of eight or nine Daubechies' favorite hobby was to sew clothes for her dolls because it fascinated her that flat pieces of material could be worked into curved surfaces that fit the angles of the doll's body. But she also fascinated with machinery and mathematical axioms. Daubechies used to lie in bed and compute the powers of two, or test the mathematical law that any number divisible by nine produces another number divisible by nine when the digits are added together. Reading has been a lifelong hobby.

Daubechies spent her entire childhood and school years in Belgium. She was educated at the Free University Brussels, earning a B.S. degree in 1975 and a Ph.D. in 1980, both in physics. Her thesis was entitled "Representation of Quantum Mechanical Operators by Kernels on Hilbert Spaces of Analytic Functions." Between 1978 and 1980 Daubechies wrote ten articles based on her own original research. While pursuing her own studies, she taught at the Free University Brussels a total of 12 years. Daubechies first visited the United States in 1981, staying for two years, then returned to Belgium believing she would not come back to America.

In 1984, Daubechies was the recipient of the Louis Empain Prize for physics. The prize is given every five years to a Belgian scientist for scientific contributions done before the age of 29. She returned to the United States in 1987 and joined AT&T Bell Laboratories, where she was a technical staff member for the Mathematics Research Center. During her employment with AT&T, she concurrently took leaves of absences to teach at the University of Michigan and later at Rutgers University. In 1993, Daubechies became a full professor at Princeton University in the Mathematics Department and Program in Applied and Computational Mathematics, where she has remained to date. Daubechies is the first woman to obtain this position at Princeton. Her responsibilities include teaching both undergraduate and graduate courses, directing Ph.D. students in thesis work, and collaborating with postdoctoral fellows in research. She has also devoted much time to creating mathematics curriculums for grades kindergarten through 12th grade that reflect present–day applications of mathematics.

The Physicist Who Became a Mathematician

Daubechies' original intent was to become a physicist (particularly in the field of engineering). But she involved in mathematical work which was very theoretical in nature. She soon found herself caught up in mathematical applications. Her designation as a mathematician was sealed through her brilliant and innovative work in wavelet theory.

In 1987, Daubechies made one of the biggest breakthroughs in wave analysis in the past two hundred years. Prior to the development of Daubechies' theorem, signal processing was accomplished by using French mathematician Jean–Baptiste Fourier's series of trigonometric functions, breaking down the signal into combinations of sine waves. Sine waves can measure the amplitude and frequency of a signal, but they can't measure both at the same time. Daubechies changed all that when she discovered a way to break signals down into wavelets instead of breaking them down into their components; a task thought by most mathematicians to be impossible.

This discovery has changed the image–processing techniques used by the Federal Bureau of Investigation for transmitting and retrieving the information contained in their massive database of fingerprints. With more than 200 million fingerprints on file, the technique also allows for data compression without loss of information, and eliminates extraneous data that slows or clutters the procedure. Of more significance to Daubechies is the application of her discovery to the field of biomedicine. She likens a wavelets transform to "a musical score which tells the musician which note to play at what time," and this is of particular importance to medical science. Through the analysis of signals used in electrocardiograms, electroencephalograms, and other processes used in medical imaging, the medical world hopes to employ Daubechies' development to detect disease and abnormalities in patients much sooner than is presently possible. The development and implementation of wavelet imagery in medicine would improve the ability of an ECG from a simple recording of a heartbeat to a digitized record of complete heart function.

Other applications for wavelets still in the research stage include video and speech compression, sound enhancement, statistical analysis, and partial differential equations involving shock waves and turbulence, to name only a few.

Leaving a Legacy in Her Own Time

Daubechies' work has not gone unnoticed by her peers. She has been a fellow of the John D. and Catherine T. MacArthur Foundation from 1992 to 1997 and an elected member of the American Academy of Arts and Sciences since 1993. She was the recipient of the American Mathematical Steele Prize for Exposition for her "Ten Lectures on Wavelets" in 1994, and received the Ruth Lyttle Satter Prize in 1997. Daubechies is also a member of the American Mathematical Society, the Mathematical Association of America, the Society for Industrial and Applied Mathematics, and the Institute of Electrical and Electronics Engineers.

Daubechies has written more than 70 articles and papers during her career, more than 20 of them dealing with the nature, application, and interdisciplinary use of wavelets. She has held memberships in more than 17 professional organizations and committees, including her current memberships with the United States National Committee on Mathematics and the European Mathematical Society's Commission on the Applications of Mathematics. Daubechies has been a guest editor or member of the editorial board for ten professional journals and has served as editor–in–chief for the publication *Applied and Computation Harmonic Analysis.*

Daubechies married A. Robert Calderbank, a mathematician, in 1987 and has two children.

SELECTED WRITINGS BY DAUBECHIES:

"Ten Lectures on Wavelets." CBMS–NSF Lecture Notes nr. 61, *SIAM*, 1992.
(With S. Maes) "A Nonlinear Squeezing of the Continuous Wavelet Transform Based on Auditory Nerve Models," in *Wavelets in Medicine and Biology*, edited by A. Aldroubi and M. Unser, 1996.

"Where Do Wavelets Come From? A Personal Point of View," in *Proceedings of the IEEE Special Issue on Wavelets* 84, no. 4 (April 1996): 510–13.

FURTHER READING:

Periodicals

Von Baeyer, Hans Christian. "Wave of the Future." *Discover* (May 1995): 69–74.
What's Happening in the Mathematical Sciences 2 (1994): 23.

Other

Daubechies, Ingrid with Kelley Reynolds Jacquez conducted May 16, 1997.

—Sketch by Kelley Reynolds Jacquez

Norman R. Davidson
1916–
American organic chemist

One of the hallmarks of Norman R. Davidson's career has been the tendency to find new and interesting projects in areas relatively unrelated to those in which he has previously worked. Davidson received his doctoral degree shortly before the beginning of World War II and, thus, some of his earliest research was related to military programs. After returning to an academic career at the end of the war, he began a series of studies on the kinetics of ultrafast reactions. In order to study these reactions, Davidson found it necessary to develop new techniques and instruments that could detect the presence of various chemical species over time periods of less than 10^{-5} second.

By the 1960s, Davidson had found a new topic of interest, the structure and function of deoxyribonucleic acid (DNA). Again, Davidson developed methods of studying this important molecule that had previously been unavailable to chemists. Many of those techniques remain in wide use today. In recent years, Davidson has turned to yet another field of study, the structure and organization of genes. In addition to his active research career, Davidson has been active in a variety of professional organizations and, in his eighth decade, remains Executive Officer of the Division of Biology at the California Institute of Technology.

Norman Ralph Davidson was born on April 5, 1916, in Chicago, Illinois. He attended the University of Chicago, from which he earned his B.S. degree in 1937 and his Ph.D. in chemistry in 1941. He also studied at Oxford University, which awarded him a B.Sc. degree in 1939. Davidson also holds an honorary degree, a Doctor of Science degree from the University of Chicago, awarded in 1992.

Ultrafast Reactions and War Research

Davidson's first major line of research focused on ultrafast reactions. In chemistry, it is often not difficult to write chemical equations that summarize the overall changes that take place during a reaction. However, the reaction itself generally tends to be much more complex, with a number of stages occurring between initial contact of products and final formation of products. The problem in studying these reaction stages is that they often occur very rapidly, often in much less than a thousandth of a second.

Davidson developed a variety of techniques for discovering what happens during these rapid reactions. One such technique is known as flash photolysis. In flash photolysis, reactants are exposed to very brief, high intensity pulses of radiant energy. This energy excites reactants in the mixture, and they give off characteristic spectral patterns that provide clues to their identity.

Davidson's work in this field was interrupted in 1942 by World War II. He joined the Manhattan Project and was assigned to research on the production of transuranium elements at the Division of War Research at Columbia University and, later, at the University of Chicago. He was also appointed Instructor of Chemistry at the Illinois Institute of Technology in 1942.

Joins Faculty at California Institute of Technology

At the war's conclusion, Davidson began working at the Radio Corporation of America (RCA), where he became interested in the development of an early electron microscope. After only a year at RCA, he accepted an offer to work at the California Institute of Technology (Caltech) as Instructor of Chemistry. Davidson has remained at Caltech ever since, eventually becoming full professor and then Norman W. Chandler Professor of Chemistry and Biology. In 1986, he was made Emeritus Professor in the Chandler chair. Since 1990, Davidson has also served as Executive Officer of the Division of Biology at Caltech and Senior Science Consultant at the Amgen Corporation, a pioneer in the industrial applications of genetic engineering technology.

Research on DNA and Genes

One of Davidson's earliest lines of research at Caltech involved studies of the DNA molecule. He claims that this research was motivated by the realization that DNA was not "just another polymer, but that it was an informational molecule." His research was part of a widespread attempt on the part of molecular biologists to find out how genetic information is stored and transmitted in chemical molecules such as DNA and ribonucleic acid (RNA).

Among the critical breakthroughs made by Davidson was the process of DNA renaturation. Most beginning chemistry students are familiar with the process of protein denaturation, in which heat, exposure to chemicals, or other factors cause a protein molecule to lose its three-dimensional shape. A similar process occurs with DNA. Davidson discovered that DNA molecules once denatured, will renature spontaneously, that is, they will recover their original shape. The process by which renaturation occurs is a somewhat complex one whose elements Davidson was eventually able to decipher. An understanding of DNA renaturation has important applications in a number of fields, such as determining base sequences in a DNA molecule, comparing DNA from various organisms, and identifying RNA from particular species.

Davidson next turned to an analysis of the chemical composition of genes. He decoded the gene structure for ribosomal RNA, as well as transfer RNA genes for *E. coli* plasmid F14 and for *B. subtilis*, as well as for a number of other cells. The motivation for this research, he said, is to discover what chemical mechanisms are involved in the expression of various genes at various stages of development.

In recent years, Davidson and his colleagues have turned to the study of the chemical structure of molecules involved in nerve transmission. One series of studies, for example, is designed to find out how changes in the chemical structure of molecules affects the ability of the potassium ion to flow through channels in neural membranes.

Davidson has been awarded the **Peter R. Debye** Award in Physical Chemistry in 1971, the Dickson Prize for Science in 1985, the Robert A. Welch Award in Chemistry in 1989, and the National Medal of Science in 1997. He was elected to the National Academy of Sciences in 1960 and to the American Academy of Arts and Sciences in 1984.

SELECTED WRITINGS BY DAVIDSON:

Books

Statistical Mechanics, 1962.

Periodicals

(With N. Dascal, W. Schreibmayer, N. F. Lim, W. Wang, C. Chavkin, L. DiMagno, C. Labarca, B. L. Kieffer, C. Gaveriaux-Ruff, D. Trollinger, and H. A. Lester) "Atrial G Protein-Activated K+ Channel: Expression Cloning and Molecular Properties." *Proceedings of the National Academy of Science* 90, (1993): 10235-10239.

(With S. Mager, C. Min, D. J. Henry, C. Chavkin, B. J. Hoffman, and H. A. Lester) "Conducting States of a Mammalian Serotonin Transporter." *Neuron* 12, (1994): 1-20.

(With H. Hsu, E. Huant, X.-C. Yang, A. Karschin, C. Labarca, A. Figl, B. Ho, and H. A. Lester) "Slow and Incomplete Inactivation of Voltage-Gated Channels Dominate Encoding in Synthetic Neurons." *Biophysical Journal* 65, (1993): 1196-1206.

FURTHER READING:

Other

"Henry Lester & Norman Davidson." http://www.caltech.edu/.biology/brochure/faculty/lesdav.html.

—*Sketch by David E. Newton*

Elaine Diacumakos
1930–1984
American biologist

A cell biologist, Elaine Diacumakos worked in obscurity most of her career. She developed the first technique for safely inserting into and removing material from cells, using a tiny glass needle. In addition to developing the method, Diacumakos made the actual tubes through which this process worked. In the mid-1970s, medical doctor and genetics researcher French Anderson heard about Diacumakos's work, and working together, they adapted her cell insertion method for gene therapy. This resulted in one of the early breakthroughs in the development of gene therapy.

Diacumakos was born on August 11, 1930, in Chester, Pennsylvania, to Gregoris G. and Olga (nee Dezes) Diacumakos. She had one brother, Basil. Diacumakos earned her undergraduate degree in zoology at the University of Maryland (at College Park) in 1951, and did her graduate work at New York University, earning her M. S. in cell physiology and embryology in 1955, and her Ph.D. in 1958. Two other significant events happened in Diacumakos's life in 1958: she received the Founders Day Award by

New York University, and she married James Chimondies in November.

While completing her graduate work, Diacumakos began working as a research associate at New York University, holding this position until 1964. After earning her Ph.D., Diacumakos held a two-year long fellowship at Rockefeller University. From 1962 until 1964, she worked in the areas of biochemistry and genetics under **Edward Tatum**, a prominent geneticist and a Nobel Prize winning scientist.

It was while working at New York University that Diacumakos also became associated with the Sloan-Kettering Division of the Graduate School of Medical Studies at Cornell University in New York City. She worked as a Research Associate there from 1959 until 1963, when she was promoted to Instructor, a post she held until 1971. Diacumakos was also associated with the related entity, the Sloan-Kettering Institute for Cancer Research, in similar positions, from 1958 until 1971.

In 1971, Diacumakos returned to Rockefeller University, becoming a senior research associate in biochemistry and genetics. She held this position until 1975; in 1976 she became head of the Laboratory of Cytobiology. When Diacumakos began working at Rockefeller, she again worked with Tatum. His unexpected death in 1975 led to her promotion in the Cytobiology Laboratory. However, Tatum was able to get more funding than she was, and the work did not progress as well.

Diacumakos began developing her cell insertion techniques and instruments while working with Tatum. The pair was interested in discovering if a cell's organelles contained any inheritable genetic material. She continued to refine her technique and her needles over the years. Diacumakos made the instruments by her own hand with glass bent by the heat of a Bunsen burner. The results were glass needles that were thinner than a strand of human hair.

After **French Anderson**, a geneticist and medical doctor, heard of Diacumakos's accomplishment, they worked in concert for several years. Anderson says of her in Larry Thompson's book, *Correcting the Code*, "She was a nice little lady, a pure scientist. All she did is sit in front of a microscope all day, and play with chromosomes and things. No one took her seriously . . . She went in and micro injected a microdrop of silicone [oil] right into the nucleus. It absolutely amazed me. She was doing it, but nobody knew or cared." With her method, in 1979, they were able to repair a mouse's genetic defect by placing a functioning gene into a deficient cell. Eleven years later, the first successful gene therapy was done on a human being.

This was not Diacumakos's only scientific accomplishment. In collaboration with other scientists at Memorial Sloan-Kettering Center, she studied cancer cells. She also did work in the area of cells and their resistance to drugs. Before her death, Diacumakos's research focused on cloning plants via their cells.

Less than a week before her death, Diacumakos and her research contributions were recognized by the Metropolitan Chapter of the Association for Women in Science, one of many professional organizations with which she was affiliated. (Others included the American Genetic Society, the American Society for Cell Biology, and Cell Cycle Society.) Diacumakos died on June 11, 1984, of a heart attack in her Manhattan home.

SELECTED WRITINGS BY DIACUMAKOS:

Periodicals

(With French Anderson) "Genetic Engineering in Mammalian Cells." *Scientific American* (July 1981): 106.

FURTHER READING:

Books

Thompson, Larry. *Correcting the Code: Inventing the Genetic Cure for the Human Body.* New York: Simon & Schuster, 1994.

Periodicals

Thompson, Larry. "French Anderson's Genetic Destiny." *The Washington Post Magazine* (January 20, 1991): W23.
Waggoner, Walter. "Elaine Diacumakos, Held a Leading Role in Cell Microsurgery." *The New York Times* (June 15, 1984): D19.

—*Sketch by Annette Petrusso*

Gladys (Henry) Dick
1881–1963
American medical researcher and physician

Before 1922, not much was known about the then-endemic disease of scarlet fever, which primarily affected children in Europe and North America, killing about 25% of the children who contracted it. Additionally, scarlet fever had many complications, some of which were severe and could be crippling. Gladys Dick, with her husband, George Dick, successfully isolated the bacteria which caused scarlet fever, developed a test for human vulnerability to the

disease, and devised preventive methods. The couple patented their findings, specifically the way their scarlet fever toxin and antitoxin were prepared, although this decision was controversial at the time.

Dick was born Gladys Rowena Henry in December 18, 1881, in Pawnee City, Nebraska, to William Chester Henry, a grain dealer and banker who also raised carriage horses, and Azelia Henrietta (Edson) Henry. She had one older brother and one older sister. Dick was raised in Lincoln, Nebraska, where her family moved when she was an infant. She graduated in 1900 from the University of Nebraska, earning a Bachelor of Science degree. Dick wanted to study medicine, but could not persuade her mother to agree to such a radical notion. In the interim, Dick taught biology at a high school in Carney, Nebraska, and took some graduate courses at her alma mater.

When Dick's mother finally granted permission, Dick enrolled at the Johns Hopkins University School of Medicine, and graduated in 1907. She practiced medicine for several years at Johns Hopkins, first as an intern, and later as a staff physician. She then traveled to Berlin to do a year of postgraduate work, which was completed in 1910. While in medical school, Dick became interested in biomedical research. Blood chemistry and experimental cardiac surgery were her first experiences in research, and her studies in Berlin reinforced this interest.

Teamed with George Dick

After returning from Berlin, Dick moved to Chicago in 1911, where her mother then lived. She began working at the University of Chicago on the pathochemistry of kidneys and scarlet fever etiology. Dick was teamed with George F. Dick, her future husband, in the etiological research. They married on January 28, 1914. After returning from their honeymoon, Dick went into private practice and was employed as Evanston Hospital's pathologist, while her husband went to work at the University of Chicago-affiliated John R. McCormick Institute for Infectious Diseases. Dick began working at the Institute a short time later.

Most of Dick's research on scarlet fever (always in conjunction with her husband) was accomplished at McCormick. In 1923, the Dicks published papers in which they proved that scarlet fever was caused by hemolytic streptococcus. Within a few years, the Dicks also published papers on how to prevent, test, diagnose, and treat scarlet fever. Their ground-breaking work insured that the disease was finally understood and brought under control.

Dick and her husband announced the development of what came to be known as the Dick test in 1924. This skin test showed whether the patient was susceptible or immune to scarlet fever. The test involved injecting a toxin-containing substance in the arm and determining if the skin around the area became inflamed. If it did, the patient was vulnerable to scarlet fever. This test was also useful in predicting if pregnant women would develop puerperal infection during childbirth.

The essence of the Dicks' discovery—the toxin and antitoxin—became controversial because the couple took a patent out on their preparation and manufacture methods. They patented these processes in the United States in 1924 and in Great Britain two years later. The controversy revolved around accusations of commercial opportunism; the health organization of the League of Nations argued as late as 1935 that the patent forced unnecessary restrictions on research and prevented biological standardization. Another aspect of contention was the issue of whether the discovery was original and/or an invention. The Dicks defended their actions, asserting that they did so to ensure that quality standards would be met and not for financial gain. In fact, Dick did bring suit against a manufacturer, Lederle Laboratories, in the late 1920s for negligent production procedures and patent infringement. After a long court battle, she won the lawsuit.

Nominated for Nobel Prize

With her husband, Dick was nominated for the 1925 Nobel Prize in Medicine for her work on scarlet fever, but no prize was awarded that year. The couple did receive the University of Edinburgh's 1933 Cameron Prize and the University of Toronto's 1926 Mickel Prize for their success. Their work remained important for the next 20 years until the discovery of antibiotics during World War II. The new treatments became the preferred standard, and the Dicks' work became outdated.

Scarlet fever research was not Dick's sole accomplishment, however. She began investigating polio, and worked as a bacteriologist for the United States Public Health Service during World War I. Dick also maintained a lifelong interest in children and their welfare. She founded what is arguably the first professional adoption organization in the United States, the Cradle Society, headquartered in Evanston, Illinois. She worked with the Cradle Society from 1918 until 1953. Dick took this issue quite personally, and in 1930, she and her husband adopted two children, Roger Henry Dick and Rowena Henry Dick.

In addition to the honors with her husband, Dick received numerous accolades during her lifetime. Honorary degrees were conferred on her by the University of Nebraska (1925) and Northwestern (1928). Dick retired in 1953, and the couple moved to Palo Alto, California. During the last years of her life, Dick suffered from cerebral arteriosclerosis, which

had severely limited her activities. She died of a stroke on August 21, 1963, in Menlo Park, California.

SELECTED WRITINGS BY DICK:

Books

(With George Dick) *Scarlet Fever*. 1938.

Periodicals

(With George Dick) "Scarlet Fever." *Edinburgh Medical Journal* (1934): 1-13.

FURTHER READING:

Books

Bailey, Martha J. "Gladys Rowena Henry Dick." *American Women in Science: A Biographical Dictionary*. Denver: ABC-CLIO, 1994, p. 86.
Rubin, Lewis P. "Gladys Rowena Henry Dick." In *Notable American Women, 1607-1950: A Biographical Dictionary*. Edited by Edward T. James. Cambridge, MA: The Belknap Press of Harvard University Press, 1971, pp. 191-2.
Siegel, Patricia Joan and Kay Thomas Finley. "Gladys Rowena Henry Dick." *Women in the Scientific Search: An American Bio-bibliography, 1724-1979*. Metuchen: The Scarecrow Press, Inc., 1985, pp. 246-48.

Periodicals

"Deaths. Dick, Gladys Rowena Henry." *Journal of the American Medical Association* (December 28, 1963): 120.
"Gladys Dick, Scarlet Fever Expert, Dies." *Chicago Tribune* (August 23, 1963): 2A.

—Sketch by Annette Petrusso

Robert Henry Dicke
1916–1997
American physicist

Robert H. Dicke was one of those rare physicists whose contributions to fundamental theories, exact laboratory work, and new devices are similarly important. His radar improvements during World War II, extremely accurate measurements of physical constants, and anticipation of both the theory and practice of the laser would each by itself have made a successful career for any physicist. Dicke is best

Robert Henry Dicke

known for his alternative to **Albert Einstein**'s theory of gravity, even though more recent experiments confirm Einstein to a high degree of precision. Dicke also is often mentioned among "scientists who should have won the Nobel Prize (but didn't)" for his prediction of and work toward observation of the cosmic background radiation. When Dicke died noted astrophysicist John B. Bahcall of the Institute for Advanced Study at Princeton said of him, "The most difficult problem for the Nobel committee would have been deciding which of his many achievements most warranted a prize."

Robert H. Dicke (rhymes with "sticky") was born May 16, 1916, in St. Louis, Missouri. Dicke's parents, Oscar H. Dicke and Flora Peterson Dicke, moved several times when Dicke was young, however, and Dicke grew up in Rochester, New York. Dicke's father was an electrical engineer working in power-generating stations. When his work took him to Washington, D.C., Dicke's father studied patent law, leading to a job as a patent attorney for the General Signal Company in Rochester.

Dicke got his A.B. degree in 1939 from Princeton University, after starting college at the University of Rochester in New York. Although he had intended to be an electrical engineer like his father, his interest and success in the physics courses he had taken as electives at Rochester provided him with a scholarship to Princeton and also determined his future career direction. After Princeton, Dicke returned to

Rochester, where he obtained a Ph.D. in nuclear physics in 1941. He was quickly employed by the Radiation Laboratory at Massachusetts Institute of Technology, a federal enterprise just started in response to the expected war with Germany.

Professional Life

The Radiation Laboratory, like the much better known Manhattan Project that developed the atom bomb, was a well-kept secret during World War II. After the war, American attention was focused on the developers of the bomb, and little thought was paid to the less dramatic Radiation Laboratory. It is easy to think that all working U.S. physicists were building the bomb during the war, but in actuality the Radiation Laboratory employed about one in five of U.S. physicists. Accomplishments of the Radiation Laboratory that directly influenced the course of the war included the design of America's advanced radar systems, used both for locating enemy targets and navigation of U.S. aircraft, and LORAN, the ship navigation system. Because of the contributions of radar to both the war in the air and at sea, it has been said that the Radiation Laboratory won the war, while the Manhattan Project ended it.

Dicke was part of Group 41 at the Radiation Laboratory, the Fundamental Development Group that specialized in airborne radar. A measure of Dicke's success in this work is the remarkable number of patents that he acquired during this period, nearly 2% of all the patents obtained by the entire staff of the Radiation Laboratory. Dicke's patents were mostly for components of microwave generators or detectors; his most notable invention was a radiometer for detecting very faint microwaves that to this day is the basis of detectors used in astronomy. Dicke's co-workers at the Radiation Laboratory included three future winners of the Nobel Prize in Physics (**I. I. Rabi** in 1944, **Julian Schwinger** in 1965, and **Luis Alvarez** in 1968), while several others also became famous scientists or educators.

Photos of Dicke at the Radiation Laboratory show a handsome, tall, broad-shouldered, wavy-haired young man in a striped suit, which he wore even when he was on the roof installing a test version of his microwave radiometer. While at the Radiation Laboratory, the soft-spoken Dicke married Annie Henderson Currie on June 6, 1942, whom he had met three years earlier in Rochester. Together they had three children, a girl and two boys.

As soon as World War II ended, the Radiation Laboratory staff was given notice. Aside from a few caretaker "fragments," all jobs were to be terminated by December 31, 1945. Dicke went to Princeton, his undergraduate alma mater, in 1946 and stayed for the remainder of his life. His research there soon progressed through the fundamental mechanisms by which atoms generate electromagnetic radiation and into ways to control the radiation more closely. In the process, he and his students found new experiments to measure fundamental constants of physics with greater precision than ever before. In the 1950s Dicke developed many of the ideas and techniques that were to lead to working lasers in the 1960s, although his group did not build any of the first lasers. His work in controlling exactly the emission of electromagnetic radiation produced by vibrating atoms also led to practical atomic clocks. In 1957 he was appointed full professor.

Begins His Studies of Gravity

Dicke and coworkers at Princeton in 1964 confirmed the basis of dynamics and gravitational theory with one of the most exact measurements ever made. As early as 1586 Simon Stevinius had measured the rate at which objects of different mass fall and observed that the rate was independent of density. Galileo a few decades later reached the same conclusion. Newton's theory of gravity uses the idea that gravitational force is equal to inertial force, but takes it as an observation. Albert Einstein recognized that the observed equality of gravity and inertia had larger implications, which led him to develop the theory of general relativity. In Einstein's theory, objects of different masses are required to fall at exactly the same rate. Dicke's group measured the rate at which aluminum and gold masses fall to one part in 100,000,000 and found the rates to be equal, confirming the theory of general relativity.

Ironically, Dicke at about the same time as his confirmation of Einstein's theory (starting in 1961, in collaboration with **Carl E. Brans**), developed a complex mathematical alternative to general relativity. Dicke searched for experimental verification that his theory was a more accurate description of nature than Einstein's. One of the great successes of Einstein's theory was that calculations based on general relativity describe the observed regular changes in the orbit of Mercury, changes that cannot be explained by Newtonian gravitation. Dicke's theory produced a somewhat different amount of change, but Dicke thought that his version would be more accurate than Einstein's if the shape of the Sun were taken into account. Dicke and coworkers made careful measurements of how far the Sun deviates from being a perfect sphere. They announced in 1966 that taking the Sun's shape into consideration makes Einstein's prediction off by 8% of Mercury's behavior, but that Dicke's own theory accurately explains variations in Mercury's orbit.

Dicke's gravitational theory has not withstood further studies of its implications, however. The best-known prediction of Dicke's theory is that the gravitational force is slowly changing, but various careful

measurements do not confirm such a change. Other predictions of Dicke's theory on the evolution of the solar system also do not accord with experience. Eventually further measurements of the shape of the Sun and changes in Mercury's orbit showed better agreement with Einstein than with Dicke. Although this theory may have failed, science writer Walter Sullivan has noted that "Dicke remained a major gravity theorist throughout his life."

The story of Dicke's near brush with the Nobel Prize in Physics is complex. It begins in 1946 when Russian-American physicist **George Gamow** tried to explain the present abundance of elements as a result of the origin of the universe in what amounted to a nuclear explosion. Gamow's colleagues did the complex calculations that showed that such a "big bang" would also produce energy that would fill the entire universe, although this part of the theory was little noticed at the time. Various other theorists then tried to use the observed distribution of elements to confirm or deny the big bang hypothesis or its rivals. By 1965, after nearly 20 years of calculations, the answer was not clear, so Dicke decided to try a different tack entirely. Dicke independently recognized that there should be radiation left by any big bang. He was, after all, the inventor of the common form of radiometer, used to measure radiation from the sky, so he initiated construction of a sensitive radiometer at Princeton to determine if the background radiation predicted by the big bang theory was present or not. While the radiometer was being built, Dicke and astronomer **Jim Peebles** calculated the wavelength of radiation that should be expected if the big bang theory was correct.

Meanwhile **Arno Penzias** and **Robert Wilson** of Bell Laboratories, a few miles north of Princeton, were engaged in trying to eliminate all static in an antenna designed to receive signals from the first communications satellites. After a year of trying to eliminate all noise in their sensitive antenna by cleaning it of bird droppings and checking other possible internal sources of static, they found that the residue of noise was a signal from space that seemed exactly the same in all directions. When Penzias and Wilson called Princeton for advice, they were sent to Dicke, who told them of his project. The two groups agreed on joint publication in the July 1, 1965, *Astrophysical Journal*—a long explanatory letter from Dicke and Peebles followed by a shorter report of observations by Penzias and Wilson. Cosmologists everywhere instantly recognized that the two articles showed that the search for a confirmed theory of the origin of the universe was essentially over. The combination of the theoretical calculations of Dicke and Peebles with the observational evidence from Penzias and Wilson established the big bang theory. Subsequent evidence from different sources has only confirmed the theory or details of it.

From 1975 until his death on March 4, 1997, from Parkinson's disease, Dicke was the Albert Einstein Professor of Science at Princeton (emeritus since 1984). His work has been honored with many awards, including the Rumford Medal (1967), the U.S. National Medal of Science (1971), the NASA Medal for Exceptional Achievement and the Comstock Prize (both 1973), the Cresson Medal of the Franklin Institute (1974), the Michelson Morley Award (1987), and the Beatrice M. Tinsley Prize (1992). Princeton awards the Robert H. Dicke Postdoctoral Fellowships in his honor.

SELECTED WRITINGS BY DICKE:

Books

(with J. P. Wittke) *An Introduction to Quantum Mechanics.* 1960.
The Theoretical Significance of Experimental Relativity. Gordon & Breach Science, 1965.
Gravitation and the Universe. Philadelphia: American Philosophical Society, 1970.

FURTHER READING:

Books

Layzer, David. *Constructing the Universe.* New York: Scientific American Library, 1984.

—*Sketch by Bryan Bunch*

Irene Diggs
1906–

American anthropologist

Irene Diggs focused her anthropological work on the comparative ethnohistorical sociology of the descendants of Africans in the Americas. Her scholarship was influenced by her work with W. E. B. DuBois, a black scholar, educator, and leader. She later wrote about him and his work with original insight because of this experience. In addition to much international research and travel, Diggs was also one of the founders of *Phylon: A Journal of Race and Culture.*

She was born Ellen Irene Diggs on April 13, 1906, in Monmouth, Illinois, to Charles Henry and Alice Diggs. She was an intelligent and imaginative child who read extensively and dreamed of travelling all over the world. Her working-class parents encouraged and supported her scholarly and worldly ambi-

tions. After spending a year at Monmouth College on scholarship, from 1923-24, she transferred to the University of Minnesota. While at Minnesota, Diggs experienced overt racism for the first time. This experience showed Diggs that there was a need for black role models, which in turn influenced her to pursue her education further. She earned her B.A. from Minnesota in 1928.

Diggs began graduate work at Atlanta University in 1932 and also started what would become a fruitful association with W. E. B. DuBois. It was a mutually beneficial relationship. Diggs assisted DuBois in the research and publication of some of his most important writings, including *The Dusk of Dawn,* and DuBois gave Diggs freedom and support in her own developing scholarship. Also while at Atlanta, Diggs co-founded *Phylon,* a scholarly journal published by Atlanta University, which published articles on race and culture.

In the early 1940s Diggs began to fulfill her dreams of traveling. A vacation to Cuba inspired her to return there to study. She received a Roosevelt Fellowship from the Institute for International Education at the University of Havana. There she worked with Fernando Ortiz, an ethnographer with an international reputation, and learned fieldwork skills collecting information on local cultures. In 1945 she earned her Ph.D. in anthropology from the University of Havana. After graduation and the end of World War II, she spent several years traveling throughout Central and South America; researching and writing popular travel articles. Diggs spent part of 1946 in Montevideo, Uruguay, as an exchange scholar. She continued to travel and research in South America, Europe, and the Middle East. The newspaper articles she wrote about these travels were syndicated by the Associated Negro Press.

Diggs became a professor of sociology and anthropology at Morgan State University in Baltimore, Maryland, in 1947. While maintaining a heavy and varied teaching load, Diggs travelled throughout the world, both to engage in research and write travel literature. Because of her experiences in Havana, she also has contributed significant work on blacks in Central and South America, as well as the Caribbean. In the 1950s, she published a series of articles on the Brazilian phenomenon of *quilombos,* communities formed by runaway slaves. Diggs's most important publication is the book *Black Chronology,* which, as the subtitle proclaims, outlines the contributions of black people to the world from 4000 B.C. to the abolition of slavery.

Diggs was associated with a number of professional anthropological associations, including the American Anthropological Association and the American Association for the Advancement of Science. Though she retired from Morgan State in 1976, she continued to conduct research and held an emeritus professorship at the University of Maryland. In 1978, she was honored by the Association of Black Anthropologists for her many years of service as a scholar as well as mentor to black students.

SELECTED WRITINGS BY DIGGS:

Books

Black Chronology from 4000 B.C. to the Abolition of the Slave Trade. G.K. Hall & Company, 1983.

Periodicals

"Argentine Diptych: Meliton and Schimu." *Crisis* (June-July 1953).
"DuBois and Marcus Garvey." *A Current Bibliography on African Affairs* (Spring 1973).

FURTHER READING:

Books

Deegan, Mary Jo, ed. "(Ellen) Irene Diggs (1906-)." *Women in Sociology: A Bio-bibliographic Source Book.* New York: Greenwood Press, 1991, pp. 124-30.

—*Sketch by Annette Petrusso*

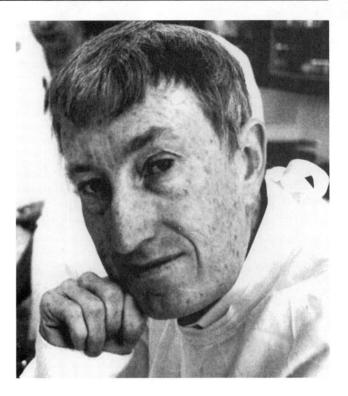

Peter C. Doherty

Peter C. Doherty
1940–
Australian immunologist and virologist

Peter C. Doherty is best known for his contribution to a discovery that transformed biologists' understanding of the immune system. With colleague **Rolf Zinkernagel**, he uncovered the way the body identifies friend and foe. This finding linked immunology, virology, and transplantation medicine in a way that has revolutionized the complex study of the immune system and the practical goal of vaccine development. This work garnered Doherty and Zinkernagel the 1996 Nobel Prize in Physiology or Medicine.

Doherty's lofty achievements have not changed a man who, perhaps in keeping with his Australian heritage, prides himself as remaining straightforward and unassuming. In numerous interviews, he has stressed the importance of non-goal-driven research to the advancement of science, and that he and Zinkernagel had not set out to make a great discovery,

only to satisfy their scientific curiosity. When an interviewer from the Australian Academy of Science pointed out that the Nobel Prize would inevitably bring many scientists and journalists to seek his opinion of scientific matters, he said simply, "I shall have to watch what I say."

Today, as a Nobel laureate, department chairman, and laboratory head at St. Jude's Hospital in Memphis, Tennessee, Doherty reportedly has not changed his lifestyle greatly, pursuing lifelong interests such as mystery stories, art, the theater, and amateur photography along with his research.

"Boys Don't Study Biology"

Born to a piano teacher and a government employee in Brisbane, Australia, on October 15, 1940, both the circumstances of Doherty's early education and his own down-to-earth nature made it seem unlikely he would become famous for theoretical work on the immune system. For one thing, the local government schools he attended did not allow boys to take biology courses. The young Doherty did posess a sharp and enquiring mind—he went to the University of Queensland to earn his bachelor's degree a year early—but shied away from the more academic pursuits. "I didn't want to spend hours analysing poetry," even though the idea appealed to him, he told the same AAS interviewer, " . . . when there were more important issues to think about—like feeding the world."

An open day at the veterinary school at Queensland decided Doherty's future—or so he thought. The prospect of becoming an agricultural veterinarian, and contributing to the fight against world hunger, seemed to the 17-year-old to be a properly useful pursuit. But with further study—he gained his B.V.Sc. from Queensland in 1962, and an M.V.Sc. in 1966—Doherty came to understand the economic complexities of world hunger much better—namely, that a single veterinarian could not make much of a contribution.

So once again, Doherty's career took an unexpected turn. By reading the books of Sir Frank Macfarlane Burnet, a countryman who had won the 1960 Nobel in medicine for his work on immune tolerance, Doherty became interested the immune system. Doherty went to the University of Edinburgh, Scotland, earning a Ph.D. there in 1970 for his studies of viral infection of sheep brains. In 1972 he returned to Australia as a research fellow at The John Curtin School of Medical Research, Australian National University, Canberra–setting the stage for his seminal discovery.

Friend or Foe?

At the Curtin school, space was at a premium. Doherty had his own laboratory for a project studying killer T cells—white blood cells that destroy virus–infected cells in the body by recognizing viral proteins on the cells' surfaces. In the nearby laboratory of Robert Blanden, which was working on a similar project, space was so short that they needed to export a worker. That worker, Rolf Zinkernagel, moved into Doherty's lab; together the two began studying how killer T cells know which cells to attack.

At the time, immunologists were very interested in a group of genes collectively called the major histocompatibility complex, or MHC. These genes, clustered together in the DNA sequence, encode a series of proteins called the MHC antigens, which determine whether a transplanted organ will be accepted or rejected by a recipient. If the MHC genes of the donor and the recipient match, the organ survives; if they do not, the organ is attacked by the recipient's immune system and dies.

A number of researchers had guessed that the rejection of MHC-mismatched organs was essentially the same process as the killing of virus-infected cells by killer T cells. Doherty and Zinkernagel demonstrated that this was true, and that the MHC antigens were necessary for killer T cells to tell friend from foe. When they investigated further, they found something unexpected. Most immunologists had expected that when virus-infected cells and killer cells were poorly MHC matched, the immune cells' killing response would be strongest, much as in badly matched transplants. But the opposite was true. In order to get

proper T-cell killing of the virus-infected cells, Doherty and Zinkernagel discovered, the cells' MHC regions had to match.

The two had discovered that T cells—indeed, the immune response in general—can only recognize viral proteins when they are displayed in the context of properly matched MHC antigens. The immune system, which had evolved to recognize "self" from "other" did not react most strongly to "other," but to a third state, "altered self." This discovery finally put transplant rejection into biological context: the body does not purposely reject mismatched organs because they are different, it rejects them because it mistakenly identifies the mismatched MHC antigens as "self" antigens that have been altered by interaction with viral proteins. The finding also opened the way to better methods for heading off transplant rejection, for creating vaccines, and for further unraveling the workings of immunity; vulnerability to certain infections; and autoimmune disease, where the body mistakenly attacks its own tissues.

A Bully Pulpit

While immunologists recognized that Doherty's and Zinkernagel's 1973-1974 discovery was important, its true significance took time to sink in. The successful collaborators went their separate ways, with Doherty heading for the Wistar Institute in Philadelphia, as an associate professor in 1975. He returned to the Curtin school in 1982 as professor and head of the Department of Experimental Pathology, leaving once again in 1988 to be chairman of the Department of Immunology at St. Jude Children's Research Hospital, Memphis, Tennessee. At St. Jude's, in addition to heading the hospital's immunology research program, he has maintained his own laboratory work on viruses that cause cancer as well as the Epstein-Barr virus, which causes severe infections in the compromized immune systems of AIDS patients.

Along the way, international recognition of Doherty's work grew. In 1983 he was given the Paul Ehrlich Prize in Germany; in 1986, he gained the International Award of the Gairdner Foundation of Canada; and in 1995 he received the Albert Lasker Medical Research Award, often a prelude to a Nobel, which came in 1996.

Doherty regards the notoriety brought by his Nobel with no small amount of caution. He has also capitalized on it, chiefly to sound an alarm that governments may not be spending enough on the type of curiosity-driven, long-term research that proved so fruitful for him and for immunology in general. While he has said that applied research, with its relatively short deadlines and well-defined goals, is crucial, he also believes governments and foundations need to strike a balance, because basic research produces the pieces of the puzzle that applied research puts together.

Doherty says that he plans to remain an active researcher for at least another 10 years or so. While he admits that another big breakthrough would be nice, he characteristically points out that basic research breakthroughs are partly a matter of luck and few researchers have been lucky enough to produce two advances of the magnitude of his Nobel-winning discovery. Despite this humility—or perhaps because of it—his fellow countrymen have been proud to call him theirs, giving him the Australian of the Year Award in 1997.

After retirement, Doherty has said that he would like to try his hand at writing—first a book on his big discovery, and then perhaps one on viral immunology. He would also like to write fiction, toying with the idea of a novel about scientists. He has been married to his wife, Penny, for 32 years. They have two adult sons, attorney Jim and physician Michael.

Harry G. Drickamer

SELECTED WRITINGS BY DOHERTY:

Periodicals

"Cell-Mediated Cytotoxicity." *Cell* (November 19, 1993): 607-612.
(With R.A. Tripp and J.W. Sixbey) "Evasion of Host Immune Responses by Tumours and Viruses." *Ciba Foundation Symposium* (1994): 245-246; discussion 256-260.
(With R.M. Zinkernagel) "Immunological Surveillance Against Altered Self Components by Sensitized T Lymphocytes in Lymphocytic Choriomeningitis." *Nature* (October 11, 1974): 547-548.
(With R.M. Zinkernagel) "The Discovery of MHC Restriction." *Immunology Today* (January 1997): 14-17.

FURTHER READING:

Periodicals

Benowitz, Steven. "New Nobel Laureates Speak Out for Increased Research Funding." *The Scientist* (November 11, 1996): 1, 4-5.
"Reflections of a New Nobelist." *St. Jude Rounds* (Winter 1996/97): 1.

Other

"David Baron Reports that the Latest Nobel Prize Goes to Rolf Zinkernagel and Peter Doherty." Audio Recording, October 7, 1996. http://www6.realaudio.com/contentp/npr/nc6o07.html (November 25, 1997).

"Doherty Wins Lasker Basic Medical Research Award." http://www.stjude.org/pr/webdoher.html (November 25, 1997).
Sarzin, Anne. "Nobel Prize-Winner Makes Plea for Basic Science." October 14, 1996. http://www.usyd.edu.au/su/exterel/news/961114News/14.11.nobel.html (November 25, 1997).
"The Australian Academy of Science Interviews Australia's Lastest Nobel Laureate, Professor Peter Doherty." November 1996. http://www.science.org.au/educatio/doherty.html (November 25, 1997).
"The Nobel Prize in Medicine 1996." October 7, 1996. http://www.nobel.se/announcement-96/medicine96.html (25 November 25, 1997).
"The Peter Doherty Story." http://www.stjude.org/Pr/pdoherty-story.html (November 25, 1997).

—Sketch by Kenneth Chiacchia

Harry G. Drickamer
1918–

American chemist

Harry George Drickamer is recognized as a world leader in the use of high pressure to investigate the electronic structure of matter. His fundamental discovery was that pressure affects different kinds of electronic orbitals to different degrees. An electronic orbital is the wave function of an electron moving in a molecule or atom, corresponding to the orbit of the electron in earlier theory. The finding of this pressure effect, known as the "pressure tuning" of electronic energy levels, had two main consequences. One, it explained how the electronic transition to a new ground state, the state of least possible energy, can lead to very different and often unanticipated physical and chemical properties in a variety of materials. Two, it provided new ways to test theories about physical and chemical phenomena using pressure as a variable.

Drickamer was born on November 19, 1918, in Cleveland, Ohio. His father, George Henry Drickamer, who died when his son was two years old, had a degree in mechanical engineering. Drickamer's mother, Louise Strempel Drickamer, had only an eighth-grade education, but she taught herself to be a secretary after her husband's death. As Drickamer later recalled in a 1997 letter to author Linda Wasmer Smith, "She had no knowledge or interest in science but was determined that my sister and I would go to college—and we had better get good grades or else."

Drickamer attended the University of Michigan, where he received a bachelor's degree in 1941 and a master's degree in 1942. Up until this point, he had shown little interest for science himself, and he had completed math through calculus plus one year each of physics and chemistry. However, on a bet, Drickamer took the written chemical engineering qualifying exams. A few months later, he learned that he had passed. Meanwhile, he had taken a job at the Pan American Refining Corporation in Texas City, Texas, where he was introduced to more advanced mathematical and science concepts. Drickamer's appetite for science was whetted.

While at Pan American, Drickamer began working toward a doctoral degree from the University of Michigan. He was granted permission to use Pan American's lab equipment on nights and Sundays for his thesis. However, he still needed 22 hours of course work. He completed the necessary courses in a single semester, receiving his Ph.D. degree in 1946. That same year, Drickamer accepted a position as assistant professor of chemical engineering at the University of Illinois. He spent the rest of his career at this institution, rising to the position of professor of chemical engineering, chemistry, and physics. Although Drickamer formally retired in 1989, he continues to play an active role in research at the college as a professor emeritus.

Uses High Pressure to Study Electronic Phenomena

When Drickamer first arrived at the University of Illinois, high pressure was still a very specialized

tool used in relatively few labs. As Drickamer noted in a 1990 paper, published in *Annual Reviews of Materials Science*, "Now [high pressure] is used in hundreds of laboratories around the world for studies in such diverse fields as physics, chemistry, geology, and biochemistry. The central feature in this development has been the realization that pressure (really compression) is a powerful, indeed essential, tool for investigating the molecular and electronic properties of matter."

Drickamer has been a key figure in this burgeoning field. Techniques were developed in his lab to study phenomena such as optical absorption, luminescence, electrical resistance, Mössbauer resonance, and x-ray diffraction under high pressure. Summing up his achievements in his letter to author Linda Wasmer Smith, Drickamer wrote: "(1) We were the first to show that pressure could be used to study atomic, molecular and electronic phenomena—the stuff of modern chemistry and physics . . . (2) We have been fortunate to pick the right techniques and the right systems to study so that one could demonstrate the wide applicability of high pressure . . . (3) We have been diligent enough to study a wide variety of materials by a variety of techniques so that the power and versatility of pressure tuning spectroscopy has become apparent."

Drickamer has received many honors over the years. He is a member of the National Academy of Sciences, the National Academy of Engineering, and the American Philosophical Society, and a fellow of the American Academy of Arts and Sciences. His numerous awards include the Colburn, Alpha Chi Sigma, William H. Walker, and Warren K. Lewis Awards of the American Institute of Chemical Engineers; the Ipatieff Prize and the **Irving Langmuir** and **Peter Debye** Awards of the American Chemical Society; the Chemical Pioneers Award and Gold Medal of the American Institute of Chemists; and the Buckley Solid State Physics Award of the American Physical Society. In 1989, Drickamer received the National Medal of Science. The citation recognized "his discovery of the 'pressure tuning' of electronic energy levels as a way to obtain new and unique information on the electronic structure of solids."

Drickamer married Mae Elizabeth McFillen on October 28, 1942. She later became a family planning nurse practitioner. The couple have five grown children: Lee, a zoologist; Lynn, a library employee; Kurt, a biochemist; Margaret, a physician; and Priscilla, a reference librarian. In his leisure time, Drickamer enjoys walking several miles a day and reading history books and mysteries. However, a quiet retirement is not his style. He maintains an active research program at the University of Illinois, where he is currently involved in studies of nonlinear optical phenomena.

SELECTED WRITINGS BY DRICKAMER:

Books

"High Pressure Luminescence Spectroscopy in Polymers." In *Photochemistry and Photophysics*, volume 1. Edited by J.F. Rabek. New York: CRC Press, 1989, pp. 137-185.

Periodicals

"High Pressure Studies of Molecular Luminescence." *Annual Reviews of Physical Chemistry* 33 (1982): 25-47.

"Forty Years of Pressure Tuning Spectroscopy." *Annual Reviews of Materials Science* 20 (1990): 1-17.

FURTHER READING:

Books

McGraw-Hill Modern Scientists and Engineers, vol. 1. New York: McGraw-Hill, 1980, pp. 308-310.

Who's Who in America, 52nd ed., 1998. New Providence, NJ: Marquis Who's Who, 1997, p. 1136.

Other

National Medal of Science, citation dated 1989.

—*Sketch by Linda Wasmer Smith*

Gerald Durrell
1925–1995
English naturalist and conservationist

Gerald Durrell's lifelong commitment to the care and preservation of animals led to his 1958 creation of a scientific zoo and wildlife trust on the Channel Island of Jersey, aimed at promoting conservation and protecting endangered species through breeding and research. The first of its kind, the zoo is still widely visited today, and Durrell's travels throughout the world to collect and protect endangered species provided the material for a number of his successful books and television documentaries.

Gerald Malcolm Durrell was born January 7, 1925, in Jamshedpur, India. His mother was Louisa Florence Dixie. His father, Lawrence Samuel, was an Anglo-Irish civil engineer working on the construction of India's fledgling system of railroads and bridges.

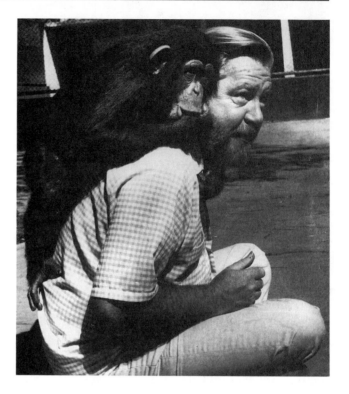

Gerald Durrell

Durrell was the youngest of four children, all individualists in their own right. One older brother, Lawrence, was a celebrated poet and novelist, remembered for *The Alexandria Quartet*. Another brother, Leslie, is a talented painter, while his sister, Margot, is a designer.

When Durrell was two, his father died. The family left India for England in 1928 and, for more than a decade, lived in a variety of cities and towns in England and on the continent. From his earliest days, Durrell enjoyed the company of animals. In fact, the first understandable word he spoke was "zoo." As he wrote in his book, *A Bevy of Beasts*, "I am an exceptionally lucky person, for at the age of two I made up my mind quite firmly and unequivocally that the only thing I wanted to do was study animals. Nothing else interested me."

Durrell's education was anything but typical. He didn't attend a formal school system; rather, he gained his schooling from private tutors in Greece, France, Italy, and Switzerland. The period of his life most impressed upon his memory were the five years he spent on the Greek island of Corfu in the late 1930s. He recounts in a trio of books (*My Family and Other Animals; Birds, Beasts, and Relatives;* and *The Garden of the Gods*) his enjoyable years there, describing his youthful adventures with local flora and fauna, and how his family reacted to his life as a budding naturalist. Fortunately, Durrell had the tutelage of the Greek scientist Theodore Stephanides during his Corfu days.

A Bevy of Beasts

It was not uncommon for the young Durrell to spend twelve hours a day wandering the hills and beaches of Corfu, filling his collection bottles with samples of the local wildlife. He recounted in *My Family and Other Animals* how his brother Larry would recoil in horror upon discovering a scorpion and her infant brood nesting in his match box, or finding snakes coiled in the bathtub. In *A Bevy of Beasts,* Gerald told how "my marmoset had tried to climb in bed with Larry in the early morning and, on being repulsed, had bitten him in the ear." Despite the rather humorous portrait Gerald painted of his brother, it was Larry who exerted a father-like influence over his younger brother. Lawrence Durrell, thirteen years older than Gerald, constantly urged his brother to spend time reading and, later, to write of his animal exploits.

When the tides of World War II reached upon the Greek island, the Durrells returned to England, where for a while, they took up residence in London. Durrell obtained a job in a local pet store and, when not engaged there, made constant visits to the London zoo. In 1945, the twenty-year old Durrell was offered the position of student keeper at Whipsnade, the Zoological Society of London's zoo for the breeding and preservation of animals in the country community of Bedfordshire. Here, he did more than the routine tasks of feeding, grooming and cage-cleaning; he initiated a systematic approach to recording animal behavior, comparing his findings with those expounded in the current literature. Durrell was aware that many of the zoo's species were extremely rare and that much of the world's wildlife faced extinction.

Becomes a Writer to Support His Calling

On his twenty-first birthday, Durrell came into an inheritance of three thousand pounds. He left the zoo and used the money to finance the first of many animal-collecting trips. On his trip to the rain forests of the British Cameroons, he collected over a hundred crates of mammals, reptiles, and birds for zoos throughout England. Between 1947 and 1949, Durrell made two expeditions to the Cameroons and one to British Guiana in search of rare animal species for local zoos. While the zoos profited from his adventures, Durrell was left with wonderful memories and a drained bank account. At a loss for a way to fund additional expeditions, Durrell took his brother Larry's advice and decided to write about his expeditions to pay for future trips. His first book, *The Overloaded Ark,* published in 1953, described his first trip to the Cameroons. It was an immediate success. The following year he published *The Bafut Beagles,* describing his second Cameroon expedition, and *Three Tickets to Adventure,* which covered his adventures in British Guiana. All three books were extremely successful

financially; Durrell had finally found a way to finance his prime interest, the gathering of and caring for animals. In his search throughout England for a place to create his own zoo, he found the local bureaucracy so difficult that he decided to look elsewhere.

In 1958, Durrell established a thirty-five-acre site on Jersey, one of the Channel Islands that lie between England and France, on which he established his own nonprofit zoo. He intended to create a wildlife preserve devoted to animal conservation, scientific research, and specialized training programs. Despite its island location, more than 200,000 people visit his zoo annually. In 1963, Durrell founded the Jersey Wildlife Preservation Trust to operate the zoo, and served as the group's honorary chairman. A decade later, he established an affiliate of his Jersey trust, a worldwide conservation group called the Wildlife Preservation Trust International, which has headquarters in Philadelphia.

Durrell's first marriage to Jacqueline Sonia Rasen in 1951 ended in a divorce in 1979. He married American zoologist Lee Wilson McGeorge the same year, and in the late 1980s, the two went on an animal-gathering expedition to Madagascar that led to a series of television shows for BBC and a book entitled *The Aye-Aye and I.* Durrell was a member of the Royal Geographical Society, the Fauna Preservation Society, the American Zoo-parks Association, and the Zoological Society of London. He held an honorary degree from the University of Durham, and was made an Officer of the Order of the British Empire.

The author of more than a dozen books, including several novels and a half-dozen children's books, Durrell continued to finance his various zoological and conservation activities with income from his writings. He made it clear that he only wrote to finance his true love—working with animals. In an interview for the *Christian Science Monitor,* he stated that "I try to get it over with as quickly as possible. Larry writes for posterity, but I write for money—it provides me with the wherewithal to do the things I really like doing, which is rushing off to Mexico to catch volcano rabbits."

SELECTED WRITINGS BY DURRELL:

Books

My Family and Other Animals. Hart-Davis, 1956.
Birds, Beasts and Relatives. New York: Viking, 1969.
Beasts in My Belfry. Collins, 1973. Published in the U.S. as *A Bevy of Beasts.* New York: Simon & Schuster, 1973.

The Garden of the Gods. Collins, 1978. Published in the U.S. as *Fauna and Family.* New York: Simon and Schuster, 1979.

The Amateur Naturalist: A Practical Guide to the Natural World New York: Knopf, 1983.

The Aye-Aye and I. New York: Arcade, 1993.

FURTHER READING:

Periodicals

Christian Science Monitor (28 November 1979).

Discover (December 1984): 42.

Hilchey, Tim. "Gerald Durrell, 70, Who Prized Animals, Dies" (obituary). *New York Times* (1 February 1995).

Lawson, Trevor. "A Rare Animal." *Geographical Magazine* 67 (April 1995): 37-38.

People (15 March 1982): 119.

Simmons, Nancy. "Zoo Pioneer Dies" (obituary). *Wildlife Conservation* 98 (May-June 1995): 21.

—Sketch by Benedict A. Leerburger

Harry Eagle
1905–1992
American medical scientist

Spanning over six decades, Harry Eagle's career as a medical researcher has been diverse and far reaching, making its mark in such disciplines as immunology, virology, pharmacology, and microbiology. Most notably, he defined the exact elements needed to grow animal cell cultures for experimental purposes. Eagle enhanced his life in research further by successfully forging an academic career as well. He rose through the ranks of such establishments as Johns Hopkins Medical School, University of Pennsylvania Medical School, and the Albert Einstein College of Medicine.

Born in New York, New York, on July 13, 1905, and raised in Baltimore, Maryland, Eagle earned both his bachelors (1923) and medical (1927) degrees from Johns Hopkins University. One year later in 1928, he married Hope Whaley with whom he had one daughter, Kay. Like his career, their marriage lasted 64 years until his death on June 12, 1992, in Port Chester, New York, from cancer. He was 86 years old.

Combats Syphilis While Director of Johns Hopkins' Venereal Disease Research Laboratory

During the 1930s and 1940s, Eagle focused his research on the serology of syphilis. As Director of Johns Hopkins' Venereal Disease Research Laboratory and Laboratory of Experimental Therapeutics, he developed a test for syphilis, which gained popularity in the 1930s. Through his expert analysis of the disease, Eagle, along with three other colleagues, were on the threshold of devising effective therapies to combat the disease in 1938. However the introduction of penicillin in the early 1940s nullified any need for other treatment forms. The foursome dropped their pursuit of clinical trials and moved on to other research. One of the therapies formulated by Eagle and his colleagues was further developed during World War II as a cure for African sleeping sickness. A further outgrowth of that therapy lead to the use of a similar injectable compound to treat arsenic poisoning.

From 1944-55, Eagle studied the differences between the new antibiotics, defining their effective treatment of syphilis as well as penicillin's ability to eradicate gonorrhea in its early stages. During this period, Eagle held positions at the National Institutes of Health (1947-61), the National Cancer Institute (1947-49), and the Experimental Therapeutics Section of the National Microbiological Institute (1949-59).

Defines Conditions Necessary for Cell Growth Cultures

By far, Eagle profoundly effected the future of experimental biology when he devised what is now known as Eagle's growth medium for use in laboratory experimentation. In his studies, Eagle determined the exact concentrations of cellular material necessary for protein synthesis to occur. Before his calculations, researchers did not precisely know what went into a culture, therefore their experimentation was not as controlled as it could have been. Eagle noted that several elements were necessary for growth: 13 amino acids, glucose, eight vitamins, six ionic species, and factors present in serum protein. The ramifications of his work on experimentation and what scientists could cull from the control cultures was unprecedented and has lead to today's breakthrough research in virology, oncology, and genetics.

Eagle's scientific endeavors were applauded by numerous accolades and appointments. He was honored with an Eli Lilly Award in Bacteriology, a Waterford International Biomedical Award, and he received citations from the American association of Medical Colleges and the American Society of Cell Biology. He was an active member of such organizations as the American Association for Cancer Research, the American Society for Pharmacology and Experimental Therapeutics, the Society for Clinical Investigation, the American Society of Biological Chemists, and the American Association of Immunologists. He was also appointed to the American Academy of Arts and Sciences in 1960 and the National Academy of Sciences in 1963.

From 1961 to 1988, Eagle was professor and then chair of the cell biology department at Albert Einstein College in Bronx, New York. Even after his retirement in 1988, Eagle remain engrossed in scientific endeavor until his death in 1992.

FURTHER READING:

Books

McGraw-Hill Modern Scientists and Engineers. McGraw-Hill Inc., 1980.

Periodicals

"Dr. Harry Eagle is Dead at 86; Formulated Cell-Growth Medium." *The New York Times* (June 13, 1992).

—*Sketch by Jacqueline L. Longe*

Alice Eastwood
1859–1953
Canadian-born American botanist

Alice Eastwood's life was her work as a systematic botanist, specializing in flowering plants indigenous to the California coast and Colorado Rocky Mountains. Despite a limited formal education, Eastwood's position as curator of botany at the California Academy of Sciences spanned 50 years and established the Academy's vast botanical collections. Eastwood eagerly collected and classified area plant species. She passionately shared her botanical knowledge through her work with clubs and her journal and book publications. Her many accomplishments did not go unnoticed in her lifetime.

Alice Eastwood was born to Eliza Jane (Gowdey) and Colin Skinner Eastwood, on January 19, 1859, in Toronto, Canada. She was the eldest of three children. Her mother died when Eastwood was six, and she and her siblings were sent to live with relatives while their father struggled financially. For a period of time, Eastwood lived with her uncle, William Eastwood, a doctor, and it was during this period that her interest in flora was piqued. Eastwood was educated at the Oshawa convent near Toronto, where a like-minded priest also encouraged her budding curiosity in plants. At age 14, Eastwood rejoined her father in Denver, Colorado. She graduated valedictorian from the East Denver High School in 1879, despite having to continually work to support her family. Though Eastwood's formal education ended after her high school graduation, she continued to study botany on her own.

Because of her family's financial difficulties, Eastwood was compelled to teach high school in Denver for the next 11 years. While teaching, she continued to collect and identify plant species in the nearby Rocky Mountains. By saving her money, she was able to expand her library of botany texts. Eventually, she became locally recognized for her growing botanical knowledge and collection. Such recognition led to the recommendation that she guide the famous naturalist Alfred Russel Wallace, who was visiting the area, on an expedition of Gray's Peak.

In 1890, after she and her father made a modest profit in Denver real estate, Eastwood was finally able to leave her teaching position and pursue botany full time. She visited San Francisco, California, where she met Katharine Brandegree, the curator of botany at the California Academy of Sciences. Brandegree hired Eastwood to contribute to their botanical magazine, *Zoe*, and work in the Academy's herbarium.

Eastwood returned to Denver briefly, where she finished her self-published book, *A Popular Flora of Denver, Colorado* (1893). In 1892, Brandegree offered Eastwood an assistantship position at the Academy, which she accepted. During this time, Eastwood founded the California Botanical Club, an organization in which she would remain active for many years. Eastwood became the editor of *Zoe* and the curator when Brandegree and her husband left the Academy in 1893. Eastwood continued to improved the Academy's collection through her own collecting and acquisition efforts. Eastwood published *A Handbook of the Trees of California* in 1905.

When an earthquake hit San Francisco on April 18, 1906, Eastwood chose to save as much of the Academy's botanical specimens as she was able, rather than save any personal possessions from the fires that followed. Eastwood later went on to rebuild the collection she had so carefully organized, visiting and sometimes working at other collections and herbariums in the United States and Europe. Between 1912, when the Academy reopened with Eastwood back as curator, and her retirement in 1950, Eastwood collected some 340,000 specimens and built up the Academy's library of botanical literature. The herbarium is now officially known as the Alice Eastwood Herbarium of the California Academy of Sciences.

In 1932, she founded a forum for botanical research called the *Leaflets of Western Botany* with her assistant John Thomas Howell. Eastwood is credited with over 300 published articles on botany. Such a prolific bibliography garnered her an international reputation. Because she lacked a university education, Eastwood refused all honorary degrees offered to her. In 1950, at the age of 91, the Seventh International Botanical Congress in Stockholm, Sweden, asked Eastwood to serve as their honorary president. Robust until the end, Eastwood died of cancer in San Francisco on October 30, 1953. She was 95 years old.

SELECTED WRITINGS BY EASTWOOD:

Books

Eastwood, Alice. *A Popular Flora of Denver, Colorado*. San Francisco: Zoe Publishing Co, 1893.

FURTHER READING:

Books

Bailey, Martha J. "Alice Eastwood." In *American Women in Science: A Biographical Dictionary.* Denver: ABC-CLIO, Inc., 1994, pp. 95-96.

Bonta, Marcia Myers. "Alice Eastwood: Grand Old Botanist of the Academy." In *Women in the Field: America's Pioneering Women Naturalists.* College Station, TX: Texas A & M University Press, 1991, pp. 93-102.

Ewan, Joseph. "Alice Eastwood." In *Notable American Women, The Modern Period: A Biographical Dictionary.* Barbara Sicherman and Carol Hurd Green, eds. Cambridge, MA: The Belknap Press of Harvard University Press, 1980, pp. 216-17.

Ogilvie, Marilyn Bailey. "Alice Eastwood." In *Women in Science: Antiquity through the Nineteenth Century.* Cambridge, MA: MIT Press, 1986, pp. 79-80.

Other

Eastwood, Alice. *Science Magazine* publication of a letter discribing the 1906 San Francisco earthquake. (May 7, 1906). http://www.kqed.org/fromKQED/Cell/Calhist/afterstory.html (October 5, 1997).

—*Sketch by Annette Petrusso*

John C. Eccles

John C. Eccles
1903–1997
Australian neurophysiologist

John Carew Eccles was a neurophysiologist whose research explained how nerve cells communicate with one another. He demonstrated that when a nerve cell is stimulated it releases a chemical that binds to the membrane of neighboring cells and activates them in turn. He further demonstrated that by the same mechanism a nerve cell can also inhibit the electrical activity of nearby nerve cells. For this research, Eccles shared the 1963 Nobel Prize for Physiology or Medicine with **Alan Lloyd Hodgkin** and **Andrew Huxley.**

Born on January 27, 1903, in Melbourne, Australia, Eccles was the son of William James and Mary Carew Eccles. Both of his parents were teachers, and they taught him at home until he entered Melbourne High School in 1915. In 1919, Eccles began medical studies at Melbourne University, where he participat-ed in athletics and graduated in 1925 with the highest academic honors. Eccles's academic excellence was rewarded with a Rhodes Scholarship, which allowed him to pursue a graduate degree in England at Oxford University. In September 1925, Eccles began studies at Magdalen College, Oxford. As he had done at Melbourne, Eccles excelled academically, receiving high honors for science and being named a Christopher Welch Scholar. In 1927, he received appointment as a junior research fellow at Exeter College, Oxford.

Embarks on Neurological Research

Even before leaving Melbourne for Oxford, Eccles had decided that he wanted to study the brain and the nervous system, and he was determined to work on these subjects with **Charles Scott Sherrington.** Sherrington, who would win the Nobel Prize in 1932, was then the world's leading neurophysiologist; his research had virtually founded the field of cellular neurophysiology. The following year, after becoming a junior fellow, Eccles realized his goal and became one of Sherrington's research assistants. Although Sherrington was then nearly seventy years old, Eccles collaborated with him on some of his most important research. Together, they studied the factors responsible for inhibiting a neuron, or a nerve cell. They also explored what they termed the "motor unit"—a nerve cell which coordinates the actions of many muscle fibers. Sherrington and Eccles conducted their research without the benefit of the electronic devices that would later be developed to measure a nerve cell's electrical activity. For this work on neural excitation and inhibition, Eccles was awarded his doctorate in 1929.

Eccles remained at Exeter after receiving his doctorate, serving as a Staines Medical Fellow from 1932 to 1934. During this period, he also held posts at Magdalen College as tutor and demonstrator in physiology. The research that Eccles had begun in Sherrington's laboratory continued, but instead of describing the process of neural inhibition, Eccles became increasingly interested in explaining the process that underlies inhibition. He and other neurophysiologists believed that the transmission of electrical impulses was responsible for neural inhibition. **Bernhard Katz** and Paul Fatt later demonstrated, however, that it was a chemical mechanism and not a wholly electrical phenomenon which was primarily responsible for inhibiting nerve cells.

Returns to Australia

In 1937, Eccles returned to Australia to assume the directorship of the Kanematsu Memorial Institute for Pathology in Sydney. During the late 1930s and early 1940s, the Kanematsu Institute, under his guidance, became an important center for the study of neurophysiology. With Katz, Stephen Kuffler, and others, he undertook research on the activity of nerve and muscle cells in cats and frogs, studying how nerve cells communicate with muscle or motor cells. His team proposed that the binding of a chemical (now known to be the neurotransmitter acetylcholine) by the muscle cell led to a depolarization, or a loss of electrical charge, in the muscle cell. This depolarization, Eccles believed, occurred because charged ions in the muscle cell were released into the exterior of the cell when the chemical substance released by the nerve cell was bound to the muscle cell.

During World War II, Eccles served as a medical consultant to the Australian army, where he studied vision, hearing, and other medical problems faced by pilots. Returning to full-time research and teaching in 1944, Eccles became professor of physiology at the University of Otago in Dunedin, New Zealand. At Otago, Eccles continued the research that had been interrupted by the war, but now he attempted to describe in greater detail the neural transmission event, using very fine electrodes made of glass. This research continued into the early 1950s, and it convinced Eccles that transmission from nerve cell to nerve cell or nerve cell to muscle cell occurred by a chemical mechanism, not an electrical mechanism as he had thought earlier.

In 1952, Eccles left Otago for the Australian National University in Canberra. Here, along with Fatt and J. S. Coombs, he studied the inhibitory process in postsynaptic cells, which are the nerve or muscle cells that are affected by nerve cells. They were able to establish that whether nerve and muscle cells were excited or inhibited was controlled by pores in the membrane of the cells, through which ions could enter or leave. By the late 1950s and early 1960s, Eccles had turned his attention to higher neural processes, pursuing research on neural pathways and the cellular organization of the brain.

Begins a Second Career in the United States

In 1966, Eccles turned sixty-three and university policy at the Australian National University required him to retire. Wanting to continue his research career, he accepted an invitation from the American Medical Association to become the director of its Institute for Biomedical Research in Chicago. He left that institution in 1968 to become professor of physiology and medicine and the Buswell Research Fellow at the State University of New York in Buffalo. The university constructed a laboratory for him where he could continue his research on transmission in nerves. Even at a late stage in his career, Eccles's work suggested important relationships between the excitation and inhibition of nerves and the storing and processing of information by the brain.

In 1975, he retired from SUNY with the title of Professor Emeritus, subsequently moving to Switzerland. During the final period of his career, Eccles focused on a variety of fundamental problems relating to consciousness and identity, conducting research in areas where physiology, psychology, and philosophy intersect. He died at his home in Contra, Switzerland.

Eccles received a considerable number of scientific distinctions. His memberships included the Royal Society of London, the Royal Society of New Zealand, and the American Academy of Arts and Sciences. He was awarded the Gotch Memorial Prize in 1927, and the Rolleston Memorial Prize in 1932. The Royal College of Physicians presented him with their Baly Medal in 1961, the Royal Society gave him their Royal Medal in 1962, and the German Academy awarded him the Cothenius Medal in 1963. Also in 1963, he shared the Nobel Prize for Physiology and Medicine with Alan Hodgkin and Andrew Huxley. He was knighted in 1958.

In 1928, Eccles married Irene Frances Miller of New Zealand. The marriage, which eventually ended in divorce in 1968, produced four sons and five daughters. One of their daughters, Rosamond, earned her doctorate and participated with her father in his research. After his divorce from Irene Eccles, Eccles married the Czech neurophysiologist Helena Taboříková in 1968. Dr. Taboříková also collaborated with Eccles in his scientific research.

SELECTED WRITINGS BY ECCLES:

Books

Reflex Activity of the Spinal Cord. Oxford: Oxford
  University Press, 1938.
The Neurophysiological Basis of Mind. Oxford:
  Clarendon, 1965.
The Cerebellum as a Neuronal Machine. New
  York: Springer-Verlag, 1967.
The Physiology of Nerve Cells. Baltimore: Johns
  Hopkins University Press, 1968.
*The Inhibitory Pathways of the Central Nervous
  System.* Liverpool: Liverpool University Press,
  1969.

FURTHER READING:

Books

Fox, D., and M. Meldrum, eds. *Nobel Laureates
  in Medicine or Physiology.* New York: Gar-
  land, 1990.
Fox, D., and M. Meldrum, eds. *One Hundred
  Most Important People in the World Today.*
  New York: Putnam, 1970.

—*Sketch by D. George Joseph*

J. Presper Eckert

J. Presper Eckert
1919–1995

American computer engineer

Electrical engineer J. Presper Eckert invented the
first general-purpose electronic digital computer,
called the ENIAC, with **John William Mauchly.**
Further collaboration between the two engineers led
to the development of the first commercial digital
electronic computer, the UNIVAC. Their combined
efforts ushered in the commercial computer revolution in America, a revolution that continues to change
the world in profound ways.

John Presper Eckert, Jr., was born on April 9,
1919, in Philadelphia, to John Presper Eckert and
Ethel Hallowell Eckert. His father was a self-made
millionaire businessman, whose business interests
would strongly influence his son's future. Eckert was
an only child, and spent much of his youth building
radios and other mechanical and electronic gadgets.
He wanted to attend the Massachusetts Institute of
Technology (MIT), but his mother, who was devoted
to him, did not want him so far away from home. His
father even made up a story that he could not afford
MIT's tuition. So Eckert settled instead on the Moore

Engineering School at the University of Pennsylvania.
Upon discovering his father's lie during his freshman
year, he became very angry, which had a negative
effect on his grades. But Eckert persisted at Moore,
eventually earning his undergraduate degree in electrical engineering in 1941, and his master's degree in
1943. On October 28, 1944, he married Hester
Caldwell, with whom he had two sons, John Presper
III and Christopher. Hester died in 1952. Eckert
married Judith A. Rewalt on October 13, 1962, and
they had two children, Laura and Gregory.

Eckert was widely regarded as a superb engineer
while at the Moore School, but he could be stubborn,
and his work habits were regarded as odd. As Robert
Slater wrote in *Portraits in Silicon,* "Eckert liked to
work things out orally in the presence of someone; it
didn't matter whether it was a technician or a night
watchman. He was highly nervous and would rarely
sit in a chair or stand still while thinking. Often he
would crouch on top of a desk or pace back and
forth."

Invents the First General-Purpose Electronic Computer

The first of the four computers that Eckert built
with Mauchly was the ENIAC (Electronic Numerical
Integrator and Computer). The ENIAC was comprised of over 10,000 capacitors, 70,000 resistors, and
500,000 soldered connections. Separate wire panels
defined each of its programs, which meant that

operators had to change its wiring manually by turning dials, changing switches, and moving cables every time they changed to a new program. Adding to its complexity were nearly 18,000 vacuum tubes, any one of which could burn out at any time and stopped a calculation. An expert on electric organs, Eckert thought about this problem carefully. He knew that organs contained many vacuum tubes that could be used over long periods of time without burning out, and found that if he ran the computer's tubes at a low rate of power, they too would last a long time. Eckert also instituted careful standards for the computer's circuits. He designed each one individually and insisted, for the sake of simplicity, that only his circuits be used in all areas of the computer. This enabled everyone who worked on the computer to understand exactly how it worked very quickly, which minimized confusion.

At 80 feet (24 m) long, eight feet (2.4 m) high, and three feet (1 m) deep, the ENIAC occupied a total of 1,800 square feet (167 sq. m) and weighed thirty tons. Although it was enormous, power hungry, and slow compared to the average personal computer of the 1990s, its calculating speed was one thousand times faster than any mechanical calculator built up to that time. ENIAC could calculate a trajectory for an artillery shell in thirty seconds, while it took a person using a mechanical desk calculator 20 hours to perform the same calculation, with the possibility of error. The ENIAC was a general-purpose computer that could add, subtract, multiply, divide, compare quantities, and extract square roots. The ENIAC did not become operational until after World War II. It passed its first full operational test on December 10, 1945, and was dedicated on February 16, 1946. In August 1947, it was used to solve trajectory problems and compute ballistics tables at the U.S. Army's Aberdeen Proving Ground, and was later engaged in the development of the hydrogen bomb. In 1944, while working as a research associate at the Moore School, Eckert began work with Mauchly on the EDVAC (Electronic Discrete Variable Automatic Computer), greatly advancing the functions of its predecessor. Completed in 1952, EDVAC had an internal memory for storing programs, used only 3,600 vacuum tubes, and took up a mere 490 square feet (45 sq. m).

Developing the First Commercial Computer

Shortly before the end of World War II, Eckert and Mauchly, with the grudging permission of the Moore School of Engineering, began the long process of patenting the ENIAC. However, subsequent administrators at the Moore School did not like the idea of their employees applying for patents on equipment developed for U.S. government projects. In early 1946, one administrator decided that the Moore School would retain future patents on all projects developed by employees of the school. When asked to sign a form consenting to this, Eckert and Mauchly refused, and resigned in March of 1946.

Though IBM had offered Eckert a job and his own lab for developing computers, Mauchly talked him into jointly starting the Electronic Control Company. Their first work in 1946 and 1947 was with the National Bureau of Standards and the Census Bureau. They developed the specifications for a computer eventually known as the UNIVAC (Universal Automatic Computer)—the Electronic Control Co. took this as their name in 1948. Like most start-up companies developing complex hardware, Eckert and Mauchly ran into their share of financial problems, consistently underestimating the development costs for their computers. To raise money, they signed a contract in the fall of 1947 with the Northrop Aircraft Company to create a small computer for navigating airplanes—the BINAC (Binary Automatic Computer). The BINAC, completed in August, 1949, and the UNIVAC were the first computers to employ magnetic tape drives for data storage. Smaller in size and comprised of fewer parts than the ENIAC, both machines had internal memories for storing programs and could be accessed by typewriter keyboards.

Eckert and Mauchly had been kept from bankruptcy by the support of Henry Straus, an executive for the American Totalisator Company, which manufactured the odds-making machines used at race tracks. When Straus was killed in a plane crash in October 1949, Eckert and Mauchly knew they had to sell UNIVAC. The Remington Rand Corporation acquired their company on February 1, 1950. Eckert remained in research to develop the hardware for UNIVAC, while Mauchly devoted his time to developing software applications. The first UNIVAC, delivered to the Census Bureau in March 1951, proved its value in the 1952 presidential election between Dwight Eisenhower and Adlai Stevenson, when, less than an hour after the polls closed, it accurately predicted that Eisenhower would be the next president of the United States. Eckert and Mauchly's patent on the ENIAC was eventually challenged during an infringement suit between Sperry-Rand (formerly Remington), who now owned the rights to the computer, and Honeywell. On October 19, 1973, the court invalidated the ENIAC patent and asserted that Iowa State University professor **John Vincent Atanasoff** was the true inventor of the digital electronic computer.

Eckert received his doctorate from the University of Pennsylvania in 1964. He also received 87 patents and numerous awards for his innovations, including the Howard N. Potts and John Scott Medals, both of which he shared with Mauchly, and the National Medal of Science, given to him by President Lyndon B. Johnson in 1969. He was elected to the National Academy of Engineering in 1967. Eckert remained with the Remington Rand Corporation through a number of mergers, retiring in 1989 from what eventually became UNISYS. He later served as a consultant to UNISYS and to the Eckert Scientific International Corporation, based in Tokyo, Japan. At the time of his death, Eckert was a resident of Gladwyn, Pennsylvania. He died on June 3, 1995 in Bryn Mawr, Pennsylvania.

FURTHER READING:

Books

Metropolis, N., et al., eds. *A History of Computing in the Twentieth Century.* Academic Press, 1980, pp. 525-39.

Shurkin, Joel, *Engines of the Mind.* New York: Pocket Books, 1984.

Slater, Robert. *Portraits in Silicon.* Cambridge: MIT Press, 1987.

Stern, Nancy. *From ENIAC to UNIVAC: An Appraisal of the Eckert-Mauchly Computers.* Digital Press, 1981.

Periodicals

Baranger, Walter R. "J. Presper Eckert, Co-Inventor of Early Computer, Dies at 76" (obituary). *New York Times* (7 June 1995): B12.

—Sketch by Patrick Moore

Mileva Einstein-Marić
1875–1948
Austrian-born Hungarian-Serbian physicist

Mileva Marić (or in Hungarian, Marity), wife of **Albert Einstein**, was born in Titel, a small town north of the Danube ruled at the time of her birth by Austria. Her father, Miloš Marić, was a soldier under Austrian command on the so-called Banat Military Frontier—the easternmost part of the southern line of Austrian defense against Bosnia and Serbia. (Titel passed to the civil jurisdiction of Hungary with the abolition of the Military Frontier in 1882, and it later formed part of the new state of Yugoslavia.) The Banat, north of the Danube in southeastern Hungary, was peopled by a mosaic of Austrians, Romanians, Hungarians, Slavonians, and Serbs. Marić's parents belonged to the latter community, which was seen by Austria as a buffer against invasion. Miloš Marić knew German well, from the time of his youth, but his wife Marija Ružić (whom he married in 1867) spoke only Serbian to her oldest child, Mileva. From birth

Marić suffered from a displaced hip joint, giving her a lifelong limp.

In 1882 Marić's father joined the Hungarian civil service, which moved him and his family about the southern part of the kingdom. Mileva attended elementary school in Ruma and in 1886 began secondary school in Novi Sad (Neusatz) at the Serbian Girls' School; she transferred to the Kleine Realscule in Sremska Mitrovica (Syrmia), an old school that had until 1881 taught only in German. Since at that time girls in Austria-Hungary could not attend the classical secondary schools that prepared students for university studies, Miloš Marić sent Mileva to the Royal Serbian Gymnasium in Šabac in 1890. There she deepened her knowledge of German and acquired a knowledge of French. Then she followed her father to a new posting in Zagreb. By special arrangement, Mileva was the only female student in Zagreb's all-male Köningliche Obergymnasium, and there in 1894 she received the best grade in mathematics and physics.

Living conditions were poorer in Zagreb than in Novi Sad, and Miloš Marić decided to send his daughter to complete her secondary education in Switzerland—where the physical conditions would not as readily compromise her health and where women were encouraged to attend universities. From 1894 to 1896 Marić attended the Höhere Töchtershule in Zurich, and the school's diploma (which she obtained in 1896) allowed her to enter the Swiss universities.

In 1896 Marić began studying medicine at the University of Zurich, altogether after a semester she transferred to the scientific-pedagogical division of the Federal Institute of Technology (ETH), also in Zurich, which was then one of Europe's finest science and engineering schools. The ETH dated from the early part of the nineteenth century. Marić was the fifth woman to pass through its portals as a student. There she met Albert Einstein, also at the beginning of his scientific studies.

The two attended classes together for four years (she spent a semester at the University of Heidelberg in 1897-98), although they did not become lovers until 1898-99. Einstein graduated in 1900. Marić tried twice to obtain a diploma from the ETH (in 1900 and 1901), and twice failed. But like Einstein, she began working on a doctorate, in her case at the University of Zurich under Heinrich Friedrich Weber. After two and and half and lean years of living together, during which Einstein took odd jobs, they married, over the objections of their parents. Einstein's father had died (thus removing one objector), and Einstein had received a position as a patent examiner in Berne, establishing a steady family income.

In 1902 Marić gave birth to Einstein's daughter, Lieserl, of whom there is no trace after 1903. The couple later had two sons, Hans Albert and Eduard; Hans Albert Einstein became a professor at the California Institute of Technology. Evidence in the form of letters suggests that during the years leading up to 1905, when Einstein was composing his epoch-making physics, he and his physicist wife discussed all his ideas. Although Marić never authored a scientific paper, Russian physicist Abraham F. Joffe recalled that the manuscripts of three of Einstein's famous papers of 1905 bore both Einstein's and Marić's names (Joffe worked with a professor who then coedited the journal that published the papers). Marić's biographer reports that in 1907-08 she worked with Einstein and Paul Habicht to patent an instrument for measuring small electrical voltages and describe the instrument in a published article; again, her name did not appear as a co-inventor or coauthor. Marić corrected the proofs of at least some of Einstein's papers. She formed friendships with other women physicists who were her contemporaries, **Marie Curie** and **Tatjana Ehrenfest-Afansijeva**.

Marić raised Einstein's family and kept his house until 1914, when the couple separated—he to occupy one of the highest-paid physics positions in the world at Berlin, she to live in Zurich with her two sons. At first it was temporary arrangement, but with the beginning of the First World War (and Einstein's progressively intimate friendship with his first cousin Elsa Einstein, whom he later married) Einstein cut himself off from Marić. His support for Marić and the children was inconsistent. In 1919 Marić, whose health was uncertain, accepted a divorce from Einstein on the condition that he give her any Nobel Prize money that came his way. Einstein won the Nobel Prize in Physics soon after the divorce, and Marić did indeed receive its tangible reward.

FURTHER READING:

Books

Stachel, John, et al. *The Collected Papers of Albert Einstein. Volume 1: the Early Years, 1879-1902.* Princeton University Press, 1987.

Periodicals

Pyenson, Lewis. "Einstein's Natural Daughter," *History of Science* 28 (1990): 365-79.
Troemel-Ploetz, Senta. "Mileva Einstein-Marić: The Woman Who Did Einstein's Mathematics," *Women's Studies International Forum* 13 (1990): 415-532.

—Sketch by Lewis Pyenson

Walter M. Elsasser
1904-1991
German-born American physicist and geophysicist

Walter Elsasser developed the first general model of the role of water vapor in the radiation balance of the Earth's atmosphere, which is part of the basis in understanding the greenhouse effect, as well as having various implications for weather. Earlier in his career he contributed to the development of the fields of both quantum mechanics and atomic physics. In addition to these recognized accomplishments, which have won him several nominations for Nobel Prizes, Elsasser has also applied ideas from physics to the study of biology, work that remains controversial.

Walter Maurice Elsasser was born in Mannheim, Germany, on March 20, 1904, the son of Moritz and Johanna (Masius) Elsasser. He obtained his Ph.D. in physics at Göttingen University in 1927. Elsasser moved from one University post to another for most of his life. He taught at the University of Frankfort for three years (1930-33). Elsasser left Germany for Paris after the rise of the Nazi Party, teaching at the Sorbonne between 1933 and 1936 before taking a position at the California Institute of Technology in Pasadena. There he married his first wife, Margaret Trahey, in 1937. They had two children.

Elsasser became a naturalized United States citizen in 1940. He contributed to the war effort by conducting research on radar at the U.S. Signal Corps and at the Radio Corporation of America (RCA), leaving RCA in 1947 for academia. Elsasser taught at the University of Pennsylvania (1947-50); the University of Utah (1950-56); the University of California at La Jolla (1956-62); which partially overlapped with the University of New Mexico at Albuquerque (1961-62); followed by Princeton University (1962-68); and the University of Maryland at College Park (1968-74). He found a long-term home at Johns Hopkins University (1975-91). While at Princeton he married Suzanne Rosenfeld in 1964. Elsasser died on October 14, 1991, in Baltimore.

Elsasser made his first contribution to science while at Göttingen, calling attention to the diffraction effects that should be observable in the interaction of electrons and crystals, effects that would demonstrate the wave nature of the particles. In 1925, American physicist **Clinton Davisson** had accidentally discovered an odd interaction between crystals of nickel and electrons. He asked **Max Born** at Göttingen to explain what it meant. Elsasser was then a student; his professors were Born and **James Franck**. Born and Franck assigned the problem to Elsasser, who recognized that the effects could be explained by de Broglie's theory that electrons have the properties of waves. The following year, **Ernst Schrödinger** developed his famous wave equation of 1926, which was verified by Davisson's experiments and Elsasser's calculations.

When Elsasser was in France, his work centered on the problems connected with the Bohr model of the atom, in which electrons orbited the nucleus, and the Schrödinger model, in which electron *waves* circled the nucleus. Elsasser helped develop a different model, in which electron orbits are replaced by certain probable regions called *orbitals*. This point of view remains the dominant way electrons in atoms are treated in chemistry today and has also heavily influenced the modern concept of the atomic nucleus.

Surprisingly, it is not for either of Elsasser's achievements in quantum physics that he is remembered today. When he emigrated to the United States in 1936, Elsasser became interested in the Earth's magnetic field. Although it has been known for nearly 2,000 years that small magnets line up approximately with Earth's north and south poles, the exact reason why this should occur remained a mystery. William Gilbert called the Earth "the great magnet" in 1600, but this was recognition of a magnetic field rather than a theory of why one should exist. Elsasser proposed in 1939 the explanation that is still accepted today. Deep within the Earth the liquid part of the core is composed largely of fluid iron, a metal with strong magnetic properties. Movements of that fluid caused by the rotation of the Earth induce electric currents and magnetic fields for the same reasons that movement of the iron core of a dynamo will generate electric current if placed in a magnetic field.

Elsasser's second important contribution to the theory of geomagnetism is the notion that as molten rocks cool and solidify, they trap the orientation of the Earth's magnetic field as it was at that time. Thus, one can measure this residual magnetic field to determine where the rock was in relation to Earth's geomagnetic poles at the time the rock formed. Certain sediments also trap magnetic fields as they harden. This idea led to investigations which revealed that the continents did not always have the orientation to the magnetic poles that they do today, establishing that the theory of continental drift might be correct. Also, the rocks revealed that Earth's magnetic field reverses from time to time, a concept which led to the theory of plate tectonics. Today, the magnetic reversals are among the main tools for finding the approximate time that events happened in the long past.

For the last 30 years of his life, Elsasser devoted much of his time to applying the methods of statistical mechanics to biological problems, but his theories in this regard have not made many converts.

Elsasser received the Gauss Medal in 1977, which is particularly appropriate because Gauss conducted the first modern investigations of Earth's magnetic field, and the U.S. National Medal of Science in 1987 in recognition of his "fundamental and lasting contributions to physics, meteorology, and geophysics."

SELECTED WRITINGS BY ELSASSER:

Books

Atom and Organism: A New Approach to Theoretical Biology. Princeton: Princeton University Press, 1966.
The Chief Abstractions of Biology. New York: American Elsevier, 1975.
Memoirs of a Physicist in the Atomic Age. New York: Science History Publications, 1978
The Physical Foundation of Biology: An Analytical Study. New York: Pergamon Press, 1958.
Reflections on a Theory of Organisms. Editions Orbis, 1987.

—Sketch by Bryan Bunch

Charles Sutherland Elton
1900-1991
English ecologist

Charles Elton was a well known and highly respected biologist in the field of animal ecology, an area in which he wielded extraordinary influence. Elton's entire life was dedicated to furthering the understanding of the environment's effects on animal populations. His most significant contribution to the field of science, however, was not a noted discovery, but the establishment of the Bureau of Animal Population (BAP), which became an internationally acclaimed research center on the dynamics of animal population and ecology.

Charles Sutherland Elton was born on March 29, 1900, in Manchester, England, to Professor and Mrs. Oliver Elton. Professor Elton was chair of the English Literature department at the university there at the time of the younger Elton's birth. Charles Elton was very proud of his maternal heritage. His mother, it is said, was a descendent of crofters (farmers) from the Isle of Coll in Scotland. Shortly after Charles' birth, the Eltons moved to the east coast of England, where his father joined the staff of Liverpool University. It was there, at about age nine, that the naturalist traits began to develop in Elton under the watchful eye of his older brother, Geoffrey Yorke Elton. Geoffrey had a tremendous impact on his younger brother's life and, consequently, Elton was devastated when Geoffrey died suddenly at age 33. Elton was indebted to his brother for fostering his appreciation of the beauty of the world around him. Geoffrey taught him to carefully observe all living things and to watch for the principles that regulate their lives. That is the vocation to which Charles Elton dedicated his life.

In 1918, Elton entered Oxford, where he studied zoology under the tutelage of **Julian Sorell Huxley**, grandson of Thomas Henry Huxley, who boldly defended the theory of evolution as put forth in Charles Darwin's epochal 1859 work, *On the Origin of Species.* As an undergraduate, Elton was invited to assist Huxley on Oxford's first Arctic expedition to Spitsbergen in 1921. This study proved less successful than was expected, due to extreme weather conditions. Elton was invited to go along on the second Spitsbergen expedition in 1923, in which he found only nine dry-land invertebrates out of a possible 60 or more known species for that locale. On the third expedition in 1924, Elton was placed in charge of all scientific work. He spent most of his time working from the base camp, conducting a general survey of animal life in that region. It was during this trip that Elton almost lost his life when he fell through the ice. It is thought that this accident may have actually aided Elton's scientific endeavors by increasing his consciousness of the impact of accidental occurrences in the population dynamics of animal life. All together, these expeditions resulted in numerous publications in the fields of botany, geology, and zoology.

After graduating from Oxford in 1922 with high honors, Elton accepted a part-time position there as departmental demonstrator in zoology. This position enabled him to continue his research and documentation of animal population fluctuations and the reasons behind them. Offering a modest salary, the position eventually became full-time in 1929, and Elton held the post until 1945. He had also been appointed biological consultant to the Hudson Bay Company in 1925. During the five years he held this post, Elton conducted studies on the fluctuation of fur-bearing animals and their prey. With the help of George Binney of the Hudson Bay Company, Elton established a simple yet sophisticated recording system that provided input from hundreds of observers from a wide geographic area. Combined with the company's archives, this data eventually enabled Elton to trace the population fluctuation of the Canadian lynx back to 1736.

Establishes the Bureau of Animal Population (BAP)

The Bureau of Animal Population (BAP) was created on January 25, 1932. Establishing its own library and providing an atmosphere conducive to the study of population dynamics with a minimum of distraction, it acted as a world-class research center for the next 35 years. Throughout the BAP's existence, Elton worked tirelessly to obtain funding that would secure its future. The Bureau of Animal Population worked on a budget that was inconceivably small by research standards at that time, yet the quality and depth of research conducted by its members was never compromised, due in large part to Elton's strict adherence to the goals and objectives set forth by the BAP. On December 10, 1934, almost three years after its establishment, the Bureau of Animal Population became an official unit of Oxford University with a three-year grant to continue operations. While this alleviated some of the financial concerns for the foreseeable future, Elton continued his search for additional funding that would provide for materials and instrumentation not covered by the grant.

Faced with the possibility of a war with Germany, the British government notified all scientists that they would be exempted from military service in order to carry out applicable research. Elton did not wait for the inevitable to happen. He notified the Agricultural Research Council (ARC) that the Bureau was ready to offer its services in investigating the loss of food due to rodents in the field and in storage areas. Elton's staff was already experienced in this area, because they'd faced the same problem during the First World War. Elton's plan was approved by the ARC in August 1939, and by the university shortly after the outbreak of the war. Elton's team proved to be highly successful in controlling the rodent problem and much of the Bureau's research during this period was published by the ARC after the war.

Witnesses the Demise of the BAP

The BAP's reputation grew under the powerful, but low-key leadership of Charles Elton, as did the number of those who came to the Bureau to study and conduct research. Elton made many friends within the national and international ecological network, but he tended to stay out of the university's political arena. This, in the end, contributed to the dissolution of the Bureau as a separate research institute within the university. Elton did not have a political base of support when it became apparent that the current administration was out to dismantle the BAP.

Based on a report by the committee appointed to determine the status of the BAP, it was decided that Bureau personnel would be absorbed into Oxford's zoology department without any independent status. This was announced in the *University Gazette* on August 7, 1964, and would take effect upon Elton's retirement on September 30, 1967. Once that decision was made, the university treated the BAP as a nonentity, never acknowledging its existence in any report beyond September 1965. Scientists from around the world who had ever worked with the BAP or with Charles Elton were astounded by its demise. Peter Crowcroft, in his book *Elton's Ecologists,* wrote, "For twenty years, the Bureau had sought to function as an international institute, and the presence of its alumni in important jobs worldwide was evidence that it succeeded." Elton fought and won to keep the BAP library intact after the Bureau closed, as well as for space to continue the Wytham Biological Survey.

It has been said that the Bureau of Animal Population, unlike any other ecological institution, has influenced the lives of so many people that it will continue to live on through their work and research. Charles Elton, the quiet yet resourceful founder of the BAP and its staunchest supporter, always sought to stay out of the spotlight. He told Peter Crowcroft in 1978, "I would only object to your book if it overemphasized me in the BAP picture, or tried to be biographical in a larger or more general sense." Elton went on to say, "The whole nature of the BAP performance was its mixture of team-work and freedom." Crowcroft summed up Elton's involvement with the Bureau of Animal Population very adequately, when he said, "One cannot produce *Hamlet* without the Prince of Denmark." Elton died in 1991. His honors included a Foreign Honorary membership in the American Academy of Arts and Sciences. He was awarded a Gold Medal by the Linnean Society in 1967, and the Royal Society's Darwin Medal in 1970. In 1976, Elton received the Tyler Ecology Award, and the following year he was awarded the Edward W. Browning Award for Conservation. He was a Fellow of the Royal Society.

SELECTED WRITINGS BY ELTON:

Books

Animal Ecology. London, 1927.
Animal Ecology and Evolution. London, 1930.
The Pattern of Animal Communities. London, 1966.

FURTHER READING:

Books

Crowcroft, Peter. *Elton's Ecologists: A History of the Bureau of Animal Population.* Chicago: University of Chicago Press, 1991.
Vernoff, Edward. *The International Dictionary of 20th Century Biography.* New American Library, 1987.

—*Sketch by Paula M. Morin*

Gladys Anderson Emerson
1903–1984
American biochemist and nutritionist

Gladys Anderson Emerson was a landmark biochemist who conducted valuable research on vitamin E, amino acids, and the B vitamin complex. She later studied the biochemical bases of nutrition and the relationship between disease and nutrition. An author and lecturer, Emerson helped establish dietary allowances for the United States Department of Agriculture.

Emerson was born in Caldwell, Kansas, on July 1, 1903, the only child of Otis and Louise (Williams) Anderson. When the family moved to Texas, Emerson attended elementary school in Fort Worth. She later graduated from high school at El Reno, Oklahoma, where she excelled in debate, music, languages, and mathematics. In 1925 she received a B.S. degree in chemistry and an A.B. in English from the Oklahoma College for Women.

Following graduation, Emerson was offered assistantships in both chemistry and history at Stanford University and earned an M.A. degree in history in 1926. She eventually became head of the history, geography, and citizenship department at an Oklahoma City junior high school, then a short time later accepted a fellowship in biochemistry and nutrition at the University of California at Berkeley, where she received her Ph.D. in animal nutrition and biochemistry in 1932. That same year Emerson was accepted as a postdoctoral fellow at Germany's University of Göttingen, where she studied chemistry with the Nobel Prize-winning chemist **Adolf Windaus** and **Adolf Butenandt,** a prominent researcher who specialized in the study of hormones.

In 1933, Emerson returned to the United States and began work as a research associate in the Institute of Experimental Biology at the University of California at Berkeley. She remained there until 1942, conducting pioneering research on vitamin E; using wheat germ oil as a source, Emerson was first to isolate vitamin E. In 1942, she joined the staff of Merck and Company, a pharmaceutical firm, eventually heading its department of animal nutrition. Staying with Merck for fourteen years, Emerson directed research in nutrition and pharmaceuticals. In particular, she studied the structure of the B vitamin complex and the effects of B vitamin deprivation on lab animals; she found that when vitamin B6 was withheld from rhesus monkeys, they developed arteriosclerosis, or hardening of the arteries.

During World War II, Emerson served in the Office of Scientific Research and Development. From 1950 to 1953 she worked at the Sloan Kettering Institute, researching the link between diet and cancer. From 1962 to her retirement in 1970, she was professor of nutrition and vice-chairman of the department of public health at the University of California at Los Angeles.

In 1969, President Richard M. Nixon appointed Emerson vice president of the Panel on the Provision of Food as It Affects the Consumer (the White House Conference on Food, Nutrition, and Health). In 1970, she served as an expert witness before the Food and Drug Administration's hearing on vitamins and mineral supplements and additives to food. A photography enthusiast who won numerous awards for her work, Emerson was also a distinguished board member of the Southern California Committee of the World Health Organization and was active on the California State Nutrition Council. She died in 1984.

SELECTED WRITINGS BY EMERSON:

Periodicals

"Agnes Fay Morgan and Early Nutrition Discoveries in California." *Federation Proceedings* 36: 1911-14.

FURTHER READING:

Books

Huber, Louis. *Women Pioneers of Science*. Harcourt, 1979.
Siegel, J. P., and R. T. Finley. *Women in the Scientific Search*. Metuchen, NJ: Scarecrow, 1985.
Vare, E. V., and G. Ptacek. *Mothers of Invention*. New York: Morrow, 1988.

—*Sketch by John Henry Dreyfuss*

Paul Erdös
1913–1996
Hungarian number theorist

For Paul Erdös, mathematics was life. Number theory, combinatorics (a branch of mathematics concerning the arrangement of finite sets), and discrete mathematics were his consuming passions. Everything else was of no interest: property, money, clothes, intimate relationships, social pleasantries—all were looked on as encumbrances to his mathematical pursuits. A genius in the true sense of the word, Erdös traveled the world, living out of a suitcase, to problem solve—and problem pose—with his mathematical

Paul Erdös

peers. A small, hyperactive man, he would arrive at a university or research center confident of his welcome. While he was their guest, it was a host's task to lodge him, feed him, do his laundry, make sure he caught his plane to the next meeting, and sometimes even do his income taxes. Cosseted by his mother and by household servants, he was not brought up to fend for himself. Gina Bari Kolata, writing in *Science* magazine, reports that Erdös said he "never even buttered his own bread until he was 21 years old."

Yet this man, whom Paul Hoffman called "probably the most eccentric mathematician in the world" in the *Atlantic Monthly*, more than repaid his colleagues' care of him by giving them a wealth of new and challenging problems—and brilliant methods for solving them. Erdös laid the foundation of computer science by establishing the field of discrete mathematics. A number theorist from the beginning, he was just 20 years old when he discovered a proof for Chebyshev's theorem, which says that for each integer greater than one, there is always at least one prime number between it and its double.

Erdös was born in Budapest, Hungary, on March 26, 1913. His parents, Lajos and Anna Erdös, were high school mathematics teachers. His two older sisters died of scarlet fever when he was a newborn baby, leaving him an only child with a very protective mother. Erdös was schooled at home by his parents and a governess, and his gift for mathematics was recognized at an early age. It is said that Erdös could multiply three–digit numbers in his head at age three, and discovered the fact of negative numbers when he was four. He received his higher education from the University of Budapest, entering at age 17 and graduating four years later with a Ph. D. in mathematics. He completed a postdoctoral fellowship in Manchester, England, leaving Hungary in the midst of political unrest in 1934. As a Jew, Hungary was then a dangerous place for him to be. During the ensuing Nazi reign of power, four of Erdös's relatives were murdered, and his father died of a heart attack in 1942.

In 1938, Erdös came to the United States, but because of the political situation in Hungary, he had difficulty receiving permission from the U. S. government to come and go freely between America and Europe. He settled in Israel and did not return to the United States until the 1960s. While in the country, he attended mathematical conferences, met with top U. S. mathematicians such as Ronald Graham, Ernst Straus and Stanislaw Ulam, and lectured at prestigious universities. His appearances were irregular, owing to the fact that he had no formal arrangements with any of the schools he visited. He would come for a few months, receive payment for his work, and move on. He was known to fly to as many as fifteen places in one month—remarking that he was unaffected by jet lag. Because he never renounced his Hungarian citizenship, he was able to receive a small salary from the Hungarian Academy of Sciences.

An Erdös Number Conveys Prestige

So esteemed was Erdös by his colleagues that they invented the term "Erdös number" to describe their close connections with him. For example, if someone had coauthored a paper with Erdös, they were said to have an Erdös number of one. If someone had worked with another who had worked with Erdös, their Erdös number was two, and so on. According to his obituary in the *New York Times*, 458 persons had an Erdös number of one; an additional 4,500 could claim an Erdös number of two. It is said that **Albert Einstein** had an Erdös number of two. Ronald Graham, director of information sciences at AT&T Laboratories, once said that research was done to determine the highest Erdös number, which was thought to be 12. As Graham recalled, "It's hard to get a large Erdös number, because you keep coming back to Erdös." This "claim to fame" exercise underscores Erdös's monumental publishing output of more than 1,500 papers, and is not only a tribute to his genius but also to his widespread mathematical network.

Throughout his career, Erdös sought out younger mathematicians, encouraging them to work on problems he had not solved. He created an awards system as an incentive, paying amounts from $10 to $3,000

for solutions. He also established prizes in Hungary and Israel to recognize outstanding young mathematicians. In 1983, Erdös was awarded the renowned Wolf Prize in Mathematics. Much of the $50,000 prize money he received endowed scholarships made in the name of his parents. He also helped to establish an endowed lectureship, called the Turán Memorial Lectureship, in Hungary.

Perfect Proofs from God's "Great Book"

Erdös's mathematical interests were vast and varied, although his great love remained number theory. He was fascinated with solving problems that looked—but were not—deceptively simple. Difficult problems involving number relationships were Erdös's special forte. He was convinced that discovery, not invention, was the way to mathematical truth. He often spoke in jest of "God's Great Mathematics Book in the Sky," which contained the proofs to all mathematical problems. Hoffman in the *Atlantic Monthly* says "The strongest compliment Erdös can give to a colleague's work is to say, 'It's straight from the Book.'"

Mother's Death Brings on Depression

Erdös's mother was an important figure in his life. When she was 84 years old, she began traveling with him, even though she disliked traveling and did not speak English. When she died of complications from a bleeding ulcer in 1971, Erdös became extremely depressed and began taking amphetamines. This habit would continue for many years, and some of his extreme actions and his hyperactivity were attributed to his addiction. Graham and others worried about his habit and prevailed upon him to quit, apparently with little result. Even though Erdös would say, "there is plenty of time to rest in the grave," he often talked about death. In the eccentric and personal language he liked to use, God was known as S. F. (Supreme Fascist). His idea of the perfect death was to "fall over dead" during a lecture on mathematics.

Erdös's "perfect death" almost happened. He died of a heart attack in Warsaw, Poland, on September 20, 1996, while attending a mathematics meeting. As news of his death began to reach the world's mathematicians, the accolades began. Ronald Graham, who had assumed a primary role in looking after Erdös after his mother's death, said he received many electronic–mail messages from all over the world saying, "Tell me it isn't so." Erdös's colleagues considered him one of the 20th century's greatest mathematicians. Ulam remarked that it was said "You are not a real mathematician if you don't know Paul Erdös." Straus, who had worked with Einstein as well as Erdös, called him "the prince of problem solvers and the absolute monarch of problem posers," and compared him with the great 18th–century mathematician Leonhard Euler. And, Graham remarked, "He died with his boots on, in hand–to–hand combat with one more problem. It was the way he wanted to go."

SELECTED WRITINGS BY ERDÖS:

At his death, Paul Erdös had written more than 1,500 mathematical papers. He had collaborated with so many mathematicians still at work on problems that it was expected that an additional fifty to 100 papers would be published after his death. Erdös was once asked in the early 1980s if he had any particular mathematical works of which he was especially proud. He replied that two were the Erdös–Kac and the Erdös–Wintner theorems. He also mentioned a theory on elementary geometry. Sources which discuss these theorems are listed below:

Kac, M. *Statistical Independence in Probability, Analysis and Number Theory.* Mathematical Association of America, 1959 (Carus Monograph #12).

Kubilius, J. *Probabilistic Methods in the Theory of Numbers.* American Mathematical Society, 1964 (Translation of Mathematical Monographs, #11).

FURTHER READING:

Books

Albers, Donald J. and G. L. Alexanderson, editors. *Mathematical People, Profiles and Interviews.* Chicago: Contemporary Books, Inc., 1985.

Honsberger, R. "Stories in Combinatorial Geometry: A Theorem of Erdös." *Two–Year College Mathematics Journal* 10 (1979): 344–347.

Ulam, S. M. *Adventures of a Mathematician.* New York: Charles Scribner's Sons, 1976.

Periodicals

Hoffman, Paul. "The Man Who Loves Only Numbers." *The Atlantic Monthly* (November 1987): 60–74.

Kolata, Gina Bari. "Mathematician Paul Erdös: Total Devotion to the Subject." *Science* (April 8, 1977): 144–145.

———. "Paul Erdös, 83, a Wayfarer in Math's Vanguard, Is Dead." *The New York Times.* September 24, 1996, A: 1:5 ; B: 8: 5.

Other

"In Memoriam: Paul Erdös." February 11, 1997. http://www.cs.uchicago.edu/groups/theory/erdos.html (July 20, 1997). This web site includes hyperlinks, images, obituaries, and explications of Erdös' most important theories.

—Sketch by Jane Stewart Cook

Agner Krarup Erlang
1878–1929
Danish mathematician

Erlang is regarded as the founder of queuing theory and of operations research. His formulas, designed and published in 1917, enabled early telephone switching systems to become operational. These formulas give the probability that a user will encounter a busy signal instead of a dial tone, or the length of waiting time for a system that can hold calls. They are used to calculate the number of circuits needed to give a specified level of service. Erlang's formulas may be applied to any system with a limited number of servers and customers that arrive at random times.

Agner Krarup Erlang was born on January 1, 1878, at Lonborg, near Tarm in Jutland, the mainland of Denmark. His parents were Hans Nielson Erlang, the parish clerk and schoolmaster, and Magdalene Krarup Erlang. Many of his mother's family were clergymen. Erlang had an older brother, Frederik, and two younger sisters, Marie and Ingeborg. Erlang studied at his father's school, then was tutored at home by his father and the assistant school teacher, P.J. Pedersen, for his preliminary examination. Erlang passed with distinction, although at age 14 he needed special permission to take the examination. Erlang served as assistant teacher at his father's school for two years, then stayed for two years with M. Funch, in Hillerod, to prepare for his university examination at the Frederikborg Grammar–school. In 1896, Erlang passed this examination and attended the University of Copenhagen. He studied mathematics, astronomy, physics and chemistry, and completed an M.A. in 1901.

After graduation, Erlang taught at a number of schools. He joined a Christian students' association where he met his friend H.C. Nybolle, who later became a professor of statistics at Copenhagen University. Erlang also was a member of the Mathematics Association. In 1904, he won a distinction for his answer to the University mathematics prize question about Christiaan Huygen's methods of solving infinitesimal problems. At the Mathematics Association, Erlang met J.L.W.V. Jensen of the Copenhagen Telephone Company. Jensen introduced Erlang to Fr.

Johannsen, his managing director, who hired Erlang in 1908 as scientific collaborator and leader of the laboratory.

Johannsen had already published two essays on the barred access and waiting time problems inherent in telephone systems. He suggested that Erlang study these problems further. Erlang demonstrated in a 1909 paper that the number of calls to arrive during a period of time follows a Poisson distribution, and treated the problem of waiting time when holding times are constant, for the simplest case of one circuit. In 1917, Erlang's most important paper was published, in which he gives his B–formula for the probability of barred access, or a busy signal, for a group of circuits, and formulas for waiting time. His proof of the B–formula is based on the idea of statistical equilibrium, that transitions between pairs of states are in balance. In 1922 and 1926 Erlang published lectures on the contents of his earlier papers; the 1922 paper containing a new interconnection formula. In 1924 he wrote about a principal of K. Moe for deciding whether to add circuits to large or small groups of circuits. Erlang often presented his results as tables as well as formulas. He wrote several papers about producing accurate tables and published tables produced by his methods.

Erlang also wrote about cables, the induction coil in a telephone, and about a device for measuring transmission in cables. Also interested in more theoretical matters, Erlang used the idea of statistical equilibrium to prove Maxwell's Law in the kinetic theory of gases, and wrote short papers on geometry and on proportional representation in voting.

Erlang, who never married, lived with his sister Ingeborg in Copenhagen. He had a large collection of books on science and mathematics. Erlang's sister founded a home for mentally ill women, which he supported generously. Erlang died after a brief abdominal illness on February 3, 1929, at 51 years of age.

In addition to his widely used formulas, Erlang's name is attached to the gamma probability distribution. In 1946, the C.C.I.F. (La comite consultatif des communications telephoniques a grande distance) adopted the Erlang as the unit of telephone traffic. The average traffic in Erlangs is the sum of the lengths of calls originating during an interval of time, divided by the length of the time interval. ERLANG is also the name of a programming language which was developed at Ericsson and Ellemtel Computer Science Laboratories for programming telecommunications switching systems.

SELECTED WRITINGS BY ERLANG:

"Principal Works of A. K. Erlang." *Transactions of the Danish Academy of Technical Sciences* 2 (1948): 131–267.

FURTHER READING:

Books

The Biographical Dictionary of Scientists. Second Edition. New York: Oxford University Press, 1994.
Dansk Biografisk Leksikon. Kobenhavn: Gyldendal, 1980.
James, Robert C. *Mathematics Dictionary.* Fifth Edition. New York: Van Nostrand Reinhold, 1992.
Mathematical Society of Japan. *Encyclopedic Dictionary of Mathematics.* Second Edition. Edited by Kiyosi Ito. Cambridge, MA: MIT Press, 1987.

Periodicals

Brockmeyer, E. and H. L. Halstrom. "The Life of A. K. Erlang." *Transactions of the Danish Academy of Technical Sciences* 2 (1948): 9–24.
Brockmeyer, E. "A Survey of A. K. Erlang's Mathematical Works." *Transactions of the Danish Academy of Technical Sciences* 2 (1948): 101–126.
Halstrom, H. L. "A Survey of A. K. Erlang's Electrotechnical Works." *Transactions of the Danish Academy of Technical Sciences* 2 (1948): 127–30.

—Sketch by Sally M. Moite

James C. Evans
1900–1988
American engineer

James C. Evans is one of America's first outstanding African American engineers. After taking his college and postgraduate degrees at Massachusetts Institute of Technology, Evans became an award-winning researcher in electronics as well as an inventor and patent-holder. He came to prominence during World War II as a high-ranking civilian aide to the U.S. Secretary of War, after which he taught electrical engineering at Howard University.

James Carmichael Evans was born in Gallatin, Tennessee, on July 1, 1900. When he was eighteen years old, he enlisted in the U.S. Army and served as an instructor in the Student Army Training Corps. After receiving his B.A. from Roger Williams University in Memphis, Tennessee, in 1921, he realized that he was not fully prepared to go on to graduate school and pursue a professional technical career. He then re-enrolled at the undergraduate level at the Massachusetts Institute of Technology in Cambridge. Four years later, in 1925, he graduated with a B.S., and in 1926 he received his master's degree. He took a job in electrical and construction engineering upon graduating and also taught for a year at the Booker T. Washington High School in Miami, Florida. In 1928 Evans accepted a position he would hold until 1937. He was named professor of technical industries at West Virginia State College as well as its director of the trade and technical division. The year he joined West Virginia State College was also the year he married his wife, Roselline, with whom he later had two children, James and Rose. In 1937 he became administrative assistant to that university's president, and he remained there until 1942.

With the outbreak of World War II in Europe, Evans took on the responsibility of coordinating pilot training programs for civilians and military personnel, and in 1941 he became a technical training specialist with the War Production Board. In 1943, however, he moved from the technical side of things when he accepted a position as a civilian aide to the U.S. Secretary of War. After war's end he remained connected with the federal government through 1949, serving Secretary of Defense Louis Johnson as his highest adviser on racial relations at a time when the Army, Navy, and Air Force were studying their personnel policies to assure equal treatment and opportunity for all their members. It was during these postwar years that he became affiliated with Howard University. He joined that university in 1946 as a professor of electrical engineering and remained there until his retirement in 1970. He died on April 14, 1988, at his home in Washington, D.C.

Early in his career, Evans did research in pre-radar electronics, and in 1926 he received the Harmon Award for scientific research in electronics. He was also interested in aeronautical problems, and he held a patent on a method of using airplane exhaust gases to prevent ice from forming on aircraft. In 1953 Evans was given the Dorie Miller Foundation Award, and he also received the Career Service Award in 1959 from the National Civil Service League. He was a member of various professional organizations, including the National Institute of Science and the National Education Association, as well as several honor societies. He was also a widely known member of the National Technical Association and served as its national executive secretary for twenty consecutive years, from 1932 to 1952.

FURTHER READING:

Books

Christmas, Walter, ed. *Negroes in Public Affairs and Government.* Educational Heritage Inc., 1966, p. 334.

William Maurice Ewing

Periodicals

"James C. Evans, Professor, 87" (obituary). *New York Times* (23 April 1988): 11.

—*Sketch by Leonard C. Bruno*

William Maurice Ewing
1906–1974
American geophysicist and oceanographer

Maurice Ewing's research profoundly influenced modern geology, although Ewing never formally studied the discipline. He directed most of the research that led to the creation of the theory of plate tectonics, but was among the last of the geophysicists to embrace the concept. His greatest achievements are from his emphasis on data collection and storage. Ewing invented the techniques needed to establish the shape, thickness, composition, and magnetism of the floor of the ocean. Before Ewing, the ocean floor had been almost unknown. He attacked the lack of knowledge by using bombs, air guns, underwater surveillance, and a small navy to get the data he wanted.

William Maurice Ewing was born on May 12, 1906, in Lockney, Texas, far from the ocean that would become his life's work. His father Floyd Ford Ewing combined farming with selling farm implements and hardware. Ewing's mother, Hope Hamilton Ewing, gave birth to 10 children of whom William Maurice was the fourth, but the first to survive infancy. There was considerable emphasis on education in the family, unusual for that time and place. Maurice and five of his siblings received college degrees. The youngest, John, also became a geophysicist and eventually worked with Maurice.

Maurice was skilled in mathematics and interested in science, so he studied physics at Rice Institute in Houston, for which he had obtained a scholarship. During summer vacations, Ewing worked on oil prospecting crews. He studied petroleum possibilities under lakes in Louisiana and fired charges of blasting gelatin from a whaleboat off the Gulf Coast to obtain seismic profiles. Ewing spent six years at Rice, during which time he obtained his B.A. (in 1926), M.A. (1927), and Ph.D. (awarded in 1931), all in physics. His first teaching job was on the physics faculty at the University of Pittsburgh in Pennsylvania in 1929, but a year later he moved to Lehigh University, in Bethlehem, Pennsylvania. Ewing continued teaching physics at Lehigh until World War II, but from 1935 on he also conducted oceanographic research part of each year at the Woods Hole Oceanographic Institute in Cape Cod, Massachusetts. At the onset of the war, Ewing began to work full time at Woods Hole, which like virtually all of the United States was engaged in the war effort. Near the end of the war Ewing moved to the geology department of Columbia University in New York City, finally discarding physics for geophysics, geology, and oceanography. He stayed at Columbia until 1972, mostly as the first director of the Lamont Geological Observatory (now Lamont-Doherty Earth Observatory) on the Hudson River a few miles north of New York City. Then he returned to Texas, to the University of Texas at Galveston, not far from Rice Institute in Houston. On May 4, 1974, he died suddenly of a cerebral hemorrhage.

Ewing's scientific career had an auspicious beginning. A paper he wrote as an undergraduate was published in *Science* in 1926 and his doctoral thesis on methods of calculating the paths of earthquake waves was also published as two journal papers. At Lehigh he continued to study how waves travel through rock and sediments. (Such waves are called seismic waves, and can be generated by explosions as well as by earthquakes.) His published analyses of seismic waves in Lehigh Valley limestone deposits and within ice of a frozen pond soon established Ewing as an expert. In 1934, he was asked by the U.S. Coast and Geodetic Survey and the American Geophysical Union to investigate the geology of the submerged edge of the North American continent. Ewing later commented, "If they had asked me to put seismographs on the moon instead of the bottom of

the ocean, I would have agreed, I was so desperate for a chance to do research." Ewing developed new methods for analyzing the sediments from aboard a ship at sea. Thereafter, he conducted or directed much of his research from ocean-going vessels.

Ewing Advances Modern Oceanography

The history of oceanography is very short and Ewing's discoveries are surprisingly near the beginning. Modern oceanography dates from the 1850 map of U.S. Navy Captain Matthew Maury that first revealed hints of a ridge along the middle of the Atlantic, but little else was studied before Ewing began his research. Not only did Ewing develop the shipborne seismic survey technique in 1935 and variations on it starting in 1949, but he also improved methods of sampling ocean sediments with long cores (starting in 1948), developed methods to use earthquake waves to study oceanic crust (1949), improved techniques for investigating gravitational (1936) and magnetic (1952) anomalies beneath the sea, and introduced the use of sound waves (1949) and underwater photography (1947) to oceanography. The concept that today's geologists have of Earth's crust is almost entirely based on Ewing's techniques and to a large extent on data gathered by Ewing or his staff at Lamont.

During World War II, Ewing studied the transmission of sound through the oceans, a topic of vital importance to the war effort since sound was involved in locating and hiding submarines, improving navigation. His 1937 discovery of a channel in the oceans that could carry the sound of even a small explosion across the entire Atlantic Ocean aided in the rescue of downed airplane crews and sailors. At one time the U.S. Navy equipped planes with special small bombs that could be dropped into the sea if the plane crashed. Five stations around the ocean could then detect the explosion and use Ewing's sound channel to locate the downed plane.

Shortly after Ewing came to Columbia at the end of the war, a gift of land and money enabled the University to start the Lamont Geological Laboratory in Palisades, New York, on the west bank of the Hudson River. Ewing became its director, a post he held for a quarter of a century. During the laboratory's infancy, Ewing and the Lamont team relied on a large sailing ship from Woods Hole for data collection at sea. In 1953, however, Lamont acquired its own three-masted schooner, the *Vema,* a former luxury yacht that had been stripped down by the Navy during the war. Ewing very nearly lost his life on January 13, 1954, when he, his brother John, and two crew members were tossed overboard from the *Vema* during a gale off Cape Hatteras. One crew member drowned, but the Ewings and the other crew member were eventually retrieved.

Not all the research took place at sea. Ewing determined that he could profile the floor of the sea by analyzing earthquake waves. Lamont started a seismology laboratory for that purpose and also developed a network of such laboratories around the world. Today, Lamont remains at the forefront of earthquake studies, as well as oceanography.

With Frank Press, Ewing used earthquake waves to show for the first time that the crust beneath the ocean is much thinner than that beneath the continents, on average only 3 miles (5 km) thick. The continental crust ranges from 20-55 miles (30-90 km) in thickness. This was announced in 1949 and may be taken as the beginning of the revolution that led to plate tectonics, the now accepted view that the crust of the Earth is split into large plates that slowly shift position with respect to each other.

Ewing was a great collector of data of all kinds. His first major expedition at Lamont in 1947 traced the canyon at the mouth of the Hudson River for 200 miles (320 km) and established that it led to a vast, abyssal plain. Under his direction at Lamont starting in 1952, ships began towing magnetometers to observe changes in the magnetic field trapped in ocean sediments. Others followed suit, and the collected data became one of the key links in the chain of reasoning that led to the theory of plate tectonics. The trapped magnetic fields were confirmed in ocean cores taken by the *Vema* as well as by cores from other vessels. Ewing and **Bruce Heezen** of Lamont had been the first to note, about 1960, that there appear to be great mid-ocean ridges that circle the globe. The *Vema* used echo-sounding to confirm this speculation. Similarly, profiles of the Mid-Atlantic Ridge collected by Lamont led to the Ewing, Heezen, and Marie Thorp discovery of its central rift valley in 1959 and earthquake activity associated with it, another link in the chain. Ewing himself did not accept plate tectonics until 1966, when enough evidence had accumulated, much of it due to Ewing's own work and that of his staff, to make an ironclad case for the theory.

Ewing's own theory of note was that changes in the circulation of the Atlantic Ocean influenced by variations in ice cover in the Arctic caused the ice ages. Although some details are now thought to be different, Ewing's theory from 1956 is quite similar to many recent proposals on ice-age causation.

Among Ewing's many honors were the Arthur L. Day Medal of the Geological Society of America (1949), the Agassiz (1955) and Carty (1963) medals of the U.S. National Academy of Sciences, the William Bowie Medal of the American Geophysical Union (1957), the first gold medal of the Royal Astronomical Society in geophysics (1965), and the U.S. National Medal of Science (1973). A primitive mollusc discovered by scientists aboard the *Vema* in 1958, *Neopilina ewingi,* was named in his honor.

Ewing was a tall man (six foot two), large but not overly heavy, with unruly brown hair and blue eyes shining behind large spectacles. An amateur musician whose trombone playing attracted the attention of his first wife, Avarilla Grace Hildenbrand, while they were students at Rice, Ewing eventually married three times and fathered five children. During the his marriage to Avarilla, from 1928 to 1941, they produced one son, William Maurice Jr. His second marriage, from 1944 through 1965 to Margaret Kidder, whom he met at Woods Hole, resulted in two daughters, Hope Hamilton and Margaret, and two sons, Jerome H.K. and Peter Duryee. In 1965, after his divorce from Margaret, Ewing married Harriet Green Bassett, who survived Ewing after his death at age 67 in 1974.

SELECTED WRITINGS BY EWING:

Periodicals

"Seismic Shooting at Sea." *Scientific American.* (May 1962): 116-B26.

FURTHER READING:

Books

Ericson, David B. and Goesta Wollin. *The Ever-Changing Sea.* New York: Alfred A. Knopf, 1967.

Miller, Russell, et. al. *Planet Earth:* Continents in Collision. Alexandria, VA: Time-Life Books, 1983.

—Sketch by Bryan Bunch

Charles Fabry

Charles Fabry
1867–1945
French physicist

The focus of Charles Fabry's professional life was the optics branch of physics, and he shared his enthusiasm for the subject with the general populace as well aspiring scientists. While teaching at universities in Paris and Marseilles, Fabry did much important research. With Alfred Pérot, he invented the Fabry-Pérot interferometer, which is used to measure light's wavelength. Using his invention, Fabry conducted many experiments in the interferometer's applications throughout different scientific disciplines. Fabry proved that ozone exists in Earth's upper atmosphere by using the interferometer. Ozone screens the Earth from the sun's ultraviolet radiation and its negative effects.

Most of Fabry's major research accomplishments happened early in his career, for by its end, he juggled several teaching appointments with a directorship. Though Fabry was always busy, he was interested in spreading scientific knowledge among laypeople. He

lectured and wrote books and articles to support this effort.

Fabry was born in Marseilles, France, on June 11, 1867, to Charles Fabry and his wife Marie Estrangin. Fabry was one of five (some sources say four) brothers, of whom two others became prominent scientists. Eugene Fabry was a respected mathematician, teaching at the University of Marseilles and the University of Montpellier, while Louis Fabry became an astronomer. Their interests influenced Fabry in his research, and he shared a love of astronomy with both of them.

Like his brothers, Fabry received his education at the École Polytechnique in Paris, where he earned his university teaching degree (agrégation) in physics in 1892, and his doctorate (doctorat ès sciences) in 1892. (Some sources say he received both degrees at the University of Marseilles; others say he received his doctorate from the University of Paris, the Sorbonne.) After earning his doctorate (some sources say before) Fabry was a lycée (high school) teacher for two years in several cities, including Paris, Bordeaux, Nevers, and Marseilles.

Focuses on Optical Field

In 1894, Fabry began his university science teaching and research career in his home town at the University of Marseilles. He did most of his important research at this university before he left it in 1920. Fabry's research focused on the same subject as his doctoral thesis, optics and the effects of optical interference, with a focus on interference fringes and localization. Indeed, Fabry worked at Marseilles in an optics-focused laboratory, and built many of his own instruments.

Invents the Fabry-Pérot Interferometer

At Marseilles, Fabry worked with Alfred Pérot, and together they invented what came to be known as the Fabry-Pérot interferometer in 1896. The instrument is used to measure the wavelength of light from a single source, based on the concept of light's multiple beam reflection possibilities. The Fabry-Pérot Interferometer is made of two lightly silvered flat glass plates, set to be perfectly parallel. It works by reuniting rays from a single light source, after they have undergone a number of reflections. Upon reunion, they can either produce light bands, if the rays cohere, or dark bands, if the rays interfere. An interferometer can have a resolving power accuracy of one million.

Though Fabry undoubtedly knew the importance of his and Pérot's invention, he was known to humbly refer to it as "this interferometer whose name I have the honor to bear myself." Indeed, Fabry and Pérot improved on work done by earlier by American **Albert Michelson**; their instrument was superior, in part, because it exhibited sharper fringes. Their interferometer was also useful in spectroscopy, for it can copy superior aspects of diffraction grating.

For about ten years after they invented the Fabry-Pérot interferometer, Fabry and Pérot used their device in spectroscopy as well as meteorology. In one experiment, they worked to ascertain a sequence of standard wavelengths. During this fruitful period of research, in 1904, Fabry was elected to the Chair of Industrial Physics at the University of Marseilles.

In 1906, Fabry began collaborating with Henri Buisson, again using the Fabry-Pérot interferometer. Their research continued along the same lines as Fabry's work with Pérot. With Buisson, Fabry confirmed a prediction of the kinetic theory of gases. In this theory, lines should broaden when dealing with the spectra of gases like krypton, neon, and helium.

Buisson and Fabry continued to do relevant work, and by 1914, they had devised a laboratory-based way to confirm the Doppler effect for light. Until their breakthrough, the relevant measurement had to be made by using stellar sources.

Proves the Ozone Layer Exists

Influenced by his brothers' interest in astronomy, Fabry used his interferometer in this realm, beyond the Doppler effect. He examined the sun and the stars' spectra. He used photometry to measure the night sky's brightness. Fabry's work in this area led to his 1913 discovery of ozone in the upper atmosphere, and his conclusion that ozone is responsible for the absorption of ultraviolet light. This layer of ozone is important to life on Earth because it filters out most of the Sun's harmful ultraviolet radiation. The ozone layer's erosion became an important scientific and political issue in the 1990s.

In 1914, following the outbreak of World War I, Fabry was brought to Paris by the French government's Ministry of Inventions. In Paris, Fabry studied light and sound waves and related interference phenomena, receiving several awards for his work. During this period, Fabry realized that France needed a national Optics Institute. Several years later, this idea materialized, and Fabry was named the first director of the Paris-based Institut d'Optique.

Appointed to a Professorship at the Sorbonne

By 1920 or 1921, having chosen Paris as his permanent residence, Fabry was appointed to a physics professorship at the University of Paris (Sorbonne). He simultaneously held his directorship at the Institut d'Optique. At both institutions, Fabry implemented important changes, linking training with laboratory work, and building up educational experiences of students and staff. In 1926, Fabry added another position to his already full work load, and assumed the Chair of Physics at École Polytechnique. Throughout the 1920s and 1930s, then, as Fabry's teaching and leadership roles increased, his involvement in research decreased.

Still, his peers recognized Fabry's work on all fronts. In 1927, he was elected to the French Academy of Sciences. Later, Fabry spent several years as a member of the prestigious Bureau de Longitudes' International Committee on Weights and Measures. He was elected President in 1944, but illness prevented him from holding the post for more than several months.

Fabry was not just concerned with education and research within in the academy and related scientific community. He was also interested in bringing science to the general public—through popular lectures, articles, and books. A gifted speaker, Fabry was a highly appreciated lecturer among both the student community and the general public. In a tribute to Fabry, Jean Lecomte related the following story from Fabry's time at the University at Marseilles. "The use of electricity in factories and private homes was a topical matter, so his lectures attracted workers and electricians interested in the study of the phenomena they were utilizing, as well as a scientific audience. The lectures began at 9 in the evening, but the doors of the Faculty had to be closed half an hour before as it was already impossible to enter the lecture room."

By 1945, Fabry was seriously ill and disheartened by the havoc caused by World War II. After a lifetime of dedicated scientific work, Fabry died in Paris on December 11, 1945.

SELECTED WRITINGS BY FABRY:

Books

Les applications des interférences lumineuses. Paris, 1923.
Optique. Paris, 1926.
Oeuvres choisis. Paris, 1938.
Les radiations. Paris: A. Colin, 1946.
L'ozone atmosphérique. Paris: CNRS, 1950.

FURTHER READING:

Books

Asimov, Isaac. "Fabry, Charles." In *Asimov's Biographical Encyclopedia of Science and Technology.* New rev. ed. Garden City: Doubleday, 1972, p. 535.

"Fabry, Charles." In *Biographical Dictionary of Scientists.* 2nd ed. New York: Oxford University Press, 1994, pp. 221-22.

"Fabry, Charles." In *Dictionary of Scientific Biography*, vol.4. New York: Scribner's 1976, pp. 513-14.

Periodicals

Lecomte, Jean, et al. "Charles Fabry." *Applied Optics* (June 1973): 1117-29.

Nye, Mary Jo. "Physique et physiciens en France, 1918-1940–book reviews." *Science* (8 February 1985): 628.

—Sketch by Annette Petrusso

William Fairbank

William Fairbank
1917–1989
American physicist

As an experimental physicist, William Fairbank traversed several controversial areas, making an impact not just on the physics community, but beyond it. Fairbank's best known work is as a quark hunter. Quarks are theorized to be the smallest subatomic particles. Many scientists believe that quarks are the components, the building blocks, of all conventional subatomic particles. Fairbank has essentially proven the existence of single quarks.

Fairbank's other research has had broader application. He has also studied superconductivity (perfect electrical conduction found in materials that have no resistance to electric currents) and its nature, as well as the essence of magnetism, specifically gravity waves and monopoles. A multi-million dollar project involving an orbiting gyroscope has grown out of Fairbank's work. The project intends to answer questions that have arisen from predictions based on Einstein's relativity theory.

He was born William Martin Fairbank on February 24, 1917, in Minneapolis, Minnesota. His elder brother Henry was also a physics professor, primarily at Duke University. Fairbank started his college education at Whitman College in Walla Walla, Washington, where he earned two undergraduate degrees,

an A.B. in chemistry in 1939, and an A.B. in physics a year later. He met his future wife, Jane Davenport, at Whitman, where she was also a student. After they married, they had three sons together, William Jr., Robert, and Richard. The couple then did a year and a half of graduate work at the University of Washington. Towards the end of World War II, the couple worked for a short time at the Massachusetts Institute of Technology's (MIT) radiation laboratory, where Fairbank did experiments in radar, specifically on overwater tests. He completed his graduate work at Yale University, where he was awarded his Ph.D. in 1948.

Fairbank began his teaching career a year earlier at Amherst College in Maryland, where he taught until 1952. After spending the rest of the 1950s at Duke University, Fairbank secured an appointment as a physics professor at Stanford University in 1959. He remained there until his death 30 years later.

As early as 1977, Fairbank (working with a team that included George Larue) announced that his experiments had generated evidence that quarks existed. Though Fairbank was always cautious in his claims, his findings were always subject to debate as some scientists did not believe that quarks could be produced in his experimental environments. Because of the highly controversial nature of his findings, Fairbank continually tried to refine his experimental set-up to try to eliminate possible irregularities. Fairbank continued to publish his improved results, once in 1981, and again in 1985. Although Fairbank's respectability as a researcher gave credence to his controversial "quark" claims among his peers, to date, no one has been able to reproduce his quark-related experiments.

In 1947, Fairbank conducted his first superconductivity experiments with his brother Henry. These pioneering investigations were some of the earliest experiments on superconductivity. Throughout his career, Fairbank continued to experiment with low-temperature superconductivity. His work focused on materials that when cooled to near absolute zero have no resistance to an electric current. Fairbank's findings have led to worldwide scientific experiments. At Stanford, a superconducting accelerator has been developed, which led to innovative work that produced the first free-electron laser.

Fairbank sometimes had the opportunity to apply the results of his physics experiments to practical matters. In 1975, for example, he developed the Medical Pion Generator, a cancer-killing machine that worked on mouth and throat cancer, as well as some brain and lung cancers, without damaging surrounding tissues. The generator killed cancer cells with tiny nuclear explosions.

Though Fairbank's work has been speculative, the nature of his experiments and theories, as well as the care with which he executed them, brought him accolades. In back-to-back years in the 1960s, Fairbank was named California Scientist of the Year. He was awarded the Oliver E. Buckley Prize (American Physical Society) for research in 1963. Fairbank's work had so many widespread applications that a conference was held in his honor of his 65th birthday. A book titled *Near Zero: New Frontiers in Physics* was published based on the 56 papers presented at the conference. The conference and book exemplify the extensive nature of Fairbank's contributions throughout physics and science.

Though Fairbank retired in 1987, becoming emeritus professor at Stanford, he continued to work. Fairbank died on September 30, 1989, while jogging near the Stanford University campus. Fairbank had worked in his laboratory until the night before his death on his quark experiments, using superconductivity to help prove their existence. In his *San Francisco Chronicle* obituary, colleague Francis Everett was quoted as saying, "When he went into retirement, he decided to concentrate on proving this experiment." Indeed, Everett said, during retirement, Fairbank "worked about twice as hard as the ordinary person."

FURTHER READING:

Books

Biographical Encyclopedia of Scientists. 2nd ed. Bristol: Institute of Physics Publishing, 1994, pp. 277-78.

Fairbank, J. D. et al, eds. *Near Zero: New Frontiers of Physics*. New York: W. H. Freeman, 1988.

Periodicals

Cabrera, Blas, and C. W. F. Everitt. "Obituaries: William M. Fairbank." *Physics Today* (February 1991): 112-113.

Cabrera, Blas. "William Martin Fairbank (1917-1989)." *Nature* (November 9, 1989): 125.

Garcia, Dawn. "William Fairbank, Stanford Pioneer of Superconductors." *The San Francisco Chronicle* (October 2, 1989): B6.

"Obituary of Prof William Fairbank." *The Daily Telegraph* (October 14, 1989): 17.

"Physics Researcher William Fairbank." *Chicago Tribune* (October 6, 1989): 15.

Taubes, Gary. "Is Anything Left out There? Discoveries in Particle Physics." *Discover* (April 1987): 42.

Trefil, James S. "Closing in on Creation." *Smithsonian* (May 1983): 33-51.

"William Fairbank, 72; Stanford Expert on Superconductivity." *Los Angeles Times* (October 3, 1989): sec. 1, p. 22.

—Sketch by Annette Petrusso

Etta Zuber Falconer
1933–
American algebraist

Etta Zuber Falconer has encouraged hundreds of young people, particularly African–American women, to study mathematics and the sciences through her classroom teaching and program work at Spelman College in Atlanta, where, she told author Fran Hodgkins in an interview, she "was able to crystallize my desire to change the prevailing pattern of limited access and limited success for African American women in mathematics." Falconer received the **Louise Hay** Award for her contributions to mathematics education in 1995.

Falconer was born in Tupelo, Mississippi, in 1933, the younger of two daughters of Dr. Walter A. Zuber and Zadie L. (Montgomery) Zuber. She attended Tupelo public schools and graduated from George Washington High School in 1949. At Fisk University in Nashville, she found two of her three life mentors: Dr. **Evelyn Boyd Granville** and Dr. Lee Lorch. Granville taught just one year at Fisk. For Falconer, seeing an African American woman teaching at the college level was inspiring; most instructors were men. She

Etta Zuber Falconer

had intended to teach high–school mathematics after graduation, but Lorch, who served as chair of the mathematics department, encouraged her to go on to graduate school. Falconer graduated *summa cum laude* with a bachelor of science degree in mathematics in 1953, and went on to earn her master's degree in mathematics from the University of Wisconsin in 1954.

From 1954 to 1963, she taught mathematics at Okolona Junior College in Okolona, Mississippi. While teaching there, she met and married her husband, Dolan Falconer. They would have three children, Dolan Jr., an engineer; Alice (Falconer) Wilson, a physician; and Walter, also a physician.

In 1963, Falconer left Okolona to teach at Chattanooga Public School. Two years later, she joined the faculty of Spelman College in Atlanta as an instructor. In 1969, she earned her Ph.D. in mathematics from Emory University, where she studied under her third mentor, Trevor Evans, who encouraged her growth in algebra and her study of quasigroups and loops. Her dissertation was titled "Quasigroup Identities Invariant Under Isotopy." Out of her dissertation came two published papers, "Isotopy Invariants in Quasigroups" and "Isotopes of Some Special Quasigroup Varieties." After receiving her doctorate, Falconer held an associate professorship at Norfolk State College from 1971 to 1972. She received a master's degree in computer science from Atlanta University in 1982, and also attended the

National Science Foundation Teacher Training Institute at the University of Illinois from 1962 to 1965.

Falconer has spent most of her professional career at Spelman College, her mother's alma mater. She has held the positions of instructor/associate professor (1965–71), professor of mathematics and chair of the mathematics department (1972–82), chair of the division of natural sciences (1982–90), director of science programs and policy (1990), and associate provost for science programs and policy (1991–present). Falconer has been Spelman's Fuller E. Callaway Professor of Mathematics since 1990.

Falconer has devoted her career to encouraging African American students, particularly women, to study mathematics and the sciences. She is the director of Spelman College's NASA Women in Science and Engineering Scholars program (WISE), which fosters promising women students and encourages them to continue into graduate school. Among students' fields of study are applied mathematics, chemistry, and industrial engineering. Approximately 150 women have taken part in the program since its inception in 1987, and the program will soon celebrate the first of its alumnae receiving her Ph.D. Falconer also coordinates the university's NASA Undergraduate Scholar Awards program, which, like WISE, allows undergraduate students to conduct research at NASA facilities. In addition, she is one of the founders of the National Association of Mathematicians, which promotes the concerns of African American students and mathematicians, and the Atlanta Minority Women in Science Network.

Falconer has received many awards in recognition of her work on behalf of the next generation of scientists. In addition to the Louise Hay Award from the Association for Women in Mathematics (AWM), she also received the Giants in Science Award from the Quality Education for Minorities Network (1995). Her other honors include: Spelman College Presidential Faculty Award for Distinguished Service (1994); Spelman College Presidential Award for Excellence in Teaching (1988); United Negro College Fund Distinguished Faculty Award (1986–87); Achievement and Service Award, presented by the Atlanta Minority Women in Science Network and the Auxiliary to the Atlanta Medical Association; and the National Association of Mathematicians' Distinguished Service Award (1994). Falconer also received an honorary doctor of science degree from the University of Wisconsin at Madison in 1996. She is a member of Phi Beta Kappa, Pi Mu Epsilon (honorary mathematics fraternity), and Beta Kappa Chi (honorary scientific society). In addition, she has served in a variety of roles in the following organizations: the American Association for the Advancement of Science, the American Mathematical Society, the AWM, the Mathematical Association of America, the National

Association of Mathematicians, and the National Science Foundation.

SELECTED WRITINGS BY FALCONER:

"Isotopy Invariants in Quasigroups." *Transactions of the American Mathematical Society* 151 (1970): 511–526.
"Isotopes of Some Special Quasigroup Varieties." *Acta Mathematica* 22 (1971): 73–79.
"Women in Science at Spelman College." *Signs* 4 (1978): 176–177.
"A Story of Success: The Sciences at Spelman College." *SAGE* 6 (1989): 36–38.
"Views of an African American Woman on Mathematics Meetings." *A Century of Mathematics Meetings.* Edited by Bettye Anne Case. American Mathematical Society, 1996.

FURTHER READING:

Bailey, Lakiea. "Etta Falconer." *Biographies of Women Mathematicians.* June 1997. http://www/scottlan.edu/lriddle/women/chronol.htm (July 21, 1997).
Falconer, Etta Zuber, interview with Fran Hodgkins conducted May 1, 1997.

—*Sketch by Fran Hodgkins*

Joseph C. Farman
1930–
English atmospheric chemist

Joseph C. Farman is best known for his discovery of the hole in the stratospheric ozone layer over Antarctica in 1984. This was a momentous scientific breakthrough, revealing unequivocally that human activity, in particular the production of chlorofluorocarbons (CFCs), has altered the protective atmosphere that surrounds the Earth, posing an unprecedented threat to the future of living organisms.

Farman's work with the British Antarctic Survey was once in danger of being eliminated because it was thought too "unsophisticated." In the wake of his discovery, Farman has been active in speaking to governments and lay groups about the dangers of ozone depletion, as well as the negative consequences of commercial exploitation of Antarctica. Within three years of the publication of Farman's observations on ozone depletion, international agreements were formulated to slow worldwide production of CFCs.

Farman was born in Norwich, England, in 1930, the son of a builder. He studied mathematics and natural sciences at the University of Cambridge, worked briefly in aerospace, and in 1956 joined the Falkland Islands Dependency Survey, now the British Antarctic Survey. The Survey is an agency of the National Environmental Research Council, and Farman became its section head of atmospheric dynamics. Farman initially worked in the Falkland Islands and in Edinburgh, Scotland, then in 1976 moved to Cambridge with the Survey; at that time he was married to a history teacher and was responsible for training young scientists.

Discovers "Hole" in the Earth's Ozone Shield

One of the activities of the British Antarctic Survey since 1957 has been to monitor levels atmospheric ozone (O_3) through the use of instruments mounted on balloons and with ground-based spectrophotometers. The ozone "layer," concentrated in the stratosphere about 14 mi (23 km) from the Earth's surface, shields the Earth from damaging ultraviolet (UV) rays. Ground-based instruments measure ozone indirectly, via the amount of ultraviolet light that is incident upon them. Normal readings for ozone in the Antarctic usually fluctuated around 400 Dobson units (DU), and in 1982 Farman's ground-based instruments at Halley Bay and the Argentine Islands readings as low as 130 DUs.

"In 1982, we noticed strange depletions in the layer above the Antarctic," Farman wrote in the November 12, 1987 issue of *New Scientist* magazine. "However, ozone levels are notorious for bouncing about and our instruments were then rather old. The Americans with their satellite viewing of the Antarctic continent from 800 kilometers up had not spotted anything, so we decided to check the figures with newer instruments. By October 1984, we were sure something dramatic was happening above Antarctica." It was learned that the computer processing data from the U.S. satellite Nimbus had been programmed to ignore readings that varied by more than one-third. Farman's examination of past records showed that ozone had been declining since 1977. He and his colleagues B. G. Gardiner and J. D. Shanklin published their findings in *Nature* in May 1985. They implicated CFCs in ozone depletion, suggesting that the very low temperatures prevailing in midwinter makes the Antarctic particularly sensitive to the buildup of destructive inorganic chlorine.

Ozone is naturally created and destroyed in an atmospheric cycle that has been in equilibrium for millions of years. Accelerated ozone destruction due to CFCs (chemicals used primarily in refrigeration and air conditioning equipment, and cleaning solvents) was foreseen in the 1970s. At that time, aerosol cans were responsible for most releases, and laws were passed in the United States, Canada, and Europe to ban nonessential uses. Use of CFCs continued, however, and the time between manufacture of a CFC and its release into the atmosphere has averaged about three years. CFCs are stable in the lower atmosphere, but as they diffuse outward toward the stratosphere, intense UV radiation causes them to release chlorine (Cl) atoms that destroy ozone.

The Mechanism of Ozone Destruction

Ozone is created primarily in the equatorial regions by UV acting on oxygen molecules. The ozone is then spread over the Earth via atmospheric circulation, and is thinnest at the poles.

Farman's discovery stimulated a great deal of research activity related to the chemical reactions involved in ozone destruction and creation of the ozone hole. Antarctic ozone depletion occurs primarily when temperatures in the ozone layer get cold enough for icy clouds to form. These clouds increase the UV activation of chlorine.

The process leading to ozone destruction is a catalytic reaction; that is, the chlorine is not used up in the process, but continues to destroy more ozone for many years. The chlorine atoms are produced in the atmosphere during the daytime because of the action of UV; consequently, the ozone hole starts each year in midwinter at the sunlit edge of Antarctica. Growth of the ozone hole is exacerbated by the winter polar vortex, a huge pool of stable air that sits over the Antarctic pole. In October, at the polar winter's end, the vortex collapses and ozone-containing air is drawn in from elsewhere.

In 1993, as much as 70 percent of the ozone over the Antarctic was destroyed and the "hole" grew to an area the size of North America. At the same time, losses of greater than 25 percent were seen in the Arctic. Ozone losses mean increased levels of UV radiation reach the Earth, which in turn are directly related to increased levels of mutations, skin cancers, and cataracts. UV also kills phytoplankton, the basis of the Antarctic food chain, and reduces crop yields, portending widespread negative effects on living organisms.

Lobbies for Restrictions of CFCs

Farman has been an outspoken advocate of the enviromental future of Antarctica, urging that the continent be declared a world park for nature and science, and has lobbied strongly for increased restrictions on the manufacture and use of CFCs. " [The warning from scientists] is that CFCs are dangerous and that enough is enough," he wrote in 1987. "The chemical industry may think it has many years in which to discover and to introduce substitutes for CFCs, but we need them now, not tomorrow." At a 1989 conference in Helsinki, 81 nations agreed to phase out CFC production by the end of the twentieth century, a deadline that was later tightened. However, even with complete halting of CFC production, many decades will be required to significantly restore the ozone layer.

Farman has retired from the British Antarctic Survey, but continues to work as a consultant for the European Ozone Research Coordinating Unit.

SELECTED WRITINGS BY FARMAN:

Periodicals

"What Hope for the Ozone Layer Now?" *New Scientist* (November 12, 1987): 50-54.
(With B.G. Gardiner and J. D. Shanklin) "Large Losses of Total Ozone in Antarctica Reveal Seasonal ClO_x/NO_x Interaction." *Nature* (May 16, 1985): 207-210.

FURTHER READING:

Books

The Cambridge Dictionary of Scientists. Cambridge: Cambridge University Press, 1996, p. 107.

Periodicals

Barker, Dennis. "Man Who First Sent Up Balloon." *Guardian* (June 28, 1990): 3.
Brown, Paul. "Scientists Flay Antarctic Policy." *Guardian* (April 19, 1991): 5.

—Sketch by Jill Carpenter

Mary Celine Fasenmyer
1906–1996
American computer analyst

Sister Fasenmyer spent most of her professional life teaching at various schools in Pennsylvania, but even her doctoral research was already setting the stage for the brave new world of computer–driven mathematical proofs.

Fasenmyer was born in central Pennsylvania on October 4, 1906. Her parents, George and Cecilia, lived in Crown, where George had an oil lease he tended as a business. Cecilia died only a year after

Sister Mary Celine Fasenmyer

geoning field of computer technology was already being drawn upon to aid the superhuman tasks of high mathematics computations.

Discrete Math

Even today, the new science of proving hypergeometric identities via computer programming is influenced by Fasenmyer's work. Herbert Wilf, Marko Petkovsek, and Doron Zeilberger acknowledge her influence on their project in their 1996 book *A=B*. Wilf, of the University of Pennsylvania, was responsible for posting the only testimonial on the Internet devoted to Fasenmyer after his book's publication. Wilf only found out about Fasenmyer's sudden death on December 27, 1996, just after New Year's, 1997. Fasenmyer's colleagues at Mercyhurst College, where Fasenmyer held a full professorship for decades, had been going through her papers when they discovered a memento from a Discrete Math convention in Florida in 1994. Sister M. Eustace Taylor was moved to write the three authors, to thank them for continuing to apply Fasenmyer's methods in their work.

Fasenmyer was not highly celebrated in her day, though she clearly molded generations of students and engaged her peers through the Mathematical Association of America. With the world of computers still growing in terms of capacity and ability, however, her reputation may well grow along with it.

SELECTED WRITINGS BY FASENMYER:

Fasenmyer, Sister Mary Celine. "On Recurrence Relations," *American Mathematical Monthly* 56 (1949): 14.

FURTHER READING:

American Men & Women of Science. Thirteenth edition. New York: R.R. Bowker, Co., 1976.

Other

Wilf, Herbert. "Remarks on the life of Sister Mary Celine Fasenmyer." http://www.cis.upenn.edu/~wilf/celine (July 1997).

—*Sketch by Jennifer Kramer*

Fasenmyer was born, but George remarried a few years later to a much younger woman named Josephine. Fasenmyer's earliest formal education took place less than 30 miles from her hometown, in Titusville, at a school called St. Joseph's Academy. She graduated at age 17 and began teaching.

The Community

Fasenmyer was strongly impressed by her Catholic education, as she wound up a ten–year phase of her life teaching her strongest subject by gaining an A.B. degree from Mercyhurst, a Catholic college in Erie, Pennsylanvia. She was already pledged to the Sisters of Mercy there by 1933, as she soon embarked to teach at St. Justin's, a high school in Pittsburgh, at the order's behest. Her community of sisters later decided to send Fasenmyer to the University of Pittsburgh for an M.A. This she earned in 1937 with a major in mathematics and a minor in physics. A change of pace came between 1942 and 1946, during which Fasenmyer studied under Earl Rainville at the University of Michigan.

Rainville directed Fasenmyer's doctoral thesis on the subject of algorithmic deduction. Algorithms have been studied since medieval times, but here they were applied to more novel mathematical entities known as hypergeometric polynomial sequences. Thanks to a postdoctoral paper published in the *American Mathematical Monthly*, Fasenmyer's refined methodology reached a wide audience of experimenters. The bur-

Käte Fenchel
1905–1983
German–born Danish algebraist

Without benefit of more than an undergraduate education in mathematics, Käte Fenchel published four treatises on pure mathematics in her lifetime. Suffering through poverty compounded by persecution because of her Jewish heritage, Fenchel maintained her passion for mathematics by studying and researching on her own. Her primary interests lie in finite nonabelian groups and algebra. Fenchel's accomplishments leave a profound legacy of perseverance for women mathematicians as well as Danish mathematics.

Fenchel was born Käte Sperling in Berlin, Germany, on December 21, 1905, to Otto and Rusza Sperling. Fenchel's father worked in publishing and her mother was a bookkeeper. Her parents separated when she was young, and she and her older sister grew up in semi–poverty. Though she grew up in less fortunate circumstances, Fenchel won scholarships that allowed her to attended a private girls school. In high school Fenchel realized she wanted to be a mathematician.

From 1924 to 1928, Fenchel received the rest of her formal education at the University of Berlin's Mathematical Institute. In addition to her primary area of interest, pure mathematics, she studied philosophy and physics. Although Fenchel could have written a thesis, and perhaps gone on to earn a doctorate, her economic circumstances combined with an astute perception that she probably would not be employed in research because of her gender dissuaded her from further study of this type.

Instead, Fenchel did the course work required to become a high school mathematics teacher. She taught for two years (1931–1933) before she was dismissed because of the growing Nazi oppression of Jews. After tutoring students privately for a short time, she and her fiance, fellow mathematician and Jew Werner Fenchel, escaped to Denmark. The couple married in Denmark in December 1933.

Although Fenchel's formal education had long ceased, she kept working on her algebra research on her own time. In Denmark, she worked as a secretary for a Danish mathematics professor from 1933 to 1943. In 1937, Fenchel published her first mathematical paper (on vectormodules) in a mathematics journal. Three years later, she gave birth to her only child, a son, Tom. As the Germans closed in on Denmark during World War II, Fenchel's employment and her mathematical activities temporarily ceased when the Fenchel family eluded Nazi persecution by moving to Sweden. The family moved back to Denmark in 1945 after the war ended.

Fenchel did not publish on mathematics again until 1962. In that year, she published two papers. One examined odd order groups and group decomposition; the other focused on structure matrix and group representation theory. Fenchel returned to teaching soon thereafter, and served as a lecturer at Aarhus University in Denmark, from 1965 to 1970.

She published her last paper in 1978 on Frobenius's theorem and group theory, five years before her death during the night of December 18–19, 1983.

SELECTED WRITINGS BY FENCHEL:

"An Everywhere Dense Vectormodule with Discrete One–Dimensional Submodules." *Matematisk Tidsskrift* (1937): 94–96.
"Eine Bemerkung über Gruppen ungerader Ordnung." *Mathematica Scandinavica* (1962): 182–88.
"Beziehungen zwischen der Struktur einer endlichen Gruppe und einer speziellen Darstellung." *Monatshefte für Mathematik* (1962): 397–409.
"On a Theorem of Frobenius." *Mathematica Scandinavica* (1978): 243–50.

FURTHER READING:

Books

Høyrup, Else. "Käte Fenchel," in *Women of Mathematics: A Bibliographic Sourcebook.* Edited by Louise S. Grinstein and Paul J. Campbell. New York: Greenwood Press, 1987, pp. 30–32.

Other

"Käte Fenchel." *Biographies of Women Mathematicians.* June 1997. http://www.scottland.edu/lriddle/women/chrono.htm (July 22, 1997).

—*Sketch by Annette Petruso*

Margaret Clay Ferguson
1863–1951
American botanist

Margaret Clay Ferguson, the first woman president of the Botanical Society of America, made important scholarly and educational contributions to the field of botany. As a scholar, her early work focused on the life history of plants, especially the reproductive process. Her study of the North American pine became a standard for plant life histories used by countless other botanists. Ferguson's later work concerned plant genetics. In addition to her productive work as a botanist, Ferguson's role as an educator, mostly at Wellesley College, was equally influential. She improved the curriculum for undergraduate botany education, and welcomed an unparalled number of female botanists to the field.

Ferguson was born on August 29, 1863, in Orleans, New York, to Robert Bell and Hannah (Warner) Ferguson. Her parents were farmers, and she had five siblings. From the age of 14, Ferguson taught in local public schools while continuing her own education at the Genesee Wesleyan Seminary in Lima, New York. She graduated from the Seminary in 1885. Ferguson was a special student at Wellesley College, where she studied botany and chemistry, from 1888 until 1891.

From 1891-93, Ferguson served as the head of the science department in the Gambier, Ohio, Harcourt Place Seminary. Though Ferguson earned no degree while at Wellesley, department head Susan Hallowell was so impressed with her work that she invited Ferguson to be an instructor there in 1893. Ferguson later earned both her B.S. and Ph.D. from Cornell University in botany. Her thesis began her life's academic work concerning the life history and reproductive process of plants. After earning her Ph.D. in 1901, Ferguson rose through the ranks at Wellesley from instructor to associate professor to full professor, and finally to head of the botany department in 1930.

The first focus of Ferguson's scholarly achievements concerned the physiology of the spores of fungi. Next, she expanded on her thesis, exploring native pine and its functional morphology and cytology. Her detailed analysis in these areas was vital, especially to fellow botanists who used her work as a standard for their own. By the mid-1920s, Ferguson moved on to plant genetics and inheritance. She found the genus *Petunia* useful for a higher plant genetics study. Through this study Ferguson proved that plant flower color and pattern are variable in that they do not follow Mendelian laws of inheritance, which state that the hybridized offspring of plants have a statistically determined appearance.

Ferguson's work as an educator was equally important. She modernized Wellesley's botany facilities and improved the course of study, molding Wellesley into an important institution for undergraduate education in plant sciences. As a teacher, Ferguson believed in the then-radical idea that botanists should study other sciences—such as chemistry, zoology, and physics—because of their relevance to botany. Ferguson also introduced lab work in the greenhouse as an important part of botany education. Her efforts included raising funds and designing a new botany building and greenhouses. In 1943, the greenhouses were named in her honor.

After stepping down from her administrative position in 1930, Ferguson spent two years as a research professor at Wellesley before retiring in 1932. She continued to receive accolades, such as an honorary degree from Mount Holyoke in 1937, and in 1943, she was named a fellow of the New York Academy of Sciences. Ferguson ended her research in 1938, when she moved to Seneca Castle, New York, to be near family. She later moved to Florida, then San Diego, California. Ferguson, who never married, suffered a heart attack and died on August 28, 1951 in San Diego.

SELECTED WRITINGS BY FERGUSON:

Periodicals

"Contributions to the Knowledge of the Life History of *Pinus* with Special Reference to Sporogenesis, the Development of the Gametophytes and Fertilization." *Proceedings of the Washington Academy of Sciences* (1906): 101-02.

FURTHER READING:

Books

Bailey, Martha J. *American Women in Science: A Biographical Dictionary.* Denver: ABC-CLIO, 1994, pp. 112-13.
Hirsch, Ann M. and Lisa J. Marroni. *Notable American Women, The Modern Period.* Edited by B. Sicherman and C.H. Green, Cambridge: The Belknap Press of Harvard University Press, 1980, pp. 229-30.
Ogilvie, Marilyn Bailey. *Women in Science: Antiquity through the Nineteenth Century.* Cambridge: MIT Press, 1986, pp. 84-85.
Siegel, Patricia Joan, and Kay Thomas Finley. *Women in the Scientific Search: An American Bio-bibliography, 1724-1979.* Metuchen: The Scarecrow Press, Inc., 1985, pp. 96-97.

—*Sketch by Annette Petrusso*

Mary Peters Fieser
1909–1997
American organic chemist

Mary Peters Fieser's substantial contributions to the field of organic chemistry include her work on the Harvard research team headed by her husband, **Louis Fieser,** and her authorship of numerous key texts and reference books in the field. She was involved in numerous important areas, including the synthesis of vitamin K, the development of an antimalarial drug, and the synthesis of cortisone and carcinogenic chemicals for medical research. For her research, publications, and skill in teaching chemistry students how to write, she was awarded the prestigious Garvan Medal in 1971.

Fieser was born in 1909 in Atchison, Kansas, to Robert Peters, an English professor, and Julia (Clutz) Peters, a bookstore owner and manager. Her father accepted a position at what is now Carnegie-Mellon University, and Fieser grew up in Harrisburg, Pennsylvania. Her family believed strongly in educational and professional achievement for women: Fieser's mother did graduate work in English, and her sister, Ruth, became a mathematics professor. Her grandmother, who had educated her seven children herself at home until they were college age, impressed upon Fieser the importance of using her education constructively.

After attending a private girls' school, Fieser went to Bryn Mawr College, where she earned a B.A. in chemistry in 1930. There, she met her future husband, **Louis Fieser**, who was a chemistry instructor at the college. She enjoyed his courses, finding his emphasis on experimental rather than theoretical chemistry to be especially interesting. When Louis left Bryn Mawr in 1930 to teach at Harvard, she went with him. There, she performed chemistry research in his laboratory while earning a master's degree in organic chemistry, which she received in 1936.

When the couple married in 1932, Fieser continued her professional association with her husband on his research team. This arrangement benefited Fieser enormously in her professional career, because bias against women in the field of chemistry very strong at that time. For instance, her analytical chemistry professor at Harvard, Gregory Paul Baxter, refused to allow her to perform her experiments in the laboratory with the rest of the class. Instead, Fieser had to perform experiments in the deserted basement of another building, with little or no supervision. Once married, however, she was free to conduct research on her husband's team unhampered. As she commented during an interview with the *Journal of Chemical Education,* there were too many obstacles to an academic career in chemistry as a single woman, but after she was married, "I could do as much chemistry as I wanted, and it didn't matter what Professor Baxter thought of me."

Contributes to Vitamin K Synthesis

As part of Louis Fieser's research team, Mary Fieser helped develop a practical method of obtaining substantial amounts of vitamin K. The antihemorrhagic properties of vitamin K had been discovered during the 1930s by **Henrik Dam** in Copenhagen. Researchers had discovered this vitamin in green plants and especially in dried alfalfa, but the amount available from these sources was too small to be of

practical use in medical therapy. The Fieser research group developed a method of synthesizing large amounts of vitamin K in a short period of time. The vitamin's blood-clotting characteristic has proved useful in prenatal therapy and other therapeutic purposes as well.

The Fiesers also focused on the use of naphthoquinones as antimalarial drugs. Quinine was one of the standard drugs used to treat malaria. When Japan invaded the East Indies during World War II, most of the world's supply of quinine became inaccessible to the Allies. The Fieser research team undertook a study of naphthoquinones as an alternative treatment. The Fiesers' research focused on isolating and identifying intermediate compounds along the reaction pathway. Their work ultimately contributed to the synthesis of the antimalarial drug lapinone.

Fieser worked on numerous other projects, including studies of the chemical causes of cancer. She helped develop methods of synthesizing various carcinogenic chemicals for use in medical research. She also played an important role in one of the Fiesers' more well-known projects: their contribution to the synthesis of cortisone, a steroid hormone used in the treatment of rheumatoid arthritis.

Publishes Major Textbooks and Reference Works

Fieser was highly regarded by her colleagues for her skill as a research chemist. Harvard chemist William von Doering is quoted in the *Journal of Chemical Education* as saying that she was "a very gifted experimentalist" and an "active, influential part of the team." In addition to her research, Fieser wrote or co-wrote with her husband a dozen chemistry texts and reference books, beginning in 1944 with the best-selling textbook *Organic Chemistry.* One of their most widely used publications, *Reagents for Organic Synthesis,* was the first reference work of its kind for researchers in organic chemistry. It was the result of a comprehensive, international review of organic chemistry literature from which Mary Fieser culled the results of studies in chemical synthesis.

Fieser's books were especially noteworthy because of her expert writing skills—an unusual ability for a chemist at that time. Fieser attempted to improve the quality of writing in her field by publishing *Style Guide for Chemists.* She and her husband, also a skilled writer, often argued at length over minor stylistic issues, such as the placement of a comma. These differences over writing style prompted Fieser's sister, Ruth, to suggest that their by-line "Fieser and Fieser" be changed to "Fieser versus Fieser."

In 1971, Fieser was awarded the Garvan Medal for her research contributions, her writing, and her skill in teaching chemistry students how to write. The Garvan Medal was established to "honor an American woman for distinguished service in chemistry." Her colleagues also noted that the awards her husband received were due at least in part to her efforts in the laboratory. In her leisure time, Fieser enjoyed indulging her strong competitive streak by organizing games for her husband's research group after work hours and setting up contests in ping-pong, badminton, and horseshoes for the graduate students. She and her husband owned many cats, including one named in honor of their work on synthesizing vitamin K. Their cats' photographs were used in their published work and came to be their trademark. Mary Fieser died on March 22, 1997 in her home in Belmont, Massachusetts.

SELECTED WRITINGS BY FIESER:

Books

Organic Chemistry. New York: Wiley, 1944.
Style Guide for Chemists. Reinhold, 1959.
Reagents for Organic Synthesis. Vols. 1-16. New York: Wiley, 1967.

FURTHER READING:

Books

O'Neill, Lois Decker, ed. *The Women's Book of World Records and Achievements.* New York: Doubleday, 1979, p. 168.

Periodicals

Long, Tom. "Mary Fieser, Organic Chemist, Writer Had Harvard Career; at 87" (obituary). *Boston Globe* (26 March 1997): E17.
O'Neill, Lois Decker, ed. "Mary Fieser: Garvan Medal." *Chemical & Engineering News* (14 December 1970): 64.
Pramer, Stacey. "Mary Fieser: A Transitional Figure in the History of Women." *Journal of Chemical Education* (March 1985): 186-91.

—Sketch by Donna Olshansky

James L. Flanagan
1925–

American electrical engineer

James Flanagan's most important work applies the principles of electrical engineering to the solution of communication problems, including areas such as

James L. Flanagan

speech processing, recognition, and synthesis; human-computer communication; acoustic systems; and digital communications.

Flanagan was born in Greenwood, Mississippi, on August 26, 1925. After completing military service with the U.S. Army in 1946, Flanagan completed a bachelor of science degree in electrical engineering at Mississippi State University in 1948. He enrolled at the Massachusetts Institute of Technology (MIT) and completed his master of science in electrical engineering in 1950 and a doctor of science degree in electrical engineering in 1955.

From 1948 to 1957, Flanagan held a variety of posts as he pursued graduate studies. From 1948 to 1950, he was a research engineer in the Acoustics Laboratory at MIT; from 1950 to 1952 he was an assistant professor of electrical engineering at Mississippi State University. He returned to the MIT Acoustics Laboratory as a research engineer from 1953 to 1954, then joined the U.S. Air Force Cambridge Research Center as an electronic scientist, where he remained until 1957.

In 1957 Flanagan joined the technical staff of Bell Laboratories in Murray Hill, New Jersey. This was the beginning of a 33-year career with Bell, during which Flanagan conducted and directed research in digital communications and communication systems.

Flanagan was in the scientific vanguard of researchers who recognized the value of computers in telecommunications. He pioneered the use of digital computers for acoustic signal processing and helped develop the signal coding algorithms that are now used in telecommunications and voice mail.

Flanagan remained with the technical staff of Bell Laboratories until 1961. He then accepted the position of head of the Speech and Auditory Research Department, which he held until 1967. From 1967 until 1985, Flanagan served as the head of the Acoustics Research Department of AT&T Bell Laboratories, and in 1985, he was named director of the Information Principles Research Laboratory at the AT&T laboratories in New Jersey.

Launching a Second Career

After more than three decades of achievement, Flanagan retired from AT&T in 1990. He immediately accepted a post with Rutgers University in Piscataway, New Jersey, as director of the Center for Computer Aids for Industrial Productivity (CAIP).

CAIP conducts research aimed at crafting solutions to communications challenges in industry. The center works closely with the business community to develop workable systems with broad-based industrial applications.

Flanagan is the principal investigator for a project that is typical of the type of work undertaken at CAIP—the Distributed System for Collaborative Information Processing and Learning (DISCIPLE). The DISCIPLE project's goal is to develop methods and tools for presenting, manipulating, and analyzing multimedia objects, regardless of the type of computer platform or network protocol involved.

Flanagan's research team is developing a structure that will enhance data analysis and the comparison and delivery of multimedia objects from the source to participants who may be using a variety of groupware programs. The investigative group is involved in designing software that is flexible, but sophisticated enough to support high-level protocols and systems.

DISCIPLE also reflects Flanagan's reputation in its sources of funding; the project is supported by several contracts, including one from the National Science Foundation, and funds from the New Jersey Commission on Science and Technology.

Flanagan is also pursuing research in computer speech generation. He is studying ways to more accurately define speech signals by quantifying the characteristics and mechanics of human speech. He is developing computational methods based on fluid flow analysis (the Navier-Stokes description) rather than conventional linear models to define vocal cord sound generation and resonance in the human vocal tract. Flanagan anticipates developing a revolutionary set of parameters that will support new methods of speech synthesis that will be close to the sound quality of human speech and sound natural to listeners.

Flanagan is a member of numerous professional organizations, many of which he has served in an administration capacity. He is a member of the National Academy of Engineering and the National Academy of Sciences; a fellow of the American Academy of Arts and Sciences, the Institute of Electrical and Electronics Engineers, and the Acoustical Society of America; has served as president of the IEEE Acoustics, Speech and Signal Processing Society and the Acoustical Society of America; and has served on the scientific advisory boards of the Committee on Voice Communications, National Security Agency; Institute of Defense Analyses; the United States Air Force; and Callier Center at the University of Texas at Dallas.

Flanagan has also served on the advisory panel on White House Tapes, the Board of Governors of the American Institute of Physics, the executive council of the Committee on Hearing and Bioacoustics of the National Research Council, and the membership committee of the National Academy of Sciences.

Flanagan's work has garnered numerous awards, including the 1996 National Medal of Science; the Medal of the European Speech Communication Association, 1991; the Gold Medal of the Acoustical Society of America, 1986; the Edison Medal of the IEEE, 1986; the L.M. Ericsson International Prize in Telecommunications, 1985; the IEEE Centennial Medal, 1984; the distinguished Service Award in Science from the American Speech and Hearing Association, 1977; and the Achievement Award of the IEEE Acoustics, Speech and Signal Processing Society, 1970. He has been recognized with honorary doctorates by the University of Paris and Polytechnic University of Madrid, the Marconi International Fellowship, and the James Clark Maxwell Lectureship, IEE.

Flanagan has published more than 200 technical papers and holds 48 U.S. patents.

SELECTED WRITINGS BY FLANAGAN:

Books

Speech Analysis Synthesis and Perception. New York: Springer-Verlag, 1972.

Periodicals

"Technologies for Multimedia Communications." *Proceedings IEEE,* Volume 84, No. 4, 1994, 590-603.
(With K. Ishizaka and K. I. Shipley) "Synthesis of Speech from a Dynamic Model of the Vocal Cords and Vocal Tract." *Bell Systems Technical Journal* 544 (1975): 485-506.

Other

(With I. Marsic) "Issues in Measuring the Benefits of Multimodal Interfaces." Invited paper for the ICASSP-97, Munich, Germany, April, 1997.

(With A. Shaikh, S. Juth, A. Medl, I. Marsic, and C. Kulikowski) "An Architecture for Multimodal Information Fusion." Presented at the Workshop on Perceptual User Interfaces, Fanff, Alberta, Canada, October 1997.

FURTHER READING:

Books

American Men & Women of Science. New Providence, New Jersey: R. R. Bowker Publishing, 1992 - 93. P. 1153.

Eckes, Kristin A., ed. *Who's Who in Science and Engineering.* New Providence, New Jersey: Reed Reference Publishing, 1996.

Other

"DISCIPLE Distributed System for Collaborative Information Processing and Learning." September 24, 1997. http://www.caip.rutgers.edu/multimedia/grooupware/index.html (December 12, 1997).

"Computational Models for Speech Generation." http://www.cs.tufts.edu/-jacob/isgw/Flanagan.html (December 12, 1997).

—Sketch by Angie Mullig

Karl A. Folkers
1906–1997
American biomedical researcher

Karl Folkers' work in vitamins, hormones, and antibiotics has advanced basic knowledge in biochemistry, as well as helped people lead healthier lives. His career, spanning more than 60 years, concentrated on the identification of chemicals related to the life processes, and on linking chemistry and clinical medicine. As a leader in basic research at Merck, he isolated, elucidated the structure, and synthesized a number of organic compounds, including vitamin B_6, vitamin B_{12}, mevalonic acid and coenzyme Q, and gave impetus to commercial production of these chemicals. He also served as president of the Stanford Research Institute, and was founding director of the Institute for Biomedical Research at the University of

Karl A. Folkers

Texas, Austin. At the time of his death, at age 91, he was emeritus Ashbel Smith Professor at University of Texas, Austin and president of the Karl Folkers Foundation for Biomedical and Clinical Research.

Karl August Folkers was born on September 1, 1906, in Decatur, Illinois, the only child of August William and Susan Black Folkers. He decided early on to become a chemist. During the summer following his junior year at the University of Illinois, he worked in the laboratory of John Johnson for 40 cents an hour, paid from Johnson's personal funds. In his senior year, he worked on a research project in organic synthesis with the biochemist Carl "Speed" Marvel. When Folkers graduated from Illinois in 1928 with honors in chemistry, Marvel encouraged him to go to the University of Wisconsin to pursue a Ph.D. degree. At Wisconsin, Folkers' Ph.D. advisor was Homer Adkins, who required students to work independently. They sank or swam, and Folkers swam. He received his degree in 1931, then went to Yale University's Sterling Chemistry Laboratory for postdoctoral work with professor Treat B. Johnson.

At Yale, Folkers met and married Selma Leona Johnson. They had two children, Cynthia Carol and Richard Karl.

First Career at Merck

In 1934 Folkers left Yale to work at Merck & Co., in Rahway, New Jersey, at a salary of $200 a month.

At Merck, he became a leader in basic research, and rose steadily in the company. In 1938 he became assistant director of research; in 1945, associate director of research and development; in 1953, director of organic and biological chemical research; in 1956, executive director of fundamental research; and in 1962, vice-president for exploratory research.

In 1937, vitamin B_6 was first isolated at Merck; within three years Folkers and his associates had determined its structure and synthesized it. The vitamin plays an important role in protein and carbohydrate metabolism and has a variety of medical values. Folkers isolated vitamin B_{12} in 1947, and spent the following eight years elucidating its complex 183-atom structure; it is used in the treatment of pernicious anemia. He synthesized pantothenic acid in 1940, and biotin in 1945, and also worked on antibiotics. He was the first to synthesize penicillin, and worked out the structure of streptomycin and novobiocin, contributing to their purification and the introduction of new forms. He also isolated and synthesized mevalonic acid, an important chemical in the body's metabolism of cholesterol. He has worked on peptide hormones, including corticotropin B, which controls metabolism, and alkaloids such as morphine and curare. In the late 1950s, Folkers and fellow researchers at Merck identified and synthesized coenzyme Q, found in every cell of the body; for many years he has devoted his energies to research on CoQ and its use in clinical medicine. Folkers was always open to innovation, and in many instances found that the development of new instrumentation helped move his work forward.

In 1939 Folkers and his colleagues were presented the Mead Johnson and Company Award for work on vitamin B_6, and in 1949 they received the award for similar work on vitamin B_{12}. Folkers was elected to the National Academy of Sciences in 1948, at age 42. In 1951 the Board of Directors of Merck presented him with a scientific award that also endowed a lecture series in his name at the universities of Illinois and Wisconsin. Folkers has received many awards from the American Chemical Society (ACS). In 1941 he was honored by ACS for meritorious work in pure chemistry. In 1949 he was chosen by the Rochester Section as Harrison-Howe Lecturer. He served as ACS president in 1962 and in 1985, he won ACS's highest award, the Priestley Medal. In 1960 he received the Perkin Award from the Society of Chemical Industry. In 1972 he became the first recipient of the Robert A. Welch International Award and Medal for Research on Life Processes, and in 1981 received a MacArthur Foundation "genius" award. He was the recipient of five honorary degrees, and received two presidential citations: the Presidential Certificate of Merit from Harry S. Truman, and the National Medal of Science from George Bush. In the latter he was cited for "combining basic chemical research and clinical medicine to achieve new treatments of diseases . . . "

A Stint at Stanford, and the Biomedical Institute at University of Texas, Austin

In 1963 Folkers was invited to go to California as president of the Stanford Research Institute (SRI) at Menlo Park. In reflection, Folkers (1984) said, "leaving Merck was impossible and to the Stanford Research Institute was irresistible." He was there for five years, serving also as professor of chemistry at Stanford and as lecturer in vitamin chemistry at the University of California at Berkeley. During his presidency, SRI staff increased from 2,000 to 3,000, research and development increased, revenue doubled, and a $12 million building program was instituted.

In 1968 Folkers moved again, accepting an invitation from President Norman Hackerman to develop an Institute for Biomedical Institute at the University of Texas at Austin. The Institute assembled scientists from diverse disciplines to conduct basic biochemical and biomedical research and discover new treatments of diseases, particularly those without effective treatments. Basic research at the institute has led to many clinical applications. Thyrotropin releasing hormone was identified, and is now used as a synthetic. Coenzyme Q was shown to have therapeutic value in patients with advanced cardiomyopathy, as well as in muscular dystrophy. Vitamin B_6 was found to be valuable in treating arteriosclerosis and carpal tunnel syndrome, and the acute effects experienced in Chinese Restaurant Syndrome were shown to be caused by a vitamin B_6 deficiency. Research at the Institute has also addressed therapies for prostate and breast cancer, psoriasis, and Parkinson's disease.

In 1997 Folkers addressed the Health-Trends 2000 Conference in Copenhagen, Denmark, about his research on vitamin Q_{10}. He died on December 9, 1997, at his home in Sunapee, New Hampshire. He had just returned from a trip to Sweden.

SELECTED WRITINGS BY FOLKERS:

Periodicals

"Contemporary History Series: Perspectives on Vitamins and Hormones." *Journal of Chemical Education* (September 1984): 747-756.

FURTHER READING:

Books

American Men & Women of Science. 19th Edition, 1995-1996. Vol. 2. New Providence, New Jersey: R. R. Bowker, 1365.

William A. Fowler

Galambos, Louis. *Values and Visions: A Merck Century.* Merck, 1991, 68, 71-72.

Periodicals

Baum, Rudy M. "Karl Folkers Wins ACS's Highest Award in Chemistry." *Chemical & Engineering News* (June 17, 1985): 36-38.

Other

Tishler, Max. "Sidelights on the Medalist." Perkin Medal Award Introduction (February 5, 1960), provided by corporate public affairs, Merck & Co., Rahway, New Jersey.

—Sketch by Jill Carpenter

William A. Fowler
1911–1995

American physicist

William A. Fowler is noted for his theories explaining how stars produce heat and light based on his explanations of the synthesis of chemical elements in the universe. Fowler received the 1983 Nobel Prize in physics in recognition of "his theoretical and experimental studies of the nuclear reactions of important in the formation of the chemical elements in the universe." His contributions have been of benefit to the fields of astronomy, astrophysics, cosmology, and geophysics in addition to nuclear physics.

Fowler was born on August 9, 1911, in Pittsburgh, Pennsylvania, to John MacLeod, an accountant, and Jennie Summers (Watson) Fowler. The Fowlers had two other children, Arthur Watson, born in 1913, and Nelda, born in 1919. When William was two years old, his family moved to Lima, Ohio, where he attended Horace Mann Grade School and Central High School. At Central, Fowler was president of the senior class, a varsity football and baseball player, and valedictorian of the graduating class of 1929.

Fowler received his bachelor's degree from Ohio State University in 1933 and his Ph.D. in nuclear physics at the Kellogg Radiation Laboratory at the California Institute of Technology (Cal Tech) in 1936. Immediately, he was offered a job as research fellow at Kellogg and then, over the next forty-five years, was promoted from assistant to full professor. He retired from the California Institute of Technology in 1982 and was named emeritus professor of physics.

Fowler entered Ohio State University in the fall of 1929 intending to major in ceramic engineering. Two years later, however, he switched to engineering physics, a field in which would earn his bachelor of science. Although he had to work throughout his college years in order to support himself, Fowler was able to record the highest grade point average in his graduating class.

Begins Nuclear Research at Cal Tech

Upon graduation from Ohio State, Fowler decided to enter the California Institute of Technology for his graduate work. There, he was assigned to assist the director of the W. K. Kellogg Radiation Laboratory, C. C. Lauritsen, whom Fowler credited as being the greatest influence in his life, according to an article in *Physics Today.* For his doctoral dissertation, Fowler studied the production of radioactive isotopes as the result of bombarding light elements with protons and deuterons. He was granted his Ph.D. in physics *summa cum laude* in 1936.

Lauritsen was well satisfied with the work of the young Fowler and asked him to stay on as a research fellow in nuclear physics. Three years later, Fowler began his climb up the academic ladder with an appointment as assistant professor at Cal Tech and then, in 1942, with a promotion to associate professor. At this point, World War II interrupted the normal research taking place at Cal Tech. Lauritsen and Fowler were assigned to work in Washington, D.C., on the development of proximity fuses for bombs, shells, and rockets. Later in the war, Fowler became involved in the development of the atomic bomb. He attained the rank of full professor in 1946. For his wartime contributions, Fowler was given the U.S. Government Medal for Merit in 1948.

Explains the Origins of the Elements

Scientists have long been intrigued by the question of how the chemical elements are formed in the universe. A major revelation took place in 1939, when physicist **Hans Albrecht Bethe** at Cornell University and **Carl F. Von Weizsäcker** at the University of Berlin proposed a mechanism whereby hydrogen is converted into helium in a star. The CN cycle (for the carbon and nitrogen involved in the process) not only explained the conversion of hydrogen to helium, but also showed how energy is released in the process.

The question remained, however, as to how elements heavier than helium can burn, and thus be formed in a star. At one point, **George Gamow** had suggested a simple and reasonable explanation. The capture of a neutron by one atom could result in the formation of a new atom one atomic number greater than the original. But the problem with Gamow's hypothesis was that it could not be confirmed experimentally. Researchers at Kellogg had demonstrated that no stable mass of five or eight could exist. With these gaps, Gamow's theory became untenable.

By the early 1950s, Fowler had become convinced that the production of heavier elements can take place through the fusion of helium atoms. By 1954, the details of that process were becoming clear. Fowler spent the 1954-55 academic year at Cambridge University working with the eminent astrophysicist **Fred Hoyle** and the husband and wife team of **Geoffrey Burbidge** and **Margaret Burbidge**. Together, the four researchers identified a process whereby helium can be converted to carbon, carbon to iron, and eventually iron to the heavier elements (by neutron capture).

In 1975, Fowler, Hoyle, and the Burbridges published one of the classic papers of modern science, "Synthesis of the Elements in Stars," which often referred to the authors' initials as B_2FH. The ideas presented in the paper were the basis for the Nobel Prize committee's decision to award a share of the 1983 physics prize (along with **Subrahmanyan Chandrasekhar**) to Fowler.

The mechanisms by which elements are formed in the universe continued to dominate Fowler's research agenda for another two decades. Working often with Hoyle, he developed hypotheses about the formation of elements in bodies other than stars, such as the recently discovered radio galaxies. He also became increasingly interested in the study of neutrinos and other astronomical phenomena.

Fowler, was in great demand as a lecturer and visiting scholar. He was been a Fulbright lecturer and Guggenheim Fellow at the University of Cambridge twice, in 1954-55, and again in 1961-62. Fowler also lectured at St. John's College, the University of Washington, the Massachusetts Institute of Technology, and the Institute of Theoretical Astronomy at Cambridge. He received honorary doctorates from the University of Chicago, Ohio State University, Denison University, Arizona State University, the University of Liège, and the Observatorie de Paris. Fowler's other honors include the National Medal of Science, which he received in 1974, and the Légion d'Honneur, which he received in 1989. In 1970, he was named Institute Professor of Physics, a position he held until his retirement in 1982.

Fowler was married to the former Ardiane Foy Olmsted on August 24, 1940. They had two daughters, Mary Emily and Martha Summers. After his wife died in 1988, he married again. Fowler's colleague Bethe, writing in *Science,* described him as "full of humor and cheerfulness," and noted that Fowler's most outstanding characteristic was that he loved people. 1982. He died on March 14, 1995 at Huntington Memorial Hospital in Pasadena.

SELECTED WRITINGS BY FOWLER:

Books

Nucleosynthesis in Massive Stars and Supernovae.
    Chicago: University of Chicago Press, 1965.
Nuclear Astrophysics. Philadelphia: American Philosophical Society, 1967.

Periodicals

"Synthesis of the Elements in Stars." *Review of Modern Physics* 92 (1957): 547-650.

FURTHER READING:

Books

McGraw-Hill Modern Scientists and Engineers.
    Vol. 10. New York: McGraw-Hill, 1980, pp. 388-90.

Periodicals

Barnes, Charles, A. "William A. Fowler" (obituary). *Physics Today* 48 (September 1995): 116-18.
Bethe, Hans. A. "The 1983 Nobel Prize in Physics." *Science* (25 November 1983): 881-83.
————. "Nobel Prize to Chandrasekhar and Fowler for Astrophysics." *Physics Today* (January 1984): 17-20.

Erik Ivar Fredholm

Dicke, William. "William A. Fowler, 83, Astrophysicist, Dies" (obituary). *New York Times* (16 March 1995): B14.

—*Sketch by David E. Newton*

Erik Ivar Fredholm
1866–1927
Swedish number theorist

Erik Ivar Fredholm developed the modern theory of integral equations. His work served as the foundation for later critical research performed by **David Hilbert**, and several concepts and theorems are attributed to him. Fredholm was born on April 7, 1866, in Stockholm, Sweden. His family was upper-middle-class; his father was a well-to-do merchant, and his mother came from a cultured background. He was privy to the highest quality education available in his country and proved gifted. In 1885 he began studies at the Polytechnic Institute in Stockholm, where he developed what turned out to be a lifelong interest in problems of practical mechanics. He remained at the Institute for only one year and enrolled in the University of Uppsala in 1886, receiving his bachelor's degree in 1888.

Fredholm received his doctorate from Uppsala in 1898, although he conducted the bulk of his studies under Mittag–Leffler at the University of Stockholm. At that time, Uppsala was the only university in Sweden that offered a doctoral degree. Fredholm conducted his doctoral thesis on partial differential equations, and his work became significant to the study of deformation of anisotropic media, such as crystals.

After receiving his doctoral degree Fredholm accepted a position as lecturer in mathematical physics at the University of Stockholm and in 1906 became a professor of rational mechanics and mathematical physics. The research he conducted during this time yielded a fundamental integral equation that now bears his name. The equation, which is highly relevant in physics, was contained in a seminal research paper for which Fredholm was honored with the Wallmark Prize of the Swedish Academy of Sciences and the Poncelet Prize of the Académie des Sciences.

Much of Fredholm's research on integral equations was based on the work of American astronomer **George William Hill**. Fredholm laid the foundation for this renowned research in a 1900 paper, *Sur une nouvelle méthode pour la résolution du problèm de Dirichlet*. It was in this paper that Fredholm developed the essential component of the theory that led to what is now called Fredholm's Integral Equation. Fredholm then went on to develop what came to be known as the Fredholm Equation of the Second Type, which involved a definite integral. He also discovered the algebraic analog of his theory of integral equations. While Fredholm's contributions to mathematics and physics were significant, his research resume is sparse. Biographers attribute his small output to the mathematician's strict attention to detail, a characteristic that earned Fredholm an excellent reputation throughout Europe.

Fredholm's work was carried on by David Hilbert, who learned of Fredholm's work through Erik Holmgren, a colleague of Fredholm's whom Hilbert met in Göttingen. Hilbert incorporated Fredholm's ideas into his own theories, including the theory of eigen–values and the theory of spaces involving an infinite number of dimensions. These theories, in turn, laid the foundation for the study of quantum theory and the discovery of what are now termed Hilbert spaces.

Fredholm remained at the University of Stockholm until his death on August 17, 1927.

SELECTED WRITINGS BY FREDHOLM:

Sur nouvelle méthode pour la résolution du problèm de Dirichlet, 1900.

Oeuvres complètes de Ivar Fredholm, 1955.

FURTHER READING:

Bernkopf, M. "Ivar Fredholm," in *Dictionary of Scientific Biography*. Volume V. Edited by Charles Coulston Gillispie. New York: Charles Scribner's Sons, 1970, pp. 150–52.

—*Sketch by Kristin Palm*

G

Aleksandr Osipovich Gelfond

Aleksandr Osipovich Gelfond
1906–1968(?)
Russian mathematician

Aleksandr Gelfond made significant contributions to the theory of transcendental numbers and the theory of interpolation and approximation of the functions of a complex variable. He established the transcendental character of any number of the form a^b, where a is an algebraic number different from 0 or 1 and b is any irrational algebraic number, which is now known as Gelfond's theorem.

Gelfond was born in St. Petersburg (later Leningrad); his father was a physician who also dabbled in philosophy. Gelfond entered Moscow University in 1924 and completed his undergraduate degree in mathematics in 1927. He pursued postgraduate studies from 1927 to 1930 under the direction of A.J. Khintchine and V.V. Stepanov.

Gelfond's first teaching assignment was at the Moscow Technological College. He quickly won a more prestigious appointment at Moscow University, where he began teaching mathematics in 1931. He became a professor of mathematics in 1931, a position he held until his death. For several years, Gelfond served as the chairman of the mathematics department specializing in the theory of numbers. His enthusiasm for the history of mathematics was reflected not only by his own works on Leonhard Euler, but by incorporating a history of mathematics division into the theory department he chaired.

In 1933, Gelfond was also appointed to a post in the Soviet Academy of Sciences Mathematical Institute. He completed a doctorate in mathematics and physics in 1935 and was elected a corresponding member of the Academy of Sciences of the U.S.S.R. in 1939.

Back to the Future

Gelfond found his greatest inspiration in the past. In 1748, Euler proposed that logarithms of rational number with rational bases are either rational or transcendental; in 1900, **David Hilbert** developed a 23–problem series on the rationality or transcendence of the logarithms of such numbers. For three decades, mathematicians were unable to trace a solution to the puzzle posed by Hilbert's seventh problem—the assumption that a^b is transcendental if a is any algebraic number other than 0 or 1 and b is any irrational algebraic number.

In 1929, Gelfond established connections between the properties of an analytic function and the arithmetic nature of its values, publishing his first paper on the topic, "Sur les nombres transcendant," in 1929. He built on this discovery to unravel Hilbert's seventh riddle by using linear forms of exponential functions. Gelfond published the results of his work, "Sur le septieme probleme de Hilbert," in 1934. He continued his explorations, using his knowledge of functions to develop theorems related to rational integers, transcendental numbers (he was able to construct new classes in this area), mutual algebraic independence, and analytic theory.

Gelfond's interest in function theory was probably shaped by the Luzitania—an informal academic and social organization clustered around Nikolai Nikolaevich Luzin, a noted mathematician in the 1920s. Gelfond was a contemporary and colleague of **Nina Karlovna Bari**, a Luzin protegee; although Gelfond's name does not appear on the list of those who declared themselves Luzitanians. Luzin's prominence and the intellectual vigor of the students he attracted influenced the philosophy and direction of mathematics at the university. By 1930, the Luzitania movement sputtered and died, and Luzin left Moscow State for the Academy of Science's Steklov Institute.

Politician Pragmatism

In 1936, during the dictatorship of Josef Stalin, Luzin was charged with ideological sabotage. Luzin's trial was abruptly and surprisingly canceled, but he was officially reprimanded and withdrew from academia. Luzin's fall demonstrated—in a way that could not be ignored—the inextricable interweaving of politics and academic achievement. Gelfond was permitted to pursue his studies in peace in part because of his political connections.

"He was a member of the Communist Party," wrote Ilya Piatetski-Shapiro, for whom Gelfond was an instructor, mentor and advisor. "His father was personally acquainted with Lenin . . . he said that his father and Lenin had disagreements in public life, but in private life they were friends. Being a member of the Communist Party, Gelfond felt that he had some influence. . . ." Such influence could not overcome the deep wave of anti-Semitism that swept over Russia after World War II. Despite Gelfond's recommendation, Piatetski-Shapiro, who was Jewish, was denied admission to Moscow University's graduate school by the party committee of the mathematics department.

But Gelfond "was a very warm person, very humane and sensitive to me and to the other students," Piatetski-Shapiro wrote, and Gelfond was reluctant to let a promising student—winner of the Moscow Mathematical Society award for young mathematicians—languish. Although his sponsorship could have had dire implications for his own career, Gelfond persisted, and finally secured admission to the graduate program for Piatetski-Shapiro at the Moscow Pedagogical Institute.

Gelfond's most comprehensive publications were released in 1952. *Transtsendentnye i albegraicheskie chisla* provided an overview of his work in transcendental numbers, and his work on the theory of the functions of a complex variable is compiled in *Ischislenie knoechnyko raznostey.*

In 1968, Gelfond was named a corresponding member of the International Academy of the History of Science. He also served as chair of the scientific council of the Soviet Academy of Sciences Institute of the History of Science and technology, which refereed works on the history of physics and mathematics.

Gelfond's drive to expand the understanding of mathematics theory persisted to the day of his death. "When he died . . . I was present in the hospital," wrote Piatetski-Shapiro. "I remember he was trying to write some formula and tell me something which was clearly related to the zeta function. He could not because he was already paralyzed."

Gelfond died in Moscow; most sources list the year of his death as 1968, but Piatetski-Shapiro records it as 1966.

SELECTED WRITINGS BY GELFOND:

Ischislenie konechnykh raznostey, 1952; third edition, 1967.
Transtsendentynye i algegraicheskie chisla (1952; translated and published as *Transcendental and Algebraic Numbers,* 1960).
(With Y.V. Linnik) *Elementarnye metody v teorii chisel,* 1962.

Periodicals

"Sur les nombers transcendants." *Comptes rendus hebdomadaires des seances de l'Academie des sciences,* 189 (1929): 1224–28.

FURTHER READING:

Bell, E.T. *Men of Mathematics.* New York: Simon and Schuster, 1965, p. 463.
Youschkevitch, A. P. "Aleksandr Osipovich Gelfond," in *Dictionary of Scientific Biography.* Volume V. Edited by Charles Coulston Gillispie. New York: Charles Scribner's Sons, 1973, pp. 342–43.
Zdravkovska, Smilka and Peter L. Duran, editors. *Golden Years of Moscow Mathematics.* Providence, RI: American Mathematical Society, 1993, pp. 200–203.

—*Sketch by A. Mullig*

Ruth Gentry
1862–1917
American mathematician

Ruth Gentry wrote her doctoral thesis, "On the Forms of Plane Quartic Curves," in 1896, before receiving her Ph.D. in Mathematics from Bryn Mawr College. Bryn Mawr was the first school to offer resident fellowships to women who aspired to earn a graduate degree. Gentry was one out of only 10 women to receive Ph.D.s in mathematics during the 19th century. Her teaching career consisted of teaching at Vassar College and schools for girls and young women.

Prior to her graduate work, Gentry attended Charlotte Angas Scott College, a private liberal arts college, in Decatur, Georgia. She enrolled at the college soon after its founding in 1889. She was one of the first two graduate students from Agnes Scott to attend Bryn Mawr in Pennsylvania. Gentry was the second recipient of the Association of College Alumnae European Fellowship, as well as the first mathematician to ever receive the honor. From 1891 to 1892, she used the fellowship to attend lectures at the University of Berlin; however, Gentry barred from enrollment. At that time, women were not admitted to German universities.

During her stay in Germany, Gentry wrote to Christian Felix Klein at the University of Göttingen, asking him whether or not she could be admitted to his lectures the following year. Klein replied that she could not. In 1893, however, Klein did suggest a trial program of admitting a few women into the mathematics program at the University of Göttingen. The program went forward, but Gentry was not selected to attend.

Throughout the 19th century myths were rampant about why women appeared to be inferior to men in science and mathematics. By the 1860s, people generally believed that the frontal lobe inside male brains, thought to be where intelligence is located, were larger than the female brain. However, discoveries in the 1870s dispelled that myth, and scientists brushed the information aside when it was revealed that women actually had the larger frontal lobe.

Perhaps because of such myths of that era, and because of basic cultural differences, Gentry, as a woman mathematician, struggled to be recognized for her work.

SELECTED WRITINGS BY GENTRY:

On the forms of plane quartic curves, 1896.

FURTHER READING:

Books

Dunham William. *The Mathematical Universe: An Alphabetical Journey through the Great Proofs, Problems, and Personalities.* New York, 1994.
Fenster, Della and Karen Parshall. "Women in the American Mathematical Research Community: 1891–1906," in *The History of Modern Mathematics* Volume. III. Edited by Eberhard Knobloch and David Rowe, pp. 229–261.

Periodicals

Green, Judy and Jeanne LaDuke. "Women in the American Mathematical Community: The pre–1940 Ph.D.'s." *The Mathematical Intelligencer* 9, no.1 (1987): 11–22.

Josiah Willard Gibbs

Kenschaft, Patricia. "The Students of Charlotte Angas Scott." *Mathematics in College* (Fall 1982): 16–20.

Other

"Ruth Gentry." *Biographies of Women Mathematicians.* June 1997. http://www.scottlan.edu/lriddle/women/chronol.htm (July 22, 1997).
"Women in Mathematics Myths." http://www.telplex.bsu.edu/home/nshadle/web/myths.html. (June 2, 1997).

—*Sketch by Monica L. Stevens*

Josiah Willard Gibbs
1839–1903
American mathematical and chemical physicist

J. Willard Gibbs is not as famous as the Europeans who discovered and lionized him. James Clerk Maxwell was the first and for a time nearly the only major scientist among his contemporaries to fully understand Gibbs's publications and what they implied. **Albert Einstein** called him "the greatest mind in American history." Gibbs's studies of thermodynamics and electromagnetics and discoveries in statistical mechanics made Einstein's later theories conceivable. He is also largely responsible for the field of physical chemistry, which impacted the steel and ammonia industries. Gibbs is known as the "father of vector analysis" for replacing **William Rowan Hamilton**'s quaternions in the field of mathematical physics. Thanks to him there are such ideas as the Gibbs phase rule, the Gibbs adsorption isotherm regarding surface tension, Gibbs free energy, and Gibbsian ensembles. Even two short letters to *Nature* in the late 1890s defined what is now known as the "Gibbs phenomenon" in the convergence of a Fourier series. Gibbs's deployment of probability set the stage for quantum mechanics to come about some decades after his death. For all of these achievements, he was elected to the Hall of Fame for Great Americans in 1950.

The Gibbs family was originally from Warwickshire, England, having emigrated to Boston in the 17th century. Josiah, born on February 11, 1839, bears the same name as his father but was not known as Josiah Willard Gibbs, Jr. The two men eventually differentiated themselves according to their use of initials. Gibbs's father, a professor of biblical or "sacred" literature at Yale University, went by J.W. Gibbs. His wife Mary Anna's maiden name was Van Cleve.

Josiah was the only boy in the family. Of his four sisters he would remain closest to Anna, who also never married, and Julia, who married Addison Van Name, a member of the Connecticut Academy that first published Josiah's articles. The Van Name home in New Haven, Connecticut, where Josiah would stay later in life until his death, was within walking distance of the house where he was born.

A Practical Education

Josiah's childhood was marred by scarlet fever, which left him sensitive to illness in adulthood. However, his home life was otherwise supportive. It has been assumed that the young Gibbs's latent scientific talents were actually inherited from his mother, who was an amateur ornithologist. Her wit and charm were widely acknowledged, and her ingenuity extended to building dollhouses for her girls that included realistic plumbing and kitchen equipment. His father, who was considered a prodigy in his day, was an exemplary scholar and teacher in the humanities who received an honorary degree from Harvard after his retirement. Tragedy came later, as two sisters and both parents eventually died by the time Gibbs was a graduate student.

Gibbs began school at the age of nine, in a private boy's school known informally as "Mr. Farren's School." From there he transferred to Hopkins Grammar School, no more than half a block from the family home. At Yale, it seemed likely that Gibbs would follow his father into philology. He was a highly decorated Latin student often chosen to give orations at university functions. Like his father, he earned a bachelor's degree at 19.

The American academy at that time valued and rewarded only applied science and mathematics, so when Gibbs continued his studies at Yale he wrote a fairly pedestrian doctoral thesis on spur gear design in 1863. This made him one of three Ph.D. recipients that year at the first American institution to offer the degree. His doctorate in particular was the first in engineering and the second in science ever conferred in the United States. After a short stint as a Latin tutor, he returned to his chosen field. Gibbs was awarded a patent for his redesigned railway car brakes in 1866. That same year he took his one major trip abroad. For three years he attended physics lectures at Paris, Berlin, and Heidelberg's universities given by the field's foremost practitioners. Gustav Kirchhoff and Hermann von Helmholtz were of particular influence. Luckily, Gibbs could subsist on monies inherited from his parents, because upon his return to Yale he was appointed a professor of mathematical physics at no pay. This has been explained as resulting from his lack of published works. Gibbs would keep that unpaid post until an offer from Johns Hopkins University in 1880 of three thousand dollars a year forced Yale authorities to counteroffer two thousand.

A Late Bloomer

In 1873 Gibbs devised a geometrical representation of the surface activity of thermodynamically active substances, and wrote "Graphical Methods in the Thermodynamics of Fluids," his first publication. Although the publishers of *Transactions of the Connecticut Academy* did not fully understand this or his other papers, they raised money specifically to print his material, which was sometimes lengthy. Much has been made of the fact that he was by then 34 years old. Most mathematicians or scientists peak at a much younger age. However, Gibbs had apparently been developing his theories for quite a long time, and was only just beginning to articulate his discoveries. He built on principles previously set down by Helmholtz, Jules Joule, and Lord Kelvin, but whereas his predecessors had been specifically concerned with an immediate example like the heat engine, Gibbs preferred to keep it mathematically general. His diagrams treated entropy, temperature, and pressure, in their relations to volume, as coordinates. When he considered a three–dimensional surface, the coordinates he chose were entropy, volume, and energy.

By mathematically formulating the second law of thermodynamics regarding entropy and mechanical energy, Gibbs made thermodynamics scientifically viable. His phase rule is a simple looking formula: $f = n + 2 - r$. In that sequence f represents the total degrees of freedom in temperature and pressure, *n* the total of chemical elements in the object's makeup, and *r* the number of phases the object may take over time—solid, liquid, or gas in any combination. This rule was central to his reconception of the thermodynamics of a complex of systems into a single system over time—the probability of the existence of any possible system in "phase–space" overall.

By doing so, and by applying the first and second laws of thermodynamics to complex substances, Gibbs set the theoretical basis for physical chemistry. This relatively new specialty deals with phenomena like hydrodynamics, and novel types of mathematical modeling like electrochemical simulations and genetic algorithms. Gibbs's "single system" method is now a fundamental part of statistical mechanics in the form of Gibbsian ensembles. These are defined as large numbers of thermodynamically equivalent macroscopic systems. By using these ensembles, laboratory and factory researchers save themselves the tedium and risk of trial and error experimentation when synthesizing new compounds or alloys.

"Gibbs free energy" refers to the likelihood of any one chemical reaction taking place, which takes into account both entropy—the disorder in a system—and enthalpy, its heat content. At least one biographer considers Gibbs's clarification of Rudolf Clausius's original definition of entropy, as it became ranked with other thermodynamic properties such as energy, temperature, and pressure. His ideas of chemical potential and free energy now take precedence in the conception of how chemical reactions take place.

The American Lavoisier

Although he drew mixed reviews as a teacher, Gibbs was clearly concerned with his relationship with his students and with involving them in mathematics. In 1877 he founded the Math Club at Yale, the second of such informal groups there. He served as executive officer for ten years, and more than likely gave his first impressions of vector analysis and perhaps even the multiple algebra or matrix studies that gave birth to vectors. There are other indications that he used his classes as seminars.

For his vector analysis Gibbs drew from Hermann Grassman as well as William Hamilton. Even in its early stages he could use it to calculate the orbits of planets and comets such as Swift's, improving upon Karl Gauss's method, and also applied vectors to problems in crystallography. Gibbs accounted for most of the properties of light as an electromagnetic phenomenon according to Maxwell's theory, in purely theoretical terms, during the 1880s. In doing so, he succeeded in treating the relation between force and displacement waves in electricity in the same way as others had for mechanical and acoustic waves. All this was an outgrowth of Gibbs's courses from 1877 to 1880, including the first college–level course in vector analysis with concentration on electricity and magnetism and the first public usage of vector methods. His analyses have not had to be corrected since.

Gibbs's ideas could not be disseminated in Europe until they were translated, because no one on the Continent at that time followed American scientific or mathematical journals consistently. Consequently, both Helmholtz and Karl Planck unknowingly duplicated some of Gibbs's findings, and Jacobus Van't Hoff independently conceived of chemical thermodynamics. This situation changed when Friedrich Ostwald translated Gibbs into German in 1891. Ostwald was followed near the end of that decade by Henri Le Chatelier, who translated Gibbs into French. Edwin Wilson, who also wrote posthumous biographical commentaries on his professor, wrote a textbook published in 1901 entitled *Gibbs' Vector Analysis* that succeeded in reaching a larger audience. The book was edited from class notes used between 1881 and 1884.

Such efforts led to great fame for Gibbs near the last years of his life. After reading Gibbs in translation, one French scientist called him America's answer to Antoine Lavoisier. Gibbs was awarded honorary Doctor of Science degrees from Erlangen, Williams College, and Princeton University. Scientific and mathematical societies in Haarlem, Göttingen, Amsterdam, Manchester, and Berlin made him an honorary or foreign member. He was also given the Copley Medal by the Royal Society of London two years before he died. Before the advent of the Nobel Prize in 1901, the Copley Medal was the highest honor conferrable in the scientific world.

Gibbs became a member of the American Mathematical Society in March of 1903, one month before his death. He had also recently signed a contract to reprint his "Equilibrium" series with approximately 50 pages of additions. Because of his childhood illness, he had taken on a lifetime's regimen of mild outdoor activities such as long walks, horseback riding, and camping with close friends like fellow professor Andrew Phillips. His teaching schedule sometimes required "enforced rest" leaves of absence, but he never went against his doctor's advice. In fact, according to Wheeler's biography, Gibbs' health was excellent for more than 30 years before his final illness. However, an apparently mild illness could not be shaken off, and he died on April 28, 1903, the night before he was to resume his duties. Gibbs' last resting place, two blocks from his brother–in–law's house, is marked with a headstone identifying him only as a Yale professor.

SELECTED WRITINGS BY GIBBS:

Books

Elementary Principles in Statistical Mechanics Developed with Special Reference to the Rational Foundation of Thermodynamics, 1981.

The Scientific Papers of J. Willard Gibbs. Edited by H.A. Bumstead and R. G. Van Name, 1906.

The Collected Works of J. Willard Gibbs, 1948.

Periodicals

"Graphical Methods in the Thermodynamics of Fluids." *Transactions of the Connecticut Academy* 2 (1873): 309–42.

"A Method of Geometrical Representation of the Thermodynamic of the Thermodynamic Properties of Substances by Means of Surfaces." *Transactions of the Connecticut Academy* 2 (1873): 382–404.

"On the Equilibrium of Heterogeneous Substances." *Transactions of the Connecticut Academy* 3 (1875–78).

FURTHER READING:

Books

Asimov, Isaac. *Asimov's Biographical Encyclopedia of Science and Technology.* Second Revised Edition. Garden City, NY: Doubleday, 1982, pp. 485–86.

Eaves, Howard. *Great Moments in Mathematics (After 1650).* Washington, D.C.: Mathematical Association of America, Inc., 1980, pp.106–07.

Fien, Donald M. "Josiah Willard Gibbs," in *The Great Scientists.* Edited by Frank N. Magill. Danbury, CT: Grolier, 1989, pp. 117–23.

Grabiner, Judith V. "Mathematics in America: The First Hundred Years."

The Bicentennial Tribute to American Mathematics 1776–1976. Edited by Dalton Tarwater. Washington, D.C.: Mathematical Association of America, Inc., 1977.

Wheeler, L.P. *Josiah Willard Gibbs: The History of a Great Mind.* New Haven, CT: Yale University Press, 1951.

Other

"Josiah Willard Gibbs." *MacTutor History of Mathematics Archive.* http://www–groups.dcs.st–and.ac.uk/~history/index/.html (July 1997).

—*Sketch by Jennifer Kramer*

Alfred Goodman Gilman

Alfred Goodman Gilman
1941–
American biochemist and pharmacologist

Alfred Goodman Gilman is known for discovering, along with **Martin Rodbell**, new proteins in biological cells, called G-proteins. For this discovery they shared the 1994 Nobel Prize in Medicine. Communication between cells has been understood for a long time, but how signals were transmitted inside the cells was not known until Gilman and Rodbell found the inter-cellular proteins. G-proteins are important because disruption of their function can lead to disease.

Gilman was born in 1941 in New Haven, Connecticut, the same year his father, Alfred Gilman Sr., published the landmark textbook, *The Pharmacological Basis of Therapeutics,* along with Louis Goodman, while they were faculty members of Yale's pharmacology department. Gilman grew up in White Plains, New York, where his father was on the faculty of The College of Physicians and Surgeons of Columbia University and then later a founding chairman of the Pharmacology Department at the new Albert Einstein College of Medicine. Gilman's childhood was filled with music and culture. His father could play many musical instruments and his mother, Mabel Schmidt Gilman, was a pianist. In his autobiography published on the Nobel Foundation's web site, Gilman fondly remembers trips to museums in New York City, especially the Hayden Planetarium, which peaked his interest in astronomy. But visits to his father's laboratory peaked his interest in biology. Gilman was also able to observe intricate pharmacological experiments designed for medical students. Gilman notes in his autobiography that it was probably surprising that he turned to biochemical approaches to pharmacology, despite all the musical and visual influences in his life.

In 1955 Gilman was sent to the Taft School in Watertown, Connecticut, a prep school for boys. Gilman was not happy about being sent away, nor did he enjoy the rigid structure of the boys' school. However, he received an excellent education in chemistry, math, and physics, a well as English, his least favorite subject. He remembered receiving a comment of "not bad" from an instructor who claimed his papers sounded like lab reports.

Gilman described college life as actually easier and more fun than Taft. He majored in biochemistry at Yale university. Gilman describes his first laboratory project, to test Francis Crick's adapter hypothesis, as "wildly overambitious." The experience was rewarding for him though, because of the encouragement he received from his lab instructor Melvin Simpson. Gilman met his future wife Kathryn Hedlund during this time. Gilman recalled in his autobiography that she should have "smelled the competition" the many evenings she spent with him in the lab while he worked on projects.

After receiving his B.A. from Yale in 1962, Gilman worked for Burroughs Wellcome in New York and published his first papers. He knew he wanted to go into research when he entered a unique M.D.-Ph.D. program at Case Western Reserve University in the fall of 1962. He and Kathryn Hedlund were married during this time and would have three children, Amy, Anne, and Ted. His thesis advisor Ted Rall's commitment to projects often made Gilman late for dinner. Gilman conducted research on the thyroid gland and was also interested in studying cells and genetics. He earned an M.D. and Ph.D. in pharmacology in 1969. His interest in genetics led him to the Pharmacology Research Associate Training Program at the National Institute of General Medical Sciences, where he researched cyclic adenosine monophosphate (AMP), a genetic regulator that moderates hormone actions. His work with Nobel laureate Earl Sutherland was the beginning of his interest in cell communication.

Discovers G-proteins

In 1971 Gilman accepted a position as an assistant professor of pharmacology at the University of Virginia in Charlottesville. It was here that Gilman began his Nobel Prize-winning work. Gilman de-

scribed the atmosphere at the university as intellectually supportive. Gilman and his colleagues knew about Martin Rodbell's work at the National Institutes of Health with guanine nucleotides, which are components of deoxyribonucleic acid (DNA) and ribonucleic acid (RNA). Rodbell and his research associates at the NIH ascertained that the guanine nucleotides were somehow related to cell communication, but could not prove it. Gilman's research began where Rodbell left off, and in the late 1970s, he and his colleagues started looking for the chemicals that would confirm Rodbell's work. Gilman used genetically altered leukemia cells to detect the presence of G-proteins. He found that without the G-protein, the cells did not respond to outside stimulation the way a normal cell would. In 1980 they found the G-proteins, named because they bind to the guanine nucleotides.

G-proteins are instrumental in the fundamental workings of a cell. They allow us to see and smell by changing light and odors to chemical messages that travel to the brain. Understanding how G-proteins malfunction could lead to understanding serious diseases like cholera or cancer. Scientists have linked improperly working G-proteins to everything from alcoholism to diabetes. Pharmaceutical companies are developing drugs that would focus on G-proteins.

In 1979 Gilman was asked to chair the department of pharmacology at the University of Texas Southwestern Medical Center in Dallas. But he was too immersed in his research, as well as editing the sixth edition of his father's textbook, *The Pharmacological Basis of Therapeutics*, to accept the position. Martin Rodbell almost took the job, but when he declined, they asked Gilman again; this time he accepted. There he built up the pharmacology department, recruiting many old colleagues.

His time at Southwestern was filled with many other awards in addition to the Nobel in 1994, among them the Poul Edvard Poulson Award from the Norwegian Pharmacological Society in 1982 and the Gairdner Foundation International Award in 1984. In 1987 he shared the Richard Lounsbery Award from the National Academy of Sciences with Martin Rodbell in 1987, foreshadowing the Nobel. In 1989 he won the Albert Lasker Basic Medical Research Award. Gilman has been in the forefront of G-protein research since his discovery. He predicts that eventually scientists will be able to map cell communication in a way that will allow scientists to predict how cells will respond to a variety of signals, leading the way to major advances in the treatment of disease.

SELECTED WRITINGS BY GILMAN:

Books

Fidia Research Foundation Neuroscience Award Lectures, 1986-1987, Raven Press, 1988.

Periodicals

(With R. K. Sunahara and C. W. Dessauer)
"Complexity and Diversity of Mammalian
Adenylyl Cyclases." *Annual Review of Pharma-
cology And Toxicology*, Volume 36, 1996.

FURTHER READING:

Periodicals

Begley, Sharon. "The Biological Switchboard."
Newsweek, October 24, 1994, pp. 65-66.
Marx, Jean. "Medicine: A Signal Award for Dis-
covering G Proteins." *Science*, October 21,
1994, pp. 368-69.
McFarling, Usha L.. "Two from U.S. Share Nobel
Prize in Medicine: 'G Proteins' Seen Key to
Cell Links." *Boston Globe*, October 11, 1994,
p. 5.
Rensberger, Boyce. "Two Americans Win Nobel
Prize for Medicine." *Washington Post*, October
11, 1994, p. A4.

—*Sketch by Pamela Proffitt*

Peter Goldreich
1939–

American astrophysicist

Peter Goldreich probably said it best when he
described himself as an "all-purpose theoretician," in
the fields of astrophysics and the planetary sciences.
Certainly a list of his career achievements reads like a
guide to the galaxy. Seated in his armchair, Goldreich
has steered his way through the rings of Saturn, the
moons of Uranus and beyond into pulsars and
neutron stars in deep space, with little other than
pencil and paper to guide him in his explorations.
From this vantage position, he provided theoretical
explanations for a diverse range of astronomical
phenomena observed, but not completely understood,
by others.

Stellar Lift-off

Despite the fact that he made his first significant
contributions to astrophysics by the time he was 22,
Goldreich said that his interest in the field did not
develop until he was in college. Born July 14, 1939, in
New York City to high school biology teachers Paul
Goldreich and Edith Rosenfeld Goldreich, his first
love was for competitive sports. He was attracted to
physics and mathematics while in his first year at

Cornell University in Ithaca, New York, and thus,
graduated in 1960 with a B.S. in engineering physics.
He then obtained a Ph.D. in physics under the
guidance of renowned physicist **Thomas Gold**. Even
before graduating in 1963, Goldreich had made his
mark as a theoretician by providing the explanation
for the rotation patterns of planets and their natural
satellites (moons).

For many years astronomers had been aware of
the property of resonance in satellites—namely a
tendency to settle into a pattern of rotation such that
the ratio between the orbital frequency around its
own axis and its frequency of revolving around the
parent planet was close to a ratio of small integers.
However, scientists did not know what forces were
instrumental in establishing the particular resonance
of a planet-satellite pair. Working in conjunction with
Gold, Goldreich was able to explain the patterns in
terms of tidal forces.

A body in space exerts a gravitational force or
attractions that is proportional to its mass (or size)
and inversely proportional to the distance from that
body. When the astral bodies are rather massive—as
is the case with planets and moons—then the force is
unevenly distributed so that the attraction felt by the
side of a planet closer to the moon is more than that
facing away from the moon. The differential forces
are responsible for distorting the shape of the astronomical bodies. These distortions are referred to as tidal
forces.

What Goldreich conjectured and then showed by
his calculations to be true, was that these tidal forces
were in turn responsible for creating resonance in
satellite pairs. Three years later, along with his
colleague Stan Peale, he showed how the planet
Mercury got trapped into 3:2 resonance with its
orbital period around the Sun. In other words,
Mercury goes through a cycle of 3 days every two
years. (It should be noted here that the duration of a
day on Mercury is not the 24 hours we are used to
here on Earth.) During this interval, Goldreich spent
one year as a postdoctoral fellow at Cambridge in
England and then moved to University of California
at Los Angeles. In 1966 he accepted a position at the
California Institute of Technology in Pasadena, where
he stayed for the remainder of his career.

Roving in Space from the Armchair

In an interview with the author in 1995, Goldreich described his scientific approach as that of a
rover, typically working on a problem—invariably
with some other colleague—for a few years, writing
up his results and moving on to other topics of
interest. This manner of wandering was evident right
from the beginning. In 1965, while still engaged in
working out problems of tidal forces, he also published a paper with D. Lynden-Bell, in which he

described a mechanism for the growth of gravitational instabilities in sheared discs. Today this paper holds its own as one of the classics in astrophysics and is regarded by many as central to understanding the spiral structures of galaxies. He also made seminal contributions to the modern understanding of the formation and behavior of neutron stars, and in 1969 published a paper providing the key bit of insight to understanding the magnetospheric properties of pulsars.

In yet another publication in 1969, Goldreich provided an elegant explanation of the role of Io, one of Jupiter's moons, in governing radio bursts from its mother planet. And in the mid-1970s, he predicted that planets like Saturn and Uranus must posses undiscovered moons that helped to shepherd planetary debris floating in space into the rings that encircle these planets. Each of these predictions was dramatically confirmed by the *Voyager* spacecrafts, which detected a million-ampere current flow between Io and Jupiter, and photographed moons around Saturn's F-ring and Uranus' epsilon ring. In later years he turned his attention to the phenomenon of turbulence in magnetized fluids and tackled a problem in the area of cosmology—the theory of the development of large scale structures in the universe. As the citation for his 1995 National Medal of Science proclaims, "There are few areas of importance in contemporary theoretical astrophysics that have not been influenced by his research."

It is a measure of his colleagues' high regard for his contributions that he was elected to the National Academy of Sciences by the time he was 32. Meanwhile, despite myriad honors and achievements, Goldreich himself managed to stay remarkably down to earth. Throughout his life, he has maintained an avid interest in all manner of competitive sports, and at different times participated competitively in baseball, soccer, judo, wrestling, running, tennis, and squash. He married Susan Kroll, an occupational therapist with whom he had two sons. The only time he truly impressed his wife with his work, he said once, was when he won the National Medal and the family traveled to the White House for the honors ceremony.

SELECTED WRITINGS BY GOLDREICH:

Periodicals

"Tides and the Earth-Moon System," *Scientific American* (April 1972): 43-52.

—*Sketch by Neeraja Sankaran*

Peter Gorer
1907–1961
English immunologist

A research medical doctor, Peter Gorer performed important work in the fields of genetics, immunology, and transplantation. His discovery of the first major histocompatibility complex—the H-2 system in mice—would have important implications for organ and tissue transplantation. Found in almost all mammalian species, the major histocompatability complex (MHC) refers to a specific group of genes and the proteins they encode which aid the immune system in differentiating between an individual's own cells and the cells of an outside invader. This discovery provided the first insight into why transplanted organs are often rejected by the recipient's body. Because the MHC of every individual (except identical twins) is unique, the immune system of a transplant recipient will attack and destroy a donated organ as an invader unless powerful immunosuppressants are administered. Gorer's research, though not recognized for nearly a decade, would later help lay the foundation of modern immunology.

Peter Alfred Gorer was born on April 14, 1907, in London, England. His father, Edgar Gorer, was a wealthy art expert who died on the *Lusitania* when the ship was torpedoed and sunk by a German submarine during World War I. Gorer spent his primary education at Charterhouse, then went on to receive his medical training at Guy's Hospital Medical School in London, beginning in 1924. He earned his B.Sc. in 1929.

Begins Work in Research Medicine

By the time Gorer qualified as doctor in 1932, he had chosen a career in research medicine over clinical practice. One of his early interests was the physiology of hibernation, and he published a paper on the subject. However, he changed his focus to genetics after studying the subject for a year at University College in London under the direction of the famous geneticist **J. B. S. Haldane**.

In 1934, Gorer joined the Lister Institute under the auspices of the British Empire Cancer campaign, and remained there until 1940. While at Lister, he began his study of the genetic factors that influence the rejection or acceptance of foreign tissue. In the past, scientists had observed that a malignant tumor from one mouse would shrink when it was implanted into the body of another, unrelated mouse. However, if a tumor was implanted into a twin or another closely related individual, it would continue to grow. Gorer and his mentor Haldane believed that the reason for this phenomena lay in the immune response of the host animal. It is the responsibility of the immune system to protect the body from foreign substances, or antigens. When the immune system perceives a substance as foreign, it releases antibodies to attack and destroy the substance. In the case of the mouse tumors, the two scientists hypothesized that the cells of both the donor and the host contained antigens, the characteristics of which were controlled by genes. It would then follow that a host's immune system would attack the tumor of an unrelated donor, since its antigens would be very different from its own. By the same token, a tumor implanted into the body of a twin or closely related individual would continue to grow since the antigens of the tumor and the antigens of the host would be exactly the same or closely matched. Gorer and Haldane also believed that these antigens would fall into groups according to blood type.

Discovers H-2 system

While Haldane moved on to other subjects, Gorer set about proving their hypothesis experimentally. He first had to overcome that fact that no one had yet typed mouse blood. Unlike the blood of such other mammals as humans or rabbits, mouse blood had proven extremely difficult to type in the past, such seemingly insignificant factors as what tubes were used and how long the blood was refrigerated having an effect on the necessary experiments. However, after much trial and error, Gorer was able to determine the existence of three major types of mouse red blood cells, based on their reaction to his own blood serum. He then went about injecting tumor cells from one blood type into mice of the same type, another type, and hybrids which were related in varying degrees to the donor mouse. The resulting tumor growth or death fulfilled Gorer's expectations, and he was able to detect the presence of an antigen by observing the antibodies produced by the host animals. He published the results of these experiments in 1936. A year later he determined the chromosomal location of the genes that controlled the production of this antigen and therefore determined the compatability of host and donor tissue.

Gorer continued to work on this immunological discovery for many years, and, when combined with the efforts of others, proved to be the accepted basis of knowledge about transplant acceptance or rejection. It took ten years before anyone reacted to this ground-breaking discovery, and, though he was disappointed that his work went largely unrecognized for so many years, Gorer never expressed bitterness. In 1940, Gorer received his D.Sc. degree and returned to Guy's Hospital Medical School to work as an assistant in morbid histology and hematology. A year later Gorer married Gertrude Kahler, who died of tuberculosis the end of World War II.

Works with George Snell in Bar Harbor

In 1947 Gorer accepted a year-long appointment as a visiting professor at the Roscoe B. Jackson Memorial Laboratory based in Bar Harbor, Maine. Part of Harvard University, Bar Harbor had been set up for the study of mammalian genetics, and it proved a fruitful ground for Gorer's research. He worked primarily with American immunogeneticist **George Snell**, who had expressed his admiration of Gorer's work in earlier correspondence, and together they further elucidated the genetic basis of histocompatability in mice. While at Bar Harbor, Gorer also met his second wife, Elizabeth Bruce Keucher, who was the librarian and secretary to a scientist at laboratory. Together, they had two children, one son, Peter, and one daughter, Rachel.

Returns to Guy's Hospital

In 1948, Gorer returned to London and to Guy's Hospital Medical School. He became a reader in experimental pathology, a position he held until his death. Shortly before he died, Gorer worked with leukemia cells in mice, finding a group of antigens specific to them. Over the course of his career, he also studied immunology as it related to non-pathological tissue. In 1960, he was named a fellow of the Royal Society, though he only published about 50 papers. Gorer died of lung cancer the next year, on May 11, 1961, in London. In retrospect, one of his former associates, D. Bernard Amos, says of Gorer, "Besides being ingenious, Gorer was an extremely generous scientist. This was manifested at the personal level by his willingness to give me sole authorship of work performed with his guidance. He also put the interests of science above his own interests."

In 1980, his former Bar Harbor associate George Snell won a share of the Nobel Prize in Medicine, based in part on Gorer's discoveries. In an article in *The New York Times*, Snell gives Gorer credit for discovering the H-2 antigen. "A key discovery was made by the late Dr. Peter Gorer of Guy's Hospital in London. Dr. Snell said he 'would love to have seen him share the prize.' However, Nobel Prizes are not awarded posthumously."

SELECTED WRITINGS BY GORER:

Periodicals

"The Detection of a Hereditary Antigenic Difference in the Blood of Mice by Means of Human Group A Serum." *Journal of Genetics* (1936): 17-31.
"The Genetic and Antigenic Basis of Tumour Transplantation." *Journal of Pathology Bacteriology* (1937): 691-97.

FURTHER READING:

Books

Daintith, John, et al. "Gorer, Peter Alfred." *A Biographical Encyclopedia of Scientists*, Vol. 1. New York: Facts on File, Inc., 1981, p. 326.

Periodicals

Amos, D. Bernard. "Recollections of Dr. Peter Gorer." *Immunogenetics* (1986): 341-44.

Borders, William. "3 Cell Researchers Win Medicine Nobel." *The New York Times* (October 11, 1980): §2, p.1.

Boyse, Edward A. "Working with Gorer, 1957-1960." *Immunogenetics* (1986): 350-51.

Klein, Jan. "Seeds of Time: Fifty Years Ago Peter A. Gorer Discovered the *H-2* Complex." *Immunogenetics* (1986): 331-38.

"Obituary: P. A. Gorer." *British Medical Journal* (May 20, 1961): 1467-68.

"Obituary: Peter Alfred Gorer." *The Lancet* (May 20, 1961): 1120-21.

Snell, George D. "Some Recollections of Peter Gorer and His Work on This Fiftieth Anniversary of His Discovery of *H-2*." *Immunogenetics* (1986): 339-40.

Tucker, Anthony. "Of Mice and Men and Supergenes; Obituary: George Snell." *The Guardian*, London (July 1, 1996): 11.

—*Sketch by Annette Petrusso*

Herbert E. Grier, Jr.

Herbert E. Grier, Jr.
1911–

American engineer

In a career that spanned more than 50 years, Herbert E. Grier was both a pioneering scientist and a successful corporate manager. A leader in the development of ultra-high-speed electronic stroboscopy, he also played a pivotal role in the Manhattan Project, which developed the first atomic bomb. As the cofounder and first president of EG&G engineering company, he helped develop it into a multibillion dollar corporation. Described as talented and unassuming, Grier's craftsman-like approach to research and management led to his demand as a consultant on many projects, including overseeing critical safety elements in the first *Columbia* space shuttle flight.

Grier was born in Chicago, Illinois, on July 3, 1911, to Herbert E. Grier, Sr., and Martha Sleeter Grier, who also had three daughters. The family lived in Chicago until Grier was 11 and then moved to New York City. "Engineering came easily to me but I also got channeled [into the field] through my father," Grier told contributor contributor David Petechuk in a November 18, 1997, interview. A die chemist, Grier's father urged his son to attend the Massachusetts of Institute of Technology (MIT).

Embarks on Pivotal Partnership

Grier earned his bachelor of science and master of science degrees in electrical engineering at MIT. His thesis paper on stroboscopic photography led him to collaborate with MIT faculty member **Harold Edgerton** and Kenneth Germeshausen. Together, the scientists pioneered ultra-high-speed photography and the then unique stroboscopic and flash lighting techniques, including a portable flash unit for news photographers.

In a history of EG&G produced by the corporation, Grier points out that the partnership was first formed "to achieve, as a group, more than we could as individuals." With no written agreement, the scientists simply pooled their resources for a variety of consulting projects. As their abilities became more widely known, they prospered. "The effort worked very well; at least we ate," recalled Grier, "and in those days in the early thirties, that was somewhat of problem."

To the Nation's Defense

With the onset of World War II, the partnership of Edgerton, Germeshausen, and Grier permanently changed direction. Both Edgerton and Grier became involved in night aerial photography. Grier eventually worked on manufacturing the firing sets for the atomic bomb. The Manhattan Project, which was working on developing an atomic weapon before Germany, turned to Grier because of work with flash photography involving high-current short-time discharges of electricity, which was needed for firing.

In his book, *Nuclear Hostages*, Bernard O'Keefe, a subsequent partner in EG&G, credits Grier's scientific and technological acumen as a major contribution to the atomic bomb's development. He credits Grier's insights and leadership as helping to shorten World War II and saving countless American lives. "We were essentially workers with a goal insight," Grier told contributor Petechuk. "Time was of the essence, and a distinct push was on. I am proud to be part of the team that put an end to the war."

After the war, the team of Edgerton, Germeshausen, and Grier reunited with a new focus on atomic energy. Through a contract with MIT, the trio became involved in further developing firing sets for nuclear weapons. They formed EG&G in 1947, with Grier serving as the company's first president. In 1953, Grier headed up a group of EG&G scientists assigned by the Atomic Energy Commission to work on nuclear test operations at its Nevada Test Site. The company eventually designed, built, and operated equipment that armed, timed, fired, photographed, and acquired performance data on nearly all nuclear test blasts in Nevada and the Pacific. They also worked on instrumentation and photographic equipment for nuclear rocket test activities and became a major contractor at the Kennedy Space Center.

Although Grier proved to be an astute manager in helping build EG&G, he remained, at heart, a scientist who most valued the informal relationship he had built up with his partners over the years. In *Nuclear Hostages*, O'Keefe recalls when the group began a serious debate about the company growing too large and losing quality. "When we get that big, we'll have to start writing memos to each other," said Grier. "If we have to start writing memos, we should quit."

Despite Grier's trepidations, EG&G continued to grow into a multibillion dollar company. In 1965, Grier became President and cofounder of CER Geonuclear Corporation, a company formed by EG&G and others. CER developed and implemented the use of nuclear explosives in commercial application, primarily in the area of extracting underground natural resources. From 1969-1971, he also served as President and Chairman of the Board of Reynolds Electrical & Engineering Co. Inc., which was a major

contractor at the Atomic Energy Commission Nevada Test Site. Although he officially retired in 1976, Grier continued to work as a consultant, especially in the area of space flight.

During his career, Grier acquired numerous patents and wrote many publications in the area of high-speed lighting equipment and techniques, weapon design, timing and firing, and other areas. In 1973, he was appointed to the National Aeronautics & Space Administration (NASA) Aerospace Safety Advisory Panel. His many awards include a Commendation of the President (1948), Presidential Certificate of Appreciation (1971), and the NASA Distinguished Service Medal (1985).

The father of three, Grier retired with his second wife to La Jolla, California, where he spends most of his time gardening. "Most of us in science do our best work when we're young," said Grier, looking back on his career. "As you get older and see more of the big picture, you inevitably graduate toward management. I've been very fortunate in that I've always worked for myself in an occupation and with people I enjoyed."

FURTHER READING:

Books

O'Keefe, Bernard J. *Nuclear Hostages*. Boston: Houghton Mifflin Company, 1983.

Other

Corporate Communications and Information Department. *EG&G Inc. A History of the Company*. Massachusetts, EG&G Inc., 1991.

—*Sketch by David Petechuk*

Mary Jane Guthrie
1895–1975
American zoologist

As a scientist, Mary Jane Guthrie was an expert in cytology (cell biology). Within cytology, Guthrie was interested in the cytoplasm of the female reproductive system. Guthrie also did research into endocrinology, specifically the cytoplasm of the endocrine glands; experimental pathology; and organ culture.

Mary Jane Guthrie was born on December 13, 1895, in Bloomfield, Missouri, to George Robert Guthrie and his wife Lula Ella Loyd. She earned her undergraduate degree (A.B.) at the University of Missouri in 1916 and her A.M. in 1918 at the same institution. Guthrie attended Bryn Mawr College for her Ph.D., which she was awarded in 1922. While engrossed in her doctoral studies, she was a demonstrator in the biology department from 1918 until 1920, then worked as an instructor from 1920-21.

In 1922 Guthrie returned to the University of Missouri to teach. She moved through the ranks in the zoology department, spending nearly 30 years at Missouri. She was named an assistant professor in 1922; an associate professor in 1927; and finally a full professor in 1937. Like many female scientists of her generation, Guthrie had problems getting funding for her research projects. Though she was respected as a scientist, for example, she was told in 1934 by a Rockefeller Foundation official that women scientists had to have more confirmation of their scientific prowess than men to get grants.

Guthrie did not lack for employment, however. While at the University of Missouri, she collaborated with several other scientists on textbooks for Zoology. With Winterton Conway Curtis, she wrote the *Textbook of General Zoology*. With John M. Anderson, she wrote two books of note: *General Zoology* and *Laboratory Directions in General Zoology*.

In 1951 Guthrie moved to Detroit, Michigan, and was first associated with the Detroit Institute of Cancer Research as research associate. She also did research at Wayne State University (in Detroit), until four years later, in 1955, when Guthrie became a professor at Wayne State, while retaining her position at the Institute of Cancer Research. She retired from both posts in 1960.

Guthrie belonged to numerous professional societies over the course of her career. They included the American Society of Zoologists, the American Association of Anatomists, Genetics Society, American Society of Mammologists, Tissue Culture Association, American Association for the Advancement of Science, and the American Society of Naturalists.

Guthrie had many interests outside of science. She enjoyed collecting stamps and furniture, reading, theater, golf, and horseback riding. Guthrie died in 1975 at the age of 80.

SELECTED WRITINGS BY GUTHRIE:

Books

(With John M. Anderson) *General Zoology*. New York: Wiley & Sons, 1957.
(With John M. Anderson) *Laboratory Directions in General Zoology*. New York: Wiley & Sons, 1958.
(With Winterton Conway Curtis) *Textbook of General Zoology*. 3d ed. New York: Wiley & Sons, 1938.

FURTHER READING:

Books

Bailey, Martha J. "Guthrie, Mary Jane." *American Women in Science: A Biographical Dictionary*. Denver: ABC-CLIO, 1994, p. 145.

—Sketch by Annette Petrusso

Norman Hackerman
1912–
American chemist

Norman Hackerman is internationally recognized as an expert in metal corrosion. He has devoted most of his scientific study to the electrochemistry of oxidation, and his work has resulted in the development of a number of processes—invaluable to the metals industry—which slow or prevent corrosion.

Hackerman was born March 2, 1912, in Baltimore, Maryland. He earned his undergraduate (1932) and doctoral degrees (1935) in chemistry at Johns Hopkins University and immediately embarked on a career as an educator by accepting an assistant professorship in the physical chemistry department at Loyola College in Maryland. Hackerman also worked concurrently as a research chemist for the Colloid Corporation until 1940, when he accepted a position as an assistant chemist with the United States Coast Guard.

Hackerman briefly returned to academic life in 1941 as an assistant professor of chemistry at Virginia Polytechnic Institute. Two years later, Hackerman accepted a post as a research chemist for the Kellex Corporation. In 1945, he accepted a post as assistant professor of chemistry with the University of Texas at Austin. During his 25-year tenure at the university, Hackerman served in numerous capacities, including chairman of the department of chemistry (1952-1962), director of the corrosion research laboratory and dean of research and sponsored programs (1961-1962), vice president and provost (1962), vice chancellor of academic affairs (1963-1967), and university president from 1967 to 1970. In 1970, he joined the faculty of Rice University as a professor of chemistry and served as president of the university, holding both appointments until his retirement in 1985. Rice University named him emeritus president and distinguished emeritus professor of chemistry in 1985, and the University of Texas at Austin honored him as an emeritus professor of chemistry in the same year.

Committed to educating the next generation of scientists—many of his students have earned the recognition of the international science community—Hackerman continued to pursue his own research despite the demands of teaching and administrative duties.

Connecting the Classroom to the Laboratory

Hackerman's research has focused on the electrochemistry of corrosion. His goal has been to probe how solid metals react at the point of contact with solutions and the process of oxidation. By studying how the structures of molecules affect their function, the action of electrons, and how absorption strains molecular bonds, Hackerman has contributed to the development of products that retard corrosion and metal manufacturing techniques that produce corrosion-resistant metals. His research made it clear that simply preventing physical absorption does not prevent corrosion. Such understanding was crucial to manufacturing concerns that had emphasized protective coatings, for example, paint on automobiles, rather than the electrochemical nature of metals and the complex process of corrosion.

While continuing his work at Rice University, Hackerman broadened his research arena by accepting an appointment with the Robert A. Welch Foundation in 1982. As chairman of the foundation's Scientific Advisory Board, Hackerman again juggled administrative responsibilities with scientific investigation.

Although he retired from his academic post more than a decade ago, Hackerman continues his research with the Welch Foundation. His current investigations focus on thermally grown surface oxides, the electronic structure of surface films, and suppressing corrosion through passive and inhibitory techniques.

Serving the Broader Community

Since the beginning of his career, Hackerman has accepted the obligation to serve his profession and his nation as an integral part of his work. During World War II, he put his considerable talents at the disposal of the U.S. Coast Guard. A member of the national science board of the National Science Foundation since 1968, he served as board chairman from 1974 to 1980. Hackerman has also been a member of the National Board of Graduate Education and participated in Texas Governor's Task Force on Higher Education. He was the chairman of the board of energy studies for the National Academy of Science/NRC Commission on Natural Resources, a member of the Energy Research Advisory Board, and a member of the environmental pollution panel of the President's Scientific Advancement Committee.

Active in a number of academic and scientific organizations, Hackerman's numerous professional affiliations ranged from the chairmanship of the Gordon Research Conference on Corrosion in 1952 to serving as editor of the *Journal of Electrochemistry* since 1969. He is a member of the American Chemical Society, a member and former president of the Electrochemical Society and a member of the National Academy of Sciences.

Hackerman's work has been recognized with numerous awards and honors, including the Whitney Award from the National Association of Corrosion Engineers in 1956, the Palladium Medal from the Electrochemical Society in 1965, the Gold Medal of the American Institute of Chemists in 1978, the Charles Lathrop Parsons Award from the American Chemists Society in 1987, and the National Medal of Science in 1993. He is the author of more than 200 articles.

SELECTED WRITINGS BY HACKERMAN:

Periodicals

"The Theory and Practice of Corrosion and Its Control in Industry." *Langmuir* 3, no. 6, (1987): 922-924.

(With S. Tebbal) "Effect of the Liquid Film Thickness on the CO_2Corrosion of Steel." *Corrision* 45, no. 7, (1989): 558.

(With M. Bartos) "Inhibition Action of Propuryl Alcohol During Anodic Dissolution of Iron in Hydrochloric Acid." *Journal of the Electrochemical Society* 139, (1992): 3428.

FURTHER READING:

Books

American Men and Women of Science, 18th Edition, New Providence, NJ: R. R. Bowker, 1992-93, Volume 3, p. 428.

Eckes, Kristin A., ed. *Who's Who in Science and Engineering,* New Providence, NJ: Reed Publishing, 1996; pp. 383-384.

Other

Hackerman. "Norman Hackerman." http://pcheem1.rice.edu/Faculty/Staff/Hackerman/html (November 11, 1997).

—Sketch by A. Mullig

George S. Hammond
1921–
American chemist

George S. Hammond is noted for creating and developing the field of organic photochemistry, the study of the interaction between light and various organic materials. He is also credited with training many of the important American organic photochemists over a period of three decades. Some of the products that resulted from work in this field include catalysts used in the production of vinyl plastics, chemicals used to form the intricate circuit patterns on computer chips, and materials used in solar cells to convert the sun's energy to electrical power.

George Simms Hammond was born in Auburn, Maine, on May 22, 1921. His father, Oswald Kenric Hammond, was a farmer. His mother's maiden name was Marjorie Thomas. George attended Bates College in nearby Lewiston, Maine, where he graduated magna cum laude with a B.S. degree in chemistry in 1943. After graduation he was employed as a chemist with Rohm and Haas Corporation for two years, followed by a position with the Office of Scientific Research and Development at Harvard University, where he worked on the development of insect repellents. In 1945 he married Marian Reese. During their marriage they had five children, Kenric, Janet, Steven, Barbara, and Jeremy.

In 1947 Hammond received both his M.S. and Ph.D. degrees in chemistry from Harvard University. After postgraduate work with the Office of Naval Research at the University of California, Los Angeles, he joined the faculty of Iowa State University in 1948. He stayed there until 1958, rising to a full professor in the chemistry department.

Lays the Foundation for Photochemistry

While working at Iowa State, he began his studies of photochemical reactions. One area that especially interested him was the concept of sensitization. In a sensitized reaction, light is absorbed by one chemical in a solution, called a photoinitiator, and the resulting increase in energy is then passed on to another chemical to start the reaction. The use of a photoinitiator "sensitizes" a solution and allows chemical reactions to be triggered by certain frequencies of light. This concept is widely used in the production of integrated circuits on computer chips. In this process, a photosensitive chemical on the surface of the chip reacts with ultraviolet light passing through a mask, or pattern, to form the image of the desired circuit.

In 1958 Hammond accepted a position as professor of organic chemistry at the California Institute of Technology, where he continued his work on photochemical reactions. Many of his papers published in the *Journal of the American Chemical Society* during the period 1959-1962 established the foundation for modern photochemistry.

During the 1960s, Hammond and his students made many important observations on various photochemical reactions. One of the areas of study was the chemistry of azo-bis-isobutrynitrile (AIBN). They observed that many of the components of this chemical were held in place by the surrounding solvent molecules and ended up reacting with each other, rather than with neighboring chemicals. They found that this "cage effect" could be altered to control the amount of reaction between the AIBN components and other chemicals. Based on this discovery, AIBN became one of the most frequently used catalysts to start and control the chemical reactions required for the production of vinyl plastics.

In 1964 Hammond was named the Arthur Amos Noyes Professor of Chemistry at Caltech, and in 1968 he became Chairman of the Division of Chemistry and Chemical Engineering. He was elected to the National Academy of Sciences in 1963 and to the American Academy of Arts and Sciences in 1965. The American Chemical Society honored Hammond three times while he was at Caltech: first with the award in petroleum chemistry in 1961, then with the James Flack Norris Award in Physical Organic Chemistry in 1967, and finally with the award in chemical education in 1972.

Hammond left Caltech in 1972 to become a professor of chemistry and vice-chancellor for natural sciences at the University of California, Santa Cruz. He gave up his position as vice-chancellor in 1974 in order to spend half his time as foreign secretary of the National Academy of Sciences, while continuing his research and teaching duties at the university. In 1976 the American Chemical Society honored him with their highest award, the Priestley Medal, for his distinguished service to the profession of chemistry. In 1977 Hammond's first marriage ended in divorce. He married Eva L. Menger shortly thereafter. Eva had two children by a previous marriage, Kirsten Menger-Anderson and Lenore Menger-Anderson.

In 1978 Hammond left the academic world to join Allied Signal Corporation in Morristown, New Jersey, as Associate Director of Corporate Research. Allied Signal was engaged in the manufacture of aerospace and automotive products, chemicals, fibers, plastics, and advanced materials. Hammond became Director of Integrated Chemical Systems in 1979, and Executive Director of Bioscience, Metals, and Ceramics in 1984.

Hammond retired from Allied Signal in 1988 to become a consultant. In 1991 he joined the faculty of Bowling Green State University in Bowling Green, Ohio, as Director of Materials Science, and in 1992 he

was named a Distinguished Visiting Research Professor. In 1994, while holding the position of Senior McMaster Fellow at the Center for Photochemical Sciences at Bowling Green, Hammond was awarded the prestigious National Medal of Science for his work in organic photochemistry. He was also awarded the Seaborg Medal the same year.

Today, Hammond continues his research work at Bowling Green and is active in several scientific groups.

SELECTED WRITINGS BY HAMMOND:

Books

(With D. J. Cram) *Organic Chemistry*, 1959.
(With J. J. Osteryoung, T. J. Crawford, and H. B. Gray) *Models in Chemical Science*, 1971.
(With J. S. Fritz) *Quantitative Organic Analysis*, 1957.

FURTHER READING:

Books

American Men and Women of Science, 19th edition, 1995-96. Reed Publishing, 1994.

Other

"George S. Hammond of Bowling Green State University's Center for Photochemical Sciences Wins National Medal of Science." 1994. http://www.nsf.gov/nsf/nmos/hammond.html (October 29, 1997).
http://ernie.bgsu.edu/~iivanov/hammond.html. This website lists many of the more than 280 papers Hammond authored or co-authored.

—*Sketch by Chris Cavette*

Ethel Browne Harvey
1885–1965
American marine biologist and embryologist

Ethel Browne Harvey was responsible for discovering many of the mechanisms of cell division, some of which generated interest in the popular press. In 1937, Harvey announced that she had was able to stimulate fragments of sea urchin eggs—which contained no cell nucleus—to divide. This caused a public furor because it was seen as reproduction without parental inheritance. This was a radical notion and affected the whole theory of cell division and genetics. Harvey spent most of her career researching cell division and development, using sea urchin eggs as her primary subject model.

Ethel Browne Harvey was born in Baltimore, Maryland, on December 14, 1885, the youngest child of Bennet Browne, and obstetrician/gynecologist and professor, and his wife Jennie Nicholson Browne. Ethel had two brothers and two sisters. Her parents were progressive and believed in education for girls, so the young Browne girls attended Baltimore's Bryn Mawr School, the first American all-girls prep school.

With her parents' support, Harvey received a full college education. She graduated from what was then known as Women's College of Baltimore (later Goucher College) in 1906. After graduation, Harvey had her first experience at the Marine Biological Lab at Woods Hole, Massachusetts, a relationship that would span nearly 60 years. She earned her MA at Columbia University on a Goucher Fellowship a year later, studying zoology. In 1909, she was elected to Corporation Membership at the Marine Biological Lab. At Columbia, Harvey earned her Ph.D. in 1913, again studying zoology. While a graduate student, Harvey published six papers. She had already expressed an interest in the basic forms of life, researching embryology and cytology.

Between 1913 and 1931, Harvey bounced between positions and research, with yearly excursions to the lab at Woods Hole. For example, she spent a year on fellowship at the University of California (1914-15), teaching for several years at New York University (1928-32). Her research during the 1920s focused on sea urchin embryology, and she did much experimental work on the subject. In this period, Harvey married Princeton professor Edmund Newton Harvey in 1916. He was also a marine biologist, but they did not work together. They had two sons together, Edmund Jr. and Richard.

In 1931, she joined the biology department at Princeton as an Investigator. It was here that she announced her most important work on sea urchin eggs. Her 1937 announcement illustrated that the eggs could be divided without a nucleus when redistributed by centrifugal force. At the time, the popular press picked up on her discovery emphasizing that, as the headline in the September 13, 1937, issue of *Life* proclaimed, "New Life is Created without Sex," while the December 6, 1937, *Newsweek* stated that, "Birth without Parents: Woman's Findings Add to Doubt on Accepted Genetics Theory."

Harvey did other work on the sea urchin. She was the first to devise a way to determine the sex of a sea urchin. She published a book in 1956 which laid out all her work on the sea urchin and its embryology, entitled *The American* Arbacia *and Other Sea Urchins*. It is still used as a reference book. Though her

work received wide attention, Harvey was never a faculty member at Princeton. Indeed, she only had a corner of her husband's lab at both Princeton and Woods Hole. The only support she received for her sea urchin work was a 1937 grant from the American Philosophical Society.

Before her retirement in 1959, Harvey received numerous accolades from her peers, including membership in many biological societies around the world. The Marine Biological Laboratory elected her a trustee from 1950-56, after a lifelong relationship. She was the first woman in 50 years to be elected to the board. Harvey died of peritonitis on September 2, 1965, in Falmouth, Massachusetts.

SELECTED WRITINGS BY HARVEY:

Books

The American Arbacia *and Other Sea Urchins*. Princeton: Princeton University Press, 1956.

FURTHER READING:

Books

Bailey, Martha J. "Harvey, Ethel Browne." *American Women in Science: A Biographical Dictionary*. Denver: ABC-CLIO, 1994, pp. 154-55.

Haraway, Donna J. "Harvey, Ethel Browne." *Notable American Women, The Modern Period: A Biographical Dictionary*. Barbara Sicherman and Carol Hurd Green, eds. Cambridge, MA: The Belknap Press of Harvard University Press, 1980, pp. 319-21.

Kass-Simon, G. and Patricia Farnes, eds. "Ethel Browne Harvey: Induction and Merogony." *Women of Science: Righting the Record*. Bloomington: Indiana University Press, 1990, pp. 217-20.

Siegel, Patricia Joan and Kay Thomas Finley. "Ethel Browne Harvey." *Women in the Scientific Search: An American Bio-bibliography, 1724-1979*. Metuchen, NJ: The Scarecrow Press, Inc., 1985, pp. 364-67.

Periodicals

Butler, E. G. "Memorials—Ethel Browne Harvey." *The Biological Bulletin* (August 1967): 9-11.

"Dr. Ethel Harvey, Biologist, Was 79." *The New York Times* (September 3, 1965): 27.

"New Life Is Created Without Sex." *Life* (September 13, 1937): 70-72.

"Science. Birth Without Parents: Woman's Findings Add to Doubt on Accepted Genetics

Theory." *Newsweek* (December 6, 1937): 36-37.

—Sketch by Annette Petrusso

Hermann Haus
1925–

Slovenian-born American electrical engineer

Hermann Haus is one of a handful of researchers to be accorded the honor of membership to both the National Academy of Sciences and the National Academy of Engineers, which are the highest honors afforded to American scientists and engineers by their peers. An electrical engineer by training, he has made pioneering and influential contributions to the fields of electromagnetics, quantum electronics, and laser optics. His fundamental research has found practical applications in a variety of areas, including long distance communications and the development of instrumentation and techniques for eye surgery.

Shaping Forces

According to an interview Haus gave to the *Boston Globe* in 1995 on the occasion of his winning a National Medal of Science, he chose engineering in keeping with a long-standing family tradition: "Sons and daughters never do the same things as their parents." His father, Otto Maximilian Haus, was an Austrian medical doctor from Slovenia, which was part of the multi-national Yugoslav state from 1918 to 1991, where his family immigrated in the eighteenth century, when it belonged to the Austrian Empire. Otto Haus served as a medical officer during in the Austro-Hungarian army in World War I, during which time he met and married Helene Hynek, a refugee from eastern Hungary. After the war they settled down in the Slovenian town of Ljubljana.

Born August 8, 1925, Hermann Haus grew up under turbulent times, with his hometown passing through several hands, including those of Mussolini's fascists and Josip Broz Tito's communist partisans. The shifting political climate played havoc with his early collegiate education. He had barely entered the University of Ljubljana to study engineering in 1941, when the war intensified and the Italians closed the university down. To avoid the draft, Haus took up a job as an electrician in an aluminum factory. When Tito's communists came to power in Yugoslavia in December, 1945, Haus and his mother were arrested and imprisoned for 14 days before the new Minister for Education, a former patient of his father's whom the family had protected from the Nazis during the

war, arranged for their release. Some six months later the family, as German-speaking minorities, became "victims of Tito's overall ethnic cleansing program."

Recounting these experiences during a retirement dinner at the Massachusetts Institute of Technology (MIT) in 1996, Haus remembered being shipped across the border to Austria in an unheated cattle-cart in the dead of night in December. "On the train was a professor of chemistry, who bemoaned the fact that he had lost the notes of ten years of research. It was then I decided to choose a field of work the results of which one can mostly remember in one's head."

In Austria, Haus and his mother were reunited with their father who, heeding a warning by the partisans, had walked across the border to Austria during the communist takeover of Yugoslavia, and had become the head of a tuberculosis hospital near the town of Graz. Haus resumed his education, entering the local university to study electrical power engineering. But after a few semesters there, he decided that the field of electrical engineering had more to offer and thus switched to the University of Vienna. A course on microwave field theory and the then newly invented traveling wave tubes made him decide on his field of interest. "It was the kind of knowledge you can carry in your head as opposed to chemistry," he recalled thinking.

Haus's undergraduate education was not formally completed in Austria. In 1948, he came to the United States to Union College, in Schenectady, New York where he obtained a B.S. within one year. He went on to receive Master's degree from the Rensselaer Polytechnic Institute in 1951, and then a Ph.D. from MIT in 1954, where he took up a faculty position the same year. In 1951, he married a young woman whom he had met at Boston University. Haus and his wife Eleanor have four children. Perhaps in reaction to his peripatetic education, Haus spent his entire career at MIT, only leaving for sabbaticals, visiting appointments, and related events. He became a United States citizen in 1956.

Measuring Noise and Molding Light

Haus's early work was in the field of electronics, where he produced the first definitive analyses of noise fluctuations in electronic beams and introduced the concepts of noise measure to engineering. He went on to publish a number of now classic papers on noise, and was the first person, along with his colleague C. Freed, to report the measurement of quantum noise in a laser oscillator.

During the 1970s, Haus's fundamental insights into the behavior of laser beams enabled him to conceive of a technique called "additive pulse mode-locking" that generates ultra short laser pulses—less than 10,000 times as small as a billionth of a second.

These lasers pulses are now used in many different ways, from precision eye surgery to fiber optic communications. The latter industry has also benefited greatly from Haus's later research in the field of solitons.

Solitons are solitary waves (hence their name) that can travel for long distances without any distortion in its shape or speed. The traveling patterns of waves are determined by two main conditions, wavelength (beyond a certain size the speed of waves accelerates), amplitude or height (taller waves travel faster and will overtake shorter ones). Solitons are formed when the two effects balance each other. The earliest observation of a soliton was reported as early as in 1838 by the Scotsman J. Scott Russell, who saw such a "heap of water" generated by the sudden stopping of a canal boat and actually chased it on horseback for more than a kilometer. Waves like this are in fact a ubiquitous phenomenon and may be observed in a number of different objects, such as plastics—wall-like transition regions in long-chain polymers—and as undistorted voice and data signals in the fiber-optic cables used for long distance communications.

Despite Russell's observant eye, the soliton phenomenon was not studied by scientists until the later half of the twentieth century. The idea that solitons could be propagated by optical fibbers came around 1973. Haus, along with several colleagues at the Bell Telephone Laboratories, developed the practical means by which these waves could be generated and propagated efficiently. Solitons have greatly accelerated and even simplified long distance communication, where earlier a signal had to be detected and regenerated ever 100 km (62 mi) to prevent their deterioration, a soliton can carry it for several hundred kilometers without any distortion or deterioration.

Despite his formidable achievements, Haus himself always stressed the importance of the cooperation of his colleagues for his successes. At the time he got his Medal, he was in his seventies but still maintained a vigorous routine, bicycling to and from work, a round trip of nearly 30 miles. It was then, he told the reporter, that "the real ideas come."

SELECTED WRITINGS BY HAUS:

Books

Adler, R.B. *Circuit Theory of Linear Noisy Networks.* Cambridge: MIT Press, 1959.
Melcher, J. R. *Electromagnetic Fields and Energy.* Prentice-Hall, 1989.
Penfield, P., Jr. *Electrodynamics of Moving Media.* Cambridge: MIT Press, 1967.
Waves and Fields in Optoelectronics. Prentice-Hall, 1984.

Periodicals

"Molding Light into Solitons." *IEEE Spectrum* (March 1993): 48-53.

FURTHER READING:

Periodicals

Sankaran, Neeraja. "National Medal of Science Winners Contributed to Birth of Their Fields." *The Scientist* (30 October 1995): 3.
Sullivan, Mark. "Simple Approach, Grand Results." *Boston Globe* (8 October 1995): 21, 24.
———. "Haus, Rich to Get Medal of Science." *MIT Tech Talk* (27 September 1995): 1-2.

—*Sketch by Neeraja Sankaran*

Louise Schmir Hay
1935–1989
French–born American mathematician

Louise Hay's mathematical specialty was recursively enumerable sets, which are studied in mathematical logic and the theory of computation. She was head of the mathematics department at the University of Illinois at Chicago, and a founding member of the Association for Women in Mathematics.

Hay was born in Metz, France, on June 14, 1935. Her father, Samuel Szmir, who had emigrated to France from Poland, was in the clothing business. Her mother, Marjem Szafran Szmir, was also from Poland. Hay's mother died in 1938, and her father married Eva Sieradska Szmir late that year. There were three children in the family, Gaston, born in 1933, Louise, and Maurice, born in 1943. (Gaston Schmir became a professor of biochemistry at Yale University, and Maurice Schmir became an anesthesiologist.) The Szmirs were Jewish family and spent World War II from the Germans. In March 1944, Hay and her older brother managed to get to Switzerland, where they remained for the next year. They rejoined the others after the liberation of France, then emigrated to the United States in 1946, where the family name was changed to Schmir. Hay's father owned a delicatessen in New York from 1950 to 1965.

Hay attended William Taft High School in the Bronx, New York. She had no interest in mathematics until her tenth grade geometry teacher, David Rosenbaum, had her read a book about non–Euclidean geometry, which fascinated her. He also helped her get tutoring work. In her senior year, Hay won third prize in the Westinghouse Science Talent Search for a project in non–Euclidean geometry. She was also class valedictorian. The prize enabled her to get a scholarship to attend Swarthmore College, as well as summer jobs at the National Bureau of Standards. She also had a part time job at the Moore School of Electrical Engineering at the University of Pennsylvania. At the end of her junior year, she married John Hay, whose field was experimental psychology. Hay completed her B.A. at Swarthmore in 1956. She joined her husband at Cornell University, where she studied mathematical logic. After two years she left Cornell to go to Oberlin with her husband, and wrote a master's thesis, on infinite valued predicate calculus, for J. Barkley Rosser. Hay earned a M.A. from Cornell in 1959. Because of some unexpected results in the thesis, it was deemed publishable and appeared in the *Journal of Symbolic Logic.*

Hay held a visiting teaching position at Oberlin. Next, she worked at the Cornell Aeronautical Laboratory in Buffalo, New York, for a year. The Hays moved to Massachusetts, where John Hay had a job at Smith College. Hay taught part–time at a junior college for one year, after which she taught for three years at Mt. Holyoke College. Again inspired by a book, Artin's *Geometric Algebra,* Hay attended seminars at Cornell in the summer of 1962, where her husband was participating in a research project. She taught at Mt. Holyoke that fall, and in the following year her first son, Bruce, (now a law professor) was born. A discussion with algebraist **Hannah Neumann** about raising children while pursuing a mathematical career convinced Hay to stay on at Cornell, where she and her husband had again gone for the summer, while her husband returned to Smith. Hay landed a research assistantship, took three courses, passed her preliminary examinations, worked on her dissertation for Anil Nerode, and gave birth to twins, Philip and Gordon (both sons studied mathematical finance) in 1964, completed her thesis in recursion theory and received her Ph.D. from Cornell in 1965. After staying home for a year, Hay taught as an assistant professor at Mt. Holyoke from 1965 to 1968, spending 1966 to 1967 at M.I.T. on an N.S.F. fellowship, and going "through at least 15 sitters." In 1968, she and John Hay divorced.

Hay went to the University of Illinois at Chicago as an associate professor in 1968. She married Richard Larson, a colleague in the mathematics department in 1970. In 1975, she was promoted to professor. In the late 1960s and the 1970s especially, Hay wrote a series of papers dealing with the classification of index sets of recursively enumerable sets, and she introduced the idea of a "weak jump." She enjoyed "the peculiar thrill of briefly knowing a sliver of mathematical truth that *nobody* else knows." Hay also wrote reviews of papers in recursion theory for the *Mathematical Reviews.*

Hay was involved in the Association for Women in Mathematics, giving one of their first invited addresses on a mathematical topic in January 1974. She also supported and encouraged women students at her school, and had two graduate students, Nancy Johnson and Jeanleah Mohrherr. Hay and her husband were awarded Fulbright fellowships to the Philippines in 1978. Hay's interests, according to her brother, Gaston Schmir, included "travel, good food, guitar playing, the feminist movement, and math education for women."

Hay became acting head of the mathematics department in 1979, and headed the department from 1980 until 1988. Personally warm and caring, she was a popular administrator, who democratized the department, made strong appointments, and saw the department name changed to include mathematics, statistics, and computer science. Hay served as secretary of the Association for Symbolic Logic from 1977 to 1982, and on the executive board of the Association for Women in Mathematics from 1980 to 1982.

Hay was diagnosed with cancer in 1974 and suffered a recurrence in 1988. She died on October 28, 1989 in Oak Park, Illinois, at the age of 54. A scholarship was established in Hay's honor at Oak Park/Forest River High School for senior women who intend to major in mathematics. In addition, the Association for Women in Mathematics gives an annual award named for Louise Hay. The award is given to a woman who has made an outstanding contribution to mathematics education.

SELECTED WRITINGS BY HAY:

Periodicals

"Axiomatization of the Infinite–valued Predicate Calculus." *Journal of Symbolic Logic* (March 1963): 77–86.

"The Co–simple Isols." *Annals of Mathematics* 83, no. 2, (1966): 231–56.

"On the Recursion–Theoretic Complexity of Relative Succinctness of Representations of Languages." *Information and Control* 52 (1982): 2–7.

"How I Became a Mathematician (or How It Was in the Bad Old Days)." *Newsletter of the Association for Women in Mathematics* 19, no. 5, (1989): 3–4.

FURTHER READING:

Books

Green, Judy and Jeanne Laduke. "Women in American Mathematics: A Century of Contributions." *A Century of Mathematics in America*, Part II. Edited by Peter Duncan. Providence, RI: American Mathematical Society, 1989, pp. 379–398.

Mathematical Society of Japan. *Encyclopedic Dictionary of Mathematics*. Second Edition. Edited by Kiyosi Ito. Cambridge, MA: MIT Press, 1987.

Soare, Robert I. *Recursively Enumerable Sets and Degrees*. Berlin: Springer–Verlag, 1987.

Periodicals

Blum, Lenore. "A Brief History of the Association for Women in Mathematics: The Presidents' Perspectives." *Notices of the American Mathematical Society* (September 1991): 738–54.

Hughes, Rhonda. "Fond Remembrances of Louise Hay." *Newsletter of the Association for Women in Mathematics* (January–February 1990): 4–6.

"Louise S. Hay, Professor, 54." (Obituary) *The New York Times* (October 31, 1989): II, 10:5.

Soare, Robert I. "Louise Hay: 1935–1989." *Newsletter of the Association for Women in Mathematics* (January–February 1990): 3–4.

Other

American Mathematical Society. *Mathematical Reviews: MathSci Disc* (CD–ROM). Boston: SilverPlatter Information Systems.

Association for Women in Mathematics. "AWM Homepage." http://www.math.neu.edu/awm.

"Louise Hay." June 1997. *Biographies of Women Mathematicians*. http://www.scottlan.edu/riddle/women/hay.htm (July 22, 1997).

Schmir, Gaston L. (brother of Louise Hay), interview with Sally M. Moite conducted April 11–April 28, 1997.

—*Sketch by Sally M. Moite*

Ellen Amanda Hayes
1851–1930
American mathematics educator

Ellen Amanda Hayes was born on September 23, 1851. Her maternal grandparents, originally from Granville, Massachusetts, founded the small town of Granville, Ohio, in 1805 and it was in their home that Hayes was born. Hayes's grandparents, as well as her parents, would set the stage for her love of learning, career, and political interests.

Hayes's father, Charles Coleman Hayes, made his living as a tanner after serving as an officer in the Civil War. Her mother, Ruth Rebecca (Wolcott), taught all six of her children to read, gave them a smattering of astronomy, and instructed them in botany, supplying them with the names plants in Latin. Both generations, parents and grandparents, believed in education without regard to gender. Hayes's mother had been trained as a teacher and graduated from the Granville Female Academy, a school that enjoyed the support of, and accepted as a trustee, Hayes's grandfather, Horace Wolcott. Although Hayes's father was uneducated, he too encouraged the education of his children.

Hayes left the home instruction supplied by her mother when she was seven and went to the Centerville school. That school had only one room for all levels of instruction and kept no grades. At age 16, Hayes was herself a teacher at a country school, saving the money she earned to attend college. After entering Oberlin College in 1872 as a preparatory student, Hayes began her college career as a freshman in 1875. Her endeavors mainly centered on the fields of mathematics and science, but she also became well versed in English literature, Greek, Latin, and history. Her mother's introduction to astronomy must have left a lasting impression because Hayes spent time at the Leander McCormick Observatory at the University of Virginia in 1887–1888, where she studied the Minor Planet 267, confirming its definite orbit, and producing other important papers on Comet *a* and planetary conic curves.

After graduating from Oberlin with a bachelor of arts degree, Hayes spent a year as the principal of the women's department at Adrian College in Michigan. In 1879, she became a teacher of mathematics at Wellesley College. By 1888, she was a full professor and had assumed the role of chair of the department. In 1897, a department of applied mathematics was created at Wellesley and Hayes took the helm. Her responsibilities included giving instruction in seven levels of applied mathematics.

A Controversial Woman

Although Hayes spent 37 years at Wellesley, the association was often far from congenial because of Hayes's view on education and politics. She was never silent or restrained about either subject. Hayes was adamant about females taking mathematics and science courses and highly critical of the school for allowing students to choose electives that would make it possible for them to evade these studies. Reforms concerning working conditions, politics, and the education of women was something Hayes worked toward all her life. Her views on and support of the union movement and workers rights caused her to receive threats and to be arrested. She closely studied the Russian Revolution of 1917 as it unfolded, writing and speaking openly about the situation. Although Hayes never affiliated herself with the Communist party and disagreed with many of its doctrines, her association with socialist causes did much to brand her a radical and incite serious criticism from Wellesley College. Upon her retirement from Wellesley, Hayes was denied the honorary position of Professor Emeritus usually bestowed on teachers for lengthy and faithful service.

Legacy of a Life Well Spent

At the age of 72, Hayes began her own newspaper. The *Relay* was published monthly and was devoted to giving publicity to facts and movements that Hayes believed were not accurately presented in the mainstream press. Her description of the publication was that "the *Relay* plans to camp in a hut by the side of the road and to keep a lamp or two burning—in the hope of being a friend to wayfarers and especially to the limping Under Dog." Other books written after her retirement include *The Sycamore Trail Know?*, a book which asks readers to question the origin of their beliefs and superstitions, and study the nature of evidence. Most of Hayes' work was self–published.

Upon her death in 1930, Hayes' brain was donated to the Wilder Brain Collection at Cornell University. The epitaph assigned to her by her friends was her favorite quotation: "It is better to travel hopefully, than to arrive."

SELECTED WRITINGS BY HAYES:

Books

Lessons on Higher Algebra, 1891, revised edition 1894.
Elementary Trigonometry, 1896.
Algebra for High Schools and Colleges, 1897.
Calculus with Applications: An Introduction to the Mathematical Treatment of Science, 1900.

Periodicals

"Comet *a* 1904." *Science* 19 (May 27, 1904): 833–34.

FURTHER READING:

Books

Brown, Louise. *Ellen Hayes: Trail–Blazer.* West Park, NY: 1932.

Moskol, Ann. "Ellen Amanda Hayes," in *Women of Mathematics: A Biobibliographic Sourcebook.* Edited by Louise S. Grinstein and Paul J. Campbell. Westport, CT: Greenwood Press, 1987, pp. 62–66.

Periodicals

Gordon, Geraldine. "Ellen Hayes: 1851–1930." *The Wellesley Magazine* (February 1931): 151–52.
Merrill, Helen A. "Ellen Hayes." *Scrapbook of the History Department of Mathematics* (1944): 41–46. Archives, Wellesley College.

Other

"Ellen Amanda Hayes." *Biographies of Women Mathematicians.* June 1997. http://www.scotlan.edu/lriddle/women/chronol.htm (July 22, 1997).

—*Sketch by Kelley Reynolds Jacquez*

Olive Clio Hazlett
1890–1974
American algebraist

Olive Clio Hazlett was one of the most active women working in mathematics prior to 1940. She is best known for her work in the area of linear algebra. The majority of her research was conducted in linear algebra and also in modular invariants, making important contributions in both areas.

Hazlett received her undergraduate degree from Radcliffe College in 1912. She began work on her Ph.D. at the University of Chicago in 1913, receiving her doctorate there in 1915. She conducted additional study and research work at Harvard University and in Rome, Zurich, and Göttingen as a Guggenheim fellow. Hazlett taught mathematics for more than 40 years. She began her career in 1916 at Bryn Mawr College in Pennsylvania, remaining there for two years before accepting a position as assistant professor at Mount Holyoke College in Massachusetts. Hazlett taught at Mount Holyoke for eight years, attaining the position of associate professor in 1924. In 1925, she took a position at the University of Illinois, enticed there by the excellent library facilities and the assurance of sufficient research time to develop her mathematical theories. She completed her career at the University of Illinois, retiring as emeritus associate professor in 1959.

Career Advancement Denied

Although recognized for her outstanding and prolific accomplishments, Hazlett's career did not reflect her mathematical brilliance. As was common with many gifted women mathematicians of her era, she was denied advancement in her profession. She attained the level of associate professor, and remained at that level throughout her career. This meant Hazlett often was relegated to teaching introductory courses and undergraduates, long after her male peers had advanced to full professorships and graduate students. In spite of this, her name appeared in seven editions of *American Men and Women of Science*. Hazlett also took an active role in the professional associations of her profession, including the American Mathematical Society, and served as associate editor of the *Transactions of the American Mathematical Society* for 12 years, from 1923 to 1935. She was also a member of the Society's council from 1926 to 1928, and a member of the New York Academy of Sciences. The award of a Guggenheim Fellowship in 1928 allowed her to study in Europe for one year.

While at the University of Illinois, Hazlett suffered a series of mental breakdowns during the 1930s and 1940s. Margaret Rossiter, in her book *Women Scientists in America*, states that Hazlett never fully recovered from her illness. "Isolated and moderately successful but with aspirations of full equality, [she] denied the potential psychological dangers in [her] situation."

Hazlett died on March 11, 1974, in a Keene, New Hampshire, nursing home at age 83. She had never married, and lived out her life on what Rossiter termed a "pitiable pension," resulting from the low pay she had received throughout her career.

FURTHER READING:

Books

Bailey, Martha J. *American Women in Science: A Biographical Dictionary*. Santa Barbara, California: ABC–CLIO, Inc., 1994, p. 159.

Rossiter, Margaret W. *Women Scientists in America: Struggles and Strategies to 1940*. Baltimore: The Johns Hopkins University Press, 1982.

Periodicals

Obituary. *The New York Times*. March 12, 1974, p. 40:4.

Other

Riddle, Larry. "Olive Clio Hazlett." *Biographies of Women Mathematicians*. June 1997. http:www/ scottlan.edu./lriddle/women/chronol.htm (July 21, 1997).

—Sketch by Jane Stewart Cook

Bruce C. Heezen
1924–1977
American oceanographer

A pioneer in mapping ocean floors, Heezen determined how turbity currents act to shape the ocean floor. He also collaborated with fellow oceanographers Marie Tharp and **William Maurice Ewing** to establish the existence of the continuous, world-encircling rift that follows the Mid-Oceanic Ridge. This discovery helped prove the now widely accepted theories of continental drift and plate tectonics. He and Tharp also produced the first world ocean floor map.

Bruce Charles Heezen (pronounced (HEY-zen) was born in Vinton, Iowa, on April 11, 1924, the son of Charles Christian Heezen, a county agricultural adviser, and Esther (de Schirding) Heezen. His paternal great-grandfather had emigrated to Iowa from The Netherlands in 1857. After attending the public schools in Muscatine, Iowa, Heezen entered the University of Iowa in 1944 and received his B.A. in geology in 1948. He became a Roberts Fellow at Columbia University, and received his M.A. in 1952 and his Ph.D. in geology in 1957.

Lifetime of Seagoing Science

Heezen's lifelong study of the ocean floor began unexpectedly in 1947 while he was still an undergraduate geology major. Maurice "Doc" Ewing, an American oceanographer who had brought modern seismic techniques to the study of the ocean floor, came to give a lecture at the University of Iowa; he also wanted to recruit promising graduate students as unpaid seagoing technicians on his research expeditions. Heezen attended the lecture, then went to the podium to meet Ewing. In 1986, Marie Tharp related the story of this first encounter between the two men. She recalled that Heezen only wanted to express his admiration; however, Ewing suddenly offered, "Young man, would you like to go on an expedition to the mid-Atlantic Ridge? There are some mountains out there and we don't know which way they run." The undergraduate was so startled that his Iowa professor had to answer yes for him. Heezen would spent the next thirty years of his life pursuing the implications of Ewing's offer.

In 1948, Heezen became a student of Ewing's at Columbia University, and over the next two years took part in three expeditions to the Mid-Atlantic Ridge aboard the *Atlantis I*, the research vessel belonging to the Woods Hole Oceanographic Institution. On these voyages, the scientific crew surveyed the ridge with an echo sounder. Unlike earlier techniques, which often involved dropping explosives from a speeding ship and timing the resulting echo, this radar-like device provided uninterrupted profiles of the ocean bottom. For his part, Heezen proved to be much more than a helpful, unpaid seagoing technician, and Ewing eventually made him chief scientist.

Proves Ocean Turbidity Currents

While a graduate student at Columbia, Heezen began working at Palisades, New York, at the newly established Lamont Observatory (later the Lamont-Doherty Geological Observatory of Columbia University) where Ewing was its director. Since both were interested in the role of turbidity currents in transporting the sands of the abyssal plains out to sea, Heezen decided to learn more about this process. In his 1952 master's thesis, he demonstrated for the first time exactly how occasional turbidity currents (a suspension or dense mixture of sand and sea water that speeds downslope) are triggered by earthquakes and can erode and move large quantities of sand far out at sea. His studies showed that such currents act like underwater landslides and can move as fast as 50 mph (80 kph), carrying great quantities of sediment to the ocean plains below. Heezen was able to provide the data for his conclusions by his creative use of the precise records of failures along the Great Banks line of transatlantic cables that were compiled as a result of the 1929 earthquake.

Links Continuous Rift to Seismic Activity

That same year, Heezen was working with another Columbia graduate student, Marie Tharp, on a possible connection between earthquake epicenters and a deep valley that appeared to follow the crest of the Mid-Atlantic Ridge. It was Tharp who first believed that such a valley existed, and with Heezen, sought to understand its significance. By then, Heezen had been on enough Atlantic cruises to have compiled information on most of the underwater features of the western Atlantic Ocean, so with Tharp, he began to make a physiographic (three-dimensional) diagram of the ocean floor. When they had finished, they found that their work postulated the existence of a continuous, worldwide "rift," a crack or fault caused by seismic or earthquake activity. Since this notion was dangerously close to the then-heretical notion of continental drift, they kept their theory to themselves (and Ewing) until 1956.

In February of that year, Heezen presented this new idea at a National Academy of Sciences symposium organized by **Harry Hess**, professor of geology at Princeton University. Later in 1956, Heezen and Ewing published an abstract of this discovery at an American Geophysical Union meeting in Toronto, Canada. In 1959, the French ocean explorer, **Jacques Cousteau**, actually filmed the rift valley, proving conclusively its existence. By 1961, Heezen and his colleagues had produced physiographic diagrams that showed a seismically active rift zone at the crest of the Mid-Atlantic Ridge that extended into the Arctic and Indian oceans as well as the African rift valleys.

Heezen's work had revolutionary implications for the earth sciences since it was intimately connected to the notion that the continents or land masses were moving. It would be many years before the continental drift theory would be accepted and evolve into the modern theory of plate tectonics. However, Heezen's work was finally proven correct with the inevitable demonstration that the Mid-Oceanic Ridge grows by accretion (as new material emerges from the rift or crack), and that subduction (one plate descending or folding beneath another) occurs at the continental margins.

On June 21, 1977, Bruce Heezen died at sea. While aboard a Navy research submarine being towed behind a support ship, Heezen had a fatal heart attack. He was to take part in a planned dive over the mountains of the Reykjanes Ridge southwest of Iceland. Ever a man to take advantage of new technology, Heezen had begun using nuclear-powered submarines to explore the sea floor, since they could remain submerged for very long periods. The recipient of several medals and awards, and a member of many national and international societies, Heezen never married and enjoyed photography, opera, and the theater. As a Midwesterner from the landlocked state of Iowa, he was most at home in the middle of the sea.

SELECTED WRITINGS BY HEEZEN:

Books

(With Charles D. Hollister) *The Face of the Deep.* New York: Oxford University Press, 1971.

Periodicals

"The Rift in the Ocean Floor." *Scientific American* (October 1960): 98-110.

FURTHER READING:

Books

Daintith, John et al. *Biographical Encyclopedia of Scientists.* Bristol, Eng.: Institute of Physics Publishing, 1994, pp. 398-399.

Charles Hermite

McGraw-Hill Modern Scientists and Engineers. New York: McGraw-Hill, 1980, pp. 36-38.
The National Cyclopedia of American Biography. Volume 60. Clifton, NJ: James T. White & Company, 1981, p. 35.

Periodicals

Sullivan, Walter. "Dr. Bruce C. Heezen, 53, Dies; Mapped Ocean Floors." *The New York Times* (June 23, 1977), II, p. 4.

Tharp, Marie and Henry Frankel. "Mappers of the Deep." *Natural History* (October 1986): 48-62.

—*Sketch by Leonard C. Bruno*

Charles Hermite
1822–1901
French mathematician

Charles Hermite was one of the founders of analytic number theory. This discipline uses the techniques of analysis (the calculus) to handle questions about positive whole numbers. Hermite is also remembered for having shown that one of the central constants of mathematics, e, the base of natural logarithms, belongs in the class of transcendental numbers.

The son of Ferdinand Hermite and Madeleine Lallemand, Hermite was born on Christmas Eve, 1822. His ancestry was both French and German and the town Dieuze, Hermite's birthplace, was at one time claimed by both France and Germany. Nevertheless, Hermite considered himself French all his life and became one of the mainstays of the French academic establishment.

Hermite attended the Collège Henri IV and proceeded from there to the Collège Louis–le–Grand, where he was taught mathematics by the same instructor who had supervised the work of the ill–fated French genius **Èvariste Galois**. When Hermite decided to continue his studies at the École Polytechnique, he was admitted 68th in his class, thanks to his having neglected geometry. Throughout his life Hermite had a dislike for examinations and preferred to pick up material spontaneously rather than under the pressure of a deadline. Hermite enjoyed corresponding with the best mathematicians of Europe, including Karl Jacobi, and some of the material in Hermite's letters is remarkably sophisticated. In particular, Hermite generalized a result of Niels Abel that applied elliptic functions to the class of hyperelliptic functions as well.

Hermite's family life reflected his increasingly central position in the French mathematical establishment. His wife was the sister of the mathematician Joseph Bertrand, and one of his daughters married the eminent analyst Émile Picard (who was to edit Hermite's works after his father–in–law's death). From the time he became admissions examiner at the École Polytechnique in 1848, Hermite devoted much of his effort to working with students at every level. In addition to Picard, his other distinguished students included **Henri Poincaré**, Camille Jordan, and Paul Painlevé. This record attests to his eagerness in welcoming students as colleagues. **Émile Borel** is said to have remarked that no one made people love mathematics so deeply as Hermite did.

On a professional level, Hermite accomplished some formidable tasks with the analytic apparatus which he had mastered. The solution of the general quadratic (second–degree) equation had been known since ancient times. Solutions to the cubic and quartic equations had been developed during the Italian Renaissance. When Galois showed that ordinary algebraic methods could not solve the general quintic (fifth–degree) equation, the subject appeared to have reached a dead end. Using once again the techniques of elliptic functions, Hermite showed that fifth–degree equations could be solved after all.

The Transcendence of e

The single result for which Hermite is best known was the transcendence of e. A number is said to be algebraic if it is the solution of a polynomial equation with integer coefficients. For example, the square root of 2 is algebraic, since it is a solution of the equation $x^2-2=0$. A real number that is not algebraic is called transcendental. The French mathematician Joseph Liouville had shown that there were transcendental numbers but no familiar examples were known. Hermite was able to show that e could not be written as the solution of a polynomial equation and therefore had to be transcendental. His technique was used shortly thereafter to show that π was also transcendental, although Hermite does not seem to have recognized just how useful his technique was.

After his appointment as professor analysis at both the Ècole Polytechnique and the Sorbonne, Hermite took to writing textbooks that were widely used and appreciated. Although he resigned his chair at the Ècole Polytechnique after only seven years in 1876, he remained at the Sorbonne for another 21 years. Hermite attached a great value to insight and did not include much rigor in his teaching of elementary material. If his papers suffer from a fault, it is the occasional tendency to allow the details to get in the way of the overall picture. A large number of his ideas were developed by others and the complex generalization of quadratic forms named for him proved to be central in the formulation of quantum mechanics.

At the time of his 70th birthday, the adulation Hermite received from across Europe attests to his reputation as an elder mathematical statesman. His interests were never narrow, and he was awarded an impressive collection of decorations both at home and abroad. Hermite died on January 14, 1901, leaving a solid basis of mathematics and an unmatched collection of students to carry on his work.

SELECTED WRITINGS BY HERMITE:

Oeuvres, 4 vols. Edited by Èmile Picard, 1905–17.

FURTHER READING:

Bell, Eric. *Men of Mathematics*. New York: Simon and Schuster, 1937, pp. 448–465.
Freudenthal, Hans. "Charles Hermite," in *Dictionary of Scientific Biography*. Volume XI. Edited by Charles Coulston Gillispie. New York: Charles Scribner's Songs, 1973, pp. 306–309.
Prasad, Ganesh. *Some Great Mathematicians of the Nineteenth Century*. Volume 2. Benares, India: Benares Mathematical Society, 1934, pp. 34–59.

—*Sketch by Thomas Drucker*

Alfred Day Hershey

Alfred Day Hershey
1908–1997
American microbiologist

By seeking to understand the reproduction of viruses, the simplest form of life, Alfred Day Hershey made important discoveries about the nature of deoxyribonucleic acid (DNA) and laid the groundwork for modern molecular genetics. Highly regarded as an experimental scientist, Hershey was perhaps best known for the 1952 "blender experiment" that he and Martha Chase conducted to demonstrate that DNA, not protein, was the genetic material of life. This discovery stimulated further research into DNA, including the discovery by **James Watson** and **Francis Crick** of the double-helix structure of DNA the following year. Hershey's work with bacteriophages, the viruses that prey on bacteria, was often carried out in loose collaboration with other scientists working with bacteriophages. Hershey shared the Nobel Prize in Physiology or Medicine in 1969 with **Max Delbrück** and **Salvador Edward Luria.** The Nobel Committee praised the three scientists for their contributions to molecular biology. Their basic research into viruses also helped others develop vaccines against viral diseases such as polio.

Hershey was born on December 4, 1908, in Owosso, Michigan, to Robert Day Hershey and Alma Wilbur Hershey. His father worked for an auto manufacturer. Alfred attended public schools in Owosso and nearby Lansing. He received his B.S. in bacteriology from Michigan State College (now Michigan State University) in 1930 and his Ph.D. in chemistry from the same school in 1934. Hershey's interest in bacteriology and the biochemistry of life was already evident when he was a graduate student. His doctoral dissertation was on the chemistry of *Brucella,* the bacteria responsible for brucellosis, also known as undulant fever. Undulant fever is transmitted to humans from cattle and causes recurrent fevers and joint pain. After receiving his Ph.D., Hershey took a position as a research assistant in the Department of Bacteriology at the Washington University School of Medicine in St. Louis. There, he worked with Jacques Jacob Bronfenbrenner, one of the pioneers in bacteriophage research in the United States. During the sixteen years he spent teaching and conducting research at Washington University, from 1934 to 1950, Hershey was promoted to instructor (1936), assistant professor (1938), and associate professor (1942).

Bacteriophages—known simply as phages—had been discovered in 1915, only nineteen years before Hershey began his career. Phages are viruses that reproduce by preying on bacteria, first attacking and then dissolving them. For scientists who study bacteria, phages are a source of irritation because they can destroy bacterial cultures. But other scientists are fascinated by this tiny organism. Perhaps the smallest living thing, phages consist of little more than the protein and DNA (the molecule of heredity) found in a cellular nucleus. Remarkably efficient, however, phages reproduce by conquering bacteria and subverting them to the phage particles' own needs. This type of reproduction is known as replication. Little was known about the particulars of this process when Hershey was a young scientist.

By studying viral replication, scientists hoped to learn more about the viral diseases that attack humans, like mumps, the common cold, German measles, and polio. But the study of bacteriophages also promised findings with implications that reached far beyond disease cures into the realm of understanding life itself. If Hershey and other researchers could determine how phages replicated, they stood to learn how higher organisms—including humans—passed genetic information from generation to generation.

Exposing the Secret Life of Viruses

Hershey's study of phages soon yielded several discoveries that furthered an understanding of genetic inheritance and change. In 1945, he showed that phages were capable of spontaneous mutation. Faced with a bacterial culture known to be resistant to phage attack, most, but not all, phages would die. By mutating, some phages survived to attack the bacteria

and replicate. This finding was significant because it showed that mutations did not occur gradually, as one school of scientific thought believed, but immediately and spontaneously in viruses. It also helped explain why a viral attack is so difficult to prevent. In 1946, Hershey made another discovery that changed what scientists thought about viruses. He showed that if different strains of phages infected the same bacterial cell, they could combine or exchange genetic material. This is similar to what occurs when higher forms of life sexually reproduce, of course. But it was the first time viruses were shown to combine genetic material. Hershey called this phenomenon genetic recombination.

Hershey was not the only scientist who saw the potential in working with bacteriophages. Two other influential scientists were also pursuing the same line of investigation. Max Delbrück, a physicist, had been studying phages in the United States since he fled Nazi Germany in 1937. Studying genetic recombination independently of Hershey, he reached the same results that Hershey did in the same year. Similarly, Salvador Edward Luria, a biologist and physician who immigrated to the United States from Italy in 1940, had independently confirmed Hershey's work on spontaneous mutation in 1945. Although the three men never worked side by side in the same laboratory, they were collaborators nonetheless. Through conversation and correspondence, they shared results and encouraged each other in their phage research. Indeed, these three scientists formed the core of the self-declared "phage group," a loose-knit clique of scientists who encouraged research on particular strains of bacteriophage. By avoiding competition and duplication, the group hoped to advance phage research that much faster.

The "Blender Experiment"

In 1950, Hershey accepted a position as a staff scientist in the department of genetics (now the Genetics Research Unit) of the Carnegie Institute at Cold Spring Harbor, New York. It was at Cold Spring Harbor that Hershey conducted his most influential experiment. Hershey wished to prove conclusively that the genetic material in phages. Analysis with an electron microscope had showed that phages consist only of DNA surrounded by a protein shell. Other scientists' experiments had revealed that during replication some part of the parental phages was being transferred to their offspring. The task before Hershey was to show that it was the phage DNA that was passed on to succeeding generations and that gave the signal for replication and growth.

Although Hershey was not alone in having reached the belief that DNA was the stuff of life, many scientists were unconvinced. They doubted that DNA had the complexity needed to carry the blueprint for life and believed instead that the genetic code resided in protein, a far more elaborate molecule. Furthermore, no one had yet demonstrated the technical skill needed to design an experiment that would answer the question once and for all.

With Martha Chase, Hershey found a way to determine what role each of the phage components played in replication. In experiments done in 1951 and 1952, Hershey used radioactive phosphorus to tag the DNA and radioactive sulfur to tag the protein. (The DNA contains no sulfur and the protein contains no phosphorus.) Hershey and Chase then allowed the marked phage particles to infect a bacterial culture and to begin the process of replication. This process was interrupted when the scientists spun the culture at a high speed in a Waring blender.

In this manner, Hershey and Chase learned that the shearing action of the blender separated the phage protein from the bacterial cells. Apparently while the phage DNA entered the bacterium and forced it to start replicating phage particles, the phage protein remained outside, attached to the cell wall. The researchers surmised that the phage particle attached itself to the outside of a bacterium by its protein "tail" and literally injected its nucleic acid into the cell. DNA, and not protein, was responsible for communicating the genetic information needed to produce the next generation of phage.

Clearly DNA seemed to hold the key to heredity for all forms of life, not just viruses. Yet while the blender experiment answered one question about DNA, it also raised a host of other questions. Now scientists wanted to know more about the action of DNA. How did DNA operate? How did it replicate itself? How did it direct the production of proteins? What was its chemical structure? Until that last question was answered, scientists could only speculate about answers to the others. Hershey's achievement spurred other scientists into DNA research.

In 1953, a year after Hershey's blender experiment, the structure of DNA was determined in Cambridge, England, by James Dewey Watson and Francis Harry Compton Crick. Watson, who was only twenty-five years old when the structure was announced, had worked with Luria at the University of Indiana. For their discovery of DNA's double-helix structure, Watson and Crick received the Nobel Prize in 1962.

Career Honored with a Belated Nobel Prize

Hershey, Delbrück, and Luria also received a Nobel Prize for their contributions to molecular biology, but not until 1969. This seeming delay in recognition for their accomplishments prompted the *New York Times* to ask in an October 20, 1969, editorial: "Delbrück, Hershey and Luria richly de-

serve their awards, but why did they have to wait so long for this recognition? Every person associated with molecular biology knows that these are the grand pioneers of the field, the giants on whom others—some of whom received the Nobel Prize years ago—depended for their own great achievements." Yet other scientists observed that the blender experiment merely offered experimental proof of a theoretical belief that was already widely held. After the blender experiment, Hershey continued investigating the structure of phage DNA. Although human DNA winds double-stranded like a spiral staircase, Hershey found that some phage DNA is single-stranded and some is circular. In 1962, Hershey was named director of the Genetics Research Unit at Cold Spring Harbor. He retired in 1974.

Hershey was "known to his colleagues as a very quiet, withdrawn sort of man who avoids crowds and noise and most hectic social activities," according to the report of the 1969 Nobel Prize in the October 17, 1969 *New York Times*. His hobbies were woodworking, reading, gardening, and sailing. He married Harriet Davidson, a former research assistant, on November 15, 1945. She later became an editor of the *Cold Spring Harbor Symposia on Quantitative Biology*. She and Hershey had one child, a son named Peter Manning. Born on August 7, 1956, Peter was twelve years old when Hershey won the Nobel Prize. Hershey died on May 22, 1997 at his home in Syosset, New York.

In addition to the Nobel Prize, Hershey received the Albert Lasker Award of the American Public Health Association (1958) and the Kimber Genetics Award of the National Academy of Sciences (1965) for his discoveries concerning the genetic structure and replication processes of viruses. He was elected to the National Academy of Sciences in 1958.

SELECTED WRITINGS BY HERSHEY:

Periodicals

"Reproduction of Bacteriophage." *International Review of Cytology* 1 (1952): 119-34.
"Nuclear Acid Economy in Bacteria Infected with Bacteriophage T2. 2. Phage Precursor Nucleic Acid." *Journal of General Physiology* 37 (1953): 1-23.
"Upper Limit to the Protein Content of the Germinal Substance of Bacteriophage T2." *Viruses* 1 (1955): 108-27.

FURTHER READING:

Books

Fox, Daniel M., ed. *Nobel Laureates in Medicine or Physiology: A Biographical Dictionary.* New York: Garland, 1990.

Magner, Lois N. *History of the Life Sciences.* New York: Dekker, 1979.
_____. *McGraw-Hill Modern Scientists and Engineers.* New York: McGraw-Hill, 1980.
Wasson, Tyler, ed. *Nobel Prize Winners* New York: H. W. Wilson, 1987.

Periodicals

"A. Hershey: Chemist Won Nobel for DNA Work" (obituary). *Los Angeles Times* (24 May 1997).
"Alfred Hershey" (obituary). *Times (London)* (2 June 1997).
Altman, Lawrence K. "Alfred D. Hershey, Nobel Laureate for DNA Work, Dies at 88" (obituary). *New York Times* (24 May 1997).
Wasson, Tyler. *New York Times* (17 October 1969): 24; (20 October 1969: 46.
_____. *Science* (24 October 1969): 479-81.
_____. "Three Americans Share Nobel Prize for Medicine for Work on Bacteriophage." *Chemical and Engineering News.* (27 October 1969): 16.
_____. *Time* (24 October 1969): 84.

—*Sketch by Liz Marshall*

Jacqueline N. Hewitt
1958–

American astrophysicist

Jacqueline Hewitt, a professor of physics at Massachusetts Institute of Technology (MIT), has made historic contributions to the study of gravitational lensing. Hewitt was the first to discover what Einstein predicted in 1936—ring-shaped objects produced by distant galaxies. Einstein rings are an example of gravitational lensing, in which electromagnetic radiation (including light) is affected by its passage through a gravitational field, similar to the way light is lensed as it passes through glass. In an Einstein ring, the way the radiation is distributed is very symmetrical, producing a striking ring image. Einstein rings are beneficial as a means of measuring the size of galaxies and the volume and apportionment of dark matter in the universe. Hewitt's discovery of the Einstein rings may provide a key to understanding the universe.

Hewitt was born on September 4, 1958, in Washington, D.C. Her father, Warren E. Hewitt, retired from the State Department, where he was employed as an international lawyer. Her mother, Trudy G. (Graedel) Hewitt was a homemaker through Jacqueline's childhood. Math was Hewitt's favorite subject as a child, but she did not decide to become a scientist until later in life. She majored in economics at Bryn Mawr and graduated magna cum laude in 1980. An astronomy course her sophomore year sparked her interest in science, and she decided to continue her education at the Massachusetts Institute of Technology in Cambridge, Massachusetts. She earned a Ph.D. in physics in 1986. "Astronomy is mostly physics, so that made me want to study physics, which I thoroughly enjoyed," Hewitt explained in a November 11, 1997, letter to contributor Pamela Proffitt. While completing her Ph.D., Hewitt worked as a research assistant in the Department of Physics at MIT. That same year Hewitt married Robert P. Redwine, a nuclear physicist. They have two children, Keith, born in 1988, and Jonathan, born in 1993.

Hewitt's postdoctoral appointment was with the Very Long Baseline Interferometry (VLBI) at MIT from 1986 to 1988. After her postdoctoral appointment, until 1989, Hewitt was a research staff member in the Department of Astrophysical Sciences at Princeton, New Jersey. In 1989 she returned to MIT as an assistant professor to teach physics and was promoted to associate professor of physics at MIT in 1994. Hewitt believes there is a close interaction between teaching and research. "I often use examples of my research in my teaching," she explained in her 1997 letter, "and the teaching often will give me ideas for research and keeps me from forgetting the underlying physics!" In addition to her teaching duties, Hewitt is a principal investigator for the Radio Astronomy Group of the Research Laboratory of Electronics at MIT.

Discovers Einstein Rings

Hewitt began studying the stars while attending MIT. Frank Ockenfels, writing for *Esquire* magazine, quoted Hewitt as saying that, "To discover something there, she felt, would be like coming upon a new continent on earth." With MIT professor, Bernard F. Burke, Hewitt began gathering data using the Very Large Array radio telescope near Socorro, New Mexico. She decided to use a radio telescope instead of an optical one because optical images of gravitational lenses are very faint. The gravitational lenses emit large amounts of energy at radio wave lengths and are easier to detect. Hewitt recorded about four thousand radio images and hoped these would provide her with a database of information that might contain gravitational lenses.

In the fall of 1986, while at her postdoctoral appointment with the Very Long Baseline Interferometry group at MIT's Haystack Observatory, Hewitt was looking at the data she had collected at the VLA in New Mexico when saw a ring on her computer screen. *Discover* magazine, in the July 1988 issue, described the object as "a faint, glowing, elliptical ring about [two] arc seconds across at its widest (the full moon spans about 1,800 arc seconds), accompanied by two bright spots." The objects were found in the constellation Leo.

In her 1997 letter Hewitt said that she was " . . . doing a deliberate search for gravitational lenses with the VLA, but wasn't expecting to find the Einstein ring because we expected them to be very rare. In fact, it is not quite as rare as we thought it would be. It is actually quite reasonable to expect that several Einstein rings would be found with the VLA, as they have been now." The discovery of the Einstein ring could answer questions regarding the size of the universe and the ultimate fate of the universe, whether it will keep on expanding or whether it will collapse in on itself.

Award-winning Physicist

Hewitt has found her many awards an important source of encouragement when her career, combined with raising two children, was at times overwhelming. Of all her awards, Hewitt cites the David and Lucile Packard Fellowship in 1990 as the one that gave her the confidence and financial support to begin her work. In addition to several other awards, Hewitt was elected by faculty colleagues from MIT to receive the 1995-1996 Harold E. Edgerton Award for her contributions to the study of gravitational lenses. In 1995, Hewitt was awarded the Maria Goeppert-Mayer Award for her contribution in radio astronomy.

On the subject of being a woman in physics, Hewitt is happy to report that her colleagues have been supportive and nondiscriminating. However, she has found it particularly difficult to balance her scientific career and raising children within the structure of the traditional university academic system. Hewitt hopes there will be substantial societal changes that will make it easier for women who want a family as well as a career in science.

SELECTED WRITINGS BY HEWITT:

Books

(With J.M. Moran) *Gravitational Lenses: Proceedings of a Conference Held at the Massachusetts Institute of Technology, Cambridge, Massachusetts, in Honour of Bernard F. Burke's 60th Birthday, June 20, 1988.* Springer-Verlag, 1989.

Periodicals

(With C. B. Moore) "15 GHz Monitoring of the Gravitional Lens MG 0410+0534." *The Astrophysical Journal* (November 1997).

(With C.A. Katz and C.B. Moore) "Multifrequency Radio Observations of the Gravitional Lens System MG 0414+0534." *The Astrophysical Journal* (February 1, 1997).

(With D.B. Haarsma, J. Lehár, and B. F. Burke) "The 6 cm Light Curves of B0957+561, 1979-1994: New Features and Implications for the Time Delay." *The Astrophysical Journal* (April 10, 1997).

(With E.L. Turner, D.P. Schnieder, B. F. Burke, G. I. Langston, and C. R. Lawrence) "Unusual Radio Source MG1131+0456: a Possible Einstein Ring." *Nature* (June 9, 1988).

FURTHER READING:

Books

Kayser, R., T. and L. Nieser Schramm, eds. *Gravitational Lenses, Proceedings of a Conference Held in Hamburg, Germany 9-13 September 1991.* Berlin; New York: Springer-Verlag, 1992.

Quasars and Gravitational Lenses: Proceedings of the 24th Liege International Astrophysical Colloquium, June 21-24, 1983. Liege, Belgium: Universitâe de Liáege, Institut d'Astrophysique, 1983.

Mellier, Y., B. Fort, and G. Soucail, eds. *Gravitational Lensing (Lecture Notes in Physics, Vol. 360).* Berlin; New York: Springer-Verlag, 1990.

Periodicals

Einstein, Albert. "Lens-like Action of a Star by the Deviation of Light in the Gravitational Field." *Science.* vol. 84 (1936): 506.

"Finding Einstein's Ring." *Discover.* vol. 9 (July 1988): 15.

Ockenfels, Frank. "Jacqueline Hewitt." *Esquire.* (December 1988): 102.

Verschuur, Gerrit L. "A New 'Yardstick' for the Universe." *Astronomy.* vol. 16 (November 1988): 60-3.

Waldrop, M. Mitchell. "Einstein's Impossible Ring: Found." *Science.* vol. 240 (June 24, 1988): 1733.

Other

"Hewitt wins 1995 Edgerton award." http://rleweb.mit.edu/fiscal/news/hewitt.html. October 6, 1997.

"Maria Goeppert-Mayer Award." http://hq.aps.org/praw/mgm/descrip.html. October 11, 1997.

"MIT Radio Astronomy Group Publications." http://space.mit.edu/RADIO/papers.html. October 6, 1997.

"1995 MGM Prize Recipient." http://www.aps.org/
    praw/mgm/95winner.html. October 10, 1997.
Web site of The Radio Astronomy Group of the
    Research Laboratory of Electronics: http://rlew-
    eb.mit.edu

— *Sketch by Monica Stevens and Pamela Proffitt*

Hope Hibbard
1893–1988
American zoologist

As a scientist, Hope Hibbard focused on cell
biology (cytology), specifically studying cytoplasmic
inclusions and cell structures. Her other primary
interests where marine biology and invertebrate animals. Though Hibbard was recognized by her peers
for her research, she was also respected for her writing
and teaching, especially at the school where she spent
the bulk of her career, Oberlin College in Ohio.

Hibbard was born in Altoona, Pennsylvania, on
December 18, 1893, the daughter of Herbert Wade
Hibbard, a professor of mechanical engineering, and
his wife Mary Scofield. She earned her A.B. from the
University of Missouri in 1916. Hibbard did her
graduate work in zoology at Bryn Mawr College,
where she earned her A.M. in 1918, and her Ph.D. in
1921. While earning her Ph.D., Hibbard worked as a
demonstrator in the biology department for a year,
1919-20. Her dissertation, "Cytoplasmic Inclusions in
the Egg of Echinarachnuius Parma," concerned sea
urchin eggs and their fertilization.

After completing her graduate work, Hibbard
worked as an associate professor at Elmira College for
four years from 1921-25. In 1925 Hibbard went to the
University of Paris (the Sorbonne) where she did
post-graduate work on the Sarah Berliner fellowship
of the American Association of University Women.
After the year-long fellowship ended, she stayed on in
Paris, working at the Sorbonne as a preparateur in a
comparative anatomy techniques laboratory. In 1927
Hibbard earned another year-long fellowship through
the International Education Board. The following
year, 1928, she was awarded her D.es.Sc. in zoology
from the Sorbonne.

Hibbard began teaching zoology at Oberlin College in 1928, and through the next 30 or so years, she
worked through the ranks: assistant professor, 1928-
30; associate professor, 1930-33; and full professor in
1933. In 1952 she was named the Adelia A. Field
Johnston Professor of Biology. She was appointed
chair of zoology department the following year, 1953,

and held the post for four years, until 1957. Hibbard
retired in 1961, earning an emeritus professorship.

Hibbard belonged to several scientific societies,
including the American Society of Zoologists, American Association for the Advancement of Science, and
the American Society of Naturalists. She was especially active in the American Association of University
Women, which had awarded her the fellowship that
allowed her to go to Paris. She was named an
honorary life member of this organization in 1987.
Hibbard died a year later, in 1988.

FURTHER READING:

Books

Bailey, Martha J. "Hibbard, Hope." *American
    Women in Science: A Biographical Dictionary.*
    Denver: ABC-CLIO, 1994, p. 161.

— *Sketch by Annette Petrusso*

Peter Ware Higgs
1929–
English theoretical physicist

The name "Higgs" is familiar to anyone who
follows current scientific research, since the Higgs
particle is now the most sought-after predicted entity
of particle physics. Although the Higgs particle has
been an essential element of the theory known as the
standard model since 1964 and has enjoyed considerable fame in physics since 1980, the man who
predicted it, Peter Ware Higgs, is not well known
outside his profession.

Peter Ware Higgs was born May 29, 1929, in
Bristol, England, the son of Thomas Ware Higgs and
Gertrude (Coghill) Higgs. He attended Kings College
in London, obtaining a Ph.D. in 1954. After fellowships at Edinburgh University, the University of
London, and Imperial College in London, he taught
mathematics from 1958 through 1960 at the University of London. In 1960 he settled at Edinburgh
University, where he has remained. Since 1980, he
has been professor of theoretical physics at Edinburgh. In 1963 he married Jo Ann Williamson, an
American from Illinois; they have two sons. Higgs
likes to walk and swim for exercise and, like many
mathematicians and theoreticians, especially enjoys
music.

The Higgs particle—sometimes called the Higgs
mechanism or Higgs boson, and closely related to the

Higgs field—emerged in 1964 as a solution to a major problem in the foundations of what was to become the standard model of forces and particles. Nearly all of the predecessors to the standard model that had been developed in the early 1960s predicted particles that no one had observed. Two otherwise very promising theories, known as Yang-Mills field and spontaneous symmetry breaking, both seemed doomed because they persistently indicated that there should be massless particles other than the two or three already known (photon, graviton, and perhaps neutrinos). Such predictions are generally not a problem when particles with a high mass (high for a subatomic particle, that is) are involved, since the predicted but unobserved high-mass particles might quickly break down to become previously seen particles of lower mass. However, theories that predict particles of zero mass are hard to accept, since zero-mass particles cannot break into particles of smaller mass and, therefore, have to linger where they can be observed.

This dilemma came to attention of **Philip Anderson** of Bell Laboratories, a theoretician in a different branch of physics. In 1963 Anderson wrote in *Physical Review* that under certain circumstances two massless particles can interact with each other to produce mass. Furthermore, the precise circumstance under which mass appears is the situation for which one massless particle is produced by a Yang-Mills field and the other by spontaneous symmetry breaking. Few particle physicists in 1963 thought that Anderson was correct, but some studied the idea further, Higgs among them.

Higgs soon worked out the details of the mechanism by which a third particle appears from the zero-mass particles of a Yang-Mills field and spontaneous symmetry breaking, a particle that develops mass. Better yet, the particle imparts mass in a specific way to other particles. The idea of treating mass in this way still seemed strange to other particle physicists in 1964. As a result, Higgs had trouble getting his first two papers published. One journal told him that his mechanism was irrelevant to particle physics, but the first paper was eventually published in the *Physical Review Letters* of October 19, 1964, and the second in *Physics Review,* May 27, 1966.

As with much of modern particle physics, the true nature of the Higgs particle emerges in the form of mathematics, rather than in terms of physical entities that fit the experience humans have with objects at the scale we can observe with our own senses. Higgs particles come into existence at the comparatively low temperatures that exist in the universe today—low compared, that is, to the very high temperature of the big bang at the start of the universe. The Higgs particles fill all of space, however, under present-day conditions. Other particles that interact with the Higgs are impeded by all the Higgs

that are everywhere. This drag on particles shows up as mass. Only particles that do not interact with the Higgs, such as the photon, escape having mass. It is not known why particles interact with the Higgs to the degree they do, however, so the Higgs mechanism as understood at this time fails to explain why the proton has 2,000 times the mass of the electron, or the other mysteries of mass.

Throughout the 1960s, theoreticians continued to work on these ideas, but there was little acceptance. By 1971 enough work had been done to make some specific numerical predictions of effects that would be found. Undiscovered particles called W and Z were predicted, particles for which the Higgs mechanism could account for mass in what would otherwise be massless particles. Also, an effect called a neutral current was predicted. Experiments were set up and the particle-accelerator physicists began the search. Within two years the neutral current was found, and some of the theoreticians involved received the Nobel Prize for Physics in 1979—but not Higgs. The following year, another particle-accelerator experiment produced the massive W and Z particles, leading to a Nobel Prize for the experimenters. The Higgs particle in observable form is thought to be too massive for today's particles accelerators to create. Physicists pin their hopes for raising a Higgs particle out from the universal sea of such particles on new accelerators yet to be built.

Higgs was elected a Fellow of the Royal Society in 1983. His medals include the Hughes Medal of the Royal Society (1981), the Rutherford Medal of the Institute of Physics (1984), and the James Scott Prize (1993).

SELECTED WRITINGS BY HIGGS:

Periodicals

"Broken Symmetries and the Masses of Gauge Bosons." *Physical Review Letters* 13 (October 19, 1964): 508.

FURTHER READING:

Books

Crease, Robert E. and Charles C. Mann. *The Second Creation.* New York: Macmillan, 1986.
Lederman, Leon M. and David N. Schramm. *From Quarks to the Cosmos: Tools of Discovery.* New York: Scientific American Books, 1989.

—Sketch by Bryan Bunch

George William Hill

George William Hill
1838–1914
American mathematical astronomer

George Hill practiced mathematics only as it aided his astronomical research, but his methods and findings enriched both mathematical theory and the practice of celestial mechanics. He was the first to use infinite determinants in his calculations of "periodic orbits," a phrase and concept he initiated, and created his own detailed tables to describe the motions of Jupiter and Saturn. Hill also contributed to our knowledge of the three and four body problems with his painstaking studies of the effect of the moon's motion on other planets and vice versa. He served as vice–president of the American Mathematical Society in 1893–1894, during the organization's fifth anniversary, and was elected president the next year. Hill is considered the most famous mathematical graduate of Rutgers University in New Jersey, and his achievements are commemorated by the Hill Center on the Busch campus of the university.

George William Hill was born in New York City on March 3, 1838. His father, John William Hill, was an English–born artist who designed and produced engravings. His mother, the former Catherine Smith, was of French Huguenot extraction. Hill had at least one brother, with whom he kept close ties until his death. When Hill was eight years old, the family relocated to a farm in West Nyack, New York. He first attended school in the town of West Nyack, and for college he chose Rutgers in New Jersey. There, Hill came under the influence of Dr. Theodore Strong. Dr. Strong was running the math department singlehandedly, as he had been since taking over the university's only endowed chair for the discipline in 1827. He had no great preference for natural philosophy, as physics was then called, but he emphasized the great classical works on celestial mechanics in his classes. Thus, Hill was exposed to the works of Leonhard Euler, Sylvestre Lacroix, Pierre Simon Laplace, Joseph–Louis LaGrange and Adrien–Marie Legendre. He graduated with an A.B. in 1859 and received his master's degree three years later. Hill published his first paper in 1859, while still an undergraduate at Rutgers. In 1861, his third paper, "On the Confirmation of the Earth," appeared in *Mathematical Monthly*, earning Hill a prize and the attention of the journal's editor J. D. Runkle.

Distinguished Career

Hill became an assistant in the offices of the *American Ephemeris and Nautical Almanac*, headquartered in Cambridge, Massachusetts, in 1861. After a year or two, his employers allowed him to work from home in West Nyack. In 1874, Hill became a member of the National Academy of Sciences. Important studies of the moon soon followed. His 1877 paper, "On the Part of the Motion of the Lunar Perigee Which Is a Function of the Mean Motions of the Sun and Moon," depended upon the infinite determinant for its intricate yet superior calculations. Hill's second important paper in astronomy, "Researches in the Lunar Theory," appeared in the premier issue of *American Journal of Mathematics* in 1878. This paper introduced both the periodic orbit and the surface of zero velocity, ideas that would soon influence **Jules Henri Poincaré**. Hill recorded his 1880 canoe trip from the Great Lakes to Hudson Bay in maps and photographs that were published soon after. As with all his excursions, Hill traveled alone.

In 1882, Hill undertook his most ambitious work at the urging of Simon Newcomb, director of the *American Ephemeris*. This study of Jupiter and Saturn would eventually take Hill a decade to complete. For this project he relocated with the office of the *Nautical Almanac* to Washington, D.C. to conduct observations. Hill had previously calculated the orbits of Jupiter and Saturn to 12 decimal places for the *Nautical Almanac*, but this project culminated in a new theory of why and how the two planets travel as they do. After completing the landmark study in 1892, Hill left the *Nautical Almanac*. Hill's work on the orbits of Jupiter and Saturn is widely considered to be one of the most significant 19th century contributions to mathematical astronomy.

Hill was appointed a lecturer in celestial mechanics at Columbia University in 1892. After a hiatus to assume the presidency of the American Mathematical Association from 1894–1896, he returned to Columbia to teach until his retirement in 1901. Hill refused to take a salary for his academic activities at Columbia. As he expressed it, this was less the result of largesse than convenience—he considered the fee too much trouble to collect.

Hill's work was greatly appreciated in England. The London Royal Astronomical Society made him a foreign associate and also gave him their gold medal in 1887. The University of Cambridge offered him his second honorary doctorate in 1892. (He received his first honorary doctorate from Rutgers in 1872.) By 1902, the Royal Society made him a fellow, and in 1909 they awarded him their Copley Medal, considered the highest British honor in the field of science. More than one country extended recognition, however. Hill also won the Paris Academy's Damoiscan Prize in 1898.

Hill cultivated few relationships, preferring to work and think alone, an outlook that fostered his reputation as a deeply innovative theorist. He never married and, in later life, he lived comfortably on his farm, indulging his passion for books and botany. His married brother lived nearby and Hill often visited him for meals.

Hill died on April 16, 1914. When his collected papers were reprinted in four volumes, they were prefaced by Hill's most famous adherent, Jules Henri Poincaré. Today the position of George W. Hill Professor of Mathematics and Physics at Rutgers is underwritten by the New Jersey Board of Governors. Although his 1886 linear differential is now known as the Hill Equation, the fact that Hill was inducted into the Rutgers Alumni Hall of Fame in 1996 as an astronomer indicates that his application of mathematics to solve astronomical problems is what won him his place in history.

SELECTED WRITINGS BY HILL:

Books

The Collected Mathematical Works of George William Hill, 4 volumes, 1905–07.

Periodicals

"Researches in the Lunar Theory." *American Journal of Mathematics* 1, no. 1 (1878).

FURTHER READING:

Books

Brown, E.W. "George William Hill." *Dictionary of American Biography*. New York: Charles Scribner's Sons, 1928, pp. 32–3.

Elliott, Clark A., comp. *Biographical Index to American Science: The Seventeenth Century to 1920*. Westport, CT: Greenwood Press, 1990, p. 106.
National Cyclopaedia of American Biography. Volume 13. Reprint. Ann Arbor, MI: University Microfilms, 1967–71, p. 442.
Tarwater, Dalton, editor. *The Bicentennial Tribute to American Mathematics 1776–1976*. Washington, DC: Mathematical Association of America, 1977.

Other

"George William Hill." *MacTutor History of Mathematics Archive*.
http://www–groups.dcs.st–and.ac.uk/~history/Mathematicians/index.html (July 1997).
Weibel, Charles. "A History of Mathematics at Rutgers." http://www.math.rutgers.edu/~weibel/history.html#hill (July 1997).

—Sketch by Jennifer Kramer

Robert Hill
1899–1991
English biochemist

Though he never held an appointment at a university, Robert Hill, known as Robin to his colleagues and friends, was a pioneer in the field of biochemistry, deducing how certain key processes of photosynthesis functioned. Two of his major contributions were the Hill Reaction (1937) and the Z Scheme (1960). In short, Hill demonstrated that when chloroplasts (also known as green particles) in broken plant cells were exposed to light and a chemical compound/electron acceptor such as ferricynanide or ferric oxlate, these cells could produce oxygen from water. This reaction of electrons is known as the Hill Reaction.

Hill was born on April 2, 1899. He received his primary education at Bedales School, before attending Emmanuel College at Cambridge. After graduating, Hill worked in the Royal Engineers' anti-gas department for a year, 1917-18, at the end of World War I. In 1922 Hill became associated with the newly formed biochemistry department at Cambridge. All of his research was supported by grants and fellowships. In fact, the Agricultural Research Council funded him from 1943-66.

Although he was more interested in plant pigments, Hill spent his early years in the newborn department at Cambridge focusing on hemoglobin.

(Hemoglobin is oxygen-holding pigment found in the red blood cells.) Hill discovered that hemoglobin could be broken down into two parts, globin and heme. Globin is a large protein, and heme is a molecule that contains iron. He also was able to recombine the two parts after breaking them down. Hill also came up with a simple way to measure the range of the oxygen dissociation curve of hemoglobin. This measurement method enabled Hill to work out what would later be known as the Hill Reaction. Basically, Hill's research illustrated how something could be broken down to its basic level in order to further its study. His research also led to a greater understanding of iron and its crucial role in hemoglobin.

Hill Reaction and Z Scheme Further Explain Photosynthesis

Though Hill was compelled by his boss F. G. Hopkins (the first Professor of Biochemistry) to study hemoglobin, he harbored a long-time interest in plants and plant pigments. His research turned in this direction as soon as his experimentation on hemoglobin had ended. In 1937 Hill published his discovery of the Hill Reaction. That is, the ability of chloroplasts, when isolated from leaves and exposed to light, to derive oxygen from water, yet not make sugar from carbon dioxide.

Hill's findings contradicted the long-held belief that a molecule of chlorophyll had to be exposed to light and interact directly with carbon dioxide for photosynthesis to take place. Hill opened up the study of photosynthesis at the sub-cellular level. Hill himself continued to study photosynthesis and its processes.

In 1960, Hill published (with Fay Bendall) his findings on the "Z scheme," another significant finding related to photosynthesis. The Z scheme explained that light was a part of two separate steps in the photosynthesis process. They worked in union, sequentially, to split water into its basic components of oxygen and hydrogen, then shift the hydrogen to carbon dioxide. The Z scheme was important because it was the first to show that in plants, light energy was converted to electrical energy, then to chemical energy, thereby proving a thermodynamic basis for this conversion. Hill's discovery is still important today to our comprehension of these processes.

Lifelong Fascination with Gardening and Natural Plant-Extracted Dyes

Hill brought his interest in biochemistry of plants into his home as well. He and his family lived on a farm, called Vatches Farm, slightly outside of Cambridge in Barton. In Hill's garden, he grew what he called his biochemical plants. Knowledgeable visitors thought these plants were better specimens than found in most botanical gardens. Related to this was Hill's lifelong fascination with plant dyes and dyeing processes. He first became interested in this subject at school at Bedales. He grew plants for dyes, made pigments from them by his own hands, then painted watercolors with the pigments. He was an accomplished watercolorist.

Invents Robin Hill Camera to Support His Interest in Thunderstorms

Hill's interests spread beyond plants as well. He invented what became known as the Robin Hill camera, which featured a fish-eye lens of his own creation. This lens allowed whole-sky photographs to be taken. Hill developed this camera because of his fascination with thunderclouds.

His accomplishments, especially in the area of photosynthesis, did not go unnoticed by his scientific peers. In 1963, Hill received a number of honors. The Society of American Plant Physiologists gave him their first award designated for photosynthesis. He was also named a Honorary Fellow of Emmanuel College. The Royal Society elected him as a Fellow, and he won the Royal Medal from them that year. In 1987, the Royal Society honored Hill again, by awarding him its Copley Medal. Hill was also elected to the U.S. National Academy of Sciences in 1975, as a Foreign Associate.

In 1978 his laboratory space at Cambridge was taken away when the department was restructured, and Hill moved his work to a room at his farm. Though a painfully shy individual, Hill's fascination with the natural world and the science that he culled of it can not be denied. Hill died in Cambridge on March 15, 1991, leaving his wife Priscilla, two sons, and a daughter.

In a tribute to him, colleague Peter R. Rich wrote that "Robin's breadth of knowledge of, and affinity with, The Natural Sciences, his unassuming nature, and his remarkable intellect, made him a unique individual." In his honor, the University of Sheffield founded The Robert Hill Institute, which brought together scientists from several departments (molecular biology, biotechnology, and animal and plant sciences) to study photosynthesis in plants and microorganisms.

SELECTED WRITINGS BY HILL:

Periodicals

"Oxygen evolved by isolated chloroplasts." *Nature* (1937): 881-82.

(With Fay Bendall) "Function of the two cytochrome components in chloroplasts, a working hypothesis." *Nature* (1960): 136-37.

David Da-I Ho

FURTHER READING:

Books

"Hill, Robert (Robin)." *Biographical Dictionary of Scientists*. 2nd ed. New York: Oxford University Press, 1994, 242.

Periodicals

Bendall, D. S. "Obituary: Robin Hill." *The Independent*. London (March 21, 1991): 27.
"Dr Robert Hill." *The Times*. London (March 21, 1991).
Robin Hill Tribute issue. *Photosynthesis Research* (December 1992) 319-40.

—*Sketch by Annette Petrusso*

David Da-I Ho
1952–

Chinese–born American medical scientist

David Ho, one of the world's foremost researchers of acquired immune deficiency syndrome (AIDS),

made his greatest contribution to science when he demonstrated the power of combinations of new state-of-the art AIDS drugs. Ho's research showed that by administering these drugs to patients within weeks after they caught the human immunodeficiency virus (HIV), the virus could be halted in its tracks. Ho's work is considered a major breakthrough in the battle against AIDS, offering increased hope that a cure and vaccine will eventually be found.

Ho, the first chief executive officer and scientific director of the Aaron Diamond AIDS Research Center, the largest AIDS research center in the world, was also the fourth scientist to identify the virus that causes AIDS. He was named *Time* magazine's Man of the Year in 1996. Ho attributes his success in AIDS research to his tenacity, instilled in him by his Chinese immigrant family. "You always retain a bit of an underdog mentality," he explained in *Time* magazine. "People get to this new world, and they want to carve out their place in it. The result is dedication and a higher level of work ethic."

Ho was born in Taiching, Taiwan, the oldest child of Paul and Sonia Ho. At birth, he was given the name Da-I, meaning "Great One," a name that conveyed the family's expectations for their oldest son. In Taiching, the family lived in a small four-room house with a ditch serving as outdoor toilet. To create a better life for his family, Paul Ho left Taiwan for America, sacrificing time spent with his wife and growing son. The family, now consisting of Sonia, Paul, Da-I, and his younger brother, reunited nine years later in Los Angeles. Paul Ho then began studying for his engineering degree at the University of Southern California. A devout Christian, he chose new American names from the Bible for his sons—David and Philip. A third son, Sidney, was born after the family's move to central Los Angeles, where they settled in a predominately African-American neighborhood.

As a child, Ho was inspired to excel academically by the example of his father and other relatives, all scientists and engineers. By the time he had reached age 10, he had already developed a keen interest in science, conducting amateur scientific experiments in the family garage. At first, though, David's new American schoolmates called him "stupid" because he was practically mute; he couldn't communicate because he spoke only Chinese. This experience, however, made him determined to excel, and in later years he would become upset if he didn't make As in every subject. Six months after he started school, Ho began speaking English well enough to communicate with schoolmates after being enrolled in an English as second language program. He and his brothers also picked up English words by watching television comedies such as *The Three Stooges*.

After high school, Ho studied physics at the Massachusetts Institute of Technology and then the California Institute of Technology, where he graduated summa cum laude with a B.S. degree. Deciding that gene splicing was the most exciting area of research, he then attended medical school at Harvard, earning an M.D. degree in 1978. He started his residency in internal medicine in 1981 at Cedars-Sinai Medical Center, later serving for one year as chief resident.

Seeks Virus that Causes AIDS

While at Cedars-Sinai, Ho began seeing increasing numbers of homosexual men with a mysterious illness that targeted the body's defense mechanism—the immune system. The men began dying from infections that do not normally take hold in people with healthy immune systems, such as *Pneumocystis* pneumonia, a disease of the lungs, and toxoplasmosis, a disease that attacks the brain. At the time, doctors attributed the cause to everything from recreational drugs to allergic reactions to too many sex partners. Ho, like some other researchers, suspected a virus—and decided to specialize in research on the disease, which would later become known as AIDS.

In 1982, he started work at Massachusetts General Hospital in the infectious disease lab of Martin Hirsch, a virologist with a sharp interest in the mysterious disease. Ho now calls Hirsch his mentor. Ho wanted to be the first to isolate the virus, but that honor fell to **Luc Motagnier** of the Pasteur Institute in Paris, France. Ho was the fourth scientist to identify the virus, with **Robert C. Gallo**, a scientist at the National Cancer Institute and Jay Levy, who worked at the University of California Medical Center in San Francisco, being respectively second and third.

Yet Ho made important contributions in Hirsch's lab. "While working in Hirsch's lab, Ho became expert at detecting HIV in places where few were able to find it," *Time* said in its 1996 article on the scientist. "He was the first to show that it grows in long-lived immune cells called macrophages and among the first to isolate it in the nervous system and semen. Just as important, he showed that there isn't enough active virus in saliva for kissing to transmit the disease." In 1986, Ho moved back to Los Angeles to work in the infectious disease department of Cedars-Sinai Medical Center. He also became an assistant professor at the University of California, Los Angeles, School of Medicine. In 1989 he was approved for the post of associate professor.

By the time Ho joined Cedars-Sinai, scientists knew that HIV decimates the immune system by targeting T cells—cells that help keep disease from taking hold. They also had determined that HIV slips into T cells by attaching and unlocking CD4 receptor proteins, which are located on the surfaces of these cells. Some scientists then suggested that massive infusions of CD4 particles into the bodies of HIV patients might fool the virus, preventing it from latching on to the true receptors.

Ho and Robert Schooley of the University of Colorado Medical Center in Denver tried out this theory by testing soluble CD4 in two dozen AIDS patients. Unfortunately CD4 proved ineffective against the virus because some HIV viruses, termed "wild viruses," could tell which CD4 molecules were decoys and avoid them. But by embarking on this experiment, Ho and Schooley discovered that there were tens of thousands of infectious virus particles in their patients' bodies, much more than had ever been thought to exist in HIV patients.

Ho then decided to return to researching HIV in the earliest stages of infection to investigate the virus's mysteries. He and his team at UCLA found four homosexual men suffering from flu-like symptoms similar to an early HIV infection, and turned to a newly devised genetic tool—the PCR test—to find out how much virus was in his patients' blood. To many scientists' surprise, he discovered that there were millions of viral particles coursing through the patients' blood, even when patients showed no symptoms. And there were as many virus particles in these men with early stage disease as there were in those in the latest stages. His studies, like those conducted by Robert W. Coombs at the University of Seattle, demonstrated that the virus was always actively reproducing even in early stages, and never went into hiding as previously believed. His work also disproved earlier theories by revealing that HIV did direct damage to the immune system, rather than destroying it through an autoimmune reaction—a reaction to an invader substance in which the immune system attacks itself.

In 1990, Ho received a chance to embark on even more challenging research when philanthropist Irene Diamond named him the chief executive officer and scientific director of the new Aaron Diamond AIDS Research Center. "I said 'I don't want a star. I want a wonderful scientist,'" Diamond recalled telling people who criticized her then-unknown choice, as relayed in *Time* magazine. At the same time, Ho also became professor of medicine and microbiology at the New York University School of Medicine and co-director of the Center for AIDS Research.

Uses New AIDS Drugs to Battle the Illness

With the Diamond Research Center's funds, Ho was able to attract more than 50 world-class researchers to the center. As he began his research at the new center, Ho began to theorize that the virus load in AIDS patients might be much bigger than was apparent because the immune system could be killing off some of the viral particles. Eventually, he reasoned, the immune system becomes exhausted, letting the AIDS virus overtake the immune system's ability to combat it. Ho sought to determine whether the virus could be contained, and if so, whether the immune system could recover enough to restore health to HIV patients.

In 1994, drug researchers developed protease inhibitors and demonstrated for the first time that drugs could actually halt HIV's replication. Ho then embarked on a study with HIV-infected patients which indeed revealed that the immune system created billions of white blood cells as HIV replicated—evidence that the immune system works hard to combat the virus.

Then in a ground-breaking study in 1995, Ho shocked the AIDS research world by showing that a combination of three drugs, including protease inhibitors, halted the AIDS virus, allowing the body's immune system to reduce the number of viral particles in patients to undetectable levels—in patients in both early and late stages of the disease. By using several drugs in addition to the protease inhibitors, the scientists could drastically reduce the chances of HIV virus particles' mutating to survive and become resistant to the therapy.

The news astounded the research community, though scientists were careful to note that the therapy was not a cure for AIDS, and more research needed to be done to test the long-term effectiveness of the new drug combinations, called "drug cocktails." Scientists make two important cautions regarding the advances gained by Ho and his colleagues. First, even though HIV is apparently eliminated from the blood of patients who have been treated shortly after having contracted the virus, further experimentation is needed to determine whether it has been eliminated permanently from such body organs as the brain, lymph nodes, and testes. Second, the drugs cannot reverse the damage done to the bodies—particularly the immune systems—of patients who have suffered with AIDS for years. Nonetheless, Ho's work has provided both a scientific basis of hope for a cure and a direction for future research. "We basically have, for the first time, staggered the virus, and the new optimism comes from the fact that we now realize maybe, just maybe, the virus is not as invincible as we previously thought," Ho said in a 1997 CNN television interview.

Ho—who is married to Susan Kuo, an artist, and has three children, Kathryn, Jaclyn, and Jonathan—has found time during his research career to author or co-author 110 scientific articles. He has been awarded many scientific prizes, including the Scientific Award of the Chinese-American Medical Society, the Ernst Jung Prize in Medicine, and the New York City Mayor's Award for Excellence in science and technol-ogy. He and his family reside in a suburb of New York City.

SELECTED WRITINGS BY HO:

Periodicals

"Quantitation of Human Immunodeficiency Virus Type 1 in the Blood of Infected Persons." *New England Journal of Medicine* (December 14, 1989): 1621-1625.
"Rapid Turnover of Plasma Virions and CD4 Lymphocytes in HIV-1 Infection." *Nature* (January 12, 1995): 123-126.

FURTHER READING:

Periodicals

Chua-Eoan, Howard. "The Tao of Ho." *Time* (December 30, 1996): 69-70.
Gorman, Christine. "The Disease Detective." *Time* (December 30, 1996): 56-62.
Johnson, Hillary. "Dr. David Ho and the Lazarus Equation." *Rolling Stone* (March 6, 1997): 49.

—*Sketch by Barbara Boughton*

Dorothy Crowfoot Hodgkin
1910-1994
English chemist and crystallographer

Dorothy Crowfoot Hodgkin employed the technique of x-ray crystallography to determine the molecular structures of several large biochemical molecules. When she received the 1964 Nobel Prize in chemistry for her accomplishments, the committee cited her contribution to the determination of the structure of both penicillin and vitamin B_{12}.

Hodgkin was born in Egypt on May 12, 1910 to John and Grace (Hood) Crowfoot. She was the first of four daughters. Her mother, although not formally educated beyond finishing school, was an expert on Coptic textiles, and an excellent amateur botanist and nature artist. Hodgkin's father, a British archaeologist and scholar, worked for the Ministry of Education in Cairo at the time of her birth, and her family life was always characterized by world travel. When World War I broke out, Hodgkin and two younger sisters were sent to England for safety, where they were raised for a few years by a nanny and their paternal grandmother. Because of the war, their mother was unable to return to them until 1918, and at that time

Dorothy Crowfoot Hodgkin

brought their new baby sister with her. Hodgkin's parents moved around the globe as her father's government career unfolded, and she saw them when they returned to Britain for only a few months every year. Occasionally during her youth she travelled to visit them in such far-flung places as Khartoum in the Sudan and Palestine.

Hodgkin's interest in chemistry and crystals began early in her youth, and she was encouraged both by her parents as well as by their scientific acquaintances. While still a child, Hodgkin was influenced by a book that described how to grow crystals of alum and copper sulfate and on x rays and crystals. Her parents then introduced her to the soil chemist A. F. Joseph and his colleagues, who gave her a tour of their laboratory and showed her how to pan for gold. Joseph later gave her a box of reagents and minerals which allowed her to set up a home laboratory. Hodgkin was initially educated at home and in a succession of small private schools, but at age eleven began attending the Sir John Leman School in Beccles, England, from which she graduated in 1928. After a period of intensive tutoring to prepare her for the entrance examinations, Hodgkin entered Somerville College for women at Oxford University. Her aunt, Dorothy Hood, paid the tuition to Oxford, and helped to support her financially. For a time, Hodgkin considered specializing in archaeology, but eventually settled on chemistry and crystallography.

Crystallography was a fledgling science at the time Hodgkin began, a combination of mathematics,

physics, and chemistry. **Max Laue**, **William Henry Bragg** and **William Lawrence Bragg** had essentially invented it in the early decades of the century (they had won Nobel Prizes in 1914 and 1915, respectively) when they discovered that the atoms in a crystal deflected x rays. The deflected x rays interacted or interfered with each other. If they *constructively* interfered with each other, a bright spot could be captured on photographic film. If they *destructively* interfered with each other, the brightness was cancelled. The pattern of the x ray spots—*diffraction pattern*—bore a mathematical relationship to the positions of individual atoms in the crystal. Thus, by shining x rays through a crystal, capturing the pattern on film, and doing mathematical calculations on the distances and relative positions of the spots, the molecular structure of almost any crystalline material could theoretically be worked out. The more complicated the structure, however, the more elaborate and arduous the calculations. Techniques for the practical application of crystallography were few, and organic chemists accustomed to chemical methods of determining structure regarded it as a black art.

After she graduated from Oxford in 1932, Hodgkin's old friend A. F. Joseph steered her toward Cambridge University and the crystallographic work of J. D. Bernal. Bernal already had a reputation in the field, and researchers from many countries sent him crystals for analysis. Hodgkin's first job was as Bernal's assistant. Under his guidance, with the wealth of materials in his laboratory, the young student began demonstrating her particular talent for x-ray studies of large molecules such as sterols and vitamins. In 1934, Bernal took the first x-ray photograph of a protein crystal, pepsin, and Hodgkin did the subsequent analysis to obtain information about its molecular weight and structure. Proteins are much larger and more complicated than other biological molecules because they are polymers—long chains of repeating units—and they exercise their biochemical functions by folding over on themselves and assuming specific three-dimensional shapes. This was not well understood at the time, however, so Hodgkin's results began a new era; crystallography could establish not only the structural layout of atoms in a molecule, even a huge one, but also the overall molecular shape which contributed to biological activity.

Research and Recognition at Oxford

In 1934, Hodgkin returned to Oxford as a teacher at Somerville College, continuing her doctoral work on sterols at the same time. (She obtained her doctorate in 1937.) It was a difficult decision to move from Cambridge, but she needed the income and jobs were scarce. Somerville's crystallography and laboratory facilities were extremely primitive; one of the features of her lab at Oxford was a rickety circular staircase that she needed to climb several times a day to reach the only window with sufficient light for her polarizing microscope. This was made all the more difficult because Hodgkin suffered most of her adult life from a severe case of rheumatoid arthritis, which didn't respond well to treatment and badly crippled her hands and feet. Additionally, Oxford officially barred her from research meetings of the faculty chemistry club because she was a woman, a far cry from the intellectual comradery and support she had encountered in Bernal's laboratory. Fortunately, her talent and quiet perseverance quickly won over first the students and then the faculty members at Oxford. Sir **Robert Robinson** helped her get the money to buy better equipment, and the Rockefeller Foundation awarded her a series of small grants. She was asked to speak at the students' chemistry club meetings, which faculty members also began to attend. Graduate students began to sign on to do research with her as their advisor.

An early success for Hodgkin at Oxford was the elucidation of cholesterol iodide's molecular structure, which no less a luminary than W.H. Bragg singled out for praise. During World War II, Hodgkin and her graduate student Barbara Low worked out the structure of penicillin, from some of the first crystals ever made of the vital new drug. Penicillin is not a particularly large molecule, but it has an unusual ring structure, at least four different forms, and crystallizes in different ways, making it a difficult crystallographic problem. Fortunately they were able to use one of the first IBM analog computers to help with the calculations.

In 1948, Hodgkin began work on the structure of vitamin B_{12}, the deficiency of which causes pernicious anemia. She obtained crystals of the material from Dr. Lester Smith of the Glaxo drug company, and worked with a graduate student, Jenny Glusker, an American team of crystallographers led by Kenneth Trueblood, and later with John White of Princeton University. Trueblood had access to state of the art computer equipment at the University of California at Los Angeles, and they sent results back and forth by mail and telegraph. Hodgkin and White were theoretically affiliated with competing pharmaceutical firms, but they ended up jointly publishing the structure of B_{12} in 1957; it turned out to be a porphyrin, a type of molecule related to chlorophyll, but with a single atom of cobalt at the center.

Increasing Recognition Culminates in Nobel Prize and Order of Merit

After the war, Hodgkin helped form the International Union of Crystallography, causing Western governments some consternation in the process because she insisted on including crystallographers from behind the Iron Curtain. Always interested in the cause of world peace, Hodgkin signed on with several organizations that admitted Communist party members. Recognition of Hodgkin's work began to increase markedly, however, and whenever she had trouble getting an entry visa to the U.S. because of her affiliation with peace organizations, plenty of scientist friends were available to write letters on her behalf. A restriction on her U.S. visa was finally lifted in 1990, shortly before the Soviet Union collapsed.

In 1947, she was inducted into the Royal Society, Britain's premier scientific organization. Professor Hinshelwood assisted her efforts to get a dual university/college appointment with a better salary, and her chronic money problems were alleviated. Hodgkin still had to wait until 1957 for a full professorship, however, and it was not until 1958 that she was assigned an actual chemistry laboratory at Oxford. In 1960, she obtained the Wolfson Research Professorship, an endowed chair financed by the Royal Society, and in 1964 received the Nobel Prize in chemistry. A year later, she was awarded Britain's Order of Merit, only the second woman since Florence Nightingale to achieve that honor.

Hodgkin still wasn't done with her research, however. In 1969, after decades of work and waiting for computer technology to catch up with the complexity of the problem, she solved the structure of insulin. She employed some sophisticated techniques in the process, such as substituting atoms in the insulin molecule, and then comparing the altered crystal structure to the original. Protein crystallography was still an evolving field; in 1977 she said, in an interview with Peter Farago in the *Journal of Chemical Education,* "In the larger molecular structure, such as that of insulin, the way the peptide chains are folded within the molecule and interact with one another in the crystal is very suggestive in relation to the reactions of the molecules. We can often see that individual side chains have more than one conformation in the crystal, interacting with different positions of solvent molecules around them. We can begin to trace the movements of the atoms within the crystals."

In addition to her scientific work, Hodgkin served as chancellor of Bristol University, a position she held until her retirement in 1988. She died on July 30, 1994 at her home in Shipston-on-Stour, Warwickshire, England.

In 1937, Dorothy Crowfoot married Thomas Hodgkin, the cousin of an old friend and teacher, Margery Fry, at Somerville College. He was an African Studies scholar and teacher, and, because of his travels and jobs in different parts of the world, they maintained separate residences until 1945, when he finally obtained a position teaching at Oxford. Despite this unusual arrangement, their marriage was a happy and successful one. Although initially worried that her work with x-rays might jeopardize their ability to have children, the Hodgkins produced three: Luke, born in 1938, Elizabeth, born in 1941, and Toby, born in 1946. The children all took up their parents scholarly, nomadic habits, and at the time of the Nobel Ceremony travelled to Stockholm from as far away as New Delhi and Zambia. After her retirement, she continued to travel widely and expanded her lifelong activities on behalf of world peace, working with the Pugwash Conferences on Science and World Affairs.

SELECTED WRITINGS BY HODGKIN:

Periodicals

"The X-Ray Analysis of Complicated Molecules." *Science* 150 (19 November 1965): 979-88.

FURTHER READING:

Books

McGrayne, Sharon B. *Nobel Prize Women in Science.* Wasington, DC: Carol Publishing, 1993.
Opfell, Olga S. *The Lady Laureates.* Metuchen, NJ: Scarecrow Press, 1986.

Periodicals

Opfell, Olga S. *Journal of Chemical Education* 54 (1977): 214.
_____. *Nature* (24 May 1984): 309.
_____. *New Scientist* (23 May 1992): 36.
Pace, Eric. "Dorothy Hodgkin, 84, Is Dead; Briton Won Nobel in Chemistry" (obituary). *New York Times* (1 August 1994).
Pearson, Richard. "Dorothy Crowfoot Hodgkin, Chemist Who Won Nobel Prize, Dies at 84" (obituary). *Wasington Post* (1 August 1994): B4).

—*Sketch by Gail B. C. Marsella*

Robert William Holley
1922–1993
American biochemist

Robert Holley was best known for his isolation and characterization of transfer ribonucleic acid (tRNA). Essentially, tRNA "translates" the genetic instructions within cells by first "reading" genes, the fundamental units of heredity, and then creating proteins—the building blocks of the body—from

Robert William Holley

amino acids. Holley, along with **Har Gobind Khorana** and **Marshall Warren Nirenberg**, was awarded the 1968 Nobel Prize in medicine or physiology for determining the sequence of tRNA. But Holley's work on tRNA was only the beginning of a distinguished scientific career. Subsequently, he has investigated the molecular factors that control growth and multiplication of cells. His work in this area has had profound impact on understanding the processes that lead to cancer.

Robert William Holley was born in Urbana, Illinois, on January 28, 1922. His parents, Charles Elmer Holley and Viola Esther (Wolfe) Holley, were both teachers. They had three other sons—Charles Jr., Frank, and George. Holley grew up in Illinois, California, and Idaho, and early developed a life-long love of the outdoors and fascination with living things. The latter years of his childhood were spent in Urbana, where he attended high school and, in 1938, enrolled at the University of Illinois. He majored in chemistry, and was the photographer for the school's yearbook.

After obtaining his B.A. in 1942, Holley took up graduate studies in organic chemistry at Cornell University. He served in various positions at both the university and the medical college for the next several years. In 1945 he married Ann Lenore Dworkin, a chemist and high school mathematics teacher. They had one son, Frederick.

During the mid-1940s Holley participated as a civilian in war research for the United States Office of

Research and Development. He was a member of the team of researchers that first succeeded in making penicillin synthetically. Supported by a fellowship from the National Research Council, he completed his doctorate in organic chemistry at Cornell University in 1947 and did a year of postdoctoral work at Washington State College (now University) in Pullman before returning east. In 1948, he became assistant professor at the New York State Agricultural Experiment Station, a branch of Cornell, in Geneva. He became associate professor in 1950 and full professor in 1964.

Focuses Research on Mechanisms of Protein Synthesis

During a sabbatical on a Guggenheim Memorial Fellowship at the California Institute of Technology in 1955-1956, Holley started to investigate protein synthesis. In the wake of **James Watson**'s and **Francis Crick**'s discovery that DNA contained the information of heredity, Holley targeted the chemistry of nucleic acids, which carry and transmit genetic information. His course may have been inspired, at least in part, by Crick's suggestion that "adaptor molecules" of some sort must be involved in the translation of genetic information into proteins. Towards the end of his year away from Cornell, Holley began to look specifically at the structure of transfer RNA, the start of a nine-year effort to unlock its secrets.

Back at Cornell in 1957, Holley was appointed research chemist at the United States Plant, Soil, and Nutrition Laboratory, where he continued his studies on tRNA. Heading up a research team, he meticulously planned and carried out a painstaking series of experiments. He and his colleagues spent three years developing a technique to isolate and partially purify different classes of tRNAs from yeast. Finally they succeeded in isolating a pure sample of alanine transfer RNA. The next five years were devoted to elucidating the sequence and structure of this particular transfer RNA.

To appreciate the profound impact of Holley's work on research into the biochemistry of life, it is useful to review some fundamental concepts. Cells carry the instructions for all of their necessary tasks in their chromosomes. Chromosomes within a cell are made up of very long molecules called deoxyribonucleic acid (DNA). Genes, the basic units of heredity for all living things, are small sections of the long strands of DNA. Genes themselves are made up of a series of units called nucleotides. Nucleotides are molecules composed of a particular sugar (either ribose or deoxyribose), a phosphate group (one phosphorous atom combined with three oxygen atoms), and one of five specific bases. These bases—guanine, adenine, cytosine, thymine, and uracil—thus distinguish the nucleotides from one another. They are, in essence, the alphabet from which all of our genetic instructions are composed.

Cells and bodies, however, are built not of genes but of proteins. Proteins are the structural elements of cells, providing form and stability. Equally important, certain proteins, called enzymes, mediate critical biochemical reactions, allowing the formation and breakdown of innumerable chemicals that cells use during growth, functioning, and division. Proteins are sequences of amino acids. The amino acids are a group of about twenty different molecules that share certain chemical characteristics (e.g., the presence of an amine group).

Holley's work centered on the question of how sequences of nucleotides in DNA specify sequences of amino acids in proteins. It had been known that DNA did not directly create protein, but copied itself instead (in a complementary, or negative sense) into strands of RNA. But it was not known how these long strands of RNA, called messenger RNA or mRNA, functioned in the creation of proteins. Holley believed that the much smaller tRNA molecules played a key role. He knew that a triplet of bases, or codon, specifies each of the twenty amino acids. Examining the sequence of bases within alanine tRNA (which specifies creation of the amino acid alanine), he found an anti-codon for alanine. This anti-codon would be able to bond chemically with an alanine codon on an mRNA strand.

By studying the molecular sequence of alanine tRNA, Holley and his students were able to determine its structure and then to deduce how it functioned. A tRNA anti-codon would bind to its matching codon along a strand of mRNA. The corresponding amino acid, held at the opposite end of the tRNA, would then be positioned to link up in series with the amino acid specified by the adjacent codon on the mRNA. In this manner, the series of nucleotides in a molecule of DNA would be translated into a series of amino acids that would make up a protein.

For his illumination of this vital process, Holley won a share of the 1968 Nobel Prize for physiology or medicine. He was also honored with the prestigious Albert Lasker Award for Basic Medical Research in 1965. In other honors include a National Academy of Science award in molecular biology in 1967, as well as fellowships from the Guggenheim Foundation, the National Science Foundation, the National Research Council, and the American Chemical Society.

Redirects Research on Cell Growth and Replication Factors

From 1966 to 1967 Holley was on sabbatical at the Salk Institute for Biological Studies and the Scripps Clinic and Research Foundation in La Jolla, California. The following year he joined the Salk

Institute as a resident fellow. Like his earlier sabbatical, Holley's move proved pivotal for his research, as he launched an investigation of the molecular factors that regulate growth and multiplication of cells. Rooted somewhat in his previous work on how the protein molecules underlying cell growth are formed, the new investigations had quite different interpretations and implications.

The control of cell growth and division is critical to normal functioning. Cancerous growths are characterized by uncontrolled cell division. Normally, a balance of stimulatory and inhibitory molecular factors keeps cellular multiplication at the proper rate; the number of new cells produced roughly equals the number of cells that wear out and die. Rapid cell proliferation might be caused by over-production of the stimulatory factors, excessive cell sensitivity to the stimulatory factors, a lack of the inhibitory factors, or some combination of these causes.

Holley examined the roles of hormones, bloodborn chemicals—usually proteins—that are released by various tissues and organs and that interact with one another. Hormones can either stimulate or inhibit cell proliferation, or even, as Holley would later show, do both.

Holley discovered that the concentration of two types of hormones, known as peptide and steroid hormones, in a solution with dividing cells would determine the rate of cell division and ultimately, cell density. Further, he found that types of cells prone to develop into tumors responded dramatically to these growth factors, dividing rapidly in response to very low hormone levels. Subsequent experiments demonstrated that peptide and steroid hormones could act synergistically: several of these growth factors together in solution would produce a greater growth rate than the sum effects of each individually. Holley also found that different types of cells responded differently to particular hormones, and that their responses could change with the cells' population density. At low densities, cells take up and utilize growth factors more efficiently than they do under conditions of high density. Cellular receptors for certain growth-promoting hormones increased under conditions of low cell density, whereas receptors for certain other hormones increased as cell density increased.

Holley also studied the effects of non-hormonal factors, such as certain sugars and amino acids, on cell proliferation. He found that while cell growth patterns were quite insensitive to the levels of many amino acids, they were strongly regulated by others, notably glutamine.

Looking at the other side of the coin, Holley and his collaborators also identified growth inhibitors. Some of these compounds suppress cell growth by blocking DNA replication. Holley discovered that, in addition to blocking DNA activity, growth inhibitors stimulated production of specific proteins whose functions were unknown. Growth factors, too, were found to have an associated protein synthesis in addition to stimulating DNA activity. Interestingly, Holley noted that while growth and inhibitory factors canceled out each others' effects on DNA replication, they had no effect on each others' secondary production of hormones. With particular factors that increase both cell size and rate of cell division, Holley had noted similar effects. Adding a growth inhibitor would stop the cells from dividing, but not stop the individual cells from growing larger.

As he and his co-workers had done with tRNA, Holley's team eventually sequenced certain of the growth factors. These are considerably larger molecules than tRNA, but the techniques of molecular biology had improved so much over the years that these sequences were obtained much more readily. Holley identified the sequence of amino acids of a growth-inhibiting factor for a specific type of monkey cell. The sequence turned out to be identical to that for the human growth factor (TGF-beta 2).

Holley's work during the later phase of his career has shed new light on the factors that control how cells grow, differentiate, and divide. His research has striking implications for the development of drugs to suppress tumor growth and for understanding the fundamental causes of cancer. This entire field of investigation continues to be active, as new techniques and technologies allow researchers to ask questions of increasing sophistication. As an American Cancer Society research professor of molecular biology at the Salk Institute for Biological Studies, Holley was in the forefront of the ongoing struggle to learn about and to control unchecked cell growth. Shortly before his death, he was studying the timing of cell division. Holley died on February 11, 1993 at his home in Los Gatos, California.

SELECTED WRITINGS BY HOLLEY:

Periodicals

"An Alanine-Dependent, Ribonuclease-Inhibited Conversion of AMP to ATP, and its Possible Relationship to Protein Synthesis." *Journal of the American Chemical Society* 79 (1957): 658-62.

"Chemistry of Amino Acid-Specific Ribonucleic Acids." *Cold Spring Harbor Symposia on Qualitative Biology* 28 (1963): 117-21.

"Purification of Kidney Epithelial Cell Growth Inhibitors." *Proceedings of the National Academy of Sciences, U.S.A.* 77 (1980): 5989-92.

Ariel Cahill Hollinshead

FURTHER READING:

Books

Judson, H. F. *Eighth Day of Creation.* New York: Simon & Schuster, 1979.

Magill, F. N., ed. *The Nobel Prize Winners: Physiology or Medicine.* Volume 2, *1944-1969.* Englewood Cliffs, NJ: Salem Press, 1991, pp. 1007-17.

Periodicals

Lambert, Bruce. "Robert W. Holley Is Dead at 71; Won Nobel for Work in Genetics" (obituary). *New York Times* (14 February 1993).

—*Sketch by Ethan E. Allen*

Ariel Cahill Hollinshead
1929–

American pharmacologist and research oncologist

Ariel Cahill Hollinshead is president of the Laboratory for Virus and Cancer Research, a non-profit institution she founded in Washington, D.C. Trained in pharmacology, she has focused her research on the chemotherapy of viral diseases, and on immunotherapeutic treatments for various cancers. Her work was the first to show indisputable evidence of the involvement of viruses in cancer. With T. H. S. Stewart, she has isolated antigens specific to many kinds of cancers and has worked on specific active immunotherapy as well as combination immunochemotherapy trials for cancer patients. She is currently pursuing a project involving immunochemotherapy for human immunodeficiency virus, the cause of AIDS.

Hollinshead was born August 24, 1929, into a Quaker family of Allentown, Pennsylvania. Her father, Earl Hollinshead Sr., had an engineering degree from Lehigh University and later became head of John Galbreath Co. in Pittsburgh; her mother, Gertrude Cahill, was president and valedictorian of her class at Barnard College. As a student at Bethel Park High School, Ariel performed in musical productions and edited the school's newspaper. Early on she was interested in science. At age 15, she read *Microbe Hunters,* Paul de Kruif's 1926 dramatization of the lives of the early bacteriologists, and determined to be a scientific researcher. With money from her first summer job, she bought a Zeiss microscope and began studies of cells. She designed a science fair project on the response of nerve cells to stimuli, for which she received prizes in Pennsylvania and in national competition.

Studies Pharmacology at Ohio University

As a freshman she entered Swarthmore College, a traditional choice for students from Quaker families. The following year she and her brother, Earl (who later became a lawyer), entered Ohio University in Athens. The science curriculum was more extensive there, and Hollinshead studied with zoologist Rush Elliott and chemist Jesse Day. She also played piano and bass fiddle and sang in several musical productions. She received an A.B. degree in zoology in 1952, then began studies at the George Washington University in Washington, D.C., where she earned a master's degree in 1955 and a doctoral degree in 1957, both in pharmacology.

In 1958 Hollinshead went to Baylor University Medical Center in Houston, Texas, as a postdoctoral fellow and assistant professor of virology and epidemiology. After a year at Baylor working with Joseph Melnick, she returned to Washington, D.C., to join her new husband, attorney Montgomery K. Hyun. Hollinshead joined the faculty of the George Washington University (GWU) in 1959 as assistant professor of pharmacology, beginning a long association with that institution. In 1961 she was named assistant professor of medicine, in 1964 associate professor of medicine, and in 1974 professor of medicine. In 1991 she became professor emerita. At GWU, she taught courses in pharmacology, virology, immunology, and oncology, and in 1964 established the Laboratory for Virus and Cancer Research.

Hollinshead managed to combine raising a family with her career in science. When her two sons were babies, she used most of her salary to pay for a nanny, because maternity leave did not exist. She took them to the laboratory with her in the evenings and on weekends. At home in the kitchen, she used a conversion chart to change "teaspoons and pounds into milliliters and grams," since she was more familiar with chemistry than with cooking. "I had a devoted husband," she notes, "and we enjoyed each other's company. Busy women seem always to be able to do more." Her sons attended Sidwell Friends, a Quaker school. William is now a scientist at University of California, San Francisco, and Christopher is a lawyer in New York. Her husband retired as Chief Administrative Law Judge of the Federal Trade Commission.

Works on Relationship Between Cancer and Viruses, Tumor-Associated Antigens

Hollinshead has more than 260 scientific papers to her credit, reflecting basic research in pharmacology, virology, and oncology, as well as clinical trials of anti-cancer therapies. In a major contribution to the field of virology, she has demonstrated that viruses are associated with cancers in humans, a discovery that has led to the development of vaccines as a method of immunotherapy. Her work has provided insight into a spectrum of cancers, and into mechanisms used by the immune system to combat solid tumors.

Early in her research career, she was the first to identify purine and pyrimidine analogs effective in the chemotherapy of viral diseases, and the first to demonstrate the development of drug resistance to these compounds. She then became the first, along with her colleague T. H. M. Stewart, to isolate, purify, and identify animal and human tumor-associated antigens (TAAs). She has developed techniques for testing antibodies of cancer patients to monoclonal antibody-derived antigens (epitopes) "scissored" from intact TAAs. Hollinshead has developed and patented through her university a unique reverse enzyme immunoassay for measuring humoral antibodies in patient sera. She and Stewart have shown that TAA immunogens will produce long-lasting cell-mediated immunity.

In recent studies, Hollinshead has defined the effect of certain anti-cancer drugs on the immune system, and gained information useful in designing new strategies and regimens of combination immuno-chemotherapy, in which vaccines and anti-cancer

drugs are used in concert. In 1994 she developed a breast cancer drug sensitivity test, using gene products. She has developed a clinical protocol for a vaccine-drug combination to attack the human HIV virus, and is continuing to test it.

Promotes Women in Science

Hollinshead is an outspoken advocate of women in science. As president of Sigma Delta Epsilon Graduate Women in Science in 1968-1969, she worked to encourage young women to pursue careers in science. She established Professional Opportunities for Women in Science (POWS), which focuses on training women for part-time work in science. She speaks frequently to lay groups about women in science, science education, and women's health.

In 1975 Hollinshead was named Medical Woman of the Year by the Joint Board of American Medical Colleges. She was chosen for the award from among 250 women who were nominated, and was described a "one of the few women in our country who . . . will receive lasting distinction by applying the principles of basic research to the diseases of humanity." In 1976 she received the Alumni Association Certificate of Merit from Ohio University. In 1977 she was appointed to chair the Review Board of Oncology for the Veterans Administration, becoming the first woman to hold the post. In 1978 Ohio University presented her with an honorary doctorate. In 1980 she received the Star of Europe Medal, and in 1990 the Scholar Speciale Medicina Silver Medal from Italy. She has been twice honored with Distinguished Scientist awards from the Society for Experimental Biology and Medicine. She has collaborated with scientists worldwide, and in 1982 was an honorary consultant to the Beijing Thoracic Tumor Research Institute.

Hollinshead has served on the board of the Medical College of Pennsylvania. She is a reviewer for professional oncology, virology, and immunology journals, and is a member of number of professional organizations, including the American Association for the Advancement of Science (Fellow 1966, Life Member 1967, Distinguished Scientist award), New York Academy of Sciences (Life Member 1967), the Society for Experimental Biology and Medicine (Washington, D.C., chapter president 1980-81), and Sigma Xi scientific research society (Life Member 1968). She has served on task forces, advisory boards, and committees for the National Cancer Institute, the National Institutes of Health, National Academy of Sciences, the USDA, FDA, and NASA, among others.

Music remains an important avocation for Hollinshead, both as a performer and an audience member. She is active in a variety of political and community organizations, and finds time for writing poetry, painting, and hiking. "The life of a scientist is demanding," she says, "and there are often twelve-hour work days. But I enjoy what I do, and I enjoy what I hurry home to."

FURTHER READING:

Books

O'Neill, Lois Decker, ed. *The Women's Book of World Records and Achievements.* Garden City, New York: Anchor Press/Doubleday, 1979, pp. 222-223.

Shearer, Benjamin F., and Barbara S. Shearer, eds. *Notable Women in the Life Sciences: A Biographical Dictionary.* Westport, Connecticut: Greenwood Press, 1996.

Periodicals

"Honor Degrees to be Awarded." *Athens [Ohio] Messenger* (June 1977).

—*Sketch by Jill Carpenter*

Charles B. Huggins

Charles B. Huggins
1901–1997
American surgeon

Charles B. Huggins was awarded the Nobel Prize for physiology or medicine in 1966 for his discovery in the 1930s of the role played by hormones in the onset and growth of prostate and breast cancer. This breakthrough led Huggins to make a number of important medical advances, including the subsequent development of hormone therapy, the first non-radioactive, non-toxic chemical treatment for cancer. In other studies, Huggins found that cancer cells are not necessarily self-reliant and self-perpetuating, and that some cancers actually depend on normal hormone levels to develop and grow. He then developed a blood test to measure two particular enzymes to determine the extent of the cancer and the effect of hormone therapy. In addition, Huggins discovered the compensatory action of adrenal glands after hormone therapy and performed the first surgical removal of the adrenal glands to combat cancer regrowth. He also developed cortisone replacement therapy to compensate for the loss of normal adrenal gland function.

Charles Brenton Huggins, the oldest of two sons, was born on September 22, 1901, in Halifax, Nova Scotia, to pharmacist Charles Edward and Bessie Marie (Spencer) Huggins. He earned his B.A. from Acadia University, Wolfville, Nova Scotia, in 1920, graduating in a class of twenty-five students. That same year, he moved to the United States to attend Harvard Medical School, graduating in four years with both an M.A. and M.D. He did his internship at the University of Michigan Hospital and was appointed instructor in surgery at the University's Medical School in 1926. The following year, he became instructor of surgery on the original faculty of the University of Chicago Medical School, and in that same year, he married Margaret Wellman. The couple had a son, Charles Edward, and daughter, Emily Wellman. Huggins was promoted to assistant professor in 1929, then to associate professor in 1933, the year he became an American citizen, and he attained the rank of full professor of surgery in 1936. In 1946, he spent a brief period with the Johns Hopkins University as professor of urological surgery and director of the department of urology. He was director of the University of Chicago's Ben May Laboratory for Cancer Research from 1951 to 1969, continuing his research at the university until 1972, when he returned to Acadia University to become chancellor. He retired from the post in 1979 and moved to Chicago.

Research on Urinary Tract Leads to Prostate Studies

Huggins' initial specialty was urology, but his interest in cancer was actually sparked in 1930, when he met German Nobel Prize-winning cancer researcher **Otto Warburg**. Upon his return to the University of Chicago in the early 1930s, Huggins and his colleagues experimented with changing normal connective tissue elements into bone, using cells from the male urinary tract and bladder. His interest soon turned to the male urogenital system, particularly the role played by chemicals and hormones in the prostate gland, the male accessory reproductive gland located at the base of the urethra. He and his colleagues developed what Paul Talalay and Guy Williams-Ashman in *Science* called "an ingenious surgical procedure . . . [which] isolated the prostate gland of dogs from the urinary tract." This procedure, introduced in 1939, allowed the analysis and measurement of secretions of the gland which form much of the ejaculatory fluid. The research was at times frustrated by the formation of prostate tumors in some of the dogs, the only animal other than man known to develop cancer of the prostate. Higgins, however, saw the the obstacle as an opportunity. He turned his energy to studying the development and growth of prostate cancer, a painful and often fatal disease prevalent in men over the age of fifty that causes obstruction of the urinary tract and, if left untreated, metastasizes (spreads) to the bone and liver.

Huggins discovered high levels of testosterone, a male sex hormone, in secretions from a cancerous prostate. He also discovered that reducing male hormone secretions by either orchiectomy (castration) or estrogen (a female hormone) therapy, or both, drastically reduced testosterone levels and inhibited the growth of advanced metastatic prostate cancer. In his first human trials, four out of twenty-one patients treated with this method survived for twelve years. He also developed a blood test to measure acid phosphatase, which is secreted by the prostate, and alkaline phosphatase, which is secreted by bone-forming cells in bone tissue, both of which showed increased levels in patients with metastasized prostate cancer. Using these measurements, he could determine the extent of the cancer and the effect of the hormone treatments.

Huggins found that although the level of androgens (male sex hormones) dropped drastically after orchiectomy, in some cases they rose again, often to a level higher than before the surgery. Investigations led him to believe that the adrenal glands were producing androgens of their own, apparently compensating for the lowered levels induced by the hormone therapy. These androgens, too, encouraged the growth of the cancer. In 1944, he performed the first bilateral adrenalectomy, (removal of the two adrenal glands located above the kidneys), producing some positive results, even before cortisone was readily available for replacement therapy. In 1953, Huggins reported that, when used in combination, adrenalectomy and cortisone replacement had a beneficial effect on fifty

percent of patients suffering from either prostate or breast cancer, but had no effect on other types of cancer. This was a radical treatment, however, and used only as a last resort.

Focuses on Breast Cancer

In the 1950s, Huggins left the clinical environment to return to the laboratory. While delivering the tenth Macewen Memorial Lecture at the University of Glasgow in 1958 he referred to breast cancer as "one of the noblest of the problems of medicine." In his lecture, entitled *Frontiers of Mammary Cancer,* he said, "Cancer of the breast in the United States has the highest prevalence rate of any form of neoplastic disease in either sex . . . Commonly, the disease advances with dreadful speed and ferocity." Huggins and two students, D. M. Bergenstal and Thomas Dao, developed a treatment for cancer that entailed removal of both ovaries and both adrenal glands. Combined with cortisone replacement therapy, the treatment brought about improvement in thirty to forty percent of the patients with advanced breast cancer, sometimes with quite definite and prolonged improvement.

Breast cancer research was being hampered, however, because of the long delay between stimulation and growth of artificially-induced mammary tumors in animals. In 1956, Huggins discovered that a single dose of 7,12-dimethylbens(a)anthracene (DMBA) would quickly induce mammary tumors in certain types of female rats and that many of these tumors were, like some in humans, hormone dependentand responded to regulation of the hormonal environment. Huggins' rat tumors soon became the focus of experiments in laboratories all over the world.

In the mid-1960s, a major scientific controversy developed around whether birth control pills encourage cancer of the breast and other reproductive organs. Huggins, who by that time had spent more than thirty years researching the relationship between hormones and cancer, studied data collected from thousands of women taking birth control pills. He believed that "the pill" did not encourage such cancers in women. Some specialists later came to believe some evidence indicating that the pill may even discourage the growth of some types of cancer.

For his research on hormones and cancer, Huggins shared the 1966 Nobel Prize with **Peyton Rous**, who was honored for his work fifty-five years earlier on viral causes of cancer. Only one person previously had been awarded the Nobel for cancer research—**Johannes Fibiger** in 1926 for developing a method of growing artificial tumors. Colleagues agreed that both Huggins and Rous should have received the award many years earlier. In addition to the Nobel Prize, Huggins was awarded one of the highest honors to be bestowed by American medicine, the Lasker Clinical Research Award, in 1963. He was also the first recipient of the Charles L. Mayer Award in cancer research from the National Academy of Sciences in 1943. Huggins also was awarded two gold medals for research from the American Medical Association, the Order of Merit from Germany, and the Order of the Sun from Peru. He was made honorary fellow of the Royal College of Surgeons in both Edinburgh and London, and is the recipient of numerous honorary degrees.

A devoted family man, a lover of the music of Bach and Mozart, and a self-admitted workaholic, Huggins was also known for his wry wit. He died at his home in Chicago.

SELECTED WRITINGS BY HUGGINS:

Books

Frontiers of Mammary Cancer. Jackson, 1961.
The Scientific Contributions of the Ben May Laboratory for Cancer Research. Chicago: University of Chicago Press, 1961.
Experimental Leukemia and Mammary Cancer: Induction, Prevention, Cure. Chicago: University of Chicago Press, 1979.

FURTHER READING:

Books

Current Biography. New York: H. W. Wilson, 1965, pp. 205-08.
Nobel Prize Winners: An H. W. Wilson Biographical Dictionary. New York: H. W. Wilson, 1987, pp. 486-88.
The Nobel Prize Winners: Physiology or Medicine. Englewood Cliffs: Salem Press, 1991, pp. 967-72.

Periodicals

New York Times (16 October 1966).
Talalay, Paul, and Guy Williams-Ashman. "1966 Nobel Laureates in Medicine or Physiology." *Science* (21 October 1966): 362-64.
Altman, Lawrence. "C. B. Huggins, Nobel Prize Winner for Cancer Work, 95" (obituary). *New York Times* (15 January 1997): B7.
Heise, Kenan. "Nobel Prize Winner Dr. Charles Huggins" (obituary). *Chicago Tribune* (15 January 1997): 11.

—*Sketch by David Petechuk*

John Hughes

John Hughes
1942–
English pharmacologist

John Hughes, working with Hans W. Kosterlitz, discovered the enkephalin peptides, opiate-like substances produced naturally by the brain. This discovery helped scientists understand the means by which opiate drugs, such as heroin and morphine, fight pain. It also helped explain the mechanism behind narcotic addiction. For this achievement, Hughes shared the 1978 Albert Lasker Medical Research Award for basic research, one of the most prestigious prizes in medicine. The Lasker citation recognized "his demonstration of the specific structure of the enkephalins and the identification of their natural origin."

Hughes was born in London, England on January 6, 1942. He is the son of Joseph Henry Hughes and Edith Annie Hope Hughes. As a boy, Hughes attended the Mitcham County Grammar School. When it came time for college, he chose Chelsea College at the University of London, where he received a bachelor's degree in biochemistry and pharmacology in 1964. For graduate study, Hughes attended Kings College at the University of London. His supervisor there was Sir **John Vane**, who later went on to win a Nobel Prize in Physiology or Medicine. After completing his Ph.D. in 1967, Hughes began two years of postdoctoral research at the Yale University School of Medicine.

In 1969, Hughes moved to the University of Aberdeen in Scotland. There he served first as a lecturer in therapeutics and pharmacology and later as deputy-director of the Unit for Research on Addictive Drugs. It was at Aberdeen that Hughes and Kosterlitz undertook their best-known work together. In an obituary for Kosterlitz, Hughes later recalled that, by 1969, "the interest in opiates was intense." In 1973, this interest grew even stronger when Solomon H. Snyder and his coworkers at Johns Hopkins University discovered that the brain contains receptor sites for opiate drugs. Hughes and Kosterlitz were among those who wondered why the body would have receptors for these foreign substances. Could it be that similar substances existed naturally in the body? A scientific race was soon underway to be the first to identify an opiate-like substance made by the body.

Discovery of the Body's Own Opiates

In 1975, Hughes and Kosterlitz isolated two such substances in pig brains. They dubbed these substances "enkephalins," from the Greek words for "in the head." Scientists soon suggested that people who have a high tolerance for pain might be able to produce large amounts of these kinds of compounds, while those who have a low tolerance for pain might be deficient in either their ability to produce these compounds or in the number of receptor sites for them. Scientists also proposed a mechanism, based on these sorts of compounds, that might explain narcotic addiction. Under normal circumstances, the body's natural opiate-like substances fill a certain number of receptor sites. When a person takes morphine or a related drug, it acts by filling the remaining sites. However, too much morphine overloads the system, causing the body to cut off its production of natural opiates. If the morphine is later withheld, the receptor sites are left empty, accounting for the symptoms of withdrawal.

Hughes's research interests have included the biochemistry of stress and drug abuse, the role of various compounds in the brain, and the design of drugs to treat brain and nervous system disorders. He has published over 200 papers and reviews on these topics. In addition to sharing the $15,000 Lasker prize with Kosterlitz and Snyder, Hughes has received a number of other honors. These include the Pacesetter Award from the U.S. National Institute of Drug Abuse, the Sandoz Prize and the Gaddum Medal from the British Pharmacological Society, and the Lucien Dautrebande Prize from the Belgium Foundation of Pathophysiologie. Hughes was elected a member of Great Britain's Royal Society in 1993. He is also a foreign member of the Academie Royale de Medicine of Belgium and a member of honor of the Rumanian Academy of Medical Sciences.

In 1977, Hughes returned to the University of London, where he rose to the position of professor of pharmacological biochemistry. Then in 1983, he took a job as director of the Parke-Davis Research Centre in Cambridge, England. The center, which is operated in collaboration with the University of Cambridge, has about 60 permanent staff as well as a very active postdoctoral and Ph.D. student training program. It has an annual budget of more than £6 million. Hughes later was given the additional title of vice president of research for Warner-Lambert/Parke-Davis, the global pharmaceutical company that runs the center. At the same time, he is an honorary professor of neuropharmacology at the University of Cambridge and a fellow of Wolfson College at Cambridge.

Hughes married Madeleine Jennings in 1967. The couple had one daughter, Katherine Bryony, before their divorce in 1981. Hughes later married Julie Pinnington. Their children are Georgina Anne, Joseph Francis, and John Stephen. In addition to spending time with his family, Hughes enjoys gardening, the countryside, theater, and literature.

SELECTED WRITINGS BY HUGHES:

Periodicals

(With T. W. Smith, H. W. Kosterlitz, L. A. Fothergill, B. A. Morgan, and H. R. Morris) "Identification of Two Related Pentapeptides from the Brain with Potent Opiate Agonist Activity." *Nature* (December 18, 1975): 577-580.

"Hans Kosterlitz (1903-96)." *Nature* (December 5, 1996): 418.

FURTHER READING:

Books

Muir, Hazel, ed. *Larousse Dictionary of Scientists.* New York: Larousse, 1994, p. 264.

Periodicals

"The Painkillers: Brain Chemists Are Honored." *Time* (December 4, 1978): 96.

Other

"Previous Lasker Award Winners: Basic Research Awards." http://www.laskerfoundation.com/prev1.html (October 2, 1997).

—Sketch by Linda Wasmer Smith

Hugh Esmor Huxley

Hugh Esmor Huxley
1924–

English-born American molecular biologist

Hugh Huxley has devoted his career to answering the question of how muscles contract. Although his initial answer—the sliding filament theory—has since become part of every standard biology and physiology textbook, Huxley has relentlessly pursued the finer details of muscle contraction well into his seventies.

Huxley was born to a middle-class Welsh family in Birkenhead, Cavendish, England, in 1924. His father, Thomas, was an accountant for the post office. But both he and Huxley's mother, Olwen (Roberts), "were people of remarkable intellect, great readers, lovers of music and with great moral strength and power of judgment," Huxley wrote in an autobiographical essay in 1996. "They instilled in my sister and me the idea that if we worked hard and tried hard enough we would win scholarships to University, perhaps even to Cambridge." As a boy, Huxley developed an interest in physics, and tinkered with electric motors, shocking coils, and short-wave radio receivers. "Atomic physics, relativity and quantum theory—or what little I knew of it—were to me then subjects of magical interest, offering glimpses of the ultimate nature of reality." When not puttering with science projects, he took long bicycle rides in the countryside.

Huxley entered Cambridge University in 1941 as World War II intensified. After two years of physics, however, he began to feel "very restive at playing no direct part in, nor even being very near to, the great wartime events that were taking place," and joined the Royal Air Force as a radar officer in 1943. During his four-year tour of duty, Huxley participated in the development of several radar advancements, work which later resulted in his being made a member of the Order of the British Empire.

Enters Molecular Biology Field

The bombing of Hiroshima and Nagasaki in 1945 devastated Huxley, causing him to fundamentally question his idealistic view of nuclear physics. He later wrote, "There was dismay and disillusionment that the first practical consequences of all that beautiful work in atomic and nuclear physics had been the atom bomb, and my reluctant conclusion that I would never be able to enjoy working in that field without feelings of guilt." He considered switching his course of study to economics, but then elected to finish his physics training, returning to Cambridge in 1947. "I wanted to do scientific research involving physics," he wrote, "but far away from its wartime uses." Believing he could make a contribution to the life sciences by applying physics techniques to biology and medicine, Huxley secured a place as a student researcher at the renowned Cavendish Laboratory at Cambridge, where such scientists as **James Watson** and **Francis Crick** then conducted their work as part of a small, newly formed research group of molecular biologists. At Cavendish, Huxley worked on his thesis, using x-ray crystallography to analyze the structure of muscle tissue.

Discovers Sliding Filament Structure

Upon receiving his Ph.D. in molecular biology in 1952, Huxley came to the Massachusetts Institute of Technology (MIT) to work with the newly invented electron microscope. Huxley soon realized that the images produced by x-ray crystallography and electron microcopy could provide much more information about the molecular structure of cells if they were analyzed together rather than separately. Huxley also became intrigued by the work of Jean Hanson, a fellow British researcher at MIT who had been using phased-contrast light microscopy to investigate the contraction of rabbit and insect muscle fibers. The two researchers combined their efforts and, as they produced increasingly improved images of their specimens, they slowly realized that muscle fibers were organized into bundles of overlapping filaments made from two proteins, actin and myosin. They published their findings in the journal *Nature* in 1953, but on the advice of their supervisor, did not include any of their ideas as to how the structure might work to make a muscle contract.

Later that year, Huxley met British physiologist **Andrew Huxley** (no relation), who was to win the 1963 Nobel Prize in Medicine or Physiology for his work on how nerves stimulate muscles to contract. Andrew Huxley, on a visit to MIT, expressed great interest in Hugh Huxley's theory of a sliding-filament structure, and said that he had been conducting research on the same idea. Their concept was that, in the presence of the biochemical adenosine triphosphate (ATP), the myosin and actin fibers would slide past each other, effectively shortening the muscle. In 1954, by agreement, the two Huxleys published adjacent papers in *Nature* describing their views on the principle. Time, improved instruments, and countless experiments have proven them correct, but Hugh Huxley's contribution, which was first published in a smaller paper that appeared after the 1953 paper with Hanson and before the 1954 *Nature* piece, has been obscured. Perhaps because of confusion over their last name or Andrew Huxley's greater prominence as a Nobel Prize winner, some science historians have mistakenly attributed the sliding filament theory to only Andrew Huxley. "I think I'm credited with the first mention of the sliding mechanism in print in 1953," Hugh Huxley said in a 1997 interview with contributor Karl Leif Bates.

In 1956, Hugh Huxley returned to Great Britain as a Medical Research Council external staff member at University College, London. Four years later, he moved to the Medical Research Council Laboratory of Molecular Biology at Cambridge, an institution which had grown out of the original Cavendish research group. Huxley eventually became department director in 1977 and served in that capacity until 1987 when he accepted a professorship at Brandeis University and their Rosensteil Basic Medical Sciences Research Center. He also became the director in 1988, a post he held until 1994.

More Precise Investigations

In the decades following his discovery of the sliding filament structure, Huxley devoted his career to first providing definitive experimental proof of his theory and then to understanding the exact chemical and physical process of the sliding mechanism or cross-bridge function. In the late 1950s, he spent several years trying to generate more detailed images of the fine structures of the fibers. As a diversion from this often frustrating work, he applied his skills to the study of virus structures. In the process he developed new staining techniques that, when later applied to his

muscle studies, resulted in his first significant images of the sliding mechanism. By the early 1970s, the efforts of Huxley and others had led in the widespread acceptance of the sliding filament theory. "In fact, several people asked me what I was going to work on next, now that the muscle problem was essentially solved, and were puzzled and disappointed when I said I would continue working on muscle because I did not think the evidence was really there yet," Huxley wrote in his autobiographical article.

Indeed, since that time Huxley has continued to probe the structure of the actin and myosin proteins themselves and how the chemical impulse from ATP is turned into motion by these large molecules. Determining how myosin and actin behave has been a persistent problem since it is very difficult to observe the molecules change their shape in microseconds. Huxley resorted to using more and more powerful x-ray beams for diffraction studies at the Cornell University and Argonne National Lab synchrotrons. Also, myosin itself proved a difficult protein to map. Its full structure was not determined until 1993. "It looks like it was built to change shape, but we still don't know how it does," Huxley told Bates. "It's a fascinating problem. Very intractable. And the problem continues to be important," Huxley added, "because researchers over the years have identified proteins very similar to actin and myosin that are responsible for all kinds of motion in non-muscle cells, like cells that change their shape. It's a very basic problem, and it's about time we figured it out."

SELECTED WRITINGS BY HUXLEY:

Periodicals

"A Personal View of Muscle and Motility Mechanisms," *Annual Review of Physiology*, (1996) Vol. 58: 1-19.

(With Jean Hanson) "Structural Basis of the Cross-Striations in Muscle," *Nature* 172 (Sept. 19, 1953): 530-532.

"The Mechanism of Muscular Contraction," *Science* 164 (June 20, 1969): 1356-1366.

FURTHER READING:

Other

Hugh Huxley. July 25, 1997. http://www.bio.brandeis.edu/pages/faculty/Huxley.html

—Sketch by Karl Leif Bates

Sof'ja Aleksandrovna Janovskaja (also transliterated as Sofia Yanovskaya)
1896–1966
Russian mathematician

Sof'ja Aleksandrovna Janovskaja made her mark in the mathematical community not for what she discovered but what she promoted: the legitimacy of mathematical logic as an independent and worthy discipline. A Bolshevik during Russia's civil war (1918–1921), Janovskaja believed mathematical logic was a science with real–world applications, distinctly different from the philosophical idealism that she considered an exclusively bourgeoisie concept.

Janovskaja was born on January 31, 1896, in Pruzhany, Poland (now part of Belarus). Although scholars know little about Janovskaja's early life, some evidence suggests that the Janovskajas were native Poles, perhaps belonging to the local gentry. When Janovskaja was just a few years old, the family moved to Odessa, where she was educated in the classics and mathematics. In 1915, Janovskaja enrolled in the Higher School for Women in Odessa, where she studied until the 1917 Revolution disrupted life throughout Russia.

Janovskaja began aiding anti–royalist political prisoners in 1917 as a member of the underground Red Cross, and in November of 1918 she joined the Bolshevik faction of the Russian Communist Party—a risky move, as the party remained illegal in Odessa until late the following year. In 1919 she served as a political commissar in the Red Army and edited the *Kommunist*, Odessa's daily political newspaper that was printed out of the city's catacombs. Janovskaja was a worker in the Odessa Regional Party until 1923, when she decided her duty as a party member would be better served by using the sciences to support the tenets of the revolution.

Pursues Career in Mathematics

In the early years of the Soviet Union, the principles of the revolution gave way for the advancement of women in professional—especially scientific—fields. Talented and dedicated, Janovskaja quickly established herself in the Soviet mathematical community. From 1924 to 1929, she studied at the Institute of Red Professors in Moscow and took seminars at Moscow State University. She began directing a seminar on mathematical methodology at Moscow State University in 1925, and she officially joined the faculty a year later. By 1931, she was a professor, and she earned her doctorate from the Mechanical–Mathematical Faculty of Moscow State University in 1935.

With the breakout of World War II, Janovskaja was evacuated to Perm, where she taught at Perm University from 1941 to 1943. She returned to Moscow in 1943 to take the post as director of Moscow State University's seminar on mathematical logic, and three years later she became the first faculty member to teach mathematical logic in the philosophy department.

Joins the Debate on Mathematical Logic

For years, Western dialectical philosophers dismissed mathematical logic as being idealist—that is, based on preconceived (or *a priori*), abstract notions of number. Such a logic, these philosophers charged, lacked any material applications, and therefore the pursuit of mathematical logic would not further the proletarian cause. Because the concepts used in mathematical logic were said to be predetermined in an ideal realm removed from the material world, mathematical logic appeared to lack the Marxist–Leninist worldview derived from historical experience.

Janovskaja disagreed with these dialecticians about the nature of mathematical logic. The notion of numbers, Janovskaja contended, came from observing groups of things in the material world, and from those many experiences arriving at the general idea of numbers. Other concepts and rules used in mathematical logic were similarly induced from the collective human experience in the material world. Janovskaja saw parallels between the laws governing logic and the Communist Party's monistic philosophy; her writings frequently include the statement by Lenin that all laws are the result of billions of experiences. Janovskaja not only promoted mathematical logic as a pure science, she became a mathematical historian, studying how mathematical methods had evolved throughout time. Janovskaja believed the value of both pursuits would be in their applicability to real–world problems.

Contributions as Educator

Janovskaja produced no original works, but her translations and commentaries made the works of **René Descartes**, Georg Hegel, and Karl Marx accessible to Russian students. She wrote several lucid articles for the *Great Soviet Encyclopedia*, explaining formalism, logistics, and mathematical paradoxes in simple language accessible to most readers. Still, scholars consider Janovskaja's greatest contributions to be her two journal articles on the history of mathematical logic in the Soviet Union: "The Foundations of Mathematics and Mathematical Logic" (1948) and "Mathematical Logic and Foundations of Mathematics" (1959).

In the classroom Janovskaja did not prove abstract theorems. She preferred to explore actual problems such as the hangman's paradox, in which a man sentenced to death must use his final request to put the hangman in a logical bind. Janovskaja taught at least two courses each school year, incorporating new ideas and material in such a way that she never taught the same course twice. According to Boris A. Kushner, a student who knew Janovskaja at Moscow State University during the 1960s, students found Janovskaja's style engaging and the faculty were not incensed by her lack of original work. "Her whole personality, kind, open and deep, the tremendous and dangerous war she conducted against demagogic dialecticians—all that commanded respect," Kushner wrote in his remembrance of the teacher in *Modern Logic*.

Janovskaja was recognized for her years of contribution to the field in 1951, when she received the prestigious Order of Lenin award. Her efforts to create a department of mathematical logic at Moscow State University were successful, and she was named the department's first chair on March 31, 1959. She died on October 24, 1966.

In many ways, Janovskaja is considered more of a philosopher than a mathematician. Her work is more concerned with the nature of problems and the methods to be used than with the answers themselves. In her 1963 paper, "On Philosophical Questions of Mathematical Logic," Janovskaja listed logical concepts and problems and described how they were philosophical in nature. "These questions have not been listed in order to offer any answers at all. I do not know sufficiently the questions to allow myself to do so."

SELECTED WRITINGS BY JANOVSKAJA:

"Foundations of mathematics and mathematical logic" *Matematika v SSSR za tridcat let 1917–1947* (1948): 11–45.

"Mathematical logic and foundations of mathematics" *Matematika v SSSR za sorok let 1917–1957* (1959): 13–120.

FURTHER READING:

Books

Anellis, Irving H. "Sof'ja Janovskaja," in *Women in Mathematics*. Edited by Louise S.Grinstein and Paul J. Campbell. New York: Greenwood Press, 1987, pp. 80–85.

Periodicals

Anellis, Irving H. "The Heritage of S.A. Janovskaja." *History and Philosophy of Logic* 8 (1987), 45–56.
Bashmakova, I.G., et. al. "Sofia Aleksandrovna Yanovskaya." *Russian Mathematical Surveys* 21 (May–June 1966), 213–221.
Bochenski, J.M. "S.A. Janovskaja." *Studies in Soviet Thought* 13 (1973), 1–10.
Kushner, Boris A. "Sof'ja Aleksandrovna Janovskaja: A Few Reminiscences." *Modern Logic* 6 (January 1996): 67–72.

Other

"Sof'ja Janovskaja." *Biographies of Women Mathematicians*. Http://www.scottlan.edu/lriddle/women/chronol.htm (July 22, 1997).

—Sketch by Bridget K. Hall

Alec John Jeffreys
1950–
English geneticist

Alec John Jeffreys is a geneticist who gave the world one of its most important tools for identifying human beings—a tool now used to catch criminals, establish paternity, and detect gene mutations. It's called "genetic fingerprinting"—a procedure for analyzing each individual's genetic code, the collection of genes in our cells that gives us our individual characteristics. Each human being has about 100,000 genes in the chemical form of deoxyribonucleic acid (DNA). The genetic information coded in these genes—ranging from the color of our hair to disorders like hemophilia—varies greatly between individuals. No two humans, except for identical twins, have the same genetic code.

Alec John Jeffreys

Jeffreys was born on January 9, 1950, in Oxford, England, the son of Sidney Victor Jeffreys and Joan (nee Knight) Jeffreys. He attended Luton Grammar School and Luten Sixth Form College. Jeffreys then went to Merton College in Oxford to study molecular biology, achieving a B.A. in 1972. He also earned an M.A. and D.Phil. at Merton in 1975. Jeffreys then became a European Molecular Biology Organisation Research Fellow at the University of Amsterdam. There he worked with Richard Flavell, another British molecular biologist, studying mammalian globin genes. Flavell is noted for his research on human globin genes, especially the molecular defects found in a group of diseases called thalassaemia, a group of genetic anemias.

After becoming more involved in the science of genetics with Flavell, Jeffreys moved to the University of Leicester, where he became a lecturer in 1977, a reader in 1984, and professor of genetics in 1987. It was at Leicester that he made his most important contribution to science, discovering the unique genetic "fingerprint" in 1984. Jeffreys was studying the gene that codes for the protein myoglobin, trying to identify regions of DNA that varied distinctively between families. (Myoglobin transports oxygen into muscle tissue in both animals and humans.) He knew that a number of short sequences in the gene repeated several times. And in fact, Jeffreys had found that the number of times these "chunks" repeated seemed to vary from tmdividual to individual. At first, Jeffreys only thought he had stumbled onto a way to identify

markers for the myoglobin gene. But eventually he came to believe that these repeated segments of genes were unique to each individual—just like a fingerprint.

Hunting down the Human DNA Fingerprint

Strangely enough, Jeffreys's work on myoglobin began in an unusual place—a deep freeze locker at the British Antarctic Survey's Cambridge headquarters. It was here, among frozen meat and tissue samples contributed by polar researchers, that Jeffreys found the raw materials for his experiments. "To do the work we needed large amounts of myoglobin-rich tissue, which is why we went to the British Antarctic Survey—for whales and seals are world record holders in the amounts of myoglobin they contain. They need lots of the stuff to supply their muscles with oxygen during their long dives," Jeffreys said in an interview with author Robin McKie and geneticist Walter Bodmer in a book on genetics and the Human Genome Project called *The Book of Man.*

Armed with grey seal tissue, Jeffreys set out to identify the myoglobin gene. Then he found its counterpart in human genes and devised a way to capture the distinctive "fingerprint" of each person's repeated fragments in a photograph. He used a special detergent to break open the human cells and release the DNA code into solution. Then a restriction enzyme was used to break the chain of DNA codes at the sites near where they started to repeat. The fragments of DNA were then combined with a membrane and allowed to attach to a radioactive probe. X rays were taken of the membrane to show where the radioactive probes attached. By taking these x rays, Jeffreys could see the repeated segments of DNA as black images on film. He had, in essence, created the first DNA fingerprint.

"It was a very rare occurrence in science," Jeffreys said in *The Book of Man.* "It was a blinding flash. In those five golden minutes (of pulling the film out of the developing tank) my research career went whizzing off in a completely new direction. I was channeled away from looking at disease genes and was thinking about something new—DNA fingerprinting. The last thing that had been on my mind was anything to do with identification, family analyses, forensics, paternity suits and all that. However, I would have been a complete idiot not to spot the applications."

In 1988 scientist Henry Erlich added to Jeffreys's work when he developed a method of DNA fingerprinting so sensitive that it could be used to identify an individual from an extremely small sample of hair, blood, semen, or skin. Erlich's technique used Jeffreys's traditional method and combined it with a technique called polymerase chain reaction (PCR). First discovered by **Kary Mullis**, PCR was used to duplicate DNA and thus copy the genetic code. Erlich was able to duplicate and heat separate the DNA fragments from a single human hair root many times using PCR. PCR multiplied the DNA from one single hair to an amount equivalent to that found in a million identical strands of hair. The amplified DNA was then to be used to obtain a DNA fingerprint.

Jeffreys Achieves Worldwide Fame

Jeffreys continued to work in the field of genetic fingerprinting, participating in some of the most famous murder and manhunt cases of this century. In a famous murder case in Cardiff, England, in 1989, PCR was combined with Jeffreys's traditional technique for the first time to extract and identify DNA from a miniscule amount of bone. Workmen at a victorian house in Cardiff had dug up an old carpet, containing a black plastic bag that surrounded a skeleton. The victim's hands had been tied at the back, so the police launched a murder investigation. Several social workers stepped forward to identify the victim as Karen Price, a 15-year-old girl who had been missing since 1981. But the police had to be sure.

They sent the bone for DNA sampling to Erika Hagelberg, a scientist at the Oxford Institute of Molecular Medicine. Working with Jeffreys, Hagelberg tried to identify the DNA from the skeleton—but found it had been in the ground so long and disintegrated so much that PCR could not generate the necessary lengths of DNA required for a fingerprint. So a different form of genetic fingerprinting had to be developed.

Working with Jeffreys, Hagelberg was able to find repeating DNA sequences other than the large ones usually present in a genetic fingerprint. In fact some of the repeats they discovered in the skeleton's DNA were only a couple of base pairs long. These repeats varied from person to person and could be amplified millions of times and grown in a laboratory. After taking blood samples from Karen Price's parents, and amplifying Karen's bones many times, Jeffreys was finally able to show that the probability that the skeleton was Karen's was 99.9%. Police soon closed in on Karen's acquaintances and two of them, Idris Ali and Alan Charlton, were put on trial for murder. Though a witness also testified against them, it was the strength of the genetic evidence that finally sent them to prison—in Ali's case, for life.

At about the same time, Hagelberg and Jeffreys had been working on this new type of PCR typing to solve an even more sinister problem—the whereabouts of one of World War II's most evil war criminals, Josef Mengele. He was known as the "angel of death" at Aushwitz for sending thousands of Jews to the gas chambers as well as making thousands the subjects of "medical research"—meaning surgery

without anesthetics, and experiments involving castration and radiation exposure.

Mengele fled Aushwitz as it was being overrun by Soviet forces in 1945 and disappeared into a network of Nazi sympathizers in South America. Finally, he was traced to a grave in southern Brazil. Though pathologists found that the man's exhumed skeleton and teeth matched those of the doctor, Israeli police chiefs questioned whether the body was Mengele.

The police sent a sample of bone to Jeffreys. Working with Hagelberg, he was able to identify a tiny amount of DNA from the sample, which had been in the ground for six years. Meanwhile, Rolf Mengele, Josef's son, agreed to give a blood sample. It matched the sample from the South American grave with a 99.8% certainty. "We could only extract about thirty cells worth of DNA but that was enough to create a profile using about ten different PCR probes," Jeffreys said in *The Book of Man*.

Jeffreys Improves Techniques for Fingerprinting

The process of genetic fingerprinting can take as long as four to six weeks in a commercial laboratory today. Jeffreys made scientific history again in 1991 when he announced the development of a refined version of the test allowing results to be obtained much faster—in as little as two days.

Jeffreys technique of genetic fingerprinting has been used in a wide variety of ways—to solve crimes like rape and murder, to identify the remains of soldiers, to identify people killed in Argentina by the military junta in the 1980s, and by biologists to protect endangered species. In a landmark study, Jeffreys and other researchers used the technique to assess the gene mutations apparent in children whose families had been exposed to radiation during the Chernobyl meltdown in the Ukraine. Working with Russian researcher, Yuri Dubrova, Jeffreys found that children living in irradiated areas had twice the frequency of mutation when compared to a control groups in England. The study made headlines in April 1996, when Jeffreys and Dubrova announced their results near the tenth anniversary of the Chernobyl accident. Jeffreys and Dubrova do not know whether the genetic mutations will mean continued health problems for the Ukraine families studied, but they are continuing their research.

Though genetic fingerprinting has come in for its share of criticism—the O. J. Simpson case, for instance, turned on supposed mistakes made by lab personnel in creating the fingerprints—Jeffreys remains a proponent of his original method. The problem is that DNA fingerprints have evolved to mean any one of a number of techniques—including ones using single probes—while Jeffreys' original method used more accurate multi-locus probes, which indeed provided a truly unique "fingerprint." The single probe tests do not have the absolute, rigid accuracy of Jeffreys original procedure. "Lawyers have stood up and said these tests do not have the individual specificity of ordinary fingerprints," Jeffreys said in *The Book of Man.* "Then they allege that we are guilty of misleading the public and the judiciary. We are not, and that really annoys me."

Jeffreys married Susan Miles in 1971. They have two daughters. His leisure interests include walking, swimming, postal history, and reading "unimproving novels."

Jeffreys is an international research scholar at the Howard Hughes Medical Institute, a nonprofit source of support for biomedical research, as well as working at the University of Leicester. He became Wolfson Research Professor of the Royal Society in 1991. He won the Davy Medal from the Royal Society in 1987 and the Analytica Prize from the German Society of Chemistry in 1988.

SELECTED WRITINGS BY JEFFREYS:

Periodicals

"Human Minisatellite Mutation Rate after the Chernobyl Accident." *Nature* (April 25, 1996): 683-86.

FURTHER READING:

Books

Bodmer, Walter and Robin McKie. "Probing the Present" chapter in *The Book of Man: The Human Genome Project.* Scribner: New York, 1985.

—*Sketch by Barbara Boughton*

William P. Jencks
1927–
American biochemist

William P. Jencks has made a number of important contributions to the field of physical organic chemistry. One of the first topics he studied was the mechanisms by which enzymes catalyze reactions and how these mechanisms affect changes in living organisms. He also studied the way in which nucleophilic substitution reactions with carbon take place, a topic of considerable interest since such reactions are

William P. Jencks

common both in organic chemistry and in biochemistry. Beginning in the 1970s, Jencks also became interested in the way chemical changes in muscle cells make physical movement possible. He developed a four-step explanation for this process.

Jencks was born in Bar Harbor, Maine, on August 15, 1927. His father was a concert pianist, but eventually left performing in order to devote his time to composing. Jencks describes his father's works as "very modern and very difficult, both to perform and to appreciate. Whether his music is just another collection of dissonant notes, or an important but mostly unknown contribution to modern music remains a major question."

Jencks attended St. Paul's High School in Baltimore, Maryland, and, upon graduation, enrolled at Harvard College. Although he took some courses in chemistry, he did not find them very interesting and graduated with a degree, instead, in English. After graduation, Jencks decided to enroll in the Harvard Medical School because he "couldn't think of what else to do." After his first year at medical school, he spent a summer at the Marine Biological Laboratory at Woods Hole, Massachusetts. There he not only studied with eminent scholars, such as **Albert Szent-Gyorgyi** and **George Wald**, but also met his future wife, Miriam Ehlrich. The Jencks later had two children.

Upon the recommendation of his friend, George Wald, Jencks decided to spend two years of postdoctoral study with the eminent German-American biochemist **Fritz Lipmann**. It was at Lipmann's suggestion that Jencks began his studies of enzymes. He began by studying the way in which an enzyme called coenzyme A transferase converts fatty acids to thiol esters, an important step in the metabolism of fatty acids. Jencks was able to work out the steps by which this process occurred and showed how it was possible for a very large molecule such as coenzyme A transferase to provide the energy required to make this series of reactions occur.

Jencks' work with Lipmann was interrupted in 1953 when he was drafted into the U.S. Army. On Lipmann's recommendation, he was assigned to the Army Medical Service Graduate School at Walter Reed Hospital in Washington, D.C. There he carried out some interesting studies on the relative concentrations of various proteins in the blood serum of 1,516 patients.

After Jencks was discharged from the Army in 1955, he returned to Harvard and a third postdoctoral year with Lipmann. He then spent a year as a U.S. Public Health Service Fellow in the laboratory of Nobel Laureate **Robert B. Woodward**. Jencks tells that he spoke with Woodward only three times during his year in the laboratory, once upon arrival, once upon departure, and once during a chance meeting in a hallway.

During this period, however, Jencks became interested in one of the most common, most interesting, and most thoroughly studied reactions in chemistry, nucleophilic substitution on a carbon atom. Although this reaction usually can be expressed by means of a very simple chemical equation, the reaction itself tends to be very complex with a number of intermediary steps, each of which has a very different reaction rate. Jencks was able to provide additional insight as to how such reactions occur and how their mechanisms differ depending on pH, concentration, solvent, and other factors.

In 1957, Jencks was invited to join the faculty at Brandeis University in Waltham, Massachusetts, as Assistant Professor of Biochemistry. The appointment was something of a challenge since Brandeis was a relatively new university, and it had essentially no organized biochemistry department. Jencks has written of the exciting times he spent with the eight faculty members in the new department trying to decide how they were going to make it succeed. He eventually rose to the position of Associate Professor in 1960, to Professor in 1963, and finally to Professor Emeritus in 1996. He also served as Acting Chairman of the Department of Biochemistry from 1968 to 1970.

Over the last 20 years, Jencks has devoted much of his research efforts to understanding the mechanisms by which chemical changes in muscle cells lead to the movement of muscles. He was able to show how the hydrolysis of adenosine triphosphate (ATP) is involved in the physical movement of calcium ions through a cell. Jencks points out that the mechanism he worked out for muscle activation also applies to a number of other biochemical and physical changes in the body.

Jencks has summarized and reported on his research findings in over 400 papers, books, reviews, and other publications. Some of the honors he has received include election to the National Academy of Sciences (1971) and to the Royal Society (1992), as well as the American Society of Biological Chemists Award for 1993, the American Chemical Society's James Flack Norris Award in Physical Organic Chemistry in 1995, and the American Chemical Society Repligen Award for Chemistry of Biological Processes in 1996. Jencks has also held the Gyula and Katica Tauber Chair in Biochemistry and Molecular Pharmacodynamics at Brandeis since 1977. He has been selected to present 35 invited lectures in 15 states and four foreign countries. He has also served on more than 20 editorial and advisory boards and committees, including those of publications such as *Chemical Reviews*, *Biochemistry*, *Journal of the American Chemical Society*, and the *Journal of Biological Chemistry*.

SELECTED WRITINGS BY JENCKS:

Books

Catalysis in Chemistry and Enzymology. New York: McGraw-Hill Book Co., 1969; reprinted by Dover Publication, 1987.
(With R. H. Abeles and P. A. Frey) *Biochemistry.* New York: Jones & Bartlett, 1992.

Periodicals

"From chemistry to biochemistry to catalysis to movement." *Annual Review of Biochemistry* 66 (1997): 1-18.
(With S. Eldin) "Lifetimes of iminium ions in aqueous solution." *Journal of the American Chemical Society* 117 (1995): 4851-4857.
(With T. T. Simopoulos) "Alkaline phosphatase is an almost perfect enzyme." *Biochemistry* 33 (1994): 10375-10380.

FURTHER READING:

Periodicals

"James Flack Norris Award in Physical Organic Chemistry." *Chemical & Engineering News* 17 (October 1994): 71.

Niels K. Jerne

Jencks, William P. "From chemistry to biochemistry to catalysis to movement." *Annual Review of Biochemistry* 66 (1997): 1-18.

—*Sketch by David Newton*

Niels K. Jerne
1911–1994
Danish immunologist

Considered both the founder of modern cellular immunology and its greatest theoretician, Niels K. Jerne shared the 1984 Nobel Prize for medicine or physiology with Cesar Milstein and Georges J. F. Köhler for his body of work that explained the function of the immune system, the body's defense mechanism against disease and infection. He was best known for three theories showing how antibodies— the substances which protect the body from foreign substances such as viruses and poisons—are produced, formed, and regulated by the immune system. His theories were initially met with skepticism, but they later became the cornerstones of immunological knowledge. By 1984, when he received the prize, colleagues agreed that he should have been recognized for his important contributions to the field much earlier than he was. Jerne's theories became the

starting point from which other scientists, notably 1960 Nobel Prize winner **Frank MacFarlane Burnett**, furthered our understanding of how the body protects itself against disease.

Niels Kaj (sometimes transliterated Kai) Jerne was born on December 23, 1911, in London, England, to Danish parents Else Marie Lindberg and Hans Jessen Jerne. The family moved to the Netherlands at the beginning of World War I. Jerne earned his baccalaureate in Rotterdam in 1928 and studied physics for two years at the University of Leiden. Twelve years later, he entered the University of Copenhagen to study medicine, receiving his doctorate in 1951 at the age of forty. From 1943 until 1956 he worked at the Danish State Serum Institute, conducting research in immunology.

In 1955, Jerne traveled to the United States with noted molecular biologist **Max Delbrück** to become a research fellow at the California Institute of Technology at Pasadena. The two worked closely together, and it was not until his final two weeks at the Institute that Jerne completed work on his first major theory— on selective antibody formation. At this time, scientists believed that specific antibodies (molecules that defend the body from infection) do not exist until an antigen (any substance originating outside the body such as a virus, snake venom, or transplanted organs) is introduced and acts as a template from which cells in the immune system create the appropriate antibody to eliminate it. (Antigens and antibodies have surface patches, called combining sites, with distinct patterns. When an antibody and antigen with complementary combining sites meet, they become attached, fitting together like a lock and key.) Jerne's theory postulated instead that the immune system inherently contains all the specific antibodies it needs to fight specific antigens; the appropriate antibody, one of millions that are already present in the body, attaches to the antigen, thus neutralizing or destroying the antigen and its threat to the body.

Not until some months after developing his theory did Jerne share it with Delbrück, who sent it to the *Proceedings of the National Academy of Sciences* for publication. Jerne later noted that his theory probably would have been forgotten, except that it caught the attention of Burnett, leading him to the development in 1959 of his clonal selection theory, which built on Jerne's hypothesis to show how specific antibody-producing cells multiply to produce necessary quantities of an antigen's antibody. The following year, Jerne left his research in immunology to became chief medical officer with the World Health Organization in Geneva, Switzerland, where he oversaw the departments of biological standards and immunology. From 1960 to 1962, he served on the faculty at the University of Geneva's biophysics department.

From 1962 to 1966, Jerne was professor of microbiology at the University of Pittsburgh in Pennsylvania. During this period he developed a method, now known as the Jerne plaque assay, to count antibody-producing cells by first mixing them with other cells containing antigen material, causing the cells to produce an antibody that combines with red blood cells. Once combined, the blood cells are then destroyed, leaving a substance called plaque surrounding the original antibody-producing cells, which can then be counted. Jerne became director of the Paul Ehrlich Institute, in Frankfurt, Germany, in 1966, and, in 1969, established the Basel Institute for Immunology in Switzerland, where he remained until taking emeritus status in 1980.

In 1971, Jerne unveiled his second major theory, which deals with how the immune system identifies and differentiates between self molecules (belonging to its host) and nonself molecules (invaders). Noting that the immune system is specific to each individual, immunologists had concluded that the body's self-tolerance cannot be inherited and is therefore learned. Jerne postulated that such immune system "learning" occurs in the thymus, an organ in the upper chest cavity where the cells that recognize and attack antigens multiply, while those that could attack the body's own cells are suppressed. Over time, mutations among cells that recognize antigens increase the number of different antibodies the body has at hand, thereby increasing the immune system's arsenal against disease.

Jerne introduced what is considered his most significant work in 1974—the network theory, wherein he proposed that the immune system is a dynamic self-regulating network that activates itself when necessary and shuts down when not needed. At that time, scientists knew that the immune system contains two types of immune system cells, or lymphocytes: B cells, which produce antibodies, and T cells, which function as "helpers" to the B cells by killing foreign cells, or by regulating the B cells either by suppressing or stimulating their antibody producing activity. Further, antibody molecules produced by the B cells also contain antigen-like components (idiotypes) which can attract another antibody (anti-idiotype), allowing one antibody to recognize another antibody as well as an antigen. Jerne's theory expanded on this knowledge, speculating that a delicate balance of lymphocytes and antibodies and their idiotypes and anti-idiotypes exists in the immune system until an antigen is introduced. The antigen, he believed, replaces the anti-idiotype attached to the antibody. The immune system then senses the displacement and, in an attempt to find the anti-idiotype a "mate," produces more of the original antibody. This chain-reaction strengthens the body's immunity to the invading antigen. Experiments later demonstrated that immunization with an anti-idiotype will stimulate the production of the required antibody. It may well be that because of Jerne's network theory, vaccinations of the future will administer antibodies rather than antigens to bring about immunity to disease.

Jerne retired to southern France with his wife, Ursula Alexandra Kohl, whom he married in 1964; the couple had two sons. A citizen of both Denmark and Great Britain, Jerne received honorary degrees from American and European universities, was a foreign honorary member of the American Academy of Arts and Sciences, a member of the Royal Danish Academy of Sciences, and won, among other honors, the Marcel Benorst Prize in 1979 and the Paul Ehrlich Prize in 1982. A devoted scientist, Jerne had little interest in politics. He disliked clocks and other technological devices. In his spare time, he enjoyed literature, music, and French wine. At a reception in Basel to celebrate his Nobel Prize, Jerne, as reported in the *New York Times,* joked: "It would have been nice if it had come earlier to convince my brothers and sisters that I am not the oddball they regarded me for a long time. I will enjoy the prize and enjoy life." Jerne died on October 7, 1994 at his home in Pont du Gard, southern France.

SELECTED WRITINGS BY JERNE:

Periodicals

"The Natural Selection Theory of Antibody Formation: Ten Years Later, Cold Springs Harbor Laboratory of Quantitative Biology." *Phage and the Origins of Molecular Biology* (1966): 301-12.

"The Natural Selection Theory of Antibody Formation." *Proceedings of the National Academy of Sciences, U.S.A.* 41 (1955): 849-56.

"Antibodies and Learning." *The Neurosciences* (1967): 200-05.

"The Immune System." *Scientific American* 229 (1973): 52-60.

"Plaque-Forming Cells: Method and Theory." *Transplantation Reviews* 18 (1974): 130-91.

"Toward a Network Theory of the Immune System." *Annales d'immunologie* C125 (1974): 373-89.

FURTHER READING:

Books

Wasson, Tyler, ed. *Nobel Prize Winners.* New York: H. W. Wilson, 1987, pp. 509-11.

Nobel Prize Winners: Physiology or Medicine. Englewood Cliffs, NJ: Salem Press, 1991, pp. 1447-54.

William Summer Johnson

Periodicals

New York Times (16 October 1984): C2.
"Niels K. Jerne, Nobelist in Medicine, Dies" (obituary). *Washington Post* (9 October 1994): B8).
"Nobel Prize for Inventors of Monoclonals." *New Scientist* (18 October 1984): 3-5.
Pace, Eric. "Niels K. Jerne, 82, Authority on Immunology" (obituary). *New York Times* (8 October 1994).
Ur, Jonathon W. "The 1984 Nobel Prize in Medicine." *Science* (30 November 1984): 1025-28.

—*Sketch by David Petechuk*

William Summer Johnson
1913–1995

American organic chemist

William S. Johnson devoted his career to developing methods that improved the manufacture of synthetic biological chemical compounds such as steroids, hormones, and vitamins. His work made important scientific and social breakthroughs such as birth control pills possible.

Johnson was born in New Rochelle, New York on February 24, 1913. He attended Amherst College and graduated with a bachelor's degree in 1936. Johnson accepted a post as a chemistry instructor at Amherst after graduation, but left in 1937 to pursue advanced studies.

Johnson enrolled at Harvard and earned a doctorate in organic chemistry in 1940. He joined the faculty of the University of Wisconsin as an instructor in 1940, and during his 14-year tenure moved through the ranks to a full professorship. In 1954, he was named the Homer Adkins Professor at the university, a title he held until he moved to Stanford University in 1960.

Johnson made his mark early. Pressured by the desperate need for better ways to treat wounds during World War II in the 1940s, researchers had developed a process for synthesizing corticoid steroids to reduce inflammation in wounds. The process, however, was cumbersome and uncertain. Johnson studied the problem and devised a new method to create corticoid steroids in the laboratory; Johnson's process eliminated two-thirds of the steps required in the earlier technique used to synthesize corticoid steroids.

Unique Approach Met with Skepticism

Johnson's breakthrough was a result of his unique approach to the study of biological chemical compounds. Johnson abandoned the classic approach to synthesis; instead, he looked for ways to imitate the biological processes that produced the compounds. Johnson dubbed his research strategy the "biomimetric approach to total synthesis."

The scientific community greeted his approach with some skepticism. The structures of the compounds Johnson hoped to synthesize were so complex, and the chain of reactions that produced the compounds in living organisms so intricate, that many contemporary researchers perceived Johnson's work as a dead end. His initial success with corticoid steroids, however, proved the doubters wrong, and Johnson's method of investigation began to shape methods of research in laboratories around the world.

Johnson's techniques sparked an explosion of productivity throughout the 1950s. His work—both the research he conducted and the influence of his methods—resulted in the successful synthesis of nearly all the biologically important steroids identified at the time. As a class, steroids include the adrenal hormones, vitamin D, bile acids, and the anti-inflammatory corticoid steroids. Steroids also include male and female sex hormones. Johnson's work with these steroids made effective oral contraceptives possible. Although the synthesis of anti-inflammatory agents and vitamins had profound significance from a medical standpoint, Johnson's contribution to the development of oral contraceptives had a huge impact beyond science. Safe, reliable, inexpensive, and easy-to-use birth control has influenced women's roles, economics, and the structure of families in ways that are being still being evaluated. In 1958, Johnson earned the American Chemical Manufacturers Award for Creative Research in Organic Chemistry.

Builds Stanford's Chemistry Department

In 1960, Johnson left the University of Wisconsin to accept a post with Stanford University as a professor and executive head of the chemistry department. It was the era of the Cold War, and science education was a national priority spurred by both the weapons and space races. Resources and support for ambitious science programs were abundant, and Johnson was recruited with promises of a new building and plans to expand Stanford's chemistry faculty.

Johnson tackled the Stanford challenge with energy. From 1960 to 1969, he added 13 faculty members to the chemistry department, attracting and selecting some of the top minds in the field. His finds included **Carl Djerassi**, **Harden McConnell**, **Paul Flory**, and **Henry Taube**. Flory and Taube would win Nobel Prizes for their work. Johnson's reputation, coupled with the respect his enlarged faculty enjoyed, helped Stanford evolve as an international center for academic scientific research. During this time, Johnson earned many awards, including the Synthetic Organic Chemical Manufacturers Award for Creative Research in Organic Chemistry in 1963 and the Nichols Medal Award in 1968.

Johnson resigned from his position as head of Stanford's chemistry department in 1969. He was named to an endowed chair, serving as the Jackson-Wood Professor of Chemistry until 1978. Under this title, he won the Roussel Prize from France in 1970 and the ACS Roger Adams Award in 1977. Named professor emeritus in 1978, Johnson continued his research work and was involved in laboratory projects until just a few months before his death.

The author of more than 250 scholarly articles, Johnson continued to earn recognition after he retired. He won the National Medal of Science in 1987 and was honored by numerous universities with honorary degrees and named lectures. In 1985, Stanford University established the William S. Johnson Symposium in Organic Chemistry, an annual conference that attracts presenters and participants from around the world.

His numerous professional affiliations included membership in the International Congress of Pure and Applied Chemistry, the National Academy of Science, the National Science Foundation, the American Chemical Society, and the executive board of the *Journal of Organic Chemistry*.

Johnson died on August 19, 1995, the result of circulatory and heart problems. At the time of his death, he was studying asymmetric synthesis methodology. The body of his work was only one of his bequests. During his career, Johnson mentored more than 300 pre- and post-doctoral students, training a cadre of new talent to accept the challenge of continuing and expanding his work.

SELECTED WRITINGS BY JOHNSON:

Periodicals

"Biomimetric Polyene Cyclizations." *Angew Chemical International,* 1976.
"Biomimetric Polyene Cyclizations. Asymmetric induction by a chiral center remote from the xx center 11Alpha-methylprogestterone." *Journal of the American Chemical Society*, 1976.
"Direct Formation of the Steroid Nucleus by Nonenzyme biogenetic–like Cyclization. Cyclization and Proof of Structure and Configuration of Products." *Journal of the American Chemical Society*, 1973.

FURTHER READING:

Books

American Men and Women of Science, 18th Edition, New Providence, New Jersey: R. R. Bowker, 1992-93, Vol. 4, p.117.
Eckes, Kristin A., ed. *Who's Who in Science and Engineering,* New Providence, New Jersey: Reed Publishing, 1996, p.483.

Periodicals

"William S. Johnson, 82, Chemist Who Devised Synthesis Methods" Obituary. *The New York Times*, August 29, 1995, p. A-11.
Obituary. *Stanford Alumni News*, August 30, 1995.

—Sketch by Angie Mullig

Mary Ellen Jones
1922–1996
American biochemist

Mary Ellen Jones, a prominent biochemist and enzymologist, became known for isolating carbamyl phosphate, one of a number of molecules that are the building blocks of biosynthesis. By synthesizing this substance, Jones helped lay the groundwork for major advances in biochemistry, particularly in research on deoxyribonucleic acid (DNA) and ribonucleic acid (RNA). She has explored enzyme action, how the products of metabolism (metabolites) control enzyme activity, and metabolic pathways. The metabolic pathway is essential for cell division and differentiation, and studies of it are crucial to the understanding of the developing fetus and child, of cancer, and of some mutations in humans. Jones was recognized for her work by being named the first woman Kenan Professor and department head in the School of Medicine at the University of North Carolina at Chapel Hill in 1980.

Mary Ellen Jones was born on December 25, 1922, in La Grange, Illinois, to Elmer Enold and Laura Anna (Klein) Jones. She earned her bachelor of science degree from the University of Chicago in 1944. She then went on to receive her Ph.D. in biochemistry at Yale University, where she was a U.S. Public Health Service Fellow in the department of physiological chemistry from 1950 to 1951.

Jones solidly established herself as an enzymologist during her postdoctoral studies with **Fritz Lipmann**, a 1953 Nobel Prize winner for physiology or medicine, who was then director of the Chemical Research Laboratory at Massachusetts General Hospital. In the 1950s, he and a team of researchers discovered a group of molecules that were considered the building blocks of biosynthesis. It was during this time that Jones isolated carbamyl phosphate, one of the most important of these essential molecules. The synthesis of this molecule made important advances in biochemistry possible. Carbamyl phosphate is present in all life. Knowledge of it led to scientific understanding of two universally essential pathways of biosynthesis, the production of a chemical compound by a living organism.

Jones and Lipmann noticed that during certain biosynthetic reactions, the energy-releasing reaction was a splitting of adenosine triphosphate (ATP) that yielded a mononucleotide and inorganic pyrophosphate. The discovery suggested that DNA and RNA synthesis might occur with the liberation of inorganic pyrophosphate from ATP and other trinucleotides—a suggestion that was later proven true by the biochemist **Arthur Kornberg**. Jones remained in the Biochemical Research Laboratory at Massachusetts General Hospital until 1957 and served as a faculty member in the Department of Biochemistry at Brandeis University until 1966.

In 1966, Dr. Jones joined the University of North Carolina as an associate professor of biochemistry, was promoted to professor two years later, and in 1968 was appointed professor in the department of zoology. She left Chapel Hill in 1971 for the University of Southern California and was a professor of

biochemistry there until 1978. She returned to the University of North Carolina as a professor and chair of the biochemistry department and was named a Kenan Professor in 1980.

Author of over ninety papers related to biochemistry, Dr. Jones received international recognition for her creative scientific research. Having become a member of the Institute of Medicine in 1981, she was inducted into the National Academy of Sciences in 1984, and in 1986 served as president of the American Society of Biological Chemists and was named the North Carolina American Chemical Society distinguished chemist. She was awarded the Wilbur Lucius Cross Medal in 1982 by the graduate school at Yale University for her work as a "gifted investigator of the chemistry of life." In 1989, she resigned as department head, but continued teaching and working on research projects until her retirement in 1995. She died on August 23, 1996 in Waltham, Massachusetts.

SELECTED WRITINGS BY JONES:

Books

Purine and Pyrimidine Nucleotide Metabolism. Academic Press, 1978.
Structural and Organization Aspects of Metabolic Regulation. New York: Wiley, 1990.

FURTHER READING:

Other

Jones, Mary Ellen. Correspondence with Janet Kieffer Kelley. 6 March 1994.

Periodicals

Fountain, Henry. "Mary Ellen Jones, 73, Crucial Researcher on DNA" (obituary). *New York Times* (7 September 1996): 13.

—Sketch by Janet Kieffer Kelley

Ernst Pascual Jordan
1902–1980
German mathematical physicist

As a young man Pascual Jordan was an essential mathematical presence in the founding of two of the main branches of quantum theory, while his later career mixed politics and popular writing along with theoretical work in biology, mathematics, geology, and cosmology. During the 1930s and 1940s, he came under the spell of Adolf Hitler's National Socialist Party, an attitude that limited his influence outside of Germany. He was rehabilitated after World War II and even served in West Germany's legislature.

Ernst Pascual Jordan, known as Pascual all his life, was born on October 19, 1902, in Hannover, Germany. His father, also named Ernst Pascual Jordan, was a successful painter of portraits, buildings, and landscapes. Pascual's mother, Eva Fischer Jordan, was interested in mathematics and biology, interests that her son continued throughout his life. Pascual Jordan decided to pursue mathematics and physics while he was in the Hannover gymnasium (equivalent to an American high school), which led to two years at the Hannover polytechnic school (*Technische Hochschule*). Although the level of instruction at the polytechnic school was low, Jordan was able to transfer into Göttingen University, at that time perhaps the greatest center of applied mathematics in the world. He obtained his Ph.D. at Göttingen in 1924 and stayed at the University for several years assisting professors. One such assignment, before he obtained his degree, was to have profound reverberations. He assisted mathematician Richard Courant in preparing volume one of what was to become the "bible" of applied mathematics, Courant and David Hilbert's *Methods of Mathematical Physics*. This work put Jordan in touch with what were then the latest mathematical techniques and showed how they connected to applications.

Jordan was a shy, unambitious graduate assistant at Germany's famous Göttingen University when he began the work that brought him his greatest fame. At that time, he had studied physics for less than four years, and not done all that well at it either. Like many theoreticians, he was not very astute in the laboratory and had even failed the introductory physics lab. His doctoral thesis proposed modifications in the conclusions of **Albert Einstein's** early work with quantum theory, but Einstein himself pointed out Jordan's errors.

Despite this unauspicious beginning, Jordan became one of the founding fathers of quantum mechanics. Jordan's main input into quantum mechanics developed as a result of his interplay with the much more famous physicist **Werner Heisenberg**, as well as his employment as **Max Born's** assistant. Born was 20 years older than Jordan and already one of the leading physicists in the world. Heisenberg, almost as young and inexperienced as Jordan, had previously been an assistant to Born as had **Wolfgang Pauli** another young physicist who created large parts of the quantum theory.

In July 1925 Heisenberg had announced a new formulation for the laws of the electron. Heisenberg's computations seemed to be a breakthrough, although very difficult to apply—Heisenberg's mathematics were unorthodox and poorly understood by other physicists. Nevertheless, Heisenberg was immediately invited to conferences all over Europe to discuss further his ideas, which were the first version of quantum mechanics.

When Heisenberg returned to Göttingen after a busy summer of exploring his new formulation with leading physicists, Born and Jordan had a surprise for him. Mathematicians, they reported, had already developed a theory that applied exactly to the unorthodox behavior of the electron as worked out by Heisenberg. The mathematical system is called matrix multiplication, and it had been developed in the nineteenth century by French and English mathematicians for reasons that had nothing to do with subatomic particles, which were then unknown.

Jordan was familiar with matrix algebra from working with Courant. Born also knew the matrix concept and had recognized while Heisenberg was traveling that matrices greatly simplified how Heisenberg's calculations could be written. Furthermore, matrix theory implies physical properties that can be observed. Born was greatly excited by this discovery and, with Jordan, began calculating all the basic ideas of the electron in terms of matrices while Heisenberg was still on the road. Almost immediately Born underwent a minor mental breakdown as a result of the excitement and hard work, leaving Jordan to complete the difficult calculations. When Heisenberg returned to Göttingen in September, Jordan had put Heisenberg's ideas into the matrix format, and matrix quantum mechanics was soon formally launched with a joint paper signed by Born and Jordan, although largely written by Jordan. Within a few weeks, a more complete synthesis signed by all three collaborators became one of the two founding documents of quantum mechanics. At almost exactly the same time, an entirely different formulation, using a wave equation instead of matrices, was published by **Erwin Schrödinger**—the other founding document. Shortly after those two papers, **Paul Adrien Maurice Dirac** also created a description of quantum mechanics using an entirely different approach from either the matrices or the wave equation.

Late in 1926 both Jordan and Dirac independently demonstrated, starting from quite different premises, that Heisenberg and Schrödinger were each saying exactly the same thing in different mathematical language. Dirac also showed that his version of quantum mechanics was equivalent to the other two formulations.

During the next year, Jordan and Dirac continued to work independently on extending quantum mechanics and repeatedly obtained equivalent solutions despite different starting points. Dirac's work reached a wider audience and became better known, but Jordan was actually the first to develop the quantum theory in a way that takes special relativity into account. Neither Jordan nor Dirac were completely successful in this endeavor, which was not satisfactorily resolved until twenty years later, when a new generation of physicists finally found a way around the difficulties.

Jordan worked with many of the leaders of the quantum revolution. In addition to Heisenberg, Born, and Pauli, he spent the summer of 1927 with Oskar Klein, developing the details of how photons and similar particles interact under the rules of quantum mechanics. On his return to Göttingen, Jordan collaborated with **Eugene Wigner** in extending these ideas to the interaction of photons and other particles, often considered the birth of quantum electrodynamics. Wigner later nominated Jordan for the Nobel Prize in Physics for his fundamental work in quantum theory.

In 1927 Jordan analyzed the question of what could be observed about atoms and electrons and what could not. It seemed to quantum physicists of the time that the motions of atoms prevented any exact observation. In February 1927 Jordan proposed that lowering the temperature of a microscope to absolute zero might enable one to observe atoms exactly. At that temperature, atoms and molecules would be stationary. Jordan's idea, making measurements with instruments cooled as closely as possible to absolute zero, is now the common practice for most experimental physics. While Jordan was correct that better observations are possible close to absolute zero, he went beyond this to say that at absolute zero the position and momentum of an atom or of an electron could, in theory, be measured exactly. As with his paper on Einstein's quanta, Jordan once again directly challenged the ideas of a recognized authority, in this case his collaborator Heisenberg.

Heisenberg was already convinced that the properties of subatomic particles could not be observed directly, but he was spurred by Jordan's paper to rethink the whole idea. In analyzing Jordan's notion, Heisenberg recognized that the very act of observing an electron's position with light would change the momentum of the electron when the quantum of light (the photon) bounced off the electron. Furthermore, he also recognized that a peculiar property of matrix multiplication could be interpreted as showing that there was a definite positive number associated with measuring the position and momentum of a particle. This positive number is simply the amount of uncertainty in the position and momentum. Thus, Jordan's speculation about the microscope at absolute zero led Heisenberg to formulate his famous uncertainty principle.

At the end of the 1920s, Jordan began to obtain better positions in the German university system, becoming an professor at the University of Rostock in

1929, where he remained until 1944. He was now financially more secure, and in 1930 Jordan married Hertha Stahn, with whom he was to have two children. The University of Rostock was a venerable institution, dating from 1429, located in northern Germany. While at Rostock, Jordan developed a type of algebra that is still of some mathematical interest. These nonassociative systems are called Jordan algebras. Less successfully during these years, Jordan tried to show that biological systems have a smallest unit of action that could be termed the quantum of life. This approach was useful with some topics, such as genetics and color vision, but was not perceived as a major breakthrough by biologists.

The political situation in Germany during the 1930s became very intense with the policies of Adolf Hitler. Both Born and Schrödinger left Germany as soon as Hitler came to power. Some physicists who followed the Nazi party line began to denounce modern physics, in part because a number of prominent physicists were Jews. While Jordan defended quantum mechanics, he otherwise became a Nazi collaborator, spying on other physicists and working for the German air force during World War II.

After the war, Jordan gradually returned to academic life, becoming a professor at the University of Hamburg, where he stayed for the remainder of his life. During this period he, like several other leading physicists of the day, tried to reformulate the laws of gravity on the assumption that the constant of gravitational force changes over long periods of time. Jordan worked in the context of a universe with more than four dimensions, an idea that continues to be popular today. In exploring the consequences of slowly diminishing gravitational force, Jordan recognized that a lower gravitational constant would cause expansion of Earth. In 1961 he concluded that continents would break apart and become separated, providing a force that would explain the idea of plate tectonics, which was becoming accepted at this time. Careful measurements have shown, however, that the gravitational constant is not changing in any measurable fashion. Geologists have found other mechanisms to support the theory of plate tectonics.

Jordan's work was recognized by the Max Planck Medal in 1942 and the Gauss Medal of the German Physical Society in 1955. Several of his books for the general reader were popular in Germany and in translation, mostly during the 1950s and 1960s. Jordan died in Hamburg on July 31, 1980, at the age of 77.

SELECTED WRITINGS BY JORDAN:

Books

Science and the Course of History. (Translated by Ralph Manheim) New Haven: Yale University Press, 1955. (German original published in 1952.)

The Expanding Earth: Some Consequences of Dirac's Gravitational Hypothesis. Pergamon Press. (German original published in 1966.)

FURTHER READING:

Books

Crease, Robert P. and Charles C. Mann. *The Second Creation: Makers of the Revolution in Twentieth-Century Physics.* New York: Macmillan, 1986.

—Sketch by Bryan Bunch

Eric R. Kandel

Eric R. Kandel
1929–
Austrian-born American neurobiologist

Eric Kandel is one of the world's foremost experts in learning and behavior. He has performed a number of trailblazing studies that have added to our knowledge of the brain processes that underlie short- and long-term memory. Most recently he has made great strides toward understanding the molecular mechanisms of learning though his study of invertebrates and vertebrates in cell culture.

Kandel was born in Vienna, Austria, on November 7, 1929. He immigrated to the United States in 1939. He received a B.A. at Harvard College in 1952 and an M.D. at the New York University School of Medicine in 1956. After an internship at the Montefiore Hospital in New York City, he did three years of postdoctoral research in the Laboratory of Neurophysiology at the National Institutes of Health, working on the cell biology of the hippocampus, a part of the brain involved in memory. From 1960 to 1962 he was a resident in training in psychiatry at the

Massachusetts Mental Health Center at Harvard Medical School. Then in 1962, he began what would later become the focus of his most important research—the gill-withdrawal reflex of *Aplysia*, a marine snail—with Ladislav Tauc. He then returned to the Harvard Medical School in 1963 as a faculty member of the Department of Psychiatry. In 1965 Kandel moved to New York University as associate professor and attained the rank of professor in 1968.

Founding Director of Neurobiology Center

Kandel was recruited to the College of Physicians and Surgeons of Columbia University in 1974 as the founding Director of the Center for Neurobiology and Behavior. He became a university professor there in 1983 and a senior investigator of the Howard Hughes Medical Institute, a private non-profit research institution supporting scientific studies around the world, a year later. In addition to being a professor in psychiatry, physiology, and molecular biophysics, Kandel is currently a professor in the department of biochemisty and biophysics at Columbia.

It was when be began work at Columbia University in 1974 that Kandel's lab started producing groundbreaking studies on the processes of memory. His longstanding studies have been vital in contributing to new knowledge—chiefly that two different types of memory share a molecular switch that turns them "on." One type of memory is vital for remembering details and places, people, and things, while another helps us with perceptual and motor skills. Different forms of a molecule that controls certain genes—a molecule called cyclic AMP-response element-binding protein (CREB)—actually act together to switch both forms of memory from short-term (such as what we had for dinner the night before) to long-term memory that stays with us for months or years.

Kandel wanted to find out how long-term memory operated. He and other researchers in his lab found that the process called cyclic adenosine monophosphate (AMP) was important in short-term memory. He discovered this fact while studying the gill-withdrawal reflex of *Aplysia. Aplysia*, it seemed, had both long-term and short-term memory, just like human beings.

But how did cyclic AMP turn on protein synthesis, the synthesis that led to long–term memory? Kandel decided to investigate the role of CREB. Pramod Dash, a neuroscientist working with Kandel, discovered that if you blocked the action of CREB you also blocked long-term, but not short-term memory. "That was the first demonstration that CREB was critically important for the long-term process," Kandel told the *New Scientist.*

Later Kandel and other scientists in his lab found another molecule related to CREB called CREB-2 that seemed to block the action of CREB. "When you remove CREB-2, it is easier to put information in long-term memory," Kandel said. "If you just test your own experience you realize that the ease with which you put information in long-term memory varies a great deal." One phenomenon that explains this difference is the degree to which CREB-2 blocks long-term memory—or acts as a repressor of CREB.

Breakthrough Studies of Brain Process Called LTP

Kandel also made waves in the science community with his contribution to knowledge about LTP or long-term potentiation. LTP is a process that beefs up the strength and efficiency of signals sent throughout our brains by our neurons, or nerve cells. LTP is especially vital in regions of the hippocampus involved in storing memories about places, people, and things. According to most scientists, both receiving and sending neurons play a role in LTP. Most scientists believed until recently that the signal being sent across these neurons was nerve cell nitrous oxide, however Kandel and other scientists in his lab proved this theory was wrong by testing a mouse without the gene for nerve cell nitrous oxide. They found the animal still had LTP.

Kandel's research may eventually help us understand how nerve cells develop as well as how they function. Certainly his work will eventually help science probe into the progression of diseases involving loss of memory, including devastating genetic disorders such as Alzheimer's disease. He believes that his research has only benefited from a recent renaissance in basic biological research. "As problems in other areas of biology become partially solved, many young people are focusing their interest on neural science, which still has so many unsolved questions," he said to the *New Scientist.*

Kandel, now a U.S. citizen, married in 1956 and has two children. He has been honored with many distinguished awards, including the Albert Lasker Basic Medical Research Prize, the National Medal of Science presented to him by former President Ronald Reagan, the Gairdner International Award for Outstanding Achievement in Medical Science, the Harvey Prize of the Technion in Israel, and the Bristol-Myers Squibb Award for Distinguished Achievement in Neuroscience Research.

During 1997, Kandel was recognized for his experiments with genetically modified mice, such as the study involving LTP. Thus, in 1997, he received the Dana Award in Neuroscience and the Gerard Prize of the Society of Neuroscience.

SELECTED WRITINGS BY KANDEL:

Books

(With James H.Schwartz and Thomas M. Jessel) *Principles of Neural Science*, Norwalk, Conneticut: Appleton and Lange, 1991.

Periodicals

"C/EBP is a Immediate Early Gene Required for the Consolidation of Long-Term Facilitation in Aplysia." *Cell* 76 (1994): 1099-1114.
"Impaired Long-Term Potentiation, Spatial Learning and Hippocampal Development in Fyn Mutant." *Science* 258 (1992): 1903-1910.
"Injection of the Cyclic AMP Responsive Element Into the Nucleus of Aplysia Sensory Neurons Blocks Long-Term Facilitation." *Nature* 345 (1990): 718-721.

FURTHER READING:

Books

American Men and Women of Science. New Providence, NJ: R. R. Bowker Co., 1994.
Who's Who in Science and Engineering. New Providence, NJ: Marquis Who's Who, 1996.

Periodicals

Kreeger, Karen Young. "New Molecular Tools Revealing Mysteries of the Mind." *The New Scientist* (February 3, 1997):13-14.

—*Sketch by Barbara Boughton*

Richard M. Karp
1935–
American computer scientist

An intellectual force in the development of computer science, Richard M. Karp has pioneered linking theoretical advances in the field to real-world problems. When he received the prestigious Turing Award, Karp gave a lecture in which he likened his interest in combinatorial search problems to "jigsaw puzzles, where one has to assemble the parts of a structure in a particular way . . ." from placing and

Richard M. Karp

interconnecting components on an integrated circuit chip to "scheduling of the National Football League, and the routing of a fleet of school buses."

Known for his comprehensive understanding of the field, as well as his fertile creativity, Karp has gained worldwide recognition for his inspired work in complexity theory and determining the inherent difficulty in solving problems with computers. Dedicated to his field, Karp considers himself fortunate to be among the first generation of scientists that came to maturity after the digital computer's invention. "If I had been born at an earlier time, I don't know what career I would have pursued," Karp told contributor David Petechuk in a 1997 interview. "However, if not for computer science, I do know I would have had a much less satisfying career."

Karp was born in Boston, Massachusetts, in 1935 to Abraham Lewis and Rose Karp. Karp's father was a junior high school math teacher and school principal. On rare occasions, Karp would attend his father's classes, which fostered his interest in math and teaching. As evidence of this early influence on his life, Karp dedicated his Turing Award Lecture to his father. Karp also credits his high school math teacher, Jack Dobbyn, as instilling him with confidence in his talent.

Karp attended the Boston Latin School and, appropriately, Latin was his second favorite subject after mathematics. By the age of 10, Karp began to demonstrate his skill in mathematics, entertaining

and astounding his friends with his ability to multiply four-digit numbers in his head. He was so awed by the "power and elegance" of the formal proofs involved in plane geometry, that he would pretend to be sick so he could stay home and solve geometry problems.

Growing up at the height of the Cold War and the beginning of the "Space Race" between the Soviet Union and the United States, Karp's school years coincided with a time of significant breakthroughs in and enormous support for science education and research in the United States. Admittedly overconfident after his success at Boston Latin School, Karp quickly discovered that he had to work to succeed at Harvard University. He soon learned that he had no taste for laboratory science and that his written communication skills were "workmanlike."

Karp, who had no desire to pursue a career in pure mathematics, recalls the exact moment when he realized his true vocation. A fellow student, Bill Eastman, revealed to him the Hungarian Algorithm for solving the Assignment Problem. He was fascinated by the elegant simplicity with which the algorithm, using only addition and subtraction, "converged inexorably upon the optimal solution." For his Ph.D. dissertation at Harvard, Karp probed the idea that a directed graph can represent the flow of control in a computer program.

A Brief Interlude in Industry

After graduating in 1959, Karp went to work for the Mathematical Sciences Department at the IBM Thomas J. Watson Research Center located on the Lamb Estate, which was previously a sanitarium for wealthy alcoholics. Karp enjoyed the informal atmosphere and lunchtime frisbee games on the estate's enormous lawns. However, more importantly, IBM's research division had attracted some of the best minds in combinatorial mathematics. Assigned to work on algorithms for logic circuit design, Karp began his lifelong study of combinatorial algorithms and parallel processing.

Karp, however, felt stifled by life in corporate suburbia. He decided on a career that would allow him to pursue research and to follow in his father's footsteps as a teacher. In 1968 he joined the University of California at Berkeley. He considered this move the end of his scientific apprenticeship, as he would become a mentor to students while increasing his professional visibility.

The NP Solution

When Karp joined Berkeley, the university was poised to become an important center for research in computer science. With a strong core faculty, the university began attracting outstanding graduate students. As a teacher, Karp looked at each relationship with a student as unique and avoided "assigning" thesis problems, opting instead to work with students in helping develop their own interests and directions.

In 1971 Karp came across a paper by Steve Cook called "The Complexity of Theorem-Proving Procedures." Karp, who had worked in combinatorial optimization and was familiar with difficult combinatorial problems, like the classic "traveling-salesman problem," was impressed with Cook's theorem. Excited by the belief that he had discovered an area of work that could greatly influence computer science, he began developing a new class of computing problems. Primarily, Karp was concerned with problems in computer science for efficiently routing and scheduling. These problems had many real-world applications, ranging from the routing of electronic "traffic" over the countless wires needed in microprocessing to scheduling classes and the traveling salesman problem of finding the shortest route for a salesperson to use while touring cities.

In 1972 Karp received international recognition for his work in demonstrating the existence of an entirely new class of difficult theoretical computing problems called NP-completeness. Essentially, the NP-complete theory divides most problems in computer science into two groups, problems that can be solved efficiently by a computer and problems that probably cannot. Karp and colleagues had discovered that many of the most commonly studied combinatorial problems are disguised versions of a single underlying problem and, thus, are all of essentially the same computational complexity. The theory revolutionized computer science and still serves as the fundamental basis of scientific thought on computers' capabilities and limitations. Interesting, after his 1972 paper on the subject, Karp did little work on NP-completeness proofs. He says he moved on to leave the problems in the hands of "virtuosi of the subject."

Turns to Computational Molecular Biology

After spending 27 years at Berkeley, Karp retired and then took a faculty position at the University of Washington. The university had a rapidly growing research environment based on the human genome project, in which scientists from around the world are working on mapping the entire human genome. Karp was an avid reader of general literature concerning molecular biology and genetics and believed that his expertise in algorithms could prove valuable help in properly ordering the three billion symbols in the human genome.

Karp's work at the University of Washington has focused on strategies for sequencing the human genome, the physical mapping of large DNA molecules, the classification of tumors on the basis of gene expression data, and other combinatorial problems arising in molecular biology. "We want to take the human out of the loop as much as possible," said Karp in a *New York Times* article on DNA sequencing efforts at the University of Washington. Pointing out that running sequencing experiments is "deadly boring," Karp has set out to automate the process (for example, designing robotic systems to do most of the work) and developing algorithms so computers can analyze the data.

"Many biologists consider the acquisition of sequences to be boring," said Karp in the *Times* article. "But from a computer science point of view, these are first-rate and challenging algorithmic questions."

Karp, who is married and has a son, feels fortunate in having found a profession that was just beginning to flourish and which suited his interests perfectly. Besides his work in computer science research, he is most proud of his career as a teacher. Having supervised 35 Ph.D. candidates at Berkeley, Karp developed a definitive philosophy on teaching. In addition to his emphasis on preparation and structuring material to provide students with a "road map" of study, he developed an in-class code that included relaxing before the beginning of class, always making eye contact with his students, and being willing to share his own experiences and opinions with students while avoiding "ego trips."

For his groundbreaking efforts in computer science, Karp has received many awards, including the Turing Award, computer science's most prestigious honor, and the National Medal of Science (1997). [Karp] "has the most respect of any computer scientists I know," said Tandy Warnow, a computer scientist for the University of Pennsylvania, in the *New York Times*. "He's helping to change the ways we think about what we are doing as computer scientists."

SELECTED WRITINGS BY KARP:

Books

"Reducibility among Combinatorial Problems." *Complexity of Computer Computations.* New York, Plenum Press, 1972.

Periodicals

"Combinatorics, Complexity and Randomness" (Turing Award Lecture). *Communications of the ACM* 6 (1986): 35-48.
"Probablistic Analysis of Partitioning Algorithms for the Traveling-Salesman Problem in the Plane." *Mathematics of Operations Research* 2 (1977): 209-244.

Linda Keen

FURTHER READING:

Periodicals

Kolata, G. "Biology's Big Project Turns Into Challenge for Computer Experts." *The New York Times* (June 11, 1996): B5, B10.

—*Sketch by David Petechuk*

Linda Keen
1940–

American mathematician

Linda Keen devotes her time and energies to some of the hottest topics of the day. Her work in complex analysis and dynamical systems deals with the mathematics responsible for the vibrant graphics seen in science shows, fractal art, and lifelike computer animations. For more than 30 years, her research has been funded by grants and fellowships from the National Science Foundation (NSF). Keen has helped evaluate other postdoctoral fellowships for the NSF as well as for NATO. She is also active in the mathematical community, through her professional participation on various editorial boards and steering committees. Her influence has been felt at local and national levels

regarding such pressing issues as women and minority involvement, librarianship, project funding, educational and test standards, research goals, and professional ethics. Among her most visible posts have been the presidency of the Association for Women in Mathematics (1985–1986), and the vice–presidency of the American Mathematical Society (1992–1995).

Linda Keen was born Linda Goldway in New York City on August 9, 1940. Her father was an English teacher who did not take his daughter's interest in the comparatively obscure language of mathematics personally. In fact, he encouraged her to study at a local magnet school, the Bronx High School of Science. She would stay in New York throughout her early academic career, earning a B.S. in 1960 from City College, an M.S. from New York University (NYU) two years later, and a Ph.D. from the Courant Institute of Mathematical Sciences in 1964.

"The Children's Lunch"

Keen was fortunate to have as her Ph.D. advisor the celebrated **Lipman Bers.** "Lipa," as he was called, was a political refugee throughout the 1930s, coming to the U.S. from Latvia via Prague. At NYU, he was a colleague and friend as much as an authority on complex analysis. In 1964, it was still quite rare for a male mathematician to be even tolerant of women. Yet, as Bers said himself in an interview with Donald Albers and Constance Reid, it never occurred to him that women could be intellectually inferior to men. While studying with Bers, Keen focused on the analytic aspects of Riemann surfaces.

Keen's obituary for Bers highlighted his lack of pretense and approachability. Classes were held Friday afternoons, so Bers extended the time with his students to include lunch—the "children's lunch" as he called it. Keen, who was almost always the youngest at the table, would be given the check to divide in her head. Once, when the "children" all insisted that the oldest person take the chore, Bers was unprepared and his calculations were incorrect.

Committee on Professional Ethics

Bers' commitment to political activism and human rights, resulting from his years of living beneath the shadow of dictatorships, seems to have influenced Keen as well. From 1992 to 1996, she chaired the special advisory committee to write Ethical Guidelines and Procedures for the American Mathematical Society (AMS) Committee on Professional Ethics (COPE). The document developed by the special advisory committee provides professional mathematicians with guidance about ethical issues including giving credit for new findings, refereeing papers responsibly, protecting "whistle blowers," and social responsibility.

Among the issues with which the committee's report grappled are those arising from work in industry and with the government, as well as standards of conduct within professional organizations such as the AMS. Protecting confidentiality, anonymity, and privileged information is given top priority. As the guidelines state, "Freedom to publish must sometimes yield to security concerns, but mathematicians should resist excessive secrecy demands whether by government or private concerns." Those AMS members who advise graduate students are now expected to paint a realistic picture of employment prospects, and not to exploit their students by giving them heavy workloads at low pay. The guidelines also include a standard nondiscrimination policy. The special advisory committee's proposed guidelines were ratified in 1995 by a 25 to 3 vote.

Keen has served her profession in similar capacities a number of times. She began her involvement with COPE in 1986, and became a member of various policy boards for the AMS throughout the 1990s. Keen has also worked with the International Mathematics Union. She was of a member of the panels charged with evaluating the mathematics departments of the State University of New York–Potsdam and Rutgers University–Newark, and the minority program at the University of Minnesota. Keen was also a charter member of the Mayor's Commission for Science and Technology of the City of New York, serving on this commission from 1984–1985.

Keen's professional career has taken her to various institutions in her home state, including Hunter College and the City University of New York. When Lehman College, formerly the Bronx campus of Hunter, became independent in 1968, Keen remained on the faculty. She was promoted to full professor at Lehman in 1974 and presently holds a dual appointment in the Graduate Center Doctoral Faculties in Computer Science and in Mathematics. Keen has also held visiting professorships at the University of California at Berkeley, Columbia University, Boston University, Princeton, and MIT, as well as at mathematical institutions in several foreign countries, including Germany, Brazil, Denmark, Great Britain, and China. Keen's editorial services are equally international. Currently she serves on editorial boards for the *Journal of Geometric Analysis* and the *Annales* of the Finnish Academy of Sciences.

Throughout her career, Keen has preferred working collaboratively with other mathematicians to working alone. During the 1980s she worked with Caroline Series on the geometric aspects of Riemann surfaces, and, more recently, she contributed to the field of dynamical systems in cooperation with Paul Blanchard, Robert Devaney, and Lisa Goldberg. As Keen puts it, "I am basically a social person and enjoy people." She currently counts her husband and two children as her chief supporters, worthy successors in this regard to her father and Lipman Bers.

SELECTED WRITINGS BY KEEN:

Books

The Legacy of Sonya Kovalevskaya: Proceedings of a Symposium, 1987.
(Edited with R. Devaney) *Chaos and Fractals: The Mathematics Behind the Computer Graphics,* 1989.
(Edited with J. Dodziuk) *Lipa's Legacy,* (in publication).

Periodicals

"Lipman Bers (1914–1993)." *AWM Newsletter* 24 (1994): 5–7.

FURTHER READING:

Books

Albers, D.J., G.L. Alexanderson, and C. Reid, editors. *More Mathematical People: Contemporary Conversations.* Boston: Harcourt Brace Jovanovich, 1990.
American Men & Women of Science. Nineteenth edition. New Providence, NJ: Bowker, 1994, p. 262.

Other

"Linda G. Keen." http://www.math.neu.edu/awm/ NoetherBrochure/Keen93.html
"Linda Keen." *Biographies of Women Mathematicians.* June 1997. http://www.scottlan.edu/lriddle/women/chronol.htm (July 1997).

—*Sketch by Jennifer Kramer*

Evelyn Fox Keller
1936–
American biologist and physicist

A scientist who has openly addressed the issue of discrimination against women in the scientific community, Evelyn Keller is known for her work in designing mathematical models of biological processes. Over the last ten years, however, she has focused on the historical and philosophical issues of developmental genetics.

Evelyn Fox was born March 20, 1936, in New York City. Her parents, Albert and Rachel, were working-class Russian Jewish immigrants. During her childhood, Keller, the youngest of three children, was not interested in science. But when she learned about the "unconscious" from her older sister Frances, her interest was fired. She decided to become a psychoanalyst.

Discovering Science

After graduating from high school, Keller enrolled at Queens College in Brooklyn, with the goal of going to medical school. Her calculus professor, impressed by his brightest student, asked why she wasn't majoring in mathematics. She replied that she didn't want to be an accountant. "Well then," he said, "why don't you major in physics?" To which she replied, "What's that?"

At the end of the term, she was ready to transfer out–preferably to Antioch College or Reed College. However, as a transfer student, she was ineligible for most forms of financial aid, and because of her family's economic status, the plan was impossible. "This was a big blow. I felt I had shot myself in the foot," she says. "It was infuriating." Nevertheless, she was determined to leave—just as much as her parents were determined that she stay. Her brother Maurice came up with a compromise, Brandeis University in Massachusetts.

Keller thrived at Brandeis. "She simply devoured the math," recalls physics professor Sam Schweber, with whom she worked independently during her senior year. "She had no difficulty at all with the technical material, which is unusual." During her studies, she "fell in love" with theoretical physics, and applied for and won a National Science Foundation Fellowship, which would allow her to attend Harvard graduate school. She received her bachelor's degree in physics magna cum laude in 1957.

A Shock to the System

For Keller, the years at Harvard would be filled with "almost unmitigated provocation, insult, and denial." Students and professors told her that she couldn't possibly understand physics, and that her lack of fear was proof of her ignorance. Keller reported that she was told not to concern herself "with the foundations of quantum mechanics (the only thing that did concern me) because, very simply, I was not, could not be, good enough."

Despite the criticism, she did well in her courses. When she turned in especially good work, professors suspected her of plagiarism. "On one such occasion, I had written a paper the thesis of which had provoked much argument and contention in the department. This I learned, by chance, several weeks after the

debate was well underway. In an effort to resolve the paradox created by my results, I went to see the professor for whom I had written the paper. After an interesting discussion, which incidentally resolved the difficulty, I was asked, innocently and kindly, from what article(s) I had copied my argument."

She passed her orals and decided to forego physics and return to her original plan to be a psychoanalyst. However, in the interim, she spent the summer with her brother and his family at Cold Spring Harbor, New York, where Maurice worked for the Long Island Biological Laboratories. The biologists welcomed her. She worked beside them in the labs, and discovered an idea for her physics thesis—molecular biology. She went back to Harvard and found a physics professor who himself was switching to molecular biology. **Walter Gilbert**, a 1980 Nobel laureate, agreed to be her advisor. Keller earned her Ph.D. in theoretical physics in 1963.

In the fall of 1962, she went to work as an assistant research scientist for Joseph Bishop Keller, in the Courant Institute of Mathematical Sciences at New York University. They married in 1963, had a son, Jeffrey, in 1964 and a daughter, Sarah, in 1966.

From New York University, Keller joined a new department of mathematical biology at Cornell Medical College. She left there in 1969 to become an associate professor in mathematics at New York University, where she remained until 1972, when she joined the Division of Natural Science at the State University of New York at Purchase. From 1972 to 1974, she served as chair of the division's mathematics board of study. She became a professor of mathematics and humanities at Northeastern University in 1982, remaining at that position until 1988, when she went to the University of California at Berkeley. Since 1992, she has been a professor of the history and philosophy of science at the Massachusetts Institute of Technology.

Creates Mathematical Model of a Biological Process

During the early 1960s and much of the 1970s, Keller's early work with Lee Segel in mathematical biology reflected the renaissance of the subject at that time. Together, they created mathematical models of chemotaxis, the movement of cells toward or away from chemicals, and of slime mold aggregation.

According to Keller, it was not so much an inspiration that led her to apply mathematics to these questions, but rather her training as a theoretical mathematician. Her work drew deeply on parallels between biology and physics. In her "Mathematical Aspects of Bacterial Chemotaxis," she writes, "The individual cells may execute a random motion, which, when averaged over a large population, gives rise to a macroscopic flux in the direction of the gradient. Physics provides us with a well known analogy in Brownian motion."

During the 1980s, she devoted much of her time to gender issues in science. Her book on **Barbara McClintock**, *A Feeling for the Organism*, was called "a welcome and useful addition to the growing literature on the recent history of . . . women's achievement in science." She considers her highest achievement to be *Reflections on Gender and Science*, which was published in 1985, reissued in 1995 as the tenth anniversary edition, and was translated into more than seven languages.

In the 1990s, she turned her attention to contemporary issues in developmental biology. Some of her new work appeared in *Refiguring Life: Metaphors of 20th Century Biology*, which Columbia University Press published in 1995. "It's really exciting," Keller says. "Molecular biology is subverting its own paradigm." As of 1997, she was at work on a book about explanations in developmental biology, which has the working title,"Making Sense of Life: Explanations in Developmental Biology."

Keller received a MacArthur Foundation grant in 1992. She has also received honorary degrees from Technical University of Luleå, in 1996; Rensselaer Polytechnic Institute, in 1995; Simmons College, in 1995; the University of Amsterdam, in 1993; and Mount Holyoke College, in 1991. Her numerous awards include include the 1991 Alumni Achievement Award from Brandeis, the 1990 AAUW Achievement Award, the 1985 Radcliffe Graduate Society Medal, and the 1981-82 Mina Shaughnessy Award.

SELECTED WRITINGS BY KELLER:

Books

"The Anomaly of a Woman in Physics." In *Working it Out*, edited by S. Rudick and P. Daniels. New York: Pantheon, 1977.
A Feeling for the Organism: The Life and Work of Barbara McClintock. 2nd ed. New York: W. H. Freeman, 1993.
"Mathematical Aspects of Chemotaxis." In *Chemotaxis*, edited by S. Sorkin. Farmington, CT: S. Karger, 1974, pp. 79-93.
Reflections on Gender and Science. New Haven: Yale University Press, 1985
Secrets of Life, Secrets of Death. New York: Routledge, 1992.

Periodicals

"Assessing the Keller-Segel Model: How Has it Fared?" *Lecture Notes in Biomathematics* 38 (1980): 379-87.

"The Force of the 'Pacemaker' Concept in Theories of Aggregation in Cellular Slime Mold." *Perspectives in Biology and Medicine* 26, no. 4 (1983); 515-2.
"A Mathematical Description of Biological Clocks." *Currents of Modern Biology* 1 (1968): 279-84
(With Lee A. Segel) "A Model for Chemotaxis." *Journal of Theoretical Biology* 30 (1971): 225-234.
(With Lee A. Segel) "Slime Mold Aggregation Viewed as an Instability." *Journal of Theoretical Biology* 26 (1970): 399-415.
(With M. Meselson) "Unequal Photosensitivity of the Two Strands of DNA in Bacteriophage Lambda." *Journal of Molecular Biology* 7 (1963): 583-89..
"Women in Science: An Analysis of a Social Problem." *Harvard Magazine* (October 1974): 14-19.

FURTHER READING:

Periodicals

Horning, Beth. "The Controversial Career of Evelyn Fox Keller." *Technology Review*. (January 1993).

—Sketch by Fran Hodgkins

Motoo Kimura
1924–1994
Japanese geneticist

Motoo Kimura achieved international recognition for his numerous contributions to the fields of evolution and population genetics. He is considered the founder of the neutral theory of molecular evolution. According to this theory, evolutionary change and most of the variability within a species are caused at the molecular level by the random drift of mutant genes. By comparison, English naturalist Charles Darwin's theory of natural selection was based on the concept that evolution occurs at the species level, with those individuals best adapted to the environment most fit to survive. Kimura focused on the molecular changes that occur in the nucleotides of DNA, and concluded that the resulting mutant genes are neutral and subject to random drift, or changes, in gene frequencies due to pure chance. Kimura developed his theory quantitatively and thus, according to James F. Crow, writing in *Population Genetics and Molecular Evolution,* "laid a very strong foundation for a mathematical theory of evolution." At first these ideas were met with considerable skepticism by many other geneticists. With the accumulation of more evidence, however, they gained more acceptance.

Kimura was born on November 13, 1924, in Okazaki, Japan, to Issaku Kimura and Kana Kaneiwa. After receiving his M.Sc. degree from Kyoto University in 1947, he served as an assistant at the university for the next two years. In 1949 he was appointed as a research member of the National Institute of Genetics in Mishima. He then came to the United States in 1953, where he was a graduate student at Iowa State College. In 1956, he received his Ph.D. from the University of Wisconsin, where he worked in the laboratory of James F. Crow. Shortly afterward he returned to the National Institute of Genetics and became the laboratory head, a position he was to hold until 1964. In that year, he was appointed head of the department of population genetics, serving until 1988, when he became professor emeritus. Kimura married Hiroko Mino in 1957, and the couple had one son, Akio.

Advances Study of Population Genetics

During his career, Kimura established a mathematical approach to the field of population genetics. This branch of science deals with the distribution of genes in a population, where all individuals are considered to share the same gene pool. As the individuals interbreed, genes are exchanged, resulting in many recombinations and consequent variations among members. The significance of gene frequency in evolution of species was first recognized in 1908 by **Godfrey Harold Hardy** and **Wilhelm Weinberg** when they independently arrived at the same conclusion. Their findings, now summarized in the Hardy-Weinberg law, state that the gene pool of a population remains constant from generation to generation under the following conditions: the population is large and characterized by random matings, and there are no new factors such as mutations or migration. When these theoretical conditions are not present, gene frequencies change, leading to the emergence of new species.

Kimura used computer technology to calculate the genetic composition of populations and the gene frequencies to be expected under various conditions over hundreds of generations. He prepared mathematical equations to depict a variety of possible influences such as inbreeding, mutations, crossbreeding, selection, chromosomal aberrations, natural selection, and random drift. In so doing he was able for the first time to establish a mathematical basis for the entire process of change in the gene frequency of populations.

Over the years Kimura published more than one hundred research papers. He was elected to foreign

membership in the U.S. National Academy of Sciences, l'Académie des Sciences of Toulouse, the Genetical Society of Great Britain, and the Royal Society of London. He served as visiting professor at the Universities of Wisconsin, Pavia (Italy), Princeton, and Stanford. Kimura was honored with a number of Japanese awards, including a D.Sc. from Osaka University, the Genetics Society of Japan Prize, the Japan Academy Prize, the Japan Society of Human Genetics Prize, the Order of Culture National Medal from the Emperor, the Honorary Citizen of Okazaki award, and the Asaki Prize. Abroad, he received additional awards from Oxford University, the French government, the U.S. Academy of Sciences, as well as the International Prize for Biology, honorary degrees from the universities of Chicago and Wisconsin, and the Darwin Medal of the Royal Society. In his spare time Kimura raised and hybridized *Paphtopedilum*, lady's slipper orchids. He died in Tokyo on November 13, 1994.

SELECTED WRITINGS BY KIMURA:

Books

Introduction to Population Genetics Theory. New York: Harper & Row, 1970.
The Natural Theory of Molecular Evolution, Cambridge: Cambridge University Press, 1983.

Periodicals

"Evolutionary Rate at the Molecular Level." *Nature* 217 (1968):, pp. 624-26.
"How Genes Evolve: A Population Geneticist's View." *Annales de génétique* 19 (1976): 153-68.
"The Neutral Theory of Molecular Evolution." *Scientific American* (November 1979): 98-124.
"The Neutral Theory of Molecular Evolution." *New Scientist* 107, no. 1464 (1985): 41-46.
"DNA and the Neutral Theory." *Philosophical Transactions of the Royal Society of London* 312 (1986): 343-54.

FURTHER READING:

Books

Crow, James F. "Population Genetics and Molecular Evolution." In *The Neutrality-Selection Controversy in the History of Evolution and Population Genetics*, edited by T. Ohta and K. Aski. New York: Springer-Verlag, 1985, pp. 1–18.
Wright, Sewall. *Evolution and the Genetics of Population.* Vols. 1-4. Chicago: University of Chicago Press, 1978.

Periodicals

"Motoo Kimura, Japanese Geneticist" (obituary).
New York Times (16 November 1994): D25.
"Motoo Kimura, Japanese Geneticist" (obituary).
Washington Post (15 November 1994): B7.

—*Sketch by Maurice Bleifeld*

Helen Dean King
1869–1955
American geneticist and zoologist

Helen Dean King bred 150 generations of rats for laboratory experiments. This breeding operation gave scientists the ability to breed pure strains of animals, and it expanded King's research in such areas as sex determination, regeneration, inbreeding, and heredity. In the process, King also discovered several new types of rat, including the waltzing rat, and worked to domesticate the Norway rat. Her findings in inbreeding were applicable to other fields, including the breeding of race horses.

She was born on September 27, 1869, in Owego, New York, to George Alonzo King and his wife Leonora Louise Dean King. The Kings were a locally prominent family. Her father was president of a leather company, the King Harness Company. As a youth, she attended the Owego Free Academy. King earned her undergraduate degree from Vassar College in 1892. She did her graduate work at Bryn Mawr College, earning her Ph.D. in 1899, majoring in morphology and minoring in paleontology and physiology.

While a graduate student, King worked as a fellow in the biology department for one year, 1896-97. After earning her Ph.D., King taught science at the Baldwin School in Bryn Mawr, Pennsylvania, from 1899 until 1907. Simultaneously, King worked as an assistant in biology at Bryn Mawr, until 1906. While associated with Bryn Mawr, King's research focused on embryological issues such as regeneration and developmental anatomy, mostly involving amphibians.

In 1909, King joined the staff at the Wistar Institute of Anatomy and Biology in Philadelphia. She moved through the ranks from an assistant in anatomy and biology in 1909 to an assistant professor of embryology by 1913. King spent the rest of her career at Wistar, though she was never promoted to a full professorship. (This was not uncommon for female professors in this era.) Still, she was a key member of the staff, as well as a member of the Wistar Advisory board for 24 years.

King's most fruitful work was done at Wistar. In her first year, King began her inbreeding experiments to ensure a uniform stock of laboratory rats. Among other subjects, she spent time analyzing the effects of close inbreeding, and concluded that, if the stock has certain characteristics (among them strong health), inbreeding has certain advantages over outbreeding. Her findings became a source of popular debate in newspapers throughout the United States in the late 1910s and 1920s, as the implications of incest was exploited.

While conducting her inbreeding and generation breeding experiments on rats in 1919, King also worked on the domestication of the wild Norway rat. She focused on their life processes, carefully studying and isolating their mutations. Because of her work in this area, subsequent researchers knew how to breed pure strains of animals for their studies.

In 1932, King was awarded the Ellen Richards Prize from the Association to Aid Scientific Research of Women for her research accomplishments. Sixteen years later, she retired from Wistar. King died on March 7, 1955, in Philadelphia.

SELECTED WRITINGS BY KING:

Periodicals

"Studies on Inbreeding I. The Effects of Inbreeding on the Growth and Variability in the Body Weight of the Albino Rat." *Journal of Experimental Zoology* (July 1918): 335-78.
"Studies on Inbreeding III. The Effects of Inbreeding with Selection, on the Sex Ratio of the Albino Rat." *Journal of Experimental Zoology* (October 1918): 1-35.

FURTHER READING:

Books

Bailey, Martha J. "King, Helen Dean." *American Women in Science*. Denver: ABC-CLIO, 1994, pp. 192-93.
Bogin, Mary. "King, Helen Dean." *Dictionary of Scientific Biography*, Vol 17, Sup. II. Frederic L. Holmes, ed. New York: Charles Scribner's Sons, 1990, pp. 474-77.
Ogilvie, Marilyn Bailey. "King, Helen Dean." *Women in Science: Antiquity through the Nineteenth Century*. Cambridge, Massachusetts: MIT Press, 1986, pp. 108-110.
Siegel, Patricia Joan, and Kay Thomas Finley. "Helen Dean King." *Women in the Scientific Search: An American Bio-Bibliography, 1724-*

1979. Metuchen, NJ: The Scarecrow Press, Inc., 1985, p. 358.

—*Sketch by Annette Petrusso*

Louisa Boyd Yeomans King
1863–1948
American horticulturist

Louisa King was one of the prominent figures responsible for the garden club phenomenon at the turn of the twentieth century. She popularized home gardening in America and advocated a break away from the formality of the then-popular Victorian garden (which featured plants grown and pruned into highly stylized arrangements), in favor of a more artistic, well-planned natural garden. She modernized gardening and was recognized in the United States as well as abroad (especially Great Britain) for her efforts.

Louisa Boyd Yeomans King was born on October 17, 1863, to Alfred Yeomans, a Presbyterian minister, and his wife, Elizabeth Blythe Ramsay, in Washington, New Jersey. She was one of five children, two daughters and three sons. Formally educated in private schools, King's love of literature and art were nurtured at home as well. At her childhood home in Orange, New Jersey, King first learned about gardening from her mother. At one point, after the family moved to Illinois, Elizabeth Yeomans' formal garden featured an herb garden with over 200 plant varieties. King learned much about the basics of plants and soil from her mother.

Louisa married Francis King of Chicago, Illinois, in Orange, New Jersey, on June 12, 1890. They had three children, Elizabeth, Frances, and Henry William. After King and her husband moved to Alma, Michigan, in 1902, she planted her first garden. By 1910, King's interest in gardening had become her life's passion. She began to advocate the use of color and design in the home garden. It was her focus on color schemes as a deciding factor for garden design that encouraged seed companies to organize their seed packets by color. In 1913, King was one of the founders of the Garden Club of America, and she served as Vice President for a time. She was also president of the Women's National Farm and Garden Association from 1914 until 1921.

In addition to publishing many magazine articles in such periodicals as *House Beautiful* and *McCall's Magazine*, King published 10 gardening books. The first, published in 1915, was entitled *The Well-Considered Garden*. In her articles and books, King emphasized the aesthetics of gardening and gave information on new plant types.

With her popularity as a writer and leader in gardening organizations, King was also frequently engaged as a speaker on designing and maintaining home gardens. King's efforts were recognized by a number of organizations. In 1921, she was the first woman awarded the George White Medal from the Massachusetts Horticultural Society, the highest honor available for gardeners in the United States. Two years later she received the Garden Club of America's Medal of Honor.

King's friendship with prominent British gardeners, among them Gertrude Jekyll and Ellen Willmott, led to her recognition in Britain. She was voted a fellow of Great Britain's Royal Horticultural Society and named a Vice President of the Garden Club of London.

After King's husband died in 1927, she moved to South Hartford, New York, where she established the state's first plowing contest. King died from a coronary thrombosis on January 16, 1948, at her daughter's home in Milton, Massachusetts. Following her wishes, King's ashes were spread over her South Hartford garden, and in her honor dogwoods were planted at the National Arboretum in Washington, D.C.

SELECTED WRITINGS BY KING:

Books

The Well-Considered Garden. New York: Charles Scribners' Sons, 1915.

FURTHER READING:

Books

Bailey, Martha J. "King, Louisa Boyd Yeomans." *American Women in Science: A Biographical Dictionary.* Denver: ABC-CLIO, 1994, pp. 193-94.

Hollingsworth, Buckner. *Her Garden was Her Delight.* New York: MacMillan, 1962.

James, Edward T. "King, Louisa Boyd Yeomans." *Notable American Women, 1607-1950: A Biographical Dictionary.* Cambridge: The Belknap Press of Harvard University Press, 1971, pp. 334-35.

Read, Phyllis, J. and Bernard L. Willieb. "Louisa King." *The Book of Women's Firsts.* New York: Random House, 1992, p. 242.

Periodicals

"Mrs. King, 84, Dies; A Garden Expert." *The New York Times*, 18 January 1948, 60.

—*Sketch by Annette Petrusso*

Reatha Clark King
1938–
American chemist

Reatha Clark King is an African American chemist whose early research in fluoride chemistry aided NASA's space program. A large part of her career has been devoted to academic and scientific administration.

Reatha Belle Clark King was born in Pavo, Georgia, on April 11, 1938, the second of three daughters born to Willie and Ola Watts Campbell Clark. Her father, an illiterate farm worker, and her mother, a domestic servant, divorced when King was a young child. Shortly afterward, King moved with her mother and sisters to Moultree, Georgia. There, her life centered around activities at the Mt. Zion Baptist Church and her studies at school. During summers and spare time, King and her sisters earned money by gathering tobacco and picking cotton. Having no role models in scientific professions, they aspired to be hairdressers, teachers, or nurses. King graduated from high school in 1954, the valedictorian of her class.

Discovers Chemistry

Awarded a scholarship to Clark College in Atlanta, King originally set out to become a home economics teacher. This changed when she enrolled in an introductory chemistry class, a requirement for a home economics major. The course was taught by Alfred Spriggs, an African American chemist who had received his Ph.D. from Washington University, and the subject, coupled with the professor's dynamic personality, inspired King to change her career path. As King's new mentor, Spriggs encouraged her to continue beyond college and obtain a Ph.D. After completing her undergraduate work, she received a Woodrow Wilson Scholarship and enrolled in the chemistry graduate program of the University of Chicago. There she was drawn to the study of physical chemistry and developed a strong interest in the area of thermochemistry. In the spring of 1963, she received her Ph.D. in chemistry.

Research in Thermochemistry

Six months after leaving the University of Chicago, she accepted a research position at the National Bureau of Standards, in Washington D.C., and began work on developing materials that could safely contain the highly corrosive compound oxygen difluoride. Her research on other fluoride and intermetallic compounds had important applications for the use of rockets in the NASA space program. Her reputation at the bureau was one of professionalism and perseverance; she often stayed in the lab overnight to supply quickly needed analyses. Her superiors cited King with an outstanding performance rating, and she won the Meritorious Publication Award for a 1969 paper on fluoride flame calorimetry.

Administrative Career

In 1968 King left the Bureau of Standards to taking a teaching position at York College in New York City. Two years later she was appointed Assistant Dean of Natural Sciences and Mathematics. Shortly after her promotion to Associate Dean, she took a leave of absence from York College to obtain an M.B.A. from Columbia University. In 1977 she became the president of Metropolitan State University in St. Paul, Minnesota. Under her leadership the small college increased its number of graduates five-fold, added a graduate program in management, and expanded its general curriculum. In 1988, King left academia to become the President and Executive Director of the General Mills Foundation. She also serves on several corporate boards, including that of Exxon Corporation.

King has received a host of honorary doctorate degrees from institutions, including Alverno College, Carleton College, Empire State College, Marymount Manhattan College, Nazareth College of Rochester, Rhode Island College, Seattle University, Smith College, and the William Mitchell College of Law. In 1988 she was named the Twin Citian of Year for Minneapolis-St. Paul, Minnesota. She is married to N. Judge King, with whom she has two sons, N. Judge III and Scott.

FURTHER READING:

Books

Jenkins, Edward S. *To Fathom More: African American Scientists and Inventors.* University Press of America, 1996.

—Sketch by Leslie Reinherz

Christian Felix Klein
1849–1925
German mathematician

Felix Klein is arguably one of the most influential mathematicians of the 19th century. He is best known for building the mathematical community at the University of Göttingen which became a model for research facilities in mathematics worldwide.

Christian Felix Klein was born on November 25, 1849 in Dusseldorf, the son of an official in the local finance department. Klein graduated from Gymnasium (the German equivalent of an academic high school) in Dusseldorf and began studying at the University of Bonn in 1865. At Bonn, he fell under the influence of Julius Plücker, one of the best-known geometers of the century. Plücker had moved the center of his interest to physics, and it had been in physics that Klein originally wanted to work, but Plücker returned to his original interest in geometry and took Klein with him. After Plücker's death in 1867, Klein became responsible for finishing a manuscript of Plücker's, which gave him an early introduction to the scholarly community and, in particular, to Alfred Clebsch, another prominent geometer of the time.

After receiving his doctorate in 1868 Klein spent a year traveling between Göttingen, Berlin, and Paris. Of the three, he enjoyed Göttingen immensely, did not like Berlin, and had to leave Paris ahead of schedule because of the outbreak of the Franco-Prussian War. Some of his travels were spent with the young Norwegian mathematician Marius Sophus Lie, whose ideas on geometry and analysis were much in common with Klein's. Klein's patriotism led him to enlist as a medical orderly during the war, but before the year was over he had returned to Dusseldorf, suffering from typhoid fever. The next year Klein qualified as a lecturer at Göttingen, but the following year he accepted a chair at the University of Erlangen. The complexities of academic promotion within the German university system at the time frequently required moving about from one university to another, merely for the sake of promotion within the original university.

Imposes Order on Geometry

It was the custom for a new professor to deliver an inaugural address at a German university, and in 1872 Klein followed suit at Erlangen. At the time, it was difficult to speak of one geometry, as recent developments had led to a collection of geometries whose relation to one another was unclear. There was the familiar Euclidean geometry, based on the ordinary axioms including the parallel postulate (which stipulated that there was exactly one parallel to a line through a point not on that line). There were at least two non-Euclidean geometries, one denying the existence of any parallels through a point not on a line, the other allowing the existence of an infinite number of parallels. Finally, projective geometry, which had been known since the 17th century, had been given a more quantitive turn in the work of Arthur Cayley, among others.

As outlined by Klein, geometry is the study of the properties of figures preserved under the transformations in a certain group. Which group of transformations one started with determined the geometry in which one was working. For example, if the transformations were limited to rigid motions, then one had Euclidean geometry. If projections were allowed, then one had projective geometry. If an even wider class were included, then one could end up with topology. This view (called the Erlangen program) has infused the spirit, not just of geometry, but of mathematics as a whole ever since.

Also, in 1872 Klein took over editing *Mathematische Annalen* after the death of Clebsch. Under his editorship this was the leading mathematical journal in the world and it was to remain so until World War II. By 1875, Klein had left Erlangen for the Technische Hochschule in Munich and then in 1880 he went to the University of Leipzig. In 1884 he was invited to take the place of James Joseph Sylvester at Johns Hopkins University in Baltimore, but he declined. He did make several visits to the United States subsequently, where both his personal influence and those of his students were strong. Finally, in 1886, Klein achieved the goal of a chair at Göttingen.

Builds a Home for Mathematics

Two factors in particular led Klein to successfully create a mathematical center at Göttingen. One was personal, as he was married to Anne Hegel, a descendant of the German philosopher Georg Wilhelm Friedrich Hegel. Her striking beauty may have been a draw even for those who were not yet convinced of the mathematical attractions of her husband. In the course of their married life the Kleins had one son and three daughters.

The other factor was not so pleasant. One of the subjects on which Klein had been working while at Leipzig were automorphic functions, transformations of the complex plane into itself that satisfied certain conditions. Unfortunately, for Klein the year 1884 turned into a competition with the younger French mathematician **Henri Poincaré** seeking fundamental results. Although Klein's work during this period was of a high quality, he felt that he had not lived up to expectations and suffered a nervous breakdown.

Thereafter, Klein immersed himself in creating a major mathematical center at Göttingen. The mathematical discussions did not stop with the classroom walls, but continued at the Kleins' home or on walks into the woods around Göttingen. One feature of the institute was a room filled with geometrical models to help with visualization. The presence of such a room was a reminder of Klein's antipathy to the abstract style of analysis favored by Karl Weierstrass at Berlin. Klein wanted his mathematics to have intuitive content, which explains why he was anathema to

Weierstrass. Klein attracted many of the leading German mathematicians to Göttingen, the most outstanding being **David Hilbert**. Göttingen's creative atmosphere encouraged the presence of women in the lecture hall and foreign visitors.

At the time of Klein's retirement shortly before the outbreak of World War I, he could take pride in having brought together a mathematical research community the like of which the world had never seen. In 1912, he received the Copley medal of the Royal Society, one of just many honors. His last years were saddened by the death of his son on the battlefield during the war, and he died on January 22, 1925.

Within ten years of his death the Nazi government had undertaken the dismantling of the research community in Göttingen. When the Institute for Advanced Studies was founded at Princeton in the 1930s, it modeled itself after Göttingen. The dream which Klein had brought into reality lived on.

SELECTED WRITINGS BY KLEIN:

The Evanston Colloquium, 1911.
Gesammelte Mathematische Abhandlungen, 1921–1923.
Elementary Mathematics from an Advanced Standpoint. Translated by E.R. Hedrick and C.A. Noble, 1939.

FURTHER READING:

Burau, Werner, and Bruno Schoeneberg. "Felix Klein," in *Dictionary of Scientific Biography*. Volume VII. Edited by Charles Coulston Gillispie. New York: Charles Scribner's Sons, 1973, pp. 396–400.
Reid, Constance. *Hilbert*. New York: Springer–Verlag, 1970.
Yaglom, I.H. *Felix Klein and Sophus Lie*. Translated by Sergei Sossinsky. Boston: Birkhauser, 1988.

—*Sketch by Thomas Drucker*

Mimi A. R. Koehl
1948–
American biologist

Mimi Koehl combines research principles of engineering and biology in an effort to broaden the understanding of how mechanics—such as the movement of air and water—affect the way living organisms develop and change. An artist's eye for form, a scientist's drive to understand function, and a researcher's determination to solve puzzles frequently combine to land Mimi Koehl in unlikely places with unique laboratory materials. In her efforts to understand how the mechanics of fluids and solids have shaped biological evolution, Koehl has dropped plastic frogs from her home's deck, crafted wings from construction paper and aluminum foil, and baked balsa wood models under a heat lamp.

Born in 1948 to a mother who was an artist and a father who was a physicist, Koehl grew up in an atmosphere that blended science and art. She originally enrolled at Gettysburg College as an art student, but switched to a biology major when a required class introduced her to the multitude of fascinating and perplexing shapes of living creatures. Koehl graduated from Gettysburg College with a bachelor's degree in biology in 1970. She then entered the graduate program of zoology at Duke University. Stephen Wainwright, her graduate adviser, encouraged her to move beyond the type of thinking that narrowly defines research questions in specialized fields. Wainwright encouraged student researchers to think outside the box by working backwards. He urged students to take nature's answers—for example, wings—and try to determine the basic problems that such an engineering response would solve. This emphasis on "why" instead of "what" helped hone Koehl's thinking and shaped her creative approach to scientific research.

Koehl completed her doctorate at Duke in 1976. She was named a postdoctoral fellow at the University of Washington in 1976 and accepted another postdoctoral fellowship at the University of York, England in 1977. An assistant professor of biology at Brown University from 1978 to 1979, Koehl also taught at Oxford University and the Zoologisches Institut der Universitat Basel as a visiting professor. In 1979, she joined the Department of Zoology at the University of California, Berkeley, as an assistant professor; in 1987, she was appointed a professor in the renamed Department of Integrative Biology at Berkeley.

Koehl simultaneously established herself as an educator and earned recognition as a researcher. Among her fellowships and grants are the North Atlantic Treaty Organization (NATO) Postdoctoral Fellowship in Science, the Presidential Young Investigator Award, the John Simon Guggenheim Memorial Foundation fellowship, and several National Science Foundation grants. She was assured international recognition in 1990 when she was selected to receive a MacArthur Foundation fellowship grant, often referred to as a MacArthur "genius award."

Model Solves Mystery of Flying Frogs

The plummeting plastic frog experiment is typical of Koehl's ingenious approach to research. When a colleague—Sharon Emerson, an evolutionary biologist—asked Koehl to help her unravel the mystery of Borneo's flying frogs, Koehl tackled the puzzle from her "how" perspective. The scientists knew the "what:" this subset of frogs flew. The researchers wanted to know how the frogs flew and how flying solved some problem for the creatures.

Koehl and Emerson made molds from the bodies of Borneo frogs, then used plastic dental gel, wire, and thread to make models. They rigged up a cardboard wind tunnel to simulate the force of air rushing past a frog as it launches itself and tossed the models off Koehl's deck to watch how the frog models turned and twisted in flight. What Emerson and Koehl discovered was that the flying frog's large webbed hands and feet, rubbery skin flaps, and spread-eagle flight launch actually made the frogs poor fliers. But those special features helped flying frogs turn in mid-air, float rather than plummet to the ground, and land on their feet. Flying frogs are not built for flying but for falling safely—an evolution of structure in response to environment, Koehl noted. The frogs live in forests and must maneuver from the safety of the trees, around branches and tree-trunk hugging-predators, to the forest floor in order to breed. The ability to dodge tree limbs and hungry enemies and land unhurt increases the frogs' chances of survival.

Biomechanics Called into Question

Biomechanics is a relatively new scientific specialty that focuses on solving medical problems with engineering techniques. Most research in this area is conducted with a view to solving a specific health problem—designing a better artificial hip joint, a more comfortable prosthetic leg, or a smaller, more efficient artificial heart. But Koehl uses the principles of biomechanics to identify how a particular physical trait solves an organism's problems. "I love surprises—when people think they understand something and it actually works another way," Koehl was quoted as saying in *Notable Women in the Life Sciences.* "At one point I was studying appendages on zooplankton that looked like combs, and were thought to be used for filter feeding. During my study, I found that water wouldn't go through the gaps because they were so tiny and the water was too sticky. So these appendages were not filters at all, as had been previously assumed." Such research is more than an academic exercise. Copepods are a vital link in the ocean food chain, so understanding how they feed may help maintain the delicate ecological balance that sustains life both in the sea and on land and may help shape the politics of environmental protection. How marine organisms survive constant pummeling in the ocean may provide clues on how to build structures and vessels for the sea. Understanding how living structures function, evolve, and develop physical traits to cope with environmental challenges will add new insight to fields ranging from genetic engineering of farm animals to man's ability to adapt to conditions in space.

Koehl focuses her research efforts on ocean life. A believer in field as well as laboratory work, she spent the latter part of 1997 conducting research in the waters around Hawaii. She is continuing her study of copepods and investigating how the mechanics of sea anemones affect and are affected by fluid flow.

SELECTED WRITINGS BY KOEHL:

Periodicals

"The Interaction of Moving Water and Sessile Organisms." *Scientific American* 247 (1982): 124-134.
"Aerodynamics, Thermoregulation, and the Evolution of Insect Wings: Differential Scaling and Evolutionary Change." *Evolution* 39 (1985): 488-504.
"The Interaction of Behavior and Morphology in the Evolution of a Novel Locomotor Type: Flying Frogs." *Evolution* 44 (1990): 1931-1946.
(With J. G. Kingsolver) "Selective Factors in the Evolution of Insect Wings." *Annual Review of Entomology* 39 (1994): 425-451.
"When Does Morphology Matter?" *Annual Review of Ecological Systems* 27 (1996): 501-542.
"Mechanisms of Particle Selection by Tentaculate Suspension Feeders During Encounter, Retention and Handling." *Journal of Experimental Marine Biology and Ecology* 209 (1997): 47-73.

FURTHER READING:

Books

Sherrer, B. F., and Sherreer, B. S., eds. *Notable Women in the Life Sciences.* Westport, CT: Greenwood Publishing, 1996, pp. 239-243.

Periodicals

Franklin, Deborah. "The Shape of Life." *Discover* (December 1991): 10-16.
Smith, A. D. "Bay Area Brain Trust: 101 Achievers Who Make This the Smartest Place on Earth." *San Francisco Focus Magazine* 42 (1995): 30-47.

Georges Köhler

Other

Koehl. "Mimi A. R. Koehl." 10/27/97. http://ib.berkeley.edu/faculty.Koehl, MAR.html (29 Oct. 1997).

—*Sketch by A. Mullig*

Georges Köhler
1946–1995
German immunologist

For decades, antibodies—substances manufactured by our plasma cells to help fight disease—were produced artificially by injecting animals with foreign macromolecules, then bleeding the animals and separating the antiserum in their blood. The technique was arduous and far from foolproof. But the discovery of the hybridoma technique by German immunologist Georges Köhler changed all that, making antibodies relatively easy to produce and dramatically facilitating research on many serious medical disorders such as the acquired immunodeficiency syndrome (AIDS) and cancer. For his work on what would come to be known as monoclonal antibodies, Köhler shared the 1984 Nobel Prize in medicine. He was only 38 years old at the time.

Born in Munich, in what was then occupied Germany, on April 17, 1946, Georges Jean Franz Köhler attended the University of Freiburg, where he obtained his Ph.D. in biology in 1974. From there he set off to Cambridge University in England, to work as a postdoctoral fellow for two years at the British Medical Research Council's laboratories. At Cambridge, Köhler worked under Dr. **César Milstein,** an Argentinean-born researcher with whom Köhler would eventually share the Nobel Prize. At the time, Milstein, who was Köhler's senior by nineteen years, was a distinguished immunologist, and he actively encouraged Köhler in his research interests. Eventually, it was while working in the Cambridge laboratory that Köhler discovered the hybridoma technique.

The Experiment in the Basement

Dubbed by the *New York Times* as the "guided missiles of biology," antibodies are produced by human plasma cells in response to any threatening and harmful bacterium, virus, or tumor cell. The body forms a specific antibody against each antigen; and César Milstein has told the *New York Times* that the potential number of different antigens may reach "well over a million." Therefore, for researchers working to combat diseases like cancer, an understanding of how antibodies could be harnessed for a possible cure was of great interest. And although scientists knew the benefits of producing antibodies, until Köhler and Milstein published their findings, there was no known technique for maintaining the long-term culture of antibody-forming plasma cells.

Köhler's interest in the subject had been aroused years earlier, when he had become intrigued by the work of Dr. Michael Potter of the National Cancer Institute in Bethesda, Maryland. In 1962 Potter had induced myelomas, or plasma-cell tumors in mice, and others had discovered how to keep those tumors growing indefinitely in culture. Potter showed that plasma tumor cells were both immortal and able to create an unlimited number of identical antibodies. The only drawback was that there seemed no way to make the cells produce a certain *type* of antibody. Because of this, Köhler wanted to initiate a cloning experiment that would fuse plasma cells able to produce the desired antibodies with the "immortal" myeloma cells. With Milstein's blessing, Köhler began his experiment.

"For seven weeks after he had made the hybrid cells," the *New York Times* reported in October 1984, "Dr. Köhler refrained from testing the outcome of the experiment for fear of likely disappointment. At last, around Christmas 1974, he persuaded his wife," Claudia Köhler, "to come to the windowless basement where he worked to share his disappointment after the critical test." But disappointment turned to joy when Köhler discovered his test had been a success. Astoundingly, his hybrid cells were making pure antibodies against the test antigen. The result was dubbed "monoclonal antibodies." For his contribution to medical science, Köhler—who in 1977 had relocated to Switzerland to do research at the Basel Institute for Immunology—was awarded the Nobel in 1984. Said the blond-haired, bespectacled scientist when he found out about the honor: "My knees are still trembling."

Opening the Door of Immunology Wide

The implications of Köhler's discovery were immense, and as Milstein has told the *New York Times,* monoclonal antibodies have resulted in "a windfall of basic research." In the early 1980s Köhler's discovery had led scientists to identify various lymphocytes, or white blood cells. Among the kinds discovered were the T-4 lymphocytes, the cells destroyed by AIDS. Monoclonal antibodies have also improved tests for hepatitis B and streptococcal infections by providing guidance in selecting appropriate antibiotics, and they have aided in the research on thyroid disorders, lupus, rheumatoid arthritis, and inherited brain disorders. More significantly, Köhler's work has led to advances in research that can harness monoclonal antibodies into certain drugs and toxins that fight cancer, but would cause damage in their own right. Researchers are also using monoclonal antibodies to identify antigens specific to the surface of cancer cells so as to develop tests to detect the spread of cancerous cells in the body.

Despite the significance of the discovery, which has also resulted in vast amounts of research funds for many research laboratories, for Köhler and Milstein—who never patented their discovery—there was little remuneration. In fact, during the years following the discovery until they won the Nobel Prize, Köhler received only a single honorary doctorate. Following the award, however, he and Milstein, together with Michael Potter, were named winners of the Lasker Medical Research Award.

In 1985, Köhler moved back to his hometown of Freiburg, Germany, to assume the directorship of the Max Planck Institute for Immune Biology. He died on March 1, 1995.

SELECTED WRITINGS BY KÖHLER:

Periodicals

"Continuous Cultures of Fused Cells Secreting Antibody of Predefined Specificity." *Nature* 256 (1975): 495.
"Immunoglobulin Production by Lymphocyte Hybridomas." *European Journal of Immunology* 8 (1978): 82.

"Immunoglobulin Chain Loss in Hybridoma Lines." *Proceedings of the National Academy of Sciences U.S.A.* 77 (1980): 2197.
"The Technique of Hybridoma Production." *Immunological Methods* 2 (1981): 285-90.
"Resistance of Mice Deficient in IL-4 to Retrovirus-Induced immunodeficiency Syndrome." *Science* 262 (8 October 1993): 240-42.

FURTHER READING:

Periodicals

"A Discovery and Its Impact: Nine Years of Excitement." *New York Times* (16 October 1984): C3.
"Five Named as Winners of Lasker Medical Research Awards." *New York Times* (15 November 1984): A28..
"Georges Köhler, 48, Medicine Nobel Winner" (obituary). *New York Times* (4 March 1995).
"The Nobel Prize in Medicine." *Science* (30 November 1984): 1025.
"Three Immunology Investigators Win Nobel Prize in Medicine." *New York Times* (16 October 1984): A1.

—Sketch by Joan Oleck

Daniel E. Koshland, Jr.
1920–
American biochemist

Daniel E. Koshland, Jr. has made major contributions in the fields of enzyme action, short- and long-term memory, and science education. In the 1950s, Koshland proposed that the then-popular lock-and-key theory of enzyme action was inadequate to explain all forms of enzyme action. To augment that theory, he proposed an induced-fit theory of enzyme action. Since the 1970s, his interest has turned to the mechanism by which cells "remember" situations and events. His experiments on bacterial chemotaxis have led to important new understandings as to how organisms develop short-and long-term memory. Koshland has also been involved in a variety of programs for the promotion of scientific understanding among the general public. From 1985 to 1995 he was editor-in-chief of the prestigious journal *Science.*

Daniel E. Koshland, Jr., was born in New York City on March 30, 1920. His parents were Daniel Edward Koshland and the former Eleanor Haas, heirs to part of the fortune of Walter Haas, founder of Levi

Daniel E. Koshland, Jr.

Strauss and Company. In 1997, *Forbes* magazine estimated the younger Koshland's financial worth to be $795 million, inherited from his parents.

Koshland claims that his early life was "a landscape of boredom from sea to shining sea." It included none of the "material that generates good novels: no broken homes, no misunderstood childhood, no criminal youth gangs, no disastrous liaisons." He first became interested in science in the eighth grade when he read *Microbe Hunters*, by Paul DeKruif, and *Arrowsmith*, by Sinclair Lewis. These books so fascinated him that he decided to become a scientist and took all the courses in mathematics and science that his high school had to offer.

After graduating from high school, Koshland enrolled at the University of California at Berkeley. Once there, Koshland was influenced by some of the leading chemists in the world, including **Gilbert Newton Lewis** and Wendell Latimer. He describes one experience in an advanced inorganic chemistry class with Latimer when he turned in his final examination paper for a three-hour exam. Latimer asked Koshland if an 'A' would be sufficient for the course. Koshland had already earned straight As on three previous examinations in the course. As he asked the question, Latimer prepared to tear up Koshland exam paper. Koshland says that he "reacted angrily" and pointed out to Latimer that he had studied hard in preparation for the examination. "You owe it to me to correct it," he said to Latimer.

As expected, Koshland also earned an 'A' on that exam and in the course.

The Manhattan Project

Koshland received his B.S. in chemistry from Berkeley in 1941 and then accepted a job at the Shell Chemical Company in Martinez, California. When World War II broke out, he tried to enlist in the Navy, but found that his eyesight was 20/400, "legally blind" as far as the Navy was concerned. His offer to work in assignments where vision was not critical was rejected, and he remained with Shell.

Shortly thereafter, Koshland received a call from Latimer saying that **Glen Seaborg** was recruiting scientists to work on the Manhattan Project at the University of Chicago. Koshland had no idea, of course, what the Manhattan Project involved, but accepted the offer when Latimer told him that the work as "the most important job in the world." During his tenure with the Manhattan Project, Koshland's primary responsibilities involved the purification of plutonium for the construction of the first plutonium-based fission bomb.

At the war's conclusion, Koshland decided to remain at the University of Chicago and enter a Ph.D. program in biochemistry. At the time, the notion of applying the principles of chemistry to biological phenomena was still fairly new, and he was regarded the "odd man out" in his department. His research involved the use of radioactive carbon-14 for the study of chemical reactions in the metabolism of glucose. For this work, he was awarded his Ph.D. in chemistry in 1949.

Research Endeavors Lead to Brookhaven National Laboratory

For his postdoctoral work, Koshland moved to Harvard University, where he worked under the direction of Paul Bartlett. It was at Harvard that Koshland became interested in research on enzymes and enzymatic reactions. When he completed his two-year tenure at Harvard, Koshland found that he was virtually unable to find a job. He was already 31 years old, had published little, and was engaged in the relatively narrow and unknown field of biochemistry. He finally accepted an appointment at the Brookhaven National Laboratory, a post where he thought he might remain "for a year or so and then go back to a university." In fact, he stayed at Brookhaven for 14 years, as associate biochemist, biochemist, and senior biochemist.

It was at Brookhaven that Koshland developed his induced fit theory of enzymatic action. For more than a hundred years, the behavior of enzymes had been explained by a theory developed by the German chemist **Emil Fischer**. Fischer suggested that an enzyme molecule reacts with other molecules, called substrate molecules, that fit exactly into one or another portion of the enzyme molecule. While the enzyme and substrate molecules are joined to each other, bonds within the substrate molecules break. When the substrate molecule finally breaks loose from the enzyme molecule, it does so in a new and altered form of two new molecules.

Koshland's research had led him to conclude that Fischer's theory did not explain a number of enzymatic changes. He developed the notion that enzyme molecules sometimes have to change their shape in order to accommodate a substrate molecule. For example, a substrate molecule might move into a cavity in an enzyme molecule and then be captured as the enzyme molecule closed in around it.

Koshland found that traditional chemistry journals were largely uninterested in publishing his ideas about enzyme action. He was finally able to have his first paper on the subject published in the *Proceedings of the National Academy of Sciences*, under the sponsorship of D. D. Van Slyke, a member of the Academy. Even then, Koshland's theory was not widely accepted. One scientist wrote that "The Fischer Key-Lock theory has lasted 100 years and will not be overturned by speculation from an embryonic scientist." In spite of that view, the induced fit theory of enzymatic action is now widely accepted as an explanation of the behavior of many enzymes.

In 1964, Koshland was offered an appointment in the Department of Biochemistry at the University of California at Berkeley. He and his wife were very uncertain about the offer. They had become very happy in New York, and the prospect of picking up and moving their family of five children was not an entirely good one. Koshland points out, however, that his college days at Berkeley had been so exciting and so interesting, that he was strongly motivated to return. His wife, an Easterner, had strong reservations, but finally agreed to the move. He assumed his new position as Professor of Biochemistry in 1965, a post he has held since. He also served as chair of the department between 1973 and 1978.

In 1984, Koshland was offered the position of editor at *Science* magazine. *Science* is the largest and one of the most prestigious journals of science for general readers in the world. It has more than four times as many subscribers as its next nearest competitor, the British-published *Nature* magazine. Koshland held the post of editor-in-chief at *Science* for 10 years, during which time he was best known for his incisive and witty editorials.

Among Koshland's many honors are the Pauling and Edgard Fahs Smith awards of the American Chemical Society, the Rosenstiel Award, the Wateford Prize, and honorary degrees from the Weizmann Institute of Science, the Carnegic Mellon University,

and Simon Fraser University. Koshland's wife of 52 years, Marian, was an eminent immunologist at Brookhaven and Berkeley. She died of lung cancer in 1997.

SELECTED WRITINGS BY KOSHLAND:

Periodicals

(With B.H. Morimoto) "Conditional activation of cAMP signal transduction by protein kinase C." *Journal of Biological Chemistry* 269. pp. 4065-4069.

(With M. Shapiro and D. Panomitros) "Interactions between the methylation sites of the *Escherichia coli* aspartate receptor mediated by the methyltransferase." *Journal of Biological Chemistry* 270 (2): 751-755.

(With T. Zhang) "Modeling substrate binding in Thermus thermophilus isopropymalate dehydrogenase." *Protein Science* 4, pp. 84-92.

FURTHER READING:

Books

Press, Jacques Cattell. *American Men & Women of Science: Physical and Biological Sciences.* 14th Ed., Vol. IV, p. 2738.

Periodicals

Koshland, Daniel E. Jr. "How to Get Paid for Having Fun." *Annual Review of Biochemistry* (1996): 1-13.

Schoch, Russell. "A conversation with Daniel E. Koshland, Jr." *California Monthly* (December 1991): 44-48.

Other

Podduturi, Anil. "Colleagues Recall Professor Known As 'Superwoman'" *Daily Californian.* http://www.dailycal.org/archive/10.31.97/news/koshland.html (31 October 1997).

Wong, Sylvaine. "Koshland Masters Science of Teaching," *Daily Californian.* February 2, 1997. http://www.dailycal.org/archive/02.21.97/koshland.html

—Sketch by David Newton

William B. Kouwenhoven
1886–1975
American electrical and biomedical engineer

Though William Kouwenhoven was trained as an electrical engineer, his most enduring contributions to science came from the medical arena. Using his background in electrical engineering, Kouwenhoven invented three different defibrillators and developed CPR (cardiopulmonary resuscitation) techniques. (A defibrillator uses electricity to restore a heart's normal rhythm. Because defibrillators are not always easily accessible, Kouwenhoven developed CPR, which is an external method of cardiac massage that keeps oxygen circulating. Kouwenhoven's inventions have saved countless lives in the second half of the twentieth century.

He was born William Bennett Kouwenhoven on January 13, 1886, in Brooklyn, New York, to Tunis Garet Bergen Kouwenhoven, and his wife Phebe Florence (nee Bennett). Kouwenhoven was educated locally, and earned his bachelor's and his master's degree in electrical engineering from the Brooklyn Polytechnic Institute in 1906 and 1907, respectively. After earning his bachelor's degree, Kouwenhoven began teaching at Brooklyn Polytechnic Institute as an assistant in physics. After earning his master's, Kouwenhoven taught physics and electrical engineering as an instructor at the same institution until 1910.

In the spring of 1910, Kouwenhoven married Abigail Baxter Remsen. They had one child, a son named William Gerrit Kouwenhoven. After their wedding, the couple lived in Germany for several years while Kouwenhoven continued his electrical engineering studies in Baden. He earned his *Diplom Ingerieur* from the Karlsruhe Techinsche Hochschule in 1912, and his *Docktor Ingernieur* the following year.

Upon completion of his education in Germany, the couple moved back to the United States. Kouwenhoven taught electrical engineering for a year at Washington University, before moving to Baltimore's Johns Hopkins, where he spent the rest of his career. Between 1914 and his retirement to professor emeritus status in 1954, Kouwenhoven moved through the ranks from an instructor in electrical engineering to Dean of the School of Engineering.

Invents Three Types of Defibrillators

In the late 1920s, Kouwenhoven's interest crossed between electrical engineering and medicine. His engineering work focused on the high tension wire transmission of electricity. Kouwenhoven observed that linesmen, who died from shock-related incidents, seemed to die from fibrillation (ventricular arrest). He became interested in electricity's possible role in reviving animals (and later people), especially in restarting the heart. He knew that, when applied to the heart, electric current could start it again.

The defibrillators Kouwenhoven invented used this principle to restore normal ventricular fibrillation. From 1928 until the mid-1950s, Kouwenhoven developed three different defibrillators, the open-chest defibrillator, the Hopkins AC Defibrillator, and the Mine Safety Portable. Though Kouwenhoven developed a defibrillator that required direct contact with the heart before World War II, it did not become widely used until after the War ended.

Develops Cardiopulmonary Resuscitation (CPR)

The defibrillators Kouwenhoven invented where intended to be used within two minutes of the start of ventricular fibrillation. Indeed, at least one of his early defibrillators required direct contact with the heart, which was not feasible if the patient was not near a medical treatment facility. Beginning in 1956, Kouwenhoven began developing a non-invasive method to help restart the heart. (In the same year, Kouwenhoven became a lecturer at the Johns Hopkins Medical School.) With the assistance of then-graduate student Guy Knickerbocker and Doctor James Jude, Kouwenhoven used dogs to develop this new procedure.

During one such experiment on a dog, Kouwenhoven realized that the weight of the defibrillator's paddles themselves made the animal's blood pressure rise. Based on this principle, by 1959, Kouwenhoven came up with what he called CPR. It was also known as external heart massage or closed chest cardiac massage. Widely used today, Kouwenhoven's procedure involves putting pressure on the breastbone at timed intervals to avert cardiac arrest.

Because Kouwenhoven's CPR method does not involve surgery, it can be used in many emergency situations involving heart-stoppages or breathing-stoppage. Indeed, when properly used in combination with a mouth-to-mouth resuscitation procedure (which was also developed at Johns Hopkins), CPR can sustain a person's life for up to one hour.

Kouwenhoven taught his CPR techniques to Johns Hopkins staff and Baltimore City Fire Department Ambulance Corps. By the early 1960s, the procedure was being used throughout the United States. Kouwenhoven's ground-breaking work with defibrillators and CPR were recognized by both the medical community and the electrical engineering establishment in the early 1960s. He was awarded the American Medical Association's (AMA) Ludwig Hekton Gold medal in 1961, and the American Institute of Electrical Engineering's Edison Medal in 1962. Johns Hopkins also honored him by bestowing an honorary M.D. on Kouwenhoven in 1969. Kouwenhoven is the only person to ever receive this honor.

Though Kouwenhoven's non-medical contributions to electrical engineering are not as well known, they did exist. Kouwenhoven was interested in other aspects of electricity, including electrical measurements, electric welding, and electrical shock, as well as magnetic analysis. Indeed, for a year, 1919-20, Kouwenhoven took a leave of absence from Johns Hopkins to work as the engineering superintendent for Winchester Repeating Arms Company.

Kouwenhoven's profound contribution to medicine and engineering were also recognized in the 1970s. Before his death in 1975, Kouwenhoven won another AMA award, the Scientific Achievement Award in 1972; a year later, he won the Albert Lasker Clinical Research Award. Kouwenhoven died in Baltimore, Maryland, on November 10, 1975. In his obituary, colleague W. R. Milnor praised Kouwenhoven as "A rare combination of practical man and scholar, his scientific standards were uncompromising, yet his goals were in the everyday world."

FURTHER READING:

Books

"Kouwenhoven, William Bennett." *A Biographical Encyclopedia of Scientists*, 2nd ed. Bristol: Institute of Physics Publishing, 1994, p. 497.

Periodicals

"The lifesaver known as CPR." *FDA Consumer* (February 1986): 16.
Milnor, W. R. "William Bennett Kouwenhoven, 1886-1975." *The Johns Hopkins Medical Journal* (March 1976): 109-10.

—*Sketch by Annette Petrusso*

Fred Russell Kramer
1942–

American molecular biologist

Fred Kramer started his scientific career with an eye toward outer space, but he has instead become a pioneer of inner space, exploring the complex chemical machinery inside the cell.

In the late 1990s, Kramer's work focused on "hybridization probes," custom-made segments of deoxyribonucleic acid (DNA) with fluorescent molecules attached that seek out and bind to their exact complement in a cell's DNA. Using this highly specific marker, Kramer can detect the presence of a target gene quickly and accurately. An acquired immune deficiency syndrome (AIDS) test developed by Kramer's lab, which is based on this technique, is sensitive enough to find one human immunodeficiency virus (HIV)-infected cell among one million uninfected cells.

Attends Bronx High School of Science

Kramer was born on July 7, 1942 in New York City. He was raised in New York and completed his public school education at a magnet school, the Bronx High School of Science. He was able to skip a year and graduate at 16. His father, Paul M. Kramer, was a professional photographer who worked for newspapers and commercial studios and taught photography at the U.S. government's Armed Forces Information School. His mother, Janet (Mendelson) Kramer, was a secretary in the New York Public Schools.

Kramer had been interested in science even in grade school. As a sixth-grader, he remembers going around to third-grade classes to teach students about the properties of air pressure, what air was made of, and how it worked. "I guess I really liked science and technology," he told contributor Karl Leif Bates in an October 1997 telephone interview. It was the dawn of the space age, and Kramer was already aware of what lay ahead when the Russians launched the first Sputnik probe in 1957. "When it went up I already knew what it was and how it worked."

Shifts Focus from Astronomy to Biology

Not surprisingly, his interest led him to pursue astronomy, and when he went to the University of Michigan as a freshman he intended to become an astronomer. But that same year, "the entire astronomy department moved to Harvard," Kramer said. He became a student in an experimental curriculum called the Unified Science Program, which exposed students to chemistry, physics, and mathematics, and had them perform independent research. Most of Kramer's research was in physics, but he did get involved in one life sciences experiment involving sorting proteins for an immunology investigation.

When he wasn't in the labs, Kramer also found time to become editor of the student paper, *The Michigan Daily*. "It did a lot to prepare me for what I'm doing now," Kramer said. "You have to make decisions all the time there, you have to build consensus and work with people." The Daily won a national award as best college paper during Kramer's fourth year of school.

Kramer had declared a mathematics major, but even that fell through. "By the time I was coming to the end of my junior year, I realized I wasn't good enough to be a full-time, creative mathematician," he said. His senior year, he took biology and philosophy. "I was looking for something different. And I really loved biology." Kramer ended up staying at Michigan for a fifth year, and taking almost all biology courses.

Upon graduation in 1964, he left Ann Arbor for Rockefeller University to attend graduate school in biology. "I was probably the least-prepared graduate student there," Kramer told Bates. "Everybody else had been doing biology since grade school." He completed his Ph.D. in 1969 in molecular biology, and immediately took a post-doctoral fellowship at Columbia University's Institute of Cancer Research.

He stayed at Columbia and rose through the ranks for the next 17 years, becoming an instructor, then an assistant professor and finally a research scientist, before leaving in 1986. He joined the Molecular Genetics department of the Public Health Research Institute in New York, then, in addition, the faculty of New York University's medical school as a research professor in microbiology the year after that.

Develops Molecular Probe as Diagnostic Tool

Kramer's research came to focus on ribonucleic acid (RNA), the molecule that translates information from the DNA in genes to manufacture proteins for the cell's structure or its chemical reactions. Using a technique called "Q-beta replicase" to quickly produce huge numbers of copies of gene products, Kramer's lab became adept at reading the specific code of genes. From that, he started to develop the probes that could be useful for diagnostic medicine, detecting genes or pathogens quickly in a living organism. Since the genes of any given species are different from the genes of any other species, one can make probes complementary to very specific DNA sequences. The probes will bind only to that target sequence, if it is present.

Kramer's lab developed an improved probe called a "molecular beacon" which only fluoresces when it has successfully attached to the target DNA sequence. "This is a major physical change when a probe binds to its target," Kramer said. And the amount of light released reveals just how much of the target sequence is present. Hundreds of different diagnostic beacons based on this work became available.

One test developed by Kramer's lab can determine the drug-resistance of a strain of tuberculosis within 48 hours, greatly speeding up a physician's ability to administer the proper drug to fight the infection, and eliminating the trial-and-error approach of prescribing antibiotics for a TB patient.

Kramer and his research colleagues hold more than 20 patents, many of which have been licensed to outside firms for commercialization.

SELECTED WRITINGS BY KRAMER:

Periodicals

(With S. Tyagi) "Molecular Beacons: Probes that Fluoresce upon Hybridization." *Nature Biotechnology* 14: 303-308.

(With S. Tyagi, U. Landegren, M. Tazi, and P.M. Lizardi) "Extremely Sensitive, Background-free Gene Detection using Binary Probes and QB Replicase." *Proceedings of the National Academy of Sciences* 93: 5395-5400.

FURTHER READING:

Other:

Fred Russell Kramer, "Fred Russell Kramer, PhD" 1997. http://www.med.nyu.edu/people/F.Kramer.html.

—*Sketch by Karl Leif Bates*

Cecilia Krieger
1894–1974
Polish–born Canadian mathematician

Cecilia Krieger is best known as the woman who translated the work of **Waclaw Sierpiński** from Polish to English, returning to her native land to see him in 1931 while working on the project. She was also awarded the third mathematics doctorate ever in Canada, and the third woman in the world to earn a Ph.D. Though she never rose above the rank of assistant professor, Krieger taught for over thirty years and is credited with urging **Cathleen Synge Morawetz** to take up a career in mathematics. Her studies in set theory and topology as originated by **Georg Cantor** reach into the heart of what we now know as the interdimensional geometry of fractals.

Cypra Cecilia Krieger was born in Poland on an unknown date in 1894. She was one of five children born to a Jewish merchant named Moses and his wife Sarah. There were three daughters; Cecilia as she was called, Regina, and Rae. The sons were Samuel, who would later sponsor Cecilia's immigration to Canada in 1920, and Nathan. After early schooling in Poland, Krieger studied mathematical physics at the University of Vienna for a year. When she arrived in Toronto, however, she did not know a word of English.

"It Is Really Easy"

Much was made in the local Canadian press about the fact that only four years later Krieger took her B.A. at the University of Toronto, supporting herself by working at the Muskoka Inn in the lake district. Her master's degree in modern elliptical functions, number and set theory, and the minimum principles of mechanics followed one year later. During the years 1928 and 1929, Krieger was a Ph.D. instructor in math and physics. She became the first woman in Canada to take a Ph.D., the same year she was promoted to lecturer, in 1930. Her advisor, W. J. Webber, was chiefly responsible for the growth and development of graduate studies in his department during this time.

Krieger had already begun publishing in 1928, but her 1934 translation of Sierpiński's second volume on topology, the first into English, was earned her recognition. When asked how difficult it had been to come to Canada, learn English, and obtain her degrees in such a short period of time, Krieger demurred, prompting the reporter to declare her "a miracle of modesty." She replied that other languages are harder to learn than English. Krieger's English version of *General Topology* also included a 30–page outline of volume one in Sierpiński's series "The Theory of Aggregates," called *Transfinite Numbers*. The full–length volume one only existed in Polish and French at that point.

Unfortunately her father did not live to see this triumph, having died at age 70 in 1929 from complications following a streetcar accident.

Touched Twice by the Holocaust

Following the death of her father in 1929, Krieger did her best to help her family, supporting her unmarried sisters throughout the 1930s and the early 1940s. Krieger also "adopted" the family of Alex Rosenberg, immigrant Jewish refugees, during World War II. After 12 years at the University College, in 1942, she received her last promotion to assistant professor. Krieger averaged a course load of 13 classes a week, ranging from six to 75 students per class.

Krieger married late in life to a Holocaust survivor, the physician Zygmund Dunaij, in 1953. She continued to teach, but also spent some time in the United States and was good friends with the Synge family in New York. However, this period is not widely documented. Her husband died in 1968. Krieger then taught in a private boy's preparatory school in upper Canada from 1969 until her death at age 80.

After spending her early life during a formative period for university mathematics, being female was just one of many firsts in the field for Krieger. When asked about women's prospects for success in mathematics, she had declined to generalize. "It depends upon the individual," she concluded.

SELECTED WRITINGS BY KRIEGER:

Books

(Translator) *General Topology*, by Waclaw Sierpiński, 1934.

Periodicals

"On the Summability of Trigonometric Series with Localized Properties." *Royal Society of Canada Transactions* 22, no. 3 (1928): 139–147.

"On Fourier Constants and Convergence Factors of Double Fourier Series." *Royal Society of Canada Transactions* Series 3 24, section 3 (May 1930): 161–196.

FURTHER READING:

Books

Anand, Kailash K. "Cypra Cecilia Krieger and the Human Side of Mathematics." *Despite the Odds: Essays on Canadian Women and Science.* Edited by Marianne Ainley. Montreal, P.Q., Canada: Vehicule Press, 1990, pp. 248–251.

"Cathleen S. Morawetz." *More Mathematical People.* Edited by D.J. Albers, G.L. Alexanderson and C. Reid, pp. 221–238.

Periodicals

The Toronto Monthly and other Toronto periodicals, 1924–1934, in the collection of the Thomas Fisher Rare Book Library, University of Toronto Archives.

Other

"Cecilia Krieger." *Biographies of Women Mathematicians.*
http://www.scottlan.edu/lriddle/women/chronol.htm (July 20, 1997).

—*Sketch by Jennifer Kramer*

Harold Walter Kroto
1939–
English physical chemist

University of Sussex professor Harold Walter Kroto was awarded the 1996 Nobel Prize for Chemistry along with Rice University professors **Robert F.**

Curl, Jr., and **Richard E. Smalley** for their discovery of a new form of the element carbon, called Carbon 60. The third molecular form of carbon (the other two forms are diamonds and graphite), C60 consists of 60 atoms of carbon arranged in hexagons and pentagons and is called a "buckminsterfullerene," "fullerene," or by its nickname "Buckyball" in honor of Buckminster Fuller, whose geodesic domes it resembles. Kroto made the discovery in 1985, and Curl and Smalley confirmed his findings.

Harold Kroto was born on October 7, 1939, in Wisbech, Cambridgeshire, England to Heinz and Edith Kroto. Raised in Bolton, Lancashire, England, he graduated with a degree in chemistry from the University of Sheffield in 1961 and received his Ph.D. there in 1964. In 1963 he married Margaret Henrietta Hunter, with whom he would have two children. His Ph.D. work involved high-resolution electronic spectra of free radicals produced by flash photolysis—chemical decomposition by the action of radiant energy. His postdoctoral work was conducted at the National Research Council in Ottawa, Canada. After completing this work he spent a year at Bell Laboratories in New Jersey, where he also studied quantum chemistry. He began teaching and researching at the University of Sussex in 1967. He was appointed full professor in 1985 and a Royal Research Professor in 1991.

In the 1970s Kroto launched a research program at the University of Sussex to look for chains of carbon in interstellar space. Kroto worked with scientists at the National Research Council, where he did his postdoctoral studies, to find the space molecules and did actually find several chains in the years between 1975-78. He speculated that the molecules might be products of red-giant stars, but did not know how the chains themselves were formed. His search to find an explanation led him to not only the carbon-60 molecule, but also resulted in new areas of carbon chemistry study. In 1992 Kroto won the Italgas Prize for Chemistry for this work.

Travels Overseas to Confirm Hunch

In 1984 Kroto borrowed from his wife's bank account and flew to Houston find out exactly how the carbon chains were formed. He had heard of the work being done in laser spectroscopy by Richard Smalley and Robert Curl at Rice University in Texas and thought he could use their laser apparatus to simulate the temperatures in space needed to create the carbon chains. Smalley and Curl had been looking at semiconductors like silicon and germanium in the laser apparatus, and had no reason to look at simple carbon. But that September, the scientists turned the laser beam on a piece of graphite and found something they were not looking for, a molecule that had 60 carbon atoms. Carbon had previously been known

to have only two molecular forms, diamond and graphite. They surmised correctly that this was a third form of carbon, and that it had a cage-like structure resembling a soccer ball, or a geodesic dome. They named the structure buckminsterfullerene, which became fullerene, and also by the nickname "buckyballs."

Wins Nobel Prize with Smalley and Curl

Two things made this find unusual. One reason is that fundamental research led to the discovery, and the second is that a corporation did not fund it. Evidence for the existence of large carbon clusters had existed before, but Smalley, Curl, and Kroto were the first scientists to fully identify and stabilize carbon-60. In October of 1996, all three were recognized for this remarkable discovery with the Nobel Prize in Chemistry. At the time of the announcement Kroto thought he might be winner, but decided to go to lunch instead of waiting. He had been depressed because just two hours before the announcement he had been turned down for research funding by the British government for the very same research that had won him the Nobel Prize. That same year Kroto was knighted for winning the Nobel Prize.

The Royal Swedish Academy of Sciences, which grants the Nobel, heralded the breakthrough. "From a theoretical viewpoint, the discovery of the fullerenes has influenced our conception of such widely separated scientific problems as the galactic carbon cycle and classical aromaticity, a keystone of theoretical chemistry," stated the Academy citation. Aromaticity refers to the chemical stability of organic compounds.

Kroto's research team in Sussex continues fundamental work on the fullerene, looking at its basic chemistry as well as the way it has changed how carbon-based materials are viewed. Interdisciplinary work is also being conducted on the interstellar applications of carbon microparticles. But Kroto is not one to speculate on the uses of carbon-60. In an interview in the newsletter *Science Watch*, Kroto explains that "fundamental scientists are not necessarily the best people to ask about applications. People like myself have, in a sense, spent a lifetime avoiding applications. We're puzzled about interesting things for their own sake, and we follow up on them." Kroto compares the discovery of the fullerene to the discovery of lasers; it was almost a decade before scientists discovered a practical use for lasers.

When Kroto began his research into carbon chains, his primary interest was finding carbon-60 in space. "It was discovered by simulating certain astrophysical conditions, after all," Kroto explained in the *Science Watch* interview. This desire was fulfilled when geochemist Jeffrey Bada of the Scripps Institution of Oceanography in La Jolla, California found fullerenes inside rocks extracted from a 1.8 billion-year-old meteor crash in Canada. Bada thought that the molecules had been formed by their proximity to a red-giant star. Kroto himself had suggested almost 20 years ago that this might be the place to find carbon chains.

SELECTED WRITINGS BY KROTO:

Books

The Fullerenes : New Horizons for the Chemistry, Physics and Astrophysics of Carbon. Edited by D. R. M. Walton. Cambridge University Press, 1988.

(With John E. Fischer and David E. Cox) *The Fullerenes.* Pergamon Press, 1993.

Molecular Rotation Spectra. Dover, 1992.

Periodicals

"C60: Buckminsterfullerene, the Celestial Sphere that fell to Earth." *Chemistry*, International Edition (1992).

"Formation of Carbon Nanofibers" *Physical Chemistry* (1992).

"Fullerene Physics" *Physics Today* (1992).

"Space, Stars, C(60) and Soot." *Science* (1988).

"The Structural Characterisation of Buckminsterfullerene Compounds." *Molecular Structure* (1993).

FURTHER READING:

Books

Andreoni, Wanda, ed. *The Chemical Physics of Fullerenes 10 (And 5) Years Later: The Far-Reaching Impact of the Discovery of C60* (NATO Asi Series). Kluwer Academic Publications, 1996.

Periodicals

Zimmer, Carl. "Buckyballs from space." *Discover*, (August 1996).

Other

"Chemistry, physics Nobel winners announced." *CNN Interactive.* 1996. http://cnn.com/WORLD/9610/09/nobel.physics/index.html (09 Oct. 1996).

"1992 Winner for Chemistry." *Harold W. Kroto.* 1996. http://www.italgas.it/prize/premiati/1992_1.html (09 Oct. 1996).

—*Sketch by Pamela Proffitt*

Krystyna Kuperberg
1944–
Polish mathematician

Krystyna Kuperberg is a researcher and educator best known for disproving the famous Seifert conjecture in topology. Her counterexample, first announced in the mid–1990s, was termed a "small miracle" of geometry by Ian Stewart. It was quickly generalized and should prove central to the continued development of dynamic systems theory, by way of the vector fields used to study physical and statistical phenomena.

Kuperberg was born Krystyna M. Trybulec in Tarnow, a city in southern Poland, on July 17, 1944. Her parents, Jan W. and Barbara H. (Kurlus) Trybulec, were both trained pharmacists. Her brother, Ardrzej, also became a mathematician. After receiving a master's degree from Warsaw University in 1966, Kuperberg had to wait until settling in the United States to earn her Ph.D. This was awarded by Rice University in 1974. Upon graduating she accepted her first post at Auburn University. Kuperberg remains a member of the faculty at Auburn, and has been a full professor there since 1984. She has also held visiting positions at Oklahoma State University, the Courant Institute of Mathematical Sciences in New York, the Mathematical Sciences Research Institute at Berkeley, and l'Universite de Paris–Sud, Centre d'Orsay.

In 1974, the first counterexample to the famous Seifert conjecture was found by P. A. Schweitzer. His "plug" was devised to cancel out any circular orbit, but it broke down to two minimal sets. Kuperberg, who had begun publishing papers in 1971, was already interested in dynamical systems. She resolved a conjecture about fixed points in 1981 with Coke Reed, and built upon the methods used in this work to find a new kind of counterexample with only one minimal set. What she eventually found served to disprove the Siefert conjecture for all three–dimensional manifolds.

Hairy Donuts

The Seifert conjecture is a higher–dimensional extension of the "hairy billiard ball" theorem for the two–dimensional surface of a sphere. The idea that you cannot comb down all the hairs on a fully hairy ball without getting a cowlick is really a geometric statement about a dynamical system. The one–dimensional version, the circle or "1–sphere," is "combable," allowing for a smooth vector field. The 2–sphere is combable because it contains at least one "bald spot" consisting of a fixed point around which the trajectories can flow. The fact that there is always some place on Earth where the wind is not blowing is a real–world example of this "bald spot."

More complex surfaces proved more difficult to analyze. In the case of a torus–shaped vector field or "hairy donut," for instance, whether a trajectory is fixed or not depends upon how it advances along the circumference of the torus as it flows. This explains why it was impossible to prove a simple conjecture about one of the three–dimensional shapes for more than 40 years. In 1950, Herbert Seifert had proposed that in the three–dimensional case any smooth vector field will have at least one "closed" or periodic orbit. It was already known that 3–spheres did not have any "bald spots," but it seemed reasonable enough to think that they would have at least one closed orbit.

Kuperberg disproved this conjecture in 1993 by constructing a smooth vector field with no closed orbits, and her construction applies not only to 3–spheres, but to all three–dimensional manifolds. To do this she used a Wilson plug, a kind of topological tool, to break up any closed orbits that might be present. This plug is a three–dimensional shape that traps the trajectories of one or more formerly closed orbits inside itself. The trick is to apply the plug without creating any new closed orbits. To accomplish this, Kuperberg modified the plug so that it "eats its own tail" like a snake. Thus, the trajectories that enter get trapped in an infinite spiral and no new closed orbits can be formed. In addition to disproving the Siefert conjecture, Kuperberg's construction produces a "minimal set" that may be of an entirely new kind, according to John Mather, a dynamical systems theorist at Princeton. Since minimal sets are basic components of dynamical systems, Kuperberg's plug may help mathematicians better understand the range of things that can happen in these systems.

Since her success in disproving the Siefert conjecture, Kuperberg has been especially in demand as a speaker at events devoted to topology or dynamical systems, and at honorary symposia worldwide. She delivered the MSRI–Evans lecture at Berkeley in 1994, and addressed the American Mathematical Society and Mathematical Association of America meetings in 1995 and 1996.

Kuperberg's husband and frequent collaborator, Wlodzimierz, received his Ph.D. in mathematics from Warsaw University. He is also a professor at Auburn University. Krystyna and Wlodzimierz were married in Poland and lived there until 1969. Their son, Greg, born in Poland in 1967, is also a mathematician; he received a Ph.D. in mathematics from the University of California at Berkeley. Their daughter, Anna, born two years later in Sweden, holds a M.F.A. from the San Francisco Art Institute.

In addition to awards from Auburn University for her research and professorship, and National Science Foundation grant support, Kuperberg also won the Alfred Jurzykowski Foundation Award in 1995 from the Kosciuszko Foundation in New York. In 1996, Kuperberg was elected to the American Mathematical Society council as a member at large for a three–year term. She also currently edits the *Electronic Research Announcement* of the American Mathematical Society.

SELECTED WRITINGS BY KUPERBERG:

Books

Collected Works of Witold Hurewicz, 1995.
(With H. Cook, W.T. Ingram, A. Lelek, and P. Minc) *Continua with the Houston Problem Book*, 1995.

Periodicals

"A Smooth Counterexample to the Seifert Conjecture." *Annals of Mathematics* 140 (1994): 723–32.
(With W. Kuperberg) "Generalized Counterexamples to the Seifert Conjecture." *Annals of Mathematics* 144 (1996): 239–68.

FURTHER READING:

Periodicals

Cipra, Barry. "(Vector) Field of Dreams." *What's Happening in the Mathematical Sciences* 2 (1994): 47–51.
Stewart, Ian. "Hairy Balls in Higher Dimensions." *New Scientist* (November 13, 1993): 18.

Other

"Krystyna Kuperberg." *Biographies of Women Mathematicians.* June 1997. http://www.agnesscott.edu/lriddle/women/chronol.html (July 1997).

—*Sketch by Jennifer Kramer*

Polycarp Kusch
1911–1993
German-born American physicist

Polycarp Kusch entered the field of physics along the newly established path of quantum electrodynamics. But like all great scientists, he left the known path to blaze a trail. His work helped to reshape the basic principles of atomic theory by demonstrating conclu-

Polycarp Kusch

sively that the magnetic properties of the electron were not in agreement with existing theories. These studies of the so-called magnetic moment of the electron earned him the Nobel Prize in physics in 1955, which he shared with **Willis E. Lamb, Jr.** The discovery also led to the development of an even more sophisticated theory of how light and matter interact, that is, the theory of quantum electrodynamics.

Kusch was born on January 26, 1911, in Blankenburg, Germany, to John Matthias Kusch, a Lutheran missionary, and his wife, Henrietta. He was named for Saint Polycarp, a second-century bishop and martyr, whose feast day is January 26. Polycarp's father brought the family to the United States in 1912, where they led a somewhat unsettled existence until John Kusch took a position with a book publisher in Cleveland, Ohio.

Young Polycarp, who became a naturalized citizen of the United States in 1923, attended public schools in Cleveland, and in 1927 matriculated at Cleveland's Case School of Applied Science (later renamed Case Western Reserve University), where he intended to study chemistry. He became a physics major instead, and received his B.S. in 1931. Polycarp was one of only a few in his school who majored in physics. Years later, Kusch told the *Columbia Alumni News,* "From the start I felt more adapted to physics than to something like engineering. To me engineering was a matter of cook books and heavy economic

motivations." He continued his study of physics at the University of Illinois, where he held a graduate assistantship; he earned his M.Sc. degree in 1933 and his Ph.D. in 1936. While at the university, he met Edith Starr McRoberts, whom he married on August 12, 1935, and with whom he had three daughters, Kathryn, Judith, and Sara.

In 1937 Kusch became a research assistant to John T. Tate at the University of Minnesota. He became skilled at using mass spectroscopy, a technique that determines relative atomic masses by shooting electrically charged atoms and molecules through a magnetic field, where they are deflected with a force that depends on their mass. Through the support of Tate, Kusch received an appointment as an instructor at Columbia University in 1937, and went to work in the laboratory of **I. I. Rabi**. He had the fortune to participate in the first magnetic resonance absorption experiment, a type of spectroscopy with various applications in which atoms placed in a magnetic field and irradiated with electromagnetic energy in the radio wave region absorb part of the radiation. Different atoms absorb at different frequencies, which are monitored by a detector. The research garnered Rabi a Nobel Prize in 1944. Kusch stayed at Columbia until 1941, when he joined a team of researchers at the Westinghouse Laboratories in Bloomfield, Pennsylvania. There, he contributed to the development of vacuum tubes, a critical component of radar that greatly assisted the U.S. defense effort during World War II. Kusch returned to Columbia in 1942 as a research associate, later moving to Bell Telephone Laboratories to work on vacuum tubes and microwave generators. Four years later, at the invitation of Rabi, Kusch accepted a position as associate professor of physics, and once again returned to New York. He was made a full professor in 1949 and served as chairman of the physics department from 1949 to 1952.

Lays Foundation for New Field in Physics

In 1947, while doing research in quantum mechanics (the branch of physics that deals with the behavior of matter at atomic and subatomic levels), Kusch completed his studies on the magnetic properties of electrons, work for which he received the Nobel Prize. Kusch and Henry Foley, his colleague at Columbia, changed the energy levels of atoms in a magnetic field by exposing them to high-frequency radio waves. Kusch and Foley observed the atoms, identifying those with electrons that had a specific magnetic abnormality that would make them easily identifiable. Through this magnetic and radio wave manipulation of atoms, the two researchers were able to observe minute variations in the magnetic characteristics of the electrons spinning around the atomic nuclei. Subsequent calculations based on this data demonstrated that earlier calculations by Nobel Prize winner **Paul Dirac** had underestimated the strength of the electron's magnetic charge by at least 0.125%.

The discovery led to the development of a set of scientific principles that formed the basis of a new field in physics. This new field, established by Dirac, **Werner K. Heisenberg**, and **Wolfgang Pauli,** is called quantum electrodynamics, the study of properties of electromagnetic radiation and its interaction with electrically charged matter, specifically, atoms and their electrons. The importance of quantum electrodynamics is immeasurable, in the sense that almost all phenomena readily perceived by the human senses are thought to be ultimately reducible to and understandable in terms of its laws.

Becomes Active in Administration and Public Policy

Kusch held the chair of the department of physics at Columbia again from 1960 to 1963. In May 1968, he was appointed to the executive committee of the faculty, which represented the faculty to the university during deliberations on the future of the university. In June 1968, the committee appointed a fact-finding commission headed by Archibald Cox to investigate the causes of a student uprising on campus that occurred during the restive school year and reflected changing attitudes of students to the role of universities in society, the responsibility of government to people, and the increasingly unpopular war in Vietnam.

Following the death of his first wife in 1959, Kusch married Betty Jane Pezzoni in 1960, with whom he had two daughters, Diana and Maria. Kusch was promoted to academic vice president and provost in 1969, a post he held until 1972.

While he was at Columbia, Kusch's meticulous work in the laboratory was reflected in his approach to teaching freshman and sophomore physics and graduate seminars. Rather than dispensing large amounts of scientific information, he preferred to give students a strong grounding in scientific technique in the context of a more limited amount of data. In fact, as a member of the Columbia College Committee on Instruction, he blocked the institution of broad, undergraduate survey courses in the sciences, insisting that such a course of instruction would tempt instructors to make too many dogmatic statements. He preferred instead to offer analyses of selected scientific problems.

His knack for using science to solve problems was reflected in his prescient comments to the *New York Times Magazine* in 1962 concerning the role physics would play in the development of future technologies. Kusch ventured that advances in solid-state physics—the electric, magnetic, and other properties of solid substances—would expand beyond the simple transistor, computers, and tiny hearing aids. He predicted the development of wristwatch radio transmitters and receivers and television-telephones, two devices that by the early 1990s were being touted by scientists as inevitable. Kusch also predicted the current flurry of research into new materials such as metals and ceramics that have previously unattainable strength, as well as the appeal of superconductive materials that lose resistance to electrical flow at extremely low temperatures.

Kusch's interests ranged far from the laboratory, however, and included problems of overpopulation. In 1961, during the celebration of Columbia College's fiftieth annual Dean's Day reported in the *New York Times,* Kusch noted that "there is often a foolish, a pathetic or downright dangerous belief in the power of science to do anything at all. . . . No amount of scientific skill can find a way of feeding an indefinite expansion of the world's population." In 1966, he joined three other Nobel laureates testifying before a Senate Government Operations subcommittee on the need to curb the growth of the world's population in order to avoid starvation, social disruption, and the consequent interruption of scientific and intellectual progress. In 1972, Kusch accepted a professorship at the University of Texas, Dallas, where he was Eugene McDermott Professor from 1974 to 1980, becoming Regental Professor Emeritus in 1982. He died at his home in Dallas in March 1993.

Kusch was elected to the National Academy of Sciences in 1956, and in 1959 Columbia University's Society of Older Graduates (graduates of Columbia College and the School of Engineering who received their degrees at least thirty years before) awarded Kusch its Great Teacher Award at the society's forty-ninth annual dinner meeting. According to the *New York Times,* the award citation read in part, "His search is not only for new knowledge but for those budding scientists from whom will come the important discoveries of a new generation." Columbia honored him again in 1961 by bestowing upon him the Alexander Hamilton Medal, presented annually by the Association of the Alumni of Columbia College to alumni or faculty members for "distinguished service in any field of human endeavor."

He received the Illinois Achievement award from the University of Illinois (1975) and was a fellow of both the Center for Advanced Study in Behavioral Sciences (1964–65), and the American Physical Society, a member of the American Association for the Advancement of Science, American Academy of Arts and Sciences, and the American Philosophical Society.

SELECTED WRITINGS BY KUSCH:

Periodicals

"The Magnetic Moment of the Electron." *Physical Review* 74, no. 3 (1948): 250-63.

"Hyperfine Structure by the Method of Atomic Beams: Properties of Nuclei and of the Electron." *Physics* 17, nos. 3-4 (1951): 339-53.

"Analysis of the Band System of the Sodium Molecule." *Journal of Chemical Physics* 68 (1978).

FURTHER READING:

Books

Magill, Frank N., ed. *The Nobel Prize Winners: Physics.* Vol. 2, 1938-1967. Englewood Cliffs, NJ: Salem Press, 1989, pp. 665-72.

Periodicals

Browne, Malcolm W. "Polykarp Kusch, Nobel Laureate in Physics in 1955, Is Dead at 82" (obituary). *New York Times* (23 March 1993).

Columbia Alumni News. (January 1952).

"Columbia Names Dr. Kusch, Nobel Physicist, as Vice President." *New York Times* (5 March 1969): 1.

Cooley, Donald G. "Scientist's Show Goes on the Road." *New York Times Magazine* (16 February 1958): 38.

———. "Dark Age Feared in Population Rise." *New York Times* (20 January 1966): L21.

Galton, Lawrence. "Science Stands at Awesome Thresholds." *New York Times Magazine* (2 December 1962): 38-39; 90-94.

Pfeiffer, John. "The Basic Need for Basic Research." *New York Times Magazine* (24 November 1967): 23; 93-98.

—Sketch by Marc Kusinitz

Women's Medical College of the New York Infirmary for Women and Children. It was 1896. Within three years she had achieved her degree; she also married David L'Esperance, a lawyer, while she was still a student.

L'Esperance wanted to be a pediatrician, so after interning at New York Babies Hospital she opened her own practice in Manhattan, where she continued until 1908. During this time, she became interested in research on tuberculosis, and as a member of the Tuberculosis Research Commission, became increasing drawn to pathology.

After deciding to specialize in that field in 1910, she took a job as assistant to Dr. James Ewing, a cancer specialist at Cornell University Medical School, who had previously refused to employ a woman. Apparantly L'Esperance changed his mind about women doctors; after two years she was promoted to instructor of pathology. "It was only a technician's job," she said of her assistant's job with Ewing to a reporter at the New York *World-Telegram.* "But I knew I could pick up a tremendous amount of information from one of the greatest pathologists in the world." After becoming an instructor, she achieved the rank of assistant professor in 1920, the first woman to hold that position on the Cornell faculty. In April of 1950 she became a full professor in the department of preventive medicine.

In 1932, L'Esperance and her sister, May Strang, used an inheritance from their uncle, Chauncey Depew, to establish the first of three clinics in New York City devoted to detecting cancer. The clinic, the Kate Depew Strang Tumor Clinic at the New York Infirmary for Women and Children, was named for the L'Esperance's mother, who had died of cancer. L'Esperance filled the clinic with a staff made up entirely of women physicians who were dedicated to treating women and children. "We thought they (the cancer clinics) made more sense than a stained glass window," she told Margaret Follin Eicks, a reporter at the New York *World-Telegram* about the decision to open the clinics. After establishing the New York infirmaries, Strang embarked on an extensive campaign to educate the public about cancer prevention. Largely through her work, the value of early cancer detection became accepted by both physicians and the public.

L'Esperance believed cancer could be defeated if it was caught early—even in seemingly healthy people. Her first clinic proved so popular that a second was opened in 1940. Several others were then opened

Elise Depew Strang L'Esperance

Elise Depew Strang L'Esperance
1879–1959
American pathologist

Elise Depew Strang L'Esperance was one of the first crusaders against cancer to emphasize detection and prevention of this disease. She established the first cancer prevention clinic at the New York Infirmary for Women and Children, which later became the model for similar clinics in New York and other large American cities. She also was the first women to achieve the rank of full professor in preventive medicine.

L'Esperance was born in 1879 in Westchester, New York, the second daughter of physician Albert Strang and Kate Depew Strang. Kate Depew Strang was the sister of Chauncey Depew, a famed financier and United States Senator. L'Esperance attended St. Agnes Episcopal School in Albany and upon graduation decided to follow in her father's footsteps and study for the M.D. degree. At age 16, she entered the around the country and expanded to care for men and adolescents. The clinics developed and used new techniques for detecting cancer, including the Pap smear. By 1950, the clinics had treated 35,000 healthy patients, and cancerous conditions had been found in about one percent. L'Esperance believed that if doctors only knew how to look for premalignant cancers, it would be possible to prevent fully malignant tumors.

The distinguished pathologist published more than 30 peer-reviewed papers in medical journals during her career and was editor of the *Medical Women's Journal* and the *Journal of the American Medical Women's Association*. She received many awards, including the Elizabeth Blackwell Citation in 1950 and the Albert Lasker Award of the American Public Health Association in 1951, an extremely prestigious honor.

L'Esperance also bred show horses, owned her own stable, and drove her harness ponies in the National Horse Show at Madison Square Garden in New York yearly. During her elderly years she resided with her sister in Westchester, New York. She was often described as "a tall, fast-moving, strongly built woman" who liked to wear unusual hats even while seeing patients in her office. "There never was any place to hang the thing (in the x-ray room)," she once said. "So I kept it on. Got in the habit. Now I'd feel headless without it."

L'Esperance died on January 21, 1959. She was 80 years old.

SELECTED WRITINGS BY L'ESPERANCE:

Periodicals

"The Strang Cancer Prevention Clinics: A Symposium." *Journal of the American Medical Women's Association* (April, 1948): 131-146.

FURTHER READING:

Books

Notable Women in the Life Sciences. Greenwood Press, 1996.

Periodicals

"Dr. L'Esperance, Specialist, Dead." *New York Times* (Jan. 22, 1959):31
"Medicine. Prevention Is Her Aim." *Time* 55 (April 3, 1950): 78-79

—*Sketch by Barbara Boughton*

Edmund Landau
1877–1938
German number theorist

Edmund Landau profoundly influenced the development of number theory. His primary research focused on analytic number theory, especially the distribution of prime numbers and prime ideals. An extremely productive author of at least 250 publications, Landau's writings had a distinct style. His prose was carefully crafted, highlighted by lucid, comprehensive argumentation and a thorough explanation of the background knowledge required to understand it. Landau's writing style became more succinct over the course of his career. He was forced to retire from teaching at the behest of Nazi anti–Semitic policies.

Born in Berlin on February 14, 1877, Landau was the son of Leopold, a gynecologist, and Johanna (Jacoby) Landau. Johanna Landau came from a wealthy family with whom the Landaus lived in an affluent section of Berlin. Although Leopold Landau was an assimilated Jew and a German patriot, in 1872 he helped found an Judaism academy in Berlin. Landau himself studied in Berlin at the *Französische Gymnasium* (French Lycée), graduating two years early at age 16. He promptly began studying at Berlin University. Landau had published twice before receiving his Ph.D; both pieces explored chess related mathematical problems.

Under the tutelage of Georg Frobenius, Landau was awarded his doctorate at Berlin University in 1899 at the age of 22 years old. His dissertation dealt with what became his life's work: number theory. Landau began teaching at Berlin in 1901, when he earned the advanced degree which allowed him to teach mathematics. He proved to be a popular lecturer at the university because of his personal excitement of the carefully prepared material he presented to his students.

Landau's first major accomplishment as a mathematician came in 1903, when he simplified and improved upon the proof for the prime number theorem conjectured by Karl Gauss in 1796, and demonstrated independently by **Jacques Hadamard** and **C.J. de la Vallée–Poussin** in 1896. In Landau's proof, the theorem's application extended to algebraic number fields, specifically to the distribution of ideal primes within them.

Landau married Marianne Ehrlich (daughter of **Paul Ehrlich**, a friend of Landau's father, who won the 1908 Nobel prize in medicine or physiology) in 1905 at Frankfurt–am–Main, and fathered two daughters and two sons (one of whom died before age five). He served as a professor of mathematics at Berlin until 1909.

Landau published his first major work in 1909, the two–volume *Handbuch der Lehre von der Vertiolung der Prizahalen*. The volumes were the first orderly discussion of analytic number theory, and were used for many years in universities as a research and teaching tool. Landau's texts are still considered important documents in the history of mathematics.

In the same year, Landau became a full professor at the University of Göttingen. Although the faculty at Berlin tried twice to keep Landau on staff, the government wanted to make Göttingen a center of German mathematical learning. They succeeded in their objective, and Landau stayed there until 1934. In 1913, Landau even declined an offer from a university in Heidelberg for a chair position. Although he was still a charismatic, inspiring teacher by the 1920s he was criticized for his rigid, almost perfectionistic lecture style. A demanding lecturer, he insisted that one of his assistants sit through his presentations so any errors could be immediately corrected.

Landau continued his father's support of Jewish institutions. In 1925, he gave a lecture on mathematics in Hebrew at the Hebrew University in Jerusalem, an institution Landau heartily embraced. His activities there continued when he took a sabbatical from Göttingen and taught a few mathematics classes in 1927–28. Landau even contemplated staying in Jerusalem at one point.

Landau also published another important treatise in 1927, the three volumes of *Vorlesungen über Zahlentheorie*. In these texts, Landau brought together the various branches of number theory in one comprehensive text. He throughly explored each branch from its origins to the then–current state of research. Two years later, the widely respected Landau received a honorary doctorate of philosophy from the University of Oslo in Norway. The next year, Landau published another landmark book, entitled *Grundlagen der Analysis*. Beginning with **Giuseppe Peano**'s axioms for natural numbers, this volume presented arithmetic in four forms of numbers: whole, rational, irrational, and complex.

The Nazi Party and their policies of discrimination against Jews led to a premature end to Landau's academic career. In late 1933, he was forced to cease teaching at Göttingen, although he was one of the last Jewish professors to be purged from that institution. While technically not subject to the 1933 non–Aryan clause attached to Nazi civil servant laws, all Jewish mathematical professors were forced to leave Göttingen. Landau stayed on through the summer and fall terms of 1933, but he could only teach classes through assistants. Landau would sit in the back of every class, ready to teach at any moment if his ban was raised.

On November 2, 1933, Landau attempted to resume teaching his class. The students, alerted to this impropriety in advance, boycotted his lecture. SS Guards were stationed at the entrance in case a student did not want to boycott; only one got in. When it was clear he would not be allowed to lecture, Landau returned to his office. The boycotting students explained by letter that they no longer wanted to be taught by a Jew and be indoctrinated in his mode of thought.

In 1934, Landau was given his retirement leave, and he and his family moved back to Berlin. Although he never taught in Germany again, he did lecture out of the country at universities such as Cambridge in 1935 and Brussels in 1937. Landau died in Berlin of natural causes on February 19, 1938, and was buried in the Berlin–Weissensee Jewish cemetery.

SELECTED WRITINGS BY LANDAU:

Differential and Integral Calculus. Third Edition. Translated by Melvin Hausner and Martin Davis, 1965.

Elementary Number Theory. Translated by Jacob E. Goodman, 1968.

Foundations of Analysis: The Arithmetic of Whole, Rational, Irrational, and Complex Numbers. Third edition. Translated by F. Steinhardt, 1966.

FURTHER READING:

Books

Schoeneberg, Bruno. "Edmund Georg Hermann," in *Dictionary of Scientific Biography.* Volume VII. Edited by Charles Coulston Gillispie. New York: Charles Scribner's Sons, 1970, pp. 615–16.

Periodicals

Chowdhury, M.R. "Landau and Teichmuller." *The Mathematical Intelligencer* (Spring 1995): 12–14.

Norbert, Schappacher. "Edmund Landau's Göttingen: From the Life and Death of a Great Mathematical Center." *The Mathematical Intelligencer* (Fall 1991): 12–18.

—*Sketch by Annette Petruso*

Robert P. Langlands

Robert P. Langlands
1936–
Canadian–American mathematical physicist

Robert Langlands' subspecialities are group representations, number theory, and automorphic forms. His earliest theories faced skepticism, but he eventually persuaded fellow mathematicians of the possibility of links between algebra and analysis, promising what some have termed a "unifying principle" for all mathematics. More than 25 years ago, Langlands saw that seemingly disparate fields of mathematics are related in often unexpected ways. For example, one of his conjectures, ostensibly dealing with Lie groups, also by implication involves number theory and algebraic geometry.

In 1982, Langlands was awarded the American Mathematical Society Cole Prize for his work in automorphic forms. He received the first National Academy of Sciences Award in Mathematics in 1988 for the "extraordinary vision that has brought the theory of group representations into a revolutionary new relationship with the theory of automorphic forms and number theory." He shared the 1995 Wolf Prize with **Andrew Wiles**, again for work involving group representations, number theory, and automorphic forms. Without Langlands earlier work, Wiles would not have been able to accomplish his recent solution of Fermat's Last Theorem. However,

not all of Langlands' work is in pure mathematics. His activities in the realm of applied mathematics, often lauded for a spirited use of metaphors, directly grapple with the common pitfalls that await those who use pure mathematical models to guide physics experiments.

Robert Phelan Langlands was born in New Westminster, British Columbia, Canada on October 6, 1936, to Robert and Kathleen (Phelan) Langlands. Little is known of his early life. Though he eventually earned his Ph.D. (1960) at Yale University in the United States, he received his B.A. (1957) and M.A. (1958) from the University of British Columbia. He married Charlotte Lorraine Cheverie on August 13, 1956, and they eventually had four children—William, Sarah, Robert, and Thomasin.

Langlands joined the faculty of Princeton University as an instructor. He worked his way up to associate professor at Princeton before returning to Yale as a full professor in 1967. While at Princeton, he began his relationship with the nearby Institute for Advanced Study (IAS), where he eventually became a professor when he left Yale in 1972. During this time, Langlands was also busy writing and publishing nearly 30 papers that formulated a set of still unsolved problems and still unproven conjectures now loosely termed "the Langlands program."

"A Driving Force"

Langlands has always been welcoming to other researchers. In 1977, he invited **Pierre Deligné**, who was at the time working on several elements of the Langlands program, to the U.S. to organize a conference with him. Li Guo, now with Rutgers University, did postdoctoral research during 1995 with Langlands as a mentor. Though the program had run out of funds and there was officially no room for Guo, Langlands personally intervened so the young mathematician could work at the Institute for Advanced Study for half a year. For these and many other reasons, he has been termed "a driving force in mathematics" by Enrico Bombieri, an IAS School of Mathematics colleague.

Langlands remains a professor at the Institute for Advanced Study. To celebrate his 60th birthday, the Institute organized the Langlands Conference on automorphic forms, geometry, and analysis in 1996. Langlands possesses dual American and Canadian citizenship, and holds memberships in both the American Mathematical Society and the Canadian Mathematical Society.

SELECTED WRITINGS BY LANGLANDS:

Books

"Einstein Series, the Trace Formula, and the Modern Theory of Automorphic Forms," in *Number Theory, Trace Formulas, and Discrete Groups.* Edited by K.R. Aubert, et al, 1988.

(With D. Ramakrishnan) *The Zeta Functions of Picard Modular Surfaces*, 1992.

"Representation Theory: Its Rise and Its Role in Number Theory," in *Proceedings of the Gibbs Symposium, AMS*, 1990.

Periodicals

"The Factorization of a Polynomial Defined by Partitions." *Comm. Math. Physics* 124 (1989): 251–284.

"Some Holomorphic Semi–Groups." *Proceedings of the National Academy of Sciences* 46 (1960): 361–363.

(With Ph. Pouliot, and Y. Saint–Aubin.) "Conformal Invariance in Two–Dimensional Percolation." *Bulletin of the American Mathematical Society* 30 (1994): 1–61.

FURTHER READING:

Books

American Men & Women of Science. Nineteenth edition. New Providence, NJ: Bowker, 1994, p. 627.

McMurray, Emily J., editor. *Notable Twentieth Century Scientists*. Detroit, MI: Gale Research, 1995.

Who's Who in Science and Engineering. New Providence, NJ: Reed Publishing, 1994, p. 504.

Periodicals

"Langlands Conference: Robert Langlands's 60th Birthday." *Institute for Advanced Studies Newsletter* (Fall 1996): 1–2.

Other

Guo, Li., in a telephone interview with Jennifer Kramer, conducted July 14, 1997.

—Sketch by Jennifer Kramer

Mary Leakey
1913–1996
English paleontologist and anthropologist

For many years Mary Leakey lived in the shadow of her husband, **Louis Leakey,** whose reputation, coupled with the prejudices of the time, led him to be credited with some of his wife's discoveries in the field of early human archaeology. Yet she established a substantial reputation in her own right and came to be recognized as one of the most important paleoanthropologists of the twentieth century. It was Mary Leakey who was responsible for some of the most important discoveries made by Louis Leakey's team. Although her close association with Louis Leakey's work on Paleolithic sites at Olduvai Gorge—a 350-mile ravine in Tanzania—led to her being considered a specialist in that particular area and period, she in fact worked on excavations dating from as early as the Miocene, (an era dating to approximately 18 million years ago) to those as recent as the Iron Age of a few thousand years ago.

Developing an Interest in Archaeology

Mary Leakey was born Mary Douglas Nicol on February 6, 1913, in London. Her mother was Cecilia Frere, the great-granddaughter of John Frere, who had discovered prehistoric stone tools at Hoxne, Suffolk, England, in 1797. Her father was Erskine Nicol, a painter who himself was the son of an artist, and who had a deep interest in Egyptian archaeology. When Mary was a child, her family made frequent trips to southwestern France, where her father took her to see the Upper Paleolithic cave paintings. She and her father became friends with Elie Peyrony, the curator of the local museum, and there she was exposed to the vast collection of flint tools dating from that period of human prehistory. She was also allowed to accompany Peyrony on his excavations, though the archaeological work was not conducted in what would now be considered a scientific way—artifacts were removed from the site without careful study of the place in the earth where each had been found, obscuring valuable data that could be used in dating the artifact and analyzing its context. On a later trip, in 1925, she was taken to Paleolithic caves by the Abbé Lémozi of France, parish priest of Cabrerets, who had written papers on cave art. After her father's death in 1926, Mary Nicol was taken to Stonehenge and Avebury in England, where she began to learn about the archaeological activity in that country and, after meeting the archaeologist Dorothy Liddell, to realize the possibility of archaeology as a career for a woman.

By 1930, Mary Nicol had undertaken coursework in geology and archaeology at the University of London and had participated in a few excavations in order to obtain field experience. One of her lecturers, R. E. M. Wheeler, offered her the opportunity to join his party excavating St. Albans, England, the ancient Roman site of Verulamium; although she only remained at that site for a few days, finding the work there poorly organized, she began her career in earnest shortly thereafter, excavating Neolithic (early Stone Age) sites in Henbury, Devon, where she worked between 1930 and 1934. Her main area of expertise was stone tools, and she was exceptionally skilled at making drawings of them. During the 1930s Mary met Louis Leakey, who was to become her husband. Leakey was by this time well known because of his finds of early human remains in East Africa; it was at Mary and Louis's first meeting that he asked her to help him with the illustrations for his 1934 book, *Adam's Ancestors: An Up-to-Date Outline of What Is Known about the Origin of Man.*

In 1934 Mary Nicol and Louis Leakey worked at an excavation in Clacton, England, where the skull of a hominid—a family of erect primate mammals that use only two feet for locomotion—had recently been found and where Louis was investigating Paleolithic geology as well as fauna and human remains. The excavation led to Mary Leakey's first publication, a 1937 report in the *Proceedings of the Prehistoric Society.*

Excavating at Olduvai Gorge

By this time, Louis Leakey had decided that Mary should join him on his next expedition to Olduvai Gorge in Tanganyika (now Tanzania), which he believed to be the most promising site for discovering early Paleolithic human remains. On the journey to Olduvai, Mary stopped briefly in South Africa, where she spent a few weeks with an archaeological team and learned more about the scientific approach to excavation, studying each find *in situ*—paying close attention to the details of the geological and faunal material surrounding each artifact. This knowledge was to assist her in her later work at Olduvai and elsewhere.

At Olduvai, among her earliest discoveries were fragments of a human skull; these were some of the first such remains found at the site, and it would be twenty years before any others would be found there. Mary Nicol and Louis Leakey returned to England. Leakey's divorce from his first wife was made final in the mid-1930s, and he and Mary Nicol were then married; the couple returned to Kenya in January of 1937. Over the next few years, the Leakeys excavated Neolithic and Iron Age sites at Hyrax Hill, Njoro River Cave, and the Naivasha Railway Rock Shelter, which yielded a large number of human remains and artifacts.

During World War II, the Leakeys began to excavate at Olorgasailie, southwest of Nairobi, but because of the complicated geology of that site, the dating of material found there was difficult. It did prove to be a rich source of material, however; in 1942, Mary Leakey uncovered hundreds, possibly thousands, of hand axes there. Her first major discovery in the field of pre-human fossils was that of most of the skull of a *Proconsul africanus* on Rusinga Island, in Lake Victoria, Kenya, in 1948. *Proconsul* was believed by some paleontologists to be a common ancestor of apes and humans, an animal whose

descendants developed into two branches on the evolutionary tree: the *Pongidae* (great apes) and the *Hominidae* (who eventually evolved into true humans). *Proconsul* lived during the Miocene, approximately 18 million years ago. This was the first time a fossil ape skull had ever been found—only a small number have been found since—and the Leakeys hoped that this would be the ancestral hominid that paleontologists had sought for decades. The absence of a "simian shelf," a reinforcement of the jaw found in modern apes, is one of the features of *Proconsul* that led the Leakeys to infer that this was a direct ancestor of modern humans. *Proconsul* is now generally believed to be a species of *Dryopithecus,* closer to apes than to humans.

Discovering "Dear Boy:" *Zinjanthropus*

Many of the finds at Olduvai were primitive stone hand axes, evidence of human habitation; it was not known, however, who had made them. Mary's concentration had been on the discovery of such tools, while Louis's goal had been to learn who had made them, in the hope that the date for the appearance of toolmaking hominids could be moved back to an earlier point. In 1959, Mary unearthed part of the jaw of an early hominid she designated *Zinjanthropus* (meaning "East African Man") and whom she referred to as "Dear Boy;" the early hominid is now considered to be a species of *Australopithecus*—apparently related to the two kinds of australopithecine found in South Africa, *Australopithecus africanus* and *Australopithecus robustus*—and given the species designation *boisei* in honor of Louis Leakey's sponsor Charles Boise. By means of potassium-argon dating, recently developed, it was determined that the fragment was 1.75 million years old, and this realization pushed back the date for the appearance of hominids in Africa. Despite the importance of this find, however, Louis Leakey was slightly disappointed, as he had hoped that the excavations would unearth not another australopithecine, but an example of *Homo* living at that early date. He was seeking evidence for his theory that more than one hominid form lived at Olduvai at the same time; these forms were the australopithecines, who eventually died out, and some early form of *Homo*, which survived—owing to toolmaking ability and larger cranial capacity—to evolve into *Homo erectus* and, eventually, the modern human. Leakey hoped that Mary Leakey's find would prove that *Homo* existed at that early level of Olduvai. The discovery he awaited did not come until the early 1960s, with the identification of a skull found by their son Jonathan Leakey that Louis designated as *Homo habilis* ("man with ability"). He believed this to be the true early human responsible for making the tools found at the site.

Working on Her Own

In her autobiography, *Disclosing the Past,* released in 1984, Mary Leakey reveals that her professional and personal relationship with Louis Leakey had begun to deteriorate by 1968. As she increasingly began to lead the Olduvai research on her own, and as she developed a reputation in her own right through her numerous publications of research results, she started believing that her husband felt threatened by her. Louis Leakey had been spending a vast amount of his time in fund-raising and administrative matters, while Mary was able to concentrate on field work. As Louis began to seek recognition in new areas, most notably in excavations seeking evidence of early humans in California, Mary stepped up her work at Olduvai, and the breach between them widened. She became critical of his interpretations of his California finds, viewing them as evidence of a decline in his scientific rigor. During these years at Olduvai, Mary made numerous new discoveries, including the first *Homo erectus* pelvis to be found. Mary Leakey continued her work after Louis Leakey's death in 1972. From 1975 she concentrated on Laetoli, Tanzania, which was a site earlier than the oldest beds at Olduvai. She knew that the lava above the Laetoli beds was dated to 2.4 million years ago, and the beds themselves were therefore even older; in contrast, the oldest beds at Olduvai were two million years old. Potassium-argon dating has since shown the upper beds at Laetoli to be approximately 3.5 million years old. In 1978, members of her team found two trails of hominid footprints in volcanic ash dated to approximately 3.5 million years ago; the form of the footprints gave evidence that these hominids walked upright, thus moving the date for the development of an upright posture back significantly earlier than previously believed. Mary Leakey considered these footprints to be among her most significant finds. She died in Nairobi, Kenya, on December 8, 1996.

In the late 1960s, Mary Leakey received an honorary doctorate from the University of the Witwatersrand in South Africa, an honor she accepted only after university officials had spoken out against apartheid. Among her other honorary degrees are a D.S.Sc. from Yale University and a D.Sc. from the University of Chicago. She received an honorary D.Litt. from Oxford University in 1981. She has also received the Gold Medal of the Society of Women Geographers.

Louis Leakey was sometimes faulted for being too quick to interpret the finds of his team and for his propensity for developing sensationalistic, publicity-attracting theories. Late in her career, Mary Leakey has been critical of the conclusions reached by her husband—as well as by some others—without adding her own interpretations to the mix. Instead, she remained more concerned with the act of discovery itself; she had written that it was more important for her to continue the task of uncovering early human remains to provide the pieces of the puzzle than it was to speculate and develop her own interpretations. Her legacy lies in the vast amount of material she and her team unearthed; she left it to future scholars to deduce its meaning.

SELECTED WRITINGS BY LEAKEY:

Books

Stone Age Africa: An Outline of Prehistory in Africa. Oxford: Oxford University Press, 1936. Reprint, Negro Universities Press, 1970.
Some String Figures from North East Angola. Lisboa, Portugal, 1949.
Excavations at the Njoro River Cave: Stone Age Cremated Burials in Kenya Colony. Oxford: Clarendon Press, 1950.
Olduvai Gorge. Volume III: Excavation in Beds I and II, 1960-63. With a foreword by J. D. Clark. Cambridge: Cambridge University Press, 1971.
Olduvai Gorge: My Search for Early Man. Collins, 1979.
Africa's Vanishing Art: The Rock Paintings of Tanzania. New York: Doubleday, 1983.
Disclosing the Past: An Autobiography. New York: Doubleday, 1984.

FURTHER READING:

Books

Cole, Sonia. *Leakey's Luck: The Life of Louis Seymour Bazett Leakey, 1903-1972.* Harcourt, 1975.
Isaac, Glynn, and Elizabeth R. McCown, eds. *Human Origins: Louis Leakey and the East African Evidence.* Benjamin-Cummings, 1976.
Johanson, Donald C., and Maitland A. Edey. *Lucy: The Beginnings of Humankind.* New York: Simon & Schuster, 1981.
Leakey, Louis. *By the Evidence: Memoirs, 1932–1951.* Harcourt, 1974.
Leakey, Richard. *One Life: An Autobiography.* Salem House, 1984.
Malatesta, Anne, and Ronald Friedland. *The White Kikuyu: Louis S. B. Leakey.* New York: McGraw-Hill, 1978.
Moore, Ruth E., *Man, Time, and Fossils: The Story of Evolution.* New York: Knopf, 1961.
Reader, John. *Missing Links,* New York: Little, Brown, 1981.

Periodicals

Begley, Sharon. "Witness to the Creation: Mary Leakey, 1913-1996" (obituary). *Newsweek* (23 December 1996).

David M. Lee

Payne, Melvin M. "The Leakeys of Africa: Family in Search of Prehistoric Man." *National Geographic.* (February 1965): 194-231.

Wilford, John Noble. "Mary Leakey, 83, Dies: Traced Human Dawn" (obituary). *New York Times* (9 December 1996).

—*Sketch by Michael Sims*

David M. Lee
1931–
American physicist

David M. Lee shared the 1996 Nobel Prize for Physics with colleagues **Robert C. Richardson** and **Douglas D. Osheroff** for their discovery of superfluidity in helium-3, a rare isotope of helium, in the early 1970s. Highly esteemed for his pioneering work in cryogenics, the physics of extremely low temperatures, has also investigated the effects of low temperatures on metals and other materials.

Lee was born in Rye, New York, on January 20, 1931, the son of Marvin Lee and Annette (Franks) Lee. In 1960, he married Dana Thorangkul; they have two sons. After earning a B.A. at Harvard University in 1952, Lee served in the U. S. Army until 1954. The

following year, he completed his M.S. at the University of Connecticut. In 1959, having received his Ph.D. from Yale University, Lee joined the Department of Physics at Cornell University as an instructor; he was named professor of physics in Cornell's College of Arts and Sciences in 1968.

From 1966 to 1967, Lee was a visiting scientist at Brookhaven National Laboratory in Upton, New York. He was also visiting professor at several institutions, including the University of Florida at Gainesville, from 1974 to 1975 and again in 1994, and the University of California in San Diego, in 1988. He also lectured in China, at Beijing University, in 1981. In 1994, he was named to a professorship at Joseph Fourier University in Grenoble, France.

Lee Explores Cryogenics

Low-temperature physics, Lee's field, explores the behavior of materials at very low temperatures, almost at absolute zero, the lowest temperature possible, 0 K (Kelvin), equalling -459.67°F (-273.15°C). Quantum mechanics, formulated in the context of quantum theory, and based on the concept of a particular quantity, or quantum, of energy needed to effect a change, enables scientists to explain phenomena, such as the behavior of subatomic particles, which defy classical mechanics. Even in the unusual and mysterious world of quantum physics, where strange phenomena seem to be the rule rather than the exception, low-temperature, or condensed-matter, physics apparently enjoys a special status. Physicists who explore this area are creating conditions that have never existed anywhere in the universe. Indeed, as researchers have discovered, in the separate universe of cryogenics, liquids reach the state of superfluidity, exhibiting such properties that can hardly be imagined in the world of "normal" liquids. For example, superfluids, because their atoms have stopped moving in a random fashion, lose all inner friction, and, as a result, appear uncontainable. In other words, left in a container, a superfluid will spontaneously overflow it.

Line of Research Yields Surprising Discovery

Interestingly, when Lee and his colleagues at Cornell (Richardson was a fellow-senior researcher, while Osheroff was a graduate student) embarked on their study of helium-3, in the late 1960s, superfluidity was not their goal. Instead, they were searching for a phase transition–which in the macroscopic world, for example, would refer to the transition of a body from a solid to a liquid state—of frozen helium-3 to a magnetic order. However, the series of experiments that Lee and his collaborators conducted on frozen helium-3 eventually led to the discovery—reported in 1972—of superfluidity in helium-3. In fact, the scientists eventually found that superfluid helium-3 occurs in two different superfluid states.

In order to appreciate the magnitude of this discovery, it is necessary to explain the difference between the two isotopes of helium, helium-4 and helium-3. A common isotope, helium-4, also called a boson, has a nucleus, consisting of two protons and two neutrons, and two electrons. Bosons, which have an even number of particles, behave in accordance with Bose-Einstein condensation, in which a significant amount of particles are in the lowest-energy single quantum state. Consequently, helium-4 reaches the state of superfluidity at 2.17 K, which was confirmed experimentally in the 1930s by the Russian physicist **Pyotr Leonidovich Kapitza**, who, incidentally, coined the term *superfluid*. However, helium-3, called a fermion because of its unique structure (nucleus consisting of one neutron and two protons; two electrons) seemed impossible to bring to a superfluid state. For decades following the discovery of the superfluidity of helium-4, researchers, realizing that Bose-Einstein condensation does not work for fermions, assumed the helium-3 would always resist efforts to make it superfluid. Indeed, Lee and his team cooled the helium-3 ice to 2.7 millikelvins, which means the temperature of superfluid helium-4 is roughly a thousand times higher than that of helium-3 in a superfluid state.

Discovery Sheds Light on Birth of the Universe

A remarkable breakthrough in condensed-matter physics, the discovery made by Lee and his colleagues also has profound implications for cosmology. Namely, scientists have connected helium-3 superfluidity with the creation of cosmic strings, which may have played a role in the formation of galaxies. According to scientists, cosmic strings, whose existence is hypothetical, may have emerged in the wake of phase transitions a fraction of a second after the Big Bang. Experiments in which superfluid helium-3 was rapidly heated and subsequently cooled yielded vortices which are believed to correspond, on a microscopic scale, to cosmic strings. These events involving helium-3 may replicate, scientists believe, the birth of our universe.

Twice awarded a John Simon Guggenheim Fellowship, in 1966 and 1974, Lee became a Fellow of the American Physical Society and the American Association for the Advancement of Science, in 1982. Along with his colleagues Richardson and Osheroff, Lee received the 1976 Sir Francis Simon Memorial Prize from Britain's Institute of Physics. In 1981, the three scientists were awarded the Oliver E. Buckley Solid State Physics Prize by the American Physical Society for their discovery of superfluidity in helium-3.

SELECTED WRITINGS BY LEE:

Periodicals

(With N. David Mermin) "Superfluid Helium 3." *Scientific American* (December 1976): 56-71.

FURTHER READING:

Books

Leggett, A. J. *The Problems of Physics.* Oxford: Oxford University Press, 1987.
Tilley, Donald E., and Walter Thumm. *College Physics with Applications to the Life Sciences.* Menlo Park, CA: Cummings, 1971, pp. 542-43.

Periodicals

Browne, Malcolm W. "Discoveries of Superfluid Helium, and 'Buckyballs,' Earn Nobels for 6 Scientists." *New York Times* (10 October 1996): D21.
Lounasmaa, O. V., and G. R. Pickett. "The ^{3}He Superfluids." *Scientific American* (June 1990).
Peterson, Ivars. "Superfluidity Finding Earns Physics Nobel." *Science News* 150, no. 16 (19 October 1996): 247.
Richardson, R. C. "Low Temperature Science–What Remains for the Physicist?" *Physics Today* (August 1981): 46.
Special Issue: He^3 and He^4. *Physics Today* (February 1987).

Other

Nobel Foundation WWW Server Posting (9 October 1996). http://www.nobel.ki.se

—*Sketch by Jane Stewart Cook and Zoran Minderovic*

Rita Levi-Montalcini
1909–1989
Italian-born American neurobiologist

Rita Levi-Montalcini is recognized for her pioneering research on nerve cell growth. During the 1950s she discovered a protein in the nervous system, which she named the nerve growth factor (NGF). Her subsequent collaboration with biochemist **Stanley Cohen** at Washington University in St. Louis, Missouri, led to the isolation of that substance. Later applications of their work have proven useful in the

Rita Levi-Montalcini

study of several disorders, including Alzheimer's disease, cancer, and birth defects. Levi-Montalcini's and Cohen's work was recognized in 1986 when they were jointly awarded the Nobel Prize for physiology or medicine. Levi-Montalcini became the fourth woman to receive the Nobel in that field.

Levi-Montalcini, the third of four children of Adamo Levi and Adele Montalcini, was born into an upper-middle-class Jewish family in Turin, Italy, in 1909. She grew up in a traditional family and was steered by her father to pursue an education at an all-girls' high school that prepared young women for marriage. She graduated from high school when she was eighteen, having demonstrated exceptional intellectual ability, but was unable to enter a university because of the limited education that had been offered to her. Levi-Montalcini was uncertain what she wanted to do with her life (though she was certain she did not want to marry and have children), and it wasn't until three years later, when her beloved governess was stricken with cancer, that she decided to become a doctor.

After having convinced her father she wanted to enter medical school, Levi-Montalcini passed the entrance exams with distinction. She enrolled in the Turin School of Medicine in 1930, where she studied under Dr. Giuseppe Levi, a well-known histologist and embryologist who introduced Levi-Montalcini to research on the nervous system. She graduated from medical school in 1936 and became Levi's research assistant. With the rise of Fascism in the late 1930s, Jews were restricted from academic positions as well as the medical profession, and Levi-Montalcini was forced to resign from her academic and clinical posts in 1938. The following year, she accepted a position at the Neurological Institute in Brussels, where she worked until the Nazi invasion in 1939 precipitated her return to Italy.

Conducts Research in Hiding

Upon returning to Italy, she took up residence in Turin with her family. Restrictions imposed upon Jews had increased during her absence, and Levi-Montalcini was forced to set up a private laboratory in her bedroom. Again working with Levi, who had also been banned from his academic post, Levi-Montalcini began researching the nervous system of chicken embryos. In a memoir published in *Women Scientists: The Road to Liberation,* Levi-Montalcini recalls, "Looking back to that period I wonder how I could have found so much interest in, and devoted myself with such enthusiasm to, the study of a small neuroembryological problem, when all the values I cherished were being crushed, and the triumphant advance of the Germans all over Europe seemed to herald the end of Western civilization. The answer may be found in the well-known refusal of human beings to accept reality at its face value, whether this be the fate of the individual, of a country, or of the human race." Her research at the time, in fact, laid the groundwork for her discovery of NGF.

By 1942 the Allied bombing of Turin forced Levi-Montalcini and her family to move to the countryside, where she continued experimentation on chicken embryos to study the mechanisms of nerve cell differentiation, or the specialization of nerve cells. Contrary to previous studies conducted by the respected neuroembryologist **Viktor Hamburger**, who theorized that nerve cells reached their destinations because they were directed by the organs to which they grew, Levi-Montalcini hypothesized that a specific nutrient was essential for nerve growth. When Nazi troops invaded northern Italy in 1943, Levi-Montalcini was again forced to relocate, this time to Florence, where she remained for the duration of the war under an assumed name. Following the liberation of Florence in 1944, Levi-Montalcini worked as a doctor in a refugee camp, and, when northern Italy was liberated the following year, she resumed her post as research assistant to Levi in Turin. Hamburger, who was interested in a paper Levi-Montalcini had published on her wartime experiments, contacted her in 1946, inviting her to fill a visiting research position at Washington University in St. Louis. This temporary position ultimately lasted over three decades.

Fortuitous Collaborations Yield Results

Levi-Montalcini's early work at Washington University concerned further experimentation on the growth processes of chicken embryos in which she observed a migratory sequence of nerve cells. Her observations validated her theory on the existence of a "trophic factor," which provided the essential nutrients for nerve cell differentiation. In 1950 she began studying mouse tumors that had been grafted onto chicken embryos, and which Elmer Bueker had earlier demonstrated were capable of eliciting a proliferation of nerve cells. After repeating Bueker's results, Levi-Montalcini reached a different conclusion. Instead of maintaining that the nerve cells proliferated in response to the presence of the tumor, she deduced that the nerve cells grew out of the tumor and that, thus, the tumor released a substance that elicited the growth. Traveling to Rio de Janeiro in 1952, Levi-Montalcini further tested her hypothesis using tissue cell cultures. Her tissue culture experiments regarding the presence of a substance in the tumor proved highly successful. However, there remained the important step of isolating this substance, which she called "the nerve-growth promoting agent" and later labled nerve growth factor. Upon returning to Washington University, Levi-Montalcini began working with American biochemist Stanley Cohen between 1953 and 1959. During that time, they extracted NGF from snake venom and the salivary glands of male mice. Through these experiments, Cohen was able to determine the chemical structure of NGF, as well as produce NGF antibodies. Levi-Montalcini maintained her interest in the research of NGF; and, when she returned to italy in 1961, she established a laboratory at the Higher Institute of Health in Rome to perform joint NGF research with colleagues at Washington University.

A Lifetime of Accomplishments Is Recognized

By 1969 Levi-Montalcini established and served as director of the Institute of Cell Biology of the Italian National Research Council in Rome. Working six months out of the year at the Institute of Cell Biology and the other six months at Washington University, Levi-Montalcini maintained labs in Rome and St. Louis until 1977, at which time she resumed full-time residence in Italy. During this time she received numerous awards for her work, including becoming the tenth woman to be elected to the National Academy of Sciences in 1968. Despite her success, Levi-Montalcini was the only director of a laboratory conducting NGF research for many years. Later researchers, realizing the significance of understanding the growth of nerve fibers in treating degenerative diseases, have continued the work that Levi-Montalcini began in the late 1930s.

Levi-Montalcini remained active in the scientific community in her later years, upholding status as professor emeritus at Washington University from 1977 until her death in 1989, as well as contributing greatly to scientic studies and programs in her native country. After winning the Nobel Prize in 1986, she was appointed president of the Italian Multiple Sclerosis Association and also became the first woman to attain membership to the Pontifical Academy of Sciences in Rome. In 1987 she was awarded the National Medal of Science, the highest honor among American scientists.

Levi-Montalcini kept abreast with current scientific trends into her last years, conducting further research at the Institute of Cell Biology in Rome that focused on the importance of NGF in the immune and endocrine systems. Additionally, with her twin sister, who is an artist, Levi-Montalcini established educational youth programs that provide counseling and grants for teenagers interested in the arts or sciences. Recognized not only for her astute intuitive mind and her dedication to fully understanding the mechanisms of NGF, Levi-Montalcini, frequently described by her congenial manner and wit, influenced three generations of scientists during her own lifetime.

SELECTED WRITINGS BY LEVI-MONTALCINI:

Books

"Reflections on a Scientific Adventure," in *Women Scientists: The Road to Liberation,* edited by Derek Richter, Macmillan Press, 1982, pp. 99–117.
Molecular Aspects of Neurobioloay, Springer-Verlag, 1986.
In Praise of Imperfection: My Life and Work, Basic Books, 1988.

Periodicals

Scientific American, The Nerve Growth Factor, June, 1979, pp. 68–77.
Science, The Nerve Growth Factor 35 Years Later, Volume 237, 1987, pp. 1154–61.

FURTHER READING:

Periodicals

Holloway, Marguerite, *Scientific American,* Finding the Good in the Bad, January, 1993, pp. 32, 36.
Levine, Joe, *Time,* Lives of Spirit and Dedication, October 27, 1986, pp. 66–8.

Claude Lévi-Strauss

Marx, Jean L., *Science,* The 1986 Nobel Prize for Physiology or Medicine, October 31, 1986, pp. 543–44.

Randall, Frederika, *Vogue,* The Heart and Mind of a Genius, March, 1987, pp. 480, 536.

Schmeck, Harold M., Jr., *New York Times,* Two Pioneers in Growth of Cells Win Nobel Prize, October 14, 1986, pp. Al, C3.

Suro, Roberto, *New York Times,* Unraveler of Mysteries, October 14, 1986, p. C3.

—Sketch by Elizabeth Henry

Claude Lévi-Strauss
1908–

Belgian-born French anthropologist

Claude Lévi-Strauss is widely viewed as one of the dominant intellectual figures of the twentieth century. A master of French prose, he is revered, particularly in the French-speaking world, as a great *savant*—that is, a writer whose vast knowledge enables him to address a wide range of issues across a number of academic disciplines. In the English-speaking world, however, Lévi-Strauss is better known as anthropologist. Scholars have asserted that Lévi-Strauss deserves the credit for placing anthropology on solid scientific foundations, thus creating the highly successful and influential field of structural anthropology.

Claude Gustave Lévi-Strauss was born on November 28, 1908, in Brussels, Belgium. His father was an artist. After completing his lycée, or high school, studies, he entered the University of Paris, obtaining advanced degrees in philosophy, literature, and law. Lévi-Strauss then accepted a teaching post at a lycée. However, he perceived his subject, philosophy, as intellectually constraining, and sought a new vocation. He found it in anthropology.

Teaches and Studies in Brazil

Eager to learn about new cultures, Lévi-Strauss gladly accepted an offer to teach sociology at the University of Sao Paulo, Brazil. In addition to working at the university, where he remained from 1935 to 1938, Lévi-Strauss performed ethnological field work in Central Brazil, studying a variety of tribes and building the empirical foundations for his subsequent theoretical work. In Brazil, where he remained until 1939, Lévi-Strauss worked as an anthropologist, entering and describing the mental world of so-called "primitive" cultures. In addition, living in exile, he experienced a certain distancing from his own culture, placing human cultures in general in the wider context of scientific objectivity.

An Exile in New York

After leaving Brazil, Lévi-Strauss returned to a Europe on the verge of World War II. As a French patriot, he served in France's short defensive war against Nazi Germany. When France fell to Nazism, Lévi-Strauss, as a Jew, found himself in an extremely precarious position. Fortunately, he was able to emigrate to the United States, obtaining, in 1942, a teaching position at the New School for Social Research in New York. Vastly different from his Brazilian exile, Lévi-Strauss's stay in New York, and particularly his work at the New School, brought him in touch with the international community of European intellectuals, many of them Jewish, who were able to escape from the advancing tide of Nazi terror in Europe. For example, Lévi-Strauss's colleague at the New School was the great Russian linguist Roman Jakobson (1896-1982), whose research in structural linguistics, particularly phonology, inspired Lévi-Strauss to start comparing various systematic rule operatives in society, such as, for example, the relationship of kinship to language. In phonology, Jakobson had observed, many structural patterns can be formulated in terms of polar opposites, represented by the mathematical symbols for "plus" and "minus." The structure of polar opposites, according to Jakobson, is obvious in phonology, where all sounds can be divided into vowels and consonants, and consonants into voiced (+) and unvoiced (-) consonants. Taking his cue from Jakobson, but also relying on the wider theoretical context provided by the Swiss linguist Ferdinand de Saussure (1857-1913), who defined language as a system of abstract rules, Lévi-Strauss basically posited that all human systems, including kinship systems and mythological motifs, conform to the essentially binary logic of language.

Lévi-Strauss returned to France in 1945, following the liberation of France, but came back to the United States the following year to represent his country as a councilor for culture at the French embassy, remaining at that post until 1947. He subsequently embarked on a brilliant academic career, serving as director of studies at the Ecole Pratique des Hautes Etudes in Paris from 1950 to 1974. In 1959, he was appointed to the Chair of social anthropology at the College de France, where he taught until 1982.

Writer and Scientist: *Tristes Tropiques* and *The Savage Mind*

In 1955, Lévi-Strauss published *Tristes Tropiques*, the highly acclaimed memoir of his life in Brazil. Viewed by many as a literary work, Lévi-Strauss's beautifully written book is replete with nostalgic, melancholy reminiscences about the vanishing natives cultures of Brazil. While frequently focusing on strictly anthropological issues, *Tristes Tropiques* is a work in which Lévi-Strauss supplements his scientific insights with both personal and philosophical reflections, with specific emphasis on the fundamental sadness associated with the essentially solitary and transient destinies of individuals and societies.

In *The Savage Mind*, which, as scholars maintain, should have, in keeping with the author's choice of term, been translated as *Savage Thought*, Lévi-Strauss attacked the traditional dichotomy of "primitive" and "modern" thought. For Lévi-Strauss, "primitive" (or mythical) and "scientific" thought are merely two distinct systems of organizing the world, neither one "superior" or "inferior" in relation to the other. Lévi-Strauss defined mythical thought as concrete, object-oriented—in a literal sense—but bound, just like scientific (theoretical) thought, to rigorous logical laws. A mythological world view may, according to Lévi-Strauss, rely on a set of rules that would not work for scientific thought, but the inner logic of mythology is in no way less rigorous than that of science.

A Structuralist Tackles History

In the 1960s, Lévi-Strauss, although secure in his position as the leading anthropologist in France, faced criticism from scholars, particularly those with a leftist political agenda, who tended to view structuralism's apparent disregard of history with suspicion. In essence, these scholars, among whom was also the celebrated philosopher Jean-Paul Sartre, accused Lévi-Strauss of ignoring the historical dimension of societies. By emphasizing structure as such, they charged, Lévi-Strauss disregarded society's potential for positive political change. At first glance, the criticism seemed justified, since it implied that Lévi-Strauss, following de Saussure's distinction between *synchronic* (describing a situation at a given time) and *diachronic* (describing a process of a certain duration) terms, subscribed to a fundamentally dualistic view of the world, a view, in fact, informed by a synchronic perspective. However, as Kenneth Leach observed in his book *Claude Lévi-Strauss*, according to Lévi-Strauss, "the study of history diachronically and the study of anthropology cross-culturally but synchronically are two alternative ways of doing the same kind of thing."

In support of this observation, Leach quotes the following paragraph from *The Savage Mind*. "The anthropologist respects history, but he does not accord it a special value. He conceives it as a study complementary to his own; one of them unfurls the range of human societies in time, the other in space. And the difference is even less great than it might seem, since the historian strives to reconstruct the picture of vanished societies as they were at the points which for them corresponded to the present, while the ethnographer does his best to reconstruct the historical stages which temporarily preceded their existing form."

Mythology and Mythologics

Lévi-Strauss, who successfully used the insights and methodologies of linguistics in his early studies of mythology, introduced in his *Mythologiques* series the idea of a profound kinship between myth and music. A highly abstract, self-referential system which notably lacks the symbolic and narrative potential of language, music seems hardly capable of relating to mythology. Lévi-Strauss, however, found that, if language figures as the fundamental paradigm, many enlightening parallels between myth and music come to the fore. In his 1977 lectures for CBC radio, published as *Myth and Meaning*, Lévi-Strauss said, "If we try to understand the relationship between language, myth, and music, we can only do so by using language as the point of departure, and then it can be shown that music on the one hand and mythology on the other both stem from languages but grow apart in different directions, that music emphasizes the sound aspect already embedded in language, while mythology emphasizes the sense aspect, the meaning aspect, which is also embedded in languages."

Lévi-Strauss's rich, multi-faceted anthropological research has traversed the vast universe of human activities, also plumbing the depths of the human mind. Admired and criticized, Lévi-Strauss's monumental works remain, like any human project, incomplete. However, not even his staunchest critics can deny the profundity and power of his descriptions, analyses, and illuminations of humankind's most profound quest—the quest for meaning, which, as Lévi-Strauss has brilliantly demonstrated, is manifested in humankind's struggle, both conscious and unconscious, to rise above chaos and create an ordered world. Finally, Lévi-Strauss's work has been as praised as a unique attempt to formulate a universal anthropology of humankind, and as such, one of the great intellectual accomplishments of the twentieth century.

Lévi Strauss's numerous honors include the Grand Croix de la Légion d'Honneur and the Médaille d'Or de recherche scientifique. In addition, he is Commandeur de l'Ordre national de mérite, Commandeur des Palmes académiques, and Commandeur des Arts et des Lettres. In 1973, he was elected to the Académie française, inheriting the seat of the writer Henri de Montherlant, who had died the previous year. That year, he received the Erasmus Prize. He is also a member of several major European and American academies of science. The distinguished institutions of learning which have bestowed honorary doctorates on Lévi-Strauss include the following universities: Brussels, Oxford, Yale, Harvard, Chicago, Columbia, Uppsala, and Johns Hopkins.

SELECTED WRITINGS BY LÉVI-STRAUSS:

Books

Tristes tropiques. Paris: Plon, 1955. Translated by John and Doreen Weightman as *Tristes Tropiques.* New York: Penguin Books, 1992.

Anthropologie structurale. Paris: Plon, 1958. Translated by Monique Layton as *Structural Anthropology.* Chicago: University of Chicago Press, 1983.

La pensée sauvage. Paris: Plon, 1962. Translated as *The Savage Mind.* Chicago: University of Chicago Press, 1966.

Mythologiques I. Le cru et le cuit. Paris: Plon, 1964. Translated by John and Doreen Weightman as *The Raw and Cooked.* Chicago: University of Chicago Press, 1983.

Mythologiques II. Du miel au cendres. Paris: Plon, 1966. Translated by John and Doreen Weightman as *From Honey to Ashes.* Chicago: University of Chicago Press, 1983.

Mythologiques III. L'origine des manières de table. Paris: Plon, 1968. Translated by John and Doreen Weightman as *The Origin of Table Manners.* Chicago: University of Chicago Press, 1990.

Mythologiques IV. L'Homme nu. Paris: Plon, 1972. Translated by John and Doreen Weightman as *The Naked Man.* Chicago: University of Chicago Press, 1990.

Myth and Meaning: Five Talks for Radio. University of Toronto Press, 1978. Reprinted as *Myth and Meaning: Cracking the Code of Culture.* New York: Schocken, 1995.

Histoire de Lynx. Paris: Plon, 1991. Translated by Catherine Tihanyi as *The Story of Lynx.* Chicago: University of Chicago Press, 1995.

Regarder, écouter, lire. Paris: Plon, 1993. Translated by Brian C. J. Singer as *Look, Listen, Read.* New York: Basic Books, 1997.

Periodicals

"The Social Use of Kinship Terms among Brazilian Indians." *American Anthropologist* 45, no. 3 (July-September 1943): 398-409.

"The Name of the Nambikwara." *American Anthropologist* 48, no. 1 (1946): 139-40.

"Future of Kinship Studies." *Proceedings of the Royal Anthropological Institute of Great Britain and Ireland* (1965): 13-22.

"Anthropology: Its Achievements and Future." *Nature* 209 (1 January 1966):

"The Disappearance of Man." *New York Review* (28 July 1966).

"Structuralism and Ecology." *Barnard Alumnae* (Spring 1972): 6-14.

"Science Forever Incomplete." *Society* 16, no. 5 (July-August 1979): 16-18.

FURTHER READING:

Books

Champagne, Roland A. *Claude Lévi-Strauss.* Boston: Twayne, 1987.

Doniger, Wendy. Foreword to *Myth and Meaning: Cracking the Code of Culture* by Claude Lévi-Strauss. New York: Schocken, 1995.

Eco, Umberto. *The Open Work.* Cambridge: Harvard University Press, 1989.

Geertz, Clifford. *Works and Lives: The Anthropologist as Author.* Stanford: Stanford University Press, 1988.

Henaff, Marcel. *Claude Lévi-Strauss and the Making of Structural Anthropology.* Minneapolis: University of Minnesota Press, 1998.

Leach, Edmund. *Claude Lévi-Strauss.* Chicago: University of Chicago Press, 1970.

Pace, David. *Claude Lévi-Strauss: The Bearer of Ashes.* London: Routledge, 1983.

Periodicals

Doniger, Wendy. "Structuralist Universals versus Psychoanalytic Universals." *History of Religions* 28 (February 1989): 267-81.

Edward B. Lewis

Johnson, Christopher. "Anthropology and the Sciences Humaines: The Voice of Lévi-Strauss." *History of the Human Sciences* 10 (August 1997): 122-33.
Maybury-Lewis, David. "Claude Lévi-Strauss and the Search for Structure." *Wilson Quarterly* 12, no. 1 (1988): 82-95.

—Sketch by Zoran Minderovic

Edward B. Lewis
1918–
American developmental geneticist

Edward B. Lewis, sometimes called the father of developmental genetics, has dedicated a lifetime of research to the study of gene clusters responsible for early embryonic development. His tenacity resulted in important discoveries and led to formal recognition of his work. In 1995, Lewis was awarded the Nobel Prize in Physiology or Medicine for his groundbreaking genetic research. He shared the prize with two other scientists, **Eric Wieschaus** of Princeton University and **Christiane Nüsslein-Volhard** of the Max Planck Institute for Developmental Biology in Germany. Working independently of his co-recipients, Lewis studied "master control" gene clusters in

fruit flies and subsequently discovered their corresponding human counterparts. Such a discovery promises to explain and eventually prevent congenital human malformations (about 40% of all human birth defects). It may also lead to improved in-vitro fertilization techniques, as well as a better understanding of substances harmful to early pregnancy.

Edward B. Lewis was born May 20, 1918, in Wilkes-Barre, Pennsylvania, to Edward B. Lewis and Laura (Histed) Lewis. His early years were spent trying to satiate his thirst for scientific knowledge in an environment that did not lend itself to learning. Books were not commonplace at home and as he remembered, "the high school library had nothing at all on genetics." Lewis found solace in playing the flute. He practiced daily, and during high school played with the local symphony orchestra. His musical abilities led to a scholarship at Bucknell University; however, Lewis transferred to the University of Minnesota, which offered course work in genetics. In 1939, Lewis received a Bachelor of Arts degree in biostatistics from the University of Minnesota. He went on to earn a Doctor of Philosophy degree in genetics at the California Institute of Technology (Caltech) in 1942 and a Master of Science degree in meteorology the following year. After serving as a weatherman in the Army during World War II, Lewis married Pamela Harrah on September 26, 1946; they had met in the laboratory at Caltech. They have two sons, Hugh and Keith. A third son, Glenn, was killed in a climbing accident at the age of 13. Lewis and his wife established a prize in his name at San Marino High School in California.

For much of his career, which has spanned more than fifty years, Lewis has been affiliated with his alma mater, the California Institute of Technology. After his 1947-48 appointment as Rockefeller Foundation Fellow at Cambridge University, Lewis established himself at the Biology Department of the California Institute of Technology. From 1966 to 1988, Lewis served as **Thomas Hunt Morgan** Professor of Biology and in 1988 was named Thomas Hunt Morgan Professor Emeritus. During the years 1975-76, Lewis was a guest professor at the Institute of Genetics at the University of Copenhagen.

High School Fruit Fly Purchase Leads to Nobel Prize

Since the 1940s, Lewis has been a pioneer in the field of developmental genetics. The direction of his research was already set as a sophomore in high school: with the encouragement of a biology teacher, Lewis and a friend, Edward Novitski, purchased 100 fruit flies from Purdue University for one dollar. Lewis and Novitski let the flies breed, checking each day for any unusual new hatchlings. Their eagerness to learn something from a living specimen sparked careers in biology for both boys. In Lewis it created a lifelong obsession with the genetic workings of the fruit fly. In fact, it was a mutated fruit fly discovered by Novitski that led to Lewis's first postulations about the genetic factors causing mutations in the flies. Like Lewis, Novitski spent his professional life immersed in genetics research. Now retired, he resides in Eugene, Oregon.

Continuing his work with fruit fly specimens, Lewis was able to collect, crossbreed, and ultimately study an enormous amount of mutant flies. By mutating fly embryos so that the flies developed extra pairs of wings, Lewis was able to discern that it was not only the wings that were duplicated but the whole body segment that contained the wings. Because the fruit fly has only eight chromosomes (humans have 23 sets), Lewis was able to pinpoint the gene sequence responsible for the development and order of each fly-body segment. His findings were published in a 1978 *Nature* paper entitled "A Gene Complex Controlling Segmentation in Drosophila." Since then, geneticists have discovered that the gene sequences are almost identical for all other animal species as well. According to Bruce Alperts, the head of the National Academy of Sciences, Lewis's work "is a great example of how basic research answering apparently esoteric questions about flies and other lower organisms has fundamental importance for understanding humans."

Fifty Years of Scientific Accomplishment

Lewis has often received recognition for his contributions to developmental genetics. In 1981, he was honored with a Doctor of Philosophy degree from the University of Umeå in Sweden. He received the Thomas Hunt Morgan Medal from the Genetics Society of America in 1983. He was awarded the Canadian Gairdner Foundation International Award in 1987 and Israel's Wolf Prize in Medicine in 1989. In 1990, he received three separate awards: the Lewis S. Rosenstiel Award in basic medical research, the National Medal of Science, and an honorary membership in the Genetical Society in Great Britain. Lewis won the prestigious Albert Lasker Basic Medical Research Award in 1991, the Louisa Gross Horwitz Prize in 1992, and was given an honorary Doctor of Science degree from the University of Minnesota in 1993. Although the accolades nicely cap an illustrious career in science, recognition is second to discovery for Lewis; in his own words, "There's nothing as exciting as that."

Outside of the laboratory, Lewis is considered something of a Renaissance man. He swims daily, supports the arts with season tickets to the opera, and still plays the flute every day. Fellow scientists at the California Institute of Technology biology department often hear the sound of flute music resonating throughout the building. Lewis also raises tortoises with his wife Pamela in California.

SELECTED WRITINGS BY LEWIS:

Periodicals

"A Gene Complex Controlling Segmentation in Drosophila." *Nature* 276, 1978, pp. 565-70

"Clusters of Master Control Genes Regulate the Development of Higher Organisms." *Journal of the American Medical Association* 267, March 18, 1992, p. 1524

—Sketch by Jacqueline Longe

Carl Louis Ferdinand von Lindemann
1852–1939
German mathematician

The classic problem of squaring the circle had intrigued mathematicians since the time of Euclid. Only in 1882, however, when Ferdinand Lindemann proved that π is a transcendental number, was this problem finally resolved. While Lindemann is best known for this one result, he also played an important role in the development of mathematics in Germany during the turn of the 20th century.

Lindemann was born in Hanover, Germany, on April 12, 1852. His father was a teacher of modern languages and later a manager of a gas works while his mother was the daughter of a famous teacher of classical languages, so it is not surprising that their son finished first in his class upon graduating from his gymnasium in 1870. France and Germany had recently gone to war, but Lindemann's poor health prevented him from being called into the army. Instead, he enrolled at the University of Göttingen to study mathematics.

Göttingen attracted many of Europe's leading mathematicians. During his time there Lindemann attended lectures by Alfred Clebsch on analytic spatial geometry, algebraic curves, elliptic functions, and the theory of algebraic forms. He also met **Felix Klein**, who was then a lecturer at the university. In 1872 Klein became a full professor at the University of Erlangen; Lindemann joined him as Klein's second Ph.D. student, receiving his degree in 1873 with a thesis on non–Euclidean geometry and its connection with mechanics. In addition, after Clebsch's sudden death in 1872 and with Klein's encouragement,

Lindemann edited and revised Clebsch's geometry lectures which he published as a textbook in 1876. The Clebsch–Lindemann text won wide acclaim and was used for several decades.

Proves π Is Transcendental

Lindemann spent part of the 1876–77 academic year in Paris, where he began a long friendship with **Charles Hermite**. Because of the success of the Clebsch–Lindemann text, he was introduced to many of the leading French mathematicians. He returned from Paris to become associate professor at the University of Freiburg after a promised position at the University of Würzburg never materialized. During his six years at Freiburg, Lindemann published several minor papers on special functions and Fourier series, and also wrote a paper on the vibration of strings, inspired by the recent invention of the microphone. But his main success came with his work on the number π. During Lindemann's visit to Paris in 1876, Hermite had shown him his proof that the number e is transcendental, that is, that e is not the root of any polynomial with integer coefficients. Building upon his friend's earlier work, Lindemann finally succeeded in 1882 in proving that π is also transcendental. He sent his paper "Über die Zahl π" (Concerning the number π) to Klein for publication in the *Mathematische Annalen*. Klein sent the paper to **Georg Cantor**, who could find no errors, and who passed the paper on to Karl Weierstrass in Berlin for final verification of the proof. With Lindemann's permission, on June 22, 1882, Weierstrass presented the result to the Berlin Academy of Sciences to great acclaim.

The problem of squaring the circle, that is, constructing a square with the same area as that of a given circle, fascinated mathematicians for more than two thousand years. A solution had been found by Dinostratus around 350 B.C., but no one had ever been able to find a solution using just the classical Euclidean tools of the straightedge and compass. Mathematicians knew that if a number was transcendental, and hence not algebraic, then no line of that length could be constructed using these tools. Lindemann's proof that π was transcendental, and hence unconstructible, finally established unequivocally that the squaring of the circle was impossible by means of straightedge and compass alone.

Teacher, Advisor, and Adminstrator

With the fame of his work on π freshly behind him, Lindemann accepted an appointment as full professor at the University of Königsberg in 1883. After ten years, he moved one final time to take a chair in mathematics at the University of Munich. He never again published a paper to rival the importance of his work on π. Nevertheless, Lindemann had a successful career as a teacher, an advisor of students, and an administrator. He supervised more than 60 German and foreign Ph.D. students, including **Hermann Minkowski** and **David Hilbert**. During his years in Munich, Lindemann served as dean of the arts and sciences, as rector of the university (an elected position comparable to that of president), and for 25 years as the director of the university's administrative committee. For several years Lindemann was also a confidential advisor to the king's court. In 1918, he received the Knight's Cross of the Order of the Bavarian Crown, an honor that granted nobility and the right to be known as Ferdinand Ritter von Lindemann.

In 1887, Lindemann married Lisbeth Küssner, a successful actress from Königsberg. They had two children, both born in Königberg, a son in 1889 and a daughter in 1891. Their son died tragically at the age of 22 during a mountain climbing trip in the Alps. Lisbeth apparently had mathematical as well as acting talents as she collaborated with her husband in translating and revising some of the works of the French mathematician **Henri Poincaré**. Lindemann died on March 6, 1939, three years after his wife. In his article on the man who discovered the transcendence of π, Fritsch writes that "he still published mathematical papers and thought about problems up to the day before his death."

SELECTED WRITINGS BY LINDEMANN:

"Alfred Clebsch: 'Vorlusungen über Geometrie," bearbeitet and herausgegeben von Dr. Ferdinand Lindemann, 1876.
"Über die Zahl π," in *Mathematische Annalen* 20 (1882): 212–25.
"Wissenschaft und Hypothese" (translation of Henri Poincaré's "La Science et l'hypothèse"), 1904.

FURTHER READING:

Dunham, William. *Journal through Genius: The Great Theorems of Mathematics*. New York:John Wiley & Sons, Inc., 1990.
Fritsch, R. "The Transcendence of π Has Been Known for about a Century—but Who Was the Man Who Discovered It?" *Results in Mathematics* 7 (1994): 164–83.
Wussing, H. "Carl Louis Ferdinand Lindemann," in *Dictionary of Scientfic Biography*. Volume VIII. Edited by Charles Coulston Gillispie. New York: Charles Scribner's Sons, 1974, pp. 367–68.

—Sketch by Larry Riddle

Elizaveta Fedorovna Litvinova
1845–1919(?)
Russian mathematics educator

Elizaveta Fedorovna Ivashkina Litvinova, a daughter of a landowning family in Russia's Tula region, was born in 1845. At a time when education for girls was generally limited to housekeeping and etiquette, Litvinova attended the Marinskaia in St. Petersburg, a progressive all–girls academy that offered some basic academic instruction. Still, the course of study available at the Marinskaia was far less comprehensive than the academic programs available at institutions for boys.

As a young woman living in St. Petersburg during the 1860s, Litvinova discovered a radical group that based its philosophy on nihilism. Members of this cultural movement believed that the natural sciences would provide the foundation for peaceful social change. For an intellectually vigorous young woman like Litvinova, such a philosophy was irresistible. She joined nihilist discussion groups and wrote revolutionists' poetry. And, as a nihilist, Litvinova embraced her duty to pursue advanced studies in the natural sciences.

Her family adamantly refused to support her in her efforts to earn a place in a university. Litvinova also had to work, furiously and independently, to make up the deficiencies in her academy training so she could pass the certification examination for graduates of male academies, a requirement for university admission. Some sympathetic university professors held seminars for women in the homes of wealthy nihilist supporters. Litvinova studied mathematics with A. N. Strannoliubskii, an academician who donated his spare time to helping women qualify for university admission and who counted Sofia Kovalevskaia, who would become Russia's most famous female mathematician, as one of his protegees.

In 1865, Russian women began to emigrate to institutions in Geneva, Bern, Heidelberg and Paris, which were opening their doors to women. The University of Zurich became a magnet for Russian women pursuing advanced degrees. As others flocked to Switzerland, Litvinova was barred from following them by an obstacle of her own making. In 1866, she married. Little is known about her husband, Dr. Litvinov (even his first name is not recorded) except for his objection to his wife's academic aspirations. Russian women needed the approval of a father or husband to obtain passports, and Dr. Litvinov consistently refused to give his wife permission to leave Russia. By 1870, Litvinova had passed the required competency examination. Still, she languished in

Russia; then, as she wrote in her diary, "fate itself" intervened. She was somehow freed of her husband—whether he died, disappeared, or divorced her, Litvinova never disclosed it. She managed to obtain a passport, and in 1872 she left Russia for Zurich.

A Colony of Scholars in Zurich

Litvinova arrived in Zurich as a typical college student—short on money but rich with enthusiasm. But the Swiss viewed the colony of Russian female students with suspicion. They were cynical about the morals of women who had left husbands and families to pursue education, and they deplored the perceived assault on femininity by this cohort of Russian women who were invading the natural sciences. Instead of studying at the university, where the growing number of women students inspired some tolerance, Litvinova enrolled at the Polytechnic Institute. In many of her lectures, Litvinova was the only woman among hundreds of males; later, she wrote that she feared to raise her eyes because the men would think her a woman of loose morals.

Despite such social pressures, Litvinova was happy in Zurich. Her studies absorbed her, and some of her professors were kind. She studied with the French professor Mequet; she not only attended lectures by mathematical analyst Hermann Schwarz, but was occasionally invited to share family tea in Schwarz's home.

Litvinova moved to Zurich with a four–year plan for completing her baccalaureate. But for some time, the autocratic Russian government had eyed the female Zurich colony with distrust. These women had not only defied Russian social conventions—they tended to embrace unconventional, even revolutionary political philosophies. In 1873, the tsar issued an edict that required all women studying abroad to return to Russia by January 1, 1874. Those who ignored the tsar's *ukase* would be banned from entering Russian universities (when and if they began admitting women) and would be barred from sitting for all licensing and civil service exams. Litvinova refused to obey. She remained in Zurich and completed her baccalaureate degree in 1876, then earned a doctorate from Bern University in 1878. She could not know at the time that her dissertation in function theory would be the only mathematical paper she would publish.

The Price of Defiance

Following her return to Russia in 1878, Litvinova immediately faced the consequences of her rebellion. The doctorate, the Swiss teaching certification, and the stack of glowing recommendations from her Zurich professors meant nothing. She was prohibited from sitting for teachers' licensing exams, and she was banned from full–time posts in any state–licenced institution. Litvinova was reduced to teaching in the lower classes of a women's academy. As an unlicenced teacher, she had no rights to a pension, vacation, or salary. She was paid by the hour and supplemented her meager earnings by writing popular accounts of the lives of mathematicians and philosophers, including a biography of Sofia Kovalevskaia.

After nine years, Litvinova finally won the right to teach upper level courses, becoming the first woman in Russia to teach the equivalent of high school mathematics. Still, she was denied the rights, privileges, and compensation afforded men at the same teaching rank. Her interest in teaching itself grew. Litvinova began using word problems in her classes and emphasized alternative approaches to proofs. She encouraged her students to use mathematics as a guide to logical thinking, making generalizations, and identifying underlying principles by studying groups of individual cases. During her 35–year teaching career, she managed to publish more than 70 papers on the philosophy and method of teaching mathematics.

Little is known about Litvinova's life after she retired from teaching. It is believed she lived with a sister in the country and died in 1919, but the date of her death has never been confirmed.

SELECTED WRITINGS BY LITVINOVA:

Books

Lösung einer Abbildungsaufgabe, 1879 (doctoral thesis).
Rulers and Thinkers: Biographical Essays, 1897
S. V. Kovalevskaia (Woman–Mathematician): Her Life and Scientific Work, 1894.

Periodicals

"'Little One' (From the Life of the Zurich Women Students)," in *Pervyi Zhenskii Kalendar'na 1912.* (1912): 112–116.

FURTHER READING:

Koblitz, Ann Hibbner. "Elizaveta Fedorovna Litvinova," in *Women of Mathematics: A Biobibliographic Sourcebook*. Edited by Louise S. Grinstein and Paul J. Campbell. Westport, CT: Greenwood Press, Inc., 1987, pp. 129–134.
————. *A Convergence of Lives: Sofia Kovalevskaia: Scientist, Writer, Revolutionary*. Boston: Birkhauser Boston Inc., 1983.

Thomas Eugene Lovejoy

————. "Elizaveta Fedorovna Litvinova (1845–1919): Russian Mathematician and Pedagogue." *Association for Women in Mathematics Newsletter* 14, no. 1 (January–February 1984): 13–17.

Other

"Elizaveta Fedorovna Litvinova." *Biographies of Women Mathematicians*. June 1997. http://www.scottlan.edu/lriddle/women/chronol.htm (July 22, 1997).

—*Sketch by A. Mullig*

Thomas Eugene Lovejoy
1941–
American biologist

Thomas Lovejoy became an advocate for the preservation of the Amazonian rain forest long before it was trendy to do so. As the assistant secretary for environmental and external affairs at the Smithsonian Institution, he is an effective administrator as well as an innovative scientist. His unique, 20-year experiment in the Amazon, known as the Minimum Critical Size of Ecosystems (MCSE) Project, has become the centerpiece of the newly-emerging discipline of conservation biology, of which he is one of the more visible and effective leaders.

Lovejoy was born on August 22, 1941, in New York City into a life of wealth and privilege. His father, Thomas Eugene Lovejoy, was a life insurance executive whose family once held most of the stock of the Manhattan Life Insurance Company. His mother was the former Audrey Helen Paige. While attending the Millbrook School in New York, Lovejoy was first made aware of the wonders of the natural world. The school's founder, Frank Trevor, inspired the teenage Lovejoy to study field biology, especially birds, and in only a few weeks time he was swept away. "It was Trevor," Lovejoy told contributor Leonard Bruno in a December 4, 1997, interview, "who awakened me to the fascination of nature and biology." After entering Yale University in 1959, he was able to study under the eminent ecologist **G. Evelyn Hutchinson** who, said Lovejoy, "provided the intellectual inspiration that stretched my mind permanently." After receiving his B. S. in 1964, he married Charlotte Seymour in 1966 with whom he had three daughters, Elizabeth Paige and Katherine Seymour (twins), and Anne Williams. The couple divorced in 1978. While in pursuit of his Ph.D., Lovejoy lived in Belem, Brazil, for two years as part of a Smithsonian project and introduced the technique of bird-banding to that country. His doctoral thesis also proved to be the first major long-term study of birds in the Amazon.

Initiates Ambitious Large-Scale Amazon Experiment

Before receiving his Ph.D. in biology from Yale in 1971, Lovejoy also participated in a prehistoric expedition to Nubia and collected birds in Kenya for the Peabody Museum of Natural History in New Haven, Connecticut. In 1972 he assisted both the science director and the vice president for resource and planning at the Academy of Natural Sciences of Philadelphia before becoming program director for the World Wildlife Fund of the United States in 1973. There, Lovejoy found he was able to blend his interests in science and conservation, and he remained with that group for 14 years, eventually becoming its executive vice president. In 1987, Lovejoy joined the Smithsonian Institution to become the assistant secretary for environmental and external affairs. In 1995, he became counselor to the secretary for biodiversity and environmental affairs.

Lovejoy moved to the Smithsonian in part because of its impartial reputation, realizing that since it was not considered to be an advocacy group, his words and work would have more credibility. While at the Smithsonian, he was able to continue a long-term experiment he had begun at the World Wildlife Fund in 1976. In 1978 he initiated a 20-year

experiment to attempt to determine the best strategy for conserving biological diversity. Called the Minimum Critical Size of Ecosystems (MCSE) Project, it has been described by Harvard's **E. O. Wilson** as "one of the boldest scientific experiments and one of the most original in the field of biodiversity." Its goal is to discover whether biological diversity is better favored by conserving a single large piece of land or by preserving a large number of smaller plots. This issue needs to be resolved scientifically if an optimum conservation strategy is to be devised, yet it seemed beyond the realm of actual field experimentation until December 1976.

That month, while participating in a National Science Foundation brainstorming session, Lovejoy realized that recent practices taking place in Brazil would allow scientists to actually field test the two approaches. The Brazilian government had begun to encourage development of the Amazonian basin near Manaus by using tax incentives, but it required developers to clear only 50% of the rain forest, leaving the remaining half untouched. Since this arbitrary type of land clearing would result in a patchwork of large and small plots of untouched forest, Lovejoy quickly noted that science had the raw materials for a large-scale experiment at hand. In order to take advantage of this unique situation, Lovejoy moved to organize support and funding for what he proposed would be a 20-year experiment. After persuading the host nation and its National Institute for Amazonian Research of the worth of the project, he worked long and hard to assure its financial backing. The World Wildlife Fund supported the joint project during its first decade, after which it was supported by the Smithsonian.

Lovejoy's grand experiment consists of 24 separate reserves that vary in size from 1 to 200 hectares (2.5 to 500 acres). The largest site has 10,000 hectares (25,000 acres). As it nears the completion of its first two decades of research, the joint project has yielded valuable results, the most interesting of which is called the "edge effect." This phenomenon, in which the trees at the edge of the reserve die off and the bird and butterfly populations decline, suggests that a reserve should always be made larger than is required to support its biological diversity since an inevitable shrinkage of life-supporting land will occur after clearing. More recent results indicate that this biomass loss occurs quite deep into the surrounding environment. Lovejoy expects that this long-term experiment, also called The Biological Dynamics of Forest Fragments Project, will extend beyond its 20-year term and hopefully become an institutionalized effort.

Promotes Conservation through Debt-for-Nature Swap

After getting his MCSE or Forest Fragments project underway, Lovejoy proved he is also a scientist who can think creatively in a political context. Seeking to promote his goal of international conservation, he offered his original idea of a "debt-for-nature" swap. In 1985 he outlined his concept of partially forgiving a country's debt if it would initiate conservation projects. This unique method offered developing nations a mechanism for reducing their debt while helping the environment at the same time.

Role as One of the Chief Spokespersons for the Environment Comes Easy

Besides his intense involvement with saving the rain forest through his ongoing, joint experiment in the Amazon and his "debt-for-nature" plan, Lovejoy also has become involved in broader environmental issues such as global warming and the loss of biodiversity. Unlike many scientists who remain within the technical confines of their subject, Lovejoy is intellectually and temperamentally suited to reach out and involve a wider and more influential audience who he hopes will become supporters. It is not unusual therefore for Lovejoy to personally lead a band of politicians, journalists, and even actors on a tour of the Amazon to experience first-hand both its awesome beauty and its steady destruction.

The list of national and international environmental groups of which he is an active member is staggering, and Lovejoy can also add to this list an equally impressive number of honorary degrees, publications, awards, and honors. In his 1997 Bruno interview, he said that he is most proud of receiving the Wilbur L. Cross Medal from his graduate school and in 1987, being decorated by the government of Brazil. Today, he is recognized as one of the most effective major players in the science and conservation of biological diversity.

SELECTED WRITINGS BY LOVEJOY:

Books

(With A. W. Diamond) *Conservation of Tropical Forest Birds.* Cambridge, England: International Council for Bird Preservation, 1985.
(With R. L. Peters) *Global Warming and Biological Diversity.* New Haven, CT: Yale University Press, 1992.

Periodicals

"Will Expectedly the Top Blow Off? Environmental Trends and the Need for Critical Decision Making." *Bioscience* Special Supplement (June 1995): S3-S7.

FURTHER READING:

Books

Katz, Linda Sobel, Sarah Orrick and Robert Honig. *Environmental Profiles: A Global Guide to Projects and People.* New York: Garland Publishing, Inc., 1993, p. 555.
Olendorf, Donna. *Contemporary Authors* 143. Detroit: Gale Research, 1994, pp. 248-250.

Periodicals

Sun, Marjorie. "How Do You Measure the Lovejoy Effect?" *Science* (March 9, 1990): 1174-1176.

—*Sketch by Leonard C. Bruno*

Jane Lubchenco
1947–
American marine ecologist

Jane Lubchenco has been active in research and public policy related the environment. Specifically, she studies evolutionary population and community ecology, focusing on experimental marine ecology. The depth and breadth of her scientific work has lead to numerous grants, including the MacArthur Foundation's "genius" grant in 1993. Lubchenco is interested in biodiversity, conservation biology, evolutionary population, and community ecology. In terms of more specific organisms, Lubchenco studies marine and algal ecology, the life histories of algal, plant-herbivore interactions, predator-prey interactions, and the related area of competition.

However, Lubchenco is not only interested in ecology solely for pure scientific study. She is concerned with real-world implementation—the very survival of the earth despite human pollution—and her work has affected research policy. Lubchenco is also concerned with supporting women's ambitions in science, and has published a personal account of how she and her husband, Bruce Menge, have successfully balanced career and family.

Lubchenco was born on December 4, 1947, in Denver, Colorado. Her mother worked as a part-time pediatrician while Lubchenco and her five sisters were young. Watching her mother try to juggle career and family influenced Lubchenco's later decisions about her own career. She earned her undergraduate degree in 1969 from Colorado College.

Lubchenco began her graduate work at the University of Washington, where she earned her M.S.

in 1971. That same year she married another ecologist, Bruce Menge. Lubchenco continued her graduate work at Harvard University, where she earned her Ph.D. in ecology in 1975. After graduation, Lubchenco continued to work at Harvard as an assistant professor. In 1976, she began an association with the National Science Foundation working as a Principal Investigator.

Applies for Unique Position

While Lubchenco was at Harvard, she and her husband, who was also a professor in the Boston area, made an important decision about their future. They were thinking about having children and decided they wanted to balance this future family with their jobs. They applied jointly for one, full-time position that they could split, a unique request at the time. In the April 1993 of *BioScience* the couple wrote, "We wanted to have it all but not go crazy in the process. We sought not what later came to be called 'the mommy track,' in which career goals would be sacrificed, nor the so-called 'fast track,' which we were already on and for us would have precluded having sufficient time with our children, but rather what we intended as a 'sane track.' The ideal arrangement seemed to be one in which we could each work part-time but do so in mainstream positions."

Oregon State University was willing to try the experiment, and they were both hired as half-time assistant professors in 1978. They eventually had two sons, Alexei, born in 1979, and Duncan, born in 1982. Throughout the '80s, Lubchenco continued to be active in her field. Concurrently from 1978 on, she was affiliated with the Smithsonian Institution as a research associate. In 1978, she began a relationship with the Ocean Trust Foundation, serving as a science advisor there until 1984. In 1988 she became an associate professor, then a full professor in the Zoology Department. She held a full-time position on her own beginning in 1989. From 1989 until 1992, she served as Chair of the department. While working at Oregon State, Lubchenco continued field research in Panama that she began in 1977, and continued through 1983.

She held many different visiting positions and advisorships. From 1981-88, she was the science advisor in West Quoddy Marine Station. In 1985, she was a visiting professor at Chile's Universidad de Antofagasta; in 1987, she held a similar position at China's Institute of Oceanography. This varied research earned Lubchenco several grants from the Andrew W. Mellon Foundation, from 1989-91, and again in 1993.

Wins "Genius" Grant

In 1991, Lubchenco was a key figure in the Ecological Society of America's Biosphere Initiative.

Lubchenco and other scholars published an agenda for future research, emphasizing global change and biological diversity. From 1992-93, she was president of the Ecological Society, after having served as its vice president from 1988-89. This is but one of many honors Lubchenco earned in the '90s. She also earned a fellowship in 1992, when she was named a Pew Scholar in Conservation and the Environment. In 1993, Lubchenco worked as a section coordinator for the United Nations Environmental Program's Global Biodiversity Assessment, and she received an honorary doctorate of science from her alma mater, Colorado College. She also was awarded a John D. & Catherine T. MacArthur fellowship, the so-called "genius" grant, in 1993. In 1995, Lubchenco was elected president of the American Association for the Advancement of Science.

In July 1997 Lubchenco published what could be called a manifesto in *USA Today* magazine. In this article, Lubchenco links science, especially ecology, to the everyday world, and challenges her fellow scientists to reprioritize their "social contract." She also sums up the scope of her own work when she writes, "It no longer is sufficient to talk just about sustainable agriculture, sustainable forestry, or sustainable fisheries. It is the sustainability of the biosphere that is the proper concern. This is an entirely new world."

SELECTED WRITINGS BY LUBCHENCO:

Periodicals

(With Bruce A. Menge) "Split Positions can Provide a Sane Career Track–Personal Account." *BioScience* (April 1993).

"Needed: a New Social Contract with Science." *USA Today Magazine* (July 1997).

"The Role of Science in Formulating a Biodiversity Strategy." *BioScience* (June 1995).

FURTHER READING:

Books

Holman, Jill. "Jane Lubchenco." *Notable Women in the Life Sciences: A Biographical Dictionary.* Benjamin F. Shearer and Barbara S. Shearer, eds. Westport, CT: Greenwood Press, 1996, pp. 267-70.

—Sketch by Annette Petrusso

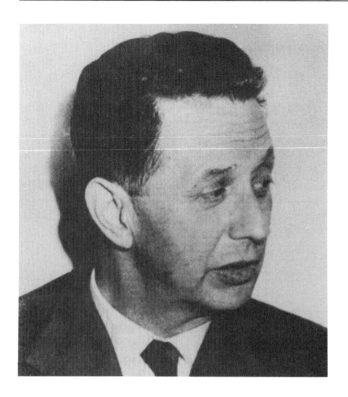

André Lwoff

André Lwoff
1902–1994
French microbiologist

André Lwoff was a French microbiologist whose seminal work in the genetic control of virus synthesis helped guide successive generations of scientists toward a new outlook on cell physiology. Lwoff's primary contributions have come from his study of the biology of viruses, including the genetics of bacteria and the mechanisms of viral infection and replication. An erudite man who painted and was well-versed in philosophy and literature, Lwoff was one of the foremost teachers and mentors to guide a generation of scientists who would move biology to a new frontier. Lwoff, who was Jewish, actively participated in the French Resistance during World War II.

André Michel Lwoff was born in Ainay-le-Château, in central France, on May 8, 1902. His parents were Russian immigrants who had come to France in the late nineteenth century. His father, Solomon Lwoff, was a physician in a psychiatric hospital; his mother, Marie Siminovitch, was a sculptor. Although Lwoff—who early on loved to paint, listen to music, and read—inherited his mother's artistic temperament, his interest in science was cultivated by his father, who often took the boy with him on his daily rounds. Lwoff spent most of his younger years in a rural community near Paris.

On the advice of his father, Lwoff attended the University of Paris (the Sorbonne) to study medicine, a field in which he could earn a comfortable living. But his real interest lay in his other major field of study, biology. Lwoff spent his summers at the Marine Biology Laboratory at Roscoff, in Britanny. He graduated with a bachelor's degree in the natural sciences in 1921 and, at the age of nineteen, became an assistant at the Pasteur Institute in Paris, working under microbiologists Édouard Chatton and Félix Mesnil. While conducting research part-time at the Institute, Lwoff continued to work toward his medical degree, which he received in 1927. He received his doctorate in natural science in 1932.

Lwoff's keen intellect was first applied to morphological studies of protozoa, one-celled animals that often live as parasites on other animals. Lwoff focused specifically on ciliates, which are covered with cilia (hair-like structures), and discovered a new species of ciliated protozoa. These studies eventually culminated in the discovery of the extranuclear inheritance characteristic of these organisms and earned Lwoff recognition as a leader in protozoology. Lwoff next turned his attention to an even simpler form of life, bacteria. The scientific community at that time primarily studied bacteria in terms of their role in putrefaction, fermentation, and the biological factors involved in disease. Lwoff, however, was more interested in the general biological properties of bacteria. Focusing on the ways such simple organisms get nutrition, he discovered how to produce chemically defined media for their growth—a discovery that led him to identify specific growth factors identified as vitamins.

Lwoff's discovery astounded the scientific community because it pointed to the bacterium as an organism much like higher organisms that need nutritional factors to grow and survive. Lwoff continued his research on vitamins, analyzing how vitamin deficiencies cause interruptions at certain points during metabolic processes. In 1936, in collaboration with his wife, Marguerite, whom he had married in 1925 and with whom he worked throughout his life, Lwoff published what was to become an extremely influential paper on how vitamins function as coenzymes, small molecules that help the larger enzyme molecules perform their catalytic functions. These discoveries revealed Lwoff's remarkable intuitive approach to research and demonstrated the unity of biochemical action in all living things. In 1938, the Pasteur Institute made Lwoff the chief of a new program focusing on the emerging field of microbial physiology.

During the 1930s, Lwoff developed a friendship with Eugène Wollman, a pioneer researcher of lysogenic bacteria, which have the hereditary power to produce bacteriophage, or bacterial viruses. In effect, these bacteriophage parasitize other bacteria and can cause bacterial lysis or cell destruction, which releases a host of bacteriophage particles, or phages. Initial interest in bacteriophages stemmed from scientists who thought it might be possible to use bacteriophages to fight specific diseases. Although this approach was, for the most part, ineffective, scientists were intrigued by the phenomenon since the appearance and disappearance of phages was highly unpredictable. Wollman, working with his wife, Elisabeth, had theorized that bacteriophages may be types of "lethal genes" that were reintroduced into the genetic makeup of an organism.

Active in French Resistance

By the early 1940s, however, lysogeny had become an area that was considered of little importance by the young school of American bacterial virologists and many others, who now focused their work on T strains of *Escherichia coli,* in which lysogeny did not occur. The advance of World War II further disrupted the study of lysogeny. The Wollmans, who were Jewish, were captured by the Gestapo in Paris in 1943 and sent to the notorious Auschwitz concentration camp in Poland, never to be heard from again. Lwoff, meanwhile, had joined a resistance group in France that focused primarily on gathering intelligence for the Allies. He managed to escape capture when his underground network was destroyed by the Gestapo, who arrested many of Lwoff's compatriots. But Lwoff was soon involved in another underground network. He also hid American airmen in his apartment as they tried to make their way to unoccupied France after having being shot down over Nazi territory. After the war, Lwoff was awarded the Médaille de la Résistance, and was made Commander of the Légion d'Honneur for his efforts in resisting the Nazi occupation of France.

At war's end, Lwoff chose to continue the work of his friends the Wollmans. At the time, scientists who still worked in the field of bacterial lysogeny maintained that the haphazard release of phages probably occurred because of one of two reasons: the release of phages either resulted from bacteria mutation that spontaneously created phages (virus particles), or that the lysogenic bacteria leaked the phages without bursting. Furthermore, **Félix d'Hérelle** had hypothesized that bacteria are resistant to phages released by other bacteria and only absorb the phage from like bacteria. He also theorized that cells in cultured lysogenic bacteria carry "free" phages on their surface, which further strengthen the phage-host association that render bacteria resistant to later viral destruction. He believed that the increase of phages in a lysogenic bacterial culture was due to a few susceptible, or phage-sensitive, bacteria.

Lwoff began working with a lysogenic strain of soil bacteria called *Bacillus megaterium* and a second

strain of bacteria susceptible to phage infection. Lwoff exhibited remarkable dexterity and skill in the extremely difficult procedure of growing individual bacteria in a microdrop and then fishing out the newly divided bacteria with a capillary pipette—only a few microns in diameter—without contaminating the specimen. He would then transfer the bacteria to a new non-contaminated medium. Although the approach was time-consuming and cumbersome, Lwoff was able to show that, contrary to D'Hérelle's theory, lysogenic bacteria could multiply for nineteen successive generations without the intervention of exogenous, or cell surface, phages. These successive generations were also lysogenic, which proved that lysogeny was a genetic trait. Lwoff's discoveries once again made lysogeny a viable area of study. Lwoff had also dispelled the notion that the host-virus relationship was one that always ended in morbidity, showing that the two could coexist.

Through his experiments, Lwoff also determined that lysogenic bacteria release the phages they produce by lysing, or breaking down, the cell. Still, Lwoff had not explained what actually took place during lysogeny. He did, however, go on to confirm Wollman's earlier finding that when the enzyme lysozyme was used to artificially break open lysogenic bacteria without affecting the phages, no phage particles could be found. He soon discovered what he called "prophages," which, unlike normal bacteriophages, were noninfectious. Furthermore, Lwoff discovered that the prophages acted as "bacterial genes" that integrated themselves into the chromosome of the host, where the genes are located. Reproduction of the phage particle was halted by a regulatory gene in the phage's deoxyribonucleic acid (DNA).

Lwoff next theorized that some external environmental stimulus could interfere with the dormant merger of phage particles and host DNA and thus cause the production of bacteriophage. After months and months of experiments, Lwoff and his colleagues at the Pasteur Institute decided to irradiate the bacteria with ultraviolet light, which normally kills bacteria and bacteriophages. To their surprise, they found that ultraviolet light caused the phage to multiply and eventually destroy the bacterial cell. Lwoff would later note this discovery as one of the most thrilling of his scientific career. Further research showed that other stimuli, including chemicals that were known to cause cancers, could produce the same effect.

Lwoff's studies of lysogeny provided a viable model for a viral theory of cancer; and, in 1953, Lwoff proposed that "inducible lysogenic bacteria" might serve as a way of testing cancerous and noncancerous activity in cells. Although this proved difficult and engendered much debate over the possible viral origins of some cancers, Lwoff was correct in postulating that viruses' protein coats contain carcinogenic properties that can be activated by outside factors such as ultraviolet light. His research on lysogeny also led Lwoff to study poliomyelitis virus. He demonstrated that, unlike vaccine strains of the virus, some strains of the polio virus were not affected by temperature fluctuations.

Wins Nobel Prize for Studies of Lysogeny

Lwoff was awarded the Nobel Prize for physiology or medicine in 1965 for his lysogeny studies. He shared the award with fellow Pasteur Institute scientists **Jacques Lucien Monod** and **François Jacob.** These three were the first French scientists to win the Nobel Prize in thirty years, and Lwoff and his fellow Nobel Prize winners were largely unknown in France until they received the award. But this was not the case in the United States, where Lwoff had traveled and conducted some of his most important scientific dialogues. Soon, many young scientists came from the United States to visit Lwoff and learn as much about his expertise in the field of microbiology as possible. They were also drawn to Lwoff because his line of research was fundamentally similar to that used in studying the genetic manipulation of microorganisms. Lwoff's influence was also enhanced because he spoke fluent English.

Unfortunately for many of his devotees, Lwoff was in no position to take them under his wing. His quarters in the attic of the Pasteur Institute were cramped and crowded with equipment. At the Institute, Lwoff was not obligated to teach and preferred to dedicate his time to his research. Even François Jacob had to plead with Lwoff on several occasions to work with him at the Institute. Despite this obstacle, many students and fellow scientists formed close relationships with Lwoff over the years. Lwoff had also helped Monod early in his career by allowing Monod to work with him in his laboratory at the Institute. In one series of studies, scientist Alice Audureau isolated a genus of bacterium taken from the gut of Lwoff; Monod eventually named the genus *Moraxella lwoffii* in Lwoff's honor.

In the book *Of Microbes and Life,* many of Lwoff's former students and colleagues contributed essays in celebration of the "fiftieth anniversary of [Lwoff's] immersion in biology." In the book, **Salvador Edward Luria** aptly described Lwoff's Renaissance nature, which made him so interesting to so many of his fellow scientists. "André Lwoff—scientist, painter, master of language, leader of one of the great schools of biology—is a prototype scientist-humanist, in whom the 'two cultures,' supposedly divergent and losing touch of each other, remain happily married." Lwoff was also noted for his marvelous sense of humor and enthusiasm, which, to the careful reader, would often shine through in even his most scientific papers. Lwoff retired from the Pasteur Institute in 1968 and became director of the Cancer Research Institute at Villejuif, near Paris, a position he held until 1972. He died in October 1994.

SELECTED WRITINGS BY LWOFF:

Books

L'Evolution physiologique. Herman, 1944.
Problems of Morphogenesis in Ciliates. New York: Wiley, 1950.
The Kinetosomes in Development, Reproduction, and Evolution. New York: Wiley, 1950.
Biological Order. Cambridge: Massachusetts Institute of Technology Press, 1962.

Periodicals

"Lysogeny." *Bacteriological Reviews* 17 (1953): 269-337.

FURTHER READING:

Books

Monod, Jacques, and Ernest Borek. *Of Microbes and Life.* Columbia University Press, 1971.

Periodicals

"André Lwoff, Nobel Prize Winner, Dies." *Washington Post* (4 October 1994): B7.
"André Lwoff, 92, Biologist, Dies; Shared Nobel for Study of Cells." *New York Times* (4 October 1994).
Stent, Gunther S. "1965 Nobel Laureates in Medicine or Physiology." *Science* 150 (1965): 462-64.

—Sketch by David Petechuk

Sheila Scott Macintyre
1910–1960
Scottish mathematician

Although Sheila Scott Macintyre's career ended prematurely by cancer, she successfully juggled professional and family responsibilities while continuing to publish in her field. Her success in academics reflected the growing tolerance in Western society towards women entering higher education and specializing in previously male–dominated subjects. Macintyre's relationship with her husband, Archibald James Macintyre, was professional as well as personal, a successful role model for working couples of today. They worked on joint papers, served the British war effort together, and taught at the same universities, moving as a family from one post to the next. Macintyre helped produce a bilingual mathematics dictionary that went through two editions.

An Only Child

Helen Myers Meldrum and James Alexander Scott, both natives of Scotland, had their only child on April 23, 1910. Macintyre was first sent to school at Trinity Academy in Edinburgh, where her father would serve as rector from 1925 to 1942. In 1926, she entered what was then known as Edinburgh Ladies' College, and in two years she became a "dux," or valedictorian, in mathematics and in her studies overall. This attracted the attention of the faculty of the University of Edinburgh, who granted Macintyre two bursaries. She was also awarded the Bruce of Grangehill Mathematical Scholarship.

Macintyre's M.A. was granted in 1932 with first class honors in mathematics and natural philosophy, and Edinburgh's faculty encouraged her to enter Cambridge University to pursue another B.A. of higher esteem. By the early 1930s women were allowed to be "wranglers," or top–rung math students, at Girton, the women's college of Cambridge. In two years Macintyre placed as a wrangler. This qualified her for a year–long research project, supervised by **Mary Lucy Cartwright**, who specialized in integral functions. The year bore fruit with Scott's first publication at the age of 25.

Another year of research followed, which was not equally satisfying. The next five years Scott spent teaching at girl's schools in Scotland, among them St.

Leonard's, in the town of St. Andrews, and James Allen's School for Girls.

New and Original Problems

Archibald James Macintyre had earned a Ph.D. at Cambridge, but he did not meet his future wife until 1933, when they were introduced by a fellow academic in Scotland. After a lengthy courtship, they married on December 27, 1940. By this time, World War II took precedence for all citizens of Great Britain. The Macintyres worked in the same department at Aberdeen and taught courses sanctioned by the War Office and the Air Ministry. Macintyre took a year off between 1943 and 1944 for the birth of her first child, Alister William, before resuming her duties. She was retained for a permanent post as assistant lecturer at that time and simultaneously launched a thesis project. Her second son, Douglas Scott, was delivered almost the same day as her doctorate on the Whittaker constant. Unfortunately, this child succumbed to enteritis just before his third birthday.

A year later the Macintyres' daughter, Susan Elizabeth, was born. Over the next five years Macintyre raised their two children, continued to teach, and published a handful of papers on various problems related to the theory of functions of a complex variable. At least one commentator noted her ability to find "new and original problems" as well as her knack for refining older techniques and existing proofs. Macintyre also joined up with a member of the German department to produce a bilingual dictionary of mathematical terms, published in 1955.

The year 1958 seemed to mark a new phase of the Macintyres' careers. Long active in the Edinburgh Mathematical Society, Macintyre was elected a full Fellow of the Royal Society of Edinburgh. She published her last paper, on Abel's series. Macintyre and her family, with her father, joined Archibald at the University of Cincinnati. The couple served as visiting research professors there for a few years, where she was particularly successful and popular with her students. Macintyre died at age 50 on March 21, 1960.

SELECTED WRITINGS BY MACINTYRE:

Books

(With Edith Witte) *Mathematical Vocabulary (German–English).* Second Edition, 1966.

Periodicals

"On the Asymptotic Periods of Integral Functions." *Proceedings of the Cambridge Philosophical Society* 31 (1935): pp. 543–554.

"A Functional Inequality." *Journal of the London Mathematical Society* 23 (1948): pp. 202–209.

(With A.J. Macintyre) "Theorems on the Convergence and Asymptotic Validity of Abel's Series." *Proceedings of the Royal Society of Edinburgh* A63 (1952): pp. 222–231.

FURTHER READING:

Books

Fasanelli, Florence D. "Sheila Scott Macintyre," in *Women of Mathematics*. Edited by Louise S. Grinstein and Paul J. Campbell. Westport, CT: Greenwood Press, 1987, pp. 140–143.

National Cyclopaedia of American Biography. Volume 48. New York: James T. White & Co., 1965.

Periodicals

Cartwright, Mary L. "Sheila Scott Macintyre." *Journal of the London Mathematical Society* 36 (1961): pp. 254–256.

Cossar, J. "Sheila Scott Macintyre." *Edinburgh Mathematical Notes* 43 (1960): p. 19.

Wright, E.M. "Sheila Scott Macintyre." *Year Book of the Royal Society of Edinburgh* (1961): pp. 21–23.

Other

"Sheila Scott Macintyre." *MacTutor History of Mathematics Archive*. http://www–groups.dcs.st–and.ac.uk/~history/Mathematicians/ Macintyre.html (July 1997).

"Shelia Scott Macintyre." *Biographies of Women Mathematicians*. June 1997. http://www.scottlan.edu/lriddle/women/chronol.htm (July 20, 1997).

—*Sketch by Jennifer Kramer*

Madge Thurlow Macklin
1893–1962
American geneticist

Madge Thurlow Macklin pioneered the field of genetics. Based on her thorough data, Macklin emphasized how important family history of disease—especially for several cancers—was in the diagnosis of patients, and she crusaded to have genetics added to the curriculum of all North American medical schools. Despite these important contributions and perhaps because of her support of eugenics (a medical movement advocating improvement of the species through controlled breeding practices), Macklin was largely unrecognized for her work.

Madge Macklin was born in Philadelphia, Pennsylvania, on February 6, 1893, to William Harrison Thurlow, an engineer, and his wife Margaret De Grofft Thurlow. She had three sisters and one brother. While still young, the family moved to Baltimore, Maryland, where she also received her undergraduate education at Goucher College. She graduated in 1914 with an A.B. Macklin won a fellowship to attend Johns Hopkins medical school. She studied physiology and then went on to the medical school proper at the same institution. While in medical school, she married Charles Macklin in 1918. She was awarded her M.D., with honors, in 1919. She and her husband had three daughters, Carol (born 1919), Sylva (born 1921), and Margaret (born 1927).

After graduation, she and her husband moved to London, Ontario, Canada, where he had an appointment in histology and embryology at Western Ontario University. While her husband was a full professor, she received only part-time, one-year appointments at Western Ontario beginning in 1921, to teach embryology. She also helped teach his histology classes. Though her controversial support of eugenics may have been a factor in her lack of support by the University, it was also nearly unheard of for husband-wife teams to hold academic appointments together.

At Western Ontario, Macklin began her quest to have genetics added to medical school curricula. She supported her point with her carefully conducted research. As a scientist, she valued experiments that were controlled and used sound statistical techniques. Because of her disciplined approach to scientific research, Macklin laid important early groundwork in human genetics and related statistical methodology.

As a genetics researcher, Macklin's most significant studies showed that some cancers—stomach and breast, for example—are affected by both heredity and the environment. This knowledge was an important consideration in cancer prevention. Though her undergraduate alma mater bestowed an honorary degree on her in 1938 for her work, she never taught genetics while at Western.

During her time at Western Ontario, Macklin also was an outspoken supporter of eugenics. She believed eugenics to be another method of preventive medicine. Though debunked by the 1930s, Macklin supported eugenics for many years. In 1930, she helped found the Canadian Eugenics Society.

After years of short appointments, Macklin's appointment was not renewed at Western Ontario in 1945. She was immediately hired as a National Research Council Associate at Ohio State University. While her husband continued his work at Western Ontario, Macklin moved to Columbus where she worked as a research associate and lectured on medical genetics. She returned for holidays and vacations to their London home during her appointment. In 1957, she was awarded the American Medical Women's Association's Elizabeth Blackwell Medal.

Macklin retired in 1959, and returned to London to care for her ailing husband, who died shortly thereafter. During that same year, she was elected president of the American Society for Human Genetics. She held this post until her death, caused by a heart attack, on March 17, 1962.

SELECTED WRITINGS BY MACKLIN:

Books

The Role of Inheritance in Disease. Baltimore: Williams & Wilkins, Co., 1935.

Periodicals

"The Value of Accurate Statistics in the Study of Cancer." *Canadian Public Health Journal* (1934): 369-73.

FURTHER READING:

Books

Bailey, Martha J. "Macklin, Madge Thurlow." *American Women in Science: A Biographical Dictionary.* Denver, Colorado: ABC-CLIO, 1994, p. 228.
Mehler, Barry. "Macklin, Madge Thurlow." *Notable American Women: The Modern Period, A Biographical Dictionary.* Barbara Sicherman & Carol Hurd Green, eds. Cambridge, Massachusetts: The Belknap Press of Harvard University Press, 1980, pp. 451-52.
Siegel, Patricia Joan, and Kay Thomas Finley. "Madge Thurlow Macklin." *Women in the Scientific Search: An American Bio-bibliography, 1724-1979.* Metuchen, New Jersey: The Scarecrow Press, Inc., pp. 242-44.

Periodicals

Soltan, Hubert C. "Madge Macklin–Pioneer in Medical Genetics." *The University of Western Ontario Medical Journal* (October 1962): 6-11.

—*Sketch by Annette Petrusso*

Robert MacPherson
1944–
American mathematician

MacPherson's mathematical writings cover a number of topics related to the relatively new field of topology, including combinatorics and group theory. His areas of interest also include catastrophe theory and random numbers. MacPherson has received numerous grants from the National Science Foundation, as well as honorary doctorates from the Universite de Lille and Brown University. In 1992, he was honored with the National Academy of Sciences award in mathematics.

Robert MacPherson is dedicated to teaching, but his highest profile in the mathematics community comes through his international outreach activities, especially within Russia and the former Soviet satellite nations. He has served on a number of committees devoted to aiding mathematicians caught in the collapse of the U.S.S.R., even raising and distributing much needed cash personally. MacPherson's most successful book, *Stratified Morse Theory*, has been translated into Russian for publication by Mir Press of Moscow.

Robert Duncan MacPherson was born in Lakewood, Ohio, to Herbert G. and Jeanette (née Wolfenden) MacPherson on May 25, 1944. He graduated from Swarthmore College in 1966, and his B.A. was conferred with highest honors. Upon being granted a Ph.D. from Harvard University in 1970, MacPherson joined the faculty of Brown University. He remained at Brown for 17 years, holding a number of positions including Florence Pirce Grant University Professorship (1985–1987). From 1987 to 1994, MacPherson was a full–professor at MIT, and in 1994 he joined the staff of the Institute for Advanced Study (IAS) in Princeton, New Jersey.

Because the IAS is not a teaching facility, MacPherson accepted a concurrent, non–paying post at nearby Princeton University in order to maintain interaction with students. Research activities with the more than 20 Ph.D. candidates he has advised have often informed his presentations, if a recent talk on oriented matroids and topology is any indication. In the abstract, MacPherson notes that the talk is "mainly a report on work of Laura Anderson, Eric Babson, and Jim Davis," two of whom were his graduate students.

Foreign Aid

During the spring of 1980, MacPherson worked at the Steklov Institute of Mathematics in Moscow as part of a National Academy of Sciences exchange program. Since then he has become involved with a number of joint international planning and advisory committees devoted to helping mathematicians weather the political and financial upheavals of post–Communism. MacPherson currently serves on the governing board of the Moscow Mathematical Institute and chairs the American Mathematics Society's Former Soviet Union Aid Fund Advisory Committee.

As noted in a 1995 issue of the *Notices of the AMS*, MacPherson was largely responsible for bringing attention to the financial plight of mathematicians in the former Soviet Union. In response, AMS established an aid program, to which members contributed. George Soros arranged for matching grants from the International Science Foundation and the Sloan Foundation, resulting in aid for 400 students and working mathematicians ranging from $50 to $80 per month.

As MacPherson remembers it, this activity sometimes involved a bit of skulduggery. When no quick, inexpensive way could be found to transfer the money they had raised to the intended recipients, MacPherson and Tim Goggins of the AMS carried $25,000 into Russia secretly. After smuggling the money past the border guards, the two men distributed it at meetings in Russia's major cities, an almost unheard of example of direct financial aid.

In 1997, MacPherson was elected to the chair of the mathematics committee of the National Research Council, a group that advises the United States government on scientific matters. He serves on the editorial boards of *Compositio Mathematica* and *Advances in Mathematics*, is an editor of the *Annals of Mathematics* and associate editor of *Selecta Mathematica*. MacPherson is also active in GLBMATH, an organization for gay and lesbian mathematicians. As he recently pointed out, "There are very few openly gay scientists, and young gays have no role models." In part through his GLBMATH activities, MacPherson hopes to change this situation.

SELECTED WRITINGS BY MACPHERSON:

Books

(With W. Borho and J.L. Brylinski) "Primitive Ideals and Cone Bundles," in *Progress in Mathematics 78*, 1989.

(With M. Goresky) *Stratified Morse Theory*, 1988.

(With M. McConnell) "Projective Geometry and Modular Varieties," in *Algebraic Analysis, Geometry, and Number Theory*, 1989.

Periodicals

(With W. Fulton) "A Compactification of Configuration Space." *Annals of Mathematics* 139 (1994): 183–225.

(With W. Fulton) "Intersection Theory on Spherical Varieties." *Jouranl of Algebraic Geometry* 4 (1995): 181–93.

(With S. Gelfand and K. Vilonen) "Perverse Sheaves and Quivers." *Duke Math. Journal* 83 (1996): 621–643.

FURTHER READING:

Books

Who's Who in Science and Engineering. New Providence, NJ: Reed Publishing, 1994, p. 549.

Other

MacPherson, Robert, in an electronic mail interview with Jennifer Kramer, conducted July 14, 1997.

—Sketch by Jennifer Kramer

Ada Isabel Maddison
1869–1950
English algebraist

In spite of her accomplishments and education, Ada Isabel Maddison remained a shy woman throughout her life. In fact, while serving as an assistant at Bryn Mawr to President M. Carey Thomas in 1913, she received a note from Thomas invoking her to "[Speak] distinctly. When you get embarrassed, your voice gets lower and lower. I am sure the Faculty thinks it is shyness, as it is. You must conquer it."

Maddison was born on April 13, 1869, in Cumberland, England. Her parents were John and Mary Maddison. She took college preparatory courses at Miss Tallies School in Cardiff, South Wales, then entered the University of South Wales where she studied from 1885 to 1889. After leaving the University of South Wales she attended Girton College, Cambridge, for another three years. While at Girton she met and befriended **Grace Chisholm Young**, the first woman to receive a doctorate in Germany.

During their first year at Girton, both women attended a lecture given by Arthur Cayley, a mathematician who played a central role in founding the modern British school of pure mathematics and author of more than 900 published articles addressing almost every aspect of modern mathematics. Later, while at Bryn Mawr attending graduate lectures, Maddison studied Cayley's papers on modern algebra.

Maddison succeeded at passing the examinations of the Honour School at Oxford in 1892, and in the same year passed the Cambridge Mathematical Tripos Examination, first class. The examination was equivalent to the highest class of honors at Cambridge, 27th Wrangler, but the accomplishment did little to secure a degree since Maddison was not allowed to receive one.

Between 1892 and 1893 Maddison attended lectures given by Dr. **Charlotte Angas Scott** at Bryn Mawr. During the same time, she began her investigation into the singular solutions of differential equations, which was later published in 1896 in the *Quarterly Journal of Pure and Applied Mathematics* in 1896. Scott was sufficiently impressed by Maddison to write: "[She] has a powerful mind and excellent training." In acknowledgment of Scott's teaching skill, Maddison wrote an article on her for the *Bryn Mawr Alumnae Bulletin* in January 1932 entitled "Charlotte Angas Scott: An Appreciation."

In 1893, Maddison received her Bachelor of Science degree with Honours from the University of London. She was also given a resident mathematics fellowship at Bryn Mawr for the 1893–1894 school year. In 1895, she became the first person awarded the Mary E. Garrett Fellowship by Bryn Mawr to be used for study abroad. Maddison chose to attend the University of Göttingen, where she renewed her acquaintance with Grace Chisholm Young and met Annie Louis MacKinnon, who in 1894 had received her Ph.D. in mathematics from Cornell University. Both Maddison and MacKinnon were elected to the American Mathematical Society in 1897. Maddison concentrated on the lectures of **Felix Klein**, author of the *Erlanger Programm*, and **David Hilbert**, considered the greatest influence on geometry since Euclid. These lectures must have had an impact on Maddison because her field of specialization became algebraic geometry. In 1896, she published a translation of Felix Klein's work, "The Arithemitizing of Mathematics," in the *Bulletin of the American Mathematical Society*.

Mathematician Turned Administrator

Maddison completed the work for her Ph.D. at Bryn Mawr and received the degree in 1896. Her dissertation was entitled "On Singular Solutions of Differential Equations of the First Order in Two Variables, and the Geometric Properties of Certain Invariants and Covariants of Their Complete Primitives." Concurrent with her studies, Maddison acted as assistant secretary to the president of Bryn Mawr. She then stepped into the dual role of reader in mathematics and secretary to the president, serving both positions for more than seven years. In 1904, she again accepted the tasks associated with two positions, becoming an associate professor and assistant to the president.

Although Maddison had never studied in Dublin, she was awarded a B.A. degree by the University of Dublin in 1905. That university was the first to award degrees to women in the British Isles. The degree was conferred on Maddison based on her work at Girton College.

Between 1910 and 1926, when she retired from teaching, Maddison remained the assistant to the president and jointly held the administrative position of Recording Dean. These duties left her little time for mathematics or research, which must have given her some cause for regret because in 1937 she wrote, "I confess to feeling ashamed of having deserted mathematics for a less rarified atmosphere of work among people and things." She always considered mathematics "the most perfect of the sciences" and felt that her loyalty remained steadfast with the discipline.

In 1897 Maddison became a member of the Daughters of the British Empire and in the same year she was elected to the American Mathematical Association. Maddison also joined the London Mathematical Society and remained a member throughout her lifetime. In spite of her considerable responsibilities as an administrator, Maddison found time to aid in the compilation of a study on women who had graduated from college. The study dealt with such issues as marriage, children, and occupations.

After her retirement from Bryn Mawr, Maddison returned to England. After a time she came back to Pennsylvania, and it was there that she died in 1950. Upon her death, Bryn Mawr was bequeathed ten thousand dollars, with instructions that the gift is used for nonfaculty members as a pension fund in honor of the woman with whom she had such a long working relationship, President M. Carey Thomas.

SELECTED WRITINGS BY MADDISON:

"On Certain Factors of C– and P–Discriminants and Their Relation to Fixed Points on the Family of Curves," in *Quarterly Journal of Pure and Applied Mathematics* 26 (1893): 307–21.

"Note on the History of the Map Coloring Problem," in *Bulletin of the American Mathematical Society* 3 (1897): 257.

Handbook of Courses Open to Women in British, Continental, and Canadian Universities 1896; supplement 1897; Second edition 1899; supplement 1901.

FURTHER READING:

Books

Whitman, Betsy S. "Ada Isabel Maddison," in *Women of Mathematics*. Edited by Louise S. Grinstein and Paul J. Campbell. Westport, CT: Greenwood Press, 1987, pp. 144–46.

Periodicals

Whitman, Betsy S. "Women in the American Mathematical Society before 1900." *Association for Women in Mathematics Newsletter* 13, no. 5 (September–October 1893): 7–9.

Williams, Mary. "Ada Isabel Maddison." (Handwritten manuscript, 5 pp. n.d.) The Mary Williams Collection, Schlesinger Library, Radcliffe College, Cambridge, Massachusetts.

Other

"Ada Isabel Maddison." *Biographies of Women Mathematicians*. http://www.scottlan.edu/lriddle/women/chronol.htm (August 1997).

—*Sketch by Kelley Reynolds Jacquez*

Vivienne Malone–Mayes
1932–1995
American mathematics educator

Vivienne Lucille Malone–Mayes was a prominent mathematics educator who taught at Baylor University in Waco, Texas, for nearly three decades. As a black woman who grew up in a segregated society, she was a pioneer in her field and an inspiration for younger students. Malone–Mayes was the fifth African American woman to receive a doctorate in pure mathematics in the United States, and she was the first black full-time professor at Baylor.

Malone–Mayes was born on February 10, 1932, in Waco, Texas. Her father, Pizarro Ray Malone, was a visiting teacher in the Waco public schools for many years and also worked for the Urban Renewal Agency. Her mother, Vera Estelle Allen Malone, was a junior high school teacher. It is little wonder, then, that education was stressed in their home. Malone–Mayes later recalled that the only lie her parents ever encouraged her to tell was about her age when she started school. She was only five years old, but her parents told her to say she was six so that she would be admitted. Always an excellent student, Ma-

lone–Mayes graduated from her racially segregated high school in 1948 at age 16.

Leaving her home in Waco, Malone–Mayes traveled to Nashville, Tennessee, where she became a student at Fisk University. Her first ambition was to be a physician. However, she changed that goal after meeting her future husband, James Jeffries Mayes, a dental student. He convinced her that two doctors in the same family would never see each other, so Malone–Mayes switched her major from pre-med to mathematics. She received a B.A. degree in 1952. On September 1 of that year, she and Mayes were married.

Two years later, Malone–Mayes received an M.A. degree in mathematics, also from Fisk University. She promptly moved back to Waco, where she became chairperson of the math department at Paul Quinn College and her husband opened a dental practice. Malone–Mayes eventually spent seven years at Paul Quinn. She later chaired the math department at Bishop College in Dallas for a year. She and her husband had one daughter, Patsyanne. The couple divorced in 1985.

A Career Filled with Firsts

By 1961, Malone–Mayes was eager to refresh her education and she applied to Baylor University. Her application was rejected on grounds of race. She turned instead to the University of Texas at Austin, which had already been required by federal law to desegregate. Malone–Mayes endured much emotional stress and social ostracism as a black female graduate student. She later recalled that many classmates liked to gather at a cafe that would not serve blacks; the closest she came to joining them was marching in picket lines protesting the cafe's policy. For her thesis topic, Malone–Mayes chose "A Structure Problem in Asymptotic Analysis." In 1966, she received a Ph.D. from the University of Texas, making her the second black, and the first black woman, to earn a doctorate in math from that institution.

Malone–Mayes was immediately hired as a professor by Baylor, the same university that had rejected her as a student just five years before. She remained in that position until 1994, when she was forced to retire due to ill health. During her years as a professor, Malone–Mayes continued to break racial barriers, becoming the first African American elected to the executive committee of the Association for Women in Mathematics. She also served on the board of directors of the National Association of Mathematicians, a group oriented toward the black community. In 1988, she participated in a panel featuring prominent female mathematicians that was part of the American Mathematics Society's Centennial Celebration in Providence, Rhode Island.

Malone–Mayes had an active life outside of academia. For many years she served as youth choir director and organist at her local Baptist church. She also volunteered for a number of charitable organizations, and she served as advisor for a traditionally black sorority at Baylor. Her last years were marred by health problems, however. She was plagued by lupus, a chronic inflammatory disease that can damage multiple systems of the body. On June 9, 1995, Malone–Mayes died of a heart attack in Temple, Texas. In an obituary in the *Association for Women in Mathematics Newsletter*, **Etta Falconer** and Lee Lorch wrote of their friend and colleague: "With skill, integrity, steadfastness and love she fought racism and sexism her entire life, never yielding to the pressures or problems which beset her path. She leaves a lasting influence."

SELECTED WRITINGS BY MALONE–MAYES:

Books

(With Howard Rolf) *Pre-calculus,* 1977.

FURTHER READING:

Periodicals

Falconer, Etta and Lee Lorch. "Vivienne Malone–Mayes: In Memoriam." *Association for Women in Mathematics Newsletter* (November–December 1995).

Simpson, Elizabeth. "'You Had to Make It All Alone': Black Baylor Teacher Recalls Road to Success." *Waco Tribune–Herald* (August 22, 1988): 1A, 3A.

Other

Falconer, Etta, Dr., and Dr. Lee Lorch. "Vivienne Malone–Mayes: In Memoriam." *Biographies of Women Mathematicians.* June 1997. http://www.scottlan.edu/lriddle/women/chronol.htm (July 22, 1997).

Miscellaneous newspaper clippings and press releases. The Texas Collection, Baylor University Library, Waco, TX.

—*Sketch by Linda Wasmer Smith*

Walter S. McAfee
1914–1995

American astrophysicist

Walter S. McAfee was best known as the mathematician for the U.S. Army's Project Diana. As

Walter S. McAfee

mathematician for the project, he was responsible for making the essential calculations that led to the first human contact with the moon, a radar signal sent in January 1946.

Walter Samuel McAfee was born in Ore City, Texas, on September 2, 1914. He was the second of nine children born to Luther F. McAfee, a carpenter, and Susie A. Johnson McAfee. He received a bachelor's degree from Wiley College in 1934 and earned an M.S. from Ohio State in 1937. Unable to afford further graduate work, McAfee turned to teaching, and from 1939 to 1942 he taught physics at Champion Junior High School in Columbus, Ohio. There, he met Viola Winston, a French teacher, whom he married in 1941; they had two daughters. In 1946, McAfee was awarded a Rosenwald fellowship and enrolled in the doctoral program at Cornell University. There, he studied with theoretical physicist **Hans Bethe**, receiving a doctorate in physics from Cornell in 1949.

In May 1942, McAfee joined the theoretical studies unit of the Electronics Research Command, part of the U.S. Army's Signal Corps at Fort Monmouth, New Jersey. A civilian physicist, he remained with the group in various capacities for more than forty years, studying and experimenting in theoretical nuclear physics and electromagnetic theory, quantum optics, and laser holography. From 1958 to 1975 he also taught graduate and undergraduate courses at nearby Monmouth College as a lecturer in nuclear physics and electronics. He retired in 1985.

Project Diana Pioneers Space Communications

Project Diana was an effort to bounce a radar signal off the moon's surface. It was not known at the time if a high-frequency radio signal could penetrate the Earth's ionosphere or stratosphere. Early experiments with low- and medium-frequency radio waves had failed. In sending a signal, Project Diana scientists needed to account accurately for the moon's speed, which varies from 750 miles (1,200 km) per hour slower than the earth's rotation to 750 miles (1,200 km) per hour faster. As mathematician for the project, McAfee made the necessary calculations. On January 10, 1946, a radar pulse was sent through a special forty-foot square antenna toward the moon. Two and a half seconds later, a faint radar echo was heard, and Project Diana was recorded a success. Made public two weeks later by the Signal Corps, the experiment provided an important breakthrough in space exploration, establishing that communication was possible across the enormous distances of outer space.

The official news report of the accomplishment did not include McAfee's name, nor give any hint of the role he had played. Public recognition did not come until twenty-five years later, at the anniversary of Project Diana in 1971. Subsequently, however, he was honored by the Stevens Institute of Technology and by Wiley College, which in 1982 inducted McAfee into its Science Hall of Fame, founded to inspire students to excel in the sciences. In an interview at the time, quoted in *ERADCOM Currents,* he said, "If the [Hall of Fame] program bears fruit, and if my presence helped in some small way, then that shall have been reward enough." McAfee subsequently established a math and physical science fellowship at Wiley College to encourage minority students in math and science. He was member of the American Association for the Advancement of Science, the American Astronomy Society, the American Physical Society, the American Association of Physics Teachers, and was a senior member of the Institute of Electrical and Electronics Engineers. McAfee died on February 18, 1995, at his home in South Belmar, New Jersey.

SELECTED WRITINGS BY MCAFEE:

Periodicals

"Determination of Energy Spectra of Backscattered Electrons by Use of Everhart's Theory." *Journal of Applied Physics* 47, no. 3 (1976): 1179-84.

"Electron Backscattering from Solids and Double Layers." *Journal of Vacuum Science Technology* 13, no 4 (1976): 843-47.

FURTHER READING:

Periodicals

Accardo, Carl A. "Walter S. McAfee" (obituary). *Physics Today* (June 1995): 72; 74.

Gould, Jack. "Contact with Moon Achieved by Radar in Test by the Army." *New York Times* (25 January 1946): 1; 19.

————. "McAfee Named to Wiley's Science Hall of Fame." *ERADCOM Currents* (May 1982).

————. "Original Participants Mark Diana's 25th Anniversary." *Army Research and Development Newsmagazine* (January-February 1971).

Other

McAfee, Walter S. Interview by F. C. Nicholson. 9 February 1994.

—Sketch by F. C. Nicholson

Margaret Dusa McDuff
1945–
English mathematician

State University of New York at Stony Brook professor and Royal Society fellow Dusa McDuff won the first Ruth Lyttle Satter Prize in Mathematics in 1991. This prize recognizes outstanding contribution to mathematics research by a woman in the previous five years. Even as a graduate student McDuff was particularly creative. Her Ph.D. thesis used operator theory to solve a well–known problem about the factors of Von Neumann algebras. As interpreted by Pam Davis in her poster "Squeezing the Phase Space," McDuff's current work in geometry applies to the classical physics of orbiting bodies in space. Which properties are intrinsic to geometric shape, and which to the descriptive coordinates used for the entire system, are still being determined.

McDuff was born Margaret Dusa Waddington on October 18, 1945, and her earliest aspiration was to be a farmer's wife. Although she was born in London, she grew up in Scotland, where both her parents worked. Her father was a professor of genetics and an author, and her mother, who came from a long line of intelligent, productive women, was an architect who worked for the civil service. Dusa bears the name of her maternal grandmother, a writer and political activist. McDuff's sister became an anthropologist at King's College, Cambridge. Despite the fact that so

Margaret Dusa McDuff

many women in her family were successful in their chosen occupations, McDuff herself felt isolated. At the girl's school she attended she discovered mathematics, a field that did not at the time seem to offer her any role models.

McDuff's earliest years of formal study in mathematics were marked by some passivity. Instead of accepting a scholarship to Cambridge, she took a bachelor of science degree at the University of Edinburgh in order to stay with her boyfriend, whom she later married and whose surname she adopted. However, he returned the favor when she became a graduate student, and followed her to Cambridge. McDuff's Ph.D. under G. A. Reid in functional analysis was published, and stood as her best work for many years.

While her husband was in Moscow for a time conducting archival research in Russian poetry, McDuff was able to study with the group theorist Israel M. Gel'fand. She was inspired to write two mathematical papers in Russian that were published in Soviet journals during 1970.

Expanding Professional Horizons

Upon returning to Cambridge to formally receive her doctorate, McDuff found it difficult to channel her energies. The still predominantly male institution did not seem welcoming to a young, married, and soon-pregnant woman. To escape from this situation, McDuff accepted a job at York University. While running the household and caring for her infant, McDuff found the time to collaborate with Graeme Segal to produce what she considered tantamount to a "second Ph.D." on homology fibrations and the group–completion theorem. This paper was published in 1976, the year McDuff moved to Warwick University for another lectureship.

Meanwhile McDuff's professional horizons were expanding. In 1974 she was invited to visit MIT to fill a position reserved for a female. There she found the company of other women mathematicians invigorating. She was encouraged to apply to the Institute for Advanced Study and also won a spot there for a year. McDuff soon trusted her instincts enough to give up her tenure–track job at Warwick for an untenured position at SUNY–Stony Brook. During this period the McDuffs had divorced.

McDuff's "Autobiographical Notes" specifically mention that "there are only a few people who are interested in what I did," indicating that even today some of her work is obscure to many mathematicians. She had to struggle alone to solidify her early work into a foundation for her subspeciality in foliations. After some years of dealing with a commuter relationship, McDuff married mathematician **John Milnor** and gave birth to another child. Around this time she became involved in the field of symplectic topology. She gained a full professorship in 1984, and took a sabbatical in Paris the next year to investigate her newest speciality. In 1991 McDuff began a two–year stint as head of the mathematics department at SUNY–Stony Brook.

The forums at which McDuff presents her findings are socially as well as scientifically noteworthy. In 1994, she took part in "A Celebration of Women in Mathematics," a two–day conference at MIT featuring all female speakers. A lecture McDuff gave at Oregon State University in 1996 was sent out over the Internet in between rounds of The First Micro–Robot World Cup Soccer Tournament. Her talk was accompanied by interactive notes later posted on the World Wide Web. Another online project is part of a series funded by the National Science Foundation, called "Visualizing Women in Mathematics, the Physical Sciences and Technology." For it McDuff, artist Pam Davis, and fellow SUNY faculty member Tony Phillips collaborated on a Web installation. McDuff's set of activities are coordinated around the construction of a hypercube from plastic straws. These studies in projective geometry and trigonometry are not only physically accessible to anyone with Internet access. Their levels of difficulty range from elementary school to college–level topics.

McDuff is also active in the offline world. She helps oversee publication of the *Journal of the American Mathematical Society* as an associate editor. In

1994 she was inducted into the Royal Society of London, one of two female mathematicians in its ranks. She was elected a foreign honorary member of the American Academy of Arts and Sciences in 1995, one of only eight mathematicians chosen that year. Most recently, she was given an honorary doctorate by the University of Edinburgh. McDuff is a proponent of calculus reform and is an active mentor in the WISE (Women in Science and Engineering) program at SUNY–Stony Brook. WISE offers support to female undergraduates who plan careers in mathematics, science, or engineering.

SELECTED WRITINGS BY MCDUFF:

Books

(With D. Salamon) *J–Holomorphic Curves and Quantum Cohomology*, 1994.
(With D. Salamon) *Introduction to Symplectic Topology*, 1995.

Periodicals

"A Countable Infinity of II_1 Factors." *Annals of Mathematics* 90 (1969): 362–71.

Other

"An Introduction to the Vocabulary of Dimension." *Squeeze the Phase Space*. Online Introductory Activities to Accompany the Posters of Dusa McDuff. http://math.math.sunysb.edu/~tony/visualization/dusa/activities.html
"Some Autobiographical Notes." http://math.math.sunysb.edu/~tony/visualization/dusa/dusabio.html
"Symplectomorphisms and the Flux Homomorphism." *Pacific Northwest Geometry Seminar*. Online Lecture Notes for the 1996 Fall Meeting. http://www.math.washington.edu/~lee/PNGS/96-fall/

FURTHER READING:

Books

American Men & Women of Science. Nineteenth edition. New Providence, NJ: Bowker, 1994.

Other

Love, Lauren. "Dusa McDuff." *Biographies of Women Mathematicians*. June 1997. http://www.agnesscott.edu/lriddle/women/chronol.htm (July 1997).

Phillips, Tony. "Dusa McDuff: Biographical Sketch." http://math.math.sunysb.edu/~tony/visualization/dusa/bio.html

—Sketch by Jennifer Kramer

Hugues Charles Robert Méray
1835–1911
French number theorist

Hugues Charles Robert Méray was not considered a leading mathematician by his contemporaries, but is renowned for one significant contribution to his field. In 1869 Méray was the first to publish a theory of irrational numbers that correctly anticipated the later, more popular theory developed by **Georg Cantor**, whose theory is one of the main steps in the arithmetization of analysis. In developing his theory of irrational numbers, Méray consciously built upon the earlier work of Joseph–Louis LaGrange, believing he could firmly establish what LaGrange had merely proposed.

Méray was born on November 12, 1835 in Chalon–sur–Saône, France, and received his formal mathematical training at the École Normale Supérieure there, commencing studies in 1854. From 1857 until 1859 he taught at the lycée of St. Quentin and then retired for seven years to a small village near his birthplace. In 1866 he came out of retirement to accept a position as a lecturer at the University of Lyons and, the following year, accepted a position as professor at the University of Dijon, where he remained for the rest of his teaching career.

Méray first presented his theory of irrational numbers in an article entitled "Remarques sur la nature des quantités définies par la condition de servir de limites à des variable données," published in *Revue des sociétés savantes des départements* in 1869. The article captured little attention, however, partially because the journal was relatively obscure. Today, although credit for the theory is commonly given to Cantor, Méray's work is considered of great historical significance. While Karl Weierstrass had introduced the theory in his lectures, Méray's article marked the first time the theory had been published. Méray's theory was again published in 1873 in his *Nouveau précis d'analyse infinitésimale*, but again his theory was largely ignored. The focus of the *Nouveau précis* was the presentation of a theory of functions of complex variables. The theory was based on the notion of a power series, another concept developed earlier by Weierstrass, although it is not believed that

Méray was aware of Weierstrass's work either in this area or, specifically, with regard to the theory of irrational numbers. The *Nouveau précis* is also noted for its rigorous structure, an approach not yet common in Méray's time.

Méray died in Dijon in 1911.

SELECTED WRITINGS BY MÉRAY:

"Remarques sur la nature des quantités définies par la condition de servir de limites à des variable donnéss," 1869.
Nourveau précis d'analyse infinitésimale, 1873.

FURTHER READING:

Books

Djugak, P. "The Limit Concept and Irrational Numbers: Ideas of Charles Méray and Karl Weierstrass," in *Studies in the History of Mathematics.* Moscow, 1973, 176–80.
Robinson, Abraham. "Hugues Charles Robert Méray," in *Dictionary of Scientific Biography.* Volume IX. Edited by Charles Coulston Gillispie. New York: Charles Scribner's Sons, 1970, pp. 307–08.

Other

"Hugues Charles Robert Méray." *MacTutor History of Mathematics Archive.* http://www–groups.dcs.st–and.ac.uk/~history/Mathematicians/index.html. (August 1997).

—*Sketch by Kristin Palm*

Helen Abbot Merrill
1864–1949
American mathematician

Helen Abbot Merrill took up mathematics as a vocation and avocation at a time when women were rarely visible in the field. She was most active as an instructor, co-writing textbooks as well as publishing articles on pedagogy. Merrill also wrote a "mathematical amusement" book, a populist work for young readers entitled *Mathematical Excursions.* Even in her spare time she was devoted to broader aspects of her profession, joining many mathematical, academic, and scientific organizations, and serving as vice–president of both the Mathematical Association of America and the American Mathematical Society.

Merrill was born March 30, 1864 in Orange, New Jersey, near Thomas Edison's facilities at Llewellyn Park. Her family traced its ancestry back to 1633, when Nathaniel Merrill settled in Massachusetts. Her father, George Dodge Merrill, had many business concerns, including being an inventor. Her siblings included a sister, Emily, and two brothers, Robert and William, who both grew up to become Presbyterian ministers.

An Experimental Situation

Merrill began high school in 1876 at Newburyport, and entered Wellesley College six years later in one of the first graduating classes in the history of the college. Originally, her major was classical languages, an interest she would keep up throughout her life. However, as a freshman she committed to mathematics. At that time, Wellesley was still considered something of an experiment, but Merrill responded to the close–knit atmosphere and wrote a history of her graduating class as a commemorative booklet. Merrill graduated with a B.A. after four years and began her career as a teacher. Working at the Classical School for Girls in New York, Merrill was allotted courses in Latin and history as well as mathematics. She was assigned to a variety of students, including "mill girls" from New Brunswick, New Jersey, and immigrant children in the Germantown section of Philadelphia.

In 1893, Merrill was asked to return to Wellesley, this time as an instructor, in exchange for a stipend and housing. Helen Shafer, who had hired Merrill, allowed her time off intermittently for graduate studies at the universities of Chicago, Göttingen, and eventually Yale. Merrill earned a Ph.D. from Yale in 1903 and her thesis on "Sturmian" differential equations was published the same year. Merrill moved up from instructor to associate professor status at Wellesley. The college benefitted directly from Merrill's excursions, as she introduced courses in functions and descriptive geometry for her undergraduate students based on her graduate work.

"Flowery," Not Thorny Paths

Merrill dedicated herself to providing a "flowery path" for her young charges to follow into the normally thorny subject of mathematics. She did not lower her standards for undergraduates; in fact, the courses Merrill taught were often in subjects generally offered only at the graduate level. However, she was quick to offer tailored assistance to any young woman she considered a diamond in the rough.

After being promoted to full professor in 1916, Merrill was appointed head of the mathematics department the next year. She was particularly active as associate editor of the Mathematical Association of American's monthly newsletter, member of the executive council, and later vice president in 1920. With a fellow MAA member, Clara E. Smith, who would also serve as vice president of the group, Merrill authored two textbooks. Merrill remained at Wellesley until her retirement, when she was named a Lewis Atterbury Stimson professor.

Merrill was also an amateur historian, fulfilling archival duties at Wellesley. She was elected as an executive committee member of the National Historical Society. Her interest in music and language led her to become as student again, taking summer courses at the University of California at Berkeley. She also traveled across Europe and the Americas. Merrill retired as professor emerita in 1932, and died at her home in Wellesley on May 1, 1949.

SELECTED WRITINGS BY MERRILL:

Books

(With Clara E. Smith) *Selected Topics in College Algebra*, 1914.
(With Clara E. Smith) *A First Course in Higher Algebra,* 1917.
Mathematical Excursions: Side Trips along Paths Not Generally Traveled in Elementary Courses in Mathematics, 1933.

Periodicals

"On Solutions of Differential Equations Which Possess an Ooscillatoin [*sic*] Theorem," in *Transactions of the American Mathematical Society* 4 (1903): 423–33.
"Why Students Fail in Mathematics," in *Mathematics Teacher* 11 (1918): 45–56.
"Three Mathematical Songs," in *Mathematics Teacher* 25 (1932): 36–37.

FURTHER READING:

Books

Green, Judy and Jeanne LaDuke. "Women in American Mathematics: A Century of Contributions." *A Century of Mathematics in America*, Volume 2. Edited by Peter Duren. Providence, RI: American Mathematical Society, 1989, pp. 384, 386.
Henrion, Claudia. "Helen Abbot Merrill." *Women of Mathematics*. Edited by Louise S. Grinstein and Paul J. Campbell. Westport, CT: Greenwood Press, 1987, pp. 147–151.

The National Cyclopedia of American Biography. Volume 42. Reprint. Ann Arbor, MI: University Microfilms, 1967–71, pp. 171–72.
Siegel and Finley. *Women in the Scientific Search: An American Bio–bibliography, 1724–1979*. Metuchen, NJ: The Scarecrow Press, Inc., 1985, pp. 214–15.

Periodicals

"Helen A. Merrill of Wellesley, 85." *The New York Times* (May 3, 1949): p. 25.
"Helen Abbot Merrill." *Yale University Obituary Record* (July 1, 1949): 142.

Other

"Helen Abbot Merrill." *Biographies of Women Mathematicians*. June 1997. http://www.scottlan.edu/lriddle/women/chronol.htm (July 22, 1997).

—*Sketch by Jennifer Kramer*

Winifred Edgerton Merrill
1862–1951
American mathematics educator

Winifred Edgerton Merrill forever secured her place in history by becoming the first woman to be awarded a Ph.D. in mathematics. This accomplishment is more significant because she was the first woman to receive any sort of degree of any type from Columbia University. Merrill was born September 24, 1862, in Ripon, Wisconsin, to parents Emmet and Clara (Cooper) Edgerton. Merrill's American ancestry dates back to 1632, when Richard Edgerton left England and settled in Saybrook, Connecticut. Richard Edgerton is credited as one of the founders of Norwich, Connecticut.

Merrill was educated by private tutors before entering Wellesley College in Massachusetts. Wellesley was founded in 1871 as a seminary for women to be educated mainly as teachers. Because of the Civil War, the number of male students had decreased; coupled with the growing system of education initiated in the United States, and the fact that female teachers were paid about one–third that of male teachers, women were in high demand as teachers for public schools. Merrill graduated in 1883. She married Frederick J.H. Merrill, a mining geologist, in 1887 and they raised four children, Louise, Hamilton, Winifred, and Edgerton.

Victory and Recognition

When Merrill graduated from Wellesley, she astonished the academic community by applying to Columbia University. Women were expected to, at most, secure a bachelor's degree then become instructors in the public school system. Merrill's admission to Columbia was granted only after the trustees met on several occasions to discuss the situation. As a condition of being the first woman to participate in the graduate mathematics program, she was obligated to keep the instruments used by the men as well as herself dust free and to pursue her studies in such a way that it would not discomfit her male peers. The academic trustees also made it clear that her admission was by no means meant "to set a precedent" and Merrill's acceptance was merely an "exceptional case." The male students in one of her classes were so disturbed by the idea of studying alongside a woman that they entered into a conspiracy with the professor, asking him to choose the most difficult textbook available for the course. The professor agreed to the choice. The plan gave Merrill no cause for concern, however, since she had already studied the book while at Wellesley College.

Merrill was awarded her Doctor of Philosophy degree *cum laude* in 1886 "in consideration of the extraordinary excellence of the scientific work" even though the university had not yet approved the dispensing of degrees to women. Merrill's doctorate dissertation was entitled "Multiple Integrals: a.) Their Geometrical Interpretation in Cartesian Geometry, in Trilinears and Triplanars, in Tangenials, Quaternions, and in Modern Geometry; b.) Their Analytic Interpretation in the Theory of Equations Using Determinants, Invariants, and Covariants as Instruments in the Investigation."

An Educator and Pioneer for Women's Education

At about the same time that Merrill entered Columbia she began teaching at Sylvanus Reed's School in New York City. Three years later, in 1886, she was appointed vice principal and held the position until she married. In 1888, Merrill was one of five who helped in the founding of Barnard College, located on land adjacent to Columbia University. Barnard became part of Columbia in 1900 and remains the undergraduate liberal arts school for women. The music, classics, mathematics, physics, and religion departments are joint departments with Columbia. Merrill served on the Board of Trustees for a number of years but gave up her membership after her husband objected to frequent obligatory meetings with two male lawyers in private offices.

The demands of married life and child rearing kept Merrill away from teaching for a time. She taught for one year at the Emma Willard School in Troy, New York in 1894, then did not resume her career until 1906, when she accepted a position in Yonkers at Highcliff, then founded her own girls' school, Oakesmere, when she was in her forties and served as its principal for 13 years. The school was located in New Rochelle, New York, then later moved to Mamaroneck. Merrill directed the school until 1928, watching the enrollment increase over the years from eight to 148 students. The school was recognized for its high academic standards and in 1912 another school, Oakesmere Abroad, was founded in Paris, France. After 1928, Merrill made her home in New York City, assuming the role of director for the Three Arts Wing of the Barbizon Club. During the same time, she served as an alumna trustee and fundraiser for Wellesley College. She served as editor for the publications *Historical Vistas* and *Renaissance Vistas* in 1930. Her experience and interest in education also prompted her to write articles and give public speeches on various issues of education. Merrill was a member of many educational and political associations, including the Women's Graduate Club of Columbia University, the Woman's Organization for National Prohibition, and the American Association for the Advancement of Science.

In 1933, the college that had her donning a dust cloth 50 years earlier honored her as the inaugural woman graduate of Columbia, and recognized her efforts in furthering the education of women by installing her portrait in the Philosophy Hall. An inscription under the portrait reads, "She opened the door." The portrait was presented by Merrill's 1883 graduating class from Wellesley. Merrill died on September 6, 1951, in Stratford, Connecticut.

FURTHER READING:

Books

Farnes, Patricia and G. Kass–Simon. *Women of Science: Righting the Record*. Bloomington: Indiana University Press.
National Cyclopedia of American Biography. Volume 41. New York: James T. White & Co., 1956.

Periodicals

Green, Judy and Jeanne LaDuke. "Women in the American Mathematical Community: The Pre–1940 Ph.D.'s." *The Mathematical Intelligencer* 9, no. 1 (1987): 11–13.

Other

"Winifred Edgerton Merrill." *Biographies of Women Mathematics*. June 1997. http://

—*Sketch by Kelley Reynolds Jacquez*

Ynes Mexia
1870–1938
American botanist

Although Ynes Mexia came to botany late in life, she made many important contributions to botanical science and herbariums via numerous collecting expeditions. In her trips to Alaska, and more importantly, Central and South America, Mexia collected about 150,000 specimens which were eventually housed in some of the finest botanical collections in the world, including the Field Museum in Chicago and Harvard University's herbarium. She discovered a new genus of Compositae (the largest family of flowering plants which includes common weeds, chrysanthemums, and sunflowers), which was named *Mexianthus mexicanus* in her honor, as well as hundreds of other previously unknown plant species.

Ynes Enriquetta Julietta Mexia was born on May 24, 1870, in Washington, D.C. Her grandfather was José Antonio Mexia, a general under Santa Anna. Her father, Enrique Antonio Mexia, was probably representing Mexico in Washington when his daughter was born to him and the former Sarah Wilmer. The Mexia family lived primarily in Texas where they owned land near what is now the town of Mexia. Mexia attended schools in Texas, Philadelphia, Mexico City, Ontario, Canada, and Maryland, including private Quaker schools in Philadelphia and Maryland. In 1897, Mexia married Herman de Laue, who died in 1904. She married Augustin A. de Reygados in 1907, but divorced him a year later. She had no children. After her divorce, she moved to San Francisco and was employed as a social worker.

In 1921, Mexia was admitted to the University of California in Berkeley as a special student. Focusing on the natural sciences, Mexia took several classes in botany. These classes led Mexia to devote her remaining years to botany and collecting botanical specimens. Though Mexia never finished her degree, she continued to attend classes throughout her life.

Beginning in 1925 with a trip to Mexico, Mexia collected botanical specimens in remote locations in South America, including Brazil, Peru, Ecuador, Bolivia, Argentina, and Chile. With the help of her agent and curator Nina Floy Bracelin, Mexia paid for her expeditions by selling specimens to herbariums and other institutions. Her Mexican-American background aided her in understanding the language and culture of the people living in the remote areas where she collected. Her knowledge of South American culture also helped future researchers when they traveled to these areas. A keen observer, Mexia studied more than plants; she also studied the local animals, especially birds.

In her brief, ten-year career as a botanical collector, Mexia accomplished more than any woman before her in terms of numbers of plants collected and range of travel. Her work was important to completing many a botanical collection. She was also proud to claim that she had never lost a specimen. She was praised by scientific contemporaries for her many discoveries and her meticulous collection of rare specimens. Mexia's 1928 expedition to Mt. McKinley National Park in Alaska was the first general collecting trip in this area. Mexia was happiest in the field and she stayed active late into her life. She survived many accidents, including a fall off a cliff, but illness finally stopped her during her last collecting trip to Mexico in 1937-38. She became ill with a stomach problem and had to return home early. She died of lung cancer a few months later, on July 12, 1938, in Berkeley, California.

SELECTED WRITINGS BY MEXIA:

Books

(With Edwin Bingham Copeland) *Brazilian Ferns Collected by Ynes Mexia*. Berkeley: The University of California Press, 1932.

Periodicals

"Botanical Trails in Old Mexico." *Madroño* (September 1929).

FURTHER READING:

Books

Bailey, Martha J. *American Women in Science: A Biographical Dictionary*. Denver: ABC-CLIO, 1994, pp. 248-49.
Ewan, Joseph. *Notable American Women, 1607-1950: A Biographical Dictionary*. Ed. E.T. James. Cambridge, MA: The Belknap Press of Harvard University Press, 1971, pp. 533-34.
Siegel, Patricia Joan and Kay Thomas Finley. *Women in the Scientific Search: An American Bio-bibliography, 1724-1979*. Metuchen: The Scarecrow Press, Inc., 1985, pp. 101-04.

Periodicals

"Biographical Notes. Mexia, Ynes." *Leaflets of Western Botany* (January 1957): 95-96.

—*Sketch by Annette Petrusso*

Peter D. Mitchell

Peter D. Mitchell
1920–1992
English biochemist

Peter D. Mitchell was awarded the 1978 Nobel Prize in Chemistry for his chemiosmotic theory, which explained how organisms use and synthesize energy. In his Nobel Prize address, Mitchell honored his long association with Professor David Keilin of Cambridge University, whose work provided the takeoff point for Mitchell's discoveries. Keilin had discovered cytochromes—electron-carrier proteins that assist in energy transfer via a respiratory chain. Mitchell's revolutionary chemiosmotic hypothesis changed the way scientists view energy transformation, and though it was initially viewed as controversial, it eventually won almost universal acceptance.

In 1961, when Mitchell's idea was first introduced, it was greeted by some in the scientific community with skepticism: what he was proposing was radically different than the prevailing thought on energy conversion at that time, and those opposing his conclusions questioned the validity of his research. Also, although Mitchell viewed his small research staff and unconventional laboratory at Glynn House mansion in Cornwall as positive elements conducive to productive research, others viewed his unorthodox working environment with suspicion. Mitchell's chemiosmotic theory generated intense

debate, but the positive result for science as a whole was the creation of much additional scientific experimentation and productivity attempting to prove or disprove his theory, and advancing the discipline of bioenergetics—the study of energy exchanges and transformations between living things and their environments—in the process.

Peter Dennis Mitchell was born in Mitcham, Surrey, England, on September 29, 1920, the son of Christopher Gibbs Mitchell, a civil servant, and Kate Beatrice Dorothy Taplin Mitchell. He received his secondary education at Queens College in Taunton, England, and was admitted to Jesus College at Cambridge University in 1939. A graduate student of James F. Danielli in the department of biochemistry at Cambridge, Mitchell earned his doctorate degree in 1951. He taught biochemistry at Cambridge from 1951 until 1955, when he left to develop a chemical biology unit at Edinburgh University. He remained there until 1963, when poor health caused him to look for a calmer working atmosphere.

Mitchell found a peaceful environment in an eighteenth-century manor house in Cornwall. The manor house, called Glynn House, was in disrepair, and was restored by Mitchell and converted to family living quarters and a research laboratory. Glynn Research Laboratories was organized and directed in 1964 by Mitchell and his colleague, Jennifer Moyle, whose background work was instrumental to Mitchell's development of the chemiosmotic hypothesis. By the time Mitchell received the Nobel Prize, the laboratory had grown to require a staff of six.

Development of the Chemiosmotic Theory

The intriguing question of how organisms take energy from their surroundings and transform it for use in specialized functions, such as movement and respiration, was thought to have been answered by a theory called chemical coupling. This theory postulated that energy was carried down the respiratory chain by an unknown high-energy intermediate compound formed during oxidation. The energy derived from the intermediate compound was thought to form a "universal energy currency" known as adenosine triphosphate (ATP).

The search was on to identify the energy-rich intermediary when Mitchell upset prevailing thought by proposing that the process was an electrical, not a chemical, one. He coined the term "proticity" to explain the process by which protons flow across cell membranes to synthesize ATP. Mitchell likened this process to the way electricity moves from a high concentration to a concentration low enough to power an electric appliance. Laboratory experiments crucial for the support of his chemiosmotic theory were successfully carried out during the 1960s by Mitchell and Moyle at Glynn Research Laboratories, as well as in other research labs throughout the world. These experiments included identifying the membrane protons that provide a link to the movement of other molecules across the cell membrane and showing that the membrane also serves to halt the movement of other molecules.

Recognition for his work on cell energy transfer culminated in Mitchell's receipt of the Nobel Prize in 1978. Later, Mitchell and his staff at the Glynn laboratory studied the biochemical actions involved in energy transfer within cells, seeking precise details of this complex process. Those contributions advanced scientific knowledge of how cells use, transform, and generate energy. Mitchell maintained that he was just one more link in science's intellectual and historical chain. He believed that the practice of science was a continuing process, whereby one scientist builds on the discoveries and knowledge of another, and was quick to give credit to those whose past work had advanced and made possible his own. In the December 15, 1978 issue of *Science,* Frank Harold quoted Mitchell as saying, "Science is not a game like golf, played in solitude, but a game like tennis in which one sends the ball into the opposing court and expects its return."

Many awards other than the Nobel Prize were presented to Mitchell. Among them were the CIBA Medal and Prize, Biochemical Society, England; the Warren Triennial Prize, Massachusetts General Hospital; the Louis and Bert Freedman Award of the New York Academy of Sciences; the Lewis S. Rosenstiel Award for Distinguished Work in Basic Medical Research of Brandeis University; and the Copley Medal of the Royal Society. He held memberships in various professional societies and received honorary degrees from universities in Berlin and Chicago, as well as from numerous British institutions. Although immersed in his work, Mitchell found time to participate in local affairs, respond to environmental issues, and restore medieval farmhouses. He and his wife, Mary Helen French, were married in 1958; they had six children: Jeremy, Daniel, Jason, Gideon, Julia, and Vanessa. Peter Mitchell died at Glynn House, Bodmin, on April 10, 1992.

SELECTED WRITINGS BY MITCHELL:

Periodicals

"Coupling of Phosphorylation to Electron and Hydrogen Transfer by a Chemi-Osmotic Transfer of Mechanism." *Nature* 191 (1961).
"Chemiosmotic Coupling in Oxidative and Photosynthetic Phosphorylation." *Biological Reviews.* 41 (1966).
"Vectorial Chemistry and the Molecular Mechanics of Chemiosmotic Coupling: Power Transmission by Proticity." *Transactions of the Biochemical Society* 4 (1976).

"Vectorial Chemiosmotic Processes." *Annual Review of Biochemistry.* 46 (1977).
"David Kellin's Respiratory Chain Concept and Its Chemiosmotic Consequences." *Science* 206 (1979).
"Compartmentation and Communication in Living Systems. Ligand Conduction: A General Catalytic Principle in Chemical, Osmotic, and Chemiosmotic Reaction Systems." *European Journal of Biochemistry.* 95 (1979).

FURTHER READING:

Books

Wasson, Tyler. *Nobel Prize Winners.* New York: H. W. Wilson, 1987.

Periodicals

"Dr Peter Mitchell" (obituary). *Times (London)* (15 April 1992).
Gwynne, Peter. "Nobel Quartet." *Newsweek* (30 October 1978): 105-06.
Harold, Franklin M. "The 1978 Nobel Prize in Chemistry." *Science* (15 December 1978): 1174; 1176.

—Sketch by Jane Stewart Cook

Louis Joel Mordell
1888–1972
American–born English mathematician

Louis Mordell, who is best known for his work in pure mathematics and the development of the finite basis theorem, became fascinated with mathematics at an early age. Born in Philadelphia, Pennsylvania on January 28, 1888 to Hebrew scholar Phineas Mordell and Annie Feller Mordell, both Jewish immigrants from Lithuania, Mordell was introduced to complex mathematical concepts through used books he purchased at a bookstore. He already had a solid grasp of mathematics when he entered Central High School in Philadelphia at the age of 14, and he completed that school's four–year mathematics course in two years.

In 1907, Mordell placed first on Cambridge University's scholarship examination and accepted a scholarship to St. John's College at the British school. His interest in Cambridge dated back to his self–taught days, when the used books he studied presented numerous examples from Cambridge scholarship and tripos papers. Two years later, he took the first part of the mathematical tripos and placed third,

Louis Joel Mordell

behind P. J. Daniell and E. H. Neville. Following this success, he pursued research in the theory of numbers. There was little interest in this area of study in England at that time, and Mordell was largely self–taught. His focus was the integral solutions of the Diophantine equation $y^2 = x^3 + k$, which dates back to the 1600s and the mathematician Pierre de Fermat. Mordell, however, greatly expanded the work in this area, determining the solubility for many new values of k, among other things. His work earned him a Smith's Prize but this high honor did not immediately lead to a college fellowship.

Mordell continued his research and acted as a tutor, and in 1913 joined the faculty of Birkbeck College in London. In 1916 he married Mabel Elizabeth Cambridge, with whom he later had a daughter and a son. Mordell remained at Birkbeck College until 1920, and much of his work there focused on modular forms, which resulted in two important advances. His first discovery involved the tau function—the set of coefficients of a specific modular form—which had previously been introduced by **Srinivasa Ramanujan**. Mordell proved Ramanujan's theory that the tau function has the property of multiplicativity. The theory was studied, proven, and popularized by Erich Hecke in 1937. The second discovery involved the representation of integers as the sum of a fixed number of squares of integers. Mordell's work in this area was also furthered by Hecke.

Mordell accepted a lecturer position at Manchester College of Technology in 1920, where he remained

for two years. It was during this period that Mordell developed the finite basis theorem, based on earlier work by **Jules Henri Poincaré**. It is this work for which Mordell is best known, and it was later furthered by **André Weil**. In his theorem, Mordell determined that there exist a finite number of rational points on any curve of genus greater than unity. "Mordell's conjecture," as this determination was commonly called, was proven by Gerd Faltings in 1983.

In 1922, Mordell transferred to the University of Manchester, and in 1923 was named Fielden professor of pure mathematics and head of the mathematics department at that school. In 1924, while still a citizen of the United States, he was named to the Royal Society. Mordell became a British subject in 1929. Mordell remained at Manchester until 1945 and the school became known as a leading center for mathematics during his tenure. Mordell himself explored the theory of numbers and made significant advances in the area of the geometry of numbers while at Manchester. His work during this period was political as well as scientific, as he devoted much time to assisting European refugees. Mordell even secured temporary and permanent positions at the university for some of the immigrants.

Mordell left Manchester in 1945 to succeed **Godfrey Harold Hardy** as Sadleirian professor of pure mathematics at Cambridge. At this time he also became a fellow of St. John's College at Cambridge. Mordell advanced Cambridge's reputation as a highly reputable research school before his retirement in 1953. He continued to work with other mathematicians, especially beginners, but also used the time to travel. Cambridge continued to be his home, however, and he died there after a brief illness in 1972.

SELECTED WRITINGS BY MORDELL:

Books

Diophantine Equations, 1969.

Periodicals

"The Diophantine Equation $y^2 - k = x^3$," in *Proceedings of the London Mathematical Society,* second series, 13 (1913): 60–80.
"Reminiscences of an Octogenarian Mathematician," in *American Mathematical Monthly* 78 (November 1971): 952–961.

FURTHER READING:

Periodicals

Cassels, John W.S., "Louis Joel Mordell." *Biographical Memoirs of Fellows of the Royal Society* 19 (1973): 493–520.

Ann Haven Morgan

Davenport, Harold. "Louis Joel Mordell." *Acta Arithmetica* 9 (1964): 1–22.

—*Sketch by Kristin Palm*

Ann Haven Morgan
1882–1966
American zoologist and ecologist

Ann Haven Morgan was known to her students as "Mayfly Morgan" because of her passion for the mayflies that were the subject of her Ph.D. dissertation. Her passions extended much further, however. A promoter of conservation, or applied ecology, she wrote about animal adaptations and noted the impact of human populations on wilderness and natural habitats. Morgan's long career at Mount Holyoke College was coupled with a lifelong commitment to conservation education. In addition to scientific papers, she produced a textbook and two popular field guides notable for their clarity and grace of language.

Morgan was born May 6, 1882, in Waterford, Connecticut, to Stanley Griswold and Julia Alice Douglass Morgan. The eldest of three children, she took pleasure in exploring the woods and streams near her home, and throughout life professed her fondness for "oozy mudholes." In 1902, after graduation from Williams Memorial Institute at New London, she entered Wellesley College. Finding it confining, in 1904 she transferred to Cornell University, where in 1906 she received an A.B. degree. She spent the subsequent three years at Mount Holyoke College in South Hadley, Massachusetts, as a biology assistant and instructor, then returned to Cornell to study for a doctoral degree under the aquatic biologist James George Needham. It was at Cornell that her freshman biology students christened her "Mayfly Morgan." At about the same time she received the Ph.D. in 1912, she changed her name from "Anna" to "Ann."

Upon graduation Morgan returned to Mount Holyoke, where her promotions were rapid. She was named associate professor in 1914, chairman of the zoology department in 1916, and full professor in 1918. Morgan's career at Mount Holyoke was punctuated by postgraduate work at the University of Chicago and summer research and teaching at Cornell and the Marine Biological Laboratory at Woods Hole, Massachusetts. In 1920 Morgan was a visiting fellow at Harvard and, in 1921, at Yale. She spent the summer of 1926 at William Beebe's tropical laboratory in Kartabo, British Guiana. Her studies of aquatic life focused primarily on the American Northeast, ranging from land-locked salmon in New Hampshire to water bugs in a pond near Northampton.

Field Book on Ponds and Streams Becomes Popular Favorite

Morgan's *Field Book of Ponds and Streams: An Introduction to the Life of Fresh Water*, published in 1930 with her own drawings and photographs and a foreword by Needham, described the "lively populations" of freshwater habitats as well as methods of collection and preservation. It was an instant success and became a longtime favorite of fishermen and amateur naturalists as well as professional biologists. In 1935 she published Field Book of Animals in Winter; it was based on a course she had taught, and it inspired an educational film produced by Encyclopedia Brittannica Films.

The pioneering zoologist Cornelia Clapp considered Morgan her successor at Mount Holyoke. Morgan was an outstanding teacher, inspiring many students to enter biological fields. In the 1930s, she and her colleague, A. Elizabeth Adams, won funding from the National Academy of Sciences, the National Research Council, Sigma Xi, the American Association for the Advancement of Science, and the Rockefeller Foundation. In 1933, when Morgan was 50, she was one of three American women "starred" in recognition of their excellence, in James McKeen Cattell's *American Men of Science. Time* magazine, reporting on the honor, noted that her recent publications dealt with spotted newts, although mayflies remained her favorite subjects. The diminutive Morgan was portrayed as moving briskly about her laboratories in her physician's coat, and lecturing her classes "in clear, crisp tones."

After retirement from Mount Holyoke in 1947, Morgan continued her energetic pace, conducting workshops for teachers and promoting conservation education—appreciation and intelligent care of living things and the environment—as integral to science programs. As members of the National Commission on Policies in Conservation Education, Morgan and Adams traveled to the western United States and Canada to study conservation programs, and Morgan returned to apply what she had learned to the Connecticut River Valley. In 1955 Morgan published *Kinships of Animals and Man*, a textbook that treats zoological structure and function, animal behavior, evolution, and ecology. It is a comprehensive work, a culmination of her teaching career, and is considered a classic text.

Morgan died of stomach cancer on June 5, 1966, at her home in South Hadley. She was buried at Cedar Grove Cemetery in New London.

SELECTED WRITINGS BY MORGAN:

Books

Field Book of Ponds and Streams: An Introduction to the Life of Fresh Water. New York: G. P. Putnam's Sons, 1930.
Field Book of Animals in Winter. New York: G. P. Putnam's Sons, 1939.
Kinships of Animals and Man: A Textbook of Animal Biology. New York: McGraw-Hill, 1955.

FURTHER READING:

Books

Bonta, Marcia Myers. *Women in the Field: America's Pioneering Women Naturalists.* College Station, TX: Texas A&M University Press, 1991, pp. 245-249.
Rossiter, Margaret W. *Women Scientists in America: Struggles and Strategies to 1940.* Baltimore: Johns Hopkins University Press, 1982, pp. 19, 145, 174, 294.
Shearer, Benjamin F., and Barbara S. Shearer, eds. *Notable Women in the Life Sciences: A Biographical Dictionary.* Westport, CT: Greenwood Press, 1996, pp. 293-297.
Sicherman, Barbara, and Carol Hurd Green, editors. *Notable American Women: The Modern Period, A Biographical Dictionary.* Cambridge: Belknap Press of Harvard University Press, 1980, pp. 497-498.

Nevill Francis Mott

Periodicals

"Best Women." *Time*, March 20, 1933, pp. 38.

—*Sketch by Jill Carpenter*

Nevill Francis Mott
1905–1996
English physicist

Sir Nevill Francis Mott began his career applying the then-recently discovered laws of quantum mechanics and ultimately became a leading figure in solid state physics. He shared the 1977 Nobel Prize with **Philip Warren Anderson** and **John Van Vleck** for work on semiconductors, the materials that drove the modern revolution in electronics and led to improved electronic circuits and increases in the memory of computers. Mott also worked on theories explaining the physical underpinnings of the properties of many materials, and with R. W. Gurney, developed a theory explaining how a photographic image is formed when the film is exposed to light.

Mott was born on September 30, 1905, in Leeds, England, the first of two children of Charles Francis and Lilian Mary (Reynolds) Mott, both of whom worked for a time in the Cavendish Laboratory at

Cambridge University under **J. J. Thomson**, who had just discovered the electron. His parents moved to Stafford when Mott was six years old, but Mott studied at home with his mother until he was ten because of concerns about his health. He wrote in his autobiography that he wanted to be a physicist from the time he understood what physics was. At age thirteen, he began five years of secondary study at Clifton College. In 1927, he received a baccalaureate degree in mathematics from Cambridge, where he did his first work in theoretical physics, studying the scattering of electrons by nuclei. He continued those studies during a 1928 term in Copenhagen with **Niels Bohr**, who in 1913 had put forth the theoretical model of the atom. Mott went on to teach at Manchester University during the 1929-1930 school year and received an introduction to solid state physics from **William Lawrence Bragg**, who with his father, **William Henry Bragg,** won a Nobel Prize for his work in X-ray crystallography. In 1930, Mott returned to Cambridge, received a master's degree, became a lecturer at Cambridge's Gonville and Caius College, and made his first big discovery in the scattering of particles by atoms and nuclei. These collisions between charged particles are now known as Mott scattering. Mott became Melville Wills Professor of Theoretical Physics at Bristol in 1933, and held this position until he became chair of the physics department there in 1948. Mott's group of researchers at Bristol led the world in the development of solid state physics. Mott's approach focused on using physics to explain the properties of materials, particularly metals and alloys. As he wrote in *Scientific American* in 1967, "In solid state perhaps more than anywhere else quantum mechanics has ceased to be restricted to pure science and has become a working tool of technology."

Mott's studies of electrons in metals and dislocations and defects in crystals resulted in the 1936 publication of the seminal work, *Theory of the Properties of Metals and Alloys*, which he wrote with Harry Jones. Mott, with Gurney, also became the first to formulate a theory explaining how photographic plates work, an explanation that led to improvements in the field. They theorized that free electrons produced when light strikes the plates became trapped at dislocations or other imperfections and attract silver ions, which become silver atoms and form a latent image.

Work in Semiconductors Leads to Nobel Prize

Mott then became interested in semiconductors, which are materials that can act as insulators or conductors and are used in many electronic devices. In 1940, Mott wrote *Electronic Processes in Ionic Crystals* with Gurney, and did important work on transition metals, becoming the first to theorize that all electrons in such materials are involved in electri-

cal conductivity. He also postulated that certain nonmetals can act like metals when placed under pressure and that all electrons become free to move at once; these processes are called Mott transitions.

In 1954, Mott became Cavendish Professor of Physics at Cambridge, a post he held until his retirement in 1971. He also served as the master of Gonville and Caius College from 1959 to 1966. Mott was involved in confirming by observations with the electron microscope the existence of moving dislocations, or tiny defects, responsible for hardening in alloys. During the mid-1960s, Mott became interested in non-crystalline, or amorphous, semiconductors, a research shift that stemmed in part from his work on metal-insulator transitions and eventually brought him the Nobel Prize. Mott added considerably to science's knowledge of the electronic properties of amorphous (disordered) materials such as glasses, alloys and impure semiconductors, where atoms are not arranged in regular arrays. Adding impurities to semiconductors, for example, can improve conductivity. Mott remained active in science after his retirement, applying his knowledge to the generation of affordable solar energy. A scientist whose interests included philosophy and theology, Mott was baptized in the Church of England when he was 80. He died on August 8, 1996, at a hospital near his home in Apsley Guise, not far from London.

Mott married Ruth Horder in 1930 and had two daughters, Elizabeth and Alice. During his career, he was involved in scientific publishing and a number of social and philosophical issues, including the control of nuclear armaments. A popular public speaker who organized and participated in many scientific conferences, Mott was elected a fellow of the Royal Society of London in 1936 and knighted in 1962. In addition, he was a member of several foreign societies, including the U.S. National Academy of Sciences. Mott received the Royal Society's Hughes Medal in 1941, the Royal Medal in 1953, and the Copley Medal in 1972, in addition to many other awards and honorary degrees.

SELECTED WRITINGS BY MOTT:

Books

The Theory of Atomic Collisions. Oxford: Clarendon Press, 1933.
The Theory of the Properties of Metals and Alloys Oxford: Clarendon Press, 1936.
Electronic Processes in Ionic Crystals. Oxford: Clarendon Press, 1940.
Electronic Processes in Non-Crystalline Materials. Oxford: Clarendon Press, 1971.

Periodicals

"The Solid State." *Scientific American* (September 1967): 80-89.
"Metal-Insulator Transitions." *Physics Today* (November 1978): 42-47.

FURTHER READING:

Books

Contemporary Authors. Vol. 129. Detroit: Gale, 1990.
Modern Scientists and Engineers. New York: McGraw-Hill, 1980, pp. 332-33.
Mott, Sir Nevill. *A Life in Science.* Taylor and Francis, 1986.
Wasson, Tyler. *Nobel Prize Winners.* New York: H. W. Wilson, 1987.

Periodicals

Cohen, Marvin L., and L. M. Falicov. "The 1977 Nobel Prize in Physics." *Science* (18 November 1977): 713-15.
Saxon, Wolfgang. "Sir Nevill Francis Mott, 90, a Pioneer Physicist" (obituary). *New York Times* (10 August 1996): A30.
Weil, Martin. "Nobel-Winning Physicist Nevill Francis Mott Dies" (obituary). *Washington Post* (11 August 1996): B6.

—*Sketch by Julie Anderson*

Barbara Moulton Browne

Barbara Moulton Browne
1915–1996
American bacteriologist

If not for the efforts of Barbara Moulton Browne, the practice of drug companies influencing government approval of their products might still be commonplace, despite the potential harm that untested medications could pose to the public. Moulton's testimony before a Senate subcommittee in the early 1960s helped put a halt to that practice and fostered the creation of the drug-approval process now in place.

Barbara Moulton was born in Chicago on August 26, 1915. She was the second child of Harold Moulton and Frances Christine (Rawlins) Moulton; she had an older brother, John Rawlins Moulton. Her father, an economics professor at the University of Chicago, moved his family to Washington, D.C., when he became president of the Brookings Institution. Barba- ra attended both Smith College and the University of Vienna before receiving her bachelor's degree in 1937 from the University of Chicago. She spent 1938 and 1939 at the university studying bacteriology and developing an interest and expertise in infectious disease. She went on to study at George Washington University in Washington, D.C., and received her master's degree in 1940 and then her M.D. in 1944.

From 1945 to 1947 she served her surgical residency at St. Luke's Hospital in Chicago, and at Suburban Hospital in Bethesda, Maryland. After completing her residency, she spent a year at George Washington University as an anatomy instructor and then entered general practice with the Group Health Association of Washington, D.C. She also worked as a physician in student health services at Washington State College. In 1950, Moulton left Washington, D.C. and returned to Illinois, where she became the assistant director of student health services at Illinois State Normal University; from there, she went on to become the assistant medical director of Chicago's Municipal Contagious Diseases Hospital. During 1953, she taught medicine at the University of Illinois.

In 1955, Moulton became a medical officer with the Food and Drug Administration (FDA), then part of the Department of Health, Education, and Welfare. Charged with investigating the validity of drug manufacturers' claims concerning their new products, Moulton soon found the objective environment she needed to conduct her job to be compromised by the considerable influence of the very companies she was asked to investigate. They wanted their products approved carte blanche by the government, and Moulton's superiors often did not object to this convenient arrangement.

A blatant manifestation of this understanding was the marked difference between protocol for approving a drug and that for rejecting one. A medical officer like Moulton could approve a new drug without any input from colleagues or superiors; however, rejecting a new drug was far more difficult. The medical officer needed, at the very least, the approval of the chief of the new drug branch, the Bureau of Medicine's director, and the FDA commissioner. The approval of the general counsel and the director of the enforcement bureau were usually needed as well. Given this environment, it is not surprising that many medical officers took the path of least resistance. Moulton could not.

Resigns to Testify

In 1960, Moulton resigned her position at the FDA in order to testify before a Senate subcommittee regarding the abuses she had witnessed. The Kefauver Subcommittee on Monopoly and Antitrust was investigating the actions of the drug industry, and had become focused on the actions of the head of the FDA's antibiotics division, Henry Welch, who had been accused of accepting a million dollars from drug manufacturers over a seven-year period. The subcommittee was especially interested in his involvement with the marketing of the drug Sigmamycin.

Moulton testified about how she had expressed her concerns about Welch and Sigmamycin to her superiors, only to have them warn that Welch's reputation "added luster to the name of the Food and Drug Administration, and nothing could or should be done against him." Besides noting the FDA's attitude toward Welch, Moulton also described the difficulty of evaluating drugs while the manufacturer representatives watched. She called their attentions "an almost insurmountable handicap." Partly due to Moulton's testimony, the subcommittee proposed a bill that placed more stringent controls on the drug approval process. It later became law as the Kefauver-Harris Amendment to the Food Drug and Cosmetic Act.

A Career Continues

Moulton never returned to the FDA, but did stay in government work, joining the Federal Trade Commission (FTC) in 1961. In the FTC's Bureau of Deceptive Practices, she worked as a medical officer in the Division of Scientific Opinions. She remained with the FTC until her retirement, and during that time, she worked tirelessly to protect consumers from fraud and deceptive practices. Even after her retirement, she continued to serve the public, spending several years working for the General Accounting Office. In 1967, she received the Federal Woman's Award in recognition of her contributions.

Moulton was a member of many organizations. She became a fellow of the American Association for the Advancement of Science in 1963, and a member of the American Public Health Association, the American Society of Microbiology, the American Society of Hematology, and the American Medical Women's Association.

On March 30, 1962, Barbara Moulton married E. Wayles Browne, Jr., an economist working with the Senate subcommittee during the time she testified. When not in Washington, they devoted some of their time to the herd of registered Holsteins that Barbara and her father had assembled on a farm in West Virginia. They sold the property in 1972 and disbanded their 138-head herd.

Barbara Moulton Browne died May 12, 1996, in an Arlington, Virginia, nursing home of Alzheimer's disease. Her legacy lives on in the many consumer protection groups that now exist and in the stringent rules that govern the approval of new medications and the interaction of business and government.

SELECTED WRITINGS BY MOULTON BROWNE:

"Antibiotics in the Treatment of Viral Diseases." *Antibiotics Annual*, 1955-56: 719-726.

FURTHER READING:

Books

Levin, Beatrice. *Women in Medicine.* Lincoln, NB: Media Publishing, 1988.
Who's Who of American Women, 1974-75. Chicago: Marquis, 1975.

Periodicals

Lear, John. "Drugmakers and the Govt.—Who Makes the Decisions?" *Saturday Review*, July 2, 1960, 37-42.

—Sketch by Fran Hodgkins

Koji Nakanishi

Koji Nakanishi
1925–

Japanese-born American chemist

Koji Nakanishi believes in conventional values, like devotion to family and respect for authority. Yet, his career and life have been anything but conventional. In his autobiography, *A Wandering Natural Products Chemist,* Nakanishi describes himself as a "hybrid" who grew up in Europe, Egypt, and Japan and whose philosophy and behavior in life have been influenced by both Eastern and Western thought. A dedicated, world-renowned organic chemist with wide-ranging interests, Nakanishi is also an amateur magician who delights in mystifying his audience and likes "drinking in quiet bars with friends." Although he has spent the past 30 years primarily in the United States conducting research and teaching, Nakanishi has always maintained strong ties with his homeland.

In his autobiography, Nakanishi says that his wife accuses him of having too many professional interests instead of specializing. He also modestly asserts that he does not consider himself "brilliant."

However, with the dedicated help of his students and colleagues, Nakanishi has made important contributions in elucidating the structures of natural bioactive compounds and their modes of action. For example, his work in the isolation and structural studies of visual pigments has led to new insights into the mechanism of vision. As a result, he has gained international respect and numerous honors, including the Imperial Prize and the Japan Academy Prize, which represent the highest honors for a Japanese scholar.

Nakanishi was born in the hills of Hong Kong on May 11, 1925, the eldest of Yuzo and Yoshiko Nakanishi's four sons. In Japanese, the characters for KO in Nakanishi's first name are identical to Hong, which means perfume. (Hong Kong means perfume harbor.) Nakanishi's father, Yuzo, worked in international banking, and the family moved to Lyon, France, soon after Nakanishi's birth. His father was then transferred to England, where Nakanishi learned English at a young age and "proper English manners." The family eventually relocated to Alexandria, Egypt, and then to Japan in 1935.

During the next 10 years, Nakanishi was to experience one of the most tumultuous times in Japanese history. A fanatic militarism was on the rise in Japan, culminating in World War II and ultimate defeat at the hands of the Allies. While he was interested in chemistry and biology, Nakanishi chose chemistry as a major without any specific plans or ambitions. After high school, he applied to Tokyo Imperial University and was the only applicant from his school not to be accepted. "The failure was devastating to both my mother and myself," he writes. Because of the country's military build-up, Nakanishi and his family knew he would be drafted unless he went to college.

Nakanishi eventually was accepted by Nagoya Imperial University, located between Tokyo and Kyoto. He enjoyed the university's pastoral setting and the young and bright staff. It was also here that he met his future wife, Yasuko, who was a laboratory assistant. He eventually moved in with his future wife's family after his apartment was bombed during an air raid. In his autobiography, Nakanishi recounts the numbing effects of war, describing his engagement to Yasuko as "strangely emotionless because I did not think we would live to be married."

Embarks on Career in Natural Products

Following the war, Nakanishi and his colleagues quickly emersed themselves in chemistry, trying to catch up on lost time. In 1946, he joined the research group of Fujio Egami, who was carrying on Japan's tradition of excellence in natural products chemistry. After completing his graduate work in structural studies of the red crystalline antibiotic actinomycin, Nakanishi went on to become a Garioa Fellow at Harvard. Unfortunately, because of his financial situation, he was forced to leave his wife and newly born daughter Keiko in Japan for two years. (Nakanishi also has a son, Jun.) He returned to Nagoya University in 1952 as an assistant professor of chemistry. Shortly afterward he was diagnosed with tuberculosis and required to rest for several months. Nakanishi used this time to complete his translation of *Organic Chemistry* (the original work was coauthored by his mentor at Harvard, Louis Fieser) in a three-volume set. The book, which became a best-selling chemistry book well into the 1960s, brought financial security to Nakanishi and his family.

In 1969, after stints as a professor of chemistry at Tokyo Kyoiku and Tohoku universities in Japan, Nakanishi accepted a professorship at Columbia University in New York. "I had no pressing reason to leave Tohoku University except that, subconsciously, I was interested in trying out life abroad," writes Nakanishi. This interest would drastically change the Nakanishis' life. Although his plan was to conduct advanced research in chemistry for 10 years in the United States and then return to Japan to upgrade his home country's efforts in the field, Nakanishi has spent 30 years at Columbia. Yet, he still found time to direct the Suntory Institute for Bioorganic Research (SUNBOR) in Japan and fulfilled his dream of improving Japanese science by starting the first true international postdoctoral system in Japan in 1980.

Helping Solve the Molecular Mysteries of Life

Over his career, Nakanishi has been noted for his multidisciplinary and international collaborations. He has directed research that has characterized more than 180 natural products, including antimutagens from plants and metal-sequestering compounds from sea squirt blood. He has also worked with visual pigments and wasp toxins, an effort that has led Nakanishi and colleagues to synthesize a series of compounds structurally similar to the venom of a type of Egyptian wasp. These synthetic compounds are 33 times more powerful than the natural venom and will help in obtaining pure samples of glutamic acid receptors on the surface of nerve cells for further study.

Like wasp venom, many of the compounds Nakanishi has worked with can be found only in minuscule amounts. As a result, much of his research has focused on methods stressing isolation and purification of such compounds and on new approaches to structure elucidation. Beginning in the late 1980s, his worked has centered on investigations into the interaction of bioactive molecules with receptor molecules.

A man of many interests professionally, Nakanishi also enjoyed building miniature railroads for many years and collects paintings and sculptures of bulls and cows. "Cows are pastoral, never appear to be rushing about, and give one a peaceful feeling; I am the opposite," he writes. But his favorite hobby has been magic, which he took up as a way to entertain people at graduations, weddings, and parties. When he received the prestigious Imperial Prize, Nakanishi performed magic rope tricks for Japan's Crown Prince during the reception and dinner.

As for the future of chemistry, Nakanishi is optimistic. "Medicines and pharmacy are built completely around organic compounds," he writes in his autobiography. "In this interdisciplinary era, if we want to solve the mode of action of bioactive compounds for the purpose of uncovering the mysteries of life and to develop more active compounds, chemistry simply has to play a central role."

SELECTED WRITINGS BY NAKANISHI:

Books

A Wandering Natural Chemist. Washington, DC: American Chemical Society, 1991.

Periodicals

"Bioorganic Studies of Receptors with Philantoxin Analogs." *Pure and Applied Chemistry* 66 (1994): 671-678.

FURTHER READING:

Periodicals

"Koji Nakanishi Receives Mosher Award." *Chemical and Engineering News* (February 21, 1994): 38.
Rouhi, Maureen. "Nakanishi Wins Welch Award in Chemistry." *Chemical and Engineering News* (May 20, 1996): 9.
Wheeler, David. "Research Notes." *Chronicle of Higher Education* (September 9, 1991): A16.

—Sketch by David Petechuk

John Forbes Nash
1928–
American algebraist and game theorist

John Forbes Nash is considered one of America's most eminent mathematicians, having been

John Forbes Nash

awarded the 1994 Nobel Prize in Economic Science for his work in game theory, which he shared with economists John C. Harsanyi and Reinhard Selten.

A Genius of the Postwar Era

Nash was born in Bluefield, West Virginia, and came of age during the Depression. His mother, Lillian, was a Latin teacher, and his father, John Sr., an electrical engineer. The Depression did not affect the Nash family as severely as other families in West Virginia; they lived in a upper–class home down the road from the local country club. Nash and his younger sister, Martha, were both well educated. He was an avid reader, skilled at chess, and enough of an accomplished whistler to whistle complete melodies of Bach. Always curious, problem solving was his passion even as a child. One of Nash's mathematics teachers told his parents he was having trouble in class when in actuality the young prodigy was solving math problems in a different way than his teacher could formulate.

In 1945, Nash entered the Carnegie Institute of Technology (now Carnegie–Mellon University), in Pittsburgh, Pennsylvania. Nash completed the requirements for a bachelor of science degree in two years, and immediately began graduate study. In 1948, Nash began his doctoral work at Princeton University, at that time the home of such renowned scholars as **Albert Einstein** and **John von Neumann**. It was in his second year at Princeton that Nash wrote his thesis paper which laid the mathematical foundations of game theory and, 45 years later, earned him the Nobel Prize.

What Is Game Theory?

Game theory was first invented by John von Neumann and Oskar Morgenstern, an economist at Princeton, who wrote of their discovery in *The Theory of Games and Economic Behavior* in 1944. Game theory became a very popular concept during the Cold War. As the nuclear arms race between the United States and the USSR escalated, a methodology which could predict the possible outcome of a worst or best case scenario was a priceless commodity. Von Neumann and Morgenstern provided a theory based on pure rivalries where the gain for one side exactly balances the loss for the other side (called a "zero–sum situation"). In his doctoral thesis, Nash focused on nonzero–sum noncooperative games involving two or more players when the players are in direct competition. He proved that under appropriate conditions, there always exists stable equilibrium strategies for the players. In such a collection of strategies, no player can increase his gain by changing his strategy while the other players' strategies remain fixed. This concept is now known as the Nash equilibrium.

In 1952 Nash became an instructor at the Massachusetts Institute of Technology and began working on a series of papers, the first of which involved real algebraic varieties. His work was important to a theorem of Artin and Mazur concerning how the number of periodic points for a smooth map can increase as a function of the number of points. Nash's work allowed Artin and Mazur to translate the problem into an algebraic one of counting solutions to polynomial equations.

Nash also tackled one of the fundamental problems in Riemannian geometry, the isometric embedding problem for Riemannian manifolds. What Nash did was to introduce an entirely new method into nonlinear analysis, which enabled him to prove the existence of isometric embeddings. Nash also developed deep and significant results about basic local existence, uniqueness, and continuity theorems for parabolic and elliptic differential equations.

Nash was diagnosed with paranoid schizophrenia at the age of 30 and spent the greater part of what could have been his most productive years in and out of mental institutions. In 1966, during a period of remission, Nash published his last paper, which was a continuation of his work on the isometric embedding theorem.

In 1994, Nash shared the Nobel Prize in Economic Science for his work in game theory. Of his achievements **John Milnor** writes: "It is notoriously difficult to apply precise mathematical methods in the social sciences, yet the ideas in Nash's thesis are simple and rigorous, and provide a firm background, not only for economic theory but also for research in evolutionary biology, and more generally for the study of any situation in which human or nonhuman beings face competition or conflict."

SELECTED WRITINGS BY NASH:

Books

(With C. Kalisch, J. Milnor, and E. Nering) "Some Experimental *N*–Person Games," in *Decision Processes,* edited by R.M. Thrall, C.H. Coombs, and R.L. Davis, 1954.

Periodicals

"Equilibrium Points in *N*–person Games." *Proceedings of the National Academy of Sciences USA* 36 (1950), 48–49.

"The Bargaining Problem." *Econometrica* 18 (1950): 155–162.

"Real Algebraic Manifolds." *Annals of Mathematics* 56 (1952): 405–421.

"Two–Person Cooperative Games." *Econometrica* 21 (1953): 128–140.

"Results on Continuation and Uniqueness of Fluid Flow." *Bullentin of the American Mathematical Society* 60 (1954): 165–166.

"A Path Space and the Stiefel–Whitney Classes." *Proceedings of the National Academy of Sciences USA* 411 (1955): 320–321.

"The Imbedding Problem for Riemannian Manifolds." *Annals of Mathematics* 63 (1956): 20–63.

"Continuity of Solutions of Parabolic and Elliptic Equations." *American Journal of Mathematics* 80 (1958): 931–954.

"Analyticity of the Solutions of Implicit Function Problems with Analytic Data." *Annals of Mathematics* 84 (1966): 345–355.

FURTHER READING:

Books

Casti, John L. *Five Golden Rules, Great Theories of 20th–Century Mathematics—and Why They Matter.* New York: John Wiley & Sons, Inc., 1996.

Periodicals

Milnor, John. "A Nobel Prize for John Nash." *The Mathematical Intelligencer* 17, no. 3 (Summer 1995): 11–17.

Yuval Ne'eman

Nasar, Sylvia. "The Lost Years of a Nobel Laureate." *New York Times* (November 13, 1994).

Warsh, David. "Economist Share Nobel Trio Pioneered Use of Game Theory in the Field." *The Boston Globe* (October 12, 1994): 43.

—*Sketch by Tammy J. Bronson*

Yuval Ne'eman
1925–
Israeli theoretical physicist

Few scientists in the twentieth century have had a more colorful career than Yuval Ne'eman. Ne'eman had been a colonel the Israeli Army and Deputy Director of Military Intelligence before he became a physicist. His work in physics helped revolutionize our view of the structure of the universe. While continuing to work in physics, Ne'eman also became involved in his country's politics and held a seat in its chief parliamentary body and also served as a cabinet minister.

Ne'eman was born on May 14, 1925, in Tel Aviv, Palestine, the son of Gedalia and Zipora (Ben Ya'acov) Ne'eman. While Ne'eman obtained degrees in engineering from the Israel Institute of Technology

(Technicon) in Haifa (he received a B.Sc. in 1945 and an M.Sc. in 1946), he was already a member of the Jewish Underground. After graduation, he worked for a time on hydrodynamical design at a pump factory, but in 1946 progress in creating the Jewish state of Israel stalled, and Ne'eman joined the Underground full time. At this time the Underground mainly engaged in smuggling Jews into Palestine and in acts of sabotage. Finally in 1947 the General Assembly of the United Nations voted to partition Palestine into Jewish and Arab states. The state of Israel officially came into being on Ne'eman's birthday in 1948, but was immediately invaded by its Arab neighbors. Ne'eman moved from the Underground into the regular armed services. Although all-out war lasted officially only about a year, the Middle East remained tense. Ne'eman continued in the Israeli Defense Forces until 1955, advancing to the rank of colonel. During this period he also married Dvora Rubinstein (1951), with whom he has two children, and obtained a Staff College Diploma at the Ecole Superieure de Guerre in Paris, France (1952). A second Arab-Israeli war broke out in 1956; by that time, Ne'eman had moved into the intelligence division, where he was deputy director.

In 1957, after Israel's victory in the war, Ne'eman asked Moshe Dayan, then Israeli Chief of Staff, for a leave to study physics. Dayan did not grant the leave, but did offer Ne'eman a less demanding post as defense attaché in London. This job allowed Ne'eman the time to take physics courses on the side. Ne'eman accepted and arrived in London at the beginning of 1958.

Kings College, where Ne'eman hoped to study relativity, was too far from the embassy for Ne'eman to travel back and forth to classes. Imperial College, however, was only a five-minute walk. But when Ne'eman told his first advisor at Imperial that he wanted to study gravitational field theory, he learned that there was no one there working on that subject. The advisor had heard, however, that theoretical physicist **Abdus Salam** was working with field theory at Imperial College. Ne'eman applied to study with Salam, an Islamic Pakistani. Salam agreed to supervise the apparently unqualified Ne'eman because Salam felt that Islamic science owed a debt to medieval Jewish scholars. The field theory that Salam and his group at Imperial College were studying was called gauge theory, which applied to particle physics.

Beginning with the Iraqi revolution in 1958, Ne'eman was required to spend all his time on military duties for almost two years. But after complaining to a new Israeli Chief of Staff and reminding him of Dayan's promise that he would be allowed to study physics, Ne'eman was finally released from the armed services in 1960; he now could devote himself to physics completely for a few years. At that time one of the main problems in particle theory was the recent

discovery of unexpected particles that seemed to fit nowhere in existing theories. Their odd decay patterns had earned them the name "strange particles." Ne'eman wanted to apply a mathematical tool called group theory to the task of classifying these strange particles. Salam, an excellent mathematician as well as a physicist, was able to direct Ne'eman to the proper mathematical resources. Within six months, in the fall of 1960, Ne'eman thought that he had the answer. Meanwhile, in the United States, at almost exactly the same time, Caltech physicist **Murray Gell-Mann** had found the same answer as Ne'eman.

At the start of the 1960s, however, observations seemed to doom the group-theoretical ideas of Ne'eman and Gell-Mann. But the whole picture changed in June, 1962, when new data indicating the existence of two new particles were presented at a large physics conference. Both Ne'eman and Gell-Mann were at the conference and both recognized that their theory had been vindicated. Ne'eman used the new data to show some friends how his group-theory predicted the existence of exactly one more strange particle. The next day Gell-Mann made the same prediction before the whole conference. At that point Ne'eman and Gell-Mann met for the first time. They had not known of each other's work before the conference. When the particle that Ne'eman and Gell-Mann had predicted was found two years later, the theory was proven. By then Ne'eman and Gell-Mann were fast friends and even collaborated on a book about their theory, which Gell-Mann had named "the eightfold way" after one of the basic tenets of Buddhism. The name was a kind of joke, since the only connection is that the mathematical group involved contains parts with eight members, called octets.

It was not clear at first how the eightfold way applied to particle classification. Scientists believed that the basis of the group used in the eightfold way should be the set of three strange particles. Ne'eman recognized that the three particles should be the basis of the whole group and proposed the existence of additional particles with fractional charges. But Ne'eman did not work out all the implications of this idea, which proved to be correct. Two years later, Gell-Mann described in some detail three previously unknown particles with fractional charges, which he named quarks, as the basis of the eightfold way.

Ne'eman received a D.I.C. from Imperial College and his Ph.D. in physics from London University in 1962, but by then he had already returned to Israel to head a research group of the Israeli Atomic Energy Commission. In 1965 he became the first head of the physics department at Tel-Aviv University. From 1972 through 1975 he worked as president of the university, and he currently holds its Wolfson Extraordinary Chair of Theoretical Physics. Ne'eman has also directed the Center for Particle Theory at the

University of Texas in Austin since 1968. In 1981 Ne'eman entered politics and was elected to Israel's parliament, the Knesset, taking the cabinet post of Minister of Science during 1982-84 and again in 1990-92. He has also served as Minister of Energy in the Israeli Cabinet. Ne'eman has been awarded the Israel Prize (1969), the Einstein Medal (1970), and the Wigner Medal (1982).

SELECTED WRITINGS BY NE'EMAN:

Books

(With Murray Gell-Mann) *The Eightfold Way.* 1964.

(With Yoram Kirsh) *The Particle Hunters.* Cambridge, UK: Cambridge University Press, 1986 (original Hebrew version published by Masada in Israel in 1983).

(With Elena Eizenberg) *Membranes and Other Extendons: p-branes.* Singapore: World Scientific, 1995.

FURTHER READING:

Books

Crease, Robert, and Charles C. Mann. *The Second Creation.* New York: Macmillan, 1986.

—Sketch by Bryan Bunch

Joseph Needham

Joseph Needham
1900–1995
English biochemist

After distinguishing himself as a research scientist with his work on the biochemistry of embryonic development, Joseph Needham embraced an entirely different career before his 40th year and devoted himself to a life-long, comprehensive study of the development of science in China. In 1954, he produced the first volume of his monumental *Science and Civilisation in China*, a seminal work that reached 17 volumes by the time of his death, and which is continued by a team of scholars at the Needham Institute at Cambridge. Needham was undoubtedly the greatest Western sinologist or student of China of the 20th century.

Born in London, England, on December 9, 1900, Noel Joseph Terence Montgomery Needham was the only child of Joseph Needham, a successful physician, and Alicia Adelaide Montgomery, a gifted musician.

Although his parents had distinctly different styles and temperaments—his father was a practical, serious man who loved learning and possessed a fine library, and his mother was an artistic type who was also a successful songwriter—they shared strict Victorian standards of decorum. They agreed upon little else however, and with his father calling his son Noel and his mother calling him Terence, the solitary, introspective boy decided to call himself Joseph—a traditional family name that always went to the first-born son. During his early school years at Dulwich College Preparatory School, Needham had few companions except for his Parisian governess. At the beginning of World War I, he was sent to Oundle School in Northamptonshire in 1914. During the war, he served as surgeon sub-lieutenant in the Royal Navy Volunteer Reserve, assisting at the overcrowded military hospitals. In 1918 he entered Gonville and Caius College, Cambridge to study natural sciences and obtained his B.A. in 1921.

Gives Up Medical Career and Pursues Biochemistry

At this point in his life, Needham turned away from pursuing a career in medicine as a surgeon. Once he began as a postgraduate at the Cambridge Biochemical Laboratory and studied under Sir **Frederick Gowland Hopkins**, who essentially founded modern biochemistry in England and who would win a Nobel Prize in 1929, Needham realized that surgery did not offer the intellectual challenge he desired, and that the future lay, as one colleague put it, with atoms and molecules. In 1924 he married a fellow student, Dorothy Mary Moyle, whose work on the biochemistry of muscles led to her being elected a fellow of the Royal Society in 1948. The two became the first married couple (besides Queen Victoria and Prince Albert) to be so elected. After receiving his Ph.D., Needham joined the staff of Caius College, which would remain his academic home for the rest of his life. There he would establish himself as a chemical embryologist of distinction, eventually publishing a three-volume work, *Chemical Embryology*, that offered the untraditional thesis that embryonic development is controlled chemically. Had Needham continued his work in biochemistry, he no doubt would have continued to pursue his correct idea that only structural chemistry could fully explain the complex changes that take place during the development of an organism.

Although always generally interested in the history of science, Needham found himself drawn more to that field in 1937 when he met three young Chinese biochemistry students who had come to Cambridge for study. He became especially close to one of these students, Lu Gwei-Djen, whose father was a pharmacist in China and who herself was interested in traditional Chinese science. She was to become the dominant influence in Needham's life and proved to be the catalyst in his deciding to change from being a research scientist and become a historian of science in China. Drawn suddenly to all things Chinese, Needham learned the Chinese language as a labor of love and began a life-long collaboration with Lu Gwei-Djen who became his wife in 1989, two years after his first wife, Dorothy, died.

Travels to China and Lays Foundation for Life's Work

As Needham began to educate himself about the development of Chinese science, he found himself puzzled by what scholars later came to describe as "the Needham question." The question he posed was why modern science never developed in China the way it did in the West. As Needham learned the Chinese language, he found that although China had produced such breakthroughs as gunpowder, printing, and the magnetic compass centuries before the West, the scientific and industrial revolutions had occurred in the West and not in China. Attempting to find the answer to this question became the guiding theme of his life.

By 1942 the world was once again engulfed in a global conflict, and when England decided to send a scientific mission to China, it chose Needham as its head. As a British scientist who spoke Chinese and understood its history and culture, he was by far the most qualified. For the next six years, he traveled throughout China, immersing himself in Chinese life and learning more and more about China's approach to science and technology. In 1946, after the war, Needham went to Paris to direct the department of natural sciences at the newly established United Nations Educational, Scientific and Cultural Organization. It is Needham who is often credited with literally putting the "S" in UNESCO.

Begins Pioneering Work of Synthesis on Chinese Science

By the early 1950s, Needham finally was able to begin the work he and his close colleague, Lu Gwei-Djen, had originally conceived around 1939. When he first began to explore the issue of why modern science originated only in Europe and not in China, Needham thought he would probably produce a single small volume. However, as his work began to expand to a planned seven volumes and each volume itself was then projected as having multiple parts, the work grew so extensive that he and dozens of associates worked on it for the next five decades. The first volume of *Science and Civilisation in China* appeared in 1954, and by the time of Needham's death in 1995, 17 large volumes had been published. Twenty-five total volumes are planned, and the work is being continued by the Needham Research Institute at Cambridge.

Recognized as the Greatest Sinologist of the Twentieth Century

By spending nearly a lifetime writing and editing his monumental history of scientific development in China, Needham became almost universally acclaimed as the foremost Western interpreter of China. The factual information alone contained in his monumental work guarantee its lasting value. Still, Needham has had his critics who argue that he emphasizes only the positive aspects of Chinese culture, while others say he tries too hard to put science in a socioeconomic context.

Indeed, Needham was from his earliest adult years a socialist who, in a provocative and controversial manner, tried to blend his science, socialism, and religion. Contradiction and paradox were often found in his life and work, as he proved to have a mind that was open to all forms of cultural experience. In the 1920s, Needham and his wife, Dorothy, considered each other's extramarital affairs unobjectionable and to be entirely consistent with their radical politics. Needham also held deep religious feelings, and while a firm Christian, he also described himself to be an "honorary Taoist." He also called himself a Marxist, humanist, and scientist. In a 1992 interview in the *Scientific American*, Needham offered a partial answer to the question that drove his life's work, saying that the bureaucratic nature of Chinese society was partly responsible for inhibiting modern science, however he also referred to the second part of his conclusion which he said did not please him. "I think the answer is going to be that modern science arose with capitalism, and I don't like that, because I have been a socialist all of my life." When Joseph Needham died on March 24, 1995 at the age of 94, his pioneering work of scientific synthesis was immediately compared to that of Gibbons and Toynbee.

SELECTED WRITINGS BY NEEDHAM:

Books

Chemical Embryology. 3 vols. Cambridge, England: The University Press, 1931.
Order and Life. Cambridge, England: The University Press, 1935.
Science and Civilisation in China. Cambridge, England: The University Press, 1954-1994.

FURTHER READING:

Books

Goldsmith, Maurice. *Joseph Needham: 20th-Century Renaissance Man.* Paris: UNESCO Publishing, 1995.
Porter, Roy, ed. *The Biographical Dictionary of Scientists.* New York: Oxford University Press, 1994, pp. 507-508.

Periodicals

Holloway, Marguerite. "Joseph Needham: The Builder of Bridges." *Scientific American* (May 1992): 56-57.
Lyall, Sarah. "Joseph Needham, China Scholar From Britain, Dies at 94." *The New York Times* (March 27, 1994): B, 10.

—*Sketch by Leonard C. Bruno*

Evelyn Nelson
1943–1987
Canadian algebraist

Though Evelyn Nelson's mathematical career was cut short by cancer, she published about 40 papers on her main research topics, algebra, and theoretical computer science. She was specifically concerned with equational compactness, model theory, and formal language theory. A generous teacher and researcher, Nelson spent her career at McMaster University.

Nelson was born Evelyn Merle Roden in Hamilton, Ontario, Canada, the daughter of Russian immigrants. A gifted student, Nelson attended Westdale High School in Hamilton. With her parents' constant encouragement, she began her undergraduate education at the University of Toronto in the Honours course of Mathematics–Physics–Chemistry. Two years later, she transferred to the Honours Mathematics program at McMaster University in Hamilton. Soon after her transfer she married Mort Nelson, and they had two daughters together. They later divorced.

Nelson began publishing her research quite early, beginning with her master's thesis. It was published in 1967 as "A finiteness criterion for partially ordered semigroups and its application to Universal Algebra," in *Canadian Journal of Mathematics.* She completed her university education at McMaster, earning her Ph.D in 1970 with a thesis titled "The lattice of equational classes of commutative semigroups." It was also published, though in a modified form, in the *Canadian Journal of Mathematics.*

Nelson wrote over 40 papers, primarily in the general area of universal algebra. The topic of her thesis, the lattice of equational classes of semigroups, continued to be explored in her first five papers. Her other papers ranged from various aspects of equations compactness to partially ordered universal algebra subject to conditions originating in theoretical computer science.

Nelson also taught mathematics at her alma mater, McMaster, throughout her career. She first lectured as a postdoctoral fellow (1970–73), then as a research associate (1973–78). She was finally promoted to the tenure track level as an associate professor in 1978 and became a full professor in 1983. Nelson also served as chair of the Computer Science Unit from 1982 to 1984, but could not continue in the position when Computer Science became a full–fledged department because of her increasing illness.

Nelson served the mathematical community and McMaster University in other ways. She edited the prestigious journal *Algebra Universalis,* and refereed articles and reviewed other scholar's work for several other journals. She also held many memberships in academic societies, among them the American Mathematical Society and the Canadian Mathematical Society. She also served on some committees for the latter. Nelson was active in the McMaster community outside of the mathematics department as well.

In 1987, Nelson died of cancer after battling the disease for many years.

SELECTED WRITINGS BY NELSON:

"Finiteness of semigroups of operators in Universal Algebra." *Canadian Journal of Mathematics* 19 (1967): 764–68.
"The lattice of equational classes of commutative semigroups." *Canadian Journal of Mathematics* 19 (1971): 875–95.

FURTHER READING:

Adamek, Jiri. "A Farewell to Evelyn Nelson." *Cahiers de topologie et géométrie différentielle catégoriques* (1988): 171–74.
Banaschewski, B. "Evelyn M. Nelson: An Appreciation." *Algebra Univeralis* 26 (1989): 259–64.
"Evelyn Nelson." *Biographies of Women Mathematicians.* June 1997. http://www.scottlan.edu/lriddle/women/chronol.htm (July 22, 1997).

—*Sketch by Annette Petruso*

Hanna Neumann

Hanna Neumann
1914–1971
German algebraist

Hanna Neumann was a well–traveled mathematician who instilled a humble sense of dignity to the mathematics programs that she headed. She fled Nazi Germany to England, where she obtained a doctorate in mathematics and went on to solve many problems, including the finite basis problem for varieties generated by a finite group.

Born in Berlin on February 12, 1914, Neumann was the youngest of three children of Hermann and Katharina von Caemmerer. Her father was a historian who was killed in World War I, leaving only a war pension to support the family. To earn extra money, Neumann coached younger children in academics and evolved into an organized and studious pupil as a result. She entered the University of Berlin in 1932 and became inspired by her mathematics professor, Ludwig Bieberbach. He influenced her studies toward geometry, but it would be professors Erhard Schmidt and Issai Schur that would introduce her to analysis and algebra. Her future husband, Bernhard H. Neumann, was also a mathematics student at the university. They became secretly engaged in 1934, but due to the rise of Nazism in Germany, Bernhard (who was Jewish) moved to England, and their plans were put on hold. Neumann remained in Germany and lost her job at the Mathematical Institute as a result of her activities to protect other Jewish lecturers. Neumann

was advised that because of her political stance, she should avoid the oral exam on "political knowledge," which was required for a doctorate, and switch to the *Staatsexamen* final. This exam was a written essay, and she chose as her topic the epistemological basis of numbers in Plato's later dialogues. She graduated with distinctions in mathematics and physics.

Teaches in England

To escape the Nazis, Neumann moved to England and began working in Bristol. Her natural talent for learning new languages benefitted her career by being able to read journals and books in a number of different languages. She experimented with finite plane geometries, wrote several papers, and presented them at lecture courses. Neumann also contributed an explanation of the two types of quadrangles found in finite planes: those whose diagonal points are collinear, and those that are not (the Fano configuration).

In 1938, Neumann moved to Cardiff, England, and married Bernhard in secret to protect his parents, who were still living in Germany, from any reprisals. In 1939, their first child, Irene, was born. The family was soon uprooted because of their classification as "least restricted" aliens, whom are barred from living along the coast. Moving to Oxford, Neumann resumed her doctoral studies while pregnant with her second child, Peter. The acute housing shortage grew as European refugees swamped England, forcing Neumann and her children to move into a rented caravan in 1942. It would be here, by candlelight, that she would write her doctoral thesis, submitting it in 1943. Her third child, Barbara, was born shortly after, and when the war ended the entire family were able to move back to Cardiff. Bernhard was decommissioned from the army and returned to his job at the University College in Hull, where Neumann began her teaching career as a temporary assistant lecturer of applied mathematics. Their fourth and fifth children, Walter and Daniel, were born in 1946 and 1951, respectively. She continued to work at Hull for the next 12 years, changing the curriculum toward the more pure mathematics that she herself had been trained in.

In 1955, Neumann received a D.Sc. from Oxford based on her research and papers, two of which were published in the *American Journal of Mathematics*. A highly motivated individual, she chose to work as the secretary of a local United Nations Association in her spare time. Her husband had moved to Manchester to lecture in 1948. As she continued to search for a job that would bring her and her husband closer together, the faculty of Technology of the University of Manchester finally added an honors program that would enable her wish to come true.

Breaks New Ground

Neumann was hired as senior lecturer at the University of Manchester in 1958 and set about making very abstract ideas more accessible for her students. She worked with a model building group, lectured on prime numbers and the dissection of rectangles into incongruent squares, and advised several graduate students. Neumann went beyond the confines of a teacher/student relationship and regularly invited staff and students over to her home for coffee and discussions. She mentored many individuals who would themselves go on to become successful mathematicians, including John Bowers, Jim Wiegold, and Chris Houghton.

In the following summer, Neumann toured the universities in Hungary, lecturing on her research on groups and analysis. She also attended the 12th British Mathematical Colloquium, held in 1960, and was asked to speak about wreath products (a group construction). A group theory, such as the wreath products, consists of a set of elements subject to one binary operation and meeting these three requirements: (1) It is a closed system; (2) It obeys the associative law; (3) There is an identity element, e, such that e Θ x = x for any element x in the group; (Θ is the binary operation).

Upon her return to England, Neumann began preparing for a joint study leave with her husband to the Courant Institute of Mathematical Sciences in New York. Her three sons accompanied them and the oldest, Peter, began to study under Gilbert Baumslag,

one of the professors at Courant. During the course of the year, Peter and his parents solved the problem of the structure of the semigroup of varieties of groups, demonstrating that it is free. Neumann also presented a number of lectures and taught a graduate course on varieties of groups. During this time, Bernhard Neumann was invited to organize a research department of mathematics at the Australian National University and Hanna was offered a post as a reader.

The Next Frontier

Neumann began her new job in Australia in 1964. She overhauled the department and trained its teachers on subject matter covered in the new syllabuses. The material reflected the changes in mathematics worldwide, including more emphasis on pure mathematics and take–home assignments that promoted the use of ideas and theorems firsthand. Due to the difficulty of the subject matter, Bernhard's research students helped part–time with tutoring.

A conference on the theory of groups was organized by Neumann in 1965. The next year, she finished a monograph about group varieties. With the royalties, she was finally able to buy a good camera and revive her hobby of photography, collecting shots of flowers and trees. She also enjoyed extensive bike rides, later taking to four wheel drives with her husband in the outback.

In January of 1966, the Australian Association of Mathematics Teachers was formed and Neumann was elected to the position of vice–president. She took on the responsibility of bringing together math teachers representing all areas of Australia. In 1967, she became president of the Canberra Mathematical Association and helped prepare pamphlets for teachers; her most famous one was on probability. During a sabbatical leave in 1969, Neumann wrote letters to publicize the inadequacy of Australian mathematics programs compared to the rest of the world and the need for reorganization of the content in many courses. She also visited the United States on a National Science Foundation Senior Foreign Scientist Fellowship. During her stay at Vanderbilt University in Nashville, Tennessee, Neumann and Ian Dey solved the problem on the free product of finitely many finitely–generated Hopf groups.

Neumann's return to Australia was short-lived, for she accepted a lecture tour of Canada in 1971, speaking at the universities of British Columbia, Calgary, Alberta, Saskatchewan, and Manitoba. All of this travel and intense lecturing exhausted her, and she fell ill on November 12, checking into a hospital only to lapse immediately into a coma. Neumann did not regain consciousness and died two days later at age 57. After her death, a memorial fund was created from supporters all over the world to further Neumann's courageous and inspiring teaching.

FURTHER READING:

Newman, M. F. "Hanna Neumann," in *Women of Mathematics: A Biobibliographic Sourcebook.* Edited by Louise S. Grinstein and Paul J. Campbell. Westport, CT: Greenwood Press, 1987, pp. 156–160.

Newman, M.F. and G. E. Wall. "Hanna Neumann." *Journal of the Australian Mathematical Society* 17 (1974): 1–28.

Records of the Australian Academy of Science 3, no. 2. (1975).

Other

"Hanna Neumann." *Biographies of Women Mathematicians.* June 1997. http:www.scottlan.edu/lriddle/women/chronol.htm (July 22, 1997).

—*Sketch by Nicole Beatty*

Seth Barnes Nicholson

Seth Barnes Nicholson
1891–1963

American astronomer

Nicholson is best known for his discovery of four satellites of Jupiter, an accomplishment equaled in number only by Galileo. He also gained prominence for his documentation of sunspot cycles and for his estimations of planetary and lunar temperatures.

Seth Barnes Nicholson was born on November 12, 1891, in Springfield, Illinois, to William Franklin and Martha (Ames) Nicholson. His father, who had a master's degree in geology from Cornell University, was an elementary school teacher and principal. He worked first in Springfield, then when his son was seven years old, moved the family to a farm near Toulon, Illinois, for health reasons. Six years later he returned to teaching, eventually becoming principal of Toulon Academy, a high school in the small farming community. Nicholson had one older sister, Neva, who became a missionary in India, and two younger sisters, Carrie and Helen, who became schoolteachers in California. Although Nicholson grew up in a rural environment, he possessed a great interest in science, something his father instilled in him early in life. He later recalled that his father "was interested in science of all kinds and from him I learned the names of the stars, flowers, birds, and rocks. . . .Electricity was my favorite hobby and my father showed me how to make toy motors, telegraph instruments, and induction coils."

Discovers a Love of Astronomy

In 1908 Nicholson entered Drake University in Des Moines, Iowa, having no special interest in astronomy. At Drake however, he came under the influence of D. W. Morehouse, a professor of astronomy who had discovered a comet two years earlier. When Halley's Comet appeared in 1910, Nicholson took what came to be considered some of the classic photos of that famous comet using Drake's 8-in (20-cm) telescope. It was at Drake also that Nicholson met Alma Stotts, a classmate in astronomy whom he would marry after graduation in 1913, the same year they both enrolled in the graduate department of astronomy at the University of California at Berkeley. The eventually had three children, Margaret, Donald, and Jean.

It was at Berkeley that Nicholson would do his most significant astronomical work. As a graduate student there in 1914, it was Nicholson who was chosen to remain at Lick Observatory to study a recently discovered satellite of Jupiter that had an oddly retrograde rotation. Most other staff members were making a trip to Russia, one of the few locations where an eclipse of the sun would be visible. Nicholson took his orders seriously and, to be safe, decided to make an extra-long photographic exposure using what was then the largest telescope in the world. Because of this, he was able to barely detect yet another tiny satellite heretofore unknown. Thus at the age of 23, Nicholson had discovered the ninth known moon of Jupiter. This satellite later proved to be a twin of Jupiter's eighth moon, and it provided Nicholson with a sufficiently original topic for his doctoral dissertation, in which he offered calculations of its orbit and position. After receiving his Ph.D. in 1915, Nicholson joined the staff of the Mount Wilson Observatory, which was run by the Carnegie Institution and operated primarily as a solar observatory. Ironically for Nicholson, this position determined that the bulk of his career would be spent observing the sun instead of the planets.

Studies Lunar and Planetary Temperatures and Discovers Three More of Jupiter's Moons

Nicholson remained at Mount Wilson until his retirement in 1957, and because of his long-term and detailed observations of the surface features and spectrum of the sun, he was able to conduct highly delicate and sensitive measurement studies of its temperatures. He also issued regular reports on sunspot activity and studied their effects on Earth's atmosphere, eventually compiling a continuous solar history maintained over several sunspot cycles. His skill with temperature studies was eventually applied to the moon and the planets, and in 1927, he demonstrated that the moon's temperature dropped as much as 390°F (200°C) when it was in Earth's shadow. Applying such newly discovered facts to questions of the origin and composition of the planets, Nicholson then was able to make several insightful and correct theoretical observations.

Besides his important work on the temperatures of planetary bodies, Nicholson served as an observer on several solar eclipse expeditions in the 1920s and 1930s. In 1938, Nicholson returned to observing Jupiter when, in a replay of his graduate days, most of the Mount Wilson astronomers traveled to Stockholm to attend a meeting of the International Astronomical Union. This allowed him sufficient time to not only reconfirm his 1914 discovery but, surprisingly, to discover two more satellites orbiting Jupiter. These became the tenth and eleventh of Jupiter's moons. Finally, in 1951, while intending to observe the tenth moon, he discovered Jupiter's twelfth moon. All four of the satellites found by Nicholson were very faint and extremely difficult to locate, and when he was asked about the "thrill" of such discoveries, he replied that he experienced no such feelings, since confirmation of an actual discovery took such a long time.

Throughout his career and even after his retirement, Nicholson was an engaging and highly effective lecturer, and was deeply involved with all aspects of the astronomical community on the West Coast. From 1935 to 1960, he served as president of the Astronomical Society of the Pacific, as well as editor of its *Publications* from 1940 to 1955. A regular hiker of mountain trails, he also enjoyed tennis and ping-pong. After his retirement in 1957, he continued to work for the United States Weather Bureau. The recipient of several awards and honorary degrees, Nicholson died of cancer in Los Angeles, California, on June 2, 1963.

SELECTED WRITINGS BY NICHOLSON:

Periodicals

"Discovery, Observations and Orbit of the Ninth Satellite of Jupiter." *Lick Observatory Bulletin*, 1915, Volume 8, pp. 100-103, 147-49.
"The Ninth Satellite of Jupiter." *Proceedings of the National Academy of Sciences*, 1917, Volume 3, pp. 147-49.

FURTHER READING:

Books

Asimov, Isaac. *Asimov's Biographical Encyclopedia of Science and Technology*. Doubleday & Company, 1972, p. 639.
Gillispie, Charles Coulston, ed. *Dictionary of Scientific Biography*. Charles Scribner's Sons, 1981, p. 107.
Herget, Paul. "Seth Barnes Nicholson." *Biographical Memoirs. National Academy of Sciences*. Columbia University Press, 1971, pp.200-227.

Periodicals

"Seth Nicholson, Astronomer, Dies." *The New York Times* (July 3, 1963): 25.

—*Sketch by Leonard C. Bruno*

Alfred O. C. Nier
1911–1994
American physicist

Alfred O. C. Nier's research and discoveries were in the area of examining and defining isotopes through mass spectroscopy, particularly in the areas of uranium isotopes used in nuclear fission and the use of isotopes for geological dating methods. Nier invented the double-focusing mass spectrometer which was used in the *Viking* Spacecraft's visit to Mars, bringing back the first on-site data from that planet.

Alfred Otto Carl Nier was born on May 28, 1911, in St. Paul, Minnesota. His parents were August C.

and Anna J. Stoll Nier, both immigrants to the United States from Germany. Nier attended the University of Minnesota, from which he received a bachelor of science degree in 1931 and a master of science degree in 1933, both in the field of electrical engineering. He then changed his major to physics and earned his Ph.D. in that subject in 1936.

Begins Studies in Mass Spectroscopy

From his days as a graduate student, Nier's career reflected his ability to look at problems from two perspectives: that of the technologically-oriented engineer, and that of the research-oriented physicist. Much of his work involved the use of mass spectrometers to analyze the isotopic composition of elements.

The principle of mass spectroscopy was developed in the first decade of the twentieth century by **Francis W. Aston**. In a mass spectrometer, atoms are ionized and then accelerated through electrical and magnetic fields. Since these fields act with different force on ions of different mass, the spectrometer can be used to separate particles according to their masses. That separation is relatively clear-cut when mass differences are large, but becomes less clear as the masses of two particles become closer in size.

An important objective of Nier's work was to refine the mass spectrometric process so that it can distinguish smaller and smaller mass differences. One such refinement is the double-focusing mass spectrometer. In Nier's version of the double-focusing mass spectrometer, a beam of ions is accelerated first through an electrical field at an angle of ninety degrees, and then through a magnetic field at an angle of sixty degrees. Nier found that this arrangement could be used to achieve a high degree of separation of ions with similar masses at a cost much less than that of conventional mass spectrometers.

Mass Spectrometer Used to Discover Important Isotopes

Nier's first major discovery, the radioactive isotope potassium-40, was made while he was still a graduate student in Minnesota. That discovery was of considerable importance, since potassium is one of the most abundant elements in the Earth's crust, and potassium-40 is, therefore, an important source of background radiation. In 1934, Nier and Lyman T. Aldrich were able to show how the decay of potassium-40 to argon–40 can be used to measure the age of very old objects. That technique has since become extraordinarily useful in the dating of geological objects and materials.

From 1936 to 1938, Nier worked at Harvard University under a National Research Council fellowship. While there, he used the mass spectrometer to determine the isotopic composition (the percentage of each isotope of a given mass) for a number of elements. During this work he discovered a number of new isotopes whose abundance is so low that they had never been identified previously. These included sulfur-36, calcium-46, calcium-48, and osmium-186. He also carried out studies on the relative abundance of two isotopes of carbon, carbon-12 and carbon-13, and showed that the ratio of the two is a function of the source from which the carbon is taken. This research has been put to use in recent attempts to estimate the temperature of past geological years.

Nier's most important research was his study of the isotopes of uranium. His earliest research was aimed at determining the relationship between the radioactive isotopes of this element and the isotopes of lead, some of which are formed during the decay of uranium. This work eventually provided scientists with a second method for estimating the age of rocks, a method based on the ratio of radiogenic lead (from uranium) to non-radiogenic lead.

The early uranium studies led to even more significant research during World War II. In 1938, **Otto Hahn** and **Fritz Strassmann** discovered that fission occurs when uranium is bombarded by neutrons. Physicists immediately understood the enormous potential of this discovery as a source of energy for both peaceful applications and, more relevant at the time, for the development of weapons. One practical problem of the development of nuclear fission as a source of energy was the uncertainty as to which isotope of uranium actually undergoes fission. Nier answered this question in 1940, working with J. R. Dunning, E. T. Booth, and A. V. Grosse at Columbia University, as they were able to show that it is the relatively uncommon uranium-235, rather than the more common uranium-238, that undergoes fission. During and after the war, Nier was active in the development of methods for separating these two isotopes from each other.

In 1938, at the conclusion of this postdoctoral work at Harvard, Nier returned to Minnesota. He remained there for the rest of his academic career as assistant professor, from 1938 to 1940, associate professor from 1940 to 1944, professor, from 1944 to 1956, and Regents' Professor of Physics, from 1956 until his retirement in the early 1980s. Continuing his scientific work after his retirement, Nier supervised a study of cosmic dust in the 1990s. He died on May 16, 1994 in Minneapolis.

Nier's research using mass spectographs to measure isotopes and other atomic masses led to his invention of the first double-focusing mass spectrometer, miniature versions of which were later used on satellites observing the lower thermosphere. Nier was appointed by the National Aeronautics and Space Administration to lead the Entry Science team to study the composition and structure of the Martian atmosphere during the *Viking* spacecraft's descent to the planet's surface. On this mission, Nier's mass spectrometer provided the first on-site information known about the make-up of the atmosphere of Mars.

Nier was married twice, first to Ruth E. Andersen in 1937, and then to Ardish L. Hovland in 1969. He had one son and one daughter. His work was recognized by the American Geological Society's Arthur L. Day Medal (1956), the Goldschmidt Medal of the Geochemical Society (1984), the U.S. Atomic Energy Commission's Field and Franklin Award (1985), and the Thomson Medal of the International Mass Spectrometry Conference (1985).

FURTHER READING:

Books

McGraw-Hill Modern Scientists and Engineers. Vol. 2. New York: McGraw-Hill, 1980, pp. 361-63.

Periodicals

"Alfred Nier; Helped Build Atom Bomb" (obituary). *Los Angeles Times* (19 May 1994): A20.
"Alfred O. C. Nier, 82, Physicist Who Helped Develop Atomic Bomb" (obituary). *Boston Globe* (18 May 1994): 33.
Hilchey, Tim. "Alfred Nier, 82; Physicist Helped Foster A-Bomb" (obituary). *New York Times* (18 May 1994): B8.
Johnson, Walter H., Jr., and Konrad Mauersberger. "Alfred Nier" (obituary). *Physics Today* 48 (January 1995): 68-69.

—*Sketch by David E. Newton*

Max Noether
1844–1921
German algebraist

Today, Max Noether's career as a mathematician is perhaps overshadowed by his more famous daughter, **Emmy Noether**. Still, at the height of his career, Noether led the German school of algebraic and geometric mathematics from the University of Erlangen. Noether's primary interests were algebra and algebraic geometry, and he is responsible for the development of algebraic function theory. His work on curves and related theorems inspired many Italian geometrists.

Max Noether

Noether was born in Mannheim, Germany, on September 24, 1844, the son of Hermann (an iron wholesaler) and Amalia (nee Würzburger) Noether. With his four siblings, Noether began his education in Mannheim. He contracted polio at age 14, and could not use his legs for two years. Because of this illness, Noether was handicapped for life. He continued his education at home, following the Gymnasium curriculum.

In 1865, Noether began his university studies in astronomy at the Mannheim Observatory, although he did not stay there long. He entered the University of Heidelberg in 1865, studying mathematics. He also studied at the University of Gissen and the University of Göttingen, before earning his doctorate (without a dissertation) from Heidelberg in 1868. Noether was the first member of his family to earn this degree. Noether began teaching at Heidelberg as a (privatdozent) lecturer from 1870 to 1874. In 1874, Noether became an associate professor at the University of Erlangen.

The mathematical research Noether did in this early part of his career, from approximately 1869 to 1879, is arguably his most important. His 1869 paper, "Über Flächen, welche Scharen rationaler Kurven besitzen" ("Concerning Surfaces which have families of Rational Curves"), began this work, containing what came to be known as Noether's fundamental theorem. In 1871, he published a proof that improved on work done by one of his inspirations as a mathematician, Antonio Cremona. In it, Noether proved the result that a plane Cremona transformation can be built up from a sequence of quadratic and linear transformations. Two years later, Noether published another theorem, perhaps his most famous result, concerning two algebraic curves and their intersection under certain so–called Noether conditions. The conditions concern the complexity of contact of curves and their common multiple points. This result could also be extended to surfaces and hypersurfaces, though Noether himself did not prove it.

After 1880, Noether's private life became more domesticated, perhaps accounting for the changes in Noether's research. Noether married Ida Amalia Kaufmann in 1880. Together they had four children, three of whom became scientists. His eldest daughter, Amalie Emmy Noether, born in 1882 and familiarly called Emmy, became a mathematician whose work built on and surpassed her father's. She had three younger brothers: Alfred, born in 1883, who became a chemist; Fritz, born in 1884, also a mathematician; and Gustav, born in 1889.

Still, Noether continued to do his original research and teaching at Erlangen, where he served as an associate professor until 1888. That year he became a full professor. From about 1879 onward, his mathematical work focused on refining his earlier publications. This work also inspired and opened up fields for other mathematicians, especially in Italy.

Some of Noether's later publications that are widely known include the 1882 publication on algebraic curves, *Zur Grundlegung der Theorie der Algebraischen Ramkurven*. In 1894 he coauthored *Bericht über der Entwicklung der algeraischen Funktionen*, with Alexander von Brill. This treatise concerned algebraic functions.

Noether was also involved with the journal *Mathematische Annalen*. In addition to publishing in it almost continuously from 1870–1921, he served as its director for a time. Noether also wrote many of the biographic obituaries for this journal, and other publications. These pieces also gained recognition and were known for their thoroughness and insight.

Noether's important mathematical contributions did not go unnoticed by his peers. In 1903, he became a member of the French Académie Royale des Sciences. He was also a member or honorary member of many other academic societies, among them the London Mathematical Society, the Academy of Berlin, and the Royale Accademia dei Lincei.

The last decade of his life saw Noether lose his wife and retire from teaching. When Ida Noether died 1915, Noether's daughter Emmy started to fill in for her father's lectures as necessary. Four years later, in 1919, he retired from teaching, and was given an emeritus professorship.

Noether died in Erlangen on December 13, 1921. In his obituary published in the *Proceedings of the London Mathematical Society*, the author describes the three main ways Noether contributed to his field: "By the new and fruitful ideas contained in his original researches, by the patient investigation and encouragement he gave to other writers, and by his acutely critical and detailed historical work."

SELECTED WRITINGS BY NOETHER:

"Über Flächen, welche Scharen rationaler Kurven besitzen" ("Concerning Surfaces Which Have Families of Rational Curves"), 1869.
Zur Grundelgung der Theorie der Algebraischen Ramkurven, 1882.
(With Alexander von Brill) *Bericht über der Entwicklung der algeraischen Funkionen*, 1894.

FURTHER READING:

Kimberling, Clark. "Emmy Noether and Her Influence," in *Emmy Noether: A Tribute to Her Life and Work*. Edited by James W. Brewer and Martha K. Smith. New York: Marcel Dekker, Inc., 1981, pp. 3–8, 20.
Kramer, Edna E. "Max Noether," in *Dictionary of Scientific Biography*. Volume X. Edited by Charles Coulston Gillispie. New York: Charles Scribner's Sons, 1970, pp. 137–39.
"Max Noether." *Proceedings of the London Mathematical Society*. Volume 21, 2nd Series (1921): xxxvii–xlii.

—*Sketch by Annette Petruso*

Tetsuo Nozoe
1902–
Japanese organic chemist

Tetsuo Nozoe is an organic chemist whose work on the synthesis and structure of tropolones helped found a new field in chemistry, the study of novel aromatic compounds.

Tetsuo Nozoe was born on May 16, 1902, in Sendai, Japan, the middle child of eleven children born to Juichi and Toyoko Nozoe. His father practiced law in Sendai and served as a member of the House of Representatives. During Nozoe's childhood he suffered from a variety of illnesses, including typhoid fever, beriberi, and pneumonia. Because his primary schooling was frequently interrupted by poor health, his mother employed a private tutor for him. Nozoe's interest in chemistry began to develop when he entered middle school. Around this time he constructed a makeshift chemistry laboratory in a garden storage shed, assembling various pieces of glassware, chemicals, and an alcohol lamp from a local pharmacy. His parents, who wanted him to pursue a medical career, were fearful he would set fires or injure himself in his shed, though no such mishaps occurred.

In 1923 Nozoe entered Tohoku Imperial University in Sendai, where he began pre-medical studies. Soon he convinced his family he was more suited to the study of chemistry. At Tohoku he came under the tutelage of Riko Majima, one of the leading Japanese organic chemists of his day. Nozoe's thesis work on the synthesis of the thyroid hormone, thyroxine, became the subject of his first scientific publication, which appeared in 1927 in the *Journal of the Chemical Society of Japan*. Shortly after his graduation in 1926, the Government Monopoly Bureau Research Laboratories in Formosa (now Taiwan) offered him a position as an industrial organic chemist. His journey from Sendai to Formosa took five days by train and ship.

Begins Study of Organic Compounds

By the summer of 1926, Nozoe had settled in the city of Taipei and begun research on the *taiwanhinoki,* a local tree that was economically important to the region. His work focused on identifying the organic components of the essential oils derived from the tree's leaves. In 1929 he received an appointment as an assistant professor of chemistry at the newly created Taihoku Imperial University in Taipei. His research shifted to the chemistry of another economically important plant, *Barringtonia asiatica*, a type of mangrove. In the seeds of this plant he isolated saponins, a class of chemicals that are used as soap substitutes and fish poisons. Saponins and the related sapogenins would become one of the primary subjects of research for Nozoe until the early 1940s. In 1936, he submitted a summary of his early work on the structure of organic natural products to Majima, who had recently been appointed Dean of the Faculty of Science at the newly established Osaka University. As a result of this summary, Nozoe became the first recipient of the D.Sc. degree awarded by the university.

In 1936 Nozoe also began a new line of research, studying the components of wool wax. He was intrigued by the fact that wool wax, an animal product, contained triterpenoids, which are usually found in plants. His work on wool wax helped elucidate the physical properties of its commercially valuable components. Another research project that Nozoe pursued simultaneously was the investigation

of hinokitin and hinokitiol, essential oils that he derived from several of the island's coniferous trees. In 1938 it was discovered that hinokitiol had an antibacterial effect against the tubercle bacillus.

Discovery of Tropolones

War activities from 1942 to 1945 brought a temporary end to Nozoe's organic chemistry research. In 1946 he resumed his studies of hinokitiol and experimentally demonstrated that it was a new type of aromatic compound, different from traditional benzene type aromatics, which was later named "troplone." Since Formosa had been re-occupied by the Chinese, Taihoku Imperial University was now known as National Taiwan University. Most of the Japanese faculty members left their posts and returned to Japan, but because of his importance to the chemistry department, Nozoe was not granted permission to leave until the spring of 1948.

In the fall of 1948 he took a post in the Chemistry Department of Tohoku Imperial University, back in Sendai. Continuing his investigation of the non-benzenoid aromatic hinokitiol, he resolved the structure and aromatic properties of its various derivatives. He also began work on the synthesis of tropolones from hinokitiol. His study of tropolones and other troponoids was to become his most important contribution to the field of organic chemistry. Many of the tropolones have fungicidal properties, and colchicine, a tropolone derivative, is a useful both as a medicine and as an agent for biomedical research. Nozoe retired from Tohoku University in 1966, but continued for several decades to conduct research on non-benzenoid aromatics.

Nozoe received many awards throughout his career. He received the Majima Award for Organic Chemistry in 1944, the Asahi Cultural Award in 1952, the Japan Academy Award in 1953, the Order of Cultural Merit Medal in 1958, and the 1980 Wilhelm August von Hofman Memorial Medal. He became a foreign member of the Royal Sweden Academy of Sciences in 1972 and was also made an honorary member of the Swiss Chemical Society.

Shortly after taking his first post in Formosa, Nozoe married Kyoko Horiuchi. Together they had four children, one son, Shigeo, and three daughters, Takako, Yoko, and Yuriko. Nozoe pursued a variety of hobbies during his career, including stamp collecting and autograph collecting. His personal autograph books include signatures, cartoons, and written commentary from many of the leading chemists of the twentieth century. He is also an accomplished photographer. During his early years in Formosa, his forays into the countryside to collect plant samples brought him in contact with the indigenous tribes of the island, and Nozoe's photographs of tribal dance and dress remain important documents of the region's anthropological history.

SELECTED WRITINGS BY NOZOE:

Books

Nozoe, Tetsuo. *Seventy Years in Organic Chemistry.* American Chemical Society, 1991.

—*Sketch by Leslie Reinherz*

Christiane Nüsslein-Volhard
1942–

German genetic researcher

Christiane Nüsslein-Volhard, winner of the 1995 Nobel Prize in Physiology or Medicine, is the first German woman to win in this category. She is most noted for her contribution to research in identifying genes that control the early stages of embryonic development in fruit flies. Nüsslein-Volhard and two other scientists, **Edward B. Lewis** and **Eric F. Wieschaus**, paved the way for the study of the human counterparts to genes that influence human development, including ones responsible for birth defects.

Nüsslein-Volhard was born on October 20, 1942, in Magdeburg, Germany. The daughter of Rolf Volhard, an architect, and Brigitte (Hass) Volhard, a musician and painter, Christiane decided at a young age that she wanted to be a scientist. She stood out in a family of artists and architects—two of her four siblings are architects, and all of the children are amateur painters and musicians (Nüsslein-Volhard herself plays the flute and sings). If her family had any doubts about her chosen career, the earliness of her decision helped them to grow accustomed to the idea. Teachers also adjusted to her determination, and she moved easily through school.

Embarks on Scientific Career

Even though few women of her generation chose scientific careers, Nüsslein-Volhard found that being female in a male-dominated field presented little in the way of an obstacle to her studies. She received degrees in biology, physics, and chemistry from Johann-Wolfgang-Goethe-University in 1964 and a diploma in biochemistry from Eberhard-Karls University in 1968. In 1973 she earned a Ph.D. in biology and genetics from the University of Tübingen. Nüsslein-Volhard was married for a short time as a young woman and never had any children. She

decided to keep her husband's last name because it was already associated with her developing scientific career.

In the late 1970s Nüsslein-Volhard finished postdoctoral fellowships in Basel, Switzerland, and Freiburg, Germany, and accepted her first independent research position at the European Molecular Biology Laboratory (EMBL) in Heidelberg, Germany. She was joined there by Eric F. Wieschaus who was also finishing his training. Because of their common interest in *Drosophila*, or fruit flies, Nüsslein-Volhard and Wieschaus decided to work together to find out how a newly fertilized fruit fly egg develops into a fully segmented embryo.

Nüsslein-Volhard and Wieschaus chose the fruit fly because of its incredibly fast embryonic development. They began to pursue a strategy for isolating genes responsible for the embryos' initial growth. This was a bold decision by two scientists just beginning their scientific careers. No one had done anything like this before, and it wasn't certain whether they would be able to actually isolate specific genes.

Unique Strategy Creates Useful Mutants

Their experiments involved feeding male fruit flies sugar water laced with deoxyribonucleic acid (DNA)-damaging chemicals. When the male fruit flies mated with females, the females often produced dead or mutated embryos. Nüsslein-Volhard and Wieschaus studied these embryos for over a year under a microscope which had two viewers, allowing them to examine an embryo at the same time. They were able to identify specific genes that basically told cells what they were going to be—part of the head or the tail, for example. Some of these genes, when mutated, resulted in damage to the formation of the embryo's body plan. Nüsslein-Volhard became known for her ability to spot the slightest deviation from the norm and know whether it was significant to the way the embryo would develop.

Nüsslein-Volhard and Wieschaus published the results of their research in the English scientific journal *Nature* in 1980. They received a great deal of attention because their studies showed that there were a limited number of genes that control development and that they could be identified. This was significant because similar genes existed in higher organisms and humans and, importantly, these genes performed similar functions during development. Nüsslein-Volhard and Wieschaus's breakthrough research could help other scientists find genes that could explain birth defects in humans. Their research could also help improve in-vitro fertilization and lead to an understanding of what causes miscarriages. With this important work recognized by the scientific community, Nüsslein-Volhard began lecturing at universities in Germany and the United States. She was the

Silliman Lecturer at Yale University and the Brooks Lecturer at Harvard.

Launches Controversial New Research

In 1991 she and Wieschaus received the Albert Lasker Medical Research Award, which is considered second only to the Nobel. During this time Nüsslein-Volhard had begun new research at the Max Planck Institute in Tübingen, Germany, similar to the work she did on the fruit flies. This time she wanted to understand the basic patterns of development of the zebra fish. She chose zebra fish as her subject because most of the developmental research on vertebrates in the past was on mice, frogs, or chickens, which have many technical difficulties, one of which was that one couldn't see the embryos developing. Zebra fish seemed like the perfect organism to study because they are small, they breed quickly, and the embryos develop outside of the mother's body. The most important consideration, however, was the fact that zebra fish embryos are transparent, which would allow Nüsslein-Volhard a clear view of development as it was happening.

Despite her prize-winning research on fruit flies, she received skeptical feedback on her zebra fish work. Other scientists claimed it was risky and foolish. When she submitted papers about her laboratory's work for publication, one reviewer even asked her why she was bothering. Nüsslein-Volhard was not one to be stopped by criticism or to rest on her laurels. Even though her reputation was built on her fruit fly research, her love of new challenges pushed her to take on this risky new project and set her sights to the future.

Unique Research Wins Nobel

Then on October 9, 1995, in the midst of criticism about her new research, Nüsslein-Volhard, Wieschaus, and Edward B. Lewis of the California Institute of Technology won the Nobel Prize in Physiology or Medicine for their work on genetic development in *Drosophila*. Lewis had been analyzing genetic mutations in fruit flies since the forties and had published his results independently from Nüsslein-Volhard and Wieschaus.

It has yet to be proven if zebra fish will actually provide any answers to the complex genetic questions Nüsslein-Volhard has raised. But her love of genetics compels her to continue. Her home country of Germany recognizes her as a national treasure, despite her controversial research. Nüsslein-Volhard herself dismisses public fear about gene research on embryos. "No one has in their grasp the genes that make humans wiser, more beautiful, or that make blue eyes," she said when she accepted the Nobel Prize. Her research, she says, has helped people "become wiser, understand biology better, understand how life functions."

SELECTED WRITINGS BY NÜSSLEIN-VOLHARD:

Periodicals

"Embryology Goes Fishing." *Nature,* May 22, 1986, pp. 380-1

"Determination of Anteroposterior Polarity in Drosophila." *Science,* December 18, 1987, pp. 1675-81

"From Egg to Organism: Studies on Embryonic Pattern Formation." *The Journal of the American Medical Association,* October 2, 1991, p. 1848

"Large-Scale Mutagenesis in the Zebrafish—In Search of Gene-Controlling Development in a Vertebrate." *Current Biology,* March 1, 1994, pp. 189-202

"Of Flies and Fishes." *Science,* October 28, 1994, p. 572

—Sketch by Pamela Proffitt

Gerard K. O'Neill

Gerard K. O'Neill
1927–1992
American physicist

As an experimental physicist, Gerard O'Neill invented and developed the technology of storage rings that became the basis of today's high-energy particle accelerators. Not content to be only a pioneer of physics, O'Neill went on to become a visionary teacher and educator who advocated large-scale human colonization of outer space, as well as an entrepreneur who founded several corporations devoted to developing new space-based technologies.

Gerard Kitchen O'Neill was born in New York City on February 6, 1927. The only child of Edward Gerard and Dorothy Lewis (Kitchen) O'Neill, he was raised in Connecticut and upstate New York. He attended the Newburgh Free Academy in Newburgh, New York, and edited the school newspaper. During this time, he also earned money broadcasting news for a local radio program. After graduating from high school in 1944, he joined the U. S. Navy on his birthday. There he was trained as a radar technician

and was sent to the Pacific theater just as the war ended. Following his discharge in 1946, he entered Swarthmore College in Pennsylvania to study physics and mathematics, graduating Phi Beta Kappa in 1950. During the war, O'Neill had realized the potentially destructive role physicists could play in society, and decided to use his knowledge of physics only to benefit human beings. Upon graduation, he received an Atomic Energy Commission fellowship and entered Cornell University in Ithaca, New York. He received his Ph.D. in physics in 1954 and accepted a faculty position at Princeton University the same year.

Pioneers High-Energy Physics with his Colliding-Beam Principle

During only his second year as an instructor in the Princeton physics department, O'Neill published a two-page letter in *Physical Review* titled "Storage-Ring Synchrotron: Device for High-Energy Physics Research." Discussing this important paper in a 1993 article, British physicist **Freeman Dyson** stated, "it laid down the path that high-energy physics has followed for the next 36 years. If you read the letter now, you can see that almost everything in it is right." However, in 1956 when his letter was written, O'Neill encountered a highly skeptical physics community. His special storage ring design for increasing the collision energies of atomic beams from particle accelerators was simply a theory that had not been proven. Finally obtaining financial support in 1959 from the Office of Naval Research and the Atomic Energy Commission, O'Neill and his colleagues built two particle storage rings at Stanford University that used his high-vacuum technique and successfully demonstrated his colliding-beam theory. Physicists around the world concurred immediately and soon hurried to build their own. O'Neill became a full professor at Princeton in 1965.

Embraces "Humanization" of Outer Space

In 1966, when the National Aeronautics and Space Administration (NASA) opened its astronaut program to civilian scientists, O'Neill immediately applied and, following months of training and testing, was selected as a finalist. Although NASA later discontinued this program, O'Neill used the experience to reform the teaching of physics at Princeton. Seeking to replace the same traditional problems that students of classical physics had always considered, he encouraged them to apply physics to something real and relevant like the *Apollo* moon missions that were taking place in 1969. After asking his class to consider his question, "Is the surface of the planet earth really the right place for an expanding technological civilization?" O'Neill found himself as intrigued and enthusiastic about the notion of a possible human habitat in space as were his students. This led him to a prolonged study of the technical issues of building human colonies in space, such as energy, land area, size and shape, atmosphere, gravitation, and sunlight. By 1974, O'Neill wrote an article, "The Colonization of Space," that led to his most significant book, *The High Frontier: Human Colonies in Space*, published in 1977.

This lively book expanded upon his thesis that a "breakout" from Earth was inevitable, and that this future colonization, or "humanization," of space would ultimately determine the continuance of intelligent life. The book proved to be both a popular and a critical success, winning the Phi Beta Kappa Science Book of the Year Award. It has since seen six English editions and been translated into six languages. As he continually reevaluated and revised his ideas, O'Neill shifted his emphasis for colonizing space from relieving population pressure to providing Earth with a limitless supply of clean, inexpensive energy. His plans included ambitious space manufacturing programs, and he argued that several potentially profitable space-based industries could exist.

Founds the Space Studies Institute

O'Neill realized that because of political influences and budgetary constraints, NASA could not be a reliable and steady supporter of the kind of basic research he felt needed to be done. Therefore, in 1977 he sought and obtained private support for a new, non-profit corporation called the Space Studies Institute. Located at Princeton University, the Space Studies Institute supports technical research on the science and engineering of living and working in space with grants made possible by members' contributions.

In addition to providing dependable funding, the Space Studies Institute was intended to usher in a new style of space technology development. Ever the individualist, O'Neill believed fervently that small, private groups were superior to large, governmental bureaucracies in developing the tools of exploring space. He felt strongly that the settlement of space offered such potential benefits to mankind that it was too important to be left in the hands of national governments. In 1983, he founded the Geostar Corporation which, based on O'Neill's own patent, developed the first private satellite navigational system to guide travel on earth. The company, however, went out of business in 1991, despite having developed a satellite-based navigational and position locating system.

O'Neill died on April 27, 1992, of leukemia. He also left behind three children, Janet Karen, Eleanor Edith, and Roger Alan, from his 1950 marriage to Sylvia Turlington. Divorced in 1966, he married Renate Steffen in 1973, with whom he founded the Space Studies Institute. O'Neill's son, Roger, became Chairman of the Institute's Board of Directors and is working to carry on his father's tradition. Before his death, O'Neill wrote in *Who's Who*: "To me the ideals of human freedom, of individual choice, and of concern for others have always been of the greatest importance. I hope that at the end of my life I can look back on work honestly done and on fair dealings with others."

In April 1997, a Pegasus rocket carried O'Neill's ashes into space along with those of 21 others, including *Star Trek* creator Gene Roddenberry, counter-culture guru Timothy Leary, and Harvard psychologist Krafft Ehricke. His remains should circle the earth for up to a decade before reentering the atmosphere and burning up harmlessly.

SELECTED WRITINGS BY O'NEILL:

Books

The High Frontier: Human Colonies in Space. New York: Morrow, 1977.
2081: A Hopeful View of the Human Future. New York: Simon and Schuster, 1981.
The Technology Edge: Opportunities for America in World Competition. New York: Simon and Schuster, 1983.

FURTHER READING:

Periodicals

Daniels, Lee A. "Gerard K. O'Neill, Professor, 69 (sic); Led Studies on Physics and Space." *The New York Times.* April 29, 1992, D: 24.
"Gerard K. O'Neill." *Current Biography* (1979): 290-293.
"Interview: Gerard K. O'Neill." *Omni* (July 1979): 77–79, 113-115.

—Sketch by Leonard C. Bruno

Severo Ochoa

Severo Ochoa
1905–1993
Spanish biochemist

Spanish-born biochemist Severo Ochoa spent his life engaged in research into the workings of the human body. In the 1950s, he was one of the first scientists to synthesize the newly discovered ribonucleic acid (RNA) in the laboratory. This feat marked the first time that scientists managed to combine molecules together in a chain outside a living organism, knowledge that would later prove to be an essential step in enabling scientists to create life in a test tube. For this work, Ochoa received the Nobel Prize in 1959. In addition to his laboratory work, Ochoa, who was trained as a physician in Spain, taught biochemistry and pharmacology to many generations of New York University medical students.

Severo Ochoa was born on September 24, 1905, in Luarca, a small town in the north of Spain. Named after his father, a lawyer, Ochoa was the youngest son in the family. He lived in this mountain town until the age of seven, when his parents decided to move to Málaga, Spain. The move gave young Severo access to a private school education that prepared him for entrance into Málaga College, which is comparable to an American high school. By this time, Ochoa had decided on a career in the sciences; the only question in his mind was in which field he would specialize.

Because Ochoa found mathematics at Málaga College very taxing, he decided against pursuing an engineering career. Instead, he chose biology. After Ochoa received his B.A. from Málaga in 1921, he spent a year taking the prerequisite courses for medical school—physics, chemistry, biology, and geology. In 1923 he matriculated at the University of Madrid's Medical School.

Acquires a Medical Education

At Madrid, Ochoa had dreams of studying under the Spanish neurohistologist Santiago Rámon y Cajal, but these were quickly dashed when he discovered that the 70-year-old histology professor retired from teaching, although he still ran a laboratory in Madrid. Ochoa hesitated in approaching Cajal even at the lab, however, because he thought the older man would be too busy to be bothered by an unimportant student. Nonetheless, by the end of his second year in medical school, Ochoa had confirmed his desire to do biological research and jumped at one of his professor's offers of a job in a nearby laboratory.

The Medical School itself housed no research facilities, but Ochoa's physiology teacher ran a small research laboratory under the aegis of the Council for Scientific Research a short distance away. Working with a classmate, Ochoa first mastered the relatively routine laboratory task of isolating creatinine—a white, crystalline compound—from urine. From there, he moved to the more demanding task of studying the function and metabolism of creatine, a nitrogenous substance, in muscle. The summer after his fourth year of medical school he spent in a Glasgow laboratory, continuing work on this problem. Ochoa received his medical degree in 1929.

In an attempt to further his scientific education, Ochoa applied for a postdoctoral fellowship under **Otto Meyerhof** at the Kaiser-Wilhelm Institute in a suburb of Berlin. Although the Council for Scientific Research had offered him a fellowship to pursue these studies, Ochoa turned down their offer of support because he could afford to pay his own way. He felt the money should be given to someone more needy to himself. Ochoa enjoyed his work under Meyerhof, remaining in Germany for a year.

On July 8, 1931, he married Carmen García Cobian, a daughter of a Spanish lawyer and businessman, and moved with his newlywed wife to England, where he had a fellowship from the University of Madrid to study at London's National Institute for Medical Research. In England, Ochoa met Sir **Henry Hallett Dale**, who a few years later won the 1936 Nobel in medicine for his discovery of the chemical transmission of nerve impulses. During his first year at the Institute, Ochoa studied the enzyme glyoxalase, and the following year he started working directly under Dale, investigating how the adrenal glads affected the chemistry of muscular contraction. In 1933, he returned to his alma mater, the University of Madrid, where he was appointed a lecturer in physiology and biochemistry.

Spanish Civil War Forces Him to Flee Native Country

Within two years, Ochoa accepted a new position. One of the heads of the Department of Medicine was planning to start an Institute for Medical Research with sections on biochemistry, physiology, microbiology, and experimental medicine. The institute was partially supported by the University of Madrid, which offered it space in one its new medical school buildings, and partially supported by wealthy patrons, who planned to provide a substantial budget for equipment, salaries, and supplies. The director of the new institute offered the young Ochoa the directorship of the section on physiology, which he accepted, and provided him with a staff of three. However, a few months after Ochoa began work, civil war broke out in Spain. In order to continue his work, Ochoa decided to leave the country in September 1936. He and his wife immigrated to Germany, hardly a stable country in late 1936.

When Ochoa arrived, he found that his mentor Meyerhof, who was Jewish, was under considerable political and personal pressure. The German scientist had not allowed this to interfere with his work, though Ochoa did find to his surprise that the type of research Meyerhof conducted had changed dramatically in the six years since he had seen him last. As he wrote of the laboratory in a retrospective piece for the *Annual Review of Biochemistry:* "When I left it in 1930 it was basically a physiology laboratory; one could see muscles twitching everywhere. In 1936 it was a biochemistry laboratory. Glycolysis and fermentation in muscle or yeast extracts or partial reactions of these processes catalyzed by purified enzymes, were the main subjects of study." Meyerhof's change in research emphasis influenced Ochoa's own work, even though he studied in the laboratory for less than a year before Meyerhof fled to France.

Before Meyerhof left, however, he ensured that his protege was not stranded, arranging for Ochoa to receive a six-month fellowship at the Marine Biological Laboratory in Plymouth, England. Although this fellowship lasted only half a year, Ochoa enjoyed his time there, not the least because his wife Carmen started working with him in the laboratory. Their collaboration later led to the publication of a joint paper in *Nature.* At the end of six months, though, Ochoa had to move on, and friends at the lab found him a post as a research assistant at Oxford University. Two years later, when England entered the war, Oxford's Biochemistry Department shifted all its efforts to war research in which Ochoa, an alien,

could not take part. So in 1940 the Ochoas picked up stakes again, this time to cross the Atlantic to work in the laboratory of **Carl Ferdinand Cori** and **Gerty T. Cori** in St. Louis. Part of the Washington University School of Medicine, the Cori lab was renowned for its cutting edge research on enzymes and work with intermediary metabolism of carbohydrates. This work involved studying the biochemical reactions in which carbohydrates produce energy for cellular operations. Ochoa worked there for a year before New York University persuaded him to move east to take a job as a research associate in medicine at the Bellevue Psychiatric Hospital, where he would for the first time have graduate and postdoctoral students working beneath him.

Appointed Chair of NYU's Pharmacology Department

In 1945, Ochoa was promoted to assistant professor of biochemistry at the medical school. Two years later when the pharmacology chair retired, Ochoa was offered the opportunity to succeed him and, lured by the promise of new laboratory space, he accepted. He remained chairperson for nine years, taking a sabbatical in 1949 to serve as a visiting professor at the University of California. His administrative work did not deter him from pursuing his research interests in biochemistry, however. In the early 1950s, he isolated one of the chemical compounds necessary for photosynthesis to occur, triphosphopyridine nucleotide, known as TPN. Ochoa continued his interest in intermediary metabolism, expanding the work of **Hans Adolf Krebs,** who posited the idea of a cycle through which food is metabolized into adenosine triphosphate, the molecule that provides energy to the cell. The Spanish scientist discovered that one molecule of glucose when burned with oxygen produced 36 ATP molecules. When the chairman of the biochemistry department resigned in 1954, Ochoa accepted this opportunity to return to the department full-time as chair and full professor.

Once more ensconced in biochemistry research, Ochoa turned his attentions to a new field: the rapidly growing area of deoxyribonucleic acid (DNA) research. Earlier in his career, enzymes had been the hot new molecules for biochemists to study; now, after the critical work of **James Watson** and **Francis Crick** in 1953, nucleic acids were fascinating scientists in the field. Ochoa was no exception. Drawing on his earlier work with enzymes, Ochoa began investigating which enzymes played roles in the creation of nucleic acids in the body. Although most enzymes assist in breaking down materials, Ochoa knew that he was looking for an enzyme that helped combine nucleotides into the long chains that were nucleic acids. Once he isolated these molecules, he hoped, he would be able to synthesize RNA and DNA in the lab. In 1955, he found a bacterial enzyme in sewage that appeared to play just such a role. When he added this enzyme to a solution of nucleotides, he discovered that the solution became viscous, like jelly, indicating that RNA had indeed formed in the dish. The following year, **Arthur Kornberg**, who had studied with Ochoa in 1946, applied these methods to synthesize DNA.

Wins Nobel for Synthesis of RNA

In 1959, five years after he assumed the directorship of the biochemistry department, Ochoa shared the Nobel Prize for Physiology or Medicine with Kornberg, for their work in discovering the enzymes that help produce nucleic acids. Ochoa was particularly delighted to share the prize with his old colleague; by this time, he was no stranger to academic plaudits. The holder of several honorary degrees from both American and foreign universities, including Oxford, Ochoa was also the recipient of the Carl Neuberg Medal in biochemistry in 1951 and the Charles Leopold Mayer Prize in 1955. Ochoa served as chairperson of NYU's biochemistry department for 20 years, until the summer of 1974, just before his seventieth birthday. When he retired from this post, he rejected the department's offer to make him an emeritus professor, preferring to remain on staff as a full professor. But even that could not keep Ochoa sufficiently occupied. In 1974, he joined the Roche Institute of Molecular Biology in New Jersey.

In 1985, he returned to his native Spain as a professor of biology at the University Autonoma in Madrid to continue his lifelong fascination with biochemical research. At the age of 75, Ochoa wrote a retrospective of his life, which he titled "Pursuit of a Hobby." In the introduction to this piece, he explained his choice of title. At a party given in the forties in honor of two Nobel laureate chemists Ochoa listed his hobby in the guest register as biochemistry, although he was at the time professor of pharmacology at New York University. Sir Henry Dale, one of the party's honorees, joked, "now that he is a pharmacologist, he has biochemistry as a hobby." Ochoa concluded this tale with the statement, "In my life biochemistry has been my only and real hobby." He died in Madrid on November 1, 1993.

SELECTED WRITINGS BY OCHOA:

Books

Pullman, Maynard, ed. *An Era in Biochemistry: A Festschrift for Sarah Ratner.* New York: New York Academy of Sciences, 1983.

Periodicals

"The Pursuit of a Hobby." *Annual Review of Biochemistry.* 48 (1980): 1-30.

George A. Olah

FURTHER READING:

Books

Moritz, Charles, ed. *Current Biography.* New York: H. W. Wilson, 1962.

Wasson, Tyler, ed. *Nobel Prize Winners.* New York: H. W. Wilson, 1987.

Periodicals

"Biochemist Severo Ochoa Dies; Won Nobel Prize" (obituary). *Washington Post* (3 November 1993): D4.

"Severo Ochoa, Biochemist, A Nobel Winner, 88, Dies" (obituary). *New York Times* (3 November 1993): D25.

—Sketch by Shari Rudavsky

George A. Olah
1927–
Hungarian-born American chemist

The recipient of the 1994 Nobel Prize for Chemistry, Olah is primarily known for his crucial work on reactive intermediates in hydrocarbons. The complex chemistry of hydrocarbons, compounds of carbon and hydrogen, includes the study of numerous reactions, which are sometimes extremely difficult to record. Reactive intermediates, or substances acting as the intermediate steps of a chemical reaction mechanism, are so short-lived and elusive that chemists used to regard them as purely hypothetical entities.

Before there was empirical evidence for the existence of reaction intermediates, chemists believed that carbon ions, or positively charged atoms, played an intermediary role in hydrocarbon reactions; the action of these intermediaries, however, was imagined to be so rapid, maybe measurable in millionths of a second, that scientists only postulated their existence. Olah, however, did not doubt the existence of reactive intermediates were real, deciding, in fact, to empirically prove their existence. In order to identify a reactive intermediate, Olah needed a substance that would somehow arrest the reaction mechanism, thus enabling the observer to capture processes which cannot be seen under normal circumstances. The substances that worked, he found, were superacids (a superacid is an extremely powerful acid—for example, more than a trillions times the strength of sulfuric acid). Olah subsequently created a superacid which could extract individual atoms from hydrocarbon compounds. What remained when a hydrocarbon compound was exposed to a superacid, Olah noticed, was an alkyl (an alkyl is a univalent group created when a hydrogen atom is removed from an open-ended hydrocarbon compound) carbon ion, which, although unstable, was measurable. The carbon ion, or *cation*, was the reaction intermediary.

Born in Budapest, Hungary, on May 22, 1927, the son of Julius Olah and Magda Krasznai, Olah received his Ph.D. from the Technical University of Budapest in 1949. That year, he married Judith Lengyel; they have two sons. Olah taught at the Technical University from 1949 to 1954, subsequently joining the Hungarian Academy of Sciences, where he served as associate director of the Central Chemical Research Institute from 1954 to 1956. When the Soviet Union crushed the Hungarian revolt in 1956, Olah and his family fled to the West. In 1957, he joined Dow Chemical in Sarnia, Ontario, where he worked as a research scientist from 1957 to 1965. From 1965 to 1977, he was professor of chemistry at Case Western University. Since 1977, he has worked as professor of chemistry and director of the Hydrocarbon Research Institute at the University of Southern California.

Discovery Finds Applications in Industry

Following his discovery, in 1962, that superacids could neutralize the extreme reactivity of cations,

Olah has worked on developing new superacids to be used in both industry and fundamental research. As Olah's work has opened vast areas of research, many younger chemists have contributed to the search for new superacids. Significantly, the study of intermediate reactants has also resulted in numerous industrial applications, particularly in fuel synthesis. For example, the synthesis of high-octane gasoline is one of the notable industrial uses of Olah's original research. In essence, Olah has created the scientific instruments for creating cleaner and more efficient fuels.

Olah's awards include the 1966 Baekeland Award, the 1989 American Chemical Society Award, the 1993 Pioneer of Chemistry Award given by the American Institute of Chemists, and the Mendeleev Medal, which he received from the Russian Academy of Sciences in 1992.

SELECTED WRITINGS BY OLAH:

Books

Superacids. New York: Wiley, 1985.
Cage Hydrocarbons. New York: Wiley, 1990.
Chemistry of Energetic Materials. San Diego: Academic Press, 1991.
Synthetic Fluorine Chemistry. New York: Wiley, 1992.
Hydrocarbon Chemistry. New York: Wiley, 1995.
Onium Ions. New York: Wiley, 1998.

FURTHER READING:

Periodicals

Baum, Rudy. "George Olah Reflects on Chemical Research." *Chemical and Engineering News* 73, no. 9 (27 February 1995):44-48.
Brown, David. "Chemical 'Intermediates' Work Honored." *Washington Post* (13 October 1994): A3.
Flam, Faye. "Snaring an Elusive Quarry–and a Prize." *Science* 226, no. 5184 (21 October 1994): 369-70.
Lipkin, Richard. "Hydrocarbon Research Garners Nobel Prize." *Science News* 146, no. 17 (22 October 1994): 261.

—*Sketch by Zoran Minderovic*

Olga Oleinik
1925–

Russian mathematical physicist

Olga Oleinik is a prolific writer and educator with eight books and nearly 60 graduate students to

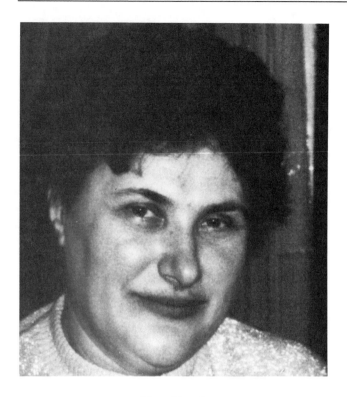

Olga Oleinik

her credit. She teaches mainly in Russia at Moscow State University, but she also travels to colloquia in America, and has held classes as a visiting scholar at such institutions as the University of South Carolina. Oleinik has also contributed more than 300 papers to a variety of professional journals and is a member of the Russian Academy of Sciences. She has made important findings in the area of algebraic geometry in projective space.

Olga Arsenievna Oleinik was born in Kiev, Ukraine on July 2, 1925. Her parents, Arseniy Ivanovich and Anna Petrovna lived in an area known as Matusov. Olga's early years spanned times of great upheaval and difficulty in the Soviet Union, especially World War II. She did, however, earn a degree from Moscow State in 1947. She received her doctorate in 1954, and shortly thereafter began the professorship in mathematics at Moscow State University that she holds today.

In 1972 Oleinik was promoted to the head chair of differential equations in her department. Her specialty is partial differential equations. Although her classes can carry such intimidating titles as "Asymptotic Properties of Solutions of Nonlinear Parabolic and Elliptic Equations and Systems," she is generous with her ideas and more than willing to give her students the right start, according to one former student. Igor Oleinik remembers how much time his "PDE" professor was willing to give to her students despite her busy schedule. Because they were fellow

Ukrainians, and Oleinik is as common a name there as Smith is in America, Igor had to put up with a little teasing from fellow class members who joked that he was really Olga Oleinik's grandson.

Oleinik's studies in mathematics cover broad areas of physics, such as the interactivity of liquids or gases in porous substances, the thermodynamics of bodies in different phases, as well as problems in elasticity and homogenization.

Oleinik is married and has one son, Dmitri. She holds an honorary doctorate from Rome University, granted in 1981, and is also an honorary member of the Royal Society of Edinburgh. She is a member of various societies throughout Europe. Her awards include the medal of the College de France and a "first degree" medal from Prague's Charles University, as well as various prizes from Russian institutions.

SELECTED WRITINGS BY OLEINIK:

Books

Homogenization of Differential Operators and Integral Functionals, 1994.
Mathematical Problems in Elasticity and Homogenization, 1992.
Some Asymptotic Problems of the Theory of Partial Differential Equations, 1995.

FURTHER READING:

Books

Who's Who in the World, 1993–1994. Eleventh edition. New Providence, NJ: Marquis, 1992.

Other

Oleinik, Igor, in an electronic mail interview with Jennifer Kramer, conducted July 12, 1997.
"Olga Oleinik." *The Emmy Noether Lectures of the American Association for Women in Mathematics. Profiles of Women in Mathematics.* http://www.math.neu.edu/awm/noetherbrochure/Oleinik96.htm

—Sketch by Jennifer Kramer

Douglas D. Osheroff
1945–
American physicist

Douglas D. Osheroff, co-recipient of the 1996 Nobel Prize for Physics with his colleagues **David M.**

Douglas D. Osheroff

Lee and **Robert C. Richardson**, is known for his important role in the work that led to the discovery of superfluidity in helium-3, a rare isotope of helium. A junior member of the Cornell scientific team that made the discovery (he was a doctoral student of his co-workers Lee and Richardson), Osheroff has continued work with helium-3, focusing on the two transitions occurring in the superfluid state.

Osheroff was born in Aberdeen, Washington, on August 1, 1945, the son of William Osheroff and Bessie Anne (Ondov) Osheroff. He married Phyllis S. K. Liu in 1970. After obtaining a B.S. at the California Institute of Technology in 1967, he came to Cornell University, where he collaborated in low-temperature physics research with his doctoral mentors. In 1973, Osheroff completed his doctorate. He remained at Cornell, while concurrently working at Bell Laboratories, where he stayed until 1982. At Cornell, he headed the Solid State and Low Temperature Department from 1982 to 1987. Osheroff left Cornell in 1987 to accept a full professorship at Stanford University. Chair of Stanford's Physics Department from 1993 to 1996, he was named J. G. Jackson and C. J. Wood Professor of Physics in 1992.

Notices Crucial Clue Leading to Historic Discovery

When Osheroff and his colleagues started the research that would eventually lead to discovery of helium-3 in a superfluid state, they were actually looking for the transition of frozen helium-3 to a

magnetic state. As a sample of helium-3 cooled to the temperature of 2.7 millikelvins, it was Osheroff who noticed significant, and unexpected, deviations in the cooling rate of the sample. Realizing that the results of the experiments were pointing in a new direction, the scientists abandoned the magnetic state hypothesis, theorizing instead that the helium-3 may have attained a particular solid state. However, additional observation led Osheroff and his colleagues to conclude that their sample had reached the state of superfluidity. In fact, the scientists found that helium-3 can exist in two distinct states of superfluidity.

Physicists find superfluidity fascinating because substances in a superfluid state exhibit behaviors that are much different than those observed in other states. For instance, a superfluid in an open cup-like container will spontaneously overflow. While classical mechanics cannot account for such phenomena, superfluidity does not violate the principles of quantum mechanics. When, for example, a liquid is cooled to a temperature near absolute zero, it loses its inner resistance, or friction, because its atoms, which at "normal" temperature move around in a random fashion, fall into a rigid structure. The lack of inner resistance is responsible for the liquid's unusual behavior. However, more important is the light that superfluidity can shed on microscopic and macroscopic quantum physics. In addition to widening the horizons of quantum theory, superfluidity may also explain certain puzzles pertaining the genesis of the universe. For example, scientists have used superfluid helium-3 to experimentally replicate certain helium reactions that, having occurred in the first microseconds following the Big Bang, may account for the hypothetical cosmic strings, which, scientists believe, played an important role in the formation of galaxies.

Osheroff is a Fellow of the American Physical Society. His memberships include the National Academy of Sciences and the American Academy of Arts and Sciences. A recipient of the 1981 John D. and Catherine T. MacArthur Fellowship, Osheroff also won a Walter J. Gores Award for Excellence in Teaching. With his colleagues Lee and Richardson, Osheroff received Britain's Institute of Physics Sir Francis Simon Memorial Prize in 1976. In recognition for their discovery, the three scientists also received the 1980 Oliver E. Buckley Solid State Physics Prize.

SELECTED WRITINGS BY OSHEROFF:

Periodicals

(With M. C. Cross) "Novel Magnetic Properties of Solid Thelium-3." *Physics Today* (February 1987): 34.

FURTHER READING:

Books

Leggett, A. J. *The Problems of Physics.* Oxford: Oxford University Press, 1987.

Tilley, Donald E., and Walter Thumm. *College Physics: A Text with Applications to the Life Sciences.* Menlo Park, CA: Cummings, 1971.

Periodicals

Browne, Malcolm W. "Discoveries of Superfluid Helium, and 'Buckyballs,' Earn Nobels for 6 Scientists." *New York Times* (10 October 1996): D21.

Lounasmaa, O. V., and George Pickett. "The ^{3}He Superfluids." *Scientific American* (June 1990): 104-11.

Peterson, Ivars. "Superfluidity Earns Physics Nobel." *Science News* 150, no. 16 (19 October 1996): 247.

Other

Nobel Foundation WWW Server Posting (9 October 1996). http://www.nobel.ki.se

—*Sketch by Jane Stewart Cook and Zoran Min-derovic*

P

David Packard

David Packard
1912–1996
American electrical engineer

David Packard was an electrical engineer and entrepreneur who had a profound impact on politics and industry in the United States. With **William Hewlett**, he founded Hewlett-Packard in 1939, one of the nation's first high-technology companies. He served as Deputy Secretary of Defense under President Nixon, and as vice chairman of the President's Commission on Defense Management, known as the Packard Commission, under President Reagan. He also made large charitable contributions through the David and Lucile Packard Foundation.

Packard was born in Pueblo, Colorado, on September 7, 1912, the second child of Sperry and Ella (Graber) Packard. His mother was a high school teacher of German descent, and his father was a lawyer descended from New England colonialists. Packard was educated at Somerlid Grade School, where he first became interested in electrical engineering, and at Centennial High School in Pueblo. He

later attended Stanford University, where he first met Hewlett. Packard played football and received his B.A. in electrical engineering in 1934. In 1935, he was hired by the General Electric company to work in the vacuum-tube engineering division at Schenectady, New York. Offered a fellowship by an engineering professor, **Frederick Terman,** he returned to Stanford and in 1939 took a master's degree in electrical engineering with a focus on radio engineering.

Co-founds Hewlett-Packard Company

In 1939, Packard and Hewlett, two of the most successful partners in the history of industry, used $538 to start their firm in Packard's garage in Palo Alto. Many of their early inventions were related to work that Hewlett had done at Stanford. One of Packard and Hewlett's first projects was production of a new kind of audio oscillator, called a "resistance-capacitance oscillator," the design of which was the subject of Hewlett's master's thesis at Stanford. The oscillator, named the 200A, produced electrical signals in the range of human hearing, from 20 to 20,000 cycles per second. The device was used primarily to measure the intensity of recorded sound. Hewlett and Packard presented the oscillator, which sold at a quarter the cost of similar instruments of its day, at a 1938 meeting of the International Radio Engineers in Portland, Oregon. Here, they met Walt Disney; later, the chief sound engineer at Disney Studios ordered eight of these devices for use in making the landmark film *Fantasia.*

Hewlett-Packard was incorporated a year later, and the two men flipped a coin to see whose name would go first. Packard co-founded the West Coast Electronics Foundation in 1942 and was awarded the Medal of Honor of the Electronics Industry for his involvement. Packard, who was more the businessman than Hewlett, served as president of Hewlett-Packard from 1947 to 1964, and as chairman of the board and chief executive officer from 1964 to 1968. During World War II, the company grew rapidly as the result of defense contracts; forced to reorganize and redefine their objectives after the war, Hewlett and Packard decided to focus development and marketing efforts on the engineering industry. The company specialized in instruments for measuring and testing; they were also one of the first companies to make use of semiconductors, and in 1966 they introduced their first computer.

Hewlett-Packard was a highly successful technology firm by the 1960s, but almost none of their market was outside of industry; their first successful product in the popular market was the hand-held calculator, introduced in 1968 as the HP 9100. Growth at Hewlett-Packard was the result of continuing technological innovation, but as *Fortune* magazine observed in a 1988 profile of Packard, "No single product . . . has brought the company as much distinction as its management style." An informal management style, which often involved what Hewlett remembered as "wandering around," cultivated loyalty and commitment from their work force and encouraged creative participation.

Becomes Involved in National Politics

Packard was chairman of the board of trustees of Stanford University in 1958 and 1959. Packard was also a friend of Herbert Hoover, and in keeping with Hoover's wishes, he prevented a takeover by liberal faculty of the Hoover Institution, where he sat on the advisory board. He became acquainted with Richard Nixon during this period and supported him for president in the election of 1968. In 1969, Packard was asked by the Secretary of Defense, Melvin Laird, to serve under Nixon as Deputy Secretary of Defense, a post he held until 1971. During his tenure at the Pentagon, Packard made sure he did not benefit from any changes in the value of Hewlett-Packard stock; during the three years he was in his office, the value of his stock rose over twenty million dollars, but he arranged his holdings so he never received this increase.

Another California politician to whom Packard developed strong ties was Ronald Reagan. In 1985, he was chosen by President Reagan to head the Packard Commission, which was charged with making recommendations to overhaul defense-procurement policies. This was during a period when government was spending a great deal of money on defense, and Packard was appointed in the midst of a scandal over the prices many defense contractors were charging the Pentagon. In the report his committee submitted to the president, Packard recommended strengthening the role of the chair of the Joint Chiefs of Staff and stimulating better long-term planning, as well as appointing what *U.S. News and World Report* called "a high-level civilian procurement czar to oversee the services' buying plans." After the report was released, Packard told *U.S. News and World Report:* "There's no question that, because of long-term structural problems, we've wasted tens of billions of dollars out of the more than a trillion that's been spent." The Reagan administration submitted to Congress most of the recommendations he included in his report.

Both Packard and Hewlett retired from active leadership of their company in 1978, but they returned to take the helm at Hewlett-Packard in 1990, guiding the company through difficulties caused by

mismanagement and changing circumstances in the computer industry. They restructured the divisions of the company and reduced the power of the centralized bureaucracy, and Hewlett-Packard was posting a profit again within two years. Packard remained chairman of the company until 1993, when he took the title of chairman emeritus.

On April 8, 1938, Packard married Lucile Laura Salter, a Stanford classmate; the couple had four children. His wife, who died in 1987, shared many of his interests, and they founded the David and Lucile Packard Foundation to support scientific and health research, as well as a broad range of social and educational programs. The foundation made a $70 million contribution to the children's hospital at Stanford University. The Packards were also the major contributors to the construction of the Monterey Bay Aquarium, where Packard designed a machine to simulate tidal movements. He once financed a project to salvage four U.S. Navy Sparrowhawk biplanes that had gone down in 1,500 feet (450 m) of water off the Pacific coast in 1935 aboard the U.S.S. Macon. In 1988, Packard announced that he would give most of his fortune, which was estimated to amount to over two billion dollars, to the David and Lucile Packard Foundation. Their children supervise many of the foundation's programs, particularly those in archaeology and marine biology. Packard died on March 27, 1996 at Stanford University Hospital.

SELECTED WRITINGS BY PACKARD:

Periodicals

"The Real Scandal in Military Contracts." *Across the Board* (November 1988): 17-23.

FURTHER READING:

Books

Kanter, Rosabeth Moss. *The Change Masters.* New York: Simon & Schuster, 1983.
Peters, Thomas J., and Robert H. Waterman. *In Search of Excellence.* New York: Warner Books, 1982.
Schoenbaum, Elenora, ed. *Political Profiles: The Nixon/Ford Years,* New York: Facts on File, 1979.

Periodicals

"Calling for a Pentagon Shake-Up." *U.S. News and World Report* (10 March 1986): 23-24.
Goff, T. J. "The Best in Business: 1986." *California Business Magazine.* (December 1986): 40-45.

Guzzardi, Walter, Jr. "The U.S. Business Hall of Fame." *Fortune*, (14 March 1988): 142-44.
———. "Packard's Big Giveaway." *Time* (9 May 1988): 70.
———. "A Pentagon Manifesto." *Newsweek* (10 March 1986).
———. "A Quartet of High-Tech Pioneers." *Fortune* (12 October 1987): 148-49.
———. "Silicon Valley's Troubled Olympus." *California* (February 1991): 12-13.
Barnes, Bart. "David Packard Dies at 83; Founded Hewlett-Packard" (obituary). *Washington Post* (27 March 1996): D4.
Fisher, Lawrence M. "David Packard, 83, Pioneer of Silicon Valley, Is Dead" (obituary). *New York Times* (27 March 1996): D20.
King, Peter H. "One Who Took The High Road." *Los Angeles Times* (31 March 1996): A3.

Other

Packard, David. Interview by John Henry Dreyfuss. 9 February 1994.

—*Sketch by John Henry Dreyfuss*

Arthur C. Parker
1881–1955

American anthropologist

Anthropologist Arthur C. Parker was instrumental in preserving the culture of the Seneca people through his directorship of the Rochester (New York) Municipal Museum. At the same time, he also did much to promote Native Americans as members of American society. Most remarkably, he accomplished his scientific achievements without the aid of a college degree.

Arthur Caswell Parker was born April 5, 1881, on the Cattaraugus Indian Reservation near Iroquois, New York. His father, Frederick Ely Parker, who was half Seneca, was a railroad worker and a descendent of General Ely Parker, Ulysses S. Grant's civil war military secretary. His mother, Geneva Hortense Griswold, had been a teacher on the Cattaraugus and Allegheny reservations.

Arthur spent much of his childhood on the reservation. Even after his father was transferred to White Plains, New York, in 1892, the family returned often. Because clan and tribal affiliations among the Seneca were passed down through the mother's side of the family, neither Arthur nor his father had affiliations, however they were both later adopted into the Seneca's Bear Clan. In his early twenties, Parker

received the adult name *Gawasowanah*, which means Big Snowsnake.

Parker and his sister attended public schools. He graduated from high school in White Plains in 1897, and briefly attended Centenary College in Hackettstown, New Jersey, in 1899. Later that year, he went to the Williamsport (Pennsylvania) Dickinson Seminary, but left without graduating in 1903.

During his time at the seminary, Parker was exposed to anthropology through lectures given by Harvard University anthropologist Frederick Ward Putnam at the American Museum of Natural History in New York. In 1900 he worked for a short time as an anthropological assistant at the museum.

Between 1900 and 1903, Parker worked as a field anthropologist for Putnam and Harvard's Peabody Museum. His first field project was collecting the myths, stories, and oral history of the Seneca people on the Cattaraugus Reservation. In 1904, the year he took a temporary job collecting cultural materials with the New York State Library and Museum, he married his first wife, an Abenaki Indian named Beatrice Tahamont. He married his second wife, Anna Theresa Cooke, on September 17, 1914. Together, they had two daughters and a son.

Continues Anthropological Endeavors After Meeting with Franz Boas

While in New York, Parker was able to meet some of the most intriguing people who would influence the course of his professional life. Among them was Franz Boas, considered the father of American anthropology, who was at the time lecturing at Columbia College. Boas specialized in the study of the Northwest Indians. He encouraged Parker to formally pursue a degree in anthropology, but Parker eventually decided against it. His decision was made in part because he disagreed with Boas's stance on the evolutionary theories of Lewis Henry Morgan, an anthropologist who, like Parker, had been adopted by the Seneca. Although he never earned a degree, Parker would go on to write over 300 articles and numerous books.

Besides Boas, Parker also met many scholars through his acquaintance with Harriet Maxwell Converse. "Aunt Hattie" was an amateur scientist whose special interest was Iroquois culture. Like Parker and Morgan, she too had been adopted by the Seneca.

In 1905 Parker passed the civil service examination and became an archaeologist with the New York State Museum. During his nine years there, he extensively researched and published on folklore, ethnology, archaeology, museology, and race relations. While at the state museum, Parker became active in the Society of American Indians (SAI), a newly formed group that promoted cooperation among Native Americans. The SAI—and Parker—believed that Native Americans could adapt successfully to mainstream American culture without losing their cultural identity. He remained active with the group until 1920, when he became president of the New York State Indian Welfare Association. From 1919 to 1922, Parker served as secretary to the New York State Indian Commission.

In 1924 Parker became the director of the Rochester (New York) Municipal Museum, a professional affiliation he would maintain for the rest of his life. While director, he obtained federal funding for an Indian arts and crafts program. Able to pay wages to Iroquois artists and craftsmen for a variety of traditional items, Parker both created an outstanding collection for his museum and helped maintain an important part of Seneca culture.

Recognized for Establishing and Contributing to Many Native American Organizations and Publications

Parker was unafraid of new ventures. During his career he founded several organizations and publications, and even initiated American Indian day, a holiday celebrated on the second Saturday in May. Parker founded and edited the SAI's *Quarterly Journal* as well as *American Indian* magazine, *Museum Service,* and *Research Records of the Rochester Municipal Museum.* He founded both the Albany Philosophical Society and the New York State Archeological Association. Besides the SAI, he was a member of the Indian Rights Association, the New York State Indian Welfare Association, the American Association of Museums, the American Anthropological Society, the American Ethnological Society (of which he was a fellow), and the New York State Historical Society (trustee). He was also a member of the Royal Order of Scotland and was a 33rd degree Mason.

Parker also enjoyed collecting coins (he was a member of the American Numismatic Association), collecting manuscripts and autographs, hiking, and camping. Besides his work on behalf of Native Americans, he also actively promoted the establishment of public parks and forest preserves.

Parker may never have earned a college degree, but he received several honorary degrees. The University of Rochester presented him an honorary master's degree in 1922. In 1940 Union College gave him an honorary doctorate in science, and in 1945 he received an honorary doctorate in human laws from Keuka College. In 1916 he received the Cornplanter Medal for his ethnographic research.

Arthur C. Parker died of a heart attack on New Year's Day, 1955.

SELECTED WRITINGS BY PARKER:

Books

Excavations in an Erie Indian Village, 1906.
Code of Hansome Lake, 1913.
Seneca Myths and Folk Tales, 1923.
Analytical History of the Senecas, 1925.
Rumbling Wings, 1929 (a children's book of legends).

FURTHER READING:

Books

Liberty, Margot, ed. "Arthur C. Parker—Seneca, 1881–1955." *American Indian Intellectuals, 1976 Proceedings of the American Ethnological Society.* West Publishing Co., 1978, pp. 128-138.
Saari, Peggy and Stephen Allison, eds. *Scientists: The Lives and Works of 150 Scientists.* Detroit: UXL, 1996.

—*Sketch by Fran Hodgkins*

Eugene Newman Parker
1927–
American astrophysicist

Eugene Parker's career changed the then-prevailing notion of space as a silent, still vacuum. In the space that Parker explored, stars like our Sun blow energetic streams of protons and electrons through interstellar space at a million miles per hour like a powerful wind. In Parker's universe, stars, planets, and even galaxies are surrounded by huge magnetic fields that attract or repel the elements in these solar winds. Though he first published these ideas in the 1950s, numerous space-based scientific missions in the 1990s were still trying to get precise measurements of the solar wind and its interaction with Earth's magnetic field.

Parker was the first-born child of Glenn Parker, an engineer, and Helen MacNair. He was born in Houghton, Michigan, where his mother went in June of 1927 to be with her mother for the birth and care of the newborn child. Parker's father was then in graduate school at Purdue University in West Lafayette, Indiana, pursuing a degree in aeronautical engineering. "It was a hand-to-mouth business in those years," Parker told contributor Karl Leif Bates in a November 7, 1997 interview. His father worked for a series of airplane makers, but by 1935, he had

Eugene Newman Parker

joined the Chrysler Motor Company in Detroit, Michigan, to work in automotive engineering.

"I was always terribly curious about everything and how things work," Parker said. "I remember being curious about how a railroad locomotive worked and how the signal on the tracks worked, and my father of course was well prepared to answer." Parker remembers being given a microscope as a gift when he was about six years old, and exploring the little worlds inside a drop of stagnant pond water. But the life sciences were not for him, Parker decided. "You have to remember so many darn things."

He majored in physics at Michigan State University, graduating in 1948. Then it was off to the California Institute of Technology for a Ph.D. in physics in 1951. Parker's first job was as an instructor in the mathematics department at the University of Utah in Salt Lake City, but it was not a tenure-track position, nor did it allow any time for research. In 1953 he switched departments to become a research assistant to Utah physicist **Walter M. Elsasser**, a pioneer in the field of studying Earth's magnetic field. Magnetism was not a subject that was unknown to Parker, as he had done his Ph.D. dissertation on the magnetic field lines seen in the dust surrounding the Pleiades, or Seven Sisters star cluster, in the constellation Taurus. Working with Elsasser turned out to be a key turning point in Parker's career.

Further Explains Earth's Magnetic Field with Illustrations and Math

Elsasser was advancing the notion that Earth's magnetic field resulted from a dynamo effect; the planet's spinning liquid core created an electro-magnetic current much as the windings in an electric generator do. Parker further refined that concept by showing how the azimuthal (or equatorial) fields produced by such a dynamo would be converted to the dipole (or north and south) field lines we experience so strongly on Earth's surface. "Once I got to it, it was a matter of a month or so," Parker said of this breakthrough. "You draw a sketch of it on a piece of paper and suddenly it hits." The math to prove his concept took most of the time. "It turns out that the process seems to work quite generally in the universe," Parker added. He quickly showed that this same sort of "cyclonic effect" was at work in our Sun as well. Parker published this paper in 1955, but it was ignored for some time.

Solves Solar Wind Riddle

In 1957 Parker moved to the University of Chicago to work under physicist John Simpson, who was exploring cosmic rays. Simpson had some new instruments that would measure the radiation of interplanetary space. "That's what got me thinking about interplanetary space," he told Bates.

In 1958 Parker solved the riddle of what is now known as solar wind. Though the Sun's gravity is a massive force, some of the hot gases being accelerated by the star's magnetic fields are able to escape, roaring across our solar system as streams of charged particles. "You take the equation $F = ma$ (force equals mass times acceleration). It follows," Parker said. "Plasma moving fast enough is simply able to escape the Sun's gravity." Though solar wind is impossible to measure from within Earth's protective atmosphere and magnetosphere, interplanetary probes launched in the 1960s provided confirmation of Parker's idea.

Combining Parker's two ideas, it is understood today that Earth's magnetosphere prevents the solar wind from penetrating the atmosphere, but that in doing so, the magnetic field is blown back in an extreme teardrop shape that extends nearly 1,000 Earth diameters on the dark side of the planet. Having exhausted his study of solar wind, Parker turned his attention to the magnetic fields of the Milky Way galaxy, and returned to the study of magnetic fields and dynamos throughout the 1970s.

In an age when many astronomers and physicists are pushing the limits of understanding further and further into space, Parker said he still prefers to stay close to home. "You can do hard physics only when you have enough detailed observations to figure out what the processes are," he said. "I like to needle my

C. Kumar N. Patel

friends that they have a theory for everything that is not resolved in the telescope." In fact, he said, much of the theoretical physics being done in the 1990s will never be confirmed by measurement. In June 1995, at age 68, Parker retired from the University of Chicago.

SELECTED WRITINGS BY PARKER:

Periodicals

"Magnetic fields in the cosmos." *Scientific American* (August 1983): 44-54.
"Why do stars emit x rays?" *Physics Today* (July 1987): 36-42.

—*Sketch by Karl Leif Bates*

C. Kumar N. Patel
1938–
Indian-born American physicist and engineer

As a scientist and administrator, C. Kumar N. Patel has shown leadership qualities that have made him one of the leading spokesmen in both academic and industrial research. Considered one of the most extraordinary scientists in America, Patel holds 35

major patents, including groundbreaking contributions in gas lasers, nonlinear optics, molecular spectroscopy, pollution detection, and laser surgery. Eloquent and thoughtful, Patel has also spearheaded a shift in the university research environment, stressing the need for more industrial-sponsored research rather than government- and military-sponsored research.

Although Patel's scientific accomplishments cover a broad spectrum, he is especially noted for his work in lasers. His invention of the carbon dioxide laser resulted in numerous industrial, scientific, medical, and defense applications. The first person to carry out infrared nonlinear optics experiments, Patel literally created the field. His inventions include the spin-flip Raman laser, which was the first tunable Raman laser in any wavelength region, and a tunable laser opto-acoustic measurement technique for detection of pollutant gases in extremely small concentrations.

Patel was born in Baramati, India, on July 2, 1938, to Naran Phai and Mani Ben Patel. He has one older brother and a younger sister. Naran, Patel's father, a civil engineer employed by the government, was transferred often, and Patel was tutored at home until he was 11 years old. A good student, Patel was placed in the eighth grade with older students when he started formal schooling. He received his bachelor's degree in telecommunications from the College of Engineering in Poona, India, when he was 20 years old.

The Accidental Scientist

Upon graduation, Patel planned to enter the Indian Foreign Service but had to wait until he reached age 25 to be hired. Not one to waste his time, Patel decided to earn his Ph.D. in the interim. With financial support guaranteed by his father for the first year of graduate school, Patel enrolled in Stanford University in the United States.

"After the first year, I really got interested in research," Patel told contributor David Petechuk in a December 8, 1997, interview. "It was such fun, much more than I ever imagined. I guess you could say I was an 'accidental scientist.'"

Patel's gift for independent, innovative thinking was nurtured early at Sanford, where he was given free reign to develop his own Ph.D. research agenda in electrical engineering. After receiving his Ph.D. in 1961, thoughts of the foreign service had long fallen by the wayside. Patel, who became a naturalized U.S. citizen, was to embark on a remarkable research career.

The Bell Laboratory Years

After graduation, Patel joined Bell Laboratories, which would prove to be ideal for Patel's independent way of thinking. "Bell Laboratories really valued science, technology, and independence," Patel told Petechuk. "They wanted us to be discoverers and inventors. We were given a free hand and basically told to 'just go do it.'"

However, along with the autonomy came the burden of providing results. Patel did not disappoint. In two short years, he discovered and invented efficient vibrational energy transfer between molecules, which led to experiments with carbon dioxide lasers and their use in a wide range of industrial and scientific applications. Because of Patel, the carbon dioxide laser has had a greater impact on society than any other laser.

Patel followed up this success by creating the field of infrared nonlinear optics in 1966 and, in 1970, invented the spin-flip Raman lasers (a class of tunable infrared lasers). In 1970 he developed a tunable laser opto-acoustic measurement technique that could detect minute concentrations of pollutant gases in the atmosphere and that became the standard for measuring small absorptions in gases. He also invented an opto-acoustic detection technique capable of measuring small optical absorptions in liquids, solids, thin films, and powders. In the area of spectroscopy, Patel's opto-acoustic spectroscopy studies of cryogenic liquids and solids have supplied important data for understanding their practical applications.

During his 32 years at Bell Laboratories, Patel held many important management positions. He was head of the Infrared Physics and Electronics Research Department, director of the Electronics Research laboratory, director of the Physical Research Laboratory, and executive director of the Research Physics and Academic Affairs division.

Time for a Change

After 30 years in industry, Patel began to ponder a career change. "I asked myself what would happen to if I stayed [at Bell] for 15 more years," Patel told Petechuk. "Although I might become vice-president for research, which would be exciting, it would also be more of the same."

Although devoted to his laboratory work, Patel had developed a strong interest in public policy issues concerning science and the relationship of pairing industry with universities. In 1992 Patel left Bell Laboratories to become vice chancellor for research at the University of California, Los Angeles (UCLA), which recruited Patel to help the university make the transition from a defense-based economy to a high-tech consumer-oriented economy.

"Because of his background, he had other ways of looking at problems [than most academicians]," Alan Fogelman, who was on the UCLA search committee,

told Petechuk. "He has been every bit as good as his reputation."

Since moving to UCLA, Patel has played a pivotal role in helping universities rethink their approach to research. In 1994 he organized and chaired the first national conference on reinventing the research university. He has placed a special emphasis on recognizing the importance of coupling universities with small-to-medium size companies and how university research can contribute to the creation of jobs and wealth in society.

Patel, who married in 1961, has two children. Despite the demands on his time, he enjoys tennis and wind surfing and has taken up roller blading. He also enjoys French cooking, especially "eating his experiments."

Throughout his accomplished career, Patel has shown himself to be a man of vision with the ability to make his ideas come to fruition. In 1996 he received the National Medal of Science, the United States equivalent to the Nobel Prize. He is fond of quoting his favorite comic book character, Pogo, who points out that "we are surrounded by insurmountable opportunities."

"What people call insurmountable obstacles are really opportunities," Patel told Petechuk. "Some things work and some don't; but you don't know unless you try."

SELECTED WRITINGS BY PATEL:

Periodicals

"Controlled Environment Processing for Semiconductors–A Factory-in-a-Bottle (A Lean Manufacturing Alternative)." *Journal of Electronics Manufacturing* 1 (1991): 45.
"Materials and Processing: Core Competencies and Strategic Resources." *AT&T Technical Journal* 69 (1990).

FURTHER READING:

Periodicals

"Insurmountable Opportunities." *Nature* (April 1, 1993): 394-395.
"Technology Transfer." *Nature* (April 1, 1993): 395.

—Sketch by David Petechuk

Wolfgang Paul

Wolfgang Paul
1913–1993
German physicist

Wolfgang Paul's Nobel Prize-winning research included the invention of an "ion trap" (also known as an "electrical bottle" or "Paul trap") which holds particles in place by means of two electrical plates and a ring-shaped electrode for the purpose of very precise measuring and observation. Paul was widely esteemed for his research in the fields of molecular-beam physics, mass spectroscopy, high-energy physics, and radiobiology.

Paul was born in Lorenzkirch, Saxony, Germany, on August 10, 1913. He was the fourth of six children born to Theodor and Elizabeth (Ruppel) Paul. Theodor Paul was professor of pharmaceutical chemistry at the University of Munich and a colleague of the eminent theoretical physicist **Arnold Sommerfeld**. Wolfgang developed an interest in science at an early age and, after graduating from high school, entered the Technical University of Munich in 1932. Two years later, he transferred to the Technical University of Berlin, from which he received his diploma (comparable to a master's degree) in 1937.

Paul then stayed on in Berlin to work on his doctoral degree under Hans Kopfermann, a specialist in nuclear and atomic physics. He was nearly prevented from completing his degree by his induction into

the German military at the onset of World War II. His service was cut short, however, when he was allowed to return to graduate school and excused from further military obligations. Paul was granted his Ph.D. in 1939 for a thesis on the properties of the beryllium nucleus.

After completing his doctoral studies, Paul joined his former advisor Kopfermann, who was then at the University of Kiel. The two worked together for sixteen years, moving to the University of Göttingen in 1942, where Paul was appointed assistant professor two years later. He remained at Göttingen until 1952.

Works on Mass Spectrometry and Radiobiology

Paul's earliest research interest at Kiel and Göttingen was mass spectrometry, a technique in which magnetic and electrical fields are used to separate ions of different masses from each other. The devastation caused by Germany's defeat in World War II eventually made a continuation of this line of research impossible, however. It was a difficult time for physicists, with an acute lack of equipment and severe governmental restrictions on the type of research allowed. As a consequence, Paul briefly refocused his studies to the field of radiobiology, where these limitations were not as serious.

Shortly after receiving his Ph.D., Paul married Liselotte Hirsche. The couple had four children, two sons and two daughters. Mrs. Paul died in 1977. Paul later married Doris Walch, a professor of medieval literature at the University of Bonn.

Paul moved to the University of Bonn in 1952 to become a professor of physics. He remained there for three decades, until his retirement in 1983. It was at Bonn that Paul carried out the research for which he is best known and which won him the 1989 Nobel Prize for physics. That research involved the development of methods for focusing the path of ions, and was done with collaborating scientists **Norman Foster Ramsey** of Harvard University, and **Hans Dehmelt** of the University of Washington.

Develops Electric and Magnetic Lenses and Traps

The development of devices that can be used to divert the path of moving particles goes back to the invention of the mass spectrometer by the English physicists **J. J. Thomson** and **Francis W. Aston** in the first decade of the twentieth century. In the mass spectrometer, a beam of charged particles is deflected as it is forced to travel through a strong magnetic field. The device is used to separate particles of differing masses from each other since those particles are deflected differentially by the magnetic field.

In the 1950s, Paul began to work on modifications of the mass spectrometric principle known as electrical and magnetic lenses. In a lens of this type, electrical and magnetic fields are arranged to focus a beam of particles in much the same way that glass and plastic lenses can focus a beam of light. Paul's electrical and magnetic lenses have become valuable tools in the use of atomic and molecular beams used for the study of the structure and properties of atoms and molecules.

An electrical or magnetic lens is a device for limiting the movement of a particle beam in two directions. The logical extension of this device is to find a way of restricting movement in three dimensions, that is, of stopping the motion of an individual particle and holding it in a suspended state for some period of time. A device of this type is of enormous value to scientists since it makes possible very precise studies of the changes that take place within an individual atom or ion and the changes that occur when energy interacts with that particle.

In the late 1950s, Paul invented such a device. It consists of a ring-shaped electrode placed between two electrical plates. A particle placed within the ring is prevented from moving in any direction by the electrical field that surrounds it. The device has been described as an "electrical bottle" or a "Paul trap." With it, scientists have been able to observe transitions within an atom with far greater precision than had ever been possible before.

In the 1970s, Paul turned his attention to an even more challenging task, the trapping of uncharged particles. Since traditional mass spectrometric and beam focusing methods do not work on uncharged particles, Paul and his associates (including his two sons, Lorenz and Stephan) found variations on the Paul trap to use with such particles.

Paul later became interested in the study of elementary particles. He was responsible for the construction at Bonn of Germany's first particle accelerator, a 500 million-electron-volt electron synchrotron, and later for the installation of a more powerful 2.5 billion-electron-volt accelerator.

Paul served both as director of the nuclear physics division at CERN, the European Center for Nuclear Research in Geneva, and as executive director of DESY, Germany's national particle accelerator laboratory. From 1979 to 1989, he was president of the Humboldt Foundation. In addition to the Nobel Prize, Paul received the Robert W. Pohl Prize of the German Physical Society and the Gold Medal of the Czech Academy of Sciences. He died in Bonn on December 6, 1993.

SELECTED WRITINGS BY PAUL:

Periodicals

"A New Mass Spectrometer without Magnetic Field." *Zeitschrift für Naturforschung* 89 (1953): 448-50.

"Production of Elementary Particles in the Laboratory." *Naturwissenschaften* 46 (1959): 277-83.

FURTHER READING:

Periodicals

Hall, Nina. "Perfect Timing Wins Belated Nobel for Paul." *New Scientist* 21 October (1989): 29.

Levi, Barbara Goss. "Ramsey, Dehmelt, Paul Win Nobel for Helping to Set High Standards." *Physics Today* (December 1989): 17-19.

Pool, Robert. "Basic Measurement Lead to Physics Nobel." *Science* (20 October 1989): 327-28.

Whitney, Craig H. "Dr. Wolfgang Paul, 80, Is dead; German Winner of Nobel" (obituary). *New York Times* (9 December 1993): D23.

—Sketch by David E. Newton

Phillip James Edwin Peebles
1935–
Canadian-born American cosmologist

P. J. E. Peebles was an important figure in establishing the leading theory of the origin of the universe in 1965, and since then, he has conducted influential studies that reflect on how it will end.

Phillip James Edwin Peebles often signs his professional writing simply as P. J. E. Peebles and is known in the Princeton University telephone directory as Phillip J., but his coworkers call him Jim. He was born on May 25, 1935, in Winnipeg, Manitoba, Canada, where his father, Andrew Charles Peebles, worked at the Winnipeg Grain Exchange. His mother, the former Ada Marion Green, was a homemaker. Working his way through college at the University of Manitoba in Winnipeg, he initially had the vague idea of becoming an engineer, but discovered the joy of physics and switched his major. In 1958 he took his B.S.C. in physics and moved on to Princeton University in the United States, where he earned a Ph.D. in physics in 1962. He began teaching at Princeton in 1961 while he was finishing his doctorate and has continued working at the University ever since.

Early in his career at Princeton, Peebles encountered **Robert H. Dicke**, who started Peebles on a lifelong interest in gravity and cosmology. Peebles has often been termed an astronomer, but his main work and teaching, although concerned with the large-scale nature of the universe, has been in physics. He is an Albert Einstein Professor of Science at Princeton, a post in the physics department that he has held since 1984. Peebles is married to Alison Peebles. Jim and Alison have never found any connection between her Peebles family from Ireland and Jim's from southern England. They have three children, Lesley, Ellen, and Marion.

Shortly after he received his Ph.D., Peebles worked with Dicke in 1965 on the problem of the origin of the universe. At that time the big bang was only one of several competing theories about the evolution of the universe, and many believed that a different cosmology, known as steady state, was more likely. Peebles' calculations connected the temperature of the cosmic origin in a great expansion of space to the wavelength of the cooled radiation that would still be observable. He also determined the expected and observed density of matter in the universe, as well as the total amount of helium, two other numbers that would be important evidence for or against the big bang theory.

The best-known of Peebles' results from this period is his and Dicke's proposed cosmic background radiation, confirmed that year by **Arno Penzias** and **Robert Woodrow Wilson** at the same time as Peebles and Dicke were developing their theory. Penzias and Wilson had discovered and measured the radiation but did not know how to explain it. Someone told them about a seminar on the subject of background radiation given by Peebles. They phoned Princeton, spoke to Dicke, and soon the two pairs of scientists published separate papers in the same journal issue on the discovery and its meaning. Since then the big bang theory has become generally accepted and the steady-state theory almost totally abandoned. Peebles' 1965 value for the total amount of helium was another important calculation that also tended to establish the big bang theory.

Investigates the "Flatness" of the Universe

In 1979 Peebles, again working with Dicke, developed another idea with important implications for the history of the universe. They investigated what cosmologists call the "flatness" of the universe. Flatness refers to the curvature of space predicted by Einstein's theory of general relativity. Such curvature is directly related to the density of matter in the universe, which in turn tells the fate of the cosmos. If there is too much matter for the amount of space, not only will space be curved with a positive curvature, but all the universe will eventually stop expanding and collapse. However, if there is too little matter, space will have a negative curvature and the universe will expand forever, gradually thinning to nothingness. If the universe has just the right amount of matter, space will be flat and the expansion of the

universe will gradually slow down and eventually stop. In the late 1970s, although there was not enough evidence for a definite conclusion, it appeared likely to Peebles and Dicke that space actually is flat. In turn, this led to several theories by various physicists, astronomers, and cosmologists in the 1980s that purported to explain why this happens.

More recently, Peebles has reached the somewhat unpopular conclusion that the evidence now on hand indicates that the mass density of the universe is too low to produce flatness by itself. Unless there is some other factor, which some scientists think is possible, space has a negative universe and expansion should continue indefinitely. This model is known as an "open" universe instead of a flat one.

Peebles also has worked extensively on a related problem in cosmology. If the universe originated in a big bang from a uniform past, why is it not uniform today? That is, why is matter gathered into great aggregations called galactic clusters and galaxies that have large amounts of empty space between them? One of the main tools in trying to resolve this problem has been analysis of the cosmic background radiation, the very radiation that made Peebles and Dicke famous in 1965.

Published Works and Awards

Peebles has been an important author throughout his career, presenting the main ideas of cosmology, relativity, and quantum physics to two generations of physical scientists. His classic textbook *Physical Cosmology* from 1972 has only been succeeded by his more recent *Principles of Physical Cosmology*, published in 1993. He has also written a textbook for quantum mechanics as well as outlining *The Large Scale Structure of the Universe* for fellow cosmologists.

Peebles has been honored with the A.C. Morrison Award of the New York Academy of Sciences (1977), the Eddington Medal of the Royal Astronomical Society (1981), the Heineman Prize of the American Astronomical Society (1982), the Robinson Prize (1992), the Bruce Medal of the Astronomical Society of the Pacific (1995), and the Lemaître Award (1995) in addition to many honorary degrees and special lectureships.

SELECTED WRITINGS BY PEEBLES:

Books

The Large-Scale Structure of the Universe. Princeton, NJ: Princeton University Press, 1980.
Physical Cosmology. Princeton, NJ: Princeton University Press, 1972.

Rudolf Peierls

Principles of Physical Cosmology (Princeton Series in Physics). Princeton, NJ: Princeton University Press, 1993.

Quantum Mechanics. Princeton, NJ: Princeton University Press, 1992.

FURTHER READING:

Books

Voyage Through the Universe: The Cosmos. The Editors of Time-Life Books. Richmond, VA: Time-Life Books, 1988.

Wheeler, John Archibald. *A Journey into Gravity and Spacetime.* New York: Scientific American Library, 1990.

—*Sketch by Bryan Bunch*

Rudolf Peierls
1907–1995
German-born English theoretical physicist

As Rudolf Peierls lay on a hill in New Mexico on June 16, 1945, and watched through darkened glass as the first atomic bomb turned night into day, he was struck with awe. Although he was a Manhattan Project scientist and knew exactly what to expect, he later wrote that, "no amount of imagination could have given us a taste of the real thing." As a theoretical physicist who had made contributions to quantum mechanics, it was Peierls and his associate **Otto Frisch** who in 1940 wrote the scientific report that informed governmental leaders that an atomic bomb of extraordinary power was technically possible. Working first for the British, the German-born Peierls eventually moved to the United States and joined the American team assembled at Los Alamos to help build the first bomb.

Rudolf Ernst Peierls was born in Berlin, Germany on June 5, 1907. His father, Heinrich Peierls, was managing director of the cable factory Allgemeine Elektrizitaets-Gesellschaft. His mother, Elisabeth Weigert, died when he was fourteen. The youngest of three children, he was educated at the Humboldt School, Oberschoenewide. Always fascinated by machinery, he decided by the time he was eighteen to become an engineer. However, since he was rather clumsy with his hands and always had poor eyesight, he was persuaded to study the next best subject, physics. Throughout his university career, Peierls was able to study under or have as classmates some of the greatest minds of twentieth century physics. In 1925 he began at the University of Berlin, where he attended lectures on theoretical physics given by **Max Planck** and **Hermann Walther Nernst**. After two semesters there, he moved to Munich and studied under **Arnold Sommerfeld**, who many consider the greatest teacher in theoretical physics. There Peierls became good friends with **Hans Bethe** who was a year ahead of him. In early 1928, Peierls moved again, this time going to Leipzig on the advice of Sommerfeld to study under **Werner Heisenberg**. In Leipzig, he met and became good friends with fellow student, **Felix Bloch**. After a fruitful year there, he moved to Zurich, Switerland in 1929 to join **Wolgang Pauli** at the Federal Institute of Technology. Of these teachers and classmates, only Sommerfeld did not receive a Nobel Prize.

Although this was a time of intense work and study for Peierls, he did not describe it as especially difficult or burdensome when he recalled it in his 1985 autobiography, *Bird of Passage*. He mentioned the stimulating intellectual life, theater, and cabarets of Berlin, the mountain-climbing and swimming at Leipzig, and the sailing, concerts, and cinema of Zurich as often as he recalled encountering a new theory or learning something new.

Continues Associations with Nobel Winners

After receiving his Ph.D. in 1929, Peierls remained at Zurich as Wolgang Pauli's research assistant at the Federal Institute of Technology. The following year he met his future wife, a recent Ph.D. named Eugenia Nikolaevna Kannegiser, at a physics conference in the Soviet Union held at Odessa. They married in Leningrad in 1931.

After they returned to Zurich and Peierls completed his three-year stay at the Institute, he was advised by Pauli to apply for a fellowship at the Rockefeller Foundation, which he received in 1932. Peierls decided to divide the fellowship between Rome for the winter and Cambridge for the summer. Just as he had spent time with **Niels Bohr** when visiting Copenhagen, he met **Enrico Fermi** in Rome and **Ernest Rutherford** in Cambridge, where he also became friends with **Patrick Blackett**—four more colleagues who were or would become Nobel Prize winners. Throughout these years, Peierls' own research remained in the realm of theoretical physics, divided between studying electrons in metals and relativistic field theory.

As his fellowship came to end in 1933, Peierls found himself competing with many other "non-Aryan" scientists who were leaving an increasingly uncomfortable Germany and appearing in England. Unable to obtain a teaching post and already the father of a baby girl named Gaby, he accepted a two-year grant in Manchester University. There he was reunited with his friend, Hans Bethe, and worked with four more Nobel Prize winners, **William L. Bragg**, **James Chadwick**, **Paul Dirac**, and **Eugene Wigner**. During his initial year in Manchester, Peierls and Bethe first began work in the new field of nuclear physics. In early 1935, Peierls left Manchester to accept a temporary fellowship at the Royal Society's Mond Laboratory at Cambridge, which by now had become the center of physics in England. The fellowship had been established to help refugees like Peierls whose Jewish origins made his return to Germany unthinkable.

By this time, he had also become the father of a second child, Ronald (a daughter, Catherine, would be born in 1948 and another, Joanna, in 1949). After two years there, Peierls applied for and received a chair at the University of Birmingham, a position he was to hold until 1963. By 1938, the situation in Germany had deteriorated, and Peierls' father fled to the United States. In 1939, World War II broke out.

Collaboration with Frisch Leads to Startling Atomic Discovery

The discovery of nuclear fission by German scientists **Otto Hahn** and **Fritz Strassmann** was roughly coincidental with the start of World War II. Although discovered by them, it was the Austrian physicists, **Lise Meitner** and **Otto Frisch** (her nephew), who were able to explain this startling phenomenon to the world. Their laboratory work revealed that when a neutron is sent into a uranium nucleus, violent internal motions occur that cause the uranium to split into two other elements. Most importantly, the byproduct of this fission process was the release of an enormous amount of energy. Frisch named the process "fission," since it was so similar to the division of a biological cell.

Like many other physicists, Peierls became interested in fission and wrote a preliminary paper on it. He hesitated to publish however, since it could have had possible bearings on the design of a weapon. He decided to show the paper to Otto Frisch, who had come to Birmingham, England when it appeared the Nazis might overrun Denmark. In early 1940, Frisch made a fateful suggestion to Peierls about his paper. Up to this point, most physicists had considered using only natural uranium, but what, Frisch suggested to Peierls, do you suppose would happen if you used a quantity of pure 235 isotope of uranium? Working on this idea together, they produced in three days time an estimate of the energy released in such a chain reaction. Their conclusions staggered them. Where every other physicist had assumed that tons of scarce uranium would be needed to make an atomic bomb, their calculations indicted that a substantial fraction of that amount, maybe as little as a pound, would result in an energy release equivalent to thousands of tons of ordinary explosive.

The possibility that the Germans may have also made this breakthrough discovery and that Hitler might have already ordered work to begin on such a bomb terrified them and pointed immediately to their next task. In his autobiography, Peierls said, "It was our duty to inform the British government of this possibility. At the same time our conclusion had to be kept secret; if the German physicists had not yet seen the point, we did not want to draw their attention to it."

Discovery Leads to the Manhattan Project

Peierls and Frisch decided to write a memorandum in two parts: one was technical and gave the arguments, and the other was nontechnical and summarized the conclusions. After passing it on to a fellow physicist, Mark Oliphant, who promised to get it to the right person, it went to Sir **Henry Tizard** and then to G. P. Thomson, the chairman of a committee charged with studying this exact problem. The committee was about to disband itself after concluding that no such weapon was technically feasible. At first Peierls and Frisch were told that they could have no more involvement with the committee since they were "enemy aliens." Reason prevailed later and their expertise was eventually requested.

Peierls was soon relieved of his teaching duties in order to work full time on the British effort to build a bomb. By 1943, after Churchill and Roosevelt had direct talks, the British and the Americans decided that it was neither wise nor economical to have duplicate efforts. In late 1943, Peierls led the British group that went to the United States, and he eventually found himself at Los Alamos in the New Mexican desert. Peierls met many old friends from Europe there. One of these friends, Klaus Fuchs, who would later prove to be a Soviet spy, was there because Peierls himself had hired him in 1941 after he had fled the Nazis. Fuchs tricked Peierls and everyone else until his capture in early 1950. At Los Alamos, Peierls worked hard, with what he called "grim determination," and found that his special knowledge of shock waves was especially useful to the Americans. The successful atomic test at Alamogordo on June 16, 1945, meant that the new weapon would soon be ready for use. The United States would soon use this fearsome new weapon twice against Japan.

Peierls remained at Los Alamos until the war was over and then returned to England. Reflecting on his role in building the bomb, Peierls was ever the realist, stating that while he could take no pride in building a weapon that resulted in the horrors of Hiroshima and Nagasaki, he felt that once nuclear fission had been discovered, it could not be undiscovered. It was inevitable therefore, that the atomic bomb would be built, but it was unthinkable for it to be possessed first by the enemy.

Peierls remained in Birmingham until 1963 when he became Wykeham Professor of Theoretical Physics at Oxford University. From 1974 to 1977, he was Professor of Physics at the University of Washington, Seattle. His many honors include a knighthood in 1968, the Royal Medal in 1959, the Copley Medal in 1986 from the Royal Society, the Max Planck Medal from Germany in 1963, and the Enrico Fermi Award from the United States in 1980. He died in Oxford, England on September 19, 1995, after suffering from a kidney ailment.

SELECTED WRITINGS BY PEIERLS:

Books

Bird of Passage. Princeton University Press, 1985.
The Laws of Nature. Allen & Unwin, 1955.

FURTHER READING:

Books

McGraw-Hill Modern Scientists and Engineers. New York: McGraw-Hill, 1980, pp. 403-05.
Porter, Roy, ed. *The Biographical Dictionary of Scientists.* New York: Oxford University Press, 1994, p. 542.

Charles Sanders Peirce

Periodicals

Thomas, Robert M., Jr. "Rudolph Peierls, 88, Atomic Physicist, Dies in England," *The New York Times.* September 22, 1995, B7.

—*Sketch by Leonard C. Bruno*

Charles Sanders Peirce
1839–1914
American logician

Charles Sanders Peirce remains one of the enigmatic figures in the history of American science. He made substantial contributions to a number of fields, especially logic, but his use of unusual terminology makes it difficult to appraise much of his work. As the project of publishing his collected writings continues, it may become possible to do justice to this many–sided thinker.

Charles Sanders Peirce was born on September 10, 1839 in Cambridge, Massachusetts. His father, Benjamin Peirce, was not only a professor of mathematics at Harvard University but also perhaps the most accomplished American mathematician of his generation. Peirce's early education outside the home was at various private schools in Boston and Cambridge, and he showed an interest in puzzles and chess problems. By the age of 13, he had read Archbishop Whately's *Elements of Logic*, perhaps a hint of the interests to come. Peirce entered Harvard in 1855, and the results were not impressive. Although he succeeded in graduating four years later, it was with a class rank of 71 out of 91. Upon graduation Peirce obtained a temporary position with the United States Coast Survey, which was to be his employer for most of his working life. His contributions to geodesy were many, and his service to the Coast Survey have been recognized with a memorial.

In the early 1860s Peirce studied under Louis Agassiz at Harvard, but his work with the Coast Survey proved to have had its benefits. He had become a regular aide to the Survey in 1861, which resulted in his exemption from military service. He was an assistant to the Coast Survey from 1867 to 1891, but that did not prevent his continuing researches in other areas. In particular, not only did he observe a solar eclipse in the United States in 1869, a year later he led an expedition to Sicily to observe a solar eclipse from a position that he had selected.

Broadens the Scope of Logic

Peirce had developed a technical competence in mathematics that came in handy when he turned to logic. As an example of a result in mathematics itself, he succeeded in showing that of linear associative algebras (a subject to which his father had devoted a book) the only three that had a uniquely defined operation of division were real numbers, complex numbers, and the quaternions of Sir William Rowan Hamilton. Perhaps the most significant innovation he made in logic was the extension of Boolean algebra to include the operation of inclusion. The most widely influential treatise on the algebra of logic was produced by the German mathematician Ernst Schröder beginning in 1890, and he displayed a detailed familiarity with Peirce's work. In fact, had Peirce made the effort to produce a systematic account of the subject before Schröder, it would be easier to measure the importance of Peirce's contributions.

One of the factors that played a role in Peirce's interest in logic and its algebraic expression was his having taken a position in 1879 at Johns Hopkins University in Baltimore. During the five years that he worked at the university, he stayed on at the Coast Survey. As Nathan Houser remarked in an article about Peirce, "during those years Peirce was a frequent commuter on the B & O Railroad between Baltimore and Washington." Peirce's first paper on the algebra of logic was published in the *American Journal of Mathematics* in 1880. The period 1880 to 1885 saw Peirce's introduction of two ideas to mathematical logic: truth–functional analysis and quantification theory. Truth–functional analysis is

the ancestor of the technique used by the Austrian philosopher Ludwig Wittgenstein to serve as the basis for logic in his *Tractatus Logico–philosophicus*. Quantification theory was at the heart of the logical apparatus introduced by Gottlob Frege for the reduction of mathematics to logic. It is difficult to imagine two more crucial contributions at the time, although Peirce's share of the recognition suffers by virtue of the scattered nature of his contributions.

Develops an Alternative Philosophy of Science

Peirce was never one to limit his scientific investigations to a single discipline. In 1879, he determined the length of the meter based on a wavelength of light. This provided a natural alternative to the standard meter bar on deposit in Paris. Three years later, he worked on a mathematical study of the relationship between variations in gravity at different points on the Earth's surface and the shape of the Earth. Better known is his role in serving as an advocate of a philosophy of science called pragmatism. Peirce's pragmatism was heavily dependent on the idea of inference to the best explanation. In other words, what existed was determined by what was needed for successful scientific practice at the time. While neither realists nor their opponents were happy with Peirce's position, it has continued to offer an alternative. In particular, philosophers of science with an inclination to take the history of science seriously find Peirce's approach one of the few that take change in one's scientific models to heart.

In light of Peirce's contributions in so many areas of science and mathematics the puzzle remains of why he was unable to secure an academic position commensurate to his abilities. One factor may have been domestic; he married Harriet Melusina Bay in 1862 and was divorced from her in 1883, the year of his second marriage (to Juliette Froissy of Nancy, France). Peirce and his first wife had been separated since 1876, and public sentiment was on her side. More generally, however, Peirce's personality tended to go between extremes, and it was difficult for others to adjust to his mood swings. He was quick to enter into disputes (and frequently with the wrong party) and was easily influenced by others.

Peirce spent his later years in Milford, Pennsylvania, removed from the centers of intellectual life. He had been asked to resign from the Coast Survey in 1891 and for the rest of his life his income was uncertain, despite prodigious periods of writing. Even his philosophy, to which he continued to devote his best efforts, was neglected, if only as a result of his remoteness from university settings. He died in Milford on April 19, 1914, having made contributions across the intellectual map, but more to the benefit of the discipline than his own.

SELECTED WRITINGS BY PEIRCE:

Collected Papers, volumes 1–6. Edited by Charles Hartshorne and Paul Weiss, 1935.
Collected Papers, volumes 7–8. Edited by Arthur W. Burks, 1958.
Writings of Charles S. Peirce, 1982–.

FURTHER READING:

Brent, Joseph. *Charles Sanders Peirce: A Life.* Bloomington: Indiana University Press, 1993.
Eisele, Carolyn. "Charles Sanders Peirce," in *Dictionary of Scientific Biography.* Volume X. Edited by Charles Coulston Gillispie. New York: Charles Scribner's Sons, 1973, pp. 482–488.
Hookway, Christopher. *Peirce.* London: Routledge and Kegan Paul, 1985.
Houser, Nathan. "Peirce and the Law of Distribution," in *Perspectives on the History of Mathematical Logic.* Edited by Thomas Drucker. Boston: Birkhauser, 1991, pp. 10–32.
Mlsak, Cheryl I. *Truth and the End of Inquiry.* Oxford: Oxford University Press, 1985.
Weiss, Paul. "Charles Sanders Peirce," in *Dictionary of American Biography.* Volume 7. Edited by Dumas Malone. New York, Charles Scribner's Sons, 1962, pp. 398–403.

—Sketch by Thomas Drucker

Deborah L. Penry
1957–

American oceanographer

As only the second female to receive the National Science Foundation's Alan T. Waterman Award since its inception in 1976, Deborah Penry is not only an important figure within her scientific discipline, but she is also an extraordinary role model for women in the sciences. Handed out annually to outstanding scientists under the age of 35, the award was given to her in 1993 for her correlation between chemical reactors and the digestive behavior of benthic (living on the bottom of the ocean) organisms. Her digestive paradigm enhances the understanding of ocean ecology and lends broader meaning to the effects feeding and digestion have on various ecosystems.

Deborah L. Penry was born in Maryland on February 28, 1957. With a childhood spent living near Chesapeake Bay and fishing with her father, Penry's passion for oceanography blossomed early in her life. She liked to fish, but she was more intrigued by the contents of a fish's stomach when it was being gutted. It was that curiosity the led her to the University of Delaware, where she earned her B.A. in Biology in 1979. She continued her educational training at William and Mary College in Williamsburg, Virginia, and finished her master's degree in 1982. It was at this point that Penry's interest in ichthyology (the study of fish) was diverted to the organisms and invertebrates that the fish ate.

Penry chose to complete her doctoral studies under the direction of Dr. Peter A. Jumars, a Professor of Oceanography at the University of Washington. Jumars focused his research on the processes conducted by an ocean community and its individuals in order to understand why certain organisms congregate to form various ecosystems. Penry completed her Ph.D. in oceanography in 1988 and continued her post-doctorate work at the University of Washington.

In collaboration, Penry and Jumars discovered parallels between chemical reactor types and the digestive practices of benthic organisms. Like chemical reactions, the feeding/digestion of an organism consumes a material, reacts to that material, and expels that material once its nutrients are extracted. Using this model as a basis, they applied it to other types of organisms.

Finished with her post-doctoral research, Penry moved to a faculty position at the University of California, Berkeley. The biology department within which she taught and conducted research was a conglomeration of smaller departments, including zoology, paleontology, oceanography, and botany, for example. Such an integrative approach to the study of biology lends itself to a broader perspective and was unique at the time. Berkeley's Integrative Biology Department was the first of its kind in the United States as of the early 1990s.

At the University of California, Berkeley, Penry is able to spend quite a bit of time nurturing the minds of her students. She teaches undergraduate and graduate level courses. She has even personally developed a course on biological oceanography. She is a mentor to budding scientists, allowing students access to her laboratory in order to pursue their own research. In fact, the moneys she received along with the Waterman Award were used to further her students' research as well as purchase laboratory equipment.

SELECTED WRITINGS BY PENRY:

Periodicals

(With C. A. Miller and P. M. Glibert) "The Impact of Trophic Interactions on Rates of Nitrogen Regeneration and Grazing in Chesapeake Bay." *Limnol. Oceanography* 40 (1995): 1005-1011.

(With Peter A. Jumars) "Digestion Theory Applied to Deposit Feeding.*" Lecture Notes on Coastal and Estuarine Studies* 31 (1989): 114-128.

(With Peter A. Jumars) "Gut Architecture, Digestive Constraints and Feeding Ecology in Deposit-Feeding and Carnivorous Polychaetes." *Oecologia* 82 (1990): 1-11.

(With Peter A. Jumars) "Modeling Animal Guts as Chemical Reactors." *American Naturalist* 129 (1987): 69-96.

FURTHER READING:

Books

Murphy, Patricia and Leslie O'Brien. "Deborah L. Penry." *Notable Women in the Life Sciences: A Biographical Dictionary.* Benjamin F. Shearer and Barbara S. Shearer, eds. Westport, Connecticut: Greenwood Press, 1996.

Other

University of California, Berkeley Integrative Biology Department directory. http://ib.berkeley.edu/faculty/Penry,DL.html (October 30, 1997).

—Sketch by Jacqueline L. Longe

Martin L. Perl
1927–
American physicist

Martin L. Perl is known for his discovery of the tau lepton, a massive particle related to the electron. For this discovery he was awarded the 1995 Nobel Prize in Physics, along with **Frederick Reines**, discoverer of the neutrino. The tau lepton is an unstable particle that decays into other particles in less than a trillionth of a second. It weighs 3,500 times more than the electron (which is also a lepton, although a stable one). It is one of the 12 subatomic particles from which all matter is formed, the others being the muon, the electron, the three neutrinos (electron neutrino, muon neutrino, and tau neutrino), and the six quarks (up, down, charm, strange, top, and bottom).

Martin Lewis Perl was born in New York City on June 24, 1927, the son of Oscar Perl, a printer and advertiser, and Fay Rosenthal, a secretary and later a bookkeeper for a firm of wool merchants. Both parents came to the United States from Russia at the beginning of the century to escape poverty and anti-

Martin L. Perl

Semitism. America was in the midst of the Great Depression when the Perls were raising their family, but chiefly because of the family printing business, they were able to live in the better neighborhoods of Brooklyn, and the children, Martin and his sister Lila, attended better schools. Lila later became a professional writer in the United States.

Studies Chemical Engineering

Although Perl won a physics medal when he graduated from high school in 1943, he never considered a career in science. The Perls thought a career in engineering would be more profitable than a career in pure science. This was still an unusual career choice for a Jewish boy at the time because there were feelings of anti-Semitism in the engineering field, but it was an area that combined Perl's interest in mechanics, mathematics, and science. He enrolled at the Polytechnic Institute of Brooklyn. He has attributed his early interest in chemical engineering to the exciting nature of the chemical field at the time. Chemistry had captured the public imagination by introducing such popular synthetic materials as nylon.

A future in physics was still unrealized by Perl during college. A general course in physics that he took dealt only with classical mechanical physics, making the science seem dull in comparison to chemistry. Perl continued in his study of engineering and chemistry.

Perl wanted to put his education on hold and enter the United States Army at the beginning of World War II, but as a result of his accelerated graduation from high school he wasn't yet 18, and his parents refused permission for him to enlist. He was, however, allowed to enter the Kings Point Merchant Marine Academy as an engineering cadet. He served six months at sea as part of the training. The war ended in 1945, but the draft was still in effect, and Perl was drafted into the army. He spent a year in Washington, D.C., before returning to college and receiving a bachelor's degree in chemical engineering, summa cum laude, in 1948. That same year he married Teri Hoch.

Discovers Interest in Physics

After college, Perl worked for the General Electric Company in Schenectady, New York, as a chemical engineer in the electron tube division. He was involved in trouble-shooting and designing production improvements for television picture tubes. It was necessary for him to learn something about the workings of electron vacuum tubes, so he took courses at Union College in Schenectady. One day a professor he had come to know, Vladimir Rojansky, told him, "Martin, what you are interested in is called physics not chemistry!"

Perl entered the physics doctoral program at Columbia University in 1950. His background in physics amounted to only one year of elementary physics and a half year in atomic physics, nowhere near the educational preparation of his fellow students. He has said that he was "arrogant" about his ability to learn anything fast, and that by the time he realized the difficulty of the curriculum, it was too late to back out because he had a wife and child and needed the degree.

Upon graduation in 1955, Perl received job offers from the physics departments at the University of Illinois, Yale University, and the University of Michigan. He said he chose Michigan, despite the better reputations of the other two departments, because he wanted the greater freedom and opportunity for recognition that came with working in a smaller, less-established research group.

Discovers the Tau Lepton

Perl's earliest research was conducted prior to the early 1960s, while he was with the University of Michigan. While affiliated with the University he performed experiments at the Brookhaven Cosmotron in New York state, and the Berkeley Bevatron in California. These experiments were in strong interaction physics, but by 1962 his interests were moving toward lepton physics, a field he considered "simpler." In "The Discovery of the Tau Lepton," Perl

states that he had always liked simple theory "and it was clear that strong interaction theory was not becoming simpler . . . [T]he physics of leptons seemed a simpler world."

Perl accepted a position at the Stanford Linear Accelerator Center (SLAC), at Stanford University in California, in 1963. The facility was the site of the SPEAR Positron-Electron storage ring which Perl would use in his positron-electron colliding beam search for heavy leptons. A 1971 proposal for an experiment, the first to involve a search for a heavy lepton, devoted just three pages to the tau lepton search, because "to most others it seemed a remote dream."

Despite the tau lepton's lifespan of less than a trillionth of a second, Perl and his colleagues were able to prove its existence by showing that events in the experiment could not be explained away by the decay or production of any other known particles. The discovery paved the way for other physicists to find the bottom and top quarks, thereby completing the standard model of fundamental particles that explains all of the forces and interactions in matter and energy. The discovery was a total surprise to the physics community in 1975. Stanley Wojcicki, a colleague at SLAC, has called it "the best kind of discovery," and says that Perl "caught people completely out of the blue. No one anticipated it." Perl's hope is that his 1995 Nobel Prize for discovering the tau will help convince people that his current efforts to discover free quarks are "not a waste of time." Perl is still at Stanford.

SELECTED WRITINGS BY PERL:

Books

High Energy Hadron Physics. Wiley, 1974.
The Search for New Elementary Particles. World Scientific Publishing Co., 1992.
The Tau-Charm Factory. Editions Frontiéres, 1994.

—Sketch by Paul Lewon

Hans Pettersson
1888–1966
Swedish oceanographer

Hans Pettersson was born in Marstrand, on an island off the Swedish coast, on August 26, 1888, the son of Otto and Agnes (Irgens) Pettersson. His father was a scientist who was well-known in Sweden for his studies of the swift tides that run in the Skagerrak, an arm of the North Sea between Norway and Denmark. These tides flowed vigorously just outside the door of Kälhuvudet, the Pettersson's house built on a large, cabbage-shaped rock. Although Hans was to become famous for commanding a trip around the world, he seldom left the Swedish coast for long. From the start of World War I almost up to the start of the Space Age, Pettersson made his main base at the University of Göteborg, a few miles down the Skagerrak from Kälhuvudet and at the top of the Kattegat, another North Sea arm.

Before finally settling at Göteborg, however, Pettersson had bounced between physics and oceanography for a few years. His studies at the Universities of Uppsala and Stockholm and at University College in London culminated in a Doctor of Science in physics from Stockholm in 1914. During this time, he became interested in problems connected with radioactivity, which became one of his ongoing interests. Even while he was a physics student, he began to work on oceanography, publishing papers on the tides and currents of the Kattegat. One of his main concerns at this time remains a compelling topic to modern oceanographers, how the currents of the North Atlantic affect the climate of Europe. Another area of study around this time was the amount of radioactivity in sea water and in undersea sediments. Until 1930 Petersson varied his activities greatly, lecturing regularly on oceanography at Göteborg while also leading a team at the Institute of Radium Treatment in Vienna. In 1930, however, he accepted a professorship at Göteborg, where he remained until 1956.

While Pettersson was at Göteborg in the 1930s, he worked hard on making oceanography a prime concern for other Swedes. He wrote books and articles, spoke on the radio, and made many personal contacts and appeals to wealthy businessmen in Sweden. Eventually he obtained the financial backing needed to start an oceanographic laboratory at Göteborg, the Oceanografiska Institutet, of which Pettersson became the first director. By the time the laboratory was in operation, in 1939, Europe was at war. During the war, Pettersson was able to continue his promotion of oceanography in neutral Sweden. Borja Kullenberg, working for Pettersson in Sweden during World War II, developed new designs for a corer to sample the sediments on the ocean floor, and Pettersson did not neglect his wealthy patrons. As soon as hostilities ended, the Brostrom Shipping Company provided the Oceanografiska Institutet with an ocean-going ship (on loan) to be used for a round-the-world scientific expedition. Other firms, organizations, and individuals supplied the money or equipment needed for the trip, which was to last more than a year.

Round-the-World Voyage Provides Invaluable Research on Ocean Floor

The ship, the *Albatross,* could operate as a sailing ship or as a steamship, an important option for a round-the-world voyage. After a trial run in the Mediterranean, the *Albatross* embarked on July 4, 1947, aiming at a 40,000 mile (64,000 km) voyage that would be primarily in the tropics. Along the way, the crew would sample the ocean floor in many ways, not only by obtaining as many sediment cores as they could, but also by studying the ocean floor for pollen, radioactive elements, volcanic ash, and any other materials that could be dredged from the bottom of the sea, including dust from meteorites. The workers on the *Albatross* even measured the clarity of the seawater in various oceans. Furthermore, many parts of the sea floor were mapped for the first time. The Swedish Deep-Sea Expedition in the *Albatross* was among the first scientific expeditions whose main intent was to study the ocean.

At about the same time as the Swedish Deep-Sea Expedition was getting under way, similar research projects were being started in the Atlantic Ocean by the Lamont Geological Observatory under **William Maurice Ewing.** Many of the discoveries of both institutions complemented each other. Both Borja Kullenberg at Göteborg University, who sailed on the *Albatross,* and Maurice Ewing in the United States had developed new devices that could bring back cores of ocean floor, some as long as 60 ft (18 m), although 20 ft (6 m) was the average for the *Albatross* expedition. In 1948 the Swedish Deep-Sea Expedition under Pettersson's leadership discovered a deep abyssal plain south of the Bay of Bengal in the Indian Ocean. This was just a year after a similar deep plain, both of them extremely flat (depth variations a less than 6 ft [1.8 m] in a mile), had been found by Ewing in the North Atlantic.

We have today become so used to the understanding of the oceans based on the theory of plate tectonics, that it is surprising to realize how different the concept was in 1948, when Pettersson led the crew of the *Albatross* around the world. Pettersson himself had many ideas that seemed plausible at the time, but which subsequent research has shown to be invalid. He thought that volcanic activity accounted for the great plains, such as the one he discovered in the Indian Ocean, but we now think they are the result of sediment that has slid across the ocean floor and settled. Pettersson was interested in meteorites, and so he thought that the iron nodules and nickel-rich sediments he dredged up showed large bombardments of Earth by meteoroids. Today, these are explained by chemical precipitation from sea water. He tried to use radium to date the sediments on the ocean floor, which was not unlike modern methods of dating, but more difficult because of the small amount of radium present.

After the plate tectonics revolution of the 1950s and 1960s, the findings of the *Albatross* expedition were reinterpreted and provided useful data on many aspects of the sea and the sea floor.

SELECTED WRITINGS BY PETTERSSON:

Books

The Ocean Floor. New Haven: Yale University Press, 1954.
Westward Ho With the Albatross. New York: Dutton, 1953. (Swedish edition *Med Albatross over havsdjupen*, published in 1950.)

FURTHER READING:

Books

Ericson, David B. and Goesta Wollin. *The Ever-Changing Sea.* New York: Alfred A. Knopf, 1967.

—*Sketch by Bryan Bunch*

William D. Phillips

William D. Phillips
1948–

American physicist

William D. Phillips has spent his entire professional career at the National Institute of Standards and Technology (NIST), formerly the National Bureau of Standards, of the U.S. Department of Commerce. He has focused much of his research on the development of techniques for cooling atoms to very low temperatures and then studying the properties of these atoms. In 1988 he discovered that atoms could be cooled to a temperature of only 40μK, or 40 millionths of a degree Kelvin. This temperature was about six times lower than the temperature that had been predicted as the lowest possible temperature to which matter can be cooled. As a result of this discovery, he was able to study the interaction of sodium atoms in a form that had never been observed before. For his work with the cooling of matter, Phillips was awarded a share of the 1997 Nobel Prize in Physics along with **Steven Chu** and **Claude Cohen-Tannoudji**.

William Daniel Phillips was born on November 5, 1948, in Wilkes-Barre, Pennsylvania. He grew up in Camp Hill, outside Harrisburg, and attended Juniata College. He was remembered as a very good student who asked a lot of questions to get more information.

Phillips was also active in extracurricular activities, participating in the Forensic Club and the Honors Society, and was a member of the tennis team.

Phillips was awarded his B.S. degree from Juniata in 1970. He then continued his studies at the Massachusetts Institute of Technology (MIT), from which he earned a Ph.D. in physics in 1976. He then spent two years as a postdoctoral Chaim Weizmann Fellow at MIT. In 1978, Phillips accepted an appointment as a physicist at NIST, a post he retained for the next two decades.

Studies Low Temperature Phenomena

Phillips has been interested in the problem of cooling and trapping atoms since his years at MIT. This line is of growing interest among physicists because it provides a way of studying the structure and properties of individual molecules and atoms. Traditionally, scientists have been able to study only the bulk properties of matter, that is, the average properties of, at best, trillions and trillions of atoms and molecules. Yet, it is known that these average properties mask the properties of individual particles that make up a sample. The study of atoms and molecules is of interest not only for theoretical reasons, but also because of its potential practical applications on a macroscopic scale. Engineers are beginning to learn how to construct particles that consist of a relatively small number of particles, called nanostructures, with potentially revolutionary applications. In order to advance in this field of research, it has become necessary to understand how individual atoms and molecules behave.

The key to these studies is to find ways to cool atoms and molecules, that is, to reduce the speed at which they travel. At room temperature, the particles in a gas are typically traveling at speeds of a few thousand miles (kilometers) per hour. At these speeds, particles escape from a field of view so quickly that no meaningful measurements can be made. In order to keep the particles within a field of view, their velocity must be reduced. Simply cooling a gas by conventional methods (such as putting it in a refrigerator) does not solve this problem. Under those conditions, the gas particles do lose speed, but they eventually condense to form a liquid or solid. In both liquids and solids, particles are so close to each other that individual properties cannot be determined. The objective, then, is to cool down a gas without permitting it to condense.

Theoreticians were proposing methods for solving this problem since the 1950s. One of the most popular approaches was to bombard a moving particle with a photon of energy moving towards that particle. Imagine, for example, a stream of ping pong balls fired from a gun. Those ping pong balls might be compared to the particles in a gas. Then imagine that short puffs of air are directed at the stream of ping pong balls. The puffs of air correspond to photons of energy. As each puff of air strikes a ping pong ball, it transfers energy to the ball and reduces the speed with which the ball is moving in the forward direction. If this process is repeated over and over again with any given ping pong ball, the ball eventually slows down and comes to a stop.

This analogy is greatly oversimplified, however. Real particles that are struck by a photon quickly give off the energy they have absorbed and recoil in a direction that cannot be predicted. Another photon aimed at the same particle will miss contact because the particle has changed its line of flight.

Another factor to be considered is that atoms and molecules absorb only certain quantized levels of energy. A photon with the wrong energy will have no effect on any particle that it strikes. Furthermore, the energy needed to excite a particle changes as the particle moves toward or away from the source of energy. This effect is known as the Doppler effect and is familiar to anyone who has heard the pitch of a train whistle increase or decrease as it moves toward or away from an observer.

Still, given all these conditions, an experimenter should be able to design an apparatus by which bursts of energy can be used to slow down the movement of atoms and molecules. In the mid-1980s, Steven Chu and his co-workers at the Bell Laboratories in Holmdel, New Jersey, designed an "atom trap" in which particles are bombarded by three pairs of laser guns arranged at right angles to each other. This arrangement was able to slow atoms down to a speed of about 12 in per second (30 cm per second), equivalent to a temperature of about 240 microkelvin. Theoretical calculations had shown that this temperature was probably the lowest that could be reached by the methods described above.

Unexpected Results

In 1988, Phillips attained a remarkable breakthrough by repeating the kinds of experiments carried out earlier by Chu and his colleagues. Phillips' group found that they were able to attain a minimum temperature of 40 microkelvin, six times lower than that predicted by theory and observed by Chu. Phillips later wrote that his results were "at first difficult to believe, especially considering the attractive simplicity of the Doppler cooling theory (and the generally held belief that experiments never work better than one expects). This turn of events," he went on, "was both welcome and unsettling." The theoretical explanation for these observations was later provided by Claude Cohen-Tannoudji at the École Normale Supérieure in Paris, an accomplishment for which he was awarded a share of the 1997 Nobel Prize in Physics.

Phillips produced other breakthroughs in the study of low temperature behavior. In 1985, for example, he found a way to trap atoms in a maze of laser beams. The beams were arranged so as to produce constructive and destructive interference patterns. When placed into this kind of maze, gaseous atoms at very low temperatures fell into low-energy pockets in somewhat the manner that eggs fall into the depressions of the cartons in which they are sold.

Using devices such as these, Phillips has been able to create entirely new forms of matter that exist only under low temperature conditions and only for very brief periods of time. For example, in one experiment, he brought together a collection of sodium atoms that formed a molecular-like substance but that was much larger than an ordinary molecule. The collection of atoms broke apart after about 10 nanoseconds.

In addition to his position at NIST, Phillips has been Visiting Professor of Atomic Physics at the College de France (1987), Visiting Scientist at the École Normale Supérieure in Paris (1989-1990), and Adjunct Professor of Physics at the University of Maryland (1992-). He was elected to the National Academy of Sciences in 1997. He married to the former Jane Van Wynen in 1970 and has two daughters, Catherine and Christine.

SELECTED WRITINGS BY PHILLIPS:

(With H. J. Metcalf) "Cooling and Trapping Atoms." *Scientific American* (March 1987): 36-44.

(With Claude N. Cohen-Tannoudji) "New Mechanisms for Laser Cooling." *Physics Today* (October 1990): 33-40.

FURTHER READING:

Other

"Press Release: The Nobel Prize in Physics 1997." http://www.nobel.se/announcement-97/physics97.html.

"1997 Nobel Prize in Physics Awarded to Juniata College Graduate." http://www.juniata.edu/news/latest.htm.

"NIST Fellow William D. Phillips Elected to National Academy of Science." http://physics.nist.gov/News/Releases/tn6136.html.

"Physicists Get Hot New Results with Cold Atoms." http://physics.nist.gov/News/Releases/n96-02.html.

—*Sketch by David E. Newton*

George Edward Pierce
1947–

American microbiologist

George Edward Pierce is noted primarily for his application of microbiological principles to industrial pollution problems. He has linked scientific research to the corporate world in an effort to prevent pollution, produce environmentally friendly products, and to neutralize hazardous waste.

Born in Meriden, Connecticut, on June 6, 1947, Pierce completed his undergraduate degree in biology in 1969 and earned his doctorate in microbiology in 1976 at Rensselaer Polytechnic Institute, Troy, New York. He remained at the institute until 1977, working as a teaching and research assistant and postdoctoral associate in the biology department. In this early part of his career, Pierce focused on the use of microbes to aid the breakdown of petroleum and petroleum-based products.

In 1977, Pierce moved from academia to industry. He accepted a post as a biomedical researcher Battelle Columbus Division in Columbus, Ohio. He remained with Battelle until 1988, serving as a senior researcher and associate section manager. It was

during this period that Pierce firmly linked microbiology to industry. He studied the effectiveness of activated carbon and silver-impregnated filters in relationship to microbes in water systems; he investigated levels of and resistance to dichlorodiphenyltrichloroethane (DDT) in microorganisms present in soil heavily laden with the pesticide. He looked for commercially feasible methods to manufacture the more environmentally acceptable fuel ethanol and studied herbicide-degrading bacteria. Pierce left Battelle to accept a position as director of bioremediation technology with Celgene Corporation in Warren, New Jersey. Here, he continued his research in the identification and development of microorganisms that could be used to neutralize waste.

Pierce's work emphasizes the elimination of environmental toxins through environmentally friendly methods. Genetic manipulation of microorganisms poses its own potential dangers; Pierce, through his work in the laboratory, his service with regulatory agencies, and his scientific presentations, promotes long-term analysis and scientific responsibility in this area.

Promoting Optimism and Caution

In 1991, Pierce joined American Cynamid, Linden, New Jersey, as manager of technology development in the Environmental Services Group. He became more visible as a spokesman for those in the scientific community who demanded responsible use of microbiological technologies. He addressed in more depth the barriers and issues, as well as the technological advances, surrounding the use of enzymatic and microbiological treatment of industrially produced hazardous waste.

Pierce stepped up his activities in the regulatory community—a key element in developing, applying, and controlling technologies that were advancing faster than their long-term effects could be understood. In 1991, he joined the Environmental Protection Agency's Subcommittee on Pollution Prevention as co-chair, and chaired the committee in 1992. He serves as a member of the U.S. Department of Commerce Committee on Biotechnology, which he joined in 1991, and has served since 1992 as a consultant to the EPA Science Advisory Board and since 1990 as a member of the EPA's Bioremediation Action Committee.

Pierce also feels a commitment to the next generation of scientists. He held an appointment as adjunct professor with Ohio State University from 1983 to 1995 and is currently an adjunct professor at Rensselaer Polytechnic Institute.

Recognition and Professional Affiliations

Pierce is active in the American Society for Microbiology and the Society for Industrial Microbiology. He served as editor-in-chief of *The Journal of Industrial Microbiology* from 1985 to 1993 and co-chaired the 1995 annual meeting of the Society for Industrial Microbiology. Since 1985, he has served as the U.S. national delegate to the International Union of Microbiological Societies and, since 1991, has been a member of the steering committee of the American Academy of Environmental Engineers. He also served as director of the Society for Industrial Microbiology from 1982 to 1985.

Pierce currently holds seven patents in the United States, Europe, Canada, and Japan. He has been awarded patents for the microbial production of hydroxy- and keto-fatty acids; development of recombinant DNA plasmid used to degrade organic compounds; production of new bacteria lipase enzymes; biofilters; aerobic degradation; fluid phase biodegradation; and microorganisms for compound degrading. In 1993, the Society for Industrial Microbiology recognized Pierce's work with the Charles Porter Award. Pierce has also published dozens of scholarly articles and made numerous professional presentations.

Pierce is currently manager of Technology Development and Engineering in the Environmental Services Group of Cytec Industries, a company created by a series of mergers and divestitures involving American Cynamid.

SELECTED WRITINGS BY PIERCE:

Periodicals

(With C. B. Wick) "Integrated Approach to the Development of Biodegradation Systems to Treat Hazardous Organic Chemicals," *Developments in Industrial Microbiology*, 1990, Volume 31, pp. 81-98.

(With A. H. Lipkkus, K. K. Chitur, S. J. Vesper, and J. B. Robinson) "Evaluation of Infrared Spectroscopy as a Bacterial Identification Method," *Journal of Industrial Microbiology*, 1990, Volume 6, pp. 63-70.

(With J. B. Robinson, G. E. Garrett, D. K. Terman, and S. A. Sojka) "Improved Cloning and Transfer of Pseudomonas Plasmid DNA," *Developments in Industrial Microbiology*, 1985, Volume 26, pp. 793-801.

"Potential of Genetic Engineering in Microbial Degradation." *Battelle Memorial Institute Proceedings*, 1981, Volume 4, pp. 204-210.

FURTHER READING:

Books
American Men and Women of Science, 19th edition. R. R. Bowker Co., 1994, p. 1242.

Who's Who of Emerging Leaders in America, 1st edition. Marquis Who's Who, 1987.
Who's Who in Engineering and Science, 1st edition. Marquis Who's Who, 1991.

—*Sketch by Angie Mullig*

Naomi E. Pierce
1954–
American entomologist and molecular biologist

Naomi E. Pierce is best known for her studies of the interactions between butterflies and other species of insects. Her field and laboratory investigations, particularly of the relationship between the Lycaenid "mistletoe butterfly" and the farmer ants that "herd" it, have helped reveal the environmental and behavioral forces that maintain cooperation between insect species. In addition, her recent efforts to use molecular science have helped improve upon the body-structure-based methods previously used to understand the evolutionary relationships between these butterflies.

Pierce is also known for her active efforts to help women scientists train and become established in the scientific community. A MacArthur fellow and the first woman to be tenured in her department at Harvard University, Pierce is a vocal proponent of mentoring in scientific education. She says that her early, positive experiences with mentor relationships have encouraged her to take on a growing number of graduate students and other teaching responsibilities.

Hooked on Butterflies

Pierce was born on October 19, 1954, into an erudite Denver, Colorado, family. Her father was a geophysicist; her grandfather was a novelist in Japan. The latter especially influenced her, leading to a lifelong interest in novels and contemporary fiction. She did not originally want to become a scientist; for the first three years of her college education at Yale University, she majored in history, arts, and letters.

Pierce was also hedging her bets, taking science courses in case she wanted to go to medical school. A course on evolution taught by Charles Remington, which she took in her third year of college, was to trigger a profound change in her life. Intrigued by Remington's lectures touching on his work with butterflies at the Rocky Mountain Biological Laboratory in Colorado, Pierce visited his office one day to find out more about his work. She found his enthusiasm for butterflies to be infectious, and registered for summer courses at the Rocky Mountain laboratory. In her senior year of college, she changed her major to biology, graduating in 1976.

In 1976 Pierce won a John Courtney Murray Fellowship that allowed her to travel to Southeast Asia to study butterflies. There she became acquainted with the Lycaenids, especially the "mistletoe butterfly" of Australia. Half of a unique cooperative arrangement between butterfly and ant, the mistletoe butterfly's larvae are tended, protected, and herded by farmer ants, in exchange secreting a sugary liquid that the ants eat. She was so intrigued by the relationship that she made it the topic of her doctoral dissertation at Harvard University, where she worked with famous ant expert **Edward O. Wilson** as well as doctoral advisors Bert Hilldobler and R. E. Silberglied. She received her Ph.D. from Harvard in 1983.

Pierce returned to Southeast Asia in that same year, as a Fullbright Postdoctoral Research Fellow at Griffith University in Queensland. There she studied another family of Lycaenid butterflies that are carnivorous, feeding on aphids. Following her year in Australia, she continued her studies of the carnivorous Lycanidae, first as a NATO Postdoctoral Fellowship and a research lecturer at Oxford University from 1984 to 1986, then as an assistant professor at Princeton University from 1986 to 1990.

Pierce's postdoctoral work led her to study larger questions of evolution and species relationships. Dissatisfied with the depth of knowledge of the Lycaenid butterflies' relationships and life histories, Pierce determined to improve the previous phylogenetic "family trees," built mostly by comparing relationships between body structures. As one of only 31 MacArthur fellows named in 1988, Pierce had five years to conduct unrestricted research. She retrained as a molecular biologist, learning how to use genetic technologies to refine and improve upon the maps of evolutionary relationship between the Lycaenidae. In 1991 Pierce was named the first Hessel Professor of Biology at Harvard, becoming the first tenured woman in that university's Department of Organismal and Evolutionary Biology as well as the curator of the world-renowned butterfly collection at Harvard's Museum of Comparative Zoology.

Pierce's willingness and ability to branch out into new specialties and interact with scientists in different fields has characterized her work. In particular, her studies of the chemical signals by which butterflies and ants communicate have brought together field biologists, entymologists, and molecular scientists. Today, her research spans a number of disciplines having to do with the ecological, behavioral, and biochemical mechanisms underlying butterfly/ant interactions. Her work concentrates particularly with the goal of understanding how the Lycaenid butterflies evolved to fill diverse ecological niches in which they can be carnivorous or herbivorous, and cooperative or parasitic on other insect species.

Mentoring Women in Science

While earning a reputation for multidisciplinary flexibility, Pierce has also taken an active role in encouraging other women to rise in the scientific establishment. She credits her relationship with mentor Remington with helping her achieve a strong start in what can sometimes be a challenging career choice for women.

An active teacher with a preference for individual and small-group teaching, Pierce leads a laboratory that she says follows a cooperative rather than a hierarchical model. As well as helping her to add molecular techniques to her laboratory's investigatory armamentarium, her MacArthur fellowship also allowed several of her graduate students to travel and study in Australia. Pierce and her students spend three months out of each year doing field work.

Pierce's most recent "research interest," according to her web page, are her and her husband Andrew Berry's twin daughters, Kate and Megan, born in 1997.

SELECTED WRITINGS BY PIERCE:

Books

"Amplified Species Diversity: A Case Study of an Australian Lycaenid Butterfly and its Attendant Ants." *Biology of Butterflies. XI Symp R Entomol Soc (Lond).* R.I. Vane Wright and P.R. Ackery, editors. London: Academic Press, 1984, pp.197-200.
(With J.T. Costa) "Social Evolution in the Lepidoptera: Ecological Context and Communication in Larval Societies." *Social Competition and Cooperation in Insects and Arachnids, Volume II: Evolution of Sociality.* B.J. Crespi and J.C. Choe, editors. 1996.

Periodicals

"Costs and Benefits of Cooperation Between the Australian Lycaenid Butterfly, Jalmenus evagoras and its Attendant Ants." *Behav Ecol Sociobiol* (1987): 237-248.
(With B.S.W. Chang, et al.) "Cloning of the Gene Encoding Honeybee Long-Wavelength Rhodopsin: A new Class of Insect Long-Wavelength Visual Pigments." *Gene* (1996): 215-219.

David R. Pilbeam

FURTHER READING:

Periodicals

Cromie, William J. "Naomi Pierce: Butterfly Behavior Leads to Insights on Evolution." *Harvard Gazette* (November 8, 1991): 9.

Other

"Pierce Laboratory: Harvard University." October 4, 1996. http://www.oeb.harvard.edu/faculty/pierce/lab (November 25, 1997).

"Prof. Naomi Pierce." April 22, 1997. http://www.oeb.harvard.edu/faculty/pierce/npierce/npierce.html (25 November 25, 1997).

—*Sketch by Kenneth Chiacchia*

David R. Pilbeam
1940–

English-born American paleoanthropologist

In the field of physical anthropology, David R. Pilbeam stands out as a scientist whom all recognize as an authority. Pilbeam enjoys the respect of his peers in part because he has not flinched at changing his views when new evidence surfaces.

David Roger Pilbeam was born on November 21, 1940, in the seaside resort of Brighton in Sussex, England. He is the son of Ernest and Edith (Clack) Pilbeam, and was the first member of his family to attend a university. Upon completing his B.A. at Cambridge University in England in 1963, he came to the United States to study at Yale University in New Haven, Connecticut. He returned to Cambridge in 1965 to teach. After receiving his Ph.D. from Yale in 1967, Pilbeam joined the faculty at Yale, where he became Professor of Anthropology in 1974. In 1981 he moved to Harvard University in Cambridge, Massachusetts, where he now is Henry Ford II Professor of the Social Sciences, head of the Paleoanthropology research center, and an Academic Dean. He also was Director of the Peabody Museum from 1990-96. At Harvard he met his wife, Maryellen Ruvolo, who is a molecular geneticist/anthropologist and a Professor in the Anthropology Department.

Pilbeam's research has primarily been focused on interpreting the role of Miocene-period apes in the evolution of humans. During the 1960s, he identified three species of an African and European ape or hominoid genus dating back 20 million years that appeared to be ancestral to the great apes. He also concurred with a Yale colleague that a 15-million-year-old ape discovered in India, known as *Ramapithecus*, possessed teeth more like those of the human line, the hominids. At that time, this classification scheme seemed plausible, since the separation of apes and humans was thought to have occurred early in the Miocene epoch, which spans roughly from 30 million years ago to five million years ago. Pilbeam put the separation of humans from apes at about 20 to 15 million years ago. However, deoxyribonucleic acid (DNA) dating indicated that the common ancestor lived only about five million years ago, at the end of the Miocene. Pilbeam defended *Ramapithecus* and its close relatives as early hominids for a decade after the first DNA evidence appeared. Later in 1981, Pilbeam examined a partial skull from Pakistan that, along with other recently discovered evidence, changed his mind completely. This ape, known as *Sivapithecus*, dated back to approximately 10 million years ago and was clearly similar to the modern orangutan and also related to *Ramapithecus*. Consequently, Pilbeam modified his original theory, leading other anthropologists to accept a more recent date for the divergence of great apes and human ancestors.

Pilbeam's expeditions to Asia and Africa continue to produce more evidence concerning both Miocene apes and the early line leading to humans. His studies in Pakistan cover a period from early in the Miocene—about 18 million years ago—to the time of early species of *Homo,* about two million years ago, and deal not only with the apes and hominids but also with evolution of animals and their interaction with the environment. At Harvard, he has become a great synthesizer of ideas related to the evolution of hominids and hominoids. When any major new discovery concerning early human ancestry is announced, Pilbeam's phone begins to ring with queries from science writers everywhere who want to know what the new fossil might mean.

SELECTED WRITINGS BY PILBEAM:

Books

The Evolution of Man. London: Thames and Hudson, 1970.
Ascent of Man: An Introduction to Human Evolution. New York: Macmillan Publishing Company, 1972.
(with G.A. Harrison, J.M. Tanner, and P.T. Barker) *Human Biology.* New York: Oxford University Press, 1988.
(Ed. with Stephen Jones and Robert D. Martin) *The Cambridge Encyclopedia of Human Evolution.* New York: Cambridge University Press, 1993.

FURTHER READING:

Books

Lewin, Roger. *The Origin of Modern Humans.* New York: Scientific American Books, 1993.

—*Sketch by Bryan Bunch*

Vera Pless
1931–
American mathematician

Vera Pless took her early interest in the pure algebra of ring theory and applied it to the combinatorics of error—correcting computer codes in the developing field of computer science. This line of inquiry cuts to the quick of a computer's weakness—faulty data transmission. As one of the first lay people to recognize this challenge, Pless naturally became a leader in what is now being called discrete mathematics. As projects with computers demand more fidelity (as in compact discs) and greater scale (as with the Sojourner Mars mission), coding theory becomes more central to all technologies.

Vera Pless was born Vera Stepen in Chicago on March 5, 1931. Her parents were Russian immigrants who settled in the predominantly Jewish west side of the city. A friend of the family, who was a graduate student at the University of Chicago, taught Pless calculus when she was 12 years old. He saw a bright kid with a future in math, but may not have realized that she would not welcome a scholarship to the College at the University of Chicago. The fifteen–year–old Pless wanted to play the cello, but acceded to her father's wish that she study a practical subject.

Pless took some inspiration from the woman some call the founder of modern algebra, **Emmy Noether**. "I passed my master's exam two weeks after I got married," in 1952, she states plainly enough in her autobiographical essay. Although her husband was pursuing a Ph.D. in physics, Pless accepted a research associateship at Northwestern University to pursue her own Ph.D. They both relocated to Boston while she was completing her thesis on ring theory and defended her thesis two weeks before giving birth in 1957.

Unfortunately, at that time Boston academia did not welcome a female Ph.D. with two children and a working husband. "I heard people say outright, 'I would never hire a woman'," Pless remembers. However, the nearby Air Force Research Labs in Cambridge were very much in need of her algebraic skills. Error correcting codes were of most immediate use to the military's intelligence and security programs. Pless welcomed the chance to work as part of a group and found the workshops with Andrew Gleason of Harvard University beneficial as well. Later on, she was allowed maternity leave for her third child. Pless's work there included designing programs to compare tracks left behind in experimental bubble chambers.

After the U.S. Congress passed the Mansfield Amendment banning basic research within the defense sector of the government, Pless returned to the possibility of an academic career. It was a struggle to get back into the mode of papers and lecturing. Nonetheless, three years as a research associate at M.I.T., working on such subjects as encryption, led her in 1975 to a position at the University of Illinois, back in her hometown.

Greedy Codes

Pless has worked as a visiting professor, researcher, and scientist at The Technion in Haifa, the Argonne, and a number of American universities including M.I.T. The National Science Foundation (NSF) funded her stay at Caltech during 1985–86 with its visiting professorship for women grant, only the most recent example of NSF aid to Pless's career. There, she organized bimonthly coding seminars over the academic year. Over the years Pless has sat on several thesis committees and personally directed 15 graduate and postdoctoral students, sometimes three at once.

Such a busy schedule has not prevented Pless from figuring out new ways her students can use technology and innovative means of studying computer programs, as Laura Monroe attests. As Monroe's thesis advisor in 1995, Pless encouraged her to apply her ideas about "greedy codes" in computer science to some of the most powerful computers available, including a CRAY–C90 (UNICOS). "As an advisor," Monroe concluded, "she was always interested in her students' new ideas and enthusiastic about their progress."

The dual responsibilities of teaching and research have called for innovation on Pless's part. She started the CAMAC computer system at M.I.T. and brought it out west with her when she relocated in 1975, where she continues to extend and develop it with associate Thom Grace. The system has gained a measure of prominence because of its use in countless projects and being mentioned in over 20 publications. CA-MAC I proved so popular that CAMAC II was started by another colleague, Jeff Leon, with Pless's aid.

The All–Professor Team

Pless writes, reviews, referees, and edits extensively, having held concurrent editorships in several publications during the 1980s and 1990s. Some of this is borne of necessity, as her field is still very new. With Joel Berman, she designed the first college course in discrete mathematics based on their lecture notes. Pless's *Introduction to The Theory of Error–Correcting Codes* carries the highest rating in the Mathematical Association of America's Library Recommendations for Undergraduate Mathematics. From 1993 to 1994, the U.S. Department of Education retained her for a paid position as part of their Algebra Initiative.

Pless's professional service includes advisory and elected positions with a variety of mathematics and science groups, helping to oversee projects of the National Science Foundation, the National Research Council, and to review the funding of Fulbright scholars and National Security Agency proposals. As a member of the American Mathematical Society, Pless has served on committees concerning the human rights of mathematicians, academic freedom, and employment security. She is often invited and fully funded to speak at various professional meetings, seminars, and colloquia. Not all of Pless's honors are so formal. In 1993, the *Chicago Tribune* included her in their "All–Professor Team of Academic Champions."

By the middle of 1997, Pless's list of publications on aspects of information theory and code design numbered over 100, written either singly or with such illustrious figures as John H. Conway and **John Thompson**.

SELECTED WRITINGS BY PLESS:

Books

An Introduction to The Theory of Error–Correcting Codes, 1983; revised edition 1990.
(Editor) *Handbook on Coding* (in publication).

Periodicals

"Continuous Transformation Ring of Biorthogonal Bases Spaces." *Duke Mathematics Journal* 25, MR 20, No. 2630 (1958).
"Power Moment Identities on Weight Distributions in Error Correcting Codes." *Information and Control*, MR 41, No. 6614 (1963).
"Attitudes About and of Professional Women: Now and Then," in *Career Guidance for Women Entering Engineering: Proceedings of an Engineering Foundation Conference*. Edited by Nancy Fitzroy. August 1973.

Other

"Short Autobiography of Vera Pless." *Pless Papers*. University of Illinois at Chicago, January 1997.

FURTHER READING:

Periodicals

Birman, Haimo, Landau, Srinivasan, Pless, and Taylor. "In Her Own Words: Six Mathematicians Reflect on Their Lives and Careers." *Notices of the American Mathematical Society* 38 No. 7 (1991): pp. 702–706.

Other

"F. Jessie MacWilliams." *A Survey of Coding Theory*. http://www.math.neu.edu/awm/noether-brochure/MacWilliams80.html
"MAA Prizes Presented in Orlando." *Notices of the AMS* (April, 1996): http://e-math.ams.org/notices/199604/comm–maa.html
Monroe, Laura, email interview with Jennifer Kramer conducted July 10–18, 1997.

—Sketch by Jennifer Kramer

Mark Plotkin

Mark Plotkin
1955–

American ethnobotanist

One of the world's leading ethnobotanists, Mark Plotkin is an impassioned spokesman for the preservation of rain forest environments. His chosen specialty is finding the medically beneficial plant life that grows in a rain forest and cataloging its native people's medicinal uses. Since both the rain forests and their native inhabitants are threatened with annihilation, his goal is the preservation of this knowledge before it disappears. Plotkin's science is inextricably bound with such issues as conservation and the rights of indigenous peoples, and rather than shying away from such topics, he combines his research with his role of being a highly active public advocate of conservation.

Mark Plotkin was born on May 21, 1955, in New Orleans, Louisiana. One of two sons of George Plotkin, a shoe store owner, and Helene Tatar, a teacher, he attended Newman High School in New Orleans and graduated in 1973. One of his earliest formative experiences was recounted in a *Life* magazine profile which describes a very young Plotkin so enjoying his toy *Tyrannosaurus rex* that he asked his parents for a pet dinosaur, only to then learn what the word "extinct" really meant. However, growing up in New Orleans offered him the opportunity of investi-

gating the wildlife of its fertile swamps, and often Plotkin would arrive home covered with mud and carrying a pillowcase full of rat snakes. This was the type of biological investigation Plotkin had in mind when he entered the University of Pennsylvania in 1973. Instead, he found college biology to be mostly cellular and molecular, far removed from the vivid, living reality to which he was accustomed.

Drops Out of School and Discovers a Life's Passion

After dropping out of the University of Pennsylvania in 1974, Plotkin moved to Cambridge, Massachusetts, where he talked his way into an assistant's position working with the herpetology collection at Harvard's Museum of Comparative Zoology. Since his new job allowed him to take low-tuition night courses at Harvard, he joined a class with the intriguing title, "The Botany and Chemistry of Hallucinogenic Plants" taught by ethnobotanist **Richard Evans Schultes**. In the very first class, Schultes showed a slide of three men in grass skirts and barkcloth masks dancing under the effect of a hallucinogenic potion made from the bark of the tropical vine, *Banisteriopsis*. As Plotkin recalled in a 1993 interview with *People* magazine, when Dr. Schultes described them as Yukuna Indians doing the sacred kai-yah-ree dance and added dryly that the one on the left had a Harvard degree, Plotkin was hooked. "People talk about summer jobs that led to their careers. For me it was that one slide. I knew I would become an ethnobotanist." Working toward that goal, Plotkin entered Harvard's extension school and received his A.B. in 1979. Following his M.A. in 1981 from Yale University's School of Forestry, he was awarded his Ph.D. from Tufts University in 1989.

During these student years, Plotkin traveled to the remote jungles of Suriname (formerly Dutch Guiana, on the north central coast of South America) and other Amazonian countries between semesters to study the natives' use of plant-based medicinals, which was the topic of his dissertation. It was also during that time that he met his wife, Liliana Madrigal, a conservationist from Costa Rica, at a rain forest conference. The couple have two daughters, Gabrielle and Ann Lauren. In 1989, Plotkin joined the Washington-based World Wildlife Fund to become its director of plant conservation, and remained there for four years. In 1993 he joined the non-profit environmental organization Conservation International as vice-president for plant conservation, and also became a research associate at Harvard's Botanical Museum the same year.

Writes Highly Successful Book and Becomes Ethnobotany Spokesman

After the 1991 publication of the scholarly text, *Sustainable Harvest and Marketing of Rain Forest*

Products, Plotkin published in 1993 his very popular *Tales of a Shaman's Apprentice: An Ethnobotanist Searches for New Medicines in the Amazon Rain Forest*. Into its 14th edition by 1997, this crossover book is well on its way to accomplishing his goal of enlisting a new generation of students into the study of ethnobotany. The success of his book made Plotkin and his unusual subject matter more visible, allowing him to more fully use his considerable talents as a speaker. In a short time, he became the premier spokesman for the preservation of rain forest environments as well as of the native cultures that used to flourish there. Described by Conservation International colleague Russell A. Mittermeier as "the single best speaker in the conservation business," and "the one who put plant conservation on the map," Plotkin has been hammering his dual theme and achieving results. The notion that native knowledge as well as the environment must be preserved is finally beginning to resonate with his audience. With each visit to the rain forest, Plotkin witnesses the devastating results of acculturation, and stresses the urgency of preserving as much knowledge of native plant use as possible since. As he told *The New York Times* in 1991, "Each time a medicine man dies, it is as if a library has burned down." It is phrases like that, and the lasting effect they have, that underscore Plotkin's high talent for communication.

Co-Founds New Conservation Effort

In 1995, Plotkin co-founded The Ethnobiology and Conservation Team with his wife, Liliana Madrigal, and prominent Canadian environmentalist Adrian Forsyth. Plotkin is executive director of this Virginia-based organization formed to help indigenous people gain control of their environmental and cultural destinies. Plotkin also hopes to persuade drug companies to regard rain forests as he does, as libraries and store houses of future drugs and medicines. It is in this aspect of what might be called the bioprospecting aspects of his work that he remains adamant about the rights of indigenous peoples. Sensitive to the steady exploitation of these people, Plotkin was able to encourage a partnership between Suriname natives and a major pharmaceutical company to screen plants for drugs that might work on such diseases as cancer and AIDS. Through his efforts and those of companies like Shaman Pharmaceuticals, a native tribe finally will receive financial compensation for its intellectual property.

Always searching for a broader and larger audience, Plotkin has written a children's book, *The Shaman's Apprentice*, with Lynne Cherry, and will publish *Healer's Quest: New Medicines From Mother Nature* in 1999. In late 1997, the IMAX film "Amazon" opened in Los Angeles and Stockholm. Directed by award-winning Keith Merrill, this film depicts the search for new medicines from Amazonian plants. In

only the first decade of his professional career, Mark Plotkin has achieved a great deal in a highly impressive manner, attesting to the effectiveness of combining science with integrity and passion.

SELECTED WRITINGS BY PLOTKIN:

Books

(With Lynne Cherry) *The Shaman's Apprentice: A Tale of the Amazon Rain Forest*. San Diego, CA: Harcourt Brace & Co., 1998.
(With Lisa Famolare) *Sustainable Harvest and Marketing of Rain Forest Products*. Washington, DC: Island Press, 1991.
Tales of a Shaman's Apprentice: An Ethnobotanist Searches for New Medicines in the Amazon Rain Forest. New York: Viking, 1993.

FURTHER READING:

Books

Collins, Louise Mooney. *Newsmakers: The People Behind Today's Headlines*. Detroit: Gale Research Inc., 1994, pp.96-97.
Katz, Linda Sobel, Sarah Orrick, and Robert Honig. *Environmental Profiles: A Global Guide to Projects and People*. New York: Garland Publishing, Inc., 1993, pp. 648-649.

Periodicals

Allen, Karen. "Mark Plotkin: Conservation Medalist." *ZooNooz*, The Zoological Society of San Diego (January 1995).
Jackson, Donald Dale. "Searching for Medicinal Wealth in Amazonia." *Smithsonian* (February 1989): 94-103.
Reed, Susan. "Sorcerers' Apprentice." *People* (December 6, 1993): 143-146.

—*Sketch by Leonard C. Bruno*

Cyril Ponnamperuma
1923–1994
Sri Lankan-born American chemist

Cyril Ponnamperuma, an eminent researcher in the field of chemical evolution, rose through several National Aeronautics and Space Administration (NASA) divisions as a research chemist to head the Laboratory of Chemical Evolution at the University

Cyril Ponnamperuma

of Maryland, College Park. His career focused on explorations into the origin of life and the "primordial soup" that contained the precursors of life. In this search, Ponnamperuma took advantage of discoveries in such diverse fields as molecular biology and astrophysics.

Born in Galle, Ceylon (now Sri Lanka) on October 16, 1923, Cyril Andres Ponnamperuma was educated at the University of Madras (where he received a B.A. in Philosophy, 1948), the University of London (B.Sc., 1959), and the University of California at Berkeley (Ph.D., 1962). His interest in the origin of life began to take clear shape at the Birkbeck College of the University of London, where he studied with J. D. Bernal, a well-known crystallographer. In addition to his studies, Ponnamperuma also worked in London as a research chemist and radiochemist. He became a research associate at the Lawrence Radiation Laboratory at Berkeley, where he studied with **Melvin Calvin,** a Nobel laureate and experimenter in chemical evolution.

Chemical Evolution—Searching for Life from Primordial Soup

After receiving his Ph.D. in 1962, Ponnamperuma was awarded a fellowship from the National Academy of Sciences, and he spent one year in residence at NASA's Ames Research Center in Moffet Field, California. After the end of his associate year, he was hired as a research scientist at the center and

became head of the chemical evolution branch in 1965.

During these years, Ponnamperuma began to develop his ideas about chemical evolution, which he explained in an article published in *Nature.* Chemical evolution, he explained, is a logical outgrowth of centuries of studies both in chemistry and biology, culminating in the groundbreaking 1953 discovery of the structure of deoxyribonucleic acid (DNA) by **James Watson** and **Francis Crick**. Evolutionist Charles Darwin's studies affirming the idea of the "unity of all life" for biology could be extended, logically, to a similar notion for chemistry: protein and nucleic acid, the essential elements of biological life, were, after all, chemical.

In the same year that Watson and Crick discovered DNA, two researchers from the University of Chicago, **Stanley Lloyd Miller** and **Harold Urey,** experimented with a primordial soup concocted of the elements thought to have made up earth's early atmosphere—methane, ammonia, hydrogen, and water. They sent electrical sparks through the mixture, simulating a lightening storm, and discovered trace amounts of amino acids.

During the early 1960s, Ponnamperuma began to delve into this primordial soup and set up variations of Miller and Urey's original experiment. Having changed the proportions of the elements from the original Miller-Urey specifications slightly, Ponnamperuma and his team sent first high-energy electrons, then ultraviolet light through the mixture, attempting to recreate the original conditions of the earth before life. They succeeded in creating large amounts of adenosine triphosphate (ATP), an amino acid that fuels cells. In later experiments with the same concoction of primordial soup, the team was able to create the nucleotides that make up nucleic acid—the building blocks of DNA and ribonucleic acid (RNA).

Search for Life's Origins Extends to Space

In addition to his work in prebiotic chemistry, Ponnamperuma became active in another growing field: exobiology, or the study of extraterrestrial life. Supported in this effort by NASA's interest in all matters related to outer space, he was able to conduct research on the possiblity of the evolution of life on other planets. Theorizing that life evolved from the interactions of chemicals present elsewhere in the universe, he saw the research possibilities of spaceflight. He experimented with lunar soil taken by the *Apollo 12* space mission in 1969. As a NASA investigator, he also studied information sent back from Mars by the unmanned Viking, Pioneer, and Voyager probes in the 1970s. These studies suggested to Ponnamperuma, as he stated in an 1985 interview with *Spaceworld,* that "earth is the only place in the solar system where there is life."

In 1969, a meteorite fell to earth in Muchison, Australia. It was retrieved still warm, providing scientists with fresh, uncontaminated material from space for study. Ponnamperuma and other scientists examined pieces of the meteorite for its chemical make-up, discovering numerous amino acids. Most important, among those discovered were the five chemical bases that make up the nucleic acid found in living organisms. Further interesting findings provided tantalizing but puzzling clues about chemical evolution, including the observation that light reflects both to the left and to the right when beamed through a solution of the meteorite's amino acids, whereas light reflects only to the left when beamed through the amino acids of living matter on earth. "Who knows? God may be left-handed," Ponnamperuma speculated in a 1982 *New York Times* interview.

Ponnamperuma's association with NASA continued as he entered academia. In 1979, he became a professor of chemistry at the University of Maryland and director of the Laboratory of Chemical Evolution—established and supported in part by the National Science Foundation and by NASA. He continued active research and experimentation on meteorite material. In 1983, an article in the science section of the *New York Times* explained Ponnamperuma's chemical evolution theory and his findings from the Muchison meteorite experiments. He reported the creation of all five chemical bases of living matter in a single experiment that consisted of bombarding a primordial soup mixture with electricity.

Ponnamperuma's contributions to scholarship include hundreds of articles. He wrote or edited numerous books, some in collaboration with other chemists or exobiologists, including annual collections of papers delivered at the College Park Colloquium on Chemical Evolution. He edited two journals, *Molecular Evolution* (from 1970 to 1972) and *Origins of Life* (from 1973 to 1983). In addition to traditional texts in the field of chemical evolution, he also co-authored a software program entitled "Origin of Life," a simulation model intended to introduce biology students to basic concepts of chemical evolution.

Although Ponnamperuma became an American citizen in 1967, he maintained close ties to his native Sri Lanka, even becoming an official governmental science advisor. His professional life has included several international appointments. He was a visiting professor of the Indian Atomic Energy Commission (1967); a member of the science faculty at the Sorbonne (1969); and director of the UNESCO Institute for Early Evolution in Ceylon (1970). His international work included the directorship of the Arthur C. Clarke center, founded by the science fiction writer, a Sri Lankan resident. The center has as one of its goals a Manhattan Project for food synthesis.

Ponnamperuma was a member of the Indian National Science Academy, the American Association for the Advancement of Science, the American Chemical Society, the Royal Society of Chemists, and the International Society for the Study of the Origin of Life, which awarded him the A. I. Oparin Gold Medal in 1980. In 1991, Ponnamperuma received a high French honor—he was made a Chevalier des Arts et des Lettres. Two years later, the Russian Academy of Creative Arts awarded him the first Harold Urey Prize. In October 1994, he was appointed to the Pontifical Academy of Sciences in Rome. He married Valli Pal in 1955; they had one child. Ponnamperuma died on December 20, 1994 at Washington Adventist Hospital.

SELECTED WRITINGS BY PONNAMPERUMA:

Books

The Origins of Life. Dutton, 1972.
Cosmic Evolution. Houghton, 1978.
Limits of Life. Kluwer, 1980.
Comets and the Origin of Life. Kluwer, 1981.

Periodicals

Nature (25 January 1964).

FURTHER READING:

Periodicals

Boffey, Philip. "Precursors of Life Found in Meteorite." *New York Times* (30 August 1993).
————. "E. T. May Look Like Us." *USA Today Magazine* (June, 1987).
————. "Interview: Cyril Ponnamperuma." *Space World* (February 1985).
————. "Is There a Cosmic Chemistry of Life?" *Science News* (20 September 1986).
Sullivan Walter. "Cyril Ponnamperuma, Scholar of Life's Origins, Is Dead at 71" (obituary). *New York Times* (24 December 1994): A10.

—Sketch by Katherine Williams

Frank Press
1924–
American geophysicist

One of the most accomplished geophysicists of his generation, Frank Press is best known as a pioneer

Frank Press

in the use of seismic waves to explore subsurface geological structures and for his pioneering use of waves to explore Earth's deep interior. His election to the National Academy of Sciences at the age of 33 made him one of the youngest ever to gain admission to that highly selective and prestigious body. In 1977, he was chosen by President Jimmy Carter to serve as his science advisor, after which Press became the first ever to move from the White House to the presidency of the National Academy of Sciences.

Frank Press was born in Brooklyn, New York on December 4, 1924. The youngest of three sons of immigrant parents—Solomon Press and Dora Steinholtz—he was raised in the predominantly Jewish neighborhood of Crown Heights and attended Samuel J. Tilden High School in East Flatbush. It was in that neighborhood that he became friends with Leonard Garment, who would later become President Richard Nixon's lawyer. In his book, *Crazy Rhythm*, Garment recalls that, as youngsters, he and his "skinny, shy, hugely intelligent schoolmate" believed that the world was theirs to conquer. "Wide-eyed with excitement, we set out to do just that. Frank and I ran ahead of the pack. Weighing a future in science, history, and journalism, he led his classes in all three."

Publishes Landmark Paper with Ocean-Floor Pioneer

After graduating from Tilden High, Press attended the City College of New York and received his B.

S. in 1944. He earned his master's degree from Columbia University in 1946, the same year he married Billie Kallick. They would have two children, William Henry and Paula Evelyn. After receiving his master's, Press remained at Columbia and was awarded a Ph.D. in geophysics in 1949. It was at Columbia that he studied with **William Maurice Ewing**, a major innovator in modern geology, and with whom he invented in 1950 an improved seismograph. That same year, they published a landmark paper that is recognized as beginning a new era in structural seismology.

Upon receiving his Ph.D. in 1949, Press became an instructor at Columbia. He left there in 1955 as an associate professor of geophysics to serve as professor of geophysics at the California Institute of Technology. Two years later, he became director of the Seismological Laboratory at Caltech, where he remained until 1965. That year he joined Massachusetts Institute of Technology to become chairman of its department of Earth and Planetary Sciences. His quiet leadership is credited with invigorating that program and with guiding its research and teaching units to scholarly preeminence.

Leaves Academe for Position of National Significance

While at Caltech and later MIT, Press became known in public policy circles for his work on seismic detection of underground nuclear tests and for his advocacy of a national program to develop earthquake prediction capabilities. During those years, he served as a consultant or advisor to seven federal departments or agencies, as well as U.S. Delegate to the Nuclear Test Ban Conference in Geneva from 1959 to1961 and Moscow in 1963. As a member of the President's Science Advisory Committee (PSAC) from 1961 to 1964, he also served as U.S. Delegate to the United Nations Conference on Science and Technology in Underdeveloped Nations in 1963. A week after President Kennedy's assassination, Press resigned from PSAC, later telling *Science* magazine that, "I felt so down I didn't want to continue."

In 1977, however, Press was recalled to the national stage when newly elected President Jimmy Carter chose him to serve as Science Advisor to the President as well as director of the Office of Science and Technology Policy. Press's four-year tenure at the White House was characterized by his judicious, low-key approach. With the Carter administration on record as having a pro-science policy, Press can take credit for the signing of United States-China scientific cooperation agreements, as well as for increased federal support for basic research. Under his direction, measures were initiated that spurred industrial innovation and joint ventures between industry, universities, and government.

Moves from White House to National Academy of Sciences

After leaving government in 1980 and returning for a short time to MIT as Chairman of its Earth and Planetary Sciences department, Press became in July 1981 the first White House science advisor to move into the presidency of the National Academy of Sciences (NAS). As a scientist, Press brought impeccable scientific credentials to that position. As a former member of the White House, he also brought a demonstrated commitment and ability to understand and influence science policy at the highest levels. Press remained NAS President for two six-year terms during which he revamped and reinvigorated its National Research Council, the branch of the Academy that responds to government requests for scientific advice. The Academy also published several landmark studies on such subjects as biology education in the nation's schools, global warming, biodiversity, and science and creationism. Overall, Press left the Academy a more effective and smoother functioning complex, with a goal for monitoring how the nation is doing in educating its young people in science and mathematics.

In 1993, when his two-term presidency was over, Press became the Cecil and Ida Green Senior Fellow at the Carnegie Institution of Washington. He remained in residence at that institution's Geophysics Laboratory and Department of Terrestrial Magnetism until 1997, having joined the Washington Advisory Group as a partner in 1996. The recipient of 30 honorary degrees and a member of 14 major scientific societies worldwide, Press has also received numerous awards and medals. Among these is the Royal Society's Gold Medal, France's Legion of Honor, Germany's Cross of merit, and the Japan Prize. In October 1994, he was given the United States' highest scientific honor when President Clinton awarded him the National Medal of Science. Authorized by Congress in 1959 and only periodically bestowed, it was given to Press for his contributions to understanding the nature of Earth's deepest interior and the mitigation of natural disasters, as well as in recognition of his service in academia, as a government official, and at the National Academy of Sciences.

In light of his varied career, Press may best be remembered for his efforts as a successful educator. In addition to his own contributions to geophysics and the large number of students that he sent into the world as accomplished earth scientists, he co-authored, in 1974 with Raymond Siever, the classic undergraduate textbook titled *Earth*. As one of the most influential earth science texts for several generations of students worldwide, it was redone and issued in 1994 as *Understanding Earth*. It seems fitting that Press even has a mountain in Antarctica named after him in tribute to his use of seismic waves to ascertain the structure of the Antarctic ice cap and its underlying terrain.

SELECTED WRITINGS BY PRESS:

Books

(With Raymond Siever) *Understanding Earth*. New York: W. H. Freeman, 1994.

Thompson, Kenneth W., ed. *The Presidency and Science Advising*. New York: University Press of America, 1988, pp.133-143.

FURTHER READING:

Periodicals

Boffey, Philip M. "Frank Press, Long-Shot Candidate, May Become Science Advisor." *Science* (February 25, 1977): 763-766.

Culliton, Barbara J. "Frank Press to Be Nominated for NAS." *Science* (October 24, 1980): 405-406.

Other

"Frank Press Wins National Medal of Science." Press Release. National Science Foundation. September 8, 1994.

—*Sketch by Leonard C. Bruno*

Margie Profet
1958–
American biomedical researcher

As a self-made scientist, Margie Profet's approach to scientific the discipline is relatively unique. She told Terry McDermott in the *Seattle Times*, "I'm very opportunistic and if I think of a neat idea, I work on it." Profet conducts biomedical research from a Darwinian perspective, one that believes that the human body is an adaptation to its environment. In this evolutionary medical theory, bodily defense mechanisms happen for a reason, there are few accidents, and there is a balance between costs and benefits. Her theories concern everyday questions and bodily functions such as menstruation, allergies, and morning sickness in pregnancy. Because Profet lacks advanced degrees, her theories are controversial with scientists and physicians. However, Profet has been lauded for her work, and in 1993 she was awarded a MacArthur Foundation "genius" grant.

Profet was born August 7, 1958, in Berkeley, California, to Bob (a physicist) and Karen (an engineer) Profet. With her three siblings, Profet grew up in Manhattan Beach, California, where her parents worked in the aerospace industry. Profet received her first undergraduate degree from Harvard University in 1980. She majored in political philosophy, and it was while writing her senior thesis that she decided she wanted to devote her intellectual life to original thought. After graduation, Profet went to Europe, where she worked for a year as a computer programmer in Munich, Germany, from 1980 to 1981. After returning to the United States, Profet decided to pursue her lifelong interest in biology. She entered the University of California, Berkeley, and earned another B.A. in 1985, this time in physics. Profet was unhappy with the structures, limitations, and regimentations of academia, and decided to pursue her interests on her own time. She has never taken a college-level biology class.

Living in San Francisco, Profet supported herself with a series of part-time jobs while she pursued her own research. Beginning in 1986, Profet derived what became her first published theory, which concerned morning sickness and pregnancy. It was inspired by conversations she had with pregnant friends and relatives. Profet concluded, after much research and reflection, that morning sickness happens for a reason. She believes that certain foods contain toxins that could harm a developing embryo in the first trimester, when the fetus is most vulnerable and when most significant birth defects can develop.

Profet believes that the nausea caused by certain foods and scents is a defense mechanism to protect the vulnerable embryo when it needs it the most. After the first trimester, when the embryo is less susceptible because it has begun to develop its own defenses, there is usually little to no morning sickness. In 1995, Profet published a book, *Protecting Your Baby-to-Be*, explaining this idea for women in their first trimester of pregnancy. In it, she outlines specific foods to avoid.

While working through her morning sickness theory for publication, Profet had her second insight, inspired by her own experiences with allergies. Beginning with the observation that certain allergic reactions are often immediate—scratching, sneezing, vomiting, etc.—Profet formulated a hypothesis that argues allergies are reactions to toxins. She believes that the human body's immune system battles these environmental toxins—plant-borne compounds—that are potentially harmful to cells. The toxins themselves can cause allergies, or a toxin and allergen can be linked. The toxins must be immediately expelled by the body, hence the immediacy of a sneeze or a scratch. Additionally, Profet theorizes that allergic reactions do not happen to everybody because they are a last ditch defense method against toxins.

Because other, first-line defenses work in some people, they do not need to have allergic reactions. Profet published these findings in 1991 in the *Quarterly Review of Biology*.

During this period, Profet was hired by Professor **Bruce Ames**, a toxologist at the University of California at Berkeley, to be a biology research associate in his laboratory. In June 1993, she was awarded a five-year $225,000 grant by the John D. & Katherine T. MacArthur Foundation. Soon after receiving the grant, Profet moved to Seattle, Washington, and became affiliated with the University of Washington and its molecular biotechnology department.

In the fall of 1993, Profet published her seminal theory on why women menstruate in the September issue of the *Quarterly Review of Biology*. This was a subject that had intrigued her since the age of seven when she first learned what it was. Profet wondered why women's bodies cast off so much blood and tissue, including the nutrients therein, and concluded that it is an evolutionary adaptation. She believes the process of menstruation defends the uterus, fallopian tubes, and related organs from pathogens and other potentially damaging microbes that append themselves to sperm. By menstruating, the body sheds the uterus's outer lining where these pathogens persist. The blood that douses the area is full of immune cells that can neutralize any remaining microbes.

Profet's approach to science has been called visionary, because she questions phenomenons for which there are already accepted answers. Still, Profet has many critics to her ideas, methodology, and lack of graduate education. She explained to Terry McDermott that her view is "No matter what aspect of physiology you look at the core question is: What's it there for? Maybe it is just a fluke or a by-product. But maybe it has a function. You have to know that. Otherwise, you're doing blind medical intervention."

SELECTED WRITINGS BY PROFET:

Book
Protecting Your Baby-to-Be. New York: Addison-Wesley Publishing, 1995.

Periodicals

"The Function of Allergy: Immunological Defense Against Toxins." *Quarterly Review of Biology* (March 1991): 23.
"Menstruation as a Defense against Pathogens Transported by Sperm." *Quarterly Review of Biology* (September 1993): 335.

FURTHER READING:

Periodicals

Angier, Natalie. "Biologists Advise Doctors to Think like Darwin." *The New York Times* (December 24, 1991): C1.

"Radical New View of Role of Menstruation." *The New York Times* (September 21, 1993): C1.

Bloch, Hannah. "School Isn't My Kind of Thing." *Time* (October 4, 1993): 72.

McDermott, Terry. "Darwinian Medicine—It's a War Out There and Margie Profet, A Leading Theorist in a New Science, Thinks the Human Body Does Some Pretty Weird Things to Survive." *The Seattle Times* (July 31, 1994): 10.

McNichol, Tom. "Bleach Blanket Biologist." *USA Weekend* (October 8, 1995): 14.

Oliwenstein, Lori. "Dr. Darwin: Darwinian Medicine Studies the Evolutionary Purpose of Disease." *Discover* (October 1995): 110.

Rudavsky, Shari. "Margie Profet. (Researcher of Evolutionary Physiology)." *Omni* (May 1994): 69.

Williams, Emily. "Allergies First Attracted Notice in Modern Times." *The Dallas Morning News* (October 11, 1993): 6F.

—*Sketch by Annette Petrusso*

Stanley B. Prusiner

Stanley B. Prusiner
1942–
American neurologist

In many ways, it was the classic case of the underdog overcoming adversity, of the lone voice vindicated. A brash young "maverick scientist," according to Lawrence K. Altman in the *New York Times,* flew in the face of conventional medical wisdom to propose a radical new form of infective agent. If proven to exist, such an agent would be the "most remarkable form of life on the planet" and one that "would require a dramatic rewriting of the dogma of molecular biology, a redefinition of the meaning of life itself," as Gary Taubes wrote in *Discover*. For a quarter of a century this scientist stuck to his guns in the face of criticism and sometimes ridicule to be honored for his work in 1997 by the Nobel Prize. For Stanley B. Prusiner, the prize was an indication that his life's work had been validated. However, as he told the *Washington Post* after receiving the award, he still felt that "science should be reticent to accept new ideas. Ninety-nine percent

of new ideas are wrong. We have to be very tough on our colleagues."

The furor over Prusiner's work was caused by his novel theory of an infective agent which was neither bacterial, nor viral, nor fungal. Building on the work of British scientists, Prusiner hypothesized in 1981 that a type of protein particle, which he dubbed the prion (pronounced *pree-on*), was responsible for a host of fatal neurodegenerative disorders, including Creutzfeldt-Jakob disease (CJD) as well as diseases of animals such as scrapie and mad cow disease. Prusiner's hypothesis and subsequent research was revolutionary in that it posited the ability of a protein—which lacks genetic material and thus the ability to reproduce—to function as a pathogenic agent and to spread infectious disease. Prusiner's ground-breaking work won him the 1997 Nobel Prize in Physiology or Medicine because it "provides important insights that may furnish the basis to understand the biological mechanisms underlying other types of dementia-related diseases, for example Alzheimer's disease," noted the Karolinska Institute in its announcement of the prize. The Nobel committee went on to say that Prusiner's work also "establishes a foundation for drug development and new types of medical treatment strategies."

Death of Patient Spurs Early Research

Prusiner was born on May 28, 1942, in Des Moines, Iowa. He earned his B.A., *cum laude*, at the

University of Pennsylvania, in 1964, and then went on to receive an M.D. in 1968 from the same university. Already during his medical studies, he was interested in biochemical research. Prusiner then served his internship and residency at the prestigious University of California at San Francisco (UCSF) from 1968 to 1969, where he later served a residency in neurology, "the last great frontier of medicine," as he was quoted as saying in *Discover.* Married and the father of two children, Prusiner soon became interested in neurodegenerative diseases. This interest was in part developed after one of his patients died of CJD, a disease of the cerebral cortex which leads to dementia and eventual death.

As a result of this experience, Prusiner learned that an entire category of diseases was yet to be elucidated. At the time, researchers thought many neurodegenerative diseases were caused by so-called slow viruses, which would take years and sometimes decades to incubate in the host. As early as 1967, a British team working at Hammersmith Hospital had proposed the existence of an infective agent that lacked nucleic acid in the sheep disease known as scrapie. Their hypothesis grew out of the fact that when the genetic substance was destroyed in known infected material, extracts from the infected material were still able to spread the disease. This led to the conclusion that perhaps the infective agents in such animal diseases as scrapie (so called because infected sheep tend to scrape the wool off their bodies) and kuru (a disease of the cannibalistic Fore people of New Guinea which had been traced to the ritual eating of the brains of departed relatives) were non-viral.

Prusiner combined a zeal for research with a disarming political sense to win grants for the study of such diseases, including CJD, scrapie, kuru, fatal familial insomnia, and bovine spongiform encephalopathy (BSE), or mad cow disease. Over three decades, he managed to gain funding totaling 56 million dollars from the National Institutes of Health (NIH).

Three Decades of Research Lead to Prion

Expanding on work by British researchers as well as the NIH's Rocky Mountain Laboratories, which had shown similarities between kuru and scrapie, Prusiner set up a research team at UCSF employing ultimately a quarter million mice infected with diseased brain matter in an attempt to isolate the infective agent in neurodegenerative diseases. Such research was laborious and time-consuming, for the incubation period in mice took upwards of 200 days. Early breakthroughs occurred when Prusiner switched from mice to hamsters, as the onset of illness in those animals would occur twice as fast. By 1981, Prusiner was able to conclude that a protein was the causative

agent in these brain diseases, and he dubbed this agent the prion. Such proteins were resistant to any modification of nucleic acids. When he and his team added enzymes that destroy nucleic acids in genes, they discovered that there was no reduction in the infective power of prions.

This early pronouncement caused a stir in the scientific community, with critics finding it implausible that infectious diseases could be transmitted by a substance incapable of reproducing itself. Prusiner answered this criticism with his theory that prions existed in the white blood cells and on the surface cells in the brains of all mammals and were, in their normal state, non-infectious. Such normal particles he called the prion protein, PrP; so-called "rogue" prions which spontaneously altered their form to cause scrapie, he called scrapie PrP, or PrPSc. PrP's consist primarily of alpha helices, that is, as Prusiner described it in *Scientific American,* "regions in which the protein backbone twists into a specific kind of spiral."

Research showed, however, that PrPSc, or the scrapie form of prion, contains beta strands in which the backbone seems to be fully extended. Such PrPSc's accumulate in beta sheets. Prusiner concluded that prion-induced diseases spread when such a rogue prion attaches itself to healthy prions and causes a sort of chain reaction in healthy proteins, cascading them into malignant clusters that cause dementia, loss of muscular control, and insomnia, depending upon which part of the brain these renegade prions attack. Smaller than viruses and resistant to the body's immune system because they have been present since birth, these disease-causing prions ultimately destroy parts of the brain by killing brain cells and forming a porous or spongy area. Thus the class of neurodegenerative disorders they cause is called spongiform encephalopathies. Prusiner was also able to demonstrate that such diseases may be inherited, may be transmitted within species and possibly between species, and may also occur in as-yet unknown ways spontaneously.

In 1992, Prusiner's research more clearly demonstrated the nature of the interaction between prion proteins. Prusiner showed that when the gene encoding for the prion protein in mice was destroyed, such mice (called prion knock-out mice) proved resistant to the diseases when injected with preparations of disease-causing prion protein. Later, when the prion gene was re-activated and the same mice were injected with diseased matter, they again became susceptible to infection. Though the role of prion proteins is unclear, what has become clear is the close causative effect of rogue prions in a variety of neural diseases.

The diseases which Prusiner studied are life-threatening to only a tiny fraction of the world's population–the annual death toll of CJD in the

United States annually, for example, is about 225, less than the number of traffic fatalities in two days. However, as the Nobel committee noted, Prusiner's researches could lead to new therapies for a larger array of neurological disorders such as Alzheimer's and Parkinson's disease, which may or may not be caused by protein-based infective agents. In the case of prion-based diseases, Prusiner has suggested gene therapy to curtail the production of prion proteins and thus eliminate the spread of such diseases, as was done with his prion knock-out mice.

Critics Remain Unconvinced

Prusiner still has his critics. Some say that there is still no conclusive proof that a viral agent is not involved in neurodegenerative diseases, claiming that Prusiner's work does not rule out the possibility of viral particles working in tandem with prions. Also, only a week before the awarding of the Nobel, *Nature* magazine, in its October 2, 1997 issue, ran an article that suggested a viral cause for transmission of CJD to humans from BSE, or mad cow disease. Prusiner had attributed a cross-species infection from a wild prion for the 21 cases of a new variant of CJD. Other critics note that the variety of strains of each of these neural diseases points to the existence of an agent that is able to adapt and change its reproductive coding. For example, 15 different strains are recognized for scrapie and at least one variant for CJD. Prusiner answers such critics with the explanation that prion folding or the shape-changing of rogue prions could be responsible for such a variety of disease strains; different alpha helix mutations could also explain the phenomena of disease strain variety for prion-based infections. Still other critics complain that Prusiner has extrapolated his findings past credibility, and that he has simply incorporated the work of others into his own, changing terminology so as to make him appear the lone pioneer in the field. Some also assert that his findings are often published in journals without adequate peer review.

When awarding Prusiner with the Nobel, the Karolinska Institute deviated from its norms in two ways. Usually the award is shared by several researchers in one field. Prusiner is the first individual winner since 1987. Also, the committee usually withholds the Nobel until all controversies have been resolved. But as Dr. Lars Edstrom, a member of the Nobel award committee, noted in Altman's *New York Times* article, "There are still people who don't believe that a protein can cause these diseases, but we believe it.... From our point of view, there is no doubt." Other award committees have felt the same. Prusiner has won, among other prominent scientific awards, the Gairdner Foundation Award for Outstanding Achievement in Medical Science in 1993, the Albert Lasker Award for Basic Medical Research in 1994, and the Wolf Prize in Medicine in 1996. But only

time will demonstrate if Prusiner or his critics are right. As Prusiner himself said in an interview reported in Altman's *New York Times* article, "No prize, not even a Nobel Prize, can make something true that is not."

SELECTED WRITINGS BY PRUSINER:

Books

Prions, Prions, Prions. Springer, 1995.

Periodicals

(With others) "Evidence for Isolate Specified Allotypic Interactions between the Cellular and Scrapie Prion Proteins in Congenic and Transgenic Mice." *Proceedings of the National Academy of Science U.S.A.* 91 (1994): 5690-5694.
(With others) "Degeneration of Skeletal Muscle, Peripheral Nerves, and the Central Nervous System in Transgenic Mice Overexpressing Wild-Type Prion Proteins." *Cell* 76 (1994): 117-129.
(With others) "Structural Clues to Prion Replication." *Science* 264 (1994): 530-531.
(With others) "Transmission of Creutzfeldt-Jakob Disease from Humans to Transgenic Mice Expressing Chimeric Human-Mouse Prion Protein." *Proceedings of the National Academy of Science U.S.A.* 91 (1994): 9936-9940.
"The Prion Diseases." *Scientific American* 272 (1995): 70-77.

FURTHER READING:

Periodicals

Altman, Lawrence K. "U.S. Scientist Wins Nobel Prize for Controversial Work." *New York Times* (October 7, 1997): A1, A12.
Taubes, Gary. "The Game of the Name Is Fame. But Is It Science?" *Discover* (December 1986): 44-56.
Weiss, Rick. "Nobel Prize Vindicates U.S. Scientist." *Washington Post* (October 7, 1997): A1.

Other

The Nobel Assembly at the Karolinska Institute. "Press Release: The 1997 Nobel Prize in Physiology or Medicine." October 6, 1997. http://www.nobel.se/laureates/medicine-1997.html (October 2, 1997). This web site provides hyperlinks to a vast array of material on Prusiner, his research, and writings.

—*Sketch by J. Sydney Jones*

Theodore T. Puck

Theodore T. Puck
1916–
American biologist

Theodore Puck helped lay the foundations of cytogenetics with his ground-breaking technique of culturing mammalian cells and his subsequent research into the genetic basis of human cell development, differentiation, and mutation. His work has led to modern methods of radiation therapy and genetic screening, as well as helped pave the way toward recent advances in genetic engineering and cancer research.

Theodore Thomas Puck was born September 24, 1916, in Chicago, Illinois to Joseph and Bessie (Shapiro) Puckowitz. He attended Chicago Public Schools and graduated with a bachelor's degree in chemistry from the University of Chicago in 1937. In 1940, he earned his Ph.D. in physical chemistry from the university.

Launches a Career

After receiving his doctorate, he became a research fellow in the university's department of medicine. Working there from 1941 to 1945, Puck focused on aerosol dynamics and the prevention of infections caused by airborne viruses and bacteria. During his investigations, he discovered that particular aerosols could kill contagions by condensing onto their surfaces to quickly create a sterilizing concentration. Puck applied his findings to his work as a member of the U.S. Army's Commission on Airborne Infections during World War II. In 1945, he joined the faculty of the University of Chicago's departments of medicine and biochemistry as an assistant professor. While at the university he married Mary Hill on April 17, 1946, in Santa Fe, New Mexico.

In 1947, Puck left the Midwest for a senior fellowship at the California Institute of Technology. After a year, he joined the University of Colorado Medical Center as professor and chairman of its new department of biophysics. He remained there from 1948 to 1967, when he joined the medical center's department of biophysics and genetics.

Builds on Single-Cell Plating Techniques

In the years before Puck conducted his research, biologists discovered that if they isolated an individual cell from certain plants or animals and placed it in a specific artificial medium, it could thrive and ultimately be encouraged to asexually replicate, or clone, itself. Using this method, known as single-cell plating, scientists could bypass the time-consuming process of sexual reproduction and grow large colonies of cells in a short time. However, while the cells of many complex species had been replicated, no one had yet devised a way to grow mammalian cells in this manner. Puck made this a research priority and, with his students at the University of Colorado Medical Center, devised a simple and effective means to asexually reproduce mammalian cells in petri dish cultures.

This achievement opened the way to a wide range of investigations into the qualities of mammalian—and ultimately human—cells. Puck and other researchers could measure genetic processes as well as isolate and create reserves of various mutated cells for use in experiments. Puck was also able to observe how a wide range of chemical, biological, and physical conditions could possibly affect the cells and their genetic material. Among his most important discoveries in this regard was his determination of the mean dose of radiation that would kill a mammalian cell. His experiments demonstrated that it took only 100 rads of radiation to kill a cell—a fraction of what had previously been thought of as the lethal dose. This work held important implications for cancer patients undergoing radiation therapy, for they would not have to be subjected to such high doses as had been believed necessary.

Investigates Genes

Another significant finding made by Puck and his laboratory involved the number of chromosomes in a human cell. Able to sample and maintain the cells of a wide range of individuals, Puck eventually concluded that the standard number of chromosomes in a human cell is 46, not 47 or 48 as had previously been believed. The first complete analysis of human chromosomes, Puck's research helped pave the way for the later study of chromosomal and genetic abnormalities.

While these accomplishments may have been sufficient for another scientist, they inspired Puck to continue his work. He turned his attention to studying cell biochemistry and the factors that caused cell differentiation. He and his laboratory also produced the first single-gene mutants in mammalian cells and created a hybrid cell that contained both human and hamster chromosomes. In addition, he also investigated the effect of cyclic adenosine monophosphate (cyclic AMP) on cancer cells, work that has since formed the basis of new theories regarding the disease.

Is Honored for His Work

Theodore Puck has received many honors in recognition of his work. Many universities have invited him to speak, and professional organizations have honored him often. Among his many awards are the Albert Lasker Award in Medical Research (1958), the Borden Award in Medical Research (1959), the General Rose Memorial Hospital Award (1960), the American Clinical and Climatological Association's Gordon Wilson Medal (1977), the Ann Award from the Environmental Mutagen Society (1984), and the E. B. Wilson Medal from the American Society of Cellular Biologists, also in 1984. In 1969, his alma mater presented him with its distinguished alumni award.

Among his many memberships are the National Academy of Science, the Institute of Medicine, the Commission on Physicians for the Future, and the American Academy of Arts and Sciences (1972, fellow). In 1966, the American Cancer Society named him its distinguished research professor.

Currently, Puck is director of the Eleanor Roosevelt Cancer Center in Colorado. He has also been a visiting fellow at Los Alamos National Laboratories in New Mexico since 1987 and a member of the National Institutes of Health's Advisory Committee on Radiologic Health.

FURTHER READING:

Books

National Cyclopedia of American Biography. New York: James T. White & Company, 1930. Volume N-63, pages 79-80.

—*Sketch by Francis Hodgkins*

Edward Mills Purcell

Edward Mills Purcell
1912–1997
American physicist

Edward Mills Purcell spent much of his lifetime studying the basic particles of matter. Ultimately focusing on the frequencies of atomic particles spinning in magnetic fields, he developed a method of measuring their magnetic moments and investigating their atomic structures. For his simultaneous but independent development of this method, known as nuclear resonance absorption, he shared the 1952 Nobel Prize in physics with physicist **Felix Bloch.** The principle of nuclear magnetic resonance itself has been applied to a wide range of applications, from studying space through radio astronomy to measuring magnetic fields with magnetometers.

Purcell was born on August 30, 1912, in Taylorville, Illinois, to Edward A. and Mary (Mills) Purcell. His mother was a high school teacher, and his father was a former country school teacher, who, during Purcell's boyhood, was the general manager of an independent telephone company. Purcell read the Bell System technical magazine that his father received and decided to become an electrical engineer. In addition, he inherited his parents' interest in teaching.

Purcell received a bachelor's degree in electrical engineering from Purdue University in 1933. During his undergraduate days, Purcell's interest in physics was encouraged and strengthened by Karl Lark-Horowitz, a professor from Vienna, who was building Purdue's physics department. After graduation, Purcell spent a year at the Technische Hochschule in Karlsruhe, Germany, as an international exchange student. He received a master's degree from Harvard in 1935 and a Ph.D. in physics in 1938. He remained at Harvard as a physics instructor until 1941, when he became leader of the Fundamental Developments Group at the Massachusetts Institute of Technology's Radiation Laboratory, contributing to the World War II effort by working on advanced radar for night fighting. At MIT, he worked with **I. I. Rabi** and some of Rabi's Columbia University colleagues, who were developing the field of nuclear moments and resonance. The work Purcell and his group did with higher frequencies and shorter wavelengths also played a role in Purcell's later research. He returned to Harvard as an associate professor in 1946, advancing to professor of physics in 1949. He served as Donner professor of science from 1958 to 1960, and Gerhard Gade University professor from 1960 until his retirement in 1977.

Shares Nobel Prize for Nuclear Measurement Method

During the 1930s, Rabi had experimented with a method of determining nuclear magnetic moments, the rotating force exerted on nuclei when placed in a magnetic field. Purcell pursued a similar methodology by placing atoms in the field of a strong electromagnet and a second magnet activated by radio waves. He aligned the atoms in the magnetic field and then introduced varying frequencies of radio waves to change their orientation, allowing him to determine the one signature frequency at which the atoms absorbed energy, showing nuclear magnetic resonance. As Purcell wrote in his Nobel lecture, "Commonplace as such experiments have become in our laboratories, I have not yet lost a feeling of wonder, and of delight, that this delicate motion should reside in all the ordinary things around us, revealing itself only to him who looks for it . . . . To see the world for a moment as something rich and strange is the private reward of many a discovery."

Discovery Leads to Invention

Purcell put his discovery to work, when, with Harold Ewen, he built a radio telescope. In 1951, they detected for the first time radiation emitted by hydrogen clouds in space, noting a signature wavelength of 21 cm (8.3 in). Thus, they were able to exact a frequency by which radio astronomers could use to track hydrogen clouds. Purcell also found that the nuclear magnetic resonance signatures could change in substances like crystals or liquids because of the influence of their surroundings, a change known as a chemical shift. This phenomenon provided a means of studying molecular structures. Later in his career, Purcell ventured into biophysics to study bacterial behavior and locomotion, particularly the physics of swimming microscopic organisms.

In 1937, Purcell married Beth C. Busser, with whom he had two sons, Frank and Dennis. In addition to his work at Harvard, Purcell served on the scientific advisory board to the U.S. Air Force in 1947 and 1948, and from 1953 to 1957. A member of the President's Science Advisory Committee from 1957 to 1960 and 1962 to 1966, he was elected to the National Academy of Science in 1951 and received an honorary doctorate in engineering from Purdue in 1953. Purcell was a member of a number of scientific organizations and received the National Medal of Science from the National Science Foundation in 1978. Purcell died on March 7, 1997 in Cambridge, Massachusetts.

SELECTED WRITINGS BY PURCELL:

Books

Electricity and Magnetism. New York: McGraw-Hill, 1965.

Periodicals

"Nuclear Magnetism in Relation to Problems of the Liquid and Solid States." *Science* (30 April 1948): 433-40.
"Research in Nuclear Magnetism." *Science* (16 October 1953): 431-36.

FURTHER READING:

Books

McGraw-Hill Encyclopedia of Science and Technology. New York: McGraw-Hill, 1993, pp. 157–66.
Modern Scientists and Engineers. New York: McGraw-Hill, 1980, pp. 445-46.
Pioneers of Science: Nobel Prize Winners in Physics. Philadelphia: The Institute of Physics, 1980, pp. 145-46.
Wasson, Tyler, ed. *Nobel Prize Winners.* New York: H. W. Wilson, 1987.

Periodicals

Calnan, Patrick. "Edward M. Purcell, Won Nobel for Work on Atomic Nuclei" (obituary). *Boston Globe* (9 March 1997): D24.
"Dr. Edward Purcell, 84, Dies; Shared Nobel Prize in Physics" (obituary). *New York Times* (10 March 1997): B9.

Science News Letter (15 November 1952): 307.

Torrey, Volta. "Changing Partners in the Atom Dance." *Saturday Review* (6 May 1961): 68-69.

Weil, Martin. "Nobel-Winning Pysicist Edward Purcell Dies" (obituary). *Washington Post* (9 March 1997): B8.

—Sketch by Julie Anderson

Calvin F. Quate
1923–
American engineer

Calvin Quate owns at least part of 42 different patents; he has published or co-published more than 160 articles. Quate is known for developing two important microscopes, the scanning acoustic microscope and an atomic force microscope. The latter has numerous applications and is used throughout many industries. Atomic force microscopy has become an industry unto itself. In addition to microscopy, Quate has also made innovations in physical acoustics, digital information and its storage, as well as solid state devices and microwave electronics.

Quate had relatively humble beginnings. He was born Calvin Forrest Quate on December 7, 1923, in Baker, Nevada, to Graham Shepard Quate and Margie Lake. Quate began his education in a one-room school. He received his undergraduate education at the University of Utah, earning his B.S. in electrical engineering in 1944. The following year he married Dorothy Marshall on June 28th. The couple eventually had four children together, Robin, Claudia, Holly, and Rhodalee. From 1944 to 1946 Quate served as a lieutenant in Navy Reserves. Afterwards he completed his graduate work at Stanford University, where he earned his Ph.D. in electrical engineering in 1950.

After graduation, Quate did not immediately enter academia. He spent approximately ten years working for industrial companies. From 1949 to 1958, he was a member of the technical staff at Bell Telephone Laboratories, in Murray Hill, New Jersey, then at the Sandia Corporation in Albuquerque, New Mexico. He spent two years at Sandia, first as director of research, from 1959 to 1960, then as vice president of research from 1960 to 1961. Quate spent a great deal time at Bell and Sandia's laboratories scrutinizing electronics. This proved productive as it had a profound effect on his long-term research methodology.

It was during this work at Bell and Sandia that Quate became intrigued by a phenomenon he observed when investigating acoustics and microwaves. Quate saw that in optical microscopes the light waves were at a wavelength equal to that of acoustical waves. He continued this research into microscopes when he became a professor.

Wins Guggenheim and Fulbright Awards

In 1961, Quate returned to Stanford University, where he was appointed to a professorship in the applied physics and engineering department. He served as chair of this department from 1969 to 1972, and again from 1978 to 1981. He also held administrative positions at Stanford, serving as the associate dean of the School of Humanities and Sciences twice, from 1972 to 1974, then again from 1982 to 1983. Quate won a Guggenheim fellowship and a Fulbright Scholarship to work as a member of the Faculty of Science in Montpellier, France, from 1968 to 1969.

Part of his first 12 years at Stanford involved continuing his research into acoustics and microscopes. Together with scientist Ross Lemons, Quate announced the creation in 1973 of a scanning acoustic microscope that could see through opaque items. The microscope worked by emitting sound waves which, after passing through a sapphire crystal and spherical lens, traveled through a liquid cell containing the object to be analyzed. The microscope did not merely peer through things like silicon chips; it also gave a sense of the object's other characteristics like softness or hardness.

Throughout the 1980s, Quate received numerous accolades. In 1981, he was awarded the Morris N. Liebmann Award from the Institute of Electrical and Electronic Engineers (IEEE), of which he is a member. He has also won several additional honors from the IEEE, the Rank Prize for Opto-electronics in 1982, the Achievement Award in 1986, and the Medal of Honor in 1988.

Quate continued to build up professional positions in the 1980s as well. While maintaining his relationship with Stanford, he began working at the Xerox Palo Alto Research Center as a senior research fellow in 1984. In 1986, he was appointed to a concurrent position at Stanford as the Leland T. Edwards Professor of Engineering in 1986.

Develops Groundbreaking Microscope

It was during the mid-1980s that Quate began research into what came to be known as the atomic force microscope. After reading about the new scanning tunneling microscope, developed in Switzerland, Quate got the idea for a similar instrument that could work on an atomic level. After much work and conversation, some of it with the scientists who developed the scanning tunneling microscope, Quate built his microscope, using it to scale boron nitrade's atomic structure. As he and his team experimented with the atomic force microscope, they discovered it had an anomaly concerning its cantilever. This finding expanded the microscope's application possibilities, and made it a multi-million dollar industry unto itself. The atomic force microscope has practical applications in such far-ranging fields as electrochemistry and biology. Ironically, when Quate first sent his paper on the microscope to a professional journal, it was rejected because the concept behind the microscope was considered too improbable.

Quate's groundbreaking work continued to be lauded in the 1990s. In 1992, he was awarded the National Medal of Science, the highest honor a scientist can receive from the United States government. In 1995, Quate was voted into the Royal Society of London as well as named *R & D* magazine's scientist of the year. Quate is described as a shy and soft-spoken man, well regarded by his colleagues. In a story published in the July 1995 issue of *R & D* magazine in conjunction with the award, a colleague in the scientific instrument business, Sang-il Park, said, "Cal is a major force in microscopy—I've been watching him in action for 13 years. Whenever I hear his ideas, they're always hard to believe. But he makes

them work. He has real insight. He's taken microscopy beyond optics and electricity to a third generation."

SELECTED WRITINGS BY QUATE:

Periodicals

"Atomic Force Microscopy of an Organic Monolayer." *Science* (1988).
"Electrons that Make Waves." *Nature* (1988).
"Switch to Atom Control." *Nature* (1991).
"Variations on an Original Theme." *Nature* (1989).

FURTHER READING:

Periodicals

Koprowski, Gene. "AR & D Magazine's Scientist of the Year." *R & D* (July 1995): 22-25.
"National Medals of Science Given to 1992's Honorees." *Physics Today* (August 1992): 79.

—Sketch by Annette Petrusso

R

Mina S. Rees

Mina S. Rees
1902–1997
American mathematician

Mina S. Rees was the founding president of the Graduate Center of the City University of New York, and the first woman elected to the presidency of the American Association for the Advancement of Science. She was recognized by both the United States and Great Britain for organizing mathematicians to work on problems of interest to the military during World War II. After the war she headed the mathematics branch of the Office of Naval Research, where she built a program of government support for mathematical research and for the development of computers.

Rees was born in Cleveland, Ohio, on August 2, 1902, to Moses and Alice Louise (Stackhouse) Rees. Educated in New York public schools, Rees received her A.B. *summa cum laude* from Hunter College in New York City in 1923, and taught at Hunter College High School from 1923 to 1926. She completed an M.A. at the Teacher's College of Columbia University

in 1925, and became an instructor at the Mathematics Department of Hunter College the following year. She continued her training in mathematics at the University of Chicago, where she received a fellowship for 1931 to 1932, and earned a Ph.D. in mathematics in 1931 with a dissertation on abstract algebra. Returning to Hunter, Rees was promoted to assistant professor in 1932 and associate professor in 1940.

In 1943, in the midst of World War II, Rees joined the government as a civil servant, working as executive assistant and a technical aide to Warren Weaver, the chief of the Applied Mathematics Panel (AMP) of the National Research Committee in the Office of Scientific Research and Development. The AMP, located in New York City, established contracts with mathematics departments at New York University, Brown, Harvard, Columbia, and other universities. Under these contracts, mathematicians and statisticians studied military applications such as shock waves, jet engine design, underwater ballistics, air-to-air gunnery, the probability of damage under anti-aircraft fire, supply and munitions inspection methods, and computers. In 1948, in recognition for her wartime service, Rees received a Certificate of Merit from President Truman, as well as the Medal for Service in the Cause of Freedom from King George VI.

Joins Office of Naval Research

From 1946 to 1953, Rees worked for the Office of Naval Research (ONR), first as head of the mathematics branch and then, from 1950, as director of the mathematics division. Under Rees, the ONR supported programs for research on hydrofoils, logistics, computers, and numerical methods. Rees emphasized the study and development of mathematical algorithms for computing. The ONR supported the development of linear programming and the establishment in 1947 of an Institute for Numerical Analysis at the University of California at Los Angeles, and also worked with other military and civilian government agencies on the acquisition of early computers. In addition, the ONR funded university research programs to build computers, such as Project Whirlwind at MIT, lead by **Jay Forrester**, and the Institute for Advanced Study project under **John Neumann**. The ONR also awarded grants to support applied and basic mathematical research.

In 1953, Rees returned to Hunter College as Dean of Faculty and Professor of Mathematics. She was married in 1955, to Dr. Leopold Brahdy, a physician. In 1961, she was appointed dean of graduate studies for the City University of New York (CUNY), which established graduate programs by pooling distinguished faculty from the City Colleges, including Hunter. The following year, Rees became the first recipient of the Award for Distinguished Service to Mathematics established by the Mathematical Association of America. Rees was appointed provost of the Graduate Division in 1968 and the first president of the Graduate School and University Center in 1969. By the time Rees retired as emeritus president in 1972, CUNY's graduate school had created twenty-six doctoral programs and enrolled over two thousand students. During her post-war years at Hunter and CUNY, Rees served on government, scientific, and educational advisory boards and held offices in mathematical, scientific, and educational organizations. She became the first female president of the American Association for the Advancement of Science in 1971. In 1983 Rees received the Public Welfare Medal of the National Academy of Sciences, an award that confers honorary membership in that organization. She died on October 25, 1997, at the Mary Manning Walsh Home in Manhattan.

SELECTED WRITINGS BY REES:

Periodicals

"The Nature of Mathematics." *Science* (5 October 1962): 9-12.

"The Mathematical Sciences and World War II." *American Mathematical Monthly* (October 1980): 607-21.

"The Computing Program of the Office of Naval Research, 1946-1953." *Annals of the History of Computing* 4, no. 2 (April 1982): 102-20.

FURTHER READING:

Books

Dana, Rosamond, and Peter J. H. Hilton. "Interview with Mina Rees." In *Mathematical People,* edited by Donald J. Albers and G. L. Alexanderson. Cambridge, MA: Birkhauser, 1985, pp. 256-65.

Periodicals

————. "Award for Distinguished Service to Mathematics." *American Mathematical Monthly* (February 1962): 185-87.

Saxon, Wolfgang. "Mina S. Rees, Mathematician and CUNY Leader, Dies at 95" (obituary). *New York Times* (28 October 1997): B10.

—*Sketch by Sally M. Moite*

Alexander Rich

Alexander Rich
1924–
American biophysicist

In any account of the history of molecular biology, Alexander Rich must occupy a prominent place as one of the prime architects who shaped the discipline to its modern form. Entering the field in its infancy, Rich made fundamental discoveries about nucleic acids—deoxyribonucleic acid (DNA) and ribonucleic acid (RNA)—molecules that encode the specific information needed by all organisms for performing the various functions of living. His findings have helped answer questions about the basic functions of DNA and RNA molecules.

Rich was born in Hartford, Connecticut, on November 15, 1924, to Max Rich and Bella Shub Rich. His parents had both immigrated to the United States from Russia in the first decade of the twentieth century and his father worked in the dry cleaning industry. Rich grew up in Hartford and served in the U.S. Navy from 1943 to 1945, before going to Harvard University for a bachelor's degree in biochemical sciences. He went on to receive a Doctor of Medicine degree from Harvard Medical School in 1949, but never practiced medicine. Instead, upon completing his degree, he undertook a four year postdoctoral fellowship in physical chemistry in the laboratory of **Linus Pauling** at the California Institute of Technology in Pasadena. He got married in 1952 to Jane Erving King, a nursery school teacher from Cambridge, Massachusetts.

It was in Pauling's laboratory that Rich first began to work on nucleic acid chemistry. During that time, **James Watson** and **Francis Crick** were just formulating their proposal for the double helix structure of DNA, which they published in 1953. Rich, who moved to Bethesda in 1954 as chief of the section of physical chemistry at the National Institute of Mental Health, provided some of the earliest experimental evidence to back up Watson and Crick's structural model.

When Two Strands Meet

As we now know, a DNA molecule is made up of two complementary chains wound around each other to form a double helix. Each chain is a polymer comprised of molecular units called nucleotides made up of a deoxyribose sugar, phosphate groups, and either a purine or pyrimidine side chain. The sugar and phosphate molecules make up the backbone of each strand, while side chains form the basis of DNA specificity and complementarity. A total of four possible side chains—adenine, guanosine, thymine and cytosine (A, G, T, C)—are arranged in specific sequences to make up different genes. An A in one strand binds to a T in the complement while G bind to C, via hydrogen bonds. In contrast to DNA, RNA molecules contain a ribose sugar in the backbone, and have uracil (U) residues instead of T. While they exist, for most part, as single-stranded polymers, they can, and often do, form double helical structures as well.

Working with artificially synthesized single polynucleotide chains—in this case one string each of A and U residues on ribose phosphate backbones—Rich found that when mixed together in solution, these strands wound around each other to form a double helix. The experiment showed that not only was the base pairing possible in nature, but that in fact, it was the configuration that nucleic acids assumed by default if the strands were complementary. Clearly the molecules did not require the help of an enzyme to form a helix, a fact which, Rich recounted later, greatly surprised his colleagues. Furthermore, these experiments showed that contrary to Watson's predictions, RNA molecules too, could form double helices. The reaction, which is known as hybridization, is the basis for many modern molecular biological techniques. For example, using a sequence from a gene in one organism, scientists can probe the DNA from other species or organisms to see if they contain similar sequences.

While experimenting with hybridization, Rich found that when one type of strand was present in excess over the other rather than in equal quantities, the nucleic acids were capable of adopting a triple-stranded configuration. The implications of this finding went largely ignored for many years, and it is only recently that biotechnologists have begun to investigate the therapeutic value of DNA triple helices by attempting to use them to prevent the expression of specific, disease-inducing genes.

Milestones at MIT

Moving to the Massachusetts Institute of Technology (MIT) in 1958, Rich continued to work on the structure and behavior of nucleic acids. In 1960 he discovered that hybridization was also possible between DNA and RNA strands, a finding that had fundamental theoretical implications far beyond its obvious practical applications. "It suggested how DNA might transfer its information to RNA," Rich recounted in an interview in 1995. Yet again, Rich's experiments provided experimental support for a very important biological principle, in this case the "Central Dogma" of biology, which was formulated during the late 1950s to describe the flow of information in living organisms—from DNA to RNA to proteins.

Still more details about this information path came to light from Rich's lab throughout the 1960s. His group isolated and characterized polysomes—clusters of ribosomes and messenger RNA (m-RNA) and transfer RNAs (t-RNAs)—which gave scientists a dynamic picture of how protein synthesis proceeded inside the cell. They went on to solve the crystal structure of a yeast t-RNA specific for the amino acid phenylalanine. This was the first time anyone had elucidated the three-dimensional structure of any nucleic acid. During this time they also crystallized a single base-pair unit of DNA, which Rich described as "the first crystal structure in which the atomic details of double helical nucleic acid can be visualized."

In 1979 Rich's laboratory announced the discovery of a new configuration of DNA, in which the helix is wound in a left-handed orientation, opposite to the conventional helix proposed by Watson and Crick. While the exact role of Z-DNA is as yet unknown, evidence from different labs indicate it is involved in a wide variety of fundamental biological activities including transcription and cell division. His attention then turned to different compounds that interacted with DNA, and was responsible for solving the structure of several DNA binding drugs during the 1980s.

His achievements in basic sciences aside, Rich also involved himself in arenas that touched people's lives more directly. Beginning in the late 1960s, Rich worked with the National Aeronautics and Space Administration (NASA) in various capacities. He was a member of the Lunar and Planetary Missions Board from 1968 to 1970, in the Life Sciences Committee from 1970 to 1975, and a member of the biology team for the Viking Mars Mission since 1969. In recognition of his service, NASA awarded him with their Skylab Achievement Award in 1974.

As befits a long productive career marked by many firsts, Rich received scientific honors and awards too numerous to name. He was elected as a member of the National Academy of Science—the highest honor for an American scientist—in 1970, and in 1995 received the National Medal of Science from the President. Probably the best summary of his career came from Northwestern University chemist Irving Klotz at a symposium celebrating 40 years of DNA in 1995, "The young Alexander Rich, a freshly hatched M.D., arrived in Pasadena in 1949, just at the onset of the 'giant leaps forward' in protein and nucleic acid structure, and has been at the very center of the field ever since."

SELECTED WRITINGS BY RICH:

Periodicals

"The Nucleic Acids, A Backward Glance." *DNA: The Double Helix. Perspective and Prospective at Forty Years.* Vol. 758 of *Annals of the New York Academy of Sciences.* Edited by Donald A. Chambers, 1995.

FURTHER READING:

Periodicals

Sankaran, Neeraja. "National Medal of Science Winners Contributed to Birth of Their Fields." *The Scientist* (October 30, 1995): 3.

—Sketch by Neeraja Sankaran

Robert C. Richardson
1937–
American physicist

A pioneer in low-temperature physics, Robert C. Richardson received part of the 1996 Nobel Prize in Physics for his role in the work that led to the discovery of superfluidity in helium-3, a rare isotope of helium. He shared the prize with **David M. Lee** and **Douglas D. Osheroff**; their collaboration at Cornell University culminated in their condensation, reported in 1972, of helium-3 to a superfluid state. Superfluidity, an unusual state of matter occurring at extremely low temperatures, close to absolute zero (the lowest possible temperature according to theoret-

ical physics), is a strange phenomenon by everyday standards. For example, a substance in the state of superfluidity will not stay in a cup-like container; it will spontaneously overflow. This behavior, which does not contradict the principles of quantum mechanics, results from the rigid organization of a substance's normally randomly moving atoms, which enables the liquid in superfluid form to flow without any inner resistance. Richardson's important discovery not only shattered the widely-held belief that helium-3 could not reach a superfluid state, but also opened new fields of research, both in low-temperature physics and cosmology. Working with Lee, Richardson is currently studying the behavior of metals and other materials at low temperatures.

Richardson was born in Washington, D.C., on June 26, 1937, to Robert Franklin and Lois (Price) Richardson. He married Betty Marilyn McCarthy in 1962; they have two daughters. Having completed his undergraduate studies at Virginia Polytechnic Institute, Richardson earned his B.S. in 1958; two years later, he completed his M.S. After receiving a Ph.D. in physics from Duke University in 1966, he joined the physics department at Cornell University as a research associate. He was named assistant professor of physics in 1969, associate professor in 1972, and full professor in 1975. He became Floyd R. Newman Professor of Physics in 1987, and assumed the directorship of Cornell's Laboratory of Atomic and Solid State Physics three years later. In addition, Richardson has served as a member of the editorial board of the *Journal of Low Temperature Physics* since 1984.

Participates in Historic Discovery

At Cornell, Richardson and Lee conducted experiments in an effort to investigate the behavior of substances at the lowest possible temperatures, just thousandths of a degree above absolute zero. As senior researchers, the scientists included Douglas Osheroff, a graduate student, in their team. In the late 1960s, Richardson and his colleagues, who had constructed their own cooling apparatus, experimented with frozen helium-3, hoping to identify a phase transition to a magnetic order. The outcome, however, was quite different. The team discovered helium-3 in a superfluid state, a discovery which not only significantly enhanced research in condensed-matter physics, but also suggested new ideas to cosmologists, who, using the behavior of superfluid helium-3 as a model, proposed new theories about the genesis of the universe, and suggested possible parallels between the hypothetical behavior of helium-3 a fraction of a second after the Big Bang and particular processes obtained in a laboratory.

A recipient of the John Simon Guggenheim Fellowship in 1975 and 1982, Richardson is a member of the National Academy of Sciences. In 1981, he was elected Fellow of the American Association for the Advancement of Science; two years later, Richardson became a Fellow of the American Physical Society. In 1976, Richardson and his two colleagues shared the Sir Francis Simon Memorial Prize, given by Britain's Institute of Physics. The three scientists also received the 1980 Oliver E. Buckley Solid State Physics Prize from the American Physical Society for their successful research in superfluidity.

SELECTED WRITINGS BY RICHARDSON:

Books

(With Eric N. Smith, et al.) *Experimental Techniques in Condensed Matter Physics at Low Temperature.* Addison-Wesley, 1988.

Periodicals

"Low Temperature Science–What Remains for the Physicist?" *Physics Today* (August 1981): 46.

FURTHER READING:

Books

Leggett, A. J. *The Problems of Physics.* Oxford: Oxford University Press, 1987.

Periodicals

Browne, Malcolm W. "Discoveries of Superfluid Helium, and 'Buckyballs,' Earn Nobels for 6 Scientist." *New York Times* (10 October 1996): D21.
Lounasmaa, O. V., and G. R. Pickett. "The ³He Superfluids." *Scientific American* (June 1990): 104-11.
Peterson, Ivars. "Superfluidity Finding Earn Physics Nobel." *Science News* 150, no. 16 (19 October 1996): 247.
Special Issue: He3 and He4. *Physics Today* (February 1987).

Other

Nobel Foundation WWW Server Posting (9 October 1996). http://www.nobel.ki.se

—*Sketch by Jane Stewart Cook and Zoran Minderovic*

Martin Rodbell

Martin Rodbell
1925–
American biochemist

Known for his part in the discovery of G-proteins, Rodbell has done ground-breaking work in cell biology, determining the mechanism whereby cells communicate. For his work in this area, Rodbell shared the Nobel Prize in Medicine with scientist **Alfred Gilman.**

Rodbell was born on December 1, 1925 in Baltimore, Maryland. He attended a special high school in Baltimore that accepted boys from all over the city and prepared students to enter college as sophomores. The school emphasized languages, and Rodbell thought he might continue his language studies when he entered Johns Hopkins University in 1943. However, he was more interested in chemistry.

Rodbell was happy to go into the Navy during World War II. He was bored with classes at Johns Hopkins and being Jewish, was motivated to fight Hitler. Most of the war, however, he spent in the South Pacific. He was a radio operator in the Philippine jungles until he contracted malaria. When he recovered, he stayed on ships, traveling to Korea and China. In his autobiography published on the Nobel Foundation's web site, Rodbell describes his experiences in the war as extremely influential. " . . . My interactions with so many different types of people under trying conditions provided me with a healthy respect for the human condition."

When he came back from the war, he continued his studies at Johns Hopkins and was unsure about what direction he wanted to go. He was interested in French literature and existentialist philosophy, and his father wanted him to go to medical school. He was not interested in medical school because of the competition for grades, but a biology class given by James Ebert turned his attention back toward the sciences. When he was close to graduating he went to Professor Bently Glass for advice, who told him to study biochemistry. He hadn't had any course in chemistry, so he stayed at Johns Hopkins an extra year and took every available chemistry course.

Rodbell received a B.A. from Johns Hopkins University in 1949. That same year he met his future wife, Barbara Lederman, a ballet dancer from Holland who had lost her family in the Auschwitz concentration camp. They married a year later, and Rodbell credits his wife for immersing him the world of the arts. Rodbell and his new wife traveled to Seattle, where Rodbell began his graduate studies in biochemistry at the University of Seattle. He studied the chemistry of lipids (the fatty substances in cells), and his thesis was on the biosynthesis of lecithin (fats found in cell membranes) in the rat liver. Unfortunately, his thesis was disproved by another scientist working on the same subject. This experience taught him not to assume that biological chemicials are pure, something that would help him later in his Nobel Prize-winning work.

Chooses Research Over Teaching

Rodbell finished his Ph.D. in 1954 and then went to the University of Illinois for his post-doctoral fellowship. His research involved the biosynthesis of chloramphenicol, an antibiotic. When his fellowship advisor, Herbert Carter, asked him where he wanted to teach, Rodbell had to answer nowhere. After having taught a lecture course to freshman, only a few of whom passed his exams, Rodbell decided that teaching was not his calling. He accepted a position at the National Heart Institute in Bethesda, Maryland, and continued his research into fats, identifying important proteins that pertained to diseases concerning lipoproteins.

In the 1960s he returned to his original interest in cell biology and was awarded a fellowship to work at the University of Brussels. There he learned new lab techniques and enjoyed European culture with his family. He returned to the United States and accepted a postion at the NIH Institute of Arthritis and Metabolic Diseases in the Nutrition and Endocrinology lab. He developed a simple procedure that would separate and purify fat cells. He was also able to remove the fat from a cell, conserving most of the structure of the cell. He named these cells "ghosts."

Conducts Nobel Prize Winning Research

In several groundbreaking experiments, Rodbell and his colleagues at the NIH showed that cell communication involves three different working devices: (1) a chemical signal; (2) a "second messenger" like a hormone; and (3) a transducer, something that converts energy from one form to another. Rodbell's major contribution was in discovering that there was a transducer function. He and his colleagues also speculated that guanine nucleotides, components of deoxyribonucleic acid (DNA) and ribonucleic acid (RNA), were somehow involved in cell communication, something that would later be confirmed by Alfred Goodman, the biochemist with whom he would share the Nobel Prize. Gilman searched for the chemicals involved with guanine nucleotides and discovered the G-proteins.

G-proteins are instrumental in the fundamental workings of a cell. They allow us to see and smell by changing light and odors to chemical messages that travel to the brain. Understanding how G-proteins malfunction could lead to a better understanding of serious diseases like cholera or cancer. Scientists have already linked improperly working G-proteins to diseases like alcoholism and diabetes. Pharmaceutical companies are developing drugs that would focus on G-proteins.

Rodbell served as director of the National Institute of Environmental Health Sciences in Chapel Hill, North Carolina, from 1985 until his retirement in 1994. Ironically, only a few months before receiving the Nobel Award, Rodbell opted for early retirement, because there were no funds to support the research he wanted to do. Upon receiving the Nobel Prize, Rodbell was vocal in his criticism of the government because of its unwillingness to provide adequate support for fundamental research. He criticized them for favoring projects that yield obviously tangible and potentially profitable results, like drug treatments. Rodbell's other awards include the NIH Distinguished Service Award in 1973 and the Gairdner Award in 1984.

SELECTED WRITINGS BY RODBELL:

Books

(With Robert S. Adelstein and Claude B. Klee) *Advances in Second Messenger and Phosphoprotein Research.* Raven Press, 1988.
(With Robert S. Adelstein and Claude B. Klee) *Advances in Second Messenger and Phospho-*

protein Research/Sixth International Conference/Formerly Advances in Cyclic Nucleotide and Protine Phosphoryl. Raven Press, June 1988.

Periodicals

"Glucagon-Sensitive Adenyl Cyclase System in Plasma Membranes of Rat Liver. Obligatory Role of of Guanyl Nucleotides in Glucagon Action." *Journal of Biological Chemistry*, 1971.

FURTHER READING:

Periodicals

Begley, Sharon. "The Biological Switchboard." *Newsweek*, (October 24, 1994): 65-66.

Bronstein, Scott. "South Carolinian, Texan Win Nobel for Showing How Cells 'Talk'." *Atlanta Constitution*, (October 11, 1994): A3.

Friend, Tim. "U.S. Duo Receive Nobel Prize for Cell Research." *USA Today*, (October 11, 1994) : 3D.

Marx, Jean. "Medicine: A Signal Award for Discovering G-Proteins." *Science*, (October 21, 1994): 368-69.

Silverman, Edward R.. "Colleagues Laud 1994 Nobelists As Overdue for Coveted Prize." *The Scientist*, (November 28, 1994): 1.

—Sketch by Pamela Proffitt

Leon Raymand Roddy
1921–1975
American entomologist and arachnologist

Around Louisiana, Leon Roddy was known simply as "The Spider Man." The transplanted Texan taught entomology—the study of insects—for 20 years at Southern University in Baton Rouge and became known nationally as the man to see when you had a strange spider on your hands. When he finished his Ph.D. in entomology at Ohio State University in 1953, he was probably one of only three African-American insect specialists in the United States.

A systematist who specialized in identifying and categorizing insects, Roddy single-handedly organized and catalogued the Southern University collection of more than 1,000 previously unknown insects. But his real passion became spiders, family *Acracnida*. After cleaning up and identifying Southern's small collec-

tion of spiders, Roddy began scouring the bayous and woods of Louisiana, looking for new species, often in difficult conditions. He identified many new species and published several well-received papers on spiders. As his reputation grew, he also consulted with worried homeowners and the U.S. Army. Though his position at Southern was primarily a teaching post, he continued his research energetically, often at his own expense, throughout his life. "In my opinion, research is one of the tools of a good teacher," he told an *Ebony Magazine* interviewer in 1962.

Earning a Chance at Education

Roddy was the second son of Floyd and Mattie Roddy of Whitewith, in western Texas. His father worked in the flour mill in Amarillo and got his son summer work there, in the hopes that Leon would follow in his footsteps. But Leon had other ideas, starting with college. After graduating from Sherman High School in nearby Sherman, Texas, Leon had to scrape together the money he needed to attend Texas College, a Methodist school in Tyler. Thanks to strong grades in biology, English, math, and foreign languages, Roddy also earned a small scholarship for college. He continued to work two jobs while attending college, but still managed to earn good grades.

Just one week shy of graduation from Texas College, Roddy, along with hundreds of thousands of other young Americans incensed by the Japanese attack on Pearl Harbor, enlisted in the armed forces. He was in basic training for the U.S. Army when Texas College granted Roddy a bachelor's degree *in absentia*. The Army shipped him out to Europe, where he fought for 18 months in an artillery unit that saw action in the "Battle of the Bulge."

After an honorable discharge in 1945, Roddy resumed his studies as a graduate student at the University of Michigan, with financial support from the federal government under the GI Bill. An encounter there with a dragonfly researcher changed Roddy's focus and made him pursue insects full time, and he moved to Ohio State University's stronger entomology program for his Ph.D.

However, Roddy was supporting a wife and child at the time, and he had to interrupt his studies in Columbus after only one term to earn some money. He accepted a teaching position in biology at Tillotson College in Texas, and stayed there for two years before returning to Ohio State. His Ph.D. was finished in only a year and a half. Roddy apparently had several job offers to choose from upon graduation, but he settled on Southern, one of three traditionally black colleges in the south that made him an offer. "Somehow, I felt needed back home," he told biographer Edward S. Jenkins in *To Fathom More: African American Scientists and Inventors*.

Roddy had three daughters with his wife Marian Daniel Roddy, who was a nurse, and a son, Leon, by an earlier marriage. He died of cancer on June 22, 1975, at the age of 54.

SELECTED WRITINGS BY RODDY:

Periodicals

"New Species, Records of Clubinoid Spiders." *Transactions of the American Microscopic Society* 85: 399-407.

FURTHER READING:

Books

Jenkins, Edward Sidney. *To Fathom More: African American Scientists and Inventors.* Lantham, Maryland: University Press of America, 1996.

Periodicals

"Man Who Understands Spiders." *Ebony* (March 1962): 65-70.

—*Sketch by Karl Leif Bates*

Mary Ellen Rudin
1924–

American mathematician

Mary Ellen Rudin's mathematical specialty is set theoretic topology, a modern, abstract geometry that deals with the construction, classification, and description of the properties of mathematical spaces. Rudin's approach is often to construct examples to disprove a conjecture. As an incoming freshman at the University of Texas, Rudin was chosen by the topologist R. L. Moore and trained almost exclusively by the unorthodox "Moore method" of active and competitive mathematical problem–solving. Rudin credits Moore with building her confidence that given the axioms, she should be able to solve any problem, even if it involves building a complicated structure.

Rudin was born December 7, 1924, in Hillsboro, Texas, to Irene Shook and Joe Jefferson Estill. Her father was a civil engineer and her mother, before she married, was a teacher. Rudin's parents were from Winchester, Tennessee, and both of her grandmothers were graduates of Mary Sharp College in Winchester. Advanced education was valued in both families, and her parents expected that she would go to the university to "do something interesting."

Rudin grew up in Leakey, Texas, a small isolated town in the hills of southwest Texas, where her father worked on road building projects. Her childhood surroundings were simple and primitive, and as a child she had lots of time to think and to play elaborate, complicated, and imaginative games, something she says contributed to her later success as a mathematician. Rudin's performance was generally in the middle of her class of five students, and she expected she would make Cs at the university; she made As.

Is Trained by the R. L. Moore "Method"

Rudin had no special course of study in mind when she went to the University of Texas at Austin. On her first day, Moore helped her register for classes, asked about her mathematical background, and enrolled her in his mathematics class. Although she took courses in other fields and was good at them, she continued to study with Moore through her B.S. degree in 1944 and her Ph.D. degree in 1949, and had a class from him every single semester. Rudin has said, "I am a mathematician because Moore caught me and demanded that I become a mathematician."

Moore, known for his unorthodox Socratic teaching style, preferred his students to be naive; he required that they be unspoiled by mathematical terminology, notation, methods, results, or ideas of others. He also required his students to actively think, rather than passively read. Moore forbade them to read the work of others and sometimes removed books from the library so that his students would not see them. He never referred to the work of others; rather, he gave definitions and required his students to prove theorems, some that had been solved, some that had not. Students were required to think about problems just as research mathematicians do. In the classroom, Moore called on the weakest students first, then proceeded through the class to the top students. Rudin was generally at the top of the class.

Rudin solved one of the unsolved problems as her thesis research, finding a counterexample to a well–known conjecture. At the time she wrote her thesis, she had never seen a mathematics paper. While the Moore method produced students who were independent, confident and creative, there were lacunae in their knowledge of mathematics and deficient in their mathematical language. Rudin has used a more traditional approach in her own teaching, requiring her students to learn as much as possible about what has been done by others, but she acknowledges that her students are not always as confident as she was.

Research at Duke, Rochester, and Wisconsin

After Rudin received her Ph.D. in 1949, Moore told her she would be going to Duke University. At Duke, she worked on a problem related to Souslin's conjecture and began to be known for her work. She also met mathematician Walter Rudin at the university and married him in 1953. Together, they went to the University of Rochester where Walter had a position, and Rudin taught part–time and researched mostly as she pleased until 1958, when they moved to Madison, Wisconsin. Rudin held a similar position at the University of Wisconsin; she was a lecturer from 1959 to 1971, when she was appointed full professor.

Rudin has likened facility in research in mathematics to a career in music. "It must be done every day," she says. "If you don't play for three years, you're not likely to be of concert pianist quality when you start playing again, if ever again." She also notes that mathematical research requires a high tolerance for failure; successes are much less frequent than failures; she may have three exciting breakthroughs in a year. Rudin prefers to work on topological problems while lying on the couch in her Frank Lloyd Wright–designed home, surrounded by the activities of her family. Rudin's productivity has been strong and consistent; she has almost 90 scientific papers and book chapters to her credit.

Rudin's counterexamples, she says, are "very messy" topological spaces that show that some ideas you thought were true, are not. She compares her many–dimensional examples, which are difficult for some people to imagine, to a business problem that has 20 aspects. The aspects are the dimensions of the problem, the number of factors taken into account.

Rudin has been at the University of Wisconsin since 1959, where she assembled a strong research group in topology. She is the first to hold the **Grace Chisholm Young** Professorship, which she assumed in 1981. Her visiting professorships include stints in New Zealand, Mexico, and China. Moore imbued Rudin with a sense of responsibility for publication and responsibility to the mathematical community, and she has held offices and worked on numerous committees of the American Mathematical Society, the Mathematical Association of America, the Association for Women in Mathematics, and the Association for Symbolic Logic. Over the years she has received several research grants from the National Science Foundation, and has served on mathematical advisory boards for the National Academy of Sciences, the National Science Foundation, and the United Nations.

Rudin and her husband have four children, and she notes that they are all skilled in pattern recognition. Now professor emerita, Rudin continues to lecture widely, produce vital papers in her field, and to promote and speak about women in mathematics.

She is a Fellow of the American Academy of Arts and Sciences, has received the Prize of Niewe Archief voor Wiskunk from the Mathematical Society of the Netherlands, and has been awarded four honorary doctorates. In 1995 Rudin was elected to the Hungarian Academy of Sciences.

FURTHER READING:

Books

Albers, Donald J., Gerald L. Alexanderson and Constance Reid. *More Mathematical People: Contemporary Conversations.* Boston: Harcourt Brace Jovanovich, 1990, pp. 282–303.

Periodicals

Ford, Jeff. "Geometry with a Twist." *Research Sampler* (Spring 1987): 20–23.

Other

Carr, Shannon. "Mary Ellen Rudin." *Biographies of Women Mathematicians.* June 1997. http://www.scottlan.edu/lriddle/women/chronol.htm (July 21, 1997).

—*Sketch by Jill Carpenter*

S. K. Runcorn
1922–1995
English geophysicist

Geophysicist S. K. Runcorn made significant contributions to the understanding of several areas within his field, including the earth's magnetic field and the theory of continental drift. During the 1950s, he helped establish the discipline called paleomagnetism—the study of the intensity and direction of residual magnetization found in ancient rocks. More recently, his research has encompassed lunar magnetism. In a prolific career marked by the publication of more than one-hundred and eighty papers and the editing of over two dozen books, Runcorn exerted a wide-ranging impact on his field.

Stanley Keith Runcorn was born on November 19, 1922 in Southport, England. He was the eldest of two children born to William Henry Runcorn, a businessman, and Lily Idina Roberts Runcorn. As Runcorn related to contributor Linda Wasmer Smith in a letter, "My interest in science as a child was certainly stimulated . . . by excellent maths and physics teaching in my grammar school." In 1941,

Runcorn began studies at Gonville and Caius College of Cambridge University. He passed the tripos, or final honors examination, in mechanical sciences two years later. Runcorn earned a B.A. degree from Cambridge in 1944 and an M.A. in 1948, before transferring to Manchester University to obtain a Ph.D. in 1949. Later, he returned to Cambridge, where he received an Sc.D. degree in 1963.

Advances the Theory of Continental Drift

Runcorn's early years at college coincided with World War II. From 1943 through 1946, he worked on radar research for the ministry of supply at Malvern. For three years afterward, he was a lecturer in physics at Manchester University. His department head there was **Patrick Maynard Stuart Blackett,** who won the 1948 Nobel Prize in physics. Under Blackett's leadership, Runcorn first began a long line of investigations into geomagnetism, which extended well past his move back to Cambridge as assistant director of geophysics research in 1950.

At the time, the idea was rapidly gaining currency in England that many rocks contain within them a fossilized record of the magnetic conditions under which they were formed. This is the basic assumption behind paleomagnetic research. Runcorn compared the results of tests done on rocks from Great Britain and the United States. His analyses seemed to support the hypothesis that over hundreds of millions of years the earth's magnetic poles had undergone large-scale movement, or polar wandering. However, the polar migration routes were different depending on whether the tested rocks came from Europe or North America. This suggested that the continents themselves had actually moved. Thus Runcorn became a proponent of the theory called continental drift. Although this idea had first been put forth in 1912, it had not up to that point won widespread acceptance. It was not until the mid-1950s that Runcorn and his colleagues published convincing evidence for its existence.

Advocates of continental drift argued that the direction of magnetization within rocks from different continents would align if only the land masses were oriented differently. However, this suggestion was not immediately embraced by most scientists, partly because a physical mechanism to explain continental drift had yet to be found. By the early 1960s, though, Runcorn had proposed that, under very high temperature and pressure, rocks beneath the earth's cold, outer shell—the lithosphere—might gradually "creep," or flow. The resulting upward transfer of heat by convection currents could be the force that moved continents. This idea contributed to the modern theory of plate tectonics, which posits that the earth's shell is divided into a number of rigid plates floating on a viscous underlayer.

In 1956, Runcorn accepted a post as professor and head of the physics department at King's College, part of the University of Durham. Seven years later, King's College became the University of Newcastle upon Tyne, and Runcorn was appointed head of the school of physics there, a position which he held until 1988. During this period, Runcorn was also a visiting scientist or professor at several institutions around the world, including the University of California, Los Angeles and Berkeley; Dominion Observatory, Ottawa; the California Institute of Technology; the University of Miami; the Lunar Science Institute, Houston; the University of Texas, Galveston; and the University of Queensland, Australia.

Proposes New Ideas on Lunar Magnetism

By the late 1960s, Runcorn's attention had turned toward the moon. At the time, the moon was generally presumed to be a dead body. As early as 1962, though, Runcorn had suggested that the moon, too, might be subject to the forces of convection—an idea that was initially rejected by most scientists. However, examination of lunar samples brought back by the Apollo missions showed that some of them were magnetized, which implied that they had been exposed to magnetic fields while they were forming. Runcorn and his colleagues concluded that the moon had probably once possessed its own strong magnetic field, generated within an iron core.

Not only that, but this magnetic field seemed to have pointed in different directions at different times in lunar history. When Runcorn and his co-workers calculated the strengths and directions of this ancient magnetism, they found evidence of polar wandering. Runcorn subsequently proposed that the wandering could have been caused by the same impacts that created large basins near the moon's equator. According to this hypothesis, the force of the impacts could have shifted the moon's entire surface, so that regions once near the poles might have been relocated closer to the equator. However, attempts to confirm this notion have so far proved inconclusive.

Runcorn's remarkable skill as a theorist was widely recognized. In 1989, he assumed an endowed chair in the natural sciences at the University of Alaska in Fairbanks, a position he held until his death. He also received honorary degrees from universities in Utrecht, Netherlands; Ghent, Belgium; Paris; and Bergen, Norway. Among the many prestigious awards he received are the Napier Shaw Prize of Britain's Royal Meteorological Society in 1959, the John Adams Fleming Medal of the American Geophysical Union in 1983, the Gold Medal of Britain's Royal Astronomical Society in 1984, and the Wegener Medal of the European Union of Geosciences in 1987.

In addition, Runcorn was elected a fellow or member of such respected associations as the British Royal Society, the American Physical Society, the European Geophysical Society, the Royal Netherlands Academy of Science, the Indian National Science Academy, the Royal Norwegian Academy of Science and Letters, the Pontifical Academy of Science, and Academia Europaea.

Runcorn, who never married, was an aficionado of sports and the arts. Among his favorite pastimes was rugby, which he enjoyed as a participant until he was past fifty and as a spectator thereafter. In a letter to Wasmer Smith, Runcorn described himself also as an avid fan of "squash rackets and swimming, . . . visiting art galleries, seeing opera and ballet, reading history and politics, hiking in the country, and seeing architecture in my travels." He was murdered in San Diego, on December 5, 1995.

SELECTED WRITINGS BY RUNCORN:

Books

Methods and Techniques in Geophysics. Vols. 1 and 2. New York: Interscience, 1960 and 1966.
Continental Drift, Academic Press, 1962.
Mantle of the Earth and Terrestrial Planets. New York: Interscience, 1967.

Magnetism and the Cosmos. Oliver & Boyd, 1967.

Periodicals

"The Moon's Deceptive Tranquility." *New Scientist* (21 October 1982): 174-80.
"The Moon's Ancient Magnetism." *Scientific American* 257 (1987): 60-68.

FURTHER READING:

Books

A Biographical Encyclopedia of Scientists. Vol. 2. New York: Facts on File, 1981, p. 693.
McGraw-Hill Modern Scientists and Engineers. Vol. 3. New York: McGraw-Hill 1980, pp. 50-51.

Periodicals

Creer, Kenneth M. "Stanley Keith Runcorn" (obituary). *Nature* 379 (11 January 1996): 119.
Dalton, Rex. "UK Geophysicist Killed in San Diego" (obituary). *Nature* 378 (14 December 1995): 657.
Sullivan, Walter. "Leading Expert in Geophysics is Found Slain in Hotel Room" (obituary). *New York Times* (7 December 1995): B17.

—Sketch by Linda Wasmer Smith

Carl Sagan

Carl Sagan
1934–1996
American astronomer and exobiologist

One of the first scientists to take an active interest in the possibility that life exists elsewhere in the universe, and an astronomer was both a best-selling author and a popular television figure, Carl Sagan was one of the best-known scientists in the world. He made important contributions to studies of Venus and Mars, and he was extensively involved in planning NASA's Mariner missions. Regular appearances on the *Tonight Show* with Johnny Carson began a television career which culminated in the series Sagan hosted on public television called *Cosmos,* seen in sixty countries by over 400,000,000 people. He was also one of the authors of a paper that predicted drastic global cooling after a nuclear war; the concept of "nuclear winter" affected not only the scientific community but also national and international policy, as well as public opinion about nuclear weapons and the arms race. Although some scientists considered Sagan too speculative and insufficiently committed to

detailed scientific inquiry, many recognized his talent for explaining science, and acknowledged the importance of the publicity generates by Sagan's enthusiasm.

Sagan was born in Brooklyn, New York, on November 9, 1934, the son of Samuel Sagan, a Russian emigrant and a cutter in a clothing factory, and Rachel Gruber Sagan. He became fascinated with the stars as a young child, and was an avid reader of science fiction, particularly the novels by Edgar Rice Burroughs about the exploration of Mars. By the age of five he was sure he wanted to be an astronomer, but, as he told Henry S. F. Cooper, Jr., of the *New Yorker,* he sadly assumed it was not a paying job; he expected he would have to work at "some job I was temperamentally unsuited for, like door-to-door salesman." When he found out a few years later that astronomers actually got paid, he was ecstatic. "That was a splendid day," he told Cooper.

Sagan's degrees, all of which he earned at the University of Chicago, include an A.B. in 1954, a B.S. in 1955, an M.S. in physics in 1956, and a doctorate in astronomy and astrophysics in 1960. As a graduate student, Sagan was deeply interested in the possibility of life on other planets, a discipline known as exobiology. Although this interest then considered beyond the realm of responsible scientific investigation, he received important early support from scientists such as Nobel laureates **Hermann Joseph Muller** and **Joshua Lederberg.** He also worked with **Harold C. Urey,** who had won the 1934 Nobel Prize in chemistry and had been **Stanley Lloyd Miller**'s thesis adviser when he conducted his famous experiment on the origin of life. Sagan wrote his doctoral dissertation, "Physical Studies of the Planets," under **Gerard Peter Kuiper,** one of the few astronomers who was a planetologist at that time. It was during his graduate student days that Sagan met Lynn Margulis, a biologist, who became his wife on June 16, 1957. She and Sagan had two sons; they divorced in 1963.

From graduate school, Sagan moved to the University of California at Berkeley, where he was the Miller residential fellow in astronomy from 1960 to 1962. He then accepted a position at Harvard as an assistant professor from 1962 to 1968. On April 6 he married the painter Linda Salzman; Sagan's second marriage, which ended in a divorce, produced a son. From Harvard, Sagan went to Cornell University, where he was first an associate professor of astronomy at the Center for Radiophysics and Space Research. He was then promoted to professor and associate director at the center, serving in that capacity until 1977 when he became the David Duncan Professor of Astronomy and Space Science.

Suggestions About Mars and Venus Confirmed by Spacecrafts

Sagan's first important contributions to the understanding of Mars and Venus began as insights while he was still a graduate student. Color variations had long been observed on the planet Mars, and some believed these variations indicated the seasonal changes of some form of Martian plant life. Sagan, working at times with James Pollack, postulated that the changing colors were instead caused by Martian dust, shifting through the action of wind storms; this interpretation was confirmed by *Mariner 9* in the early 1970s. Sagan also suggested that the surface of Venus was incredibly hot, since the Venusian atmosphere of carbon dioxide and water vapor held in the sun's heat, thus creating a version of the "greenhouse effect." This theory was also confirmed by an exploring spacecraft, the Soviet probe *Venera IV*, which transmitted data about the atmosphere of Venus back to Earth in 1967. Sagan also performed experiments based on the work of Stanley Lloyd Miller, studying the production of organic molecules in an artificial atmosphere meant to simulate that of a primitive Earth or contemporary Jupiter. This work eventually earned him a patent for a technique that used gaseous mixtures to produce amino acids.

Sagan first became involved with spaceflight in 1959, when Lederberg suggested he join a committee on the Space Science Board of the National Academy of Sciences. He became increasingly involved with NASA (National Aeronautics and Space Administration) during the 1960s and participated in many of their most important robotic missions. He developed experiments for the Mariner Venus mission and worked as a designer on the *Mariner 9* and the *Viking* missions to Mars, as well as on the *Pioneer 10*, the *Pioneer 11*, and the *Voyager* spacecrafts. Both the *Pioneer* and the *Voyager* spacecrafts have left our solar system carrying plaques which Sagan designed with Frank Drake as messages to any extraterrestrials that find them; they have pictures of two humans, a man and a woman, as well as various astronomical information. The nude man and woman were drawn by Sagan's second wife, Linda Salzman, and they provoked many letters to Sagan denouncing him for sending "smut" into space. During this project Sagan met the writer Ann Druyan, the project's creative director, who eventually became his wife. Sagan and Druyan had two children.

Sagan continued his involvement in space exploration in the 1980s and 1990s. The expertise he developed in biology and genetics while working with Muller, Lederberg, Urey, and others, is unusual for an astronomer, and he extensively researched the possibility that Jupiter's moon, Titan, which has an atmosphere, might also have some form of life. Sagan was also involved in less direct searches for life beyond Earth. He was one of the prime movers behind NASA's establishment of a radio astronomy search program that Sagan calls CETI, for Communication with Extra-Terrestrial Intelligence.

A colleague of Sagan's working on the Viking mission explained to Cooper of the *New Yorker* that this desire to find extraterrestrial life is the focus of all of Sagan's various scientific works. "Sagan desperately wants to find life someplace, anyplace—on Mars, on Titan, in the solar system or outside it. I don't know why, but if you read his papers or listen to his speeches, even though they are on a wide variety of seemingly unrelated topics, there is always the question 'Is this or that phenomenon related to life?' People say, 'What a varied career he has had,' but everything he has done has had this one underlying purpose." When Cooper asked Sagan why this was so, the scientist had a ready answer. "I think it's because human beings love to be alive, and we have an emotional resonance with something else alive, rather than with a molybdenum atom."

During the early 1970s Sagan began to make a number of brief appearances on television talk shows and news programs; Johnny Carson invited him on the *Tonight Show* for the first time in 1972, and Sagan soon was almost a regular there, returning to discuss science two or three times a year. However, it was *Cosmos,* which Public Television began broadcasting in 1980, that made him into a media sensation. Sagan narrated the series, which he wrote with Ann Druyan and Steven Soter, and they used special effects to illustrate a wide range of astronomical phenomena such as black holes. In addition to being extremely popular, the series was widely praised both for its showmanship and its content, although some reviewers had reservations about Sagan's speculations as well as his tendency to claim as fact what most scientists considered only hypotheses.

Warns About the Possibility of Nuclear Winter

Sagan was actively involved in politics; as a graduate student, he was arrested in Wisconsin for soliciting funds for the Democratic Party, and he was also involved in protests against the Vietnam War. In December, 1983, he published, with Richard Turco, Brian Toon, Thomas Ackerman, and James Pollack, an article discussing the possible consequences of nuclear war. They proposed that even a limited number of nuclear explosions could drastically change the world's climate by starting thousands of intense fires that would throw hundreds of thousands of tons of smoke and ash into the atmosphere, lowering the average temperature ten to twenty degrees and bringing on what they called a "nuclear winter." The authors happened upon this insight accidentally a few years earlier, while they were observing how dust storms on the planet Mars cooled the Martian surface and heated up the atmosphere. Their warning provoked a storm of controversy at first; their article was then followed by a number of studies on the effects of war and other human interventions on the world's climate. Sagan and his colleagues stressed that their predictions were only preliminary and based on certain assumptions about nuclear weapons and large-scale fires, and that their computations had been done on complex computer models of the imperfectly understood atmospheric system. However, despite numerous attempts to minimize the concept of a nuclear winter, the possibility that even a limited nuclear war might well lead to catastrophic environmental changes was confirmed by later research.

The idea of nuclear winter not only led to the reconsideration of the implications of nuclear war by many countries, institutions, and individuals, but it also produced great advances in research on Earth's atmosphere. In 1991, when the oil fields in Kuwait were burning after the Persian Gulf War, Sagan and others made a similar prediction about the effect the smoke from these fires would have on the climate. Based on the nuclear winter hypothesis and the recorded effects of certain volcanic eruptions, these predictions turned out to be inaccurate, although the smoke from the oil fires represented about 1% of the volume of smoke that would be created by a full-scale nuclear war.

In 1994, Sagan was diagnosed with myelodysplasia, a serious bone-marrow disease. Despite his illness, Sagan kept working on his numerous projects. His last book, *The Demon-Haunted World: Science as a Candle in the Dark,* was published in 1995. At the time of his death, Sagan was co-producing a film version of his novel *Contact.* His partner in this project was his wife, Ann Druyan, who had co-authored *Comet.* Released in 1997, the film received popular and critical acclaim as a testimony to Sagan's enthusiasm for the search for extraterrestrial life. Sagan, who lived in Ithaca, New York, died at the Fred Hutchinson Cancer Research Center in Seattle on December 20, 1996.

Carl Sagan won a Pulitzer Prize in 1978 for his book on evolution called *The Dragons of Eden.* He also won the A. Calvert Smith Prize (1964), NASA's Apollo Achievement Award (1969), NASA's Exceptional Scientific Achievement Medal (1972), NASA's Medal for Distinguished Public Service (twice), the International Astronaut Prize (1973), the John W. Campbell Memorial Award (1974), the Joseph Priestly Award (1975), the Newcomb Cleveland Prize (1977), the Rittenhouse Medal (1980), the Ralph Coats Roe Medal from the American Society of Mechanical Engineers (1981), the Tsiolkovsky Medal

of the Soviet Cosmonautics Federation (1987), the Kennan Peace Award from SANE/Freeze (1988), the Oersted Medal of the American Association of Physics Teachers (1990), the UCLA Medal (1991), and the Mazursky Award from the American Astronomical Association (1991). Sagan was a fellow of the American Association for the Advancement of Science, the American Academy of Arts and Sciences, the American Institute for Aeronautics and Astronautics, and the American Geophysical Union. Sagan was also the chairman of the Division for Planetary Sciences of the American Astronomical Society (from 1975 to 1976) and for twelve years was editor-in-chief of *Icarus,* a journal of planetary studies.

SELECTED WRITINGS BY SAGAN:

Books

The Cosmic Connection: An Extraterrestrial Perspective. New York: Doubleday, 1973.
Other Worlds. New York: Bantam, 1975.
The Dragons of Eden: Speculations on the Evolution of Human Intelligence. New York: Random House, 1977.
Broca's Brain: Reflection on the Romance of Science. New York: Random House, 1979.
Cosmos. New York: Random House, 1980.
Comet. New York: Random House, 1985.
Contact: A Novel. New York: Simon and Schuster, 1985.
A Path where No Man Thought: Nuclear Winter and the End of the Arms Race. New York: Random House, 1990.
Shadows of Forgotten Ancestors: A Search for Who We Are. New York: Random House, 1992.
Pale Blue Dot. New York: Random House, 1994.
The Demon-Haunted World: Science as a Candle in the Dark. New York: Random House, 1995.

Periodicals

"The Radiation Balance of Venus." *California Institute of Technology Laboratory Technical Report* 32–34 (1960).
"Comets and the Origin of Life." *Astronomy* 20 (February 1992).

FURTHER READING:

Books

Contemporary Authors: New Revision Series. Vol. 11, Detroit: Gale, 1984.
Goodell, Rae. *The Visible Scientists.* New York: Little, Brown, 1975.

Periodicals

Barnes, Bart. "Carl Sagan, the Man Who Reached for the Stars" (obituary). *Washington Post* (21 December 1996): A12.

Baur, Stuart. "Kneedeep in the Cosmic Overwhelm with Carl Sagan." *New York* (1 September 1975): 28.

Cooper, Henry S. F. "A Resonance with Something Alive." *New Yorker* (21 June 1976): 39–80; (28 June 1976): 29–57.

Dicke, William. "Carl Sagan, an Astronomer Who Excelled at Popularizing Science, Is Dead at 62" (obituary). *New York Times* (21 December 1996): A26.

Friend, Tim. "Carrying on without Carl Sagan." *USA Today* (30 June 1997): 1D.

Heise, Kenan. "Carl Sagan, 62; Took Mystery out of Cosmos" (obituary). *Chicago Tribune* (21 December 1996): A21).

Hernbest, Nigel. "Organic Molecules from Space Rained Down on Early Earth." *New Scientist* (25 January 1992): 27.

Hogan, A. R. "Carl Edward Sagan: Astronomer and Popularizer of Science." *Ad Astra* 3 (1991): 30.

Lewin, Roger. "Shadows of Forgotten Ancestors." *New Scientist* 137 (16 January 1993): 40.

Myrna, Oliver. "Astronomer Sagan Dies; Helped Popularize Science" (obituary). *Los Angeles Times* (21 December 1996): A1.

Ridpath, Rian. "A Man Whose Time Has Come." *New Scientist* 63 (4 July 1974): 36.

Ruina, Jack. "A Path Where No Man Thought." *Nature* 352 (29 August 1991): 765.

Zimmer, Carl. "Ecowar." *Discover* 13 (January 1992): 37.

—*Sketch by Chris Hables Gray*

Ruth Sager
1918–1997
American biologist and geneticist

Ruth Sager devoted her career to the study and teaching of genetics. She conducted groundbreaking research in chromosomal theory, disproving nineteenth-century Austrian botanist Gregor Johann Mendel's once-prevalent law of inheritance—a principle stating that chromosomal genes found in a cell's nucleus control the transmission of all inherited characteristics. Through her research beginning in the 1950s, Sager revealed that a second set of genes (nonchrosomomal in nature) also play a role in one's genetic composition. In addition to advancing the

Ruth Sager

science of nonchromosomal genetics, she worked to uncover various genetic mechanisms associated with cancer.

Born on February 7, 1918, in Chicago, Illinois, Ruth Sager was one of three girls in her family. Her father worked as an advertising executive, while her mother maintained an interest in academics and intellectual discourse. As a child, Sager did not display any particular interest in science. At the age of sixteen, she entered the University of Chicago, which required its students to take a diverse schedule of liberal arts classes. Sager happened into an undergraduate survey course on biology, sparking her interest in the field. In 1938, she graduated with a B.S. degree. After a brief vacation from education, Sager enrolled at Rutgers University and studied plant physiology, receiving an M.S. in 1944. Sager then continued her graduate work in genetics at Columbia University and in 1946 was awarded a fellowship to study with botanist Marcus Rhoades. In 1948 she received her Ph.D. from Columbia, and in 1949 she was named a Merck Fellow at the National Research Council.

Two years later, Sager joined the research staff at the Rockefeller Institute's biochemistry division as an assistant, working at first in conjunction with Yoshihiro Tsubo. There she began her work challenging the prevailing scientific idea that only the chromosomal genes played a significant role in genetics. Unlike many of her colleagues of the time, Sager speculated that genes which lay outside the chromosomes behave in a manner akin to that of chromosomal genes. In 1953 Sager uncovered hard data to support this theory. She had been studying heredity in *Chlamydomonas*, an alga found in muddy ponds, when she noted that a gene outside the chromosomes was necessary for the alga to survive in water containing streptomycin, an antimicrobial drug. Although the plant—which Sager nicknamed "Clammy"—normally reproduced asexually, Sager discovered that she could force it to reproduce sexually by withholding nitrogen from its environment. Using this tactic, Sager managed to cross male and females via sexual fertilization. If either of the parents had the streptomycin-resistant gene, Sager showed, the offspring exhibited it as well, providing definitive proof that this nonchromosomal trait was transmitted genetically.

During the time she studied "Clammy," Sager switched institutional affiliations, taking a post as a research associate in Columbia University's zoology department in 1955. The Public Health Service and National Science Foundations supported her work. In 1960 Sager publicized the results of her nonchromosomal genetics research in the first Gilbert Morgan Smith Memorial Lecture at Stanford University and a few months later in Philadelphia at the Society of American Bacteriologists. Toward the end of the year, her observations were published in *Science* magazine. As she continued her studies, she expanded her knowledge of the workings of nonchromosomal genes. Sager's further work showed that when the streptomycin-resistant alga mutated, these mutations occurred only in the non-chromosomal genes. She also theorized that nonchromosomal genes differed greatly from their chromosomal counterparts in the way they imparted hereditary information between generations. Her research has led her to speculate that nonchromosomal genes may evolve before the more common deoxyribonucleic acid (DNA) chromosomes and that they may represent more closely early cellular life.

Sager continued announcing the results of her research at national and international gatherings of scientists. In the early 1960s Columbia University promoted her to the position of senior research associate, and she coauthored, along with Francis J. Ryan, a scientific textbook titled *Cell Heredity*. In 1963 she travelled to the Hague to talk about her work, and the following year she lectured in Edinburgh on nonchromosomal genes. In 1966 she accepted an offer to become a professor at Hunter College of the City University of New York. She remained in New York for nine years, spending the academic year of 1972 to 1973 abroad at the Imperial Cancer Research Fund Laboratory in London. The following year she married Dr. Arthur B. Pardee. Harvard University's Dana Farber Cancer Institute lured her away from Hunter in 1975 with an offer to become

professor of cellular genetics and head the Institute's Division of Cancer Genetics.

In the past twenty years, Sager's work has centered on a variety of issues relating to cancer, such as tumor suppressor genes, breast cancer, and the genetic means by which cancer multiplies. Along with her colleagues at the Dana Farber Institute, Sager has been researching the means by which cancer multiplies and grows, in an attempt to understand and halt the mechanism of the deadly disease. She has likened the growth of cancer to Darwinian evolution in that cancer cells lose growth control and display chromosome instability. In 1983 she told reporter Anna Christensen that if researchers discover a way to prevent the chromosomal rearrangements, "we would have a potent weapon against cancer." More recently, she has speculated that tumor suppressor genes may be the secret to halting cancer growth.

Sager continued to publish and serve on numerous scientific panels until her death. In 1992 she offered scientific testimony at hearings of the Breast Cancer Coalition. A member of the Genetics Society of America, the American Society of Bacteriologists, and the New York Academy of Sciences, Sager was appointed to the National Academy of Sciences in 1977. An avid collector of modern art, she was also a member of the American Academy of Arts and Sciences. Sager died of bladder cancer on March 29, 1997, at her home in Brookline, Massachusetts.

SELECTED WRITINGS BY SAGER:

Books

Cell Heredity. New York: Wiley, 1961.

Periodicals

"Tumor Suppressor Genes: The Puzzle and the Promise." *Science.* (15 December 1989): 1406–12.

FURTHER READING:

Periodicals

Christensen, Anna. "Potential Weapon in War on Cancer." *United Press International* (7 February 1983).
Pace, Eric. "Dr. Ruth Sager, 79, Researcher on Location of Genetic Material" (obituary). *New York Times* (4 April 1997).

—*Sketch by Shari Rudavsky*

Abdus Salam

Abdus Salam
1926–1996
Pakistani physicist

Abdus Salam's major field of interest in the 1950s and 1960s was the relationship between two of the four basic forces governing nature then known to scientists, the electromagnetic and weak forces. In 1968, Salam published a theory showing how these two forces may be considered as separate and distinct manifestations of a single more fundamental force, the electroweak force. Experiments conducted at the European Center for Nuclear Research (CERN) in 1973 provided the empirical evidence needed to substantiate Salam's theory. For this work, Salam shared the 1979 Nobel Prize in physics with physicists **Sheldon Glashow** and **Steven Weinberg**, who had each independently developed similar theories between 1960 and 1967. Salam's long-time concern for the status of science in Third World nations prompted him in 1964 to push for the establishment of the International Center for Theoretical Physics (ICTP) in Trieste, Italy. The Center provides the kind of instruction for Third World physicists that is generally not available in their own homelands.

Salam was born on January 29, 1926, in the small rural town of Jhang, Pakistan, to Hajira and Muhammed Hussain. Salam's father worked for the local department of education. At the age of sixteen, Abdus

Salam entered the Government College at Punjab University in Lahore, and, in 1946, he was awarded his master's degree in mathematics. Salam then received a scholarship that allowed him to enroll at St. John's College at Cambridge University, where he was awarded a bachelor's degree in mathematics and physics, with highest honors, in 1949.

Attempts to Return to Pakistan

Salam remained at Cambridge as a graduate student for two years, but felt an obligation to return to Pakistan. Accepting a joint appointment as professor of mathematics at the Government College of Lahore and head of the department of mathematics at Punjab University, Salam soon discovered that he had no opportunity to conduct research. "To my dismay," he told Nina Hall for an article in the *New Scientist,* "I learnt that I was the only practicing theoretical physicist in the entire nation. No one cared whether I did any research. Worse, I was expected to look after the college soccer team as my major duty besides teaching undergraduates."

As a result, Salam decided to return to Cambridge, from which he had received a Ph.D. in theoretical physics in 1952. He taught mathematics for two years at Cambridge and, in 1957, was appointed professor of theoretical physics at the Imperial College of Science and Technology in London. He held that post for most of his life.

Attacks the Problem of Force Unification

Beginning in the mid–1950s, Salam turned his attention to one of the fundamental questions of modern physics, the unification of forces. Scientists recognize that there are four fundamental forces governing nature—the gravitational, electromagnetic, strong, and weak forces—and, that all four may be manifestations of a single basic force. The unity of forces would not actually be observable, they believe, except at energy levels much greater than those that exist in the everyday world, energy levels that currently exist only in cosmic radiation and in the most powerful of particle accelerators.

Attempts to prove unification theories are, to some extent, theoretical exercises involving esoteric mathematical formulations. In the 1960s, three physicists, Salam, Steven Weinberg, and Sheldon Glashow, independently derived a mathematical theory that unifies two of the four basic forces, the electromagnetic and weak forces. A powerful point of confirmation in this work was the fact that essentially the same theory was produced starting from two very different beginning points and following two different lines of reasoning.

One of the predictions arising from the new electroweak theory was the existence of previously unknown weak "neutral currents," as anticipated by Salam and Weinberg. These currents were first observed in 1973 during experiments conducted at the CERN in Geneva, and later at the Fermi National Accelerator Laboratory in Batavia, Illinois. A second prediction, the existence of force-carrying particles designated as W^+, W^-, and Z^0 bosons was verified in a later series of experiments also carried out at CERN in 1983. By that time, Salam, Glashow, and Weinberg had been honored for their contributions to the electroweak theory with the 1979 Nobel Prize in physics. Salam was the first Muslim to win the Nobel prize.

Theoretical physics was only one of Salam's two great passions in life. The other was an on-going concern for the status of theoretical physicists in Third World nations. His own experience in Pakistan was a lifelong reminder of the need for encouragement, instruction, and assistance for others like himself growing up in developing nations. His concern drove Salam to recommend the establishment of a training center for such individuals. That dream was realized in 1964 with the formation of the ICTP in Trieste, Italy, which invites outstanding theoretical physicists to teach and lecture aspiring students on their own areas of expertise. In addition, the Center acts, according to Nina Hall, as a "sort of lonely scientist's club for Brazilians, Nigerians, Sri Lankans, or whoever feels the isolation resulting from lack of resources in their own country." Salam also served as a member of Pakistan's Atomic Energy Commission (1958–1974) and its Science Council (1963–1975), as Chief Scientific Advisor to Pakistan's President (1961–1974) and as chairman of the country's Space and Upper Atmosphere Committee (1962–1963).

Salam, director of ICTP since its founding, has been involved in a host of other international activities linking scientists to each other and to a variety of governmental agencies. He was a member (1964–1975) and chairman (1971–1972) of the United Nations Advisory Committee on Science and Technology, vice president of the International Union of Pure and Applied Physics (1972–1978), and a member of the Scientific Council of the Stockholm International Peace Research Institute (1970–). Salam was awarded more than two dozen honorary doctorates and has received more than a dozen major awards, including the Atoms for Peace Award for 1968, the Royal Medal of the Royal Society in 1978, the John Torrence Tate Medal of the American Institute of Physics in 1978, and the Lomonosov Gold Medal of the U.S.S.R. Academy of Sciences in 1983. He was also awarded an honorary knighthood by Queen Elizabeth.

Salam died on November 21, 1996 at his home in Oxford, England. He had been suffering from a neurological disorder for some years before his death at the age of 70.

SELECTED WRITINGS BY SALAM:

Books

Aspect of Quantum Mechanics. Cambridge: Cambridge University Press, 1972.
Ideas and Realities: Selected Essays of Abdus Salam. World Scientific, 1987.

Periodicals

"The Electroweak Force, Grand Unification, and Superunification." *Physical Sciences* 20 (1979): 227–34.

FURTHER READING:

Books

Wasson, Tyler, ed. *Nobel Prize Winners.* New York: H. W. Wilson, 1987, pp. 914–16.
Weber, Robert L. *Pioneers of Science: Nobel Prize Winners in Physics.* American Institute of Physics, 1980, pp. 263–64.
————. *The Way of the Scientist.* New York: Simon & Schuster, 1962, pp. 67–76.

Periodicals

Browne, Malcolm W. "Abdus Salam is Dead at 70; Physicist Shared Nobel Prize" (obituary). *New York Times* (23 November 1996).
Coleman, Sidney. "The 1979 Nobel Prize in Physics." *Science* (14 December 1979): 1290–91.
Hall, Nina. "A Unifying Force for Third World Science." *New Scientist.* (27 January 1990): 31.
————. "Nobel Prizes: To Glashow, Salam and Weinberg for Physics. . ." *Physics Today* (December 1979): 17–19.
————. "Nobels for Getting It Together in Physics." *New Scientist.* (18 October 1979): 163–64.

—Sketch by David E. Newton

Katherine Koontz Sanford
1915–
American biologist and medical researcher

Throughout her accomplished career, Katherine Koontz Sanford remained a private person committed to her research in cell biology, genetic predisposition to cancer, and neurodegenerative disease. Described as a gracious colleague who readily shared credit with her coworkers, Sanford demonstrated amazing stamina in a career than spanned more than half a century. Even after she retired from the National Cancer Institute (NCI) at the age of 80, Sanford continued to conduct research at the institute and work on manuscripts.

In the late 1940s, Sanford was a young woman entering what had traditionally been a man's world. However, Sanford's keen and resourceful intellect earned her colleagues' admiration and respect. She went on to become a world leader in research of tissue culture and in vitro carcinogenesis (cancer) and was the first person to clone a mammalian cell. Part of Sanford's success can be attributed to her ability to work well with people and her willingness to listen to their ideas and suggestions. Occasionally, she could be blunt and outspoken. "She never hesitated to tell me when she thought I was wrong," said Dr. Ram Parshad, of Howard University School of Medicine. "Yet, she was always willing to share credit, even with technicians who contributed to her work. Her example caused me to think about my own values."

Sanford was born in Chicago, Illinois, on July 19, 1915, to William James and Alta Rache Koontz. She attended college in Massachusetts, receiving her B.A. from Wellesley College, which she attended along with her two sisters. She earned her M.A. and Ph.D. in zoology from Brown University in 1942 and was one of an elite group of women at that time who graduated from the university's biology graduate program and went on to distinguished scientific careers. After graduation, Sanford spent two years as a biology instructor, first at Western College in Oxford, Ohio, and then at Allegheny College in Meadville, Pennsylvania. From there, she became an assistant director of the science program at the John Hopkins University Nursing School in Baltimore, Maryland.

In 1947, Sanford accepted a position that was to define her career. Joining the tissue culture section of the National Cancer Institute's (NCI) Laboratory of Biology, she began her lifelong focus on cancer research. Working with the section's director Virginia Evans and others, she developed techniques for establishing tissue cultures, with a strong focus on cancerous transformation in cultured cells.

Develops Vital Tool for Studying Cancer-Causing Mechanisms in Cells

Sanford made her mark in cell biology and cancer research early in her career at NCI. As the first person to isolate and clone a single mammalian (rodent) cell *in vitro* (in an artificial environment outside the living body), Sanford paved the way for a new field of research on the *in vitro* malignant transformation of cells. Sanford's isolated single cell could propagate itself to produce a colony of geneti-

cally identical cells. Although Sanford's method was cumbersome and hard to duplicate, scientists had a method they could further develop to produce pure cell lines with known metabolic and genetic properties. This "cloning" method would eventually lead to virus cultures, vaccine research, and new approaches for studying metabolic disorders. In 1954, she received the Ross Harrison Fellowship Award for her accomplishment.

Discovers Test for Cancer and Alzheimer's Disease

While most noted for her cloning discovery, Sanford, who married Charles Fleming Richards Mifflin on December 11, 1971, continued to make important contributions in the field of cancer and cell research. In the 1990s, she developed the first laboratory tests to distinguish people with Alzheimer's disease (a neurodegenerative disorder) and those with a predisposition to cancer. The test, or assay, involves exposing a person's skin fibroblasts, or blood lymphocyte cells, in culture to fluorescent light that causes deoxyribonucleic acid (DNA) damage. After treatment with DNA repair inhibitors, the cells are compared for chromatid breaks. Alzheimer's and cancer patients' cells have exhibited many more chromatid breaks under certain conditions. Although somewhat controversial because of other scientists' difficulty in repeating it, the test has correlated well with identifying genetic predispositions to some forms of cancer.

"The cytogenetic assay developed by Dr. Sanford is a great contribution," said Sanford's longtime colleague, Dr. Ram Parshad, in an article in the *NIH Record*. "It has the potential to be used as both a marker of cancer predisposition and for certain neurodegenerative disorders."

As early as 1985, Sanford had developed a cytogenetic test to evaluate DNA repair of mammalian cells in culture. This test showed that people genetically predisposed to cancer have a common defect in the processing of x-ray-induced DNA damage to their tumors and unaffected skin fibroblasts or to blood lymphocytes. In 1995, Sanford and colleagues found that phenolic compounds derived from green tea and a plant phenolic called curcumin can inhibit the DNA damaging effects of fluorescent light on cultured cells.

Sanford "Officially" Retires

In 1974, Sanford was appointed head of NCI's cell physiology and oncogenesis section, in the Laboratory of Biochemistry. In 1977, she became chief of the in vitro carcinogenesis section at the institute's Laboratory of Cellular and Molecular Biology. After a 49-year career at NCI, Sanford announced her retirement in late 1995. However, her energy was far from spent. Committed to completing her research into the new cytogenetic test, Sanford continued over the next year to work five days a week and sometimes on weekends in an unofficial capacity at the institute. Even after leaving her government laboratory for good in 1996, she continued to work from her home in Delaware with colleagues on manuscripts concerning the test. She also continued to be sought out and consulted by scientists from around the world.

"She is a first-class scientist, leaving behind a good set of experiments still to be done," said Charles W. Boone of NCI's Division of Cancer Prevention and Control in the *NIH Record*. "Her research will endure and will not be lost in the molecular woodlands."

SELECTED WRITINGS BY SANFORD:

Periodicals

"Studies On the Difference in Sarcoma-Producing Capacity of Two Lines of Mouse Cells Derived *in vitro* from one cell." *Journal of the National Cancer Institute* (1958): 121.
"Fluorescent Light-Induced Chromatid Breaks Distinguish Alzheimer Disease Cells from Normal Cells in Tissue Culture." *Proceedings of the National Academy of Science, USA.* (May 1996): 5146-50.
"Familial Clustering of Breast Cancer: Possible Interaction between DNA Repair Proficiency and Radiation Exposure in the Development of Breast Cancer." *International Journal of Cancer* (February 1995): 107-14.

FURTHER READING:

Books

Parry, Melanie, ed. *Biographical Dictionary of Women.* Chambers, 1996.
Kass-Simon, G. and Patricia Farnes, eds. *Women of Science: Righting the Record.* Bloomington: Indiana University Press, 1990.

—*Sketch by David A. Petechuk*

Alice T. Schafer
1915–
American algebraist

Alice T. Schafer was born in Richmond, Virginia, on June 18, 1915. Her mother died during childbirth, and Schafer was sent to the countryside area of Scottsburg, Virginia, to live with family friends. She was raised by Pearl Dickerson, a woman Schafer considered her mother and who was supportive of Schafer's ambitions throughout her life.

As a child, Schafer wanted to write novels, but by the third grade she became intrigued with mathematics after a teacher expressed concern that she would not able to master long division. Schafer not only mastered long division, but took math courses throughout her years of primary education. In her senior year of high school Schafer asked the principal to write a letter of recommendation for a scholarship to study mathematics in college. He was only willing to write the letter if she would promise to major in history instead.

After graduating from high school Schafer enrolled at the University of Richmond, where, at the time, the classes for men and women were held on separate sides of the campus. Mathematics classes were not offered on the female side of the campus, however, and as the only woman majoring in math, Schafer had to walk to the men's area of the campus to receive instruction. Women were also not allowed in the main library at the university. Books had to be sent over to the women's section of the campus upon request. In Schafer's junior year she questioned this policy and was finally allowed to sit in the library to read *Cyrano de Bergerac*, a book that was not available for circulation. After reading the book, Schafer was asked not to make any more requests to visit the library. The following summer she was offered a job in the library alphabetizing books. Schafer later quipped that she took the job because she needed the money.

Also in her junior year at Richmond, Schafer won the mathematical prize competition in Real Analysis but received no congratulatory praise from the chairman of the prize committee. Schafer graduated Phi Beta Kappa in 1936 when she was 21 years old with a degree in mathematics.

A Long and Varied Career

Schafer was offered a position at a high school in Glen Allen, Virginia, where she taught for three years. In 1939 she was awarded a fellowship at the University of Chicago and attained her Ph.D. in 1942. (Her dissertation was titled "Projective Differential Geometry.") While at the university, Schafer studied with Ernest P. Lane and Adrian Alberts.

Schafer's first teaching job as a Ph.D. was at Connecticut College, where she taught such classes as linear algebra, calculus, and abstract algebra for two years before accepting a position with Johns Hopkins University in the Applied Physics Laboratory doing research for the war effort. She was the only woman on the five member team of scientists.

Schafer married Richard Schafer, a professor of abstract algebra at MIT, in 1942. They have two children, Richard Stone Schafer, born in 1945, and John Dickerson Schafer, born in 1946. Between the years 1945 and 1961 Schafer taught at such institutions as the University of Michigan, the Drexel Institute of Technology, and Swarthmore College, among others. In 1962, she joined the staff at Wellesley College and stayed there until her forced retirement at the age of 65 in 1980. The retirement proved to be short-lived, however, when in that same year Schafer went to Harvard University as a consultant and teacher of mathematics in the management program. She again became a professor of mathematics, this time at Marymount University, in 1989 and retired in 1996.

A Trailblazer for Women

Schafer has been a visiting professor and lecturer at various colleges, including Brown University and Simmons College. Schafer was the first woman to receive a Honorary Doctor of Science degree from the University of Richmond in 1964 and was presented with the Distinguished Alumna Award, Westhampton College, at the University of Richmond in 1977. During her tenure at Wellesley College, Schafer and two other women professors succeeded at implementing the black studies department there. She is also a cofounder of the Association for Women in Mathematics (AWM), along with Mary W. Gray, and others. The organization was established in 1971 to encourage women to study and seek careers in the mathematical sciences; currently, it boasts a membership of 4,500 from the United States and abroad. More than 300 academic institutions are supporting members of AWM in the United States. The AWM is open to both women and men. Schafer served as its president from 1973 to 1975 and remains active on various committees. A prize was established in her name in 1989 and is given annually to an undergraduate woman for excellence in mathematics.

Schafer is the author of eight articles concerning the progress of women in the field of mathematics and affirmative action. Her other articles include research on space curves and theorems on finite groups. A book published by the American Mathematical Society includes talks given by Schafer at their "100 Years of Annual Meetings Celebration." Her fields of specialization are abstract algebra (group theory). Schafer has three times been the leader of the delegation of women mathematicians to China, the last of which was the U.S.–China Joint Conference on Women's Issues held in Beijing between August 24 and September 2, 1995.

Schafer currently lives in Arlington, Virginia, with her husband.

SELECTED WRITINGS BY SCHAFER:

Books

"Women and Mathematics," in *Mathematics Tomorrow*. Edited by Lynn Arthur Steen. New York: Springer–Verlag, 1981.

Periodicals

"The Neighborhood of an Undulation Point of a Space Curve." *American Journal of Mathematics* 70 (1948): 351–363.
"Mathematics and Women: Perspectives and Progress." *American Mathematical Notices* (September 1991).
(With M.W. Gray) "Guidelines for Equality: A Proposal." *Academe* (December 1981).
"Two Singularities of Space Curves." *Duke Mathematical Journal* (November 1994): 655–670.

Other

"Alice T. Schafer." *Biographies of Women Mathematicians.* June 1997. http://www.scottlan.edu/lriddle/women/chronol.htm (July 22, 1997).
Schafer, Alice T., interview with Kelley Reynolds Jacquez conducted May 8, 1997.

—*Sketch by Kelley Reynolds Jacquez*

Berta Scharrer
1906–1995
German-born American biologist

Berta Scharrer, together with her husband Ernst Scharrer, pioneered the field of neuroendocrinology —the interaction of the nervous and endocrine systems. Fighting against the then-accepted belief that nerve cells were only electrical conductors, as well as against the prejudice toward women in the sciences, Berta Scharrer established the concept of neurosecretion through her research with insects and other invertebrates. A highly respected educator, she was also among the founding faculty of the department of anatomy at the Albert Einstein College of Medicine in New York.

Berta Vogel Scharrer was born in Munich, Germany on December 1, 1906, the daughter of Karl Phillip and Johanna (Greis) Vogel. She developed an early interest in science, and attended the University of Munich, earning her Ph.D. in 1930 in biology for research into the correlation between sweetness and nutrition in various sugars. Upon graduation, Scharrer took a position as research associate in the Research Institute of Psychiatry in Munich, and in 1934 she was married to Ernst Albert Scharrer, a biologist. Together they formed an intellectual and domestic partnership that would last until Ernst Scharrer's death in 1965.

In 1928 Ernst Scharrer had discovered what he termed nerve-gland cells in a species of fish and made the rather startling hypothesis that some nerve cells actually were involved in secreting hormonal substances just as cells of the endocrine system do. It was a thesis sure to upset the more conservative members of the scientific community, as the synaptic function between neurons or nerve cells was then thought to be purely electrical. The idea of neurons having a dual function was looked on as something of a heresy: either cells secreted hormones, in which case they were endocrine cells belonging to the endocrine system, or they conducted electrical impulses, making them nerve cells, part of the nervous system. But what Ernst and Berta Scharrer demonstrated was that there existed an entire class of cells which performed both functions. The nerve-gland or neurosecretory cells are actually a channel between the nervous system and the endocrine system—an interface between an organism's environment and its glandular system. Some of the neurohormones secreted by neurosecretory cells actually control the release of other hormones via the anterior pituitary gland. To elucidate such action fully, the Scharrers divided up the animal kingdom between them: Ernst Scharrer took the vertebrates and Berta Scharrer the invertebrates.

Working as a research associate at the Neurological Institute of the University of Frankfurt, where her husband had been named director of the Edinger Institute for Brain Research, Berta Scharrer discovered other nerve-gland cells: in mollusks in 1935, in worms in 1936, and in insects beginning in 1937. But if research into neurosecretion was going well, life in Germany under Hitler was far from positive. The Scharrers decided, in 1937, to immigrate to the United States.

Introduces Neurosecretion to American Neuroscientists

The Scharrers travelled the long way to America, via the Pacific, collecting specimens for research along the way. They joined the Department of Anatomy at the University of Chicago for a year, and then moved on to New York where Ernst Scharrer was visiting investigator at the Rockefeller Institute from 1938 to 1940. Berta Scharrer continued her insect research in New York, and together the Scharrers prepared the results of their research for presenta-

tion at the 1940 meeting of the Association for Research in Nervous and Mental Diseases, the first presentation of the concept of neurosecretion in the United States, and one that was warmly received. That same year, Ernst Scharrer took a position as assistant professor in the anatomy department of Western Reserve University School of Medicine in Cleveland, Ohio, a post he would hold until 1946. Berta Scharrer was offered a fellowship assisting in the histology laboratory, which gave her research facilities, but scant professional standing. It was during these years that she accomplished some of her most important research into the localization of neurosecretory cells and their role in animal development, using the South American cockroach *Leucophaea maderae* as her research subject.

After the Second World War, Ernst Scharrer accepted a position at the University of Colorado Medical School in Denver, and Berta Scharrer won a Guggenheim Fellowship to continue her research, becoming an assistant professor in Denver in 1947. The next years were some of the Scharrers' most fruitful, as they loved the mountains, skiing, and horseback riding. Professionally these were also important times, for the theory of neurosecretion was beginning to be accepted around the world, especially after a German scientist was able to successfully stain neurosecretory granules—the packaging for neurohormones which some neurons secrete. Thus it became possible to study the fine structure of such granules and follow their course upon secretion. Neurosecretion became an accepted fact, in fact the cornerstone of the emerging field of neuroendocrinology. By 1950 it had also become an accepted fact that a chemical transmission took place at the synapse along with electrical charge. These advancements not only confirmed the Scharrers' work, but also paved the way for advances in their research. Berta Scharrer applied the new findings to her own work on the maturation of the ovarian systems of her South American cockroaches with results that verified earlier findings in the endocrinology of invertebrates.

Wins Full Professorship at Albert Einstein College

In 1955 the Scharrers were offered joint positions at the new Albert Einstein College of Medicine at Yeshiva University in New York: Ernst as department head of anatomy, and Berta as full professor in the same department. This was the first real professional recognition for Berta Scharrer, and the couple left Denver for New York. Here she taught histology —the microscopic structure of tissues—and continued with research into insect glands. Using the electron microscope, she was able to accomplish some of the earliest detailing of the insect nervous system and especially the neurosecretory system. Together with her husband, she published *Neuroendocrinology* in 1963, one of the basic texts in the new discipline.

Tragically, her husband died in a swimming accident in Florida in 1965, but Berta Scharrer carried on with their research, acting as chair of the department for two years until a successor could be found. She also went on to elucidate the fine structure of the neurosecretory cell—composed of a cell body, projecting dendrites, the extending long axon, and synaptic contacts at one end, just as in other neurons or nerve cells. Additionally, neurosecretory cells have special fibers allowing for feedback, as well as neurohemal organs—the point at which the neurohormones pass into the blood stream. Neurosecretory cells, it was shown, can affect targets contiguous with them or distant, through the blood stream, as with other hormones. Scharrer also investigated the make-up of the secretory material, discovering that it was a peptide or polypeptide—a combination of amino acids. Scharrer's later research deals with the immunoregulatory property of neuropeptides, or the relationship between the immune and nervous systems in invertebrates.

Continuing with her research and instruction, as well as co-editing *Cell and Tissue Research,* Scharrer became an emeritus professor of anatomy and neuroscience at Albert Einstein College of Medicine in 1978. She was honored with a National Medal of Science in 1983, for her "pioneering contributions in establishing the concept of neurosecretion and neuropeptides in the integration of animal function and development." She also won the F. C. Koch Award of the Endocrine Society in 1980, the Henry Gray Award of the American Association of Anatomists in 1982, and was honored by her former country with the Kraepelin Gold Medal from the Max Planck Institute in Munich in 1978 and the Schleiden Medal in 1983. She was a member of the National Academy of Sciences and held honorary degrees from colleges and universities around the world, including Harvard and Northwestern. Reading and music were among Berta Scharrer's free-time activities, and she continued scientific research virtually till her death. Scharrer died on July 23, 1995, at her home in Bronx, New York. She was 88.

SELECTED WRITINGS BY SCHARRER:

Books

Neuroendocrinology. New York: Columbia University Press, 1963.
An Evolutionary Interpretation of the Phenomenon of Neurosecretion. New York: American Museum of Natural History, 1978.

Periodicals

"Comparative Physiology of Invertebrate Endocrines." *Annual Review of Physiology* 25 (1953): 456-72.

"The Fine Structure of the Neurosecretory System of the Insect Leucophaea Maderae." *Memoirs of the Society of Endocrinology* 12 (1962): 89-97.
"Insects as Models of Neuroendocrine Research." *Annual Review of Entomology.* 32 (1987): 1-16.
"Neurosecretion: Beginnings and New Directions in Neuropeptide Research." *Annual Review of Neuroscience* 10 (1987): 1-17.
"Peptidergic Neurons: Facts and Trends." *General and Comparative Endocrinology* (January 1978): 50-62.
"Recent Progress in Comparative Neuroimmunology." *Zoological Science* (December 1992): 1097-10.

FURTHER READING:

Periodicals

"Honorary Degrees Given By Harvard." *New York Times* (16 October 1982): 9.
"Medal of Science to Berta Scharrer." *Einstein* (Spring 1985): 2.
Saxon, Wolfgang. "Berta Scharrer, 88, Research Scientist and Roach Expert" (obituary). *New York Times* (25 July 1995).

Other

Palay, Sanford L. "Presentation of the Henry Gray Award to Professor Berta Scharrer at the Ninety-Fifth Meeting of the American Association of Anatomists" (speech). 5 April 1982.

—*Sketch by J. Sydney Jones*

Bela Schick
1877–1967
Hungarian-born American pediatrician

Bela Schick was a pioneer in the field of child care; not only did he invent the diphtheria test, which helped wipe out this disease in children, but he also formulated and publicized child care theories that were advanced for his day. Schick also defined the allergic reaction, was considered the leading pediatrician of his time, and made contributions to knowledge about scarlet fever, tuberculosis, and infant nutrition. Schick received many honors for his work, ncluding the Medal of the New York Academy of Medicine and the Addingham Gold Medal, a British

Bela Schick

award. Schick was also the founder of the American Academy of Pediatrics.

Schick was born on July 16, 1877 in Boglar, Hungary, the child of Jacob Schick, a grain merchant, and Johanna Pichler Schick. He attended the Staats Gymnasium in Graz, Austria, graduating in 1894. He then received his M.D. degree at Karl Franz University, also in Graz. After a stint with the medical corps in the Austro-Hungarian army, Schick started his own medical practice in Vienna in 1902. From then on he devoted his ample energies to teaching, research, and medical practice at the University of Vienna, where he served from 1902 to 1923, first as an intern, then as an assistant in the pediatrics clinic, and finally as lecturer and professor of pediatrics.

It was in 1905 that Schick made one of his most significant contributions. While working with collaborator Clemens von Pirquet, Schick wrote his first research study describing the phenomenon of allergy, which was then called "serum sickness." The study not only described the concept of allergy, but also the best ways to treat it.

Develops Diphtheria Test

At age 36, Schick moved on to make one of the most important discoveries of the twentieth century—the test for diphtheria. The test, announced in 1913, was a remarkably simple one that could tell whether a person was vulnerable to the disease. It showed whether a patient had already been exposed to the diphtheria toxin, which would make him immune from getting it again. A tiny amount of the diluted toxin was injected into the patient's arm. If the spot turned red and swollen, the doctors would know whether or not the patient been exposed to the disease. The treatment was then injection with an antitoxin.

Diphtheria was a common disease in the early twentieth century and afflicted thousands of children in every city throughout the world. It was especially common in Europe, where the close quarters of many cities made infection more likely. At the time Schick embarked on his research, scientists had already isolated the microbe or toxin that caused diphtheria. A horse serum had also been developed that could prevent or even cure the disease. But the serum had so many side effects that doctors were unwilling to prescribe it unless they knew a patient was seriously in danger of catching diphtheria. Thus, Schick's discovery made it easier for them to treat those who were the most vulnerable.

In 1923, an antitoxin without side effects was developed and was then given to babies during their first year of life. Later on, the Schick test would show whether the baby's immunity lasted. Schick's test technique was also used years later to treat people with allergies, using the same technique of injecting small doses of an antitoxin.

Schick left Vienna in 1923 to become pediatrician-in-chief at Mt. Sinai Hospital in New York City. Schick became an American citizen that same year and two years later married his wife, Catherine C. Fries. He held his post at Mt. Sinai Hospital until his retirement in May 1943, when he became a consulting pediatrician. During his career, he also worked simultaneously at other hospitals, acting as director of pediatrics at Sea View Hospital in Staten Island, New York and consulting pediatrician at the Willard Parker Hospital, the New York Infirmary for Women and Children, and Beth Israel Hospital. He also taught as a professor of the diseases of children at Columbia University's College of Physicians and Surgeons, starting in 1936.

Schick directed a private practice in New York City as well. His office held a collection of dolls and animals that he had acquired in travels throughout the world. He would often play the piano in his office, or take out one of his doll or animal figures to calm a child. He never displayed a stethoscope until he made sure a child was relaxed. At one time, he estimated that he had treated over a million children. Often visitors would be surprised to see him on the floor with his small charges, making faces at them. "To be a good pediatrician, it helps to be a little childish yourself," he often said.

Childless himself, he had a great fondness for children and in 1932 authored a popular book containing his firm beliefs about how children should be raised, *Child Care Today.* Many of his ideas were advanced for his time. He advocated little punishment for children and no corporal punishment. He also said that trauma in a child's early life often had a lasting effect.

Schick and his wife lived in a large apartment in New York City and were frequent travelers around the world. On a cruise to South America with his wife during his later years, Schick fell ill with pleurisy. Eventually brought back to the United States to Mount Sinai Hospital, he died on Dec. 6, 1967. He was 90 years old.

SELECTED WRITINGS BY SCHICK:

Books

Child Care Today. Greenberg, 1932.
(With C. F. Von Pirquet) *Serum Sickness.* Williams and Wilkins, 1951.

FURTHER READING:

Books

Gronowicz,, Antoni. *Bela Schick and the World of Children.* New York: Abelard-Shuman, 1954.

Periodicals

Whitman, Alden. "Schick, Who Devised Diphtheria Test, Dies." *New York Times* (Dec. 7, 1967): 1, 47.

—*Sketch by Barbara Boughton*

John Henry Schwarz
1941–
American theoretical physicist

Murray Gell-Mann, the Nobel-Prize winning theorist who described and named quarks, said in 1985 of superstring theory—the main work of John H. Schwarz—that a version of it would someday be understood as the theory underlying the whole universe. "It's *the* candidate," he said.

The story of superstrings begins with string theory, an attempt to construct a theory of nuclear forces. While trying to overcome some of the difficul-

ties of this approach, Pierre Ramond, André Neveu, and Schwarz combined string theory and another idea, known as supersymmetry, in 1971. Even in this modified form there remained an another apparent difficulty for the theory; it predicted a kind of zero-mass particle that was not possible for nuclear forces. In 1974, however, Schwarz and coworker Joël Scherk showed that the zero-mass particle had the right properties to be the particle that transmits the gravitational force, known as the graviton. This particle, although not yet observed, is thought to exist. At that point, string theory graduated from being a theory of strong nuclear forces only to being a theory candidate for a unified theory of all fundamental particles and gravity. Schwarz introduced the term *superstring* in 1982 to describe theories that combine strings and supersymmetry.

One problem with early superstring theories was that the most likely versions showed mathematical inconsistencies, called *anomalies,* when applied to quantum theory. Superstring unification did not become popular until Schwarz and another collaborator, Michael Green, showed in 1984 that there was a subtle mechanism that causes the anomalies to cancel. This mechanism only worked for two choices of symmetry structures. Schwarz and Green also showed that one of these structures seemed promising as a basis for a realistic model of particle interactions. Almost immediately, superstring theory became a part of mainstream theoretical physics.

Since 1994 there has been another period of dramatic progress. What once appeared to be five different superstring theories are actually different realizations of a unique underlying concept, which has been named M theory. Spinoffs of M theory have brought about deeper understanding of black holes and of supersymmetric versions of quantum theory. Schwarz and many other physicists believe that M theory is a conceptual revolution as profound as those associated with relativity and quantum theory.

John Henry Schwarz was born on November 22, 1941, in a hospital in North Adams, Massachusetts, near to his parent's home in Williamstown, where his father managed a branch of the company now known as Agfa-Gevaert. John's parents were both Hungarians from a Jewish background. His father, George Schwarz, was a research chemist specializing in photographic processes, and his mother, Madeline "Magda" (Haberfeld) Schwarz was trained as a physicist. Both parents received Ph.D.s from the University of Vienna, where they met. They and John's elder sister Mimi had been living in Antwerp, Belgium, when the Germans invaded in May, 1940. After some narrow escapes, the Schwarz family reached the United States a year before John was born.

Schwarz's family moved to Glen Head, Long Island, New York in 1951, where Schwarz graduated in the first class of the then-new North Shore High School. Schwarz entered Harvard University in Cambridge, Massachusetts, where he got his A.B. in mathematics in 1962. A National Science Foundation fellowship helped Schwarz obtain a Ph.D. in physics at the University of California, Berkeley, in 1966, from which he returned east to teach physics and continue his research at Princeton University in New Jersey. He began working on string theory in 1969 while at Princeton.

In 1972 Schwarz headed back west to the California Institute of Technology, which has been his base ever since. Currently Schwarz is the Harold Brown Professor of Theoretical Physics at Caltech. One of his main retreats from Caltech has been a summer program at the Aspen Center for Physics in Colorado. His breakthrough with Green came at Aspen; it was in Aspen on July 11, 1986, that Schwarz married Patricia Moyle, whom he had met a year and a half before at a physics conference that they both attended in Jerusalem.

The theory of superstrings is still being developed by the continuing work of Schwarz and other theoreticians, but its goals are already reasonably clear: to explain the origin of the forces and subatomic particles observed in nature, including their masses and other properties. They also hope to understand the structure of space and time and to explain the origin of the universe. Their theoretical structures so far resemble reality in many ways, making scientists optimistic that superstring theory will eventually succeed in these goals. Because of this broad program, superstring theory is sometimes labeled a "theory of everything," although Schwarz does not like this label.

The underlying nature of superstring theory can only be understood through its mathematics, but the superstring description of reality can be described roughly as follows. The fundamental entities from which everything is built are very short curves, or strings, with one dimension-length-instead of point-like particles. The strings are typically as short compared to an atom as an atom is compared to the solar system. Some strings have ends while others form loops. The strings exist in ten dimensions, including the three familiar space dimensions of length, width, and height, a time dimension, and six other space dimensions that must be wound up so tightly that we do not observe them. Strings interact by joining or splitting. This can be described by a two-dimensional surface in spacetime called the *worldsheet* of the string. Such surfaces are classified and studied by known mathematical techniques. The view of superstrings just described is the one technically called *perturbative* superstring theory. M theory and other newer versions also employ additional methods, and sometimes even an eleventh dimension.

Schwarz's work has been recognized by the MacArthur Foundation with one of its "genius grants" for the period 1987-92, which are awarded to encourage the brightest and most creative young people by giving them a large measure of financial freedom. In 1989 Schwarz received the Dirac Medal, and in 1997 he was elected to the U.S. National Academy of Sciences.

SELECTED WRITINGS BY SCHWARZ:

Books

(With Edward Witten and Michael B. Green) *Superstring Theory.* two volumes. New York: Cambridge University Press, 1988.

Periodicals

(With A. Neveu) "Factorizable Dual Models of Pions." *Nuclear Physics* B31 (1971): 86-112.
(With J. Scherk) "Dual Models for Nonhadrons." *Nuclear Physics* B81 (1974): 118-144.
(With M. B. Green) "Anomaly Cancellations in Supersymmetric D=10 Gauge Theory and Superstring Theory." *Physics Letters* 149B (1984): 117-122.
"Lectures on Superstring and M Theory Dualities." *Nuclear Physics B (Proceeding Supplement)* 55B (1997): 1-32.

FURTHER READING:

Books

Crease, Robert, and Charles C. Mann. *The Second Creation.* New York: Macmillan, 1986.
Weinberg, Steven. *Dreams of a Final Theory.* New York: Vintage Books, 1994.

—Sketch by Bryan Bunch

Charlotte Angas Scott
1858–1931
English mathematician

Charlotte Angas Scott was the first mathematics department head at Bryn Mawr College and a member of its founding faculty. She developed the curriculum for graduate and undergraduate math majors and upgraded the minimum mathematics requirements for entry and retention at Bryn Mawr. Scott also initiated the formulation of the College Entrance

Charlotte Angas Scott

Examination Board in order to standardize such requirements nationwide. At one time, she was the only woman featured in the first printing of *American Men of Science*, and the only mathematician in another venerable reference book, *Notable American Women 1607–1950*. Scott was one of the main organizers of the American Mathematical Society and the only female to leave such an extensive mark on its first 50 years of existence.

Breaking "The Iron Mould"

Scott was born in Lincoln, England, on June 8, 1958, to Caleb and Eliza Exley Scott. As the daughter of the president of Lancashire College, she was provided with mathematics tutors as early as age seven. Her father and grandfather, Walter, were both social reformers as well as educators, and encouraged her to "break the iron mould" and seek a university education. At the age of 18 Scott won a scholarship to Hitchin College, now known as Girton College, the women's division of Cambridge University.

As the 19th century drew to a close, Girton was still an anomaly. Scott and her classmates numbered 11. The young women had to walk three miles to Cambridge to attend classes with those lecturers who allowed them in their classroom, but they had to sit behind a screen where they could not see the blackboard. At that time, a woman caught unescorted on Cambridge campus grounds could be sent to The Spinning House, a prison for prostitutes both active

and suspected. A hint of the future could be seen in the changing attitudes of male undergraduates and graduate students, however. Tutors offered to prepare female undergraduates for the "Tripos," a grueling oral examination that lasted over a week's time. The first female student took the mathematics Tripos in 1872, and thereafter more women applied for permission to take the tests along with their male counterparts. Scott took the examination in January 1880, placing eighth. Although university policy kept her accomplishment a secret, the news spread throughtout the campus. The awards ceremony was disrupted by a crowd of young men shouting "Scott of Girton!" over the name of the man honored in her place. Scott was later "crowned with laurels" in a private ceremony. In February 1881 Cambridge reversed its policy and women were allowed to take examinations with the male students.

Double Duty

Scott remained at Girton as a lecturer for four years while finishing her graduate studies at the University of London. The algebraist Arthur Cayley, a leader in coeducational reform, became Scott's mentor and recommended her for jobs as well as guiding her graduate research. Her doctorate was the first of its kind to be earned by a British female. In the nascent specialty of analysis within algebraic geometry, Scott focused on analyzing singularities in algebraic curves. Both of Scott's degrees at London were of the highest rank.

In 1885 Scott emigrated to the United States, where she joined the faculty of Bryn Mawr College in Pennsylvania. Founded that same year by the Society of Friends, Bryn Mawr was the first women's college to offer graduate degrees. Between 1885 and 1901 Scott successfully lobbied for a series of reforms to the admissions policies and entrance procedures at Bryn Mawr. Once the College Entrance Examination Board was instituted with her help, she served as Chief Examiner from 1902 to 1903. Scott's dedication was finally rewarded in 1909 with Bryn Mawr's first endowed chair and a formal citation.

Helps Organize the AMS

In 1891 Scott was one of the first women to join the New York Mathematical Society, which later evolved into the American Mathematical Society (AMS) in 1895. Scott served on the council that oversaw this transition and received an "acclaimed review" from the group. She would serve on the AMS council again (between 1899 and 1901), and as vice–president in 1905.

Also, in 1899 Scott became the coeditor of the *American Journal of Mathematics*. She would continue to edit and peer review for this publication until two years after her official retirement from Bryn Mawr. Her influence spread internationally with her proof of **Emmy Noether**'s "fundamental theorem," an accomplishment which helped place Bryn Mawr and American mathematics on the world map.

"Auntie Charley"

During her long sojourn in America, Scott was visited regularly by her father and younger brother, Walter, while her sisters remained in England. "Auntie Charley," as Scott was called, would travel to Europe during spring and summer breaks to visit with her expanding circle of relatives and with mathematicians in major European cities. Scott's own personal life was more circumspect, clouded further by the fact that all her personal correspondence was apparently disposed of or lost. She traveled often to Baltimore to visit her close friend Frank Morley, but she never married.

As Scott aged, the deafness that had plagued her since her student days became a stumbling block. However, even rheumatoid arthritis could not dampen her ambitions although it disrupted her publications' schedule for many years. On the advice of a physician Scott took up gardening, only to breed a new species of a chrysanthemum.

Scott retired at age 67, after a 40–year career as one of the many European women who could only find work as scientists and mathematicians in the United States. She stayed on voluntarily at Bryn Mawr until the following year, however, when her last doctoral student graduated. Scott continued mentoring younger mathematicians and inspired another generation of women to follow in her footsteps. She died in November 1931 in Cambridge, England, and was buried next to her cousin Eliza Nevins in St. Giles's Churchyard. Her textbook on analytical geometry, having gone through a second edition in 1924, would be reissued in a third edition 30 years after her death.

SELECTED WRITINGS BY SCOTT:

Books

An Introductory Account of Certain Modern Ideas and Methods in Plane Analytical Geometry. First Edition, 1894 (republished as *Projective Methods in Plane Analytical Geometry* in 1961).
Cartesian Plane Geometry, Part I: Analytical Conics, 1907.

Periodicals

"A Proof of Noether's Fundamental Theorem." *Mathematische Annalen* 52 (1899): 592–97.

FURTHER READING:

Books

Eves, Howard. *An Introduction to the History of Mathematics.* Sixth Edition. Philadelphia, PA: Saunders College Publishing, 1990.
Green, Judy and Jeanne LaDuke. "Contributors to American Mathematics: An Overview and Selection," in *Women of Science: Righting the Record.* Edited by G. Kass–Simon and Patricia Farnes. Bloomington and Indianapolis: Indiana University Press, 1990.
_____. "Women in American Mathematics: A Century of Contributions," in *A Century of Mathematics in America.* Volume 2. Providence, RI: American Mathematical Society, 1989, pp. 379–389.
Kenschaft, Patricia Clark. "Charlotte Angas Scott," *Women of Mathematics.* Edited by Louise S. Grinstein and Paul J. Campbell. New York: Greenwood Press, 1987, pp. 193–203.
Lehr, Marguerite. "Charlotte Angas Scott." *Notable American Women, 1607–1950.* Volume 3. Cambridge, MA.: Belknap Press of Harvard University, 1971, pp. 249–250.
Ogilvie, Marilyn Bailey. "Charlotte Angas Scott," *Women in Science.* Cambridge, MA.: MIT Press, 1986, pp. 158–59.
Rossiter, Margaret W. *Women Scientists in America: Struggles and Strategies to 1940.* Baltimore, MD: Johns Hopkins University Press, 1982.

Periodicals

Katz, Kaila and Patricia Kenschaft. "Sylvester and Scott." *The Mathematics Teacher* 75 (1982): 490–494.
Kenschaft, Patricia C. "The Students of Charlotte Angas Scott." *Mathematics in College* (Fall 1982): 16–20.
_____. "Why Did Charlotte Angas Scott Succeed?" *Association for Women in Mathematics Newsletter* 17, no. 2 (1988): 9–11.
_____. "Charlotte Angas Scott 1858–1931." *College Mathematics Journal* 18 (March 1987): 98–110.
Maddison, Isabel and Marguerite Lehr. "Charlotte Angas Scott: An Appreciation." *Bryn Mawr Alumni Bulletin* 12 (1932): 9–12.

Other

Chaplin, Stephanie. "Charlotte Angas Scott." http://www.agnesscott.edu/lriddle/women/chronol.htm (July 1997).

"Charlotte Angas Scott." http://
www–groups.dcs.st–and.ac.uk/~history /Mathe-
maticians/Scott.html (July 1997).

—*Sketch by Jennifer Kramer*

Atle Selberg
1917–

Norwegian number theorist

Atle Selberg's most newsworthy achievement
came in 1950, when he won the Fields Medal for an
elementary proof of the 18th century conjecture
known as the Prime Number Theorem. Since this
achievement, Selberg has been affliated with the
Institute for Advanced Studies (IAS) at Princeton,
New Jersey. However, he continues to venture out to
visit with children in their early teens, and to take
part in special math–oriented programs held around
the country.

Selberg was born in Langeslund, Norway, on
June 14, 1917, to Ole Michael and Anna Kristina (nee
Skeie) Selberg. He received all his early schooling
there and earned a Ph.D. from the University of Oslo
in 1943. Selberg was resident fellow at the university
for a total of five years. However, he would soon
become part of that wave of European emigres who
enriched American mathematics after World War II.

Selberg married Hedvig Liebermann on August
13, 1947, the year he relocated to the United States.
They would eventually have two children, Ingrid
Maria and Lars Atle. Aside from a year–long stint at
Syracuse University in New York, Selberg did not
teach full–time in America. He was granted membership to the IAS and by 1951 was a member of the
faculty there. Selberg was one of the three top
European number theorists working in America,
including Hungarian mathematician **Paul Erdös**, with
whom he discovered the proof for the Prime Number
Theorem.

Originally, Selberg and Erdös agreed to publish
back to back papers in the same journal, but Selberg
jumped ahead at the last minute. The fact that he
published first led to his being awarded the Fields
Medal by the International Mathematics Union.
Selberg received more awards, including the Wolf
Prize in 1986 and an honorary commission of Knight
Commander with Star from the Royal Norwegian
Order of St. Olav in 1987. He also holds an honorary
doctorate from the University of Trondheim in his
home country.

Math Camp

As Selberg approached age 80, he traveled widely, taking part in commemorative and experimental
events. For example, Selberg was invited to give the
keynote address at the 1996 Seattle Mathfest celebrating the 100th anniversary of the Prime Number
Theorem. That same month, he visited the "Math
Camp" at the University of Washington. The Math
Camp is an annual summer workshop designed to
bring together and inspire bright youngsters from the
Americas, Europe, and Asia. Selberg was one of many
distinguished speakers invited, who had made significant strides in their particular areas of mathematics.

Selberg's specialty is in generalizing the works of
others, an important step towards solidifying the
foundations of number theory. He arrived at generalizations of Viggo Brun's sieve methods, and also
summarized the Prime Number Theorem to include
all prime numbers in an arbitrary arithmetic progression. His investigations also hinge on group theory
and analysis. Not all of Selberg's work follows others,
though; his conjecture that Lie groups are arithmetical
was eventually proven in 1968 by Russian mathematicians Gregori Aleksandrovitch Margulis and D.A.
Kazhdan.

SELECTED WRITINGS BY SELBERG:

Books

"The General Sieve–Method and Its Place in
Prime–Number Theory," in *Proceedings of the
International Congress of Mathematicians,
Cambridge, MA, 1950, Volume 1*, 1952, pp.
286–292.
"Recent Developments in the Theory of Discon-
tinuous Groups of Motions of Symmetric
Spaces," in *Proceedings of the 15th Scandina-
vian Congress, Oslo, 1968*. Lecture Notes in
Mathematics, Volume 118, 1970, pp. 99–120.

Periodicals

"On the Zeros of Riemann's Zeta–Function."
*Skrifter utgitt av Det Norske Viden-
skaps–Akademi i Oslo I. Mat.–Natruv. Klasse*
no. 10 (1942): 1–59.
"An Elementary Proof of the Prime Number Theorem." *Annals of Mathematics* 50, no. 2
(1949): 305–15.

FURTHER READING:

Books

Albers, Alexanderson, and Reid. *International
Mathematical Congresses: An Illustrated Histo-
ry 1893–1986*. Revised edition. New York:
Springer–Verlag, 1986.

Sands, Karen. "Gregori Aleksandrovitch Margulis," in *Notable Twentieth Century Scientists.* Volume 3. Edited by Emily J. McMurray. Detroit, MI: Gale Research, Inc., 1995, p. 1318.

Tarwater, Dalton, editor. *The Bicentennial Tribute to American Mathematics: 1776–1976.* Mathematical Association of America, Inc. 1977.

World Who's Who in Science. First Edition. Edited by Allen G. Debus. Chicago: Marquis, 1968, p. 1519.

Other

Peterson, Ivars. "Math Camp." *Ivars Peterson's MathLand* (August 26, 1996). http://www.maa.org/mathland/mathland_8_26.html

"Atle Selberg." *MacTutor History of Mathematics Archive.* http://www–groups.dcs.st–and.ac.uk/~history/Mathematicians/Erdös.html (July 1997).

—*Sketch by Jennifer Kramer*

Roger N. Shepard
1929–

American psychologist

Roger Newland Shepard is a psychologist whose work has advanced our understanding of how the human mind perceives the physical world. Shepard made great progress in studying mental processes that were previously thought to be beyond the scope of rigorous research. In the process, he changed the way scientists and the public alike view mental imagery, and he influenced fields ranging from psychology and neuroscience to philosophy and computer science. His basic research laid the groundwork for a number of practical applications by others. These include the design of better organized cockpit displays, the development of improved ways to detect breast cancer, and the discovery of more accurate ways to predict the skill of future pilots.

Shepard was born on January 30, 1929, in Palo Alto, California. He was the elder of two children born to Orson Cutler Shepard, an engineering professor at Stanford University, and Grace Newland Shepard, a homemaker. Writing to author Linda Wasmer Smith in 1997, Shepard recalled that as a boy he "was enthralled by science, but less from exposure in school than from early exposure through my father." He also enjoyed drawing, a hobby he traced to his mother, who dabbled in watercolor, weaving, and needlework. These interests endured, as did Shepard's childhood penchant for perceptual pranks.

In his 1990 book, *Mind Sights*, Shepard noted that the types of pranks that especially appealed to him "were those whose essential elements were perceptual incongruity and surprise." For example, he once surreptitiously removed the rug, curtains, and all the furniture from his sister's bedroom, so as to shock her when she tried to go to bed.

As an undergraduate at Stanford, Shepard had trouble deciding upon a major course of study. His agile mind was alternately attracted by art, music, philosophy, and physics. He finally settled on psychology, however, and he received a B.A. degree in that field in 1951. One factor shaping his decision was a growing conviction that there were general principles of the mind not unlike the universal laws of physics. Shepard wanted to apply mathematical methods to studying the mind, something that had rarely been done in the past. For graduate school, Shepard moved to Yale University, where he completed a M.S. degree in 1952 and a Ph.D. in 1955. For postdoctoral training, Shepard moved once again, this time to Harvard University, where he served as a research fellow from 1956 to 1958. At both schools, he sought out the guidance of mathematically oriented professors, such as cognitive psychologist George A. Miller at Harvard.

In 1958, Shepard accepted a post with the technical staff at Bell Telephone Laboratories in Murray Hill, New Jersey. There he had access to state-of-the-art computer facilities. Shepard used these facilities to develop a method for converting qualitative data into quantitative representations. This method, which came to be known as nonmetric multidimensional scaling, has since been applied to a wide range of behavioral, social, and medical problems. Also while at Bell Labs, Shepard used the computer to generate an auditory illusion: a repeating series of tones that sound as if they are forever rising in pitch. These "Shepard tones" have since been incorporated into the works of several composers as well as used in studies of human auditory perception.

The Art and Science of Mental Imagery

In 1966, Shepard returned to Harvard as a psychology professor. Then in 1968, he joined the faculty at Stanford, in the same year that his father retired from that university. Three years later, he published the first of many papers coauthored with graduate students that explored what came to be known as mental rotation. Shepard showed that, when people visualize objects, they imagine them moving in much the same way that the physical objects might be rotated. He also showed that these mental movements can be measured. The idea that mental imagery could be analyzed in a rigorous manner was a revolutionary concept at the time. Shepard and graduate student

Lynn A. Cooper covered this topic in their 1982 book, *Mental Images and Their Transformations*.

The direction that Shepard's work has taken over the years has been guided by his personal beliefs. In his letter to author Linda Wasmer Smith, he explained his philosophy. "Having evolved in a world governed by general laws, we have internalized a knowledge of these laws, both through natural selection of our genes and through individual learning. This knowledge is deeply built into our perceptual and representational systems at a level that is not accessible to conscious introspection." Yet Shepard says we have some access to this knowledge through "thought experiments," in which we do mental manipulations based upon our inborn but unconscious wisdom about the fundamental nature of the physical world. One thing Shepard believes we have internalized is a principle of generalization. This lets us recognize, for example, that poodles and collies are both dogs. In 1987, he proposed a "universal law of generalization," in which he argued that generalization is the most basic principle of behavioral and cognitive science.

In 1995, Shepard was presented the National Medal of Science by President Bill Clinton. The citation noted, among other things, "his creative theoretical and experimental work elucidating how the human mind perceives and represents the physical world." His other awards include the 1976 Distinguished Scientific Contribution Award from the American Psychological Association. Shepard has been elected to the National Academy of Sciences and the American Academy of Arts and Sciences. He has also been named a Guggenheim fellow as well as a fellow of the Center for Advanced Study in the Behavioral Sciences.

Shepard married Barbaranne Bradley, an early childhood educator, on August 18, 1952, in her hometown of Redfield, South Dakota. The couple have three grown children, Newland, Todd, and Shenna. Shepard is not only a scientist but also a skilled artist, and several of his drawings of visual illusions appear in the book *Mind Sights*. His recreational passions are as varied as his professional ones. He enjoys composing music, writing poetry, taking photographs, hiking, in-line skating, and reading about science.

SELECTED WRITINGS BY SHEPARD:

Books

(With Lynn A. Cooper) *Mental Images and Their Transformations*. Cambridge, MA: MIT Press, 1982.

Mind Sights: Original Visual Illusions, Ambiguities, and Other Anomalies, with a Commentary on the Play of Mind in Perception and Art. New York: W.H. Freeman, 1990.

FURTHER READING:

Periodicals

"Roger N. Shepard." *American Psychologist* (January 1977): 62-65.

Salisbury, David. "For Roger Shepard, It's All in the Mind." *Stanford Report* (September 27, 1995): 5-6.

Salisbury, David F. "Visualization: The Secret Key to Progress." *Stanford Observer* (March-April 1994): 13.

Stites, Janet. "Roger Shepard." *The Bulletin of the Santa Fe Institute* (Summer 1994): 13-15.

Other

National Medal of Science, citation dated September 11, 1995.

"Psychologist Receives National Medal of Science." http://www.apa.org/psa/novdec95/shep.html (October 22, 1997).

"The Mind's Eye: Finding Truth in Illusion." *Frontiers Newsletter* (June 1996). http://www.nsf.gov/od/lpa/news/publicat/frontier/6-96/6illusio.htm (October 22, 1997).

—*Sketch by Linda Wasmer Smith*

Clifford Glenwood Shull
1915–
American physicist

Shull won a share of the 1994 Nobel Prize in Physics for his pioneering development of neutron scattering techniques. Like **Bertram N. Brockhouse**, the Canadian physicist with whom he shared the prize, Shull was recognized belatedly for research conducted more than 40 years earlier. Working at one of the first nuclear reactors in the United States, Shull found that the atomic structure of solid or fluid matter could be determined by directing waves of neutrons at a sample and measuring the angle at which they bounce off, or are scattered by, the atoms in the sample. This discovery has had significant impact on a wide range of scientific fields, since neutron scattering, also known as neutron diffraction, has been used to analyze the atomic structure of such diverse substances as viruses, polymers, and super-conductive materials.

The youngest child of David and Daisy Shull, Clifford Glenwood Shull was born on September 23, 1915, in the Glenwood section of Pittsburgh, Pennsylvania. Several years earlier, his parents had moved from rural, central Pennsylvania to the city and opened a small business that eventually became a hardware store and home repair service. Along with his older brother and sister, Shull attended neighborhood schools, then enrolled in Schenley High School, which was 45 minutes away by streetcar. At Schenley, a dynamic instructor sparked Shull's interest in physics, causing him to reconsider his initial ambition to be an aeronautical engineer. After graduating, he won a partial scholarship to the Carnegie Institute of Technology, now Carnegie Mellon University, and immersed himself in his studies. During Shull's freshman year, however, his father died suddenly, precipitating not only an emotional, but a financial crisis for the family. As a result, Shull's older brother, Perry, quit his job as an art teacher and ran their father's business until his younger sibling had graduated from college.

Works with Accelerators

After receiving his B.A. from Carnegie, Shull entered the graduate physics program at New York University. Early on he became associated with the nuclear physics research group and took part in several different experiments using particle accelerators. For his Ph.D. thesis he used the department's newly constructed Van de Graaff accelerator to determine whether or not electrons have a spin or polarization. While at the university, he also met Martha-Nuel Summer, a native of South Carolina and graduate student in early American history. They married in 1941 after completing their studies and eventually had three sons, John, Robert, and William.

A month after receiving his Ph.D. from New York University, Shull accepted a research position at The Texas Company, now Texaco, in Beacon, New York. There, he used gas absorption as well as x-ray diffraction and scattering to analyze catalysts used in the production of high-performance aviation fuel. This research took on great importance following the entry of the United States into World War II. However, Shull, like many other young physicists of the time, was very interested in the Manhattan Project. He had seen several of his former university friends and professors join in the race to produce the first nuclear weapon and longed to take part as well. Yet when an attempt was made to recruit him, The Texas Company blocked his way, eventually convincing a government manpower board that his research for them was more crucial to the wartime effort.

Develops Neutron Scattering Techniques

At the end of the war Shull was free to pursue his interest in nuclear physics, and in 1946 he left The Texas Company for the Clinton Laboratory in Oak Ridge, Tennessee. Eventually renamed the Oak Ridge National Laboratory, it had been one of the top-secret sites of the Manhattan Project, and its nuclear reactor had supplied a significant portion of the plutonium used in the atomic bombs dropped on Hiroshima and Nagasaki. At the time Shull arrived, the laboratory's administrators had begun to shift its focus from military to civilian uses, and he was assigned to work with Ernest Wollan. Wollan, who had been with the laboratory since its inception, had begun to investigate how the neutron beams produced by the reactor could be used to analyze the structure of matter. Over the next decade, the two scientists developed a method of neutron diffraction that eventually became the foundation of an entirely new branch of physics research.

Shull and Wollan discovered that neutrons, upon hitting the atoms within a fluid or solid sample, ricochet in a characteristic fashion. Specifically, the angle at which the neutrons are deflected shows how the atoms are arranged. In other words, neutron scattering effectively determines the atomic structure of a sample. Neutron scattering was a truly revolutionary discovery, opening new avenues of research as it shed new light on important substances, such as the element hydrogen, that had been resistant to earlier methods of analysis. Sadly, by the time that the Nobel committee recognized the significance of their work, Wollan had died. Shull wrote in his autobiography for the Nobel Foundation, "I regret very much that Wollan's death in 1984 precluded his sharing in the Nobel honor . . . since his contributions were certainly deserving of recognition."

Shull left the Oak Ridge National Laboratory in 1955 to become a professor of physics at the Massachusetts Institute of Technology, retiring as emeritus professor in 1986. His other awards include the Buckley Prize, which he received in 1956.

FURTHER READING:

Periodicals

Allen, Scott. "MIT Physicist Shares Nobel for Analysis of Matter with Neutrons." *Boston Globe*, October 13, 1994, p. 261.

Peterson, Ivars. "Physics Nobel for Neutron-Scattering Work." *Science News*, October 22, 1994, p. 261.

Silverman, Edward R. "Colleagues Laud 1994 Nobelists As Overdue for Coveted Prize." *The Scientist*, November 28, 1994.

Suplee, Curt. "Molecular Research Wins Prize, American, Canadian Share Physics Nobel." *Washington Post*, October 13, 1994, p. A3.

— *Sketch by Bridget Travers*

Waclaw Sierpiński
1882–1969
Polish mathematician

Waclaw Sierpiński and his colleagues are credited with revolutionizing Polish mathematics during the first half of the 20th century. They took a couple of relatively new fields of mathematics and devoted whole journals to them. Although detractors had opined that such an experiment could not succeed, the mathematical heritage of the Polish community between the world wars has left a legacy of results, problems, and personalities, chief among them being Sierpiński.

Sierpiński was born in Warsaw on March 14, 1882. His father was Constantine Sierpiński, a successful physician, and his mother was Louise Lapinska. Sierpiński received his secondary education at the Fifth Grammar School in Warsaw, where he studied under an influential teacher named Wlodarski. From there, he entered the University of Warsaw and began studying number theory under the guidance of G. Voronoi. In 1903, Sierpiński's work in mathematics was recognized by a gold medal from the university, from which he graduated the next year. After graduation, he taught in secondary schools, a standard career path due to the shortage of positions available to Poles under Russian rule. In that capacity, he was involved in the school strike that occurred during the revolution of 1905. Even though the strike was not wholly unsuccessful, Sierpiński resigned his teaching position and moved to Kraków.

In 1906 Sierpiński received his doctorate from the Jagiellonian University in Kraków. Two years later he passed the qualifying examination to earn the right to teach at Jan Kazimierz University in Lwów, to which he had gone at the invitation of one of the faculty. There, Sierpiński offered perhaps the first systematic course in set theory, the subject of his investigations for the next 50 years. In 1912 he gathered his lecture notes and published them as *Zarys Teorii Mnogósci* ("Outline of Set Theory"). Sierpiński's texts were recognized by prizes from the Academy of Learning in Kraków.

With the outbreak of World War I in 1914, Sierpiński was interned by the Russians, first at Vyatka, then in Moscow. This internment was not particularly severe, for while he was in Moscow, Sierpiński was accorded a cordial reception by the leading Russian mathematicians of the era. In fact, he was able to conduct some joint research with N. Lusin during this period in the field of set–theoretic topology.

Blends Set Theory with Topology

The area of set–theoretic topology in which Sierpiński worked depended on a few basic notions. One of these is that of a closed set, or a set that includes its boundary. A simple example is the interval of real numbers between 0 and 1, including both endpoints. Related to the notion of a closed set is that of an open set, one which does not include its boundary. An example of an open set is the interval between 0 and 1, not including either 0 or 1. If one takes that interval and includes 0 but not 1, then the set is neither closed nor open. Much time was spent investigating the results of combining open and closed sets in various infinite combinations. The entrance of infinity is what required the use of methods and ideas from set theory.

When the war ended Sierpiński returned to Lwów, but in the fall of that year he was appointed to a position at Warsaw. He devoted a number of papers to the set–theoretic topics of the continuum hypothesis and the axiom of choice. The continuum hypothesis, which had been known to **Georg Cantor**, claimed that there were no infinite numbers between the number of integers and the number of real numbers. If the continuum hypothesis is present, it reduces the complexity of the hierarchy of infinite numbers. The axiom of choice had been a matter for much discussion at the turn of the 19th century, allowing for the possibility of making an infinite number of choices simultaneously. Some distinguished French mathematicians like **Émile Borel** questioned the meaningfulness of such a choice, and one of the early consequences of investigation into the axioms of set theory was the discovery that the axiom of choice was equivalent to a number of other propositions of set theory. Sierpiński took an agnostic position with respect to the axiom, using it in proofs and also trying to eliminate it wherever possible.

It was during the period between the world wars that Sierpiński, in conjunction with several Polish colleagues, created what has since become known as the Polish school of mathematics. The subjects that dominated the Polish school were logic and set theory, topology, and the application of these subjects to questions in analysis. To make certain that there would be an audience for the work in these areas, the journal *Fundamenta Mathematicae* was founded in 1919. Although by the end of the 20th century a profusion of specialized journals within mathematics had sprung up, *Fundamenta* was the first of its kind and was greeted with some suspicion about its likelihood for survival. The quality of its papers was high, the contributors were international, and the problems proposed and solved were substantial. As a permanent record of the Polish mathematical school, *Fundamenta Mathematicae* supplements the reminiscences of those who took part in the work.

Presides over the Polish Mathematical Community

Sierpiński often led the Polish delegations to international congresses and conferences of mathematicians. One of the most ambitious projects in which he was involved was a Congress of Mathematicians of Slavic Countries, whose very existence attests to a political consciousness side–by–side with the mathematical one. The event took place in Warsaw in 1929 and was chaired by Sierpiński.

During World War II Sierpiński was in Warsaw, holding classes in whatever secret settings were available. A good deal of the discussion went on in Sierpiński's home, where his wife did her best to make guests feel as comfortable as possible in such troubled times. In 1944, the Nazis took control of Warsaw and Sierpiński was taken by the Germans to a site near Kraków. After the latter city was liberated by the Allies, he held lectures at the Jagiellonian University there before returning to Warsaw.

The period after the war was marked by further honors to Sierpiński as his students dominated the mathematical landscape. He served as vice president of the Polish Academy of Sciences from its inception and was awarded the Scientific Prize (First Class) in 1949, as well as the Grand Cross of the Order of Polonia Restituta in 1958. There were not many mathematicians in any country who approached his publication records of more than 600 papers in set theory and approximately 100 articles about number theory.

Sierpiński died in Warsaw on October 21, 1969. His mathematical textbooks educated an entire generation, and he helped to lay the foundations of the discipline of set–theoretic topology. Sierpiński's legacy was in establishing a Polish mathematical community, a contribution at the same time to mathematics and to national identity.

SELECTED WRITINGS BY SIERPIŃSKI:

Hypothèse du continu, 1934.
Cardinal and Ordinal Numbers, 1958.
Elementary Theory of Numbers, 1964.

FURTHER READING:

Kuratowski, Kazimierz. *A Half Century of Polish Mathematics*. Warsaw: Polish Scientific Publishers, 1980, pp. 167–173.

Kuzawa, Sister Mary Grace. *Modern Mathematics: The Genesis of a School in Poland*. New Haven, CT: College and University Publishers, 1968.

—*Sketch by Thomas Drucker*

Ellen Kovner Silbergeld
1945–
American toxicologist

Ellen Silbergeld is an American environmental toxicologist and public health policy advocate. She has conducted research and advised policy makers on the toxicological effects of such substances as lead, mercury, dioxin, dibenzofurans, manganese, and Agent Orange.

Ellen Kovner Silbergeld was born on July 29, 1945, in Washington D.C., the first girl and second child of Joseph Kovner, a lawyer, and Mary Gion Kovner, a journalist. Joseph Kovner fell victim to the witch hunts of the House Committee on un-American Activities during the early 1950s and was forced to leave his government job, an event that left a lasting impression on Silbergeld. When she was seven years old, her family moved to Concord, New Hampshire, where her father took up private legal practice. In nearby Boston, one of her father's closest childhood friends, civil liberties lawyer Reuben Goodman, became a mentor to the young Silbergeld. His commitment to civil rights, his rigorous intellect, and his zest for life were, according to Silbergeld, a constant source of stimulation. She was also influenced intellectually by a her mother's friends, who eventually played a role in her decision to attend a women's college. When Silbergeld was in the eighth grade, her family returned to Washington D.C. Although as a young student she enjoyed mathematics and puzzle solving, she avoided the study of science as much as possible and believed she had no talent in the subject.

In 1967, Silbergeld began her undergraduate work in history at Vassar College, in Poughkeepsie, New York. Graduating in 1967, with an A.B. degree in modern history, she accepted a Fulbright Fellowship to England and began a doctoral degree program at the London School of Economics. A year later, disenchanted with the field of economics, she returned to Washington D.C. and took a position as a secretary and program officer for the Committee on Geography at the National Academy of Sciences. It was in this post that Silbergeld first began to develop an interest in science. She remained at the National Academy of Sciences until 1970. By then Silbergeld had begun graduate studies in environmental engineering at Johns Hopkins University in Baltimore. In 1972 she received her Ph.D. and assumed a postdoctoral fellowship in environmental medicine and neurosciences, also at Johns Hopkins University. Her graduate and post-graduate research on the topic of lead neurotoxicity prompted Silbergeld to get involved in public policy regarding lead exposure.

In 1975, Silbergeld became a staff fellow in the Unit on Behavioral Neuropharmacology at the National Institutes of Health (NIH) in Bethesda, Maryland. There, she continued her research on lead and began investigating the toxicology of food dyes. She also conducted research on neurological disorders such as Huntington's disease and Parkinson's disease. In 1979, she became Chief of the Section on Neurotoxicology at NIH, a post she held until 1981. As Section Chief, Silbergeld directed research on the mechanisms of neurotoxic agents such as lead and manganese. She also directed research into the effects of estradiol on the central nervous system.

From 1982 until 1991, she served as the Chief Toxic Scientist and Director of the Toxic Chemicals Program for the Environmental Defense Fund in Washington, D.C. Simultaneously, she maintained research programs at several institutions. As a guest scientist at the National Institute of Child Health Development, from 1982 to 1984, she researched the effects of polycyclic aromatic hydrocarbons (PAHs) on ovarian function.

From 1985 till 1987, as Visiting Professor at the University of Maryland School of Medicine, she studied the effects of tetrachlorodibenzo-p-dioxin (TCDD) on glucocorticoid receptors, and from 1987 to 1989 she investigated lead toxicity and the genetic effects of TCDD as a Visiting Professor in the Program for Toxicology at the University of Maryland. In 1987, as an Associate Faculty member in the Johns Hopkins School of Hygiene and Public Health, she began supervising research into lead toxicity and risk assessment. Her affiliation with Johns Hopkins continued in 1991 as an Adjunct Professor. Ongoing programs of research on the neural and reproductive effects of lead and on the molecular mechanism of TCDD were begun at the University of Maryland School of Medicine in 1989.

Other appointments at the University of Maryland include an affiliate professorship in the School of Law, begun in 1990, a professorship in the Department of Pathology, begun in 1991, and a professorship in the Department of Epidemiology and Preventive Medicine, begun in 1992. Since 1993, Silbergeld has been a Senior Consultant Toxicologist for the Environmental Defense Fund, and since 1996, the Director of the Program in Human Health and the Environment at the University of Maryland.

Silbergeld has published over 200 research and policy articles and is a member of the editorial board for more than half a dozen journals related to environmental health and toxicology. She has served as an advisor and consultant for environmental and health causes throughout her career. She has organized a variety of international symposia and workshops on chemically induced diseases and lead toxicology. Highly commended for both her scientific research and her environmental advocacy, she was designated one of the Four Outstanding Women of Maryland by the Maryland Education Association in 1987. That same year, she received the Warner-Lambert Award for Distinguished Women in Science. In 1990, she received the Governor's Citation for Excellence, in 1991, the Abel Wolman Award, and in 1992, the Barsky Award. The MacArthur Foundation made her a Fellow in 1993, and that year she also received the Earth Month Award of the Maryland Department of the Environment. In 1994, she was an honoree in the Maryland Women's History Project, and, the following year, Chatham College named her one of the Women Who Make a Difference. That year, Silbergerld was awarded a patent for a lead detection procedure.

In 1969, she married Mark Silbergeld, with whom she has two children. Sophia, their daughter, was born in 1981, and their son Nicholas Reuben, named after Reuben Goodman, was born in 1985.

SELECTED WRITINGS BY SILBERGELD:

Books

"Risk assessment and risk management: an uneasy divorce." In *Acceptable Evidence: Science and Values in Risk Management*, Deborah G. Mayo and Rachelle D. Hollander, eds. New York: Oxford University Press, 1991.

FURTHER READING:

Books

Shearer, Benjamin F., and Barbara S. Shearer. *Notable Women in the Life Sciences.* Westport: Greenwood Press, 1996.

—Sketch by Leslie Reinherz

Howard Ensign Simmons, Jr.

Howard Ensign Simmons, Jr.
1929–1997
American organic chemist

Howard Ensign Simmons Jr. built a fruitful scientific career exploring the relationship between chemical structures and chemical activity, contributing to both organic chemistry practice and theory. Simmons' contributions extended to corporate administration as well. As director and later vice president of central research for E. I. du Pont de Nemours and Company, he led a major expansion of the company's research and development program. In addition to his career achievements, Simmons is remembered for his interests in foreign languages, prehistoric Native American cultures, and boating. He held visiting professorships in chemistry at Harvard University, in 1968; the University of Chicago, in 1978; and the University of Delaware, from 1970 until his death.

Simmons was born on June 17, 1929, in Norfolk, Virginia, to a merchant marine captain and a homemaker. He received a B.S. in chemistry from Massachusetts Institute of Technology (MIT) in 1951, followed three years later by an organic chemistry Ph.D. from MIT. In 1954 he joined du Pont, launching a 37-year career topped by scientific and administrative achievement.

Contributions to Chemical Toolbox and Thinking

Simmon's most significant pre-du Pont discovery was benzyne, the chemically unstable key to a large family of reactions for adding or removing chemical groups from the benzene molecule. Along with later work at du Pont that demonstrated the chemical structure of benzyne, this research allowed organic chemists to better understand and control these industrially important reactions. Du Pont colleague R. D. Smith and Simmons also developed the Simmons-Smith reaction—an efficient method of synthesizing the chemical workhorse cyclopropane and its derivatives, in a manner that controls the structure of the final product. In later work, Simmons and collaborator Chung Ho Park synthesized a new class of large cyclic molecules that are today being used to create synthetic enzymes and catalysts.

Simmons also contributed greatly to organic chemical theory. In a 1989 monograph, Simmons and Richard E. Merrifield introduced a new theoretical field to the chemical community, topological chemistry, which predicts chemical activity by computing the exact shapes and surfaces of reactant molecules without resorting to the usual physics necessary for such predictions. Recognition for Simmons' research has come in the form of membership in the American Academy of Arts and Sciences and the National Science Foundation in 1975, Columbia University's Chandler Medal of chemistry in 1991, the National Medal of Science in 1992, and the American Chemical Society Priestley Medal in 1994.

Successful Administrator As Well As Scientist

As Simmons was compiling research achievements, he was also rising in the du Pont organization. Named a research supervisor in the company's Central Research Department in 1959, he rose to associate director of research in 1970 and then overall director of the department in 1974. Arguably, his greatest administrative contributions to the company came during his tenures as director of the Central Research and Development Department from 1979 to 1983, and vice president of the department from 1983 to 1990. This period saw a dramatic growth in the department, including the strengthening of du Pont's already world-class programs in organic and physical chemistry and an expansion into the fields of life science, materials science, and electronics. In 1990 he was made vice president and senior science advisor at du Pont; he retired in 1991.

Simmons also served his country in key administrative positions, including a term on the National Science Board (NSB), a 24-member committee that determines policy for the National Science Foundation. He served on the NSB from 1990 to 1996.

Simmons died on April 26, 1997, of congestive heart failure. He was survived by his wife, the former Elizabeth Warren; sons Howard E., III, and John W., both chemists at du Pont.

SELECTED WRITINGS BY SIMMONS:

Books

Orbital Symmetry Papers. American Chemical Society, 1974.
(With Richard E. Merrifield) *Topological Methods in Chemistry.* John Wiley, 1989.

Periodicals

"Basic Research–A Perspective." *Chemical & Engineering News* (March 14, 1994): 27-31.

FURTHER READING:

Periodicals

Kreeger, Karen Young. "Du Pont Chemist Receives Priestley Medal." *The Scientist* (March 21, 1994): 23.
Milford, Phil. "Award-Winning Du Pont Scientist Dies." *Wilmington News Journal* (April 28, 1997): B1.
"Simmons, Howard." *The New York Times* (May 5, 1997): A30.

Other

"Howard Ensign Simmons, Jr." http://www.dupont.com/corp/r-and-d/lavoisier/simmons (November 20, 1997).
"Five Du Pont Scientists Honored with Lavoisier Medals (Eleuterio, Ibrahim, Kwolek, Shivers, and Simmons)." April 27, 1995. http://www.dupont.com/corp/whats-new/releases/95archive/950427.html (November 22, 1997).
"ACS Awards: List of Awards Administered." September 5, 1997. http://www.acs.org/acsgen/awards/quicklst.htm#53 (November 22, 1997).

—*Sketch by Kenneth Chiacchia*

Clive Marles Sinclair
1940–
English electronics engineer

A self-taught electronics specialist, Clive Sinclair developed and introduced the first widely available

Clive Marles Sinclair

pocket calculator and a host of other innovative products, including watches, miniature televisions, a motor-powered three-wheeled bicycle, and a line of personal computers.

The son of a mechanical engineer, Sinclair was born at Richmond, Surrey, England on July 30, 1940. Both his father and grandfather, also an engineer, encouraged Sinclair's interest in designing and building. As a youngster, Sinclair planned and built a submarine, using government surplus fuel tanks; in his teens, he discovered electronics. His room at home "a tangle of wires, radio parts and circuit components" was viewed with amused tolerance by his family.

In his early teens, Sinclair invented a calculating machine that he programmed with punch cards, using a binary system to perform calculations. Although fascinated by mathematics and electronics, Sinclair had no desire to attend a university. After completing courses at Box Grove Preparatory School, he attended several secondary schools before completing a course of study at Highgate School, supplemented with advanced course work in physics and mathematics at St. George's College in Weybridge. At the age of 17, Sinclair considered his formal education complete.

Almost immediately, Sinclair landed a job as an editorial assistant with *Practical Wireless*, a magazine dedicated to radio and sound technology. Shortly after Sinclair joined the magazine staff, the editor retired, and Sinclair took over as editor (at the age of

18) of the publication. In addition to his editorial duties, Sinclair churned out technical works and how-to manuals for radio enthusiasts. He published plans for his own circuit designs, which emphasized reduced size and inexpensive components.

Following the Entrepreneurial Urge

Sinclair's duties at the magazine allowed him time to tinker and think. He wanted to manufacture and distribute the items he designed, and in 1961, he officially registered his own business as Sinclair Radionics Ltd. He planned to launch his new company with the introduction of a miniature transistor radio kit, but unable to find an investor for his design and short of funds, he accepted a position as technical editor with *Instrument Practice* in 1962.

Sinclair continued to develop ideas for his fledgling business. He began to advertise products of his own design, such as a micro amplifier, the Sinclair Slimline (the miniature transistor radio on which he founded his firm), and a host of radio and high-fidelity products.

In 1972 Sinclair introduced the Sinclair Executive, his first pocket calculator, which won a Design Council Ward for Electronics in 1973. That was followed with the Cambridge Scientific Calculator in 1974, which won two Queen's Awards for Industry, and by 1975, Sinclair Radionics was the largest European manufacturer of calculators.

But Sinclair's triumph was short-lived. He introduced a series of commercial disappointments, including a quartz digital watch and a pocket television, and it became clear that his inventive genius did not extend into the realm of marketing. By 1979 Sinclair Radionics was on the brink of financial disaster and the firm was split into various components and sold.

Research Successes, Business Failures

When Sinclair Radionics went under, Sinclair formed his own research firm, called Sinclair Research, and began to explore the personal computer market. In 1980 Sinclair Research introduced the ZX80, followed by the ZX81. By 1982 Sinclair Research was producing 500,000 computers a year, but Sinclair, in the quest for an inexpensive, small, versatile, and reliable home computer, continued to refine the microcomputer design. In 1982 he introduced the ZX Spectrum, his most commercially successful microcomputer and one which developed a cadre of devotees.

Although knighted for his achievements in 1983, the pattern that had plagued his first firm recurred in his second venture. Sinclair failed to negotiate important contracts to supply microcomputers; then, in 1984, he introduced the QL model. Sinclair's firm belief in the QL's merits did not impress the now fiercely competitive consumer marketplace. The QL was a commercial disaster, and in 1986, Sinclair was again forced to preside over the dismemberment and sale of his firm, turning over the computer product line to Amstrad.

In a 1985 interview with the *Observer*, Sinclair said "I am not a management type. I am an inventor. I am awful at managing established businesses." The lack of business acumen has not diminished Sinclair's inventiveness. In 1985 he introduced an environmentally friendly, financially disappointing electric tricycle; the Z88 computer in 1987; miniaturized integrated circuits, satellite TV antennas, inexpensive portable telephones, the LC3 (an inexpensive color computer), and a second electric cycle.

In a 1984 address to the U.S. Congressional Clearinghouse on the Future, Sinclair said "It often seems that each new step in technology brings misery rather than contentment . . . By the end of this decade manufacturing decline will be almost complete . . . and technical change will virtually remove all employment. . . . The future promises a better solution."

Sinclair's vision includes a future in which computer systems and artificial intelligence will perform routine calculating and decision-making tasks "such as navigating a car" and free the human mind to tackle both abstract and concrete challenges that require the kind of intuition that has fueled much of Sinclair's own work.

A retiring man who is happiest in a laboratory, Sinclair avoids public attention. Ironically, the man responsible for popularizing computer technology and focusing the spotlight on the potential of such systems has no electronic mail address. "I don't think I want to have my stuff spewing all over the Internet," he said in an interview with *Cyberia Magazine*.

FURTHER READING:

Books

Jenkins-Jones, S., ed. *Hutchinson Dictionary of Scientists*. Oxford, England: Helicon Publishing Ltd., 1996, p. 441.

Porter, Roy, ed. *Biographical Dictionary of Scientists*. New York: Oxford UniveristyPress, 1994, pp. 448-49.

Other

"After the Fall: Sir Clive Looks Back." August 1986. (July 6, 1995) http://www.nvg.unit.no/spectrum/sellout.html (November 24, 1997).

Dale, Rodney. "The Sinclair Story, Part 1: Early Days." (July 7, 1995). http://www.nvg.unit.no/spectrum/clive1.html (November 24, 1995).

Godlovitch, Ilsa. "Netted–Sir Clive Sinclair." http://www.magazine./cyberiacafe.net/issue4/features/features.3.html (November 24, 1997).

Scolding, Bill. "Riding High: Sir Clive on the Future." 1985. (March 6, 1995) http://ttp.nvg.unit.no/spectrum/intervieww.html (November 24, 1997).

"Sir Clive Addresses Congress." 1984. (July 7, 1995). http://www.nvg.unit.no/spectrum/speech.html (November 24, 1995).

—*Sketch by A. Mullig*

Jens C. Skou
1918–
Dutch biochemist

Jens C. Skou was one of three men who shared the 1997 Nobel Prize in Chemistry. Skou received the award in recognition of discovering the first "molecular pump," Na^+, K^+ ATPase, an enzyme that promotes movement through the membrane surrounding a cell and maintains the balance of sodium ions (Na^+) and potassium ions (K^+) in a living cell.

Jens Christian Skou was born October 8, 1918, in Lemvig, Denmark, to Magnus Martinus Skou, a timber merchant, and Ane-Margrethe (Jensen Knak) Skou. He received his M.D. degree (cand.med.) from the University of Copenhagen in 1944. Ten years later, he received his Doctor of Medical Sciences degree (dr.med.) from Aarhus University. In 1948 he married Ellen-Margrethe (Nielsen); they have two children, Hanne and Karen.

After receiving his M.D., Skou went for clinical training at the Hospital at Hjørring and Orthopaedic Clinic at Aarhus, Denmark. He remained there until 1947, when he became an assistant professor in the University of Aarhus's Institute of Physiology. In 1954 the same year he received his Doctor of Medical Sciences degree, he became associate professor at the institute. In 1963 Skou became a full professor and was named chairman of the Institute of Physiology. From 1978-1988, he was professor of biophysics at the University of Aarhus.

Skou has devoted his career to both education and research. He has served as an advisor for many Ph.D. and doctor of medical science students and as an examiner at doctoral dissertation presentations. He has published more than 90 papers on his research, which has investigated the actions of local anesthetics and what mechanisms made them work, as well as the work that earned him the 1997 Nobel Prize, the transport of sodium and potassium ions through the cell membranes.

A Delicate Balance

A cell's health depends on maintaining a balance between its inner chemistry and that of the cell's surroundings. This balance is controlled by the presence of the cell membrane, the wall between the cell's inner workings and its environment.

For more than 70 years, scientists have known that one of the delicate balances that are maintained involves ions (electrically charged particles) of the elements sodium (Na) and potassium (K). A cell maintains its inner concentration of sodium ions (Na^+) at a level lower than that of its surroundings. Similarly, it maintains its inner concentration of potassium ions (K^+) at a level higher than its surroundings.

This balance is not static, however. In the 1950s, English researchers **Alan Hodgkin** and Richard Keynes found that sodium ions rush into a nerve cell when it is stimulated. After the stimulation, the cell restores its original sodium/potassium levels by transporting the extra sodium out through its membrane. Scientists suspected that this transport involved the compound adenosine triphosphate (ATP). ATP was discovered in 1929 by German chemist Karl Lohmann. Further research by **Franz Lippman** between 1939 and 1941 showed that ATP carries chemical energy in the cell. It has been called the cell's "energy currency." Scientists noticed that, when ATP's presence was inhibited, cells did not rid themselves of the extra sodium that they absorbed during stimulation.

Begins Investigating Problem with Crab Cells

In the 1950s, Skou began his investigations into the workings of ATP. For his experimental material he chose finely found nerve membranes from crabs. He wanted to find out if there was an enzyme in the nerve membranes that degraded ATP, and that could be involved with the transport of ions through the membrane.

He did find such an ATP-degrading enzyme, which needed ions of magnesium. In his experiments, Skou found that he could stimulate the enzyme by adding sodium ions—but there was a limit to the stimulation he could achieve. Adding small amounts of potassium ions, however, stimulated the enzyme even more. In fact, Skou noted that the enzyme—called ATPase—reached its maximum point of stimulation when he added quantities of sodium and potassium ions that were the same as those normally found in nerve cells. This evidence made Skou hypothesize that the enzyme worked with an ion "pump" in the cell membrane.

Skou published his first paper on ATPase in 1957. Years of further experimentation followed. In them, Skou learned more about this remarkable enzyme. He learned that different places on the enzyme attracted and bound ions of sodium and potassium.

When ATP breaks down and releases its energy, it become adenosine diphosphate (ADP) and releases a phosphate compound. Skou's work discovered that this freed phosphate bound to the ATPase as well, a process known as phosphorylation. The presence or absences of this phosphate changed the enzyme's interaction with sodium and potassium ions, Skou discovered. When the ATPase lacked a phosphate group, it became dependent on potassium. Similarly, when it has a phosphate, it became dependent on sodium.

This latter discovery was key to learning just how ATPase moved sodium out of the cell. ATPase molecules are set into the cell membrane, and they consist of two parts, one which stabilizes the enzyme and the other which carries out activity.

Part of the enzyme pokes inside the cell. There, one ATP molecule and three sodium ions can bind to it at a time. A phosphorus group is taken from the ATP to bind to the enzyme, and the remaining ADP is released. The enzyme then changes shape, carrying the attached sodium ions with it to the outside of the cell membrane. There, they are released into the cell's surroundings, as is the attached phosphorus. In place of the three sodium ions, two potassium ions attach themselves to the enzyme, which again changes shape and carries the K^+ into the cell's interior.

This activity uses up about one-third of the ATP that the body produces each day, which can range from about half of a resting person's body weight to almost one ton in a person who is doing strenuous activity.

Thanks to this molecular pump, the cell is able to maintain its balance of potassium ions on the inside and sodium ions on the outside, maintaining the electrical charges that allow cells to pass along or to react to stimulation from nerve cells.

This enzyme is important for other reason as well. For example, the pump's action on the balance of sodium and potassium makes it possible for the cell to take in nutrients and to expel waste products. If the molecular pump were to stop—as it can when a lack of nourishment or oxygen shuts down ATP formation—the cell would swell up, and it would be unable to pass along nerve impulse. If this were to happen in the brain, unconsciousness would rapidly follow.

Since Skou discovered ATPase, scientists have found other molecular pumps hard at work in the cell.

They include H^+, K^+-ATPase, which produces stomach acid, and Ca^{2+}-ATPase, which helps control the contraction of muscle cells.

Other Honors and Awards

In addition to the Nobel Prize, Skou has received much recognition for his work. He is a regular participant and organizer of symposia on transmembrane transport. In addition, he has received the Leo Prize, the Novo Prize, the Swedish Medical Association's Anders Retzius gold medal, and the Dr. Eric K. Ferntroms Big Nordic Prize.

He is a member of the Danish Royal Academy, and has served on a number of its committees and science foundation board. He is also a member of the Danish Royal Society, the Deutsche Akademie der Naturfoscher, Leopoldins, and the European Molecular Biology Organization (EMBO). He is a foreign associate of the American National Academy of Sciences. In addition, Skou is an honorary member of the Japanese Biochemical Society and the American Physiological Society. He received and honorary doctorate from the University of Copenhagen. Skou lives in Denmark.

SELECTED WRITINGS BY SKOU:

Books

(With Boyer, P.D.) "The binding change mechanism of ATP synthesis." *Membrane Bioenergetics.* C.P. Lee, G.Schatz, and L. Ernester, eds. Reading, MA: Addison-Wesley, 1979, p. 461-479.

Periodicals

"The influence of some cations on an adenosine triphosphatase from peripheral nerves." *Biochimica et Biophysica Acta* 23 (1957): 394-401.
(With M. Esmann). "The Na, K-ATPase." *Journal of Bioenergetics and Biomembranes* 24 (1992): 249-261.

FURTHER READING:

Periodicals

Broad, William. "Six Researchers Awarded Nobel Prizes in Chemistry and Physics." *The New York Times* (October 16, 1997).
Lingrel, J.B. "Na-K-ATPase: Isoform Structure, Function, and Expression." *Journal of Bioenergetics and Biomembranes* 24 (1992): 263-270.
Lutsenko, S. and J. H. Kaplan. "Organization of P-type ATPases: Significance of structural diversity." *Biochemistry* 34 (1996): 15607-15613.

Møller, J.V., Juul, B., and le Maire, M. "Structural organization, ion transport, and energy transduction of P-type ATPases." *Biochimica et Biophysica Acta* 1286 (1996): 1-51.

Other

1997 Nobel Prize in Chemistry announcement. www.nobel.se/announcment-97/chemistry97.html (January 5, 1998).

Curriculum vitae, Jens C. Skou. Posted on Aarhus University's web site at http://www.au.dk/uk/sun/biofysik/nobel/cv.htm (January 5, 1998).

The Nobel Prize Internet Archive. "Jens C. Skou." URL: http://www.almaz.com/nobel (January 5, 1998).

—Sketch by Fran Hodgkins

Richard Errett Smalley
1943–
American chemist and physicist

American scientist Richard E. Smalley is best known as one of the winners of the 1996 Nobel Prize for Chemistry, along with fellow Rice University professor **Robert F. Curl, Jr.**, and Briton **Harold W. Kroto** from the University of Sussex, for the discovery of a new carbon molecule, the buckminsterfullerene. It was given that name, or more simply "fullerene," in honor of architect Buckminster Fuller, whose geodesic dome the carbon molecule resembles. A pioneer of supersonic beam laser spectroscopy, Smalley is also renowned for his elaborate supersonic beam experiments, which use lasers to produce and study clusters, aggregates of atoms that occur for a short time under specific conditions. The discovery of fullerenes promises to be the basis for not only a new area of carbon chemistry, but also a way to produce remarkably strong and lightweight materials, new drug delivery systems, computer semiconductors, solar cells, and superconductors.

Smalley was born in Akron, Ohio, on June 6, 1943. Smalley's mother, Esther Virginia Rhoads, was from a furniture manufacturing family. Smalley credits his mother with sparking his interest in science. He spent many hours with her collecting samples from a local pond and looking at them under the microscope. His mother taught him to love literature and nature and the practical skill of mechanical drawing. His father, Frank Dudley Smalley, Jr., was the CEO of a trade journal for farm implements, *Implement and Tractor*. His father taught him machinery repair as well as woodworking. In his autobiogrpahy published on-line through Rice University's web site, Smalley believes that these childhood activities were the perfect preparation for a scientific career.

Several more events inspired Smalley to become a scientist. One was the launching of Sputnik in 1957. Another was his aunt, Dr. Sara Jane Rhoads, who was one of the first women in the United States to achieve a full professorship in chemistry. Smalley used to refer to this bright, active woman as "the Colossus of Rhoads." She encouraged Smalley to study chemistry and one of Smalley's best memories is of working in her organic chemistry laboratory at the University of Wyoming.

Learns Real-World Applications of Chemistry

Smalley's aunt also encouraged him to attend Hope College in Holland, Michigan, which was known for its undergraduate programs in chemistry. Smalley spent two years at Hope College but decided to transfer to the University of Michigan after one favorite professor died and another retired. When Smalley graduated in 1965, he decided to take a job rather than go directly to graduate school. He worked for three years at Shell Chemical Company's polypropylene manufacturing plant and at their Plastics Technical Center in Woodbury, New Jersey. There Smalley learned what he called in his autobiography "real-world applications of chemistry." It was also there that Smalley met his wife, Judith Grace Sampieri, a secretary for Shell. They were married on May 4, 1968.

Smalley enjoyed his work at Shell but he knew it was time to begin graduate school. His graduate school prospects became entangled with several near misses in the Vietnam War draft. He was close to accepting an offer from the University of Wisconsin when he discovered that graduate students were no longer automatically deferred from the draft. His industrial deferment was still valid, so he decided to stay at Shell. However, that deferment eventually expired, so he decided to reapply to graduate school anyway and take his chances. He applied to Princeton University because his wife's family lived there. In the fall of 1968 he was in fact drafted, but within a week of that event, his wife became pregnant and he was reclassified. The Smalley's son Chad Richard was born on June 9, 1969.

That fall the Smalleys moved to Princeton, New Jersey, and Smalley began his Ph.D. work. Here Smalley learned a concentrated style of research as well as chemical physics and molecular systems. In 1973 Smalley began his postdoctoral research with Professor Don Levy at the University of Chicago. Part of his oral exam was three original research proposals; in researching topics, Smalley became interested in the work of Nobel Prize winner **Yuan Lee** and Stuart Rice. Yuan Lee had built a universal molecular beam apparatus and had used it to slow down molecules. This was the germ of Smalley's future Nobel Prize-winning work. His collaboration with Don Levy on supercooled molecules led to supersonic beam laser spectroscopy. This technology allowed scientists to examine molecules with the kind of detail only achieved before on atoms.

Smalley became an assistant professor in the chemistry department of Rice University in Houston, Texas, in 1976. He was aware of Rice University professor Robert Curl's work with laser spectroscopy and had wanted to collaborate with him. Smalley's first work was building a supersonic beam apparatus similar to one he had used at the University of Chicago. His first proposal to the National Science Foundation was for a larger apparatus that would allow him to increase the beam's intensity and be able to study a larger variety of molecules.

Interruption Leads to Discovery of "Buckyballs"

At the same time Smalley was using his laser apparatus to examine molecules, a professor at Sussex University in England, Harold Kroto, was researching chains of carbons in space. Kroto thought these chains might be the products of red-giant stars, but was not sure how the chains actually formed. In 1984, Kroto traveled to the United States to use Smalley's beam apparatus. He thought that he could use the machine to simulate the temperatures in space needed to form the carbon chains. Smalley and Curl had had no reason to look at simple carbon in their complex laser apparatus. It was something of a favor as well as a break in their research when Kroto asked them to look at carbon in order to verify his research. So that September, the scientists turned the laser beam on a piece of graphite and found something they were not looking for, a molecule that had 60 carbon atoms. Carbon had previously been known to have only two molecular forms, diamond and graphite. They surmised correctly that this was a third form of carbon and that it had a cage-like structure resembling a soccer ball, or a geodesic dome. They named the structure buckminsterfullerene, which later became known as fullerene, and also by the nickname "buckyball."

Evidence for the existence of large carbon clusters had existed before, but Smalley, Curl, and Kroto were the first scientists to fully identify and stabilize carbon-60. In October of 1996, all three were recognized for this remarkable discovery with the Nobel Prize in Chemistry.

Fullerene research took off quickly, and today scientists can manufacture pounds of buckyballs in a day. Extraordinarily stable because of their molecular structure and resistant to radiation and chemical destruction, fullerenes have many potential uses.

Smalley's research group is now looking at the tubular versions of fullerenes. In his autobiography Smalley writes that he is "convinced that major new technologies will be developed over the coming decades from fullerene tubes, fibers, and cables, and we are moving as fast as possible to bring this all to life."

SELECTED WRITINGS BY SMALLEY:

Periodicals

"Lasers, Supersonic Beams, NO₂, and New Possibilities for Molecular Spectroscopy," National Meeting of the Division of Electron and Atomic Physics of the American Physical Society (invited paper), 1974.

(With T. Guo and C. Jin) "Doping Bucky: Formation and Properties of Boron-Doped Buckminsterfullerene," *Journal of Physical Chemistry*, 1991.

(With D.M. Poirier, T.R. Ohno, G.H. Kroll, Y. Chen, P.J. Benning, J.H. Weaver, and L.P.F. Chibante) "Formation of Fullerides and Fullerene-Based Heterostructure," *Science*, 1991.

(With A.P. Ramirez, R.C. Haddon, O. Zhou, R.M. Fleming, J. Zhang, and S.M. McClure) "Magnetic Susceptibility of Molecular Carbon: Nanotubes and Fullerite," *Science*, 1994.

"Solar Generation of the Fullerenes." *Journal of Physical Chemistry* 97, 1994.

"Discovering the Fullerenes" Nobel Lecture, *Reviews of Modern Physics*, 1997.

(With J.Liu, H.J. Dai, J.H. Hafner, D.T. Colbert S.J. Tans and C. Dekker) "Fullerene Crop Circles" *Nature*, 1997.

FURTHER READING:

Periodicals

Nash, Madeleine. "SCIENCE: Great Balls of Carbon." *Time* (May, 6 1991).

Wu, Corinna. "Buckyballs Bounce into Nobel History." *Science News*, Vol. 150 (October 19, 1996): 247.

Zimmer, Carl. "Buckyballs From Space." *Discover Magazine* (August 1, 1996).

Other

"Chemistry, physics Nobel winners announced." *CNN Interactive.* 1996. http://cnn.com/WORLD/9610/09/nobel.physics/index.html (December 17, 1997).

"Richard E. Smalley." Rice Chemistry Department. http://pchem1.rice.edu/FacultyStaff/Smalley.html (December 17, 1997).

—*Sketch by Pamela Proffitt*

Solomon H. Snyder

Solomon H. Snyder
1938–

American neuroscientist

Solomon H. Snyder is best known for his work in locating opiate receptors in the human brain and isolating opiate-like substances made by the body. It is for this achievement that he shared the 1978 Albert Lasker Medical Research Award for basic research, one of the most prestigious prizes in medicine. However, Snyder's contributions extend to many other areas of neuroscience as well, including the development of techniques to study receptors, the identification of a protein that plays a role in odor detection, the demonstration of adult brain cell reproduction in the lab, and the discovery of what may be a novel class of neurotransmitters. In a *Scientific American* profile, author Marguerite Holloway described Snyder as "one of the country's most prolific and creative neuroscientists."

Solomon Halbert Snyder was the second of five children. He was born on December 26, 1938, in Washington, D.C. His father, Samuel Simon Snyder, was a cryptanalyst for the National Security Agency who helped break enemy codes during World War II. Later his father pioneered the use of computers for code-breaking. His mother, Patricia Yakerson Snyder, was a real estate broker and avid contest participant. When Snyder was just nine years old, his father taught

him to program computers. As a teenager, though, he was more interested in reading, writing, and philosophy than science. He was also a serious student of classical guitar, and his parents suggested that he attend a music conservatory after high school. He chose to train for a medical career, however, partly because many of his friends wanted to become doctors, and partly because he was attracted to the writings of Sigmund Freud.

Rises Quickly From Intern to Laboratory Director

In 1955, Snyder enrolled in the premedical program at Georgetown University in Washington, D.C. Three years later, he was admitted to Georgetown Medical School, before he had even completed a bachelor's degree. He received his M.D. degree in 1962, when he was just 23 years old. He spent the next year as an intern at the Kaiser Foundation Hospital in San Francisco. Then starting in 1963, Snyder worked for two years at the National Institute of Mental Health as a research associate in the laboratory of Nobel Prize-winner **Julius Axelrod**. In the preface to *Biological Aspects of Mental Disorder*, Snyder later recalled that he took this position "largely in an effort to avoid the doctor draft. However, working in the stimulating environment of this Nobel laureate's laboratory addicted me to the basic research enterprise. Research in a laboratory at the forefront was vastly different from the boring science of classes and textbooks." Despite this he was determined to become a psychiatrist, and in 1965, he began a residency in psychiatry at Johns Hopkins Hospital in Baltimore.

Thus began a long and fruitful association with Johns Hopkins University School of Medicine. In 1966, while still a resident, Snyder joined the faculty there as an assistant professor of pharmacology. He quickly rose through the ranks, and since 1980, he has held the position of distinguished service professor in neuroscience, pharmacology, and psychiatry, as well as director of the neuroscience department. Like Axelrod before him, Snyder does not have a permanent staff of researchers in his lab. Instead, he relies on an ever-changing pool of graduate students. Since he gives the training of young scientists high priority, he collaborates on various projects with up to a dozen students at a time. Many ideas for projects come from the students themselves during brainstorming sessions with Snyder. Others come from Snyder's voracious reading habits. As Gina Kolata reported in *The New York Times*, "Snyder says that his secret is to read widely, keeping up with research that seems completely unrelated to studies of the brain, and then to think about ways the findings might apply to the brain."

Collaboration Leads to New Insights into Addiction and Stroke

Snyder's most famous collaboration began in 1972, when he and graduate student Candace Pert embarked on a search for opiate receptors. Scientists at the time assumed that there must be receptors in the brain for heroin and other opiate drugs, but this had never been proven. Such receptors were thought to function as molecular locks, with opiates being the keys that would fit these locks, starting a sequence of events leading up to a feeling of euphoria or a reduction in pain. By devising a technique to study receptors, Snyder and Pert were able to pinpoint the locations of opiate receptors and study the way drugs bind to these sites. In 1973, just nine months after starting their quest, the pair published their findings in *Science*. Their work paved the way for greater understanding of the communication system within the brain, the actions of drugs such as painkillers, and the dynamics of narcotic addiction.

More recently, Snyder and his colleagues launched an investigation into novel neurotransmitters, substances that transmit impulses between nerve cells. They found that a gas called nitric oxide seems to deliver messages from one nerve cell to another, even though it bypasses traditional receptors. Carbon monoxide is another gas that appears to carry messages within the brain, raising the possibility of a whole new class of neurotransmitters. Snyder and his colleagues also showed that nitric oxide may be a critical link in the chain of biochemical events that leads to brain cell death after a stroke.

Snyder has been married to psychotherapist Elaine Borko since June 10, 1962. The couple have two grown daughters, Judith and Deborah. Snyder still plays classical guitar, and he swims every morning before work. He is also actively involved in his synagogue. Writing in *The New York Times*, Kolata described Snyder as "soft-spoken" and "self-effacing." Yet she noted that "in his quarter of a century in science Dr. Snyder has made some breathtaking discoveries about how the brain works."

SELECTED WRITINGS BY SNYDER:

Books

(Editor) *Perspectives in Neuropharmacology: A Tribute to Julius Axelrod.* New York: Oxford University Press, 1972.
Madness and the Brain. New York: McGraw, 1974.
(With Steven Matthysse) *Opiate Receptor Mechanisms: Neurochemical and Neurophysiological Processes in Opiate Drug Action and Addiction.* Cambridge, MA: MIT Press, 1975.
The Troubled Mind: A Guide to Release from Distress. New York: McGraw, 1976.
Biological Aspects of Mental Disorder. New York: Oxford University Press, 1980.

Periodicals

(With Candace B. Pert) "Opiate Receptor: Demonstration in Nervous Tissue." *Science* (March 1973): 1011-1014.

Other

"Neurotransmitters, Second Messengers and Drug Action in the Nervous System." http://www.med.jhu.edu/neurosci/web_text_neurosci-PRIMARY-SNYDER.html (October 10, 1997).

FURTHER READING:

Books

Graham, Judith, ed. *Current Biography Yearbook 1996.* New York: H.W. Wilson, 1996, pp. 523-527.

Periodicals

Holloway, Marguerite. "The Reward of Ideas That Are Wrong." *Scientific American* (August 1991): 29-30.
Kolata, Gina. "Brain Researcher Makes It Look Easy." *The New York Times.* 25 May 1993, C: 1, 8.
Stutz, Christine. "Master of Science: Inside the Mind of Sol Snyder." *Baltimore Jewish Times.* December 27, 1996.

Other

"New Discovery May Offer Protection Against Stroke." September 30, 1997. http://hopkins.med.jhu.edu/NewsMedia/news.release.html (October 10, 1997). This Web site includes several press releases and news reports from Johns Hopkins Medicine about Snyder's research.

—*Sketch by Linda Wasmer Smith*

Roger W. Sperry
1913–1994
American psychobiologist

Roger W. Sperry, a major contributor to at least three scientific fields—developmental neurobiology, experimental psychobiology, and human split-brain studies—conducted pioneering research in the functions of the left and right hemispheres of the brain. He was awarded the Nobel Prize for physiology or

Roger W. Sperry

medicine in 1981 for his work. The system of split-brain research that he created has enabled scientists to better understand the workings of the human brain.

Sperry was born on August 20, 1913, in Hartford, Connecticut, to Francis Bushnell Sperry, a banker, and Florence Kramer Sperry. When Sperry was 11 years old, his father died and his mother returned to school and got a job as an assistant to a high school principal. Sperry attended local public schools through high school and then went to Oberlin College in Ohio on a scholarship. There, he competed on the track team and was captain of the basketball squad. Although he majored in English, Sperry was especially interested in his undergraduate psychology courses with R. H. Stetson, an expert on the physiology of speech. Sperry earned his B.A. in English in 1935 and then worked as a graduate assistant to Stetson for two years. In 1937 he received an M.A. in psychology.

Thoroughly committed to research in the field of psychobiology by that time, Sperry went to the University of Chicago to conduct research on the organization of the central nervous system under the renowned biologist Paul Weiss. Before Weiss's research, scientists believed that the connections of the nervous system had to be very exact to work properly. Weiss disproved this theory by surgically crossing a subject's nerve connections. After the surgery was performed, the subject's behavior did not change. From this, Weiss concluded that the connections of the central nervous system were not predetermined,

so that a nerve need not connect to any particular location to function correctly.

Challenges Mentor's Theories

Sperry tested Weiss's research by surgically crossing the nerves that controlled the hind leg muscles of a rat. Under Weiss's theory, each nerve should eventually "learn" to control the leg muscle to which it was now connected. This did not happen. When the left hind foot was stimulated, the right foot responded instead. Sperry's experiments disproved Weiss's research and became the basis of his doctoral dissertation, "Functional results of crossing nerves and transposing muscles in the fore and hind limbs of the rat." He received a Ph.D. in Zoology from the University of Chicago in 1941.

Sperry did other related experiments that confirmed his findings and further contradicted Weiss's theory that "function precedes form" (that is, the brain and nervous system learn, through experience, to function properly). In one experiment, Sperry rotated a frog's eyeball and cut its optic nerve. If Weiss's theory was correct, the frog would reeducate itself, adjust to seeing the world upside down, and change its behavior accordingly. This did not happen. In fact, the nerve fibers became tangled in the scar tissue during healing. When the nerve regenerated, it ignored the repositioning of the eyeball and reattached itself correctly, albeit upside down. From this and other experiments, Sperry deduced that genetic mechanisms determine some basic behavioral patterns. According to his theory, nerves have highly specific functions based on genetically predetermined differences in the concentration of chemicals inside the nerve cells.

In 1941, Sperry moved to the laboratory of the renowned psychologist Karl S. Lashley at Harvard to work as a National Research Council postdoctoral fellow. A year later, Lashley became director of the Yerkes Laboratories of Primate Biology in Orange Park, Florida. Sperry joined him there on a Harvard biology research fellowship. While there, he disproved some Gestalt psychology theories about brain mechanisms, as well as some theories of Lashley's.

During World War II, Sperry fulfilled his military service duty by working for three years in an Office of Scientific Research and Development (OSRD) medical research project run by the University of Chicago and the Yerkes laboratory. His work involved research on repairing nerve injuries by surgery. In 1946, Sperry returned to the University of Chicago to accept a position as assistant professor in the school's anatomy department. He became associate professor of psychology during the 1952–53 school year and also worked during that year as section chief in the Neurological Diseases and

Blindness division of the National Institutes of Health.

In 1954, he transferred to the California Institute of Technology (Caltech) to take a position as the Hixon Professor of Psychobiology. At Caltech, Sperry conducted research on split-brain functions that he had first investigated when he worked at the Yerkes Laboratory. It had long been known that the cerebrum of the brain consists of two hemispheres. In most people the left hemisphere controls the right side of the body and vice versa. The two halves are connected by a bundle of millions of nerve fibers called the corpus callosum, or the great cerebral commissure.

Neurosurgeons had discovered that this connection could be cut into with little or no noticeable change in the patient's mental abilities. After experiments on animals proved the procedure to be harmless, surgeons began cutting completely through the commissure of epileptic patients in an attempt to prevent the spread of epileptic seizures from one hemisphere to the other. The procedure was generally successful, and beginning in the late 1930s, cutting through the forebrain commissure became an accepted treatment method for severe epilepsy. Observations of the split-brain patients indicated no loss of communication between the two hemispheres of the brain.

From these observations, scientists assumed that the corpus callosum had no function other than as a prop to prevent the two hemispheres from sagging. Scientists also believed that the left hemisphere was dominant and performed higher cognitive functions such as speech. This theory developed from observations of patients whose left cerebral hemisphere had been injured; these patients suffered impairment of various cognitive functions, including speech. Since these functions were not transferred over to the uninjured right hemisphere, scientists assumed that the right hemisphere was less developed.

Discovers Role of Right Brain

Sperry's work shattered these views. He and his colleagues at Caltech discovered that the corpus callosum is more than a physical prop; it provides a means of communication between the two halves of the brain and integrates the knowledge acquired by each of them. They also learned that in many ways, the right hemisphere is superior to the left. Although the left half of the brain is superior in analytic, logical thought, the right half excels in intuitive processing of information. The right hemisphere also specializes in non-verbal functions, such as understanding music, interpreting visual patterns (such as recognizing faces), and sorting sizes and shapes.

Sperry discovered these different capacities of the two cerebral hemispheres through a series of experiments performed over a period of several decades. In one such experiment, Sperry and a graduate student, Ronald Myers, cut the nerve connections between the two hemispheres of a cat's brain. They discovered that behavioral responses learned by the left side of the brain were not transferred to the right, and vice versa. In an article published in *Scientific American* in 1964, Sperry observed that "it was as though each hemisphere were a separate mental domain operating with complete disregard—indeed, with a complete lack of awareness—of what went on in the other. The split-brain animal behaved in the test situation as if it had two entirely separate brains." It was evident from this experiment that the severed nerves had been responsible for communication between the two halves of the brain.

In another experiment on a human subject, he showed a commissurotomy patient (one whose corpus callosum had been surgically severed) a picture of a pair of scissors. Only the patient's left visual field, which is governed by the nonverbal right hemisphere, could see the scissors. The patient could not verbally describe what he had seen because the left hemisphere, which controls language functions, had not received the necessary information. However, when the patient reached behind a screen, he sorted through a pile of various items and picked out the scissors. When asked how he knew the correct item, the patient insisted it was purely luck.

Sperry started published technical papers on his split-brain findings in the late 1960s. The importance of his research was recognized relatively quickly, and in 1979 he was awarded the prestigious Albert Lasker Basic Medical Research Award, which included a $15,000 grant. The award was given in recognition of the potential medical benefits of Sperry's research, including possible treatments for mental or psychosomatic illnesses.

Awarded Nobel Prize for Split-Brain Studies

Two years later, Sperry was honored with the 1981 Nobel Prize in physiology or medicine. He shared it with two other scientists, **Torsten N. Wiesel** and **David H. Hubel**, for research on the central nervous system and the brain. In describing Sperry's work, the Nobel Prize selection committee praised the researcher for demonstrating the difference between the two hemispheres of the brain and for outlining some of the specialized functions of the right brain. The committee, as quoted in the *New York Times,* stated that Sperry's work illuminated the fact that the right brain "is clearly superior to the left in many respects, especially regarding the capacity for concrete thinking, spatial consciousness and comprehension of complex relationships."

In his acceptance speech, as quoted in *Science* in 1982, Sperry talked about the significance of his discovery of the previously unrecognized skills of the nonverbal right half-brain. He commented that an important gain from his work is increased attention to "the important role of the nonverbal components and forms of the intellect." Because split-brain research increased appreciation of the individuality of each brain and its functions, Sperry believed that his work helped to point out the need for educational policies that took into consideration varying types of intelligence and potential.

Sperry rejected conventional scientific thinking that viewed human consciousness solely as a function of physical and chemical activity within the brain. In his view, which he discussed in his Nobel Prize lecture, "cognitive introspective psychology and related cognitive science can no longer be ignored experimentally. . . . The whole world of inner experience (the world of the humanities) long rejected by twentieth-century scientific materialism, thus becomes recognized and included within the domain of science."

Known as a private, reserved person, Sperry was, quite characteristically, camping with his wife in a remote area when the news of his Nobel Prize award was announced. He had married Norma Gay Deupree in 1949, and they had two children, Glenn Tad and Janet Hope. In addition to camping, Sperry's avocational interests included sculpture, drawing, ceramics, folk dancing, and fossil hunting. He retired from Caltech in 1984 as Professor Emeritus. In 1989, Sperry was awarded a National Medal of Science. He died in Pasadena.

In addition to the Nobel prize, Sperry received many awards and honorary doctorates. He was member of many scientific societies, including the Pontifical Academy of Sciences and the National Academy of Sciences. Sperry was always held in high regard by his students. One of them, Michael Gazzaniga, described him in *Science* as "exceedingly generous" to many students at Caltech. Gazzaniga also defined Sperry as a teacher "constitutionally only able to be interested in critical issues," who drove his "herd of young scientists to consider nothing but the big questions."

SELECTED WRITINGS BY SPERRY:

Books

Problems Outstanding in the Evolution of Brain Function. New York: American Museum of Natural History, 1964.
Science and Moral Priority: Merging Mind, Brain, and Human Values. New York: Columbia University, 1983.

Periodicals

"The Great Commisure." *Scientific American* (January 1964).

"Mental Unity Following Surgical Disconnection of the Cerebral Hemispheres." *Harvey Lectures* 62 (1968): 293–322.

FURTHER READING:

Books

Wasson, Tyler, ed. *Nobel Prize Winners.* New York: H. W. Wilson, 1987.
Weintraub, Pamela. *The Omni Interviews.* New York: Ticknor & Fields, 1984.

Periodicals

"Brain Mappers Win a Nobel Prize." *Newsweek* (19 October 1981): 110.
Gazzaniga, Michael S. "1981 Nobel Prize for Physiology or Medicine." *Science* (30 October 1981): 517–18.
———. "The Nobel Prizes." *Scientific American* (December 1981): 80.
Heise, Kenan. "Roger Sperry, 80; Studied Functions of Human Brain" (obituary). *Chicago Tribune.* (23 April 1994): 15.
Oliver, Myrna. "Roger Sperry, Nobel Prize Winner, Dies" (obituary). *Washington Post* (19 April 1994): 22.
Pearson, Richard. "Roger Sperry, Nobel Prize Winner, Dies" (obituary). *Washington Post.* (20 April 1994): B4.
Puente, Antonio E. "Roger Sperry" (obituary). *American Psychologist* 50 (1 November 1995): 940–41.
Schmeck, Harold M., Jr. "Three Scientists Share Nobel Prize for Studies on the Brain." *New York Times* (10 October 1981): 1; 50–51.
Sperry, Roger W. "Nobel Prize Lecture." *Science* (24 September 1982).
Wade, Nicholas. "Roger Sperry, A Nobel Winner for Brain Studies, Dies at 80" (obituary). *New York Times* (20 April 1994): D27.

—*Sketch by Donna Olshansky*

Lyman Spitzer, Jr.
1914–1997
American astrophysicist

Lyman Spitzer, Jr., through his research into galactic structure, made important insights into the understanding of star formation. Through continued investigations into the nature of stars, he pioneered

Lyman Spitzer, Jr.

theoretical research into the techniques of achieving controlled nuclear fusion in a laboratory setting.

Spitzer was born in Toledo, Ohio, on June 26, 1914. He studied at Phillips Academy in Massachusetts before moving on to Yale University, where he received a B.A. in Physics in 1935. He broadened his academic development as a Henry fellow, spending a year in Cambridge, England, studying with Sir **Arthur Stanley Eddington**. After returning to the United States, Spitzer worked with **Henry Norris Russell** at Princeton where he received his Ph.D. in astrophysics in 1938. He immediately obtained a National Research Council fellowship for a year of study at Harvard after which he returned to Yale as an instructor in physics and astronomy. As was the case with many young Americans, Spitzer's fast-rising career was interrupted by World War II. From 1942 to 1946, he supervised projects at Columbia University in underwater warfare research, including the development of sonar. When the war ended, Spitzer continued at Yale for a year or so. In 1947 he moved to Princeton, where he became the chair of the astronomy department. He was later appointed Charles A. Young Professor in 1951 and elected to the National Academy of Sciences in 1952.

By 1950, with the disruptions and distractions of war behind them, astronomers were poised for a new leap forward in knowledge. Helping them was the massive new 200-inch (508-cm) Hale telescope on Mount Palomar, which had just come on line in 1949

and promised to deliver a treasure trove of new data for scientists to ponder. Also, theories concerning the expansion of the universe in the first half of the century and more recent work on the process of stellar evolution both served to help knit the sum of astronomical progress into an emerging, coherent "story." What was missing was an understanding of how stars formed in the first place.

It was apparent from studies of the Milky Way and nearby spiral galaxies that hot, massive stars seemed to be generated almost constantly from within the spiral arms. Calculations verified that the massive stars burned their fuel at so furious a rate that they could only live for a few tens of millions of years, a short time by cosmic standards, before burning themselves out. The fact that astronomers could observe these brilliant stars at all meant that some process was continually at work replacing the burned out stars with new ones. The arms of spiral galaxies had the most plentiful abundance of such massive stars, so it became obvious that some feature or attribute of the spiral arms was responsible for star formation. The one major feature that characterizes the spiral arms of galaxies is their large concentration of gas and dust. Lyman Spitzer, along with others, attempted to untangle the mystery of how clouds of gas and dust could combine to form stars.

Spitzer analyzed the characteristics of ionized gas clouds which existed near massive, hot stars and compared them with the cooler regions of interstellar molecular clouds. He found that the hot gas, or plasma, regions exerted a strong thermal pressure, created by temperatures of 10,000 degrees Kelvin. The pressure was sufficient to churn the nearby molecular clouds. This explained the high gas velocities observed in such regions. With instability introduced into an otherwise quiescent gas cloud, the stage was set for the cloud's gravitational collapse and the onset of star formation.

Pioneering Work on Nuclear Fusion Begins

Spitzer analyzed the effects of interstellar magnetic fields on plasma clouds and became one of the leading contributors to the burgeoning field of plasma physics. He calculated that it would be possible to contain hydrogen gas plasma at the incredible temperature of 100 million degrees Kelvin by keeping the plasma within magnetic fields. The trapped, superheated hydrogen would then fuse into helium, releasing a tremendous amount of energy. Indeed, nuclear fusion is the energy source that powers the stars, wherein the tremendous pressure of gravity at the star's core transforms hydrogen into helium at high temperatures. Spitzer's insight was to show how a hydrogen plasma could be fused to produce energy without requiring the presence of a massive star to do it. The implications of this idea, which is nothing less than the creation of energy by controlled thermonuclear fusion, is still being studied in laboratories around the world and stems directly from the work of Spitzer.

Something of the depth of Spitzer's contributions to astronomy and physics can be glimpsed from the numerous awards he received during his long career, including the Rittenhouse Medal of the Franklin Institute in 1957, the Exceptional Science Achievement Medal from NASA in 1972, The Bruce God Medal from the Astronomical Society of the Pacific in 1973, the Henry Draper Medal from the National Academy of Sciences in 1974, the James Clerk Maxwell Prize from the American Physics Society in 1975, the Distinguished Public Service Medal from NASA in 1976, the Gold Medal of the Royal Astronomical Society in 1978, the Jules Janssen Medal from the Société Astronomique de France in 1980, and the Franklin Medal from the Franklin Institute in 1980.

Spitzer also speculated on the possibility of artificial, earth-orbiting satellites and telescopes . As head of the Princeton University Observatory, he was among the first to promote the use of rockets for scientific research. Princeton played a leading part in his endeavor with programs designed to perform studies using high-altitude balloons and rockets. The critical role that orbiting observatories play in current astronomical research is testimony to Spitzer's vision. Lyman Spitzer Jr. died March 31, 1997, at his home in Princeton, New Jersey. The 82-year-old had suffered from heart disease.

SELECTED WRITINGS BY SPITZER:

Books

Physics of Fully Ionized Gases. New York: Interscience Publishers, 1956.
Diffuse Matter in Space. New York: Interscience Publishers, 1968.
Physical Processes in the Interstellar Medium. New York: Wiley, 1978.
Searching between the Stars. New Haven, CT: Yale University Press, 1982.
Dynamical Evolution of Globular Clusters. Princeton, NJ: Princeton University Press, 1987.

FURTHER READING:

Periodicals

Saxon, Wolfgang. "Lyman Spitzer, Jr., Dies at 82; Inspired Hubble Telescope" (obituary). *New York Times* (2 April 1997): A19.

—*Sketch by Jeffery Bass*

Richard Stanley

Richard Stanley
1944–
American mathematician

Richard Stanley is a pioneer in the field of combinatorics, a specialty not highly regarded when Stanley was emerging as a mathematician, but one that has gained greater acceptance throughout his career. His *Enumerative Combinatorics,* which is based on concepts presented in commutative algebra, homological algebra and algebraic topology, is one of the seminal texts in this area.

Stanley was born in New York City on June 23, 1944, to Alan Stanley, a chemical engineer, and Shirley Stanley, a homemaker. Stanley did not remain in New York City long, spending his early childhood in Tahawus, New York, a city that was later moved to another location building by building. During his time in Tahawus, he explains in a document on his early years available on his World Wide Web site on the Internet, he dreamed of being a ventriloquist. As an adolescent, then living in Lynchburg, Virginia, he set his sights on astronomy, which triggered his interest in mathematics as well. He credits an elderly resident of Lynchburg—who taught him the standard synthetic algorithm for finding the square root of a positive real number—with getting him started. Around the same time, he also began to read the mathematics section of his father's *Handbook of Chemistry and*

Physics, which detailed the cube root algorithm. Just before his family's move to Savannah, Georgia, when the younger Stanley was 13, he shifted his interest from astronomy to nuclear physics until he met a classmate who was working on determining synthetic algorithms for finding roots higher than the cubic. His interest was piqued, and he began to read widely on mathematical topics in addition to his high school mathematics courses. Stanley often worked independently of his classmates since only basic courses were available at his school.

Stanley earned his Bachelor of Science degree in mathematics in 1966 from the California Institute of Technology and went on to receive a Ph.D. in mathematics from Harvard University in 1971, with G.C. Rota, a professor at the Massachusetts Institute of Technology (MIT), as his thesis advisor. He also worked as the C.L.E. Moore Instructor of Mathematics at MIT in the final year of his Ph.D. program. While at Harvard, Stanley met his wife Doris, who became a French teacher. The Stanleys have two children.

After receiving his Ph.D., Stanley conducted postdoctoral studies through a Miller Research Fellowship at the Berkeley campus of the University of California. In 1973, he returned to MIT as an assistant professor in mathematics and, in 1979 was named a full professor of applied mathematics, eventually serving as chair of the Applied Mathematics Committee. He relinquished that post when he accepted a visiting professor position at Berkeley, where he spent a year as the Chern Visiting Professor in the Mathematical Sciences Research Institute, over which Stanley served as chair from 1993 to 1997. Stanley also spent a year as a visiting professor at the University of California at San Diego for the 1978–79 academic year.

Stanley has held other visiting professor positions across the world, including short stints at the University of Stockholm, University of Augsburg, and Tokai University in Japan. In addition, Stanley spent a semester as the Göran Gustafsson Professor at the Royal Institute of Technology and the Institute Mittag–Leffler in Sweden in 1992. He was recruited for this position by Anders Björner, one of Sweden's leading mathematicians, for whom Stanley had served as an advisor when Björner spent time at MIT as a visiting student.

Among his awards and honors, Stanley received a Guggenheim Fellowship in 1983, which he used to fund research on reduced combinatorics. He has published widely on the topic of combinatorics, including authoring the definitive text on the topic, *Enumerative Combinatorics*. As of 1997, he was at work on a second volume of *Enumerative Combinatorics*, which he had spent 11 years researching at that time. In addition to teaching, Stanley works as a consultant for Bell Telephone Laboratories in Murray Hill, New Jersey, and serves on editorial boards for several prestigious mathematical journals, including the *Journal on Algebraic and Discrete Methods*, *Studies in Applied Mathematics*, and *PanAmerican Mathematics*.

In an interview with Kristin Palm, Stanley discussed the qualities that drew him to his profession. "To me it's just a very elegant, beautiful structure. It's been developed for thousands of years. You can go exploring on your own with it and add to it," he explained.

SELECTED WRITINGS BY STANLEY:

Combinatorics and Commutative Algebra, second edition, 1996.
Enumerative Combinatorics, 1986.

FURTHER READING:

Richard Stanley. http://www–math.mit.edu/~rstan (August 26, 1997).

Other

Stanley, Richard, in an interview with Kristin Palm, conducted July 11, 1997.

—Sketch by Kristin Palm

Joan Argetsinger Steitz
1941–
American biochemist and geneticist

Joan Steitz is an American biochemist and geneticist, best known for her discovery of small nuclear ribonucleoproteins or snRNPs, which play an important role in converting the information encoded in mammalian DNA into instructions for building protein molecules. Her work has led to a deeper understanding of the way in which genetic transcription and translation is controlled.

Joan Argetsinger Steitz was born on January 26, 1941, in Minneapolis, Minnesota. Her father, Glenn Davis Argetsinger, a high school guidance counselor, and her mother, Elaine Magnusson Argetsinger, a speech pathologist, encouraged her to pursue her intellectual interests, and she developed an interest in science at an early age. Steitz attended Antioch College, in Yellow Springs, Ohio, and received a bachelor of science degree in chemistry in 1963. In addition to her college chemistry studies, she had taken classes in molecular genetics, a field that was undergoing rapid development as a result of the 1953 discovery of the double helical structure of the deoxyribonucleic (DNA) molecule. **James Watson**, **Francis Crick**, and **Maurice Wilkins** had received the 1962 Nobel Prize in Medicine for this important work. Two of these three laureates were soon to become her mentors.

Under the direction of James Watson at Harvard University, Steitz received a Ph.D. in 1967. Her graduate research centered on the *in vitro* assembly of R17, a ribonucleic acid bacteriophage (a type of virus that attacks bacteria). This research led to a better understanding of how the protein and nucleic-acid components of viruses interact. From 1967 till 1970, Steitz pursued post-doctoral studies under the direction of Francis Crick, at the Medical Research Council Laboratory of Molecular Biology, in Cambridge, England. There, her research focused on the way in which bacterial ribosomes, intracellular organelles that play a role in building proteins within the cell, locate themselves on messenger ribonucleic acid (RNA), the molecule that carries the protein building instructions from a cell's nucleus to its cytoplasm.

In 1970, Steitz returned to the United States, accepting an assistant professorship in the Department of Molecular Biophysics and Biochemistry at Yale University, in New Haven, Connecticut. Her work in molecular genetics yielded, within the decade, a discovery which she considers her most significant, that of small nuclear ribonucleoproteins or snRNPs (pronounced "snurps"). The intricate molecular process by which the double stranded DNA molecule dictates protein synthesis begins with a step known as transcription. During this step, DNA information is transferred to a single stranded heterogeneous nuclear RNA molecule, called hnRNA. Typically, a DNA molecule contains a vast amount of "nonsense," encoded instructions that are not useful during the process of protein synthesis. The snRNPs that Steitz discovered play a significant role in insuring that this nonsense is removed from the hnRNA. They coordinate a process called RNA splicing, in which the hnRNA molecule is snipped into pieces and its useful parts rejoined. The end result of this splicing is that a messenger RNA molecule is formed.

Steitz has identified many different types of snRNPs and helped to determine how they operate within the nucleus. Currently, she is examining snRNPs that are formed when certain herpes viruses infect their host cells. Her research into the structure and function of snRNPs has already seen direct clinical application, especially in the area of diagnosis and treatment of rheumatic disorders.

Steitz was promoted to full professorship at Yale in 1978, and has been a Henry Ford II Professor there

since 1988. During the 1976-77 academic year, while on sabbatical as a Josiah Macy Scholar, she conducted research at the Max Planck Institute for Biophysical Chemistry in Göttingen, Germany, and at the Medical Council Center Laboratory of Molecular Biology in Cambridge, England. As a Fairchild Distinguished Fellow she spent the 1984-85 academic year on sabbatical at the California Institute of Technology in Pasadena.

The list of scientific honors that have been bestowed upon Steitz is extensive, beginning in 1975 with the Passano Foundation Young Scientist Award, and followed in 1976 by the Eli Lilly Award in Biological Chemistry. In 1982, Steitz received the U.S. Steel Foundation Award in Molecular Biology, and the following year she shared the Lee Hawley, Sr. Award for Arthritis Research with J. A. Hardin and M. R. Lerner. For her pioneering work on snRNPs, President Ronald Reagan presented her with the National Medal of Science in 1986. She received the Radcliffe Graduate Society Medal for Distinguished Achievement in 1987, and the Dickson Prize for Science, from Carnegie Mellon University, in 1988. Steitz shared the Warren Triennial Prize with Thomas R. Cech in 1989, and in 1992 she received the Christopher Columbus Discovery Award in Biomedical Research. The Antioch College Alumni Association presented her with the Rebecca Rice Award for Distinguished Achievement in 1993. Steitz considers one of her greatest honors to be the Weizman Women and Science Award, which she received in 1994. In 1996, she received the Distinguished Service Award at the Miami Bio-Technology Winter Symposium, as well as the City of Medicine Award.

Steitz has been granted honorary doctoral degrees from various academic institutions, including Lawrence University, the University of Rochester School of Medicine, Mount Sinai School of Medicine, Trinity College, and Harvard University. She has served on the editorial boards of several of the leading journals in the field of genetics and is a member of the National Academy of Sciences, the American Philosophical Society, and the American Academy of Arts and Sciences. She became the director of the Jane Coffin Childs Memorial Fund for Medical Research, a fund that supports post-doctoral fellows, in 1991. Steitz is married to a fellow scientist, with whom she has one son.

FURTHER READING:

Books

Shearer, Benjamin F., and Barbara S. Shearer. *Notable Women in the Life Sciences.* Westport: Greenwood Press, 1996.

—*Sketch by Leslie Reinherz*

George R. Stibitz
1904–1995

American mathematician and computer scientist

George R. Stibitz joined the Bell Telephone Laboratories as a mathematical engineer in 1930. His work at Bell Labs convinced him of the need to develop techniques for handling a large number of complex mathematical operations much more quickly than was currently possible with traditional manual systems. His research eventually led to the development of one of the first binary computers ever built. Stibitz was also the first to transmit computer data long-distance. Later in his life the mathematician became especially interested in the application of mathematics and the computer sciences to biomedical problems.

George Robert Stibitz was born on April 20, 1904, in York, Pennsylvania. His mother was the former Mildred Amelia Murphy, a math teacher before her marriage, and his father was George Stibitz, a professor of theology. Stibitz's childhood was spent in Dayton, Ohio, where his father taught at a local college. Because of the interest in and aptitude for science and engineering that he had exhibited, Stibitz was enrolled at an experimental high school in Dayton established by **Charles Kettering**, inventor of the first automobile ignition system.

For his undergraduate studies, Stibitz enrolled at Denison University in Granville, Ohio. After earning his bachelor of philosophy degree there in 1926, he went on to Union College in Schenectady, New York, where he was awarded his M.S. degree in 1927. After graduating from Union, he worked as a technician at General Electric in Schenectady for one year before returning to Cornell University to begin his doctoral program. Stibitz received his Ph.D. in mathematical physics from Cornell in 1930.

Stibitz's first job after graduation was as a research mathematician at the Bell Telephone Laboratories in New York City. His job there was to work on one of the fundamental problems with which modern telecommunication companies have to deal: How to carry out the endless number of mathematical calculations required to design and operate an increasingly complex system of telephones. At the time, virtually the only tool available to perform these calculations was the desktop mechanical calculator. It was obvious that this device would not long be adequate for the growing demands of the nation's expanding telephone network.

In the fall of 1937 Stibitz made the discovery for which he is now best known, the use of relays for automated computing. A relay is a metallic device that can assume one of two positions—open or closed—when an electrical current passes through it. The relay acts as a kind of gate, therefore, that will control the flow of electrical current, and was a common device used to regulate telephone circuits.

Stibitz Designs the "K-Model" Computing Machine

In November 1937 Stibitz decided to see if relays could be used to perform simple mathematical functions. He borrowed a few of the metal devices from the Bell stockroom, took them home, and assembled a simple computing system on his kitchen table. The system consisted of the relays, a dry cell, flashlight bulbs, and metal strips cut from a tobacco can. He soon had a device in which a lighted bulb represented the binary digit "1" and an unlighted bulb, the binary digit "0." The device was also able to use binary mathematics to add and subtract decimal numbers. Stibitz's colleagues later gave the name "K-Model" to this primitive computer because it was built on his kitchen table.

When Stibitz first demonstrated his K-model computer for company executives, they were not very impressed. "There were no fireworks, no champagne," he was quoted as saying in *The Computer Pioneers.* Less than a year later, however, Bell executives had changed their minds about the Stibitz invention. An important factor in that decision was the increasing pressure on Bell to find a way of solving its increasingly complex mathematical problems. The company agreed to finance construction of a large experimental model of Stibitz's invention. Construction on that machine began in April 1939, and the final product was first put into operation on January 8, 1940. Called the Complex Number Calculator (CNC), the machine had the capacity to add, subtract, multiply, and divide complex numbers—just the kinds of problems that were particularly troublesome for engineers at Bell.

Nine months later, Stibitz recorded another milestone in the history of computer science. At a meeting of the American Mathematical Society at Dartmouth College, he hooked up the new Complex Number Calculator in New York City with a telegraph system. He then sent problems from Dartmouth to the CNC in New York, which solved the problems and sent the answers back to Dartmouth by means of the telegraph. This type of data transmission has now become commonplace in a modern day society of modems and fax machines.

During World War II, Bell Labs permitted Stibitz to join the National Defense Research Council. There the demands of modern military artillery convinced Stibitz even more of the need for improved computer hardware, and he spent most of the war working on improved versions of the CNC, also known as the Model 1. The Model 2 computer, for instance, used punched tapes to store programs that would give the computer instructions; in this manner the computer could perform the same complex calculations many times on different sets of numbers. This proved useful in calculating weapons trajectories.

At the end of World War II, Stibitz decided not to return to Bell Labs. Instead he moved with his family to Vermont where he became a consultant in applied mathematics. After two decades in this line of work Stibitz was offered a job at Dartmouth's Medical School, where he was asked to show how computers can be used to deal with biomedical problems. He accepted that offer and was appointed professor of physiology at Dartmouth; in that capacity he investigated the motion of oxygen in the lungs and the rate at which drugs and nutrients are spread throughout the body. In 1972 he retired from his position and was made professor emeritus; nevertheless, he continued to contribute his knowledge to the department.

Stibitz was married on September 1, 1930, to Dorothea Lamson, with whom he had two daughters, Mary and Martha. Among the awards he has received are the Harry Goode Award of the American Federation for Information Processing (1965), the Piore Award of the Institute of Electrical and Electronic Engineers (1977), and the Babbage Society Medal (1982). He was also the recipient of honorary degrees from Keene State College and Dartmouth College. The holder of 35 patents, Stibitz was named to the Inventors Hall of Fame in 1983. He died in his Hanover, New Hampshire, home on January 31, 1995. He was 90.

SELECTED WRITINGS BY STIBITZ:

Books

Mathematics and Computers. New York: McGraw-Hill, 1957.
Mathematics in Medicine and the Life Sciences. Year Book Medical Publishers, 1966.

FURTHER READING:

Books

Ceruzzi, Paul E. *Reckoners: The Prehistory of the Digital Computer, from Relays to the Stored Program Concept, 1935–1945.* Westport, CT: Greenwood Press, 1983, pp. 78–79.
Cortada, James W. *Historical Dictionary of Data Processing: Biographies.* Westport, CT: Greenwood Press, 1987, pp. 240-42.
Ritchie, David. *The Computer Pioneers: The Making of the Modern Computer.* New York: Simon & Schuster, 1986, pp. 33–52.

George Gabriel Stokes

Periodicals

Loveday, Evelyn. "George Stibitz and the Bell Labs Relay Computer." *Datamation* (September 1977): 80–83.
Saxon, Wolfgang. "Dr. George Stibitz, 90, Inventor of First Digital Computer in '40" (obituary). *New York Times* (2 February 1995): B11.

—*Sketch by David E. Newton*

George Gabriel Stokes
1819–1903
British mathematical physicist

Sir George Gabriel Stokes made important advances in the fields of hydrodynamics and optics. He also did significant work in wave theory, as well as the elasticity and light diffraction of solids. With his work on viscous fluids, he helped develop the theoretical foundation for the science of hydrodynamics. These equations, known as the Navier–Stokes equations (he shared credit with Claude Navier) describe the motion of viscous fluids. The word "fluorescence" entered the English language when Stokes first used it to explain his conclusions about the blue light emitting from the surface of colorless, transparent solutions. He then applied the phenomena of fluorescence to study light spectra. An important practical use for fluorescence was in the pharmacy, where British chemists used it—instead of relying on the availability of sunlight—to tell the difference among chemicals. Stokes is also considered a pioneer in scientific geodesy (publishing a major work on the variation of gravity at the Earth's surface in 1849), and spectrum analysis. In 1849, he assumed the Lucasian chair at Cambridge University, which he held until his death. Stokes was also very active in various scientific and academic societies. He served as president of the Cambridge Philosophical Society from 1859 to 1861, and was president of the Royal Society of London from 1885 to 1890. In 1887, he became a member of Parliament, representing the University of Cambridge, serving until 1891. The Royal Society awarded Stokes the Rumford Medal in 1852 for his work with fluorescence; he was also awarded the Copley Medal in 1893. His scientific contributions were recognized by a knighthood in 1889.

Stokes was born in Skreen, County Sligo, Ireland, on August 13, 1819. His family was of Anglo–Irish extraction, whose forebears included many clergy in the Church of Ireland. His father, Gabriel, was rector in Skreen, and his mother, Elizabeth Haughton Stokes, was the daughter of a rector. Stokes was the youngest of six children. He was educated by his father as a young boy, later attending a Dublin school. He went to Bristol College in England to prepare for university.

Begins Long Tenure at Cambridge

In 1837, he entered Pembroke College, Cambridge, to study mathematics. He graduated in 1841, winning senior Wrangler and 1st Smith's prizeman academic honors. He was given a fellowship at Pembroke and remained at Cambridge the rest of his life. His appointment as Lucasian professor coincided with teaching at the Government School of Mines in London, which he did to increase his income—his Cambridge position being poorly endowed at that time. He married Mary Susanna Robinson in 1857, giving up his fellowship to marry, as was the custom at that time. They became the parents of three children, two sons and a daughter. He was able to regain a fellowship in 1859 when a change in University rules regarding married professors was made.

Introduces Advances in Hydrodynamics

Pure mathematics was never the sole focus of Stokes' inquiry—his experimental work was equally important. For him, theory was placed in the service of answering specific physical questions, and his mathematical papers reflect his interest in developing problem–solving methods or proving out existing formulas. His investigations into hydrodynamics led

him to test out and publish his theories on the internal friction of fluids. Although French physicists (Claude Navier in particular) had already done work in this area, Stokes introduced new applications for their mathematical equations. In 1846, he presented a paper on hydrodynamic advances to the British Association for the Advancement of Science, which greatly enhanced his reputation. Later hydrodynamic experiments involved a study of the propagation of oscillatory waves in water, and led to a method of calculating their shape.

In 1850, Stokes published a major paper on hydrodynamics that included Stokes' Law governing the fall of an object through a liquid, using the action of pendulums to test out his fluid theories. Based on his observations, and also using the experiments conducted by others in the field, he was able to explain how clouds formed in the atmosphere. These conclusions, combined with his studies on surface gravity, caused Stokes to be regarded in England as an authority on the emerging science of geodesy. In 1854 he published Stokes' Theorem, a three–dimensional generalization of Green's Theorem in vector calculus.

To compliment his study of hydrodynamics, Stokes also delved into the principles of sound. He analyzed how sound was produced and the effect of wind on its intensity. Using this information, he explained why stringed instruments required sounding boards in order to transmit sound. Stokes also explained how sound is produced through telegraph wires.

Examines Concept of Light Propagation

The wave theory of light also captured Stokes' attention. His early mathematical studies revolved around the nature of ether—then a concept for explaining how light is propagated. Although he attempted to work around conceptual flaws by connecting his work on elastic solids to the properties of ether, its existence was eventually disproved in later experiments by other scientists. However, Stokes' work in light diffraction bore fruit in many other areas. For example, in 1849, he developed instruments which allowed him to measure the amount of astigmatism in the human eye, and in 1851 he invented a device to analyze polarized light. Stokes subsequently published, in 1852, a mathematical formula for the characteristics and behavior of polarized light, known as Stokes' Parameters.

Important Light Experiments Involve Fluorescence

Stokes used the results of his many experiments with fluorescence for further investigation into the properties of light and other elements of nature. One example is his use of fluorescence to study ultraviolet spectra. He eventually was able to determine that the dark spectral lines discovered by Joseph von Fraunhofer were lines of elements which absorbed light from the sun's outer crust. Stokes' last major work was the mathematical study on the dynamical theory of double refraction, which were presented to the British Association for the Advancement of Science in 1862.

Stokes is regarded as having great influence on later Cambridge physicists, not only through his own research, but also through his knowledge of the work physicists outside Britain were doing. His promulgation of French mathematical physics—at a time when Cambridge had little knowledge of it—is one example.

Because of the time-consuming administrative duties Stokes was responsible for in the several scientific societies of which he served as an officer, his scholarly output was curtailed toward the end of his career. Stokes was, however, quick to respond to the many queries he received from other physicists regarding the progress and problems of their work. His voluminous correspondence with his contemporaries, notably George Green, James Challis, and William Thomson, details his influence and guidance. From 1883 to 1885, he delivered a series of lectures on light at the University of Aberdeen, and a series of lectures on theology at Edinburgh from 1891 to 1983. These lectures were later published. Stokes died at Cambridge on February 1, 1903.

SELECTED WRITINGS BY STOKES:

Books

Mathematical and Physical Papers, 5 volumes, 1880–1905.
Burnett Lectures. On Light. In Three Courses Delivered at Aberdeen in November, 1883, December, 1884, and November, 1885.
Natural Theology. The Gifford Lectures Delivered Before the University of Edinburgh in 1891.

FURTHER READING:

Books

Asimov, Isaac. *Asimov's Biographical Encyclopedia of Science and Technology.* Garden City, NY: Doubleday & Company, Inc., 1972.
Daintith, John, editor. *Biographical Encyclopedia of Scientists.* Volume 2. New York: Facts on File, Inc., 1981, pp. 759–760.
Debus, Allen G., editor. *Who's Who In Science.* Chicago: Marquis Who's Who, Inc., 1968, p. 1616.

Parkinson, E.M. "George Gabriel Stokes," in *Dictionary of Scientific Biography.* Edited by Charles Coulston Gillespie. Volume XIII. New York: Charles Scribner's Sons, 1976, pp. 74–79.
Porter, Roy, editor. *The Biographical Dictionary of Scientists.* New York: Oxford University Press, 1994, pp. 647–648.
Wilson, D.B. *Kelvin and Stokes: A Comparative Study in Victorian Physics,* 1987.

—Sketch by Jane Stewart Cook

Alicia Boole Stott
1860–1940
Irish–born English mathematician

Alicia Boole Stott is considered noteworthy for her famous relatives as much for her own discoveries that translate Platonic and Archimedean solids into higher dimensions. She is more likely described when mentioned in other contexts as the daughter of mathematician and Royal Medal recipient George Boole and Mary Everest Boole.

Stott was born on June 8, 1860, in Cork, Ireland, where her father held a professorship at Queen's College. When George Boole died of a fever in 1864, Stott's sisters were dispersed to live with relatives while their mother struggled to support herself in London. Stott was shuttled between her grandmother in England and a great-uncle in Ireland, and was not reunited with her sisters until she was more than 10 years old.

Cardboard Models

Stott was well into her teens by the time she became seriously interested in mathematics. A family friend named Howard Hinton, soon to become her brother-in-law, introduced her to the tesseract, or four-dimensional hypercube. He not only offered Stott intellectual stimulation, he got her a job as secretary to an associate, John Falk. At that time, Hinton was working on a book that would eventually see publication in 1904.

In 1900, Stott (with the encouragement of Walter Stott, an actuarian whom she later married) published an article on three-dimensional sections of hypersolids. They led an ordinary middle-class existence following their marriage and had two children, Mary and Leonard. Walter took note of his wife's interests and introduced her to the work of Pieter Hendrik Schoute of the University of Groningen. The Stotts took a chance and wrote to him describing Stott's work.

Upon viewing photographs of Stott's cardboard models, Schoute elected to relocate to England from the Netherlands in order to collaborate with her. Over their 20–year relationship, Schoute arranged for the publication of Stott's own papers and cowrote others. Stott refined her approach towards deriving the Archimedean solids from the Platonic solids to improve upon Johannes Kepler's. She also coined the term "polytope" as a name for a four–dimensional convex solid form.

Schoute's university colleagues were impressed enough to invite Stott to their tercentenary celebration in 1914, to bestow upon her an honorary doctorate. Unfortunately, the 71–year–old Schoute died before the event. At a loss, Stott resumed her role as homemaker for nearly 20 years.

Stott found another collaborator, H.S.M. Coxeter, a writer who specialized in the geometry of kaleidoscopes, in 1930. She was quite taken with these "magic mirrors" and the challenge they would present to more old–fashioned mathematicians. Stott was inspired to devise a four–dimensional analogue to two of the Archimedean solids, which she called the "snub 24–cell." This construction was not original to her, having been discovered earlier by Thorold Gosset. However, her cardboard models of it in its "golden ratio" relationship with the regular 24–cell are still stored at Cambridge University.

Stott was an animal lover who enjoyed bird watching. She became ill around the time England entered World War II and died on December 17, 1940.

SELECTED WRITINGS BY STOTT:

"On Certain Sections of the Regular Four–Dimensional Hypersolids," in *Verhandelingen der Koninklijke Akademie van Wetenschappen* (1.sectie) 7 (3) (1900): 1–21.
"Geometrical Deduction of Semiregular from Regular Polytopes and Space Fillings," in *Verhandelingen der Koninklijke Akademie van Wetenschappen* (1.sectie) 11 (1) (1910): 1–24.

FURTHER READING:

Books

Coxeter, H.S.M. "Alicia Boole Stott," in *Women of Mathematics*. Edited by Louise S. Grinstein and Paul J. Campbell. Westport, CT: Greenwood Press, 1987, pp. 220–24.

Verner E. Suomi

Other

Frost, Michelle. "Mary Everest Boole." *Biographies of Women Mathematicians*. http://www.scottlan.edu/lriddle/women/chronol.htm (July 1997).
"Alicia Boole Stott." *MacTutor History of Mathematics Archive*. http://www-groups.dcs.st-and.ac.uk/~history/Mathematicians/Stott.html (July 1997).

—*Sketch by Jennifer Kramer*

Verner E. Suomi
1915–1995
American meteorologist

Verner E. Suomi helped pioneer the use of space satellites to study weather on earth and other planets. A meteorologist with a knack for building gadgets, Suomi invented the spin-scan camera which takes pictures of earth from a spinning satellite. He also developed a global data system called McIDAS (Man-computer Interactive Data Access System) that gave scientists worldwide access to the satellite data. The images and information gathered in space through his developments have improved forecasting and contributed to a greater understanding of weather systems.

Verner Edward Suomi was born in the small mining town of Eveleth, Minnesota, on December 6, 1915. His father, John E. Suomi, was a carpenter for a mining company. His mother, Anna Emelia Sundquist Suomi, had seven children, five girls and two boys. At the age of 22, Suomi began teaching science and mathematics at a Minnesota high school. The following year, he earned a bachelor's degree at Winona Teachers' College. Suomi married Paula Meyer in 1941, and the couple eventually had three children: Lois, Stephen, and Eric.

As an aviation student, Suomi's interest in meteorology was sparked by student handbook charts that described how the atmosphere and the amount of water in the atmosphere differed according to altitude. But it was World War II that changed the course of Suomi's career. Prompted by a radio message from noted meteorologist **Carl-Gustaf Rossby** for meteorologists to help in the war effort, Suomi returned to school. At the University of Chicago he studied under Rossby himself, an arrangement that Suomi called "a happy accident," in *Omni* magazine in 1989.

Suomi's dissertation, "The Heat Budget of a Cornfield," was a study that gave him a background that would be useful in a more ambitious project in the future: measuring the heat budget of the entire planet. Although Suomi earned his Ph.D. in 1953, he had belonged to the faculty at the University of Wisconsin at Madison since 1948. He co-founded the Space Science and Engineering Center at the University of Wisconsin in 1966 and acted as its director from its inception until his retirement in 1988.

Suomi's activities at the University of Wisconsin extended well beyond the classroom. Before any U.S. weather satellite had been launched into space, Suomi developed an instrument called a radiometer that measured the amount of heat going into and coming out of the earth's atmosphere. The radiometer was made of four metallic balls with the temperature sensors at the tips of long antennas. From a satellite orbiting the planet, it would measure the heat coming to the earth from the sun, as well as the heat reflected back into space by clouds, snow, and water. Suomi watched as the Vanguard Rocket carrying his invention was launched in 1959. Unfortunately, the rocket crashed. "When . . . my gadget fell into the ocean, it was almost like a death in the family," Suomi told *Omni* magazine. Undeterred, he built another radiometer, but it too exploded along with the Juno rocket that it was aboard.

When the first successful U.S. meteorological satellite was finally launched on the *Explorer VII* in 1959, another of Suomi's radiometer s was on board. Suomi set up a radio station in his bedroom to collect data as the satellite orbited the earth. The information

he gathered showed that the energy changes in the atmosphere varied much more than scientists previously believed. Although clouds and other materials such as snow reflect sunlight, they also absorb energy. Thus, from the satellite the earth appeared dark, because it was reflecting much less solar energy back into space than people had come to believe.

One of Suomi's most noted contributions was the spin-scan camera that took pictures of the planet from a rapidly spinning satellite 22,000 miles above the earth. The images displayed dynamic weather patterns and brought about a revolution in forecasting. The satellite, designed to travel at the same speed as the earth, hovered over a given region. With each spin, the satellite viewed a narrow swath of the earth. As the satellite tilted gradually, the camera could take pictures of the entire earth in 2400 revolutions. Previous satellites had been able to take pictures, but the spin-scan camera, introduced in 1963, took sequential photos that showed how the weather was changing. Those first sets of images from the spin-scan camera caught many meteorologists by surprise. They had expected the atmosphere to appear turbulent and chaotic. Instead, the images showed organized weather patterns—"clouds that looked like someone was pulling taffy across the sky," Suomi told *Omni* magazine in 1989. The camera provided images that enabled meteorologists to study patterns of air motion, cloud growth, and atmospheric pollution which resulted in improved forecasting of storms.

In 1959 Suomi and three others founded the Global Atmospheric Research Program which attempted to form a central location for the atmospheric data which was collected by more than sixty nations. To make the best use of the immense amounts of data gathered by weather satellites, Suomi developed the Man-computer Interactive Data Access System (McIDAS) in 1972 to manage the data for research and weather forecasting. The system also made data readily accessible to other nations. In 1978 the Global Atmospheric Research Program sponsored an experiment with the spin-scan camera that doubled the amount of time for which meteorologists could forecast accurately.

In 1971, Suomi proposed an ambitious experiment to study the atmosphere's temperature and water vapor using infrared technology, but the experiment was not launched until nine years later. The results showed how storms developed over a region of several hundred thousand square miles, and the infrared technique became useful for warnings of storms and hurricanes. Looking beyond our own planet, Suomi also used satellite technology to study the atmospheres of Venus, Jupiter, and Saturn. With colleagues at the Space Science and Engineering Center, he designed and built an instrument that entered the atmosphere of Venus and discovered an intense vortex over each pole.

In addition to the directorship of the Space Science and Engineering Center at the University of Wisconsin, Suomi's other positions included a term as president of the American Meteorological Association in 1968 and a year as chief scientist of the United States Weather Bureau in 1964. Though honored for his inventions that revolutionized the way meteorologists forecast the weather, colleagues and students thought of Suomi foremost as an educator. His contributions went beyond developing technology to include fostering an interest in meteorology among several generations of students.

Suomi received the Carl-Gustaf Rossby Award in 1968, the highest honor bestowed on an atmospheric scientist by the American Meteorological Society. He was also presented with the National Medal of Science by President Carter in 1977. Suomi died on July 30, 1995, of congestive heart failure at a Madison, Wisconsin, hospital. He was 79.

FURTHER READING:

Periodicals

Bagne, Paul. "Verner Suomi." *Omni* (July 1989).

Broad, William J. "A 30-Year Feud Divides Experts on Meteorology." *New York Times* (24 October 1989): C1.

Stout, David. "Verner E. Suomi, 79, Pioneer in Weather Forecasting, Dies" (obituary). *New York Times* (1 August 1995): D20.

—*Sketch by Miyoko Chu*

Richard Synge
1914–1994
English biochemist and physical chemist

Richard Synge made important contributions in the fields of physical chemistry and biochemistry. He is best known for the development of partition chromatography, a collaborative effort undertaken with **A. J. P. Martin** in the late 1930s and early 1940s. As a result of their work, Synge and Martin received the 1952 Nobel Prize in chemistry.

Richard Laurence Millington Synge was born on October 28, 1914, in Liverpool, England, to Laurence Millington Synge, a stockbroker, and Katherine Charlotte (Swan) Synge. He was the oldest of three children and the only son. After growing up in the Cheshire area of England, he attended Winchester College, a private preparatory school, where he won a classics scholarship to attend Trinity College at

Richard Synge

Cambridge University. After listening to a speech given by the noted biochemist **Frederick Gowland Hopkins,** however, he decided to forego his education in the classics and instead pursue a degree in biochemistry at Trinity.

Synge undertook graduate studies at the Cambridge Biochemical Laboratory in 1936, receiving his Ph.D. in 1941. His doctoral research concerned the separation of acetyl amino acids. It was at this time that Synge first met Archer Martin, who was engaged in building a mechanism for extracting vitamin E. They began to work together on a separation process, which was delayed when Martin left for a position at the Wool Industries Research Laboratories in Leeds, England. Synge was able to join Martin there in 1939, when he received a scholarship from the International Wool Secretariat for his work on amino acids in wool.

The Development of Partition Chromatography

Synge and Martin's work built on the adsorption chromatography techniques first developed by **Mikhail Tswett**, a Russian botanist, who evolved the procedure in his work on plant colors. Like Tswett, Synge and Martin's goal was to separate the various molecules that make up a complex substance so that the constituent molecules could be further studied. In order to achieve this goal, Tswett had filled a glass tube with powder, then placed a sample of the complex material to be studied at the top of the tube. When a solvent was trickled into the tube, it carried the complex material down into the powder. As the solution moved through the tube, the molecules of the different substances would separate and move at different speeds depending on their chemical attraction to the powder. While Tswett's technique was useful, it did not have universal application; there were a limited number of materials that could be used for the powder filling, and therefore only a limited number of substances could be identified in this manner.

In addition to Tswett's adsorption chromatography, there also existed the process of countercurrent solvent extraction. This technique involves a solution of two liquids that do not mix, such as alcohol and water. When a complex substance is applied to this solution, the molecules separate depending on whether they are more attracted to the water or the alcohol. Synge and Martin's breakthrough involved the combination of adsorption chromatography and countercurrent solvent extraction. This was achieved by using a solid substance adsorbent such as fine cellulose paper in place of Tswett's powder. In one application of the procedure, a complex mixture of molecules is spotted on one end of the paper, then that end is placed in a solution that might contain alcohol and water or chloroform and water. As the liquids flow through the paper, transporting the complex substance, the molecules in the substance separate depending both on their rate of adsorption by the paper and also by their affinity for either of the two liquids. When the process is completed, a series of spots is visible on the strip of paper. Each spot depicts one type of molecule present in the complex substance.

Synge and Martin had made early progress on partition chromatography during their time at Cambridge, but the need by industry and medicine for a more reliable technique spurred further research. At Leeds, they built a forty-unit extraction machine and experimented with various solvents and filtering materials. Their collaboration continued after Synge left to become a biochemist at the Lister Institute of Preventive Medicine in London in 1943, and by 1944 the improved cellulose filter method resulted. Later, they developed a two-dimensional chromatography process wherein two solvents flow at right angles to one another. This technique yielded an even sharper degree of molecular separation.

Partition chromatography was readily adopted by researchers for a variety of biochemical separations, especially those involving amino acids and proteins. Using the process in his doctoral research, Synge was able to separate and analyze the twenty amino acids found in protein. The technique was used in studies of enzyme action as well as in analyses of carbohydrates, lipids, and nucleic acids. Partition chromatography also became a useful tool for the food, drug, and chemical industries. Further experimentation with the process allowed proteins to be identified through the use of radioactive markers. The result of this marking was the ability to produce a photograph of the biochemical separation. The marking technique was used extensively by other biochemists, notably **Melvin Calvin** for his work in plant photosynthesis, and **Walter Gilbert** and **Frederick Sanger** for their research into DNA sequencing. All three would later receive the Nobel Prize for discoveries made using partition chromatography.

Later Research Builds on Chromatography Knowledge

Continuing his research of amino acids and peptides, Synge traveled to the Institute of Biochemistry at the University of Uppsala, Sweden, in 1946. There, he and **Arne Tiselius**, the Swedish biochemist, studied other separation methods, especially electrophoresis and adsorption. Back home, Synge applied this knowledge toward the isolation of amino acids in rye grass in order to study their structure, a subject he collaborated on with J. C. Wood. He also used the new techniques to study the molecular makeup of plant juices, examining the juices' role as a stimulator in bacteria growth. Partition chromatography was an important factor in other research carried on by Synge at that time. With D. L. Mould, he separated sugars through electrokinetic ultrafiltration in order to study the metabolic process. With Mary Youngson, he studied rye grass proteins. He and E. P. White were able to isolate a toxin called sporidesmin, which produces eczema in sheep and other cud-chewing animals. Synge's findings in all of these areas benefited efforts by agriculture, industry, and medicine to improve human health and well-being.

In 1948 Synge accepted a position as director of the Department of Protein Chemistry at Rowett Research Institute in Scotland. From 1967 until his retirement in 1976, he was a biochemist with the Food Research Institute in Norwich. He closed out his academic career as an honorary professor in the School of Biological Sciences at the University of East Anglia from 1968 until 1984. In addition to the Nobel Prize, Synge received the John Price Wetherill Medal of the Franklin Institute in 1959. He held memberships in the Royal Society, the Royal Irish Academy, the American Society of Biological Chemists, and the Phytochemical Society of Europe. He married Ann Stephen, a physician and the niece of writer Virginia Woolf, in 1943. They had seven children. Synge died on August 18, 1994, of myelodysplastic syndrome.

SELECTED WRITINGS BY SYNGE:

Periodicals

"A New Form of Chromatography Employing Two Liquid Phases." *Biochemical Journal* 35 (1941): 1358-68.

"Partition Chromatography." *The Analyst* 71 (1946).

"Methods for Isolating Amino-Acids: Aminobutyric Acid from Rye Grass." *Biochemical Journal* 48 (1951).

"Applications of Partition Chromatography." Nobel lecture, 1952.

"Note on the Occurrence of Diaminopimelic Acid in Some Intestinal Micro-organisms from Farm Animals." *Journal of General Microbiology* 9 (1953).

"Experiments on Electrical Migration of Peptides and Proteins Inside Porous Membranes: Influences of Adsorption, Diffusion and Pore Dimensions." *Biochemical Journal* . 65 (1957).

"A Retrospect on Liquid Chromatography." *Biochemical Society Symposium,* no. 30 (1969).

FURTHER READING:

Books

The Nobel Prize Winners, Chemistry. Vol. 2: 1938–1968. Edited by Frank N. Magill. Englewood Cliffs, NJ: Salem Press, 1990, pp. 598-607.

Wasson, Tyler, ed. *Nobel Prize Winners.* New York: H. W. Wilson, 1987, pp. 1033-34.

Other

Facts on File World News Digest (8 September 1994).

—*Sketch by Jane Stewart Cook*

Gabor Szegö
1895–1985
Hungarian–born American mathematician

Gabor Szegö was a product of the German–Hungarian mathematical school, something of a child prodigy who, by age 20, had published a seminal paper in an internationally recognized mathematical journal. By the age of 30, he had published some 30 noteworthy papers, and also coauthored with **George Polyá**, a fellow Hungarian, a famous mathematical problem book, *Problems and Theorems in Analysis.* Szegö most important theoretical work was in orthogonal polynomials and Toeplitz matrices, and he was, according to **Richard Askey** and Paul Nevai writing in *The Mathematical Intelligencer,* "one of the most prominent classical analysts of the twentieth century." Forced to immigrate to the United States to avoid Nazi persecution, Szegö helped build the mathematics department at Stanford University, where he taught from 1938 until his retirement.

Szegö was born on January 20, 1895 in Kunhegyes, then part of Austro–Hungary, to Adolf Szegö and Hermina Neuman. Szegö completed elementary school in the town of Szolnok, some 60 miles southeast of Budapest, and in 1912 enrolled in the Pázmány Péter University in the capital, now known as Eotvos Lorand University. It was in that same year that he won his first mathematic prize, the coveted Eotvos Competition. As Askey and Nevai noted in their article, it was fortunate for Szegö that he won such a prize at the outset of his studies, for as a Jew, he might not otherwise have secured a university post. He followed this impressive beginning with a further prize the next year, this time for a paper on polynomial approximations of continuous functions.

World War I Interrupts Studies

Szegö's first publication in a notable journal came in 1913 when he published the solution of a problem given by George Polyá in *Archiv der Mathematik und Physik.* His first research paper, on the limit of the determinant of a Toeplitz matrix formed from a positive function, was published in 1915 and again inspired by a conjecture by Polyá. As Askey and Nevai stated, "Szegö spent another 45 years working on sharpening, extending, and finding applications of the results published in this article." It was during this time also that Szegö became a tutor to another mathematical prodigy, **John von Neumann.**

With the onset of World War I, however, this life of research came to a temporary halt. Szegö joined the cavalry, though he was a self–admitted poor horseman. He remained in the army from 1915 to 1919, even after the collapse of the Austro–Hungarian Empire. He was able, while posted in Vienna, to finish his doctorate, and after the war he married Erzébet Anna Neményi, herself the holder of a Ph.D. in chemistry. The couple had two children, Peter and Veronica. But the effects of the war did not end with the Armistice. The early 1920s were a turbulent time in much of Central Europe, and Hungary was no exception. Szegö worked for a time as an assistant at the Technical University of Budapest, but by 1921 he and his family were forced to move to Germany in search of a more secure living. In Berlin, Szegö secured a post with the university for his work on orthogonal polynomial series, and became friends and worked with Issai Schur and **Richard von Mises**, among others. He continued his research and won the Julius Konig Prize in 1924, yet was only an associate professor without tenure at the University of Berlin.

Writes a Classic Problem Book

Together with his old acquaintance Polyá, Szegö collaborated on "the best–written and most useful problem book in the history of mathematics," according to Askey and Nevai. In 1925, the two published *Aufgaben und Lehrsatze aus der Analysis*, a two–volume work later translated into English as *Problems and Theorems in Analysis*. Students are introduced to mathematical research via a series of problems in analysis, number theory, combinatorics, and geometry, such that the solution to a group of problems prepares the reader for independent research in that area. Publication of this book rightly placed Szegö as not only a noted researcher, but also as an educator with innovative ideas.

The following year, Szegö was invited to assume to position of full professor at the University of Königsberg, succeeding Knopp in that position. He remained at Könisgberg for eight years, but increasingly the situation for Jews in Germany was becoming untenable. It slowly became apparent to Szegö and his wife that they would need to move once again, and this time not simply to a neighboring country.

Emigrates to America

In 1934, Szegö secured, through the intercession of friends, a teaching position at Washington University in St. Louis. The money to pay for his salary was raised by a Rockefeller Grant, and by grants from local Jewish merchants as well as the Emergency Committee in Aid of Displaced Scholars. Szegö remained in St. Louis until 1938, during which time he advised five Ph.D. students, and worked on his seminal book, published in 1939, *Orthogonal Polynomials*. This book has become a standard reference work for both pure and applied mathematicians. Orthogonal polynomials are polynomials that first appeared in connection with numerical analysis and approximation theory. It was Szegö's accomplishment to reduce many of these problems to the asymptotic behavior of certain Toeplitz determinants, which come into consideration as a variable reaches a limit, most usually infinity. Applications of Szegö's theory have proved of significance in the fields of numerical methods, differential equations, prediction theory, systems theory, and statistical physics. Also, Szegö's work on Toeplitz matrices led to the concept of the Szegö reproducing kernel and the Szegö limit theorem.

Builds Stanford Mathematics

In 1938, Szegö accepted an offer to lead the department of mathematics at Stanford University, in Palo Alto, California. He remained Head until 1953, and during those 15 years he succeeded in building the department to one of the most renowned in the world, bringing people such as Polyá, Loewner, Bergman, and Schiffer to the school, and helping to train an entire generation of new mathematicians. It was while he was at Stanford also, in 1940, that Szegö became a naturalized American citizen.

Szegö retired from Stanford in 1960 as Professor Emeritus. His wife died in 1968, and Szegö remarried in 1972 to Irén Vajda in Budapest. Ten years later, his second wife also died. In 1985, after several years of declining health, Szegö passed away, leaving behind a body of work of some 140 articles and six books authored or coauthored, as well as a generation of trained mathematicians to carry on his research in orthogonal polynomials, a field which he pioneered. In 1995, the centenary of his birth, Szegö was posthumously honored by the dedication of a statue in his hometown of Kunhegyes, replications of which were also installed at Washington University and at Stanford.

SELECTED WRITINGS BY SZEGÖ:

Books

Orthogonal Polynomials, 1939.
(With George Polya) *Problems and Theorems in Analysis*. Volumes 1 and 2. Translated by Dorothee Aeppli and C. E. Billingheimer, 1972–76.
Gabor Szegö: Collected Papers. Volumes 1–3. Edited by Richard Askey, 1982.

FURTHER READING:

Books

Askey, Richard, "Gabor Szegö: A Short Biography." *Gabor Szegö: Collected Papers*. Volume 1. Edited by Richard Askey. Boston, Basel: Birkhauser, 1982, pp. 1–7.

Periodicals

Askey, Richard, and Paul Nevai. "Gabor Szegö: 1895–1985," in *The Mathematical Intelligencer* 18, no. 3 (1996): 10–22.

—Sketch by J. Sydney Jones

Olga Taussky-Todd

Olga Taussky-Todd
1906–1995

Austro–Hungarian–born American number theorist

Olga Taussky-Todd is best remembered for her research on matrix theory and algebraic number theory. Matrix theory is the study of sets of elements in a rectangular array that are subject to operations such as multiplication or addition according to specified rules. Number theory is the study of integers and their relationships. During a long, productive career, Taussky-Todd published over 200 research papers and other writings on a wide range of mathematical topics. In 1964 she was named "Woman of the Year" by the *Los Angeles Times*, and in 1970 she received the Ford Prize for an article on sums of squares. Taussky-Todd was also well known for her lectures. In 1981, she gave the **Emmy Noether** Lecture at the annual meeting of the Association for Women in Mathematics, taking as the subject of her talk the many aspects of Pythagorean triangles.

Taussky–Todd was born on August 30, 1906, in Olmütz, Austria–Hungary (now Olomouc, Czechoslovakia). She was the second of three daughters born to Julius David Taussky and Ida Pollach Taussky. Her father was an industrial chemist who also worked as a newspaper journalist. He encouraged his daughters to take their education seriously. Her mother was an intelligent person as well, but had little formal education. In an autobiographical essay published in *Mathematical People: Profiles and Interviews*, Taussky–Todd recalled of her mother: "She was rather bewildered about our studies and compared herself to a mother hen who had been made to hatch duck eggs and then felt terrified on seeing her offspring swimming in a pool." However, Taussky–Todd also noted that her mother was more willing than her father to accept the notion of girls actually using their educations later in life to earn a living.

Shortly before Taussky–Todd turned three, her family moved to Vienna. Midway through World War I, the family moved again, this time to Linz in upper Austria. Her father was manager of a vinegar factory there, and he often asked Taussky–Todd to help with such chores as calculating how much water to add to mixtures of various vinegars to achieve the right acidity. Taussky–Todd's best subjects in school were grammar and expository writing. As a girl in Linz, she began a lifelong hobby of writing poems.

First Forays into Number Theory

During Taussky–Todd's last year of high school, her father died, leaving the family without an income. Taussky–Todd took jobs tutoring and working at the vinegar factory. The next year she entered the University of Vienna, determined to prove that her plan to study mathematics was a practical one. Among her professors was noted number theorist Philip Furtwängler. When the time came for Taussky–Todd to decide upon a thesis topic, Furtwängler suggested class field theory. In mathematics, a field is a set that has two operations, addition and multiplication. For each operation, the set is closed, associative, and commutative, and it has an identity element and inverses. As Taussky–Todd wrote in *Mathematical People*, "This decision had an enormous influence on my whole future . . . It helped my career, for there were only a very few people working in this still not fully understood subject. It was definitely a prestige subject."

In 1930, Taussky–Todd received her doctoral degree in mathematics. Based on her thesis, she was promptly offered a temporary post at the University of Göttingen in Germany, where she helped edit **David Hilbert**'s writings on number theory. She also edited Emil Artin's lectures on class field theory. By 1932, the growing political tensions in Germany made it unwise for Jews such as Taussky-Todd to stay there. She returned to Vienna, where she worked as a mathematics assistant. Among those she assisted was Hans Hahn, one of her former professors. Hahn had first introduced Taussky-Todd to functional analysis, the study of a particular type of function.

Travels to United States and England

Taussky-Todd applied for and received a three-year science fellowship from Girton College at Cambridge University in England. It was agreed that she could spend the first year of the fellowship at Bryn Mawr College in Pennsylvania. Taussky-Todd took a few English lessons and embarked for the United States in 1934. At Bryn Mawr, she had the chance to work with Emmy Noether, whom she had earlier met at Göttingen. Noether, who was 24 years older than Taussky-Todd, was already an established figure in modern abstract algebra. Taussky-Todd enjoyed accompanying the older woman on her weekly trips to Princeton University whenever possible. However, she also found that Noether had a critical side. As Taussky-Todd recalled in *Mathematical People*, "She disliked my Austrian accent, my less abstract thinking, and she was almost frightened that I would obtain a [permanent] position before she would."

In 1935, Taussky-Todd traveled to Girton College at Cambridge, where she spent the last two years of her fellowship. The mathematical interests of her colleagues there did not quite match her own. However, she did get some much-needed practice at teaching in English. In 1937 she took a junior-level teaching position at one of the women's colleges at the University of London. The hours were arduous, but she still found time to attend professional seminars. It was at one such seminar that she met fellow mathematician John (Jack) Todd. The two were married in 1938.

Growing Interest in Matrix Theory

Soon thereafter World War II broke out, bringing not only political but also personal upheaval. The newlyweds moved 18 times during the war. For a while, the couple lived in Belfast, Ireland, where Taussky-Todd first began to focus on matrix theory while teaching at Queen's University. A year later Taussky-Todd returned to work at her London college, which had since been relocated to Oxford for safety reasons. In 1943, she took a research job in aerodynamics with the Ministry of Aircraft Production. There she joined a group that was studying flutter problems in combat aircraft. Flutter refers to the self-excited oscillations of part of an airplane such as the wings. A corresponding problem in mathematics involves the stability of certain matrices. As a result, this job just strengthened Taussky-Todd's growing fascination with matrix theory.

In 1947 Taussky-Todd's husband accepted an invitation to come to the United States for a year and work for the National Bureau of Standards. Taussky-Todd also joined the staff of the bureau field station at the University of California at Los Angeles. After this first year, the couple briefly went back to London. They soon returned to work again for the National Bureau of Standards, however, this time in Washington, D.C. Taussky-Todd's title at the Bureau was mathematical consultant, and as she noted in *Mathematical People*, "this I truly was, because everybody dumped on me all sorts of impossible jobs, from refereeing every paper that was written by a member or visitor to the group, to answering letters from people . . . to helping people on their research."

Ends Personal Odyssey at CalTech

Taussky-Todd and her husband made one last major career move in 1957, accepting positions at the California Institute of Technology. In an autobiographical essay in *Number Theory and Algebra*, Taussky-Todd wrote: "It seemed to me as if an odyssey of 20 years (I left Cambridge, England, in 1937) had ended. I could at last work again with academic freedom and have Ph.D. students." Some of her students went on to play starring roles in the burgeoning of matrix theory that has occurred since the 1960s. In 1977, Taussky-Todd was made a professor emeritus at Caltech.

Taussky-Todd received a number of honors in the course of her prolific career. Upon her retirement, two journals, the *Journal of Linear Algebra* and the *Journal of Linear and Multilinear Algebra*, published issues dedicated to her. Going a step further, the *Journal of Number Theory* published an entire book, *Algebra and Number Theory*, dedicated to Taussky-Todd and two others. Taussky-Todd received the Gold Cross of Honor from the Austrian government in 1978. A decade later she was awarded an honorary D.Sc. degree by the University of Southern California.

Taussky-Todd died on October 7, 1995, at her home in Pasadena, California. An obituary by Myrna Oliver in the *Los Angeles Times* referred to her as "one of the most prominent women mathematicians in the United States." Indeed, a lifetime of contributions to both pure and applied mathematics across several specialty areas had earned her the respect of mathematicians of both genders and many nationalities.

SELECTED WRITINGS BY TAUSSKY–TODD:

"Olga Taussky–Todd: An Autobiographical Essay." *Mathematical People: Profiles and Interviews.* Edited by Donald J. Albers and G.L. Alexanderson, 1985, pp. 310–336.

FURTHER READING:

Books

Luchins, Edith H. "Olga Taussky–Todd." *Women of Mathematics: A Biobibliographic Sourcebook.* Edited by Louise S. Grinstein and Paul J. Campbell. Westport, CT: Greenwood, 1987, pp. 225–235.
"Olga Taussky–Todd." *Number Theory and Algebra: Collected Papers Dedicated to Henry B. Mann, Arnold E. Ross, and Olga Taussky–Todd.* Edited by Hans Zassenhaus. New York: Academic Press, 1977, pp. xxxiv–xlvi.

Periodicals

Oliver, Myrna. "Olga Taussky–Todd: Noted Mathematician." *Los Angeles Times* (December 3, 1995): A44.

Other

Davis, Chandler. "Remembering Olga Taussky Todd." *Biographies of Women Mathematicians.* June 1997. http://www.scottlan.edu/lriddle/women/chronol.htm (July 22, 1997).

—*Sketch by Linda Wasmer Smith*

Maria Telkes
1900–1995
Hungarian-born American physical chemist

Maria Telkes devoted most of her life to solar energy research, investigating and designing solar ovens, solar stills, and solar electric generators. She was responsible for the heating system installed in the first solar-heated home, located in Dover, Massachusetts. The importance of Telkes's work has been recognized by numerous awards and honors, including the Society of Women Engineers Achievement Award in 1952 (Telkes was the first recipient) and the Charles Greely Abbot Award from the American Section of the International Solar Energy Society.

Maria de Telkes, the daughter of Aladar and Maria Laban de Telkes, was born in Budapest,

Maria Telkes

Hungary, on December 12, 1900. She grew up in Budapest and remained there to complete her high school and college education. Studying physical chemistry at Budapest University, she obtained a B.A. degree in 1920, then a Ph.D. in 1924. The following year, on a visit to her uncle in the United States, Telkes was hired as a biophysicist at the Cleveland Clinic Foundation investigating the energy associated with living things. Her studies looked at the sources of this energy, what occurs when a cell dies, and the energy changes which occur when a normal cell is transformed into a cancer cell. In 1937, the year she became an American citizen, Telkes concluded her research at the clinic and joined Westinghouse Electric as a research engineer. She remained at Westinghouse for two years, performing research and receiving patents on new types of thermoelectric devices, which converted heat energy into electrical energy.

In 1939, Telkes began working on solar energy, one of her greatest interests since her high school days. Joining the Massachusetts Institute of Technology Solar Energy Conversion Project, she continued her research into thermoelectric devices, with the heat energy now being supplied by the sun. She also researched and designed a new type of solar heating system which was installed in a prototype house built in Dover, Massachusetts, in 1948. Earlier solar heating systems stored the solar energy by heating water or rocks. This system differed in that the solar energy was stored as chemical energy through the crystallization of a sodium sulphate solution.

Telkes's expertise was also recruited by the United States government to study the production of drinking water from sea water. To remove salt from sea water, the water is vaporized to steam, then the steam is condensed to give pure water. Utilizing solar energy for vaporization of the water, she designed a solar still which could be installed on life rafts to provide water. This design was enlarged for use in the Virgin Islands, where the supply of fresh water was often a problem.

In 1953, Telkes moved to New York University and organized a solar energy laboratory in the college of engineering where she continued her work on solar stills, heating systems, and solar ovens. Transferring to the Curtiss-Wright company in 1958, she looked into the development of solar dryers and water heaters as well as the application of solar thermoelectric generators in space. Her position there, as director of research for the solar energy lab, also required her to design a heating and energy storage system for a laboratory building built by Curtiss-Wright in Princeton, New Jersey.

Working at Cryo-Therm from 1961 to 1963, Telkes developed materials for use in the protection of temperature sensitive instruments. Shipping and storage containers made of these materials were used for space and undersea applications in the Apollo and Polaris projects. In 1963, she returned to her efforts of applying solar energy to provide fresh water, moving to the MELPAR company as head of the solar energy application lab.

Telkes joined the Institute of Energy Conversion at the University of Delaware in 1969, where her work involved the development of materials for storing solar energy and the design of heat exchangers for efficient transfer of the energy. Her advancements resulted in a number of patents—both domestic and foreign—for the storage of solar heat. Her results were put into practical use in Solar One, an experimental solar heated building at the University of Delaware.

In 1977, the National Academy of Science Building Research Advisory Board honored Telkes for her contributions to solar heated building technology; previous honorees included Frank Lloyd Wright and Buckminster Fuller. In 1978, she was named professor emeritus at the University of Delaware, and retired from active research. She was, however, active as a consultant until about three years before her death. Telkes died on December 2, 1995, on a visit to Budapest in her native Hungary.

SELECTED WRITINGS BY TELKES:

Books

"Thermodynamic Basis for Selecting Heat Storage Materials." In *Solar Materials Science,* edited by L. E. Murr. Academic Press, 1980, pp. 405-38.

Periodicals

"Storing Solar Heat in Chemicals—a Report on the Dover House." *Heating and Ventilation* (November 1949): 80-86.
"A Review of Solar House Heating." *Heating and Ventilation.* (September 1949): 68-74.
"Fresh Water from Sea Water by Solar Distillation." *Industrial & Engineering Chemistry* 45 (1953): 1108-15.
"Solar Thermoelectric Generators." *Journal of Applied Physics.* 25 (1954): 765-77.

FURTHER READING:

Books

"Maria Telkes." *Current Biography 1950.* New York: H. W. Wilson, 1950, pp. 563-64.
O'Neill, Lois Decker, ed. *The Woman's Book of World Records and Achievements.* New York: Doubleday, 1979, p. 189.

Periodicals

"Maria Telkes Pioneering Researcher Built Early Solar Home." *Miami Herald* (15 August 1996): B6.

Other

4 January 1994. Correspondence with Jerome P. Ferrance. University of Delaware Archives.

—Sketch by Jerome P. Ferrance

Max Tishler
1906–1989
American chemist

Max Tishler is noted for taking the formulation of pharmaceutical chemicals out of the laboratory and onto the production floor. During his long career as an industrial research chemist, he received patents relating to more than 100 medicinal chemicals, vitamins, antibiotics, and hormones. In doing so he significantly improved human health and nutrition and laid the foundation for modern, large-scale process chemistry of complex compounds.

Tishler was born on October 30, 1906, in Boston, Massachusetts. His father's name was Samuel, and his mother's maiden name was Anna Gray. He attended Tufts College in Medford, Massachusetts, where he earned a B.S. in chemistry in 1928. During his high school and college years, he worked part time in a pharmacy, where he first became interested in the use of pharmaceutical chemicals to treat health problems.

After graduation from Tufts, Tishler studied organic chemistry at Harvard University, where he was a teaching fellow from 1930 to 1934. He received an M.A. degree from Harvard in 1933 and a Ph.D. in 1934, both in organic chemistry. Shortly after he graduated, he married Elizabeth M. Verveer. They had two sons during their marriage, Peter Verveer Tishler, who went on to become a noted physician specializing in the genetics associated with diseases, and Carl Lewis Tishler.

Makes Significant Contributions to Process Chemistry

Tishler stayed on at Harvard, first as a research associate from 1934 to 1936 and then as an instructor in chemistry from 1936 to 1937. In 1937 George Merck, president of the pharmaceutical firm Merck and Company, persuaded Tishler to leave his teaching position at Harvard and become a research chemist at the company's laboratories in Rahway, New Jersey. One of Tishler's first assignments was to develop a method for making riboflavin, which would, in turn, allow economical production of vitamin B_2. His success in solving this problem led to processes for making other vitamins, such as vitamin A, vitamin K_1, and pantothenic acid.

In 1941 Tishler was named head of process development at Merck, and in 1944 he was promoted again to director of developmental research. During this period, Tishler continued to study complex chemical reactions and reduce them to definable processes for production in quantity. One of his investigations led to the development of a new drug, sulfaquinoxaline, which was used as a feed-additive to effectively combat parasite infections in poultry. This allowed a significant expansion of the poultry industry and opened up an entirely new field of pharmaceutical research specifically aimed at developing drugs to promote animal health.

In the late 1940s Tishler and his colleagues took on the difficult project of making the new therapeutic chemical cortisone in large quantities. In the laboratory the conversion of desoxcholic acid to cortisone was a complex process involving 42 separate steps which yielded less than one percent of the final product. By altering the chemical reactions, Tishler and his team at Merck were able to simplify the operations to work in a production environment, while at the same time increasing the product yield to 30 percent. Tishler's success proved that even the most sophisticated chemical process could be modified to work in a large-scale production facility, and his work made him one of the leaders in modern process chemistry.

In 1951 Tishler was awarded the Board of Directors' Scientific Award of Merck and Company, Inc. for his achievements. Tishler used the money from this award to establish the Max Tishler Visiting Lectureship at Harvard University and the Max Tishler Scholarship at Tufts University. In 1953 he was elected to the National Academy of Sciences.

Tishler was named vice president of scientific activities at Merck in 1954, and in 1956 he became president of the Merck laboratories. He held that position until 1969, when he took over as senior vice president of research and development until his retirement in 1970. During his 33 years at Merck, Tishler was responsible for the development of a wide range of new drugs for the treatment of infections, growth disorders, heart disease, hypertension, mental depression, and several inflammatory diseases, such as arthritis.

Tishler was honored for his contributions to industrial research when he was awarded the Industrial Research Institute Medal in 1961, and the Chemical Industry Award of the American Section of the Society of Chemical Industry in 1963. He received the Chemical Pioneer Award and the Gold Medal Award from the American Institute of Chemistry in 1968. In 1970 he was awarded the Priestley Medal, the highest award of the American Chemical Society.

Returns to the Academic World

After he retired from Merck in 1970, Tishler accepted a position as a professor of chemistry at Wesleyan University in Middletown, Connecticut, where he taught and conducted research into the chemistry of various natural substances. Some of the chemical compounds he investigated were leukomycin and prumycin, which are natural antibiotics, and cerulenin, a microbe which inhibits the production of fats. Tishler took over as chairman of the chemistry department during 1973-1974, and was named professor of the sciences emeritus in 1975. Concurrent with his work at Wesleyan, Tishler held advisory and directory positions with the Weizmann Institute of Science, the American Cancer Society, and the Sloan Kettering Institute.

Among his many honors, Tishler received nine honorary doctorate degrees and numerous lecture awards. In 1987, he received the National Medal of Science "for his profound contributions to the nation's health and for the impact of his research on the practice of chemistry." Max Tishler died on March 18, 1989, at the age of 82.

SELECTED WRITINGS BY TISHLER:

Books

(With J. B. Conant) *Chemistry of Organic Compounds.* [publisher unknown], 1937.

Alexander Todd

(With S. A. Waksman) *Streptomycin.* [publisher unknown], 1949.
(Editor-in-chief) *Organic Synthesis,* vol. 39. [publisher unknown], 1959.

FURTHER READING:

Books

American Men and Women of Science, 16th edition. Reed Publishing, 1986.

—*Sketch by Chris Cavette*

Alexander Todd
1907–1997
English chemist

Alexander Todd was awarded the 1957 Nobel Prize in chemistry for his work on the chemistry of nucleotides. He was also influential in synthesizing vitamins for commercial application. In addition, he invesitgated active ingredients in cannabis and hashish and helped develop efficient means of producing chemical weapons.

Alexander Robertus Todd was born in Glasgow, Scotland, on October 2, 1907, to Alexander and Jane Lowrie Todd. The family, consisting of Todd, his parents, his older sister, and his younger brother, was not well-to-do. Todd's autobiography, *A Time to Remember,* recalls how through hard work his parents rose to the lower middle class despite having no more than an elementary education, and how determined they were that their children should have an education at any cost.

Education and Early Career

In 1918, Todd gained admission to the Allan Glen's School in Glasgow, a science high school; his interest in chemistry, which first arose when he was given a chemistry set at the age of eight or nine, developed rapidly. On graduation, six years later, he at once entered the University of Glasgow instead of taking a recommended additional year at Allan Glen's. His father refused to sign an application for scholastic aid, saying it would be accepting charity; because of superior academic performance during the first year, though, Todd received a scholarship for the rest of course. In his final year at university, Todd did a thesis on the reaction of phosphorus pentachloride with ethyl tartrate and its diacetyl derivative under the direction of T. E. Patterson, resulting in his first publication.

After receiving his B.Sc. degree in chemistry with first-class honors in 1928, Todd was awarded a Carnegie research scholarship and stayed on for another year working for Patterson on optical rotatory dispersion. Deciding that this line of research was neither to his taste nor likely to be fruitful, he went to Germany to do graduate work at the University of Frankfurt am Main under Walther Borsche, studying natural products. Todd says that he preferred Jöns Berzelius's definition of organic chemistry as the chemistry of substances found in living organisms to Gmelin's definition of it as the chemistry of carbon compounds.

At Frankfurt he studied the chemistry of apocholic acid, one of the bile acids (compounds produced in the liver and having a structure related to that of cholesterol and the steroids). In 1931, he returned to England with his doctorate. He applied for and received an 1851 Exhibition Senior Studentship which allowed him to enter Oxford University to work under **Robert Robinson**, who would receive the Nobel Prize in chemistry in 1947. In order to ease some administrative difficulties, Todd enrolled in the doctoral program, which had only a research requirement; he received his D.Phil. from Oxford in 1934. His research at Oxford dealt first with the synthesis of several anthocyanins, the coloring matter of flowers, and then with a study of the red pigments from some molds.

After leaving Oxford, Todd went to the University of Edinburgh on a Medical Research Council grant to study the structure of vitamin B_1 (thiamine, or the anti-beriberi vitamin). The appointment came about when George Barger, professor of medical chemistry at Edinburgh, sought Robinson's advice about working with B_1. At that time, only a few milligrams of the substance were available, and Robinson suggested Todd because of his interest in natural products and his knowledge of microchemical techniques acquired in Germany. Although Todd and his team were beaten in the race to synthesize B_1 by competing German and American groups, their synthesis was more elegant and better suited for industrial application. It was at Edinburgh that Todd met and became engaged to Alison Dale—daughter of Nobel Prize laureate **Henry Hallett Dale**—who was doing postgraduate research in the pharmacology department; they were married in January of 1937, shortly after Todd had moved to the Lister Institute where he was reader (or lecturer) in biochemistry. For the first time in his career, Todd was salaried and not dependent on grants or scholarships. In 1939 the Todds' son, Alexander, was born. Their first daughter, Helen, was born in 1941, and the second, Hilary, in 1945.

The Maturing of a Scientist

Toward the end of his stay at Edinburgh, Todd began to investigate the chemistry of vitamin E (a group of related compounds called tocopherols), which is an antioxidant—that is, it inhibits loss of electrons. He continued this line of research at the Lister Institute and also started an investigation of the active ingredients of the *Cannabis sativa* plant (marijuana) that showed that cannabinol, the major product isolated from the plant resin, was pharmacologically inactive.

In March of 1938, Todd and his wife made a long visit to the United States to investigate the offer of a position at California Institute of Technology. On returning to England with the idea that he would move to California, Todd was offered a professorship at Manchester which he accepted, becoming Sir Samuel Hall Professor of Chemistry and director of the chemical laboratories of the University of Manchester. At Manchester, Todd was able to continue his research with little interruption. During his first year there, he finished the work on vitamin E with the total synthesis of alpha-tocopherol and its analogs. Attempts to isolate and identify the active ingredients in cannabis resin failed because the separation procedures available at the time were inadequate; however, Todd's synthesis of cannabinol involved an intermediate, tetrahydrocannabinol (THC), that had an effect much like that of hashish on rabbits and suggested to him that the effects of hashish were due to one of the isomeric tetrahydrocannabinols. This view was later proven correct, but by others, because the outbreak of

World War II forced Todd to abandon this line of research for work more directly related to the war.

As a member, and then chair, of the Chemical Committee, which was responsible for developing and producing chemical warfare agents, Todd developed an efficient method of producing diphenylamine chloroarsine (a sneeze gas), and designed a pilot plant for producing nitrogen mustards (blistering agents). He also had a group working on penicillin research and another trying to isolate and identify the "hatching factor" of the potato eelworm, a parasite that attacks potatoes.

Late in 1943 Todd was offered the chair in biochemistry at Cambridge University, which he refused. Shortly thereafter he was offered the chair in organic chemistry, which he accepted, choosing to affiliate with Christ's College. From 1963 to 1978, he served as master of the college. As professor of organic chemistry at Cambridge, Todd reorganized and revitalized the department and oversaw the modernization of the laboratories (they were still lighted by gas in 1944) and, eventually, the construction of a new laboratory building.

Wins Nobel Prize for Work on Nucleotides

Before the war, his interest in vitamins and their mode of action had led Todd to start work on nucleosides and nucleotides. Nucleosides are compounds made up of a sugar (ribose or deoxyribose) linked to one of four heterocyclic (that is, containing rings with more than one kind of atom) nitrogen compounds derived either from purine (adenine and guanine) or pyrimidine (uracil and cytosine). When a phosphate group is attached to the sugar portion of the molecule, a nucleoside becomes a nucleotide. The nucleic acids (deoxyribonucleic acid, or DNA, and ribonucleic acid, or RNA), found in cell nuclei as constituents of the chromosomes, are chains of nucleotides. While still at Manchester, Todd had worked out techniques for synthesizing nucleosides and then attaching the phosphate group to them (a process called phosphorylating) to form nucleotides; later, at Cambridge, he worked out the structures of the nucleotides obtained by the degradation of nucleic acid and synthesized them. This information was a necessary prerequisite to **James Watson** and **Francis Crick**'s formulation of the double-helix structure of DNA two years later.

Todd had found the nucleoside adenosine in some coenzymes, relatively small molecules that combine with a protein to form an enzyme, which can act as a catalyst for a particular biochemical process. He knew from his work with the B vitamins that B_1 (thiamine), B_2 (riboflavin) and B_3 (niacin) were essential components of coenzymes involved in respiration and oxygen utilization. By 1949 he had succeeded in synthesizing adenosine—a triumph in itself—and had gone on to synthesize adenosine di- and triphosphate (ADP and ATP). These compounds are nucleotides responsible for energy production and energy storage in muscles and in plants. In 1952, he established the structure of flavin adenine dinucleotide (FAD), a coenzyme involved in breaking down carbohydrates so that they can be oxidized, releasing energy for an organism to use. For his pioneering work on nucleotides and nucleotide enzymes, Todd was awarded the 1957 Nobel Prize in chemistry.

Todd collaborated with **Dorothy Crowfoot Hodgkin** in determining the structure of vitamin B_{12}, the antipernicious anemia factor, which is necessary for the formation of red blood cells. Todd's chemical studies of the degradation products of B_{12} were crucial to Hodgkin's X-ray determination of the structure in 1955.

Another major field of research at Cambridge was the chemistry of the pigments in aphids. While at Oxford and working on the coloring matter from some fungi, Todd observed that although the pigments from fungi and from higher plants were all anthraquinone derivatives, the pattern of substitution around the anthraquinone ring differed in the two cases. Pigment from two different insects seemed to be of the fungal pattern and Todd wondered if these were derived from the insect or from symbiotic fungi they contained. At Cambridge he isolated several pigments from different kinds of aphids and found that they were complex quinones unrelated to anthraquinone. It was found, however, that they are probably the products of symbiotic fungi in the aphid.

A Senior Scientist and Government Advisor

In 1952 Todd became chairman of the advisory council on scientific policy to the British government, a post he held until 1964. He was knighted in 1954 by Queen Elizabeth for distinguished service to the government. Named Baron Todd of Trumpington in 1962, he was made a member of the Order of Merit in 1977. In 1955 he became a foreign associate of the United States' National Academy of Sciences. He traveled extensively and been a visiting professor at the University of Sydney (Australia), the California Institute of Technology, the Massachusetts Institute of Technology, the University of Chicago, and Notre Dame University.

A Fellow of the Royal Society since 1942, Todd served as its president from 1975 to 1980. He increased the role of the society in advising the government on the scientific aspects of policy and strengthened its international relations. Extracts from his five anniversary addresses to the society dealing with these concerns are given as appendices to his autobiography. In the forward to his autobiography, Todd reports that in preparing biographical sketches of a number of members of the Royal Society he was

struck by the lack of information available about their lives and careers and that this, in part, led him to write *A Time to Remember*. Todd died on January 10, 1997, in his home city of Cambridge, England. He was 89.

SELECTED WRITINGS BY TODD:

Books

A Time to Remember: The Autobiography of a Chemist. Cambridge: Cambridge University Press, 1983.

Periodicals

"Chemistry of Nucleotides." *Proceedings of the Royal Society* A227 (1954): 70-82.
"Chemical Structure of Nucleic Acids." *Proceedings of the National Academy of Sciences* 40 (1954): 748-55.
"The Structure of Vitamin B_{12}." *Chemical Society Special Publication,* no. 3 (1955): 109-23.

FURTHER READING:

Books

Current Biography 1958. New York: H. W. Wilson, 1958, pp. 437-39.
Nobel Lectures Including Presentation Speeches and Laureate's Biographies—Chemistry: 1942–1962. Elsevier, 1964, pp. 519–538.

Periodicals

Saxon, Wolfgang. "Lord Todd, 89, a Nobelist for Work on Nucleic Acids" (obituary). *New York TImes* (15 January 1997): B7.

—Sketch by R.F. Trimble

Clyde W. Tombaugh
1906–1997
American astronomer

Clyde W. Tombaugh, an astronomer and master telescope maker, spent much of his career performing a painstaking photographic survey of the heavens from Lowell Observatory in Flagstaff, Arizona. This led to the discovery of Pluto (1930), the ninth planet in the solar system. Although Tombaugh is best known for this early triumph, he went on to make other contributions, including his work on the geogra-

Clyde W. Tombaugh

phy of Mars and studies of the distribution of galaxies. Tombaugh also made valuable refinements to missile-tracking technology during a nine-year stint at the U.S. Army's White Sands Proving Grounds in New Mexico.

Clyde William Tombaugh, the eldest of six children, was born on February 4, 1906, to Muron Tombaugh, a farmer, and Adella Chritton Tombaugh. He spent most of his childhood on a farm near Streator, Illinois. In 1922, the family relocated to a farm in western Kansas. Tombaugh glimpsed his first telescopic view of the heavens through his uncle Leon's three-inch (7.6-cm) refractor, a kind of telescope that uses a lens to gather faint light from stars and planets. In 1925, inspired by an article in *Popular Astronomy,* Tombaugh bought materials to grind an eight-inch light-collecting mirror for a reflecting telescope. He ground that first mirror by hand, using a fence post on the farm as a grinding stand.

The finished instrument, a seven-foot-long, rectangular wooden box, was equipped with wooden setting circles for aligning it to objects of interest in the sky. Tombaugh had not ground the mirror very accurately, and thus the telescope was unsuitable for the planetary observing he had in mind. However, it launched a lifetime of building, improving, and maintaining telescopes, tasks at which Tombaugh excelled. Tombaugh biographer and amateur astronomer David H. Levy estimated that Tombaugh ground some thirty-six telescope mirrors and lenses in his

career. He continued to use a few of his early telescopes for decades after he first constructed them (for example, his nine-inch reflector, whose mechanical mounting included parts from a 1910 Buick).

Hired to Search for Ninth Planet

Tombaugh's nine-inch reflector, which he completed in 1928, led to a career as a professional observer as well as to sharper views of the planets and stars. After a 1928 hailstorm wiped out the Tombaughs' wheat crop and foiled Clyde's plans for college, the young observer turned his new telescope to Jupiter and Mars. Subsequently, he sent his best drawings of these planets to Lowell Observatory, which had been founded in the late nineteenth century by famed Mars watcher Percival Lowell.

Hoping only for constructive criticism of his drawings, Tombaugh instead received a job offer from the astronomers at Lowell. He accepted, and in January 1929 began his work on the search for the predicted ninth planet beyond the orbit of Neptune. Working full time as a professional observer (although lacking any formal education in astronomy), Tombaugh used Lowell's thirteen-inch telescope to systematically photograph the sky. He then used a special instrument, called a blink comparator, to examine the plates for telltale signs of moving bodies beyond the orbit of Earth. A blink comparator, or blink microscope, rapidly alternates—up to ten times per second—two photographic images, taken at different times, of the same field or area of the sky. Seen through a magnifying lens, moving bodies will appear to jump back and forth or "blink" as the images are switched.

Using his knowledge of orbital mechanics and his sharp observer's eye, Tombaugh was able to discern asteroids and comets from possible planets; a third "check" plate was then taken to confirm or rule out the existence of these suspected planets. On February 18, 1930, after ten months of concentrated, painstaking work, Tombaugh zeroed in on Pluto, fulfilling a search begun by Percival Lowell in 1905. The discovery of Pluto secured the twenty-four-year-old Tombaugh's reputation and his place in the history of astronomy, and he remained with the survey until 1943.

After his discovery, Tombaugh took some time off to obtain his formal education in astronomy. He left for the University of Kansas in the fall of 1932, returning to Lowell each summer to resume his observing duties. At college, he met Patricia Irene Edson, a philosophy major. They married in 1934, and subsequently had two children, Alden and Annette. Tombaugh paused only once more for formal education in science, taking his master's degree in 1938-39 at the University of Kansas. For his thesis work, he restored the university's twenty-seven-inch

(68.6-cm) reflecting telescope to full health and studied its observing capabilities.

In 1943, Tombaugh taught physics at Arizona State Teachers College in Flagstaff; that same year, the U.S. Navy asked him to teach navigation, also at Arizona State. In what little spare time remained, Tombaugh struggled to continue the planet survey. The following year, he taught astronomy and the history of astronomy at the University of California in Los Angeles. Tombaugh's stint on the planet survey ceased abruptly in 1946. Citing financial constraints, observatory director **Vesto M. Slipher** asked Tombaugh to seek other employment.

Tombaugh's contribution to the "planetary patrol" at Lowell proved enormous. From 1929 to 1945, he cataloged many thousands of celestial objects, including 29,548 galaxies, 3,969 asteroids (775 of them previously unreported), two previously undiscovered comets, one nova, and, of course, the planet Pluto. However, as Tombaugh pointed out to biographer David Levy, tiny Pluto cast a long and sometimes burdensome shadow over the rest of his career, obscuring subsequent astronomical work. For instance, in 1937, Tombaugh discovered a dense cluster of 1,800 galaxies, which he called the "Great Perseus-Andromeda Stratum of Extra-Galactic Nebula." This suggested to Tombaugh that the distribution of galaxies in the universe may not be as random and irregular as some astronomers believed at the time.

Tombaugh was also an accomplished observer of Mars. He predicted in 1950 that the red planet, being so close to the asteroid belt, would have impact craters like those on the moon. These craters are not easily visible from Earth because Mars always shows its face to astronomers fully or nearly fully lighted, masking the craters' fine lines. Images of the Martian surface captured in the 1960s by the *Mariner IV* space probe confirmed Tombaugh's prediction.

In 1946, Tombaugh began a relatively brief career as a civilian employee of the U.S. Army, working as an optical physicist and astronomer at White Sands Proving Grounds near Las Cruces, New Mexico, where the army was developing launching facilities for captured German V-2 missiles. Tombaugh witnessed fifty launchings of the forty-six-foot (14-m) rockets and documented their performance in flight using a variety of tracking telescopes. Armed with his observing skills and intimate knowledge of telescope optics, Tombaugh greatly increased the quality of missile tracking at White Sands, host to a number of important postwar missile-development programs.

Tombaugh resumed serious planetary observing in 1955, when he accepted a teaching and research position at New Mexico State University in Las Cruces. There, he taught astronomy, led planetary observation programs, and participated in the care and construction of new telescopes. From 1953 to 1958, Tombaugh directed a major search for small, as-yet-undetected objects near the Earth—either asteroids or tiny natural satellites—that might pose a threat to future spacecraft. He and colleagues developed sensitive telescopic tracking equipment and used it to scan the skies from a high-altitude site in Quito, Ecuador. The survey turned up no evidence of hazardous objects near the Earth, and Tombaugh issued a closing report on the program the year after the Soviet Union launched *Sputnik* (1957), the first artificial satellite.

Upon his retirement in 1973, Tombaugh maintained his links to New Mexico State University, often attending lunches and colloquia in the astronomy department that he helped to found. He also remained active in the local astronomical society and continued to observe with his cherished homemade telescopes. Indeed, asked by the Smithsonian Institution in Washington, D.C., to relinquish his nine-inch reflector to its historical collections, Tombaugh refused, explaining to *Smithsonian* magazine, "I'm not through using it yet!" He died on January 17, 1997 at his home in Las Cruces, New Mexico.

SELECTED WRITINGS BY TOMBAUGH:

Books

Out of Darkness: The Planet Pluto. Mechanicsburg, PA: Stackpole Books, 1980.

Periodicals

"Plates, Pluto, and Planet X." *Sky & Telescope* (April 1991): 360-61.

FURTHER READING:

Books

Levy, David H. *Clyde Tombaugh: Discoverer of Planet Pluto.* Tucson: University of Arizona Press, 1991.

Periodicals

Dicke, William. "Clyde W. Tombaugh, 90, Discoverer of Pluto" (obituary). *New York Times* (20 January 1997): B8.

Levy, David H. "Clyde Tombaugh: Planetary Observer and Telescope Maker." *Sky & Telescope* (January 1987): 88-89.

Searcey, Dionne. "Snatching Fame from the Heavens." *Chicago Tribune* (2 February 1997): Perspective1.

Sheehan, William. "Clyde Tombaugh" (obituary). *Astronomy* 25, no. 4 (April 1997): 28.

Alexsandr Vasil'evich Topchiev

Trefil, James. "Phenomena, Comments and
  Notes." *Smithsonian* (May 1991): 32-36.

—*Sketch by Daniel Pendick*

Alexsandr Vasil'evich Topchiev
1907–1962

Russian organic chemist

Alexsandr Vasil'evich Topchiev was born in Russia in 1907. When Topchiev was 10 years old, the Russian Revolution began and led soon to the formation of the Union of Soviet Socialist Republics, or the Soviet Union, a profound change that was to affect Topchiev throughout his life. Like many scientists in the Soviet Union, Topchiev found that the road to success was through politics and cooperation with the national goals of his government.

Topchiev graduated from the Moscow Institute of Chemical Technology in 1930 and two years later joined the communist party, putting him in position to join the Soviet elite. He specialized in the economically important fields of food development and petroleum chemistry, and gained his initial reputation by the discovery of catalysts for obtaining usable chemicals, such as gasoline, from raw petroleum and for other processes used in treating petroleum. His services were especially important as Europe entered into World War II at the end of the 1930s, making production of fuel from petroleum vital to the war effort.

After World War II, development first of the atomic bomb and hydrogen bomb became an important priority, and Topchiev turned to nuclear chemistry, although he also stayed active in petroleum research. Because of the general secrecy of the Soviet research on fission and fusion weapons, not much is known in detail about Topchiev's activities in this field. He first went to England in 1955 for a conference on nuclear energy and was also a delegate at the opening of the world's first large-scale nuclear power plant in England in 1956. By 1958 he was able to deliver a paper on radioactive isotope s to the Geneva Congress on the Peaceful Uses of Atomic Energy. He also became involved in the Soviet space program of the 1950s, perhaps concerned with the chemistry of rocket fuel, but that too is shrouded in secrecy.

After World War II, Topchiev became a part of the Soviet government. He was the deputy Minister of Higher Education in the period from 1947 through 1949, and he continued as a deputy in the legislative body of Russia, known as the Supreme Soviet of the Russian Federation. After 1949, Topchiev suddenly became one of the members of the Soviet scientific elite, holding various posts in the Soviet Academy of Sciences, including the key one of scientific secretary of the Academy. Consequently, he was generally addressed as "Academician Topchiev" instead of "Comrade Topchiev," the general way of speaking to a Soviet citizen. As Academician Topchiev, he was allowed to travel outside the U.S.S.R to international scientific conferences. During the post-Stalin period in the Soviet Union, Topchiev became involved with the political process known as de-Stalinization, but by 1958 his past caught up to him and he was ousted from his post as secretary of the Academy. This did not, however, end his attendance at international conferences.

In 1957 Topchiev had been the first head of the Soviet delegations to the important series of scientific meetings on control of nuclear arms known as the Pugwash Conferences. These annual meetings were named after the location of the first such conference at Pugwash, Nova Scotia, the birthplace of Cyrus Eaton, an American multimillionaire who sponsored the early conferences. Although officially the scientists attending the conference were supposed to be individuals, the Soviet Union insisted on having a delegation and on naming a leader for it. The scientists from Western nations nicknamed the burly Russian "Top Chief" for his role in the conferences. He was known for his frequent speeches in favor of international peace and cooperation. Topchiev continued as delegation head through the 1962 conference. He died a few months later on December 27, 1962.

The Moscow Petroleum Institute, which he had headed since 1940, was later renamed the A.V. Topchiev Institute of Petrochemical Synthesis. During his life, Topchiev was awarded a Stalin Prize and on two occasions received the Order of Lenin.

SELECTED WRITINGS BY TOPCHIEV:

Books

(With L.S. Polak and R. H. Holroyd) *Radiolysis of Hydrocarbons.* Amsterdam, New York: Elsevier Publishing, 1964.
(With S. V. Zavgorodnii and V.G. Krychova) *Alkylation with Olefins.* Amsterdam, New York: Elsevier Publishing, 1964.
(With S. V. Zavgorodnii and Ya. M. Paushkin) *Boron Fluoride and its Compounds as Catalysts in Organic Chemistry.* (Translated by J.T. Greaves.) New York: Pergamon Press, 1959.

FURTHER READING:

Periodicals

Tomkeieff, S. I. "Academician A. V. Topchiev." *Nature* 4870 (March 2, 1963): 847.

—*Sketch by Bryan Bunch*

Lap-Chee Tsui

Lap-Chee Tsui
1950–
Chinese-born Canadian molecular geneticist

Lap-Chee Tsui (pronounced "choy") is best known for his lead role in the discovery of the gene that causes cystic fibrosis. This inherited disease affects about 1 out of every 2,500 Caucasian children in the world. It can lead to a host of problems, including lung infections and digestive symptoms. Until recently, most people with cystic fibrosis died by age 30. In 1989, Tsui and his collaborators announced their landmark discovery of the cystic fibrosis gene in the journal *Science*. In an accompanying editorial, **Daniel E. Koshland, Jr.**, described the finding as "a milestone of major importance." Among other things, it was a crucial step in the search for a cure for this devastating disease.

Tsui was born in Shanghai, China, on December 21, 1950. He was the eldest of four children born to Jing-Lue Hsue, a salesman, and Hui-Ching (Wang) Hsue, a housewife. Tsui was raised and educated in Hong Kong. As a boy, he dreamed of being an architect. His love of drawing persists to this day, and he still creates his own diagrams and sketches. Young Tsui also liked to explore ponds with his friends, catching tadpoles and fish. One of his favorite pastimes was to buy silkworms, then feed the worms mulberry leaves. He later recalled getting into trouble for stripping the leaves from a neighbor's mulberry bush.

Explores the Nature of Diseases

Tsui went on to study biology at the Chinese University in Hong Kong, where he received a bachelor's degree in 1972 and a master's degree in 1974. By this point in his career, Tsui was already interested in studying the nature of diseases. His doctoral dissertation looked at the structure and early developmental stages of bacteriophage lamba, a virus that infects bacteria. It was not until after he had earned a Ph.D. from the University of Pittsburgh in 1979, however, that Tsui first began to focus on genetic research.

For a short time after completing his Ph.D., Tsui trained in the biology division of Oak Ridge National Laboratory in Tennessee. Then in 1981, he moved to the Hospital for Sick Children in Toronto. Initially a postdoctoral fellow at the hospital, Tsui became a staff scientist there two years later. Today he continues to do research at the hospital, where he now holds the title of geneticist-in-chief. At the same time, he is a professor of molecular and medical genetics at the University of Toronto.

Finds the Cystic Fibrosis Gene

When Tsui first arrived at the Hospital for Sick Children, scientists were just developing new ways to identify defective genes. Tsui and his coworkers were looking for a genetic marker; in other words, a variation in deoxyribonucleic acid (DNA) that is associated with the defective gene that causes cystic fibrosis. Tsui, together with Manuel Buchwald and other scientists, identified the first such marker in 1985. Four years later, Tsui led a team of scientists that found the defective gene that causes cystic fibrosis and defined the main defect involved. The gene, which sits on the long arm of human chromosome 7, was dubbed the Cystic Fibrosis Transmembrane Regulator. This discovery marked the culmination of seven years of painstaking work, much of it done in Tsui's cramped, cluttered lab at the hospital.

Having found the defective gene, Tsui and his coworkers set about determining what was wrong with it. There are 150,000,000 base pairs, or units, of DNA on chromosome 7. The mutation Tsui found involves a deletion of just three base pairs. While this is the main defect involved in cystic fibrosis, hundreds of other mutations have since been linked to the disease as well. To advance the study of such mutations, Tsui organized an information exchange among 150 research labs in 35 countries. The success of this group effort, the first of its kind, has served as a model for the study of other genetic diseases. In more recent work, Tsui and his colleagues identified a modifier gene that can affect the severity of cystic fibrosis.

Thanks to Tsui, scientists now have a much clearer picture of how cystic fibrosis does its harm. Tsui and his coworkers found that the DNA sequence with the main mutation is part of the instructions for making a particular protein. This protein, in turn, is part of the cell membrane in certain mucus-producing cells that line organs such as the lungs and pancreas. All proteins are composed of long chains of amino acids. Of the 1,480 amino acids making up this particular protein, it turns out that people with cystic fibrosis are missing a single, critical one. As a result, their bodies produce abnormally thick, sticky mucus that can clog the lungs and lead to fatal infections. The thick mucus can also block the pancreas, interfering with normal digestion.

Maps Human Chromosome 7

In addition to the cystic fibrosis work, Tsui and his colleagues have been striving to create a complete map of human chromosome 7. This map should make it easier to identify other disease-causing genes located on the chromosome. In the process, Tsui and his coworkers have developed a number of new chromosome mapping techniques. Another line of current research is a study aimed at identifying the defective gene responsible for Tourette's syndrome. This severe neurological disorder typically leads to facial and body tics and uncontrollable verbal outbursts. Tsui also manages the DNA sequencing facility for the Canadian Genetic Disease Network and a physical mapping facility for the Canadian human genome project.

Tsui has published over 250 scientific papers. He has received a number of awards for his research, including the Paul di Sant'Agnese Distinguished Scientific Achievement Award from the Cystic Fibrosis Foundation, the Award of Excellence from the Genetic Society of Canada, the Gairdner International Award, the Starstedt Research Prize, and the Medal of Honor from the Canadian Medical Association. In 1991, Tsui was presented the Order of Canada. He has also received honorary doctoral degrees from universities in Canada, Hong Kong, and the United States. Tsui is a senior scientist in the Medical Research Council of Canada and a fellow in the Royal Societies of Canada and London.

Past Mentors and Future Directions

"Great Canadian Scientists," a site on the World Wide Web, contains a page devoted to Tsui. On this page, Tsui identifies mentors who have influenced his work. They include K. K. Mark, who taught him "how to concentrate on a single thing, and be good at it;" Roger Hendricks, who taught him "how to encourage independent thinking" in students; Manuel Buchwald, who taught him "how to be critical and look at the broad perspective;" and Han Chang, who taught him "how to be flexible [and] adaptive" and helped him to understand "the Western (American) way of thinking."

Tsui married Ellen Lan Fong on February 11, 1977. The couple has two sons, Eugene and Felix. Tsui travels widely, giving lectures to scientists, physicians, and students around the world. He devotes much of his spare time to volunteer work within the Chinese community. Tsui especially enjoys good food and wine. His other leisure interests range from basketball to the music of Puccini.

In 1989, *Maclean's* magazine named Tsui to its "honor roll." Writing in the magazine, D'Arcy Jenish and Brian Willer observed that "if Tsui and his fellow researchers or others solve the mysteries of cystic fibrosis, doctors may eventually be able to administer drugs to correct the genetic defect and eliminate the symptoms. . . .The dedication of scientists such as Tsui gives victims of that disease—and of other genetic disorders—new reasons to have hope." Tsui himself is optimistic about the future of cystic fibrosis research. Writing to contributor Linda Wasmer Smith, he notes that his team's recent progress in finding modifiers of disease severity "has generated renewed excitement in disease gene research."

SELECTED WRITINGS BY TSUI:

Books

(Editor with Giovanni Romeo, Rainer Greger, and Sergio Gorini) *The Identification of the CF Cystic Fibrosis Gene: Recent Progress and New Research Strategies.* New York: Plenum Press, 1991.

Periodicals

(With Johanna M. Rommens, Michael C. Iannuzzi, Bat-Sheva Kerem et al.) "Identification of the Cystic Fibrosis Gene: Chromosome Walking and Jumping." *Science* (September 8, 1989): 1059-1065.

(With John R. Riordan, Johanna M. Rommens, Bat-Sheva Kerem et al.) "Identification of the Cystic Fibrosis Gene: Cloning and Characterization of Complementary DNA." *Science* (September 8, 1989): 1066-1073.

(With Bat-Sheva Kerem, Johanna M. Rommens, Janet A. Buchanan et al.) "Identification of the Cystic Fibrosis Gene: Genetic Analysis." *Science* (September 8, 1989): 1073-1080.

FURTHER READING:

Books

Biographical Encyclopedia of Scientists, 2nd edition. Bristol: Institute of Physics Publishing, 1994, p. 891.

Periodicals

Jenish, D'Arcy and Brian Willer. "Discoveries of Hope at the Heart of Human Life: Lap-Chee Tsui." *Maclean's* (December 25, 1989): 22-23.

Koshland, Daniel E., Jr. "The Cystic Fibrosis Gene Story." *Science* (September 8, 1989): 1029.

Other

"Lap-Chee Tsui: Molecular Geneticist." http://www.science.ca/scientists/Tsui/tsui.html (October 14, 1997).

—*Sketch by Linda Wasmer Smith*

Frederick Twort
1877–1950
English bacteriologist

As a pioneering bacteriologist, Frederick Twort was responsible for several important advances in his field. He discovered what would be known as bacteriophages, bacteria-attacking viruses. This discovery led to the advent of molecular biology. Twort was the first scientist to grow the organism that caused Jöhne's disease, a deadly cattle infection, and his efforts contributed to its elimination. Twort also discovered a nutritional element later identified as vitamin K.

Frederick William Twort was born in Camberley, Surrey, England, on October 22, 1877. His father, William Henry Twort, was a doctor. Frederick was the oldest of ten siblings. He studied medicine in London at St. Thomas's Hospital Medical School. He became qualified and licensed in 1900, though he never actually practiced clinically. Soon after graduation Twort began his work as an assistant to Louis Jenner in London's St. Thomas's Hospital, working in their clinical laboratory. In 1902, Twort found work with William Bullock as an anatomy instructor in London Hospital. It was here that his first work in bacteriology began. He spent several years familiarizing himself with the bacteriology of hospitals and soon began his own experimentation.

Twort married Dorothy Nony Banister, who helped him with his work, and with her had a son and three daughters. His son, Antony, also became a doctor as well as his father's biographer.

Devotes Life to Research

Twort's own research work became of primary importance to him in 1907. In that year, he published one of his earliest significant papers on bacteria. In it, he outlined how bacteria adapted and mutated. Two years later, in 1909, he published on bacterial growth and related growth agents. In what became a common occurrence, Twort's results were basically ignored at the time, and found to be important only decades later.

In that same year Twort was named superintendent of the Brown Institution at the University of London, an animal hospital. While working here, Twort was able to devote all his time to research. His work was limited, however, by funding and support problems, which plagued him throughout his career. Still, Twort pushed ahead with his theories. His work was considered remarkable and original from the beginning. He believed that all pathogenic, or disease-causing, bacteria developed from organisms that lived freely, while most of his contemporary bacteriologists believed pathogens originated in the body.

Scrutinizes Jöhne's Disease

Twort's first important achievement was his in-depth study, with G.L.Y. Ingram, of Jöhne's Disease, the results of which were published in the early 1900s. Twort did the earliest cultures of the organism that caused the disease. He believed that there was a connection between tuberculosis and Jöhne's Disease, so he derived what he called his "essential substance" from dead tubercle bacilli. These bacilli, when incorporated in a culture medium, proved ideal for growing Jöhne's bacillus. Twort's study of Jöhne's disease directly led to the development of the Jöhnin test. His discovery also eventually proved important to biochemistry, specifically in the study of bacteria and their nutritional needs.

Discovers Bacteriophages

In 1915, Twort discovered what came to be known as bacteriophages. Twort's discovery was something of an accident. He spent several years using artificial media to grow viruses. Twort noticed that the bacteria infecting his plates kept becoming transparent. This was the earliest recorded proof of bacteriophages, though Twort called his discovery "transmissible lytic agent."

Twort published his results, but he was not certain about what he discovered. He made several guesses in his articles, but did not commit to any specific one, a hallmark of his career that lessened his findings in the eyes of his peers. Twort's experiments in this area were also overshadowed by World War I; he served in the Royal Army Medical Corps from 1915-18.

In 1917, Canadian bacteriologist **Felix d'Hérelle** made the same discovery, independent of Twort. D'Hérelle gave his findings their now common name, bacteriophages, which translates as bacteria eater. After d'Hérelle announced his findings, there was some controversy over who made the discovery first and when, in part because of Twort's published uncertainties. The results eventually carried both their names, and became known as the Twort-d'Hérelle phenomenon. Both scientists shared a life-long obsession with their discovery, and both wanted to use it to fight diseases plaguing humans.

Before antibiotics were developed, scientists were searching for ways to fight disease. Twort and d'Hérelle thought bacteriophages might be an answer, but the viruses did not work when used on human patients. The importance of the discovery of bacteriophages did not emerge until after Twort and d'Hérelle had died. In recent years, the idea has again come to light, as bacteria continues to develop resistance to antibiotics. In 1984, it was learned that illnesses in livestock and human illnesses such as meningitis can be curbed with bacteriophages.

Based on his many accomplishments, Twort was accorded some honors. Among other distinctions, he was appointed professor of bacteriology at the University of London in 1919 and in 1929, he was elected a fellow of the Royal Society. Twort's peers found him a difficult and remote man, which perhaps limited the acceptance of him and his ideas. Still, his rather unique ability to work independently and at a high level of technical aptitude contributed to his capacities as a scientific explorer.

Abrupt End to Research

As Twort's research progessed, he became obsessed with proving, in more specific terms, that bacteria evolved from viruses, and that these viruses had evolved from more primary cellular forms. Though he spent years on this idea, he did not publish anything of consequence. Twort's research was permanently interrupted in 1944 when the Brown Institution was destroyed by enemy fire during World War II. His laboratories and specimens were completely decimated. Twort spent his last years suffering greatly from this loss.

Twort died in the city of his birth, Camberley, on March 20, 1950. Posthumously, he was remembered for his scientific accomplishments, as well as his uncompromising belief that scientific funding should not be controlled by the government. His obituary in the leading journal *The Lancet* states: "An outstanding representative of the independent research-worker, he had made valuable contributions to bacteriology, but he felt himself increasingly uneasy in the closer relationship of research and the State."

Leaves a Complicated Legacy

There was more to Frederick Twort than his scientific accomplishments and related attitudes. In a review of his biography, *In Focus, Out of Step: A Biography of Frederick William Twort* written by son Antony Twort, Bernard Dixon describes the elder Twort as "a multifaceted man, who at various times made violins and began to design a more efficient internal combustion engine, who entered the Daily Mail contest for the biggest and best sweet pea in England, threw vegetables and meat each day into a large cooking pot of stew kept continually on the hob, and later developed considerable skills as an amateur radio constructor." This giant of science was a very complicated man working, as the title of his biography so succinctly states, in his own focus and quite out of step with his times.

SELECTED WRITINGS BY TWORT:

Periodicals

"The Fermentation of Glucosides by Bacteria of the Typhoid-coli Group and the Aquisition of New Fermentings Powers by *Bacillus dysenteriae* and other Micro-Organisms, Preliminary Communication." *Proceedings of the Royal Society*, B series (1907): 329-36.

FURTHER READING:

Books

Clarke, Edwin. *Dictionary of Scientific Biography*. Ed. Charles Coulston Gillispie. Vol. 8. New York: Charles Scribner Sons, 1976, pp. 519-21.

Daintith, John et al, eds. *A Biographical Encyclopedia of Scientists*. Vol. 2. New York: Facts on File, Inc., 1981, pp. 797-98.

Muir, Hazel, ed. *Larousse Dictionary of Scientists*. New York: Larousse, 1994, p. 519.

Williams, Trever, ed. *A Biographical Dictionary of Scientists*, 2nd ed. New York: Halsted Press, 1971, pp. 521-22.

Twort, Antony. *In Focus, Out of Step: A Biography of Frederick William Twort FRS, 1877-1950*. Gloucestershire, UK: Alan Sutton Publishing, 1993.

Periodicals

Dixon, Bernard. "Attack of the Phages: Bacteriophages." *American Association for the Advancement of Science* 84 (June 1984): 66.

"Obituaries. Frederick William Twort." *The Lancet* (April 1, 1950): 648-49.

"Obituaries. Prof. F. W. Twort, F.R.S." *Nature* (June 3, 1950): 874.

Radetsky, Peter. "The Good Virus; the use of Bacteriophages to Fight Antibiotic Resistant Bacterial Diseases." *Discover* (November 1996): 50.

—*Sketch by Annette Petrusso*

Boris Petrovich Uvarov
1889–1970
Russian-born English entomologist

Boris Uvarov's enormous love of scientific inquiry and its practical applications, coupled with his intense sense of purpose, allowed him to become the world's leading expert on locust and grasshopper research. Not only did he contribute to the taxonomy of 284 genera and over 900 species and subspecies of Orthoptera, but he singlehandedly organized and activated a worldwide cooperation to combat and control locust swarms.

Boris Petrovich Uvarov was born on November 11, 1889, in Uralsk, Russia. His father, Petr P. Uvarov was a bank cashier employed by the State Bank. His mother's name was Alexandra. He was the youngest of three sons. As a child, Uvarov enjoyed collecting bugs, and he took this interest with him to the University of St. Petersburg, where he graduated with a degree in biology in 1910. After graduation, he married Anna Federova Prodanjuk; they had one son.

As a young adult in a turbulent Russia, Uvarov held several positions in the country's agricultural department. In 1911, he was stationed in the Northen Caucasus, where he was to begin his lifelong study of locust. The next year, when he was 23 years old, he was appointed director of the Entomological Bureau at Stavropol. It was during this time that Uvarov developed his theory on locust swarming and nonswarming tendencies.

At the time, it was believed that swarming and nonswarming locusts were two different species because their physical and behavioral characteristics appeared to be vastly different. Through scientific observation and data collection, Uvarov proved that swarming and nonswarming locusts were indeed the same species that were engaged in apparently different phases. Such a discovery was startling because it meant that the gross agricultural devastation caused by swarming locust could in fact be controlled by deploying a management plan. Uvarov's phase theory had monumentous effects worldwide.

In 1915, he was appointed to director of the Tiflis Bureau of Plant Protection. In 1919, he became Professor of Zology at the State University of Tiflis and Keeper of Entomology and Zoology in the State Museum of Georgia. By 1919, Russia had gone through its revolution and broken up into republics.

Tiflis was now the capital of Georgia, which was experiencing militant nationalism. Understandably, Uvarov was uncomfortable with the new instability and was having difficulties performing his duties. It was at this time that he met Patrick A. Buxton, a medical entomologist accompanying the British troops stationed in the area. It was through his friendship with Buxton that Uvarov was able to accept a position at the Imperial Bureau of Entomology in London. Even though it occupied but a small corner of the British Museum, the bureau, renamed the Commonwealth Institute of Entomology, would become the world headquarters for locust research and plague control under Uvarov's 25-year tenure.

During the 1920s, Uvarov focused primarily on identifying and classifying insects within the British Commonwealth. In 1928, Uvarov published his book *Locusts and Grasshoppers*, which became the reference work on the subject for the next 30 years. After several major locust outbreaks in Asia and Africa, Uvarov was asked to head the Locust Committees of the Economic Advisory Council in Africa. At once, Uvarov recognized the need for a global anti-locust plan. He organized anti-locust conferences, monitored investigations into locust plagues, and eventually developed an international plan to research and contain locust populations. World War II inhibited full rollout of Uvarov's methodology, however his plan was successfully implemented in break-out areas of Africa.

At the end of the World War II in 1945, the Commonwealth Institute realigned itself under the Colonial Office and was named the Anti-Locust Research Centre. Uvarov actively developed the center's laboratory by inspiring younger researchers, while at the same time encouraging global cooperation in locust control by traveling extensively. He retired as director of the center in 1959 and spent the next three years serving as president of the Royal Entomological Society of London.

Uvarov's scientific career spanned over 50 years, and in that time he received many accolades. The highest honor bestowed upon him by England was a knighthood in 1961. This was possible because Uvarov was naturalized in 1943. Other honors include an honorary doctorate in science at the University of Madrid in 1935, commandeur de l'Ordre Royal de Lion in 1948, and Fellow of the Royal Society in 1950.

Uvarov spent the 1960s revising a new edition of *Locusts and Grasshoppers*. The updated first volume was completed in 1966. In 1968, his wife of 58 years died. Uvarov passed away at his home in Ealing on March 18, 1970. At the time of his death, Uvarov was approaching completion of his updated second volume of his 1928 publication. It was eventually completed by colleagues and published in 1977.

SELECTED WRITINGS BY UVAROV:

Books

Locusts and Grasshoppers. 1928.
Insect Nutrition and Metabolism. 1928.
Insects and Climate. 1931.

FURTHER READING:

Books

Oxbury, H., ed. *Great Britons: 20th Century Lives.* 1985.
Wigglesworth, V. B. *Dictionary of Notable Biographies 1961-1970.*

Periodicals

Obituary. *The New York Times* (March 19, 1970).

—Sketch by Jacqueline L. Longe

Peter van de Kamp
1901–1995
Dutch-born American astronomer

Peter van de Kamp devoted his career to the study of planets that exist outside of our own solar system. He is perhaps best known for his controversial assertion that two planets orbit nearby Barnard's Star, a claim questioned by many astronomers. Yet, despite this debate, van de Kamp is credited with advancing the study of extrasolar planets with his pioneering work and inspiring other astronomers to pursue the existence of worlds outside of our own.

Born in the Netherlands on December 26, 1901, Peter van de Kamp studied at the University of Utrecht, where he earned his doctoral degree in 1922. He emigrated to the United States in 1923 and joined the staff of the University of Virginia. In 1924, he left for a position at the Lick Observatory, but returned to the university a year later.

Joins Swathmore College and the Sproul Observatory

In 1937, van de Kamp became professor of astronomy at Swathmore College in Pennsylvania and director of the Sproul Observatory, a post he held until he retired in 1972. At the observatory, he used the 24-in (53-cm) telescope to conduct extensive studies of the movement of Barnard's Star. This red dwarf star is named for E. E. Barnard, who first observed in 1916 that it had some peculiarities. It has a proper motion of 10.3 seconds of arc per year—very large when compared to most stars, and giving it the highest-known apparent motion of all stars. In addition, Barnard's Star is a virtual neighbor to our system, being less that six light-years away from Earth (only the Centuri system lies closer).

Over the years, as he made and compared thousands of photographic plates, van de Kamp noticed that Barnard's Star seemed to wobble very slightly. In 1969, he attributed this motion to a companion body which could not been seen via a telescope; the gravitational pull of an astronomical body can effect the motion of another, thereby creating a wobble, or sinusoidal motion. Through mathematical calculations, van de Kamp estimated that the invisible companion of Barnard's Star was too small to be another star—it had a mass roughly one and a half times that of the planet Jupiter, he

maintained, and circled the Barnard's Star once every 24 years in an elliptical orbit. He decided that, given the relatively small mass, the companion body had to be a planet. He published his results in March 1969, in a paper in the *Astronomical Journal*.

Van de Kamp, after further calculations, revised his theory that same year. In the August issue of the journal, he stated that there was not only one planet orbiting Barnard's Star, but two, each about the mass of Jupiter, one with the orbital period of 12 years, the other, 26. Six years later, he published another paper that analyzed the data he had collected from 1950 to 1974. He estimated the sizes of one of the companions to be four-tenths the size of Jupiter, with an orbital period of 22 years. The other he maintained to be about the same size as Jupiter, with orbital period of 11.5 years.

Others Question his Observations

Other researchers, however, disagreed with van de Kamp regarding the companions of Barnard's Star. George Gatewood and Heinrich Eichhorn, working with the Van Vleck Observatory's 20-in (51-cm) refractor telescope and the Allegheny Observatory's 30-in (76 cm) Thaw refractor, were unable to discern any wobbling in Barnard's Star. They published their results in 1973, a year after van de Kamp's retirement from Sproul and Swathmore. Doubts were further cast upon the companion planets by researchers Robert Harrington of the U.S. Observatory and Laurence Frederick of the McCormick Observatory, both of whom recorded no wobbles with their instruments.

In 1973, another astronomer at the Sproul Observatory, John Hershey, used the same plates that van de Kamp had analyzed in his own study. He looked at 12 stars, including Barnard's, and noticed that all of them seemed to wobble. Such an observation raised an interesting question: could all the stars have companion planets, or was the Sproul telescope in some way not correct? Could the installation of new parts, first in 1949, then in 1957, and the subsequent readjustment of the scope be the cause of the discrepancy in star positions that Hersey noted on plates made between 1949 and 1956, and those made after 1957?

Defends his Observations

Van de Kamp defended his work throughout his lifetime, maintaining that his observations had taken place over a much longer period of time and involved many more photographic plates than did any other study of Barnard's Star. In 1982, he published his last paper on the subject. Involving the analysis of thousands of plates taken between 1938 and 1982, the article reconfirmed van de Kamp's belief in the existence of two companions, one about seven-tenths and the other about half the size of Jupiter, orbiting Barnard's Star in period of 12 and 20 years, respectively. Their orbits were circular, he maintained.

Other researchers have as yet been unable to confirm or fully deny the existence of planets around Barnard's Star. Some are quite pessimistic, while others suggest that planets smaller than Jupiter may indeed be in orbit around the star. Harrington's and Gatewood's work have largely ascertained that no near-Jupiter-sized planet or larger orbits Barnard's Star.

Leaves a Legacy of Research

Despite these controversies, Peter van de Kamp's lifelong devotion to the search for extrasolar planets was by no means in vain. He was among the first to suggest that planets could be orbiting other stars, and he inspired other astronomers to search for them. Because of him, planets have been detected in orbit around the stars Peg51, Rho 1 Canceri, Rho Cornoae Borealis, Tau Bootis, Upsilon Andromedae, 47 Ursae Majoris, and 70 Virginis. Many other stars are also believed to have planets, although the presence of the planets has not yet been confirmed. Scientists have also found planets around pulsars as well.

Besides his scientific work, van de Kamp was well known on campus as a composer and musician. He directed the college's orchestra for 10 years, from 1944 to 1954. He also played the piano at campus screenings of silent movies, many of them Charlie Chaplin films from his own collection.

Peter van de Kamp died May 18, 1995, in Middenbeemster, the Netherlands.

SELECTED WRITINGS BY VAN DE KAMP:

"Alternate Dynamical Analysis of Barnard's Star." *Astronomical Journal*, 74:(2): 238-240, March 1969.
"Astrometric Study of Barnard's Star from Plates Taken with the Sproul 61-cm Refractor." *Astronomical Journal*, 80(8): 658-661, August 1975.
"The Planetary System of Barnard's Star." *Vistas in Astronomy*, 26: 141-157, 1982.

FURTHER READING:

Periodicals

Black, David. "Worlds Around Other Stars." *Scientific American*, 264:1, pp. 76-81, January 1991.
Schilling, Govert. "Peter van de Kamp and His 'Lovely Barnard's Star.'" *Astronomy*, 13 (December 1985): 26, 28.
Stoudt, David. "Peter van de Kamp, Astronomer and Musician at Swathmore, 93." *New York Times*, May 23, 1995, p. B10.

Other

Bell, George H. "The Search for Extrasolar Planets: A Brief History of the Search, the Findings and the Future Implications." On the Arizona State University web site, URL: http://www.lib.asu.edu/noble/space/exoplnt.htm

—Sketch by Fran Hodgkins

Charles Jean Gustave Nicolas de la Vallée–Poussin
1866–1962
Belgian number theorist

Charles Jean Gustave Nicolas de la Vallée–Poussin was responsible for proving the prime number theorem. A prime number is a number that can be divided by only one and itself without producing a remainder, and de la Vallée–Poussin—like many others—set out to prove the relationship between prime numbers. In an article for *MAA Online* dated December 23, 1996, Ivars Peterson asserts: "In effect, [the prime number theorem] states that the average gap between two consecutive primes near the number x is close to the natural logarithm of x. Thus, when x is close to 100, the natural logarithm of x is approximately 4.6, which means that in this range, roughly every fifth number should be a prime." De la Vallée–Poussin was additionally known for his writings about the zeta function, Lebesgue and Stieltjes integrals, conformal representation, algebraic and trigonometric polynomial approximation, trigonometric series, analytic and quasi–analytic functions, and complex variables. His writings and research, which were—and are—considered clear, stylish, and precise, were highly respected by his peers in academia and other well–placed individuals in Western society.

Despite the historical confusion posed by de la Vallée–Poussin's name (it is often rendered as Charles–Jean–Gustave–Nicolas, Charles–Jean Gustave Nicolas, Charles–Joseph, Vallée Poussin, etc.), the facts surrounding his origins are well known. De la Vallée–Poussin was born on August 14, 1866, in Louvain, Belgium. A distant relative of the French painter Nicolas Poussin, de la Vallée–Poussin's father was, like himself, an esteemed teacher at the University of Louvain. (The elder de la Vallée–Poussin, however, specialized in geology and mineralogy.) De la Vallée–Poussin's family was well–off, and as a child, he found encouragement and inspiration in fellow mathematician Louis–Philippe Gilbert (some sources identify him as Louis Claude Gilbert), with whom he would eventually work.

De la Vallée–Poussin enrolled at the Jesuit College at Mons in southwestern Belgium, where it is said he originally intended to pursue a career in the clergy. He ultimately, however, obtained a *diplôme d'ingenieur* and began to pursue a career in mathematics. In 1891, like his father and Gilbert, he became employed at the University of Louvain, where he initially worked as Gilbert's assistant. Gilbert's death the following year created an academic opening to which de la Vallée–Poussin was appointed in 1893, thereby earning him the title of professor of mathematics.

Although de la Vallée–Poussin was gaining recognition as early as 1892, when he won a prize for an essay on differential equations, he earned his first widespread fame four years later. In 1896, de la Vallée–Poussin capitalized on the ideas set forth by earlier mathematicians, notably Karl Friedrich Gauss, Adrien Marie Legendre, Leonhard Euler, Peter Gustav Lejeune Dirichlet, Pafnuty Lvovich Chebyshev, and Georg Friedrich Bernhard Riemann, and proved what is now known as the prime number theorem. (De la Vallée–Poussin shares this honor with **Jacques Hadamard**, who revealed his finding in the same year. Historians note, however, that de la Vallée–Poussin's and Hadamard's achievements were performed independently and that although both mathematicians used the Riemann zeta function in their work, they came to their conclusions in different ways.)

De la Vallée–Poussin revealed much of his groundbreaking work in a series of celebrated books and papers. His two–volume *Cours d'analyse infinitésimale* went through several printings, and the work was consistently edited between printings to offer updated information. Initially, the book was directed toward both mathematicians and students, and de la Vallée–Poussin used different fonts and sizes of types to differentiate between the audiences to whom a particular passage was directed. In the 1910s, de la Vallée–Poussin was preparing the third edition of this work, but this was destroyed by German forces, who invaded Louvain during World War I. De

la Vallée–Poussin subsequently dedicated his 1916 *Intégrales de Lebesgue fonctions d'ensemble, classes de baire* to the Lebesgue interval to compensate for the material destroyed by the Germans. De la Vallée–Poussin continued to publish well into his eighties, and, like *Cours d'analyse infinitésimale,* many of his writings went through various reprintings and revisions. Almost all of de la Vallée–Poussin's writing have been praised for their originality and the clarity of his writing style.

De la Vallée–Poussin, who married a Belgian woman whom he met while vacationing in Norway in the late 1890s, died on March 2, 1962, in the city of his birth. During his lifetime, he was accorded many honors. In addition to the celebrations commemorating his 35th and 50th anniversaries as chair of mathematics at the University of Louvain, he was elected to various prestigious institutions including the French Académie Royales des Sciences, the International Mathematical Union, the London Mathematical Society, the Belgian Royal Academy, and the Legion of Honor. In 1928, the king of Belgium also awarded him the title of baron in recognition of his years of academic tenure and his professional achievements.

SELECTED WRITINGS BY DE LA VALLÉE POUSSIN:

Books

*Cours d'analyse infinitésimale. 2 volumes, 1903–1906.
Intégrales de Lebesgue fonctions d'ensemble, classes de baire, 1916.
Leçons sur l'approximation des fonctions d'une variable réelle, 1919.
Leçons de mécanique analytique, 1924.
Les nouvelles méthodes de la théorie du potentiel et le problème généralisé de Dirichlet: Actualités scientifiques et industrielles, 1937.
Le potentiel logarithmique, balayage et représentation conforme, 1949.
*(Much of de la Vallée–Poussin's works was revised and reprinted. This work, in particular, was heavily revised, with each new edition offering substantive changes and new information.)

FURTHER READING:

Books

Burkhill, J. C. "Charles–Jean–Gustave–Nicolas de laVallée–Poussin," in *Dictionary of Scientific Biography.* Volume XIII. Edited by Charles Coulston Gillispie. New York: Charles Scribner's Sons, 1976, pp. 561–62.

Young, Laurence. *Mathematicians and Their Times: History of Mathematics and Mathematics of History.* Amsterdam: North–Holland Publishing Company, 1981, p. 306.

Periodicals

Bateman, Paul T. and Harold G. Diamond. "A Hundred Years of Prime Numbers." *The American Mathematical Monthly* 103, no. 9 (November 1996): 729–41.
Burkill, J. C. "Charles–Joseph de la Vallée Poussin." *Journal of the London Mathematical Society* 39 (1964): 165–75.

Other

Peterson, Ivars. "Ivars Peterson's MathLand: Prime Theorem of the Century." *MAA Online* (December 23, 1996). http://www.maa.org.

—*Sketch by C. J. Giroux*

Edward Bright Vedder
1878–1952
American bacteriologist

Edward Bright Vedder made invaluable contributions to early twentieth century medicine. He discovered the causes of beriberi and scurvy; both are diseases stemming from vitamin deficiencies. He also contributed to knowledge about leprosy, syphilis, and amoebic dysentery.

Vedder was born in New York, New York, on June 28, 1878, the son of Baptist clergyman Henry Clay Vedder and his wife, Minnie Lingham Vedder. Vedder attended public schools on Long Island and then graduated from the University of Rochester in New York in 1898. He earned his M.D. degree at the University of Pennsylvania in 1902. While working on his master's degree in science (which he obtained in 1903), he studied with Simon Flexner, investigating the bacteria that causes dysentery.

In 1903 Vedder joined the army and became first lieutenant and assistant surgeon for the medical corps. After attending the Army Medical School and contributing to experiments on the typhoid vaccine, he graduated in 1904. He would then serve in cities in the United States and the Philippines until 1910, even working in the Philippines under General Pershing during the guerilla war against the Moros from 1904 to 1906. Starting in 1910, he studied tropical diseases as a member of the army's scientific board in the Philippines and became an instructor in bacteriology

in 1913 at the Army Medical School, where he served until 1919.

It was while he was in the Philippines that Vedder did his most important work. While studying the disease beriberi, he deduced that it was a deficiency disease associated with the Philippine custom of eating polished rice. He had the idea of substituting half-polished rice, instead, which successfully cured the disease. Later, scientists found the disease came from a deficiency of vitamin B_1.

Vedder's groundbreaking study on beriberi was so impressive that he won the Cartwright Prize of the College of Physician and Surgeons of Columbia University in 1913. He then moved on to investigate the causes of scurvy, which he found to be a deficiency of vitamin C. Vedder celebrated his discovery of vitamin C with a paper called "Study of the Antiscorbutic Vitamin," which won him the Wellcome prize in 1932.

Vedder also added to knowledge about the treatment of leprosy and syphilis. In 1911 he showed the effectiveness of emetine in the treatment of amoebic dysentery. His study of this medicine led to its widespread use.

After leaving the Philippines, he led the Southern Department Laboratory in Fort Sam, Texas, from 1920 until 1922. Then Vedder entered a new field of research, chemical warfare. From 1922 until 1925, he was chief of medical research at the Edgewood Arsenal, Maryland, where he delved into the basics of chemical warfare. From there, he moved back to the Philippines to become a senior member of the Army's Board of Medical Research in 1926. That same year, he was promoted to the rank of colonel.

In 1928 Vedder became the Army Medical School's commandant, and then during 1931 started research on poison gas at Edgewood Arsenal.

After retiring from the army in 1933, he was appointed professor of experimental medicine at George Washington University in Washington DC. In 1942 he moved to the San Francisco Bay area of California to become director of medical education at the Alameda County Hospital and director of the Highland County Hospital's lab in Oakland. He retired in 1947.

Vedder wrote a number of noteworthy books including *Beriberi* (1913), *Sanitation for Medical Officers, War Manual* (1917), *Syphilis and Public Health* (1918), *The Medical Aspects of Chemical Warfare* (1925), and *Medicine: Its Contribution to Civilization* (1929) as well as many articles which appeared in respected scientific journals of the time. In 1924 he received an honorary Sc.D. degree from the University of Rochester.

Vedder was a Baptist and a Republican who enjoyed walking and playing tennis. On June 22,

1903, he married his wife Lily Sheldrake in Philadelphia. She was the daughter of a Philadelphia manufacturer, Henry Edward Norton. They had two children, Sibyl Norton, and Henry Clay, as well as three grandchildren.

The scientist died in Walter Reed General Hospital in Washington D.C. on January 30, 1952. Vedder was 73.

SELECTED WRITINGS BY VEDDER:

Books

Sanitation for Medical Officers. Philadelphia: Lea and Febiger, 1917.
Syphilis and the Public Health. Philadelphia: Lea and Febiger, 1918.

FURTHER READING:

Periodicals

"Col. E.B. Vedder, 73, Noted as Scientist." *The New York Times* (Febuary 2, 1952): 13.
"Deaths." *Journal of the American Medical Association* (April 5, 1952): 1236.
"Obituary." *British Medical Journal* (February 23, 1952): 441.

—*Sketch by Barbara Boughton*

Argelia Velez-Rodriguez

Argelia Velez–Rodriguez
1936–

Cuban–born American mathematics educator

Since leaving her native Cuba shortly after completing her Ph.D., Argelia Velez–Rodriguez has devoted her career to mathematics and physics education. She has been involved with math education programs of the National Science Foundation (NSF) since 1970 and became director of the Minority Science Improvement Program at the U.S. Department of Education in 1980.

After showing promise in mathematics as a girl, Velez–Rodriguez earned a bachelor's degree in 1955 from the Marianao Institute of Cuba and a Ph.D. in 1960 from the University of Havana. Her doctoral dissertation concerned the use of differential equations in figuring astronomical orbits. Her father, Pedro Velez, had worked in the Cuban Congress under Fulgencio Batista, the leader ousted by Fidel Castro in 1959.

Velez–Rodriguez's first teaching position in the United States was at Texas College, where she began teaching mathematics and physics in 1962. In 1972, she became a professor of math and served as the department's chair at Bishop College in Dallas. Velez–Rodriguez's research at the time focused on differential equations and classical analysis, and it was at Bishop that she first became involved with the NSF programs for improving science education. Velez–Rodriguez has also studied teaching strategies, with a particular focus on helping minorities and disadvantaged students learn mathematics. She directed and coordinated several NSF programs for high school and junior high school mathematics teachers.

Velez–Rodriquez was married to Raul Rodriguez in 1954 in Cuba and they had two young children when the family fled the country in 1962. "I had just finished my Ph.D.," she told contributor Karl Bates in an interview. Her son is now a surgeon, and her daughter is an engineer with a Harvard MBA. She and Rodriguez are divorced, and she is a naturalized citizen of the United States.

FURTHER READING:

"Argelia Velez–Rodriguez." *Biographies of Women Mathematicians.* June 1997. http://www.scottlan.edu/lriddle/women/chronol.htm (July 22, 1997).

Other

Velez–Rodriguez, Argelia, interview with Karl Leif Bates, conducted June 17, 1997.

—*Sketch by Karl Leif Bates*

Frederick John Vine
1939–
English geophysicist

The creation of the theory of plate tectonics cannot be ascribed to any one person or year, unlike most of the other overarching theories of science. But acceptance of the theory by most geologists stems from the convincing argument and evidence of Frederick John Vine, first developed in 1963 and presented in full form in 1966. After 1966 leading geologists around the world came to believe that the ocean floor was created at the mid-ocean ridges and slowly spread apart as large individual plates. These plates move with respect to each other, with some plate edges plunging under others to form great ocean trenches. Action of the plates accounts for chains of mountains and for patterns of earthquake or volcanic activity. Plate tectonics also produces the movement of continents with respect to each other, which is known as continental drift.

Vine's work in the 1960s did more than establish the theory of plate tectonics. It also connected that theory to evidence for periodic reversals of Earth's magnetic field and established the validity of that idea.

Vine was born in Chiswick, England, a suburb of west London. His parents were Frederick Royston Vine, an accountant, and Ivy Grace (Bryant) Vine, a personal secretary. Vine attended school in London before going to St. John's College at Cambridge University to study for a degree in natural sciences and for a Ph.D. in marine geophysics with Drummond Matthews. In 1967 he came to the United States to teach and do research in geophysics at Princeton University in New Jersey, but in 1970 returned to England to work in the Environmental Sciences department at the University of East Anglia in Norwich. He is currently Dean of Environmental Sciences at that university. In 1964 he married Susan Alice McCall. They have a daughter and a son.

Vine was a graduate student at St. John's in 1962 and already a firm believer in continental drift since the age of 14 when, like so many others before him, he was struck by the fit between the great gulf of West Africa and the bulge of Brazil. In 1962 his supervisor

at Cambridge, Drummond Matthews, traveled on *H.M.S. Owen* to the northwest part of the Indian Ocean to map the trapped magnetic pattern in the sea floor near that part of the Mid-Ocean Ridge System, which locally is termed the Carlsberg Ridge. The resulting map was not the first to observe that the magnetism of the ocean floor consists of a series of stripes. These had also been observed off the coast of California in the Pacific Ocean and near Iceland in the Atlantic Ocean. Now the magnetic banding appeared in the Indian Ocean as well. The individual stripes can be as much as 20 miles (30 km) wide. A magnetometer towed through the sea shows these as regular changes from band to band in the intensity of Earth's magnetic field.

Vine and Matthews had given considerable thought to the then-new hypothesis of sea-floor spreading, just published that year by **Harry Hammond Hess** but widely circulated among oceanographers since 1960 (the name "sea-floor spreading" was coined by Robert J. Dietz in 1961). Vine and Matthews recognized that previous interpretations of the magnetic variations on the ocean floor had overlooked an important clue. Although the magnetometer recorded the changes from band to band as variations in intensity, the same effect on the magnetometer would be produced by variations in polarity (the direction of the magnetic field; that is, which pole is observed as north). They reinterpreted their data with this in mind. If trapped magnetic fields in one band show the north magnetic pole in its expected location near the north geographic pole, a few kilometers east or west will be a band that appears to show the north magnetic pole near the south geographic pole.

This interpretation of the stripes as variations in polarity would not make much sense unless there were some mechanism that could account for the changes, but Vine and Matthews recognized that sea-floor spreading could account for the changes, provided that one also accepted another new idea that was being advanced in the early 1960s. This idea, largely the work of several young Americans led by Allan Cox, Richard Doell, and Brent Dalrymple, was based on measurements of magnetism trapped in continental rocks. Their work showed that every hundred thousand years or so something causes Earth's magnetic field to reverse its polarity. Few in the early 1960s accepted Cox, Doell, and Dalrymple's theory on geomagnetic reversals any more than they believed Hess and Dietz on sea-floor spreading.

Vine and Matthews saw how the two new concepts could work together. If the sea floor were stable, as previously believed by geologists, polarity reversals of Earth's magnetic field would place rocks of one magnetic direction on top of another, like a layer cake. But if the sea floor is being created at mid-ocean ridges and new crust is spreading away from the ridges, the polarity reversals would appear as stripes instead of as layers. Furthermore, one could expect that the stripes on each side of the ridge would be symmetrical. If the third stripe from the ridge on the east is a wide one with a north magnetic pole near the north geographic pole, then the third stripe on the west should also be wide with the same polarity. This pattern could be observed in the intensity map—not the polarity, of course, but the comparative widths.

About the same time as Vine and Matthews, a Canadian geophysicist also had this idea but could not get it published because he did not have the data to back it up, and the idea was rejected as worthy only of conversation interest. Vine and Matthews had the data and were published in *Nature* in September 1963. Combined with other data supporting sea-floor spreading, magnetic reversals of the ocean floor became the convincing evidence that led to the theory of plate tectonics. This did not happen at once, since few believed in any of the theories or even in some of the evidence in 1963.

In 1965 a chance meeting with Brent Dalrymple on a trip to the United States led Vine to forge another link in the chain of reasoning. Dalrymple told Vine in private conversation in some detail of an unannounced discovery of a previously unrecognized geomagnetic reversal, this one less than a million years ago, an eye blink in geological time. The rock that revealed the reversal was located near Jamarillo Creek in Mexico. A few months later, Vine visited the Lamont Geological Observatory (now Lamont-Doherty Earth Observatory) in New York, where he was shown new data from the South Pacific floor that also showed a geomagnetic reversal at exactly the same time as the Jamarillo event. Vine could easily see that the two were the same. Indeed, when the two magnetic records were identical. It was too good a match to have occurred unless the reversals were real events, and not some effect that occurred as a result of chance local conditions. But if the reversals were real, then so would sea-floor spreading be real, and indeed would create a whole new view of Earth.

The exact date that plate tectonics became the accepted and orthodox theory of Earth's crustal history among geologists is difficult to pin down. There is no single moment like the 1858 presentations of the theory of evolution by Darwin and Wallace. But a case can be made for a meeting of the Geological Society of America in San Francisco in December 1966, when Vine presented a paper titled "Proof of Ocean-Floor Spreading." Following that meeting, most geologists came to believe in that explanation of the apparent continental drift first proposed by **Alfred Wegener** in 1912 and mostly derided since that time. Two years later, a series of ocean cores revealed that the ages of the different stripes on the sea floor matched the ages of the geomagnetic reversals observed on continental rocks. No one could doubt the reality of sea-floor spreading after that.

Subsequently and notably with Eldridge Moores, Vine has worked on a rock formation in the Troodos Mountains of southern Cyprus that is thought to be an upthrust slice of ocean floor. Their project is to elucidate further details of the structure and physical properties of oceanic crust formed by sea-floor spreading. Vine's other work includes studies of the form of Earth's magnetic field in the past and of the electrical conductivity of the continental crust.

SELECTED WRITINGS BY VINE:

Books

(With Philip Kearey) *Global Tectonics, 2nd ed.* London: Blackwell Science, 1996.

Periodicals

(with D.H. Matthews) "Magnetic anomalies over oceanic ridges." *Nature* (1963), 199: 947-949.
"Spreading of the ocean floor; new evidence." *Science* (1966), 154: 1405-1415.
"The continental drift debate." *Nature* (1977), 266: 19-22.

FURTHER READING:

Books

Miller, Russell. *Continents in Collision.* Alexandria, VA: Time-Life Books, 1983.
Weiner, Jonathan. *Planet Earth.* New York and Toronto: Bantam Books, 1986.

—Sketch by Bryan Bunch

Arnold C. Wahl
1937–1982
American chemical physicist

Arnold Wahl was a chemical physicist who pioneered the use of computers to study the structure and properties of atoms and molecules as well as the changes these particles undergo in different physical and chemical conditions. He worked for most of his professional life at the Argonne National Laboratory in Argonne, Illinois. In the later years of his life, he was in generally poor health and left Argonne in 1977 to take a job with Science Applications, Inc. He died in 1982.

Wahl was born on February 18, 1937, in Chicago in a house only a block from Lake Michigan. His father was a brewmaster and for many years was in charge of the production of beer at a local company. After he retired, he operated a correspondence school for brewmasters. Friends say that Wahl had a natural curiosity about the world around him as a child, and his parents often allowed him to decorate portions of their house with his latest scientific "finds."

Wahl attended the Latin High School in Chicago and then enrolled at the Rensselaer Polytechnic Institute for his undergraduate studies. He worked briefly as a student aide at the Union Carbide Company in 1957. In 1959, Wahl received his bachelor of chemical engineering degree from Rensselaer, and then returned to Chicago for his doctoral studies. While at the University of Chicago, he was a university fellow (1961), a National Science Foundation fellow (1962-1963), and an Argonne fellow (1963-1964). He was awarded his Ph.D. in chemical physics in 1964.

Upon his graduation from Chicago, Wahl accepted a position as research associate and fellow at the Argonne National Laboratory. A year later, he left Argonne to take a post as assistant professor at the University of Wisconsin. However, he only remained at Wisconsin for a year before returning to Argonne as Senior Scientist and Group Leader. In addition to his work at Argonne, Wahl worked as a consultant at the Illinois Institute of Technology (1965-1966), the Center for Applied Quantum Mechanics in Paris (1966-1967), and the Lawrence Livermore Laboratory (1969-1977).

The Use of Computers for Chemical Research

Wahl's research involved the combination of two crucial fields, quantum mechanics and computer technology. In a review paper written for *Scientific American* in 1970, he outlined his view of the way these two fields could be integrated to produce a better understanding of chemical phenomena. "Assuming that one starts with a fundamentally sound theoretical model of the structure of the individual atoms or molecules, and of the nature of the forces between them, the laws of basic electrostatics, classical physics, quantum mechanics, and statistical mechanics in principle provide a means for computing the macroscopic outcome of a chemical experiment—without ever performing the experiment!"

That is, atoms and molecules are nothing other than collections of electrically charged particles. The way in which these particles interact with each other can all be described by well-known laws from classical and quantum physics. The only problem is that these interactions are incredibly complex for any but the very simplest of systems. It would take a human years to solve the relevant mathematical equations involved in the description of most atomic and molecular systems.

What Wahl realized was that the computer made it possible to perform these calculations at a speed that made the solution of complex mathematical equations a realistic possibility. Thus, it should be possible to predict the results of various interactions without ever having to try those reactions out in the laboratory. Wahl pointed out that this approach involved using the computer as a source of information, not a device for collecting and collating information from other sources. In this respect, Wahl's vision of the role of the computer in studying chemical reactions has been more than justified by the kinds of computer programs now used by chemists to draw and study chemical structures of all kinds.

One of the techniques developed by Wahl for the study of two- and three-atom systems was called MultiConfiguration Self-Consistent Field (MCSF) theory. This theory has been and remains a powerful tool in the field of theoretical chemistry.

Wahl applied his knowledge of and interest in computer-based chemistry to a number of different situations. For example, he organized a theoretical chemistry group at Argonne and supervised studies on the application of his work to atmospheric and molecular beam chemistry. He also served as a member of the Committee on Electronic Structure of Atoms and Molecules of the U.S. Air Force Office of Scientific Research. In addition, he created a number of films and wall charts representing the results of his computer studies on the properties of atoms and molecules.

SELECTED WRITINGS BY WAHL:

Periodicals

(With P. Bertoncini, K. Kaiser, and P. Land) "BI-SON: A New Instrument for the Experimentalist." *International Journal of Quantum Chemistry*, Symposium No. 3, Part 2 (1970): 499-512.

"Chemistry by Computer." *Scientific American* (April 1970): 12, 54-70.

"Chemistry from Computers." *Argonne National Laboratory Reviews* 5, Vol. 1 (April 1969): 43-69.

FURTHER READING:

Periodicals

Wahl, Arnold C. "Chemistry by Computer." *Scientific American* (April 1970): 12, 54-70.

—*Sketch by David Newton*

George Wald

George Wald
1906–1997
American biochemist

George Wald first won a place in the spotlight as the recipient of a Nobel Prize for his discovery of the way in which hidden biochemical processes in the retinal pigments of the eye turn light energy into sight. Among Wald's important experiments were the effects of vitamin A on sight and the roles played by rod and cone cells in black and white and color vision. Outside the laboratory, his splendid lectures at Harvard to packed audiences of students generated great intellectual excitement. It was as a political activist during the turbulent 1960s, however, that Wald garnered further public recognition. Wald's personal belief in the unity of nature and the kinship among all living things was evidenced by the substantial roles he played in the scientific world as well as the political and cultural arena of the 1960s.

Wald's father, Isaac Wald, a tailor and later a foreman in a clothing factory, immigrated from Austrian Poland, while his mother, Ernestine Rosenmann Wald, immigrated from Bavaria. Most of Wald's youth was spent in Brooklyn, New York, where his parents moved after his birth on the Lower East Side of Manhattan on November 18, 1906. He attended high school at Brooklyn Tech, where he intended to study to become an electrical engineer. College changed his mind, however, as he explained for the *New York Times Magazine* in 1969, "I learned I could talk, and I thought I'd become a lawyer. But the law was man-made; I soon discovered I wanted something more real."

Wald's bachelor of science degree in zoology, which he received from New York University in 1927, was his ticket into the reality of biological research. He began his research career at Columbia University, where he was awarded a master's degree in 1928, working under Selig Hecht, one of the founders of the field of biophysics and an authority on the physiology of vision. Hecht exerted an enormous influence on Wald, both as an educator and a humanist. The elder scientist's belief in the social obligation of science, coupled with the conviction that science should be explained so the general public could understand it, made a great impression on the young Wald. Following Hecht's sudden death in 1947 at the age of 55, Wald wrote a memorial as a tribute to his colleague.

In 1932 Wald earned his doctorate at Columbia, after which he was awarded a National Research Council Fellowship in Biology. The two-year fellowship helped to support his research career, which first took him to the laboratory of **Otto Warburg** in Berlin. It was there, in 1932, that he discovered that vitamin

A is one of the major constituents of retinal pigments, the light sensitive chemicals that set off the cascade of biological events that turns light into sight.

Warburg sent the young Wald to Switzerland, where he studied vitamins with chemist **Paul Karrer** at the University of Zurich. From there Wald went to **Otto Meyerhof**'s laboratory of cell metabolism at the Kaiser Wilhelm Institute in Heidelberg, Germany, finishing his fellowship in the department of physiology at the University of Chicago in 1934. His fellowship completed, Wald went to Harvard University, first as a tutor in biochemistry and subsequently as an instructor, faculty instructor, and associate professor, finally becoming a full professor in 1948. In 1968, he became Higgins Professor of Biology, a post he retained until he became an emeritus professor in 1977.

Wald did most of his work in eye physiology at Harvard, where he discovered in the late 1930s that the light-sensitive chemical in the rods—those cells in the retina responsible for night vision—is a single pigment called rhodopsin (visual purple), a substance derived from opsin, a protein, and retinene, a chemically modified form of vitamin A. In the ensuing years, Wald discovered that the vitamin A in rhodopsin is "bent" relative to its natural state, and light causes it to "straighten out," dislodging it from opsin. This simple reaction initiates all the subsequent activity that eventually generates the sense of vision.

Wald's research moved from rods to cones, the retinal cells responsible for color vision, discovering with his co-worker Paul K. Brown, that the pigments sensitive to red and yellow-green are two different forms of vitamin A that co-exist in the same cone, while the blue-sensitive pigments are located in separate cones. They also showed that color blindness is caused by the absence of one of these pigments.

For much of his early professional life, Wald concentrated his energy on work, both research and teaching. His assistant, Brown, stayed with him for over 20 years and became a full-fledged collaborator. A former student, Ruth Hubbard, became his second wife in 1958, and they had two children, Elijah and Deborah. (His previous marriage to Frances Kingsley in 1931 ended in divorce; he has two sons by that marriage, Michael and David.) Wald, his wife, and Brown together became an extremely productive research team.

Research Efforts Receive Recognition with Nobel Prize

By the late 1950s Wald began to be showered with honors, and during his career he received numerous honorary degrees and awards. After Wald was awarded (with **Haldan K. Hartline** of the United States and **Ragnar Granit** of Sweden) the Nobel Prize

in physiology or medicine in 1967 for his work with vision, John E. Dowling wrote in *Science* that Wald and his team formed "the nucleus of a laboratory that has been extraordinarily fruitful as the world's foremost center of visual-pigment biochemistry."

As Wald's reputation flourished, his fame as an inspiring professor grew as well. He lectured to packed classrooms, inspiring an intense curiosity in his students. The energetic professor was portrayed in a 1966 *Time* article that summarized the enthusiasm he brought to teaching his natural science course: "With crystal clarity and obvious joy at a neat explanation, Wald carries his students from protons in the fall to living organisms in the spring, [and] ends most lectures with some philosophical peroration on the wonder of it all." That same year, the *New York Post* said of his lectures, "His beginnings are slow, sometimes witty. . . . The talk gathers momentum and suddenly an idea *pings* into the atmosphere—fresh, crisp, thought-provoking."

Six days after he received the Nobel Prize, Wald wielded the status of his new prestige in support of a widely popular resolution before the city council of Cambridge, Massachusetts—placing a referendum on the Vietnam War on the city's ballot of November 7, 1967. Echoing the sentiments of his mentor Hecht, he asserted that scientists should be involved in public issues.

The Cambridge appearance introduced him to the sometimes stormy arena of public politics, a forum from which he never retired. The escalating war in Vietnam aroused Wald to speak out against America's military policy. In 1965, during the escalation of that war, Wald's impromptu denunciation of the Vietnam war stunned an audience at New York University, where he was receiving an honorary degree. Shortly afterward, he threw his support and prestige behind the presidential campaign of Eugene McCarthy. His offer to speak publicly on behalf of McCarthy was ignored, however, and he became a disillusioned supporter, remaining on the fringe of political activism.

Political Activism Punctuated with "The Speech"

Then on March 4, 1969, he gave an address at the Massachusetts Institute of Technology (MIT) that, "upended his life and pitched him abruptly into the political world," according to the *New York Times Magazine.* Wald gave "The Speech," as the talk came to be known in his family, before an audience of radical students at MIT The students had helped to organize a scientists' day-long "strike" to protest the influence of the military on their work, a topic of much heated debate at the time.

Although much of the MIT audience was already bored and restless by the time Wald began, even many of those students who were about to leave the room stopped to listen as the Nobel laureate began to deliver his oration, entitled, "A Generation in Search of a Future." "I think this whole generation of students is beset with a profound sense of uneasiness, and I don't think they have quite defined its source," Wald asserted as quoted in the *New York Times Magazine*. "I think I understand the reasons for their uneasiness even better than they do. What is more, I *share* their uneasiness."

Wald's discourse evoked applause from the audience as he offered his opinion that student unease arose from a variety of troublesome matters. He pointed to the Vietnam War, the military establishment, and finally, the threat of nuclear warfare. "We must get rid of those atomic weapons," he declared. "We cannot live with them." Speaking to the students as fellow scientists, he sympathized with the their unease at the influence of the military establishment on the work of scientists, intoning, "Our business is with life, not death. . . ."

The speech was reprinted and distributed around the country by the media. Through these reprints, Wald told readers that some of their elected leaders were "insane," and he referred to the American "war crimes" enacted in Vietnam. In the furor that followed, Wald was castigated by critics, many of whom were fellow academics, and celebrated by sympathizers. A letter writer from Piney Flats, Tennessee was quoted in the *New York Times Magazine* as saying, "So good to know there are still some intellects around who can talk downright horsesense." Wald summed up his role as scientist-political activist in that same article by saying, "I'm a scientist, and my concerns are eternal. But even eternal things are acted out in the present." He described his role as gadfly as putting certain controversial positions into words in order to make it, "easier for others to inch toward it."

His role as a Vietnam war gadfly expanded into activism in other arenas of foreign affairs. He served for a time as president of international tribunals on El Salvador, the Philippines, Afghanistan, Zaire, and Guatemala. In 1984, he joined four other Nobel Prize laureates who went with the "peace ship" sent by the Norwegian government to Nicaragua during that country's turmoil.

In addition to his interests in science and politics, Wald's passions included collecting Rembrandt etchings and primitive art, especially pre-Columbian pottery. This complex mixture of science, art, and political philosophy was reflected in his musings about religion and nature in the *New York Times Magazine*. "There's nothing supernatural in my mind. Nature is my religion, and it's enough for me. I stack it up against any man's. For its awesomeness, and for the sense of the sanctity of man that it provides."

In addition to the Nobel Prize, Wald received numerous awards and honors, including the Albert Lasker Award of the American Public Health Association in 1953, the Proctor Award in 1955 from the Association for Research in Ophthalmology, the Rumford Premium of the American Academy of Arts and Sciences in 1959, the 1969 Max Berg Award, and the Joseph Priestley Award the following year. In addition, he was elected to the National Academy of Science in 1950 and the American Philosophical Society in 1958. He is also a member of the Optical Society of America, which awarded him the Ives Medal in 1966. In the mid–1960s Wald spent a year as a Guggenheim fellow at England's Cambridge University, where he was elected an Overseas fellow of Churchill College for 1963–64. Wald also held honorary degrees from the University of Berne, Yale University, Wesleyan University, New York University, and McGill University.

Wald died on April 12, 1997, at his home in Cambridge, Massachusetts, at the age of 90.

SELECTED WRITINGS BY WALD:

Books

General Education in a Free Society. Cambridge: Harvard University Press, 1945.
Visual Pigments and Photoreceptors: Review and Outlook. Academic Press, 1974.

Periodicals

"The Molecular Basis of Visual Excitation." *American Scientist* (January 1954).

FURTHER READING:

Periodicals

Dowling, John E. "News And Comment; Nobel Prize: Three Named for Medicine, Physiology Award." *Science* (27 October 1967).
Dudar, Helen. "Profile. . ." *New York Post* (1 May 1966): 32.
————. "George Wald: The Man, the Speech." *New York Times Magazine* (17 August 1969): 28-29.
————. "Profile. . ." *Time* (6 May 1966).
Pace, Eric. "George Wald, Nobel Biologist, Dies at 90" (obituary). *New York Times* (14 April 1997): B9.

—Sketch by Marc Kusinitz

John E. Walker

John E. Walker
1941–

English biochemist

John E. Walker was awarded a share of the 1997 Nobel Prize in Chemistry for his research on the enzyme ATP synthase. That enzyme is responsible for the biologically critical molecule known as adenosine triphosphate (ATP) that provides the energy needed to drive a host of biochemical reactions in cells. Walker's research dovetailed with similar work carried out by the second 1997 Nobel Laureate, **Paul Boyer**, who devised a theory that explained the process by which the ATP synthase enzyme operates. Walker has been employed at the Laboratory of Molecular Biology of the Medical Research Council in Cambridge for more than two decades.

Walker was born on January 7, 1941, in Halifax, England. He attended the Rastrick Grammar School in Brighouse, Yorkshire, and then enrolled at St. Catherine's College, Oxford, in 1960. He was awarded his B.A. Degree in Chemistry by St. Catherine's in 1964. Walker then spent four years as a research student at the Sir William Dunn School of Pathology at Oxford before earning his M.A. and D. Phil. degrees from Oxford in 1969.

Upon completion of his doctoral studies, Walker spent two years as a Postdoctoral Fellow at the School of Pharmacy at the University of Wisconsin. He then spent three additional years as a NATO Fellow at CNRS, in Gif-sur-Yvette, France, and as an EMBO Fellow at the Institut Pasteur in Paris. In 1974, Walker accepted an appointment as a member of the scientific staff at the Cambridge Laboratory of Molecular Biology of the Medical Research Council. He was assigned to the Division of Protein and Nucleic Acid Chemistry of the laboratory. In 1982, Walker was promoted to Senior Scientist at the laboratory, and in 1987, he was given a Special Appointment (Professorial Grade) at the laboratory.

Structure and Function of ATP

Adenosine triphosphate (ATP) is one of the most important molecules in the cells of living organisms. It has been described as an "energy-carrying" molecule because it provides the energy needed to drive many essential biochemical reactions.

The energy carried by an ATP molecule is stored in its phosphate bonds. A molecule of ATP is produced through a series of steps in which a phosphate group is first attached to a molecule of adenosine monophosphate (AMP) to form adenosine diphosphate (ADP). ADP then adds a second phosphate group to form adenosine triphosphate (ATP). As each phosphate group is added to the growing molecule, it brings with it energy stored in the form of the chemical bonds by which the phosphate is attached to the core molecule.

ATP acts as an energy-provider because it tends to break down to form first ADP plus a phosphate group, and then AMP and a second phosphate group. Each time one of these steps occurs, energy is released. That energy is transferred to some other set of chemical reactants in a cell, making it possible for those reactants to form new compounds.

Mechanism of ATP Synthesis

Scientists have long been very interested in learning precisely how ATP is formed and how it carries out its biochemical functions. Discovered in 1929 by the German chemist Karl Lohmann, ATP was first synthesized two decades later by the Scottish chemist **Alexander Todd**. The role of ATP in providing energy to cell reactions was first elucidated by the German-American biochemist **Fritz Lipmann** in the period 1939-1941.

One important line of ATP research has focused on the mechanism by which the molecule is formed. In 1960, the American biochemist Efraim Racker found a substance in the mitochondria of cells that appeared to be responsible for the synthesis of ATP. They called the enzyme $F_0 F_1$ ATPase, although it is now better known as ATP synthase. The original name for the enzyme comes from the fact that it consists of two parts, an F_0 domain that is attached to a cell membrane, and an F_1 domain that protrudes from the membrane.

During the 1950s, the American biochemist Paul D. Boyer developed a theory to explain how ATP synthase is able to produce ATP. Essentially, he argued that a flow of hydrogen ions within the cell membrane causes the F_0 domain of the enzyme to rotate in much the same way that the wind causes the blades on a windmill to turn. Boyer hypothesized that the turning of the F_0 membrane sequentially exposed structurally different regions of the F_1 domain in such as way as to make possible the ADP + phosphate reaction to occur. Walker's research completely identified the amino acid sequence of ATP synthase and proteins attached to it and determined much of the three-dimensional structure of the molecule. It was for this research that he was awarded the 1997 Nobel Prize in Chemistry.

Honors and Awards

Walker has received a host of honors and awards in addition to the Nobel Prize. Among these have been the A. T. Clay Gold Medal for academic distinction in 1959, the Johnson Foundation Prize of the University of Pennsylvania Medical School in 1994, the CIBA Medal and Prize of The Biochemical Society in 1995, the Peter Mitchell Medal of the European Bioenergetics Congress in 1996, and the Gaetana Quagliariello Prize for Mitochondrial Research from the University of Bari, Italy, in 1997. Walker has also been elected a Fellow of The Royal Society (1995), a Fellow of Sidney Sussex College at Cambridge (1997) and an Honorary Fellow of St. Catherine's College at Oxford (1997). He has also been asked to give named lectures at the University of California at San Diego (the Nathan Kaplan Memorial Lecture), Copenhagen (the Novo-Nordic Lecture), Sheffield University (the Krebs Lecture), the Biochemical Society (the CIBA Lecture), the EBEC Conference at Louvain, Belgium (the Peter Mitchell Lecture), and the Netherlands Biochemical Society (Lecture of the Year).

For two decades, Walker has also been active in a variety of professional responsibilities. He has served on the editorial board of *The Biochemical Journal, Biochemistry International, Molecular Biology, Journal of Bioenergetics,* and *Structure.* He is the author or co-author of more than 175 papers and book chapters. Walker is married and has two children.

SELECTED WRITINGS BY WALKER:

Periodicals

"The Mechanism of ATP Synthesis," *The Biochemist,* 16 (1994): 31-35.

Ernest Walton

"The Mitochondrial Transporter Family," *Current Opinion in Structural Biology,* 2 (1992): 519-526.
"The Regulation of Catalysis in ATP Synthase," *Current Opinion in Structural Biology,* 4 (1994): 912-918.
"Structure at 2.8 ? Resolution of F121-ATPase from Bovine Heart Mitochondria," *Nature,* 370 (1994): 621-628.

FURTHER READING:

Other

"Information," at http://www.nobel.se/announcement-97/chemistry97.html.

—*Sketch by David Newton*

Ernest Walton
1903–1995
Irish experimental physicist

Ernest Thomas Sinton Walton was an Irish experimental physicist who gained renown for achieving, with physicist **John D. Cockcroft,** the first artificial disintegration of an atomic nucleus, without the use of radioactive elements. Their breakthrough was accomplished by artificially accelerating a beam of protons (basic particles of the nuclei of atoms which carry a positive charge of electricity) and aiming it at a target of lithium, one of the lightest known metals. The resultant emission of alpha particles, that is, positively charged particles given off by certain radioactive substances, indicated not only that some protons had succeeded in penetrating the nuclei of the lithium atoms but also that they had somehow combined with the lithium atoms and had been transformed into something new. Although the process was not an efficient energy producer, the work of Walton and Cockcroft stimulated many theoretical and practical developments and influenced the whole course of nuclear physics. For their pioneering work, Walton and Cockcroft shared the 1951 Nobel Prize in physics.

Ernest Thomas Sinton Walton was born October 6, 1903, in Dungarven, County Waterford, in the Irish Republic. His father, John Arthur Walton, was a Methodist minister, while his mother, Anna Elizabeth (Sinton) Walton, was from a very old Ulster family, who had lived in the same house in Armagh for over two hundred years. The young Walton was sent to school at Belfast's Methodist College, where he demonstrated an aptitude for science and math. It was no surprise, then, when in 1922 he decided to enroll in math and experimental science at Dublin's Trinity College. He graduated in 1926 with a B.A. degree, in 1928 with a M.Sc., and in 1934 with a M.A.

Joins the Cavendish During its Heyday

The following year he headed to Cambridge University, England, on a Clerk Maxwell research scholarship. There, he joined the world-famous Cavendish Laboratory, headed by the great New Zealand-born physicist, **Ernest Rutherford**. Walton was assigned cramped laboratory space in a basement room. While his quarters were less than luxurious, he was at least blessed by having roommates with whom he struck up an immediate friendship, physicists T. E. Allibone and John D. Cockcroft. Walton went on to make scientific history, in collaboration with the latter, for a project that would pave the way for the development of the atom bomb. Walton had first to learn to crawl before he could take such giant steps. At the suggestion of Rutherford, he began attempting to increase the velocity of electrons (the negatively charged particles of the atom) by spinning them in the electric field produced by a changing circular magnetic field as a method of nuclear disintegration. Although the method was not successful, he was able to figure out the stability of the orbits of the revolving electrons, and the design and engineering problems of creating an accelerating machine with minimal tools

and materials. This early work of Walton's later led to the development of the betatron, that is, a particle accelerator in which electrons are propelled by the inductive action of a rapidly varying magnetic field.

Next, Walton tried to build a high frequency linear accelerator. His goal was to produce a stream of alpha particles traveling at high speed which could be used to shed light on various aspects of the atomic nucleus. Rutherford had long been keen to get his hands on such as source of alpha particles but despaired of any short-term breakthrough. As it transpired, Rutherford's wish was granted sooner than he expected.

What was needed was a fundamentally different way of viewing the problem. Walton and his colleagues at the Cavendish were trying to accelerate electrons to a speed sufficient to enable them to penetrate an atomic nucleus. Such high velocities were necessary, they believed, in order to counteract the repulsive charge of the nuclei. The speeding electrons, they figured, would literally bully their way through. However, achieving such high speeds was easier said than done. It required the application of enormous amounts of electricity, about four million volts, which at that time was impossible to generate in a discharge tube (a tube that contains a gas or metal vapor which conducts an electric discharge in the form of light). A crucial breakthrough came in 1929, when the Russian physicist **George Gamow,** visited the Cavendish laboratory. With physicist **Niels Bohr** in Copenhagen, he had worked out a wave-mechanical theory of the penetration of particles, in which they believed particles tunneled through rather than over potential barriers. This meant that particles propelled by about 500,000 volts, as opposed to millions, could possibly permeate the barrier and enter the nucleus, if present in sufficiently large numbers. That is, one would need a beam of many thousands of millions of moving particles to produce atomic disintegrations that would be capable of being observed.

Rutherford gave Walton and Cockcroft the go-ahead to test the supposition. It was a measure of his confidence in them—the high voltage apparatus they constructed to enable them to accelerate atomic particles cost almost £1,000 (British pounds) to build. It was an enormous sum in those days, and represented almost the entire annual budget for the laboratory.

The machine, the first of its kind ever built, and today on view at the London Science Museum in South Kensington, was built out of an ordinary transformer, enhanced by two stacks of large condensers (or what would today be called capacitors), which could be turned on and off by means of an electronic switch. This arrangement generated up to half a million volts, which were directed at an electrical discharge tube. At the top of the tube protons were produced. The velocity of the protons was increased into a beam which could be used to hit any mark at the bottom of the tubes. Although it would be considered primitive by today's standards, their apparatus was, in fact, an ingenious construction, cobbled together from glass cylinders taken from old fashioned petrol pumps, flat metal sheets, plasticene, and vacuum pumps. The current generated by the discharge tube was almost one hundred-thousandth of an ampere, which meant that about 50 million million protons per second were being produced. The availability of such a large and tightly controlled source of particles—compared with that produced by, say, a radioactive source—greatly increased the odds of a nucleus being penetrated by the speeding atomic particles.

Halfway through 1931, while their experiment was still in its early stages, Walton and Cockcroft were forced to vacate their subterranean basement when it was taken over by physical chemists. They were obliged to deconstruct their installation and build it again. As it happened, it turned out to be a lucky break. Their new laboratory was an old lecture theater, whose high ceiling was much more suitable for their purposes. When Walton and Cockcroft went to reassemble their massive apparatus, they used the opportunity to introduce a few modifications. This time around, they incorporated a new voltage multiplying circuit, which Cockcroft had just developed, into their apparatus. It took them until the end of 1931 just to produce a steady stream of five or six hundred volts.

When the accelerator was finally completed, they restarted the laborious process of trying to penetrate an atomic nucleus using a stream of speeded up protons. They positioned a thin lithium target obliquely across from the beam of protons, in order to observe the alpha particles on either side of it. In order to detect the alpha particles that they hoped would be produced, they set up a tiny screen made of zinc sulfide, which they observed with a low-power microscope; a technique borrowed from Rutherford.

Walton's Scintillating Discovery

The first few months of 1932 were spent in rendering the installation more reliable and measuring the range and speed of the accelerated protons. It was not until April 13, 1932, that they achieved a breakthrough. On that fateful date, Walton first realized that their experiment had been successful. On the tiny screen, he detected flashes, called scintillations. These indicated that not only had the steam of protons succeeded in boring through the atomic nuclei but also that, in the process, a transformation had occurred. The speeding protons had combined with the lithium target to produce a new substance,

the alpha particles, which appeared on the screen as scintillations.

Walton and Cockcroft confirmed Walton's observations using a paper recorder with two pens, each operated by a key. Walton worked one key, Cockcroft the other. When either noticed a flash, he pressed his key. As both keys were consistently pressed at the same time, it was clear that the alphas were being emitted in pairs. The implication was that the lithium nucleus, with a mass of seven and a charge of three had, on contact with an accelerated proton, split into two alpha particles, each of mass four and charge two. In the transformation, a small amount of energy was lost, equivalent to about a quarter of a percent of the mass of lithium.

Walton and Cockcroft's achievement was groundbreaking and historic in many ways. It represented the first time that anyone had produced a change in an atomic nucleus by means totally under human control. They had also discovered a new energy source. Furthermore, they had confirmed Gamow's theory that particles could tunnel or burrow their way into a nucleus, despite the repulsion of the electrical charges. And finally, they furnished a valuable confirmation of physicist **Albert Einstein's** theory that energy and mass are interchangeable. The extra energy of the alpha particles, when allowance was made for the energy of the proton, exactly corresponded to the loss of mass.

Walton and Cockcroft's achievement was announced in a letter in *Nature* and later at a meeting of the Royal Society of London, on June 15, 1932. By that time, they had succeeded in splitting the nuclei of fifteen elements, including beryllium, the lightest, to uranium, the heaviest. All produced alpha particles, although the most spectacular results were obtained from fluorine, lithium, and boron. The news caused a sensation throughout the world. As a result of their discovery, Walton and Cockcroft were the star attractions at the Solvay Conference, an important gathering of international physicists, held in 1933, and at the International Physics Conference, held in London in 1934.

Walton and Cockcroft's particle accelerator spawned many more sophisticated models, including one built by their colleague physicist Marcus Oliphant at the Cavendish. It was capable of producing a more abundant supply of particles; not only protons, but also deuterons (nuclei of heavy hydrogen). With this, many groundbreaking nuclear transformations were carried out. Their invention also inspired the American nuclear physicist, **Ernest Orlando Lawrence,** to build a cyclotron, a cyclical accelerator, capable of reaching tremendous speeds. Although scientists in the close of the twentieth century may regard the equipment Walton and Cockcroft used as primitive, the basic idea behind the particle accelerator has stayed the same.

In 1932, Walton received his Ph.D from Cambridge and two years later, returned to Dublin as a fellow of Trinity College, his reputation preceding him. He remained there for the rest of his career. The year 1934 was memorable not only for Walton's shifting bases but also because it was the year he married Freda Wilson, a former pupil of the Methodist College, Belfast. They had two sons and two daughters, Alan, Marian, Philip, and Jean.

The next few years passed rather uneventfully for Walton. While his erstwhile partner, John D. Cockcroft went from one high profile position to another, Walton preferred to remain slightly aloof from the mainstream of physics. He concentrated instead on establishing his department's reputation for excellence. His efforts were rewarded in 1946 when he was appointed Erasmus Smith Professor of Natural and Experimental Philosophy.

Shares 1951 Nobel Prize with Cockcroft

In 1951, almost twenty years after achieving the breakthrough that changed the face of nuclear physics, Walton and Cockcroft finally achieved the recognition that many believed was long overdue them. The Nobel Prize for physics was awarded to them jointly for their pioneering work on the transmutation of atomic nuclei by artificially accelerated atomic particles. The following year, Walton became chairman of the School of Cosmic Physics of the Dublin Institute for Advanced Studies. He was elected a senior fellow of Trinity College in 1960.

Outside of his scientific work, Ernest Walton was active in committees concerned with the government, the church, research and standards, scientific academies, and the Royal City of Dublin Hospital. He has been described as "quiet, undemonstrative, and little given to talk," according to Robert L. Weber in *Pioneers or Science: Nobel Prize Winners in Physics.* Walton died on June 25, 1995, at a hospital in Belfast, Northern Ireland.

SELECTED WRITINGS BY WALTON:

Other

The First Penetration of Nuclei by Accelerated Particles (sound recording). Educational Materials and Equipment Co., Spring Green Multimedia, 1974.

FURTHER READING:

Books

Andrade, E. N. da C, *Rutherford and the Nature of the Atom,* Doubleday Anchor, 1964.

Ernst Weber

Andrade, E. N. da C, *Biographical Dictionary of Scientists,* Volume 2, Facts-on-File, 1981, pp. 823.

Crowther, J. G., *The Cavendish Laboratory, 1874–1974,* Science History Publications, 1974.

Crowther, J. G., *Modern Men of Science,* McGraw-Hill, 1966, pp. 509.

Oliphant, Mark, *Rutherford: Recollections of the Cambridge Days,* Elsevier Publishing Co., 1972.

Weber, Robert L., *Pioneers of Science: Nobel Prize Winners in Physics,* Bristol and London, The Institute of Physics, 1980, pp. 141.

Wilson, David, *Rutherford: Simple Genius,* MIT Press, 1983.

—Sketch by Avril McDonald

Ernst Weber
1901–1996
Austrian-born American electrical engineer

Ernst Weber is noted for his significant contributions to the development of microwave technology used in radar and communications systems. He is also noted for decades of work as an educator whose enthusiasm and method of teaching inspired several generations of students and colleagues in the field of electrical engineering.

Weber was born on September 6, 1901, in Vienna, Austria. He grew up in Vienna and graduated from the Vienna Technical University with a degree in electrical engineering in 1924. He continued his education at the University of Vienna, where he received a Ph.D. in physics in 1926. He then returned to the Vienna Technical University to earn an Sc.D. degree in electrical machinery in 1927. During this time he also worked as a research engineer, first at Osterreichische Siemens-Schuckert-Werke in Austria from 1924 to 1929, and later at Siemens-Schuckert-Werke in Germany from 1929 to 1930.

Emigrates to America and Begins a Long Career as an Educator

In 1930, Weber came to America to take a temporary position as a visiting professor of electrical engineering at the Polytechnic Institute of Brooklyn in New York. He was appointed to a permanent research professor position at the institute in 1931, where he taught electromagnetic theory, high-frequency phenomena, and other advanced subjects in electrical engineering. Many engineers working in industry were attracted to Polytechnic because of Weber's courses, and in 1936 the institute began offering the first evening doctoral program for electrical engineers in the United States. This program became so popular that by 1947 it accounted for almost half of the part-time Ph.D. candidates in the country.

In the mid-1930s, war clouds began to form over Europe. Weber decided to remain in the United States permanently, and he became a naturalized citizen in 1936. That same year he married. He and his wife had two children during their marriage. Weber continued his role at Polytechnic as a researcher and teaching professor until 1941.

Contributes to the Development of Radar During World War II

With the onset of World War II, Weber organized a research team at Polytechnic in 1941 under contract with the Office of Scientific Research and Development. Working with the Radiation Laboratory at the Massachusetts Institute of Technology, Weber and his team worked on several problems facing the development of early radar systems. One of the problems involved measurements of the very high frequency microwaves used in radar. In order to do this they had to coat glass tubes with a very thin layer of conducting metal. Weber recalled the art of decorating chinaware with gold and silver, and drew on

this ancient skill to produce some of the first successful components for testing. Later the Polytechnic team substituted a mixture of platinum and palladium to replace the gold and silver. Their designs and production techniques contributed to the overall development of radar during the war, and Weber was awarded the Presidential Certificate of Merit for his work.

In 1943, while working on the radar development project, Weber helped establish the Microwave Research Institute at Polytechnic to develop microwave components and devices. In 1945, Weber was named Director of the Microwave Research Institute and head of the electrical engineering department at Polytechnic. He held both positions until 1957. The success of the Microwave Research Institute led to the development of several commercially saleable products, and the Polytechnic Research and Development Company was formed in 1944 to market those products. Weber served as company secretary from 1944 to 1952, and as president from 1952 to 1959, in addition to his teaching, research, and other duties. The company was sold to Harris-Intertype Corporation in late 1959.

Receives Honors for His Work

Weber was named president of Polytechnic Institute of Brooklyn in 1957. He held that position for 12 years until 1969, when he retired to become president emeritus. In 1970, Polytechnic awarded him an honorary doctorate in engineering—one of six honorary doctorates he received during his lifetime. As a result of Weber's commitment to the highest quality education during his years as a professor and as president, the graduate electrical engineering program at Polytechnic was ranked sixth in the nation by the American Council of Education in 1966. Weber himself was named one of the top ten all-time educators by the Institute of Electrical and Electronic Engineers and was awarded the IEEE Education Medal by that group.

Outside of the academic world, Weber was also active. He was president of the Institute of Radio Engineers in 1959 and helped merge that group with the American Institute of Electrical Engineering to become the first president of the Institute of Electrical and Electronic Engineers in 1963. He became a founding member of the National Academy of Engineering in 1964 and was elected to the National Academy of Science in 1965.

After his retirement from Polytechnic, Weber moved to North Carolina. He joined the National Research Council in 1969 and served in various capacities until 1978, when he became a consultant to that group. In 1986 the Microwave Research Institute at Polytechnic was renamed the Weber Research Institute in honor of his work in the development of microwave technology. One year later, in 1987, Weber was awarded the prestigious National Medal of Science for his lifetime contributions to electrical engineering. In addition to his many awards, Weber also held numerous patents in microwave technology and was the author of many scientific papers and several books. Ernst Weber died on February 15, 1996, at the age of 94.

SELECTED WRITINGS BY WEBER:

Books

Linear Transient Analysis. 2 volumes. [publisher unknown], 1954-1956.
Electromagnetic Theory, Static Fields and Their Mapping. [publisher unknown], 1965.
The Evolution of Electrical Engineering–A Personal Perspective. [publisher unknown], [date unknown].

FURTHER READING:

Other

http://catt.poly.edu/polytech/alumni/cable/spring96/weber.html This website includes a notice of Weber's death, a summary of his life and work, and a photo of his receiving the National Medal of Science in 1987 from then-Vice President George Bush.

—*Sketch by Chris Cavette*

Mary Catherine Bishop Weiss
1930–1966
American trigonometrist

Mary Weiss helped to create methods of harmonic analysis that apply to higher–dimensional geometry and one problem in lacunary series that defied solution for 20 years. Her work was recognized and supported by the National Science Foundation.

Weiss was born on December 11, 1930, to Albert Bishop, a mathematics professor, and his wife, Helen, in Wichita, Kansas. Both Weiss and her brother, Errett, would follow in their father's footsteps. Mr. Bishop had become an Army officer after graduating from the United States Military Academy at West Point, but began teaching at the university level following his retirement from the military. He died

while Weiss and her brother were still very young, and the family moved to another region in Kansas to be closer to relatives. Weiss and her mother moved to the Chicago area when Errett entered the University of Chicago, where she also enrolled in the institution's experimental Laboratory School. During her undergraduate years she met and married a fellow student, Guido Weiss. They both earned their doctorates at the University of Chicago, both working in the same general area of inquiry under Antoni Zygmund. Zygmund would later become Weiss's colleague, co–writer, and editor, a collaboration which lasted until her death.

Weiss's Ph.D. thesis, completed in 1957, laid the foundation for three years of work on lacunary series, the subject of her first five published papers. During this time she provided a proof for a theorem of Raymond Paley's and solved a problem first posed by one of the founders of the Hardy–Littlewood series, John E. Littlewood. Her investigations held a lot in common with some tenets of probability theory involving random variables.

Weiss had a mathematician's temperament, in the sense that she could summon great concentration for days at a time when absorbed by some mathematical enigma. Yet she was highly sociable. During her career as a lecturer, she worked individually with students at De Paul, Washington, and Stanford universities as well as her alma mater. She read widely and held an appreciation for the fine arts, and she often participated in campus protests against the Vietnam War.

Overseas Experiences

Between 1960 and 1961, Weiss and her husband took a sabbatical to Buenos Aires and Paris, yet it was a working vacation for both of them. Guido had been wrestling with Hardy spaces in the framework of classical mathematics. Once both of them attacked the topic they extended its domain onto the complex or Gaussian plane, and also into higher dimensions. Later during this period they invited J.P. Kahane to aid their continued efforts with general lacunary power series. Upon returning from sabbatical Weiss contacted Zygmund and **Alberto P. Calderón** about their discoveries in harmonic analysis, and the three wrote a paper on Calderón–Zygmund singular integral operators in higher dimensions. Weiss's central contribution was in proving the early assumptions of Zygmund and Calderón. She also continued work with her husband on the theory of Hardy spaces in higher dimensions with E.M. Stein. Here, she applied mainly geometric methods of analysis which have yet to be fully exploited by her successors.

During the academic year of 1965–66, the National Science Foundation funded Weiss's senior postdoctoral fellowship at Cambridge University, after which she returned to America. She began work that fall at the University of Illinois, but died on October 8, a few weeks after the semester had begun. In 1967, a symposium on harmonic analysis was held at the Edwardsville campus of Southern Illinois University in Weiss's honor. At this gathering, her mentor Zygmund presented a technical summary of her published work.

SELECTED WRITINGS BY WEISS:

"The Law of the Iterated Logarithm for Lacunary Trigonometric Series." *Transactions of the American Mathematical Society* 91 (1959): 444–469.

(With Guido Weiss). "A Derivation of the Main Results of the Theory of Hp Spaces." *Revista de la Union Matematica Argentina* 22 (1960): 63–71.

(With Alberto P. Calderón and Antoni Zygmund) "On the Existence of Singular Integrals," in *Singular Intervals: Proceedings of Symposia in Pure Mathematics. Volume 10.* Edited by Alberto P. Calderón, 1967.

"A Theorem on Lacunary Trigonometric Series," in *Orthogonal Expansions and Their Continuous Analogues.* Edited by D.T. Haimo, 1968, pp. 227–230.

FURTHER READING:

Books

Pless, V. and Srinivansan, B. "Mary Catherine Bishop Weiss (1930–1966)." *Historical Encyclopedia of Chicago Women* (in production).

Weiss, Guido. "Mary Catherine Bishop Weiss," in *Women of Mathematics.* Edited by Louise S. Grinstein and Paul J. Campbell. Westport, CT: Greenwood Press, 1987, pp. 236–40.

Zygmund, A. "Mary Weiss: December 11, 1930–October 8, 1966," in *Orthogonal Expansions and Their Continuous Analogues.* Edited by D.T. Haimo. Carbondale, IL: Southern Illinois University Press, 1968, pp. xi–xviii.

Other

"Mary Catherine Bishop Weiss." *Biographies of Women Mathematicians.* http://www.scottlan.edu/lriddle/women/chronol.htm (July 1997).

—Sketch by Jennifer Kramer

Anna Johnson Pell Wheeler
1883–1966
American algebraist

A distinguished mathematics researcher and educator, Anna Johnson Pell Wheeler is best remembered for her interest and research in biorthogonal systems of functions and integral equations. Much of her work was in the area of linear algebra of infinitely many variables—an area which she studied her entire career. Wheeler struggled to gain equality with men in the field of mathematics. In 1910, she was only the second woman at the University of Chicago to receive a doctorate in mathematics. Finding a full–time teaching position was difficult, even though she was often more qualified than the male applicants. Her break came when she substituted for her incapacitated first husband, Alexander Pell, at the Armour Institute in Chicago. There, although she did not obtain a permanent position, she convinced her superiors of her competency. She was then hired as an instructor in mathematics at Mount Holyoke College in Hadley, Massachusetts, in 1911, leaving there in 1918 to take a position as associate professor at Bryn Mawr College in Pennsylvania. She remained at Bryn Mawr until her retirement in 1948, becoming head of the mathematics department in 1924. A champion of women in the field of mathematics, she urged her students to persevere toward terminal degrees despite the gender prejudices exhibited by authorities at colleges and universities at that time. It is significant, in her tenure at Bryn Mawr College, that seven of her graduate students received doctorates in mathematics.

During her career, Wheeler was active in many professional associations. She served on the council and the board of the American Mathematical Society, and was also a member of the Mathematical Association of America and the American Association for the Advancement of Science. (In 1927, Wheeler was invited by the American Mathematical Society to deliver their annual Colloquium Lectures—the only woman so honored until 1970.) In 1940, she received recognition from the Women's Centennial Congress as one of the 100 women honored who had succeeded in non–traditional careers. Continuing her support of women mathematicians, Wheeler helped **Emmy Noether**, the eminent German algebraist, to relocate to Bryn Mawr when she sought political asylum from Nazi Germany in 1933.

Wheeler, of Swedish heritage, was born in Hawarden, Iowa, on May 5, 1883. Her parents were Amelia (Frieberg) and Andrew Johnson. Her father was an undertaker and furniture dealer in the small town of Akron, Iowa. Anna attended the local high school there and received her undergraduate degree from the University of South Dakota in 1903. There, her exceptional ability in mathematics was observed by her professor, Alexander Pell (later to become her first husband). She furthered her education at the University of Iowa and at Radcliffe College, earning master's degrees from both institutions.

Fellowship Allows Study in Europe

In 1906, Wheeler received an Alice Freeman Palmer Fellowship, allowing her to continue her studies at Göttingen University in Germany. There, she was guided in her work in integral equations by such eminent mathematicians as **Hermann Minkowski**, Felix Klein, and **David Hilbert**. Her thesis was completed under Hilbert's instruction, but for some reason—speculated to have been a dispute with Hilbert—she did not receive a degree from Göttingen.

Although Wheeler accepted the fellowship with the understanding she could not marry during its term, Pell joined her in Germany at the end of the year, and they were married there in 1907. Her new husband had an interesting past. He was actually a Russian revolutionist named Sergei Degaev, who had fled his country after being implicated in the murder of an officer of the Russian secret police. After emigrating to the United States, Dagaev changed his name to Alexander Pell, and began his new life as a mathematics professor.

The Pells left Germany and returned to the University of South Dakota. Shortly after their return, Pell accepted a position to teach at the Armour Institute of Technology in Chicago. Wheeler completed the work for her Ph. D. at the University of Chicago, and when Pell suffered a stroke in 1911, she assumed his teaching duties. She had hoped for a permanent position with a Midwestern university, but was unsuccessful. Other than taking over her husband's classes, the closest Wheeler came to being employed while in Chicago was when she taught a course at the University the fall semester of 1910. When she did find permanent work, it was out east at Mount Holyoke, and later, at Bryn Mawr. Pell, who was a semi–invalid after his stroke, died in 1921. In 1925, she married Arthur Leslie Wheeler, a classics scholar who had just become professor of Latin at Princeton University in New Jersey. Wheeler continued to teach at Bryn Mawr, even though they lived in Princeton where her husband was teaching. They also enjoyed a summer home in the Adirondack Mountains, to which she often invited her students. When Arthur died suddenly in 1932, she moved back to Bryn Mawr, where she lived and taught for the rest of her life.

Strengthens School's Reputation in Mathematics

Wheeler's work at Bryn Mawr took her beyond the classroom. She was well aware of the need to strengthen the reputation of the school's mathematics department, and set about doing so. She advised reducing teaching loads so that more research could be carried out by the faculty and encouraged professional collaboration and theoretical exchanges with other schools in the Philadelphia area. During this time of increasing administrative responsibilities, Wheeler remained active in publishing the results of her research into integral equations and functional analysis. Her Colloquium Lectures, however, were never published.

Although suffering from arthritis, Wheeler continued to participate in mathematics association meetings after her retirement. She died at age 82 at Bryn Mawr on March 26, 1996, after suffering a stroke. She was eighty–two.

SELECTED WRITINGS BY WHEELER:

Biorthogonal Systems of Functions, 1911.

FURTHER READING:

Books

Bailey, Martha J. *American Women in Science: A Biographical Dictionary.* Santa Barbara, CA: ABC–CLIO, Inc., 1994, pp. 414–415.
Ogilvie, Marilyn Bailey. *Women in Science: Antiquity through the Nineteenth Century.* Cambridge, MA: MIT Press, 1986, pp. 173–174.
Sicherman, Barbara and Carol Hurd Green, editors. *Notable American Women: The Modern Period, A Biographical Dictionary.* Cambridge, MA: The Belknap Press, 1980, pp. 725–726.

Periodicals

"Dr. Anna Pell Wheeler" (obituary). *The New York Times* (April 1, 1966): 35: 1.

Other

"Anna Johnson Pell Wheeler." *Biographies of Women Mathematicians.* June 1977. http://www.scottlan.edu/lriddle/women/chronol.htm (July 22, 1997).

—*Sketch by Jane Stewart Cook*

John R. Whinfield
1901–1966
English textile chemist

John Rex Whinfield invented terylene, a synthetic polyester fiber that is equal to or surpasses nylon in toughness and resilience, and has become used universally as a textile fiber. The invention of terylene, also known as Dacron, was the culmination of many years of study and reasoning about the molecular structure and physical and chemical properties of polymers. Whinfield's major inventive work on terylene was carried out aside from his primary research in the small laboratory of a company that had little or no interest in research on fibers. He spent his life working as an industrial research chemist and eventually became director of the fibers division of Imperial Chemical Industries. Recognition for his work came in the later years of his life.

Whinfield was born February 16, 1901, in Sutton, Surrey, England, to John Henry Richard Whinfield, a mechanical engineer, and Edith Matthews Whinfield. As a boy, Whinfield showed an early interest in science and chemistry. He was educated at Merchants Taylors' School and Caius College of Cambridge, reading in natural sciences (1921) and chemistry (1922). In 1922 he married Mayo Walker, the daughter of the Rev. Frederick William Walker. She died in 1946, and in 1947 he married Nora Hodder of Worthing.

Discovers a Process to Make Terylene

Whinfield was interested in the molecular make-up and properties of synthetic fibers, and to gain experience in fibers after graduating, he worked for a year without pay in the London laboratory of C. F. Cross and E. J. Bevan, who in 1892 had invented the "viscose reaction" for the production of rayon. In 1924, Whinfield was employed by the Calico Printers' Association as a research chemist, where he worked primarily on the chemistry of fabric dyeing and finishing. He continued his studies of the physical and chemical properties of synthetic fibers, however, and followed with interest the work of **Wallace Hume Carothers** in the United States, who in 1928 published the first of a long series of papers on condensation polymerization reactions. Carothers' work led to the invention of nylon, a polyamide; he had worked on but rejected the polyester group as a source of synthetic textile fibers because he thought the melting points were too low.

Whinfield's studies and rough analogies led him to believe that a polyester might work, specifically a polyester made from terephthalic acid and ethylene glycol. The latter chemical was available commercially, but terephthalic acid had been produced only in small quantities. Whinfield pressed his company to try some fiber work; in 1940 he was finally able to devote some time to the fiber research he had been thinking about, and in March 1941 he and his assistant, James T. Dickson, discovered a method of condensing terephthalic acid and ethylene glycol to produce a compound that could be drawn into fibers.

Empirical work demonstrated—happily, because this had not been predictable from theoretical word—that the fibers had a high melting point and were resistant to hydrolytic breakdown. Whinfield and Dickson filed their patent on terylene in July 1941. Britain was engaged in World War II at the time, and terylene's potential utility for the war industry was examined briefly by the Ministry of Supply, for whom Whinfield had come to work during the war. It was known to be an important invention, but production was not thought to be practicable for the war effort, and registration of the patent was delayed until 1946, after the war.

The Calico Printers' Association decided not to develop terylene, and consequently sold their rights to the product to Imperial Chemical Industries (ICI), who obtained world manufacturing rights. Whinfield went to work for ICI in 1947. Du Pont in the United States independently prepared terylene and purchased the U.S. patent application filed by the British in 1946. Although Du Pont had been working on terylene, there was no question of the priority of its invention. Du Pont first called it "Fiber V," then "Dacron," and began full-scale production in the United States in 1953. ICI, after operating two pilot plants for several years, began commercial production of terylene fibers in 1955.

In the production of terylene, dimethyl terephthalate and ethylene glycol, derived from coal, air, water, and petroleum, are polymerized. Then the substance is "melt spun" into filaments. The filaments are stable, but springy; Whinfield found that the fibers would stretch to 10-25% of their original length before rupturing. Terylene was shown to be equal to nylon in its potential usefulness, and it contributed greatly to the popularity of "wash and wear" clothing.

Works as Chemist at ICI

At ICI, Whinfield worked first in the Fibers Development Department of the plastics division with W. F. Osborne, then in the Fibers Division, where he eventually became director. In 1954, he received a Commander of the Order of the British Empire (C.B.E.) for his work on terylene. The same year, he was engaged to advise on *Point of Departure*, an educational film on manmade fibers made by the Film Producers Guild. He was a clear explicator, but somewhat unexpectedly, he also proved to be an accomplished actor, and as a result played a leading role in the film. In 1955, he was elected an honorary fellow of the Textile Institute, and in 1956 he received the Perkin medal of the Society of Dyers and Colourists. During his tenure at ICI, Whinfield traveled widely, including to the former Union of Soviet Socialist Republics as a guest of the Russian government. He retired in 1963. In 1965, the University of

York named its chemical library and a number of traveling fellowships after Whinfield.

Whinfield died on July 6, 1966, at Dorking, at age 65. In an obituary published in *Chemistry in Britain* (1967), P. C. Allen wrote, "[He] remained until the end of his life an essentially modest and simple man. He had a host of friends and no wonder for no one could be more charming companion, or when he was in the mood, a better talker. He wrote very clearly also; his publications are a model of clarity."

SELECTED WRITINGS BY WHINFIELD:

Periodicals

"Fibres From Aromatic Polyesters." *Endeavour* XI, no. 41 (January 1952): 29-32.

FURTHER READING:

Books

Biographical Dictionary of Scientists, 2nd ed. Bristol: Institute of Physics Publishing, 1994, p. 521.
The Dictionary of National Biography: Missing Persons. Oxford: Oxford University Press, 1993, p. 709.
Jewkes, John, David Sawers, and Richard Stillerman. *The Sources of Invention.* New York: St. Martin's Press, 1959, pp. 18, 165, 388-392.

Periodicals

Allen, P. C. "John Rex Whinfield, 1901-1966." *Chemistry in Britain* 3, (1967): 26.

—*Sketch by Jill Carpenter*

Raymond L. White
1943–

American molecular biologist

Raymond L. White has contributed greatly to the understanding of how human genes are arranged on chromosomes and how they contribute to the occurrence of hereditary diseases. He is best known for developing a technique for mapping and locating genetic deoxyribonucleic acid (DNA) markers. Markers are genetic sequences that are located near defective genes and can be used to indicate the presence or absence of such genes, because they are often passed along with the defective gene. White's work, and that of others who are involved with the Human Genome Project, will help scientists in their quest to understand the genetic causes of such diseases as hemophilia, Duchenne muscular dystrophy, and breast cancer, and to discover ways to conquer or control them.

White was born on October 23, 1943, in Orlando, Florida, the son of a dentist. Although he at first intended to enter the field of medicine, he became interested in molecular biology and genetics while a student at the University of Oregon. After he received his bachelor of science degree in microbiology in 1965, White attended the Massachusetts Institute of Technology (MIT), where in 1971 he earned his Ph.D. in microbiology. From 1971 to 1972, he was a research associate and instructor at MIT. After postdoctoral work at Stanford from 1972 to 1975, White returned to Massachusetts and became an assistant professor in the microbiology department at the University of Massachusetts School of Medicine in Worcester. He held that position from 1975-1978, when he became an associate professor in the department.

In 1980, White joined the staff of the University of Utah Medical School as an associate professor in the department of cellular, viral, and molecular biology, and as an investigator at the university's Howard Hughes Medical Institute (he was an investigator there until 1994). In 1984, he was named cochair of the medical school's human genetics department. Since 1985, White has served as a professor in the departments of oncological sciences and human genetics. In addition, he is currently chairman of the department of oncological sciences at the University of Utah School of Medicine and is the executive director of the Huntsman Cancer Institute at the University of Utah. He has held both positions since 1994.

Begins Tracking Defective Genes

While at the University of Massachusetts, White began investigating a question that intrigued many scientists, namely, whether or not it was possible to discover where on certain chromosomes the genes responsible for many hereditary illnesses were located. Much of the genetic material is identical from person to person, but some parts were different, and these different parts (called polymorphisms) accounted for the variety in human hair color, eye color, and many other inherited features—including the presence or absence of such disorders as hemophilia, a genetic disease in which the blood lacks the factors that allow it to clot normally. It was possible that people who showed the effects of these defective genes would share certain polymorphisms. If so, perhaps the polymorphisms could be used to flag the defective genes.

The polymorphisms White was interested in were called restriction fragment length polymorphisms, or RFLPs. But RFLPs were scattered across 23 chromosomes that comprised about 100,000 genes, and finding them at all would be a tremendous task. Working with Arlene Wyman in 1979, he began looking for RFLPs by first eliminating all the parts of the human genome that were identical. In the end, they narrowed down their search to five sequences of DNA that contained between 15,000 and 20,000 "bases." By combining radioactively labeled copies of these sequences with the DNA from 56 donors, White and Wyman were able to find eight RFLPs.

Throughout the 1980s, White worked on proving his theory that RFLPs could be used as genetic markers. The first genetic marker was discovered by British researchers in 1981; it was an RFLP on the X chromosome that was linked to the gene that can cause Duchenne muscular dystrophy. Combined with the efforts of other researchers, White's work has allowed for the creation of a map of the human genome, and for the discovery of many genes. This genetic mapping allows scientists to predict what will happen when certain genes are present, and to take steps to develop therapies that will lessen the effects of the genes.

White's laboratory has been working with two important genes, both of which normally work in the body to suppress tumor formation. One gene, NF1, normally takes part in signal pathways for cell growth; when it is mutated, however, it causes peripheral neurofibromatosis. NF1 has also been found in tumors that are not usually associated with it, which makes researchers believe that the gene is a growth regulator. The other gene, APC, can cause adenomatous polyposis when mutated, and further mutation can lead to colon cancer. Interestingly, mutations in the different parts of the APC gene lead to different physical manifestations (phenotypes) of the illness.

Another gene White is studying is BRCA1, another tumor-suppressor gene found on chromosome 17q. This gene makes certain women predisposed to early-onset breast and ovarian cancer. By studying these genes, White and his staff may gain more information about what mechanisms in the body cause the formation of cancer, and may lead to ways in which medical professionals can help detect who is at risk for breast cancer and help prevent this disease.

The author of nearly 300 scientific papers, White is a member of the National Academy of Sciences, the American Association for Cancer Research, the Human Genome Organization, and the American Society for Human Genetics. He has served on a variety of advisory boards and committees. Among the many honors he has received in recognition of his work are the American Cancer Society's Sword of Hope Award

(Utah chapter, 1995), the Utah Governor's Medal for Science and Technology (1993), the National Health Council National Medical Research Award (1991), the National Neurofibromatosis Foundation's Friedrich von Recklinghausen Award, and the Allan Award for Cancer Research.

SELECTED WRITINGS BY WHITE:

Periodicals

"DNA in Medicine: Human Genetics." *The Lancet* 1, (December 1984):1257-62.
"Polymorphic DNA Markers on the Genomic Map: Signposts for Localization of Unknown Genes." *Somatic Cell and Molecular Genetics* 13, (1987): 361-63.
(With others) "Tightly Linked Markers for the Neurofibromatosis Type 1 Gene." *Genomics* 1, (1987): 364-67.
"Molecular Biology of the APC Protein." *Pathologie Biologie* 45 (1997):240-44.

—Sketch by Fran Hodgkins

Frank Whittle
1907–1996
English aviation engineer

Frank Whittle, along with German engineer Hans von Ohain, invented the jet engine. Neither Whittle nor von Ohain was aware of the other's work, however, until after World War II. Whittle first began working on the concept of a jet engine in the 1920s, but he was repeatedly rebuffed by those who insisted that the idea was unworkable or impractical. With persistence during the 1930s and into World War II, Whittle developed his concept into the first flyable jet airplane outside of Germany. His creation, the Gloster-Whittle E28/39, first flew on May 15, 1941.

Whittle was born to working-class parents in Coventry, England, on June 1, 1907. His father had talents as a machinist and inventor, and in 1916 he bought a small business that he called the Leamington Valve and Piston Ring Company. The young Whittle acquired some experience here in manufacturing, helping with odd jobs such as drilling valve stems or working on the lathe. Whittle later wrote in his autobiography that he inherited his inventiveness and love for things mechanical from his father.

When Whittle turned eleven he received a small scholarship to attend secondary school. His school work was spotty. Most of the subjects he liked best,

Frank Whittle

such as astronomy, engineering, and natural science, were not taught at the school. He read whatever he could find on popular science and became interested in chemistry. Still, he hated homework, and excelling at school seems to have been undermined by what Whittle himself called, in *Jet: The Story of a Pioneer,* "a natural laziness."

It was in secondary school that Whittle developed an interest in aeronautics and flying, an interest that would carry him through a brilliant and sometimes frustrating career as an aviation engineer. After graduating from secondary school, Whittle joined the Royal Air Force as an aircraft apprentice, although he had difficulty getting accepted because he stood only five feet tall. After he spent three years rigging aircraft, the RAF College at Cranwell accepted Whittle as a cadet. While at Cranwell he joined the Model Aircraft Society, which, Whittle later wrote, played a critical role in his early education as an engineer.

After graduating from the cadet college, Whittle was assigned to 111 Fighter Squadron, where he reported in August 1928. Here, along with his regular duties, Whittle continued pilot training, this time at Central Flying School at Wittering. Lectures at Wittering added to his fund of knowledge and helped nurture to maturity Whittle's ideas about jet propulsion. The problem under much discussion then was that propellers and piston engines limited an airplane's altitude and speed. The air was too thin at higher altitudes to properly engage a propeller, and

the content of oxygen in the air was too lean to keep a piston-driven engine from stalling. Whittle thought that the problem could be solved by using a turbine instead of a piston engine. This way a lean mixture of oxygen could be compressed, combined with fuel, and ignited. The expanding gases caused by igniting the mixture of compressed oxygen and fuel would result in a jet blast that would propel the aircraft forward.

Overcomes Resistance

Convincing officials in the Air Ministry, however, was perhaps as great a challenge as developing the engine itself. One of the main objections was that materials did not yet exist that could withstand the heat and stress present in a jet engine. Whittle persisted. Eventually he found supporters who were willing to give him financial backing for his project. In return for their support, Whittle promised his backers each a quarter share of the commercial rights. The result of their agreement was the formation in March 1936 of a small corporation called Power Jets.

Development and testing of prototype jet engines continued into the war years after the German invasion of Poland in September 1939. The British surmised that Germany was also working on a jet engine, but could only speculate on the nature of that work. As for Whittle, he eventually prevailed over what at times seemed like insurmountable odds posed by technical difficulties and bureaucratic infighting.

By April 1941 Whittle and the Power Jet corporation began testing their W.1 jet engine in the Gloster-Whittle E28/39 airplane (after Gloster Aircraft Company, which constructed the airplane) by making taxi runs to see how the engine handled on the ground. With this testing and confidence-building measure, the engineers were able to make further adjustments, so that by the evening of May 15, 1941, a test pilot could take the aircraft aloft. The flight lasted seventeen minutes during which the aircraft reached a speed of 370 miles (592 km) per hour at an elevation of twenty-five thousand feet (7,500 m). This easily exceeded the speed of the next fastest airplane in the Royal Air Force, the redoubtable Spitfire, which in many minds had defeated Germany's best aircraft in the Battle of Britain.

Despite the successful flight of the E28/39 with its W.1 engine (other models of this engine were also undergoing tests), more refinement was needed before they could be mass produced. With this in mind, engineers and other decision makers decided to start production of aircraft and engines in June 1942. As it was, production models of Britain's first jet did not appear in the skies until mid–1944. The production model, dubbed the Meteor I, was used against the German V–1 rockets that pummeled London late in the war.

In 1944, Great Britain nationalized the Power Jets company, which had been taken over by Rolls-Royce in 1943. The company was now called Power Jets R & D, and was limited to research and development. Whittle became chief technical advisor to the board, but because of poor health he played an increasingly marginal role, the more so since by the end of 1944 it had become clear that further development of a jet fighter would contribute little to what then seemed like the inevitable defeat of Germany. Morale sank and Whittle left the company in January, 1946.

Awarded Knighthood

By this time, Whittle's fame had become well established, and he was in demand as a lecturer in the United Kingdom. During the latter part of 1946 Whittle undertook a lecture tour in the United States, but again fell ill and required two months' hospitalization. In the United Kingdom, Whittle had received the Clayton Prize (£1,000) from the Institution of Mechanical Engineers for his work on jet engines. The Royal Commission on Awards to Inventors honored Whittle in 1945 with an interim award of £10,000, which it increased in 1948 to £100,000. That same year, King George VI granted him knighthood. Whittle's personal life was subsumed by his career, and *Jet,* his book about his work on jet propulsion, gives scant attention to life at home. Nonetheless, Whittle married Dorothy Mary Lee, whom he had known in Coventry, in 1930. Their first son, Francis David, was born in May of the following year. A second son was born, but the marriage ended in 1976.

After the war, Whittle worked for a while as a mechanical engineering specialist for the Dutch oil company, Bataafsche Petroleum Maatschappij, where he designed an oil-drilling motor called the Whittle turbo-drill. Thereafter he became a technical consultant to a number of aerospace firms, emigrated to the United States in 1976, and married his second wife, Hazel, after having accepted a lectureship with the U.S. Naval Academy. Whittle also worked on jet propulsion at Wright-Paterson Air Force Base in Dayton, Ohio, and became chief scientist at Wright-Paterson's Aero Propulsion Laboratory. Thereafter, Whittle worked as a senior research engineer at the University of Dayton Research Institute.

Whittle's research in jet propulsion revolutionized air travel and provided the technical groundwork for America's first jet airplane, the Bell XP–59A, which had its maiden flight in 1942. In recognition of Whittle's achievements, in 1991 the National Academy of Engineering in Washington, D.C., awarded him and Hans von Ohain its prestigious Charles Draper Prize, which included a grant of $375,000 to be divided between the two engineers. Whittle died at his home in Columbia, Maryland, on August 8, 1996, at the age of 89.

SELECTED WRITINGS BY WHITTLE:

Books

Jet: The Story of a Pioneer. Frederick Muller, 1953.
Gas Turbine Aero-Thermodynamics. Tarrytown, NY:Pergamon, 1981.
Whittle: The True Story. Washington, DC: Smithsonian Institution Press, 1987.

FURTHER READING:

Periodicals

"Air Commodore Sir Frank Whittle." *Times (London)* (10 August 1996: 21).
Fink, Donald E. "Jet Engine Milestone." *Aviation Week & Space Technology* (13 April 1987): 15.
Joyce, Christopher. "Jet Pioneers Win Engineering's 'Nobel Prize,'" *New Scientist* (5 October 1991): 31.
Stix, Gary. "Smaller World: The Draper Prize Recognizes the Fathers of the Jet Age." *Scientific American* (December 1991): 15.
————. "Turbojet's Inventors Earn Draper Prize." *Science News* (19 October 1991): 252.
Vietmeyer, Noel. "They Created the Jet Age." *Reader's Digest* (May 1987): 162-66.

—Sketch by Karl Preuss

Eric F. Wieschaus
1947–
American biologist

Eric F. Wieschaus won the 1995 Nobel Prize in Physiology or Medicine, along with **Edward B. Lewis** and **Christaine Nüsslein-Volhard**, for his work on identifying key genes that make a fertilized fruit fly egg develop into a segmented embryo. His research could help improve knowledge of how genes control embryonic development in higher organisms, including identifying genes that cause human birth defects.

Wieschaus was born in South Bend, Indiana, in 1947 but grew up in Alabama. He received his bachelor's degree in biology from the University of Notre Dame in 1969 and his doctorate from Yale in 1974. His doctoral dissertation involved using genetic methods to label the progeny (offspring) of single cells in fly embryos. He showed that even at the earliest cellular stages, cells were already determined to form specific regions of the body called segments.

Wieschaus married Gertrud Schupbach, who is a professor of molecular biology at Princeton. They have three children, Ingrid, Eleanor, and Laura. Over the years, Wieschaus has been described by colleagues as a dedicated, hard worker. He spends time in the lab, doing experiments himself, unlike some professors who delegate lab work to their graduate students.

Early in his career, Wieschaus was recognized with a John Spangler Niclaus Prize in 1974 for his dissertation on experimental embryology. At the University of Zurich, Switzerland, Wieschaus held a post-doctoral fellowship from 1975-78. There he studied sex determination in flies and developed techniques to create flies with mosaic ovaries composed of mutant and normal cells.

Wieschaus joined the Princeton faculty in 1981 as an assistant professor and became Squib Professor of molecular biology in 1987. In 1989 he was bestowed the National Institutes of Health Merit Award, and in 1995 he became the first professor in Princeton's Life Science Department to receive the Nobel Prize.

Experiments With Fruit Fly DNA

Wieschaus began his Nobel-winning work in the latter part of the 1970s. The Alabama native spent three years with Christiane Nüsslein-Volhard in the European Molecular Biology Lab at the University of Heidelberg, Germany, tackling the question of why individual cells in a fertilized egg develop into various specific tissues. They elected to study *Drosophila*, or fruit flies, because of their extremely fast embryonic development. New generations of fruit flies can be bred in a week. In addition, fruit flies have only one set of genes controlling development compared to the four sets humans possess. This means that testing each fruit fly gene individually takes one-fourth the time it would involve to test human genes.

To begin their experiment, Nüsslein-Volhard and Wieschaus damaged male fruit fly deoxyribonucleic acid (DNA) by applying ultraviolet light to the genes or by feeding the flies sugar water laced with chemicals. Then the team "knocked out" one gene from the fly, breeding generations of fruit flies without that particular piece of code. In this way, Nüsslein-Volhard and Wieschaus were able to isolate all the genes crucial to the early stages of embryonic development. When the male flies were bred with female fruit flies, the females produced dead embryos. These lifeless embryos resulted from only 150 different mutations of the 40,000 mutations applied. These 150 genes proved to be essential to the proper development of

the fly embryo because, when damaged, the genes caused extraordinary deformities that killed the embryo. For example, a fly with skin comprised only of nerve cells resulted from one of the mutations. By viewing the fly embryos with a two-person microscope, Wieschaus and Nüsslein-Volhard were able to simultaneously view and classify a large quantity of malformations caused by gene mutations. Next, they identified 15 different genes, that, when mutated, eliminate specific body segments in the fly embryos. Wieschaus also established that systematic categorizing of genes that control the various stages of development could be accomplished. For example, he was able to isolate the genes that form specific organs and body segments.

While working together in the 1970s, Nüsslein-Volhard and Wieschaus had their research results first published in *Nature*, an English scientific journal, in 1980. They reported that the number of genes controlling early development was not only limited, but could also be classified into specific functional groups. They also identified genes that cause severe congenital defects in flies. After additional experimentation, the principles involved with the fruit fly genes were found to apply to higher animals and humans. This led to the realization that many similar genes control human development, and this finding could have a tremendous impact on the medical world. The applications of their research extend to in vitro fertilization, identifying congenital birth defects, and increased knowledge of substances that can endanger early stages of pregnancy.

Wieschaus's research was not without its share of setbacks. One major accident involved Wieschaus bumping into a table with 40,000 test tubes full of fruit flies and watching his experiment crash to the floor. However, he did not become discouraged by this catastrophe, nor did he give up. He knew that he would have to pick up all the test tubes and start over because " . . . the only thing that really matters is to get the experiment to work," he stated. "Someday you will know something that no one has ever known before."

SELECTED WRITINGS BY WIESCHAUS:

Periodicals

"Mutations Affecting Segment Number and Polarity in Drosophila." *Nature,* Volume 287, 1980, pp. 795-801.

"Kruppel, a Gene Whose Activity is Required Early in the Zygotic Genome for Normal Segmentation." *Developmental Biology,* Volume 104, 1984, pp. 172-186.

"Mutations Affecting the Pattern of the Larval Cuticle in Drosophila melangaster." *Developmental Biology,* Volume 193, 1984, pp. 296-307.

Eugene Paul Wigner

"Embryonic Transcription and the Control of Developmental Pathways." *Genetics,* 1996 (in press)

—Sketch by Nicole Beatty

Eugene Paul Wigner
1902–1995
American mathematical physicist

Eugene Paul Wigner's enormous contribution to various branches of physics, notably quantum and nuclear, was confirmed by his receipt of the 1963 Nobel Prize for Physics (he shared the award with **Maria Goeppert-Mayer** and **J. Hans D. Jensen**). Recognizing the role of symmetry principles in predicting certain physical processes, Wigner formulated many of the laws governing this theory. Wigner is remembered as being one of the first physicists to call attention to the problems of nuclear energy, and also as one of the first scientists to forge links between science and industry around nuclear energy.

Wigner was born in Budapest, Austria-Hungary (now Hungary) on November 17, 1902, the son of a businessman. At school, Wigner discovered an interest in physics, but he realized that job opportunities

as a physicist in Hungary would be very limited. He therefore decided to study chemical engineering. After receiving a doctorate in chemical engineering from the Technische Hochschule in Berlin in 1925, Wigner returned to Budapest for a year to take up a post in a leather-tanning plant. He left Hungary for the last time in 1926 upon receiving an invitation to return to Berlin to work as an assistant to the well-known physical chemist R. Becker. "The whole of quantum physics was being created within my own eyesight," he said of physics in Germany during the 1920s, as quoted in *Pioneers of Science: Nobel Prize Winners in Physics.* Inspired by such inventiveness, Wigner began writing papers of his own; specifically, he was interested in exploring how the mathematical concept known as group theory could be used as a tool in the new quantum mechanics. On the strength of this work, Wigner was invited in 1927 to join the physics department of the University of Göttingen, as assistant to the mathematician **David Hilbert**.

At Gottingen Wigner developed his law of the conservation of parity, which states that no fundamental distinction can be made between left and right in physics. The laws of physics are the same in a right-handed system of coordinates as they are in a left-handed system. Based on Wigner's law of parity conservation, particles emitted during a physical interaction should emanate from the nucleus to the right and the left in equal numbers. In practical terms, the law meant that a nuclear process should be indistinguishable from its mirror image, that is, an electron emitted from a nucleus will be indifferent as to whether it is ejected to the left or right and will shoot off in equal numbers in both directions along the spin axes of the aligned nucleus. This theory remained steadfast until 1956 when two Chinese-American physicists, **Tsung-Dao Lee** and **Chen Ning Yang**, disproved it by showing experimentally that parity is not conserved in weak interactions. Instead, their experiments revealed that far more electrons were emitted from the south end of the nucleus than from the north. For invalidating the widely held concept of the conservation of parity, they shared the 1957 Nobel Prize for Physics.

Wigner returned in 1928 to the Technische Hochschule and continued his work on group theory until 1930, when he moved to the United States to accept a position as lecturer in mathematical physics at Princeton University. For eight years he served as a part-time professor at Princeton, until he was elevated to the position of Thomas D. Jones Professor of Mathematical Physics in 1938. The year before, Wigner had become an American citizen.

Develops Short Periodicity of Binding Energies

Wigner's tenure at Princeton afforded him the time and space to do his most important work. As a young physicist, he had become interested in symmetry principles, especially with the patterns found in atomic and molecular spectra. Important discoveries in the 1930s of the binding forces within a nucleus paved the way for Wigner's research. It was found that nuclei containing even numbers of protons (the positively charged particles in the nucleus) and neutrons (the neutral particles) are bound together more strongly than those with an uneven number of protons and neutrons. This is referred to as the short periodicity of binding energies. Longer periods of binding energy are also possible, and show especially strong binding when the number of protons or neutrons or both is 2, 8, 20, 28, 40, 50, 82, or 126. The longer binding periods are thought to be caused by the existence in the nucleus of shells or orbits, similar to those that surround the nucleus and contain the electrons, the negatively charged particles. Armed with this data, Wigner forecasted an optical spectra based on the long periodicity model. His findings were published in one of the first papers on the subject. Wigner also contributed significantly to the understanding of short periodicity in his application of mathematical group theory to the energy levels of nuclei up to atomic weight 50. His book on group theory has become a classic in the physics canon.

In 1933, the year after **James Chadwick** discovered the neutron, Wigner composed a paper which postulated the existence of an energy state of the deuteron which differed from the ground state that had been observed. A deuteron is the nucleus of an atom of deuterium, the hydrogen isotope that has twice the mass of regular hydrogen, and which occurs in water. A deuteron contains one proton and one neutron. Wigner's theory provided an explanation for a hitherto unaccounted-for phenomenon: the large deflections of slow neutrons when they pass close to protons. Although Wigner discounted the idea's importance and did not deem it worthy of publication, it proved to be the foundation for numerous other papers.

In 1936, while working with **Gregory Breit,** Wigner examined the phenomenon of neutron absorption by a compound nucleus. Their Breit-Wigner formula did much to throw light on this subject. Continuing his work around atomic nuclei, Wigner postulated in 1937 that protons and neutrons were analogous to isotopes in the periodic table of the elements. The manifestation of a particle as a proton or as a neutron could be accounted for by different degrees of spin on the particle, known as isotopic spin or isospin for short.

Turning his attention to nuclear fission in 1938, Wigner developed a number of theoretical techniques of reactor calculations, some of which formed the basis of the first controlled chain reaction carried out by the Italian physicist **Enrico Fermi.** Together with his fellow Hungarians, **Leo Szilard** and **Edward Teller,**

Wigner persuaded **Albert Einstein** to send a letter to President Franklin Roosevelt urging him to beat Hitler in the race to develop an atom bomb. The letter was crucial in convincing the American government to build nuclear reactors and was also directly responsible for the establishment of the Manhattan Project, on which Wigner played a key role.

In 1941, Wigner married Mary Annette Wheeler, with whom he had two children, David and Martha. His second marriage, to Eileen Hamilton, produced a daughter, Erika. Despite his many scientific commitments, Wigner tried to find time to devote to his family and to pursue his hobbies of bowling and figure skating.

The outbreak of war in Europe caused Wigner to turn his full attention to nuclear physics. At the Metallurgical Laboratory at the University of Chicago, he began work on the Manhattan Project as the chief engineer of the water-cooled Hanford plutonium reactors. Wigner's colleagues observed that, for a theorist, he had a remarkably precise knowledge of the engineering design of reactors. Also remarkable was the tremendous speed at which the latest scientific findings in the laboratory were converted into engineered chain reactors. After the war, Wigner accepted a position as director of research and development at the Clinton Laboratories at Oak Ridge from 1946 to 1947.

Career Honored with Copious Awards

Wigner's many contributions to physics have been recognized in a variety of prizes and honorary degrees. He was elected to the National Academy of Sciences in 1945. He was awarded the U.S. Atomic Energy Commission's Enrico Fermi Prize in 1958 and the Atoms for Peace Award in 1960. Most significantly, in 1936, Wigner won the Nobel physics prize for "systemically improving and extending the methods of quantum mechanics and applying them widely." Specifically, he was commended for his contribution to the theory of atomic nuclei elementary particles, especially for his discovery and application of fundamental principles of symmetry. This marked an unusual departure for the Nobel Committee, which normally awards the prize for a single discovery or invention.

Wigner, who retired from Princeton in 1971, was also active on behalf of other scientists. He was one of thirty-three Nobel Prize winners who sent a telegram to President Podgorny of the former Soviet Union asking that **Andrei Sakharov** be permitted to receive the Nobel Peace Prize in Stockholm. Wigner died in Princeton, New Jersey, on January 1, 1995, of pneumonia. He was 92.

SELECTED WRITINGS BY WIGNER:

Books

Nuclear Structure. Princeton: Princeton University Press, 1961.

Symmetries and Reflections. Bloomington: Indiana University Press, 1967.

Who Speaks for Civil Defense? New York: Scribner, 1968.

Survival and the Bomb. Bloominton: Indiana University Press, 1969.

Aspects of Quantum Theory, Cambridge: Cambridge University Press, 1972.

Reminiscences about a Great Physicist: Paul Adrian Maurice Dirac. Cambridge: Cambridge University Press, 1987.

FURTHER READING:

Books

Asimov, Isaac. *Atom: Journey Across the Subatomic Cosmos.* New York: Truman Talley Books, 1991.

_____. *Great American Scientists: America's Rise to the Forefront of World Science.* Prentice Hall, 1967, pp. 21–22, 119.

Weber, Robert L. *Pioneers of Science: Nobel Prize Winners in Physics.* Philadelphia: Institute of Physics, 1980, p. 188.

Periodicals

"Physicist Eugene Wigner Dies; Won Nobel, Pioneered A-bomb" (obituary). *Washington Post* (5 January 1995): B7.

—*Sketch by Avril McDonald*

Cicely Delphin Williams
1893–1992
Jamaican-English physician

Cicely Delphin Williams devoted her life to improving the health of women and children all over the world. She is known for discovering the causes of the malnutrition illness kwashiorkor, as well as Jamaican vomiting disease. She was the first female physician to be appointed by the British Colonial Medical Service to Ghana and to hold the post of head of Maternity and Child Welfare. She was also noted for her personal heroism as a prisoner of war during World War II.

Williams was born on Dec. 2, 1893, the daughter of a long-established plantation family in Jamaica, originally from Wales. Her father, James Towland Williams, was the director of education in Jamaica. Williams wanted to attend Oxford, where her father had studied, but when it came time to enter college, the family had no money to send her. She was discouraged from becoming a nurse, so Williams resigned herself to an unchallenging existence at home with her family.

William's break came during World War I, when women were admitted to Oxford because of a shortage of doctors. She decided to study tropical medicine and hygiene and was tutored by one of the famed physicians of the time, Sir William Osler. In 1929, she received her B.A. degree from Oxford.

Williams then went on to study for her M.D. degree. However, after she had taken her finals and it came time for her residency, World War I had ended and along with it the doctor shortage. Williams applied to 70 hospitals before being accepted for a gynecological surgery residency at South London Hospital for Women and Children. It was here that Williams discovered that she loved working with children. Although she found the work at South London Hospital challenging, she really wanted to work overseas. Positions for women were still scarce, so Williams decided the best course of action was to work for the overseas British Colonial Office. After two years of petitioning the office, officials finally relented and posted her in the Gold Coast (now Ghana).

In one year, Williams learned the Ghanaian language and started to develop real fondness for her patients. She was struck by how devoted they were to their children and amused at how often they brought them in to see her. Williams began to notice a common illness among toddlers in Ghanaian families. These children had swollen legs and bellies, rashes, and a red tinge to their hair. Williams thought this might be a nutritional disease, but the other doctors told her she was misdiagnosing the illness pellagra, an already identified malnutrition disease that had similar symptoms.

To test her theory, Williams wanted to do autopsies on the children who had died from the disease but was told that local burial customs would not permit it. But in truth, the families were rushing their children home after death because they could not pay the high cost of moving the body. So Williams offered to pay this fee and began to perform postmortems. She found that the Ghanaians called the disease kwashiorkor, or weaning disease, because children developed it when a new baby was born. Williams surmised correctly that the toddlers were not getting enough protein because they were no longer breast-fed and were not yet eating adult food. Convinced she had found a new type of malnutrition, she identified the disease in *Archives of Disease in Children* in 1933. She also wrote an article in the medical journal *Lancet,* which described the differences between kwashiorkor and pellagra.

While performing an autopsy in her investigations of kwashiorkor, Williams contracted blood poisoning. When she recovered she was transferred to the city of Kumasi. She was disappointed, but decided to make the best of it by writing her delayed doctoral thesis "Child Health in the Gold Coast." The thesis was accepted and she received her M.D. degree in 1936.

Williams wanted to return to Africa but was sent to Trengganu, Malaya (now Malaysia) instead. She never achieved the same fondness for Malaya as she did for the Gold Coast, and found health conditions were horrible. The local religious beliefs regarded illness as fate. Infant mortality was high, partly because Western companies were persuading new mothers to buy canned milk that had little nutrition. Williams tried to take on these companies, but was unable to stop them from sending "nurses" to visit new mothers with their products.

When the Japanese invaded Malaya in 1941, Williams escaped to Singapore. Her safety was short-lived when the Allied forces left Singapore in 1942 and the Japanese strafed the city with bombs. Williams moved children in the city's hospitals from makeshift shelter to makeshift shelter until the Japanese troops entered Singapore. Then, to save her young charges, she offered them to any family that would take them. All were placed.

During the Japanese occupation, Williams was held in the Changi prison camp in Singapore. Her life there was filled with hardship and disease. The Japanese Secret Police, the Kempaitai, began to suspect her after she became head of the women's side of the camp and arrested her. She spent her fiftieth birthday in a tiny prison cell with seven men.

In March 1944, suffering from dysentery and the psychological and physical cruelty she had endured, Williams was returned to Changi prison camp. Seven months later the prisoners saw Allied planes. Weak from dysentery and malaria, Williams survived to see the Japanese surrender.

When Williams recovered, she returned to Malaya as head of the Maternity and Child Welfare Services. It was the first powerful post to be held by a woman in the Colonial Service. In 1948, the new World Health Organization named her to be the first director of the Child and Maternal Health section. But Williams was asked to return to Jamaica to direct an investigative team studying Jamaican vomiting sickness. In a year, her team discovered the culprit was a substance in spoiled ackee fruit, and designed the life-saving treatment of glucose therapy.

In 1955, Williams entered the more sedate life of academia when she became a senior lecturer in nutrition in London University. In 1960, she was hired as professor of maternal and child health with the American University in Beirut. After four years, she went back to London to work with the Family Planning Association as an advisor. In 1965 she was awarded the James Spence Memorial Gold Medal by the British Paedeatric Association.

In 1968, she became professor of international family health at Tulane University's School of Public Health. In 1971 the American Public Health Association gave her the Martha May Eliot Award, and a year later she was awarded the Dawson Williams Prize in Paediatrics by the British Medical Association. At her retirement, she remained active and was an honorary Fellow at Somerville and Green Colleges of Oxford. At age 90, she was still making appearances and speeches. In her speeches she often encouraged young doctors to become general practitioners, citing a need for doctors who would look after people and not just diseases. She died on July 13, 1992 at age 98.

SELECTED WRITINGS BY WILLIAMS:

Periodicals

"Kwashiorkor: A Nutritional Disease of Children Associated with a Maize Diet." *Lancet* 16 (November 1935): 1151-52.

"A Nutritional Disease of Childhood Associated with a Maize Diet." *Archives of Disease in Childhood* 8 (1933): 423-33.

FURTHER READING:

Books

Craddock, Sally. *Retired Except on Demand: The Life of Cicely Williams.* Oxford: Green College, 1983.

Dally, Ann. *Cicely: The Life of a Doctor.* London: Gollancz, 1968.

—Sketch by Barbara Boughton

Evan James Williams
1903–1945
English physicist

Evan Williams is known both for his experiments involving atomic particles and for his work as an operational researcher for the British forces during

World War II. Just as Williams gained stature among his fellow physicists for his ability to choose the correct experiment and carry it out, he soon became known to the Royal Air Force as someone who rejected traditional ideas of bombing effectiveness and proposed new approaches of much greater efficiency. His untimely death a month after the end of World War II probably contributed to the lack of recognition of his important role in planning the aerial campaigns.

Evan James Williams, the son of a stonemason, was born on June 8, 1903, at Cwmsychpant, Wales. He was fortunate in his early schooling, since the headmaster of his country school had been an outstanding mathematics student at Cambridge University and was able to recognize Williams's ability and to encourage his interest in physics and mathematics. Williams graduated from the Swansea (Wales) Technical College—now part of the University of Wales—and continued his studies at the University of Manchester in England and at Cambridge University. He obtained a Ph.D. in physics from Manchester in 1926 and another degree at Cambridge in 1929, where he worked with **Ernest Rutherford** and **C. T. R. Wilson** at the Cavendish Laboratory. In 1930 Williams returned to Manchester, where, with the exception of a year at the Copenhagen Institute of Niels Bohr, he taught physics and conducted experiments until 1937. He then moved to the University of Liverpool to work with **James Chadwick**, who had won the Nobel Prize two years earlier for the discovery of the neutron.

Williams in the 1920s and '30s specialized in exacting measurements of particle paths using the Wilson cloud chamber. C. T. R. Wilson near the end of the nineteenth century had been studying cloud formation and had invented a way to create miniature clouds by suddenly expanding moist air in a small chamber. When x rays were discovered, Wilson discovered that x rays had a profound effect on his cloud chambers. By 1911 he had developed at the Cavendish Laboratory a version of the cloud chamber with which he could photograph the tracks of individual charged particles. The tracks become visible by a process similar to the one that causes jet airplanes to leave contrails. The Wilson cloud chamber became the observational device of choice for atomic scientists before World War II.

Williams's work with the cloud chamber generally consisted of making very precise measurements that could be used to confirm or deny particular theories. In 1927, for example, he calculated the stopping power of alpha and beta particles by various different gases. (The three common forms of radiation produced by a radioactive element were labeled alpha, beta, and gamma. Beta particles were found to be energetic electrons, while gamma rays are very high energy x rays. Alpha particles are the nuclei of helium

atoms propelled from the radioactive atoms.) For these experiments, Wilson replaced the air in the cloud chamber with the gases hydrogen, helium, nitrogen, oxygen, and neon, then photographed and measured the tracks. The reason for such experiments was to determine whether or not the Bohr model of the atom as a nucleus with electrons in orbit was sufficient. Wilson's work showed that the Bohr model was successful in predicting how hydrogen would stop alpha and beta particles, but that the situation was more complicated for heavier atoms and that a different theory would be needed.

In 1930 Wilson turned to another problem, which was the nature of the various decay products that were being discovered. He used the cloud chamber to observe the particle tracks produced by the substance then known as "radium E," a radioactive substance near the end of the chain of decay products of uranium. Today radium E is called bismuth-210. It decays either by emitting a beta particle to become radium F (polonium-210) or by an alpha particle and a beta particle into lead-206, the stable end of uranium decay.

In the late 1930s one of the great problems of particle physics was understanding the nature of particles found in cosmic rays. Williams and a coworker used the Wilson cloud chamber to analyze the decay pattern of the cosmic ray particles in 1940. This was exacting experimental science. They shielded the cloud chamber with a lead plate to keep out all particles but the energetic cosmic rays. The cloud chamber was kept in a strong magnetic field so that the charge of the particles and their masses could be determined. A magnet bends positively charged particles in one direction and negatively charged particles in the other. The degree of bending tells how heavy the particle is. Williams photographed the tracks made by the cosmic rays. In two photographs he obtained a clear picture of decay, from which he was able to show that the decay product was an electron.

During World War II Williams was associated with **Patrick Maynard Stuart Blackett**, later Baron Blackett, a colleague from Cavendish Laboratory days who had worked on many problems similar to those Williams had studied, including transmutation of elements and cosmic rays. They were among the chief founders of operations research. The classic example of operations research from this period concerned the use of depth bombs released by aircraft pursuing submarines. Conventional military assumed that submarines would immediately dive when a plane was spotted, so bombs should be set to explode at a depth of about 100 yds (91 m) beneath the sea. However, most submarines escaped such bomb attacks. The analysis from operations research demonstrated that if a submarine spotted an enemy airplane, it saw it far enough away to dive below 100 yds (91 m) in a direction unknown to the bomber on the plane. Yet, if the submarine had failed to notice the approaching aircraft until the bomb was about to be released, the submarine could not dive as deep as 100 yds (91 m). Thus, the best strategy for an air attack would be to use bombs that explode on the surface and only bomb submarines on the surface or just as a dive was beginning. The number of submarines sank by aerial bombardment doubled when the new strategy was adopted. After the war, the mathematical techniques of operations research became popular in analyzing business enterprises.

SELECTED WRITINGS BY WILLIAMS:

Periodicals

Correlation of Certain Collision Problems with Radiation Theory. 1927.

FURTHER READING:

Books

Ernest Rutherford, James Chadwick, and C. D. Ellis. *Radiation from Radioactive Substances.* Cambridge: University Press, 1930 (reprinted 1951).

—*Sketch by Bryan Bunch*

Heather Williams
1955–
American ornithologist

Heather Williams is a truth seeker. Whether it is as a world class orienteer (long distance running using a map and compass to find specific points and traverse a course) or as an ornithologist/neuroethologist, she challenges herself both mentally and physically in order to give greater meaning and understanding to the world in which she lives. Her tenacious approach to research and discovery has brought Williams substantial success, most notably the MacArthur Foundation award and grant in 1993 as well as recognition as one of the top female orienteers during the 1980s.

Heather Williams was born on July 27, 1955, in Spokane, Washington, to James Edward Williams and Maria Greig Williams. She has three siblings, Greig, Reid, and Alexandra. Because her father was employed by the U.S. foreign service, Williams moved frequently during her childhood. With each move, she was exposed not only to different cultures but also to

vastly different flora and fauna. While living in such places as Laos, Turkey, and Bolivia, Williams explored her surroundings and was attracted to the indigenous animal species. The fact that she was exposed to many different animals and enjoyed collecting the smaller of those species further developed her interest in biology.

Williams cultivated her interests through formal study, receiving an A.B. in biology from Bowdoin College in Maine in 1977. Always an achiever, she graduated *summa cum laude* from that institution, and her interests blossomed into a career of scientific inquiry. Williams spent 1977-78 as a Thomas J. Watson Fellow at Hebrew University in Eilat, Israel, before continuing with her masters and then doctoral degrees. While in Israel, she conducted research in marine biology. While she was pursuing her higher degrees, she found her life's work.

Williams chose to continue her studies at Rockefeller University in New York. Her mentor at Rockefeller was Fernando Nottebohm, whose own research pertained to the canary and its behavior. Expanding Nottebohm's research, Williams was award her doctorate in 1985 for her studies of the zebra finch. Her dissertation was entitled "A Motor Theory for Bird Song Perception," and it has been the basis for her scientific endeavors ever since.

Concerned with how a bird hears the sounds or songs of other birds, Williams' research pinpoints both the nerves and parts of the brain that are involved in song recognition, organization, and reconstruction. She has discovered that zebra finches learn songs in three syllable "chunks," which they reorganize to create new songs. The way in which the zebra finch executes the song is also highly stylized and fits into specific behavioral patterns. As with speech, a bird's song is a lateralized function, primarily executed by one half of the brain. The other brain hemisphere does, however, contribute to the song production. This is an interesting fact in that birds do not have a connection (corpus callosum) to coordinate the activity of each of the brain hemispheres. Williams is investigating how brain activity occurring between hemispheres is regulated. She is also interested in sexual dimorphism and its role in song perception, as well as how distinct dialects are maintained within delineated finch groups. Her work not only has insight into zebra finch behavior and biology, but it also implies parallels with other animal species and their communication. Her findings will cross the boundaries of biology to broaden our understanding of neuroscience and psychology.

During the same time period as Williams was pursuing her doctoral degree and conducting postdoctoral research, she also found the time to become the third ranking orienteer in the United States (1980-89) and marry Patrick D. Dunlavey (1986). In 1988,

Williams joined the faculty at Williams College in Williamstown, Massachusetts. Still close enough to Rockefeller University in New York, Williams was drawn to the small town atmosphere, knowing she could still confer closely with her Rockefeller colleagues. In 1993, Williams was a member of the course-mapping team for the world championships in orienteering. She and her husband have two children, Maria Greig and Alan Peter Dunlavey.

SELECTED WRITINGS BY WILLIAMS:

Periodicals

(With Jessica McKibben) "Changes in Stereotyped Central Vocal Motor Patterns are Induced by Peripheral Nerve Injury." *Behavioral and Neural Biology* 57 (1992): 67-78.

(With Kirsten Staples) "Syllable Chunking in Zebra Finch (*Taeniopygia guttata*) Song." *Journal of Comparative Psychology* 106 (1992): 278-286.

(With Linda Crane, Timothy Hale, et. al.) "Right-side Dominance for Song Control in the Zebra Finch." *Journal of Neurobiology* 23 (1992): 1006-1020.

Other

(With Franklin Mullins and Jennifer Danforth) "A Comparison of the Effects of Deafening and Vocal Disruption on the Stability of Crystallized Song." *Society for Neuroscience Abstracts* 23. 1997. http://www.williams.edu:803/Biology/ZFinch/nsci97.html (30 October 1997).

FURTHER READING:

Books

King, Kathleen Palombo. "Heather Williams." *Notable Women in the Life Sciences: A Biographical Dictionary.* Benjamin F. Shearer and Barbara S. Shearer, eds. Westport, Connecticut: Greenwood Press, 1996.

Other

Williams College faculty information directory. http://www.williams.edu:803/Biology/hwilliams.html (October 30, 1997).

—*Sketch by Jacqueline L. Longe*

Ian Wilmut

Ian Wilmut
1944–
English embryologist

Ian Wilmut, an embryologist working at the Roslin Institute in Scotland, made headline news around the world when he announced that he had cloned the first mammal—a sheep named Dolly—from an adult animal. Conducted in February 1997, his experiment was a giant step forward for animal science, genetics, and medicine. It meant animals could be cloned in order to further human medical advancements. Cloned animals could produce large quantities of proteins useful in the manufacture of certain pharmaceuticals. They might also provide a source for organs that could be transplanted to human beings.

Wilmut's work caused a sensation because it carried startling implications. If a sheep could be cloned, so could a human being. Many scientists believe that humans can be cloned. Wilmut, a quiet, intense scientist, believes it would be a mistake—and an inhumane choice—to do so. He intended for his work to benefit animal science, not to create new Frankensteins, he told a *New York Times* reporter in a 1997 interview. "I am not a fool," he said. "I know what is bothering people about this. I understand why the world is suddenly at my door. But this is my work. It has always been my work, and it doesn't have anything to do with creating copies of human beings."

Ian Wilmut was born on July 7, 1944, in Hampton Lucey, England in Warwick. He attended the University of Nottingham, where he became fascinated with embryology after meeting G. Eric Lamming, a world-renowned expert in reproduction. The meeting became a turning point for Wilmut, who set out on a singular quest—to understand the genetic engineering of animals. He graduated from Nottingham in 1967, with a degree in agricultural science.

Wilmut continued his studies at Darwin College at Cambridge University in England. There he received his doctoral degree in 1973, awarded after he completed his thesis on the techniques for freezing boar semen. A workaholic by nature, he immediately took a position at the Animal Breeding Research Station, an animal research institute supported by government and private funds. The research station eventually became the Roslin Institute. It is headquartered in Roslin, near Edinburgh, Scotland.

In 1973, after receiving his doctorate, Wilmut produced the first calf ("Frosty") born from a frozen embryo that had been implanted into a surrogate mother. The motivation for such an experiment was to harvest cows that provide the best meat and milk by implanting their embryos into other females. The average cow can birth five to 10 calves during their lifespan. With the ability to transfer embryos, cattle breeders could increase the quality of their animal stock.

Wilmut continued his research during the 1980s, despite other scientists' growing discouragement in the possibility of cloning. In 1996, Wilmut overheard a story in an Irish bar, while attending a scientific meeting, that solidified his belief in cloning. The rumor that Wilmut heard was that Dr. Steen M. Willadsen of Grenada Genetics in Texas had cloned a lamb using a differentiated cell from an already developing embryo.

Like a fertilized egg that contains enough deoxyribonucleic acid (DNA) to build an entire organism, a differentiated cell carries a full complement of the genetic material for DNA, which forms a blueprint for an animal's characteristics. To clone an animal, an adult animal cell would have to be harvested, and the nucleus placed in an embryo cell, thereby replacing the nucleus of the embryo cell. Yet the problem was how to get the new nucleus to spawn growth in the embryo cell.

Keith Campbell, a biologist at the Roslin Institute, had an insight that proved to be crucial. He deduced that an egg probably will not use genetic material from a transplanted adult cell because the cycles of each cell are not synchronized. Cells go through specific cycles, growing and dividing and making an entirely new package of chromosomes each time. In order to synchronize the cells, Campbell slowed down adult mammal cells—in fact, nearly

stopping them—so they would actually exist in synchrony with the embryos. Then each embryo could be joined with an adult cell, and in turn, they could join together and grow. To slow an already developing or adult cell down, Campbell forced it into a hibernating state by depriving it of nutrients. With this method, he and Wilmut were able to clone two sheep from developing embryo cells. They named the sheep Megan and Morag.

To clone an adult sheep, Wilmut and Campbell harvested udder, or mammary, cells from a six-year-old ewe. The cells were preserved in test tubes and starved by reducing their serum concentration for five days. Out of 277 attempts, Dolly's embryo was the only one to survive. They implanted Dolly's embryo when it was six days old into a surrogate mother, and on July 5, 1996, Dolly was born. She was named for the country singer Dolly Parton. They kept the lamb's birth secret until they had received a patent for the process that had created her. As a government employee working at Roslin, Wilmut does not own the patent on his cloning procedure. The company which runs Roslin, called PPL P.L.C. Therapeutics, will benefit from the patent proceeds, and will produce new drugs through the procedure.

Wilmut continues to work nine-hour days at the Roslin Institute, often bringing work home. He lives in a small village near Edinburgh with his wife, Vivian. They have three children, Helen, Naomi, and Dean. Wilmut is an honorary fellow at the Institute of Ecology and Resource Management at the University of Edinburgh. He enjoys walks in the Scotish highlands and an occasional single-malt scotch whisky.

Those working with Wilmut describe him as careful, diligent, honest, and thoughtful. Perhaps that is why Wilmut was puzzled and a bit angry about all the attention his work received from news reporters around the world. "People have sensationalized this in every way," he told the *New York Times.* Many public figures expressed dismay over the negative implications of cloning animals—and perhaps humans. The British government was even considering cutting the highly respected Roslin Institute's finances as a result of the cloning experiment. "People say that cloning means that if a child dies you can get that child back," he commented to the Times. "You could never get that child back. It would be something different. You need to understand the biology. People are not genes. They are so much more than that."

Wilmut remains passionate about his work. His goal is to push the work of cloning animals forward, so that it can help solve some of the world's worst medical problems. He continues his cloning projects so he and other scientists can study genetic diseases for which there are presently no cures. He sees a day when genetic engineering and cloning can produce proteins like the clotting factor that hemophiliacs lack. Other diseases, resulting from the lack of a genetic material, might also be cured.

SELECTED WRITINGS BY WILMUT:

Periodicals

"Sheep Cloned by Nuclear Transfer from a Cultured Cell Line." *Nature* 380 (1996): 64-66.

FURTHER READING:

Periodicals

Ibrahim, Youssef M. "Ian Wilmut: Secrecy Gives Way to Spotlight for Scientist." *The New York Times* (February 24, 1997): B8.
Kolata, Gina. "With Cloning of Sheep, the Ethical Ground Shifts." *The New York Times* (February 24, 1997): A1.
Specter, Michael and Gina Kolata. "After Decades of Missteps, How Cloning Succeeded." *The New York Times* (March 3, 1997): A1.

—*Sketch by Barbara Boughton*

Chien-Shiung Wu

Chien-Shiung Wu
1912–1997
American physicist

For more than thirty years, Chien-Shiung Wu was a member of the physics department at Columbia University, where she earned a reputation as one of the world's foremost nuclear physicists. Wu was best known for a classic experiment on beta decay, completed in 1957, which confirmed a prediction made a year earlier by **Tsung-Dao Lee** and **Chen Ning Yang** regarding the conservation of parity (the basic symmetry of nature) in reactions involving the weak force. A number of observers have commented on the apparent inequity of the Nobel Prize committee's not having included Wu in the 1957 physics prize, which was awarded to Lee and Yang for this work.

Chien-Shiung Wu was born on May 29, 1912, in Liu Ho, near Shanghai, China. Her father, Wu Zhongyi, was a former engineer who had abandoned his profession in 1911 to take part in the revolution that overthrew the Manchu dynasty. After the war, Wu returned to Liu Ho to open a school for girls. Still filled with revolutionary zeal, he saw it as his mission to make sure that girls as well as boys were able to have an education in the "new China." Chien-Shiung's mother, Fan Fuhua, helped her husband in this effort, providing education to their students' families in their own homes.

Wu attended her father's school until she was nine and then continued her education at the Soochow Girls School, about fifty miles (80 km) from her home. During her high school years, Wu was active in a number of political causes; her fellow classmates chose her to represent them in some of the causes because, with her stellar scholastic record, she could not readily be dismissed from school on the basis of her involvement in political issues. In 1930, Wu graduated from Soochow as valedictorian of her class and then entered the National Central University in Nanking. By that time she had decided to pursue physics as a career, and in 1934 was awarded a bachelor's degree in that field. After teaching and doing research for two years, Wu left China in 1936, intending to obtain the graduate training in physics that was not then available in her native land. Her original plans to enroll in the University of Michigan changed abruptly when she reached San Francisco and was offered an opportunity to attend the University of California at Berkeley.

Among the factors influencing Wu's decision to remain in California was the presence of **Ernest Orlando Lawrence,** inventor of the atom-smashing cyclotron (a device that accelerates the speed of nuclear particles), on the Berkeley campus. The chance to study with Lawrence was, Wu decided, too important to pass up. Another factor in her decision was the presence of "Luke" Chia Liu Yuan—a young man she met soon after arriving in San Francisco. Wu and Yuan were married in 1942 and eventually had one son, Vincent Wei-Chen Yuan.

Teaches at Smith, Princeton, and Columbia

Wu received her Ph.D. in 1940, a time of great turmoil in her homeland and in the world at large. The Japanese army had already invaded China, and U.S. involvement in World War II was only a year away. Wu stayed on as a research assistant at Berkeley for two years after receiving her degree, but spent much of that time on war-related work. In 1942 she was offered her first teaching position, at Smith College in Northampton, Massachusetts. She remained at Smith for only one year before accepting an appointment at Princeton University, where she was assigned to teach introductory physics to naval officers. She held this position for only a few months before she was offered a post at Columbia University, where she would join the Manhattan Project—through which the world's first atomic bombs were designed and built. That job, which began in March 1944, was the beginning of a long relationship with Columbia; she eventually became a research associate in 1945, associate professor in 1952, and finally full professor in 1958. She retired from Columbia in 1981.

Tests the Lee-Yang Theory of Parity Nonconservation

The work for which Wu gained fame took place in 1957. It was based on a revolutionary theory proposed by two colleagues, Tsung-Dao Lee, also of Columbia, and Chen Ning Yang, of the Institute for Advanced Study in Princeton, New Jersey. In 1956 Lee and Yang had raised the possibility that a property known as parity may not be conserved in certain types of nuclear reactions. Conservation laws had long been at the heart of physical theories. These laws said that a number of important physical characteristics—mass, energy, momentum, and electrical charge, for instance—were always conserved during physical or chemical changes. As an example, the law of conservation of electrical charge says that the total electrical charge on all particles involved in a physical change would be the same both before and after the event.

Lee and Yang found theoretical reasons to question the conservation of parity in some instances. Parity refers to the theory that the laws of nature are not biased in any particular direction, a concept long held by physicists. When beta particles are emitted by nuclei during radioactive decay, for example, classical theory predicts that they will be emitted without preference to any particular spin orientation. Lee and Yang developed a mathematical argument showing

that this might not be the case and outlined experiments through which their theory could be tested.

Lee and Yang presented their ideas to Wu, already recognized as an authority on beta decay (a radioactive nuclear transformation) and the weak force that causes it. Even before her colleagues had published a paper on their theory, Wu had begun to design experiments to test their ideas. Working with colleagues at the National Bureau of Standards's Low Temperature Physics Group, Wu labored almost without rest for six months. In January of 1957, she announced her results: clear evidence for the violation of parity conservation had been observed. Later that same year, Lee and Yang were awarded the Nobel Prize in physics—an award that many observers in the field believe might easily have been shared with Wu.

Although she did not receive a Nobel Prize, Wu has won a host of other awards, including the first Wolf Prize awarded by the state of Israel (1978), the first Research Corporation Award (1959) given to a woman, the Comstock Award of the National Academy of Sciences (1964), and the National Science Medal (1975). She was elected to the National Academy of Sciences in 1958. Wu suffered a fatal stroke in Manhattan, New York, on February 16, 1997. She was 84.

SELECTED WRITINGS BY WU:

Books

An Experimental Test of Parity Conservation in Beta Decay. New York, 1957.
Nuclear Physics, Academic Press, 1961.

FURTHER READING:

Books

Kass-Simon, G., and Patricia Farnes, eds. *Women of Science: Righting the Record.* Bloomington: Indiana University Press, 1990, pp. 205-08.
————. *McGraw-Hill Modern Men of Science.* Vol. 2. New York: McGraw-Hill, 1984, pp. 541-42.
McGrayne, Sharon Bertsch. *Nobel Prize Women in Science.* Secaucus, NJ: Birchlane Press, 1993, pp. 255-79.
Yost, Edna. *Women of Modern Science.* Dodd, 1959, pp. 80-93.

Periodicals

Dicke, William. "Chien-Shiung Wu, 84, Dies; Top Experimental Physicist" (obituary). *New York TImes* (18 February 1997): B7.

—*Sketch by David E. Newton*

J. Z. Young
1907–1997
English biologist

John Zachary, or "J. Z.," Young was a highly acclaimed biologist whose research on the squid and the octopus has helped greatly in making neurology an exact science. His studies of the regeneration of the nerves of the octopus qualified him, during World War II, to work with a team of scientists investigating the problems of peripheral nerve injuries and their surgical repair. Young was the first to prove that the giant fibers of the squid are nerves. For his work, which has shed light on the nature of memory, Young was named a fellow of the Royal Society, which also bestowed on him its Royal Medal in 1967. In 1973, he was awarded the Linnean Gold Medal, and two years later he received the London Medal from the Zoological Society.

John Zachary Young, the eldest of five children, was born on March 18, 1907 in Fishponds, Bristol, England, to Philip Young and Constance Maria Lloyd Young. His father's family were yeoman farmers in Gloucestershire and Somerset, becoming prosperous in the eighteenth and nineteenth centuries. His mother's ancestors were Welsh, and they became industrialists and bankers in Birmingham and the West Midlands.

Research on Octopus and Squid Flourishes in Naples

In 1928, Young graduated in zoology at Oxford University. His interest in octopus research led him to the Zoological Station of Naples, which was the first international marine biological observatory in Europe. Young's first paper, on the regeneration of the nerves of octopus, was published in Italian in 1929. It was also at this time that he began research that led to the discovery of the giant nerve fibers of the squid. His studies of squid, which were described in various papers published during the 1930s, provided the basis for the research into the study of nerve impulses in higher animals. "In a squid, the whole jet propulsion system is worked by just *two* nerve cells; but the learning part of the squid's brain has many millions, as has that of an octopus. Multiplicity is a prime clue to the nature of memory," Young wrote in his book, *Philosophy and the Brain.* In 1945, Young was appointed to the Chair of Anatomy at University College London (U.C.L.), a post he held until 1974. Upon his retirement, he chose to work in the Psychology Department at Oxford, where he continued to do experimental work on octopus and squid.

Young's appointment to the chair of anatomy at U.C.L. marked a departure for the college, which previously had sought traditional anatomists for this position. However, by the time of his appointment, Young had acquired a considerable reputation as a researcher on the physiology of lampreys, the nervous system of cephalopods, the autonomic nervous system, as well as the regeneration of mammalian nerves, which assumed much importance during the Second World War. During his tenure as chair, Young continued his research on the octopus. "He must be the first man to have made a really detailed study of the brain of an invertebrate. Perhaps he has reached a greater understanding of the brain of a single type of animal than any other biologist, and it was a stroke of genius on his part to choose such a fascinating and intelligent creature," wrote the editors of *Essays on the Nervous System,* a book dedicated to Young on the occasion of his sixty-seventh birthday. Young's research touched many people through his books and also through the radio lectures he gave on the British Broadcasting Corporation (BBC). The first of these, the Reith Lectures, were given in 1950 and later published in book form as *Doubt and Certainty in Science.* Young, who had sent a copy of the Reith lectures to the English writer Lewis Mumford, commented in a letter to him dated November 28, 1951, "I cannot help feeling that we are at a point where we could develop a new 'science' lying between fields as wide apart as physics, physiology and history. The more I think of it, the more convinced I become that all scientific study is a study of the behaviour of observers and reactors, which, I suppose, is the same as History."

Young's Work at U.C.L. Inspires Colleagues

At the college itself, Young's octopus research, which shed a great deal of light upon the relationship between brain structure and behavior in higher animals, inspired psychiatrists, neurologists, and engineers. One result was a model electronic brain, devised by an electrical engineer named W. K. Taylor. This model was able to discriminate between various shapes, and even between portraits of people. Young continued his work on the reaction of nerves to injury, gathering around him a group of eager young anatomists who went on to become important researchers in the fields of anatomy and neurology. Several years after Young was chosen to head the anatomy department, he persuaded the college to purchase an electron microscope, which had so impressed him at the American embassy in London. Its use threw much light on the study of cell membranes.

Research on Octopus Brain Illuminates Nature of Memory

The research that Young embarked upon in Naples as a young man continued to absorb him. Focusing on the brain of the octopus, Young also analyzed the structure and functions of the various lobes concerned in memory, differentiating between the short- and long-term memory systems. He demonstrated that there are two separate sets of lobes for recording information about visual and tactile events. Both sets are organized on the same principles, allowing the signals of the results of actions (pleasure and pain) to provide the information for inductive forecasting of the best course of future action. From this work, Young formulated a theory about the units that accumulate in the memory by the release of inhibitory substances, which limit the possible outputs for the classifying cells of the receptors. These researches have illuminated one of the most complex and most challenging of all biological problems—the nature of memory. During his tenure at U.C.L., Young divided his time between research and teaching; one of the first things he did as department chairman was to revise the teaching of gross anatomy. As a result, he substantially reduced the burden it imposed on medical students. In addition, Young played an important role in developing B.Sc. courses in anatomy at the college, thus offering opportunities to young biologists both within and without the medical field.

Young continued his research on cephalopods through his retirement. He returned to the lab to study the autonomic nervous system of bony fish, and he continued to produce new editions of his textbooks. At the time of his death, he was working with Marion Nixon on a new book to be called *The Brains and Lives of Cephalopods*.

Young married Phyllis Elizabeth Heaney in 1938. They had one son and two daughters before her death in 1987. He subsequently married Raymonde May, with whom he had one daughter. Young wrote numerous scientific papers and books, and delivered several notable lectures. He received many awards and medals and was made an honorary fellow of numerous academies and societies both in the U.K. and abroad. Young died on July 4, 1997, at the age of 90.

SELECTED WRITINGS BY YOUNG:

Books

Doubt and Certainty in Science. Oxford: Oxford University Press, 1960.
From Molecule to Man. New York: Crown, 1969.
Philosophy and the Brain. Oxford: Oxford University Press, 1987.

FURTHER READING:

Books

Bellairs, R. and E. G. Gray, eds. *Essays on the Nervous System.* Oxford: Clarendon Press, 1974.

Periodicals

"Professor J.Z. Young" (obituary). *Times (London)* (9 July 1997).

Other

Letter from J. Z. Young to Lewis Mumford, dated 28 November 1951.

—Sketch by Rayma Prince

Lai–Sang Young
1952–
Chinese mathematician

Lai–Sang Young keeps a low profile outside the field of mathematics, but her investigations into the statistical parameters of dynamical systems broke through a mathematical bottleneck that had existed for several years. For this achievement, Young received the 1993 Ruth Lyttle Satter Prize in mathematics. She also won a National Science Foundation Faculty Award for Women Scientists and Engineers, which funds her teaching and research over a number of years.

Lai–Sang Young was born in Hong Kong in 1952. Before emigrating to the United States at an unknown date, her mainly Cantonese education included English classes from a variety of schoolteachers. Her higher education was received in America, however. Young earned a bachelor's degree from the University of Wisconsin at Madison in 1973, and both her M.A. and Ph.D. from the University of California at Berkeley over the ensuing five years.

Young began a teaching career that took her from Northwestern in 1978, to Michigan State in 1980, then on to concurrent posts at the University of Arizona and the University of California at Los Angeles (UCLA). As a recipient of a Sloan Fellowship during 1985–86, she taught at the Universitat Bielefeld in Germany. Young also held visiting positions at institutions at Warwick in England and Berkeley's Mathematical Science Research Institute, and at the Institute for Advanced Study in Princeton, New Jersey, during the 1980s.

Specializes in Ergodic Theory

Young specializes in a field that is fairly new in applied mathematics. In the realm of systems analysis, a rigorous computational method to measure the complexity of non–uniform systems is under current investigation. The subspecialty devoted to the statistical properties of dynamical systems is called "ergodic theory." The probability of the recurrence of any state in a model and the chance that any sample is equally representative of the whole make up the key questions in ergodic theory. The goal is to be able to model deterministic systems in other disciplines, such as anthropology, with a model that is random yet statistically regular.

With this goal in mind, Young has focused on the dynamics of strange attractors. A Henon attractor is a fractal with two variables, an *a* parameter and a *b* parameter, that looks something like a fuzzy sketch of a boomerang. It is considered one of the simplest dynamic systems that does not possess a stable periodic cycle. In a joint paper with a colleague, Young showed that a subset of the fractal turns out to have "a common distribution to the limit." This statistical norm is what allows the interdimensional figure to show up on a computer screen as a boomerang shape. Young produced similar work with quadratic maps, another set of simple yet nonuniform systems, that clarified previously contradictory evidence. Finding predictability in chaos was an achievement termed "both unexpected and deep" in Young's Satter Prize citation.

"Embarrassing" Lack of Examples Leads to Breakthrough

Since the 1970s, mathematicians have been able to measure "uniformly hyperbolic" systems, and by the 1980s a number of researchers had come up with an ergodic theory for non–uniform counterparts. This work built a platform for generalizing about both types in terms of being able to predict an outcome for an attractor regardless of any initial condition. That means that no matter where researchers start, they wind up with the same general results. However, a natural invariant measure—the necessary statistical pattern—could not be found for a specific non–uniform case. As Young had stated during her response to the Satter Prize citation, the "lack of examples was starting to get a little embarrassing" for everyone. Investigations into the Henon attractor maps, considered the most likely suspects at that juncture, were already underway when Young was invited to join. She and a teammate constructed invariant measures for the parameters of a Henon, considered the first examples of their kind.

Young has participated in a number of events that bring mathematicians together in formal and informal settings. She delivered the invited address at the 1985 meeting of the American Mathematical Society (AMS). In 1994, she presented at a workshop on lattice dynamics and ergodic theory at the Mathematics Research Centre of Warwick. As the second recipient of the Satter Prize, Young kept the tradition, begun with **Margaret Dusa McDuff**, of helping to select the next winner, **Sun–Yung Alice Chang**, in 1995. Young was most recently part of the AMS Committee on Summer Institutes and Special Symposia, to organize the 1997 Summer Research Institute on differential geometry and control at the University of Colorado.

Gary Froyland, an Australian Ph.D. who shares Young's interest in topological entropy, was at first surprised at how approachable she was. Froyland's supervisor at the University of Western Australia asked Young, considered a world leader in her field, to spare some time at a conference. Young not only met and offered some pertinent explanations to the student, she invited him to UCLA. She also helped him find accommodations there and cover his expenses. During his stay, Froyland was impressed with Young's humor, clarity of mind, and teaching style. In her lectures and consultations Young strives to keep attention to precisely accurate detail without sacrificing the accessibility of everyday examples. Froyland reports that Young is a bit of a mimic, at least when it comes to imitating the accents of all her former English teachers, including a range of British natives and an American priest. The two mathematicians also discovered a shared interest in table tennis. A hint of Young's high personal standards came to light when she admitted she was once ranked among the top 20 female ping–pong players in the United States, but retired at the age of 25 when she felt her reflexes were beginning to slow.

SELECTED WRITINGS BY YOUNG:

(With Huyi Hu) "Nonexistence of SBR Measures for Some Diffeomorphisms that Are 'Almost Anosov'." (31K, TeX) *The Mathematical Physics Preprint Archive.* http://www.ma.utexas.edu/mp_arc/a/97–30

FURTHER READING:

Periodicals

"1993 Ruth Lyttle Satter Prize." *Notices of the American Mathematical Society* 40, no. 3 (March 1993): 229–30.

Other

Froyland, Gary, in an electronic mail interview with Jennifer Kramer conducted July 12, 1997.
Gary Froyland Web Page. http://maths.uwa.edu.au/~gary/mycv.html (August 15, 1997).
"Lai–Sang Young." *Biographies of Women Mathematicians.* http://www.scottlan.edu/lriddle/women/chronol.htm (August 15, 1997).

—*Sketch by Jennifer Kramer*

William Henry Young
1863–1942
English applied mathematician

William Henry Young made advances in several areas of mathematics, but his most significant contribution was the development of a calculus approach that has been adopted by nearly all authors of advanced calculus textbooks since 1910. Together with his wife, **Grace Chisolm Young**, he published widely on a variety of mathematical topics.

The eldest child of Henry Young and Hephzibah Jeal, Young was born in London, England, on October 20, 1863, into a family that had been prominent in banking for several generations. He received his early education at the City of London School. The headmaster of the school, Edwin A. Abbott, author of a mathematical fantasy novel entitled *Flatland*, recognized Young as a skilled mathematician. Young chose to focus on mathematics in his college career at the Peterhouse College of Cambridge University, where he commenced study in 1881. He was expected to place as the senior wrangler, or first place, on the 1884 mathematical tripos, but he only placed fourth. Young later contended that he did not place as expected because he refused to limit his scope to the intensive study of mathematics required to excel on the tripos, and, in addition to mathematics, chose to pursue other intellectual avenues as well as athletics. He studied the works of Molière and competed for a Smith prize in the field of theology rather than mathematics. Young won the prize.

From 1886 to 1892, Young was a fellow of Peterhouse, although he held no official post at the school. Rather than immersing himself in research, Young chose the more lucrative path of private mathematics instruction of undergraduates. During this time, he also laid the foundation for a professional and romantic partnership with one of his students, Grace Chisholm, a student at the Girton College of Cambridge who obtained her first class degree in mathematics in 1892 and obtained senior wrangler status on the mathematical tripos. They were married in 1896.

The Youngs lived primarily in Göttingen, Germany, where Grace earned her doctorate, until 1908, when they moved to Switzerland. They lived first in Geneva and later moved to Lausanne. Young did not seriously pursue research until after his marriage, however, beginning around 1900. Between then and 1924, however, he wrote more than 200 papers with his wife. He devoted significant time to the study of real functions, independently discovering what came to be known as Lebesgue integration. Unfortunately, he did not make the discovery until two years after **Henri Lebesgue**, and although Young's definition of integration was different in form from Lebesque's, it was basically equivalent to it. Young made significant contributions to the further development of this area of study, however, most notably by establishing a method of monotone sequences as used in the Stieltjes integral. Young also made advances in Fourier analysis and measure theory.

Young's career was also noteworthy because of his professional collaboration with his wife, whose doctorial thesis focused on algebraic groups of spherical trigonometry. The Youngs embarked on projects together prior to their marriage, with Grace conducting most of the research while William provided financial support through his private tutoring. Due to the educational climate at the time, most papers written by the couple were attributed solely to William. This arrangement, with Grace undertaking the bulk of the research, may have hindered William later in life, as his lack of research credits may have been a factor in his inability to obtain positions of the high quality he desired.

One of the most important works to come out of the Youngs' collaboration was their second textbook, *The Theory of Sets of Points*. While set study is now a foundation for studies in all areas of mathematics, it was not yet commonly regarded at the time. On the whole, the mathematical community of the time overlooked this contribution, although **Georg Cantor**, one of the foremost experts in modern set theory, hailed the work.

Young returned to instruction in 1913, when he accepted part–time chair positions at the universities of Calcutta and Liverpool, and a position as professor at Aberystwyth. He was named an honorary doctor of the universities of Calcutta, Geneva, and Strasbourg. Among his many honors was the Sylvester Medal of the Royal Society, bestowed upon him in 1928. He also served as president of the International Union of Mathematicians from 1929 to 1936.

With the travels he undertook to earn a living, Young frequently found himself away from home for extended periods of time. The spring of 1940 found Young in Switzerland and his wife in England. Although they anticipated no problems reuniting, the escalation of World War II and the downfall of France intervened. For the last two years of his life, Young was separated from his family, which in addition to Grace included two sons and three daughters (a third son was killed in 1917). He died on July 7, 1942, in Lausanne, Switzerland.

In addition to their large body of research, his and Grace's legacy included two children who continued study in the field of mathematics, Professor Laurence Chisholm Young and Dr. Rosalind Cecily Tanner, who both practiced pure mathematics.

SELECTED WRITINGS BY YOUNG:

Books

(With Grace Chisholm Young) *The First Book of Geometry,* reprinted 1969.
(With Grace Chisholm Young) *The Theory of Sets of Points,* 1906; second edition 1972.
The Fundamental Theorems of the Differential Calculus, 1910.

FURTHER READING:

Books

Pycior, Helena M., Nancy G. Slack, and Pnina G. Abir–Am, editors. *Creative Couples in the Sciences.* New Brunswick: Rutgers University Press, 1996, pp. 126–40.

Periodicals

"William Henry Young." *Journal of the London Mathematical Society* 17 (1942): 218–37.
"William Henry Young." *Obituary Notices of Fellows of the Royal Society of London* 3 (1943): 307–23.

—*Sketch by Kristin Palm*

Paul Charles Zamecnik
1912–

American physician and genetic researcher

Paul Zamecnik was one of the first scientists to explore the field of genetics. Beginning his work shortly after the structure of deoxyribonucleic acid (DNA) was discovered in 1953, Zamecnik was the first to describe how the micromachinery of each cell turns the genetic code of DNA into the proteins that build cells and make them work. His groundbreaking research, spanning more than 60 years, opened up vast new areas of inquiry in genetics and pharmaceuticals, especially the hunt for "gene therapy" and drugs that work on the genetic level.

Son of a Musical Family

Zamecnik was born in Cleveland, Ohio, on November 22, 1912. His grandfather was a bandleader and composer who had emigrated from Prague, in what is now the Czech Republic, to Cleveland, where there was a significant population of what were then known as Bohemians. Zamecnik (pronounced ZAM-es-nick) remembers sitting on his father's shoulders as his grandfather's marching band paraded past on Cleveland's Euclid Avenue.

Zamecnik's father was a banker in Cleveland, and Paul decided he wanted to be a doctor. On the advice of a high school teacher whom he admired, he went to Dartmouth College in Hanover, New Hampshire. "I was a city boy, why not try the country? I liked it there," he told contributor Karl Leif Bates in an October 1997 telephone interview. Dartmouth enabled students to complete their premedical curriculum in three years and then go on for two years of medical school there, which Zamecnik did. He then transferred to Harvard University in 1933 to finish his last two years of medical school, earning his M.D. in 1936.

Upon earning this degree, Zamecnik took a departure from the normal course of study, which was to change his career. He took a research-oriented residency at C.P. Huntington Memorial Hospital, a 24-bed cancer facility owned by Harvard. "I thought I would become a surgeon, but I was rather dazzled by the prospect of working in a laboratory and seeing some medical patients," he told Bates. "This idea of pursuing research was rather interesting." But cancer research, at the time, was thought to be a dead-end career.

Just to be sure he wasn't missing anything in medicine, or Cleveland, Zamecnik took a general medicine internship at Western Reserve University Hospital in Cleveland. But from then on, his career has been strongly focused on the lab. Following the internship, he took a fellowship post at the Carlsberg Laboratories in Copenhagen, a biochemistry lab that was "a mecca for Americans at that time." One of his professors at Carlsberg was heard telling a colleague "that young man is throwing his medical education down the sink," Zamecnik remembers. He had to leave Copenhagen in 1940, as the Nazis began to take over Europe. Americans were neutral in the war at the time, but were having trouble getting their fellowship checks from home cashed.

He returned to the States to work at the Rockefeller Institute under biochemist Max Bergmann, who was trying to figure out how proteins were made in the cell and what their structures and functions were. Zamecnik thought it was a crucial area to study to advance medicine, because surgeons could operate on a disorder after the fact, "but had to leave the rest up to nature." With only one antibiotic on the market at the time, the biochemical approach to medicine was hardly considered.

Bergmann's idea was that the same enzymes involved in breaking proteins apart were also somehow responsible for putting proteins together. He had found a set of enzymes inside cells that were complementary to known break-down enzymes of the digestive system. Bergmann thought that the proteins were so specific that they might synthesize proteins under the proper conditions. Interestingly, Bergmann had initially rejected Zamecnik's query about working in his lab because he was a medical doctor, not an organic chemist. But after his experience in Copenhagen, "I had a little stardust on my shoulders from Carlsberg, so he decided to take me." When the war reached the United States in late 1941 and early 1942, though, plans changed. Zamecnik returned to Harvard to work in the Huntington Labs on war-related research, like separating and typing blood.

Still Puzzled by Source of Proteins

As the war ended, Zamecnik was still puzzling over protein synthesis. "Nothing was known about protein synthesis, there was no map to go by. It took up one paragraph in a biochemical textbook," he said.

Why, he wondered, does a tumor cell continue to multiply wildly, when other cells seem to know when to quit? "So, I thought, 'there's something wrong with the regulation, but we've got to get inside the cell to figure out what it is.'"

Two key things had happened during the war. First, a scientist at Massachusetts General Hospital, **Fritz Lippman** proposed that proteins are made by a different set of enzymes, and second, the government's Oak Ridge Labs had developed Carbon-14, a very useful radioactive probe. "So we decided to find out whether Bergmann was right or whether Lippman was right." Using a marker made by attaching C-14 to an amino acid, Zamecnik and colleagues at Harvard found that aminos were the building blocks of proteins, but that assembly would require quite a bit of energy. He then identified where the energy for that assembly came from, adenosine triphosphate, or ATP.

"We felt quite confident that Lippman was right, and that there were a different set of enzymes involved." From 1948 to '52 he worked on finding a cell-free system which produced protein in the presence of an energy donor. This work "created a whole new area of biochemistry. One pearl after another dropped out, as the days went on. It was very exciting."

A Glimpse into the Cell

In 1953, **James Watson** and **Francis Crick** first proposed the double-helix structure of deoxyribonucleic acid (DNA). Now scientists had a better idea about how DNA could convey information and duplicate itself reliably, but still no one knew how that information was turned into action inside the cell. In late 1955, and early '56, Zamecnik proposed the existence of "transfer RNA," a ribonucleic acid like DNA that could form a complement to the genetic strand and carry its information from the nucleus of the cell out into the cytoplasm, where proteins are made. Then he announced the discovery of ribosomes, small globular bodies in the cell's cytoplasm that appear to "read" the stretch of transfer RNA and bring in the amino acid building blocks it specifies to assemble the protein. "It seemed to be a spool on which the reaction took place," Zamecnik said. Then two competing labs were able to put the finishing touches on Zamecnik's idea, decoding the language of transfer RNA and identifying yet another code, messenger RNA, which worked between DNA and transfer RNA.

For the next 20 years Zamecnik turned his attention to research which created a whole new field of inquiry for the pharmaceutical industry, fighting diseases of protein synthesis by jamming the cell's DNA signals. The mechanism for this was something now called "antisense DNA," a complementary short strand of DNA that can be used to bind to a piece of messenger RNA and stop it from working. Zamecnik targeted a virus, Rous Sarcoma Virus, which caused cancer in chickens. As he struggled to sequence the virus's genes and then make the complementary DNA sequences which would prevent it from copying itself, the tools of biotechnology took great strides forward.

By 1978, Zamecnik finally had his breakthrough against Rous Sarcoma, a strand of man-made DNA that blocked the virus' ability to copy itself. Other scientists had figured out how to sequence genes, chop them into manageable pieces, and make new sequences to order. Using these new tools, Zamecnik was finally able to make his antisense approach work. "Our results indicated that the small pieces could get in and affect the metabolism of cells. I was astonished that the (man-made sequences) did get into the cell, and blocked the replication of the Rouse's Sarcoma cells." He has been called "the father of antisense," but Zamecnik said he fought the use of the term for years, since it sounds so much like "nonsense."

Drug companies have been striving, since his 1978 breakthrough, to devise man-made antisense strands that will effectively block the genetic signals that cause protein-related diseases. While most drugs in use today treat the disorder after an errant protein has been manufactured by the cell, the antisense approach is believed to have great promise in the treatment of hepatitis, cancers, coronary artery disease and many other disorders, before they occur in the cell.

Zamecnik was a professor of oncologic medicine and director of the Huntington Lab at Harvard from 1956 to 1979. He was also a physician at Massachussets General Hospital for the same period. Upon retiring from Harvard, he joined the Worcester Foundation for Experimental Biology in Shrewsbury, Massachusetts, as principal scientist. In 1989, he founded a company, Hybridon, to pursue antisense drugs. He left the Worcester Foundation in July 1997 when it was acquired by the University of Massachusetts and went to work at Hybridon full time, keeping long hours in the lab well into his 80s. "I'm too old to retire now," he told Bates a month before his 85th birthday. "I've muffed it. I'm not very good at gardening nor at hammering nails and I don't consider this work. It's interesting. Like watching a horse race."

When he received the first ever-awarded Albert Lasker Award for Special Achievement in Medical Science in 1996, Zamecnik was cited for his "brilliant and original science that revolutionized biochemistry and created an entirely new field of scientific inquiry." He was also awarded a National Medal of Science in 1991, The National Cancer Society National Award in 1968, and several honorary degrees.

Rolf M. Zinkernagel

Zamecnik has been married to Mary Zamecnik since 1936, and she still assists him in the lab. They have three children.

FURTHER READING:

Other

"Welcome to Hybridon, Inc." Oct. 1997. http://www.hybridon.com/ (28 Oct. 1997)

Herald-Sun Newspapers (North Carolina) "Paul C. Zamecnik, M.D." http://www.herald-sun.com/cityomed/com/zamecnik.html. (16 October, 1997)

—*Sketch by Karl Leif Bates*

Rolf M. Zinkernagel
1944–

Swiss immunologist and virologist

Rolf M. Zinkernagel joined the ranks of the Nobel laureates in 1996 because of his relatively early work with colleague **Peter Doherty** defining the system by which the immune system identifies friend and foe. His work since then has built upon this discovery, revealing how the thymus gland selects only white blood cells that react properly to virus-infected cells and investigating the complex interplay by which viruses and their hosts co-evolve.

Zinkernagel has also been a vocal proponent of the promise of biotechnology in his native Switzerland. He worries that the conservatism of his countrymen may lead to the stifling of the fledgling Swiss biotechnology industry.

Zinkernagel and his ophthalmologist wife, Kathrin, live in Zumikon, Switzerland, near Zurich, where he is head of the Institute of Experimental Immunology, and she practices medicine. Their adult children, Christine, Annelies, and Martin, are all in various stages of physician training.

A Rich, Busy Childhood

Zinkernagel was born on January 6, 1944, in Basel, Switzerland. His father was a biologist and had the distinction of being both the first Ph.D. and one of the few biologists at the time hired by the Swiss pharmaceutical giant J.R. Geigy AG. His mother, who came from the French-speaking Jura mountains region of Switzerland, came from a family with ties to the Swiss watch-making and banking industries. She became a lab technician when she moved to Basel, where she met Zinkernagel's father.

Zinkernagel attended the Mathematisch-Naturwissenschaftliches Gymnasium, the same secondary school that had educated both his father and father-in-law. While there, he pursued a great number of hobbies, including exploration of prehistoric human settlements near Basel with a chemist friend of his father's, cabinet-making and smithing, dancing, and alpine mountaineering. He also voluntarily studied Latin for four years—not a requirement of his school, but prerequisite to studying law or medicine at the time. He traveled to Scandinavia, France, and England as a teen, spending a year in England in order to learn English.

Zinkernagel went to the University of Basel in 1962, deciding to study medicine rather than chemistry—his other great interest—because the former profession offered the possibility of clinical or private practice as well as research. He met his wife when they were both medical students; the two married in 1968, two weeks after their final board examinations. In 1970 the university accepted his M.D. dissertation. Rejected by the World Health Organization for travel to Africa to study and treat leprosy because of lack of experience, the couple worked for the next three years in Switzerland.

To Australia—and to Immunology

In 1969 Zinkernagel's work in the surgery department of a hospital in Basel failed to spark his interest.

He began looking around for other possible career paths. From 1970 to 1973 he worked as a postdoctoral fellow at the University of Lausanne, Switzerland, in a laboratory studying the process by which the immune system kills virus-infected cells. Zinkernagel's project, trying to monitor the destruction of bacterial cells preloaded with radioactive chromium-51, was frustrating because the method never worked properly on the bacteria—but it gave him experience with a number of experimental techniques that were to prove crucial for his Nobel-winning research.

In 1972 Robert Blanden of the John Curtin School of Medical Research, Canberra, Australia, came to the Swiss university to teach a World Health Organization course on immunology. Intrigued by the course and encouraged by senior researchers at Lausanne, Zinkernagel applied for a fellowship with Blanden at the Curtin school. Thanks to a two-year Swiss Foundation for Biomedical Fellowships grant, Zinkernagel and his young family—Christine was two, and Annelies not yet one—moved to Australia in 1973. While at the Curtin school, Zinkernagel earned a Ph.D. in immunology, finishing his dissertation in 1975.

A fortuitous accident led Zinkernagel to team up with another young postdoctoral fellow at the Curtin school, Peter Doherty. While the Blanden laboratory was cramped for space, Doherty had room in his assigned lab. Thanks in part to their shared love of operatic music—and Zinkernagel's penchant for singing it aloud while working—Zinkernagel began to work with Doherty on how white blood cells called killer T cells identify virus-infected host cells to attack. "He was tolerable, but loud," according to Doherty.

Friend or Foe?

At the time, immunologists were very interested in a group of genes collectively called the major histocompatibility complex, or MHC. These genes, clustered together in the DNA sequence, encode a series of proteins called the MHC antigens, which determine whether a transplanted organ will be accepted or rejected by a recipient. If the MHC genes of the donor and the recipient match, the organ survives; if they do not, the organ is attacked by the recipient's immune system and dies.

A number of researchers had guessed that the rejection of MHC-mismatched organs was essentially the same process as the killing of virus-infected cells by killer T cells. Zinkernagel and Doherty demonstrated that this was true, and that the MHC antigens were necessary for killer T cells to tell friend from foe. But when they investigated further, they found something very unexpected; most immunologists had expected that when virus-infected cells and killer cells were poorly MHC matched, the immune cells' killing

response would be strongest, much as in badly matched transplants. But the opposite was true. In order to get proper T-cell killing of the virus-infected cells, Zinkernagel and Doherty discovered, the cells' MHC regions had to match.

The two had discovered that T cells—indeed, the immune response in general—can only recognize viral proteins when they are displayed in the context of properly matched MHC antigens. The immune system, which had evolved to recognize "self" from "other" did not react most strongly to "other," but to a third state, "altered self." This discovery finally put transplant rejection into biological context. The body does not purposely reject mismatched organs because they are different, it rejects them because it mistakenly identifies the mismatched MHC antigens as "self" antigens that have been altered by interaction with viral proteins. The finding also opened the way to better methods for heading off transplant rejection, for creating vaccines, and for further unraveling the workings of immunity; vulnerability to certain infections; and autoimmune disease, where the body mistakenly attacks its own tissues.

Recognition—and a Chance to be Heard

Zinkernagel's and Doherty's work together took place in a fairly short amount of time between 1973 and 1974. By 1976, both were moving on, with Zinkernagel going to the Scripps Clinic Research Institute in LaJolla, California, as an associate—a rank roughly equal to an assistant professor at a university. There he studied whether or not the thymus gland—long known to play a role in the "maturation" of infection-fighting white blood cells—used MHC antigens to select which white blood cells would mature and which would die before being released to the bloodstream. The work once again proved seminal, providing the first evidence that the thymus only allows killer cells that react against slightly altered self MHC antigens to survive. This helped explain how and why killer T cells recognize altered-self antigens most strongly. The thymus prevents autoimmune disease by killing off killer cells that would otherwise attack healthy tissues and prevents a too-weak immune response by destroying those that would fail to attack any but the most profoundly changed self antigens.

Zinkernagel became a member—the equivalent of a full professor—at Scripps in 1979. But later that year he returned to Switzerland, to take an associate professorship at the University of Zurich, followed by a full professorship in 1988. During that period, his work with Doherty began to receive growing international recognition, with an Ehrlich Prize in Germany in 1983 and a Gairdner Foundation International Award in Canada in 1986. In 1992 Zinkernagel was named head of the Institute of Experimental Immunology in Zurich and also received the Christoforo Colombo Award in Italy, to be followed by an Albert Lasker Medical Research Award—often a prelude to a Nobel—in 1995.

Zinkernagel's and Doherty's Nobel Prize for Physiology or Medicine came in 1996. Zinkernagel has since used the award as a platform from which to speak out on the threat posed by what he has said is "the Swiss lack of willingness to take risks." Conservative Swiss investors, he has argued, do not fully appreciate the importance of high-risk venture investments like those necessary to establish a biotechnology industry. Worse, he has said, his country's strong animal welfare movement threatens to kill what little biotechnology Switzerland has with over-regulation. While he applauds his country's progressive laws to ensure animal welfare and is in favor of increased government oversight of the use of genetic engineering and transgenic animals, he worries that unless Swiss voters are properly educated about the risks and promise of biotechnology, outright bans will ensue.

SELECTED WRITINGS BY ZINKERNAGEL:

Periodicals

"Cytotoxic T Cells Learn Specificity for Self H-2 During Differentiation in the Thymus." *Nature* (January 19, 1978): 251-253.

(With P.C. Doherty) "Immunological Surveillance Against Altered Self Components by Sensitized T Lymphocytes in Lymphocytic Choriomeningitis." *Nature* (October 11, 1974): 547-548.

(With P.C. Doherty) "The Discovery of MHC Restriction." *Immunology Today* (January 1997): 14-17.

Other

"Rolf M. Zinkernagel." September 29, 1997. http://www.nobel.sdsc.edu/laureates/medicine-1996-2-autobio.html (November 25, 1997).

FURTHER READING:

Periodicals

Benowitz, Steven. "New Nobel Laureates Speak Out for Increased Research Funding." *The Scientist* (November 11, 1996): 1, 4-5.

Other

"David Baron Reports that the Latest Nobel Prize Goes to Rolf Zinkernagel and Peter Doherty." Audio Recording, October 7, 1996. http://www6.realaudio.com/contentp/npr/nc6o07.html (November 25, 1997).

Walter Henry Zinn

"Research for Life." April 23, 1997. http://www.unizh.ch/upd/unileute/portraet/zinkernagel-le.html (November 25, 1997).

"The Nobel Prize in Medicine 1996." October 7, 1996. http://www.nobel.se/announcement-96/medicine96.html (November 25, 1997).

—Sketch by Kenneth Chiacchia

Walter Henry Zinn
1906–
Canadian-born American physicist

Walter Henry Zinn's scientific endeavors dramatically changed the world. He, along with his colleague **Leo Szilard**, began his exploration of atomic fission at Columbia University. That same exploration led to his participation in the Manhattan Project and the conception and invention of the atomic bomb, as well as a lifelong career for Zinn. After World War II, Zinn continued his research into atomic energy, creating the world's first breeder reactor and acting as Argonne National Laboratory's first director. His work revolutionized the way energy is harnessed and used today.

Walter Zinn was originally from Kitchener, Ontario, Canada, born on December 10, 1906. After receiving his B.A. (1927) and M.A. (1929) from Queen's University in Ontario, he moved to the United States in 1930 to continue his higher education at Columbia University, and eight years later he became a naturalized American citizen in 1938. During that same period, Zinn married his first wife in 1933, received his Ph.D. in 1934, and began to pursue his lifelong interest in atomic energy.

Verifies Fission and Lays Groundwork for Atomic Bomb

Between 1932 and 1941, Zinn taught at the City College of New York, first as an instructor and then as an assistant professor. It was during this time that he and his colleague, Leo Szilard, conducted their experimentation on the possibility of atomic fission. In 1939 they successfully illustrated how uranium, when placed under pressure, will undergo fission, its atomic structure breaking apart to release a large amount of energy.

Because of his groundbreaking work with fission, Zinn moved to the University of Chicago's Manhattan Engineering District's Metallurgical Laboratory in 1942. It was there that Zinn worked with colleagues on the Manhattan Project, which created the atomic bomb.

Designs First Breeder Reactor

After World War II, Zinn continued his work at the Metallurgical Laboratory, but he switched his focus to the development of nuclear power reactors. In 1944 Zinn successfully started "the world's first heavy-water-moderated nuclear reactor" known as Chicago Pile 3 (CP-3).

Two years later, the Manhattan Engineering District's Metallurgical Laboratory was officially changed to Argonne National Laboratory, and named Zinn as its first director. One year later in 1947, Zinn is approved by the Atomic Energy Commission, Argonne's sponsor, to build the first breeder reactor. Unlike the reactor that produces energy from uranium-235 fission, the breeder reactor attains energy while at the same time converting uranium-238 to more uranium-235. It makes more energy than it needs, thereby making nuclear energy a potential fuel source. Known as experimental breeder reactor 1 (EBR-I) or "Zinn's Infernal Pile" (ZIP), the breeder reactor produced its first electricity in 1951, when it lit up four light bulbs.

Zinn also was key in establishing the National Reactor Testing Station (now, Idaho National Engineering Laboratory), a reactor proving ground. He also set up the Naval Reactor Division at Argonne in 1948, and in 1949 he discovered that the water-cooled reactor is most appropriate type of reactor for naval use. In 1956 Zinn resigned as director from Argonne.

After resigning from Argonne, Zinn held a position as special consultant to the Joint Congressional Committee on Atomic Energy. He was also a special member of the President's Scientific Advisory Committee and president of the General Nuclear Engineering Corp. from 1956-64. In 1959 he was appointed vice president of Combustion Engineering Inc., a position he held until 1971.

Zinn was a member of the National Academy of Science, the National Academy of Engineering, and the American Nuclear Society, as well as being a fellow of the American Physics Society. In 1969 he received the Enrico Fermi Award.

FURTHER READING:

Books

A Biographical Encyclopedia of Scientists. Bristol: Institute of Physics Publishing, 1994.

Asimov, Isaac. *Asimov's Biographical Encyclopedia of Science and Technology: The Lives and Achievements of 1510 Great Scientists from Ancient Times to the Present.* Garden City, NY: Doubleday & Co. Inc., 1982.

Other

Argonne National Laboratory. "Argonne Highlights." (September 27, 1996). http://www.anl.gov/OPA/history/ (December 3, 1997).

—Sketch by Jacqueline L. Longe

Selected Biographical Sources

African American Scientists, Capstone Press, 1996.

Asimov, Isaac, *Asimov's Biographical Encyclopedia of Science and Technology: The Lives and Achievements of 1510 Great Scientists from Ancient Times to the Present Chronologically Arranged*, 2nd revised edition, New York: Doubleday, 1982.

Blacks in Science: Ancient and Modern, edited by Ivan Van Sertima, New Brunswick, NJ: Transaction Books, 1983.

Dash, Joan, *The Triumph of Discovery: Women Scientists Who Won the Nobel Prize,* Englewood Cliffs, NJ: Julian Messner, 1991.

Dunlap, Jr., Orrin E., *Radio's One Hundred Men of Science: Biographical Narratives of Pathfinders in Electronics and Television,* New York: Harper, 1944.

Feldman, Anthony, *Scientists and Inventors,* New York: Facts on File, 1979.

Gaillard, Jacques, *Scientists in the Third World,* Lexington: University Press of Kentucky, 1991.

Hispanic Scientists, Capstone Press, 1996.

Larousse Dictionary of Scientists, edited by Hazel Muir, Larousse, 1996.

Lives in Science, New York: Simon and Schuster, 1957.

McGraw-Hill Modern Men of Science: 426 Leading Contemporary Scientists, New York: McGraw-Hill, 1966-68.

McGraw-Hill Modern Scientists and Engineers, New York: McGraw-Hill, 1980.

McGrayne, Sharon Bertsch, *Nobel Prize Women in Science: Their Lives, Struggles, and Momentous Discoveries,* Secaucus, NJ: Carol Publishing Group, 1993.

Native American Scientists, Capstone Press, 1996.

Out of Their Minds: The Lives and Discoveries of 15 Great Computer Scientists, Springer-Verlag, 1995.

A Passion to Know: 20 Profiles in Science, New York: Scribner, 1984.

Pioneers of Science in America: Sketches of Their Lives and Scientific Work, revised and edited by William J. Youmans, New York: Arno Press, 1978.

The Scientific 100: A Ranking of the Most Influential Scientists, Past and Present, Citadel Press, 1996.

Scott, Michael Maxwell, *Stories of Famous Scientists,* London: Barker, 1967.

Siedel, Frank, and James M. Siedel, *Pioneers in Science,* Boston: Houghton, 1968.

The Twentieth-Century Sciences: Studies in the Biography of Ideas, New York: Norton, 1972.

Van Wagenen, Theodore F., *Beacon Lights of Science: A Survey of Human Achievement from the Earliest Recorded Times,* New York: Thomas Y. Crowell, 1924.

Weisgerber, Robert A., *The Challenged Scientists: Disabilities and the Triumph of Excellence,* New York: Praeger, 1991.

Women Scientists in America: Before Affirmative Action, 1940-1972, Johns Hopkins University Press, 1995.

Autobiographical Collections

The Excitement and Fascination of Science: A Collection of Autobiographical and Philosophical Essays, Palo Alto, CA: Annual Reviews, 1965-78.

Scientists Who Believe: Twenty-One Tell Their Own Stories, edited by Eric C. Barrett and David Fisher, Chicago: Moody Press, 1984.

Studying Animal Behavior: Autobiographies of the Founders, edited by Donald A. Dewsbury, Chicago: University of Chicago Press, 1989.

Historical Collections

Elliott, Clark A., *Biographical Dictionary of American Science: The Seventeenth through the Nineteenth Centuries,* Westport, CT: Greenwood Press, 1979.

Engstrand, Iris W., *Spanish Scientists in the New World: The Eighteenth-Century Expeditions,* Seattle: University of Washington Press, 1981.

Gascoigne, Robert Mortimer, *A Historical Catalogue of Scientists and Scientific Books: From the Earliest Times to the Close of the Nineteenth Century,* New York: Garland Pub., 1984.

The Golden Age of Science: Thirty Portraits of the Giants of 19th-Century Science by Their Scientific Contemporaries, edited by Bessie Zaban Jones, New York: Simon and Schuster, 1966.

Hutcgubgs, D., and E. Candlin, *Late Seventeenth Century Scientists,* 1st edition, Oxford, NY: Pergamon Press, 1969.

Kohler, Robert E., *Partners in Science: Foundation Managers and Natural Scientists, 1900-1945,* Chicago: University of Chicago Press, 1991.

Late Eighteenth Century European Scientists, 1st edition, edited by Robert C. Olby, Oxford, NY: Pergamon Press, 1966.

Lenard, Philipp Eduard Anton, *Great Men of Science: A History of Scientific Progress,* translated from the second German edition by H. Stafford Hatfield, New York: Macmillan, 1933.

Murray, Robert H., *Science and Scientists in the Nineteenth Century,* New York: Macmillan, 1925.

North, J., *Mid-Nineteenth-Century Scientists,* 1st edition, Oxford, NY: Pergamon Press, 1969.

Dictionaries and Encyclopedias

The Biographical Dictionary of Scientists, edited by Roy Porter, Oxford: Oxford University Press, 1994.

Biographical Encyclopedia of Scientists, edited by Richard Olsen and Roger Smith, Marshall Cavendish, 1998.

Concise Dictionary of Scientific Biography, New York: Scribner, 1981.

Howard, Arthur Vyvyan, *Chambers's Dictionary of Scientists,* New York: Dutton, 1961.

Directories

American Men and Women of Science, 1998-99, 20th edition, New York: R. R. Bowker, 1998.

Cassutt, Michael, *Who's Who in Space: The International Space Year Edition,* Boston: Prentice Hall, 1993.

Ireland, Norma, *Index to Scientists of the World from Ancient to Modern Times: Biographies and Portraits,* Boston: Faxon, 1962.

Pelletier, Paul A., *Prominent Scientists: An Index to Collective Biographies,* 3rd edition, New York: Neal-Schuman, 1994.

Who's Who in Computer Education and Research: U.S. Edition, edited by T. C. Hsiao, Latham, NY: Science and Technology Press, 1975.

Who's Who in Science and Engineering, 1998-1999, 4th edition, edited by Kristin A. Eckes, New Providence, NJ: Marquis Who's Who, 1997.

Who's Who in Technology, 7th edition, edited by Kimberley A. McGrath, Detroit, MI: Gale Research Inc., 1995.

Who's Who in Science in Europe: A Biographical Guide in Science, Technology, Agriculture, and Medicine, Essex, England: Longman, 1995.

Who's Who of British Scientists, 1980-81, New York: St. Martin's, 1981.

Who's Who of Nobel Prize Winners, 3rd edition, edited by Bernard S. Schlessinger and June H. Schlessinger, Phoenix, AZ: Oryx Press, 1996.

Field of Specialization Index

Acoustic Design
Harris, Cyril **2:** 866

Aerodynamics
Prandtl, Ludwig **3:** 1610

Aeronautical Engineering
Bondar, Roberta L. **S:** 51
Draper, Charles Stark **1:** 518
Durand, William F. **1:** 534
Flügge-Lotz, Irmgard **2:** 662
Fokker, Anthony H. G. **2:** 663
Harris, Wesley L. **2:** 868
Heinkel, Ernst **2:** 889
Hunsaker, Jerome C. **2:** 980
Johnson, Clarence L. **2:** 1027
Ochoa, Ellen **3:** 1496
Piasecki, Frank **3:** 1579
Shurney, Robert E. **4:** 1839
Sikorsky, Igor I. **4:** 1843
Stever, H. Guyford **4:** 1922
van der Wal, Laurel **4:** 2078
von Kármán, Theodore **4:** 2096
von Mises, Richard **4:** 2099
Widnall, Sheila E. **4:** 2184
Williams, O. S. **4:** 2216
Wright, Wilbur **4:** 2262

Aerospace Engineering
Alcorn, George Edward **1:** 16
Armstrong, Neil **1:** 63
Bluford, Guion S. **1:** 201
Brill, Yvonne Claeys **1:** 255
Gutierrez, Orlando A. **2:** 831
Harris, Wesley L. **2:** 868
Johnson, Barbara Crawford **2:** 1026
Korolyov, Sergei **2:** 1127
Liepmann, Hans Wolfgang **3:** 1248
MacGill, Elsie Gregory **3:** 1296
Rockwell, Mabel M. **3:** 1698
Rogers, Marguerite M. **3:** 1700
Ross, Mary G. **3:** 1710
Tereshkova, Valentina **4:** 1992
Tsiolkovsky, Konstantin **4:** 2048
von Braun, Wernher **4:** 2093
Wu, Y. C. L. Susan **4:** 2268

Agriculture
Brown, Lester R. **1:** 265
Carver, George Washington **1:** 325
Evans, Alice **1:** 604
Khush, Gurdev S. **2:** 1091
Sanchez, Pedro A. **4:** 1774
Swaminathan, M. S. **4:** 1954
Tsao, George T. **4:** 2047

Anatomy
Alcala, Jose **1:** 15
Banting, Frederick G. **1:** 102
Barr, Murray Llewellyn **1:** 115
Cobb, William Montague **1:** 371
Crosby, Elizabeth Carolyn **1:** 431
Dart, Raymond A. **1:** 456
Dubois, Eugène **1:** 526
Fell, Honor Bridget **2:** 621
Hoyle, Fred **2:** 960
Keith, Arthur **2:** 1075
Lloyd, Ruth Smith **3:** 1263
Papanicolaou, George **3:** 1529
Romer, Alfred Sherwood **3:** 1704
Sabin, Florence Rena **4:** 1754
Scharrer, Berta **S:** 408
Straus, William Levi, Jr. **4:** 1936
Trotter, Mildred **4:** 2044
Vallois, Henri-Victor **4:** 2069
Weidenreich, Franz **4:** 2140

Anthropology
Dart, Raymond A. **1:** 456
Diggs, Irene **S:** 127
Keith, Arthur **2:** 1075
Leakey, Louis **3:** 1187
Leakey, Mary **S:** 273
Leakey, Richard E. **3:** 1194
Lévi-Strauss, Claude **S:** 280
Parker, Arthur C. **S:** 347
Stewart, Thomas Dale **4:** 1925
Weidenreich, Franz **4:** 2140

Astronomy
Adams, Walter Sydney **1:** 5
Baade, Walter **1:** 83
Babcock, Horace W. **S:** 23
Banks, Harvey Washington **1:** 101
Bell Burnell, Jocelyn Susan **1:** 141

Brown, Robert Hanbury **S:** 68
Cannon, Annie Jump **1:** 304
Clemence, Gerald M. **S:** 98
Davis, Raymond, Jr. **1:** 463
de Sitter, Willem **1:** 490
Eddington, Arthur Stanley **1:** 546
Faber, Sandra M. **2:** 607
Geller, Margaret Joan **2:** 742
Gold, Thomas **2:** 778
Hertzsprung, Ejnar **2:** 904
Hill, George William **S:** 206
Hogg, Helen Sawyer **2:** 943
Hubble, Edwin **2:** 969
Humason, Milton L. **2:** 979
Jeffreys, Harold **2:** 1012
Kuiper, Gerard Peter **2:** 1143
Le Cadet, Georges **3:** 1200
Leavitt, Henrietta **3:** 1196
Lemaître, Georges **3:** 1221
Lin, Chia-Chiao **3:** 1252
Lippmann, Gabriel **3:** 1256
Massevitch, Alla G. **3:** 1324
Maunder, Annie Russell **3:** 1333
Maury, Antonia **3:** 1334
Minkowski, Rudolph **3:** 1389
Moulton, Forest Ray **3:** 1434
Nicholson, Seth Barnes **S:** 327
Oort, Jan Hendrik **3:** 1510
Osterbrock, Donald E. **3:** 1519
Payne-Gaposchkin, Cecilia **3:** 1552
Ponnamperuma, Cyril **3:** 1600
Reber, Grote **3:** 1655
Roman, Nancy Grace **3:** 1703
Rubin, Vera Cooper **3:** 1725
Russell, Henry Norris **3:** 1737
Sagan, Carl **4:** 1757; **S:** 399
Sandage, Allan R. **4:** 1775
Shapiro, Irwin **4:** 1816
Shapley, Harlow **4:** 1817
Slipher, Vesto M. **4:** 1861
Stefanik, Milan Ratislav **4:** 1910
Taylor, Joseph H., Jr. **4:** 1980
Tombaugh, Clyde W. **S:** 456
van de Kamp, Peter **S:** 467
Voûte, Joan George Erardus
    Gijsbert **4:** 2104
Whipple, Fred Lawrence **4:** 2167
Wilson, Robert Woodrow **4:** 2235

Harvey, Ethel Browne S: 189
Horn, Michael Hastings 2: 954
Just, Ernest Everett 2: 1049
Ray, Dixy Lee 3: 1653
Russell, Frederick Stratten 3: 1735

Marine Engineering
Gibbs, William Francis 2: 753

Mathematical Physics
Bremermann, Hans-Joachim S: 58
Gibbs, Josiah Willard S: 175
Langlands, Robert P. S: 272
Oleinik, Olga S: 340
Poincaré, Jules Henri 3: 1592
Stokes, George Gabriel S: 440

Mathematics
Ahlfors, Lars V. S: 2
Aleksandrov, Pavel S. 1: 19
Antonelli, Kay McNulty Mauchly S: 11
Artin, Emil 1: 67
Askey, Richard S: 14
Atiyah, Michael Francis 1: 72
Baker, Alan 1: 95
Banach, Stefan 1: 100
Bari, Nina S: 28
Bari, Ruth Aaronson S: 30
Batchelor, George 1: 123
Baxter, Agnes S: 31
Bellow, Alexandra S: 33
Bernays, Paul 1: 158
Bernstein, Dorothy Lewis 1: 162
Bers, Lipman S: 41
Birkhoff, Garrett S: 44
Birkhoff, George David 1: 175
Blackwell, David 1: 190
Blum, Lenore S: 48
Bondi, Hermann 1: 212
Borel, Émile 1: 216
Born, Max 1: 221
Bott, Raoul 1: 229
Bragg, William Henry 1: 238
Brouwer, Luitzen Egbertus Jan 1: 263
Browne, Marjorie Lee 1: 270
Calderón, Alberto P. 1: 292
Cantor, Georg 1: 305
Cartan, Élie Joseph S: 81
Cartan, Henri Paul S: 82
Cartwright, Mary Lucy S: 84
Chandrasekhar, Subrahmanyan S: 86
Chang, Sun-Yung Alice S: 89
Chung, Fan R. K. S: 95
Church, Alonzo S: 97
Cohen, Paul 1: 375
Courant, Richard 1: 409
Cox, Elbert Frank 1: 418

Cox, Gertrude Mary 1: 420
Dantzig, George Bernard 1: 453
Daubechies, Ingrid S: 119
de Sitter, Willem 1: 490
Deligné, Pierre 1: 487
Dirac, Paul 1: 503
Donaldson, Simon 1: 515
Enskog, David 1: 592
Erdös, Paul S: 146
Erlang, Agner Krarup S: 148
Falconer, Etta Zuber S: 156
Feigenbaum, Mitchell 2: 619
Fenchel, Käte S: 160
Fisher, Ronald A. 2: 644
Fraenkel, Abraham Adolf 2: 681
Fréchet, Maurice 2: 693
Fredholm, Erik Ivar S: 170
Freedman, Michael H. 2: 695
Friedmann, Aleksandr A. 2: 699
Geiringer, Hilda 2: 741
Gelfond, Aleksandr Osipovich S: 173
Gentry, Ruth S: 174
Gödel, Kurt Friedrich 2: 771
Granville, Evelyn Boyd 2: 811
Grothendieck, Alexander 2: 821
Hadamard, Jacques 2: 837
Hardy, Godfrey Harold 2: 862
Hauptman, Herbert A. 2: 873
Hausdorff, Felix 2: 874
Hayes, Ellen Amanda S: 194
Hazlett, Olive Clio S: 195
Hermite, Charles S: 198
Hilbert, David 2: 925
Hoyle, Fred 2: 960
Johnson, Katherine Coleman Goble 2: 1031
Karlin, Samuel 2: 1063
Kato, Tosio 2: 1070
Keen, Linda S: 243
Kemeny, John G. 2: 1079
Klein, Christian Felix S: 250
Kodaira, Kunihiko 2: 1115
Kolmogorov, Andrey Nikolayevich 2: 1121
Krieger, Cecilia S: 260
Kuperberg, Krystyna S: 263
Kurtz, Thomas Eugene 2: 1146
Ladd-Franklin, Christine 3: 1153
Landau, Edmund S: 270
Lebesgue, Henri 3: 1199
Lemaître, Georges 3: 1221
Levi-Civita, Tullio 3: 1232
Li, Ching Chun 3: 1242
Lin, Chia-Chiao 3: 1252
Lindemann, Carl Louis Ferdinand von S: 284
Litvinova, Elizaveta Fedorovna S: 286

Macintyre, Sheila Scott S: 295
Mac Lane, Saunders 3: 1298
MacPherson, Robert S: 297
Maddison, Ada Isabel S: 298
Malone-Mayes, Vivienne S: 300
Mandelbrot, Benoit B. 3: 1307
Margulis, Gregori Aleksandrovitch 3: 1317
Markov, Andrei Andreevich 3: 1322
McAfee, Walter S. S: 301
McDuff, Margaret Dusa S: 302
Méray, Hugues Charles Robert S: 304
Merrill, Helen Abbot S: 305
Merrill, Winifred Edgerton S: 306
Milne, Edward Arthur 3: 1383
Milnor, John 3: 1385
Minkowski, Hermann 3: 1388
Morawetz, Cathleen Synge 3: 1416
Mordell, Louis Joel S: 310
Mori, Shigefumi 3: 1422
Nash, John Forbes S: 318
Nelson, Evelyn S: 324
Neumann, Hanna S: 325
Noether, Emmy 3: 1479
Noether, Max S: 330
Novikov, Sergei 3: 1489
Oleinik, Olga S: 340
Peano, Giuseppe 3: 1554
Pearson, Karl 3: 1556
Penrose, Roger 3: 1562
Péter, Rózsa 3: 1575
Pless, Vera S: 369
Pólya, George 3: 1598
Poincaré, Jules Henri 3: 1592
Polubarinova-Kochina, Pelageya Yakovlevna 3: 1596
Ramanujan, S. I. 3: 1639
Ramsey, Frank Plumpton 3: 1647
Rees, Mina S. S: 387
Robinson, Julia 3: 1694
Rudin, Mary Ellen S: 394
Russell, Bertrand 3: 1730
Sanchez, David A. 4: 1772
Schafer, Alice T. S: 407
Scott, Charlotte Angas S: 413
Selberg, Atle S: 416
Serre, Jean-Pierre 4: 1814
Shannon, Claude 4: 1814
Sierpiński, Waclaw S: 420
Simon, Herbert A. 4: 1847
Singer, I. M. 4: 1852
Smale, Stephen 4: 1864
Sommerville, Duncan McLaren Young 4: 1880
Stanley, Richard S: 436
Steinmetz, Charles P. 4: 1915
Stibitz, George R. S: 439
Størmer, Fredrik 4: 1932

Gender Index

Male

Carver, George Washington
Castro, George
Cech, Thomas R.
Chadwick, James
Chain, Ernst Boris
Chamberlain, Owen
Chamberlin, Thomas Chrowder
Chance, Britton
Chandrasekhar, Subrahmanyan
Chang, Min-Chueh
Chargaff, Erwin
Charnley, John
Charpak, Georges
Chaudhari, Praveen
Cherenkov, Pavel A.
Chestnut, Harold
Chew, Geoffrey Foucar
Child, Charles Manning
Cho, Alfred Y.
Chu, Paul Ching-Wu
Chu, Steven
Church, Alonzo
Claude, Albert
Claude, Georges
Clay, Jacob
Clemence, Gerald M.
Cloud, Preston
Cobb, William Montague
Cockcroft, John D.
Cocke, John
Cohen, Paul
Cohen, Stanley
Cohen, Stanley N.
Cohen-Tannoudji, Claude
Cohn, Zanvil
Commoner, Barry
Compton, Arthur Holly
Condon, Edward U.
Cooke, Lloyd M.
Coolidge, William D.
Cooper, Leon
Corey, Elias James
Cori, Carl Ferdinand
Cormack, Allan M.
Cornforth, John
Coster, Dirk
Coulomb, Jean
Courant, Richard
Cournand, André F.
Cousteau, Jacques
Cox, Elbert Frank
Cram, Donald J.
Cray, Seymour
Crick, Francis
Cronin, James W.
Crosthwait, David Nelson, Jr.
Crutzen, Paul J.
Curie, Pierre
Curl, Robert Floyd, Jr.

Dale, Henry Hallett
Dalén, Nils
Dallmeier, Francisco
Dalrymple, G. Brent
Daly, Reginald Aldworth
Dam, Henrik
Daniels, Walter T.
Dantzig, George Bernard
Dart, Raymond A.
Dausset, Jean
Davidson, Norman R.
Davis, Raymond, Jr.
Davisson, Clinton
de Broglie, Louis Victor
de Duvé, Christian
de Forest, Lee
de Gennes, Pierre-Gilles
de Sitter, Willem
DeBakey, Michael Ellis
Debye, Peter
Dehmelt, Hans
Deisenhofer, Johann
Delbrück, Max
Deligné, Pierre
Dennis, Jack B.
d'Hérelle, Félix
Diaz, Henry F.
Dicke, Robert Henry
Diels, Otto
Diener, Theodor Otto
Dijkstra, Edsger W.
Dirac, Paul
Djerassi, Carl
Dobzhansky, Theodosius
Doherty, Peter C.
Doisy, Edward A.
Dole, Vincent P.
Domagk, Gerhard
Donaldson, Simon
Douglas, Donald W.
Draper, Charles Stark
Drew, Charles R.
Drickamer, Harry G.
Drucker, Daniel Charles
du Vigneaud, Vincent
Dubois, Eugène
Dubos, René
Dulbecco, Renato
Durand, William F.
Durrell, Gerald
Dyson, Freeman J.
Eagle, Harry
Eccles, John C.
Eckert, J. Presper
Eddington, Arthur Stanley
Edelman, Gerald M.
Edgerton, Harold
Edison, Thomas Alva
Ehrenfest, Paul

Ehrlich, Paul
Ehrlich, Paul R.
Eigen, Manfred
Eijkman, Christiaan
Einstein, Albert
Einthoven, Willem
Eisner, Thomas
Eldredge, Niles
Elsasser, Walter M.
El-Sayed, Mostafa Amr
Elton, Charles Sutherland
Enders, John F.
Engler, Adolph Gustav Heinrich
Enskog, David
Erdös, Paul
Erlang, Agner Krarup
Erlanger, Joseph
Ernst, Richard R.
Esaki, Leo
Euler, Ulf von
Euler-Chelpin, Hans von
Evans, James C.
Ewing, William Maurice
Fabry, Charles
Fairbank, William
Farman, Joseph C.
Farnsworth, Philo T.
Fauci, Anthony S.
Favaloro, René Geronimo
Feigenbaum, Edward A.
Feigenbaum, Mitchell
Ferguson, Lloyd N.
Fermi, Enrico
Fersman, Aleksandr Evgenievich
Feynman, Richard P.
Fibiger, Johannes
Fieser, Louis
Fischer, Edmond H.
Fischer, Emil
Fischer, Ernst Otto
Fischer, Hans
Fisher, Ronald A.
Fitch, Val Logsdon
Flanagan, James L.
Fleming, Alexander
Fleming, John Ambrose
Flexner, Simon
Florey, Howard Walter
Flory, Paul
Fokker, Anthony H. G.
Folkers, Karl A.
Forbush, Scott Ellsworth
Ford, Henry
Forrester, Jay W.
Forssmann, Werner
Fowler, William A.
Fox, Sidney W.
Fraenkel, Abraham Adolf
Fraenkel-Conrat, Heinz

Franck, James
Frank, Il'ya
Fraser-Reid, Bertram Oliver
Fréchet, Maurice
Fredholm, Erik Ivar
Freedman, Michael H.
Frenkel, Yakov Ilyich
Friedman, Jerome
Friedmann, Aleksandr A.
Frisch, Karl von
Frisch, Otto Robert
Fujita, Tetsuya Theodore
Fukui, Kenichi
Fuller, Solomon
Gabor, Dennis
Gadgil, Madhav
Gagarin, Yuri A.
Gajdusek, D. Carleton
Gallo, Robert C.
Gamow, George
Garrod, Archibald
Gasser, Herbert Spencer
Gates, Bill
Gates, Sylvester James, Jr.
Gaviola, Enrique
Geiger, Hans
Gelfond, Aleksandr Osipovich
Gell-Mann, Murray
Ghiorso, Albert
Giacconi, Riccardo
Giaever, Ivar
Giauque, William F.
Gibbs, Josiah Willard
Gibbs, William Francis
Gilbert, Walter
Gilbreth, Frank
Gilman, Alfred Goodman
Glaser, Donald
Glashow, Sheldon Lee
Glenn, John H., Jr.
Goddard, Robert H.
Gödel, Kurt Friedrich
Goethals, George W.
Gold, Thomas
Goldmark, Peter Carl
Goldreich, Peter
Goldschmidt, Richard B.
Goldschmidt, Victor
Goldstein, Avram
Goldstein, Joseph L.
Golgi, Camillo
Gorer, Peter
Goudsmit, Samuel A.
Gould, Stephen Jay
Gourdine, Meredith Charles
Gourneau, Dwight
Govindjee
Granit, Ragnar Arthur
Greatbatch, Wilson

Greenewalt, Crawford H.
Grier, Jr., Herbert E.
Griffith, Frederick
Grignard, François Auguste Victor
Grothendieck, Alexander
Groves, Leslie Richard
Guillaume, Charles-Edouard
Guillemin, Roger
Gullstrand, Allvar
Gutenberg, Beno
Guth, Alan
Gutierrez, Orlando A.
Haagen-Smit, A. J.
Haber, Fritz
Hackerman, Norman
Hadamard, Jacques
Hahn, Otto
Haldane, John Burdon Sanderson
Hale, George Ellery
Hall, Lloyd Augustus
Hamburger, Viktor
Hammond, George S.
Hanafusa, Hidesaburo
Hannah, Marc R.
Hansen, James
Harden, Arthur
Hardy, Alister C.
Hardy, Godfrey Harold
Harris, Cyril
Harris, Wesley L.
Hartline, Haldan Keffer
Hassel, Odd
Hauptman, Herbert A.
Haus, Hermann
Hausdorff, Felix
Hawking, Stephen
Hawkins, W. Lincoln
Haworth, Walter
Heezen, Bruce C.
Heimlich, Henry Jay
Heinkel, Ernst
Heisenberg, Werner Karl
Hench, Philip Showalter
Henderson, Cornelius Langston
Henry, John Edward
Henry, Warren Elliott
Hermite, Charles
Herschbach, Dudley R.
Hershey, Alfred Day
Hertz, Gustav
Hertzsprung, Ejnar
Herzberg, Gerhard
Hess, Harry Hammond
Hess, Victor
Hess, Walter Rudolf
Hevesy, Georg von
Hewish, Antony
Hewlett, William
Heymans, Corneille Jean-François

Heyrovský, Jaroslav
Higgs, Peter Ware
Hilbert, David
Hill, Archibald V.
Hill, George William
Hill, Henry A.
Hill, Robert
Hinshelwood, Cyril N.
Hinton, William Augustus
Hitchings, George H.
Ho, David Da-I
Hodgkin, Alan Lloyd
Hoffmann, Roald
Hofstadter, Robert
Holley, Robert William
Holmes, Arthur
Hopkins, Frederick Gowland
Horn, Michael Hastings
Houdry, Eugene
Hounsfield, Godfrey
Houssay, Bernardo
Hoyle, Fred
Hrdlička, Aleš
Hubbard, Philip G.
Hubbert, M. King
Hubble, Edwin
Hubel, David H.
Huber, Robert
Huggins, Charles B.
Hughes, John
Hulse, Russell A.
Humason, Milton L.
Hunsaker, Jerome C.
Hutchinson, G. Evelyn
Huxley, Andrew Fielding
Huxley, Hugh Esmor
Huxley, Julian
Hyman, Libbie Henrietta
Imes, Elmer Samuel
Ioffe, Abram F.
Isaacs, Alick
Itakura, Keiichi
Iverson, F. Kenneth
Jacob, François
Jansky, Karl
Janzen, Dan
Jarvik, Robert K.
Jason, Robert S.
Jeffreys, Alec John
Jeffreys, Harold
Jeffries, Zay
Jencks, William P.
Jensen, J. Hans D.
Jerne, Niels K.
Jewett, Frank Baldwin
Jobs, Steven
Johannsen, Wilhelm Ludvig
Johnson, Clarence L.
Johnson, John B., Jr.

Johnson, Joseph Lealand
Johnson, Marvin M.
Johnson, William Summer
Johnston, Harold S.
Joliot-Curie, Frédéric
Jones, Fred
Jordan, Ernst Pascual
Josephson, Brian D.
Julian, Percy Lavon
Juran, Joseph M.
Just, Ernest Everett
Kamerlingh Onnes, Heike
Kan, Yuet Wai
Kandel, Eric R.
Kapitsa, Pyotr
Karle, Jerome
Karlin, Samuel
Karp, Richard M.
Karrer, Paul
Kastler, Alfred
Kates, Robert W.
Kato, Tosio
Katz, Bernard
Katz, Donald L.
Kay, Alan C.
Keith, Arthur
Kemeny, John G.
Kendall, Edward C.
Kendall, Henry W.
Kendrew, John
Kettering, Charles Franklin
Kettlewell, Bernard
Khorana, Har Gobind
Khush, Gurdev S.
Kilburn, Thomas M.
Kilby, Jack St. Clair
Kimura, Motoo
Kinoshita, Toichiro
Kinsey, Alfred
Kishimoto, Tadamitsu
Kistiakowsky, George B.
Klein, Christian Felix
Klug, Aaron
Knudsen, William Claire
Knuth, Donald E.
Koch, Robert
Kocher, Theodor
Kodaira, Kunihiko
Köhler, Georges
Kolff, Willem Johan
Kolmogorov, Andrey Nikolayevich
Kolthoff, Izaak Maurits
Konishi, Masakazu
Kornberg, Arthur
Korolyov, Sergei
Koshland, Daniel E., Jr.
Kossel, Albrecht
Kountz, Samuel L.
Kouwenhoven, William B.

Kramer, Fred Russell
Krebs, Edwin G.
Krebs, Hans Adolf
Krogh, August
Kroto, Harold Walter
Kuhn, Richard
Kuiper, Gerard Peter
Kurchatov, Igor
Kurtz, Thomas Eugene
Kurzweil, Raymond
Kusch, Polycarp
Lamb, Willis E., Jr.
Land, Edwin H.
Landau, Edmund
Landau, Lev Davidovich
Landsberg, Helmut E.
Landsteiner, Karl
Langevin, Paul
Langlands, Robert P.
Langmuir, Irving
Latimer, Lewis H.
Lattes, C. M. G.
Laub, Jakob Johann
Laue, Max von
Lauterbur, Paul C.
Laveran, Alphonse
Lawless, Theodore K.
Lawrence, Ernest Orlando
Le Cadet, Georges
Leakey, Louis
Leakey, Richard E.
Lebesgue, Henri
Leder, Philip
Lederberg, Joshua
Lederman, Leon Max
Lee, David M.
Lee, Raphael C.
Lee, Tsung-Dao
Lee, Yuan T.
Leevy, Carroll
Leffall, LaSalle D., Jr.
Lehn, Jean-Marie
Leloir, Luis F.
Lemaître, Georges
Lenard, Philipp E. A. von
Leopold, Aldo
Leopold, Luna
Lester, William Alexander, Jr.
Levi-Civita, Tullio
Lévi-Strauss, Claude
Lewis, Edward B.
Lewis, Gilbert Newton
Lewis, Julian Herman
Lewis, Warren K.
Li, Ching Chun
Li, Choh Hao
Libby, Willard F.
Liepmann, Hans Wolfgang
Lillie, Frank Rattray

Lim, Robert K. S.
Lin, Chia-Chiao
Lindemann, Carl Louis Ferdinand von
Lipmann, Fritz
Lippmann, Gabriel
Lipscomb, William Nunn, Jr.
Little, Arthur D.
Lizhi, Fang
Loeb, Jacques
Loewi, Otto
London, Fritz
Lorentz, Hendrik Antoon
Lorenz, Edward N.
Lorenz, Konrad
Lovejoy, Thomas Eugene
Lovelock, James E.
Luria, Salvador Edward
Lwoff, André
Lynen, Feodor
Lynk, Miles Vandahurst
Mac Lane, Saunders
MacArthur, Robert H.
MacDonald, Gordon
MacLeod, Colin Munro
Macleod, John James Rickard
MacPherson, Robert
Maillart, Robert
Maiman, Theodore
Maloney, Arnold Hamilton
Mandelbrot, Benoit B.
Mandel'shtam, Leonid Isaakovich
Marchbanks, Vance H., Jr.
Marconi, Guglielmo
Marcus, Rudolph A.
Margulis, Gregori Aleksandrovitch
Marie-Victorin, Frère
Markov, Andrei Andreevich
Martin, A. J. P.
Massey, Walter E.
Massie, Samuel P.
Masters, William Howell
Matuyama, Motonori
Mauchly, John William
Maynard Smith, John
Mayr, Ernst
McAfee, Walter S.
McCarthy, John
McCarty, Maclyn
McCollum, Elmer Verner
McConnell, Harden
McMillan, Edwin M.
Medawar, Peter Brian
Méray, Hugues Charles Robert
Merrifield, R. Bruce
Meselson, Matthew
Metchnikoff, Élie
Meyerhof, Otto
Michel, Hartmut

Risi, Joseph
Ritchie, Dennis
Robbins, Frederick
Roberts, Lawrence
Roberts, Richard J.
Robinson, Robert
Rock, John
Rodbell, Martin
Roddy, Leon Raymand
Roelofs, Wendell L.
Rohrer, Heinrich
Romer, Alfred Sherwood
Romero, Juan Carlos
Röntgen, Wilhelm Conrad
Ross, Ronald
Rossby, Carl-Gustaf
Rous, Peyton
Rowland, F. Sherwood
Rubbia, Carlo
Runcorn, S. K.
Ruska, Ernst
Russell, Bertrand
Russell, Frederick Stratten
Russell, Henry Norris
Russell, Loris Shano
Rutherford, Ernest
Ružička, Leopold
Ryle, Martin
Sabatier, Paul
Sabin, Albert
Sagan, Carl
Sakharov, Andrei
Sakmann, Bert
Salam, Abdus
Salk, Jonas
Samuelsson, Bengt
Sanchez, David A.
Sanchez, Pedro A.
Sandage, Allan R.
Sanger, Frederick
Satcher, David
Schaller, George
Schally, Andrew V.
Schawlow, Arthur L.
Schick, Bela
Schneider, Stephen H.
Schou, Mogens
Schrieffer, J. Robert
Schrödinger, Erwin
Schultes, Richard Evans
Schwartz, Melvin
Schwarz, John Henry
Schwinger, Julian
Seaborg, Glenn T.
Segrè, Emilio
Seitz, Frederick
Selberg, Atle
Semenov, Nikolai N.
Serre, Jean-Pierre

Shannon, Claude
Shapiro, Irwin
Shapley, Harlow
Sharp, Phillip A.
Sharp, Robert Phillip
Sheldrake, Rupert
Shepard, Alan B., Jr.
Shepard, Roger N.
Sherrington, Charles Scott
Shockley, William
Shoemaker, Eugene M.
Shokalsky, Yuly Mikhaylovich
Shtokman, Vladimir Borisovich
Shull, Clifford Glenwood
Shurney, Robert E.
Siegbahn, Kai M.
Siegbahn, Karl M. G.
Sierpiński, Waclaw
Sikorsky, Igor I.
Simmons, Howard Ensign, Jr.
Simon, Herbert A.
Simpson, George Gaylord
Sinclair, Clive Marles
Singer, I. M.
Sioui, Richard H.
Skoog, Folke Karl
Skou, Jens C.
Slater, John Clarke
Slipher, Vesto M.
Smale, Stephen
Smalley, Richard Errett
Smith, Hamilton O.
Smith, Michael
Snell, George Davis
Snyder, Solomon H.
Soddy, Frederick
Solberg, Halvor
Sommerfeld, Arnold
Sommerville, Duncan McLaren
    Young
Sorensen, Charles E.
Sørensen, Søren Peter Lauritz
Spedding, Frank Harold
Spemann, Hans
Sperry, Elmer
Sperry, Roger W.
Spitzer, Lyman, Jr.
Stahl, Franklin W.
Stanley, Richard
Stanley, Wendell Meredith
Stark, Johannes
Starling, Ernest H.
Starr, Chauncey
Starzl, Thomas
Staudinger, Hermann
Stefanik, Milan Ratislav
Stein, William Howard
Steinberger, Jack
Steinman, David B.

Steinmetz, Charles P.
Steptoe, Patrick
Stern, Otto
Stever, H. Guyford
Steward, Frederick Campion
Stewart, Thomas Dale
Stibitz, George R.
Stock, Alfred
Stokes, George Gabriel
Stommel, Henry
Størmer, Fredrik
Strassmann, Fritz
Straus, William Levi, Jr.
Strutt, John William
Strutt, Robert
Sturtevant, A. H.
Sumner, James B.
Suomi, Verner E.
Sutherland, Earl
Sutherland, Ivan
Sutton, Walter Stanborough
Svedberg, Theodor
Swaminathan, M. S.
Synge, Richard
Szegö, Gabor
Szent-Györgyi, Albert
Szilard, Leo
Tamm, Igor
Tan Jiazhen
Tapia, Richard A.
Tarski, Alfred
Tatum, Edward Lawrie
Taube, Henry
Taylor, Frederick Winslow
Taylor, Joseph H., Jr.
Taylor, Moddie
Taylor, Richard E.
Taylor, Stuart
Teller, Edward
Temin, Howard
Terman, Frederick
Terzaghi, Karl
Tesla, Nikola
Theiler, Max
Theorell, Axel Hugo Teodor
Thom, René Frédéric
Thomas, E. Donnall
Thompson, D'Arcy Wentworth
Thompson, Kenneth
Thomson, George Paget
Thomson, J. J.
Thurston, William
Tien, Ping King
Tildon, J. Tyson
Timoshenko, Stephen P.
Tinbergen, Nikolaas
Ting, Samuel C. C.
Tiselius, Arne
Tishler, Max

Tizard, Henry
Todd, Alexander
Tombaugh, Clyde W.
Tomonaga, Sin-Itiro
Tonegawa, Susumu
Topchiev, Alexsandr Vasil'evich
Townes, Charles H.
Trump, John G.
Tsao, George T.
Tsiolkovsky, Konstantin
Tsui, Daniel Chee
Tsui, Lap-Chee
Tswett, Mikhail
Turing, Alan
Turner, Charles Henry
Tuve, Merle A.
Twort, Frederick
Uhlenbeck, George
Urey, Harold
Uvarov, Boris Petrovich
Uyeda, Seiya
Vallée-Poussin, Charles Jean
  Gustave Nicolas de la
Vallois, Henri-Victor
Van Allen, James
Van de Graaff, Robert J.
van de Kamp, Peter
van der Meer, Simon
van der Waals, Johannes Diderik
Van Vleck, John
Vane, John R.
Varmus, Harold E.
Vedder, Edward Bright
Veksler, V. I.
Vernadsky, Vladímir Ivanovich
Vine, Frederick John
Virtanen, Artturi Ilmari
Vollenweider, Richard
Volterra, Vito
von Braun, Wernher
von Kármán, Theodore
von Klitzing, Klaus
von Mises, Richard
von Neumann, John
Voûte, Joan George Erardus
  Gijsbert
Vries, Hugo de
Wagner-Jauregg, Julius
Wahl, Arnold C.
Waksman, Selman
Wald, George

Walker, John E.
Wallach, Otto
Walton, Ernest
Wang, An
Wang, James C.
Wankel, Felix
Warburg, Otto
Washington, Warren M.
Watkins, Levi, Jr.
Watson, James D.
Watson-Watt, Robert
Weber, Ernst
Wegener, Alfred
Weidenreich, Franz
Weil, André
Weinberg, Robert A.
Weinberg, Steven
Weinberg, Wilhelm
Weizsäcker, Carl F. Von
Weller, Thomas
Went, Frits
Werner, Alfred
West, Harold Dadford
Wetherill, George West
Weyl, Hermann
Wheeler, John Archibald
Whinfield, John R.
Whinnery, John R.
Whipple, Fred Lawrence
Whipple, George Hoyt
White, Augustus
White, Gilbert Fowler
White, Raymond L.
Whitehead, Alfred North
Whittaker, Robert Harding
Whittle, Frank
Wickenden, William E.
Wiechert, Emil
Wieland, Heinrich
Wien, Wilhelm
Wiener, Alexander
Wiener, Norbert
Wieschaus, Eric F.
Wiesel, Torsten
Wigglesworth, Vincent
Wigner, Eugene Paul
Wiles, Andrew J.
Wilkes, Maurice
Wilkins, J. Ernest, Jr.
Wilkins, Maurice Hugh Frederick
Wilkinson, Geoffrey

Williams, Daniel Hale
Williams, Evan James
Williams, Frederic C.
Williams, O. S.
Williamson, James S.
Willstätter, Richard
Wilmut, Ian
Wilson, C. T. R.
Wilson, Edmund Beecher
Wilson, Edward O.
Wilson, J. Tuzo
Wilson, Kenneth G.
Wilson, Robert R.
Wilson, Robert Woodrow
Windaus, Adolf
Wirth, Niklaus
Witten, Edward
Wittig, Georg
Wolman, Abel
Wood, Harland G.
Woodland, Joseph
Woodward, Robert B.
Woodwell, George M.
Wozniak, Stephen
Wright, Almroth Edward
Wright, Louis Tompkins
Wright, Orville
Wright, Sewall
Wright, Wilbur
Yang, Chen Ning
Yau, Shing-Tung
Young, J. Z.
Young, William Henry
Yukawa, Hideki
Zadeh, Lotfi Asker
Zamecnik, Paul Charles
Zeeman, E. C.
Zeeman, Pieter
Zel'dovich, Yakov Borisovich
Zen, E-an
Zernike, Frits
Ziegler, Karl
Zinder, Norton
Zinkernagel, Rolf M.
Zinn, Walter Henry
Zinsser, Hans
Zsigmondy, Richard
Zuse, Konrad
Zworykin, Vladimir

Nationality/Ethnicity Index

Scientists are listed by country of origin and/or citizenship as well as by ethnicity (see African American, Asian American, Hispanic American).

Hauptman, Herbert A. **2**: 873

Haus, Hermann **S**: 191

Hawkins, W. Lincoln **2**: 879

Hay, Elizabeth D. **2**: 883

Hay, Louise Schmir **S**: 192

Hayes, Ellen Amanda **S**: 194

Hazen, Elizabeth Lee **2**: 883

Hazlett, Olive Clio **S**: 195

Healy, Bernadine **2**: 885

Heezen, Bruce C. **S**: 196

Heimlich, Henry Jay **2**: 887

Hench, Philip Showalter **2**: 893

Henderson, Cornelius Langston **2**: 895

Henry, John Edward **2**: 896

Henry, Warren Elliott **2**: 897

Herschbach, Dudley R. **2**: 898

Hershey, Alfred Day **S**: 199

Herzenberg, Caroline L. **2**: 908

Hess, Harry Hammond **2**: 909

Hewitt, Jacqueline N. **S**: 202

Hewlett, William **2**: 918

Hibbard, Hope **S**: 204

Hicks, Beatrice **2**: 924

Hill, George William **S**: 206

Hill, Henry A. **2**: 929

Hinton, William Augustus **2**: 931

Hitchings, George H. **2**: 933

Hobby, Gladys Lounsbury **2**: 934

Hoffmann, Roald **2**: 939

Hofstadter, Robert **2**: 941

Hogg, Helen Sawyer **2**: 943

Holley, Robert William **S**: 214

Hollinshead, Ariel Cahill **S**: 217

Hopper, Grace **2**: 951

Horn, Michael Hastings **2**: 954

Horstmann, Dorothy Millicent **2**: 955

Houdry, Eugene **2**: 956

Hrdlička, Aleš **2**: 963

Huang, Alice Shih-hou **2**: 965

Hubbard, Philip G. **2**: 966

Hubbert, M. King **2**: 968

Hubble, Edwin **2**: 969

Hubel, David H. **2**: 972

Huggins, Charles B. **S**: 219

Hulse, Russell A. **2**: 977

Humason, Milton L. **2**: 979

Hunsaker, Jerome C. **2**: 980

Hutchinson, G. Evelyn **2**: 982

Huxley, Hugh Esmor **S**: 223

Hyde, Ida H. **2**: 988

Hyman, Libbie Henrietta **2**: 990

Imes, Elmer Samuel **2**: 993

Itakura, Keiichi **2**: 997

Iverson, F. Kenneth **2**: 998

Jackson, Shirley Ann **2**: 1001

Jansky, Karl **2**: 1005

Janzen, Dan **2**: 1007

Jarvik, Robert K. **2**: 1009

Jason, Robert S. **2**: 1011

Jeffries, Zay **2**: 1014

Jemison, Mae C. **2**: 1016

Jencks, William P. **S**: 229

Jewett, Frank Baldwin **2**: 1020

Jobs, Steven **2**: 1022

Johnson, Barbara Crawford **2**: 1026

Johnson, Clarence L. **2**: 1027

Johnson, John B., Jr. **2**: 1029

Johnson, Joseph Lealand **2**: 1030

Johnson, Katherine Coleman Goble **2**: 1031

Johnson, Marvin M. **2**: 1032

Johnson, Virginia E. **2**: 1033

Johnson, William Summer **S**: 233

Johnston, Harold S. **2**: 1035

Jones, Fred **2**: 1041

Jones, Mary Ellen **S**: 234

Julian, Percy Lavon **2**: 1045

Juran, Joseph M. **2**: 1047

Just, Ernest Everett **2**: 1049

Kan, Yuet Wai **2**: 1055

Kandel, Eric R. **S**: 239

Karle, Isabella **2**: 1059

Karle, Jerome **2**: 1061

Karlin, Samuel **2**: 1063

Karp, Richard M. **S**: 240

Kates, Robert W. **2**: 1068

Kato, Tosio **2**: 1070

Katz, Donald L. **2**: 1072

Kay, Alan C. **2**: 1074

Keen, Linda **S**: 243

Keller, Evelyn Fox **S**: 244

Kelsey, Frances Oldham **2**: 1078

Kemeny, John G. **2**: 1079

Kendall, Edward C. **2**: 1081

Kendall, Henry W. **2**: 1082

Kettering, Charles Franklin **2**: 1085

Khorana, Har Gobind **2**: 1089

Kilby, Jack St. Clair **2**: 1094

King, Helen Dean **S**: 248

King, Louisa Boyd Yeomans **S**: 249

King, Reatha Clark **S**: 250

Kinoshita, Toichiro **2**: 1098

Kinsey, Alfred **2**: 1098

Kistiakowsky, George B. **2**: 1102

Kittrell, Flemmie Pansy **2**: 1104

Knopf, Eleanora Bliss **2**: 1106

Knudsen, William Claire **2**: 1107

Knuth, Donald E. **2**: 1109

Koehl, Mimi A. R. **S**: 252

Kolff, Willem Johan **2**: 1119

Kolthoff, Izaak Maurits **2**: 1122

Konishi, Masakazu **2**: 1123

Kornberg, Arthur **2**: 1124

Koshland, Daniel E., Jr. **S**: 255

Kountz, Samuel L. **2**: 1130

Kouwenhoven, William B. **S**: 258

Kramer, Fred Russell **S**: 259

Krebs, Edwin G. **2**: 1132

Krim, Mathilde **2**: 1136

Kuhlmann-Wilsdorf, Doris **2**: 1141

Kuiper, Gerard Peter **2**: 1143

Kurtz, Thomas Eugene **2**: 1146

Kurzweil, Raymond **2**: 1148

Kusch, Polycarp **S**: 264

Ladd-Franklin, Christine **3**: 1153

Lamb, Willis E., Jr. **3**: 1155

Lancaster, Cleo **3**: 1156

Lancefield, Rebecca Craighill **3**: 1157

Land, Edwin H. **3**: 1160

Landsberg, Helmut E. **3**: 1166

Landsteiner, Karl **3**: 1167

Langlands, Robert P. **S**: 272

Langmuir, Irving **3**: 1172

Latimer, Lewis H. **3**: 1173

Lauterbur, Paul C. **3**: 1180

Lawless, Theodore K. **3**: 1184

Lawrence, Ernest Orlando **3**: 1185

Le Beau, Désirée **3**: 1198

Leavitt, Henrietta **3**: 1196

Leder, Philip **3**: 1201

Lederberg, Joshua **3**: 1203

Lederman, Leon Max **3**: 1206

Lee, David M. **S**: 276

Lee, Raphael C. **3**: 1208

Lee, Tsung-Dao **3**: 1209

Lee, Yuan T. **3**: 1211

Leeman, Susan E. **3**: 1212

Leevy, Carroll **3**: 1214

Leffall, LaSalle D., Jr. **3**: 1215

Leopold, Aldo **3**: 1226

Leopold, Estella Bergere **3**: 1228

Leopold, Luna **3**: 1229

L'Esperance, Elise Depew Strang **S**: 269

Lester, William Alexander, Jr. **3**: 1231

Levi-Montalcini, Rita **S**: 277

Lewis, Edward B. **S**: 283

Lewis, Gilbert Newton **3**: 1236

Lewis, Julian Herman **3**: 1238

Lewis, Warren K. **3**: 1240

Li, Ching Chun **3**: 1242

Li, Choh Hao **3**: 1244

Libby, Willard F. **3**: 1245

Liepmann, Hans Wolfgang **3**: 1248

Lillie, Frank Rattray **3**: 1250

Lim, Robert K. S. **3**: 1251

Lin, Chia-Chiao **3**: 1252

Lipmann, Fritz **3**: 1253

Lipscomb, William Nunn, Jr. **3**: 1258

Little, Arthur D. **3**: 1259

Lloyd, Ruth Smith **3**: 1263

Loeb, Jacques **3**: 1264

Subject Index

References to individual volumes are listed in **boldface;** numbers following a colon refer to page numbers. A **boldface** page number refers to the full entry for the scientist.

Abbot, William R. **3:** 1657
Abbott, Edwin A. **S:** 508
Abderhalden, Emil **1:** 497
Abegg, Richard **1:** 154
Abel, John Jacob **3:** 1302
Abel, Niels Henrik **3:** 1199
Abell, George O. **3:** 1519
Abel's series **S:** 295
Abelson, Philip Hauge **1:** 1; **3:** 1352; **4:** 1804
ablation cooling **4:** 1846
ablative coatings for missile reentry **4:** 1846
abortions, spontaneous, in cows **1:** 604
Abraham, Edward P. **S:** 1
abrasives **4:** 1856
absolute motion **3:** 1593
absolute zero **2:** 1054; **3:** 1165, 1650
abstract algebra **3:** 1481
abstract spaces **2:** 694
abyssal plain **S:** 152, 362
AC
  See alternating current (AC)
accelerated flow modification **1:** 339
accommodation theory of optics **2:** 828
accretion **S:** 197
acetanilide **1:** 78
acetate **1:** 196
acetic acid **2:** 859
acetone, production of **3:** 1488
acetyl coenzyme A **2:** 1090; **3:** 1287, 1288
acetyl phosphate **3:** 1254
acetylcholine **1:** 442, 601; **3:** 1218, 1266; **S:** 138
acetylene **1:** 363, 443; **4:** 1750
acid phosphatase **2:** 976; **S:** 220
acid rain **1:** 210, 211; **3:** 1167
acid-base equilibria **1:** 260
acidimeter **1:** 132
acidity **1:** 132
acids **1:** 258, 260
Ackerman, Thomas **S:** 400
acoustic signal processing **S:** 165
acoustic system **S:** 164
Acoustic Thermometry of Ocean Climate (ATOC) **3:** 1446
acoustical design **2:** 867
acoustics **2:** 866; **S:** 385
acquired immunodeficiency syndrome (AIDS) **1:** 30, 382, 384; **2:** 613, 614,
692, 721–723, 737, 738, 1035, 1101, 1136, 1138; **3:** 1408; **4:** 1991, 1992; **S:** 209, 217, 255, 259
acquired immunological tolerance **3:** 1355
Acta Chimica Scandinavica **2:** 872
ACTH
  See adrenocorticotropic hormone (ACTH)
actin **S:** 223
actinide concept **4:** 1804
actinium radioactive decay series **3:** 1567
actinomycetes **1:** 269
actinomycin **4:** 2113
acyclovir **1:** 584
ADA
  See adenosine deaminase (ADA)
Adair, Gilbert **3:** 1573
Adams, Cyril **1:** 345
Adams, Numa P. G. **2:** 1029, 1031
Adams, Roger **1:** 4, 313; **4:** 1898
Adams, W. A. **1:** 548
Adams, Walter Sydney **1:** 5
Adamson, George **1:** 7
Adamson, Joy **1:** 7
Adams's catalyst **1:** 4, 5
adaptation **4:** 2028
adaptive landscape **3:** 1338
adaptive response **3:** 1282
addiction **1:** 510, 512; **2:** 789, 790; **S:** 221, 431
Addison's disease **4:** 1959
additives, antiknock for gasoline **3:** 1374, 1375
adenine **1:** 427; **S:** 389
adenohypophysis portion of the pituitary gland **3:** 1244
adenosine deaminase (ADA) deficiency **1:** 52
adenosine diphosphate (ADP) **S:** 427, 456, 479
adenosine monophosphate (AMP) **S:** 479
adenosine triphosphate (ATP) **3:** 1254, 1255, 1367; **S:** 230, 309, 373, 426, 456, 479, 512
adenovirus **3:** 1692
adermin **2:** 1142
adiabatic demagnetization **2:** 752

ADP
  See adenosine diphosphate (ADP)
adrenal cortex **2:** 894
adrenal glands **2:** 976; **3:** 1662; **4:** 1958; **S:** 219
adrenalectomy **2:** 976; **S:** 220
adrenaline **1:** 601; **3:** 1244, 1266; **4:** 1947
adrenaline reversal **1:** 442
adrenergic receptors **1:** 185
adrenocorticotropic hormone (ACTH) **2:** 894, 895; **3:** 1244
Adrian, Albert **3:** 1298
Adrian, Edgar Douglas **1:** 9, 153, 257; **2:** 810; **4:** 1829
adsorption **3:** 1173; **4:** 2030, 2053, 2290
AEC
  See Atomic Energy Commission (AEC)
Aëdes aegypti mosquito **3:** 1658
aenorhabditis elegans (C. elegans) nematodes **1:** 250
aerial warfare **4:** 2092
aerodynamic flutter **4:** 2303
aerodynamics **2:** 980; **3:** 1610; **4:** 2216
aeronautical engineering **2:** 980, 1027
aeronautical propulsion **1:** 534
aeronautics **2:** 662, 865, 866, 980; **4:** 1922, 2184
aeropropulsion **3:** 1663
aerosols **S:** 381
aerospace engineering **3:** 1710; **4:** 2184
aesthetics in science **2:** 939
aether
  See ether
affinities, chemical **3:** 1521, 1522
AFM
  See atomic force microscope (AFM)
African Americans, biological study of **3:** 1238, 1239
African Americans in American College of Surgeons **4:** 2259
African infantile leishmaniasis **3:** 1472
African sleeping sickness **S:** 135
aga **1:** 444
Agassiz, Louis **3:** 1420, 1705
age of rocks and minerals **1:** 447
Agent Orange **S:** 421
aging **3:** 1733
Agramonte, Aristides **3:** 1658